CONTENTS

LIST OF CONTRIBUTORS

EDITORS

Paul Cloke
University of Bristol, UK
Philip Crang
Royal Holloway, University of London, UK
Mark Goodwin
University of Exeter, UK

CONTRIBUTORS

William M. Adams
University of Cambridge, UK
Clive Barnett
The Open University, UK
Jacquie Burgess
University College London, UK
Mike Crang
University of Durham, UK
Tim Cresswell
University of Wales, Aberystwyth, UK
Luke Desforges
University of Wales, Aberystwyth, UK
Felix Driver
Royal Holloway, University of London, UK
Claire Dwyer
University College London, UK
Sally Eden
University of Hull, UK
David Gilbert
Royal Holloway, University of London, UK
Jon Goss
University of Hawaii, USA
Pyrs Gruffudd
University of Wales, Swansea, UK
Chris Hamnett
King's College London, UK
Sarah Holloway
Loughborough University, UK
Peter Jackson
University of Sheffield, UK
Nuala Johnson
Queen's University Belfast, UK

James Kneale
University College London, UK
Scott Kirsch
University of North Carolina at Chapel Hill, USA
Khalid Koser
University College London, UK
Lisa Law
University of St Andrews, UK
Roger Lee
Queen Mary, University of London, UK
Jon May
Queen Mary, University of London, UK
Don Mitchell
Syracuse University, USA
Catherine Nash
Queen Mary, University of London, UK
Miles Ogborn
Queen Mary, University of London, UK
Hester Parr
University of Dundee, UK
Richard Phillips
University of Liverpool, UK
Geraldine Pratt
University of British Columbia, Canada
Sarah A. Radcliffe
University of Cambridge, UK
Paul Routledge
University of Glasgow, UK
Joanne Sharp
University of Glasgow, UK
Susan J. Smith
University of Durham, UK
Lynn Staeheli
University of Colorado, USA
Adam Tickell
University of Bristol, UK
Michael Watts
University of California, Berkeley, USA
Sarah Whatmore
University of Oxford, UK
Katie Willis
Royal Holloway, University of London, UK
Jane Wills
Queen Mary, University of London, UK

ACKNOWLEDGEMENTS

This second edition of *Introducing Human Geographies* – 'IHG2' as it became to us – leaves us owing thanks in many directions. Most obviously, we should thank all those who bought the first edition in such numbers, collectively making it a sufficient success to bring this extended and updated second edition into being. More specifically, we are indebted to the various cohorts of first-year undergraduate students we have taught over the years, both before and after the first edition of this book appeared. The idea for *Introducing Human Geographies* began to form when we were all teaching first-year Human Geography courses at the University of Wales, Lampeter. We witnessed the students there being inspired by the preoccupations of contemporary Human Geography; but we also saw them having to develop that inspiration through materials not written or designed for them. In subsequent years – at Bristol, UCL, RHUL, Aberystwyth and Exeter – we have continued to be convinced of students' enthusiasm for engaging with new, often complex ideas and materials, so long as that complexity is not presented in a fashion that excludes all but a small clique from the conversation. We are proud that the first edition – with its emphasis on short, punchy, suggestive chapters – proved a good basis for that wider conversation, and we sincerely hope IHG2 will serve the same function even better.

With three editors and 39 other contributors, this book is inevitably a shared endeavour. The contributors deserve particular thanks. Of the chapters carried forward from the first edition, every single one has been revised and updated. The enthusiasm of the new authors we approached to get involved was inspiring. Those 16 new chapters arrived on time and further evidence the intellectual care all our authors clearly invest in their pedagogical work. Past and present editorial and production staff at Arnold also warrant our warmest thanks. Laura McKelvie worked alongside us from the very beginning of the first edition, overseeing its translation from editorial ambition to printed page. Abi Woodman worked with us on the planning and commissioning of this second edition, not least negotiating its higher production values (full-colour illustrations at last!). Liz Gooster succeeded Abi just before manuscript submission, demonstrating remarkable calm even when that tower of paper and copyright requests arrived on her desk. There are instances where we have been unable to trace or contact the copyright holder. If notified the publishers will be pleased to rectify any errors or omissions at the earliest opportunity.

On a personal note, special thanks are due, as ever, to: Viv, Liz and Will; Katharine, Esme and Evan; and Anne, Rosa and Sylvie.

INTRODUCTION

Starting a university course is always both an exciting and stressful time. Even without the changes it may bring about in your life, the academic challenges faced are in themselves enough. New ways of learning are often required. New ideas and issues are confronted. Even a subject studied at school or college is likely to look and feel very different at the university level. This is certainly the case with Human Geography. Sometimes this is wonderfully energizing, but it can also be disorientating. There is so much to take in and make sense of. The aim of this book is to help new Human Geography students have the excitement whilst minimizing the stress, to be inspired by new ideas and materials without feeling totally lost. *Introducing Human Geographies* provides you with a 'travel guide' into the academic subject of Human Geography and the worldly Human Geographies it represents. It maps out the big, foundational questions that Human Geographers past and present are fascinated by and that have shaped the discipline (Part 1); it explores in more depth the key research themes that are being pursued in the subject today (Part 2); and it takes you to some of the geographical contexts and issues in which these themes come together (Part 3).

This second edition of *Introducing Human Geographies* presents a number of improvements and updates to the first edition, which was published six years ago, in 1999. All the chapters carried over from the first edition have been revised and updated. The book as a whole is bigger, with 16 newly written chapters added. It is glossier too, particularly thanks to the presence of full-colour figures, a feature of some importance in a discipline with such a strong visual tradition as geography. There are some stylistic tweaks: definitions of key terms included not only in a consolidated glossary but in marginal notes, so you can more easily consult them as you read; discussion points at the end of chapters, around which to focus private reflection and class discussion. In addition, this new edition addresses issues of public concern that have come to the fore in the last six years, such as the 'global war on terror'. The spirit of the book, however, has not changed from its first edition.

The overall effect, we hope, is to represent a subject that is relevant, thought-provoking, challenging and dynamic. The Human Geography you will be introduced to here is a million miles from some of the popular images of the subject. It is not a dry compendium of facts about the world, its countries, capital cities, and so on. This book probably won't be a great deal of help in getting the geography questions right in a game of Trivial Pursuit. Sorry. Nor is it much concerned with the ever more sophisticated tools for managing and manipulating geographical 'information', the sort of geography so successfully marketed to commercial and political organizations. Before engaging with these technologies of information management we feel it is important to have a wider sense of geographical 'knowledge'. The book doesn't have the ethos of a travelogue either. We regard with suspicion the explorer's view of the world as divided into, on the one hand, a dull domesticity and, on the other, wider, wilder spaces for adventure and challenge. The domestic is far from dull; the wider world far more than a stage for our own projects of adventure, heroism and personal renewal. Nor do we have much space for the sorts of simplistic models of spatial laws and forms that for a while came to dominate many anglophonic school curricula. The Human Geography we want to introduce you to, and the Human Geography you will find to be predominant in the subject's intellectual arteries of research journals and books, avoids the easy and ultimately dull options of retreating into worlds of compiled fact or modelled fantasy. It engages with real life and real lives. It seeks to do more than record or model; it tries to explain, understand, question, interpret and maybe even propose improvements to these Human Geographies.

In this general introduction we want to say a little about why and how we are going to introduce this sort of Human Geography. We begin by addressing that thorny question 'What is Human Geography?', the bane but also the inspiration for all of us who have to explain to friends, family and colleagues the things we are interested in as geographers. Our response focuses in particular on how Human Geography combines substantive breadth with a coherent intellectual core. We then briefly consider the character of contemporary Human Geography, highlighting the subject's dynamism and explaining some of the key features of recent developments within it. Here, we also begin to move away from issues of content – what Human Geographers study – and on to questions of approach and styles of thought. We try to give you a feel for what is being asked of you as Human Geography students, highlighting ways of thinking about the world that you can apply across the full range of Human Geography's substantive concerns. Finally, we explain the layout of the book itself, both in terms of structure and in terms of the presentational style of the chapters. Our intention has been to produce a book that gives you the cutting edge of Human Geographical thought, but in an accessible and usable form.

WHAT IS HUMAN GEOGRAPHY?

A fairly common exercise for an early Human Geography tutorial or seminar is a request to mine a week's news coverage and to come back with an example of something that seems to you to be 'Human Geography'. Have a go at doing this now. Think about the last week's news. Draw up a shortlist of two or three stories that strike you as the kinds of things Human Geography would study. Then reflect on how you decided on these, and what you thought was geographical about them. Now read on.

Literally, if one goes back to the word's Greek origins, geography means 'to write (*graphien*) the earth (*geo*)'. It is hardly surprising, then, that both human and physical geography have a vast range of substantive topics. In this book you will find chapters addressing topics as diverse as third-world development, the international financial system, the post-9/11 'war on terror', British-Asian music and fashion, urban gentrification, global environmental change, nationalism, landscape painting and design, the Zapatista resistance movement in Chiapas, Mexico, the emergence of the Countryside Alliance in the UK, immigration and asylum policy, tourism, commemorations of the Holocaust, colonialism, shopping, global humanitarianism, love, watching television, photography, anti-globalization activists, domestic architecture, and oven-ready chickens, to pick out just a few highlights. You could, then, have picked any of these and more in your hypothetical seminar exercise. It is quite common to have mixed feelings about this range. On the one hand, many people choose to study geography because of it, appreciating the wider understanding of human life such breadth seems to offer. On the other hand, though, if this wider view is to be anything more than an intellectual pick and mix, it is also important to have a sense of what makes Human Geography cohere and what binds these apparently diverse topics together. Why are all these topics Human Geography?

One response is of course to look at these topics and to see some as more geographical than others. So you might organize this variety of subject matters into a mental landscape of central and peripheral con-

cerns. You may be doing that right now. But we need to think very carefully about how we make such judgements. Perhaps all too often we base them more on convention than on any serious and sustained thinking about the intellectual contribution of Human Geography. So, for example, because we are used to Human Geographers studying the urban planning issues of out-of-town developments or suburbanization or 'inner cities', we think of that as geography; whereas a discussion of, say, eighteenth-century landscape art or philosophies of love does not have that familiarity and hence feels less

like 'normal' and 'proper' geography. We expect geography to address issues about economic organization and regional development; we are less used to geographers talking about unpaid or paid domestic work, the organization of households, and childcare.

Especially as university-level geography is going to throw up a huge number of topics you may be unfamiliar with, we want to suggest that mere convention alone is an insufficient criterion through which to assess whether something is central to Human Geography or not. Having an understanding of the traditions of Human Geography is enormously valuable, but one of the crucial lessons we learn from that historical understanding is that what counts as Human Geography, what has been central and marginal to it, has always been subject both to change and to contestation (see Livingstone, 1992, for an excellent, sustained analysis of this). For instance, for much of its history Human Geography, reflecting the social worlds it was being produced in, largely ignored over half the world's human beings, i.e. women. It reduced human to man. Economic geographers ignored the domestic work done by women at home;

FIGURE I
Which of these photographs of work looks more like it should be in a Human Geography textbook to you? Why? Credit: (above) Jose Luis Palaez, Inc./Corbis; (below) Brownie Harris/Corbis

Masculinism, masculinist

a form of thought or knowledge that, whilst often claiming to be impartial, comprehends the world in ways that are derived from men's experiences and concerns. Many Feminist Geographers have argued that Human Geography has traditionally been masculinist (*see* FEMINISM).

Gender

a criterion of social organization that distinguishes different groups of people on the basis of femininity or masculinity. In any one location, many masculinities and femininities interact. As a concept, gender is usually used in Human Geography in distinction to that of sex (i.e. femaleness and maleness) in order to emphasize the SOCIAL CONSTRUCTION of women's and men's roles, relations and identities. Human Geographers' accounts of the world have always been shaped through understandings of gender (*see* MASCULINISM) but explicit analyses of the geographies of gender and the gendering of geographies are comparatively recent, and associated with the growth of Feminist Geography (*see* FEMINISM).

Feminism

a series of perspectives, which together draw on theoretical and political accounts of the oppression of women in society to suggest how GENDER relations and Human Geography are interconnected (*see also* PATRIARCHY).

development geographers paid too little attention to the gendered nature of both development problems and practice; issues and understandings that were seen as feminine were trivialized (see Fig. i). Human Geography was **masculinist**. At the level of research and teaching there are still more men than women in Human Geography, though it has to be said that considerable progress has been made, and certainly the contributions of women have tended to make up in quality, and hence influence, what they have lacked in simple quantity. Geography is much less exclusively masculine then it was even two decades ago. Few of you, we imagine, would today say that Human Geography should be about and done by men. But it would be naïve to pretend that the predominance of men in the research and teaching levels of the subject, both past and present, has not moulded for the worse our senses of what 'conventional' Human Geography is. Topics and ways of studying them that are seen as more 'feminine' still tend to be seen as less central to the subject. Bizarrely, given that we all have a **gender**, this can even include the whole issue of gender itself, which is all too often seen as something that concerns only a few 'feminist geographers' rather than being an absolutely central facet of what it means to be human, and hence to have Human Geographies. (To clarify, the problem here is not a product of feminist geography, though wider prejudices against the f-word (**feminism**) do have an impact, not least on student reactions. The issue is the sometime ghettoization of gender as a fringe geographical concern rather than as something all Human Geographers need to engage with – if you want to follow this up, see the review of work on 'feminist geographies' by members of the Women and Geography Study Group of the RGS–IBG (1997); the recent introduction to geographical thinking on gender by Domosh and Seager (2001) and, of course, Chapter 7 in this volume).

How, then, can we approach the question of 'What is Human Geography?' in more open and thoughtful ways? How can it be more than a matter of convention and hence inertia? To begin with, we have to move back beyond the more superficial questions of topic, by returning to that basic definition of geography – 'to write the earth' – with which we began. If we think about the meanings of the 'geo' or 'the earth' in *geo*graphy we can identify two interconnected cores to Human Geography's distinctive intellectual contribution (see also Cosgrove, 1994) (Fig. ii). First, there is the earth as 'Mother Earth' (there is gender again), as 'the living planet earth', as 'soil', as land and sea and air. A consistent preoccupation of Human Geography is therefore with the relations between human beings and the 'nature' we are also part of. Second, however, there is another meaning to 'earth', one we use when we talk about 'the whole earth' or 'the world' or, more recently, 'the global'. Here, 'geo' comes to signal something about both human universality (we all live on one world) and human diversity (when we talk about 'world music' and 'global cuisine', for example, we convey some sense of variety and difference as well as collectivity). This second set of meanings leads us into Human Geographers' fascination with the peoples and places that make up our world, with the differences and similarities between them, with the ways they are connected to or disconnected from each other, and with the processes through which the world is structured into identifiable peoples, spaces and places at all.

In summary, branching off from the 'geo' in geography, from its project of 'writing the earth', are two foundational concerns. First, human–nature relations. Here Human Geographers are concerned with how we live on and with our planet, and the 'environments' and 'natures' it provides for us; with how we impact on those environments and how they impact on us; with how we understand and value them; and with how we relate to our own natures and our existence as part of the natural world. These concerns reach across a range of scales: from global concerns with climate change to local debates over particular environments and habitats, to domestic engagements with other (once) living beings (in the form of food or pets or plants or pests), to concerns with our existence through fleshy and living/dying bodies.

Second, as this review of scales of human–nature relations demonstrates, Human Geographers are also concerned with human life's constitution through space (often termed a concern with spatiality). To express this less obtusely, all human and non-human being happens somewhere; and Human Geographers argue especially strongly that this matters. A variety of central geographical notions reflect this: location, distance, place, travel, scale, distribution, to name but a few. All try to express something about the 'where-ness' of things in the world. 'Where' we are is fundamental to what we see (and don't), what problems we face, what chances we have, what languages we speak and think in, what we do, who we identify with. All things – human and non-human – only exist in and through space. Human Geography is concerned with the implications of that abstract assertion. But this is not a purely abstract facet of our world. All of us encounter the spatiality of the world in mundane ways all of the time: we live in homes that organize the world into (more) private and public, intimate and distant realms; we live in settlements that we name individually and categorize by type (cities, suburbs and villages, for example); we belong to/in certain territories and have different claims to others (by virtue of nationality, for example); we understand a host of things and people as foreign; we talk of here and there; we have (ever more complicated) experiences and understandings of distance; we move and settle. Human Geography is about these (and many more) fundamentals of worldly existence.

These, then, are the connective threads that hold together the seemingly diverse contents of Human Geography. They are also why – returning to one of our earlier examples of a perhaps unexpected topic addressed in this book – an oven-ready chicken (Fig. iii) is doubly geographical. After all, and without wishing to steal the thunder from Michael Watts' fascinating analysis in Chapter 39, this oven-ready chicken is an embodiment of some particular ways for human beings to relate to nature: based on logics and practices of domestication, commodification, industrialized production, purposive modification and consumption that reach well beyond this one member of the animal kingdom. The oven-ready chicken is also an embodiment of some particular sorts of spatiality: one in which different people and places are all connected together through the economic systems of the chicken world (the consumers eating it, the farmers raising it, the large companies controlling its production and its distribution, the scientists genetically modifying it); but also one

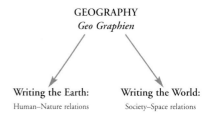

GEOGRAPHY
Geo Graphien

Writing the Earth:
Human–Nature relations

Writing the World:
Society–Space relations

FIGURE II
Human Geography: writing the earth and writing the world

Spatiality

socially produced space. This term is used by Human Geographers to emphasize how space is socially constructed and experienced, rather than being an innate backdrop to social life (*see also* SOCIAL CONSTRUCTION). As such it is a central concept of contemporary Human Geography. It is sometimes used in the plural, spatialities, in order to stress the many different ways in which space can be constructed and experienced.

Commodification

this term is used in two interrelated ways: (a) as the conversion of any thing, idea or person into a COMMODITY (the term 'commoditization' is often preferred for this sense); and (b) a wider societal process whereby an ever increasing number of things, human relationships, ideas and people are turned into commodities. Both meanings see the process of commodification as symptomatic of the penetration of CAPITALISM into the everyday lives of people and things.

in which these connections are forgotten (by many) through a distancing of production and consumption (so even avid meat eaters would be unlikely to want to see video footage of broiler production and death as they tuck into their evening meal). Again, these are geographies that have far wider resonances, offering us a lens through which to consider a world that both connects and divides up people, places and activities. So, geography is not just to be found on the library shelves or indeed in the newspaper; it is all around us, even in an oven-ready chicken.

SUMMARY

- One of Human Geography's main intellectual contributions is to understand the relations between human beings and the natural world of which we are a part.

- Another of Human Geography's main intellectual contributions is to understand how all facets of human life – the economic, the environmental, the political, the social, the cultural, the historical among others – are bound up with questions of space and place or 'spatiality'.

- These central concerns of Human Geographers are pursued across diverse and changing subject matters. We would encourage you to be open to that diversity and change rather than defining Human Geography in terms of topics and approaches that are already familiar to you.

DOING HUMAN GEOGRAPHY TODAY

FIGURE III
Human Geography? Credit: British Chicken Information Service

Our approach in this book is therefore to introduce you to a Human Geography that has a strong intellectual coherence at its heart, but that applies this with an invigorating catholicism. More particularly, in traversing the subject's substantive diversity we have been especially concerned to give you a feel for the kinds of topics and approaches that are coming to the fore in contemporary Human Geography, offering you a bridge into the debates that are being thrashed out, often in rather more obtuse and difficult languages, in research journals and books. Human Geography has always been a dynamic field of enquiry, and even in the six years between the first and second editions of this book it is notable how senses of the discipline's most pressing issues and developments have changed (for recent collections of essays setting out these kinds of issues at the 'research frontier' see Cloke et al., 2004, and Massey et al., 1999). But whilst always encouraging others (and ourselves) to be open to new ideas, we also need to maintain a sense of historical perspective. We should not artificially cut through longer lineages and traditions in a fetishization of current fashions. For that reason, whilst recognizing (and being pleased) that the Human Geography textbooks produced in, say, 1970 look almost nothing like this one, the character of the work in this book needs to be contextualized in longer-running trends that do reach back to at least that long ago (and one could argue well before). Two such trends are especially important: a questioning of the 'factual' character of Human Geographies; and a commitment to 'critical' thinking. Expressed like this, these are fairly abstract, so let us elaborate, using as an illustrative sketch how they might frame our understandings of the Human Geographies of a country such as the United States of America.

We begin with Human Geography's move beyond the factual. The Trivial Pursuit model of the Human Geography of the USA would be that it involves learning key geographical facts: names and locations of states and state capitals perhaps; population distributions, maybe divided up into categories such as racial and ethnic groups, age bands (showing the retirement belts of Florida, for example) and class; locations of different industries and forms of employment, and so on. Now, knowing these kinds of facts is of some value, not least because the activities required to find them out – reading decent newspapers, finding useful sites amongst the deluge of information on the Internet, reading books – promote a more generally inquiring attitude to the world we live in. But in themselves they are a pretty pathetic sort of geographical knowledge. They convert Human Geographies into the thinnest of forms, not even beginning to scratch the surface of people's real lives, their values and beliefs, their daily preoccupations, their hopes and dreams, their loves and hates. For that one has to look to much more people-centred approaches, trumpeted in Human Geography under the label humanistic geography (for exemplary collections, see Ley and Samuels, 1978; Meinig, 1979; for a more recent revisiting of such humanistic work see Holloway and Hubbard, 2000).

As simple geographical facts they also tell us nothing about how these geographies have come into being and how and why they might change in the future. For that we have to think about how ways of relating to nature and of organizing activities spatially are bound up with wider American ways of life: ways of making a livelihood; ways of seeking enjoyment through leisure; ways of politically organizing, and so on (for an accessible example of American ways of relating to nature, see Wilson, 1992). In a country such as the USA this centrally involves understanding capitalist ways of life; something that has been the broader project for the last 30 years of what are termed political–economic approaches in Human Geography (for a summary review, see Peet and Thrift, 1989). It would also involve understanding America's foundation through processes of European colonialism, colonization and, of course, displacement (for recent work on this theme, see Anderson and Domosh, 2002).

Simple geographical facts also tell us nothing about the phenomena they claim to measure and how they have come into being as categories of thought and life. For that we have to turn to various discursive approaches (for a collection of these, see Barnes and Duncan, 1992). We have to think carefully about how so-called facts – like race or ethnicity – are actually produced and contested as part of human life, rather than being aspects of it that Human Geographers can map as obvious and unproblematic. The USA, for example, has different understandings of race and ethnicity from those in Africa, Asia or even the UK. Even the geographical units of the USA – both its regions and its own status as a nation-state – cannot simply be assumed. They are part of what needs investigating. After all, the regions of the USA are not simple facts of nature but dynamic political, economic and vernacular constructions (see Shortridge, 1991; Warf, 1988). And the USA itself has to be questioned as a 'fact' to focus on, in so far as developments within it can only be understood in terms of its relationship to the wider world political-

Humanistic Geography

a theoretical approach to Human Geography that concentrates on studying the conscious, creative and meaningful activities and experiences of human beings. Coming to prominence in the 1970s, Humanistic Geography was in part a rebuttal of attempts during the 1960s to create a law-based, scientific Human Geography founded on statistical data and analytical techniques (see SPATIAL SCIENCE). In contrast, it emphasized the subjectivities of those being studied and, indeed, the Human Geographers studying them. Human meanings, emotions and ideas with regard to place, space and nature thus became central.

Political-economic, political economy

the study of how economic activities are socially and politically structured and have social and political consequences. Political-economic approaches in Human Geography have paid particular attention to understanding capitalist economies and their geographical organization and impact (see CAPITALISM and also MARXIST GEOGRAPHY). Central to such analyses have been questions concerning the class-based nature of the human geographies of capitalist societies (see CLASS).

Colonialism

the rule of a NATION-STATE or other political power over another, subordinated, people and place. This domination is established and maintained through political structures, but may also shape economic and cultural relations. See also NEO-COLONIALISM and IMPERIALISM.

Colonization

the physical settling of people from a colonial power within that power's subordinated colonies (see COLONIALISM). See also DECOLONIZATION.

Discourse, discursive

drawing on the work of the French philosopher Michel Foucault, Human Geographers define discourses as ways of talking about, writing or otherwise representing the world and its geographies (*see also* REPRESENTATION). Discursive approaches to Human Geography emphasize the importance of these ways of representing. They are seen as shaping the realities of the worlds in which we live, rather than just being ways of portraying a reality that exists outside of language and thought. They are also seen as connected to questions of practice – that is, what people actually do – rather than being confined to a separate realm of images or ideas. More specifically, Human Geographers have stressed the different ways in which people have discursively constructed the world in different times and places, and examined how it is that particular ways of talking about, conceptualizing and acting on people and places come to be seen as natural and common-sensical in particular contexts.

economy (this argument is developed at length in Agnew, 1987b; recent elaborations in the light of current American foreign policy are made in Harvey, 2003, and Gregory, 2004). The general point here is that geographical entities (like a region or a nation or a continent) are always 'imaginative', framed through particular ways of thinking, speaking and acting (see Chapter 10 for a more sustained account of this argument and its intellectual lineages).

So, long-standing trends in Human Geography – towards humanistic, political-economic and discursive approaches – have emphasized kinds of geographical knowledge that go well beyond the recording and mapping of facts. One important consequence of this is that the doing of Human Geography involves far more than compiling data that provide definitively correct answers. Instead, it requires 'critical thinking'. It is easy to misunderstand this phrase. When we say someone is being critical often we mean they are being negative, just finding fault; and at times it can seem that what academics most love to do is indeed to nit-pick, demonstrating their own intelligence by dismantling the ideas of others. But that is not what we mean here. True critical thought is as much about seeing strengths as weaknesses. What it does require is not taking things for granted, questioning the assumptions held by others and, crucially, oneself. It means – and this is a tricky balance – combining a determined scepticism with a profound openness to unfamiliar ideas and voices. It means recognizing that the 'rightness' of answers to geographical questions is something that has to be justified, and is as dependent on values, beliefs and perspective as it is on the 'facts' of the matter. Within the subject, a number of intellectual movements have emphasized this – perhaps most importantly the various 'radical geographies' of feminist, **Marxist** and **post-colonial** writers (for a sense of these you could flick through past and present volumes of the 'radical journal of geography', *Antipode*; see also Blunt and Wills, 2000).

But critical thinking wears no particular political colours. It is more a style of thought, a way of doing Human Geography. Of course, at times a requirement for critical thought can be infuriating. All geography students have probably had moments, especially around exam time, when they wished there would be a simple, right answer that someone could just tell them and they could repeat. However, in the end, it is the need to think critically that makes doing a Human Geography course more than time spent learning information to be forgotten soon afterwards. It is what ensures that you really can learn something that stays with you, that changes you, which is what genuine education is all about of course.

SUMMARY

- Human Geography is a dynamic subject that has changed rapidly in the last few years. This book introduces you to the approaches and issues preoccupying Human Geographers in the early twenty-first century.

- These contemporary approaches build on longer-standing bodies of work that have emphasized

how geographical questions rarely have simple, right or wrong answers.

- Doing a Human Geography course therefore means learning to 'think critically' about the world, and your own and other people's understandings of it.

THE STRUCTURE AND STYLE OF THIS BOOK

The 43 main chapters in this book are organized into three parts – 'Foundations', 'Themes' and 'Issues' – each with its own brief editorial introduction. The nine chapters in 'Foundations' (Part 1) give you the latest thinking on some of the 'big questions' of substance and approach that have always concerned Human Geographers. Rather than deal with these through potted histories of the subject, or through abstract theoretical pieces, all the authors weave together conceptual ideas with accessible examples and illustrations. Each chapter is framed around a binary relationship. The first two binaries discussed – between culture and nature and society and space – pick up directly on the two central intellectual projects of Human Geography outlined in this introduction. Subsequent chapters – working with and beyond binaries of the local and the global, control and freedom, the self and the other, image and reality, masculine and feminine, science and art, and the relevant and the esoteric – explore both more specific facets of these relations and debates over the nature of our knowledge of them. The chapters in Part 1 are unlikely to match with particular, substantive lectures in a first-year course, and don't exist as easily locatable debates in the discipline's journals. But in many ways they deal with the most important questions to think about as a new Human Geography student, giving you a sense of why Human Geographers pursue more specific studies in the way they do and thus introducing you to ideas that you will be able to use across a range of more substantive topics.

Those substantive areas of the subject are mostly addressed in the second and largest part of this book, 'Themes'. Here, 24 chapters, themselves divided into eight sections, each with a brief editorial introduction, cover the major thematic 'sub-disciplines' of Human Geography: cultural geographies, development geographies, economic geographies, environmental geographies, historical geographies, political geographies, social geographies, and urban and rural geographies. This part of the book provides you with thought-provoking arguments on the key issues currently being debated within these sub-disciplines, as well as giving you a feel for the kind of Human Geography undertaken within each.

Thematic sub-disciplines are one of the major ways in which teaching curricula are organized and research activity structured, to the extent that geographers are often labelled according to these specialisms (as economic geographers, political geographers, and so on). However, the world we live in is (unsurprisingly) resistant to these neat classifications. Economy and politics and culture and environment (and so on) all interweave with each other. You can't go out and find something that is purely 'economic' (or political or cultural or environmental). These labels are designations of emphasis and approach, not of really existing objects of inquiry. Moreover, a lot of the most innovative work in Human Geography goes on in the border zones between these sub-disciplinary territories. For these reasons, the final part of the book, 'Issues', comprises ten chapters that are organized around questions that do not fit neatly in any one sub-discipline. Editorially, we have inflected this selection in two ways. First, we have sought to give the long-standing geographical appreciation of

Marxist

social and economic theories influenced by the legacy of the leading nineteenth-century political philosopher, Karl Marx. Highly influential in the framing of critical geography, these theories focus on the organization of capitalist society and the social and environmental injustices that can be traced to it. *See also* CAPITALISM, MODE OF PRODUCTION, ALIENATION and COMMODIFICATION for examples of the influence of Marxist thinking in Human Geography.

Post-colonial, post-colonialism

sometimes hyphenated, sometimes not, this term has two distinct meanings: (a) the post-colonial era, i.e. the historical period following a period of COLONIALISM (*see also* DECOLONIZATION); (b) post-colonial political, cultural and intellectual movements, and their perspectives, which are critical of the past and ongoing effects of European and other colonialisms.

Space of flows

a term first coined by the urban theorist Manuel Castells in distinction to the 'space of places', this self-confessed 'cumbersome expression' emphasizes how the character and dynamics of a bounded place are reliant upon a host of connections and flows that go beyond its boundaries. These include flows of people (through many forms of travel and migration), of capital and money (think of the impacts of the global networks of the international financial system, for example), of ideas, of media imagery and of objects, amongst many others. The notion of the 'space of flows' is therefore a complement and corrective to Human Geographers' long-standing interest in bounded places and territories (*see* TERRITORY), perhaps particularly important in an age of intensified GLOBALIZATION.

Diaspora

the dispersal or scattering of people from their original home. As a noun it can be used to refer to a dispersed 'people' (hence the Jewish diaspora or the Black diaspora). However, it also refers to the actual processes of dispersal and connection that produce any scattered, but still in some way identifiable, population. In this light it also can be used as an adjective – diasporic – to refer to the senses of home, belonging and cultural identity held by a dispersed population.

particular places and regions (sometimes called 'area studies') a contemporary twist, paying particular attention both to what it means to live in place and the **spaces of flows** that connect and bring those places into being (Castells, 1989). Second, we have also sought to highlight particularly current issues. Here we have in part responded to wider assessments of crucial developments in the world today, as reflected in currents of public debate. Hence chapters on the character of war in the twenty-first century, on humanitarianism and the geographies of care, on globalization and those who protest its dominant forms, on migration. But we have also sought to highlight issues that might at first glance seem less important, but which on further consideration crystallize absolutely fundamental facets of twenty-first century life: on commodification; on tourism (the world's largest industry, devoted to the production, sale and consumption of places); on the mass media; on population **diasporas**. Furthermore, we have sought to present materials on aspects of our Human Geographies that have been unduly neglected in the past, including their embodied and emotional characters.

Stylistically, every chapter obviously has its own authorial signature, but all the contributions combine discussions of challenging ideas and issues with accessible presentation. Unfamiliar academic terminology is kept to a minimum, but where central to an argument is marked in bold type and defined (by the editors) in both marginal text and the Glossary at the back of the book. The book aims to make you think but to do that through being lively and engaging. Scholarly knowledge doesn't have to be dry and self-obsessed. Chapters are deliberately short and punchy, but can easily be followed up using the suggested readings included at the end of each.

Further readings are perhaps an appropriate place for us to stop introducing *Introducing Human Geographies* for they signal that the most important contribution this book can make is to encourage readers to move on. We hope you enjoy and are just a little bit inspired by this collection, but we know we are a doorway to a much wider process of learning. At the risk of sounding like a dating agency, and mixing our metaphors, think of this book as setting you up with other Human Geographies. It would be nice if you remembered us fondly, of course, but we hope there will be a time when you want to hang out with those other books and articles in the library, maybe even getting passionate about some of them. Most importantly, use our introduction to their geographical ideas, themes and issues as an excuse to invite *them* out for a breath of fresh air. They get bored in their ivory towers. Take those geographical ideas to your favourite haunts and see what they make of them. Find out how you get on, and if you don't seem to connect, agonize over whether that is their fault or yours. Have a relationship with Human Geography. In the end, we are sure you will hit it off with some bits of the subject, learning and changing in the process. After all, as our contributors have demonstrated so admirably, Human Geography today is vibrant, lively, fun, serious and thought-provoking. At times it can be challenging and difficult, but anything worth loving is. Here's to a great relationship.

DISCUSSION POINTS

1. Look at a newspaper from the last week. Identify three stories that seem to you to address Human Geography topics. Explain your choices and why you think they are 'geographical'.

2. What makes Human Geography a distinctive subject?

3. 'Human Geography is a down-to-earth subject, concerned with facts not theories.' Discuss this assertion.

FURTHER READING

Obviously, our primary suggested reading is the rest of this book! However, the following are other useful complementary texts, that fulfil slightly different functions.

Agnew, J.A., Livingstone, D. and Rogers, A. (eds) (1996) *Human Geography: an essential anthology.* **Oxford: Blackwell.**

An excellent collection of classic geographical writings, both old and new. This anthology demonstrates the long-standing but changing Human Geographical interest in questions both of culture, nature and landscape, and of region, place and space.

Cloke, P., Cook, I., Crang, P., Goodwin, M., Painter, J. and Philo, C. (2004) *Practising Human Geography.* **London: Sage.**

An account of how research in Human Geography is done, covering both the production of geographical materials or 'data' and the production of varying kinds of geographical 'interpretations' of these data. This, and other books on geographical research and methods, provide invaluable links between the kinds of materials introduced in this volume and the opportunities that exist for you to undertake your own geographical investigations in project work and independent dissertations.

Daniels, S. and Lee, R. (eds) (1996) *Exploring Human Geography: a reader.* **London: Arnold.**

A collection of relatively recent geographical writings, giving a feel for contemporary Human Geography's 'critical' spirit and its determination to explain and understand, rather than just describe. As this is a reader, the contents are not specifically designed for a student audience, but all are relatively accessible and well set in context by the editors.

Johnston, R.J., Gregory, D., Pratt, G., Smith, D.M. and Watts, M.J. (eds) (2000) *The dictionary of Human Geography* **(4th edn). Oxford: Blackwell.**

This dictionary has concise but comprehensive definitions and explanations relevant to almost every aspect of Human Geography. As a reference tool it is invaluable and has no better. A book you will be able to use throughout your time studying Human Geography.

Kneale, P. (2003) *Study skills for geographers.* **London: Arnold.**

A guide to the basic study skills Human Geography students need at the university level. In this chapter we have suggested Human Geographers need to be able to 'think critically'. This book helps you with some of the hard work of actually doing that. Well worth a look early on in your degree programme.

Livingstone, D. (1992) *The geographical tradition.* **Oxford: Blackwell.**

A scholarly rendition of the history of Human Geography, a topic we pay comparatively little attention to in this collection. Livingstone concentrates on the longer-term history of the subject rather than on its recent developments. Throughout, one gets fascinating insights into how the concerns of Human Geographers have run in parallel with wider social currents.

Part one
FOUNDATIONS

INTRODUCTION

Sometimes the start of Human Geography textbooks, and indeed courses, can be very daunting. This is because of the perception by some of the authors of the books and courses concerned that it is necessary to throw in a load of theoretical stuff at the beginning, before getting on with the more interesting stuff. While it may indeed be preferable that certain theoretical foundations are laid before dealing with systematic issues, the net result is likely to be that the reader/course-attender can either be bored to tears or bemused by the abstract nature of those foundations. Well, here's the bad news – we have also decided to begin this book with some theoretical dimensions. But, here's the good news – we utterly reject the false division between abstract theory and the substantive issues of everyday life. Indeed, we believe that our everyday lives are simply teeming with the kinds of issues and questions that are often pigeon-holed as theory. Much of the excitement and value in Human Geography lies in addressing these issues and questions by thinking through aspects of our own lives and of the world(s) in which we live.

As an illustration, here is a very short account of a typical journey to work for one of us – Paul Cloke. Neither the story nor the journey is in any way special; that is the point of narrating it. It could be any part of your everyday experience, whoever you are or wherever you live. What it does show is that different sets of Human Geography relationships crop up all over the place, and certainly not just in the abstract treatments of theory in books and lectures. So, imagine if you can the leafy suburb of Stoke Bishop in north-west Bristol . . .

An alarm clock rings on a Monday morning. It is part of the routine to make sure that my son and daughter are awake and up in time for school. This often involves bringing them breakfast in bed! My son's room is decorated with photos of sports stars – footballers from English and Scottish clubs, and basketball players from the USA – and team shirts from US ice hockey and basketball. My daughter has grown out of wall-to-wall pictures, but one or two remnants from the international worlds of film and music remain. In both rooms, music sets the atmosphere, focusing variously on the anarchy of Chumbawumba, the politics of black American rap or the trip-hop of Bristol's music scene. A little later, I walk the dog – a border collie of Welsh farming stock – and feed the pond fish – goldfish of Japanese breeding stock.

Later again, I head for the front door, tripping over my wife's Traidcraft boxes – one of her passions is fair trade issues and she works hard as a voluntary representative, channelling fairly traded goods from 'developing' countries to people in our local church and beyond. Then, it's on the bike and up the hill to the Downs, a large tract of open parkland often thought of as a lungful of fresh air in the heart of the city. By day, this is a site of many different kinds of leisure and recreation, but by night it is a landmark in the geography of women's (and some men's) fear, not to be traversed alone on foot. At the edge of the Downs is Bristol Zoo, which attracts large visitor numbers and houses 'exotic' animals.

After the Downs, there is a welcome downhill stretch from Blackboy Hill past the police station to Whiteladies Road. The very names of the streets resonate with Bristol's history as a port and a centre of slave-trading. Maybe, in a different way, the names also suggest a present set of social differences in the city. Local shops hug the side of the road, including a knot of travel agents displaying posters of far-flung places and offering the passer-by a distinctive gaze on worlds of the imagination. They may not be 'real worlds' but they are real enough if that's the only experience of them you've got. Then comes 'the strip', Bristol's hot development of designer pubs and clubs, with Irishness here, and Henry Africas there, interspersed with the by-now unremarkable Indian and Chinese restaurants. Designer-label beer and wine from all over the world is spilt here over designer T-shirts from all over the world.

At the bottom of the hill are two strange bedfellows: BBC Bristol – home of local news broadcasting and 'nature' programming, amongst other things – stands across the road from an army headquarters building sometimes adorned with parked fieldguns and trucks in full battle-dress. A little further on come the banks and building societies, competing to serve the needs of local business and specifically placed to attract business from those connected to the university. Inside the nearby big department store are expensive items from all over the world, while outside someone sells the local newspaper, and another the *Big Issue*. This is often 'Chuck', a homeless man who is fed up with the compassion fatigue of passers-by, who are quite capable of avoiding eye contact with the humanity, and the issues, of street homelessness.

Finally, it is up to the department, passing through the multinational, but somehow overwhelmingly middle-class, throng of students in the precinct. Once inside my office, the first move is to fetch a cup of (fairly traded) coffee, switch on the PC and check my e-mails, hardly noticing the rows of shelves loaded with the production of particular knowledges about governments, policies, plans and politics, and how the lives of real people in real places intersect with so much in the geographical world.

That account, written in 1997 for the first edition of this book, has now in many ways become dated, prompting the rather obvious observation that human geographies are continually changing, although some things seem to stay the same. So while now, in 2004, many elements of my journey to work remain constant – I live in the same house, the basic layout and infrastructure of the city of Bristol has remained constant, and I end up in the same university building – there are other facets both of the way things are, and of the way I experience them that are quite different.

Gender

a criterion of social organization that distinguishes different groups of people on the basis of femininity or masculinity. In any one location, many masculinities and femininities interact. As a concept, gender is usually used in Human Geography in distinction to that of sex (i.e. femaleness and maleness) in order to emphasize the SOCIAL CONSTRUCTION of women's and men's roles, relations and identities. Human Geographers' accounts of the world have always been shaped through understandings of gender (see MASCULINISM) but explicit analyses of the geographies of gender and the gendering of geographies are comparatively recent, and associated with the growth of Feminist Geography (see FEMINISM).

Embodiment

this concept suggests that the self and the body are not separate, but rather that the experiences of any individual are, invariably, shaped by the active and reactive entity that is their body — irrespective of whether this is conscious or not. The argument, then, runs that the uniqueness of human experience is due, at least in part, to the unique nature of individual bodies.

Stigma

a social process leading to the devaluation of an individual or group(s) who over time come to be identified as embodying negative traits such as dirt, disorder, laziness, criminality or mental illness. Human Geographers are especially interested in the spatial practices by which stigmatized groups come to be separated from mainstream society — thus re-enforcing the boundaries between the 'normal' and the 'deviant'.

For example, I am older and I don't use my bike so often. I see less of the city from a car, partly because of a necessary focus on traffic management and partly because the radio tends to fill in much of the 'thinking space' of the journey with national and international issues. My kids have grown up – one now lives in Nottingham and the other is about to get her own place in Bristol. Early-morning routines have changed commensurately. I now have scope for trips to the gym, where I note that characteristics such as age, gender and embodiment become highly visible and sensitized, creating for some a place of display and confidence, but for others a place of stigma. The sounds and sights of the house have also changed. We are no longer subject to quite the same cultural invasions of US sport and music, although it would be foolish to ignore the pervasive influence of cable TV in this regard. Anyway, Chumbawumba has given way to Ash and Franz Ferdinand, and the departure of rap and hip-hop to Nottingham leaves an occasional space for Viv's Runrig or my Delerious? or Show of Hands. Also, there is a little more wall space for us to engage in nostalgic and fond reminders of precious places such as New Zealand and Khayelitsha – reminders that really do bring geographically distant situations actively into day-to-day life in Bristol, as does the more politically charged paraphernalia of the Trade Justice Movement campaign, which are also scattered around the place.

The city, too, is dynamic. The area around the university has become coffeeshopville and café/bar city, providing great venues for research meetings and thereby extending the spatial ambit of the university via cultural colonization from Milan or Seattle or Paris or Anyplace. Some serve fairly traded coffee too, allowing, where desired, a display of the moral self when in company … These and other changes reflect the pace and purpose of economic enculturation. The previously mentioned 'strip' of nearby pubs/cafés/clubs has been continually redressed and rebranded over the years so as constantly to re-energize the hedonisms of late-night youth culture. According to my local taxi driver, Whiteladies Road after midnight is more of a zoo than *the* Zoo. Other changes to the university area go almost unnoticed – for example, the demise of the department store, replaced by supermarket and bookshop at street level and gentrified apartments up above, and an expansive and expensive organic foodstore emphasizing from its city location that which is 'Fresh and Wild'. Sadly, 'Chuck' no longer sells the *Big Issue*. His death, in 2002, was barely noticed amidst continuing local political and media campaigns to clear beggars from the streets of the city. His pitch has been intermittently taken up by 'Des', who remembers Bristol as a 'city of compassion' but now reflects on how 'hard and mean' the atmosphere is in the experience of homeless people.

There is so much else that I could (and perhaps should) have mentioned. Never mind, these brief glimpses are sufficient to suggest everyday prompts about different dimensions of Human Geography. The journey encounters nature in many forms, and as Sarah Whatmore suggests in Chapter 1, nature is shaped by the human imagination and filtered by the categories and conventions – for example, pets, zoos, parklands, good and healthy food from good and healthy places – by which we represent ways of seeing the components and landscapes of nature in our culture. Culture–nature relations, then, lie at the heart of our everyday (as well as more intermittent) experiences.

So, too, are relations between society and space. In travelling from home through suburb and key street routes, my narratives are jam-packed with references to gender class and race – some of which are intended, and some suggested by your own powers of interpretation. In Chapter 2, Susan Smith shows how spatial patterns can reflect social structures, and how spatial processes can be used as an index of social relations. However, she warns that social categories cannot be taken for granted. Such categories are constructed socially, politically, culturally, and are mediated by the organization of space. Thus a leafy suburb might be thought of as geographically and socially different from an inner-city housing estate, but equally 'Chuck' and then 'Des' occupy a socially constructed position of difference from those who pass by only inches from them. Moreover, we can no longer rely on two-dimensional maps of society and space. Beyond the obvious, there is complexity, ambiguity and multi-dimensional identity. Class, race and gender, for example, will cross-cut and intersect in different ways at different times and places.

Equally, two-dimensional geographies of place can no longer suffice. Phil Crang, in Chapter 3, discusses the relations between the global and the local, and the sights, sounds, histories and commodities of the global crop up time and again in the local story of my journey to work. Local places get their distinctive character from their past and present connections to the rest of the world, and therefore we need a global sense of the local. Conversely, global flows of information, ideas, money, people and things are routed into local geographies. We therefore also need a local sense of the global.

'Structures' are often hidden in the story – the invisible skeleton that restricts and permits all kind of life-opportunities in our society. However, the actions of governments and the associated agencies of governance, the police, the army, financial institutions, and so on, can contribute structural constraints and opportunities within which human beings make their decisions and non-decisions. Mark Goodwin's account of control and freedom in Chapter 4 suggests a very important dimension of who gets what, where, how and why in the everyday human geographies of our lives and the lives of others. These geographies can be seen both from the outside looking in and from the inside looking out.

In Chapter 5, Paul Cloke explores the importance of 'self' and 'other' in these various lookings. Being reflexive about the self is a vital part of understanding how our knowledge of human geographies is situated. Our experience, politics, spirituality, identities, and so on, can add to our stories about the world, and denying their importance in search of 'objectivity' could well be dishonest. My journey to work will not be the same as yours, even if it follows much the same route. However, there is also a danger that we only see the world in terms of our selves and those who are the same as us, thus creating categories of 'otherness' according to the essential characteristics of our selves. What escapes us are other 'others' – those who we cannot categorize or pigeonhole; those who surprise us and cannot be accommodated in our organization of knowledge.

Some 'othering' is presented to us by the multitude of images that intersect with the real experiences of people and places. In Chapter 6, Mike Crang discusses the charts, graphs, maps, pictures, films, and so on, that provide ideas of bad image and good image in terms of specific people and places. In the travel agents' window, the wall posters, the output of news and entertainment media, and even the mental map of the journey to work, images can be deliberately promoted, managed or altered so as to suggest understandings of the world on which people act. People inhabit these worlds of images, and we certainly need to understand what role images play in the construction of geographical knowledge.

There are, however, other really important dimensions of how Human Geography can present understandings of how knowledge about the world is constructed. Geraldine Pratt, in Chapter 7, discusses how differences between masculine and feminine ways of bodily comportment lead to variations in self-perception and cognitive ability (especially spatial awareness). So the capacity to explore and know our environment can be conditioned, for example, by gendered (as well as racialized) geographies of fear and safety that characterize local places such as the Downs in Bristol. She argues that much of women's experience has long been ignored by Human Geographers, with the result that different types of masculinities have been formative in the production of geographical knowledge. It is therefore crucial that we seek to situate knowledge (see Chapter 5) so as to acknowledge the validity of a range of perspectives.

Another key dimension by which the knowledge base of Human Geography has been formulated has been the seeming distinction between scientific and other approaches. In Chapter 8, David Gilbert shows how we need to grasp the complex history of Human Geography so as to understand the subject not as a fixed way of seeing the world, but as a changing and contested tradition. My journey to work, then, can be presented and understood differently according to whether the focus is on travel patterns or on a more experiential view of the city. David's chapter details one significant element of this diversity of focus – the differences between those Human Geographers who are interested in scientific and quantitative approaches to spatial modelling, and those who have preferred to develop a critical social science dealing more qualitatively with issues of agency, meaning, power and positionality, and with the traditional interests of the humanities. Again, the key here is not to view such differences as entrenched, fixed positions (even if sometimes that's how they seem). These are elements of Human Geography that will continue to change and be contested, with many researchers already looking to find ways of making the boundaries between science and social science more porous.

In the final chapter in this part of the book, Lynn Staeheli and Don Mitchell tackle the question of the relevance of our human geographies. How, for example, can my research on urban homelessness connect with the practical life-issues of people like 'Chuck' and 'Des'? How can your studies in Human Geography be relevant to the 'real' world? As Lynn and Don point out, there are many ways of being relevant, but each is inherently political. Although some people link theoretical work with lack of relevance, this chapter argues that even highly theoretical work *can* be relevant, but it depends on the ability of researchers to translate their arguments into language that can be understood by the community, by business, and so on. Overall, they urge us to recognize Human Geography's politically important role in helping people to understand the worlds they live in.

The nine chapters in this part of the book on 'Foundations', then, represent the very stuff of lively, interpretative, relevant and accessible human geographies. They help us to think through some of the recurring questions and issues involved in understanding the interconnections of people and places, and they help us to place ourselves in the picture as well. Far from being the 'boring theoretical stuff', they offer some keys with which to unlock thoughtful and nuanced accounts of everyday life. Enjoy!

CHAPTER 1
CULTURE–NATURE

Sarah Whatmore

INTRODUCTION

Has anyone noticed how many television wildlife programmes seem to be scheduled around mealtimes? It's a mundane coincidence that illustrates just one of the ways in which we confront the tricky borders between culture and nature in our everyday lives. The feeding habits of the creatures on display and the food on the viewer's fork collide momentarily in millions of homes. In that moment, the cordon separating the things we call 'natural' from those we call 'cultural' loses its grip. Which is on the screen and which on the plate? At first glance, the big cat tearing into the flesh of its prey seems to embody nature at its most elemental – a world apart. But look again. This vision of nature 'red in tooth and claw' has been carefully framed by the hidden crews and technologies of film-making. They in turn are shaped by the conventions of science and television, which establish our expectations of how a particular type of animal should eat and which aspects of feeding make good viewing. The meal in front of us, on the other hand, is more obviously of human making. But on closer inspection we cannot fail to be reminded that, however *haut* the cuisine or industrial the ingredients, we share the metabolic urges of our animal kin. Culture and nature, it seems, are not so easy to pin down.

Geography, as we are constantly being reminded, asserts itself as a subject uniquely concerned with this interface between human culture and natural environment. While the overt sexism of exploring 'Man's role in changing the face of the earth' (Thomas *et al.*, 1956) may have become outmoded (or at least better disguised), this classic description of the geographical project has lost none of its appeal (see, for example, Simmons, 1996). But it has also become shorthand for one of the underlying difficulties with the way the discipline is organized. The assumption that everything we encounter in the world already belongs either to 'culture' or to 'nature' has become entrenched in the division between 'human' and 'physical' geography, and reinforced by the faltering conversation between them. As a result, even as geographers set about trafficking between culture and nature, a fundamental asymmetry in the treatment of the things assigned to these categories has been smuggled into the enterprise. Geography, like history, becomes the story of exclusively human activity and invention played out over, and through, an inert bedrock of matter and objects made up of everything else.

This division of the world into two all-encompassing and mutually exclusive kinds of things, the so-called culture–nature *binary*, casts a long shadow over the way we imagine and live in it. It has not always been so and does not hold universal sway today. Rather, it can be traced to the European **Enlightenment** which, beginning in the fifteenth and sixteenth centuries, came to embrace the world through networks of commerce, empire and science. The geographical tradition of exploration and expedition played an important role in extending and mapping these networks

Enlightenment

a philosophical and intellectual movement usually dated to the seventeenth and eighteenth centuries and centred in Europe, which advanced the view that the world could be rendered knowable and explained systematically by the application of rational thought (science). Revolutionary in its challenge to the religious beliefs and superstitions that then held sway, it has since been much criticized for projecting rationality as a universal, rather than situating reasoning processes in particular social and material contexts.

and has left us with a thoroughly *modern* sense of nature as the world that lies beyond their reach (Livingstone, 1992). From this European vantage point, nature comes to be associated with the places most remote from where 'we' are – like jungles and wildernesses or, more recently, nature reserves and national parks. The trouble is that, at the start of the twenty-first century, 'we' seem to be everywhere – from the hole in the ozone layer to the cloning of sheep. Where is this pristine nature to be found now? In this climate it is not surprising that geographers, like the rest of us, are having problems holding the line between the cultural and natural.

This chapter examines some of the ways in which contemporary Human Geography handles the relationship between culture and nature. The opening themes of food and wildlife are used to illustrate various approaches and interpretations, and to show the difference they make to the ways in which we understand and act in the world. The chapter focuses on two well-established kinds of account, which explore different aspects of the ways in which human societies have refashioned natural environments over time. It concludes by looking at the growing dissatisfaction with such accounts and their assumption that we can best make sense of the world by first setting ourselves apart from everything else in it.

SOCIAL CONSTRUCTIONS OF NATURE

We begin, then, with established efforts by Human Geographers to make sense of the ways in which the ideas, activities and devices of human societies reshape the natural world. To put it another way, Human Geographers have treated nature first and foremost as a **social construction** although, as we shall see, they disagree over what this means. Two different, but in some ways complementary, traditions of academic work have been particularly influential over the last 25 years or so. The first is the **Marxist** tradition, which has been concerned with the material transformation of nature as it is put to a variety of human uses under different conditions of production. The second is cultural geography, which has focused on the changing idea of nature, what it means to different societies and how they go about representing it in words and images.

Producing nature

Writing at the height of the industrial revolution in Europe in the mid-nineteenth century, Karl Marx observed the ways in which plants and animals were being physically transformed by farmers using careful selection and breeding methods to produce commercially more valuable crops and livestock (Marx, 1976 [1867]). The lesson he drew from this observation was that with the rise of industrial capitalism, those things that we are accustomed to think of as natural were increasingly becoming

Social construction

a set of specific meanings that become attributed to the characteristics and identities of people and places by common social or cultural usage. Social constructs will often represent a 'loaded' view of the subject, according to the sources from which, and the channels through which, ideas are circulated in society.

Marxist

social and economic theories influenced by the legacy of the leading nineteenth-century political philosopher, Karl Marx. Highly influential in the framing of critical geography, these theories focus on the organization of capitalist society and the social and environmental injustices that can be traced to it. *See also* CAPITALISM, MODE OF PRODUCTION, ALIENATION and COMMODIFICATION for examples of the influence of Marxist thinking in Human Geography.

FIGURE 1.1A
First nature. Seventeenth-century Spanish drawing of the Inca state of Tahuantinsuyu. Potatoes being laid up for storage

refashioned as the products of human labour. This apparently contradictory idea of 'the production of nature' has become a central theme for Human Geographers.

Noel Castree has identified three reasons for its geographical importance (1995). First, to acknowledge that nature is produced undermines the familiar, but misleading, idea that it is something fixed and unchanging. Instead we are forced to look at the specific ways in which human societies have interacted with natural environments in different times and places – from hunter-gatherer to post-industrial societies, from economies based on slave labour to those based on wage labour, for example. Second, it captures the double-edged sense in which the process of producing goods for human use and exchange simultaneously transforms the physical fabric of the natural world *and* people's relationship to it. For those of us whose idea of provisioning is stacking our shopping trolleys at the supermarket, it is difficult to imagine the intimate bonds that characterize societies in which the medicinal properties of plants or the seasonal habits of animals are part of everyday knowledge and practice. Third, it alerts us to the way in which capitalist production, in particular, seems to stop at nothing in its quest for profitability, turning landscapes, bodies and, these days, even the molecular structure of cells into marketable commodities.

Neil Smith's book *Uneven Development*, first published in 1983 and in a revised edition in 1990, has been one of the most influential elaborations of this analytical approach in contemporary Human Geography. Capitalism, he argues, for the first time in history puts human society in the driving seat, replacing God as the creative force fashioning the natural world. We can get more of the flavour of the argument from his own words.

" *In its constant drive to accumulate larger and larger quantities of social wealth under its control, capital transforms the shape of the entire world. No god-given stone is left unturned, no original relation with nature is unaltered, no living thing unaffected. Uneven development is the concrete process and pattern of the production of nature under capitalism. With the development of capitalism, human society has put itself at the centre of nature.* "

(1990: xiv)

This revolutionary social capacity to produce nature is termed *second nature* by Smith, and other Marxist geographers to distinguish it from nature in its 'God-given' or 'original' state, so-called *first nature*. These terms have an explicit historical dimension, marking off modern, or more particularly capitalist, societies from all those that have gone before in terms of their relationship with the natural world. In the same vein, a further transition is deemed to be going on today as we move towards postmodern social forms (see Chapter 2) accompanied by a *third nature* of computer-simulated and televisual landscapes and creatures.

The transition between first, second and third nature also has significant geographical dimensions, which are illustrated through the example of the potato in the three-part sequence of Figure 1.1. The potato arrived as an exotic curiosity from 'the new world' amongst the

FIGURE 1.1B
Second nature. Industrial potato cultivation in UK, 2000. Credit: Richard Morrell/Corbis

booty of fifteenth- and sixteenth-century explorers like Christopher Columbus and Walter Raleigh. Since then, the humble spud has become a staple of northern European diets and, in the guise of the McDonald's 'french fry', of a global fast-food cuisine. The image in Figure 1.1a dates from around 1600 and shows a drawing from Guaman Poma's encyclopaedic survey of the ancient Inca state of Tahuantinsuyu (in modern-day Peru) for the King of Spain. It shows sacks of potatoes transported by llamas being laid up for storage. It is the kind of image that from our own time seems to capture just what is meant by first nature – plants (and animals) in their 'original' state, remaining essentially unchanged by their encounter with a 'pre-modern' society. Figure 1.1b is a photograph of potato harvesting in Brittany in the 1980s. The large featureless field, the monotony of the crop and the presence of the tractor tell us that this is an industrial agricultural landscape – a readily recognizable picture of second nature, wearing its human fabrication on its sleeve. The third image, Figure 1.1c, is a cartoon illustrating some of the popular anxieties associated with the current transition to a third nature. Here, not only has the location and landscape of potato growing become a human artefact but the genetic structure of the potato plant itself has been mapped and engineered to enhance its commercial properties – in this case its size!

Representing nature

A rather different interpretation of what is meant by the social construction of nature is that associated with the cultural tradition of

"Who ordered the baked potato?"

FIGURE 1.1C
Third nature. A genetically engineered potato. Credit: Pugh/*The Times*, 31/7/97

SUMMARY

• Nature is socially constructed in the sense that it is transformed through the labour process and fashioned by the technologies and values of human production.

• From this perspective, nature–society relations are seen to have changed progressively over time from first (original) nature; to second (industrial) nature to today's third (virtual) nature.

Representation

the cultural practices and forms by which human societies interpret and portray the world around them and present themselves to others. In the case of the natural world, for example, these representations range from prehistoric cave paintings of the creatures that figured in the lives of early human groups to the televisual images and scientific models that shape our imaginations today. *See also* DISCOURSE.

Human Geography. In this geographical enterprise the natural world is understood to be shaped as powerfully by the human imagination as by any physical manipulation. This is because 'nature' does not come with handy labels naming its parts or making sense of itself, like a plant from the garden centre. Such naming and sense-making are the attributes of human cultures. The importance of this approach is that it forces us to recognize that our relationship with those aspects of the world we call natural is unavoidably filtered through the categories, technologies and conventions of human **representation** in particular times and places. As Alex Wilson, a Canadian landscape architect, puts it:

> *Our experience of the natural world – whether touring the Canadian Rockies, watching an animal show on TV, or working in our own gardens – is always mediated. It is always shaped by rhetorical constructs like photography, industry, advertising, and aesthetics, as well as by institutions like religion, tourism and education.*

(1992: 12)

For cultural geographers, then, nature itself is first and foremost a category of the human imagination, and therefore best treated as a part of culture.

This can be a rather unnerving starting point for those who look to nature as the reassuring bedrock of a 'real' world that stubs your toe when you trip over it, regardless of any attempt to 'imagine' it otherwise. And one could be forgiven for not taking it very seriously if cultural geographers were arguing that nature is 'just a figment of our imaginations'. But, of course, they are not. What they are saying is that the relationship between the 'real' and the 'imagined' is no less slippery than that between nature and culture (see Chapter 6). These arguments are brought to a head in the concept of *landscape*. In everyday speech, landscape refers both to physical places in which we encounter the natural world and to artistic representations of such encounters and places. Cultural geography builds on these ambiguities to direct attention to the ways in which the relationship between the two – the 'real' and the 'represented' landscapes of nature – is far from straightforward.

In their influential book *The Iconography of Landscape* (1988), Stephen Daniels and Denis Cosgrove suggest that landscape is a way of seeing the world which can take a variety of forms:

> *in paint on canvas, in writing on paper, in earth, stone, water and vegetation on the ground. A landscape park is more palpable but no more real, nor less imaginary, than a landscape painting or poem*

(1988: 1)

Whatever their form, these 'ways of seeing' the natural world share three common principles. The first of these is that the representation of nature is not a neutral process that simply produces a mirror image of a fixed external reality, like a photocopy. Rather, it is instrumental in constituting our sense of what the natural world is like. This is easy to accept for paintings or literature where we make allowance for 'artistic licence' in terms of the artist's vision and the technical qualities and stylistic conventions of their chosen medium – oils or poetry, say. But it holds equally well for natural history programme-making, or the geographical art of map-making, in which the nuts and bolts of the process of representation are less readily apparent or more actively hidden from view.

It follows that the second principle of landscape is not to take representations of the natural world at face value, however much they seem, or claim, to be 'true to life'. The 'real' and the 'represented' cannot be so surely distinguished or firmly held apart in the practical business of 'seeing the world'. The work of the imagination, for example, has begun before a single brush stroke has been made on the canvas. What has brought the artist to this particular spot and made it a worthy subject for painting? As much as anything else, it is an established repertoire of cultural reference points for interpreting the natural world that repeat and ricochet off one another down the ages, like the biblical imagery of the 'wilderness' or the 'ark'. Likewise, representations of the natural world shift effortlessly from being understood as depictions of what it *is* like, to being used as blueprints of what it *should be* like in the guise, for example, of management plans for the conservation or restoration of historic landscapes.

The third principle of landscape is that there are many incompatible ways of seeing the same natural phenomenon, event or environment. For example, the drawings and accounts of eighteenth- and nineteenth-century European colonists depicted Australia as a 'waste and barbarous' land. Yet this representation could hardly have been more at odds with the 'dreamtime' landscapes of its Aboriginal peoples whose communal stories and dances teem with plant and animal life. Such irreconcilable landscapes underline the importance of carefully situating different representations of the natural world, including our own, in the historical and social contexts that make them meaningful (see Chapter 11). They also alert us to the highly political nature of the representational process. British colonization and settlement of Australia were justified by treating it as an 'empty' continent. The prior claims and land rights of its Aboriginal inhabitants went unrecognized in the country's constitution and legal process until a historic ruling in the Australian High Court in 1992.

We can illustrate these points by returning to the case of natural history programmes that opened this chapter. Television wildlife documentaries are widely taken to 'tell it like it is', providing us with a direct lens on to nature's creatures and landscapes. But as David Attenborough, one of the world's leading wildlife film-makers, made clear in an interview with geographers in the early 1980s, 'there is precious little that is natural . . . in any film'. He goes on to explain why.

FIGURE 1.2
Taking a close-up of a lion. Credit: Michele Westmorland/Getty Images

> *You distort speed if you want to show things like plants growing, or look in detail at the way an animal moves. You distort light levels. You distort distribution, in the sense that you see dozens of different species in a jungle within a few minutes, so that the places seem to be teeming with life. You distort size by using close-up lenses. And you distort sound.*

(Burgess and Unwin, 1984: 103)

Figure 1.2 illustrates this more complex relationship between the 'real' and 'represented' landscapes of wildlife. On the left we catch a rare glimpse of the people and equipment that mediate between an animal and its celluloid image. It gives us some sense of the discomfort and risk that film-makers face to 'get the shot'. But look closely at the lion. She is within spitting distance of the cameraman yet completely uninterested in him and his paraphernalia. The reason is that this photograph was taken in Serengeti National Park, which has become a favoured location for filming African wildlife precisely because, after decades of intensive management and tourism, the animals have become habituated to human presence. Careful editing will be needed to make this animal and place live up to the standards of a documentary 'wildlife' landscape. Figure 1.3 adds a further twist. It shows the BBC Natural History Unit being caught out by a national newspaper over its filming of the Monarch butterfly for the series *Incredible Journeys*. In order to save money, the programme-makers decided not to travel to its native region in the Great Lakes of North America but to film captive-bred Monarchs which they had released into the comparable scenery of the English Lake District. Again, the film satisfies our sense of the wild aesthetically, but this time the representational process has left unknown consequences in its wake for both the butterflies and the regional ecology into which they were let loose.

FIGURE 1.3
The Monarch butterfly's journey to Lake Windermere. Credit: Jonathan Anstee/*The Independent on Sunday*, 17/11/96

SUMMARY

• Nature is socially constructed in the sense that it is shaped as powerfully by the human imagination as by any physical manipulation. Our relationships with nature are unavoidably filtered through the categories and conventions of human representation.

• From this perspective, the landscapes of nature are understood as 'ways of seeing' the world in which the 'real' and the 'imagined' are intricately interwoven.

ENLIVENING THE GEOGRAPHICAL LANDSCAPE

Whether their emphasis has been on its material transformation or on its changing meaning, Human Geographers have treated the natural world primarily as an object fashioned by the imperatives of human societies in particular times and places. Each perspective illuminates different aspects of the convoluted relationship between the things of human making (culture) and those that are not of our making (nature). But in different ways the creative energies of the earth itself, in rivers, soils, weather and oceans, and of the living plants and creatures assigned to 'nature', are eclipsed in both accounts. In their eagerness to stress the capitalist capacity for producing nature, the Marxist tradition, for example, too readily overlooks the active role of these natural entities and processes in making the geographies we inhabit. Likewise, the argument that our relationship to the natural world is always culturally mediated has tended to fix attention on the powers of the human imagination, ignoring the multitude of other lives and capacities bound up in the fashioning of landscapes.

In these marvellous worlds of exclusively human achievement nature appears destined to be relentlessly and comprehensively colonized by culture. Human Geography's long march from environmental determinism to social constructionism seems to have brought us, as the environmentalist Bill McKibben puts it, to 'the end of nature' (1990). Whatever their differences, both accounts of this triumph of human culture over the matter of nature are grounded in the assumption that the collective 'us' of human society is somehow removed from the rest of the world. Only by first placing it at a distance can human society be (re)connected to everything else on such asymmetrical terms as those between producer and product, or viewer and view (see also Chapter 5). These are geographies whose only subjects, or active inhabitants, are people, while everything consigned to nature becomes so much putty in our hands.

Such **humanist** geographies do not square with the anguish and infrastructure of environmental concern that characterizes the late twentieth century. In unimaginable and unforeseen ways the forcefulness of all manner of 'non-humans' has come to make itself felt in our social lives. From climate change to 'mad cow disease' there is a growing sense that our actions, and indifference to their consequences, are returning to haunt us. The popular face of this growing sensibility is illustrated by the image in Figure 1.4, which was circulating as a postcard at the Edinburgh Fringe Festival in 1995.

Likewise the pets and viruses, plants and wildlife that share the most urbanized of living spaces, and the peoples who over centuries have inhabited the deserts, jungles and swamplands where 'we' have seen only nature, make it apparent that 'the whole idea of nature as something separate from human experience is a lie' (Wilson, 1992: 13).

Over the past few years, there has been mounting unease about the ways in which geography has built this binary division between nature and

Humanist

an outlook or system of thought that emphasizes human, rather than divine or supranatural, powers in understanding the world. Associated with the ENLIGHTENMENT, humanism marks human beings off from other animals and living things by virtue of supposedly distinctive capacities for language and reasoning. While underscoring progressive social changes, like the idea of human rights, it is criticized for making universal claims about human nature; privileging the individual over the social relations of human being; and licensing human abuse of the natural world.

FIGURE 1.4
The cows come home. Credit: BSE
II/Edinburgh Festival, 1995

culture into its descriptions and explanations of the changing world. unease stems from several different concerns, not least the crippling effect this polarization had on the contribution that geography can make to informing more sustainable living practices (Adams, 1996). In Human Geography, it centres on a growing recognition of the intricate and dynamic ways in which people, technologies, organisms and geophysical processes are woven together in the making of spaces and places. Three of the most important currents in this rethinking of the 'human' in Human Geography give a flavour of things to come.

The first of these currents is concerned with showing that the idea of nature as a pristine space 'outside society' is a historical fallacy. This idea is so pervasive today that it is difficult for many of us to recognize it as a particular and contestable way of seeing the world. But historical geographers are helping to expose the ways in which the presence of native peoples was actively erased from the landscapes that came to be seen as wildernesses in colonial European eyes, and that are now revered by many environmentalists as remnants of 'pristine' nature (Cronon, 1995). Try looking again at the image of 'first nature' potatoes in Figure 1.1a, in this light.

The second current extends this historical repudiation of the separation of human society and the natural world by paying close attention to the mixed-up, mobile lives of people, plants and animals in our own everyday lives. The place of animals has largely fallen off – or, more accurately, between – the agendas of contemporary human and physical geography. But a new focus on 'animal geographies' is emerging that seeks to demonstrate the ways in which they are caught up in all manner of social networks from the wildlife safari to the city zoo, the international pet trade to factory farming, which disconcert our assumptions about their 'natural' place in the world (Philo and Wilbert, 2002).

Finally, and most provocatively, a third current of work against the grain of the nature–culture binary is trying to come to terms with the ways in which the seemingly hard-and-fast categories of human, animal and machine are becoming blurred. This blurring is achieved by technologies like genetic engineering and artificial intelligence which are seen to recombine the qualities associated with these categories in new forms, such as transgenic organisms, bionic enhancements and the like (Luke, 1997). Here, the body is emerging as an important new site for geographical research in ways that force us to rethink the 'human' in Human Geography as much as the 'nature' of the world out there (Whatmore, 1999). Returning again to the example of food, Figure 1.5 illustrates the

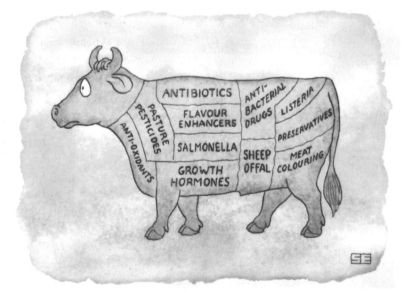

FIGURE 1.5
Mapping hybrid body spaces. Credit: Stan Eales

ways in which body spaces are being reorganized at the most intimate of scales. Where does nature end and culture start for this cow?

Human Geography has come a long way from defining itself as the study of 'man's [*sic*] role in changing the face of the earth'. The geographies now emerging challenge us to look again at how and where we draw the line between culture and nature, and to recognize that this densely and diversely inhabited planet is a much more unruly place than these categories admit.

DISCUSSION POINTS

1. In what senses has nature been understood as 'socially constructed'?

2. On what grounds have social constructionist accounts of the natural world been critiqued in recent geographical work?

3. Discuss some of the ways in which 'non-humans' are now being incorporated into the fabric of 'human' geography.

FURTHER READING

Anderson, K. (1997) A walk on the wildside. *Progress in Human Geography*, **21(4), 63–85.**

A thorough review of geographical work on domestication as one of the longest-running processes connecting human, animal and plant life worlds in new ways and helping to put the novelty of genetic engineering into historical perspective.

Cronon, W. (1995) The trouble with wilderness: or getting back to the wrong nature. In Cronon, W. (ed.) *Uncommon ground: towards reinventing nature.* **New York: W.W. Norton, 69–90.**

A very readable piece by an eminent US environmental historian, which reflects on both the intellectual and political problems of treating nature as 'outside' culture.

Luke, T. (1997) At the end of nature: cyborgs, 'humachines' and environments in postmodernity. *Environment and Planning*, **A(29), 1367–80.**

A difficult piece written with more than a hint of irony at the hyperbole with which some current writing about genetic engineering, artificial intelligence and the like are

breaking down conventional boundaries between 'nature' and 'culture'. Worth the effort to get a sense of what the geographies of 'third nature' might look like.

McKibben, B. (1990) *The end of nature.* **Harmondsworth: Penguin.**

This popular 'bestseller' argues that nature in its 'true' sense as a 'separate realm' has been eradicated by the relentless industrialization of human society. It is a passionate example of an environmental politics premised on maintaining the distinction between nature and culture. It is short and worth reading in its entirety, but the basic case is set out in Part 1.

Wilson, A. (1992) *The culture of nature.* **London: Routledge.**

Written by a Canadian landscape designer, this book is a visual and literary feast concerned with the numerous ways in which nature and culture shape each other in post-war North American landscapes. The introduction and chapters on nature films (4) and nature parks (7) are particularly good.

CHAPTER 2
SOCIETY–SPACE

Susan J. Smith

INTRODUCTION

Each of us is unique: a distinctive blend of genetic materials, physical features, personality traits and social skills with our own particular biographies and life paths. Nevertheless, there are at least some characteristics that we share with other people. Sometimes these shared characteristics have little bearing on our sense of well-being or access to resources. I am one of thousands of people who have red hair, blue eyes and write with their left hand. As far as I know, this makes no difference to my salary, housing opportunities, credit rating, health or likelihood of being burgled.

Nevertheless, there are a surprising number of shared characteristics that do affect our life chances. Whether we have particular health conditions or impairments, how the markings on our bodies are racialized and sexualized, our religious, national, local and familial affiliations, and even whether we are tall or short, can have a profound impact on what we get out of life. So although we may experience ourselves as individuals, it is important to recognize that people are often grouped, or structured, into social categories. This is not a simple process: people align with, or are assigned to multiple affiliations, and some markers matter more than others in different times and places. Nevertheless, it is always the case that people's lives can be enhanced or impaired not by how hard they work, by how nice they are or by whether they are exceptionally lucky or peculiarly accident-prone, but simply because they are assigned to, or choose to identify with, one group of people, or one set of places, rather than another.

These processes of social differentiation and unequalization do not, however, occur 'naturally'. They are a product of how power and resources – which may be both real (money, cars, homes) and symbolic (a question of how people think, and what they take for granted) – are struggled over and manipulated. Moreover, these struggles do not occur on the head of a pin. They take place. Just as history is relevant to an understanding of the present, so geography matters: in accounts of how people identify themselves; in narratives on the way they experience and reference others; in explaining why certain social characteristics are salient and others are understated, in particular places and at certain times. To illustrate this, the following pages provide an overview of the different ways in which Human Geographers have attempted to understand the links between the structuring of society and the materiality and meaning of space. These (three) ways are summarized in Table 2.1. Their strengths are discussed in the text; some limitations are flagged in Table 2.2.

FROM SOCIETY TO SPACE

Perhaps the simplest way to conceptualize the interaction of society with space is to regard spatial arrangements as a more or less straightforward reflection of social divisions. This simplicity, though deceptive, is a useful starting point. People from high income groups, for example, can afford to pay more for housing than people from low income groups. The costs and quality of housing vary over space, and it follows that those who can, will pay more for attractive homes in pleasant environments and well-serviced neighbourhoods. Because of this, people with high incomes tend to cluster in the same kinds of spaces, and these spaces are generally separated from the neighbourhoods where poorer people live. Thus it is that income inequalities are expressed in spatial arrangements. Society is mapped on to space.

In practice the picture is more complex than this, not least because the straightforward relationship between income and ability to pay is cross-cut by other factors. For example, discrimination in the housing system has, in many countries, meant that for a given income band, 'white' households secure access to better goods, services and resources than households from most other racialized groups. This is true even in societies (like the north-west European welfare states) that rely on welfare transfers to compensate in cash or kind when groups lose out because they cannot compete in the marketplace. Women, gay and lesbian, bisexual and asexual people, people whose physical or mental capabilities are impaired, and older people may be disadvantaged (relative to male, heterosexual, fit, healthy, younger people) in much the same way. Nevertheless these 'complications' do not compromise the basic argument: all these social divisions have some kind of spatial expression, in uneven residential patterns, unequal workplaces, and in the segregation of all those public, private, personal, learning, caring and recreational places positioned between labour markets and housing systems.

This first approach to linking society with space has a great deal of common-sense appeal. Indeed, the idea of reading spatial arrangements as an index of social processes formed part of the immensely exciting, fundamentally pragmatic, 'spatial turn' in sociological thought that occurred towards the end of the nineteenth century. The question on people's lips was how to handle the enormous complexity of social life in the interests not only of developing social theory but, in particular, of devising public policy. The answer, voiced most explicitly by the philosopher Georg Simmel (b. 1855) in an eclectic series of books and articles, was to position society in space. Space provided a medium that 'fixed' social processes long enough for them to be scrutinized by scholars and policy-makers.

Simmel's ideas were enthusiastically taken up by his student Robert Park, who revolutionized sociological and ecological research at the University of Chicago in the early twentieth century. He formalized the notion that spatial arrangements could be used to simplify the complexity of the social world. His argument, set out in an influential essay on 'The city as a spatial pattern and a moral order' (1926), was that spatial patterns, unlike social processes, are tangible, visible and measurable phenomena. If the teeming chaos of society could (temporarily) be fixed

Patriarchy
a social system in which men oppress and exploit women. The term was first coined in analyses of households headed by men and organized to the benefit of those 'patriarchs' (for example, through an unequal division of domestic work, or through women's marriage vows 'to obey', or through the legality of rape by husband of wife). However, the term is now used in a wider sense to think about how unequal power relations between men and women are established through realms stretching from the social organization of reproduction and childcare, to the organization of paid work, the operations of the state, cultural understandings of GENDER differences, the regulation of human SEXUALITY, and men's violence towards women.

Capitalism

an economic system in which the production and distribution of goods is organized around the profit motive (*see* CAPITAL ACCUMULATION) and characterized by marked inequalities in the social division of work and wealth between private owners of the materials and tools of production (capital) and those who work for them to make a living (labour) (*see* CLASS).

Colonialism

the rule of a NATION-STATE or other political power over another, subordinated, people and place. This domination is established and maintained through political structures, but may also shape economic and cultural relations. *See also* NEO-COLONIALISM and IMPERIALISM.

Other, Otherness

usually typographically capitalized, an Other is that person or entity that is understood as opposite or different to oneself; Otherness is the quality of difference which that Other possesses. A rather abstract conceptual couplet, potentially applicable at scales varying from the individual person to the global political bloc, these terms have been used in Human Geography to emphasize how ideas about human and geographical difference are structured through oppositions of the Self/Same versus the Other/Different. They also stress how the Other is often defined in terms of its relations to that Self – as its negative, everything it is not – rather than in its own terms. For example, a number of studies have examined how dominant ideas about GENDER are based on a logic in which Woman is Other to Man; how ideas about global politics and culture frame the East as Other to the West, and the South as Other to the North; and so on.

in space, he argued, it would be possible to learn more about social problems, and this knowledge would help devise appropriate solutions. If, as Park believed, 'human relations can always be reckoned, with more or less accuracy, in terms of distance' then it follows that 'society exhibits, in one of its aspects, characters that can be measured and described in mathematical formulas'. For Park, this pointed to 'the importance of location, position and mobility as indexes for measuring, describing and eventually explaining social phenomena'. Park's aim was not (as critics tend to suggest) to reduce society to space, but to use space pragmatically, to pick out those aspects of social life relevant to the problem at hand.

Park's pragmatism, combined with Simmel's formalism, inspired the branch of quantitative social science known as 'spatial sociology' – a term popularized by Ceri Peach in his collection of essays on urban social segregation (1975). Here Peach describes Park's (1926) essay as 'the fountainhead from which all else springs', and his own 'basic hypothesis' flows directly from it:

> the greater the degree of difference between the spatial distributions of groups within an urban area, the greater their social distance from each other . . .
>
> degrees of spatial similarity between socially defined groups are correlates . . . of the degree of social interaction between those groups . . .
>
> From the overall, spatial, residential mix of groups within urban areas, one can deduce the strengths of social divisions between those groups . . .

The basic thinking about society and space built into this approach is laid out in Table 2.1, column 1. Its mix of simplicity and quantification lent it enormous practical appeal: using a range of easy to calculate and simple to interpret indices, social researchers were able to put a figure on the extent of spatial dissimilarity, segregation and isolation of different social groups at a variety of scales. Most notably this approach was drawn into debates over the patterning of residential space where it had an important bearing on the politics of segregation. In the USA in particular, the notion that spatial separation is an index of social inequality, that residential mixing is the key to 'racial' integration, and that 'racial' integration is the route to civil rights, has been enormously influential. The findings of a spatial sociology approach to social life thus underpinned a bitter debate over school bussing as well as a mountain of legislation and case law over the imposition of barriers to open housing.

It has to be said that the scramble to use growing (though by today's standards very modest) computer power to apply new statistical techniques to newly available machine-readable census data led to a lot of inconclusive number-crunching. On the other hand, in places as far apart as Britain, Canada and the USA, not to mention the 'special' case of South Africa, analysts indebted at least partly to this line of thinking have drawn on a range of empirical evidence to argue persuasively that spatial patterns contain and express a geography of racism. In this body of work, residential segregation is exposed not just as the legacy of an imperialist, colonial and racist past but as testimony to the flexibility, adaptability and currency of

Table 2.1. Three ways of exploring the links between society and space

From society to space	The spatial construction of society	Thirdspace
Spaces are scientific and geometric, filled with an accumulation of social facts, providing an accurate but simplified representation of a more complex 'real' world.	*Spaces* have a material reality and a symbolic significance and can take on a life of their own. Spatial patterns express but also shape social relations.	*Spaces* which those marginalized by racism, **patriarchy**, **capitalism**, **colonialism** and other oppressions choose as a speaking position.
Geographies that are concrete, quantifiable and mappable.	*Geographies* that are negotiated and struggled over.	*Geographies* that were made for one purpose are appropriate for another, redefined and occupied as a strategic (real or symbolic) location.
An explanatory framework which regards spatial patterns as an index and an outcome of social and political processes.	*An explanatory framework* which regards spatial patterns as informing and interacting with socio-economic processes.	*This is about being rather than explaining* – an approach which is emancipatory rather than predictive or interpretive.
Social categories and social identities are given. The social distances between groups are expressed in spatial separation; social interaction is signalled by spatial integration.	*Social categories* and identities are constructed through spatially discriminatory material practices (markets, institutions, systems of resource allocation) and cultural politics (struggles to control imaginations).	*Social categories* are resisted by those they are imposed on. Spaces on the margin provide a position from which to build open and flexible identities. Here commonalities are emphasized and differences tolerated.

racism (as one of many enduring discriminatory essentialisms): segregation is perhaps 'the highest stage of white supremacy' (Cell, 1982; Darden, 2004; Smith, 1989). There are, then, some important ways in which the organization of residential space can be interrogated as an expression of deep-seated material and political inequalities in socially divided societies.

This line of thinking has been extremely influential, especially in relation to the idea of 'race', though in principle there is no reason why it should not apply equally to other common and emerging essentialisms. However, there are some important reservations with, and limitations to, this way of working. In the previous edition of this book – with apologies to both Lewis Carroll and Livingston and Harrison (1981) – I illustrated these limitations by drawing parallels between geographers' quest to capture social relations in the container of space, and the sailors' adventure in Carroll's *The Hunting of the Snark*. This earlier edition contains a fuller critique of the conceptual limitations of some core ideas developed under the banner of 'spatial sociology'. The points are summarized in column 1 of Table 2.2. Despite clearly formulated goals and scientifically informed precision, geography's 'spatiologists' and Carroll's sailors made the same kinds of mistake. They made an error of substance (as we shall shortly see, their 'quarry' was not what they imagined it to be); they made a practical, methodological error (their equipment was not suited to the task at hand);

Table 2.2. Errors, limitations and reservations of human geographers' approaches to society and space

From society to space	The spatial construction of society	Thirdspace
ERROR OF SUBSTANCE: Socially constructed categories are depicted as 'real', fixed and mutually exclusive.	SUBSTANTIAL LIMITATION: Social categories are depicted as socially (and politically) constructed, but research continues to emphasize the binary divides between, e.g. 'black' and 'white', male and female, sick and well.	SUBSTANTIAL RESERVATION: Is the world as flexible and as open to people defining and redefining themselves as the concept of Thirdspace suggests?
METHODOLOGICAL ERROR: Spatial patterns are seen as independent of social processes (the spatial is set up as a measure of the social, but this could only work if the two really are separate). There are social relations that cannot be studied within the kind of spatial frameworks used (notably the social relations of gender difference).	METHODOLOGICAL LIMITATION: Spatial organization is implicated in the construction of social divisions, but in order to explore this, analysts are forced to work with concepts (such as the idea of race) or frameworks (the presumption of heterosexuality) whose potency they wish to challenge.	METHODOLOGICAL RESERVATION: Boundaries, borders, peripheries and other marginal spaces have become the fashionable positions from which to resist old social categories and create new identities. In practice, the radical potential of places on the margin may be open to question.
ETHICAL ERROR: Social categories are taken for granted. The reality of 'races', the division of society into economically unequal classes, and the conventional family form are regarded as the starting point of the analysis, not as the outcome of processes which remain to be explained.	ETHICAL LIMITATION: Continues to define social categories relative to one another (black in relation to white, women in relation to men, etc.). Can therefore imply that a particular, uneven, distribution of power is inevitable. Also criticized for remaining preoccupied with marginalized 'Others' (e.g. black identities) while taking privileged selves (e.g. whiteness) for granted.	ETHICAL RESERVATION: Is it right to deny the potency of well-established points of difference just at the moment when previously powerless peoples want to put them to use?

and they made an ethical error (hunting was not the way to deal with snarks – the idea that social categories and identities can be fixed, captured and displayed on a spatial canvas is in essence remarkably naïve). No wonder spatial sociology has been 'snarked' by a new spatial turn in social thought – it has all but 'vanished' into a style of thinking that, as we shall see in the next section, refuses to take either social categories or spatial structures for granted.

However, while it is no longer credible simply to interrogate the patterning of space for clues to the structure of society, it is ethically dangerous not to continue to critique the *mechanisms* that translate social differences into spatial outcomes. Society may not be neatly projected onto and indexed by space, but on the whole people do not travel through, or end up in, particular places simply by accident. People, who are themselves active in constructing their own histories, pathways and futures, are at the same time systematically routed towards some positions and steered away, or excluded, from others; they are placed, entrapped and displaced in subtle (and not so subtle), institutionally mediated, directly and indirectly discriminatory ways. Figure 2.1 points to some of the factors that come into play: the ideological norms in which the major markets and institutions are embedded; the ways these interact with, and interrupt, the fair operation of the housing system and the labour market; the way direct and indirect, personal and institutional discrimination open up the spaces in which to live, work, learn and be creative to some people, and close them down to others.

There is, then, still a case for interrogating placings, positions and locations for what they tell us about the fissuring, fracturing and scaling of social life. But this demands a shift from a descriptive to a *discrimination model* of how society maps on to space. This model is illustrated for the case of health inequalities in Smith and Easterlow (2005). The point they make is this. The geography of health inequalities is usually interpreted contextually: as an outcome of the uneven distribution of health risks. This is undoubtedly a correct assessment. But it is only half the picture. By drawing on the established wisdom of spatial sociology – that society maps on to space – it is possible and necessary to interrogate an old health divide for a new geography of health discrimination.

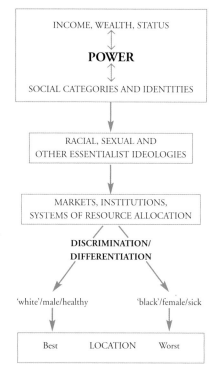

FIGURE 2.1
Exploring the mechanisms which translate social differences into spatial arrangements

SUMMARY

- One way of conceptualizing the relationship between society and space is to think of spatial patterns as a reflection of social structures, and to regard spatial processes as an index of social relations.

- This approach has, in the past, over-simplified both society and space. However, it is still useful when it focuses attention on the processes of empowerment and disempowerment, the struggles and negotiations, and the discriminatory mechanisms, that influence who ends up where, when and why.

THE SPATIAL CONSTRUCTION OF SOCIETY

The novelty of quantitative social geography wore off through the 1970s (though it is now making something of a comeback), and the theoretical limitations of social area analysis, factorial ecology and measures of spatial dissimilarity became increasingly evident. Pragmatism and policy relevance were eclipsed by radical theories that were (rightly) critical of the taken-for-granted assumptions built into a lot of empirical research. All this forced some reassessment of the relationships between society and space. For example, the question 'How are particular social groups spread across physical space?' took the character of social difference for granted. A more radical approach asked, 'How do spatial arrangements, how does place and position, *actively contribute* to the construction and reproduction of social identities?' So instead of talking about 'black' and 'white' and how they interact, juxtaposing the West against the rest, assuming (or invisibilizing) gender difference, analysts began to explore

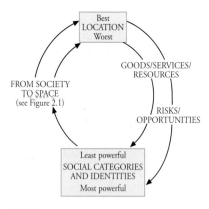

FIGURE 2.2
The spatial construction of society

where those categories came from, and how and why they are produced and reproduced. Human Geographers in particular became interested in the difference that space makes to these processes. Why, they ask, and how does geography – and specifically 'context' – matter for the construction of social life?

The nature of the difference in thinking that comes with this 'spatial constructionist' approach is illustrated in Figure 2.2, and summarized in Table 2.1, column 2. Instead of taking particular social categories for granted and mapping them on to space, analysts began to look at how socially divisive spatial arrangements mediate access to services and resources, underpin systematic differences in people's exposure both to risks and to opportunities, and so feed back into the web of power relationships that influence how people are categorized by others, and how they identify themselves.

This is both a contextual and constructionist approach to the relationship between society and space, and it is best illustrated by way of some examples.

The residential context of health

There is an enormous and growing literature on the links between health and place. Indeed to read this work you might be forgiven for thinking that the health divide is entirely a product of the uneven distribution of populations across pathogenic environments (on the one hand) and therapeutic landscapes (on the other). So health geographies offer an appealing starting point for deliberating on the way spatial inequalities shape social difference. Take, for example, the fine body of work developed by the MRC Social and Public Health Sciences Unit and the Department of Housing and Urban Research, at Glasgow University. In an extraordinary series of articles, these groups have pieced together the full range of local social, cultural, behavioural, physical and psycho-social environmental features likely to have health effects. They highlight the uneven distribution of health-relevant features across small areas, and show that these differences are reflected in neighbourhood variations in residents' health (this work is summarized in Smith and Easterlow, 2005). This amounts to a substantial platform from which to argue for the effects of place – or context – on health. Where people live matters: differential exposure to risks and unequal access to health-promoting environments underpin a spatially structured social divide in health prospects and profiles.

There is, of course, a sense in which this amounts to a rather conventional, even mildly outdated, geography (how environments affect health . . .). However, there has also always been a radical edge to this approach. Macintyre *et al.* (1991) issued a political as well as a scholarly challenge by advocating research and policies geared to collective contextual issues rather than individual attributes and behaviours. This perspective assigns responsibility to governments and collectivities, rather than individuals, for maintaining public health and it changed the tenor of core debates from a preoccupation with individual victim blaming to an interest in political responsibility. It is hard to overstate the importance of this at a time when new medical technologies, together with a wide range of diagnostic, prognostic and genetic testing, are all working towards the individualization of health histories, prospects and remedies.

Contextual geographies of health are probably the archetypical example of an approach concerned with how spatial arrangements (where people live) impact on social outcomes (their health conditions). This approach has chimed in neatly with a turn to area- and community-based policy-making. It has also inspired some interesting theorizing about the spatiality of inequality. However, it has had relatively little to say about whether and to what extent the uneven distribution of health risks (and associated health outcomes) goes on to affect people's health futures (though a new body of work on health-selective migration may be set to take this up), much less their other life chances and opportunities. This set of questions has, however, been posed by analysis concerned with more entrenched (or at least more widely recognized and researched) axes of social inequality. Let's consider these.

Geography and the construction of gender difference

Pratt and Hanson (1994) begin their analysis of women in paid work in Worcester, Massachusetts, in a fairly conventional way by developing the idea that the social characteristics of men and women help determine not only where they live and work, but also what these places are like. Society maps on to space. However, the study goes on to illustrate that once these social characteristics are rooted in space, they acquire a certain fixity. Spatial arrangements constrain social processes. In this example the characteristics acquired by different places so affect the employment prospects and practices within them that social divisions originating in the labour process are amplified through the organization of space. The result in Worcester is that social boundaries dividing men from women, and dividing different groups of women from each other, are reinforced, or hardened. Let's look at this more closely.

The case-study neighbourhoods in Worcester are differentiated by the distinctive mix of 'race', class, gender and work traditions within them. Once this mix is established, employers make locational choices on the basis of it, in order to recruit from the labour pool they regard as most suitable for their businesses. These locational decisions are partly based on stereotypes about the difference between men's and women's work, and partly on ideas about the suitability of different ethnic groups for particular kinds of task. As a result of these investment patterns, local labour markets with distinctive occupational niches develop. In this example we see how women workers in particular (because of the very local orientation of their lives) are positioned and segregated by the labour process. The most obvious social consequence of these spatial investment strategies is therefore a cementing of the gender boundary (through a spatial division of labour that plays on and feeds into the supposed differences between men and women). However, work practices are organized around class and race divisions as well, and a further outcome

Race

a criterion of social categorization that distinguishes different groups of people on the basis of particular secondary physical differences (such as skin colour). Human Geographers have studied questions of race in a number of ways including: (a) the extent, causes and implications of the spatial segregation of different racialized groups within cities, regions or nations; (b) the role played by geographical understandings of place and environment in the construction both of ideas of race per se and of ideas about particular races; and (c) the forms of racism and inequality that operate through these geographical patterns, processes and ideas. Human Geographers have played a key role in recognizing that racial categories, whilst having very real consequences for people's lives, cannot simply be assumed as biological realities, having instead to be recognized as SOCIAL CONSTRUCTIONS. *See also* ETHNICITY.

Class

a collection of people sharing the same economic position within society, and/or sharing the same social status and cultural tastes. The precise ways in which one's economic position – for example, as a worker, a capitalist or a member of the land-owning aristocracy – is related to one's social status or cultural tastes has been much debated. However, Human Geographers have studied class and its geographies from all these perspectives: as an economic, social and cultural structuring of society.

Gender

a criterion of social organization that distinguishes different groups of people on the basis of femininity or masculinity. In any one location, many masculinities and femininities interact. As a concept, gender is usually used in Human Geography in distinction to that of sex (i.e. femaleness and maleness) in order to emphasize the SOCIAL CONSTRUCTION of women's and men's roles, relations and identities. Human Geographers' accounts of the world have always been shaped through understandings of gender (*see* MASCULINISM) but explicit analyses of the geographies of gender and the gendering of geographies are comparatively recent, and associated with the growth of Feminist Geography (*see* FEMINISM).

of this particular geography of placement is a hardening of the social boundaries between different groups of women.

Pratt and Hanson's (1994) study shows, in short, that the organization of space (in this case, as shaped by the investment decisions of employees) plays a role in constructing social difference. This can take several forms, not only enhancing existing social divisions (here, between men and women) but also creating divisions within groups (in this case women) whose interests might at some level be thought of as similar. Crucially, this example shows that space and place are not simply containers in which people's social lives develop. Rather where people are placed has a direct bearing on those lives.

The spatial construction of 'race'

My own work on the politics of 'race' and residence in Britain follows a similar line of reasoning (Smith, 1989; 1993). First, it shows that there is a material basis to residential segregation. South Asians, African-Caribbeans, and their descendants are statistically over-represented in the worst homes and neighbourhoods in the inner areas of the major cities. This is a consequence both of their relative exclusion from the most buoyant sectors of the economy (resulting in low incomes and vulnerability to unemployment), and their historically limited access to the institutions of the welfare state (particularly access to the better-quality segments of public rented housing stock). Society and social inequality are mapped on to space.

However, *where* marginalized groups live is not simply a reflection of a history of social exclusion. In addition, this positioning actively affects future employment and housing options. This is because the process of economic restructuring that has occurred in the last 20 years has been spatially selective. Jobs have been lost in the regions and sectors of cities that South Asians, African-Caribbeans and other visible minorities are most likely to occupy. At the same time (and as part of the same process) these are the zones where property prices are lowest, house price appreciation is least, and where the options to move to take advantage of new employment opportunities are limited (the problem is compounded by spatial changes in the availability of public housing). So what was a spatial reflection of economic and social marginality becomes a spatial constraint on economic advance and social mobility (see Figure 2.3).

This problem of 'spatial mismatch' is also being hotly debated in relation to North American cities. Entrapment in spaces of deprivation can prevent already disadvantaged groups from taking advantage of opportunities opened up by the restructuring of the economy. In the British example, the organization of space contributes to a process of 'racialization' – of reiterating the salience of 'races' and making these social categories and the inequalities that divide them seem normal and inevitable. Space constructs society.

In this example, the process goes one step further, because in addition to the material differences that underpin patterns of segregation, British political culture has also formed an *image* of, and a discourse on, 'racial segregation'. Over the last half-century, this image has legitimized a range of public policies that – far from tackling the material inequalities that reproduce racial difference – has set the scene for things to get worse; for the divide between 'black' and 'white' Britain to harden, and for people's expectations of who should live, work and play where, to bear this in mind. (This process is not, of course, exclusive to Britain. The importance of ideas and images about the character of space for the construction and conduct of social life is, for example, further illustrated by Anderson (1991) in her work on Canadian constructions of 'Chinatown' and on the making of Sydney's 'Aboriginal Redfern'.)

The photographer Ingrid Pollard exposes the weight of this thinking in her exhibition 'Pastoral Interludes' (which is discussed at length by Kinsman, 1995). There are many ways in which the five photographs and their accompanying texts might be seen and interpreted, but for me it is the placing of 'black' figures in the 'white' English countryside that is so striking (see Figure 2.4). The juxtaposition is striking because it is not what we have been taught to expect. It is, after all, the image of the 'inner city' that most often accompanies publicly available photographs of black men and women. But Ingrid Pollard's photographs do more than simply illustrate the unexpected. They also challenge viewers to unpack the taken-for-granted assumptions that prompt them to see these images as in some way out of the ordinary. What has persuaded us – what has duped us – into thinking it is somehow 'normal' for black people to be absent from rural Britain?

FIGURE 2.3
Birmingham, England.
Credit: author's collection

FIGURE 2.4
'Pastoral Interlude' (1988) … it's as if the Black experience is only ever lived within the urban environment. I thought I liked the Lake District; where I wandered lonely as a Black face in a sea of white. A visit to the countryside is always accompanied by a feeling of unease; dread … feeling I don't belong. Walks through leafy glades with a baseball bat by my side …'
Credit: Ingrid Pollard. Courtesy of the artist.

The photographs further expose important injustices in the way we routinely conceptualize, and use, urban and rural spaces. Think, for example, about fear and anxiety. If you read newspapers or watch television, the spaces to fear – if you are 'white', which 'you' are often assumed to be – are those of the (implicitly 'black') inner city. Yet when Ingrid Pollard ventures into the countryside, she writes of an experience that 'is always accompanied by a feeling of dread'. There is another challenge here – to confront a division of space which is so socially divisive that many ordinary people feel uncomfortably out of place for much of the time.

In many ways, it could be argued that spatial constructionism is a more critical, sensitive and useful approach to the study of society and space than that adopted by the spatial sociologists. However, this approach, too, has its limitations, and these are summarized in Table 2.2, column 2. Perhaps the main reservation hinges around the tendency for academic research in this area to take privileged 'selves' for granted. 'Others' are, on the one hand, invisibilized: note the gender blindness of so much work for so many years; but consider, too, the identities of those who still lack adequate recognition. On the other hand, 'Others' may be too exclusivized. Consider, for example, the body of work concerned with the racialization and marginalization of those who are *not* 'white', yet that overlooks the extent to which this itself is the product of an equally racialized, if powerfully centralized, 'whiteness'. One response to these exclusions has been to turn attention to the meaning and materiality of 'whiteness' (see Bonnett, 1997), to the hidden agendas of masculinity, the tricky terrains of sexuality and erotic preference, the hidden essentials of ableism and healthism, and so on. A second response has been to rethink the presuppositions currently built into modern ideas about society, space, difference and inequality; to devise other ways of conceptualizing the links between them.

SUMMARY

- So far, we have identified two quite distinct ways of looking at the relationship between society and space (cf. Table 2.1, columns 1 and 2). The second of these focuses on how social categories that were once taken for granted are in fact socially and politically constructed.

- These processes of social construction are mediated by the organization of space. Both material practices (the operation of markets, institutions and systems of resource allocation) and cultural politics (disputes over the meaning of space) play a role. The result is that geographies of placement, displacement and entrapment reinforce social inequalities.

A THIRD WAY?

To overcome the limitations of both spatial sociology and spatial constructionism, feminist and post-colonial scholarship have developed a rather different way of thinking about society and space. This alternative approach encourages us to recognize not just that the social categories we once took for granted are not given in nature but made through practice, but also that this process of construction, this performance of identity, allows for the possibility of a redefinition and renegotiation of what the social world is like. People's identities may not be contained within one category or another: they may incorporate aspects of a number of categories; or they may develop in-between or on the boundary of categories; and this may make a nonsense of the idea of working with categories at all. This suggests that we need a third way of approaching the constitution of society and space.

Soja (1996) explores this third option in a book that he calls *Thirdspace*. He writes from a conviction that 'the spatial dimension of our lives has never been of greater practical and political relevance than it is today' (1996: 1). This in itself suggests that new ways of thinking about space as an element of society may be required. Indeed, Soja's book hints that the spatial turn at the end of the twentieth century may be even more radical and exciting than its nineteenth-century counterpart. At the very least, Soja argues, our old ways of thinking about space (what he calls first- and second-space thinking) can no longer accommodate the way the world works.

In practice, the third option has turned particular kinds of spaces into strategic locations on which new identities, new politics, indeed new economies, might be performed. Space has become a source of community for those oppressed by the social categories we have worked with for so long – by ideas about, and practices around, 'race', class, gender, sexuality, impairment, health, age, nation, region and colonization. Experiences of marginalization, together with spaces of exclusion, have been turned into a strategic resource. They have become a speaking position for voices that were previously unheard; a crucible of meaning, a material position, a real and imagined space in which old social categories are resisted and revised by new practices of identification.

The ideas informing this third approach are summarized in Table 2.1, column 3. Perhaps the most important point to note here is that the spaces referred to are metaphorical as well as geometric. Spaces on the margin *might* be material spaces – inner cities, spaces of unemployment, domestic spaces, segregated spaces – but they are also ways of thinking about how different groups are (and by implication how they should be) located relative to one another in the economic, political, social and cultural hierarchies. Thirdspace is created by those who reclaim these real and symbolic spaces of oppression, and make them into something else.

What does this mean for how we conceptualize society and its relationship with space? bell hooks, in her book *Yearnings* (1990), provides a useful starting point. Whereas white western scholars wrote about race and space, made black and white relational and understood black identities as a resistance to racism, bell hooks argues for African-American women that 'We must deny the oppressive other . . . *we* must determine how we will be'. To make this point, she argues that she is *choosing* marginality as the position from which to speak. She is not speaking as someone forced into a marginal position by her race and gender. She is inverting our idea of what it is to be marginal, and at the same time she is redefining what it is to be black and a woman.

This new location – this Thirdspace – articulates, and is defined by, what Homi Bhabha (1994) has called hybrid identities. All the common approaches to managing social difference in the 'western' world – the idea of 'race relations', the concept of 'multiculturalism' – are based on the assumption that when parties meet through relationships like colonialism, imperialism and the process of world economic development, their identities remain intact. But Bhabha points out that after such a meeting, no one can ever be the same. Each is changed by the other in the encounter, so all identities are hybrid.

BELL HOOKS IN THIRDSPACE

I was not speaking of a marginality one wishes to lose, to give up, but rather as a site one stays in, clings to even, because it nourishes one's capacity to resist. It offers the possibility of radical perspectives from which to see and create, to imagine alternatives, new worlds . . . [mine is] a message from that space in the margin which is a site of creativity and power, that inclusive space where we recover ourselves, where we move in solidarity to erase the category colonizer/colonized . . .
(1990: 149–52)

HOMI BHABHA IN THIRDSPACE

All forms of culture are continually in a process of hybridity. But for me the importance of hybridity is not to be able to trace two original moments from which the third emerges, rather hybridity to me is the 'third space' which enables other positions to emerge. This third space displaces the histories that constitute it, and sets up new structures of authority, new political initiatives, which are inadequately understood through the received wisdom . . . The process of cultural hybridity gives rise to something different, something new and unrecognisable, a new area of negotiation of meaning and representation . . .
(1991: 211)

FIGURE 2.5
Success, 1980 (acrylic, oil stick and gilt on wood) by Jean-Michel Basquiat (1960–1988). Credit: © ADAGP, Paris and DACS, London 1999/Bridgeman Art Library, London/New York

For Bhabha, the importance of this 'something new' is not just that it provides a different kind identity, but that it leaves the world of fixed categories and identities behind, opening up 'the possibility of a cultural hybridity that entertains difference without an assumed or imposed hierarchy' (1994: 4). This produces what Paul Gilroy describes as 'a different view of culture, one which accentuates its plastic, syncretic qualities and which does not see culture flowing into neat ethnic parcels but as a radically unfinished social process of self-definition and transformation' (1993: 61). Sometimes artists can be better than social scientists at getting this idea across. Rap music, for example, provides a space that can accommodate ideas about hybridity (Smith, 1997), while the work of Jean-Michel Basquiat – a 'black' painter entangled with a 'white' art establishment exploring his Haitian and Puerto Rican roots, his American heritage and his masculinity – reminds us forcefully of bell hooks' exhortation: 'we must determine how we will be' (see Figure 2.5).

The relevance of this third way is not limited only to identities emerging from the dichotomies drawn between 'black' and 'white' or 'colonizer'/'colonized'. Gillian Rose (1993) talks about the 'paradoxical space' occupied by feminist thought (paradoxical because of the way that feminism is trapped within, yet seeks to transcend, masculinist discourse). This, she says, is 'not so much a space of resistance as an entirely different geometry through which we can think power, knowledge, space and identity in critical and, hopefully, liberatory, ways' (1993: 159). Rose therefore talks about the performance by feminists of 'a different kind of space in which women need not be victims' (1993: 159) and in which femininity is mediated by other social identities. In the end Rose leads us towards a feminist geography that is less concerned about the man/woman boundary than about what feminism can be when it is not defined relative to masculinism or patriarchy; when it is defined in its own terms by those who identify with it, and who seek an alternative to the old gendered order.

Thirdspace seems to offer quite a different conceptualization of the constitution of society than the approaches discussed earlier. It turns our attention away from the givens of social categories and towards the strategic process of identification. It forces us to accept the complexity, ambiguity and multi-dimensionality of identity, and captures the way that class, gender, 'race' and other markers of difference, cross-cut and intersect in different ways at different times and places. The idea of Thirdspace may provide an opportunity to move beyond an historic preoccupation with social divisions – with what holds people apart – and

GILLIAN ROSE IN THIRDSPACE

These studies interpret women's lives not through the categories of production and reproduction, but through another kind of sociality . . . [this work has] created a women's space, but one which does not depend on an essentialist understanding of women, and in this manner it escapes the terms through which masculinist geography interprets space. The subject of feminism must be positioned in relation to social relations other than gender . . . in order to displace masculinism . . . There is a notion of things that are not representable in masculinist discourse but which women themselves may sense if not articulate. Feminist critique depends on a desire for something else.

(1993: 136–8)

to think about what is to be gained from a discourse of belonging. Perhaps this is what Soja (1996) has in mind when he talks of exploring Thirdspace with a view to engaging in 'some form of potentially emancipatory praxis, the translation of knowledge into action in a conscious – and consciously spatial – effort to improve the world in some significant way' (1996: 22).

Maybe the quest for belonging, the search for similarity, the hunt for commonality and community is what contains the next critical geography of society and space. Maybe it does not. Certainly the categories around which social theory, social geography and social policy have traditionally formed are being reworked in all kinds of ways. Claims to emancipation in some quarters make way in others for the recognition of neglected oppressions – around disability, health discrimination, genetic exclusion, new medicalizations, and so on.

These are complicated times, and there are already some reservations about the nature of Thirdspace. Is it really as radical and open, as liberating and as politically correct as it might at first seem (Table 2.2, column 3)? As we move from Thirdspace into the next dimension, my recommendation is that whenever we think we have something definitive to say about the vexed questions of social categorization, cultural identification or the structure of society and space, we should think about the Snark and its ill-fated pursuers. It is always a mistake to take the status quo for granted. Perhaps, with Rose (1993) we need to conclude that the best, and the least, we can hope for is 'a geography that acknowledges that the grounds of its knowledge are unstable, shifting, uncertain and, above all, contested . . .' (1993: 160).

SUMMARY

- Earlier social geographies are being challenged by groups that have, historically, been excluded from the 'mainstream' and who now claim the right to define themselves. Spaces on the margin provide a strategic location – a position of strength for those with new ideas about history, destiny, society and space.
- New performances of identity do not always coincide with the spatial, 'race', class and gender divisions that previously dominated the research agenda. A growing recognition of divisions and inequalities around genetic markers, health histories and prospects, bodily capabilities – around the politics of life itself – is forcing Human Geographers to think again about their presuppositions and their research methods.
- Thinking in thirds, performing identities, may hold the key to devising a geographically informed attempt to tackle long-standing social inequalities; but then again, it may not . . .

CONCLUSION

Like all attempts to classify knowledge into discrete bundles, the three approaches outlined in this chapter are to some extent caricatures. Every approach has some strengths; but they all come with problems and limitations. In every case there are analysts who use the approach wisely and constructively, mindful of its presuppositions and wary when interpreting results. In every case too, there are examples of bad practice, where ideas are applied uncritically or inappropriately, without adequate qualification, producing results that are theoretically and ethically suspect. It is important not to confuse the strengths and weaknesses of a particular approach with the merits or failings of particular applications.

It is tempting, nevertheless, to regard our three approaches to society and space as sequential and therefore progressive. Certainly, they developed chronologically and each new set of ideas grew out of well-founded dissatisfaction with the one that preceded it. But equally there are areas of overlap between, and debates within, these 'schools' of thought. As a result, none of the approaches is entirely redundant, and none is sufficient in itself to handle the links between society and space.

For example, labour markets and housing systems continue to segregate societies unequally with reference to ideas about race, class and gender. They can be disabling too, and there is increasing evidence that they are health-selective. To address this it is always going to be necessary to specify what forms inequality takes and how the mechanisms that produced it work. Likewise, we can only challenge the essentialism that lurks within social categories if we explore the way such categories are constructed and resisted. Finally, we can only move beyond the binary divisions between black and white, male and female, able and disabled if we recognize that old social categories can, in the end, be displaced by new forms, new practices, of identification. What we want from Human Geography today is not a consensus that any one approach to the study of society and space is inherently superior to another, but rather an awareness of when and where a particular approach is appropriate, and a sensitivity to what it can and cannot achieve.

DISCUSSION POINTS

1. Divisions around class, gender and race have been the focus of concern for both scholars and policy-makers for a century or more. How well does our understanding of the geography in these well-recognized markers of inequality prepare us for monitoring and managing some less well-known power struggles around, for example, ableism and healthism?

2. This chapter has referred to the life and work of artists to make some of its key points. To what extent can the ideas and practices of artists (exemplified in artworks and enacted through performance) add to, or elaborate on, our understandings of how space matters for societies?

3. Society and space are highly abstract concepts. What other ways of thinking help you to understand the core themes of this chapter? Does thinking with networks help link social relations into the material world, for example? Is it worth unpacking ideas around prejudice and discrimination as a way of better understanding the complex, direct and indirect, personal and institutionalized, intentional and inadvertent way in which social exclusion is practised? What theories of power help account for the differences and inequalities we have explored so far?

FURTHER READING

Peach, C. (ed.) (1975) *Urban social segregation.* **London: Longman.**

A classic collection of articles illustrating the various ways that 'spatial sociologists' have attempted to monitor social change.

Rose, G. (1993) *Feminism and geography.* **Cambridge: Polity Press.**

A cleverly argued and wide-ranging critique of how geographers have thought about space and society, mounted from a feminist perspective.

Smith, S.J. and Easterlow, D. (in press) The strange geography of health inequalities. *Transactions, Institute of British Geographers.*

An account of how the ideas in this chapter can be developed to recognize emerging inequalities.

Soja, E. (1996) *Thirdspace.* **Oxford: Blackwell.**

An important, if complex, account of the 'third way' of exploring society and space (see particularly Chapter 4).

CHAPTER 3
LOCAL–GLOBAL

Philip Crang

INTRODUCTION

Being a rather unimaginative soul, I always ask applicants to the geography course where I teach the same question: 'What would you say makes geography an interesting subject?' Unsurprisingly I also nearly always get pretty much the same answers. One of the most common is that through geography one gets to hear about, see pictures of, and maybe even go to a lot of different places. Geographers travel, whether that be literally, through an emphasis on fieldwork and various sorts of exploration, or more virtually in the form of slide shows and reportage. Pushed as to why that is a good thing, these students tend to talk about the pleasures of getting to know particular, distinctive places. They also often argue for the importance of learning about areas of the world and people of which one would otherwise be largely ignorant. These responses cut straight to the heart of the discipline, I think. They home in on a triumvirate of ideas that have long fostered Human Geography's understanding of itself as a distinctive intellectual endeavour. First, in the emphasis on the distinctive characters of particular places, they highlight the idea of the 'local'. Second, bound up with a desire to broaden horizons and foster a greater 'world awareness' is the idea of the 'global'. And third, central to this interest in both the local and global is an emphasis on 'difference' (between places and people). This chapter examines the relations between these three ideas: the local, the global and difference. It will, I hope, give a sense of how productive they have been, and can still be, for geographers. However, it also argues for critical reflection. Notions of the local, the global and difference are not as simple and obvious as they might at first seem. It is important to think carefully about each of these ideas, and perhaps even more so about how they relate to each other. If we do not, then we run the risk of simply reproducing conventional arguments about our world's geographies, without even realizing that that is what we are doing. We may close off other possible ways of thinking and acting. We may end up learning rather less about places, their particularities and their differences than we should as thoughtful 'travellers'.

I start by briefly outlining how and why ideas of the local and the global have been so important to Human Geography. I then set out three takes on local–global relations, each of which understands in its own way the differences between people and places that fascinate geographers.

LOCAL MATTERS, GLOBAL VISIONS

To start with the local, it, and associated notions such as place, locality and region, have long had a particular centrality in geographical imaginations, despite a tendency for their devaluation (at least until very recently) in other social and human sciences (Agnew, 1989). Many academic geographers have spent whole careers trying to document, understand and explain the individual 'personality' of an area (Dunbar, 1974; Gilbert, 1960). So, why is the local deemed so important to Human Geography's research and teaching? Nick Entrikin (1991; 1994) has argued that geographers have been interested in the local for three interrelated reasons. First, they have emphasized the actually existing variations in economy, society and culture between places; or what Entrikin terms the 'empirical significance of place'. Despite the homogenizing ambitions of the likes of McDonald's, everywhere is not the same. Landscapes vary. Life chances are materially affected by the lottery of location. Whether you happen to be born in Lagos or London or Los Angeles, or indeed in Compton or Beverly Hills, has an impact on the kind, and even length, of life you can expect. And location is not just something we encounter and deal with. It is part of us. Where we are is part of who we are. Most obviously, this is the case through the spatial partitioning of the world into nationalities (see Chapter 27), imaginative constructions that are part of our identities, so powerful as to get people to kill and die in their name. So, places and the differences between them can be seen to exist and have real effects.

But the local also matters in a second way. Spatial variations do not only exist. They are valued, or seen as a good thing, not least by Human Geographers. There is, then, what Entrikin calls a 'normative significance to place'. Sometimes this is expressed as a celebration of difference: whether out of a suspicion of the power of global, homogenizing forces ('the media', 'American multinationals', and so on); or out of a pleasure gleaned from experiencing variety and the unexpected. Sometimes the local is cherished for its communal forms of social organization, for embodying an ideal of small and democratic organizations (for a critical and suggestive review see Young, 1990). And sometimes this social idealization goes hand in hand with an environmental utopia of self-supporting, environmentally sustainable livelihoods (Schumacher, 1973), or at least a worry about the environmental impacts of translocal trade and supply networks (as in calls in the UK to reduce 'food miles', or the distance food travels to reach our plates, by re-localizing supply networks). But whether culturally, socially or environmentally framed, in all such arguments the local does not just matter. It matters because it is in some way 'good'.

There is a third importance attached to the local within Human Geography, according to Entrikin. This involves a concern with the impact of the local on the kinds of understanding or knowledges that geographers themselves produce; what he calls the '**epistemological** significance of place'. In part this involves a scepticism towards general theories that claim equal applicability everywhere. In equal measure it means a sensitivity to where knowledges come from (to their 'situatedness'). Geographers don't only know about localities, they produce local knowledges.

Epistemology, epistemological

epistemology is the study of knowledge, particularly with regard to its methods, scope and validity. This technical term from philosophy refers to differing ideas about what it is possible to know about the world and how it is possible to express that knowledge. Different academic disciplines and different general approaches in Geography are marked by distinctively different epistemologies. Human Geographers are interested in the epistemological questions raised by the geographical knowledges held both by academics and by ordinary people. In studying these epistemological questions Human Geographers seek to connect up questions of content (what kinds of things people know) with structures of belief (how and why they claim to know) and issues of authority (how and why these knowledges are valued and justified).

Discourse, discursive

drawing on the work of the French philosopher Michel Foucault, Human Geographers define discourses as ways of talking about, writing or otherwise representing the world and its geographies (*see also* REPRESENTATION). Discursive approaches to Human Geography emphasize the importance of these ways of representing. They are seen as shaping the realities of the worlds in which we live, rather than just being ways of portraying a reality that exists outside of language and thought. They are also seen as connected to questions of practice – that is, what people actually do – rather than being confined to a separate realm of images or ideas. More specifically, Human Geographers have stressed the different ways in which people have discursively constructed the world in different times and places, and examined how it is that particular ways of talking about, conceptualizing and acting on people and places come to be seen as natural and common-sensical in particular contexts.

Globalization

the economic, political, social and cultural processes whereby: (a) places across the globe are increasingly interconnected; (b) social relations and economic transactions increasingly occur at the intercontinental scale (*see* TRANSNATIONAL); and (c) the globe itself comes to be a recognizable geographical entity. As such, globalization does not mean everywhere in the world becomes the same. Nor is it an entirely even process; different places are differently connected into the world and view that world from different perspectives. Globalization has been occurring for several hundred years, but in the contemporary world the scale and extent of social, political and economic interpenetration appears to be qualitatively different to international networks in the past.

However, at the same time as having this local fixation, Human Geography is also determinedly global in its scope. Even as it values them, it also tries to break out of purely local knowledges through appeals to global awareness. Geographical interest in the global has been developed through a number of different 'discourses'. Let me draw out four. Figure 3.1 displays a picture of the world from each.

First, we can identify a discourse of *exploration*, driven by a desire to 'know the world'. Exploration was central to geography's early history – such that geography's development as a science, from the sixteenth century onwards, went hand in glove with European explorations to the farthest corners of the earth (Driver, 2001; Livingstone, 1992b; Stoddart, 1986). It still shapes some of the most popular parts of the subject – for example, the student and other 'expeditions' sponsored by the Royal Geographical Society in Britain, or the mass-circulation *National Geographic*'s promotional claim to give American readers a 'window to the world of exotic peoples and places' (cited in Lutz and Collins, 1993: xi). Second, there is a discourse of *development*, with its hope of 'improving the world'. Here, a world vision matters not only in order to rectify ignorance of the world's diversity, but also to explain and act against inequalities between North and South (see Chapters 13 and 14). Third, and more recently, there is the discourse of global *environmentalism*, with its passion for 'saving the world' against planetary threats such as global warming or ozone depletion (see Chapters 19, 20 and 21). Here, thinking globally is essential not only to recognize the scale of these problems, but also to understand the true environmental impacts of our local actions (so, when I switch on my electric kettle I need to be aware of the impact of my domestic energy use on CO_2 emissions). Finally, and not unrelatedly, there is a discourse of global *compression*, with an emphasis on the 'shrinking of the world' (see Harvey, 1989: 240–307). Made familiar through the corporate boasts of the likes of IBM ('solutions for a small planet'), the emphasis here is on the increasingly dense interconnections between people and places on other sides of the world from each other, whether through telecommunications, global flows of money, or migrations and other forms of travel. 'Globalization' is increasingly used as a label to describe such compression (for a very good critical review, see Allen, 1995), and in a globalized world our local lives are led on a global scale. The food we eat, the clothes we wear, the television programmes we watch, the cars we drive or bicycles we ride, all these materials of our mundane, everyday lives come to us through enormously complex and globally extensive production and retail systems.

So, there are many good reasons why Human Geography should not myopically focus on the local but also attend to the global: because global scale processes impact on, and result from, our local places and lives; because thinking globally allows us to compare, and even more usefully connect, our own lives and places to those of others; because the global stands for important, 'big' issues and processes that we cannot afford to ignore.

> *If as geographers we can get our heads out of the sands of our various minute concerns we will see the crisis which has overtaken us . . . The history of world population . . .: in 1750, . . . 730 million; 1850, . . .*

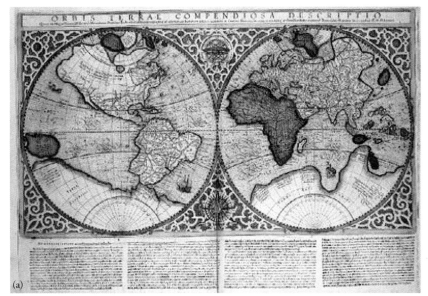

(c)

(d)

(a)

FIGURE 3.1

Four global visions. (a) the conversion of the spherical globe into a flat map is achieved here through a Mercator projection. Developed in the seventeenth century, the Mercator world map is ideal for exploration as a constant bearing appears as a straight line, but this is achieved by distorting sizes, which makes tropical regions look far smaller than they actually are. (b) the Peters projection, by contrast, is an equal area projection that distorts shape rather than size. First published in 1973, this projection was designed within development discourse to ensure the 'South' was given its proper global importance © Professor Arno Peters. (c) 'spaceship earth' is an icon of contemporary environmentalism, portraying a living whole without apparent national boundaries or other political divisions. (d) the shrinking earth of 'globalization' and telecommunicational hype. Credit: (a) Royal Geographical Society, UK/www.bridgeman.co.uk; (b) Oxford Cartographers/ Getty Images; (c) NASA; (d) Courtesy of DHL

(b)

1200 million; . . . the end of the century, 6000 million . . . Meanwhile environmental equilibrium is itself disturbed. The tropical rain forest destroyed at the rate of 1200 hectares an hour. Acid rain kills the temperate woodlands . . . Because of the greenhouse effect . . . sea-level around the world will rise . . . Quite frankly I have little patience with so-called geographers who ignore these challenges. **"**

(Stoddart, 1987: 334)

Human Geography is therefore characterized by a concern with *both* the local *and* the global. At times, these can be understood as competing scales of interest; as when calls are made for geographers to escape local trivia and address the really important global issues; or, conversely, when global accounts are criticized for their masking of local differences. But, the local and the global can also be seen as two sides of the same coin. Explorers set out across the world to find new 'locals' to study (and all too often to exploit and conquer) (on the connections of exploration, geography and imperialism, see Hudson, 1977; Driver, 1992; Smith and Godlewska, 1994). Environmentalists and multinational corporations both sloganize about 'thinking globally and acting locally'. So, how we understand and construct the global shapes our understanding of the local, and vice versa. In the second half of this chapter I therefore want to turn more directly to these relations between the local and the global. They can, I want to suggest, be thought of in a number of different ways. To illustrate, I will review three schematic accounts of local–global relations (see Fig. 3.2): the world as *mosaic*, the world as *system*, and the world as *network*.

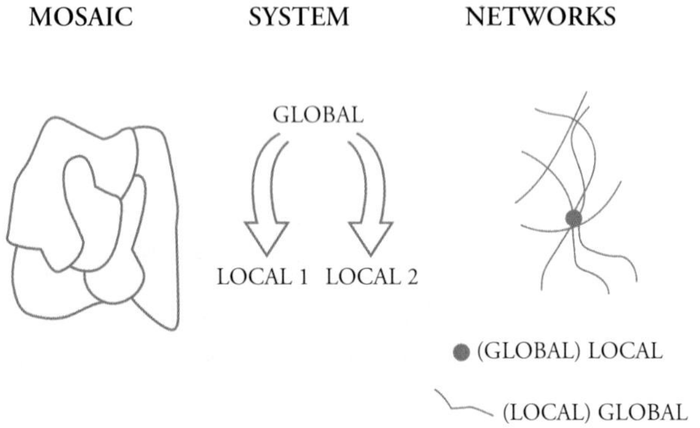

FIGURE 3.2
Figures of the local–global: mosaic, system and network

SUMMARY

- Human Geography has fashioned itself as a distinctive intellectual endeavour both through emphasizing its interest in *local* places and specificities, and through stressing various *global* concerns (for example, with exploration, development, global environmental change and global 'compression').

- Whilst the local and the global can be seen as alternative and competing scales of analysis, we need to recognize that they are always constructed in relationship to each other.

MOSAIC

One very popular way of thinking about Human Geographies is in terms of a mosaic, a collection of local peoples and places, each one being a piece in the broader global pattern. This pattern can be drawn out at a number of different scales, from neighbourhoods right up to whole continents. So, at the level of the city one could identify a patchwork of local areas, each characterized by different economies, residents and built environments. Think, for example, of portraits of the brutal contrasts in US cities between the 'hoods' and the 'subs', marked respectively by 'landscapes of decay and despair and landscapes of cash and comfort' (Riley, 1994: 151–2). Moving up a scale to the regional level, geographers, and others such as regional novelists and folklorists, have long evoked distinctive landscapes and connected them to distinct regional ways of life (Gilbert, 1972; Pocock, 1981). At the level of the nation the whole idea of nationalities depends upon constructing distinctive pieces of an international mosaic; establishing borders and distinguishing between this country and that country, our people and those foreigners. And on the supranational scale there are identifications of distinctive continental economic, political and cultural units (see Lewis and Wigen, 1997, for a critical analysis of this 'metageography').

In many ways, this notion of the geographic mosaic has been so influential (see Gregory, 1994: 34–46) that it can be hard for us to see it as anything other than common sense, a description of an obvious reality. Tourism, the world's largest industry, feeds off and actively constructs such an understanding, as it displays a world showcase of different destinations the holidaymaker can visit. But the mosaic is only one possible way of framing local–global geographies, and it is a very particular framing, with its own preoccupations and blind spots. Three features are especially important. First, it puts an emphasis on boundaries and borders. Geographical difference is seen in terms of distinct areas that can have lines drawn around them. Second, and relatedly, these areas are understood in terms of their unique characters, personalities or traditions. That is, each piece of the mosaic is seen as having distinctive 'contents', whether that be its people, culture, economic activities and/or landscape, which cohere into some sort of unified geographical identity. Third, this means that any intrusions into this distinctive area tend to be seen as a threat to its unique character. For an example one could think of worries about how the global predominance of American popular culture, from fast food to TV programmes, is destroying local cultures and producing one Americanized global monoculture, where everybody, wherever they are, eats Big Macs, drinks Coca-Cola and watches American soaps (see Peet, 1989).

FIGURE 3.3
Coca-colonization?
Credit: Anders Ryman/Corbis

All these features can be questioned evidentially. The world's geographical differences do not fit this neat model of the mosaic, and attempts to make them do so show just how rigid and unrealistic the model is. Apartheid in South Africa and ethnic cleansing in the former Yugoslavia would be examples of practices that have followed the mosaic and its logic of each different thing in its own different place to some brutal conclusions. Nor does the opening up of local places to global forces necessarily result in the destruction of difference. Take the example of American media products such as globally exported soap operas. Whilst living and researching in Trinidad the anthropologist Danny Miller was struck by the fact that he had to stop his research for an hour a day whilst everyone watched the daytime US soap *The Young and the Restless* (Miller, 1992). But this was not the sign of a homogenizing Americanization. In fact, Miller argues, 'paradoxically an imported soap opera has become a key instrument for forging a highly specific sense of Trinidadian culture' (1992: 165). For in the extensive chat about this soap, what viewers identified was not an alien American world, to be aspired to or despised, but themes that resonated with deep existing structures of Trinidadian experience. In particular, viewers liked the way it dramatized what they called 'bacchanal', or the confusion and emergence of hidden truths through scandals, something also central to other Trinidadian cultural forms such as Carnival. So, this globally distributed American soap actually helped produce a very distinctive, local Trinidadian sensibility. It was, as Miller concludes using a popular local expression, 'True True Trini'.

The problems with the figure of the mosaic are not only factual – they also stem from its political impulses and ramifications. To be fair, there are positive elements to the notion of the mosaic. Often underlying it is a desire both to recognize and respect differences; to appreciate, in both senses of the word, that everyone is not the same as you are, and that everywhere is not the same as here. But it is not enough just to applaud this appreciation of difference. We have to think about how the idea of difference is being constructed and used. To illustrate, let me take two examples of 'the world as mosaic' as constructed outside of the confines of academic Human Geography. The first is a piece of racism I overheard at a party a few years ago. I then lived in the East End of London, an area that has a significant British–Bengali population. At the party a white man was complaining about the number of 'Asian' families on the housing estate we were on (the usual racist rubbish about the smell of curries, and so on). 'I'm not a racist,' he then said, 'but they're taking over the place.' So he explained his hostility by saying it was not directed at people per se, but at people in the wrong place. People, then, who were upsetting a view of the world's mosaic in which white British people lived in the East End, and Bengalis lived in Bengal. The very idea of British, East End Bengalis did not fit. Now this, fairly typical, piece of white racism is not only nasty but nonsense. The East End has a long history of immigration, especially due to its past proximity to London's docks. Indeed, Britain as a whole is a country defined by waves of immigration and 'people taking over the place' (Romans, Normans, Saxons, Jutes, as well as hundreds of years of history of black Britons). What this appeal to a geographical mosaic does, then, is to fossilize difference and then use that fossilization as part of a defensive localism. It uses a particular way of thinking of local–global relations – recent waves of immigration upsetting a previously neat Human Geographic mosaic – to legitimate social and spatial exclusion.

A second example helps to explain how such fossilized ways of

Race

a criterion of social categorization that distinguishes different groups of people on the basis of particular secondary physical differences (such as skin colour). Human Geographers have studied questions of race in a number of ways including: (a) the extent, causes and implications of the spatial segregation of different racial groups within cities, regions or nations; (b) the role played by geographical understandings of place and environment in the construction both of ideas of race per se and of ideas about particular races; and (c) the forms of racism and inequality that operate through these geographical patterns, processes and ideas. Increasingly, Human Geographers have emphasized how racial categories, whilst having very real consequences for people's lives, cannot simply be assumed as biological realities, having instead to be recognized as SOCIAL CONSTRUCTIONS. *See also* ETHNICITY.

imagining the local–global came into being. It is the 1908 Franco-British Exhibition held at White City, London – an 'exhibition' of the world, its peoples and places, set up for both education and entertainment, and aimed at a mass market. The late nineteenth and early twentieth centuries saw a number of enormously popular exhibitions or world fairs in North America and Europe, which as they displayed scenes, objects and people from around the world also functioned to codify distinct national identities and legitimate national projects of imperialism. Figure 3.4 shows some of the pieces of the mosaic constructed for the exhibition at White City in 1908.

Colonialism

the rule of a NATION-STATE or other political power over another, subordinated, people and place. This domination is established and maintained through political structures, but may also shape economic and cultural relations. *See also* NEO-COLONIALISM and IMPERIALISM.

As Annie Coombes (1994) argues, to make sense of the Senegalese Village, the Algerian Pavilion, the Indian Palace and the Irish Village at White City, one first must recognize the logics underpinning the geographical mosaic that was being displayed – one of distinct peoples and places differentiated along ethnic and racial lines – and then contextualize these logics in the times and places of their production – in a western Europe where social elites were looking to consolidate popular affiliations to both the **nation-state** and to colonial empires (see **colonialism**). Central to these efforts was the idea of **race**. As Coombes puts it:

> *the colonial exhibition … [was] a site where the myth of a national unity was consummated in the public domain. Paradoxically, of course, the success of this ideal … relied on the painstaking elaboration of a series of 'differences' constituted along both ethnic and racial lines.*

(1994: 187)

FIGURE 3.4
Displaying a Human Geographical mosaic at the Franco–British Exhibition of 1908: the Algerian Pavilion, the Indian Palace and the Senegalese Village. Source: Coombes (1994). Credit: Hammersmith and Fulham Archives and Local History Centre

Nation-state

a form of political organization that involves (a) a set of institutions that govern the people within a particular TERRITORY (the state), and (b) that claims allegiance and legitimacy from those governed, and from other states, on the basis that they represent a group of people defined in cultural and political terms as a nation.

The appreciation of difference fostered by this exhibition involved, then, an active emphasis on the importance and interlinking of race and nationality (as echoed, 90 years later, at a party in Whitechapel, East London). The exhibition did not just display a world of differences, but through display was actively shaping them into particular forms. Those forms in turn have to be understood within a broader historical–geographical context, one where racism and national jingoism were crucial legitimations of the imperial status and ambitions of European powers.

So, whilst not without its merits – in particular its recognition of difference – the mosaic as a way of thinking about local–global relations is deeply problematic – not least because of *how* it recognizes difference. We need to think, then, about whether Human Geography can combine the local and the global in other ways.

SUMMARY

- A very common way of imagining local–global relations is to envision a world of many different local places and peoples, each being a piece in a wider Human Geographic mosaic.

- This constructs the local as a bounded area, made distinctive through the character of life and land within it. It also tends to construct global-scale processes as destructive to that local diversity.

- There are factual problems with this way of framing local–global relations. For example, local differences are not inevitably destroyed by global level processes; in fact they are often produced through them.

- There are also political dangers attached to it, in particular an impulse towards defensiveness and the exclusion of non-locals.

- The mosaic is only one way of imagining local–global relations, so rather than seeing it as a simple portrait of geographical reality the reasons for, and effects of, its use need to be analysed.

SYSTEM

One alternative way of thinking about local–global relations is to see local differences as produced by a global system. That is, the differences between places are not seen as a consequence of their internal qualities but as a result of their location within the wider world. The mosaic of geographical difference is not innate but made. We need to understand the processes and powers that make it. Perhaps the best examples of this argument come from within development studies.

To put it crudely, one way of thinking about the extreme differences, and inequalities, in wealth and life chances between different parts of the world would be to identify internal characteristics that explain these differences. So, we could say (and many do) that Europe and North America are so wealthy because of the economic innovation they have shown since the Industrial Revolution. And then we might argue that the Philippines, say, are comparatively so poor because of their lack of natural resources, or an inhospitable climate, or some deficiencies in their culture (e.g. endemic corruption or laziness). What this kind of explanation ignores, though, is the fact that Europe and the Philippines are not just separate places, they are places with long histories of interconnection through world political, economic and cultural systems. It excludes the possibility, then, that Europe and the Philippines are so different because of their relationships with each other rather than because of their internal qualities. To put it bluntly, maybe we need to think rather more about whether Europe is rich precisely because the Philippines are poor. That is a very simplistic assertion but it has its virtues. It sensitizes us to the idea that there is a set of global relations between local places. In emphasizing how global relations actively produce differences between places it reorients our efforts away from just documenting diversity (Europe and the USA are like this, the Philippines are like that) and towards understanding the processes of that *differentiation*.

Central to such efforts of understanding how and why differences are produced at the global scale has been work focused on the **world-system**. Here the world is treated as a single economic and social entity. At the heart of its operations is the capitalist world economy. This is how Jim Blaut puts it, in arguing against the idea of a special European character that has led to its relative economic success:

> *Capitalism arose as a world-scale process: as a world system. Capitalism became concentrated in Europe because colonialism gave Europeans the power both to develop their own society and to prevent development from occurring elsewhere. It is this dynamic of development and underdevelopment which mainly explains the modern world.*

(1993: 206)

World-system
an integrated international economic system, founded upon mercantile then industrial CAPITALISM, which originated in Europe around 1450 and spread to cover most of the world by 1900. World-systems analysis, which examines this system, treats the world as a single economic and social entity, the capitalist world economy.

Others will discuss the merits of this 'world-systems' approach in more detail. However, for our purposes, a more concrete example may help to show the importance, and limits, of its systemic view of local–global relations. That example is the world coconut market as portrayed by James Boyce (1992).

Boyce notes two main things about the global coconut trade in the period 1960–85: first, 'the Philippines is king' with over 50 per cent of world exports; second, the Filipino producers of coconuts do not seem to be doing very well out of this dominant market position. Understanding either of these facts requires a global systemic focus. The prevalence of coconut production in the Philippines would have to be traced back to Spanish colonization (for example, a 1642 edict for all 'indios' to plant coconut trees to supply caulk and rigging for the colonizers' galleons), to demand in the nineteenth century from European and North American soap and margarine manufacturers, and to US colonial control and post-colonial patronage in the twentieth century (which led to preferential tariff rates for Filipino coconut products in the US market until 1974). It reflects, then, an emergent international system in which the Philippines was positioned, by external powers, as a supplier of an agricultural commodity, whilst those powers used that commodity for their own purposes (for their ships or their manufacturing industries). Low rewards for this agricultural production reflect declining global terms of trade, such that each barrel of coconut oil exported in 1985 would buy only half the imports it would have in 1962 (see Table 3.1). The explanation for this decline is complex, but principally stems from the success of manufacturers of potential substitutes in the developed world – both

Table 3.1 Terms of trade for Philippine coconut oil, 1962–85

Year	(1972 = 100) Coconut oil export price index	Import price index	Terms of trade
1962	119.9	71.4	167.9
1963	133.7	76.2	175.5
1964	145.4	76.8	189.3
1965	159.8	78.1	204.6
1966	134.2	79.4	169.0
1967	142.3	81.2	175.2
1968	166.9	80.7	206.8
1969	140.1	82.7	169.4
1970	160.4	93.5	171.6
1971	143.9	95.5	150.7
1972	100.0	100.0	100.0
1973	198.8	128.8	154.3
1974	508.1	211.6	240.1
1975	208.7	219.6	95.0
1976	192.4	217.2	88.6
1977	296.8	241.2	123.1
1978	338.7	245.8	137.8
1979	512.6	270.1	189.8
1980	342.6	358.6	95.5
1981	284.3	398.6	71.3
1982	241.5	340.5	70.9
1983	286.8	342.4	83.8
1984	547.2	386.7	141.5
1985	295.7	363.8	81.3

Source: Boyce (1992)

ground nut oil producers and petro-chemical companies – at getting subsidies and protection from their governments, thereby depressing world prices for all traded fats and oils. That is, it is the political and economic power of developed-world producers and governments which means that the Filipino coconut industry gets an ever worse deal for its efforts. The world trading system not only differentiates through an international division of industries (you grow coconuts, we have petro-chemicals); it discriminates.

However, as well as stressing the global relations that have stimulated Filipino coconut production and worsened its terms of trade, Boyce's study also suggests some limits to purely global explanations. In particular, he stresses how the local trading relationships within the Philippines meant that whilst the majority of small growers reaped little reward, vast fortunes were made by a few powerful individuals. Under the guise of concern for small producers, the Marcos regime reorganized the industry to concentrate power in the hands of a single entity that controlled raw material purchases from farmers and marketing at home and overseas. This concentration was in turn used to reward a few close political associates, such as 'coconut king' Eduardo Cojuangco and the Defence Minister Juan Ponce Enrile, who siphoned off much of the dwindling national earnings from coconut trade. Thus, existing inequalities in economic and political power within the Philippines allowed actions that made these inequalities greater still. Declining global terms of trade were experienced particularly severely, and responded to in particularly unproductive ways, because of the distinctive (if not unique) political system in the Philippines. Local processes, as well as global processes, played their part in the impoverishment of coconut producers. Any attempt to rectify that impoverishment would have to deal with local and global trading relations and the political–economic structurings of each.

SUMMARY

- Differences between places are not just the result of their 'internal' characteristics. They are produced by systems of global relations between places.
- Human Geography should therefore do more than document diversity. It should investigate the *processes of differentiation* through which diversity and inequality are produced.
- These processes of differentiation operate at both global and local scales.

NETWORKS

So far we have been looking at how to think of the relations between global and local scales. In the idea of the mosaic, the global is portrayed as a collection of smaller locals. It is, paradoxically, both an arena within which those locals can be recognized (world awareness allows a comparison between places and alerts us to their differences) and the site of forces that can destroy local uniqueness (through the invasion of non-local things and people). In the model of the system, the global is portrayed as a set of relations through which local differences are produced. Here the emphasis is less on collection and comparison than on connection. In this final section I want to take the idea of connection a little further. I want to suggest that we can see both the local and the global as made up of networks or sets of connections and disconnections that any one local place has to a host of other places the world over. In consequence, we may need to view the local and the global not as different scales (small and large) but as two ways of approaching these same social and spatial networks. Networks in which the local is global, and the global is local. In which, to use a horrible piece of jargon, our Human Geographies are irresolvably 'glocal'.

Some examples may make this less opaque. Let's start with the local (and its global character). In fact, let's start by having a cup of tea. Having a cup of tea (in fact several) is often seen as a very English thing to do, whether in the setting of the upper-class afternoon tea party or the more working-class family or workplace 'cuppa'. As Stuart Hall observes, 'this is the symbolization of English identity – I mean, what does anybody in the world know about an English person except that they can't get through the day without a cup of tea?' (1991: 49). And yet, of course, tea is not simply English:

> Because they don't grow it in Lancashire, you know. Not a single tea plantation exists within the United Kingdom ... Where does it come from? Ceylon – Sri Lanka, India. That is the outside history that is inside the history of the English. There is no English history without that other history ... People like me who came to England in the 1950s [from the West Indies] have been there for centuries; symbolically, we have been there for centuries ... I am the sugar at the bottom of the English cup of tea. I am the sweet tooth, the sugar plantations that rotted generations of English children's teeth. There are thousands of others ... that are ... the cup of tea itself.

(Hall, 1991: 48–9)

Indeed, Hall's point is that it is not just the cup of tea but Englishness as a whole that is not simply English. The cup of tea is symptomatic of a wider condition; that the history of English culture, economy and society can only be understood if one analyses England's global, colonial networks

DOREEN MASSEY ON THE GLOBAL–LOCAL GEOGRAPHIES OF KILBURN, LONDON AND CAMBRIDGESHIRE

Take a walk down Kilburn High Road, my local shopping centre. It is a pretty ordinary place, north west of the centre of London. Under the railway bridge the newspaper stand sells papers from every county of what my neighbours, many of whom come from there, still often call the Irish Free State ... Thread your way through the often stationary traffic ... and there's a shop which as long as I can remember has displayed saris in the window ... On the door a notice announces a forthcoming concert at Wembley Arena: Anand Miland presents Rekha, live, with Aamir Khan, Salman Khan, Jahi Chawla and Raveena Tandon ... This is just the beginnings of a sketch from immediate impressions but a proper analysis could be done, of the links between Kilburn and the world ... It is (or ought to be) impossible even to begin thinking about Kilburn High Road without bringing into play half the world and a considerable amount of British imperialist history.

(1991: 28)

Think of the [seemingly isolated] Cambridgeshire village. Quite apart from its more recent history, integrated into a rich agricultural trade, it stands in an area which in its ancient past has been invaded by Celts and Belgae, which was part of a Roman Empire which stretched from Hadrian's Wall to Carthage ... The village church itself links this quiet place into a religion which had its birth in the Middle East, and arrived here via Rome.

(1995: 64)

(to the West Indies for sugar, to India for tea, and so on). England as a locally distinctive place, with locally distinctive features (like the ritualistic cuppa), is forged through a global web of connections, both past and present.

Doreen Massey has made a similar argument but starting from a more tightly defined local scale. Contradicting the model of a mosaic of bounded local places, she looks at how the distinctiveness of a particular place – whether that be a metropolitan urban neighbourhood or a seemingly isolated rural village – is not threatened by connections to the wider world, but actually comes from them (Massey, 1995). In consequence, she says, we need 'a global sense of place' (Massey, 1994): both in order to understand local places; and in order to appreciate them in a way that does not slip into a reactionary, defensive parochialism.

If we think of the world in terms of networks, then, we see how local places gain their different characters through their distinctive patterns of links to other places. In turn, we begin to see how the global is less some neat, all-embracing system with a single logic, than a mass of globally extensive yet locally routed practices and technologies of connection. Not only do we need to globalize the local, but we also need to localize the global. This means understanding the global as something other than a single entity or system. Arjun Appadurai (1990), for example, argues that we can imagine the global as comprised of a range of interacting but distinctive '-scapes' or morphologies of flow and movement. 'Finanscapes' comprising global networks and flows of money (often in an electronic form, routed through the major international financial centres in New York, Hong Kong, Tokyo and London); 'ethnoscapes' forged by global networks and flows of people (migrants, tourists, business travellers, even geographers), each with their own rather different patterns of movement; 'mediascapes' made up of communication technologies and product distributions; and so on. Many networks, many flows. Sometimes interconnected, but equally often with very different geographies. So, money increasingly moves across national borders with ease at the same time as the richest nations look to reinforce their disciplining of movements of people (variously categorized as legal immigrants, asylum seekers, and illegal migrants). First-world tourists expect to be able to travel the world and to be greeted with hospitality when they do so, at the same time as movements of people in the opposite direction are taken to be threats to first-world cultures, social systems and polities.

Central to this 'network' understanding of the global are questions of 'mobility' (for a pioneering account of this focus see Thrift, 1996c; for more recent reviews see Cresswell, 2001, and Urry, 1999). Particular attention has been paid to the various technologies and practices through which mobilities of people, things and ideas are produced. This includes the new communication and media technologies of today, as captured by labels such as 'virtual geographies' and 'cyberspace' (for an introduction see Crang *et al.*, 1999). It includes the kinds of geographies produced by 'older' transport technologies, whether plane, automobile or railway (for examples of studies in this vein see Augé, 1995, Merriman, 2004, and Schivelbusch, 1986). And it includes the technologies, skills and practices of much earlier explorers and traders who began 'globalizing' the world

Cyberspace

the forms of space produced and experienced through new computational and communication technologies. Exemplary are the SPATIALITIES of phenomena such as the internet, virtual reality programs, hypertext and hypermedia, or the science-fictional accounts that draw on these for inspiration. Human Geographers have approached these spatialities in at least three distinct ways: in terms of the kinds of places users encounter within them; by analysing the kinds of communicational networks they facilitate; and in terms of the geographical location of their infrastructures.

(a)

(b)

(c)

FIGURE 3.5
Three images representing a historical
geography of global mobilities and networks.
Credit: (a) NASA/Science Photo Library;
(b) Aviationphotographers.com; (c) Museum of
the City of New York/Corbis

half a millennium ago (Law, 1986; Ogborn, 2002). In a network approach, then, the global is constituted neither by a collection of placed 'locals' nor by singular, overarching systems (such as the capitalist world-economy). It comprises multiple, specific geographies of mobility, through which wider systemic networks are created, maintained and re-invented. (Chapters 36 to 40, later in this book, outline some of the issues at stake in various movements of people and things.)

Of course, as noted above, the global is constituted through unevenly distributed and experienced networks and flows. Thus the inequalities in the mobilities, connectivities and powers of different entities and people need documenting and reflection. We also need to consider how these networks both connect people, places and things together and disconnect and distance them. Take, for example, Ian Cook's account of the networked geographies of various tropical fruits, the bananas or papaya you are most likely encounter on a supermarket aisle (2000; 2004). Cook's interest is in part in the connections these fruit enact, linking as they do farm workers and farmers in the tropics (his own research focuses on the Caribbean), supermarket and fruit company technicians and managers, and 'first world' consumers. These fruit represent geographies that cannot be contained in mosaic-like distinctions of here and there: both because of their individual travels from Jamaican or St Lucian farms to British or American mouths, and through their much longer implication in processes of economic and cultural exchange and wider status as 'fruits of empire' (Walvin, 1996) (here Cook's argument parallels that of Stuart Hall on the cup of tea that we encountered earlier). But Cook is also interested in the disconnections these fruit networks usually enact: the changes the fruit undergo as they travel (for example, changing from plants to be tended for food or a wage, to everyday agricultural commodities, to 'exotic fruit', to domestic treats); and the distances made between the people and places that have these fruit in common (such that the farm worker knows the papaya or banana eater only as 'The Consumer' who dictates market pressures of demand; and the banana or papaya eater knows the farm worker only as an invisible producer or as a vague stereotype, whether that be the smiling Caribbean labourer or the oppressed 'Third World Worker'). The task of the geographer becomes not to produce knowledge of either the Caribbean or the UK; nor just to explain their differences through understanding overarching systems; but to explore the networks of connection and disconnection that bring these places into being.

In Cook's account, 'tropical fruit' are just one fragment of a global realm comprised of multi-directional, multi-fibred networks, the geographies of which are not mappable on to neat territories or neat systems. To grasp them, geographers have to get inside these networks, go with the flows and look to connect.

SUMMARY

- Local places get their distinctive characters from their past and present links to the rest of the world. In consequence, we need a 'global sense of the local'.

- All these global networks of links – with their flows of information, ideas, money, people and things – have locally routed geographies. In consequence, we need 'localized senses of the global'.

- Attending to various 'mobilities' is a particularly fruitful way of exploring these local–global networks.

CONCLUSION

Human Geography is rightly interested in both the local – the specific place, with its distinctive qualities – and the global – the wider world, with its bigger picture. A crucial question that has always faced Human Geography is how to conceptualize the relations between these two. Three general arguments have informed the discussion here. First, that appeals to ideas of diversity – a global collection of many locals – may be problematic: factually, politically and conceptually. Second, that rather than diversity the conceptual keystone of geographical work in this area should be 'differentiation' – that is, an investigation of the ongoing productions of differences between peoples and places. Third, it is debatable whether these processes of differentiation accord to singular global logics (such as, 'developed countries make other countries underdeveloped as part of their own development') and singular global systems. Rather, they may operate through the multiple networks and mobilities that constitute both the local and the global. Tracing out these networks offers a particularly fruitful way of theorizing, and actually studying, local–global geographies.

DISCUSSION POINTS

1. Why might you, as a Human Geographer, be interested in 'the local'?

2. Why might you, as a Human Geographer, be interested in 'the global'?

3. What are the strengths and weaknesses of seeing the world as made up of a mosaic of diverse local places and peoples?

4. Why are some places, like the USA, so rich and other places, like the Philippines, so poor?

5. Focusing on the place where you currently live, draw up a list and an outline sketch of the 'global networks' in which it is implicated.

FURTHER READING

Allen, J. (1995) Global worlds. In Allen, J. and Massey, D. (eds) *Geographical worlds*. Oxford: Oxford University Press, 105–42.

Taking as its focus ideas about 'global compression', this student-friendly reading deepens the discussion here on how to think of the global nature of contemporary Human Geographies.

Blaut, J.M. (1993) The myth of the European miracle and After 1492, in *The colonizer's model of the world*. New York: The Guilford Press, 50–151 and 179–213.

It is worth attempting a read of this for its powerful restatement of a world-systemic approach. It is particularly strong on debunking the idea that European 'development' stems from qualities internal to Europe itself.

Lipsitz, G. (1994) Kalfou Danjere. In *Dangerous crossroads: popular music, postmodernism and the poetics of place*. London: Verso, 1–21.

A slightly unusual suggestion, written by a non-geographer, but this consideration of the geographies of 'world music' has some lovely examples of local–global networks of political and aesthetic affiliation.

Massey, D. (1994 [orig. 1991]) A global sense of place. In *Space, place and gender*. Cambridge: Polity Press, 146–56.

Already a classic article. There are lots of ideas here about globalizing the local and localizing the global, but it is remarkably well written and really quite readable. It is also short!

Peet, R. (1989) World capitalism and the destruction of regional cultures. In Johnston, R.J. and Taylor, P. (eds) *The world in crisis* (2nd edn). Oxford: Blackwell, 175–99.

This is one of the most explicit examples of an argument for seeing global-level processes as destroying local distinctiveness. Written with real passion.

CHAPTER 4
CONTROL–FREEDOM

Mark Goodwin

INTRODUCTION

Over 150 years ago, the German philosopher and economist Karl Marx encapsulated in a few words a dilemma that has puzzled social scientists ever since. People, he wrote, 'make their own history, but not … under circumstances they themselves have chosen' (1981: 143). They also of course make their own geographies, as this book shows, but again they only do so under certain conditions and circumstances. The difficulty for those studying these geographies is to tease out just how much of their making was contributed by human agency (people making their own geographies) and how much by broader social structures (the circumstances and conditions not of their choosing). To help puzzle this one through, think for a while about the last time you went for a night out. Think about where you went and what you did; think about who you were with and what they did. You probably chatted beforehand and decided to go to see a film or have a drink, or maybe go to a club. You decided who else to invite, and once you were there you decided what to drink and when to dance, and who to dance with. You decided when to go home and how to get home. You decided whether to get a taxi or take a bus. Filling in all these questions would give you an account of your last night out. It would also give you a view that emphasizes your freedom to choose your own activities. It would place you at the centre of the night's decision-making, and would explain the events on the basis of your decisions.

Now stand back for a bit and think through the evening again. In deciding where to go how much choice did you have? How many films were on in your local area, and had you seen some of them before? Did you want to see any of the others? Which clubs were open, and how much did they cost? Could you afford to go where you really wanted to, or did you have to settle for a slightly less expensive venue? Did the choice of venue for the evening depend on whether you are male or female, or whether you are black or white – are there certain places that it is difficult for you to go, because of your gender or your race? Was the club gay or straight – did this affect where you went? Could you drink what you wanted to, or was the selection available slightly limited? Could you dance with who you wanted when you wanted, and was the right music being played? Was there a bus home at the time you left the club or film, or had the last one just gone?

Introducing these issues into the picture of the evening raises the issue of control, and of the social contexts and structures within which your actions were situated. These structures may be material, like the numbers of cinemas or the time of the last bus, or they may be immaterial such as the sets of social and cultural rules that channel behaviour in one way or another. These structures may be borne by the actors themselves in terms of the position they occupy within broader sets of social relations – being a black woman or an unemployed man, for instance – or they may be imposed by others – the bus company stopping the last bus, for instance,

FIGURE 4.1
Freedom or control over your night out?
Credit: Robert Harding Picture Library
Ltd/Alamy

or the film distributors selecting which Hollywood blockbusters should play in which cinemas. But taken together they impart some form of 'control' on your decisions and activities. The nub of the issue for the researcher is to decide whether people are 'free' to choose their own activities, or whether their actions are controlled by wider social structures.

As ever, matters are a bit more complex than this and it is not enough simply to weigh up the relative contributions of freedom and control in causing any particular social process or event. This is because, in practice, it is remarkably difficult to separate the two. Indeed, most researchers would now accept that the broader structures are both the medium and the outcome of the practices that constitute social systems. In other words, we do operate within a set of rules and resources, yet our own actions created these. Moreover, social structures are not to be conceived of purely as a barrier to action, or a control, but will be involved in helping to produce that action. The same is true of the geographies within which we operate. As Howley has reminded us, 'the urban environment shapes, and is shaped by, all those who inhabit it' (2001: 348–9). This for the geographer is at the heart of the debates over control and freedom – how do we tease out the way we shape, but at the same time are shaped by, the world in which we live?

CONTROL AND FREEDOM IN HUMAN GEOGRAPHY

This critical question has been of concern to geographers for most of the discipline's history. But perhaps because of its disciplinary beginnings in natural history, and later continuations in natural science, the human side to Human Geography was often absent. Instead there was a search for those broader natural processes that structured our geographies. Initially, an emphasis was placed on the structuring properties of climate and environment, in work which became known as **environmental determinism**. The contention in such work was that human activity, and hence Human Geography, was controlled (or 'determined') by the physical environment in which it took place. An example can be found in the writings of Griffith Taylor on the development of towns and cities in his 1949 book *Urban Geography*. In this he sets out his basic tenet – that the key to the city is 'the dominant feature of the environment' (Taylor, 1949: 9) – before going on to look at the development of individual towns and cities. Figures 4.2 and 4.3 are graphs taken from his book, which illustrate this search for the controlling factor of the environment. Figure

4.2 'suggests how great cities are controlled by temperature and rainfall' (1949: 176), whilst Figure 4.3 shows 'how the distribution of towns varies in the United States with climatic controls' (1949: 375). Some mention is made in passing of economic and political matters, but in the main Taylor writes secure in the knowledge that 'No student of human geography will deny that in the broadest sense latitude is the variable which most controls human affairs' (1949: 15). Here there is no mention of freedom, yet the word control pops up frequently – in the guise of the environment that controls us all.

Although such environmental determinism lingered in Human Geography for a long time (my copy of Taylor's book was reprinted for the fourth time in 1964), the influence of latitude and temperature and rainfall on human activity was gradually downplayed. Yet this did little to reduce the emphasis on structure, and by the 1960s Human Geography had embraced a so-called 'scientific' approach, which had as its rationale the search for universally applicable laws of human behaviour. Notions of freedom were again written out of the picture as people were reduced to little more than dots on a map or integers in an equation. We were all assumed to operate according to the same general laws – indeed, it was the very search for these controlling laws that drove this entire approach. This kind of reasoning dominated Human Geography in the 1960s and most of the 1970s, and generated the search for law-like statements of order and regularity that could be applied to spatial patterns and processes. Hence the succession of models that appeared in geography over this period – for instance, Christaller's model of settlement hierarchy, Alonso's land use model, Zipf's rank size rule of urban populations and Weber's model of industrial location. All were an attempt to use law-like statements in order to explain and predict the spatial outcomes of human activity.

One such model that Human Geographers used to explain patterns of flow between two or more centres was the so-called **gravity model**. This proposed that we can estimate the spatial interaction between two regions by multiplying together the mass of the two (equated conveniently with population size) and dividing it by some function of the distance separating them. The model was used to 'explain' all kinds of flows, from those of migration to passenger traffic, telephone conversations and commodity flows. Noticeable by their absence are any references to the actual motivations for the behaviour of the individuals who are migrating, or commuting, or speaking to each other on the phone, or purchasing the commodities. The freedom to choose one's behaviour is given no space

Environmental determinism

a school of thought which holds that human activities are controlled by the environment in which they take place. Especially influential within Human Geography at the end of the nineteenth and beginning of the twentieth centuries, when the approach was used in particular to draw a link between climatic conditions and human development. Some authors used this link to argue that climate stamps an indelible mark on the moral and physiological constitution of different races (*see* RACE). This in turn was used to assert the superiority of western civilization, and hence to justify and support the imperial drive of nineteenth-century Europe (*see* COLONIALISM and IMPERIALISM).

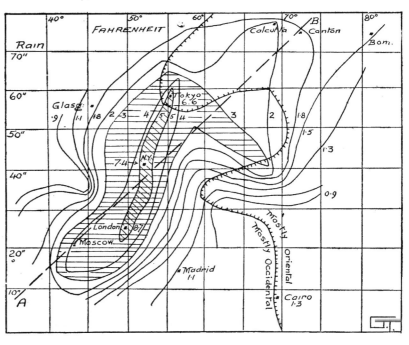

FIGURE 4.2

Cities, temperature and rainfall. A tentative isopract graph suggesting how great cities are controlled by temperature and rainfall. Figures on the isopleths indicate millions of city population. Source: Taylor, 1949, p. 176

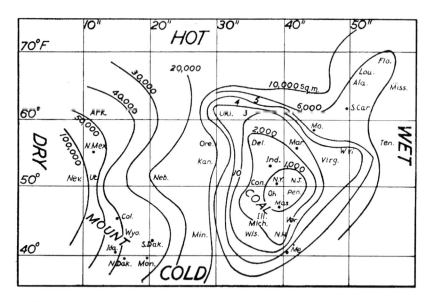

FIGURE 4.3
A tentative isopract graph showing how the distribution of towns (exceeding 17,000 folk) varies in the United States with climatic controls. Figures represent square miles allotted to each town. Source: Taylor, 1949, p. 375

Gravity model

a mathematical model based on a rather crude analogy with Newton's gravitational equation, which posited a constant relationship between the gravitational force operating between two masses, their size and the distance between them. Geographers have used this model to predict and account for a range of flows between two or more points, especially those to do with migration and transport (*see also* SPATIAL SCIENCE).

Humanistic Geography

a theoretical approach to Human Geography that concentrates on studying the conscious, creative and meaningful activities and experiences of human beings. Coming to prominence in the 1970s, Humanistic Geography was in part a rebuttal of attempts during the 1960s to create a law-based, scientific Human Geography founded on statistical data and analytical techniques (*see* SPATIAL SCIENCE). In contrast, it emphasized the subjectivities of those being studied and, indeed, the Human Geographers studying them. Human meanings, emotions and ideas with regard to place, space and nature thus became central.

whatsoever, and people's actions are assumed to conform to a general pattern – which is itself based on a model derived from a crude analogy with Newton's law of universal gravitation developed in 1687. Thus what was originally conceived as a way of accounting for the behaviour of distant bodies in the universe, was being used to explain a whole host of social, economic and cultural activities by reference to the two variables of population and distance. These, and the relation between them, were felt to govern, or control, the rate and nature of population movement.

Accounts that focused on human freedom developed in the 1970s partly as a reaction to, and critique of, the stress on determinism evident within spatial science. It was argued by **humanistic geography** that the search by spatial science for cast-iron laws underlying human behaviour effectively dehumanized such behaviour, and robbed it of the very creativity, values and meanings that drive and sustain human activity (Cloke *et al.*, 1991: 69). Instead these critics advocated an approach that studied the aspects of people 'which are most distinctively "human": meaning, value, goals and purposes' (Entrikin, 1976: 616, quoted in Cloke *et al.*, 1991: 69). As Gregory puts it in the *Dictionary of Human Geography*, such an approach is 'distinguished by the central and active role it gives to human awareness and human agency, human consciousness and creativity' (Johnston *et al.*, 1994: 263). An emphasis on human agency, and on freedom rather than control, had been placed centre stage, and the intentional human actor became the key focus of research work. A good example of the way such approaches informed research can be found in the work of Ley (1974; 1977), who sought to uncover the usually 'taken-for-granted' meanings that informed the actions of street gangs in inner-city Philadelphia. In particular he argued that place was critical in shaping these meanings, and that to speak of a place is not to speak of an object alone, but also to speak of an image and an intent. Thus in opposition to the formulations of the gravity model discussed above, he points out that

> the distant metropolis is never perceived in the perfect material terms that the gravity model with its economic determinism would have us believe. The metropolis has a meaning, it is ... a state of mind, and it is always this meaning for the subject that precedes action: creative decision-making is not pre-empted by a mechanistic gravity field.
>
> (1977: 507)

He went on to show how the most mundane and everyday features of the urban environment can represent local societal values, as symbolized in the use of graffiti to help mark and form territorial space. As Ley puts it (1974: 218–19):

> *graffiti markings represent the language of space for members of the street gang culture. Where territories meet, space is most highly contested, and aggressive behaviour is most appropriate. With increasing proximity to the core of the turf, the meaning of space changes and there is an orderly decrease in assertive behaviour, until at the core security is perceived to be maximal. In this zone, where threat is regarded by gang members as unlikely, assertive behaviour against rivals becomes unnecessary, and graffiti obscenities are almost absent.*

Through such research Ley sought to understand the everyday social world of black teenagers living in inner-city Philadelphia, and to explore what this social world means for these actors and what they meant by acting within it. He was looking, in other words, at how they shaped, and were shaped by, their environment. Within such an approach graffiti is not just part of the garbage of inner-city dereliction, but instead becomes a meaningful part of the lives of the graffiti artists for whom it carries and expresses a whole set of shared values and shared meanings (see Fig. 4.4). However, even Ley with his emphasis on creativity and meaning, recognizes that the social group (in this case the graffiti artists) is not completely autonomous in its decision-making. As he puts it, 'for some men, the macro-social structure does not permit a wide range of action' (1977: 505). In work with Cybriwsky he exemplifies this through interviews with the graffiti artists. In the words of one,

FIGURE 4.4
Mural with a message, West Houston Street, New York. Credit: Ted Russell/Alamy

> *There isn't much choice of what to do … I did it because there was nothing else. I wasn't goin' to get involved with no gangs or shoot no dope, so I started writin' on buses. I just started with a magic marker an' worked up.*

(Ley and Cybriwsky, 1974: 495)

As Ley concludes (1977: 505), 'each individual has a history and geography which imposes constraints within his lifeworld: so begins the dialectic between creativity and determinism, charisma and institution' – and we might add so begins the dialectic between freedom and control.

SUMMARY

- Accounts of human behaviour that stress the controlling influence of wider structures have predominated within Human Geography for much of its history. This is the case whether these structures refer to the physical environment or to sets of abstract laws.

- Partly in opposition to these abstract accounts, a more humanistic geography developed during the 1970s that stressed the role of creativity and human consciousness in accounting for social behaviour.

- As well as emphasizing the potential freedom of human actors, humanistic geography also sought to examine the importance and meaning of place in people's lives. In other words it looked at how we shape, and are shaped by, our human environment.

THE MULTIPLE SPACES OF CONTROL AND FREEDOM

More recent accounts have begun to explore this dialectic between 'creativity and determinism', or control and freedom, in more detail. What they have revealed is a series of very complex geographies, where the line between control and freedom is often very difficult to draw. This is partly because the same space will often serve both to constrain and enable human behaviour, and partly because geographers are constantly developing new ways of looking that draw out increasingly nuanced accounts of social activity. We will examine each of these aspects in turn, using recent empirical work on mental health and homelessness respectively, to illustrate some of the more abstract concerns that can gather around concepts such as control and freedom. Parr *et al.* (2004) have recently explored how the 'social topographies' of life in the Scottish Highlands impact on people's experiences of mental health problems. They sought to evaluate whether rural people with mental health difficulties experience inclusionary or exclusionary social relations – whether their social environment, in other words, was felt as a negative source of control, or whether it offered a more positive perspective as a place of care and relative freedom.

They found a very fluid and dynamic picture in which conceptions of the rural varied, as did the impact of living in a rural community. On the one hand, Parr *et al.* uncovered 'inclusionary practices, reflecting apparent acceptance and tolerance', operating within a space where people felt comfortable and relatively free of constraints. On the other hand, they found 'exclusionary practices reflecting rejection and intolerance', where people experienced the rural environment much more as a source of control. Interestingly they conclude that '*both* sets of practices do exist in the Highlands and that they can co-exist, in the same places and communities, even being experienced by the *same* individuals on different occasions' (2004: 408).

Practices of exclusion often hinge around the way that people with mental health problems are made to feel different. This stigmatization is arguably made easier by the difficulty of hiding mental health problems, especially in the more remote rural areas. Parr *et al.* speak of the 'sheer visibility' of rural life and rural residents, which makes it difficult for people to lead private lives. For some of those with mental health problems, this means that they constantly feel 'gazed upon'. Many of Parr *et al.*'s interviewees talked of being avoided or ignored by other residents, or even of being pointed out and verbally abused in public spaces. The dispersed communities and isolated building prevalent in the Highlands arguably made it easier for these tactics of rejection to be employed, since those with mental health problems literally had nowhere to hide – even in private they felt stigmatized when visits from family and friends became less and less frequent. As Parr *et al.* put it, 'Ignoring someone on the street of a small rural village is a powerful social act, and quite unlike avoiding the eye of someone on a busy city street' (2004: 407–8).

Yet, as Parr *et al.* point out, 'the place of people with mental health problems in rural and remote communities is ambiguous and contradictory' (2004: 411). For the same spaces that give rise to those exclusionary tactics that lead to people experiencing a lack of control over their own lives can also promote inclusion. Thus Parr *et al.*'s interviewees also spoke of the caring nature of their friends and neighbours, and of the way in which other residents show a concern for their health, in the shop or on the bus. As they point out, the dense social networks of family, friends and neighbours that characterize remote rural areas, and that can remain relatively stable from childhood to adulthood, should be 'a social environment highly conducive to assisting people living in the locality with mental health problems' (2004: 14).

FIGURE 4.5
Landscape of inclusion or exclusion?
Credit: Robert Holmes/Corbis

Parr *et al.* conclude that the 'realities of strong cultural norms, visible social lives and differing community status do not seem to "fix" those with mental health difficulties in particular positions of difference, inclusion or exclusion, but rather form a nexus of influences, shaping an instable sense of place, belonging and community for this group' (2004: 16). Thus the social and physical environment within which these people are living can help to promote processes of both inclusion and exclusion. This means that there is not one set of practices that can be mapped on to the environment in a relatively straightforward way, but instead there are a host of multiple and overlapping practices that affect different people in different ways – and even the same people in different ways at different times. Thus we have to speak of multiple rather than singular spaces through which feelings of control and freedom are experienced.

LOCATING FREEDOMS

What we look at, and how we look at it, can also affect the geographies of freedom and control that we reveal, when we study the ways in which individuals and groups shape, and are shaped by, their social and natural environments. To illustrate this I want to look at contrasting studies of the same phenomena – in this case, people's experiences of homelessness. This is a subject that has increasingly concerned geographers, as they have sought to understand the persistence, and indeed increase, of homelessness in the affluent West over the past 20 years or so. In a groundbreaking series of books and papers, Jennifer Wolch and colleagues have charted the ways in which homeless people are increasingly managed and disciplined within a series of marginal institutional spaces (Dear and Wolch, 1987; Wolch and Dear, 1993; Wolch and DeVerteuil, 2001; Wolch and Rowe, 1992). These works have shown how the geographies of the homeless have become defined through the organization of space, as they seek to develop certain routines around institutional and service nodes. Cloke *et al.* (2004b: 5) point out how these 'institutional dependencies form the basis for coping strategies with which to obtain both the materials for basic subsistence and the emotional support necessary for cognitive and psychological adjustment to being homeless'. This work has been hugely valuable in charting the geography of what Wolch and DeVerteuil (2001) call the era of 'new poverty management' – the 'organized responses by elites and/or the state to contain potentially disruptive populations' (DeVerteuil, 2003: 361). As this definition indicates, this work tends to stress the disciplining of, and control over, homeless people, as they are forced to circulate around the city between shelters, hostels, hospitals, rehabilitation centres, prisons and the street.

In contrast, other authors have looked at the same marginalized group from a different perspective. Ruddick (1996), who like Wolch conducted her fieldwork in Los Angeles, emphasizes the coping tactics of the young homeless. She stresses their day-to-day tenacity in the face of official discipline, and shows how they develop a range of place-making devices that enhance their ability to cope. In a similar vein, Cloke *et al.* (2004b) show how homeless people in Bristol use a variety of tactics to create new cartographies of the city as they seek to survive outside the institutionalized spaces of the 'new poverty management'. They relate how some homeless people consider the hostels and shelters of institutionalized space as a 'last resort', or as the 'equivalent of an open prison'. Instead of occupying such spaces they use a variety of means to travel around the spaces of the city, reinscribing those spaces with new meanings as they go. The accompanying box charts the parameters of this reinscription. It also reminds us that there is another view of the homeless at work here – one that stresses freedom rather than control, and one that looks at how,

REINSCRIBING THE TOPOGRAPHY OF THE CITY THROUGH THE TACTICS OF THE HOMELESS

It is clear that homeless people will journey to meet basic survival needs, but also to 'earn' money, and to seek leisure and restful pauses in their daily practices, sometimes gathering communally, sometimes seeking solitude. Routines of movement and pause are intimately associated not only with the landscape of city-wide services, but also with the architectures of the city. In this way, small back streets and alleyways provide channels for relatively 'invisible' movement through the city. Recesses and doorways in buildings can provide shelter and relative warmth; enclosed public spaces offering formal seating or informal surfaces (walls, ledges, steps) on which to sit, provide communal resting places; and so on. Such routines involve not only an understanding of socio-spatial possibilities in the regulated city, but also a reading of the city in terms of the possibilities of counter-inscription, of tracing over the formal understandings of city space and registering alternative signs and markers

with which to re-edit the city as 'homeless city'. For example, shop doorways become sleeping places, public lavatories become bathrooms, underground walkways and concourses become gathering points, with blankets, needle disposal bins and specific graffiti each serving as signs by which the homeless city is variously marked out. It is the intermeshing of the disciplined spaces of service provision and regulation and the less (or differently) disciplined spaces in which homeless people reinscribe the formality of space into places in which they perform their otherness, that will perhaps open up new and strange maps of being homeless in the city … in order to develop a more nuanced understanding of these journeys, places and negotiations, we also want to examine them as spaces of … creative improvisation in which multiple social identities are encoded, and also, potentially, resisted.

Source: Cloke *et al.* (2004b: 9–10)

within limits, they exercise choices, drawing on enabling knowledges as well as individual or collective creativity and capability.

SUMMARY

• There is no easy mapping of freedom and control on to the spaces that we shape and that shape us. Instead we find multiple rather than singular spaces through which feelings of control and freedom are experienced.

• The same process can often be viewed in terms of both freedom and control, depending on which aspects we examine and from which viewpoint we examine them.

CONCLUSION: SPACE AS A RESOURCE IN THE PURSUIT OF FREEDOM

Viewing the journeys of the homeless through the lens employed by Cloke *et al.* in the box opposite reminds us that the strategies of the powerful, which result in a particular kind of spatial ordering, can be resisted by the less powerful through their tactical negotiation of that ordering. Nigel Thrift has recently urged us to think of 'the pivotal role of space and time as not merely metrics but resources' (2001: 377). Through such thought we can investigate the way that space can be used as a critical resource in developing the tactics through which individuals and social groups can pursue their own freedoms. Cloke *et al.* draw out how the homeless use a whole variety of spaces in Bristol, not just for sleep and shelter, but also as places where they can obtain food, 'earn' money and socialize. Through the use of such spaces, they can escape being penned in to the new forms of poverty management favoured by the state. In this way they can use their knowledges of the alternative, and often hidden, spaces of the city to pursue their own tiny piece of freedom. Geographers have a particular role to play here – not only in uncovering and charting these alternative spaces, but also in helping to promote the possibilities that they contain. Long ago now, David Harvey wrote that the geographer's task should not entail 'mapping even more evidence of man's patent inhumanity to man' (1973: 144). Through an exploration of these alternative spaces we can begin to open out the possibility of pursuing progressive freedoms, and thus respond to David Smith's (2004: 207) more recent call that we use our geographical knowledges to help seek 'the new institutions and social arrangements required to equalize human life prospects, whoever and wherever people are'.

DISCUSSION POINTS

1. Choose a geography that is well known to you – for instance, your journey to university, your spaces of recreation, places you have worked – and chart how this space affects you in terms of both control and freedom.

2. Discuss which social groups might perceive the following spaces in terms of control, and which might experience them more in terms of freedom: the suburb; the inner city; the factory; the office; the park.

3. Choose a social group that you know to be marginalized. How might this group use space as a resource?

4. List the spaces where you feel included and those where you feel excluded. Think why this might be the case.

FURTHER READING

Livingstone, D.N. (1992) *The geographical tradition.* **Oxford: Blackwell.**

This is an excellent book, covering the history of geography as a socially constructed and contested enterprise. It contains very readable chapters on environmental determinism and spatial science, with a smaller section on humanism.

Cloke, P. *et al.* **(1991)** *Approaching Human Geography.* **London: Paul Chapman Publishing.**

Much of recent geography has looked at issues of control and freedom through the lens of structure and agency.

This book has excellent chapters on this debate, and on the development of humanistic geography.

Crang, M. and Thrift, N. (2000) *Thinking space.* **London: Routledge.**

This collection contains several chapters that provide alternative ways of thinking about the meaning and use of space.

CHAPTER 5
SELF–OTHER

Paul Cloke

INTRODUCTION: SELF-CENTRED GEOGRAPHIES?

Some people say that you should not judge a book by its cover. However, it is often interesting to pause and reflect on why books, organizations or in this case subjects such as geography are represented by particular 'cover' images. Figure 5.1 shows the cover of the 1994 Annual Report of the Royal Geographical Society, which is the organization representing academic and non-academic geographers in Britain. The image was

FIGURE 5.1
Annual report of the Royal Geographical Society, 1994. Credit: Chris Caldicott

designed to show geography in a positive light, as a subject that causes adventurous individuals to embark on exciting expeditions of learning in which they can discover the secrets of far-flung places and understand the lives of exotically different people. It is the 'us here' subjecting the 'them there' to serious geographical scrutiny.

This image, however, unintentionally poses other questions about 'us' and 'them'. The 'us' might suggest that Human Geographers can somehow be categorized as a homogeneous group of people, studying our geography in a somewhat standardized way – a bizarre supposition on a number of counts not least the 'maleness' of the encounter that is represented. The 'them' seems to have been selected on the grounds of their exotic difference to us. They, too, are in danger of being stereotyped. The strangeness of the place along with differences in skin colour, language, dress and 'culture' seem to be sufficient to mark out an appropriately 'other' subject of study. 'Us' encountering 'them' is on our terms. Exotic difference is defined by our mapping out of people and places in the world, and our assumptions about what is, and what is not, a normal view of life.

Perhaps these questions read too much from one particular image, especially since the RGS/IBG has subsequently sought to rectify in its output any previous perceptions of social or cultural insensitivity. However, these questions do reflect some of the most important themes to have arisen in Human Geography over recent years. The first is a highlighting and questioning of the geographical self. Not so many years ago, Human Geographers were taught to be 'objective' in their studies, so that anyone else tackling the same subject would come up with the same results. They were, in effect, being positioned as some kind of scientific automaton whose background, identity, experience, personality and worldview needed to be subjugated to the need for objectivity. The 'I' was personal pronoun *non grata* when it came to doing geography. However, the *self* does matter, and does influence the geography we practise. We do have different place- and people-experiences, different political and spiritual worldviews, different aspects to our identity and nature, and all of these factors will influence how we see the world, why our geographical imaginations are fired up by particular issues and, ultimately, what and how we choose to study.

The danger of *not* acknowledging and reflecting on the self is not only that we can unknowingly buy into other people's orthodoxies, but also that we can assume that everyone sees the same world as we do. We can, thereby, impose our 'sameness' on to others. The second set of questions, then, concerns a recognition of how we deal with 'others'. It is extraordinarily difficult sometimes to do anything but see things from our own perspective, however hard we try to escape from our self-centred geographies. Yet as soon as we move beyond the samenesses of self, we immediately begin to stylize and stereotype the differences of 'the other'. This has been the subject of much recent discussion across the range of human sciences, including Human Geography, under the rubric of debates on '**Otherness**' and 'Othering':

> as soon as we start to think about people who are not ourselves, we lapse into the language of 'Othering' and, as one urges oneself to consider

Other, Otherness

usually typographically capitalized, an Other is that person or entity that is understood as opposite or different to oneself; Otherness is the quality of difference which that Other possesses. A rather abstract conceptual couplet, potentially applicable at scales varying from the individual person to the global political bloc, these terms have been used in Human Geography to emphasize how ideas about human and geographical difference are structured through oppositions of the Self/Same versus the Other/Different. They also stress how the Other is often defined in terms of its relations to that Self – as its negative, everything it is not – rather than in its own terms. For example, a number of studies have examined how dominant ideas about GENDER are based on a logic in which Woman is Other to Man; how ideas about global politics and culture frame the East as Other to the West, and the South as Other to the North; and so on.

'Others' or to see the 'Other' side of the question, those who are not like 'me' can start to slide into a homogeneous mass of difference from 'me', essentially the same as each other. This is just as arrogant as the assumption that 'they' are essentially the same as 'me'. It is implicit in the terminology that the self is taken as prior. The Other is secondary, and the best that one can do for an other is to extend a liberal tolerance, a condescension flowing from a benign superiority.

(Shurmer-Smith and Hannam, 1994: 89)

Dealing with others, and with questions of difference, is therefore fraught with difficulty, and requires considerable reflection rather than an uncritical assumption about the existence and obvious nature of otherness. For example, we need to challenge any assumptions that appropriate dealings with others are somehow automatically transacted through our citizenship – both in terms of our status as 'citizens' of Human Geography, which is somehow already sufficiently attuned to issues of otherness, and in terms of our state-citizenship through which it might be thought that welfare and aid functions already take care of the need to deal with others. The French anthropologist Marc Augé has suggested that we need to adopt a two-pronged approach to understanding otherness. First, we should seek *a sense for the other*. In the same way that we have a sense of direction, or family, or rhythm, he argues that we have a sense of otherness, and he sees this sense both disappearing and becoming more acute. It is being lost as our tolerance for others – for difference – disappears. Yet it is becoming more acute as that very intolerance itself creates and structures othernesses such as nationalism, regionalism and 'ethnic cleansing', which involve 'a kind of uncontrolled heating up of the processes that generate otherness' (Augé, 1998: xv). Second, we should seek *a sense of the other*, or a sense of what has meaning for others; that which they elaborate upon. This involves listening to 'other' voices and looking through 'other' windows on to the world so as to understand some of the social meanings that are instituted among and lived out by people within particular social or identity groups. This combination of an intellectual understanding of the other, and an emotional, connected and committed sense of appreciation for the other can perhaps best be summarized in terms of attempting to achieve a solidarity with the other by participation and involvement in their worlds. Rather than converting 'them' into 'our' world, such solidarity involves a conversion of our selves for the other, hence as I have written recently:

I believe that any re-radicalised geography will be measured to some extent by the degree to which radical and critical geographers achieve a going beyond the self in order to find a sense for the other in practices of conversion for the other.

(Cloke, 2004: 101)

As the remainder of this chapter suggests, the attempt to inculcate the curricula and research of Human Geography with senses of the other, and with reflections on the self, has proved to be a complex and politicized process. Perhaps this reflects less the novelty of the ideas being worked with, than the way they speak to and critique an absolutely central concern of Human Geography: developing knowledge of people and places beyond those one already knows. This chapter argues that this critique is worthwhile, and therefore discusses some of the delights, as well as difficulties, of bringing explicit reflections of self and other into our Human Geographies.

SELF-REFLECTIONS

In many ways, 'reflexivity' has become one of the most significant passwords in Human Geography over recent years. To reflect on the self in relation to space and society has been seen as a key with which to open up new kinds of Human Geographies that relate to individuals more closely, and that individuals can relate to more closely. In particular, reflexivity has been used by feminist and post-colonial geographers in their respective political projects to persuade Human Geographers to reflect something other than male, white orthodoxies. A poem by Clare Madge urges geography to connect 'in here' rather than 'out there' by becoming a subject 'on my terms and in my terms'.

Reflexivity

a process through which we are able to reflect on what we know, how we come to know it, and how we interact with others. The key point is that we are able to change aspects of ourselves and the structures that make up society in the light of these reflections.

Feminism

a series of perspectives, which together draw on theoretical and political accounts of the oppression of women in society to suggest how GENDER relations and Human Geography are interconnected (*see also* PATRIARCHY).

Post-colonial, post-colonialism

sometimes hyphenated, sometimes not, this term has two distinct meanings: (a) the post-colonial era, i.e. the historical period following a period of COLONIALISM (*see also* DECOLONIZATION); (b) post-colonial political, cultural and intellectual movements, and their perspectives, which are critical of the past and ongoing effects of European and other colonialisms.

Clare Madge
An Ode to Geography

Geography,
What are you?
What makes you?
Whose knowledge do you represent?
Whose 'reality' do you reflect?

Geography,
You are not just space 'out there'
To be explored, mined, colonised.
You are also space 'in here'
The space within and between
That binds and defines and differentiates us as people.

Geography,
I want you to become a subject
On my terms and in my terms,
Delighting and exploring
The subtleties and inconsistencies
Of the world in which we live.

The world of pale moonlight and swaying trees in a bluebell wood.
The world of sand and bone and purple terror.
The world of bright lights flying past factory, iron and engine.
The world of jasmine scents and delicate breeze.
The world of subversion, ambiguity and resistance.
The world of head proud, shoulders defiant under the gaze of cold eyes laying bare the insecurity underlying prejudice.
The world of music, laughter and light,

Of torment and exploding violence
Of tar and steel strewn with hate
While the moon gently observes and heals.

Geography, could you be my world?
Will you ever have the words, concepts and theories
To encapsulate
The precarious, exhilarating, exquisite, unequal world in which we live?
I believe so.
By looking within and without, upside down and inside out,
Come alive geography, come alive!

(Women and Geography Study Group, 1997)

Her frustration with the subject is echoed in the book *Feminist geographies* (Women and Geography Study Group, 1997) where the writing (usually by men) in geography is critiqued, but the problems of proposing alternative forms of writing (usually by women) are starkly acknowledged:

> *Much academic writing . . . is characterised by a dispassionate, distant, disembodied narrative voice, one which is devoid of emotion and dislocated from the personal. In contrast to this, writing which is personal, emotional, angry or explicitly embodied is implicitly (and often explicitly) portrayed as its antithesis: something which (maybe) has a place in the world of fiction and/or creative writing, but which, quite definitely, is out of place in the academic world ... to be masculine often means not to be emotional or passionate, not to be explicit about your values, your background, your own felt experiences. Feminist academics wishing to challenge those exclusions from the written voice of Geography find themselves in a dilemma, however, for if academic masculinity is dispassionately rational and neutral, writing which is overly emotional or explicitly coming from a particular personalised position is often dismissed as irrational, as too emotional as too personal – as too feminine, in other words. Thus feminists who want to assert the importance of the emotional in their work, or feminists who want to acknowledge the personal particularities of their analysis, run the risk of being read as incapable of rational writing, of merely being emotional women whose work cannot be universally relevant.*

(Women and Geography Study Group, 1997: 23)

It has therefore been important for Human Geographers not only to *theorize* the self in new ways, but also to position the self appropriately in the *practising* of Human Geography, such that knowledge is situated in the conscious and subconscious subjectivities of both the author/researcher and the subjects of writing and research. In terms of new ways of theorizing the self, Steve Pile and Nigel Thrift (1995) discuss four interconnected ideas that map out the territory of the human subject.

1. *The body*: which orders our access to and mobility in spaces and places; which interfaces with technology and machinery; which encapsulates our experiences of the world around us; which harbours unconscious desires, vulnerabilities, alienations and fragmented aspects of self, as well as expressions of sexuality and gender; and which is a site of cultural consumption where choices of food and clothing and jewellery, for example, will inscribe meanings about the person.

2. *The self*: which can be understood in a variety of ways, ranging from a personal identity formed by an ongoing series of experiences and relationships, but where there is no distinctive characteristic in these experiences and relationships to suppose an inner, fixed personality, to a personal identity in which self-awareness serves to characterize each experience as belonging to a distinct self.

3. *The person*: which is a description of the cultural framework of the self, and allows for different selves in different frameworks. For example, if you were born and brought up in Rwanda, or Albania, or Cuba, your person would reflect the cultural frameworks of life in those places.

4. *Identity*: where the person is located within social structures with which they identify. Traditionally this would have been seen to involve rigid structures such as class and family, but more recently identities have tended to be constructed reflexively and therefore often flexibly leading to new identity issues – for example, focusing on alternative sexualities, ethnicities or resistance to local change.

The subject is therefore 'in some ways detachable, reversible and changeable', while in other ways it is 'fixed, solid and dependable'. It is certainly 'located in, with and by power, knowledge and social relationships' (1995: 12).

Some of these theoretical distinctions may at first be difficult to grasp, but they do serve to emphasize just how difficult it actually is to be reflexive about the self in our Human Geography. To what extent is it possible to know and to reflect on our selves, to appreciate fully how, precisely, the self is responsible for how we think, how our imaginations are prompted, how we interpret places, people and events, and so on? How much more difficult is it to understand the selves of others whom we might wish to study? These practices, which I have identified earlier as being important political and personal projects in Human Geography, are perhaps more difficult than they first appear. The multidimensionality of the body, the relationally dependent and often subconscious nature of the self, the culturally framed (and therefore flexible) person, and the changeable and overlapping influences of identity render reflexivity a most complex, and some would say impossible, task. Indeed a whole new angle on Human Geography – **non-representational theory** (see Thrift, 1996b; 2004b) has sprung up in which the focus has switched specifically to non-reflexive accounts of human being and becoming in which the instinctive, habitual and performative are emphasized.

Nevertheless, the breaking down of detached and personally irrelevant orthodoxies in Human Geography has remained a task that many continue to consider sufficiently worthwhile to warrant attempts to bring reflexivity into a prominent position in the practice of Human Geography.

Non-representational theory

introduced into Human Geography by the Geographer Nigel Thrift, this phrase – which he has since accepted may not have been 'the best-chosen of phrases' – seeks to highlight various understandings that emphasize the practical, active and EMBODIED character of the world. Rather than denying the importance of REPRESENTATIONS, non-representational theory has sought to resist an undue obsession with them (see LINGUISTIC (OR CULTURAL) TURN) through a direct focus on actions, events, moments, things.

Three interconnected and often overlapping strategies are briefly outlined here. First, a strategy of **positionality** can be identified in which 'telling where you are coming from' can be employed tactically as a contextualization of the interpretations that are to follow. Sometimes this involves the identification of key political aspects of the self, for example, a feminist positioning, which will self-evidently influence what occurs subsequently and which provides us with new positions from which to speak. On other occasions, particular spatial or social experiences will be described that are used to claim expertise or insight into particular situations. Take, for example, George Carney's autobiographical preface to *Baseball, barns and bluegrass*, his book on the geography of American folklife. Here, he describes his childhood in the foothills of the Ozarks, and how the folk knowledge accumulated during that time has been translated into a scholarly pursuit of cultural tactics of American folklife more generally. Not only does his folk heritage equip him for this work, but it also punctuates what he writes and how he writes it.

Positionality

the personal experiences, beliefs, identities and motives of the Human Geographer, which influence her or his work and the way in which her or his knowledge is situated.

GEORGE CARNEY'S AUTOBIOGRAPHICAL PREFACE

The first eighteen years of my life were spent on a 320-acre farm in Deer Creek Township, Henry County, Missouri, some six miles south of Calhoun (population 350), ten miles northwest of Tightwad (population 50), and five miles west of Thrush (population 4). My parents, Josh and Aubertine, inherited the acreage and farmstead buildings from my grandpa and grandma Carney, who retired and moved to Calhoun. The eighty acres to the north of the farmstead consisted of hardwood timber (walnut, hickory, and oak), Minor Creek, which flowed in an easterly direction as a tributary to Tebo Creek, and some patches of grazing land. The remaining 240 acres, south of the farmstead, were relatively rich farmland where my Dad planted and harvested a variety of crops ranging from corn and soybeans to alfalfa and oats. Classified as a diversified farmer, he also raised beef and dairy cattle, hogs, sheep, and chickens. Thus, my roots lay in a rural, agrarian way of life in the foothills of the Ozarks.

My early years fit the description that is often used to define the *folk* – a rural people who live a simple way of life, largely unaffected by changes in society, and who retain traditional customs and beliefs developed within a strong family structure. I was experiencing the *folklife* of the Ozarks. Folklife includes objects that we can see and touch (tangible items), such as food (Mom's home-made yeast rolls) and buildings (Dad's smokehouse). It also consists of other traditions that we cannot see or touch (intangible elements), such as beliefs and customs (Grandpa Whitlow's chaw of tobacco poultice used to ease the pain of a honeybee sting). Both aspects of folklife, often referred to as material and nonmaterial culture, are learned orally as they are passed down from one generation to the next – such as Grandpa Carney teaching me to use a broad axe – or they may be learned from a friend or neighbor – for example, Everett Monday, a neighbor, instructing me on the techniques of playing a harmonica.

Through this oral process, I learned many of the traditional ways from the folk who surrounded my everyday life – parents, relatives, friends, neighbors, teachers, preachers, and merchants. The most vivid memories associated with my early life among the Ozark folk are the six folklife traits selected for this anthology – architecture, food and drink, religion, music, sports, and medicine.

Since leaving the Ozarks for the Oklahoma plains some thirty-five years ago, I have developed a greater awareness and deeper appreciation for American folklife and all its spatial manifestations. My teaching and research interests have been strongly influenced by those folk experiences of yesteryear. Students in my introductory culture geography classes are annually given a heavy dose of lectures and slides on the folklife traits covered in this reader. My research has increasingly focused on two of these traits – music and architecture. Clearly, my roots have made a lasting impression – one that I have converted into a scholarly pursuit.

(Carney, 1998: xv–xxii)

Autoethnography

the processes by which the Human Geographer chooses to make explicit use of her or his own POSITIONALITY, involvements and experiences as an integral part of ETHNOGRAPHIC research.

Second, a more radical strategy of **autoethnography** involves interpreting people, places and events through the perspective of your own involvement. An influential figure here has been Elspeth Probyn, a sociologist from Montreal, whose use of autoethnography is carefully and critically reviewed in her book called *Sexing the self* (1993). Probyn focuses on some very personalized passages in her own life in order to discuss gendered positions in cultural studies:

> *My project here is to rethink what the self might be in and for feminism. I want to reconstitute its force and reveal the material forces behind its motion. In previous articles I have implicitly worked through my own particular self in relation to distinct concerns: anorexia; the gendering of the local; the death of my mother; and to body in general. Yet something central always seemed to evade me. It somehow seemed unseemly to speak of what drew me to these subjects: as I described these matters, I made them into objects separated from myself ... However, my idiosyncrasies aside, I must state that fundamentally I am drawn to these subjects both near and dear because I am convinced that gender must be represented as processes that proceed through experience.*

(1994: 3)

Autoethnography opens up intriguing possibilities for studying, for example, our gender, race/ethnicity, sexuality, sense of place, and also our work, leisure, tourism and other activity geographies through the medium of our personal involvement. At one and the same time, there are opportunities to practise the geographies that we understand most – our own – and yet dangers of becoming so self-obsessed that nobody else's geographies matter. Even with autoethnography, then, there are strong arguments for including 'other' voices in our own stories.

A third strategy therefore, is to acknowledge *intertextuality* in our practice of Human Geography, by finding ways of recognizing the significance of our selves as important influences that shape our geographies, whilst at the same time seeking to listen to other voices. The texts that result from such encounters are complex dialogues. The Human Geographer will shape the conversation, both by the individuality of their own subject-experience and by the questions that are asked of the 'other'. In turn, other individuals will have different, changing and even competing experiences, and will represent themselves differently to different people. The 'results' of the encounter will usually be 'interpreted' by the Human Geographer in the light of their self-positioning. This may involve a process of 'finding new places to speak from', and bringing them into the conversation, or it may involve a tactic of 'letting people speak for themselves' and seeking for a plurality of voices (a 'polyphony') to emerge. Interpretations are then usually written down, often using quoted extracts of other voices, but almost always with the author in control, exerting power over what is included and excluded, what is contextualized and how, and what storylines are used to shape the narrative of the 'findings'. In all these processes and practices, the need to recognize the interconnections between the powerful self and the 'subjected to' other is paramount.

The increasing use of ethnographic strategies and qualitative methods in Human Geography (see Cloke *et al.*, 2004) has certainly helped to provide research practices with which we can be more reflexive about our selves, and the relationships between our selves and others. In the end, however, we have to realize just how 'easy' it can become to think and write about ourselves, and how difficult it is to know enough about our selves to be reflexive in our geographies. Delvings into **psychoanalysis** (Sibley, 1995) have began to help our understandings here but there still seems to be an inbuilt desire to empower the self over the other, however much a many-voiced, polyphonic geography is being aimed at. In the more general context of the problems in the world, such preoccupations with the self might be regarded as inappropriate, if not positively dangerous!

SUMMARY

- Reflexivity – reflecting on the self in relation to society and space – is an essential process in recognizing how our individualities contribute to all aspects of our practice of Human Geography. It also gives us grounds on which to challenge seemingly 'orthodox' geographies and to make our Human Geography more relevant to us and to others.

- The difficulties involved in understanding the self are often underestimated. The human subject is a complex mix of body, self, person and identity and, for some, spirit and soul will also be important considerations.

- There is an interconnected range of strategies by which the self can consciously be included in the practice of Human Geography.

- The dangers of exaggerating the self in our reading, thinking, researching and writing about Human Geography are very real, and can divert us from important issues relating to others.

SENSING THE OTHER

There is currently what Chris Philo (1997: 22) calls 'an exciting swirl of interest' in Human Geography about the need to take serious notice of different kinds of people who are situated in different kinds of spaces and places, and who experience, mould and negotiate these spaces and places in a different way to ourselves. This interest in the differences of the other has implications for the ways in which we conceptualize and practise our Human Geographies, and also for the ways in which these geographies are politicized. Dealing with the 'other' is of course linked to dealing with the 'self'. To reiterate, the arrogance of the self is often manifest in an assumption that others must see the world in the same way as we do. Alternatively, we will often place ourselves in the centre of some 'mainstream' identity that is defined not only around our self-characteristics but also in opposition to others who are not the same as us. Think, for example, about the way white people often assume that only 'non-white' people have an ethnicity, and find their own whiteness unremarkable. As Philo further suggests, then, we are often 'locked into the thought-prison of "the same"' (1997: 22), which makes it impossible for us to appreciate the workings of the other. Indeed we will often seek either to *incorporate* the other into our sameness, or to *exclude* the other from our sameness, in order to cope with the threat that difference seems

Psychoanalysis, psychoanalytic

largely associated with the work of Freud, psychoanalytic theory concerns itself with the mental life of individuals rather than with any overt observable behaviour, and argues that the most important elements of such mental lives are the unconscious ones. It posits that the unconscious parts of the mind (the 'id') are in perpetual conflict with both the more rational and conscious elements (the 'ego') and with those parts of the mind concerned with conscience (the 'superego'). Psychological disturbances can then be traced to these conflicts, and can be remedied through psychoanalytical therapy, which is able to give an individual insight into their unconscious mental life.

to present to the perceived mainstream nature of our identity (see Sibley, 1995). Both incorporation, and exclusion are highly political acts that trap the other in the logic of the same.

The interest in recognizing 'other' Human Geographies focuses attention not only on that which is remote to us, but also should make us rethink what is close to home. Two examples serve here to highlight some of the principal themes in the recognition of otherness in proximal and remote situations. The first relates to the neglect of 'other' geographies close to home and focuses on rural geographies (see Chapter 33) although the principles involved relate to a wide range of Human Geography contexts. Philo's (1992) review of 'other' rural geographies emphasized that most accounts of rural life have viewed the mainstream interconnections between culture and rurality through the lens of typically white, male, middle-class narratives:

> there remains a danger of portraying British rural people ... as all being 'Mr Averages', as being men in employment, earning enough to live, white and probably English, straight and somehow without sexuality, able in body and sound in mind, and devoid of any other quirks of (say) religious belief or political affiliation.

(1992: 200)

Such a list is important in its highlighting of neglect for others, but also runs the risk of immediately producing a formulaic view of what is other. Thus, we can recognize that individuals and groups of people can be marginalized from a sense of belonging to, and in, the rural on the grounds of their gender, age, class, sexuality, disability, and so on. However, as David Bell and Gill Valentine (1995b) remind us, the mere listing of socio-cultural variables represents neither a commitment to deal seriously with the issues involved nor a complete sense of the *range* of other geographies. Indeed, our very recognition of *these others* serves to 'other' *different others* and exclude them from view.

A specific illustration within this rural context is offered in Chapter 2, which presents a well-known self-portrait by the photographer Ingrid Pollard (see Figure 2.4, and also Kinsman, 1995). Her autobiographical notes suggest that the photograph is a self-aware comment on race, representation and the British landscape. She sets herself in the countryside, and through juxtaposing her identity as a 'black photographer' with the cultural construction of landscape and rurality as an idyll-ized space of white heartland, she graphically expresses a sense of her own unease, dread, non-belonging – of other. The black presence in 'our' green and pleasant land says much about whiteness = sameness in this context. However, as the Women and Geography Study Group (1997) point out, the otherness in this representation is by no means a uni-dimensional matter of race. They suggest that:

> Pollard is claiming a different position from which to look at and enjoy English landscapes (albeit an uneasy pleasure); a right to be there and a right to be represented and make representations. She challenges, disrupts and complicates the notion of a generalisable set of shared ideas

about England and the implicitly white and masculinised position from which it is usually viewed. "

(1997: 185–6)

Ingrid Pollard the 'black *woman* photographer', then, exposes another critical edge of otherness in this content and clearly the multi-dimensional nature of identity is by no means exhausted by these labels. In our seemingly known worlds, therefore, we make assumptions about the nature of people and places; about who belongs where, and who doesn't fit into the sameness of our mainstream; about who, what, where and when is other (see Chapter 11).

The second illustration is even better known within Human Geography, having achieved almost cult status in attempts to formulate post-colonial approaches to the subject. Edward Said is Professor of English and Comparative Literature at Columbia University in the USA. He is a Palestinian, born in Jerusalem and educated in Egypt and America, who is most famous for his analysis of the way the West imagines the Orient or East (including the Arabic Middle East) as different to itself (for a review of these and other 'imaginative geographies' see Chapter 35). In his classic book *Orientalism* (1978; 1995) Said traces how the Arab world has come to be imagined, represented and constructed in terms of its otherness to Europe:

" *the French and the British – less so the Germans, Russians, Spanish, Portuguese, Italians and Swiss – have had a long tradition of what I shall be calling Orientalism, a way of coming to terms with the Orient that is based on the Orient's special place in European Western experience. The Orient is not only adjacent to Europe; it is also the place of Europe's greatest and richest and oldest colonies, the source of its civilisation and languages, its cultural contestant, and one of its deepest and most recurring images of the other.* "

(1995: 1)

Representations of the romantic, mystical Orient, he argues, act as a container for western desires and fantasies that cannot be accommodated within the boundaries of what is normal in the West. Yet at the same time, representations of the cruel, detached and money-grabbing nature of the Oriental Arab serve to underline the assumed hegemony of the West over political–economic and socio-cultural norms:

" *Arabs, for example, are thought of as camel-riding, terroristic, hook-nosed, venal lechers whose undeserved wealth is an affront to real civilisation. Always there lurks the assumption that although the Western consumer belongs to a numerical minority, he is entitled either to own or to expend (or both) the majority of the world's resources . . . a white middle-class westerner believes it his human prerogative not only to manage the non-white world but also to own it, just because by definition 'it' is not quite as human as 'we' are.* "

(Said, 1995: 108)

FIGURE 5.2
A guard with a zither player in an interior, by Ludwig Deutsch (1855–1935). The illustration was used on the cover of Edward Said's *Orientalism*, 1995. Credit: © Christie's Images, London, UK/Bridgeman Art Library, London/New York

Representation

the cultural practices and forms by which human societies interpret and portray the world around them and present themselves to others. In the case of the natural world, for example, these representations range from prehistoric cave paintings of the creatures that figured in the lives of early human groups to the televisual images and scientific models that shape our imaginations today. *See also* DISCOURSE.

PIERRE CLASTRES

Chronicle of the Guayaki Indians

FIGURE 5.3
Jyvukugi, chief of the Atchei Gatu. Source:
Chronicle of the Guayaki Indians by Pierre
Clastres, 1998, pp. 57–9

They really were savages, especially the *Iroiangi*. They had only been in contact with the white man's world for a few months, and that contact had for the most part been limited to dealings with one Paraguayan. What made them seem like savages? It was not the strangeness of their appearance – their nudity, the length of their hair, their necklaces of teeth – nor the chanting of the men at night, for I was charmed by all this; it was just what I had come for. What made them seem like savages was the difficulty I had in getting through to them: my timid and undoubtedly naive efforts to bridge the enormous gap I felt to exist between us were met by the Atchei with total, discouraging indifference, which made it seem impossible for us ever to understand one another. For example, I offered a machete to a man sitting under his shelter of palm leaves sharpening an arrow. He hardly raised his eyes; he took it calmly without showing the least surprise, examined the blade, felt the edge, which was rather dull since the tool was brand-new, and then laid it down beside him and went on with his work. There were other Indians nearby; no one said a word. Disappointed, almost irritated, I went away, and only then did I hear some brief murmuring: no doubt they were commenting on the present. It would certainly have been presumptuous of me to expect a bow in exchange, the recitation of a myth, or status as a relative! Several times I tried out the little Guayaki I knew on the *Iroiangi*. I had noticed that, although their language was the same as that of the Atchei Gatu, they spoke it differently: their delivery seemed much faster, and their consonants tended to disappear in the flow of the vowels, so that I could not recognize even the words I knew – I therefore did not understand much of what they said.

But it also seemed to me that they were intentionally disagreeable. For example, I asked a young man a question that I knew was not indiscreet, since the Atchei Gatu had already answered it freely: '*Ava ro nde apa?*

Who is your father?' He looked at me. He could not have been amazed by the absurdity of the question, and he must have understood me (I had been careful to articulate clearly and slowly). He simply looked at me with a slightly bored expression and did not answer. I wanted to be sure I had pronounced everything correctly. I ran off to look for an Atchei Gatu and asked him to repeat the question; he formulated it exactly the way I had a few minutes earlier, and yet the *Iroiangi* answered him. What could I do? Then I remembered what Alfred Métraux had said to me not long before: 'For us to be able to study a primitive society, it must already be starting to disintegrate.'

I was faced with a society that was still green, so to speak, at least in the case of the *Iroiangi*, even though circumstances had obliged the tribe to live in a 'Western' area (but in some sense, wasn't their recent move to Arroyo Moroti more a result of a voluntary collective decision than a reaction to intolerable outside pressure?). Hardly touched, hardly contaminated by the breezes of our civilization – which were fatal for them – the Atchei could keep the freshness and tranquillity of their life in the forest intact: this freedom was temporary and doomed not to last much longer, but it was quite sufficient for the moment; it had not been damaged, and so the Atchei's culture would not insidiously and rapidly decompose. The society of the Atchei *Iroiangi* was so healthy that it could not enter into a dialogue with me, with another world. And for this reason the Atchei accepted gifts that they had not asked for and rejected my attempts at conversation because they were strong enough not to need it: we would begin to talk only when they became sick.

Old Paivagi died in June 1963; he certainly believed that he had no more reason to remain in the world of the living. In any case, he was the oldest of the Atchei Gatu, and because of his age (he must have been over seventy) I was often eager to ask him about the past. He was usually quite willing to engage in these conversations but only for short periods, after which he would grow tired and shut himself up in his thoughts again. One evening when he was getting ready to go to sleep beside his fire, I went and sat down next to him. Evidently he did not welcome my visit at all, because he murmured softly and unanswerably: '*Cho ro tuja praru. Nde ro mita kyri wyte.* I am a weak old man. You are still a soft head, you are still a baby.' He had said enough; I left Paivagi to poke his fire and went back to my own, somewhat upset, as one always is when faced with the truth.

This was what made the Atchei savages: their savagery was formed of silence; it was a distressing sign of their last freedom, and I too wanted to deprive them of it. I had to bargain with death; with patience and cunning, using a little bribery (offers of presents and food, all sorts of friendly gestures, and gentle, even unctuous language), I had to break through the Strangers' passive resistance, interfere with their freedom, and make them talk. It took me about five months to do it, with the help of the Atchei Gatu.

Through the process of Orientalism, the societies and cultures concerned are marginalized, devalued and insulted, while the imperialism and moral superiority of the West are legitimized. Said's contestation of the othering of Orientalism points the way for wide-ranging inquiry by Human Geographers into how different people and places are similarly othered. It also shows us that at the heart of what we take to be familiar, natural, at home, actually lurk all kinds of relations and positionings to that which is unfamiliar, strange and uncanny (Bernstein, 1992).

From these illustrations it becomes clear that whether otherness is close to home or positioned in some far-off exotic space, it is often difficult to detach ourselves, both conceptually and empirically from a frame of study that validates the self, the same and the familiar as waymarkers for the understanding of others. Two sets of issues arise from this conclusion. First, there is a need to think through much more deeply about what constitutes otherness in Human Geographical study, otherwise our main contribution may only be to further emphasize the othernesses that are *reinforced by* such study. At one level, this requires a grasp of the multidimensional nature of identity. As Mike Crang (1998a) puts it:

> *very few people are the 'same' as others – everyone is different in some respects. The most we could say is that certain groups share certain things in common, so who is counted as part of a group or excluded from it will depend on which things are chosen as being significant . . . Belonging in a group depends on which of all the possible characteristics are chosen as 'defining' membership. The characteristics that have been treated as definitive vary over space and time with significant political consequences attached to deciding what defines belonging.*

(1998a: 60)

We need to recognize, therefore, that 'same' and 'other' identities are:

1. *Contingent* – in that differences which define them are a part of an open and ongoing series of social processes.

2. *Differentiated* – in that individuals and groups of people will occupy positions along many separate lines of difference at the same time; and

3. *Relational* – in that the social construction of difference is always in terms of the presence of some opposing movement.

(Jones and Moss, 1995)

Even with greater sensitivity for other identities, we are usually still trapped in a concern for what Marcus Doel (1994) calls 'the Other of the Same' – that is, we translate othernesses into our language, our conceptual frameworks, our categories of thought, and thereby effectively obscure the other with the familiarities of the samenesses of our self. The real difficulty, then, is to find ways of accessing 'the Other of the Other' – that is, the unfamiliar, unexpected, unexplainable other that defies our predictive, analytical and interpretative powers, and our socio-cultural positionings.

The second set of issues relates to the methods we employ in order to encounter 'others'. As with our self-reflections, the increasing use of **ethnographic** and qualitative methods is important to this project. However, researching the other through ethnography takes a long time. Drawing lessons from Anthropology, we would have to conclude that to carry out appropriate studies of unknown peoples and worlds can take several years. Consider, for example, the account of French anthropologist Pierre Clastres (1998), who spent two years with so-called 'savage' tribes of Indians in Paraguay in the 1960s. He acknowledges that even 'being there' with his research subjects did not break down the very considerable barriers of communication and cross-referenced understanding, until circumstances changed many months into his research. Even over this time-scale it proved difficult to form a bridge between himself (and here we might wonder whether his concept of 'savages' got in the way of effective communication) and the mythologies, embodiments and social practices that lay at the heart of the very existence of the Guayaki Indians (see box on page 72).

We need to acknowledge just how difficult it is to form a bridge between ourselves and the complicated essential existences of others, whether far off or close to home. It can be argued that the pressure to publish in the contemporary academy has run the risk of too many 'quickie' ethnographies of othered subjects. As with the Guayaki, an appreciation of the other geographies and experiences of, say, homeless

Ethnography, ethnographic
the research processes that use qualitative methods to provide in-depth explorations and accounts of the lives, interactions and 'textures' associated with particular people and places.

SUMMARY

- Sensing the other is inextricably linked with understanding the self. By assuming that others are somehow the same as us, we can be locked in to the 'thought prison' of the same, which makes it impossible to sense the other appropriately.
- Geographies of other people and places can be close to home or in far-off exotic worlds. In either case, Human Geographers should see themselves as observers who are situated *within* the objects and worlds of their observation.

- At the heart of what we take to be familiar, natural and belonging lurk all kinds of relations and positionings with that other that is unfamiliar, strange and uncanny.
- There is a need to think through much more deeply what constitutes otherness in Human Geography. It is usually very difficult to bridge over between self and other.
- There is also a need to avoid methodological shortcuts in encounters with others.

people in a city like Bristol require long-term commitment rather than brief encounters. Only by reconceptualizing otherness, and reviewing the quality of our encounters with it, are Human Geographers likely to become any more attuned to a sense for the other and a sense of the other as suggested by Augé at the beginning of this chapter.

CONCLUSION

This discussion of the interconnections of self and other raises a number of important issues about our Human Geographies. First, there is the risk that in acknowledging our selves in our work we become too self-centred and too little concerned with political and other priorities in the world around us. Second, there is the potential for losing our sense of otherness. Third, there is the conceptual and methodological complexity involved in encountering the other of the same, let alone the other of the other. Finally, there a concern over the way in which we can sometimes privilege certain kinds of otherness without giving due attention to the need for sustained, empathetic and contextualized research under appropriate ethical conditions. There can be a tendency to 'flit in and flit out' of intellectually groovy subjects, with the danger that research becomes mere tourism or voyeurism of the subjects concerned.

When we have negotiated these tricky questions, there is one further important issue of self–other interrelations to resolve. In the words of Derek Gregory, 'By what right and on whose authority does one claim to speak for those "others"? On whose terms is a space created in which "they" are called upon to speak? How are they (and we) interpellated?' (1994: 205).

In seeking to encounter the stories of other people and worlds, is it inevitable that we become mere tourists, burdened by the authority of our selves and the power of our authorship? Or are there ways in which we can be sufficiently sensitive about the postionality and intertextuality of our authorship that we can legitimately seek to understand and write about the stories of others, without polluting them with our voyeuristic or touristic tendencies, the exclusionary power of which are so graphically illustrated in Figure 5.4? I believe that in this we can learn much from Gregory's emphatic and optimistic answer:

FIGURE 5.4
The power to exclude when engaging in touristic or voyeuristic geographies. Credit: Mikkel Ostergaard/Panos Pictures

" *Most of us have not been very good at listening to others and learning from them, but the present challenge is surely to find ways of comprehending those other worlds – including our relations with them and our responsibilities toward them – without being invasive, colonizing and violent ... we need to learn how to reach beyond particularities, to speak of larger questions without diminishing the significance of the places and the people to which they are accountable. In so doing, in enlarging and examining our geographical imaginations, we might come to realise not only that our lives are 'radically entwined with the lives of distant strangers' but also that we bear a continuing and unavoidable responsibility for their needs in times of distress more.* **"**

(Gregory, 1994: 205)

In this agenda lies a pathway towards more sensitive and meaningful engagements of self and other in Human Geography.

DISCUSSION POINTS

1. What aspects of your self are significant in shaping *your* Human Geography? How do you know?

2. To what extent does non-representational theory involve a complete rethink of the self?

3. How is it possible for researchers to represent the other when they are 'so thoroughly saturated with the ideological baggage of their own culture' (Ley and Mountz, 2001)?

4. To what extent is the distinction between *the* self and *the* other crude and oversimplified, given that identity is 'always stitched together imperfectly, and therefore able to join with another to see together without claiming to be another' (Haraway, 1996)?

5. What evidence do you see in contemporary Human Geography of an emotional, connected and committed sense of the other?

FURTHER READING

Pile, S. and Thrift, N. (eds) (1995) *Mapping the subject: geographies of cultural transformation.* **London: Routledge.**

Probyn, E. (1993) *Sexing the self: gendered positions in cultural studies.* **London: Routledge.**

These two books offer comprehensive discussions of subjectivity and self, and ethnography and self, respectively.

Cloke, P. (2004) 'Deliver us from evil?' Prospects for living ethically and acting politically in Human Geography. In P. Cloke, P. Crang and M. Goodwin (eds) *Envisioning Human Geographies.* **London: Arnold, 210–28.**

Ruddick, S. (2004) Activist geographies: building possible worlds. In P. Cloke, P. Crang and M. Goodwin (eds) *Envisioning Human Geographies.* **London: Arnold, 229–41.**

Smith, D. (2004) Morality ethics and social justice. In P. Cloke, P. Crang and M. Goodwin (eds) *Envisioning Human Geographies.* **London: Arnold, 195–209.**

These present a series of manifestos on how to develop ethical Human Geographies.

Cloke, P., Cook, I., Crang, P., Goodwin, M., Painter, J. and Philo, C. (2004) *Practising Human Geography.* **London: Sage.**

Further commentary on ethnography and qualitative methodologies in Human Geography.

Crang, P. (1994) It's showtime: on the workplace geographies of display in a restaurant in southeast England. *Environment and Planning D. Society and Space* **12, 675–704.**

An excellent case study of the conceptual and practical outworking of self–other in ethnography.

Cloke, P. and Little, J. (eds) (1997) *Contested countryside cultures: otherness, marginality and rurality.* London: Routledge.

Said, E. (1995) *Orientalism.* London: Penguin (reprint with 'Afterword').

For a continuation of illustrations of rural otherness and Orientalism, respectively.

Cloke, P. (2004) Exploring boundaries of professional/personal practice and action: being and becoming in Khayelitsha township, Cape Town. In D. Fuller and R. Kitchin (eds) *Radical theory/critical praxis: making a difference beyond the academy.* Praxis (e) Press, 92–102.

For a simple illustration of self–other issues in the context of an academic and community work in a South African township.

CHAPTER 6
IMAGE–REALITY

Mike Crang

INTRODUCTION

Geographers spend a lot of time working with images. They do not, however, generally call them 'images' – they are called charts, graphs and, even, maps. The term 'images' tends to be used in a negative way. The word image is used to imply superficial, not factual, obscuring and covering up reality, conveying a biased impression. There are, it seems, 'bad' images that are things out there in the world that get in the way and mislead people (poor dears) and 'good' images that allow the geographer to grasp what is really going on. Nor is this confined to geography: Clifford Geertz comments of scientific writing in general 'that "symbolic" opposes to "real" as fanciful to sober, figurative to literal, obscure to plain, aesthetic to practical, mystical to mundane, and decorative to substantial' (in Baker 1993: 10). Image is taken to imply the opposite of real, in a series of binary pairs where two terms are opposed and we are trained through years of education to value the second terms on Geertz's list. Geography has seen many variants on this pattern, some of which are explored in more detail later. Geographers have studied '**mental maps**' to see how these diverge from 'reality', the 'perception' of risk as opposed to statistical likelihood, tourist images as glamorizing real places, facades and regenerated areas as images concealing real economic processes or literature as a 'subjective' representation of a region. The discipline has often implied that images obscure or deviate from a reality revealed by careful geographical study.

This chapter will suggest that the relationship of image and reality is rather more complex than this. We might, yes, look at how images refract, reflect and alter the world. Images have impacts on the world in terms of how they shape action by people. Images can be deliberately promoted, massaged or altered to achieve desired ends, but they all go into forming the ideas and understandings of the world, based on which people make choices and act. There are geographies of images in terms of what areas they do, or do not, show and how they move through society. Moreover, geographers produce images of the world, so we need to re-evaluate what role images play in geographical knowledge. Changes in how the world is seen can tell us something about those doing the seeing.

Mental map

a mental map describes our everyday notions about our spatial location. People rarely picture their spatial location to themselves through the images of a formal map. But of course we are all spatially located and aware. A mental map thus relates the elements we see as important and misses places we do not visit. Studies have shown that instead of a bird's eye view mental maps are organized around paths and landmarks that help us find our way in daily life. *See also* PERCEPTION.

PROCESSES OF PERCEPTION

People do not take in the whole world as they go about their business. Everyone selects and filters what they see and what they make of it. We might look at this through three ideas; biology, (physical and social) position, and cultural frames. The first highlights that human senses connect us to the world in particular ways. With the philosopher of science Donna Haraway, I would suggest walking a dog shows how specific is human experience. The dog's world is visually poor but full of odours carrying information. Our dependence on the visual, our sense of scale and our sense of location, are all based around the human body. Perception does not start as a free-floating moment, but is grounded in frailties and adaptations of the body. We are disposed to make sense of the world and make order from the sensory stimuli our body gets – think of the little parlour games of optical illusions that play on that tendency (see Fig. 6.1). Not that this is bad – just think how useful it is that we can 'see' three dimensions on a flat piece of paper.

Our orientation also plays an important part in ordering experience. The world comes to us in terms of high and low, near and far, present and absent. We understand ourselves spatially, as we recall the world in mental maps to situate ourselves. These are egocentric maps, where our life and experiences are centre stage, and the world fades off into the distance around us. We do not know every part of the planet equally, nor our country, our city, even neighbourhood. We have areas of concern or

Perception

the process through which people form mental images of the world. Often assumed to be both one-directional (from the world to us) and biological (neurologically controlled), many academic studies have emphasized the role of cultural filters or frames in altering how we form pictures of the world.

FIGURE 6.1
Things are not always as they appear.
Credit: Bettman/Corbis

FIGURE 6.2
A New Yorker's Idea of the United States of America by Daniel K. Wallingford, c. 1939.
Credit: George Glazer Gallery

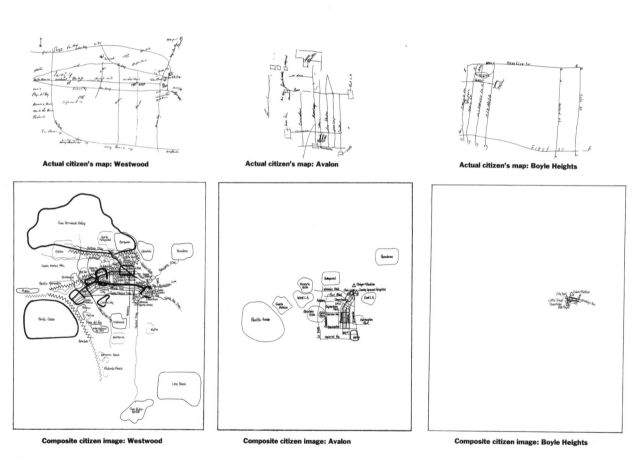

FIGURE 6.3
Cognitive maps of Los Angeles as perceived by predominantly Anglo American residents of Westwood, predominantly African American residents of Avalon, and predominantly Latino residents of Boyle Heights. Source: *The visual environment of Los Angeles*, Los Angeles Department of City Planning, April 1971, pp. 9–10

interest, and different ways of understanding these (see Fig. 6.2). As Edward Relph (1976: 5) put it, consciousness is always consciousness of something, it is not free-floating. We are inescapably immersed in the world. Thus our immediate surroundings are grasped as left and right, while more distant places are subjects of abstract images. These images may be our own experiences as they are remembered or they may be memories of images produced by others – blurring the boundaries of sensed and imagined worlds. These remembered spaces are not based on the geometrical spaces of latitude and longitude; they are shaped by our experiences, travels and the tasks we have at hand (see Figs 6.3–6.5). Our perception of the world is spatial in the way we define objects of interest as a foreground set off against a background and in relation to our viewing position. Images create a relationship between three terms: the perceiving subject, the viewed object and the relationship between them.

FIGURE 6.4
The Geographer by Jan Vermeer.
Credit: akg-images

Our images of the world are not simply our own but are derived from social sources. Different cultures have different ways of seeing the world and representing it. For example, twisted and notched sticks formed maps for travelling in the Arctic for the Inuit. Even colours can shift between cultures, so that we read Homer's 'wine dark sea', because he did not clearly distinguish blue and green (Eco, 1985: 159). Colours are described by reference to other objects ('red like fire', 'white as snow', 'yellow as cornfields'). Our descriptions refer to other things, not direct experience. Images of the world are formed, understood and communicated through materials at hand to that culture, not by a universal sensation.

MAKING PICTURES

The philosopher Martin Heidegger suggested that a crucial shift in how western people experienced the world was when it became conceived as a picture. The world became seen as separate and detached from the viewer. Up until then, Heidegger argued, people had seen themselves as part of the world. This change can be linked to the rise of new techniques for producing images, such as the camera obscura. At its simplest, this is a darkened room with a hole in one wall, while the one opposite forms a screen on which an image of the outside world appears – like a large pin-hole camera. Observers could draw directly from life. These images could be assessed by their direct correspondence to the outside world – a correspondence theory of truthfulness. It produced this image through the seclusion and detachment of the observer, separated from the world. This way of producing images thus became a model of truth that saw a world that could be known and represented through a detached observer.

The viewing position affects the knowledge created. For instance, landscape painting is a specific relationship of the viewer to the world, looking on the scene for pleasure, as an aesthetic object, not as an immersive workaday environment, reflecting how paintings were often commissioned by owners to show their estate. A famous example is Gainsborough's *Mr & Mrs Andrews* (Fig. 6.6), which depicts Mr Andrews standing by his seated wife in the left-hand corner and overlooking the house and estate. The composition is of Mr Andrews showing off his

(c)

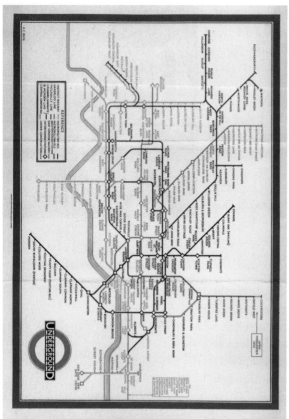

(a)

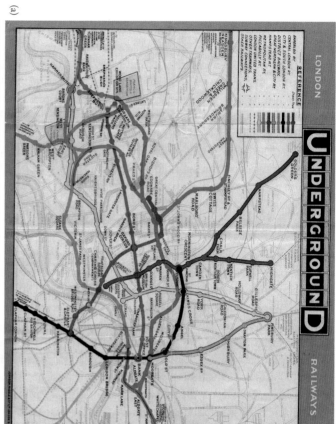

(b)

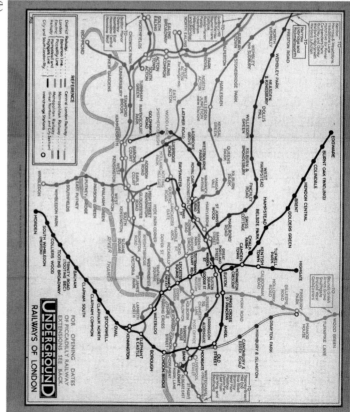

FIGURE 6.5
(a) The first London Underground Railways folding pocket map, issued free in 1908. An accurate reproduction in which lines were related to a central London map. (b) The 1932 London Underground map designed by F.H. Stingemore. This map recorded the expansion of the network into the suburbs. (c) The 1933 Underground map by Harry Beck. A diagrammatic approach that offered clarity rather than a close relationship to actual directions and locations. Credit: © London Regional Transport. Reproduced by kind permission of the London Transport Museum

belongings – with his wife included in that category. Thus it is not only the content that tells us about rural life, but also the composition of these images reveals a class-based and gendered way of looking at the world. This image relates to scenic country parks created by excluding the rural poor, removing traditional rights and privatizing the land. This was a period where villages and public rights of way were moved to create views for the owners of country houses and where new laws criminalized intrusions. Many rural

FIGURE 6.6
Mr & Mrs Andrews by Gainsborough.
Credit: © National Gallery, London, UK/
www.bridgeman.co.uk

people had traditionally hunted game, which was redefined as poaching. At the start of the nineteenth century, over a quarter of all prosecutions in England and Wales were for breaches of these 'game laws'. The image of beautiful and charming rural scenery reflects real struggles over access to the land. The detachment from the scene is also linked to patriarchal power and a masculine viewing position. Landscapes and women tend to be the objects of a male viewer separated from what is depicted, tending to link the natural and the feminine (Rose, 1997a). The art critic John Berger (1972) suggests that, in most art, men act or are viewing subjects while women appear as objects of that view. The viewing subject in this type of painting echoes the positioning in colonial photography, tending to be invisible, as though all-seeing yet not physically present, and meanwhile it turns the people depicted into distanced objects of knowledge (Gregory, 2003).

A vantage point from which the world can be made sense of is often called an 'Archimidean point'. One example is the viewpoint of maps, often suggesting an observer outside what is depicted seeing the true picture. Although apparently factual, maps can also have hidden implications of who is looking at whom from where. Thus British students are familiar with a map centred on Europe and the Atlantic, not one centred on the Americas or on the southern hemisphere (Fig. 6.7) What implicit assumptions are there in the familiar Mercator map about who is of central importance and who is not? The projection downplays the size of places near the equator and exaggerates those near the poles – making the 'West' disproportionately large. An alternative projection – the Peter's Projection – equalizes for area but is less useful for navigation (Fig. 6.8). Each emphasizes certain features of the world and not others.

Not all images rely on detached vantage points, and we can usefully consider why they may not. In art, the rise of cubism and surrealism, after the First World War, did away with realistic perspective and notions of correspondence to seen reality. What does the emergence of these images tell us about the world? Stephen Kern (1983) argues that they express changing experiences of space and time. This was a period seeing the climax of rapid changes in transport (the expansion of railways, steam ships and mass transit systems) and communication technologies (the

Patriarchy

a social system in which men oppress and exploit women. The term was first coined in analyses of households headed by men and organized to the benefit of those 'patriarchs' (for example, through an unequal division of domestic work, or through women's marriage vows 'to obey', or through the legality of rape by husband of wife). However, the term is now used in a wider sense to think about how unequal power relations between men and women are established through realms stretching from the social organization of reproduction and childcare, to the organization of paid work, the operations of the state, cultural understandings of GENDER differences, the regulation of human SEXUALITY, and men's violence towards women.

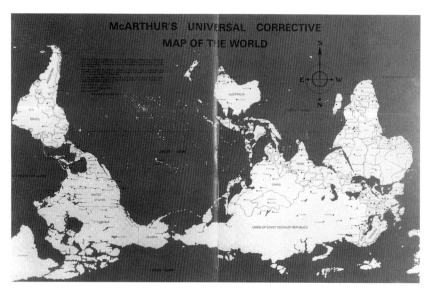

FIGURE 6.7
McArthur's corrective map of the World, by Stuart McArthur. (Further information available from Stuart McArthur, 208 Queen's Parade, North Fitzroy, 3086, Tel: 9842 1055)

telegraph, telephone, then radio). People, goods and information were circulating more rapidly, in greater numbers and over greater distances than ever before, offering no stable vantage point at which the whole picture came together or from where it could all be controlled. The great cities, modern communications and transport created a fragmented experience not a coherent whole. The world could no longer be depicted in the same way. So at this moment what we find emerging are a range of aesthetic movements and practices seeking to refashion how we might see the world, how images might portray the new experiences encountered. They tend to suggest the loss of a stable viewing point and coherent, singular perspectival view on the world – expressing the instability and fluidity found in the world. All these changes in images suggest novel ways of organizing and understanding the world and the shifts going on in society at large.

FIGURE 6.8
Peter's projection world map. Credit: Oxford Cartographers/Getty Images

SUMMARY

- The perceptual world may be more 'real' and truthful to our experiences, and thus as important in orchestrating actions, as any scientifically defined reality. As the world and our experience of it changes, the images that are produced may also change.
- Geographers need to be aware of 'from what angle', literally and metaphorically, people perceive the world. Particular ways of creating images imply relationships between the viewer and the world. The detached point of observation from which a coherent picture can be made may depend on relationships of power and control more than its 'realistic' depiction of the world.

GEOGRAPHIES OF IMAGES

There is a basic geography of making images; production facilities concentrated in Hollywood dominate the flows of images coming to Europe, while there are vibrant movie-making districts in Hong Kong and in India's 'Bollywood'. In an era of satellite pictures beamed around the world, of global news corporations and media events, the conventional geography of national broadcasters breaks up, and we need to think about the circulation of images (Aufderheider, 2000). Images circulate over increased distances at an increasing rate and in vast numbers. Much of this is controlled by multinational business, but it also offers opportunities for minority cultures to use media technology to link groups dispersed over wide distances, as in Inuit soap opera in Canada, or the circulation of videos of Australian aboriginal rituals (Ginsburg, 1991; 1993; Perlmutter, 1993). In a world of global transmission, who can control the representations of communities and their appearance through the media has become an important issue. For many minority groups, becoming visible to the world at large is an important political tool – but one that also changes the internal dynamics of groups irrevocably by altering the power and status of members who control those images (Moore, 1992; Turner, 1991; White, 2003).

Issues of power and control are highlighted when we remember that technologies of vision have been an important part of military development over the last century. Control of vision has been a vital stake – who can see and not be seen. Reconnaissance flights, high-altitude spy planes, night sights, spy satellites ... all create new images. Both Gulf Wars have seen western forces deploying advanced image-producing technology. One issue has been control of pictures: the US military blamed pictures from the Vietnam conflict for undermining support, so reporters have been tightly controlled, even in the attack on Iraq 'embedded' in military units. Although portable satellite links mean instant transmission, and the military timetable has paid heed to American network news slots, live footage has not meant free reporting. The military also provided pictures, from cameras in 'smart bombs' and war planes, ready for broadcast. Unsurprisingly they recorded successful missions, emphasizing what the military wanted and not the carpet bombing of conscripted troops in the 1991 campaign nor the literally uncounted casualities in 2002. It is revealing that the commanders had to remind viewers that these pictures were not 'video games'. The images

Hyper-reality

a phrase most associated with the Italian semiotician (*see* SEMIOTICS) and novelist Umberto Eco, which suggests the development of simulated events and representations that out-do the 'real' events they are meant to be depicting. Thus in hyper-reality the REPRESENTATION exceeds the original, being more sensational, more exciting or so forth. *See also* SIMULACRUM.

were similar, though – with troops only seeing their enemy via screens and describing missions in arcade-game terms. It becomes less clear, then, where a division of image and reality might be.

We might also look at the geography of what is made visible through popular pictures. Some of the most ubiquitous images are tourist snapshots. Estimates suggest something over a billion are taken every year (Stallybras, 1996). We could imagine a map of the world that recorded these as points of light. Think of the dense clusters around the great sights/sites – the Taj Mahal, Grand Canyon, Tower of London, and so on – tailing off into darkened hinterlands, in the slums of Mumbai, into Harlem, former mining villages around Durham. So we have a geography of what is regarded as photogenic. This geography would have to include images in brochures and on postcards. These emphasize the good points of a place: the weather is sunny, the scenery picturesque and the beaches clean. We can think of the types of place these pictures market and depict – so we might think of how they show a world where ethnic stereotypes pervade. Thus there are Amerindians in 'tribal' clothing, next to 'totem poles'; exotic cultures of Asia represented by attractive women; stereotypes of all sorts (Albers and James, 1988; Dann, 1996; Edwards, 1996). We know these images will be selective in what they portray. They illustrate and help shape the desires of tourists, what they want to see, and thus play a vital role in shaping flows of tourists even if 'inaccurate' (Bhattarcharyya, 1997; Gilbert, 1999; McGregor, 2000). We must begin to ask questions about whether images do not shape reality as much as reflect it.

GEOGRAPHIES SHAPED BY IMAGES

An example of how images shape reality comes from tourism, when places are altered to conform to expected images. More subtly, the experience of these places is shaped through images. So, in Don DeLillo's novel *White Noise*, the narrator visits the most photographed barn in America:

Simulacrum

refers to the notion of a copy without an original. If we say at the first point we have an original object, then any image represents it, or replicas are copies of it. We thus have a pattern of original and copy. However, often it is the copies themselves that are copied. The products may begin to diverge from the original. The idea of a simulacrum, or of many simulacra, takes this a step further by emphasizing the presence in contemporary POSTMODERN landscapes of many copies with no original. An example might be the shopping-mall 'Parisian café' that clearly imitates a Parisian café, but for which there is no single original it imitates; or Disneyland's main street, which is again a REPRESENTATION for which there was no original. *See also* HYPER-REALITY.

> *We counted five signs before we reached the site. There were forty cars and a tour bus in the makeshift lot. We walked along a cowpath to the slightly elevated spot set aside for viewing and photographing. All the people had cameras; some had tripods, telephoto lenses, filter kits. A man in a booth sold postcards and slides – pictures of the barn taken from the elevated spot. We stood near a grove of trees and watched the photographers. Murray maintained a prolonged silence, occasionally scrawling some notes in a little book.*

> *'No one sees the barn,' he said finally. 'Once you've seen the signs about the barn, it becomes impossible to see the barn . . . We're not here to capture an image, we're here to maintain one . . . They are taking pictures of taking pictures . . . We can't get outside the aura. We're part of the aura.'*

(Cited in Frow, 1991: 126; and Nye, 1991)

The imageworthy element of the barn is not its inherent qualities but that it appears in so many images. This is not just confined to novels, as on the Greek island of Kefalonia we find Mytros beach, one of the most-depicted beaches in tourist brochures, with its stunning white pictured from above, where there is now a large viewing platform for visitors to take similar pictures – often without actually visiting the beach itself (Fig. 6.9). We can see this taken a step further where not only not visiting, but the object of the image itself, is surpassed. For instance, we have all seen so many images of wild animals filmed with advanced equipment that actual encounters can be disappointing. Umberto Eco has called this 'hyper-reality', where the copies are more important, and realistic, than their originals. Going one step further, images become simulacra – that is, copies for which there is no original. They become entirely self-sustaining without referring to any exterior reality. Jean Baudrillard argues that this has been a long-running trend where, gradually, images have come to stand for and then replace things, calling the whole category of reality into question. Examples might include themed shopping malls that have facades conjuring up images of Parisian cafés that have never existed, or films like *The Lord of the Rings*, where tours of Aotorea/New Zealand now invite you to walk through Moria. The real landscape is imagined in terms of a film about a book that invented a fictional world.

(a)

(b)

FIGURE 6.9
Advertising for beach holidays often stresses the 'unspoiled' nature of beaches, appealing to desires for romantic solitude. However, the very success of advertising campaigns can rapidly lead to beaches becoming popular and commercialized. Credit: (a) Lorna Ainger; (b) Eye Ubiquitous/Alamy

The impacts of images shaping the world can be more direct. We can consider the global flow of news pictures and how this brought pictures of the Tianenmen Square massacre to the whole world, or the destruction of 9/11 in New York. The prominence of specific images of destruction can, though, overwhelm others, and thus the horrific destruction of New York's World Trade Center and the 4000 civilians killed in the terrorist attack there assume more global significance than the 12,000 killed in the attack on Iraq or the 6000 in Afghanistan. One example of how powerful images can be, not just in publicizing events but in shaping how they are

FIGURE 6.10
World weatherman

understood, is the Ethiopian famine of 1984. Here striking news footage of starving people in relief camps produced an enormous charitable effort, global fundraising events and a massive relief effort. The images also suggested helpless victims, fuelling stereotypes about Africa, and said nothing about the way southern Ethiopia remained a food exporter. The cause of the disaster was simplistically presented as a lack of rain and consequent decline in food availability (Fig. 6.10). These images can be criticized for inaccurately depicting the causes, yet we have to acknowledge their enormous real-world impacts.

SUMMARY

- Images selectively portray peoples and places. We need to consider who in the current global economy decides what is shown and controls how it is circulated. How peoples are represented and whether they represent themselves can be the subject of political struggles.

- Images do not just reflect reality but shape actions, experiences and beliefs. Intuitively we think reality comes first and images second. However, the relationship can be more circular. It is possible to suggest that, in some cases, this could be a closed circle of image referring to image without needing to refer to an external reality.

THE TRUTH IS OUT THERE?

Metaphor

the use of a word or symbol from one domain of meaning to apply to another. Thus a rose (a botanical term) is translated into the domain of human relationships to symbolize love. Metaphors involve this movement of concepts from their normal realm to a new realm.

These issues not only affect people 'out there', but also 'academic' images. Traditionally, geographers have seen themselves as making progressively more accurate images of the world. However, activities such as map-making have played a more active part in shaping the world – for instance, being promoted by imperial states such as Britain in order to administer conquered territories. The images produced by geographers are not exempt from the sorts of processes outlined above. We spend most of our time working with **metaphors**, images, models and so forth. How do we assume they relate to reality? Quite often the answer is in terms of some 'correspondence' theory. Yet a perfect correspondence would lead to some bizarre conclusions. The novelist Jorge Luis Borges discussed the perfect map, at a one-to-one scale, which was thus as large as the territory it depicted. More imaginatively, even if you managed to shrink this map, if it shows all the activities and features in the territory, then somewhere on it there would have to be an image of you holding it. And on that image there would have to be an even smaller image of you holding it. This is known as a problem of 'infinite regress'. It may be, then, that trying to find some underlying reality behind the images is the wrong approach. It reminds me of a story about a young pupil who approached a Lama and asked,

'Oh wise one, what is the world on which we dwell?'
The Lama paused, then replied, 'The world is a great disk with seven mountains and nine seas surrounded by the outer ocean.'
The pupil thought, then asked, 'Oh wise one, on what does the disk of the world sit?'
'It sits on the backs of four celestial elephants, and it shudders as they shift its weight on their shoulders.'
The pupil thought for a minute in silence.
'Oh wise one, on what do the four celestial elephants stand?'
'They stand, facing out towards the stars, upon the vast carapace of the world turtle.'
The pupil hesitated.
'Oh wise one . . .'
'Forget it,' said the lama, 'after that it's turtles all the way down.'

A silly example, but we have to face the possibility that we may only be able to understand reality through words or images. We need to think, then, not of how they may distort reality, but what effects and meanings they have for their beholders. In this way we need to see images as actively creating the world rather than simply transmitting a prior reality.

DISCUSSION POINTS

1. If images do not simply reflect reality and are not to be judged by how accurately they correspond to the 'world outside', then how do we discriminate which are good or bad, misleading or truthful?

2. If we see images as inevitable parts of understanding and always partial then how do we judge between them? If there is no reality to be accessed without images, then must we be 'relativists' seeing all images as equal?

3. Are there differences in how textual, pictorial or moving images work?

4. How does the control of producing images affect our knowledge of the world? What are the implications of becoming invisible or visible in the global media?

5. How does what is pictured relate to who is depicting it?

FURTHER READING

Berger, J. (1972) *Ways of seeing.* **Harmondsworth: Penguin.**

An old book but a classic, about the hidden implications of particular ways of looking at art.

Cosgrove, D. (1997) Prospect, perspective and the evolution of the landscape idea. In Barnes, T. and Gregory, D. *Reading Human Geography.* **London: Edward Arnold, 324–41.**

A careful historical survey looking especially at the invention of realistic perspective in the Renaissance.

Eco, U. (1987) *Travels in hyper-reality.* **Picador.**

Written by an Italian Professor of Semiotics (a study of images and communication) who is also a novelist – so it is readable. It documents what he sees as a trend for images to replace the originals they are supposed to depict.

Rose, G. (2001). *Visual methodologies: an introduction to the interpretation of visual materials.* **London: Sage.**

Outlines a host of ways of interrogating what images mean.

Schwartz, J. and Ryan, J. (eds) (2003) *Picturing place: photography and the geographical imagination.* **London: I.B. Tauris.**

Offers a range of essays looking at how photography has shaped geographical knowledge in a historic context.

Wood, D. (1992) *The Power of Maps.* **New York: Guilford Press.**

A nice summary of how what may appear to be factual images corresponding to reality can have many hidden assumptions.

CHAPTER 7
MASCULINITY–FEMININITY

INTRODUCTION

Come into my office and, please, do sit down. If you take a peek around, you can learn quite a bit about me. For instance, I have a child and a man in my life. The walls of my neighbours' offices are equally, or possibly even more, chatty about their family relations, especially their roles as fathers (see Fig. 7.1). Reviewing the applications for five jobs filled between 1994–98 in her geography department in the United States, Joni Seager (2000) found that twice as many male applicants revealed their marital status in their application, and those writing references for them often introduced the applicant's wife as an asset (for example, 'Simon is a friendly and well-liked individual with a charming wife'). You might ask yourself, have you ever seen in a workplace such extravagant displays of homosexual family romance?

(a)

(b)

(c)

FIGURE 7.1
Family relations come to work: (a) Geraldine Pratt's desk; (b) Derek Gregory's hallway message board; (c) Trevor Barnes' office wall

I invite you to consider the many ways that heterosexual masculinities and femininities permeate your everyday life as a geography student, and the geographical knowledges that you learn. It is likely that you come to this text as a gendered subject – just as my colleagues and I do – un-self-consciously living out particular masculine and feminine norms. Geographical knowledge itself is gendered: traditionally as masculine. But we now have many ideas of how to disrupt or unsettle this gendering of knowledge: by asking different questions, using different methods, and telling or writing different stories. I want to explore in particular the tactics of situating knowledge, exploring linkages across spheres and scales of life that typically are conceived as separate, and thinking beyond the binaries that structure much of our social life.

EMBODIED GEOGRAPHIES AND KNOWLEDGE ACQUISITION

Take a look at how you are sitting at the moment. In 1979, a German photographer, Marianne Wex, published hundreds of photographs of men and women to demonstrate feminine and masculine modes of bodily comportment. Standing, sitting or lying on the beach, women tend to hold their arms close to their sides, and their legs locked together, while men often sprawl and take up much more space. My students like to argue that Wex's photographs record a by-gone era, but artist-photographer Amelia Butler shows the enduring nature of feminine and masculine poses. Her photographs (see Fig. 7.2), taken at IKEA in Vancouver, Canada, in 2003, show customers who agreed to pose in a display room of their choice. More than their consumer fantasies are on display, however, and consider how you interpret the bodies that do not conform to feminine and masculine norms.

These bodily practices may seem trivial but it is arguable that they inhabit our psyches and shape cognitive abilities. Iris Young (1990b) has argued that masculine and feminine modes of bodily comportment reflect the fact that boys are freer to simply be in space as subjects rather than objects of visual inspection. Boys then tend to see themselves as 'creating' space and spatial relationships rather than being positioned in space. Young argues that these ways of moving the body affect self-perceptions of competence and cognitive ability. Indeed, it was documented in Britain in the late 1970s that, from age eight, (middle-class) parents tend to allow boys to explore more independently much greater distances from home (Matthews, 1987). It is immensely suggestive that it is from age nine that boys begin, in general, to perform better on tests that measure spatial aptitudes. (These are paper-and-pencil tests that measure various spatial aptitudes by asking, for example, what a two-dimensional representation of a three-dimensional figure would look like if it were rotated by 90 degrees.) Spatial aptitude is a cognitive ability for which there is some of the most persistent and robust evidence of gender difference (Self and Golledge, 1994), and some forms of spatial aptitude are prerequisites for competency in maths.

Boys' relative freedom to explore no doubt reflects their parents' fears about girls' vulnerability in public space, and there is considerable evidence that these gendered geographies of fear persist, and that women tend to be both more fearful and vulnerable to more extreme physical violence in isolated public spaces. (See Whitzman for a discussion of debates about whether this is *merely* a perceptual issue or one that demands concrete changes to the design of urban space.) Such a generalization requires qualification, however. A survey conducted amongst undergraduate students at my university, about histories of victimization on campus, indicated that racialized 'visible minority' men were as vulnerable as white women to serious physical assault. Other research suggests that parental norms may be changing due to increased fears of 'stranger danger', and that middle-class British mothers are now equally, if not more, protective of their sons (who they regard as less mature and somewhat 'dizzier' than their daughters) (Valentine, 1998). To the extent that parenting norms change, gendered differences in both freedom to explore independently and spatial aptitudes may also disappear.

There is evidence, however, that some spatial aptitudes can be developed through video games (*Globe and Mail*, 2003), and there is a gendered geographical story to tell about this as well. McNamee (1998) found that middle-class British boys tend to have better access to

SM [Interviewer]: You've got a sister, Phil. You said that your Nintendo was shared with her – do you ever fight about going on it?

Phil: Well, it's always kept in my room and there's a lot of arguments because I won't let her on it because it's in my room. I won't let her in my room.

SM: Did you say your sister was older or younger?

Phil: Younger.

SM: How much younger?

Phil: Ermm, she's 11.

SM: So you won't let her in your room, you won't let her use it?

Phil: Yeah. She starts getting real annoyed and that and starts saying 'Oh well that's it now. Next time I'm gonna trash your room' and all this lot.

SM: What does your mum say?

Phil: She tells us both to pack it in. She usually blames it on me sister.

Source: McNamee (1998: 197–8)

FIGURE 7.2
Feminine and masculine bodily comportment on display at IKEA. Source: Pratt (2004: 25), with permission of Amelia Butler

computers than do girls, and this results from gendered assumptions and territorial control within the home. In households in which there is only one computer, it is often housed in the boy's bedroom and female siblings must gain entry to this room in order to access computer technology (see box). This is another set of spatial relations, then, that contributes to gendered cognitive development.

SUMMARY
- There are masculine and feminine ways of bodily comportment and these are thought to affect self-perception and cognitive abilities, especially spatial abilities.
- Spatial mobility is conditioned by gendered (and racialized) perceptions of safety, and this affects our capacity to explore and know our environment.
- Environmental experience and organization of domestic space affect spatial aptitudes.

MASCULINIST GEOGRAPHICAL KNOWLEDGE

If you come to the discipline of geography already gendered, you are also likely to encounter knowledge that is itself gendered. The argument about the **masculinism** of geographical knowledge has been made in different ways. The first is nicely summarized by the title of an article written by Jan Monk and Susan Hanson in 1982: 'On not excluding half of the human in Human Geography'. They argued that geographers have ignored vast areas of social life, ones that are understood to be feminine. It is not only that geographers have found some questions more compelling than others (for example, the journey to work as compared to the journey to childcare); certain activities are both undervalued and effectively invisible, often reflecting a wider societal bias.

Women's labour in the home is a prime example. In most countries it is virtually impossible to obtain comprehensive information about it. Every country in the world keeps a national account of economic activity and productivity, but much of women's daily work – household work, volunteer activities, childcare and eldercare, subsistence activities, bartering – lies outside these measurements of the economy. In only a few countries, including New Zealand and Canada, governments now attempt to measure housework in the national census. It is telling that when the Canadian government began to explore the wording of such questions in order to maximize the accuracy of self-reportage, focus group discussions revealed that the term 'work' led to under-reporting (presumably because respondents did not recognize their work as work!) (Rose and Carrasco, 2000). The term 'activities' is now used to record domestic work (see box). Significantly, the Canadian government has yet to incorporate this census data into estimates of national economic activity. In 1998, the Labour government in Britain was one of the first governments to incorporate domestic labour within an estimate of the national economic activity. At that time it was estimated that the wage-equivalent value of housework in Britain exceeded the whole of the manufacturing sector. As Domosh and Seager note: 'It is interesting to note that having made this estimate, the [Labour] government did nothing with it … To formally include housework in economic valuation would require a thorough reconceptualization of the entire economic accounts system …' (2001: 45).

A second observation about the masculinism of knowledge is that when social life is recorded, it is often done so in gendered terms in subtle and unacknowledged ways. Gibson-Graham (1996), for example, argues that popular and scholarly understandings of globalization are organized

Masculinism, masculinist
a form of thought or knowledge that, whilst often claiming to be impartial, comprehends the world in ways that are derived from men's experiences and concerns. Many Feminist Geographers have argued that Human Geography has traditionally been masculinist (see FEMINISM).

through masculine representations of capitalism and a metaphor of penetration and rape of feminized, vulnerable local economies. She argues that workers have absorbed the politics of fear in ways analogous to rape victims. Following feminist efforts to re-script women's vulnerability to rape in ways other than pure victim-hood, Gibson-Graham considers ways of rhetorically diminishing the perceived power of multinational corporations by exploring their vulnerabilities as masculine bodies. We are asked to envision seminal fluid as leaky, often misdirected and wasted. Violating the norms of heterosexuality (within which the male body is seen as having well-defined borders, and (literally) an agent rather than recipient of penetration), Gibson-Graham represents the male body as penetrable. By analogy, we are also asked to consider that money (capitalism's semen) might also misfire, and that non-capitalist enterprises have the capacity to penetrate and reshape capitalism. 'Queering' globalization in this way, Gibson-Graham claims, liberates alternative ways of imagining globalization, and creates opportunities for non-capitalist economic and social forms. As a very different example of the unacknowledged gendering of objects of study, any technologies used by women (for example, 'the domestic workhorse technologies' such as microwaves) tend to be downgraded by engineers as simple and boring (compared to glamorous electronics like stereos) even when there is no rational (technological) basis for this (Cockburn, 1997). Cockburn describes how academics absorb these gendered assumptions: 'domestic technology is … something of a poor relative in the sociology of technology … In the case of the UK study of microwave cooking … I found that mention of [my] choice of subject seldom failed to raise a little smile in [my] hearers' (1997: 367).

Third, Gillian Rose (1993) has argued that Human Geography is masculinist in a more general **epistemological** sense. She identifies two traditions of masculinist geographical knowledge production, which produce and relate to constructions of femininity in specific but differing ways. She argues that masculinity and femininity are not simply social constructions but a self-reinforcing binary constructed within a masculinist frame of reference. Masculinity defines itself in opposition to what is conceived as feminine: the subjective, emotional, embodied. Social-scientific masculine knowledge represses femininity and is conceived as rational, neutral, universal, exhaustive and the product of a detached, objective observer. Aesthetic masculinity, which she attributes to **humanistic geography**, continues to operate within the dualism of masculine and feminine because it feminizes nature, landscapes and place, and posits its authority to know these places in universalizing ways.

Epistemology, epistemological

epistemology is the study of knowledge, particularly with regard to its methods, scope and validity. This technical term from philosophy refers to differing ideas about what it is possible to know about the world and how it is possible to express that knowledge. Different academic disciplines and different general approaches in Geography are marked by distinctively different epistemologies. Human Geographers are interested in the epistemological questions raised by the geographical knowledges held both by academics and by ordinary people. In studying these epistemological questions Human Geographers seek to connect up questions of content (what kinds of things people know) with structures of belief (how and why they claim to know) and issues of authority (how and why these knowledges are valued and justified).

Humanistic Geography

a theoretical approach to Human Geography that concentrates on studying the conscious, creative and meaningful activities and experiences of human beings. Coming to prominence in the 1970s, Humanistic Geography was in part a rebuttal of attempts during the 1960s to create a law-based, scientific Human Geography founded on statistical data and analytical techniques (see SPATIAL SCIENCE). In contrast, it emphasized the subjectivities of those being studied and, indeed, the Human Geographers studying them. Human meanings, emotions and ideas with regard to place, space and nature thus became central.

SUMMARY

- Much of women's experience has been ignored by geographers, and government agencies fail to collect data on many aspects of social life.
- Nonetheless, social life is often interpreted through a gendered lens.
- In the production of geographical knowledge, different types of masculinities, which produce and play upon the masculine–feminine duality in varying ways, structure epistemology.

BEYOND THE DUALITY OF MASCULINE–FEMININE

On the cover of the book in which Gillian Rose developed her critique of the masculinisms underpinning geographical knowledge is a photograph by the artist Barbara Kruger. Framing the image of a woman's face is the text: 'We won't play nature to your culture'. This is a refusal to participate in the dualisms (i.e. nature:culture, feminine:masculine) that structure masculinist knowledges. How might we refuse these dualisms, once the masculinist limits of existing geographical knowledge have been identified?

Situated knowledges

One strategy has been to rethink the concept of scientific objectivity and refuse the masculinist dualisms (objectivity:subjectivity; mind:body; scientifically detached:politically engaged) on which it has been based. Donna Haraway (1991a) has likened the traditional, detached scientific account to a 'godtrick' because it is located both nowhere and everywhere. In her view, such accounts are dangerous because they overgeneralize one way of looking at the world, and colonize other knowledges and perspectives through powerful claims to objectivity. She argues that all accounts of the world – including scientific ones – come from a social location. Scientists also typically view the world through enabling technologies (whether these be questionnaires, maps or computer modelling, to name but a few). Responsible objective descriptions of the world are situated, partial ones, that attempt to reveal the technologies upon which they are built. This is what Haraway calls 'accountable positioning'.

To give a concrete example, in 1987 Susan Hanson and I did a large social survey in Worcester, Massachusetts. A semi-structured questionnaire was 'administered' to a large representative sample of the population. Despite all of the trappings of social scientific objectivity, an important part of positioning the research was to try to understand the limitations and partiality of what we were able to see. We tried to do this by interviewing the research assistants who conducted the survey interviews (see box), and it became apparent that our observations and interpretations were coloured by our class positioning.

There are three implications that follow from the notion of situated knowledge. First, it dissolves an unfortunate dualism between quantitative and qualitative, and scientific and non-scientific, modes of research. Haraway wanted to contain the claims of scientists through the notion of situated knowledge, but she also made it clear that scientists have developed very powerful and useful technologies for seeing, and that the stakes and resources of science are too high *not* to participate in it. Her goal has been to encourage scientists to recognize the partiality and constructed nature of their knowledge claims. A non-masculinist science is one that explores its limits rather than one that dispenses with quantitative methods and the powerful visualization techniques associated

[It] was very difficult for that [domestic work done by children] to come through, the way the interview was structured. We asked about household chores in terms of 'is it either you or your spouse or someone else who does it?' The 'someone else' sounded like it was outside the family. But among my friends [growing up in Worcester] it was very common for the oldest child to make dinner.

In some interviews, it was apparent that [your] way of thinking about decisions of where to live and work was alien. I can think of one woman who found the questions very strange. The reasons why she had moved were not related to work, child care, etc., but rather, she had been thrown out of her house by her boyfriend and then in the second place she had lived, the house burnt down and so she had to move. Perhaps this reflects the class differences [between] researchers and interviewees.

(Hanson and Pratt, 1995: 83, 92)

In 1996, the Canadian census was one of the first national censuses to measure domestic labour. Every fifth Canadian household was asked to fill out a long form of the census, and they were asked three questions:

1. NAME	PERSON 1	PERSON 2
In the spaces provided, copy the names in the same order as in **Step 2**. Then answer the following questions for each person.	Family name Given name　　　　Initial	Family name Given name　　　　Initial

Remember, these questions are only for persons aged 15 and over.

HOUSEHOLD ACTIVITIES	43.	44.
Note: **Last week** refers to Sunday, May 5 to Saturday, May 11, 1996. In Question 30, where activities overlap, report the same hours in more than one part. 30. **Last week**, how many hours did this person ■ spend doing the following activities?		
(a) Doing **unpaid** housework, yard work or home maintenance for members of this household, or others. Some examples include: preparing meals, doing laundry, household planning, shopping and cutting the grass.	01 ○ None 02 ○ Less than 5 hours 03 ○ 5 to 14 hours 04 ○ 15 to 29 hours 05 ○ 30 to 59 hours 06 ○ 60 hours or more	01 ○ None 02 ○ Less than 5 hours 03 ○ 5 to 14 hours 04 ○ 15 to 29 hours 05 ○ 30 to 59 hours 06 ○ 60 hours or more
(b) Looking after one or more of this person's own children, or the children of others, **without pay**. Some examples include: bathing or playing with young children, driving children to sports activities or helping them with homework, and talking with teens about their problems.	07 ○ None 08 ○ Less than 5 hours 09 ○ 5 to 14 hours 10 ○ 15 to 29 hours 11 ○ 30 to 59 hours 12 ○ 60 hours or more	07 ○ None 08 ○ Less than 5 hours 09 ○ 5 to 14 hours 10 ○ 15 to 29 hours 11 ○ 30 to 59 hours 12 ○ 60 hours or more
(c) Providing **unpaid** care or assistance to one or more seniors. Some examples include: providing personal care to a senior family member, visiting seniors, talking with them on the telephone, and helping them with shopping, banking or with taking medication.	13 ○ None 14 ○ Less than 5 hours 15 ○ 5 to 9 hours 16 ○ 10 hours or more	13 ○ None 14 ○ Less than 5 hours 15 ○ 5 to 9 hours 16 ○ 10 hours or more
LABOUR MARKET ACTIVITIES		
31. **Last week**, how many hours did this person spend **working for pay or in self-employment**? include: ■ working directly towards the operation of a family farm or business without formal pay arrangements (e.g., assisting in seeding, doing accounts); ■ working in his/her own business, farm or professional practice, alone or in partnership; ■ working for wages, salary, tips or commission.	17 ○ None → Continue with the next question OR 18 ☐ ◄ Number of hours (to the nearest hour) ↳ Go to Question 37	17 ○ None → Continue with the next question OR 18 ☐ ◄ Number of hours (to the nearest hour) ↳ Go to Question 37

Page 18　　See the Guide or ☎ 1 800 670-3388

Source: Census (1996), long form, Statistics Canada

with them. To see what this looks like, you might visit http://www.healthgis-li.com/. This is a website that evolved out of the activism of women on Long Island, New York, who were concerned about the high rate of breast cancer among themselves, friends and family, and possible environmental causes for it. Their efforts have led to a US$27 million GIS to evaluate exposure to a large number of environmental contaminants (McLafferty, 2002). There is a clear and detailed statement on the website of the quality of the quantified data through which the maps have been created. This is an explicit effort at 'accountable positioning'.

Second, situating scientific claims opens space for other types of knowledge, constructed from different vantage points, using other technologies for seeing. These might include indigenous or community-based knowledges, or simply different research methodologies. One of the most exciting contributions of feminist geographers has been their enthusiasm for methodological experimentation with, for instance, ethnography, participatory research, video, theatre and different modes of media and writing (e.g. Moss, 2002; Pain, 2004). Consider, for example, Caitlin Cahill's participatory research with six young women of colour in the Lower Eastside of New York City. Their first project was to expose and disrupt stereotypes about young women of colour by mounting a sticker campaign in the Lower Eastside (see Fig. 7.3). They have subsequently reflected more deeply on their experiences and the meaning of these stereotypes in a newsletter, report and website (http://www.fed-up-honeys.org/). Another striking example is Gill Valentine's (1998) personal account of being stalked and receiving obscene letters. Her writing is autobiographical and deeply personal, and is both an intervention to stop the process of harassment and a fascinating description of the ways that sexual harassment re-orders the meaning of places such as the home. She describes how her new home, previously a source of pride and pleasure, became a site of great anguish. Her writing blurs all sorts of distinctions:

FIGURE 7.3
Blurring research and activism: the Fed-Up-Honeys' sticker campaign in the Lower Eastside

emotional involvement and detached assessment; scholarly reflection and activist intervention; autobiography and social geography.

Third, and most importantly, the significance of specifying scientific claims and proliferating other ways of seeing is to generate conversations across partial knowledges so that we might develop less singular, less dangerous, more complex, multidimensional and reliable understandings of the world. Situated knowledges open opportunities to learn from other perspectives and ways of knowing, and to engage in processes of translation across non-reducible knowledges. This process of translation is a laborious, halting one, and it demands a rich geographical imagination that is both knowledgeable and sensitive to the particularity of context and culture. Jane Jacobs (1994) details some of the challenges of one such process of translation, in this case between aboriginal Arrernte women and a variety of Australian feminists in the 1980s. To establish land rights and halt the construction of a dam, the Arrernte were forced to disclose information about sacred sites. Yet such disclosure transgressed important rules of secrecy surrounding the sites. At one site Arrernte deliberately shared their knowledge and allowed selective members of the press to see and photograph the site, whilst simultaneously making it clear that other ritual objects and stories, especially important to Arrernte women, would not be shown or told. In speaking of the importance of these sacred objects, Arrernte women translated them into the language of feminism: 'Like you have your women's liberation, for hundreds of years we've had ceremonies that control our conduct … They give spiritual and emotional health to Aboriginal women' (1994: 186). Jacobs describes the delicate act of disclosure and non-disclosure, and partial translation across knowledges and political aims.

Social reproduction

the processes through which societies sustain themselves in social and material terms across space and time. In purely material terms, people need to consume various commodities (housing, food, clothing, recreation, etc.) in order to sustain (reproduce) themselves, and these commodities have to be made available through various forms of exchange (e.g. wholesaling, retailing, sites of consumption like cinemas, concert venues, clubs). But, crucially, social reproduction is necessarily also a social process. It involves the development and transmission of norms and 'rules' of behaviour around the circuits of social reproduction that give direction to, and make sense of, their activities within such circuits. Social reproduction also suggests that the purpose of economic activity is not the generation of particular moments of production, consumption or exchange but the sustenance (the reproduction) of these activities over space and time.

> **SUMMARY**
> - One way of disrupting the dichotomy between subjective and objective knowledge is to reconceptualize the meaning of objectivity. Situated knowledge has been an important concept for doing this.
> - Situated knowledge is the idea that all knowledge claims – even scientific ones – are partial and located from within a particular perspective.
>
> Objectivity emerges through elaborating and understanding this partiality.
> - This opens opportunities to acknowledge the validity of other perspectives and knowledges. Situated knowledge requires a commitment to communicate across different perspectives and types of knowledge.

Exploring linkages and disrupting categories

Another strategy for disrupting the duality of masculinity–femininity is to question the classification of social life into private and public spheres, and to explore linkages across different 'spheres' of life and scales of analysis. We have already noticed that certain types of work – mostly non-waged work of **social reproduction** done in and around the home – are considered to lie outside of the formal economy, and most governments keep no record of them. It is not only women's work that disappears within the domestic sphere; many issues and relations that are fundamentally important to the equality, and material and psychological well-being of women (and other marginalized groups) have been designated as private and non-political. Much feminist analysis and activism has been dedicated to reframing and politicizing issues that have been enclaved within the private sphere – for example, childcare, domestic violence and sexual freedom.

The other side of this is to demonstrate how what is conceived as private (and feminine) is ever present in other realms of live. Reconsider the family pictures on my office desk. So, too, women's continuing overwhelming responsibility for domestic work affects where they work, whether they work full-time or part-time, and their long-term career aspirations and progress (Hanson and Pratt, 1995). Kay Anderson and Susan Smith (2001) ask us to consider how emotions permeate all aspects of public life, whether in the workplace, the housing market or urban planning decisions. They argue that recognizing this emotionality is an intensely political act. By feminizing emotions and relegating them to the private sphere, we sustain the myth that economic matters and government policies are purely rational, and set the stage for a broader neo-liberal agenda: 'the logic of efficiency *depends on* the silencing of emotions' (2001: 8).

Another aspect of disrupting conventional gendered classifications of social life involves rethinking assumptions about the scale at which particular social processes occur. Scale itself is gendered: the body, home and neighbourhood tend to be feminized, and 'large'-scale processes such as the economy, government and geopolitical security are typically viewed as masculine. These 'scalar narratives' are gendered social constructions (Marston, 2000). Not only does business and state administration involve more than rational calculation, it is accomplished at a range of scales, including the body. Alison Mountz (2003) describes how the administration of Canadian federal immigration law is embodied at a variety of scales, including very intimate ones. For instance, Canadian immigration officers interpret the criminality of refugee claimants by reading their bodies. In the case of smuggled migrants from Fujian, China, apprehended off the coast of British Columbia in 1999, immigration officers made a close study of their body tattoos as one means of differentiating 'snakeheads' (smugglers) from those who were being smuggled. Also challenging conventional narratives about scale, in this case of nation and war, Tamar Mayer (2005) argues that the war in former Yugoslavia was the paradigm for a new warfare because the rape of tens of thousands of women became not 'collateral damage', but a key means through which the war was conducted. War was conducted in the most intimate of ways as women were systematically raped, first in their homes, then in public spaces, then in detention camps, then in special rape camps, and eventually in brothels.

Proliferating genders

Finally, the duality of masculine–feminine is exhausted by proliferating the category of gender – beyond the number two. This has been

SUMMARY

- The division between public and private is a gendered classification, and what is deemed private is also often classified as feminine. The private tends to be depoliticized. Feminist analysis shows the effects of this classificatory distinction, and demonstrates the links between public and private.

- Geographical scale is also a gendered social construction. New analytical possibilities are opened by 'rescaling' our analyses (or telling other 'scalar narratives').

accomplished in different ways. One is to document the existence of many different masculinities and femininities, many different ways of 'doing' gender. In her study of the financial district in London, England, McDowell (1997) identifies two very different masculinities at work: the youthful virility of the 'Big Swinging Dick' on the trading floor and the sober, rational patriarch of corporate finance. Alison Blunt (1994) has described how Mary Kingsley, an upper-middle-class British woman who travelled to West Africa in the 1890s, was able to transgress the norms of white bourgeois femininity while travelling in Africa (and her health simultaneously improved remarkably!). Femininity could thus be lived differently in different places, and geographical mobility was key to getting some distance from Victorian norms of femininity.

One aspect of proliferating genders is to recognize that gender intersects with a range of other social identities, including race, sexuality and class. In a focus group of Asian-Canadian youth in Vancouver, Canada, in December 1997, one young woman described how she moved in and out of different femininities as she moved between languages and different spaces of the city. She described how she literally embodied different racialized femininities (see box). Sexuality also has been a rich site for proliferating and troubling gender dualisms (see Chapter 29), and to declare transgendered people to be 'the new gays' (Armstrong, 2004) exactly misses this point. Proliferating genders does more than make us think about gender in new ways; it profoundly unsettles a core dichotomy that structures our subjectivity and our patterns of thought in profound and far-reaching ways.

> When I speak Chinese, I feel very formal. I feel like I should be sitting with my back straight. It seems that when I speak Chinese, I'm trying to fit the stereotype of what I am supposed to be in Chinese culture. I am a girl. I am female. So I try to fit the identity of female when I speak Chinese. My voice when I speak English isn't extremely high pitched. It's quite low. But when I speak Chinese my voice goes up. It just shoots up. I swear. I feel like this little girl. I totally feel it. When I am speaking Chinese, I try to fit into this stereotype of what, maybe not the culture, but what I have been taught that I'm supposed to be as a Chinese female, as a Chinese woman, as a Chinese young woman.
>
> (Pratt, 2004: 134)

SUMMARY

- One strategy to move beyond gender dualism is to demonstrate that the gender itself is plural, interwoven with other social identities, and unstable across time and place.

CONCLUSION

Gender dualism structures our subjectivities as teachers and students, and the geographical knowledges that we teach and learn. A sustained critique of the masculinism of geographical knowledge over the last 25 years has led to many strategies to free our thinking from the limits imposed by this dualistic gender hierarchy. Many of these strategies are inherently geographical. They involve locating and contextualizing one's knowledge claims in particular places and times, moving across and making connections between spaces in our conceptualizations, and proliferating genders by exploring their particularity in specific places and differences across space. Human Geography, then, has not only benefited from feminist analyses and critiques of gender dualisms; a spatial imagination has much to offer to both understanding and transcending gendered norms.

DISCUSSION POINTS

1. Are you equally feminine (or masculine) in different places? Do you live different femininities (or masculinities) in different places, in relation to different people?

2. Recognizing the gendered geography of fear and its implications for access to urban space, what might we do about it? When I was doing research in Worcester, Massachusetts, one employer in an inner-city factory told us that he never hired women for the night shift because it was too dangerous for women to leave the workplace at night. This effectively blocked women from gaining the skills and knowledge for the more highly paid jobs because the night shift was the entry point for this training (Hanson and Pratt, 1995). How might we think of non-paternalist ways of dealing with gendered geographies of fear?

3. Mentally walk through various spaces (home and work), and try cataloguing your gendered assumptions about the technologies contained within them. Can you discern a spatial pattern to the locations of feminine and masculine technologies? Is a coffee pot masculine or feminine, for instance, at both home and work? What are the implications of this gendering of technology?

4. It is much easier to talk about translating across different knowledges in the abstract than in practice. Feminists have had notoriously difficult times talking across issues such as female circumcision or the rights of Islamic girls and women to wear the veil (or, more recently in France, headscarves to secular public (state) schools). Discussion usually founders on the difficulties of reconciling universal notions of women's equality (which some see as essentially western) with the desire to respect cultural differences. Consider one such controversial issue, by first elaborating the arguments for and against, and then thinking about how you might translate across these conflicting positions. How might a geographical education and attention to geographical specificity help in this process of translation?

5. Even paid domestic workers have an extremely difficult time extracting fair compensation for their work because labour in the home is not seen as work. Examine your own assumptions. Should a domestic worker be paid full wages when she is washing the dishes after dinner? Should she be paid full wages when she is caring for an employer's children around the family swimming pool? Does she need training for the job?

FURTHER READING

Haraway, D. (1991) Situated knowledges: the science question in feminism and the privilege of partial perspective. In Haraway, D., *Simians, cyborgs, and women: the reinvention of nature*. London and New York: Routledge.

This essay is not easy and it assumes some knowledge of key philosophical debates around objectivity and relativism, but it is a classic and has had a profound effect within Human Geography since the early 1990s. Don't expect to understand it fully the first time around but enjoy the writing for its great wit, passion and energy.

Hodge, D. (ed.) (1995) Should women count? The role of quantitative methodology in feminist geographic research. *The Professional Geographer* 47, 426–66.

This is a short collection of essays that explores the many useful ways that feminist geographers can use quantitative methods. It debunks the notion that quantitative methods are necessarily masculinist and thus usefully dissolves (a rather masculinist!) binary between quantitative and qualitative research strategies.

Moss, P. (ed.) (2002) *Feminist geography in practice: research and methods*. Oxford: Blackwell.

This is an edited volume that introduces undergraduate students to a range of methodologies and feminist research strategies.

Rose, G. (1993) *Feminism and geography: the limits of geographical knowledge*. Minneapolis: University of Minnesota Press.

Rose elaborates a critique of geographical knowledge as masculinist (as well as white, bourgeois and heterosexist) through case studies of time-geography, humanistic geography and traditions of studying 'the landscape' in geography.

Seager, J. (2003) *The state of women in the world atlas* (3rd edn). New York: Penguin; London: Women's Press; Paris: Autremont Editions.

This atlas demonstrates the power of mapping, for seeing patterns and generating questions. A wide range of themes and statistics are mapped – from women's formal political participation and representation, to migration patterns of domestic workers.

CHAPTER 8
SCIENCE–ART

David Gilbert

THE INDISCIPLINE OF HUMAN GEOGRAPHY

Each year, alongside the more formal teaching that I do in lectures and seminars, I work with a small group of first years. We meet weekly to discuss essays and assignments, and other issues arising from the courses that they are doing. In the last session before Christmas, we look back on the first term's work. Often this discussion concentrates on practicalities, perhaps about the differences between learning at school and university, or about moving to a British university from abroad, or about the challenges of balancing study and other commitments. But we also talk about their early impressions of 'doing geography'. Two reactions are very common – reactions that are two sides to the same coin. Some students enthuse about the diversity of what they have been doing, and about the range of subjects and approaches addressed in the first few weeks. This variety (as Philip Crang points out in Chapter 3) is often a strong motivation for taking a course in geography. But for others, this is a source of anxiety. As one (rather insightful) student put it, 'other people here at university are in disciplines, but we seem to be in an indiscipline'.

When we talk in our group we often identify a number of different dimensions to this 'indiscipline'. The first and most obvious is about the huge range of topics studied. Most of our students take broad introductory modules in both Human and Physical Geography in their first term. At 10 o'clock in the morning they may be learning about global geopolitics in a post-Cold War world, and an hour later the focus has shifted dramatically to the analysis of ice cores as evidence of long-term environmental change. Even within the confines of the Human Geography course, students have to consider a dizzying range of topics and case studies, from the lasting effects of the slave trade, through Nike's global subcontracting arrangements, to the significance of sexual identity for urban change in Manchester, and the travel writings of Alexander von Humbolt or Bill Bryson. This diversity may just be a matter of chaotic course design (I'm responsible for this module), but I suspect that something similar happens in many introductory courses to Human Geography.

However, our group discussions can go on to identify other significant differences within geography. Drawing on their experiences in classes in research methods, as well reflecting on the case studies in the lecture series, some students talk about differences in approach, as well as content. They point not just to the differences in what geographers study, but also differences in the ways that they undertake research. At the most obvious level, this is about the practices of doing geography. After they've been on their first-year field course, students are even more likely to comment on this – different kinds of geographer have very different ways of finding out about the world. This may involve the measurement of physical features (perhaps the slope profile of a beach or the size of

Quantitative methods
research methods that involve the production and analysis of numerical data.

Qualitative methods
research methods that involve the production and analysis of data that do not take a numerical form.

particles on a river bed) as a way testing the validity of a particular model of the processes creating a particular landform. Or it may involve undertaking questionnaires or interviews with local people, to be analysed afterwards using either quantitative or qualitative methods. Students are often surprised to be asked to read novels, look at paintings or watch films set in the place that they are studying. This surprise is heightened when it is suggested that this work is more than just a way of getting a background feel for the place, but a significant form of geographical research with particular methods and techniques of analysis and interpretation. (You can read more about these in Chapter 6, on 'image–reality', and Chapter 10, on 'imaginative geographies'). Closely linked to these differences in approach are differences in the technology and equipment used to do geography, and the wide variety of sites that geography takes place in. This includes not just the range of places that we call 'the field' (which might be a glacier face far from the nearest human habitation or a housing project in the heart of a giant city), but also laboratories, computer suites, libraries and archives (Crang, 1998b; Livingstone, 2000; DeLyser and Starrs, 2001).

The diversity of geography is also reflected in the ways that it is written. My first-year students experience this in a couple of ways. Alongside textbooks like this one, this is the time when many of them are taking their first look at academic journals. While all of the journals they read have the same general aim of presenting new research and ideas to the academic community, the ways in which they do this are often very different. This isn't just a difference between those journals that publish work relevant to Physical Geographers and those that publish the work of Human Geographers. There are very marked differences in style and structure between pieces in, say, *Regional Studies* and the *Journal of Historical Geography*, or even between articles in a single issue of general journals like *Transactions of the Institute of British Geographers* or *Annals of the Association of American Geographers*. Of course, students also experience this diversity actively, when they have to write essays or other assignments, and are expected to follow particular conventions of structure and writing style.

A final set of differences often comes out in these discussions with my students. Sometimes this can get a bit personal – students will talk about how different aspects of geography seem to attract different kinds of people. Very often this is done by reference to other disciplines. Some geographers are described as being like 'hard scientists', while others are seen as having much more in common with academics teaching in Sociology, History, Literature or Cultural Studies. Students point to differences in teaching styles, in the use of language, in attitudes, even in ways of dressing. Students, too, are often tempted to 'take sides', and many rapidly identify themselves as a certain kind of geographer. In many ways this is what higher education should be about. In a good geography degree

(a)

(b)

(c)

(d)

FIGURE 8.1
Images from undergraduate prospectuses show
the wide variety of practices associated with the
discipline of Geography. Different ways of
'doing Geography' are associated with different
ways of thinking about the world.
Credit: (a) Pascal Parrot/Corbis Sygma;
(b) Andrew Evans; (c) Helen Bowen;
(d) Chris Perkins

programme there's an opportunity not just to specialize in certain aspects
of the discipline, but also to develop a commitment to particular ways of
approaching the study of the world – ways of organizing evidence, solving
problems, developing theories or searching for meanings. However, all too
often this development is accompanied by a growing lack of understanding
of alternative approaches. It's not unusual to hear geographers who regard
themselves as doing 'hard science' contrasting their work with supposedly
'softer' or even 'arty-farty' approaches. Conversely, other geographers will
oppose the subtlety and sophistication of their work to the philistinism,
one-dimensionality and political naïvety of 'nerdy' scientists.

Such stand-offs are not, of course, limited to the discipline of
geography. Indeed we can find earlier examples of remarkably similar
kinds of posturing and name-calling from as long ago as the seventeenth
century, from those promoting ways of approaching the study of the
world that came to be known as the sciences and the arts or humanities.
Writing in the 1950s, the English novelist and social commentator C.P.

Snow famously pointed to this much more general division in academic life, marked by differences between 'literary intellectuals at one pole – at the other scientists, and as the most representative, the physical scientists'. Snow suggested that there was 'a gulf of mutual incomprehension' between the two groups, sometimes 'hostility and dislike, but most of all lack of understanding. Their attitudes are so different that, even on the level of emotion they can't find much common ground' (Snow, 1959: 4).

Snow was writing about what he called the problem of the 'two cultures' in the very specific context of mid-twentieth-century Britain and its universities. (For a thoughtful consideration of the limitations of Snow's arguments, and his place in the much longer history of incomprehension and hostility between the Sciences and Arts, see Gould, 2004: 69–112.) The intervening years have seen dramatic changes in universities and intellectual life more generally, most obviously in the great expansion of the social sciences, subjects like Sociology, Anthropology and Politics, characterized by a distinctive third kind of culture. Nonetheless, his remarks draw our attention to a couple of features that are particularly important in understanding the diversity of Human Geography, which seems to encompass all three intellectual cultures and more. First, he points to the ways in which academic work has a 'culture', and always takes place in particular social contexts (and indeed, as we pointed out earlier, in particular geographical contexts too). When we discuss different approaches to Human Geography we cannot talk about these in abstract – we are always talking about the work of particular groups of people, with particular interests, social networks and social characteristics. We need to think about geographical knowledge being socially and geographically situated. Second, Snow's comments draw attention to 'mutual incomprehension' and the possibility of hostility and even conflict between different approaches. In celebrating the diversity of Human Geography we shouldn't underplay the extent to which the discipline is contested – particularly in the kinds of claims about knowledge made by different approaches.

SUMMARY

• The disciplines of geography in general and Human Geography in particular are characterized by marked diversity. This diversity is expressed in the focus, methods, practices, equipment and geographical sites associated with different approaches. Different approaches to geography are also marked by very different forms of writing.

• Thinking about the diversity of Human Geography also draws our attention towards contestation and conflict between different perspectives, and between different groups of geographers.

HISTORIES OF HUMAN GEOGRAPHY

To be confronted with this 'indiscipline' at the start of a programme in geography can be more than a little daunting. This feeling isn't restricted to new undergraduates, as Noel Castree and Thomas MacMillan have pointed out, commenting on the remarkable dynamism of Human Geography in recent times. As they put it:

Modern, modernity, modernism

ideas of the modern are most commonly defined through their opposition to the old and the traditional. In this light, the adjective 'modern' is synonymous with 'newness'; 'modernity' refers both to the 'post-traditional' historical epoch within which 'newness' is produced and valued, as well as to the economic, social, political and cultural formations characteristic of that period; and 'modernism' applies more narrowly to artistic, architectural and intellectual movements that centrally explore ideas of 'newness' and develop 'new' aesthetics and ways of thinking to express these. Modernity has been most commonly located in Euro-American societies from the eighteenth century onwards, and thereby associated with their characteristic combination of capitalist economies (see CAPITALISM), political organization through NATION-STATES, and cultural values of secularity, rationality and progress (see ENLIGHTENMENT). However, increasingly, Human Geographers are recognizing that modernity is a global phenomenon that has taken many different forms in different times and places. See also MODERNIZATION.

Post-colonial, post-colonialism

sometimes hyphenated, sometimes not, this term has two distinct meanings: (a) the post-colonial era, i.e. the historical period following a period of COLONIALISM (see also DECOLONIZATION); (b) post-colonial political, cultural and intellectual movements, and their perspectives, which are critical of the past and ongoing effects of European and other colonialisms.

Masculinism, masculinist

a form of thought or knowledge that, whilst often claiming to be impartial, comprehends the world in ways that are derived from men's experiences and concerns. Many Feminist Geographers have argued that Human Geography has traditionally been masculinist (see FEMINISM).

" *Intellectual change, it seems, is now the only disciplinary constant. Some have experienced the procession of new 'isms', 'ologies', and 'turns' in Human Geography as a threat to subject identity. Others are no doubt exhausted by the ceaseless profusion of theories, methodologies, and data sources.* "

(Castree and MacMillan, 2004: 469)

The most common way of making sense of this diversity has been to examine the history of the discipline, looking at the development of major approaches, and the competition between them. The history of the discipline of geography can help us to understand its present characteristics in a number of ways. First, looking at the past shows that geography has always been characterized by diversity – as Mike Heffernan argues, 'geography, whether defined as a university discipline, a school subject, or a forum for wider debate, has always existed in a state of uncertainty and flux' (2003: 19). There was no past golden age when geography had a single stable set of questions and methods, although there have been plenty of attempts to impose a unified vision on the discipline. This historical emphasis moves us away from trying to frame an overall, everlasting definition of what geography is, or what it is that geographers study, towards thinking about a changing tradition (Livingstone, 1992). The introduction to this book suggests that we might answer the question 'What is Human Geography?' by reference to very general kinds of intellectual contribution – particularly in understanding the relations between human beings and the natural world, and in understanding questions of space and place in human life. Viewed historically, these questions can be regarded as being at the core of the geographical tradition, but we can also see how the balance between them has shifted, and how they have been framed in dramatically different ways by different groups of geographers at different times and in different places.

A second benefit of a historical approach is that it draws our attention towards the situated nature of Human Geography. Put simply, changes in the discipline need to be understood in the context of changes in the world beyond (although this isn't to make the stronger claim that such disciplinary developments are completely determined by external events). At one level this is unsurprising, particularly in respect of a rapidly changing human world. To take one very obvious example from the past 20 years, the development of the Internet, mobile telecommunications and other forms of technology has prompted geographers not only to study in detail the ways that these are used, but also to think in new ways about the nature of space and place (see Chapter 34 and Crang et al., 1999). Thinking more generally, some interpretations of the variety or fragmentation of contemporary Human Geography see this as a response to the increasingly complex nature of the **modern** (or perhaps even postmodern) world.

But we also need to think about the situatedness of Human Geography as more than just a passive response to new developments in human life, by focusing on how the discipline has been actively bound up with those developments. A very significant example of this concerns the emergence of a distinctive academic discipline in the late nineteenth century, with departments and chairs (i.e. professorships) of geography established in universities in Germany, France and Britain. This incorporation of geography into the university system came at a time of dramatic European colonial expansion, particularly in what became known as the 'scramble for Africa'. (Between 1870 and 1914, the main European powers divided up political rule of almost all of the African continent between them.) Late nineteenth-century European geography must be understood as a science of empire, valued above all for its power to map and categorize newly colonized lands and peoples. (See Chapter 23, on 'colonialism and postcolonialism', and Driver, 1992; Bell *et al.*, 1994; Godlewska and Smith, 1994.)

This example of 'imperial geography' may seem to belong to a distant past. Certainly the specific ways that geographers of the late nineteenth and early twentieth centuries framed and answered questions about human–nature relations or issues of spatial order and organization – often by searching for climatic, environmental or racial 'explanations' for the supposed superiority of European 'civilization' – now seem abhorrent. But we are in a discipline that is very clearly **post-colonial**, not just in its interest in the historical geographies of imperialism and their lasting consequences for the modern world, but also in its own long-term development as an intellectual tradition. (And indeed in the geography of Geography – while what we've identified here as core questions for Human Geography are to be found in some guise in almost all cultures, there is a marked unevenness in the extent to which these questions form the basis for a separate academic discipline called Geography or Human Geography. A world map of current university geography departments – as opposed to cartography and other technical disciplines – would have some distinct similarities with the map of the British Empire shown in Fig. 23.1.) Whilst we may share none of the views of the imperial geographers, we can trace connections back to them, through generations of academics and students in particular university institutions. There have been constant disputes about what and how geography should study, and struggles about who should be doing that study (as Gillian Rose, 1993, in her work on the **masculinist** history of geography and many others have argued, academic disciplines have a long history of elitism and exclusion), but new generations and new approaches have usually had a vested interest in continuing and developing the geographical tradition itself. Many have sought to radically transform Human Geography – relatively few have sought to dissolve it completely.

Taking a historical view also leads us to question simple notions that the discipline 'progresses'. There is a common assumption made by many new students that today's Human Geography has developed incrementally from earlier versions of the discipline through the addition of 'new' knowledge (gained by empirical research), and by the development of 'better' theories (produced from that new evidence, or possibly just by academics thinking a bit harder than their predecessors). Looking at the history of Human Geography, and indeed at the history of most other academic disciplines, indicates that change is much more episodic than this, often

Spatial science

an approach to Human Geography that became influential in the 1960s by arguing that geographers should be concerned with formulating and testing theories of spatial organization, interaction and distribution. The theories were often expressed in the form of models – of, for instance, land use, settlement hierarchy, industrial location and city sizes. Critics claim that in its attempts to formulate universally applicable laws, spatial science ignored the social and economic context within which its spatial variables were located.

involving periodic radical changes in their central interests and assumptions. One significant way of thinking about this has drawn on Thomas Kuhn's notions of paradigms and paradigmatic change (Kuhn, 1962).

Kuhn's model of scientific change was severely criticized by many philosophers and historians of science, and he made substantial adjustments to his ideas (Lakatos and Musgrave, 1970; Kuhn, 1977). Kuhn also doubted that his ideas had much applicability to the social sciences, which he saw as characterized by much less coherence and agreement about central assumptions. The history of Human Geography doesn't fit the strict model of paradigm change very well at all, and it's extremely hard to identify anything that even closely resembles a Kuhnian paradigm in contemporary Human Geography. Nonetheless, Kuhn's terminology is still used regularly to identify general approaches that are broader than specific theories and that are shared by significant sections of a discipline or, as is often the case in the social sciences and humanities, by groups of academics in different disciplines. (See Dixon and Jones, 2004, for a recent review of developments in Human Geography that uses Kuhn's terminology in this looser way.) Thinking about paradigms and paradigm shifts directs our attention to communities of Human Geographers committed to very different ways of doing geography, and to the ways that advocates of a new 'paradigm' will often promote their approach by a 'critique' (i.e. by systematic criticisms) of an existing approach.

To see the extent to which central ideas can shift in Human Geography we can compare this book with one of it predecessors. In 1972, Peter Haggett published the first edition of *Geography: A Modern Synthesis*. In many ways this was an equivalent book to this one, designed to give an introductory overview of the discipline, and to work as a bridge between study at school and university. Like this book, *A Modern Synthesis* was

PARADIGM SHIFTS

Thomas Kuhn's *The Structure of Scientific Revolutions* was first published in 1962, and despite much criticism of its detailed arguments has been an important reference point for discussion of change in academic disciplines ever since. Kuhn's work applies specifically to change within scientific disciplines (rather than disciplines in the social sciences or humanities), and was a sociological study, providing a descriptive model of the behaviour of disciplinary communities of scientists. In its broadest sense a paradigm is a stable consensus about the aims, shared assumptions and practices of a particular disciplinary community. Kuhn argued that most scientific activity works within a stable consensus ('normal science') and does not challenge these fundamental assumptions. Eventually normal science becomes disrupted by anomalies or issues that cannot be explained within the existing framework, and new innovative work may trigger a 'paradigm shift' to a new set of shared assumptions and practices. Perhaps the best-known example of this kind of change was seen in Physics, where the set of stable assumptions commonly described as Newtonian Physics, after Sir Isaac Newton, was undermined by anomalies discovered in the late nineteenth century. These led to a period of 'extraordinary research' associated with Einstein's theory of relativity and the development of quantum mechanics, and a paradigm shift to a new set of broadly held assumptions in the disciplinary community. The term 'paradigm' has entered popular usage in a looser sense since Kuhn's initial formulation, and is regularly used to refer to general approaches, theoretical frameworks and methodologies held by significant groups within disciplines and, particularly in the social sciences and humanities, across disciplines. In this far looser sense the history of Human Geography can be said to have seen significant 'paradigm shifts' and today's Human Geography can be said to be 'multi-paradigmatic'.

organized around the very general questions of human–nature relations and the significance of space in human life. Like this book Haggett recognized the diversity of geography, but as the title of the book suggests, his response was very different. *Introducing Human Geographies* celebrates not just the range of topics covered by Human Geography, but also the range of approaches to those subjects – in this sense, it can be seen to be an introduction to a multi-paradigmatic discipline (hence the reference to 'geographies' in its title). By contrast, *A Modern Synthesis* sought to find a single central approach to Human Geography that could be used to integrate the discipline (again reflected in its title). This is unsurprising as *A Modern Synthesis* was published towards the end of perhaps the most self-consciously and deliberately paradigmatic period in Human Geography's history (Haggett, 1972: 16). Peter Haggett was one of the leading advocates of what was known as spatial science, arguing that Geography should be concerned with formulating and testing theories of spatial organization using methods that looked explicitly towards those of the natural sciences. It is some measure of the extent of change over 30 years that there is little direct application in this volume of the approaches that Haggett heralded as the core of a new stable paradigm in 1972.

FIGURE 8.2
Peter Haggett's *Geography: A Modern Synthesis* (Cover of third edition from 1977.) New York: Harper & Row

HUMAN GEOGRAPHY: SCIENCE OR SOCIAL SCIENCE?

In this more general sense, Human Geography has been influenced by many paradigms over the past 30 years. A non-exhaustive list, in roughly chronological order, includes: spatial science, humanistic geography, Marxism, structuration theory, feminism, the linguistic (or cultural) turn, post-structuralism, postmodernism, postcolonialism and non-representational theory. (You can start to see why Castree and MacMillan

INTRODUCING HUMAN GEOGRAPHIES, 1972-STYLE

Just like this volume, Peter Haggett's *Geography: A Modern Synthesis* was intended as an introductory text, and opened by drawing attention to the diversity of geography:

Starting a course in a new subject at college is like driving into an unfamiliar city. We see the sprawling new suburbs, the bustling new freeways, the pockets of decay, but find it hard to get an overall impression of its structure or know where we are. Geography is a Los Angeles among academic cities in that it sprawls over a very large area, it merges with its neighbors, and we have a hard time finding its central business district.

(1972: xix)

But rather than promote a diversity of ways of approaching geography, Haggett argued for a new 'supermodel' or paradigm that could integrate or synthesize the discipline into a more coherent whole:

Modern geography is settling down again ... The last 10 years have involved a massive swing toward more analytical work in which mathematical models ... play a dominant role.

(1972: 16)

However, far from settling down, the next few years saw the development of radically new ways of approaching Human Geography that provided a fundamental critique of Haggett's suggested synthesis.

SUMMARY

- Looking at the history of geography in general and Human Geography in particular can help us to understand their variety and fragmentation, particularly through an emphasis on the historical and geographically situated nature of geographical knowledges. It also helps us to understand geography as a changing and contested tradition, rather than a fixed way of seeing the world.

- While Human Geography cannot be said to develop paradigmatically in the strict sense

suggested by Kuhn, a looser usage of the term 'paradigm' draws our attention to the existence of communities of Human Geographers who share and develop common sets of fundamental assumptions and practices. It also draws our attention to the episodic nature of change in the discipline, and to the ways that proponents of a new paradigm will often promote their approach through critique of the fundamental assumptions of existing paradigms.

talk of exhaustion!) Very brief definitions of these are to be found in the Glossary and margins of this book, and the assumptions and perspectives of many of these inform the discussions of individual chapters. The list also gives some indication of the way in which Human Geography has regularly been influenced by broader intellectual movements originating outside of the discipline (although some geographers have made very significant contributions to these movements).

By way of an introduction to some very general differences between these paradigms, it's useful to think about Human Geography's position in relation to the three broad intellectual cultures identified at the opening of this chapter. C.P. Snow drew attention to general cultural differences between these approaches, but we can go beyond this to identify different ways in which they construct knowledge about the world. **Epistemology** is a technical term used in philosophy to refer to theories of knowledge. The sciences, social sciences and humanities are marked by distinctively different epistemologies – by different ideas about their relationships with the 'real world', what it is possible to know about it, and how it is possible to express that knowledge. In very general terms we can say that the sciences work from a basic assumption that the natural world is *ordered*, and that the task of science is to uncover the fundamental regularities of that world – often in the form of statements or theories about basic laws. Science involves the use of systematic methods of investigation that are *objective*, to assemble evidence that can be used to support or challenge theories. Science's claim to objectivity is very important. Scientific enquiry should be *replicable* – that is to say, that if the methods and techniques are applied properly and consistently, then any scientist undertaking the same work will reproduce the same results. Although science often seeks to construct general theories or laws, its conclusions are also always somewhat *tentative* – new evidence or arguments can lead to theories being revised or even rejected (Giddens, 1993: 20).

Many studies of the history and social contexts of disciplines like Physics, Chemistry or Biology have emphasized the complexity of the ways they work in practice, and the twentieth century saw the development of ideas like relativity and quantum mechanics that questioned simple assumptions of an ordered natural world. In Physical Geography, too, there has been perceptive comment about the difference between any general model of scientific epistemology, and the practice of

Humanistic Geography

a theoretical approach to Human Geography that concentrates on studying the conscious, creative and meaningful activities and experiences of human beings. Coming to prominence in the 1970s, Humanistic Geography emphasized human meanings, emotions and ideas with regard to place, space and nature thus became central.

a field science where it is often impossible to reproduce the exact conditions of any measurement or observation (see, for example, Rhoads and Thorn, 1996). Nonetheless, for many there is still something very seductive about the idea that the study of human society can be modelled on the approaches of the natural sciences, and that the social sciences can produce the 'same kind of precise, well-founded knowledge that natural scientists have developed in respect of the physical world' (Giddens, 1993: 20). Because of Geography's long history as a discipline that has combined study of the physical and human worlds and its emphasis on the relationship between them, there has been additional pressure to approach Human Geography as a form of science (the paradigm of environmental determinism, significant in geography in the early twentieth century, can be seen as a different expression of this tendency). The epistemology of orthodox scientific method was adopted wholeheartedly by spatial science, so influential in Human Geography in the 1960s and 1970s. Spatial science developed a methodology based upon quantitative measurement, model building and hypothesis testing in a search for general scientific laws of spatial patterning and processes. (See Chapter 4 for a more detailed discussion of spatial science.)

The perspective that the human world can be studied using the methods of natural science is sometimes described as positivism. It is ironic that just at the time that Human Geography was turning to the positivism of spatial science, positivist assumptions were being subjected to sustained critique in disciplines like Sociology and Anthropology. By the early 1970s, this critique of positivism had been extended to Human Geography, drawing upon perspectives from across the social sciences. At the heart of this critique was an argument that there were important and necessary differences in epistemology between the sciences and social sciences. There were a number of dimensions to the challenge to positivism in Human Geography, which we can summarize as being about issues of *human agency, language and meaning, power* and *positionality*. These are core issues for what we can generally describe as 'critical social science' or 'critical social theory'. While the paradigms that have influenced Human Geography over the past 30 years have approached these issues in very different ways, it is possible to identify a very fundamental shift in the ways that Human Geographers have come to understand the nature of their discipline. As Ron Johnston puts it, 'before the 1970s, very few Human Geographers identified their discipline as a social science: two decades later, most did' (Johnston, 2003: 51).

One key difference between the epistemologies of the natural and social sciences involves the idea of *human agency*, as Mark Goodwin discusses in Chapter 4. Human beings are not like atoms, molecules or grains of sand, and studying them as if they were unthinking, unreflective objects takes away what is distinctively human about them. Unlike objects in the physical world, conscious human beings have subjectivities, and do not always act in the same way in a particular situation. This is a key issue for the social sciences. The idea of agency highlights human decision-making and creativity, but draws particular attention to epistemological issues associated with *language and meaning*. Put simply, in studying the social world we deal with objects and activities that have meaning for people. A

Structuration

an approach to social theory that stresses the interconnection between knowledgeable human agents and the wider social structures within which they operate. A key point of such theory is that the wider structural properties of social systems are both the medium and the outcome of the social practices that constitute the systems.

Linguistic (or cultural) turn

this phrase is used to describe changes in the social sciences and Human Geography over the last 30 years. It refers to the adoption of interpretative (qualitative) approaches to explore the ways in which meanings, values and knowledges are constructed through language and other forms of communication.

Epistemology, epistemological

epistemology is the study of knowledge, particularly with regard to its methods, scope and validity. This technical term from philosophy refers to differing ideas about what it is possible to know about the world and how it is possible to express that knowledge. Different academic disciplines and different general approaches in Geography are marked by distinctively different epistemologies. Human Geographers are interested in the epistemological questions raised by the geographical knowledges held both by academics and by ordinary people. In studying these epistemological questions Human Geographers seek to connect up questions of content (what kinds of things people know) with structures of belief (how and why they claim to know) and issues of authority (how and why these knowledges are valued and justified).

Environmental determinism

a school of thought which holds that human activities are controlled by the environment in which they take place. Especially influential within Human Geography at the end of the nineteenth and beginning of the twentieth centuries, when the approach was used in particular to draw a link between climatic conditions and human development. Some authors used this link to argue that climate stamps an indelible mark on the moral and physiological constitution of different races (*see* RACE). This in turn was used to assert the superiority of western civilization, and hence to justify and support the imperial drive of nineteenth-century Europe (*see* COLONIALISM and IMPERIALISM).

social scientist has to pay very careful attention to the terms that people use to describe, interpret and understand their lives. Seen in this way, even apparently obvious terms used in Human Geography, like 'city', 'urban' or 'rural', become problematic. We are in a difficult position if we choose to define a 'city' in terms of some measurable objective criterion (such as size of population) and then fail to grasp the richness and diversity of ways that people use the term in their lives to make sense of particular places and spaces. This emphasis on language and meaning is sometimes associated with the term 'hermeneutics'. While a scientific approach can be said to seek *explanation* through causal laws, a hermeneutic approach seeks *understanding* of self-aware human beings. The study of language and meaning raises difficult issues about how we can claim to understand completely what others mean by particular terms, and about the balance between individual creativity and wider social rules in the use and development of language. Different approaches to these questions (such as humanism and post-structuralism) have led to very different kinds of approaches to Human Geography.

Another distinctive issue for the epistemology of the social sciences is raised by the importance of *power* in human societies. Again, the contrast with the study of the natural world is significant. Human societies are marked by inequalities of political and economic power, and different people and groups within human society have different *interests* in particular forms of social organization. While, for example, we can talk of, say, more powerful electro-magnetic forces, it makes no sense to think of electrons or atoms having an interest in (or benefiting from) the way that the natural world is organized. Critical social sciences are concerned with uncovering orderings of power in human societies; critical Human Geographers have argued that such orderings are both expressed in their spatial arrangements, and that those spatial arrangements actively contribute to making and maintaining structured inequalities. (See Susan Smith's discussion of these issues in Chapter 2.) Very often, critical social science works through questioning simple, superficial notions of a natural order in human societies – for example, that it is 'natural' to find cities divided between rich and poor, or that it is 'natural' for women and men to have very different employment prospects and career histories (this type of argument is sometimes referred to as 'naturalization'). Instead critical social science asks questions about how a particular form of social ordering developed, in whose interests it works and how it is sustained. One important feature of critical social science is that its epistemology sees connections between knowledge and power, criticizing other approaches for serving dominant interests.

This was an important dimension of the critique of spatial science and positivist assumptions that took place in Human Geography in the 1970s. Radical geographers, particularly those influenced by **Marxist** perspectives, argued that the models of spatial science were merely descriptions of spatial patterns, rather than examinations of fundamental social processes, and that the search for explanation in terms of abstract laws of spatial organization worked to naturalize the social, political and economic ordering of capitalism. (Indeed Marxists argued that division of academic work into distinctive disciplines like geography, biology or sociology was a powerful way of fragmenting knowledge, and of obscuring the fundamental inequalities of contemporary society.) Marxist geography gave precedence to the organization of capitalist society, and particularly to class divisions in its analyses. Other forms of critical Human Geography (notably those influenced by some **feminist** and post-colonial perspectives) have rejected this reduction of all inequalities of power to a single dimension, but also work to reveal obscured or naturalized social and spatial orderings. Implicit within all approaches in critical social science, and explicit in most, is the idea that such critical knowledge has an emancipatory role; unlike the archetype of the disinterested, objective scientist, the critical social scientist seeks to change the world that they are studying.

A final feature of social science epistemology acknowledges that the social scientist is also part of the world that they are studying. This has a number of implications. On the one hand, it means that the social scientist has a great deal of almost taken-for-granted knowledge about the ways that the human world works, and how others are likely to think and feel about it. It's this kind of knowledge that makes any attempt to understand others' lives possible. On the other hand, this raises important issues about the extent to which the social scientist is able to speak for others and how their *positionality* shapes their knowledge of the world (see Paul Cloke's discussion in Chapter 5). Again, different paradigmatic approaches to Human Geography have approached this issue in different ways.

Attention to these issues of agency, meaningfulness, power and positionality has been a feature of the various paradigms that have influenced Human Geography over the past 30 years, during its period as a critical social science. We can think of each of the paradigmatic approaches in the list at the start of this section as a particular response to these epistemological challenges, and the fragmented or multi-paradigmatic character of contemporary Human Geography as the result of contestation between these approaches. However, even this doesn't fully encompass the epistemological diversity of Human Geography. While a majority of Human Geographers would endorse a critique of positivism in terms of agency, meaningfulness, power and positionality, a significant community within the discipline has continued to develop specialist techniques in spatial modelling and analysis (particularly those associated with the development and use of geographical information systems or GIS). For much of the time, there has been an uneasy stand-off between this work and those who advocate a critical social science perspective (for example, the first edition of *Introducing Human Geographies* made no reference to GIS or examples of spatial analysis after 1972. (See box, on *Rediscovering Geography*, for an opposite example.) However, there have been skirmishes between these groups in the past 20 years that have highlighted differences in epistemology, and in understandings of the relationship between academic knowledge and powerful interests in society – notably in debates around the use of GIS for military and commercial applications (see, for example, Openshaw, 1991; Pickles, 1995; Taylor, 1990).

Marxist

social and economic theories influenced by the legacy of the leading nineteenth-century political philosopher, Karl Marx. Highly influential in the framing of critical geography, these theories focus on the organization of capitalist society and the social and environmental injustices that can be traced to it. *See also* CAPITALISM, MODE OF PRODUCTION, ALIENATION and COMMODIFICATION for examples of the influence of Marxist thinking in Human Geography.

Feminism

a series of perspectives, which together draw on theoretical and political accounts of the oppression of women in society to suggest how GENDER relations and Human Geography are interconnected (*see also* PATRIARCHY).

FIGURE 8.3
Map showing 'Population size, racial composition, and land use in a Columbia, South Carolina, neighborhood' as reproduced in *Rediscovering Geography: New relevance for science and society* (Washington, National Academy Press)

DEFINING A DISCIPLINE (1): REDISCOVERING (SCIENTIFIC) GEOGRAPHY

In 1997, the 'Rediscovering Geography Committee' of the National Research Council of the United States published a report entitled, unsurprisingly, *Rediscovering Geography*. Taking advantage of widespread concern about the state of geographical awareness of the American public (as the press release for the report put it, the need to know about events in 'mysterious places – from Bosnia to China to Zaire'), the report lobbied for the extension of geographical education at all levels in the United States. While the report acknowledged the epistemological range of geography as practised in American universities, its first recommendation was the need to 'improve geographical analysis in a new era of data and analytical tool availability, related to the broader needs of science'. In selling the discipline to the US government and to the wider American public, *Rediscovering Geography* mixed enthusiasm for the new technologies of GIS and satellite remote sensing, with strong claims about the commercial and social benefits of various techniques for spatial analysis, emphasizing particularly the 'major role' played by geographers 'in collecting and analysing vast amounts of data'. *Rediscovering Geography* was an indication of the political strength of those who believed that the discipline should be organized around the collection of empirical data, the accurate representation of that data in cartographic form, and the use of that data to develop and test predictive models. *Rediscovering Geography* paid lip-service to Human Geography's engagement with critical social theory, but largely ignored its criticisms of positivist approaches to human society and its geographies.

SUMMARY

- Human Geography has been influenced by approaches with a range of epistemologies – that is to say claims about what it is possible to know about the world, and how it is possible to express that knowledge. We can draw a broad distinction between the epistemologies of the natural and social sciences.
- For the past 30 years a majority of Human Geographers have regarded their discipline as a critical social science, and have rejected positivism (or the direct use of the epistemologies of the natural sciences in the study of human society). Debates about Human Geography's epistemology have been shaped around issues of agency, meaningfulness, power and positionality.
- A significant minority of Human Geographers, particularly those closely involved in the development of GIS have maintained a research interest in spatial modelling and analysis, using epistemologies and methodologies that retain positivistic elements.

THE ART OF HUMAN GEOGRAPHY

Many new students in Human Geography are surprised at the strength of its links with the humanities, the second of C.P. Snow's 'two cultures'. Writing in 1989, the cultural geographer Denis Cosgrove suggested that 'the idea of Human Geography as a humanity is scarcely a mature or fully developed one' (1989: 121). However, Human Geography has always had some connections with some disciplines usually described as humanities – such as history, philosophy and the study of literature. In particular the sub-discipline of Historical Geography has seen important debates about its epistemologies and methods that have positioned it in relation to the approaches of both history and geography. More generally, throughout the history of their discipline, geographers have pointed to the importance of the creative imagination in the ways that we respond to places. Writing in 1962, H.C. Darby, one of the most influential geographers of his time, argued that geography needed to be both a science and an art to provide a fully meaningful description of places. He quoted these words of Margaret Anderson to promote his ideas: 'no deadly accurate, purely technical description can bring vividly to life a mountain, a great river, or even a climate, can make it our own to love and remember, as an imaginative description by a great writer can do' (Anderson, quoted in Darby, 1962: 3). Other geographers (particularly those influenced by humanistic geography) have made similar claims about the power of novels, poems and the visual arts in 'bringing alive' different places in the human world. You may have read a novel set in a place that has also been the subject of a case study in a textbook or academic journal. In conventional terms the novel is fictional while the case study is factual, but it's worth reflecting instead on the different kinds of knowledge and understanding of that place that you have taken from each of them.

What has happened in recent times is that Human Geography's engagement with the humanities has become both more extensive and more systematic. This is in part because of a more general blurring of the distinctions between the humanities and the social sciences. This has sometimes been called the 'cultural turn', a broadly based fusion between some significant perspectives in critical social theory and the traditional focus of the humanities on human creativity and the interpretation of texts, visual imagery, music and other cultural phenomena (Blunt, 2003: 73–4).

Human Geographers working within this cultural turn have drawn upon ideas of agency, meaningfulness, power and positionality to analyse written texts, such as novels and travel writing, and visual images, particularly landscape art but also other forms of visual representation such as photography, film and television (see Chapters 10–12). The 1990s were marked by a concern for the power of **representations** of the world and its geographies. Cultural geographers have used approaches such as **discourse** analysis and **iconography** (both distinctive features of the broader cultural turn in the social sciences) to ask questions about the creation of texts and images, about their formal structure and content, and about the ways that they are received and understood by their wider audiences. These interpretations have often highlighted the ways that texts and images address what we have identified as central themes for Human Geography – the ways that different cultures shape their ideas about the relationships between humans and the natural world, and the significance of space and place in human relations. One important feature of Human Geography's recent engagement with the humanities has been the increasingly explicit way that researchers in other disciplines, such as literary studies or art history, have also explored the significance of these geographical questions.

We can go one step further in thinking about Human Geography as an 'art' as well as a science or social science. An important feature of the humanities is the emphasis that they place not just on the critical analysis of texts, images and other cultural products, but also on active creativity itself. Put simply, the humanities are about 'doing' as well as about commentating and criticizing. Recent years have seen the beginnings of active collaborations between Human Geographers and practitioners in the visual and performing arts. *Cultural Geographies*, one of the main journals focusing on Human Geography as a humanity, has a regular section called 'Cultural Geographies in Practice' that reports on these collaborations. In

Representation

the cultural practices and forms by which human societies interpret and portray the world around them and present themselves to others. In the case of the natural world, for example, these representations range from prehistoric cave paintings of the creatures that figured in the lives of early human groups to the televisual images and scientific models that shape our imaginations today. *See also* DISCOURSE.

Discourse, discursive

drawing on the work of the French philosopher Michel Foucault, Human Geographers define discourses as ways of talking about, writing or otherwise representing the world and its geographies (*see also* REPRESENTATION). Discursive approaches to Human Geography emphasize the importance of these ways of representing. They are seen as shaping the realities of the worlds in which we live, rather than just being ways of portraying a reality that exists outside of language and thought.

Iconography

this term means both: (a) the study of the symbolic meanings of a picture, visual image or landscape; and, less often, (b) the system of visual meaning thereby being studied. Developed in particular within disciplines such as art history, Human Geographers have extended iconography to the analysis of landscape symbolism and meaning. This analysis combines examination of the symbolic elements of a landscape with consideration of the social contexts in which a landscape is produced and viewed (*see also* SEMIOTICS).

my own college, visual artists have joined the Geography Department as artists-in-residence and visiting fellows, to work with both Human and Physical Geographers on the staff. Commenting on these collaborations, the geographers Catherine Nash and Felix Driver, and the visual artist Kathy Prendergast, point to how they disrupted the expected distinctions between the rigorous analytical epistemologies of the academics, and the 'imaginative indeterminacy' that supposedly characterizes artistic creativity. Rather than artists simply illustrating the work of the Geographers, or the work of Geographers providing a starting point (or 'inspiration') for artists, 'the categories of the "artist" and "researcher/scientist" began to shift, realign, dissolve and sometimes re-crystallise' (Driver *et al.*, 2002: 8). What comes out of such collaborations is a recognition that there are unacknowledged creative and aesthetic dimensions to most forms of academic work, that escape standard accounts of the epistemologies of science or social science.

SUMMARY

- The recent past has seen a growing interest in Human Geography's relationship with disciplines and approaches in the humanities. This has been part of a broader engagement (known as the 'cultural turn') between critical social theory and the traditional interests of the humanities in human creativity and the interpretation of texts, images and other cultural products.

- Geographers are also developing interests in the practices associated with the humanities, notably through collaborations with artists and performers.

CONCLUSION

Human Geography, then, is a discipline that spans the epistemologies of the sciences, social sciences and humanities, which we can only make sense of as a contested tradition, subjected to episodic changes associated with new approaches (or in a loose sense, new paradigms). As Driver *et al.* suggest, 'there can be as much difficulty communicating across widely varying research areas, methodologies and theoretical approaches within geography and amongst geographers as across disciplines' (2002: 8). In many ways this is more of an issue for new students bewildered by the range and diversity of what is on offer than for those of us working as academics. We work in academic systems that encourage us to specialize, and that can bring 'star' status to those most closely associated with the development of new perspectives – put bluntly, we have a vested interest in emphasizing the distinctiveness and originality of our own work. Most Human Geographers also have close links with researchers outside the discipline who share their interests and approaches (for example, I'm as likely to present my own work at conferences in cultural studies or modern history as in geography). If there is one thing guaranteed to unite most Human Geographers (albeit in opposition), it is the suggestion that it is possible to find some overarching single epistemological approach to the discipline. Appealing as it may be to someone starting out in geography or Human Geography, this is no longer a discipline that lends itself to a 'modern synthesis'.

DEFINING A DISCIPLINE (2) – BUREAUCRATIZING DIVERSITY

In the United Kingdom in the late 1990s, the Quality Assurance Agency for Higher Education (QAA), a government-funded body with a brief to monitor the standards of teaching and learning in universities and colleges, asked academic disciplines to produce 'benchmarks'. These were meant to 'provide a means for the academic community to describe the nature and characteristics of programmes in a specific subject'. Committees of academics from disciplines were asked to produce statements of what was expected to be covered in undergraduate degree programmes. For some disciplines (particularly in the established sciences) the task was relatively easy; Chemistry, for example, produced a checklist of the core knowledge that undergraduates were expected to gain quite quickly. For other disciplines (particularly some in the humanities and social sciences) the task proved to be an occasion for extended conflict over central epistemological approaches. The Geography committee (including the author of this chapter) fairly rapidly moved away from either a checklist of particular things that geography students should know, or advocacy of a certain core epistemology for the discipline. Instead, the benchmark statement explicitly recognizes and heralds geography's 'plurality of ways of knowing and understanding the world' and argues that 'any attempts at prescription must be discarded'. The benchmark statement (rather like this book on Human Geography) offers a number of key broad themes that seem to characterize the geographical imagination – such as 'place', 'scale', 'spatial variation', 'landscapes'. The precise way that these are interpreted and taught is left to the discretion of individual departments. The geography benchmark statement can be seen as pragmatic response to an unwelcome bureaucratic initiative by a multi-paradigmatic discipline wishing to preserve its diversity and even its right to be fragmentary.

There are, I think, a couple of responses to this fragmentation that I'd recommend to a new Human Geographer. The first goes beyond simple enthusiasm about the range of courses on offer, to stress that Human Geography offers the chance not just to study different topics, but to think in different ways about the world. While the diversity of geography can encourage a clash of (intellectual) cultures – a sterile division between 'arty-farties' and 'nerds' – it can also, much more positively, encourage critical reflection on the strengths and limits of different approaches. In the terminology used in this chapter, this discipline gives an unparalleled chance to experience different epistemologies in practice. My second recommendation stems from Bruno Latour's observations about the limitations of conventional academic disciplines and ways of thinking. Latour suggests that the most significant issues of the contemporary world are **hybrids**, which escape and cross the expertise and conventional epistemological frameworks of academic disciplines. (We might add that they certainly escape and cross the various specialisms and approaches within Human Geography.) Latour asks us to think about the limits to specialism, by following the journeys made by objects in the world (an AIDS virus, a chlorofluorocarbon molecule, a rainforest tree). This strikes me as a profoundly geographical observation, not just in the way that it invites us to trace the paths of such objects through time and space, but also to look for where and how they appear (and disappear) in seemingly self-contained approaches to economic geography, climate change, geopolitics, development, cultural geography, and so on. What courses in geography offer (often as much by accident as design) is a chance to trace and follow these journeys, and to test the limits of conventional ways of thinking.

Hybrids

are the products of usually distinct things. The term comes from the description of new plant types and is often used to emphasize cultural mixing. Latour is using the term to emphasize the way that many objects in the world challenge the limits of conventional academic disciplines.

BETWEEN LOVE AND PARADISE

Between Love and Paradise is a work produced by the visual artist Kathy Prendergast, during her time as a research fellow in the Department of Geography at Royal Holloway, University of London. It is part of a longer series of works called 'mapping emotion', but also draws upon her close collaboration with the cultural geographer Catherine Nash. Aided by sophisticated cartographic software, *Between Love and Paradise* creates what at first sight is a standard topographic map of the USA. Closer inspection reveals that this is a mapping of emotional place names, used to open up questions about place and identity. In her accompanying commentary, Catherine Nash points to the ambivalence of place names:

" *I am interested in the ability of place names to suggest partial narratives of settlement, displacement, migration, possession, loss and authority. I like their taken for granted nature and their burden of meaning. There is something neat, contained and sensible about their reference to location, but there is also something that is elusive and infinite about them. … To say they have poetics and politics only begins to trace their diverse registers of meaning.* "

(Prendergast and Nash, 2002: 48)

Compare this image with the map from *Rediscovering Geographies* (Fig. 8.3). *Between Love and Paradise* works to stimulate creative speculation about the places it maps. We look at the words on the map and start to fill in stories about hopes fulfilled and hopes unfulfilled for the people that named these places. By contrast, the map of Columbia, South Carolina in Figure 8.3, seeks to shut down speculation. In its seeming precision and objectivity (particularly in its precise representation of proportions of 'white' and 'non-white' populations for each tiny block of the city), this map draws our attention away from further thought about the data that is mapped. The map draws our attention to spatial pattern, rather than to the construction of the categories of 'white' and 'non-white'.

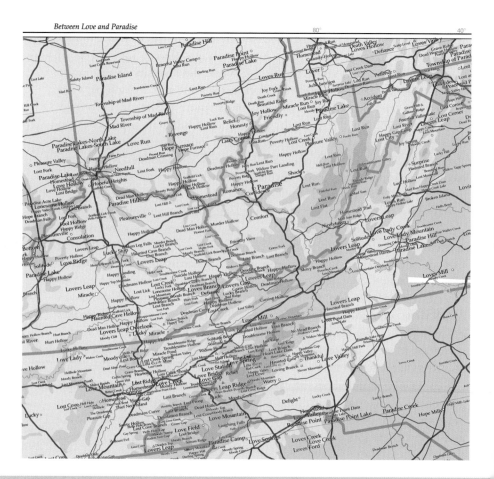

FIGURE 8.4
Extract from 'Between Love and Paradise' by Kathy Prendergast (2002) produced as part of project bringing together artists and academic geographers. (By permission of the artist.)

BRUNO LATOUR: INDISCIPLINED THINKING

On page four of my daily newspaper, I learn that the measurements taken above the Antarctic are not good this year: the hole in the ozone layer is growing ominously larger. Reading on, I turn from upper-atmosphere chemists to Chief Executive Officers of Atochem and Monsanto, companies that are modifying their assembly lines in order to replace the innocent chlorofluorocarbons, accused of crimes against the ecosphere. A few paragraphs later, I come across heads of state of major industrialized countries who are getting involved with chemistry, refrigerators, aerosols and inert gases. But at the end of the article, I discover that the meteorologists don't agree with the chemists; they're talking about cyclical fluctuations unrelated to human activity. So now the industrialists don't know what to do. The heads of state are also holding back. Should we wait? Is it already too late? Toward the bottom of the page Third World countries and ecologists add their grain of salt and talk about international treaties, moratoriums, the rights of future generations, and the right to development.

The same article mixes together chemical reactions and political reactions. A single thread links the most esoteric sciences and the most sordid politics, the most distant sky and some factory in the Lyon suburbs, dangers on a global scale and the impending local elections or the next board meeting. The horizons, the stakes, the time frames, the actors – none of these is commensurable, yet there they are, caught up in the same story. …

The smallest AIDS virus takes you from sex to the unconscious, then to Africa, tissue cultures, DNA and San Francisco, but the analysts, thinkers, journalists and decision-makers will slice the delicate network traced by the virus for you into tidy compartments were you will find only science, only economy, only social phenomena, only local news, only sentiment, only sex. Press the most innocent aerosol button and you'll be heading for the Antarctic, and from there to the University of California at Irvine, the mountain ranges of Lyon, the chemistry of insert gases, and then maybe to the United Nations, but this fragile thread will be broken into as many segments as there are pure disciplines.

(Latour, 1993: 1–3)

DISCUSSION POINTS

1. Identify three pieces of geographical writing (perhaps by looking at articles from different journals) that you would consider to be written from within a scientific, social scientific and a humanities tradition. For each, provide a short description of the ways that they approach their subjects – that is, instead of summarizing their contents, try to distinguish between them in terms of how they organize their material, the ways that they relate theories to evidence, and the kind of language that they use to make their case.

2. If you have access to a library (or an online journal service), look briefly at the contents pages and abstracts of all Human Geography articles for 1975, 1985, 1995 and 2005 in these journals: *Area; Transactions of the Institute of British Geographers; Annals of the Association of American Geographers; The Geographical Review*. Does your survey provide any evidence for paradigm shifts in the approaches, theories and methods of Human Geography?

3. Look again at the text by Bruno Latour (above). In these passages Latour uses the examples of the AIDS virus and CFCs to show the limits of conventional disciplines. Identify another example of something in the world that escapes or crosses disciplinary boundaries. Draw up a list of the different ways that it is possible to have knowledge of this object (for example, how it might be understood and interpreted by a biologist, a sociologist, a historian and an artist). What do you think a Human Geographer can bring to the study of this object?

FURTHER READING

Holloway, S, Price, S. and Valentine, G. (2003) *Key concepts in geography*. **London: Sage.**

The best next step in thinking about these issues is to look at the four essays on the disciplinary nature of geography in this book: Mike Heffernan looks at the long-term development of the discipline of geography; Keith Richards, Ron Johnston and Alison Blunt provide excellent introductory accounts of geography's relationship with the sciences, social sciences and humanities.

Johnston, R. (1997) *Geography and geographers: Anglo-American human geography since 1945 (5th edn).* **London: Arnold.**

The most comprehensive account of modern changes in the discipline of Human Geography. (As the title suggests the account is primarily limited to change in the UK and USA.) It has a useful discussion of the nature of academic disciplines, and the extent to which it is useful to draw upon the notion of paradigms in interpreting change in Human Geography. Johnston characterizes contemporary Human Geography as an 'abundance of turbulence' – and comparing the changing contents pages of the five editions of this book (from 1979, 1983, 1987, 1991 and 1997) gives a rough-and-ready indication of the intensity of that turbulence.

Openshaw, S. (1991) A view on the GIS crisis in geography, or, using GIS to put Humpty-Dumpty together again. *Environment and Planning A 23,* **621–8.**

Taylor, P. and Overton, M. (1991) Further thoughts on geography and GIS. *Environment and Planning A 23, 1087–9.*

Openshaw, S. (1992) Further thoughts on geography and GIS: a reply. *Environment and Planning A 24, 463–6.*

See the above texts for a brief and pretty bad-tempered example of geographers contesting the central assumptions of the discipline (in this case between advocates of an empirical science organized around the digital technology of geographical information systems (GIS) and advocates of a critical social science perspective).

Jones, J.-P. (2003) Reading geography through binary oppositions. In Anderson, K., Domosh, M., Pile, S. and Thrift, N. *Handbook of cultural geography.* **London: Sage.**

This will take your understanding of the idea of epistemology further than the very simple introduction presented here. John-Paul Jones identifies what he describes as spatial science, critical realism, humanism and post-structuralism as the four main 'meta-theoretical' perspectives or paradigms for geography, and shows how they differ in their epistemologies.

Driver, F., Nash, C., Prendergast, K. and Swenson, P. (2002) *Landing: eight collaborative projects between artists and geographers.* **Egham: Royal Holloway, University of London.**

Examples of the connections between Human Geography and practitioners in the visual and performing arts can be found in the regular 'Cultural geographies in practice' section in the journal *Cultural Geographies*. It's also well worth looking at the above-named text.

CHAPTER 9

Lynn A. Staeheli and Don Mitchell

RELEVANT–ESOTERIC[1]

> Questions
> What do you want to do with your studies in geography?
> How can the department help you meet those goals?
> Answers
> I want to work for an NGO in a rural part of the third world. Geography provides a good background.
> I want to do something related to sustainable development or the environment.
> The department needs more GIS classes so we can get jobs. I thought there would be more courses.
> Some of the classes are very theoretical. You can't use the things they talk about in class.
> There are no jobs for geographers, but I like the classes.

INTRODUCTION

Two years ago, one of us surveyed the undergraduate students in our department. While students indicated that they liked the department, they often felt that the course offerings did not provide a good background for the kinds of jobs they hoped to get after graduation. Their concerns were expressed in terms of the balance between a pragmatic, skills-based education and an education that emphasized theory and more conceptual approaches. In short, they questioned the relevance of their education for the kinds of jobs they hoped to attain. Their concern was that much of the material presented in classes is esoteric and understandable only to a small 'in-group' of other academics. In this way of thinking, 'relevant' and 'esoteric' are seen as opposites.

The concerns raised by the students echo those of many in the discipline who worry that the important work being done by academic geographers is not taken into the 'real' world, and that the discipline and society suffer because we do not present our work in ways that are both accessible to the public and couched in terms that demonstrate its utility in solving social and environmental problems. These calls to make geography more relevant are accompanied by debates about just what makes research relevant and questions about for whom it should be relevant.

The positions that geographers have taken on the questions of relevancy are varied. Some have seemed to assume that the relevancy of geography is self-evident, but just not communicated well to lay audiences. In this view, the discipline's focus on space, place, environment and location make geography critical to a full understanding of the world in which we live. On the other hand, some people claim that much contemporary research – particularly in Human Geography – is not as relevant as it could be. The reasons for this are variously claimed to be the institutional weakness of geography, which means that policy-makers and businesses do not automatically turn to geographers for advice (e.g. Martin, 2001), and the highly theoretical language and perhaps esoteric research foci in some critical geography (e.g. Cutter, 2000).

Underlying these arguments are differences in the ways that people understand relevance. To some, it is about informing policy; to others, It is about training students for the labour force. For others still, it is about helping people understand the world in which they live. And for yet others, it is about bringing the voices of the less powerful to the tables where decisions are made. These differences are bound up with how researchers understand the concept of relevance and where it is located: is it in the selection of topic, in helping people to understand the world around them, or in the direct application of research to policy? In turn, these differences reflect the audiences that researchers want to reach and the goals they have for any piece of research. And to say that we *as a discipline* want to make research relevant – to work in the service of society – does not address the very different political and social agendas that geographers may want to advance. As such, if geographers really want to make research relevant for a particular audience or context, it may be at the cost of seeming to be esoteric or irrelevant to other audiences and in other contexts.

In this chapter, we will explore some of these issues and argue that what makes research relevant involves a complex politics. We first highlight some of the central issues in debates about relevance. We then focus on three particular debates about relevance: the role of theory, the politics embedded in relevance, and ways in which the work we do as geographers is relevant to the lives we live as members of society.

THE PROBLEM OF RELEVANCE

While there is a lot of complaining that geography is not as relevant as it could be, there is relatively little attention to the complexity of what makes research relevant. It is difficult to understand the relevancy of a research *project* by looking at a single research *product*. Any given project, for example, may involve years of work, result in multiple publications, and be shared with participants and others in a variety of settings, including community meetings, the classroom, and in policy consultations or advocacy. Since we often only see one or two products or outcomes, it may be difficult to evaluate the relevance of an entire project. But the issue involves more than this.

Consider, for example, research on crime in urban settings. Such research has shown how mapping and other spatial information technologies have been effective in exposing neighbourhood problems and their neglect by city officials (e.g. Bunge, 1971) and in tracking and predicting crime (e.g. Rengert *et al.*, 2001). In turn, this has been important in organizing and mobilizing low-income neighbourhoods. At the same time, these studies have been criticized by some for their complicity in 'broken window' policing and in tracking anti-social behaviour – forms of policing that opponents charge with targeting people in neighbourhoods who seem 'out of place' (Fyfe, 1993). This may be important for helping neighbourhood residents feel safe, but that feeling of safety takes on different implications if the neighbourhood is an upper-income, white one that feels threatened when people of colour enter as compared with low-income neighbourhoods fighting the introduction of noxious land uses. So the *implications* of relevant research may differ based on the *contexts* in which it is implemented.

Furthermore, it is not always in the hands of the researcher to determine what constitutes the relevance of a research project or how it will be used. Indeed, stories about how research is used for unintended purposes (purposes that are sometimes the political antithesis of what a researcher hopes) are not uncommon. Neil Smith, for example, recounts the way his article on the closing of the Geography Department at Harvard University (Smith, 1987) became 'relevant' to foreign policy in the United States.[2] This seemingly esoteric article was published in the *Annals of the Association of American Geographers*, but a shorter, more publicly accessible version was included in the Harvard alumni magazine in 1989. Casper Weinberger, Ronald Reagan's defence secretary, saw it there and used it as the basis for an editorial in *Forbes* magazine, in which he argued that geography was critical to an understanding that communism was unnatural. Weinberger's argument – which he claimed was based on Smith's article about the closing of a geography department – was that the teaching of geography was the bulwark for freedom, democracy and capitalism. Smith was somewhat bemused by this, as he is a radical – indeed, a Marxist – geographer who in no way supported Weinberger or Reagan. But as he learned, once the article entered public discussion, there was no way to control the way his ideas were used. Indeed, any attempt to do so would necessarily limit the way in which research becomes relevant for other people and would constrain our attempts to change the ways in which people think about social problems (e.g. Gould, 1985).

The upshot of all this is that scholarly research is a social practice and, as such, the boundaries between what is studied and the social contexts in which it is studied are not fixed. The development of a research project – the identification of a research topic, the use of particular theoretical approaches, and the kinds of findings produced through the research – interact with the social contexts in which the research is conducted. At the same time, the sense that a project speaks to social needs and will be useful in addressing problems is also deeply social.

Several authors have helped to advance thinking about relevance, and we have listed some of them in the suggestions for further reading at the end of this chapter. Michael Dear (1999) suggests that we think about relevance in three ways: as pertinence, as commitment and as application. Research is pertinent when it addresses an issue that has significance for a particular time and place; pertinence is evaluated both in terms of the temporal and spatial context of research. Sometimes, pertinence involves addressing the 'big' issues of the day, a sort of public affairs geography. But sometimes pertinence involves helping to shape the public agenda by identifying the issues that *should* be important and to which research can contribute by drawing attention to the issue. Pertinence is, of course, fundamentally political, as it rests on a particular sense of what is, or should be, important.

This sense of what should be important also speaks to Dear's second sense of relevance: commitment. Commitment implies a pre-existing social and political agenda that research is to serve; examples include a commitment to social or environmental justice or the promotion of peace. In this case, researchers approach their topics with an explicit moral framework or set of normative values. Very often, as in much feminist, queer and anti-racist scholarship, research projects involve an attempt to directly connect values, research and political practice (e.g. Hanson, 1999).

Finally, Dear discusses relevance as application, which involves the development of tools and approaches to address specific problems. This may be the sense of relevance most people imply when they comment that research is not directly applicable to solving social problems or in the development of policy. Here there may be a distinction drawn between research that is 'merely' an intellectual exercise and research that has direct – even instrumental – applicability. As we argue in the remainder of this chapter, these meanings of relevance – and conversely, of what is esoteric – are intertwined as people evaluate how research becomes relevant.

SUMMARY

- Research is a social practice, as is the way research becomes relevant.
- There are many ways of thinking about relevance,
- including relevance as pertinence, commitment and application.
- Relevance is inherently political.

WHY WE DON'T SEE THE RELEVANCE OF RESEARCH

These ways of thinking about relevance highlight various social connections between research, practice and the societies in which we live and work. Given the diversity described here, it would seem that all research is – or could be – relevant in some way. Yet the calls for more relevant research continue, and students often wonder how the research they learn about in the classroom can be linked to future jobs or to the solution of pressing problems. Why is it that we often do not see the relevance of research? In answering this question, we highlight three specific issues that often seem to obfuscate the relevance of research: the role of theory, the inherently political nature of research, and the connections between research and daily lives.

Theory and language

Sometimes it seems as though academic researchers feel compelled to hide behind obscure theory and language, making it impossible to understand their point. Some people go so far as to argue that jargon and theory are used to mask fuzzy thinking or an absence of evidence for their arguments. We can all probably point to some article we have read that left us scratching our heads as to the point the author was trying to make. In that case, research might be pertinent, but not capable of being applied because the meaning is not clear. In response, some of the people promoting more relevant research ask that writing be sharpened and stripped down to essentials so that research becomes more accessible to policy-makers and to the lay public. These people seem to argue that geographers simply do not communicate well, whether because the authors are showing off their cleverness or because they simply have little to say.

One of the most pointed set of exchanges around these issues came in response to an article written by Michael Dear and Steven Flusty about postmodern urbanism (Beauregard, 1999; Dear and Flusty, 1998; Jackson, 1999; Sui, 1999). Amongst the critiques were arguments that this was a highly theoretical article full of neo-logisms – words that were made up on the spot – that diverted attention from pressing issues in cities, thereby making the discussion esoteric rather than real. It is true that this is a highly theoretical article with many new terms that can seem bewildering to a student or to someone who is unfamiliar with the debates addressed in the article. But the latter point is key: almost all intellectual communities develop languages and theories that they can use to talk about complex phenomena and avoid diversionary arguments. Bruno Latour (1987), for example, details the ways in which scientific languages develop out of what he calls 'controversies' – that is, specific disagreements or open questions in the literature. Technical terms – also known as jargon – are some of the resources on which scholars draw in settling these controversies. So, for example, when biogeographers write 'The PCA ordination arranges the Sierran vegetation types along two axes that are readily interpretable' (Parker *et al.*, 2001: 249), other biogeographers and physical scientists will know just what is meant. They will also know that principle components analysis (PCA) has a thorough literature behind it that tests and retests its usefulness, and that explores and exposes its limits. For biogeographers, the sentence is simple and effective in communicating ideas. For a lay audience it is jargon-ridden and opaque, and would therefore be dismissed as irrelevant. The point we wish to make is that the presentation of research often requires the use of specific languages to highlight the significance of the research *to specific audiences*.

In keeping with this point, it would be a great leap to assume that plain-speaking will constitute effective communication in the policy arena or in business, as both policy and business have developed specialized languages that are no less opaque than some theoretical languages and are no more inclusionary. Presenting research to these communities might require translating it into a different jargon that is meaningful, but still not accessible to the general public. A quick trip to a land-use planning agency, for example, will leave one bewildered as to what the various land-use regulations are, the alphabet soup of agencies that regulate planning, and the ways of talking about land. And it is not just a matter of learning the language of the bureaucracy; policy discourse sets certain motives for policy as off-limits for discussion. Policy is intended to be the means by which the public interest (as defined through rational, technical

Multicultural, multiculturalism

multicultural is an adjective used to describe a place, society or person comprised of a number of different cultures. Multiculturalism is a body of thought that values this plurality. As the Human Geographer Audrey Kobayashi has noted, both the multicultural and multiculturalism can be conceived of in a number of ways: as 'demographic', i.e. simply reflecting a diversity of population; as 'symbolic', i.e. as about the presence or absence of the symbols associated with particular cultural groups within wider societal or national culture (for example, in the media, or in museums, or in school curricula); as 'structural', in so far as institutions are established to reflect a multicultural society and pursue multiculturalism; and 'critical', to the extent that multiculturalism itself critiques the assumptions of distinct, separate cultural groups sometimes attached to notions of the multicultural. Within Human Geography, increasing emphasis is being placed on developing this 'critical multiculturalism' through examining the HYBRID or SYNCRETIC cultural forms emerging within multicultural societies.

Feminism

a series of perspectives, which together draw on theoretical and political accounts of the oppression of women in society to suggest how GENDER relations and Human Geography are interconnected (see also PATRIARCHY).

Environmentalism, environmentalist

a social and political movement aimed at harmonizing the relationship between human endeavour and the presumed limits to interference of planetary life support systems.

discussion) can be achieved (Habermas, 1970). It is hard to argue against such a goal. Rather than arguing *against* these, however, some scholars point out the exclusion that *accompanies* them – an exclusion that begins with theory and language and then has real implications in the ways that policy is designed and implemented. Citizens who are not skilled or fluent in the technical language of bureaucracy become marginalized, as are those interests that cannot be expressed in technical discourse. The exclusion of citizens can perhaps be addressed through education, but the exclusion or marginalization of ideas may be intractable. How, for example, can values of loyalty, of other-regardingness, of justice, be framed in a technical, rational discourse (e.g. Healey, 1992)? The language of rationality and the language developed in the public sector can often mask the reality of systematic exclusion. Reliance on this language also begs the questions of whose rationality, and by extension, whose relevance.

Michael Dear responds to these questions and critiques by arguing that it is important to bracket theoretical frameworks and languages when talking with different audiences.[3] For example, in his work with policy-makers, he does not talk about the 'looming hybridity of spaces' and he does not talk with people in the East LA Barrio about their 'postmodern, hybrid concoctions', even though those ideas are present in all his work. Instead, he might talk about 'diversity', about '**multiculturalism**' and about 'new cultural forms and practices'. In essence, he takes the same ideas, but expresses them in other terms to different people and in different settings. Yet theory is important in helping him frame his arguments, and plays an important role in his more academic writing. People who critique theory and jargon, then, need to appreciate the role it plays in framing arguments, and understand that jargon may often be 'translated' as researchers work with different audiences. It is the ability to make this translation that may make research relevant – or seem pertinent – not the avoidance of theory or jargon.

The role of politics

We have argued that all relevant research – indeed, probably all research – is inherently social and political. The politics of research may not be fully controlled by researchers, because ideas are used and mobilized in different settings to advance different goals. Yet there is an implication in some of the debates about relevance that research with an obvious political basis – as in **feminist**, radical, anti-racist or **environmentalist** research – limits its relevance. We suspect that some of the critics assume relevance to be indicated when research is useful either to policy-makers or to business people, and it is true that much of the critical work in geography is not widely used by these groups. Yet a host of critics raise the question of why geography and geographical research has not figured prominently in the public discussions of the pressing issues of the day. As Susan Cutter, a former president of the Association of American Geographers, asked (2000): why didn't geographers map the human genome?

In evaluating scholarly research, there is a social value accorded to objectivity, with the implication that it is possible to produce research that is entirely neutral, based on empirical facts, universal (in the sense of not being context or temporally specific), and rational. As noted above, these ideas are in accordance with the ways in which policy discourse and deliberation is supposed to proceed. The implication is that if research is to be relevant to policy-makers, it must also be value-neutral and objective.

Any number of philosophers of science have critiqued this notion, arguing that research is never value-neutral (Harding, 1991; Kuhn, 1970; Latour and Woolgar, 1979). Furthermore, the refusal to acknowledge the values and biases that underlie all research actually weakens claims to objectivity, as researchers fail to consider the ways in which their own ideas and social context shape the arguments they make on the basis of their research (Harding, 1991; Mitchell and Draper, 1982).

An example may help to clarify what happens when the political nature of research is downplayed as a discipline attempts to contribute to some of the pressing issues of the day. Our example is that of the Association of American Geographers as its leaders attempted to find a way for the discipline to contribute to efforts to understand and respond to the events of 11 September 2001. The example highlights the ways in which efforts to position research contributions as politically neutral only masks the political implications; language becomes a key means by which 'rationality' and 'objectivity' are demonstrated (see box). The events of September 11th were devastating, and geography and geographers have much to contribute in understanding them. We want to use the example, however, to show how efforts to make geography relevant to a particular policy community cannot be separated from politics – either in intent or in implication.

The description of priority research areas under 'Geospatial Data and Technologies Research' includes a call for understanding more about 'GIScience research areas such as information fusion and visualization, spatial information conflation, mobile feature modelling, feature-attribute level security, spatial scaling, feature representation and categorization, distributed spatial data interoperability, etc.'. There is an audience for whom this will be understandable, but it is not a general audience of geographers or policy-makers. Using this language, it is possible to articulate fairly specific research areas and needs, but they are not publicly accessible or understandable. Rather, these comments suggest that geography will be relevant to the extent that it can make events and the qualities of events fit into the specific, technical needs of information systems and data bases.

By contrast, other issues seem more difficult to articulate in the report, such as the means by which GIScience can be linked to area studies 'to improve data collection and understanding of the world'. This element of the agenda remains vague and unspecific by comparison with the technical elements. It is not clear why this is so. It may be that the rationale for area studies and the steps for achieving it are obvious to geographers, and they require no specification to us. But they probably do require specification for policy-makers, raising questions about the audience for the report. It may also be that the rationale for area studies cannot be articulated without a theoretical language, which the report's authors may have been loath to raise in a product intended to be read by policy-makers (even though they included theory in the section on GIS and vulnerability). Or it could be that the language masks controversies within the group as to

ASSOCIATION OF AMERICAN GEOGRAPHERS' RESEARCH AGENDA, 'THE GEOGRAPHICAL DIMENSIONS OF TERRORISM: ACTION ITEMS AND RESEARCH PRIORITIES' (AAG, 2002)

This report is intended as a statement of the discipline's ability to contribute a response to the attacks of 11 September 2001. The introduction reads, in part, as follows.

> *The project undertook a twofold research effort that 1) addressed the immediate disaster situation in a pilot study of the role and utility of geographic information and technologies in emergency management and response to the September 11, 2001 terrorist attacks; and 2) initiated a process to develop a focused national research agenda on the geographical dimensions of terrorism.*
>
> *The resulting research agenda and recommendations will be widely disseminated to national and international governmental agencies, the geographic research community, and to related disciplines. Other proposed outcomes of this on-going process include the publication of one or more books elaborating on the initial research agenda, establishment of multi-institutional research collaboration focused on implementation of the study's recommendations, and the long-term enhancement of the nation's research infrastructure to address important public policy needs and issues.*

The report identifies three key research themes and 'priority action items'. In addition, priority research issues and additional research questions were discussed. The research themes and priority action items include the following.

1. Geospatial data and technologies research

The use of geospatial data and technologies was critical during the rescue, relief, and longer-term recovery from the September 11th events. Their prominence now in planning for homeland security and international efforts to address terrorism suggest many pressing research needs, both short term and longer term, in the area of geographic information science and technology.
Priority action items are as follows.

1. Establish a distributed national geospatial infrastructure as a foundation for homeland security. This infrastructure should be designed to serve multiple other needs, such as local government, planning, environmental protection, and economic development, as well.
2. Establish a Geography Division in the Office for Homeland Security to advise on issues such as geospatial data sharing, integration of geospatial data, data security, back up systems and operations, and overall needs assessment for homeland security
3. Develop a national research center designed to better understand and anticipate the geographically variable regional economic impacts of terrorist acts …

2. Regional/international research and the root causes of terrorism

One of geography's great strengths is its ability to synthesize information about places in order to understand the linkages between regions and the manifestation of global processes at very local levels. There is a rich set of contexts advanced by regional specialists that can assist in understanding the root causes of terrorism. These should be pursued in a systematic and analytically robust manner.
Priority action items are as follows.

1. Develop and implement a major multi-institutional, interdisciplinary research program on the root causes of terrorism.
2. Develop systematic efforts to foster stronger linkages within the international community of geographic scholars to enhance regionally specific research and training.
3. Conduct a regional studies needs assessment to determine the status of training and teaching in area studies, international studies, and global studies, as a basis for identifying priorities for strengthening these programs in our universities and schools …

3. Vulnerability science and hazards research

The meaning of vulnerability has taken on new interpretations since September 11th. We need to broaden our understanding of vulnerability beyond an exposure-response framework to a more holistic view that includes exposure, susceptibility, resistance, resilience, and adaptation. We need a major effort to develop the basic data, models, and methods for conducting vulnerability assessments at all spatial scales.

Priority action items are as follows.

1. Establish a national center devoted to vulnerability science (improvements in data, models, methods) and the implementation of longer-term monitoring and modeling of disaster response and recovery efforts.

2. Compile a national tool box for local communities consisting of a set of information, data and procedures that are required for conducting pre-impact vulnerability assessments, immediate disaster response actions, and post-event activities, to insure the continuity of operations in times of crisis across all jurisdictions.

3. Establish a Quick Response program ... that enables researchers to get into the field quickly after a major world event in order to secure critical geographical data and information that would otherwise be lost ...

how far the discipline should go in promoting research that may be critical of US policy at a time when the country was still reeling from the attacks. We simply do not know, and cannot know based on the language in the report. Our point, then, is that whatever the motive, the language used in the report has political implications for geographers, for geography's contribution to understanding and responding to the attacks, and for the ways in which geographic research might be used beyond the responses to September 11th.

The report also seems to make the geographical dimensions of terrorism a series of technical issues. Even the statements about the root causes of terrorism seem to be statements about how to control terrorism and to make this a technical issue (e.g. 'What are the spatial networks and flows of information and capital that support terrorism and terrorist acts? Can we understand and ultimately model these nodes and networks?'). Such questions – those that are raised in the report, as well as those that are not raised – are inherently political; they entail a politics in the sense of a normative vision of how problems can be addressed. Politics cannot be avoided by using the language of policy. As Mitchell and Draper (1982) argue, relevant research is political and, as such, we have an ethical responsibility to acknowledge the political and moral basis of research – in other words, the nature of commitment – rather than bracket it in the name of objective, policy-oriented research.

Connecting research to daily lives

There are ways to make research relevant other than by reaching out to policy-makers, and one of these is to help ordinary people make sense of the worlds in which they live. Many researchers try to make their research 'pertinent' by working with individuals and social groups to think about the issues that confront them in their everyday lives. Many see theory as being important in helping people understand the broad structural forces that organize their lives. Some researchers also often work directly with community groups or with individuals in collaborative research in which the participants all play a role in defining research questions, implementation of various methodologies, and in analysing and presenting results. As noted earlier in the chapter, these are key stages during which the relevance of research is shaped.

It is easy to overlook this kind of research, accustomed as we are to looking at the 'big' issues of the day or to presenting research as a 'professional' product delivered to 'public' audiences. Research that examines daily life, involves regular people and is discussed in smaller groups may seem to be irrelevant to large numbers of people or to public institutions. Furthermore, some of the topics selected for study may seem to be trivial. One example that comes to mind is research on the location of public bathrooms.[4] While some might think this is not important, it is an issue that has profound implications for public health and in terms of making the public spaces of cities accessible to women, children, people with disabilities or people without permanent homes.

Research that addresses these kinds of issues – and subject populations – is often dismissed as esoteric or sometimes as putting commitment over pertinence and applicability. Yet this can be a very short-sighted approach to relevance. At one level, this is because we are often not very good about anticipating what will ultimately become important. Much of the early research on gender, for example, was dismissed as 'only' being relevant to women and focusing too much on the home. But as women have come to play increasingly visible roles in the labour force, in politics and in the use of cities, feminist research is seen as very relevant (Hanson, 1999). Continuing an earlier example, the location and design of public bathrooms has also become important as local economic development agencies strive to design city spaces that are continuously occupied. Making those bathrooms safe and accessible for women, children and disabled people is a major concern. At the same time, the use of these bathrooms by homeless people and other 'undesirables' is also a major concern (Mitchell and Staeheli, forthcoming), confounding both the politics and relevance of such research.

SUMMARY

- Highly theoretical research may still be relevant, but relevance is mediated by the extent to which researchers can 'translate' their arguments to the languages of different groups, such as the community, business, and so forth.
- All research that has relevance also is political. Rather than denying the political nature of research, it is useful to think about the ways in which politics are expressed in research, even in research that is ostensibly neutral and objective.
- An important aspect of relevance is the extent to which it helps people to understand the worlds in which they live, regardless of whether this is taken to policy or to business applications.

CONCLUSIONS

Research becomes relevant in many ways. As we indicated above, one of the most important ways it can become relevant is by helping people draw connections between social and economic processes and daily lives. We would like to conclude this chapter by arguing that this sense of relevance may be particularly important for students.

Many people we interviewed as part of a project on the relevance of research said that students were the primary audience they wanted to reach, with a goal that students would come away with tools and frameworks for understanding issues. One of the ways this was accomplished (they hoped) was through research that spoke to the lives of students in one way or another, whether it was research on college students in public spaces or on the sweatshops in which the clothes students wore were made. This ability to draw connections so as to help understand the world around us is one of the reasons some students are attracted to geography and feel that their studies are pertinent and allow them to follow their commitments. Whether this means that students gain specific skills to take into their future jobs is a different question, and addresses a sense of relevance as applicability. Ultimately, students evaluate the relevance of geography based on their own ideas about what is most important for them at a particular time as they pursue their goals. While this is to some extent an individual evaluation, it is one that is shaped by the political and social contexts in which we live, work and dream for the future. It is an evaluation that casts geographic research as either relevant or esoteric in particular times and places, and for particular issues and audiences.

DISCUSSION POINTS

1. A great deal of academic research is supported by public funds, through the salaries of academics or through research grants from public agencies. If research is always political, why should government agencies support it? If they support it, do they have the right (or responsibility) to shape the outcomes? And what if the research is something that is offensive to the public?

2. Saying that all relevant research is political may be true, but what are the *implications* of this argument? Does it make the research less accurate? Does it mean that people unthinkingly accept research results? Or is the debate over the results of research also part of the process of knowledge construction – in ways that may overshadow the politics of the research itself?

3. In multicultural, plural societies, how can arguments about the politics of research help us to understand how we can work together? Can it, for example, help to expose normative goals that might otherwise divide societies? After all, the argument seems to be another case of intellectual and political relativism.

FURTHER READING

Castree, N. and Sparke, M. (2000) Professional geography and the corporatization of the university: experiences, evaluations and engagements. *Antipode*, 32(3), 222–9.

This paper addresses various pressures on researchers and the ways these influence the kinds of research and knowledge that are produced. The paper is mostly critical of the pressures facing academics arising from bureaucratic rules within universities and from external funding sources.

Mitchell, B. and Draper, D. (1982) *Relevance and ethics in geography*. London: Longman.

This classic work argues that all research draws on the values and politics of researchers; the authors ask us to evaluate the ethical implications of this understanding.

Pacione, M. (1999) Relevance in Human Geography: special collection of invited papers. *Scottish Geographical Journal*, 115(2).

This collection of papers addresses the issue of relevance from several theoretical and political perspectives, including Marxism, humanism, feminism, postmodernism, religion and environmentalism.

NOTES

1. This chapter draws on research conducted as part of National Science Foundation grant BCS-9819828 'Changing Structures of Knowledge and Relevancy: Understanding the Sociology of Geographical Research on Public Space'. A more complete discussion of these issues can be found in Staeheli, L. and Mitchell, D. (2005), The complex politics of relevance in geography. *Annals of the AAG*, 95(2), pp. 357–372.

2. Interview with Neil Smith, 15 July 2000.

3. Interview with Michael Dear, 15 August 2000.

4. When Lynn was editor of *Gender, Place and Culture*, she received a manuscript about the locations of public bathrooms in Dunedin, New Zealand, in 1860–1940 (Cooper *et al.*, 2000). One of the reviewers initially recommended rejection of the paper, saying it was an unimportant issue and one that would make the journal look silly. After the reviewer was 'caught short' one day and could not find a safe bathroom in her home town, she revised her comments, arguing that this was an important issue in guaranteeing women's access to the public spaces of the city.

Part two
THEMES

INTRODUCTION

One of the things we have always loved about geography is the sheer range of its subject matter. Looking back, we're sure that what first attracted us to take Human Geography at university was the fact that we could legitimately study a huge diversity of human behaviour and social activity, and we're equally sure that this has played a large part in holding and stimulating our interest ever since. We always felt slightly smug at university when in conversation with other students, as their subjects seemed so narrow and limiting. The economists stuck to the study of economics and the historians to the study of history. The political scientists examined politics and the planners looked at planning. This seemed a shame, especially when by contrast we were able to study all of these areas, as well as many more. Amongst the hundreds of lectures we have attended, picked almost at random, were those on revolutions in Latin America and Asia; on welfare provision in Sweden; on urban politics in the USA; on environmental politics and policy; and on industrial development in Scotland. Amongst the thousands we have given were those on the geographies of famine and hunger in Africa; rock 'n' roll music in the USA; poverty and deprivation in urban Britain; the landscape of New York; and theme parks and shopping centres in western Europe. Other geographers could come up with similar experiences – you probably can yourself already. The point lies not in the particular subjects but in their breadth.

However, in order to make sense of this breadth, and to avoid the dangers of being jacks of all trades but masters of none, geographers tend to work in and around particular specialist areas, commonly called sub-disciplines. These sub-disciplines are the different 'themes' that we explore in this part of the book. In Part 1 we looked at some of the critical dualisms that have structured and shaped the development of geography as a whole. Now we begin to break that discipline down into its constituent parts. Those we have chosen to highlight are amongst the most vibrant areas in today's Human Geography. In each case we have selected three key aspects of these themes, which we present as individual chapters. Each is written by an acknowledged expert in their particular field who is at the forefront of contemporary geographic research. This should enable you to get some flavour of the developments taking place in the geographical literatures. Any less and we would have been trying to cover too much in each chapter; any more and the book would have become unwieldy and expensive.

Working in alphabetical order, this part of the book begins with three chapters devoted to cultural geographies, before moving on in turn to look at development, economic, environmental, historical, political, social, and urban and rural geographies. We have separated these themes in this section, although as you read through you will begin to pick out the connections – between, for instance, development geography and geopolitics; between the economy and sustainability; between the historical geographies of memory and heritage, and cultural geographies of the imagination or social geographies of identity. Indeed, one of the most exciting developments in

Human Geography in recent years has been the willingness to explore the connections and interfaces between sub-disciplines, which has raised a whole number of new avenues to study. This is taken up in more detail in the final part of the book, where these interconnections are explored in relation to a number of different contexts and issues.

For now, though, we will hold these interfaces somewhat apart in order to explore some of the key developments that have recently taken place in each sub-discipline. Each 'theme' has its own editorial introduction, briefly summarizing the key concerns of the sub-discipline and introducing the chapters in relation to these. We are not attempting to be comprehensive here, and each section is not meant to present all the work going on within any one theme. There are, inevitably, arguments to be had about the areas of each sub-discipline that we have either included or excluded. In making the choice of content, our main criterion has been to present you with a picture of, and a feel for, the excitement of contemporary Human Geography. We cannot provide an account of the whole discipline in the limited space available in this section, but we have tried to present an interesting and novel set of chapters that, individually and collectively, begin to push against the more traditional sub-disciplinary boundaries. In so doing they open up a whole series of new and vibrant issues for Human Geography to examine.

SECTION 1
CULTURAL GEOGRAPHIES

INTRODUCTION

The literary critic Raymond Williams suggested that 'culture is one of the two or three most complicated words in the English language' (1983: 87). That perhaps explains why it can be hard to define exactly what Cultural Geography is about. A starting definition – referring back to the original meaning of geography as 'the writing of the world' that was discussed in the Introduction to this book – would be that it involves the study of world cultures, or perhaps cultural worlds, or the worlds of culture. Certainly, each of these phrasings says something about the interests of Cultural Geography, but as you may have recognized, each carries a slightly different emphasis too. To understand these emphases, their differences and continuities, we need to deal with the complexity of the word 'culture' head on.

Raymond Williams did this by studying the history of the word and its usages. Rather than looking for one correct definition of culture, he argued for understanding its range of past and current meanings and their relations to each other. In that spirit we might identify three contemporary, colloquial uses of culture. First, and least common, is the usage we make of the word when talking about a 'bacterial culture', a sense that also explains the word's presence in agri*culture*. Here, culture operates as a noun of process, referring to the cultivation of crops and animals. More generally, this usage highlights the definition of culture in some relationship to nature (see also Chapter 1).

Second, the notion of culture as cultivation extends in a related direction, referring to the cultivation of the human mind. Here, culture comes to refer to something that makes people cultivated or 'cultured' or civilized, distant from their base natures. One of the dominant ways in which the word is now used comes from this set of meanings, that being our reference to *C*ulture (capitalized, reflecting its status) as the Arts, or what concerns Ministries of Culture, or what one finds in places like museums, galleries and libraries.

A third contemporary sense of the word 'culture' comes from a slightly different lineage. It is the additional sense of culture we evoke when we talk about British or American or French culture; or middle-class, elite and working-class culture; or indeed an 'organizational culture'. Here 'culture' operates as a noun of configuration, referring to the spirit that informs a whole way of life of a distinct group of people. Significantly, in this usage 'culture' can be pluralized to 'cultures', in recognition of a diversity of such ways of life.

Each of these three everyday uses and meanings of the word 'culture' points to a significant concern of Cultural Geography. What is more, the three usages of the term inform each other. Let us elaborate by relating these three sets of colloquial meanings to three intertwining strands of Cultural Geography scholarship. First, then, related to the sense of culture

Cultural landscape

traditionally this phrase has meant the impact of cultural groups in fashioning and transforming the natural landscape. More recently it has been suggested that landscape itself is a cultural image, a way of symbolizing, representing and structuring our surroundings.

in agriculture, Cultural Geography has focused on the relations between 'land and life'. This interest was established through the Berkeley School, associated with the most influential Cultural Geographer of the early twentieth century, Carl Sauer. Specific foci include: the domestication of plants and animals; the human impacts on and shapings of the natural world through such processes of cultivation; and the study of particular features of those human or **cultural landscapes**, such as built environment forms like houses.

As signalled in that summary, already apparent here was a relating of the first sense of 'culture' as material cultivation with its third sense, in the plural, as different people's ways of life. Berkeley School Cultural Geographers sought to map out and understand the differences between different cultural landscapes and different relations to nature. However, Berkeley School work tended to underplay the second colloquial sense of 'culture', as about mental cultivation, as about Culture. Today, research on land and life still has a strongly material emphasis – for example, in research on the relations between livelihoods, landscapes and ecologies (see Bebbington and Batterbury, 2001). But it also pays attention to a far wider range of ways in which culture and nature interrelate (see Sarah Whatmore's discussion in Chapter 1) including how the natural world is figured through the imaginative work in various 'Cultural' realms. These include, for instance, the visual and practical arts (for example, analysing landscape painting, photography and design; for a seminal collection see Cosgrove and Daniels, 1988), the field sciences (Crang, 2003), and the media (for example, analysing natural history television and film; see Davies, 2000).

Which brings us on to that second meaning of culture, as the cultivation of human minds. Here we can identify a second strand of Cultural Geographic scholarship, concerned with what we might call 'maps of meaning'. Cultural Geographers are interested in how people make the world and its geographies meaningful, viewing this as an essential part of what makes us human. 'Culture' designates the meaningful 'maps' (in the broadest and non-literal sense) that we compose to orientate ourselves in the world. Cultural Geographers attempt to interpret those 'maps' and their meanings. In part this has involved a focus on Culture narrowly defined – that is, those people, institutions and material forms devoted to making the world meaningful (the arts, literature, theologies, sciences, etc.). Here Cultural Geographers have studied the **representations** fashioned (in paintings, novels, sculpture, film, literal maps, and much more besides) and the practices and arrangements through which they come into being. But not all the institutions that make the world meaningful are located solely in that realm of official Culture; think of advertising or the mass media, for example. More generally, it would be absurd (though not unknown) to think that the world is only made meaningful by cultural professionals and elites, and not by all of us as part of our everyday lives. So Cultural Geographers have attended not only to narrowly defined Culture and its worldviews but also to the much wider realms of what has been variously termed (with different emphases attached to each) folk, vernacular, popular and mass cultures.

Representation

the cultural practices and forms by which human societies interpret and portray the world around them and present themselves to others. In the case of the natural world, for example, these representations range from prehistoric cave paintings of the creatures that figured in the lives of early human groups to the televisual images and scientific models that shape our imaginations today. *See also* DISCOURSE.

Which leads us back to that third everyday understanding of 'culture': the plural and diverse ways of life of different people. In focusing on 'maps of meaning', Cultural Geographers have recognized that there is not only one set of meanings about, one way of imagining, the world. There are many, many such maps of meaning, posing questions about where these are located and how they relate to each other. This signals a wider, third strand of Cultural Geography, concerned with 'culture, place and space'. Here the focus is on questions about cultural difference and its geographies. Do people differ 'culturally' (that is, in how they cultivate and imagine the world and themselves)? If so, how can such differences be mapped? Are they locatable in distinctive 'culture areas' or territories, and/or what sorts of movements of cultures are there? What does globalization mean for cultural difference? What are the relations between cultural difference and geographical distance? What role do particular places have to play in people's understandings of their own cultural identity and their differences to others? And how do we understand cultural difference in the first place? Is it an innate character of humanity for cultural diversity to exist, or is cultural difference itself a product of how we imagine the world, a cultural construction?

A range of chapters in this book speak to these cultural geographic concerns with, and approaches to, 'land and life', 'maps of meaning' and 'culture, place and space'. In part this reflects the contemporary vibrancy of Cultural Geography and its wide influence within the discipline; in part the impossibility of partitioning off the 'cultural' as a separate realm. The three chapters in this section home in on particularly influential and productive themes that have been deliberately selected to cut across the meanings of 'culture' discussed above. We begin with Felix Driver's introduction to the notion of 'imaginative geographies' (Chapter 10). Felix argues that geographical images and visual representation are not best seen as mildly diverting distractions from the geographies of the real world; they really matter. Images, he suggest, direct the sense we make of the world and how we act in it. Images aren't the opposite of reality; they *shape* realities. He develops this suggestion through the notion of imaginative geographies, advanced by the Palestinian literary and political critic Edward Said. More specifically, he considers the imagination of our identities, our senses of similarity and difference, focusing in particular on the imaginative character of 'cultures' and 'nations'. In conclusion he returns to the significance of such imaginative geographies today, showing their centrality in phenomena as diverse as the American 'war on terror' and theme parks.

In Chapter 11, Catherine Nash turns to the theme of 'landscapes'. Landscapes, she suggests, are not only material forms but also ways of thinking, seeing, being and doing. She develops this argument through an account of landscape's implications in relations of property, power, propriety and productivity. Examining the cases of English rural landscapes, British colonial landscapes and landscapes of leisure, Catherine's discussion raises consistent questions about what we might call the politics of landscape. Whose landscape is this? Who make claims to it and how? What is meant to go on in this landscape? How are the answers to these questions established and challenged? She concludes by arguing

Territory

a more or less bounded area over which an animal, person, social group or institution claims and attempts to enforce control.

Globalization

the economic, political, social and cultural processes whereby: (a) places across the globe are increasingly interconnected; (b) social relations and economic transactions increasingly occur at the intercontinental scale (*see* TRANSNATIONAL); and (c) the globe itself comes to be a recognizable geographical entity. As such, globalization does not mean everywhere in the world becomes the same. Nor is it an entirely even process; different places are differently connected into the world and view that world from different perspectives. Globalization has been occurring for several hundred years, but in the contemporary world the scale and extent of social, political and economic interpenetration appears to be qualitatively different to international networks in the past.

Imaginative geographies

representations of place, space and landscape that structure people's understandings of the world, and in turn help to shape their actions. In the work of Edward Said, the term refers to the projection of images of identity and difference on to geographical space in a way that sustains unequal relationships of power.

for cultural geographies of landscape that do not oppose material practices and imaginative representations – how we behave in and how we see landscapes – instead pointing to how the best Cultural Geographic scholarship has intertwined the two.

In Chapter 12, Philip Crang picks up on this theme of the material and imaginative nature of landscapes as part of a broader introduction to 'the geographies of material culture'. His discussion is worked through particular material forms, objects or 'bits of stuff', including houses, fences, personal stereos, interactive intelligent toys, and Italian motor scooters. The chapter uses these cases to set out four ways in which such 'stuff' can be seen as having cultural geographies: as evidence or indicators of cultural difference and distribution; as materials involved in the reproduction of distinctive cultural groups and places; as tools used in the fashioning of everyday spaces; and as a form of cross-cultural 'traffic'. The general flow of argument is away from viewing the geography of things as their distribution across space, instead moving towards cultural geographic analyses that get inside things, their meanings and uses, teasing out their role in the production of the places and spaces that people inhabit.

FURTHER READING

Cultural Geographies

Founded in 1994 under the title *Ecumene*, and renamed in 2002, this journal presents work spanning the themes of 'land and life', 'maps of meaning' and 'culture, place and space' outlined above. If you want more compressed summaries of developments in the field of Cultural Geography, the regular progress reports on Cultural Geography (and more recently on Landscape) in the journal *Progress in Human Geography* are also an excellent resource, though they can be quite dense.

Anderson, K., Domosh, M., Pile, S. and Thrift, N.J. (eds) (2002) *Handbook of Cultural Geography*. London: Sage.

This big, sprawling book collects together the latest thinking on Cultural Geography. The pitch can be uneven – sometimes explaining issues carefully, sometimes assuming a lot of knowledge – and it is currently only available in hardback, which means it is very expensive. But if your library has a copy, this is a useful resource, especially for later on in your studies.

Anderson, K. and Gale, F. (eds) (1999) *Cultural Geographies* (2nd edn). London: Longman.

The first edition of this edited collection came out in 1992 under the title *Invented Places*. In either edition, this is an excellent book with some studies that have become standards in the field contained within it.

Crang, M. (1998) *Cultural Geography*. London: Routledge.

The best introductory textbook on the field. Short, punchy and suggestive.

Foote, K.E., Hugill, P.J., Mathewson, K. and Smith, J.M. (eds) (1994) *Re-reading Cultural Geography*. Austin: University of Texas Press.

A voluminous collection of classic papers and newly commissioned pieces, representing an account of Cultural Geography's interests, approaches and history from a distinctively American perspective.

Jackson, P. (1989) *Maps of Meaning*. London: Routledge.

This book codified the re-emergence of British Cultural Geography in the late 1980s, connecting Cultural Geography to wider intellectual currents in so-called cultural studies as well to developments in Social Geography. Inevitably a little dated now, this is still an inspiring piece of work that rightly has become a standard reference.

Mitchell, D. (2000) *Cultural Geography: a critical introduction*. Oxford: Blackwell.

A combination of textbook and manifesto. This book is much longer than Crang's, and consequently simplifies much less and has a more explicit authorial agenda. It is more up to date than Jackson's. However, it can be hard going in places, and may best be encountered later in your studies.

CHAPTER 10
IMAGINATIVE GEOGRAPHIES

Felix Driver

INTRODUCTION

Geography is a subject that has always had a reputation for being down to earth. After all, its focus is on the real world, the shape of its landscapes and the pattern of its use by human beings. This sense of the rootedness of the discipline in the material world is often associated with an image of the geographer as an active inquirer, engaged with the world rather than distanced from it. Or, to put it more simply, many people would agree with the proposition that you simply can't do geography without getting your boots muddy. In the past, this image of geography as an active subject, pursued above all through fieldwork, was embodied in the figure of the intrepid explorer, determined to seek out the truth with his or her own eyes rather than rely on the speculations of 'armchair' geographers. Today, relatively few geographers consider themselves explorers in quite this sense; indeed, one has gone as far as to describe himself as an 'extrepid implorer' (Lowenthal, 1997)! Nonetheless, a sense of engagement with the world, and a more general commitment to solving real-world problems – such as environmental degradation, poverty and injustice – remains a strong feature of a modern geographical education. This is one of the main reasons why we continue to say that geography matters.

The purpose of this chapter is to consider how people imagine the geography of places, and why this matters too. The inclusion of such a topic in a geography book might seem fanciful, given the emphasis on practical fieldwork and worldly relevance that has had such an influence on modern geography. Why focus on 'imaginative' geographies when there are so many real-world problems to deal with? Can't we leave that to other disciplines, concerned with fictions rather than facts, with subjective impressions rather than objective realities? The argument of this chapter is that, far from being a diversion, the study of imaginative geographies is one of the reasons why geography remains relevant to the troubled world of the twenty-first century.

Imaginative geographies
representations of place, space and landscape that structure people's understandings of the world, and in turn help to shape their actions. In the work of Edward Said, the term refers to the projection of images of identity and difference on to geographical space in a way that sustains unequal relationships of power.

IMAGINATIVE GEOGRAPHIES AND WHY THEY MATTER

In this chapter, the term **imaginative geographies** refers to more than the subjective perceptions of individuals. While every human being is unique, in the sense that each of us experiences the world in a particular way, the images we construct are at the same time inherently social. Think of the words we use or the pictures we draw: these depend on shared systems of communication, codes or languages, which depend on a wider community. While western writers have long understood 'imagination' in subjective terms, associating it with creative licence or individual genius, there is no reason why we cannot think of imaginations in other ways.

Ever since the origins of modern anthropology in the eighteenth century, cultures have been understood in terms of shared beliefs or common ways of thinking about the world; and at least since the birth of modern psychology in the late nineteenth century, we have come to recognize that these may lie in the unconscious realm as well as in the world of thoughts and actions. Of course, there are many different ways of conceiving these ways of thinking or patterns of belief: the fundamental point here is that they are more than the work of individual minds. In other words, imaginations are social as well as individual.

Turning to the content of these imaginative geographies, let us reflect for a moment on our own place in the world: how do I conceive my own identity, or yours? I have a birth certificate that tells me where I came from, and a passport that tells me my nationality. I may also identify myself as belonging to a certain region, generation, class, gender and ethnic group. But how do these define my sense of identity? It very much depends how I imagine them to be related to each other, and how I imagine myself to belong, or not to belong, to a number of different communities; and, not least, how others identify me. These senses of identification – both subjective and imposed – may well change as I grow older. Moreover, my answer to the above question – and I suggest yours too – will vary depending on the circumstance in which it is asked: at a border post, in a bar, on a train, at home. In other words, identities are complicated things: they are shaped not just by our physical characteristics or our social positions, but also by images – those we ourselves compose to make sense of the world, those of others and those in the culture that surrounds us. In this chapter, I shall consider only a few of the ways in which cultures, nations and landscapes are imagined: the more general point is that these imaginative geographies help to shape our sense not only of the reality of places, but of our most intimate sense of our selves (Valentine, 1999).

So imaginative geographies make a difference – that is to say, they are real. Think again about passports: these are documents made up of images – words, impressions, stamps, codes, photographs – that together compose one very material form of identity. That identity shapes our lives by making certain things – residence, nationality, mobility – available to us on certain terms. It simultaneously restricts our access to these things elsewhere in the world, though this will vary according to the nature of the images involved. This is one example of the real effects that images may have. Obviously it is a particular kind of example: the images that constitute a passport are enormously powerful, and mark the extent to which our lives are bound up with the power of states. Let us then take another, less obvious, example: that of images of childhood. How do these images shape the geography of the world we inhabit? The answer to such a question is inevitably complex, especially given the wide variety of ways in which childhood is and has been imagined. In Europe, for example, images of childhood have undergone considerable change, notably in the nineteenth century, the era in which mass schooling began. Many of our ideas about what it means to be, to look like or to behave as a child have their origins in this era, which saw the gradual exclusion of young children from the world of paid work, the emergence of child protection movements and the development of ideas about juvenile delinquency. The point here is that these changes were in some measure imaginative – they required new visions of childhood – and all of them had practical consequences for the geography of children's lives. The same might be said for other aspects of identity – such as our conceptions of masculinity and femininity, or able-bodied and disabled bodies, or whiteness and blackness, or madness and sanity. Images, too, have real effects (see also Chapter 6).

SUMMARY

- The study of imaginative geographies takes images seriously: it treats words and pictures as both objects of study in their own right and as evidence for understanding the ways in which identities are constructed.

- Human Geographers are concerned with the realms of the imagination, not as a contrast to, or an escape from, the real world 'out there', but because they help to make sense of, and shape, that world.

GEOGRAPHY AND THE VISUAL IMAGE: REPRESENTATION AND PRACTICE

Visual images have long been considered important sources of geographical information. The patient, almost forensic, skills required in the interpretation of maps and aerial photographs, for example, continue to play a role within contemporary geography, nowadays alongside the use of high-precision microscopes and computer-aided analysis of remotely sensed data. But visual images are not simply frozen data banks, reflections of the patterns in the world ready to be brought to life: they also re-present information in particular forms and through particular codes that, themselves, are far from neutral or self-evident. Geographers must therefore be interested in the nature of these forms and codes of representation, how they have evolved over time, and how they may be related to the circulation of imaginative geographies of culture, landscape and identity (Harley, 2001; Rose, 2001; Schwartz, 1996).

This focus on the work of representation, particularly in the literature of cultural geography, has recently been challenged. Some critics argue that the emphasis on the ways people represent the world has diverted attention from more questions of practice and habit: it would be better to start, they suggest, with the question of what people actually do in the world, than with how they think about, or represent, what they do. The debate over what has recently been called 'non-representational theory' is not about the importance of images or imaginative geographies in themselves: it is about how worlds are actually made, and where best to begin the process of interpretation (Thrift, 1999).

The process of producing imaginative geographies involves a variety of embodied practices and knowledges: it is not simply cognitive. Take, for example, the landscape sketch in Figure 10.1, a drawing from the logbook of a young midshipman visiting the harbour of Rio de Janeiro in 1817, en route for a tour of duty in Australia. This depicts the well-known Sugar Loaf, adjacent coastal features and fortifications. Such coastal views formed part of an established way of seeing, a common visual code through which landscapes could be recognized from the sea. It is necessary to consider the precise forms through which such images took shape; the materials, techniques and skills required to produce them; the networks through which these skills were learned and applied; and the material, institutional and social contexts in which such sketches could acquire value. Coastal survey, like mapping in general, was an embodied labour, requiring particular kinds of skill and discipline. Such images as these do not reflect merely particular ways of seeing the world, projections of the mind's eye, but are also embodied and laborious engagements with that world (Driver and Martins, 2002).

FIGURE 10.1
John Septimus Roe, *Views of the Harbour of Rio de Janeiro, June 1817*. Source: logbook of the *Dick*, courtesy of the Battye Library, Perth

IMAGINING CULTURES

How are cultures 'imagined'? Consider the picture in Figure 10.2. It forms the frontispiece of a *Concise History of the World*, published in 1935 by Associated Newspapers, a book you might think of as a forerunner of the multimedia encyclopaedias now widely available. Such reference works aim to provide within a single volume – today within the space of a compact disc – the complete story of humanity, from the very beginnings to the present day. As Figure 10.2 indicates, this story is sometimes illustrated by a kind of family tree, quite literally in this case. The subsequent history of humanity is portrayed through a series of emblematic figures, each representing a distinct civilization or culture, culminating at the foot of the page with an image of the modern family, recognizable to British readers in the 1930s, complete with domesticated pet. The image as a whole condenses a larger theme in pictorial form: history as a procession of figures through age after age, culminating in the modern era.

Let us examine this curious image a little more closely. First, it represents world history as a sequence of stages, through historical time: indirectly, this owes something to the impact of evolutionary writings. More directly, H.G. Wells' famous book, *The Outline of History*, first published in 1920, set the pattern for a large number of similar works,

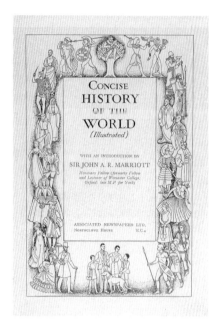

FIGURE 10.2
Frontispiece of *Concise History of the World (illustrated)*. Source: Associated Newspapers 1935

Other, Otherness

usually typographically capitalized, an Other is that person or entity that is understood as opposite or different to oneself; Otherness is the quality of difference which that Other possesses. A rather abstract conceptual couplet, potentially applicable at scales varying from the individual person to the global political bloc, these terms have been used in Human Geography to emphasize how ideas about human and geographical difference are structured through oppositions of the Self/Same versus the Other/Different. They also stress how the Other is often defined in terms of its relations to that Self – as its negative, everything it is not – rather than in its own terms. For example, a number of studies have examined how dominant ideas about GENDER are based on a logic in which Woman is Other to Man; how ideas about global politics and culture frame the East as Other to the West, and the South as Other to the North; and so on.

intended both for children and for a wider popular audience (it is very likely that your parents or grandparents will remember similar volumes). Promising nothing less than a epic history of the world, Figure 10.2 presents this spectacle in a very particular way: as a stately procession or pageant, in which colour is more important than detail. Significantly, a fundamental parting of the ways appears early in the story. The figures on the left-hand side of the image correspond to a recognizable sequence of civilizations: through the Persians, Greeks and Romans, to the medieval, the renaissance, the Victorian, and so on. Each of the figures is represented in subtly different ways, their posture and dress signifying the characteristics of their time: and there is a distinct sense of progression, from the era of martial prowess, through that of courtly ritual, to the sedate and modest world of the nuclear family. This is a story of progress by domestication: an evolutionary tale in which, ultimately, the values of the modern win out not only over the primitive, but perhaps over evolution itself. But, on the other side of the image, the same logic does not apply. Here we find a mix of cultures, including the Ancient Egyptian, Phoenician, Chinese, Japanese, Indian and Native American. There is no sense of progression in this sequence: as if to emphasize this, a thinly clad African couple have been placed at the foot of the chain, the man armed with spear and shield. The message is simple: human history has been divided into two. The West is portrayed in evolutionary terms as the domain of progress, the destiny of the human race; the rest are pictured more as a spectacle than a pageant, kept in their place, subject to geography rather than subjects of history.

Looked at in this way, Figure 10.2 can be connected to much wider traditions of thought about cultural history – and geography. For example, it could be interpreted as a popular version of more scholarly traditions of 'Orientalism', as analysed by Edward Said in a very influential book published in 1978, in which the term 'imaginative geographies' was first coined. Said argued that non-western cultures in general (and those of the 'Orient' in particular) have often been represented by western commentators as being static and backward. He also maintained that these images have played an important part in the historical construction of a contrasting image of Europe – and the West in general – as dynamic and progressive. For Said, such imaginative geographies – based on a binary opposition between the West and the Rest – have played an important role in the history of global power relationships during the last two centuries. Whatever the merits of this argument, which has been hotly debated (Gregory, 1995; MacKenzie, 1995), it does seem that something like this pattern is pictured in Figure 10.2. Said's perspective raises fundamental questions about our understandings of global history and culture, and the ways in which they may be embedded in particular imaginative geographies. It also encourages us to imagine a different picture of world history, one not structured by a binary opposition between the West and the Rest; one, for example, that paid due attention to the *interactions* between Europe and the rest of the world, and their implications for development of cultures and societies across the globe.

Edward Said's work emphasizes the role of the idea of the **Other** in the construction of imaginative geographies of culture; that is to say, he was concerned with the ways in which European history has often been conceived on the basis of an essential opposition between the civilized European and the uncivilized, or yet-to-be-civilized, non-European. While it would be far too simple to suggest that this was the *only* way in which Europeans have imagined other cultures, it is remarkable how common such stereotypes have been, even where the intention has been to challenge dominant stereotypes. Look, for example, at Figure 10.3: this image was designed to represent the philosophy of a mid-Victorian pressure group, the Aborigines Protection Society, a forerunner of modern organizations such as Anti-Slavery International and Survival International. The image contains a group of figures, each representing a different 'branch' of the human family (see also Barthes, 1972). Beneath is a motto written in Latin – *Ab Uno Sanguine* ('From One Blood') – which summarized the Society's commitment to the idea of the unity of the human race, and to the rights of indigenous (or 'aboriginal') peoples. The image portrays a single group of men, apparently united by their common humanity. Yet, on closer inspection, it seems that this is an unequal family: the white man, fully clothed, is essentially portrayed as an enlightened philanthropist, standing in relation to the others as a father does to his children. On the one hand, then, the image affirmed the unity of humanity, in marked contrast to those Victorians who maintained that there were essential and innate differences between different '**races**'; on the other hand, however, a sense of hierarchy was maintained, though this time it was cultural (learned) rather than biological (innate).

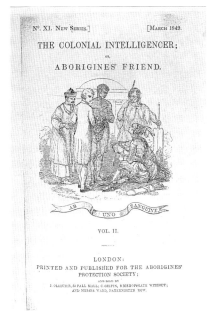

FIGURE 10.3
Frontispiece *The Colonial Intelligencer or Aborigines' Friend*. March 1849

SUMMARY

- Images of culture frequently draw upon shared collective imaginations about cultural identity and difference. This provides the starting point for Edward Said's influential book, *Orientalism*.

- Such images transmit messages about the global geography of cultures to a wider audience, in school texts, popular books, film or television, for example.

- These images can be regarded as 'real', not because they reproduce the world accurately, but because they reflect and sustain people's imagination of that world; and in turn, help to influence the worlds we now inhabit.

- Consider the image in Figure 10.4, from a missionary school book published at the end of the nineteenth century. In what ways do you think this image might reflect 'imaginative geographies' of Africa prevalent in Europe in the past or the present? For relevant arguments, see Driver (2001) and Jarosz (1992).

IMAGES OF NATIONS

Many of the images discussed so far represent distinctly English visions of civilization and culture. As this suggests, it is difficult to separate out ideas about cultural difference from ideas about nationality. Indeed, sometimes the two are treated as identical: so 'the English' are sometimes said to have a different 'culture' from the rest of Europe. We frequently find such views expressed in debates about immigration or education, especially in times of national conflict or international tension. But what is a 'national culture'? Is it something natural or created? Does it grow from within the nation, or does it depend on relations with other 'cultures'? Is it homoge-

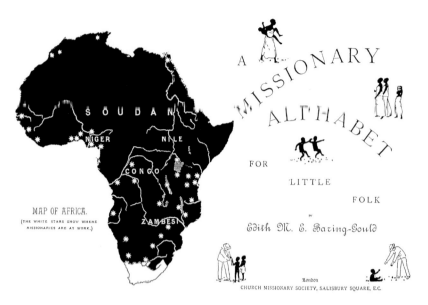

FIGURE 10.4
Frontispiece to *A Missionary Alphabet for Little Folk*. Church Missionary Society, London, 1894

nous or heterogeneous? Such questions are addressed elsewhere in this volume. Here, we shall focus on the ways in which nations, too, are imagined. They do not simply exist by virtue of location: they are constructed through the mobilization of images (Anderson, 1983).

Take the example of Englishness. How do you imagine England? Different readers may have different answers to that question: and, moreover, we will probably imagine England differently depending on where we are located, in both space and time. In other words, to speak of a single way of imagining the nation is clearly misleading: the word 'England' means different things to different people in different times and spaces (cf. Holloway and Valentine, 2000c). Nevertheless, it would be wrong to conclude from this that images of national identity are simply a matter of personal preference. Some images of national identity become more dominant than others at particular times; and frequently, though not always, these images take distinctly geographical forms. England, for example, has often been pictured through landscape imagery supposed to represent the 'essence' of the nation: sometimes these have been rural landscapes (as in the image of 'Constable country' popularized from the late nineteenth century), on other occasions they have been urban (as in the image of St Paul's during the Blitz). The task of cultural geographers working with such images is to show how they have become such potent icons of Englishness, in different ways at different times (Daniels, 1993; Matless, 1998). Two conclusions may be drawn from such work. First, the imagery of national identity is liable to constant change: while images may endure, their meanings may not. Second, the imagination of national identity is not a process that works exclusively from within, as if emerging from the heart of the nation: it is constructed relationally, by contrast with an 'other', wherever that other is located.

FIGURE 10.5
Gateway to Empire – or the Commodity Triumphant? (from R. Opie, *Trading on the British Image*, 1985)

These two points may be illustrated with reference to two contrasting examples. First, consider the role of a building such as Tower Bridge in the making of the images of British national identity. Images of this landmark continue to circulate worldwide, thanks to the tourist industry, in the form of postcards, jigsaws, tea towels, posters and models of all kinds, and the bridge has been used in many films to provide an instantly recognizable back-drop. If the building appears to represent the perfect tourist icon, it is because it simultaneously represents so many different aspects of the imagined nation. In its neo-gothic grandeur, the bridge literally towers over the Thames, dramatizing the role that the river has played in the history of London, and by extension the course of the British empire; and its location, adjacent to the Tower of London, evokes the ancient history of royal London, complete with beefeaters, jewels and princes. And yet, the bridge itself was a very late addition to this heritage landscape: in fact, it was completed little over a hundred years ago, in 1894, just in time for Queen Victoria's Diamond Jubilee. Hidden beneath the mock-medieval exterior was a thoroughly modern steel hydraulic mechanism, through which its huge bascules could be raised within minutes. The contemporary response to the appearance of the bridge was mixed, to say the least: dismissing it as 'a pretentious piece of bad medievalism', one critic complained that 'a more wretched piece of architectural falsehood and vulgarity was never perpetrated' (Driver and Gilbert, 1998: 16). For all its fakery, however, Tower Bridge soon established itself as a symbol of imperial London *par excellence*. Indeed, given its design and location, it is difficult to imagine a more appropriate monument to an age of 'invented traditions' (Hobsbawm and Ranger, 1983). A thoroughly modern building, made to look old – the last word in imperial kitsch? Images of the bridge have been appropriated in a variety of ways ever since – as a prop for commodity advertising, for example (Figure 10.5). This example illustrates a larger process, in which images of the nation are exploited for a range of different ends: once again, it is clear that such landscapes have no single, eternal meaning. They are how they are imagined.

(a)

A VILLAGE IN PUKAPUKA, UNDER HEATHENISM

(b)

THE SAME VILLAGE, UNDER CHRISTIANITY.

FIGURE 10.6
An imaginative geography of missionary work: a village in Pukapuka (a) under Heathenism and (b) under Christianity. Source: W. Gill, *Life in the Southern Isles*, 1876

Race

a criterion of social categorization that distinguishes different groups of people on the basis of particular secondary physical differences (such as skin colour). Human Geographers have studied questions of race in a number of ways including: (a) the extent, causes and implications of the spatial segregation of different racial groups within cities, regions or nations; (b) the role played by geographical understandings of place and environment in the construction both of ideas of race per se and of ideas about particular races; and (c) the forms of racism and inequality that operate through these geographical patterns, processes and ideas. Increasingly, Human Geographers have emphasized how racial categories, whilst having very real consequences for people's lives, cannot simply be assumed as biological realities, having instead to be recognized as SOCIAL CONSTRUCTIONS. *See also* ETHNICITY.

Because of their location, buildings like St Paul's or Tower Bridge have often been represented – sometimes seriously, at other times ironically – as the heart of the nation. But nations are imagined in other ways too, often by contrast with other peoples (see Ryan, 1997). For a second example, consider the images in Figure 10.6, which appeared in a book entitled *Life in the Southern Isles*, published by a missionary (and Fellow of the Royal Geographical Society) in 1876. They show two contrasting visions of a Pacific Island village scene, supposed to be before and after conversion to Christianity. The first engraving depicts the islanders engaged in a ceremonial dance, wearing grass skirts and shells, abandoned to a hedonistic life; in the second, they have been transformed into a sedate community, domesticated and cultivated, displaying the virtues of labour, exchange and civilization. Such 'before and after' images were a staple part of missionary writings during this period, and were clearly designed to promote the missionary cause in Europe: they often had little to do with the realities on the ground. Yet these images mattered, not just because they reflected the imagination of missionaries, but also because they helped to shape the actions of their sponsors 'at home'. Indeed, looking more closely at the second image, you will find that the 'heathen' natives have not simply been converted to Christianity and commerce: they and their landscape have evidently been Anglicized. The domestic scene in the second image portrays a decorous pastoral scene, reminiscent of some English landscape, in which people know their place; and the landscape is as ordered as the society (see Chapter 11). Together, the two scenes combine a historical sense of transformation (the impact of Europeans on Pacific islanders) with a geographical restructuring: the island has, imaginatively at least, become England.

SUMMARY

- Nations may be understood as imagined communities, constructed not merely on the basis of a shared location but through the mobilization of images.

- Images of the nation vary considerably over time and space; they do not have a single, eternal meaning. The processes by which some images come to be regarded as dominant is a major theme for cultural geographers.

- Images of national identity do not work exclusively from within; they are frequently constructed relationally, by contrast with an imagined 'other'. This process is particularly evident in the cultural geography of imperialism.

CONCLUSION

Images of the kind we have considered in this chapter help to compose 'imaginative geographies', representations of place, space and landscape that structure people's understandings of the world, and in turn help to shape their actions. They have a real existence and real effects; in other words, they matter. In some circumstances, particular instances of an imaginative geography may be described as false or partial – Figure 10.6, for example, clearly reflects a particular point of view, which was evidently not that of the Pacific islanders themselves. Yet to make this case is not to say that such images are inconsequential. Whether or not we regard them as essentially true or false, such imaginative geographies have significant implications for the way in which people behave. And they are certainly not simply things of the past.

The significance of imaginative geographies is starkly apparent in the recent resurgence of new forms of Orientalism in representations of military conflict in the Middle East. In the lead-up to the American invasion of Taliban-ruled Afghanistan in 2001, one military historian wrote of the essential difference between 'western' and 'Oriental' approaches to warfare:

> Westerners fight face to face, in stand-up battle, and go on until one side or the other gives in ... Orientals, by contrast, shrink from pitched battle, which they often deride as a sort of game, preferring ambush, surprise, treachery and deceit as the best way to overcome an enemy.

(Keegan, cited in Driver, 2003)

In view of the nature of modern military technology, which precisely enables unimaginable slaughter to take place without the inconvenience of 'face to face' confrontation, these remarks are cruelly ironic. Having cast doubt on the belief that a conflict between Christianity and Islam is at the root of the current 'war on terrorism', the same commentator falls back on a still cruder version of the Orientalist thesis: 'This war belongs within the much larger spectrum of a far older conflict between settled, creative productive Westerners and predatory, destructive Orientals.' As Derek Gregory argues in his book *The Colonial Present*, such claims replicate the discursive structures of Orientalism, reducing complex political situations to an essential opposition between the civilized West and its barbarian Others.

It should be noted here that Said's argument in *Orientalism* was not about the effects of ignorance so much as the power of knowledge: and he was at pains to argue that imaginative geographies were at their most powerful when they were connected to structures of authority and expertise. He thus drew parallels between British and French traditions of Orientalist scholarship in the nineteenth century, and the deployment of regional expertise in support of American foreign policy in Vietnam and the Middle East in the Cold War years. The current global crisis, in the wake of the United States-led 'war on terrorism', raises far-reaching and somewhat different questions about the actual role of imaginative geographies in the pursuit of geopolitical power. For this is a conflict in which knowledge of some things (specifically terrain, resources and technology) has been much more highly valued than that of others (culture, society and language).

Imaginative geographies, however, are not simply the property of rich and powerful institutions in the West. They continue to circulate in a wide variety of media – for example, through television, film, newspapers and magazines, school textbooks, advertising, computer games or the web. These media extend beyond texts and images to material cultures and landscapes: thus street markets, housing estates, nature reserves and theme parks could be regarded as exemplary sites for the study of imaginative geographies in the twenty-first century. What, for example, might we make of the Japanese fascination for reproductions of 'exotic' cultural landscapes in their own country? In Maruyama, a major transnational corporation was recently commissioned by the city authorities to construct a 'Shakespeare Country Park' (completed in 1997), effectively a concrete abstraction of Elizabethan culture, complete with townhouse, inn, theatre, garden and village green. We might perhaps expect this to be no more than an exercise in consumerism, the Disneyfication of a myth of 'Merrie England'. Yet it could be argued that the attention to detail manifested in the architecture and design of the site, together with the broader tradition of recreational pilgrimage within Japanese culture, may be interpreted more positively (Chaplin, 1998).

The case of the contemporary theme park raises more general methodological issues: how should we go about interpreting the meaning and effects of imaginative geographies? This is no easy task: indeed, if it were, there would be no need for you to read any further! To interpret a landscape, a text or an image, it is clearly necessary to enter the world of those who created these artefacts; to understand their ideas, values and relationships. Once we accept that the process of creation, or production, involves much more than a single intention, and usually requires the participation of many different people, the matter begins to look much more complex than at first sight. But that is not all: a theme park, like a museum, is likely to convey quite different meanings to different visitors, and they too will carry with them a wide variety of experiences, preconceptions and desires. Interpreting imaginative geographies, then, turns out to require us to think not only about their content, but about their form; and not only about what they say, but how they have said it and to whom. And while we may find it useful to think of imaginative geographies as ways of seeing, we must not forget that they are also sites of interaction and intervention. The challenge for the geographer is not to make imaginative geographies more real, but rather to make them more truly human.

DISCUSSION POINTS

1. Why should geographers concern themselves with the realms of the imagination?

2. What are imaginative geographies, and how are they generated?

3. How far does Edward Said's *Orientalism* provide a model for the understanding of cultural geographies of identity in general?

4. What role should imaginative geographies play in the making of geographical knowledge in the twenty-first century?

FURTHER READING

Daniels, S. (1993) *Fields of vision: landscape imagery and national identity in England and the United States.* **Oxford: Polity Press.**

A series of engaging studies of landscape imagery and national identity by a cultural geographer.

Gregory, D. (2004) *The colonial present: Afghanistan, Palestine, Iraq.* **Oxford: Blackwell.**

A passionate critique of the war on terror, which traces the imaginative geographies of American and British military intervention in the Middle East from the colonial past to the colonial present.

Lutz, C. and Collins, J. (1993) *Reading 'National Geographic'.* **Chicago: University of Chicago Press.**

A critical study of the world's most popular geographical magazine, focusing on the photographic representation of place, race and gender.

May, J. (1996) A little taste of something more exotic: the imaginative geographies of everyday life. *Geography,* **81, 57–64.**

An accessible account of everyday consumption in the context of multicultural urbanism.

Rose, G. (1995) Place and identity: a sense of place. In Massey, D. and Jess, P. (eds) *A place in the world?* **Oxford: Oxford University Press.**

A good account of the idea of a sense of place, exploring the role of visual and other images in the construction of national and other identities.

Said, E. (1978) *Orientalism.* **Harmondsworth: Penguin.**

The classic work on the imaginative geography of the Orient as represented in scholarly and political writings in the West.

CHAPTER 11
LANDSCAPES

Catherine Nash

INTRODUCTION

Class

a collection of people sharing the same economic position within society, and/or sharing the same social status and cultural tastes. The precise ways in which one's economic position – for example, as a worker, a capitalist or a member of the land-owning aristocracy – is related to one's social status or cultural tastes has been much debated. However, Human Geographers have studied class and its geographies from all these perspectives: as an economic, social and cultural structuring of society.

Gender

a criterion of social organization that distinguishes different groups of people on the basis of femininity or masculinity. In any one location, many masculinities and femininities interact. As a concept, gender is usually used in Human Geography in distinction to that of sex (i.e. femaleness and maleness) in order to emphasize the SOCIAL CONSTRUCTION of women's and men's roles, relations and identities. Human Geographers' accounts of the world have always been shaped through understandings of gender (*see* MASCULINISM) but explicit analyses of the geographies of gender and the gendering of geographies are comparatively recent, and associated with the growth of Feminist Geography (*see* FEMINISM).

Representation

the cultural practices and forms by which human societies interpret and portray the world around them and present themselves to others. In the case of the natural world, for example, these representations range from prehistoric cave paintings of the creatures that figured in the lives of early human groups to the televisual images and scientific models that shape our imaginations today. *See also* DISCOURSE.

The study of landscapes has been one of the longest traditions in Human Geography. Human Geographers have mapped distinctive landscapes, tried to reconstruct landscapes in the past and traced the social processes that have produced and continue to shape the landscapes of today. While the study of landscape in Human Geography in the past was part of a tradition of recording the physical and human features of particular regions, this chapter focuses on approaches to landscape that emerged in the late 1980s. This work has explored the representation and organization of landscapes as complex articulations of meaning about relationships between people (in terms of **class**, **gender**, **ethnicity**, 'race' and other categories of identity and ideas of difference) and relationships between people and places (as owners, settlers, visitors, native people, and so on). This is obviously a broad description. So one of the tasks of this introduction to the study of landscape in Human Geography is to show how the study of landscape can be a productive way of exploring themes such as gender, national identity, imaginative geographies, inclusion and exclusion, embodiment and power.

Another task is to show how landscape is a very particular sort of cultural category. Though landscape has an everyday, taken-for-granted sort of meaning, loosely connected to natural environments, mostly to the countryside, and associated with nature more generally, landscape names a particular way of thinking about, classifying and representing the world that has a specific history and geography. Landscape emerged as a meaningful category in particular times and places as part of wider shifts in ideas about how the world is organized and understood, often described in terms of **modernity** (see Chapter 24). The familiar practice of taking a photograph in such a way that the view is framed by trees or foliage, the subject is in the foreground and the view extends into the distance, evokes the western European tradition of representing landscape that developed from the sixteenth century (Cosgrove, 1985a). Cultural geographers have explored its emergence as a specific modern, European way of thinking about, organizing and representing environments and so denaturalized landscape by highlighting the social production of the concept of 'landscape' in particular times and places. They have considered how **representations** of landscape can be used to naturalize, or make very particular claims appear natural, taken for granted, right.

This probably sounds quite abstract so far. To make it more concrete, the rest of this chapter traces a series of interconnected themes that geographers have explored in their work on historical and more recent landscapes. These are themes of landscape, property and political authority; landscape, identity and difference; and landscapes of work and leisure. In their studies of landscape, geographers have used different sorts of metaphors to help explain the relationships between landscape and society. Landscape has been described as a way of seeing (Cosgrove, 1994), as a text that is authored and read (Duncan, 1995), or as a theatre where society acts out its dominant values and resistance is staged (Daniels and Cosgrove, 1993). Rather than opt for one explanatory device it might be more useful to keep certain questions in mind in addressing how landscapes are made and made meaningful. These questions are: 'Whose landscape is this?' (both in a formal or legal sense, as in legal claims of ownership and in a symbolic sense as in 'this landscape is our national heritage'); 'Who makes these claims and how?'; 'What sort of activities are taken to be moral or proper in this landscape, and by whom?'; 'How are these patterns of ownership and these arguments established and challenged?'

This chapter first explores the themes of property, power and 'politeness' in a specific tradition of viewing, depicting and arranging landscape in Britain in the late eighteenth and nineteenth centuries, that was tied to particular class, gender and 'racial' identities. Second, it connects the production of landscape imagery to themes of profit and productivity in the landscape both in Britain and in British colonial contexts. The third section moves from the theme of labour in the landscape to the theme of leisure in twentieth-century landscapes, and from ideas of improving productivity to ideas of improving people through particular sorts of activities outdoors.

Race

a criterion of social categorization that distinguishes different groups of people on the basis of particular secondary physical differences (such as skin colour). Human Geographers have studied questions of race in a number of ways including: (a) the extent, causes and implications of the spatial segregation of different racial groups within cities, regions or nations; (b) the role played by geographical understandings of place and environment in the construction both of ideas of race per se and of ideas about particular races; and (c) the forms of racism and inequality that operate through these geographical patterns, processes and ideas. Increasingly, Human Geographers have emphasized how racial categories, whilst having very real consequences for people's lives, cannot simply be assumed as biological realities, having instead to be recognized as SOCIAL CONSTRUCTIONS. *See also* ETHNICITY.

SUMMARY

- Landscapes on the ground and images of landscape reflect social meanings, ideas and values.
- Representations of landscapes are often used to express particular sorts of relationships between people, social identities and relationships between people and places.
- Landscapes can be thought about in terms of representation and practices, and in terms of questions of property, power and ideas of 'proper' behaviour.

LANDSCAPE: POWER, PROPERTY AND PICTURESQUE VISION

The late eighteenth and early nineteenth century was a particularly important period in the development of landscape traditions in Britain, especially for the style called 'picturesque'. Though this term is used nowadays to describe pretty or picture-postcard scenes, at this time the term had very specific meanings and connotations. The development of this style was linked to the new importance of images of the countryside in art. As the traditional landed classes became more involved in the active development of their estates at home and abroad, and as the middle class

FIGURE 11.1
Picturesque landscapes. Source: W. Gilpin, 1792: *Three Essays: on Picturesque Beauty, on Picturesque Travel and on Sketching*

Colonialism

the rule of a NATION-STATE or other political power over another, subordinated, people and place. This domination is established and maintained through political structures, but may also shape economic and cultural relations. *See also* NEO-COLONIALISM and IMPERIALISM.

emerged from the growing commercial and industrial sector, new frameworks for understanding their place within the world and depicting their land developed. The aristocratic owners of old landed estates commissioned paintings of the land they owned, and of their country houses within their landscaped estates in ways that presented these patterns of property and privilege as natural. There was also a new and growing metropolitan middle-class market for landscape painting and interest in travelling to see picturesque landscapes. Many guides to travel and taste were produced for this market with advice on where to visit, what to see, and how to see and sketch 'properly'. Picturesque landscapes seen on canvas or in travel were panoramic but usually framed by large trees or craggy outcrops. Organized into foreground, midground and background, they depended on the viewer looking down and out over a vista along a zig-zag path to a distant horizon and back to foreground details (see Fig. 11.1). This way of seeing emphasized a distant and elevated viewpoint, unobstructed by the branches or hills that would limit what could be seen. This approach to landscape was not confined to visual representations. Written descriptions in poetry or topographical writing could also convey ideas of an ordered, distanced and linear vision instead of a sense of immersion in the landscape and its sounds and fragrances and sights.

Being able to write about, sketch or look at landscapes in this way became a measure of good taste and proof of being cultivated, refined and of high social standing. In this way landscape was deployed to define the civilized and polite amongst those with money to buy landscape images and landscape their estates. As the estates of landed gentry and the new middle class were landscaped to make them more picturesque, landscape taste was increasingly caught up in questions of money, morality and refinement (Daniels, 1982; Daniels and Seymour, 1990). Having what was deemed to be the 'right' taste in landscape design was used as a measure of 'politeness' and refinement.

Ideas of landscapes were thus not just a matter of taste. The idea that there was a certain 'right' way of seeing landscape was not only used to distinguish amongst those with money. It was also linked to the wider development of an idea of modern subjectivity and to claims of political authority. An appreciation of the landscapes as picturesque, it was argued, was achieved by eliminating all the messy and confusing detail in the scene so that the true and abstract qualities of the landscape could be revealed. This required the viewer to be distant, objective and detached from what was being seen. The idea of being refined enough to appreciate the picturesque was thus linked to a wider idea that being civilized depended on being separate from nature. This was an exclusive as well as powerful view of modern subjectivity. Upper-class men who defined their good taste and social standing through their ability to recognize and enjoy picturesque landscapes argued that this ability to think with rational detachment, in general terms and about abstract ideas, were the skills required for positions of political authority (Barrell, 1990). But these skills depended on their class position. A private income was needed, they suggested, to both govern impartially and to see landscape with a proper distance. The lower classes and especially those who worked the land, they suggested, were not able to see landscape in this way, since they supposedly lacked the distance and objectivity that defined both the ability to govern and to see the world in appropriate ways. They were thought to be too close to the land to see it 'properly', and too caught up in making their own living to consider the good of society as a whole. When English aristocratic men made connections between landscape taste and political authority in the eighteenth century, they were attempting to define and differentiate themselves from the lower classes. But they also used ideas of landscape to claim that they were different from women and from other 'races', who were defined as 'closer to nature' in eighteenth- and nineteenth-century ideas of gender and racial hierarchies. As well as lower-class men, women in general and other 'races' were not thought to be civilized enough to be able to appreciate landscape or to govern themselves. This role of governing for the good of all, claimed by the upper classes, thus meant securing and reinforcing their own privileged position. This tradition of landscape, then, was developed by a particular section of society and used to make claims about the characteristics of different people and their place in the social order.

Modern, modernity, modernism

ideas of the modern are most commonly defined through their opposition to the old and the traditional. In this light, the adjective 'modern' is synonymous with 'newness'; 'modernity' refers both to the 'post-traditional' historical epoch within which 'newness' is produced and valued, as well as to the economic, social, political and cultural formations characteristic of that period; and 'modernism' applies more narrowly to artistic, architectural and intellectual movements that centrally explore ideas of 'newness' and develop 'new' aesthetics and ways of thinking to express these. Modernity has been most commonly located in Euro-American societies from the eighteenth century onwards, and thereby associated with their characteristic combination of capitalist economies (see CAPITALISM), political organization through NATION-STATES, and cultural values of secularity, rationality and progress (see ENLIGHTENMENT). However, increasingly, Human Geographers are recognizing that modernity is a global phenomenon that has taken many different forms in different times and places. See also MODERNIZATION.

SUMMARY
- The development of the convention of picturesque landscape in Britain was linked to issues of property and the development of specific class identities.
- Ideas of landscape taste and landscape appreciation were used to support arguments for political authority and to define an exclusive version of modern subjectivity.

LANDSCAPE: LABOUR, PRODUCTIVITY AND PROFIT

This discussion of landscape has, so far, emphasized themes of subjectivity, property and power. But as themes of property and power suggest, the aesthetic pleasures of picturesque landscapes for landowners were also about productivity and profit. Images of landscape were also often

Ethnicity

a criterion of social categorization that distinguishes different groups of people on the basis of inherited cultural differences. Ethnicity is a very complex idea that needs careful consideration. For instance, in popular usage ethnicity often becomes a synonym for RACE, but in fact there is a crucial distinction in so far as race differentiates people on the grounds of physical characteristics, and ethnicity on the grounds of learnt cultural differences. Moreover, whilst everyday understandings of ethnicity often treat it as a quality only possessed by some people and cultures (for instance, 'ethnic minorities' and their 'ethnic foods' or 'ethnic fashions') in fact these differential recognitions of ethnicity themselves need explanation. The complexities of the concept are further emphasized by recent debates within and beyond Human Geography over the extent to which new forms of ethnicity are emerging through the cultural mixing associated with processes of GLOBALIZATION (*see also* HYBRID and SYNCRETIC).

representations of labour and industriousness. The ways those who worked the land were represented in landscape representations in Britain and in British **colonial** contexts abroad reflected unequal social relations of wealth and power (Mitchell, 1994). In late eighteenth- and nineteenth-century landscape painting, the people who worked the land were seen as part of the landscape, like the trees and crops, not as viewers of it in their own right. But they were also depicted in particular ways. As the conditions of labour for the poor worsened in the early nineteenth century, the middle and upper class grew increasingly anxious about the possibility of rural unrest. At the same time there was a shift away from images in poetry and painting of a harmonious and idyllic rural world in which 'nature's' abundance required little labour (a tradition known as the Pastoral), to images that emphasized the morality and necessity of hard work (a tradition known as Georgic). With this new model of 'nature' and human relationships to the natural world, landowners could justify both their schemes of agricultural improvement to increase the profitability of the estates and their philosophy of economic individualism – the freedom to pursue profit unhindered by the constraints of tradition – often at the cost of the rural poor. Hard work was seen as natural and a productive landscape was seen as beautiful. So, if the rural poor were depicted within the landscape they had to be seen as emblems of hard and sober labour rather than as individuals with all their potential to resist a social order that oppressed them (see Fig. 11.2). Like the light and shade of landscape, society, it was suggested, was ideally and 'naturally' stratified into the rich and poor. The rural poor were located firmly 'on the dark side of the landscape' (Barrell, 1980).

These cultural conventions of the picturesque and the Georgic were also used to make particular claims of ownership and to naturalize specific patterns of privilege and labour in British colonial contexts. In the eighteenth century, attempts to make landed estates in England more productive and picturesque were frequently funded by wealth being made through colonial trade

FIGURE 11.2
John Constable, Landscape, Ploughing Scene in Suffolk (A Summerland) c. 1824. Credit: The Yale Center for British Art, Paul Mellon Collection, USA/www.bridgeman.co.uk

and overseas plantations. So as places such as Herefordshire were being depicted in painting, poetry and agricultural texts as picturesque, Georgical and national landscapes central to British economic prosperity, places such as the West Indies were also being understood and organized through English discourses of landscape productivity and beauty (Seymour *et al.*, 1994). English travel guides and topographical accounts of colonial possessions frequently concentrated on the description of places that could be most easily accommodated to the conventions of the picturesque and likened the scenery to the famous examples of European landscape painting. Like the detailed descriptions of cider making or the importance of oak trees in England within Georgical poetry, English poets encountering the West Indies wrote in similar ways of sugar cane, a crop that was increasingly the staple of English plantation agriculture in the Caribbean. These ways of understanding landscape defined the West Indies within English cultural frameworks and as British colonies. Thomas Hearne, who painted estate portraits for landowners in Britain, also depicted colonial estates through the framework of the picturesque and the Georgic (see Fig. 11.3). His image of Antigua both depicts the landscape through the conventions of the picturesque – here the palm trees frame the scene – and paints a

FIGURE 11.3
T. Hearne, A Scene in the West Indies. Credit: © The British Museum

productive landscape of sugar cane cultivation and harvesting. Slaves are depicted as happy workers.

English estates and their owners were often deeply involved in imperial systems of exploitation. Timber from estates in Herefordshire, for example, was transported to Bristol down the Wye and Severn rivers, where ships designed for the slave trade were built and sailed between Bristol, Africa and the West Indies (Seymour *et al.*, 1994: 42). In these ways, the landscapes of estates in Britain and the West Indies were connected through concerns about labour, productivity, land improvement, landscape aesthetics and **imperialism**. So though the image of a landscape empty of indigenous people was a significant feature of much European colonial travel writing and topographical description and was used to legitimize its **colonization**, when the labour of native or enslaved people was required for profitable colonial projects, the landscape conventions of the Georgic and the picturesque provided cultural frameworks for naturalizing these highly unequal relationships.

Descriptions of landscape in colonial contexts used European landscape conventions of a commanding and prospecting gaze travelling across the land, scanning 'possibilities for the future, resources to be developed, landscapes to be peopled or repeopled by Europeans' (Pratt, 1986: 144). But British colonial settlers in overseas colonies were concerned both with the potential of land to support them and with their feelings of security and belonging in these places. The African landscape, for example, was often represented as an arena through which the settler was free to roam at ease unimpeded by its native inhabitants (Bunn, 1994). In settler colonies the idea of ordered picturesque vision and free movement was linked to a concern for the order imposed by colonial settlement and the opportunities for profit afforded by free market **capitalism**. But freedom and mobility were dependent also on the idea of permanence represented in the image of the settler homestead and on reproducing at least some of the familiar features of the environment of Europe. Both visual and literary representations of the landscape used the conventions of the

Imperialism

a relationship of political, and/or economic, and/or cultural domination and subordination between geographical areas. This relationship may be based on explicit political rule (*see* COLONIALISM), but need not be.

Colonization

the physical settling of people from a colonial power within that power's subordinated colonies (*see* COLONIALISM). *See also* DECOLONIZATION.

Capitalism

an economic system in which the
production and distribution of goods is
organized around the profit motive (*see*
CAPITAL ACCUMULATION) and
characterized by marked inequalities in
the social division of work and wealth
between private owners of the materials
and tools of production (capital) and
those who work for them to make a
living (labour) (*see* CLASS).

Naturalization, naturalized

this term has two distinct and different
meanings: (a) the way in which social
relations, cultural norms or institutions
are made to seem 'natural' rather than
SOCIAL CONSTRUCTIONS; and (b)
the process through which species
become established in new
environments, sometimes also applied
to human life to refer to the formal
integration of immigrants in new
societies.

FIGURE 11.4
Encampment in the Great Namaqua Country.
Source: Francois Le Valliant, 1790: *Travels into
the Interior Parts of Africa*

SUMMARY

- In nineteenth-century British landscape painting
  the rural poor were presented in ways that
  naturalized divisions between rich and poor and
  emphasized the morality of their hard work.
- In British colonial contexts, landscapes could be
  represented as empty and therefore open to
  colonization, or as part of networks of profit and
  productivity between English estates and colonial
  plantations.
- European landscape conventions were used in
  settler contexts in the formation of gendered
  settler identities.
- The depiction of colonized people in landscape
  representations was part of wider European
  practices of colonization.

picturesque to make the landscape seem familiar (see Fig. 11.4) and the presence of British settlers natural and legitimate. These ideas of settler belonging were based on highly gendered roles for European men and women, and on the oppression of native people. By depicting the landscape as an arena for *men* to work and play, images of landscape were used to naturalize particular roles for men and women within European settler societies. White women, instead, were firmly located within the private domestic world of the home (see Fig. 11.5). In colonial landscape imagery women and men, natives and settlers were assigned different locations within both landscape representations and the landscape itself. In colonial landscape traditions, indigenous peoples frequently figured as the potential or actual workforce for European capitalist projects, as exotic fauna merged in nature or were simply missing from the landscape. These traditions continue to play their part in conflicts over the cultural value, meaning, use and ownership of land and landscape today (Huggins *et al.*, 1995; Jacobs, 1988; 1996).

FIGURE 11.5
The Bechuana boy. Source: T. Pringle, 1834: *African Sketches*

LANDSCAPE: LEISURE AND 'PROPER' BEHAVIOUR

If eighteenth- and nineteenth-century accounts of enjoying picturesque landscapes emphasized the pleasures of a distanced vision with its sense of power and authority, twentieth-century arguments about the pleasures of landscape have often come with a much stronger emphasis on the benefits of physical activity and close 'contact with nature'. David Matless has explored the ways in which ideas of nature, national identity, citizenship, subjectivity, fitness, health, order and pleasure were interwoven in arguments for the benefits of walking in the countryside and other outdoor pursuits in the period between the First and Second World Wars in England (Matless, 1995). Landscape in this period, and especially vigorous physical activity in the countryside, was seen as an antidote to the degenerating effects of urban industrial living. New transport developments opened up the countryside as a space for urban leisure and the possibilities of large numbers of people enjoying what had previously been the preserve of the wealthy. This bought new concerns as well as new opportunities. The formation of organizations like the Youth Hostels Association and the National Council of Rambler's Federations (later the Rambler's Association), both founded in 1930, reflects the widely held views of the benefits of open-air leisure in fostering physical and spiritual health. An ideal of healthy, active and energized citizenship shaped through vigorous outdoor activity in the landscape was shared across a wide range of groups and reflected in the practices of preservationists, planners, ramblers, scouts and guides, and health campaigners. Open-air recreation could regenerate the nation. Those armed with a rucksack, compass, boots and Ordnance Survey map could experience the landscape and practise the 'art of right living' (see Fig. 11.6).

FIGURE 11.6
Hiking, by J.W. Tucker, Laing Art Gallery, Newcastle upon Tyne

Yet, the possibility of extending the benefits of landscape to large numbers of people also led to anxieties about what people might do in the countryside and to attempts to educate people into appropriate environmental behaviour. The pleasure of some people – working class day-trippers, or middle-class picnickers playing music or leaving litter – was deemed intrusive and inappropriate by others who claimed the authority to define 'proper' or 'improper' behaviour. New opportunities were thus accompanied by new attempts to order activity and establish codes of conduct in the countryside often by contrasting the moral and respectable rambler with the image of the 'vulgar' working-class 'Cockney' failing to engage with the landscape in what was deemed to be an appropriate way. These broad contrasts were often inflected by local distinctions between those activities that could improve the self and those that met disapproval. David Matless (1994; 2000) has explored the ways these distinctions were made in this period in the Norfolk Broads – an area of shallow lakes, rivers and wetland in eastern England – through contrasts between sailing and motor cruising, one associated with skill, alertness, self-reliance and care for nature, the other with carelessness and immorality. Thus issues of what people did, and still do, in the landscape on holiday involves questions of morality and freedom.

> *The issue of planning for leisure, and of designating spaces [such] as national parks as sites for valued forms of leisure, entails judgements over how 'free' time should play over space, and how people might best use their play for their own good and for the good of the environment which they are in. Such judgements and tensions are inherent in and formative of landscapes of leisure and pleasure.*

(Matless, 2000: 158)

But there were other tensions within this widely shared view of the benefits of exercise in the country in inter-war England. One involved questions of property. Though the countryside was being represented as a resource for the nation, the attempts to enjoy that landscape sometimes came into conflict with those who wanted to maintain the restricted access that came with ownership. 'Open-air tensions of property and propriety arose when access was denied, and trespass was the response' (Matless, 1995: 96). The most famous example of this is the first Mass Trespass in April 1932, organized by the members of the communist British Workers Sports Federation when workers asserted the right to walk across the privately owned Derbyshire moorland of Kinder Scout. This tension between private property and the idea of a national landscape heritage was carefully managed through the idea of training the visitors in ideal codes of conduct for the new National Parks established in 1947. Another tension was a concern that the pleasures of landscape and outdoor living might spill over into excessive, dangerous and inappropriate pleasures. Suggestions of hedonistic pleasure were countered by an emphasis on a hardy, Spartan tradition in which the benefits of outdoor living were best when comfort was minimal. Youth Hostels, for example, were designed to provide basic facilities rather than indulgent luxury. The emphasis was on simple pleasures. Discipline was the answer to decadence and disorder.

As David Matless has shown, ideas of modern planning, preservation and national health were closely entwined. Open-air recreation, if properly ordered through planning and education, could ensure a nation of citizens fit for the country: morally, spiritually and physically. Arguments about walking in the countryside were part of a specific set of ideas about English national fitness, ordered experience of landscape and modern progress: 'Hygienic and efficient homes and workplaces, orderly public spaces, a planned town and country, citizens in tune with their environment, national parks for required spiritual immersion; walking took place in a larger scheme of things' (Matless, 1995: 109).

Thus the familiar idea that walking in the countryside is good for you was tied to particular cultural geographies of landscape, self and environment in inter-war England that continue to influence opinions on questions such as 'Should noise be made in the country?', 'Why is it good to be in the landscape?', 'Which practices and people are fit for the English countryside?' (Matless, 1995: 121). Recent work by geographers on landscape and leisure thus extends the earlier concerns about the ways in which images of landscape naturalized the class relations that made landscape the site of work for some and leisure for others. It also reflects

Embodied, embodiment

this concept suggests that the self and the body are not separate, but rather that the experiences of any individual are, invariably, shaped by the active and reactive entity that is their body – irrespective of whether this is conscious or not. The argument, then, runs that the uniqueness of human experience is due, at least in part, to the unique nature of individual bodies.

new interests in the body and gender. Current interests in **embodied** practices, landscape and nature add ideas of morality and 'proper' behaviour to earlier interests in power and property.

SUMMARY

- The development of the idea of landscape as a resource for creating a healthy national population in inter-war England was based on ideas of the value of nature and exercise in the countryside.

- Tensions between ideas of order and freedom, and conflicts over what counts as 'proper' behaviour are a common theme in arguments about landscape and leisure.

CONCLUSION

The development of work on landscape in Cultural Geography is sometimes described in terms of shifts from studies of the material landscape (see also Chapter 12), to explorations of the ways in which landscapes have been represented in cultural forms, to more recent work on people's physical and embodied experience of landscape in a variety of cultural practices. Yet distinctions between work on landscape as 'a way of seeing' to landscape as 'a way of being' or, to put it another way, between landscape in terms of written and visual 'texts' and landscape in terms of practice and experience, can be unhelpful. Distinctions between representation and practice like this overlook the way that much work on landscape within Cultural Geography has explored representation as a powerful practice that has been interwoven with other sorts of practices that have shaped landscapes and naturalized different sorts of social relations and identities. Landscape imagery, as Stephen Daniels has written, 'is not merely a reflection of, or distraction from, more pressing social, economic or political issues; it is often a powerful mode of knowledge and social engagement' (Daniels, 1993: 8). Conflicts over what landscapes mean or how they should be organized – in these cases, to produce profit and create wealth, or as places of leisure, order and healthy citizenship – are part of complex processes through which individuals and groups define themselves, and claim and challenge political authority. Running through these examples have been themes of identity, subjectivity, property and power.

New work on landscape continues a longer tradition of addressing the connections between images, ideas and practices. But recent studies have brought more explicit attention to the relationships between technologies, objects, images and practices in all sorts of embodied engagements with environments – walking, climbing, caving, camping. This means that 'landscape' sometimes loses its specific meaning as 'a *pictorial* way of representing, structuring or symbolising surroundings' (Daniels and Cosgrove, 1989: 1; my emphasis) and is used in a more general sense. Landscape can slip away as a neatly definable category. But part of the work of Cultural Geographers has been to explore the multiple ways in which people have tried to fix the meaning of landscape in general, or define what counts as appropriate activities for particular landscapes, and examine the effects of these temporary and contested, but often powerful, fixes of meaning.

DISCUSSION POINTS

1. In what ways are landscapes implicated in relations of 'power'?

2. How did picturesque landscapes relate to social relations of class, gender and race, either in Britain or in British colonies?

3. Why is leisure in rural landscapes a matter of public debate and argument?

4. What do we learn about landscapes by treating them as 'ways of seeing', 'texts' and 'theatres'?

FURTHER READING

Duncan, J. (1995) Landscape geography, 1993–94. *Progress in Human Geography*, 19, 414–22.

A useful introduction to the different traditions of analysing landscape as either a portion of natural and cultural environment or as a pictorial convention.

Kinnaird, V., Morris, M., Nash, C. and Rose, G. (1997) Feminist geographies of environment, nature and landscape. In Women and Geography Research Group, *Feminism and geography: diversity and difference.* **London: Longman, 146–89.**

Offers an accessible introduction to how landscape has been linked to problematic ideas of race, class, gender and sexuality.

Rose, G. (1993) *Feminism and geography: the limits to geographical knowledge.* **Cambridge: Polity, 86–112.**

Nash, C. (1996) Reclaiming vision: looking at landscape and the body. *Gender, Place and Culture: A Journal of Feminist Geography*, 3, 149–69.

The specific feminist debates about landscape, power, vision and gender are explored in depth in these texts.

Cosgrove, D. (1985) Prospect, perspective and the evolution of the landscape idea. *Transactions of the Institute of British Geographers*, 10, 45–62.

An influential article in the development of approaches to landscape in contemporary Human Geography was Denis Cosgrove's exploration of the origins of the term landscape in the culture and economy of the ruling class in fifteenth- and early sixteenth-century Italy.

Matless, D. (1992) An occasion for geography: landscape, representation and Foucault's corpus. *Environment and Planning D: Society and Space*, 10, 41–56.

This text explores in greater depth theoretical approaches to landscape interpretation.

Daniels, S. (1993) *Fields of vision: landscape imagery and national identity in England and the United States.* **Cambridge: Polity Press.**

Offers examples of the ways in which landscape and national identity have been connected.

CHAPTER 12

THE GEOGRAPHIES OF MATERIAL CULTURE

INTRODUCTION

This book represents how geography is about all sorts of stuff. In this chapter, we'll be taking that statement more narrowly and literally. We'll be thinking about how and why geographers have been interested in all kinds of different *stuff*, in the sense of things, objects and materials. In the cases discussed below, that will include buildings, fences, trees, personal stereos, toys, Italian motor scooters and a VW campervan, amongst other things. We can call this diverse world of stuff 'material culture'. This designation emphasizes the role of things in cultural processes of making distinctive ways of life and giving meaning to the world, its places and people. (For a brief summary of what the term 'culture' means, see the introduction to this section of chapters on Cultural Geography.)

Cultural Geography was for long devoted to work on material culture, documenting and explaining the spatial distributions of all manner of things from house types, to fence types, to foods (see Shortridge and Shortridge, 1999, for an excellent collection), to tools (for example, I spent much of my undergraduate studies reading up on plough and digging-stick distributions in Latin America), and much else besides. This interest never really went away, but it did become softened somewhat by a concern that a focus on things meant neglecting the more important social relations in which those things are implicated. There was a worry, then, that an interest in material culture somehow 'fetishized' things – making them the centre of our attention rather than the social, political and economic relations that brought them into being. However, more recently, there have been calls to 're-materialize' Cultural Geography (see, for example, Jackson, 2000), reflecting at least two decades of multi-disciplinary 'material culture studies' that has countered criticisms of object fetishism. This body of work (for an overview see Buchli, 2002) argues that: (a) rather than dismissing things as trivial ephemera we should recognize how their triviality and taken-for-grantedness makes them crucial **ideological** mechanisms; and (b) rather than material forms simply being the surface reflections of underlying social relations, material culture is in fact a vital constituent of our social worlds. To put that more simply, *stuff* matters.

This chapter in part traces out that fluxing history of Cultural Geography's interest in material culture, but it does so through an account of four ways in which stuff matters. First, we look at scholarship in Cultural Geography that has used material culture as an *inscription* or indicator of cultures and their spatial extents and influences. Our empirical focus will be pioneer colonization in North America. Second, we look at work that sees material culture as involved in processes of social and cultural *reproduction*, thereby making the social impacts and **cultural politics** of material forms much more evident. Here our principal substantive focus will be on one elite residential neighbourhood of the city

Ideological

a meaning, idea or thing is ideological in so far as it helps to constitute and maintain relations of domination and subordination between two or more social groups (CLASSES, GENDERS, age groups, etc.).

Cultural politics

a phrase that emphasizes the implications of culture in questions of power. On the one hand, this means reflecting on how cultural forms and judgements involve relations of power. On the other hand, it means recognizing that politics are in part undertaken through cultural relations and realms (resulting in what in the USA, especially, have been termed 'culture wars'). More specifically, a focus on cultural politics centres questions about whose culture is dominant, the role of culture in practices of resistance, whose REPRESENTATIONS portray the world, and about the IDEOLOGY of cultural forms.

of Vancouver in British Columbia, Canada: Shaughnessy Heights. Third, we turn to research that examines material culture as technologies or tools used in our *everyday space*, illustrated through the examples of personal stereos and toys. Here the focus is on what people do with things and on the powers that those things have to shape our everyday worlds. Finally, we look at material culture as a realm of cross-cultural *traffic*, highlighting work that has 'followed' things as they move around the world through the example of 'Italian' motor scooters.

THE STUFF OF CULTURAL INSCRIPTION

This summer, myself, my partner and our two children squeezed ourselves into our VW campervan and headed through the Channel Tunnel from England for a short summer holiday on 'the continent'. In the two weeks we had we didn't get very far. It's an old van and it doesn't go very fast. But even as we pottered along through northern France, the Belgian and Dutch Flanders, and the Netherlands we could not help but notice that things looked different. The road signs, the houses, the fields, all different from those in our home area of southern England and all changing as we moved around.

As I never tired of telling my co-travellers (to an understandable chorus of groans), noticing and explaining such changes is a long tradition within Cultural Geography. This is particularly true in the USA. Developing Carl Sauer's (1925) interest in the **cultural landscape** – the ways in which people shape natural landscapes into culturally distinctive forms – a fascinating body of work emerged that examined the regionalization of various material culture forms. Highlights would include the work of Fred B. Kniffen, whose particular focus was on vernacular or folk housing as well as bridges, barns and fences (see Kniffen, 1965 and 1990, for overviews). In this kind of work, emphasis is placed on observational and archival fieldwork that together can document and explain the morphology of visible material culture forms. With a particular focus on 'ordinary landscapes' (Meinig, 1979), the broad argument is that the 'built' components of those landscapes can be taken as 'un-witting autobiography' (Lewis, 1979: 12), an inscription that can be read as the imprint of cultural influences apparent in any place. An example may help elucidate this approach and the questions it centres on.

We'll look at the work of Terry Jordan and Matti Kaups on the historical geography of European settlement and 'pioneering' in North America (Jordan and Kaups, 1989). Their particular interest is on the 'backwoods' pioneers of the eighteenth century, 'a group of highly successful forest colonizers who formed the vanguard of European settlement in eastern North America' (Jordan, 1994: 215), moving European settlement westwards from the Delaware Valley far faster than the 'Yankees' in the North or the Planters in the South. Jordan and Kaups

Cultural landscape

traditionally this phrase has meant the impact of cultural groups in fashioning and transforming the natural landscape. More recently it has been suggested that landscape itself is a cultural image, a way of symbolizing, representing and structuring our surroundings.

FIGURE 12.1
Rosie, the campervan

view the success of these colonizers as stemming from a congruence between their ways of life (especially their ways of relating to land and nature) and the requirements of the pioneer environments they lived in:

> [L]iving in isolated log cabins; throwing up zigzag fences around their small ax- and fire-cleared fields of corn; skilfully hunting deer and bears in the woods; gathering berries, herbs, wild fruits, and honey; and herding small semiferal droves of pigs and cattle, these pioneers were ideally suited to the pioneer life.

(Jordan, 1994: 215)

More specifically, they identify one short-lived (1638–55) seventeenth-century colony – New Sweden in the lower Delaware Valley, and its population of ethnic Finns from the Savo-Karelian districts of Finland – as having had a vital role to play in developing this successful pioneer culture. The evidence for this surprising influence is found in American frontier material culture. Styles of log carpentry, house roof construction, house plans and architecture, other buildings such as hunting shanties and fence types are all documented and seen to bear the imprint of Savo-Karelian culture from northern Europe (see Fig. 12.2). The Värmland V-notch, the Karelian weighted board roof, the open-passage dog-trot house plan, the hunter's shanty and the zig-zag or 'worm' fence; all these specific material forms are witness, say Jordan and Kaups, to processes of cultural diffusion, being found only in northern Europe and the American backwoods frontier.

Their account is, of course, more subtle and complex than this brief summary allows. For example, they also attend to the cross-cultural contact between European pioneers and indigenous Amerindians. But, for our purposes, the central tenets of this approach to material culture and its geographies are established. Material forms can be seen as the unwitting imprint or inscription of

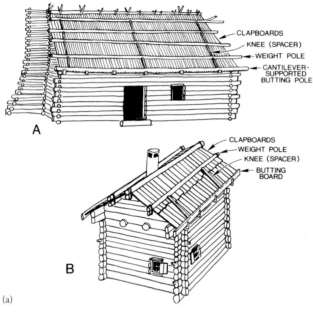

(a)

(b)

FIGURE 12.2
Imprints of Savo-Karelian culture on the North American frontier.
(a) Drawings showing similarities of backwoods pioneer and Karelian house roofs.
Key: A = America, B = Karelian Isthmus. (b) An American open-passage dog-trot cabin in Pennsylvania, showing also a Karelian board roof with weight pole and, in the foreground, a Karelian-style zig-zag rail fence with X-shaped supports.
Source: (a) *Re-reading Cultural Geography* (Foote *et al.*, 1994); (b) *Old Redstone, or historical sketches of Western Presbyterianism* (J. Smith, 1854)

distinctive cultures and peoples; tracing out the spatial distribution of those material forms therefore also evidences the spatial distribution of cultures; and thus a careful 'reading' of material traces in the landscape tells us about cultural origins, cultural diffusion and culture regions.

SUMMARY

- 'Material culture' is a term used to designate how the things or objects we make and use are related to our ways of life (our 'cultures') and our ways of making the world meaningful.
- A long-established approach to material culture in Cultural Geography is to see things or objects as markers or indicators of a culture and its influence.
- In this regard, particular attention has been paid to things and objects that can be seen in present or past landscapes (buildings and so forth), viewing these as unintentional imprints, inscriptions or etchings made by a culture on the land, which can be 'read' by the Cultural Geographer.
- Such a reading allows the Cultural Geographer to map out the spatial origins, diffusions and extents of different cultures.

THE STUFF OF CULTURAL REPRODUCTION

There are problems with seeing material culture as an unwitting imprint left by a culture on the landscape. Two are especially important. First, there is a danger of assuming 'cultures' as entities that act in and on the world, and paying too little attention to just how these 'cultures' come to be. Here, then, greater attention needs to be paid to the invention, construction and contestation of cultures and to the nature of cultural identity (see, in this volume, Chapters 10, 28 and 29 for introductory discussions). Second, and more specifically, material culture needs to be recognized as an active part of cultural life, not just as its expression. To put it another way: cultures don't only make things, things make cultures.

These worries are not unrecognized by those who look to read the materials of the cultural landscape for indicators of cultural influence – see, for example, the work of Peirce Lewis on American domestic architecture (1994), or Daniel Arreola's work on Spanish and Mexican architectural styles in the American South-West (1988). But they come to the fore in work that shifts its focus from thinking about material forms as imprints of culture to analysing their implication in processes of cultural expression and reproduction. Let me elaborate, first by referring back to me and my nuclear family in our VW campervan, and then through a more substantial case study, concerned with **class** and **ethnicity** in Vancouver City, British Columbia.

My previous mention of our family trip to the Low Countries in our campervan follows an embarrassingly common pattern – one in which, by hook or by crook, I will somehow manage to mention to people that I drive a 1970s VW Type 2 Westfalia campervan (the details can be difficult to force in, but they matter, so I make sure they get said somehow; as I just have done now!). I do this for reasons I understand only too well: this campervan is an object that I am very pleased to own (actually, my partner owns it, but I ignore that detail); I am pleased to be associated with it because I think it represents meanings that I value and says something about

Class

a collection of people sharing the same economic position within society, and/or sharing the same social status and cultural tastes. The precise ways in which one's economic position – for example, as a worker, a capitalist or a member of the land-owning aristocracy – is related to one's social status or cultural tastes has been much debated. However, Human Geographers have studied class and its geographies from all these perspectives: as an economic, social and cultural structuring of society.

Ethnicity

a criterion of social categorization that distinguishes different groups of people on the basis of inherited cultural differences. Ethnicity is a very complex idea that needs careful consideration. For instance, in popular usage ethnicity often becomes a synonym for RACE, but in fact there is a crucial distinction in so far as race differentiates people on the grounds of physical characteristics, and ethnicity on the grounds of learnt cultural differences. Moreover, whilst everyday understandings of ethnicity often treat it as a quality only possessed by some people and cultures (for instance, 'ethnic minorities' and their 'ethnic foods' or 'ethnic fashions') in fact these differential recognitions of ethnicity themselves need explanation. The complexities of the concept are further emphasized by recent debates within and beyond Human Geography over the extent to which new forms of ethnicity are emerging through the cultural mixing associated with processes of GLOBALIZATION (*see also* HYBRID and SYNCRETIC).

me that I like; and, in outline, these are something about discernment (it's not just the usual tin box), alternativeness (there's the aura of surfer culture, even though I can't actually swim a stroke) and youthfulness (when I know I am resoundingly middle-aged, a husband and father in the archetypal nuclear family unit). Further details of my tastes and self-regard need not detain us here, thank goodness. The broader argument, though, is worth an explicit re-statement: 'my' VW campervan is a fragment of material culture that plays a role in the fashioning of my cultural identity.

Chapters 28 and 18 provide further discussions of cultural identity and its relations to the consumption of material goods and their associated meanings. Here, though, let us turn to a case that shows how this understanding of material culture reconfigures how we think about the relations between culture and material landscape forms such as house types. That case is the neighbourhood of Shaughnessy Heights in Vancouver (see Fig. 12.3). In David Ley's telling (1995), in 1990 local resident Harry Liang (a pseudonym) decided to fell two large sequoia trees on the front lawn of his newly built family home. His Anglo-Canadian neighbours protested. Yellow ribbons were tied and people joined arms around the trees. The dispute became headline news in Vancouver and well beyond (for example, gaining coverage in the *South China Morning Post*, the main English-language newspaper in Hong Kong). To understand why these trees and this neighbourhood squabble generated such interest we have to reflect on the history of those sequoias and the place they played in broader cultural politics of identity.

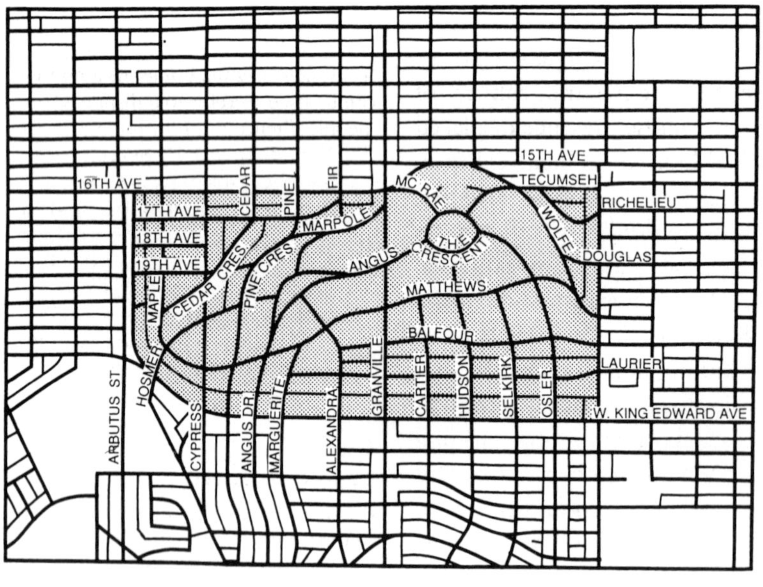

Bordering Vancouver's central business district, Shaughnessy Heights was developed as an elite neighbourhood by the Canadian Pacific Railroad from 1907 onwards. Landscaped by Frederick Todd, its layout of rolling hills, curved roads and large plots (see Fig. 12.3) materialized particular Anglophile aesthetics, reproducing eighteenth-century English elite landscape tastes for the picturesque countryside (Duncan, 1999; see also Chapter 11, on picturesque landscape aesthetics). Neo-Tudor and Victorian architecture dominated the housing stock (see Fig. 12.4). This material culture of houses, trees and streetscapes in part expressed the cultural tastes of the elite social class the development was being marketed to. But, as Jim Duncan argues, over time it also came to be implicated in the cultural reproduction of that class fraction. Residents formed the Shaughnessy Heights Property Owners Association (SHPOA) to lobby for planning regulations that would maintain the material fabric of the neighbourhood, in particular against encroachment by non-elite social groups (e.g. through property or plot sub-division). By the 1970s the SHPOA was

FIGURE 12.3
Map of Shaughnessy Heights, Vancouver (the shaded area represents Shaughnessy Heights). Source: *Cultural Geographies* (Anderson and Gale, 1999)

becoming particularly skilled at making this case in ways that did not reveal naked self-interest – for example, through appeals to **ideologies** of heritage or conservation.

More recently, the class relations implicated in this elite landscape were joined by a more explicit defence of British ethnicity. Shaughnessy Heights was constructed by and for a British **diaspora** in British Columbia. Harry Liang, by contrast, was an ethnic Chinese-Canadian, reflect-

FIGURE 12.4
A Shaughnessy mansion. Credit: Joseph Lin

ing a more recent elite migrant population into this west-coast city. Liang's newly built home was an example of what became known locally as 'monster houses', characterized by prominent symbols of wealth such as Greek columns, spiral staircases and tall cathedral entry halls, all put on public display by the clearing of vegetation from plots (hence the sequoia felling). This elite group formed a rival resident organization, the South Shaughnessy Property Owners Rights Committee (SSPORC), which as the name suggests appealed to ideologies of Canadian democracy, free markets and property rights. The competing claims on this place, and the competing landscape and housing tastes, fought it out on the letters pages of the local press and in submissions to the City Council as regards its planning policies (see box).

Paralleling Jordan and Kaups' narrative of the backwoods pioneers discussed earlier, this is once more an account of the material cultures of landscape **colonization**, first by British settlers (whose presence displaced 'first nation' peoples) and then by the so-called 'overseas' Chinese. But in the case we are discussing here, the material fabric of trees, house types, fencing, and so forth, is no longer treated as an unwitting trace of a culture and its diffusion. It is an active expression of cultural tastes (see also Duncan, 1973, and Duncan and Duncan, 2004, for a fascinating parallel study of elite cultural tastes in a town in New York state, in the eastern USA). Elements of material culture allow that expression through their meaningful nature and their implication in aesthetic judgements, and as such they need to be read not just as cultural markers but as cultural symbols and as meaningful texts. (For other excellent examples of this approach being applied to buildings see: Mona Domosh's writing on skyscrapers in New York (1994; 1999); her writing on a gendered building (1996); and Maoz Azaryahu's work on the changing place of 'water towers' in Israeli Zionist ideology and landscape (2001).)

Because of this meaningful nature, material culture is caught up in matters of cultural politics, disagreement and struggle. The same thing may not be 'read' or understood in the same way by different people. Thus Mr Liang's sequoia trees are seen as *both* a symbol of heritage and a valued urban nature, *and* as symbolic of a restriction on private freedom and a block to a clear view of and from one's new house. Furthermore, these struggles over the meanings and physical existence of things are central to

Ideology

a meaning or set of meanings that serves to create and/or maintain relationships of domination and subordination, through symbolic forms such as texts, landscapes and spaces.

Diaspora

the dispersal or scattering of people from their original home. As a noun it can be used to refer to a dispersed 'people' (hence the Jewish diaspora or the Black diaspora). However, it also refers to the actual processes of dispersal and connection that produce any scattered, but still in some way identifiable, population. In this light it also can be used as an adjective – diasporic – to refer to the senses of home, belonging and cultural identity held by a dispersed population.

Colonization

the physical settling of people from a colonial power within that power's subordinated colonies (*see* COLONIALISM). See also DECOLONIZATION.

COMPETING UNDERSTANDINGS OF THE MATERIAL LANDSCAPE OF SHAUGHNESSY HEIGHTS

" *We want the area to remain a liveable and lovely neighbourhood for the families that live here now and will live here in the future. We want to stress that this is a place to live not just a place to make money out of.* "

(Letter to City Council, 1992)

" *The face of Vancouver is changing far too quickly. We … fear the power that the Hong Kong money wields. We resent the fact that because they come here with pots of money they are able to mutilate the areas they choose to settle in. Our trees are part of our heritage.* "

(Letter to City Council, 1988)

" *I live in Shaughnessy and we built a house very much to my liking. The new zoning [planning regulations] would not allow enough space for me … I strongly oppose this new proposal. Why do I have to be inconvenienced by so many regulations? This infringes my freedom. Canada is a democratic country and democracy should be returned to the people.* "

(Translated statement at public meeting, 1988)

Source: Ley (1995)

the production and reproduction of distinctive cultural groups. Elite Anglo-Canadians use large neo-Tudor houses with tree-lined streets and lawns to materialize their cultural values and to maintain a privileged social position. Elite Chinese-Canadians need large new houses and clear plots to mark their presence in the social landscape of British Columbia. Material culture doesn't just reflect these groups; it is central to their formation.

SUMMARY

- Cultural groups do not just exist, they have to be produced and reproduced. Material culture is a means through which this (re)production can take place.
- The (re)production of cultural groups is implicated in various forms of cultural politics. Thus, so too is material culture.
- The things that make up material culture play a role in cultural (re)production in part through their meaningful and symbolic character.
- In consequence, when Cultural Geographers 'read' or interpret pieces of material culture they need to do more than culturally identify and map them – they need to tease out their multiple and contested meanings.

THE STUFF OF EVERYDAY SPACE

Did I mention that I drive a 1970s VW campervan? … Actually, I do have a good reason to talk about it again. In the preceding section, I suggested that my campervan was in part an object I relate to through its symbolic character and the meanings it can evoke for both myself and others. However, it's not only that. I do drive it. My family and I sleep in it. We go away in it. We park up and have picnics in it. The kids like playing in the pop-up top. To cut a long story short, my campervan is not just a symbolic object, it's a tool or technology put to practical use. It does things and we do things with it.

This banal observation points to a rather different approach to the geographies of material culture, one focused on practices and uses. Cultural Geographers are especially interested in how such practices and uses relate to the production and consumption of space. Let me elaborate once more through case studies of specific things. The first is the personal stereo (developed as the portable cassette player or Walkman; later becoming the Discman; and now the iPod and other MP3 players) (for a general cultural history and geography of early personal stereos see du Gay *et al.*, 1997). Why do people use personal stereos? That's the question that Michael Bull pursues in his account of what he calls 'personal stereos and the management of everyday life' (Bull, 2000). Focusing especially on urban settings, he constructs a typology that runs to at least nine common types of personal stereo use (see box). Together, these detailed observations and analyses suggest three interrelated projects in which personal stereos are used as tools: the management of interpersonal interactions with other people; the mediation of relations to the urban environment, its sights and sounds; and the activation of emotional states within the user.

All of these projects suggest the congruence of interests between work on material culture and on consumption and commodities (see Miller, 1987; 1995a; 1998b, for some of the most influential writing linking the two; see Chapters 18 and 39 for more detailed discussions on the latter themes). They suggest how the consumption of things involves far more than the economic geographies of their advertisement and purchase. Consumption is also about on-going uses. And they suggest that through these on-going uses material culture provides resources for an active inhabitation or consumption of the world and its spaces. Material culture provides tools for re-appropriating spaces and landscapes that are produced by distant bodies and forces. A range of studies has developed

FIGURE 12.5
The MP3 player is a tool used to affect everyday experiences of urban space.
Credit: Steve Connolly/Rex Features

A SUMMARY OF MICHAEL BULL'S TYPOLOGY OF COMMON USAGES OF THE PERSONAL STEREO IN URBAN SPACE

1. To block out unwelcome noises and to reimpose control over auditory environments.
2. To aid the management of interactions with strangers in the city, allowing users to signal a lack of interest in interaction and to reimpose their own senses of personal space in public.
3. To 'personalize' the user's experience of the city, replacing the city's noise with the user's own selection of music.
4. To create a pleasurable experience of the city, in particular by matching successfully music to visual scenes, creating an aesthetically convincing, cinematic experience of the city.
5. To provide some stimulation in those urban places that are dull and boring, such as crowded commuter trains, and to reclaim these repetitive, dispiriting times and spaces.
6. To avoid feeling alone in the city, by being accompanied by familiar sounds and a companionable technology.
7. To help concentration and reflection, allowing the user to organize their thoughts and adjust their moods.
8. To gain a sense of rhythm, energy and purpose from the music being listened to.
9. To listen with others via a shared player and headphone, thereby constituting an intimate and exclusive group in public space.

(see Bull, 2000; especially pages 186–90)

this idea, in particular in relation to urban space (as well as Bull on personal stereos see Borden, 2001, for a fascinating account of skateboarding in the city) and domestic space (see Blunt and Varley, 2004, for an overview of the geographies of home; Dohmen, 2004, for an account of threshold designs in southern India; Miller, 1988, for a classic account of kitchens and state housing; Miller, 2001, for a broader collection on material culture in the home; and Rose, 2003, for a brilliant study on the domestic display of family photographs). In so doing the scale of cultural geographic analysis shifts, away from just analysing landscape forms or the political arguments over them, and towards analysing how people inhabit and fashion these landscapes through particular practices and using particular 'tools'.

The other telling feature of the case of personal stereos is that it also illustrates how material cultures have technological powers to transform space and our experiences of it. Things are not just passive recipients of cultural values, meanings and projects; they have their own capacities. Thus technological changes in material culture can also involve changes in the very nature of our geographies. In attempting to trace current trends in this regard, Nigel Thrift (2003) looks to the world of toys, and in particular to the development of interactive, performative toys such as the pioneering Furby. He argues that these toys – with their abilities to sense, to communicate, to learn – presage a much wider shift in the material culture of the wealthiest societies, associated with emergent computational and artificial intelligence technologies. This shift is toward 'intelligent environments', spaces that don't just receive our projections of meaning or allow us to act on/in them but that perform and have consciousness. Thrift's prime concern is the potential for these new kinds of environments and things either to offer new possibilities for expression and empowerment to their users, or to further control them through an ever tighter designing of space and behaviour within it (see also Llewellyn, 2004). He emphasizes that the balance between these two is not determined by the technology itself, but will depend on how we develop and engage with it. In this regard, this case is illustrative of wider concerns in technology studies with both the material shaping of society and geography, and the social and geographical shaping of material forms.

SUMMARY

- We relate to the objects of material culture not only through appreciating and contesting their symbolic meanings but also through putting them to use.

- To understand the geographies of material culture we therefore need to study how objects are used, and in particular how they are used to 'inhabit' or re-fashion a range of places and spaces. Research on urban and domestic space has been pioneering in this regard.

- The stuff of material culture is diverse, and characterized by differing material and technological qualities. These qualities are important in shaping the geographical uses to which objects are put and the kinds of geographies their use produces.

THE STUFF OF CULTURAL TRAFFIC

Generally, material culture studies focus our attention on things. Rather than assuming that human geographies are only shaped and inhabited by humans, they emphasize the non-human things that are central to our worlds. A further example of this is provided by Arjun Appadurai's call to study 'the social life of things' (1986). Appadurai's particular concern is with following 'things in motion', a methodology designed to cast new light on the various social contexts through which objects move. It has been widely influential, helping to generate a range of studies that trace out the biographies and geographies of things and explore the range of places and people that these things have existed in relation to. Notable examples include: research on the production, marketing and consumption of particular products (e.g. du Gay *et al.*, 1997, on the Sony Walkman; Mansfield, 2003, on Euro-American 'imitation crab' or 'krab'); related work seeking to reconnect the producers and consumers of material commodities (Cook, 2004; Hughes and Reimer, 2004; Redclift, 2004); research on collections of objects, including in art galleries, private collections and museums (Marcus and Myers, 1995; Pearce, 1994; 1999); thinking on transnational geographies (Crang *et al.*, 2003); research on the making, selling and consuming of things marked as coming from somewhere culturally or geographically 'different' or 'foreign' (Cook and Crang, 1996; Cook and Harrison, 2003; Dwyer and Jackson, 2003; Jackson, 1999; Spooner, 1986, on 'Oriental' carpets); and accounts of the complicated lives of things that become 'second-hand' (Gregson and Crewe, 2003).

An example may help to navigate this extensive list and draw out the significance of such work for our discussions of the cultural geographies of material culture: Dick Hebdige's account of the Italian motor scooter (1988). Hebdige's interest is in the 'multiple values and meanings which accumulate around a single object over time' associated with 'different groups of users separated by geographical, temporal and cultural location' (1988: 80). His particular foci are Vespa and Lambretta motor scooters. Launched in 1946 and 1947, respectively, by the Piaggio and Innocenti engineering companies, these scooters began life intended as cheap post-war urban transport and a way of utilizing spare post-conflict production capacity, but soon became fashioned around the ideal consumer of a 'new', youthful, emancipated urban Italian woman. Both models coalesced around a design aesthetic of 'clothed' machinery (the engine and most other mechanics being hidden from view under cover panels). Motor transport was removed from the masculine realm of mechanical competence and brute force, and translated into feminine worlds of style, fashion and domestic utensils. In turn, those feminine worlds were given new geographies, the confinement of home and the passivity of being on display transformed into ideologies of active mobility and freedom. Advertising emphasized scooter-based tourism and travel, as well as the international popularity of these Italian products.

That international popularity introduced further elements to the scooter story, though. Thus, in Britain, scooters became implicated in particularly British cultural debates. At one level this was an argument

Commodity

something that can be bought and sold through the market. A commodity can be an object (a car, for example), but can also be a person (the car production worker who sells their labour for a wage) or an idea (the design or marketing concepts of the car). Those who live in capitalist societies are used to most things being commodities, though there are still taboos (the buying and selling of sexual intercourse or grandmothers, for example) (*see* CAPITALISM and COMMODIFICATION). This should not disguise the fact that the 'commodity state' is a very particular way of framing objects, people and ideas.

Transnational

an adjective used to describe Human Geographical processes that have escaped the bounded confines of the NATION-STATE. These have been identified in the realms of the economy (*see* TRANSNATIONAL CORPORATIONS), in politics (for instance, through the political agency of groups in relation to a nation-state they do not reside in; e.g. Kurdish exiles campaigning for Kurdish nationalism) and in culture (for example, through the identification of 'transnational communities' that have dispersed from an originary homeland into a number of other countries but that also have strong linkages across this DIASPORA).

between engineering and design expertise, the former (centred around the British motorcycle industry) deploring these gimmicky, unsafe and unmanly machines, the latter celebrating their aesthetics and their origins in an Italy that, for young trend-setting designers, represented 'all that was chic and modern' (Hebdige, 1988: 106). At a wider level, this polarization of reactions filtered down into the world of youth sub-cultures and wider popular tastes. On the one hand, there were the British motorbikes, American stylizations and macho masculinity of the 'Rockers', for whom scooters were nothing more than 'hair-dryers'. On the other hand, by the 1960s Italian scooters had become synonymous with the 'Mods' (short for modernist), a working-class, male-led, youth sub-culture that emerged in London in the 1950s, devoted to fashion consciousness and Continental (especially Italian) style. For the Mods, Vespas worked alongside Italian suits and coffee bars to signal an identification with foreign sophistication, discerning consumerism, youthful modernity, and a different sort of masculinity. By the 1960s this Mod(ernist) culture had mutated into the stylized scooter-boy uniform of parka anorak, jeans and Hush Puppy shoes, maybe with a beret for added continental symbolism. Scooters themselves were increasingly customized, with added chrome, mirrors, flags and even unsheathed mechanics. Fights between Mods and Rockers at British seaside resorts on bank holiday weekends became huge media stories, and have lived on through fictional renditions such as the film *Quadrophenia*.

FIGURE 12.6
The 'Italian' motor scooter was an important object to young Britons interested in design and the 'Continent' in the late 1950s and early 1960s. Credit: Popperfoto/Alamy

Thus had the scooter shifted from being cheap transport, to being an accessory of the 'new' Italian woman, to being an icon of Italian style in the UK, to being an object that was materially transformed (or customized) as part of a particularly British, working-class, male, youthful cultural opposition between Mods and Rockers.

The broader insights of this story can now be elaborated. Things move around and inhabit multiple cultural contexts during their lives. Cultural Geographers are especially interested in the changes that happen to a thing in this process: material changes; and changes or 'translations' in the thing's meanings. They are also interested in the knowledges that move with things, especially about their earlier life. How much do people encountering a thing in one context know about its life in other contexts? Who mediates this knowledge? What role do **imaginative geographies** of where a thing comes from (for example, of 'Italianicity' in the scooter's case) play in our encounters with objects, and, in reverse, what role does material culture play in wider imaginative geographies (see Chapter 10)?

Cultural Geographers are also concerned with forms of power

Imaginative geographies

representations of place, space and landscape that structure people's understandings of the world, and in turn help to shape their actions. In the work of Edward Said, the term refers to the projection of images of identity and difference on to geographical space in a way that sustains unequal relationships of power.

associated with the movement of things. Whose senses of what an object means become dominant and most powerful? What are the consequences when a thing travels cross-culturally? To what extent does one set of people end up appropriating and taking over the (material) culture of another? Thus hooks (1992) argues that 'white people' have appropriated black American culture, with a range of negative consequences for black people; and Spooner (1986) narrates the dominance of Euro-American traders and consumers in defining what counts as an authentic Oriental rug, again posing all sorts of dilemmas for those people actually making them. Or, to look at the situation rather differently, what possibilities are there for local populations to appropriate the globally distributed material culture of powerful, transnational corporations for their own ends? Thus, a range of studies has emerged that have looked at the 'indigenization' (the making local) of global products, from McDonald's (Watson, 1997) to Coca-Cola (Miller, 1996a) (more generally, see Chapter 3 and Crang, 2004).

SUMMARY

- Things travel, moving through space and time. In these travels, the meanings and material nature of things can change. Things themselves therefore have complex cultural geographies.

- Cultural Geographers have considered the understandings and knowledges that people have of where things come from as forms of 'imaginative geographies'.

- Cultural Geographers have also examined the power relations of cross-cultural movements of things. In this regard, attention has been paid to the problems of cultural 'appropriation' by dominant groups. However, on the other hand, consideration has also been given to the 'indigenization' of global things by apparently subordinate local cultures.

CONCLUSION

There is a lot of 'stuff' in cultural geography, and a lot of cultural geographies in any bit of 'stuff'. This chapter has introduced four different, but not necessarily mutually exclusive, approaches to these geographies of material culture. First, we have seen how things can be used as indicators of cultural presence, influence and distribution. Second, we have seen how material culture is implicated in processes of cultural reproduction and in their associated cultural politics. Third, we looked at how people use things as tools or technologies to re-make space in different forms. And, fourth, we thought about the cultural geographies involved in the movement of things across conventionally defined cultural–geographic borders. The general flow of argument has been away from viewing the geography of things as their distribution across the world, and towards geographical analyses that get inside things, their meanings and uses, and tease out their role in the production of the places and spaces we inhabit.

DISCUSSION POINTS

1. Construct an outline history of Cultural Geography's interest in material culture.

2. In what ways is material culture bound up with questions of cultural politics?

3. What role does the material culture of landscape play in processes of cultural reproduction?

4. Taking the example of either urban public space or domestic space, discuss the material technologies and tools we use to 'consume', 'inhabit' and 're-make' these spaces.

5. Do you think people should consume and use the material culture of other societies? Outline the potential pros and cons of such cross-cultural exchanges.

FURTHER READING

Borden, I. (2001) *Skateboarding, space and the city. Architecture and the body.* Oxford: Berg.

Written by an architectural theorist, this book is a celebration of 'street skating'. Borden argues that cities are largely produced to serve the interests of economic efficiency, but that skaters reclaim the city for their own purposes, using their boards as tools to re-make it as a stage for their own 'compositions' and 'performances'. You may find the academicism of some of this grating, but it is still a great book, offering a particularly powerful example of a performative account of material culture and space. Focusing on Chapters 1, 7 and 8 is a good start.

Duncan, J.S. and Duncan, N.G. (2004) *Landscapes of privilege: the politics of the aesthetic in an American suburb.* New York: Routledge.

A study of the town of Bedford in Westchester County, New York State, 'an archetypal upper class American suburb' according to the book's back-cover blurb. The focus is on the physical presentation of place and thus the material culture of landscape. The argument is that whilst looking natural, landscapes convey cultural codes and are implicated in the reproduction of social classes and hierarchies. A great example to use to see how the themes discussed in this chapter relate to the work on landscapes introduced in Chapter 11.

Gregson, N. and Crewe, L. (2003) *Second-hand cultures.* Oxford: Berg.

A wonderful book by two of the leading geographers in the field of consumption studies. Ranging across car-boot sales, charity shops, retro-retailers and practices of object disposal, this is a story about the changing values and meanings of things, and the places that facilitate these changes. Particularly strong in establishing what a focus on material culture and its geographies brings to consumption studies.

Hughes, A. and Reimer, S. (eds) (2004) *Geographies of commodity chains.* London: Routledge.

The title of this excellent edited collection is a little misleading. Rather than narrowly focusing on work on commodity chains (see Chapter 39 in this volume), it provides a wider discussion of the material geographies of commodities, cutting across work in both Cultural Geography and Economic Geography. The particular focus is on the relations between the producers and consumers of things.

Jackson, P. (1999) Commodity cultures: the traffic in things. *Transactions of the Institute of British Geographers*, NS24, 95–108.

A clear and thought-provoking review of what the notion of things having 'social lives' means for Cultural Geography. Sets out the key questions involved in so-called 'cross-cultural' material cultures, and summarizes some key studies in the field concisely. Invaluable.

Redclift, M. (2004) *Chewing gum. The fortunes of taste.* New York: Routledge.

A lovely little book that illustrates some of the possibilities for studies that set out to document the geographies of particular things or kinds of things. In the case of chewing gum, that involves juxtaposing the rise of chewing gum as part of American mass culture with its role in the peasant economies and revolutionary politics of southern Mexico.

Smith, J.M. and Foote, K.E. (eds) (1994) How the world looks. In Foote, K.E., Hugill, P.J., Mathewson, K. and Smith, J.M. (eds) *Re-reading Cultural Geography*. Austin: University of Texas Press, 27–163.

I have a special affection for this reader of classic papers in Cultural Geography, produced in the USA from a very American perspective. This section of the reader focuses on work that looks to 'read' material landscape forms and to understand the processes behind their production.

SECTION 2
DEVELOPMENT GEOGRAPHIES

INTRODUCTION

" *Not only is the development gap stunningly wide but also it has been getting wider. Despite considerable advances in some parts of the world, one in five people (around 1.2 billion) live on less than $1 per day. Nearly 70 per cent of these utterly impoverished people live in South Asia and Sub-Sahara Africa.* "

(Dicken, 2004b: 21)

" *At the beginning of the twenty-first century the world is more unequal than it has ever been. Three rich individuals control more wealth than the whole of Sub-Sahara Africa. In 1970, the richest 20 per cent of the world's people had 32 times the income of the poorest 20 per cent. By 1999, this group had 78 times the income of the poorest group.* "

(Christian Aid, 2004: 1)

Issues of 'development' are an inescapable part of our everyday lives. The imagined geographies of our world, as fuelled by the graphic pictures and reporting of television news and documentary, are regularly topped up with images of the latest famine, warfare, impoverishment or refugee migrations in some far off 'third world' country. Mega charity spectacles such as Children in Need and Comic Relief regularly pull at our heartstrings and purse strings in response to the victims of 'underdevelopment'. Our environmental concerns, for example, over the chopping down of rainforests or the erosion of biodiversity, bring us into direct contact with issues of how the commercial conduct of economic development (in this case of agricultural production) is often at odds with global ecological objectives. The more discerning of us may even allow the components of our everyday diet to remind us of the global geographies of food, and of the likelihood that what we are eating is directly connected with unfair trade and production conditions that benefit big international firms but impoverish those whose labour has been directly involved in food production.

Alongside opportunities for charitable giving, popular campaigns have now emerged to enable us to 'do something about' the conditions in 'third world' or 'underdeveloped countries'. For example, from small beginnings the fair trade movement has made significant strides. Since the 1970s, alternative trading organizations such as Oxfam and Traidcraft have established networks of fairly traded products, building positive trading relationships with groups of third world producers and their communities, and selling these trademarked 'fair trade' goods in countries such as the UK. Originally selling only from catalogues, charity shops, and in churches and other such organizations, the fair trade movement has now moved into the mainstream of selling in supermarkets. In 1998 the sales of Fairtrade-mark products in supermarkets and other large stores were worth £16.7 million. In 2004, sales topped £100 million. Other campaigns have also made their mark. For example, the Jubilee 2000 campaign for the cancellation of international debt mobilized millions of people worldwide to call on governments and international institutions to wipe clean the historic slate of unpayable debts owed by the poorest countries of the world. More recently, a phalanx of campaigning organizations have come together for the Trade Justice Campaign, calling for fundamental changes to the rules that govern international trade, so that they work in the interests of the world's poorest people.

Given the energy of these campaigns and the consistent media spotlight on the plight of the world's poorest and most vulnerable people, it is unsurprising that geographies of development are a vital part of bringing the global into the local – of forcing us to understand that our plenty is directly related to others' poverty. With that in mind, some of the early practice of development geography tended to be overly tied to detached indicators of the state of development in different countries. Thus, details of production, consumption, investment, demographic characteristics, health, education, income, and so on, came to dominate the agenda. However, geographers have gradually spread the news that development is diverse, complex and often contradictory, and the real-life experiences of people in the countries and regions concerned are made trivial by being reduced to a series of such indicators.

Nevertheless as Katie Willis shows us in Chapter 13, there is still more work to be done by geographers interested in development in order to unpack the in-built assumptions on which our studies are often founded. Indeed, in many ways the origins of development theory and practice – both as governmental *and academic* exercises – are inseparable from the historical process by which a *colonial* world of inter-war and post-war years has been reconfigured and transformed into a *developing* world. The unpacking of development, as the work of Arturo Escobar has demonstrated, involves both an understanding of the material realities of the development process itself, and a grasp of how development works as a social imaginary; in other words, how discourses of development are produced and circulated.

Chapter 13, then, presents a discussion of some of the most popular ideas about development, and reflects rather different understandings about the unequal nature of power relations in the world. It traces a line from development as modernization, reflecting how the 'North' has provided technical assistance to overcome the perceived obstacles to development in the 'South', to more recent neo-liberal ideas of development, with a broad reliance on market mechanisms as the most efficient ways of achieving development.

These discourses of development need to be subjected to thorough critical scrutiny, not least because they are integrally associated with the continuing disparities and uneven geographies highlighted at the start of this introduction. Sarah Radcliffe lays out some of the foundations for such a critique in Chapter 14. She demonstrates how European colonialism and neo-colonialism have shaped the experience of development, pervading contemporary development practices, and studies of those practices. Post-colonial theory, she argues, will therefore help to put nuanced geographies and histories back into essentialized binaries such as first world/third world, North/South, developed/underdeveloped and modern/traditional ways of life. Equally, feminist theory can shed new light on development practices. Although it is important to recognize multiple femininities within development, geographies of development need to address the gendered power relations that result in women working longer hours for less money and with less security than men in developing contexts. This is especially important given the increasing recognition of the role of women as active agents in development processes. Radcliffe's third strand of rethinking development recognizes that under the auspices of neo-liberalism, the role of the state in development has been reconfigured. States remain important, but NGOs and hybrid institutions are becoming more important, and so maps of development should not simply be confined to nation-states.

The unpacking of development will also need to involve listening to 'other voices' in developing countries. Paul Routledge takes us in this direction in Chapter 15. He shows how many development practices have resulted in the 'pauperization' and marginalization of indigenous people, with peasants, tribal people, women and children usually being viewed as impediments to progress and thereby being excluded from participation in the development process. It is important, therefore, to hear the voices of *these* people, who will sometimes organize themselves into place-specific social movements so as to resist threats to their economic and social survival. Routledge shows us how social movements articulate resistance within society across a range of different realms, especially the economic, political, cultural and ecological. These are not simply small localized outbursts of resistance. Many movements act across multiple scales, and are increasingly involved in globalizing networks of resistance.

Development geographies are therefore becoming more attuned to many of the wider theoretical considerations of Human Geography. Sensitivities to resistance and to gender are being allied with perspectives drawn from post-colonial and post-developmental theory. The key question is how such post-colonial and post-developmental geographies might be implemented in practice. As the socialist alternative has largely melted away, how far is it possible to engender wider access to, and participation in, capitalist development without that development merely being a vehicle for yet more pseudo-colonialism and exploitation?

Pauperization

the progressive impoverishment of people owing to the impacts of certain development programmes. For example, the displacement of peasant and tribal peoples from their sources of livelihood (e.g. land) to make way for the construction of hydro-electric dams.

FURTHER READING

Corbridge, S. (ed.) (1995) *Development studies – a reader.* **London: Arnold.**

This informative and challenging reader is an excellent 'first stop' for further reading on development geographies.

Escobar, A. (1995) *Encountering development – the making and unmaking of the Third World.* **Princeton: Princeton University Press.**

For the key contribution to post-colonial and post-developmental approaches.

Blunt, A. and McEwan, C. (eds) (2002) *Postcolonial geographies.* **London: Continuum.**

Power, M. (2003) *Rethinking development geographies.* **London: Routledge.**

For information and lively accounts of how to rethink development geographies.

Otherwise journals such as *Third World Quarterly* are worth browsing through, and regular reviews of contemporary themes in development appear in *Progress in Human Geography*.

CHAPTER 13
THEORIES OF DEVELOPMENT

Katie Willis

> " *The past 25 years have seen remarkable progress, particularly in Asia. Reforms in China have meant that over a billion people have experienced a period of unprecedented growth and poverty reduction; India has initiated far-reaching economic change. In the past 40 years, life expectancy in developing countries has increased from the mid-40s to the mid-60s … In the last quarter of a century, the number of people living on less than one dollar a day fell by 200 million at a time when the world's population grew by 1.5 billion. Yet, despite recent progress in many countries, Africa has largely been left behind, with the majority of countries experiencing little or no growth in the past 40 years, per capita income declining, and over half of the population of sub-Saharan Africa – some 315 million people – living below the $1/day poverty line.* "
>
> (British Prime Minister, Tony Blair, May 2004)

INTRODUCTION

Tony Blair's comments to the members of the Commission for Africa encapsulate many themes associated with 'development' at the start of the twenty-first century. At the heart of the concept of 'development' is the improvement of people's lives, represented in Blair's quote by reference to life expectancy and poverty reduction. However, what constitutes an 'improvement', which improvements should be addressed and how they should be achieved are highly contentious issues. In particular, it is important to consider which actors are involved in defining and achieving the 'progress' to which Blair refers. Blair also highlights how the geographies of development may differ. Within his understandings of 'progress', Asia is regarded as achieving a great deal, while millions of African people have been 'left behind'. This view of 'development' as a form of progress demonstrates the dynamism of development and how it can be understood as a process.

The World Bank divides the world's countries into three categories based on the Gross National Product per capita (GNP p.c.) of each country (see Fig. 13.1). GNP p.c. (also known as Gross National Income, GNI p.c.) is a measure of the wealth in a country divided by the population, and is often used as an indicator of development. Thus, at a global level, this measure puts western Europe, North America, Japan, Australia and New Zealand in the category of 'most developed', while most of Sub-Saharan Africa is 'least developed'. 'Development' in this case is presented as a 'goal' to be achieved. High levels of national income mean you can join the 'club' of 'developed nations'.

However, what do these national income measures tell us about the lives of individuals living within these countries? Does greater economic wealth

Development
a highly contested term that, in its most general sense, means change (usually positive change) over time. It has often been used to describe processes of becoming MODERN or ideas of progress. More specifically, development has often been defined from a particular EUROCENTRIC viewpoint, such that progress is assessed in relation to the experiences of western European societies and economies. Thus, development encompasses INDUSTRIALIZATION, urbanization and increasing standards of living in relation to health, education and housing, for example. Constructions of development are not value-free. POST-DEVELOPMENT theorists, amongst others, have highlighted the way definitions and DISCOURSES of development reflect and reinforce existing power relations.

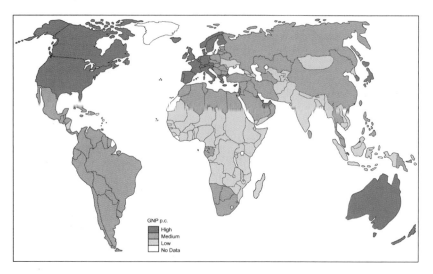

FIGURE 13.1

World Bank income classifications, 2001.
Source: Based on data from World Bank (2003)

at a national level automatically mean better standards of living for everyone? What about the 16 per cent of US citizens who did not have access to health insurance in 1998 and therefore had limited access to appropriate health treatment (PAHO, 2002: 532)? Meanwhile, in 'low income' Zambia, the richest 10 per cent of the Zambian population have access to over 40 per cent of the country's income (UNDP, 2002: 197). In addition, is greater economic wealth what everyone desires? Does 'development' have to include increased incomes, or do the environmental destruction and social upheaval that may be associated with this form of development mean that the focus on economic factors should be reconsidered? This questioning of 'development' measures can be seen in the range of indicators now adopted. These include the Human Development Index (HDI) adopted by the United Nations Development Programme (UNDP) in the early 1990s. This includes GNP p.c., but also measures of life expectancy, literacy and school enrolment.

Despite attempts to measure 'development', as exemplified by the World Bank GNP p.c. data and the HDI, 'development' is a highly complex and fluid concept. As with many concepts, we often use it without thinking how our understandings and use of the term have come about. Constructions of 'development' vary across time and space, but particular understandings become more widely used. This reflects power relations, not only at a global scale, but also within countries, communities and households.

In this chapter, I am going to discuss some of the most popular theoretical ideas about 'development' in the post-Second World War period. This temporal focus does not mean that 'development' was not theorized before the Second World War, but reflects the fact that from the mid-1940s onwards there was an explicit attempt by 'western countries' to promote 'development' in Africa, Asia, Latin America and the Caribbean. In addition, concentrating on academic theories, as well as policies implemented by governments, multilateral organizations and development agencies, does not mean that other groups of people did not have different ideas about 'development'. 'Alternative' constructions of 'development' and forms of resistance are covered in later chapters.

SUMMARY

- Definitions of 'development' vary greatly and reflect differential understandings of the world and unequal power relations.

- It is important to consider scale in any examination of 'development'.

- Development can be considered both a 'goal' and a 'process'.

MODERNIZATION

'Development' is often understood as a process of becoming 'modern'. As is discussed elsewhere in the book (Chapter 24), 'modern' can just mean 'of the moment', but in most cases there are particular understandings of what 'modern' is and should be. In 'development' terms, 'modern' has usually applied to being like 'the West'. This might be in economic terms (for example, commercial rather than subsistence agriculture), social terms (for example, the importance of class groups rather than family or tribal affiliations), or political terms (for example, democratically elected governments rather than tribal or religious forms of organization). Ideas of development as modernization can, therefore, often be viewed as Eurocentric. The idea of 'modern' being presented as desirable is based purely on the experiences and values of countries and societies in the Global North.

A number of theorists, often termed 'modernization theorists', have attempted to describe and model this form of development. The best known of these is Walt Rostow who, in 1960, published his book *The Stages of Economic Growth: A Non-Communist Manifesto*. From examining the history of a number of countries, most notably the United States of America and some European countries, he argued that there were five stages of economic growth that could be identified, ranging from 'traditional' societies to what Rostow termed 'The Age of High Mass Consumption' (see Table 13.1). While Rostow's focus was on 'economic growth' rather than 'development' per se, it is clear that the shifts in economic, social and political organization could all be encompassed within post-Second World War ideas about 'development'.

In Harry S. Truman's US presidential inauguration speech in 1949, he referred specifically to the need for assistance to be provided to the poorer countries of the world:

> For the first time in history humanity possesses the knowledge and the skill to relieve the suffering of these people [the world's poor] … I believe that we should make available to peace-loving peoples the benefits of our store of technical knowledge in order to help them realize their aspirations for a better life … What we envisage is a program of development based on the concepts of democratic fair dealing … Greater production is the key to prosperity and peace. And the key to greater production is a wider and more vigorous application of modern scientific and technical knowledge.

(Truman, 1949, in Escobar, 1995: 3)

Truman's sentiment fits into the understanding of development as modernization. Truman argued that the poverty and poor living conditions in many parts of the world were an indication of a lack of development. As the United States had the technical knowledge to promote development it should help other parts of the world. This idea of sharing knowledge to achieve development became the key to aid policies for many northern countries in the 1950s onwards. Without external aid, it was argued, the poorer countries of the world would never develop. These projects met with different degrees of success (see box).

Modern, modernity, modernism

ideas of the modern are most commonly defined through their opposition to the old and the traditional. In this light, the adjective 'modern' is synonymous with 'newness'; 'modernity' refers both to the 'post-traditional' historical epoch within which 'newness' is produced and valued, as well as to the economic, social, political and cultural formations characteristic of that period; and 'modernism' applies more narrowly to artistic, architectural and intellectual movements that centrally explore ideas of 'newness' and develop 'new' aesthetics and ways of thinking to express these. Modernity has been most commonly located in Euro-American societies from the eighteenth century onwards, and thereby associated with their characteristic combination of capitalist economies (*see* CAPITALISM), political organization through NATION-STATES, and cultural values of secularity, rationality and progress (*see* ENLIGHTENMENT). However, increasingly, Human Geographers are recognizing that modernity is a global phenomenon that has taken many different forms in different times and places. See also MODERNIZATION.

Eurocentric

adjective that describes the characteristic of believing that the western European experience is the only correct way to progress. This may be because there is no awareness of alternatives, or it may reflect a belief in European superiority. Is often used now to refer to theories and perspectives coming more generally from the Global North.

Table 13.1 Rostow's stages of economic growth

Stage	Characteristics
Traditional	Agriculture and hunter-gatherer societies; pre-Newtonian science and technology; social structures dominated by family, clan or tribal groupings; pre-nation-state.
Preconditions for Take-Off	Savings and investment rates above population growth rates; increased importance of nation-state and national institutions; elite status not based on family or clan allegiance; changes often triggered by external intrusion.
Take-Off	Triggered by internal or external stimulus, e.g. political revolution, colonialism, technical innovation; higher rates of investment and saving; substantial manufacturing sector; banks and other institutions in place.
Drive to Maturity	Expansion of use and range of technology; growth of new economic sectors; investment and savings 10–20 per cent of national income.
Age of High Mass Consumption	Widespread consumption of durable consumer goods and services; increased spending on welfare services.

Source: adapted from Rostow (1960)

THE EAST AFRICAN GROUNDNUT SCHEME

In the post-Second World War period, the British government became concerned about the reduced availability of food oils on the world market because of the potential impact on Britain's import bill. The East African Groundnut Scheme was an attempt to increase the world supply of groundnuts and oil, as well as providing opportunities for social welfare improvements and economic development in Tanganyika (now part of Tanzania) which was then part of the British Empire.

The scheme aimed to clear and cultivate approximately 1.3 million hectares, providing jobs directly and also through local multiplier effects. In addition, the project aimed to provide a demonstration effect to local people so they could see the benefits of technology and mechanization.

The UK government spent millions of pounds on equipment and seeds, but the project proved to be a disaster. By the time it was ended in 1955, only about 9000 hectares had been cleared and yields were poor. The reasons for failure were multiple. Soil, vegetation and climatic conditions in Tanganyika were unsuitable for the use of heavy machinery such as tractors. In turn, when the machinery broke down, there were insufficient spare parts or trained mechanics to mend it. There was a lack of appropriate housing and service provision for workers, and attempts to export groundnuts were hampered by problems with the railways and port facilities.

In this case, and many others, attempts to modernize agriculture in this part of East Africa using northern ideas and equipment proved to be highly inappropriate.

Source: adapted from Hogendorn and Scott (1981)

Despite external assistance, the development 'problem' was presented very much in terms of factors that were internal to the countries involved. These poorer countries did not have the skills, knowledge and capital to develop. Once they were assisted and shown how to develop, it was argued that success would follow. Rostow, for example, argued that colonialism had been crucial for the economic growth trajectory of many countries. Development obstacles were, therefore, seen as endogenous (i.e. relating to factors within countries). As I will argue in the next section, and as **post-colonial** and **post-development** theorists have argued (see later chapters), this focus on particular internal factors as explaining a lack of development has been greatly criticized.

SUMMARY

- The post-war period saw the start of large-scale 'development planning' aimed at the Global South.
- Development was understood as 'modernization' along the lines followed by the USA and western Europe.
- Northern countries were key in providing technical assistance to overcome perceived development 'obstacles' within southern countries.

STRUCTURALISM AND DEPENDENCY

While modernization theorists and northern policy-makers tended to focus on endogenous factors, other theorists and activists argued that factors external to the poorer countries (i.e. exogenous factors) were of much greater importance. Many of these ideas and theories developed in parts of the Global South, reflecting the importance of considering how understandings of and approaches to development are a product of particular temporally and spatially specific contexts.

Structuralism, most associated with Raul Prebisch and the UN Economic Commission for Latin America (ECLA), was one of the earliest theoretical approaches of this type. ECLA (known as CEPAL in Spanish) was set up in the 1940s and its aim was to promote development in Latin America. Prebisch, its first president, argued that it was important to consider the current reality of Latin America when choosing development policies, rather than following northern-based models. While free trade policies had been important in the growth of northern economies, ECLA argued that Latin American economies in the post-Second World War world needed protection from northern competition. The world economy was very different in the 1940s and 1950s than in the nineteenth century when western Europe industrialized. This approach was termed 'structuralism' because it focused on the structures of the global economy and how these might help or hinder development attempts (Clarke, 2002; Preston, 1996: 181–9).

The policy implications of this were to promote state intervention and protectionist policies in Latin America. By doing this, Latin America would be able to develop (i.e. industrialize, urbanize and increase standards of living) as western Europe had done. Thus, development as a goal was the same as described by the modernization theorists, but the process was to be slightly different.

Import-substitution industrialization (ISI) was a key element of ECLA policy recommendations. ISI policies focused on building up domestic manufacturing, rather than relying on imports from elsewhere. Because of the greater experience of European and American companies, it was important to protect Latin America's infant industries from competition. This was done through imposing import tariffs. In addition, government finance and technical support were targeted at manufacturing concerns. In many cases, these policies were successful and allowed the growth of manufacturing

Post-colonial, post-colonialism

sometimes hyphenated, sometimes not, this term has two distinct meanings: (a) the post-colonial era, i.e. the historical period following a period of COLONIALISM (see also DECOLONIZATION); (b) post-colonial political, cultural and intellectual movements, and their perspectives, which are critical of the past and ongoing effects of European and other colonialisms.

Post-developmentalism

a radical critique of DEVELOPMENTALISM, which demands the self-empowerment of poor or marginalized people in opposition to the powers of the state or capital.

Dependency theories

theories that explain levels of economic and social DEVELOPMENT with reference to global economic structures. In particular, the idea that southern countries are exploited by those of the North and will remain in subservient or dependent positions until the global economic system is changed.

industries in Latin America. For example, manufacturing production increased annually by 4.0 per cent on average in Latin America in the 1950s and 6.3 per cent per annum on average in the 1960s (World Bank, 1983, in Sheahan, 1987: 85). However, success was not always achieved. Small domestic markets and the need to import technically advanced equipment often created obstacles to self-sufficiency (Sheahan, 1987).

A similar set of theories focusing on development in the context of the global economy and exogenous limits, emerged in the 1960s and 1970s. These were termed dependency theories and were again focused on the Latin American experience. As with structuralism, dependency theorists argued that Latin America could not follow a European development path, because the global context was very different. For most dependency theorists, however, the solution was not to adopt protectionist measures as outlined by the structuralists, rather the solution was a more dramatic withdrawal from the global economic system.

The best known dependency theorist is André Gunder Frank (1967). He used the examples of Chile and Brazil to demonstrate his arguments. Since the arrival of the Europeans in Latin America, Frank argued, Latin America's peoples and resources had been exploited. Rather than being used to help the development of Latin America, profits had been taken out of the region. This had created what Frank termed 'the development of underdevelopment' – that is, Latin America's 'underdevelopment' was a direct consequence of the relationships of exploitation.

There is a strong spatial dimension to Frank's work. He highlighted how the chains of exploitation and dependency run not just from the periphery of Latin America to the core of Europe, but that within Latin America there are unequal relationships between urban and rural groups and between landowners and labourers, such that local-level exploitation and inequality reflects the inequalities on a global scale (see Fig. 13.2). Walter Rodney in his work on African 'underdevelopment' also follows a dependency argument:

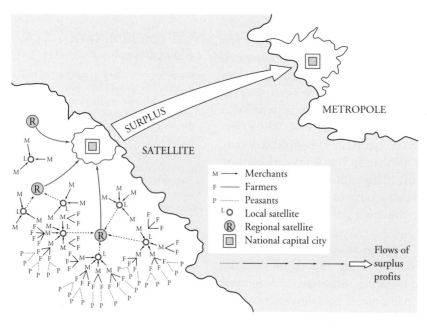

FIGURE 13.2
A graphical representation of dependency theory. Source: Potter *et al.* (2004: 111)

> " *Colonialism was not merely a system of exploitation, but one whose essential purpose was to repatriate the profits to the so-called 'mother country.' From an African view-point, that amounted to consistent expatriation of surplus produced by African labour out of African resources. It meant the development of Europe as a part of the same dialectical process in which Africa was underdeveloped.* "

(Rodney, 1974: 162)

For dependency theorists, it is the global capitalist system dominated by the northern countries that is an obstacle to autonomous development in the South. Thus, the solution and route to development is through withdrawing from the global economic system and setting up alternative forms of society and economy. Without this, southern countries are destined to remain poor and exploited, and development will not take place.

Dependency approaches attracted a great deal of criticism, not least because of their static construction of global relationships. Even as Frank and others were writing, some parts of the Global South, most notably the 'newly industrializing countries' (NICs) of East Asia (see below) were experiencing rapid economic growth and improvements in standards of living without withdrawing from global capitalism.

SUMMARY

- Structuralism and dependency approaches blamed the structure of the global political economy for low levels of economic development.
- Protectionism or withdrawal from the global capitalist system were advocated as development solutions.
- Policies based on structuralist and dependency theories experienced some success, but there were problems with their long-term viability.

NEO-LIBERALISM

As the ISI experiments based on structuralist theories began to experience severe problems, and dependency theories were increasingly unable to present realistic routes to development in the Global South, new ideas began to emerge in the late 1970s regarding new ways in which development (in a western form) could be achieved. Despite millions of dollars of aid being transferred from North to South since the late 1940s, northern governments and multilateral organizations such as the International Monetary Fund (IMF) and the World Bank were concerned that development had not reached the vast majority of peoples of the South. For these southern peoples, increasingly aware of alternative ways of life elsewhere in the world, the goal of 'development' in a western style became increasingly desirable, if unattainable.

The late 1970s and early 1980s saw the increasing prominence of **neo-liberal** ideas in government policy-making in western Europe and North America, as well as in development policies directed towards the South. At the heart of neo-liberal ideas is the belief that government intervention in the economy always leads to inefficiencies and that it is far better to let market forces determine wages, prices and what should be produced and where. The market, it is argued, is neutral and does not try to benefit one group over another (Toye, 1993).

The election of Margaret Thatcher as UK Prime Minister in 1979 and the inauguration of Ronald Reagan as US President in 1981 reflects this move to reduced state intervention in northern countries. Both leaders felt that government inefficiencies had led to poor economic performance in

Neo-liberalism, neo-liberal

pertaining to an economic doctrine that favours free markets, the deregulation of national economies, decentralization and the privatization of previously state-owned enterprises (e.g. education, health). A doctrine that, in practice, favours the interests of the powerful (e.g. TRANSNATIONAL CORPORATIONS) against the less powerful (e.g. peasants) within societies.

the 1970s, and reduced choice for individuals, families and communities. They both advocated market-led reforms such as privatization and reduced state expenditure.

These neo-liberal policies were also introduced into development policies towards the Global South, most notably through structural adjustment policies (SAPs). Just as with the modernization ideas outlined earlier, SAPs reflect the imposition of ideas and understandings of development on southern countries from those of the Global North. In the late 1970s/early 1980s most southern countries found themselves increasingly unable to meet the payments on their national debt because of rising oil prices, increasing interest rates and global recession. The debt crisis that resulted triggered the widespread implementation and adoption of SAPs. Unable to borrow money from private banks, southern governments were forced to agree to SAPs in order to gain further funding from the IMF and the World Bank.

SAPs aimed to stabilize a country's economy and then to restructure it in order to promote development in the future. Policies were aimed at reducing the role of the state and opening up national economies to foreign investment and competition, so ending ISI protectionist policies. Whilst SAPs achieved their aims of stabilization, in many cases the restructuring was associated with increasing levels of social inequality as unemployment increased and welfare provision was slashed (Mohan *et al.*, 2000). Despite these problems, SAPs continued to be promoted throughout the 1980s and early 1990s, and were also implemented in the transition economies of eastern Europe and the former Soviet Union after the collapse of the communist bloc (Bradshaw and Stenning, 2004).

The East Asian countries were often highlighted as examples of the successes of neo-liberal development policies. The NICs of Hong Kong, Taiwan, Singapore (see Fig. 13.3) and South Korea, along with other regional nations such as Thailand, the Philippines, Indonesia and Malaysia, were regarded as what the World Bank (1993) termed the 'Asian Miracle'. The World Bank argued that these nations had successfully achieved economic growth without increasing levels of inequality, by following neo-liberal market-led policies (see Fig. 13.4). These cases were used as examples for other parts of the Global South, most particularly Latin America and Sub-Saharan Africa.

Despite World Bank rhetoric, the development policies adopted by the East Asian 'miracle' countries were not as 'free market' as they were often presented. Important government subsidies and protectionist tariffs had been key in some countries. The 1997 economic crisis in the region also

FIGURE 13.3
Downtown Singapore. Source: Urban Redevelopment Authority, Singapore

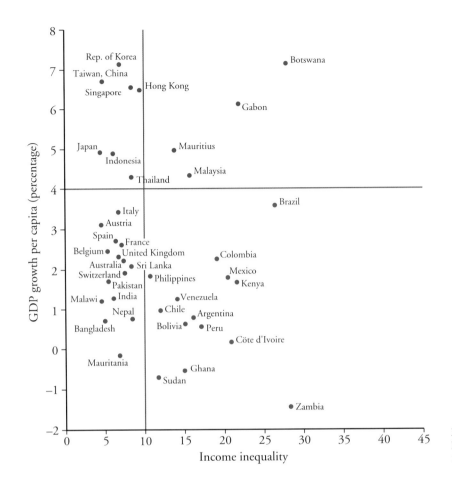

FIGURE 13.4
Income inequality and growth of GDP, 1965–1989. Source: Page (1994: 616)

led the World Bank and other multilateral organizations and northern governments to reappraise their interpretation of East Asian development in the 1970s and 1980s in order to play down the free market role. The continued intervention of an inefficient and ineffective state, it was argued, explained a great deal of the 1997 crisis. Blaming the crisis on inappropriate government activity meant that the free market model remained largely blameless (Rigg, 2003). As a result, the neo-liberal model of development continues to dominate the policies of the World Bank, IMF, European Union and key bilateral donors.

SUMMARY

- Neo-liberal theories focus on the role of the market as the most efficient route for achieving development.

- Government intervention in production and service provision is reduced, and private and voluntary organizations are supposed to replace government activities.

- The success of East Asian development has been used as an example of successful neo-liberal policies.

- Neo-liberalism remains the key theoretical grounding for government and multilateral development assistance.

GRASSROOTS DEVELOPMENT

While all the theories outlined above aimed to improve the lives of individuals, the focus of policies has been at the level of the nation-state. The argument has been that if appropriate policies are adopted nationally, then the benefits will 'trickle down' to those at grassroots level. However, in far too many cases this has not happened. Instead, national-level policies have exacerbated inequalities or have left the majority of the population without a say in what changes (if any) they would like to their lives.

The national-level focus of modernization theories, structuralism and dependency approaches and neo-liberal policies hides, however, some attempts at engaging with development at the 'grassroots'. For example, in the late 1960s and early 1970s, many multilateral organizations and northern governments began to advocate a 'basic needs approach' in their work. This was a response to the realization that many of the aid policies that had been implemented had failed to reach the very poorest. A basic needs approach identified key 'needs' that had to be met, including shelter, food, health, education and employment. Rather than focusing on the large-scale projects of earlier periods, it was argued that smaller-scale activities, such as concentrating on the work of informal-sector traders and producers in urban areas, would be much more effective in helping the economically poor (Hunt, 1989). Unfortunately, this approach was not widely adopted due to shortages of funding and fears by many southern governments that focusing on small-scale projects would hinder economic growth. For these governments, 'development' was largely economic.

Non-governmental organization (NGO)
an organization that belongs neither to the private for-profit sector, or the public or government sector.

'Helping people to help themselves' is a common slogan used by **non-governmental organizations (NGOs)** working in the development field, particularly in southern countries (see Fig. 13.5). This focus on individuals, families and communities represents a grassroots or bottom-up approach to development and has become increasingly common since the early 1980s. Development NGOs vary greatly in size, scope and membership, and can be found in both the Global North and South (Vakil, 1997). For example, Oxfam is northern-based, but it works with partner organizations in the South.

How the cow loan scheme can change lives

A family in need

Family is given cow from loan scheme

Cow produces milk and manure which is good for the crops and soil fertility

Improved diet for family from crops and milk

Milk sold at the market

A steady income from the milk

Enough money to buy food if crops fail

Money to clothe the family

Can now afford pens, paper and school uniforms so children can go to school

Female calves are returned to the scheme so another family can benefit. Male calves are kept and fed to sell

FIGURE 13.5
Oxfam cow loan scheme.

The growth of NGOs reflects the supposed benefits such organizations provide to local communities. Because they work with people at a local level, NGOs are meant to provide more efficient and appropriate services, such as healthcare, infrastructure or agricultural assistance. In comparison with the large-scale projects described earlier, NGO projects are viewed as more appropriate and therefore more likely to succeed (Edwards and Hulme, 1995). In addition, NGOs are regarded as promoting participation and empowerment amongst marginal communities and groups. It is argued that government activities often exclude the voices of the marginal, whilst NGOs are ideally positioned to engage with the needs and opinions of the poor. This may particularly be the case when they work in partnership with community-based organizations (CBOs).

Whilst many NGOs have achieved a great deal in terms of providing the services local people want in an appropriate and affordable manner, there are many cases of NGOs being unable to live up to the 'development panacea' label. Whilst the number of NGOs has increased massively in the past 25 years (Van Rooy, 1998), there are still insufficient numbers to meet the massive demand for their services. In addition, they are often spatially and socially concentrated in particular sectors. Despite supposedly meeting the needs of the most vulnerable, NGOs often work in more physically accessible communities, so contributing to spatial inequalities. In addition, because most NGOs rely on donations from individuals or governments, their work is often directed by the issues that donors regard as important, rather than those identified by local people (Hulme and Edwards, 1997).

Finally, as highlighted earlier, development policy has been dominated by neo-liberal ideologies since the early 1980s. The rise of NGOs during this period is no coincidence. As governments have reduced state expenditure and privatized many services, such as healthcare, education and infrastructure provision, poor communities have been left unable to afford these services. NGOs have, therefore, been crucial in attempts to fill the gaps left as the state has withdrawn. In addition, NGO activities often fit within neo-liberal understandings of decentralization, greater local democracy and choice. They have, therefore, been encouraged. Whilst the majority of people would regard choice and democracy as desirable, in reality, neo-liberal policies have left large numbers of marginal people even less able to access the services required to improve their lives.

SUMMARY

- Since the 1980s there has been an increasing focus on the sub-national level of development.
- NGOs have become key agents in development practice because they are regarded as providing effective, efficient and appropriate services.
- Whilst NGOs can be very important service providers and channels for consciousness-raising, there are limits to what they can do.

CONCLUSIONS

Despite its widespread use, the concept of 'development' is highly contested. Within a general understanding of improvements in individuals' lives, lies a wide variety of definitions and policies. The post-war period heralded an era of development planning, where the economically richer countries of the West tried to help the poorer countries of Africa, Asia, Latin America and the Caribbean. This help took the form of technology, education and support which mirrored that used in the 'development' of the West. Such Eurocentric theories and approaches did not remain unchallenged. Rather than seeing a 'lack of development' as a reflection of internal deficiencies, structuralist and dependency approaches argued that global structures of inequality created and exacerbated situations of poverty and marginalization. Without addressing these inequalities, development would remain a distant dream. Despite these challenges, the 1980s saw a reassertion of development theories and practices based on northern definitions and priorities with neo-liberalism. Whilst the details of these policies have been adapted since that period, neo-liberalism remains at the forefront of international development policy-making.

These major themes in development theorizing since the 1940s demonstrate the importance of considering not only how levels of development vary spatially, as demonstrated by the World Bank data in Figure 13.1, but also how understandings of 'development' are a product of particular geographies. Latin America, for example, proved a particular environment for the elaboration of structuralist and dependency ideas challenging Eurocentric theories. The politics of development policies and theories are highlighted in the following chapters.

DISCUSSION POINTS

1. What are the advantages and disadvantages of using GNP per capita as a measure of development?

2. How can external factors affect the economic development of a country?

3. Why have NGOs been regarded as appropriate agents for development and what limitations may there be to their effectiveness?

FURTHER READING

Brohman, J. (1996) *Popular development: rethinking the theory and practice of development.* **Oxford: Blackwell.**

An excellent book, which outlines the ways in which top-down development has increasingly been challenged by a range of so-called 'alternative' approaches.

Edwards, M. and Hulme, D. (eds) (1995) *Non-governmental organisations performance and accountability. Beyond the magic bullet.* **London: Earthscan.**

Useful collection of chapters on different elements of NGO activity. Provides a range of examples and highlights the ways in which NGO successes are shaped and limited.

Peet, R. with Hartwick, E. (1999) *Theories of development.* **London: The Guilford Press.**

A detailed consideration of different approaches to development in its broadest sense. Whilst a range of theories are covered, the authors make a strong case for considering radical alternatives to neo-liberal orthodoxy.

Willis, K. (2005) *Theories and practices of development.* **London: Routledge.**

Useful introductory textbook covering a range of development theories and associated policies.

WEBSITES

www.developmentgateway.org

Development Gateway: links to a range of development information, including latest news and discussion groups.

www.eldis.org

Portal for development-related information run by the Institute of Development Studies, University of Sussex.

www.imf.org

International Monetary Fund: provides information on the approaches and activities of the IMF. Useful material on structural adjustment programmes.

www.oneworld.net

One World: an excellent site for up-to-date development information. Following the 'Partners' link will provide access to information about over 1500 partner organizations.

www.worldbank.org

World Bank: details the activities of all members of the World Bank Group.

CHAPTER 14
RETHINKING DEVELOPMENT

Sarah A. Radcliffe

INTRODUCTION

At the start of the twenty-first century in what appears to be an integrated world, or a 'global village', people are living with highly differentiated experiences of, and stakes in, development. Cosmopolitan jet-setters in São Paulo live one kind of development while women in sub-Saharan Africa walking for hours to collect water experience a completely different kind of development. How do we listen to this difference? What analysis best suits this geographical diversity, whilst also linking our concerns to the obvious class, ethnic and race-based inequalities we see? Rethinking development means reconsidering the categories we use in development geography, and unpacking the power relations that shape them.

Since the explosion of post-development thinking into development studies in the mid-1990s, there has been a lot of rethinking of development going on. As noted in the other chapters in this section, development has been analysed in terms of the differentiated and highly uneven impacts of capitalist relations on countries' income and life quality levels (Chapter 13); and the past ten years have been characterized by a variety of protest movements and campaigns to provide alternatives to development (Chapter 15). Although at one time overwhelmingly economic, development studies today specifies and interrogates the interrelationship of development's political, cultural and institutional facets, which are examined in this chapter. Rethinking development is primarily concerned with thinking about the power relations bound up in development (as a process and as intervention) – its operations, its geographies, its highly uneven distribution, contradictions, and strategies for getting it, so the analysis of power is central. In the remainder of the chapter, three windows on to development's power will be examined, namely the power of writing, the power of gender and the powers of the state.

GEOGRAPHY AND POSTCOLONIALISM

Post-colonial, post-colonialism

sometimes hyphenated, sometimes not, this term has two distinct meanings: (a) the post-colonial era, i.e. the historical period following a period of COLONIALISM (see also DECOLONIZATION); (b) post-colonial political, cultural and intellectual movements, and their perspectives, which are critical of past colonialism and the ongoing effects of European and other colonialisms.

Postcolonialism has become an important framework in recent years for geographers trying to understand development, as it challenges us to write about 'developing countries' in ways that recognize the social, economic and political impacts of colonialism, whilst also drawing out the inter-connections between 'North' and 'South' (see also Chapter 23; Johnston et al., 2000). As a critique of legacies of colonialism and its rigid thinking, postcolonialism covers a broad terrain of analysis, which has been selectively used by Human Geographers in their understanding of development. Postcolonialism is thus not simply a question of independence that was gained unevenly (for example, the Spanish American colonies gained independence between the 1820s and 1898, whilst British and French colonies in Africa and Asia became independent during the middle years of the twentieth century) (McClintock, 1995) (see Fig. 14.1). A post-colonial country is one whose struggle for independence subsequently turned into the search for development, epitomized by a western-style modernization process (Schech and Haggis, 2000). Southern post-colonial countries often took development as *the* framework for national action and identity (Power, 2003), defining their identities and devising policies to reach a western-defined standard which,

inevitably, they could not replicate (Gupta, 1998). Post-colonial frameworks critique too neo-colonialism's uneven impact on the materialities of people's lives, livelihoods affected by nation-states' failure to provide services to their entire populations, income inequalities, hierarchical social relations and diverse urban structures (Power, 2003). Postcolonialism also criticizes the ways in which the West has constructed its knowledge about the South, in order to 'decolonize the mind' in Ngugi wa Thiong'o's words. By changing our 'mental maps', decolonization of

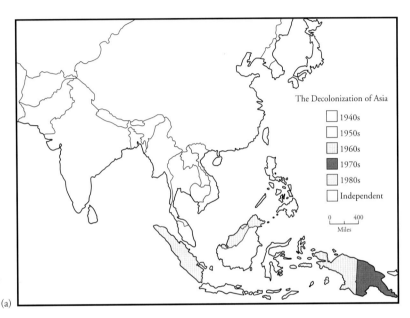

(a)

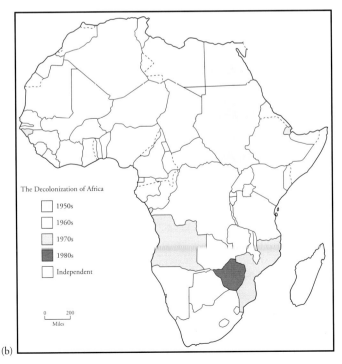

(b)

FIGURE 14.1
Decades of independence for former colonies in the South, by decade. (a) Asia, (b) Africa

the mind departs from a grounded, geographically informed understanding of the ways in which global processes of capitalism, and development interventions, intersect with local and national processes of giving meaning and living everyday lives. Moreover, postcolonialism challenges notions of a single 'path' to development. Human geographers are in a good position to provide just such a detailed, empirically rich discussion of highly differentiated post-colonial situations. By deconstructing the categories of 'poor countries' and 'third world women', the power of these categories to shape development interventions in inappropriate ways can be replaced by contextualized and empirically based knowledge, often generated by development's beneficiaries.

Postcolonialism also challenges our expectations about individuals and societies in Africa, Latin America and Asia. It throws out negative stereotypes about 'basket-case African countries' or tin-pot dictators in South America (Simon, 1997; Power, 2003), whilst forcing us to question 'our' (you as a reader might have a different stance) static view of 'tradition', seeing the third world as unchanging. Whilst post-colonial perspectives have been criticized for their over-romanticization of 'hybrid cultures' that blend local and global elements (see Chapter 3), they usefully suggest that everyday lives in the South combine a mosaic of reference points, points that link them to disparate, and often distant, places and people. For example, urban cultures in Andean countries refer – within one moment, in one place – to Brazilian soap operas, local forms of survival in the informal sector, world football teams, nationalist histories, pre-Conquest musical instruments and global youth culture. Postcolonialism throws down the challenge of documenting such grounded mosaics whilst analysing the global political economies and power structures that combine to create locally meaningful forms of poverty and inequality.

Whilst addressing the gulfs in income and well-being that characterize North–South relations (see Fig. 13.5), post-colonial approaches acknowledge the diversity of priorities in development. Needs – for clean water, adequate food, education – are not pre-given but are determined by social identities and local–regional cultures within politicized and culturally specific contexts, however self-evidently beneficial they appear at first sight. The 1980s Basic Needs Approach (BNA) to development tried to face up to the needs of 1.2 billion people in absolute poverty, yet inevitably intersected with wider political and social changes occurring in the diverse countries of Africa, Asia and Latin America. Many groups and individuals in these countries demanded clean water and electricity for their neighbourhoods (i.e. basic needs), while also pursuing demands for wider 'strategic' needs, such as political rights as citizens and participants in the development process. Whilst great strides have been made in pursuing basic goods, the politics and economics of neo-liberal development mean that these wider strategic needs often remain at the forefront of development debates in the South. Postcolonialism questions our ability as 'outsiders' to identify groups' needs, whilst reminding us that whoever claims to speak on behalf of the world's poor is already positioned vis-à-vis the very structures of political economy that produce global inequality.

Postcolonialism also encourages us to consider that we – sitting in our libraries, far from women collecting water in Nigeria – have a role to play in all of this. 'Our' identities and our worlds are made in that same global economy, as it works its uneven way around the world in ever faster circles. Development is thus not only about economic relations and income differentials, but also about the politics of needs, about a political economy of racism (how colonialism and its relations underpin our attitudes to issues as varied as AIDS, famine relief and population growth), and about how tradition can be re-invented.

SUMMARY

- Postcolonialism is a critique of the ways in which European colonialism and neo-colonialism shape the experiences of, and the writing about, development. It also hopes to contribute to new ways of 'knowing' about development.

- Post-colonial perspectives encourage us to map out a more complex geography than a world divided into first and third world, North and South, and to rethink what is meant by traditional vs modern.

CONTEXTUALIZING DEVELOPMENT: FEMINISM AND GENDER

" *In a world where women do two-thirds of the world's work, earn 10 per cent of the world's income and own less than 1 per cent of the world's property, the promise of 'postcolonialism' has been a history of hopes postponed.* "

(McClintock, 1995: 19)

In her critique of development, Anne McClintock highlights the ways in which postcolonialism celebrates too much, too soon when it comes to the position of women. National independence and the new international division of labour result in a world where women and men often experience widely differing lives, whether in terms of citizenship rights, work or kin and family relationships. To take a global view, these differences reduce women's power, visibility and access to resources.

Yet whilst McClintock points to women's continued marginalization, she represents women as a homogeneous group, which is defined more by its internal sameness than by difference. This quote from McClintock galvanizes our political solidarity with women and human rights, yet it also reiterates what the feminist film-maker Trinh Minh-ha calls the 'third world difference' – that is, a way of identifying all women in the South in a distinct category to western women. As Chandra Mohanty has argued, the third world difference portrays third world women as powerless, burdened, cloistered and oppressed by their (male) kin (Mohanty, 1991). Found in writings by colonial officials, development experts and some early geographers, this 'third world difference' is an example of a colonial legacy. A post-colonial perspective therefore attempts to examine Third World women as agents of change and as highly differentiated. **Gender** divisions of labour and a gendered distribution of resources and income

Gender

a criterion of social organization that distinguishes different groups of people on the basis of femininity or masculinity. In any one location, many masculinities and femininities interact. As a concept, gender is usually used in Human Geography in distinction to that of sex (i.e. femaleness and maleness) in order to emphasize the SOCIAL CONSTRUCTION of women's and men's roles, relations and identities. Human Geographers' accounts of the world have always been shaped through understandings of gender (*see* MASCULINISM) but explicit analyses of the geographies of gender and the gendering of geographies are comparatively recent, and associated with the growth of Feminist Geography (*see* FEMINISM).

differentiate women along lines of class, location, religion, age/generation, race/ethnicity and sexuality (Visvanathan, 1997). The gulf in living standards between women of different classes often translates into highly diverse strategies. Depending on their country, urban or rural location, family forms and sources of income, poor women face difficulties in securing income, health and a voice for themselves and their communities, whereas many high-income women enjoy careers and living standards comparable with (or better than) those of their western counterparts. Such differences are graphically illustrated by a middle-class, urban woman with a university degree and career next to her live-in maid, who is most likely from the countryside with limited formal education and few career opportunities (see Fig. 14.2; also Radcliffe, 1990).

Political coalitions across these gulfs are fraught with difficulties, especially for poor women who already face a 'triple burden' of production, reproduction and community management work (Moser, 1993). In contrast to their passive stereotype, women in the South have diverse strategies for dealing with a combination of forces, including capitalist economies that see them as the cheapest labour; racism; colonialism, and male power in families and states. As Mohanty points out, women's 'agency is ... figured in the minute, day-to-day practices and struggles' (Mohanty, 1991: 38; Radcliffe and Westwood, 1993).

FIGURE 14.2
Credit: © Angela Martin

Women who particularly face an uphill struggle in guaranteeing security for themselves under conditions of growing global inequalities and political instability are female heads of households, and refugee women. Female heads of households account for an estimated one in three of domestic units in the third world (Chant, 1997; Varley, 1996). Of the approximately 17 million refugees around the world in 1992, around 80 per cent were women and their dependants. Gender-sensitive approaches to refugee flows recognize that women must be able to gain income, become empowered, be free of sexual harassment and claim refugee status as persecuted women.

Ways of 'being female' are intimately bound up with livelihood and production relations, the form and discourse of the nation-state, cultural ideologies and political culture as well as kinship, all of which vary historically and geographically. Consequently, third world women experience their lives in the intersection of these processes; their actions are not driven 'just' by gender concerns, but by gender *in association* with struggles over class, race and ethnicity, colonial legacies and global capitalism. Third world feminism has thus challenged first world feminism for ethnocentric and racist views.

Acknowledgement of women's diverse engagements with development (both as a process and as an intervention) has only slowly entered development planning. During 'modernization', planners believed that third world women were outside development, and advocated their incorporation into the development process. Pioneer feminists of development, such as Esther Boserup, pointed out the fallacy of this argument, showing that women were disadvantaged precisely because of the 'male bias' embedded in development. 'Gender and Development' (GAD) policy attempts to rectify this bias by analysing male–female power relations in different settings. Repositioning gender and development issues around questions of rights, democracy and participation extends the long-term interest in women's empowerment in the development process (Rowlands, 1997). The establishment of women's ministries and female quotas in national elections are indicative of sustained change over the past decade in many countries of the South.

Development thinking has also begun to deconstruct the category 'men', as men's role in influencing long-term social change, supporting gender-sensitive initiatives, and male-on-male violence is increasingly recognized. Early development thinking tended to assume that male heads of households were fair to all family members. However, it was shown that in areas where historical and cultural conventions sanctioned uneven access to household goods, children and women particularly felt the consequences of illness, malnutrition and dis-empowerment. A new focus on masculinities highlights the diverse positions and attitudes of men, varying with generation, work, family role, location, and so on, to replace the notion of 'patriarchy' (universal male power). Whether development projects are targeted at women-only groups or at mixed groups, the attitudes of men in the community and their assistance or objections affect the project's outcome as well as women's confidence, as a case study from peasant associations in southern Peru illustrates (see box).

MASCULINITIES AND DEVELOPMENT: THE CASE OF SOUTHERN PERU

Indigenous ('Indian') small farmers in the Peruvian Andes are engaged in a multiplicity of livelihood activities that include subsistence farming, cash crop production, migration and local waged work. Gender divisions of labour in agriculture are clear-cut, with male farmers ploughing, while women sow, weed and harvest. Development assistance, usually in the form of credit and technical training, largely goes to men as heads of households. Small farmer confederations are the means by which men, and some women, address their concerns to government and agencies, and co-ordinate local development initiatives. Leaders are overwhelmingly men, although a small number of rural women promoted female concerns (e.g. political representation, individual land titles). Male attitudes to women's struggles and demands are crucial in determining the outcome of negotiations, either in the household or the unions. If men demonstrate *comprensión* (understanding), women travel the country, carry out promotional and organizational work, and gain support in confederations for gender-aware policies. Supportive masculinities contrast with obstructive attitudes that block women's appointment to leadership positions, marginalize their concerns and prevent female mobility. Where this happens, rural women have often established parallel, gender-specific organizations in the Andes.

Source: personal field notes (1988–90)

SUMMARY

- Gender relations in the South are diverse, as place-specific interactions of multiple femininities and masculinities offer widely diverse opportunities and create overlapping forms of disadvantage.
- Women, especially those in low-income groups and younger age groups, are – in comparison with menfolk in their society – more likely to work longer hours, earn less money for their work, and have less secure access to land or property title, credit or development assistance.
- Third world women are active agents in development, yet have been stereotyped by much writing from the North.
- Development policy needs to address gendered power relations, women's agency and the diversity of masculinities found in regional cultures.

DEVELOPMENT, POWER AND THE STATE

Neo-liberalism, neo-liberal

pertaining to an economic doctrine that favours free markets, the deregulation of national economies, decentralization and the privatization of previously state-owned enterprises (e.g. education, health). A doctrine that, in practice, favours the interests of the powerful (e.g. TRANSNATIONAL CORPORATIONS) against the less powerful (e.g. peasants) within societies.

Developmentalism

a set of propositions or policies that demand (or provide for) the transformation of pre-modern societies into MODERN societies. INDUSTRIALIZATION is often considered to play a key role in the process of development. *See also* POST-DEVELOPMENTALISM.

The nation-state remains a highly significant development actor in the South. During the middle years of the twentieth century, the state was seen as *the* institution to carry out development, as it was presumed to have its population's interests in mind and the organizational capacity to administer change. States varied, however, in their institutional make-up, political commitments and development visions. In many areas, colonization created heavily militarized priorities, political hierarchies and a limited public sphere for democratic debate, as in Latin America, Pakistan and sub-Saharan Africa. In other areas, governments – sometimes unelected – prioritized benefits for all, the reform of agriculture, and a universal education system (e.g. as in South East Asia). Where a dynamic civil society was complemented by a strong legislative structure, as in Sri Lanka, more inclusive and equitable development outcomes were possible (Martinussen, 1997). Thus, state structures and their relationship with civil society (that is, citizens) affect the negotiation and implementation of development priorities. A 'developmentalist state' is one that combines an ability to organize a productive agricultural sector (through land redistribution and taxation), together with publicly supported principles of the rule of law, guaranteed territorial sovereignty, and independent judiciaries and administrators, to bring about general well-being (Leftwich, 1996).

During the 1980s, the role of the state in development was called into question by the rise of **neo-liberal** thinking that advocated a removal of state 'interference' in favour of market mechanisms. As the neo-liberal agenda drove international development policy, particularly in the Bretton Woods institutions of the World Bank and IMF, so too third world states laid off state workers, privatized state-owned resources (mines, airlines, telecommunications, and so on), and reduced subsidies on basic food items, transport and electricity (Toye, 1993). According to the 'Washington consensus', the state was to concede its **developmentalist** role to the market through 'cutting back' its administration and oversight of development. Although it has now generally been recognized that nation-states do provide an irreplaceable role in providing some services and political guidance, the neo-liberal revolution has dramatically transformed the political landscape of development.

In addition to neo-liberalism, many countries in the South have experienced political decentralization in recent years, which is promoted as a means to create closer and more effective ties between government and the governed. Regional authorities, municipalities or ethnically defined areas have been created or strengthened with tax-raising powers and decision-making rights. For example, the Bolivian Law of Popular Participation in 1994 redirected power to local organizations – including Indian communities – in a programme to provide 'growth with equity', combining a neo-liberal economic environment with access to decision-making for mostly rural, marginalized poor populations.

FIGURE 14.3
Democratic decision-making and development.
Credit: Eric Miller/Still Pictures

As the state's role in administering development changed, new institutions and actors came on to the scene. **Non-governmental organizations (NGOs)** have become a key institution delivering development to local people. Mostly staffed by citizens of the country in which they work, NGOs have stepped into welfare provision, extension work, and credit and job-creation programmes that would, at one time, have fallen automatically to the state. NGOs vary greatly in their remit, structures and geographies, and can provide services of housing, healthcare, waste disposal and even education, often drawing on international funds. In Latin America, it is estimated that around 11,000 NGOs are working in multiple activities, from popular education to agricultural development, through to human rights work. NGOs have

Non-governmental organization (NGO)

an organization that belongs neither to the private for-profit sector, or the public or government sector.

NGOS AND NEW INSTITUTIONS IN DEVELOPMENT: ECUADOR

An example of a hybrid development institution is offered by the Ecuadorian indigenous and black peoples' development project, which has brought together a formerly disparate group of actors to oversee this poverty-alleviation project. Drawing on the experiences of grassroots groups, regional NGOs and rural federations, the Indigenous and Black Peoples' Development Project aims to bring these groups out of poverty, while empowering their decision-making and institutions. An example of a rights-based development, the project is based on the premise that indigenous and black Ecuadorians – who comprise around 40 per cent of the population – have the right to culturally appropriate

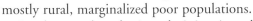

development. The project uses participatory methods to design local development projects appropriate to communities' needs. It is designed, administered and operated by a hybrid development institution, which brings together the main actors involved, namely:

- the National Council of Development Planning for Indigenous and Black People – a state agency with indigenous representatives
- local and regional management committees
- grassroots organizations – around 160 local associations for irrigation, education, production, sports, gender issues and the elderly
- indigenous national confederations, including CONAIE, FENOCIN, FEINE and FEI
- Afro-Ecuadorian organizations, such as ASONE (the Association of Ecuadorian Afro-Ecuadorians).

often been seen as closer to grassroots beneficiaries than other development agencies, and they can be innovative proponents of appropriate technology, participation and new development ideas. However, NGOs are not elected and they are often more accountable to their donors than local people, which can pressure them to work to global agendas rather than local needs. Alongside NGOs in recent decades the hybrid development institution has emerged, in which staff from (reformed) state agencies, representatives of citizen groups, NGO staff and even staff from global development agencies work together on a project (see box).

Moreover, the state's changing development role transformed the ways states and citizens interact. The 1980s and 1990s were a period of re-democratization around the world, as dictators and unelected governments fell in the wake of popular protest or collapse from within. As a result, the number of governments chosen in regular elections (and booming numbers of young voters) in the South has increased. Whilst the formal aspects of democracy are not a guarantee of citizenship rights, civilian governments have risen dramatically in number from 25 per cent globally in 1973 to 68 per cent in 1992 (Leftwich, 1993: 614), a share that has been sustained in more recent years. In order to support these trends, development policy tries to ensure that international aid is governed by transparent rules, overseen by elected representatives, and reaches its intended target groups. Within countries, too, decision-making processes have shifted to encourage more active citizen involvement in local decision-making and the implementation of development. However, certain constraints remain on this full involvement, although they are not always the same as in previous decades. Neo-liberal forms of governance induce individualized – not collective – responses to the challenges of restructuring economies and political systems. Also, exclusionary political cultures marginalize or silence certain groups, such as ethnic minorities, women, rural populations or disabled people.

SUMMARY

- The third world state is an important, but often inequitable, institution for development.
- Under neo-liberal reforms and 'roll back' policies, the state's role in development has been reconfigured.
- New development priorities have led to changes in the administration of development – although the state remains significant, NGOs and hybrid development institutions have emerged.

CONCLUSIONS

Development geographies are changing quickly. Not only are the multifaceted processes undergone by countries in the South being transformed by successive waves of political-economic change and social relations of protest and accommodation, but also the analytical frameworks we bring to bear on these varied situations have diversified in recent years. Development geographers have begun to engage with post-colonial perspectives, in ways that challenge our understanding of a neatly bounded category of 'developing countries' and that ask us to recognize the sheer diversity and groundedness of development experiences for individuals, groups and countries. The gendering of development has also been a key aspect of recent development thinking. Whereas in previous decades, development was assumed to be gender neutral and applicable to men and women, recent decades have highlighted the male bias of much development planning, and the highly differentiated impacts of development processes on diverse femininities and masculinities. Politically, the context for decision-making and the structures for administering development outcomes have also been radically re-thought in recent years. The rise in numbers of NGOs and new forms of hybrid administration, and the decentralization of (some) budgets and (some) decision-making have characterized many countries at the start of the twenty-first century. Overall, development remains a highly contested process, and however much the priority is to reduce poverty and bring an end to exclusionary political and development cultures, the means by which development is to be achieved remains the topic of highly passionate and globally significant debate. Under the umbrella of increased global integration, the complex geographies of development remain to be mapped and discussed, by participants and students of development alike.

DISCUSSION POINTS

1. Find a textbook on development and write a review of it from a post-colonial perspective.

2. Why does a gender perspective – looking at power relations between different femininities and masculinities – matter in development? Think about this question in relation to different facets of the development process (e.g. poverty; divisions of labour and availability of work; political representation and decision-making at different scales; and access to services such as education, health and training). You might find that focusing on one or two countries allows you to be more specific in your answer.

3. Discuss the relative merits of states, NGOs and other agencies in development (e.g. international NGOs such as Oxfam; hybrid development institutions, grassroots organizations). How do they compare in relation to money spent, personnel, accountability, responsiveness to development demands, and in relation to impacts? Can you find out if – and how – these different development actors co-ordinate their actions?

FURTHER READING

Martinussen, J. (1997) *Society, state and market: a guide to competing theories of development.* **London: Zed.**

An impressive and easy-to-read summary and discussion of the main theories about development, covering economics, sociology and politics.

Blunt, A. and McEwan, C. (eds) (2002) *Postcolonial geographies.* **London: Continuum.**

A new book on geographers' views on the promises and pitfalls of postcolonialism.

Mohanty, C. (1991) Cartographies of struggle: third world women and the politics of feminism. In Mohanty, C., Parker, A. and Russo, A. (eds) *Third world women and the politics of feminism.* **London: Routledge.**

A classic post-colonial feminist study of development and third world women.

Visvanathan, N. *et al.* **(eds) (1987)** *The women, gender and development reader.* **London: Zed.**

An accessible introduction to recent development thinking about women and gender issues.

Leftwich, A. (1993) Governance, democracy and development in the third world. *Third World Quarterly,* **14(3), 605–24.**

A clear summary of the arguments about why democracy is such a contested idea in the developing world, and why the issue is bound up with global financial institutions, political changes in the West, and social struggles.

CHAPTER 15
SURVIVAL AND RESISTANCE

Paul Routledge

INTRODUCTION: THE THREATS TO PEOPLE'S SURVIVAL

On New Year's Day 1994, ski-masked Mayan guerrillas emerge from the Lacandon jungle, capture the town of San Cristobal de las Casas in Chiapas, Mexico, and declare war on the Mexican state.

In late April 1997, on the horizon before Brasília, the hoes and machetes of thousands of campesinos glint in the sunshine as this movement of Brazil's landless peasants approaches the country's capital to demand land from the government.

In July 1999, on the Narmada river, India, a fleet of fishing boats, slogans written on their white sails, protest the construction of the mega-dams along the river valley, as part of a week-long 'rally for the valley'.

In November 1999, in Seattle, USA, 40,000 people from different struggles protest against the World Trade Organization and the institutions of neo-liberal globalization. A fire of rebellion is ignited that subsequently spreads to Prague, Genoa, Barcelona, Cancun and across the planet. Amongst the participants is People's Global Action (PGA), an international network of grassroots people's movements.

Whilst very different, these four moments are examples of conflicts that are occurring in both the developed and developing countries. These conflicts represent mobilizations of the dispossessed, the poor, the marginalized: those threatened with, or experiencing, displacement, **cultural ethnocide** and the grinding ravages of poverty. They speak of struggles over the allocation of resources, over self-determination, and over rights of economic and cultural survival, and it is to a consideration of these struggles that this chapter is devoted.

Within the global economy, economic development has had a variety of results. Certain locally based development practices have improved health and education services, enhanced environmental quality, and generated employment opportunities that foster equity and self-sufficiency. However, many development practices are increasingly influenced by the ideology of neo-liberalism that is committed to 'free market' principles of free trade that privilege privatization and deregulation, whilst undermining or foreclosing alternative development models based upon social redistribution, economic rights or public investment (Peck and Tickell, 2002). Within particular countries, such development has emphasized economic growth, modernization and industrialization as the panacea for poverty. Capital-intensive schemes have displaced traditional and subsistence economies that are labour intensive (often resulting in unemployment); and western values (of capitalist production, economic growth) have been emphasized at the expense of indigenous and traditional systems of knowledge, economy and culture. It has facilitated both the state's and transnational corporations' securing control over

Cultural ethnocide

the permanent disappearance of a particular ethnic group, associated with the eradication of their cultural practices, brought about by the effects of economic and/or political policies. *See also* ETHNICITY.

natural and financial resources and consolidated the power of those directing and benefiting from the development apparatus – national ruling elites and international institutions (Nandy, 1984).

Neo-liberalism entails the centralization of control of the world economy in the hands of transnational corporations and their allies in key government agencies (particularly those of the United States and other members of the G8), large international banks and international institutions such as the International Monetary Fund (IMF), the World Bank and the World Trade Organization (WTO). These institutions enforce the doctrine of neo-liberalism, enabling the unrestricted access of transnational corporations (TNCs) to a wide range of markets (including public services), whilst potentially more progressive institutions and agreements (such as the International Labour Organization and the Kyoto Protocols) are allowed to wither (Peck and Tickell, 2002). Neo-liberal policies have resulted in the **pauperization** and marginalization of indigenous peoples, women, peasant farmers and industrial workers, and a reduction in labour, social, and environmental conditions on a global basis – what Brecher and Costello (1994) term 'the race to the bottom' or 'global pillage'.

In addition to the threats posed by neo-liberal development are those posed by the practices and policies of particular states. These may be aimed at enabling development practices to take place, or they may be aimed at securing the state's political (and economic) control over resources and territory. These territories are frequently inhabited by groups who perceive such state policies as an intrusion on their political and cultural rights. The assault upon the lifeworlds of these groups – which include indigenous peoples and peasants – has led to the emergence of myriad social movements that articulate struggles for political autonomy, and cultural, ecological and economic survival. This chapter considers the four examples of contemporary popular resistance that opened this chapter: the Landless Movement of Brazil; the Zapatistas of Mexico; the Save Narmada Movement of India and People's Global Action. It investigates how geography – and geographers – can lend important insights into these struggles.

Pauperization

the progressive impoverishment of people owing to the impacts of certain development programmes. For example, the displacement of peasant and tribal peoples from their sources of livelihood (e.g. land) to make way for the construction of hydro-electric dams.

GEOGRAPHY AND RESISTANCE

Human geography can lend some important understandings to people's resistances, providing valuable insights into the place-specific character of struggles, explaining why these conflicts arise, and why they emerge where they do. This is because different social groups endow space (and its associated resources) with a variety of different meanings, uses and values. Such differences can give rise to various tensions and conflicts within society over the uses of space for individual and social purposes, and the control of space by the state and other forms economic and cultural power such as transnational corporations. As a result, particular places frequently become sites of conflict between different groups within society, which reflect concerns of ecology (e.g. struggles to prevent deforestation and pollution), economy (e.g. peasant struggles to secure land on which to grow food), culture (e.g. struggles to protect the integrity of indigenous peoples' communities) and politics (e.g. struggles for increased local autonomy). These concerns are also associated with what Gedicks (1993) terms the 'resource wars': the struggle over the remaining natural resources between indigenous and traditional peoples, state and national governments, and transnational corporations.

In response to these different concerns, people frequently organize themselves into social movements, which are ongoing collective efforts aimed at bringing about particular changes in a social order. Many of these social movements are place-specific, actively affirming local identity, culture and systems of knowledge as an integral part of their resistance. In doing so, these movements articulate localized 'terrains of resistance' with their own place-specific idioms of protest, which motivate and inform their struggles. However, resistances are also becoming increasingly global in character, spanning both national and international space. This is because with the impacts of globalization – where localities are increasingly influenced by non-local economic and cultural forces – many social movements feel obliged to focus their resistance both within and beyond the confines of their immediate locality, in order to attract as wide a support to their struggle as possible. Such 'globalized resistance' (Brecher and Costello, 1994) often involves networks of different social movements and **non-governmental organizations (NGOs)** that co-ordinate their struggles across a variety of scales in response to the emerging global economy and the actions of particular governments.

Terrains of resistance

the material and/or symbolic ground upon which collective action (e.g. by social movements) takes place. This can involve the economic, political, cultural and ecological practices of resistance movements, as well as the physical places where their resistance occurs.

Non-governmental organization (NGO)

an organization that belongs neither to the private for-profit sector, or the public or government sector.

SUMMARY

- Different social groups endow space and its resources with different meanings, uses and values arising in conflicts over the uses and control of particular places.

- Certain development practices have emphasized economic growth and industrialization as the solution to poverty, and viewed indigenous and traditional systems of knowledge as impediments to progress.

- As states and transnational corporations seek control over resources and territory for development, so the inhabitants of the areas concerned are frequently displaced and economically marginalized.

- In response to such development processes, people often organize themselves into place-specific social movements to resist threats to their economic and cultural survival. Many such movements act across multiple scales, and are increasingly involved in globalizing networks of resistance.

- Geography can provide insights into the place-specific character of resistances, explaining why these conflicts arise, and why they emerge where they do.

SOCIAL MOVEMENT STRUGGLES: RESISTANCE FOR SURVIVAL

Social movements operate on a number of interrelated 'levels' within society. At the level of the economy, they articulate conflicts over access to productive natural resources such as forests and water, as well as conducting struggles in the workplace. The economic demands of social movements are not only concerned with a more equitable distribution of resources between competing groups, and the integrity of local, traditional forms of economic practice. They are also involved in the creation of new services such as health and education in rural areas (Guha, 1989). Indeed, social movements have emerged in many areas, including civil liberties, women's rights, science and health, that are themselves often related to problems caused by neo-liberal development. At the level of culture, social movement identities and solidarities are formed – for example, around issues of class, kinship, neighbourhood and the social networks of everyday life. Movement struggles are frequently cultural struggles over material conditions and needs, and over the practices and meanings of everyday life (Escobar, 1992). Social movements frequently affirm and regenerate local (place-specific) identity, knowledge and practices, which at times are expressed in the language and character of the struggles. Local resistance may incorporate local linguistic expressions, such as songs, poems and dramas that imbue and affirm local experiences, beliefs and cultural practices.

At the level of politics, social movements challenge the state-centred character of the political process, articulating critiques of neo-liberal development ideology and the role of the state. Movements are frequently autonomous of political parties (although some have formed working alliances with trades unions, voluntary organizations and NGOs). Their goals frequently articulate alternatives to the political process, political parties, the state and the capture of state power. By articulating concerns of justice and 'quality of life', these movements enlarge the conception of politics to include issues of gender, ethnicity, and the autonomy and dignity of diverse individuals and groups (Guha, 1989). At the level of the environment, social movements are involved in struggles to protect local ecological niches – such as forests, rivers and ocean shorelines – from the threats to their environmental integrity through such processes as deforestation (e.g. for logging or cattle-grazing purposes) and pollution (e.g. from industrial enterprises). Many of these social movements are also multidimensional, simultaneously addressing, for example, issues of poverty, ecology, gender and culture, such as the survival of peasant and tribal populations.

Social movements are by no means homogenous. A multiplicity of groups including squatter movements, neighbourhood groups, human rights organizations, women's associations, indigenous rights groups, self-help movements amongst the poor and unemployed, youth groups, educational and health associations and artists' movements are involved in various types of struggle. Many of these struggles take place within the realm of civil society, i.e. those areas of society that are neither part of the processes of material production in the economy nor part of state-funded organizations, and can be either violent or non-violent in character.

Whilst social movements in the developed and developing countries share some of the broad characteristics mentioned above – for example, they articulate such issues as ecology, gender and ethnicity – there are also important differences between them. In the developed countries, social movements have often concentrated upon 'quality of life' issues, whereas in developing countries, movements have often focused on access to economic resources. An example of this difference is represented by the issues faced by ecological movements. In the developed countries, the ecology movement has taken much of the industrial economy and consumer society for granted, working to preserve nature as an item of 'consumption', as a haven from the world of work. In the developing countries, however, those affected by environmental degradation – poor and landless peasants, women and tribal peoples – are involved in struggles for economic and cultural survival rather than quality of life. Such groups articulate an 'environmentalism of the poor' (Martinez-Allier, 1990), whose fundamental concerns are with the defence of livelihoods and of communal access to resources threatened by commodification, state take-overs, and private appropriation (for example, by national or transnational corporations), and with emancipation from material want and domination by others.

Social movements rarely articulate their demands at only one level. As we shall see below, economic struggles may also contain political dimensions, political struggles may also contain cultural elements, and so on. Moreover, the responses of state authorities to social movements vary, according to the type of movement resistance, and the character of the government involved. When faced with social movement challenges, governmental responses include repression, co-option, co-operation and accommodation. Repression can range from harassment and physical beatings, to imprisonment, torture and the killing of activists.

Concerning resistance to neo-liberal development, the *Ejercito Zapatista Liberacion National* – the EZLN or the Zapatistas – in Chiapas, Mexico, has articulated resistance to the North American Free Trade Agreement (NAFTA) and the Mexican state (see Fig. 15.1). The Zapatistas, a pre-dominantly indigenous (Mayan) guerrilla movement, have emerged in Chiapas due to several factors. First, the state of Chiapas is rich in petroleum and lumber resources, which have been ruthlessly exploited causing deforestation and pollution. Second, the increasing orientation of capital-intensive agriculture for the international market has led to the creation of a class of elite wealthy farmers, and forced Indian communities to become peasant labour for the extraction and exploitation of resources, the wealth of which accrues to others. In addition, large landowners and ranchers control private armies, which are used to force peasants off their land and to terrorize those who have the temerity to resist. Third, although it is resource-rich, Chiapas is amongst the poorest states in Mexico with 30 per cent of the population illiterate and 75 per cent of the population malnourished. Fourth,

the production of two of the main crops from which *campesinos* (peasants) earn a living in Chiapas – coffee and corn – have undergone severe economic problems in recent years, and will be further damaged by NAFTA. Finally, government reforms in 1991 enabled previously protected

FIGURE 15.1
Although based in the Lacandon jungle, the Zapatistas have been able to globalize their resistance through creative use of the internet. Credit: PA Photos

individual and communal peasant landholdings to be put up for sale to powerful cattle-ranching, logging, mining and petroleum interests.

The Zapatistas initially engaged in a guerrilla insurgency by occupying the capital of Chiapas and several other prominent towns in the state, as noted at the beginning of this chapter. However, they staged their uprising in a spectacular manner to ensure maximum media coverage and thus gain the attention of a variety of audiences – including civil society, the state, the national and international media, and international finance markets. The appearance of an armed insurgency, at a moment when the Mexican economy was entering into a free trade agreement, enabled the Zapatistas to attract national and international media attention. Through their spokesperson, Subcommandante Marcos, the Zapatistas engaged in a 'war of words' with the Mexican government, fought primarily with rebel communiqués (via newspapers and the internet) rather than bullets. Through their guerrilla insurgency and their war of words the Zapatistas have attempted to raise awareness concerning the unequal distribution of land, and economic and political power in Chiapas; challenge the neo-liberal economic policies of the Mexican government; articulate an indigenous worldview that promotes Indian political autonomy; and articulate a call for the democratization of civil society. The success of the Zapatista struggle has lain in its ability, with limited resources and personnel, to disrupt international financial markets and their investments within Mexico, whilst exposing the inequities on which development and neo-liberalism is predicated (Harvey, 1995; Ross, 1995). In addition, although Zapatista guerrilla bases were in the Lacandon jungle in Chiapas, the Zapatistas were particularly concerned to globalize their resistance, and were the catalyst for the emergence of certain international networks of grassroots social movements challenging neo-liberalism, such as People's Global Action (see below).

However, despite certain successes, the movement has been faced with repression from the Mexican government. Over 15,000 army personnel have been deployed in Chiapas; villages suspected of being sympathetic to the Zapatistas have been bombed; and peasants suspected of being Zapatistas have been arrested and tortured. At present an uneasy ceasefire is in place between the Zapatistas and the government, and peace talks between them have stalled. Since their emergence in 1994, the Zapatistas have posed more than just a political challenge to the Mexican state. In their demands for equitable distribution of land, their calls for indigenous rights and ecological preservation (i.e. an end to logging, a programme of reforestation, an end to water contamination of the jungle, preservation of remaining virgin forest), they also articulate an economic, ecological and cultural struggle.

The *Movimento Sem Terra* (MST), or Landless Movement, in Brazil provides an interesting example of the organized struggle for access to land resources (see Fig. 15.2). The MST is a mass social movement of some 220,000 members that has developed during the past 17 years and is made up of Brazil's dispossessed – croppers, casual pickers, farm labourers and people displaced from the land by mechanization and by land clearances. Many of those involved are homeless, or live in roadside tents, and earn less than 60 pence a day. Of Brazil's population of 165 million people,

Neo-liberalism, neo-liberal

pertaining to an economic doctrine that favours free markets, the deregulation of national economies, decentralization and the privatization of previously state-owned enterprises (e.g. education, health). A doctrine that, in practice, favours the interests of the powerful (e.g. TRANSNATIONAL CORPORATIONS) against the less powerful (e.g. peasants) within societies.

FIGURE 15.2
Sem Terra activists hold aloft machetes and hoes
which have become symbols of their struggle
for land. Credit: © Sebastiao Selgado/Network
Photographers

fewer than 50,000 own most of the land, while four million peasants share
less than 3 per cent of the land. Whilst approximately 32 million people
in Brazil are malnourished, over 42 per cent of all privately owned land in
Brazil lies unused. Hence the principal demand amongst the dispossessed
has been for land. The MST targets Brazil's vast estates that lie unused.
First, groups of people illegally squat on the uncultivated land in 'land
invasions'. After the area has been 'secured' the MST resettles massive
numbers of people on the squatted sites, who then construct houses and
schools, and commence farming. Since 1991, the MST has occupied 518
large ranches and resettled approximately 600,000 people. The process has
been far from peaceful, as the large landowners and their private armies
have attacked and killed the squatters. For example, in one incident in
1996, in the state of Para, 19 MST activists were shot dead by police in
the pay of local landowners.

Whilst the right of the government to redistribute land that is not being
farmed is enshrined in the Brazilian constitution, successive regimes have
failed to exercise this right, due in part to the political power wielded by
the country's landowners. However, the Brazilian government has begun
to tentatively initiate agrarian reforms, providing credit for new
settlements, and confiscating some of the ranches in the state of Para to
settle some of the families of those MST members killed in 1996. This is
due, in large part, to the success of the MST in mobilizing popular
support for its cause, and its ability to develop alliances with trades unions
and other grassroots organizations, both in Brazil and internationally, as
evidenced by its participation in the People's Global Action network (see

FIGURE 15.3
During the 'Rally for the Valley' fishermen conduct a boat protest on the Narmada river.
Credit: © Paul Routledge

below). Evidence of this support was dramatically illustrated by the mass demonstration in Brasilia, in April 1997, mentioned at the beginning of this chapter, where over 120,000 landless people lined the streets to demand land reform (Vidal, 1997). In attempting to change the government's agrarian policy, the MST is also operating within the field of political action.

Another example of a 'resource war' is that of the resistance against the Narmada river valley project in India (see Fig. 15.3). This river, which is regarded as sacred by the Hindu and tribal populations of India, spans the states of Madhya Pradesh, Maharashtra and Gujarat, and provides water resources for thousands of communities. The project envisages the construction of 30 major dams along the Narmada and its tributaries, as well as an additional 135 medium-sized and 3000 minor dams. With two of the major dams already built, opposition to the project has been focused on the Sardar Sarovar reservoir, the largest of the project's individual schemes. When completed, this dam alone is expected to flood 33,947 acres of forest land, and submerge an estimated 248 towns and villages. According to official estimates (based on the outdated 1981 census), over 100,000 people – 60 per cent of whom are tribal – will be forcibly evicted from their homes and lands. The resistance to the project has been co-ordinated by the *Narmada Bachao Andolan* (Save Narmada Movement), which consists largely of peasant farmers and indigenous people, and demands the curtailment of the scheme.

The movement's repertoire of protest has included mass demonstrations, road blockades, fasts, public meetings and disruption of construction activities. In addition the movement has deployed peasant and tribal testimonies, songs and poems to give 'voice' to the struggle. Whilst the movement has been almost completely non-violent, its leaders and participants have been harassed, assaulted and jailed by police. Whilst localized protests have occurred along the entire Narmada valley, wider public attention has been drawn to spectacular events such as mass demonstrations and the 'rally for the valley' mentioned at the beginning of the chapter (Routledge, 2003a). In addition, the movement has expanded its resistance to regional, national and international levels, developing networks of solidarity and support, and participating in such initiatives as People's Global Action (see below).

However, despite this resistance, construction of the dams continues. In representing a threat to the ecology of the area surrounding the Narmada river, the construction of the dams also threatens the economic survival of the tribal and peasant peoples who will be evicted from their homes and lands – from which they earn their livelihoods – when the land is submerged. Moreover, these inhabitants have a profound religious connection to the landscape around the Narmada river. This spiritual connection to place – which eviction threatens to sever – intimately informs their customs and practices of everyday life. Hence opposition to the dam also articulates the inhabitants' desire for cultural survival. In addition, many of the villages that border the Narmada are demanding a level of regional autonomy, seeking 'our rule in our villages', thereby articulating political demands as well (Gadgil and Guha, 1995).

People's Global Action (PGA) is an example of the numerous emerging international networks of social movements resisting neo-liberalism. Established in 1998, by such groups as *Movimento Sem Terra*, Karnataka State Farmers' Association (India), Movement for the Survival of the Ogoni People (Nigeria), the *Narmada Bachao Andolan*, the *Central Sandinista de Trabajadores* (Nicaragua) and the Indigenous Women's Network (North America and the Pacific), PGA seeks to facilitate communication, solidarity and the sharing of information and resources between grassroots social movements (see Fig. 15.4). The network's main objectives are to offer an instrument for co-ordination and mutual support at the global level for those resisting corporate rule and the neo-liberal capitalist development paradigm, to provide international projection to their struggles, and to inspire people to resist corporate domination through civil disobedience and people-oriented constructive actions. It has been the PGA network along with other movements that have put out the calls for the recent global days of action against capitalism, such as the protests against the WTO in Seattle mentioned at the beginning of this chapter.

FIGURE 15.4
Members of the Bangledesh Kisani Sabha (Women Peasants' Assembly), a participant organization on the People's Global Action network. Credit © Paul Routledge

PGA is organized primarily through the internet via its website and various emailing lists. The internet acts as a communicative and co-ordinating thread in the PGA network, which weaves different place-based struggles together so that they may converge in virtual space. To decentralize the everyday workings of the network, PGA has established regional networks in Latin America, Europe, North America and Asia. In addition, PGA organizes international and regional meetings, conferences and caravans. There have been three international conferences, held in Geneva, Switzerland (1998), Bangalore, India (1999), and Cochabamba, Bolivia (2001); regional PGA conferences have been held in Europe (Milan, Barcelona, Leiden), Nicaragua, Panama, Brazil, Bangladesh, New Zealand (Aotearoa) and the United States. Such conferences and meetings enable: (i) discussions to take place that pertain to the functioning of the network; (ii) the development of joint political strategies by movements within the network; and (iii) deeper interpersonal ties to be established between different activists from different cultural spaces and struggles.

PGA also organizes activist caravans. These are buses of activists from various struggles around the world, which visit social movement struggles in countries other than their own. The PGA caravans are organized in order for activists from different struggles and countries to communicate with one another, exchange information, share experiences and tactics, participate in various solidarity demonstrations, rallies and direct actions, and attempt to draw new movements into the network. The caravans have included an Intercontinental caravan in 1999, which brought 500 Asian farmers to tour Europe; a United States caravan that culminated in the WTO protests in Seattle in 1999; and caravans before and after the PGA conferences in Bangalore, India (1999), and Cochabamba, Bolivia (2001). In addition, there have been speaking tours (e.g. that which brought Colombian activists from the Process of Black Communities to Europe in 2001), and workshops and seminars, concerning neo-liberalism and its alternatives, on several continents (Routledge, 2003b). As a network of grassroots movements, PGA articulates concerns at the political, economic, cultural and ecological levels. Moreover, PGA and each of the other struggles discussed in this chapter are examples of people's struggles that think and act both locally and globally.

SUMMARY

- Social movements articulate resistance within society in the realms of economics, politics, culture and the environment.

- At the economic level, social movements articulate conflicts over the productive resources in society, involving demands for a more equitable distribution of resources, the creation of new services and the integrity of local, traditional forms of economic practice.

- At the political level, social movements challenge the state-centred character of the political process,

articulating critiques of neo-liberal development ideology and of the role of the state.

- At the cultural level, social movements frequently affirm and regenerate local (place-specific) identity, knowledge and practices, which at times are expressed in the language and character of the struggles.

- At the ecological level, social movements struggle to protect remaining environments from further destruction, and to ensure the economic (and cultural) survival of peasant and tribal populations.

CONCLUSION: RESISTANCE AND GEOGRAPHY

The four examples described in this chapter are but a few of the resistances to neo-liberalism and repressive governments that have proliferated across the world during the past 15 years. These have involved leftist guerrillas, social movements, non-government organizations, human rights groups, environmental organizations and indigenous peoples' movements. Frequently, coalitions have formed across national borders and across different political ideologies in attempts to revitalize democratic practices and public institutions, promote economic and environmental sustainability, encourage grassroots economic development and hold transnational corporations accountable to enforceable codes of conduct. Such resistances are frequently responses to local conditions that are in part the product of global forces, and resistance to these conditions has taken place at both the local and the global level. In contrast to official political discourse about the global economy, these challenges articulate a 'globalization from below' that comprises an evolving international network of groups, organizations and social movements.

Human geography can provide valuable insights into the place-specific character of these different forms of resistance, explaining not only why conflicts emerge, but why they arise where they do. Hence, in our examples, the landless peasants of the MST focused their struggle in those areas of Brazil that have large estates with unused land; the Narmada movement has been most active in those areas threatened by submergence by the construction of dams; and the Zapatistas have emerged in Mexico's poorest and most economically and ecologically exploited state.

Geography can also provide insights into how and why movements act across multiple scales – for example, by being part of international resistance networks such as People's Global Action. As geographers, then, we can contribute to the understanding of struggles for survival in different cultural contexts. Given that we live within an increasingly interdependent world, we might also consider ways of attempting to contribute towards these struggles, to make our contribution towards an environmentally sustainable and socially just world.

DISCUSSION POINTS

1. Why, and in what ways, do challenges to neo-liberalism articulate a 'globalization from below'?

2. What opportunities and/or constraints might social movements face when they wage struggle at local as well as global levels?

3. In what ways might geographers contribute towards struggles for a more environmentally sustainable and socially just world?

FURTHER READING

Peet, R. and Watts, M. (1996) *Liberation ecologies: environment, development, social movements.* **London. Routledge.**

A fine collection of essays on the themes of development and social movements.

Brecher, J. and Costello, T. (1994) *Global village or global pillage.* **Boston: South End Press.**

A discussion of globalization and resistance.

Klein, N. (2002) *Fences and windows.* **London: Flamingo.**

Notes from Nowhere (ed.) (2003) *We are everywhere.* **London: Verso.**

Mertes, T. (ed.) (2004) *The movement of movements: a reader.* **London: Verso.**

These texts offer recent overviews of grassroots social movements and initiatives around the world.

WEBSITES

The movements discussed in this chapter have websites at:

- *Movimento Sem Terra*: **www.mstbrazil.org**

- *Narmada Bachao Andolan*: **www.nba.org**

- People's Global Action: **www.agp.org**

- The Zapatistas:
  www.eco.utexas.edu/faculty/Cleaver/chiapas95.html

Alternative news sources for articles, commentaries and reports on many issues are:

- Indymedia: **www.indymedia.org**

- ZNet: **www.zmag.org**

SECTION 3
ECONOMIC GEOGRAPHIES

INTRODUCTION

The contemporary economy is an extraordinarily complex set of processes, operating in and around a huge variety of institutions and activities. It embraces everything from a teenager receiving and spending pocket money to the most advanced manufacturing technologies in the world being employed by global corporations. It touches most of our daily lives, and directly affects what we eat, how we dress and where we sleep. We are surrounded and confronted by advertisers extolling us to purchase their products; we spend ages agonizing over which ones to buy; and huge swathes of our towns and countryside are devoted to the production of goods and services. Even the most peaceful rural scene is riven by economic relations and processes that connect the small village in the UK to a global food industry.

The usual way in which geography has dealt with such complexity is to break it down by economic activity or sector – agricultural geography, transport geography, industrial geography and the geographies of trade and services, for instance. This section introduces to you a different way of breaking up the economic world into manageable chunks – not by sectors of economic activity but into three coherent parts (production, money and finance) of a single unified process. Within the contemporary economy, the dominant sets of relations are capitalist in nature, and thus the unified process that represents most of the global economy is known as the circuit of capital, asset out diagrammatically in Figure I.i.

Money (M) is placed into the circuit at the top of the circle by those who wish to invest. This largely takes place in and through financial centres like the City of London or the New York Stock Exchange on Wall Street. Moving clockwise around our diagrammatic circle, this money, fictitious or real, is then used to purchase commodities (C) in the form of labour power (LP) – say, car workers – and the means of production (MP) – say, an assembly line and bits of steel, rubber and various other metals. These are then combined in a production process (P) – say, in a car factory – which produced further commodities (C´) – say, in the form of a car. This new commodity is then sold, for more money (M´) than was originally invested (our initial M). The difference between M and M´ is known as surplus value (S), or more usually in everyday language as profit. This amount is ready to re-invest in a further round of production. The realization of a surplus is the rationale behind the capitalist economy – those firms, organizations and individuals who do not manage to do this will quite simply go bust. Those who manage it on a regular basis will thrive and prosper. Under capitalism, therefore, production, consumption and exchange are all combined as the means to an end of making a profit – or generating surplus.

The geographies of all this are highly dynamic and mobile since one of the defining features of capitalism is that its key component parts – capital and labour – are notionally free. The creation of value, or a surplus, takes

Capitalism

an economic system in which the production and distribution of goods is organized around the profit motive (*see* CAPITAL ACCUMULATION) and characterized by marked inequalities in the social division of work and wealth between private owners of the materials and tools of production (capital) and those who work for them to make a living (labour) (*see* CLASS).

Commodity

something that can be bought and sold through the market. A commodity can be an object (a car, for example), but can also be a person (the car production worker who sells their labour for a wage) or an idea (the design or marketing concepts of the car). Those who live in capitalist societies are used to most things being commodities, though there are still taboos (the buying and selling of sexual intercourse or grandmothers, for example) (*see* CAPITALISM and COMMODIFICATION). This should not disguise the fact that the 'commodity state' is a very particular way of framing objects, people and ideas.

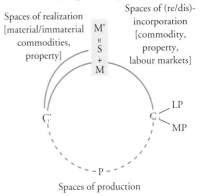

FIGURE I.I

The circuit of capital. Source: Lee (2005)

Social reproduction

the processes through which societies
sustain themselves in social and
material terms across space and time.
In purely material terms, people need
to consume various commodities
(housing, food, clothing, recreation,
etc.) in order to sustain (reproduce)
themselves, and these commodities
have to be made available though
various forms of exchange (e.g.
wholesaling, retailing, sites of
consumption like cinemas, concert
venues, clubs). But, crucially, social
reproduction is necessarily also a social
process. It involves the development
and transmission of norms and 'rules'
of behaviour around the circuits of
social reproduction that give direction
to, and make sense of, their activities
within such circuits. Social
reproduction also suggests that the
purpose of economic activity is not the
generation of particular moments of
production, consumption or exchange
but the sustenance (the reproduction)
of these activities over space and time.

place in and through specific economic spaces. We can break these spaces down into three main kinds – those of production, those of investment and those of consumption. The geographies of each of these are considered in this section. Initially, in Chapter 16, Roger Lee explores the geographies of production. He points out that production is not just confined to the formal economic spaces of the factory and the office, but instead takes place in the home around the issue of social reproduction. He also stresses how the spaces of production are increasingly dynamic and flexible, yet at the same time are vulnerable and subject to almost instant demise. In Chapter 17, Adam Tickell looks at what stimulates production in the first place by interrogating the notion of money. He shows how money, although footloose and highly mobile, has a very particular geography. A small number of world financial centres, which are the major source of investment capital, form a very tight core within the global finance industry. He then shows how this global situation is mirrored at the national level, where financial services tend, again, to be concentrated and how this in turn leads to increased social exclusion and highly unequal patterns of wealth and poverty.

By contrast, in Chapter 18 Jon Goss discusses the pervasive nature of consumption and seeks to understand the urge inside us all to consume particular products. He shows how this urge is the product of a desire to make ourselves distinctive – yet in the act of consuming we become just like millions of others. He goes on to discuss not the geographies *of* consumption, but the ways in which geography *is* consumed. By this he doesn't mean how you as students consume the discipline, but rather focuses on the ways in which spaces of consumption are increasingly based on a number of archetypal spatial settings, such as the festive marketplace.

Through the act of consumption we close one circuit of capital and help to contribute to the beginnings of the next one. But the chapters all show how this is not just an economic process, and is instead one that is rooted in key sets of social and cultural processes. The key question for geographers to explore is how these processes combine to produce and work through a whole host of very precise spatial settings. In this sense the economy only becomes realized in particular spaces. It never takes place in the abstract, but as indicated in Figure I.i, different sections of the circuit are constantly being played out to different degrees in different places. Yet as all the chapters explore, this is not a simple mapping of economic activities on to space – the spaces are themselves constitutive of the economies and are crucial to their success or failure.

FURTHER READING

Clark, G., Gertler, M. and Feldman, M. (2000) *The Oxford handbook of economic geography.* Oxford: Oxford University Press.

Sheppard, E. and Barnes, T. (2003) *A companion to economic geography.* Oxford: Blackwell.

Amongst several collections of economic geography books published recently, these are two of the best.

Peck, J., Barnes, T.J., Sheppard, E. and Tickell, A. (eds) (2003) *Reading economic geography.* Oxford: Blackwell.

Offers a companion collection of readings.

For the most up-to-date writings on economic geography you should scan recent editions of the journal *Economic Geography.* This will give you a sense of the current topics being pursued in this field.

CHAPTER 16
PRODUCTION

STORY ONE: OF CAPITAL, NETWORKS AND GLOBAL RELATIONS

" *We were in the same bed but had different dreams.* "

This cryptic remark[1] was made by a former executive of China International Capital Corporation Limited (CICC) – the first Chinese joint venture investment bank. CICC was established in 1995 by the state-owned China Construction Bank and, amongst others, Morgan Stanley – the US-based investment bank. It operates from its headquarters in Beijing and offices in Shanghai and Hong Kong and its core businesses include investment banking, and research and asset management.[2] The establishment of CICC as a joint venture between Chinese and US finance houses and the day-to-day contingencies of its work – highlighted in the comment quoted above – reveal a great deal about the contemporary geography of world development and production.

THE (TRANS)FORMATION OF NETWORKS OF PRODUCTION

The Chinese partner in this venture – the China Construction Bank – is also headquartered in Beijing and is one of the largest banks in the world.[3] It was founded in 1954 to manage the major infrastructural investments to be implemented under the first Chinese five-year national plan. Today, it combines retail operations from over 20,000 branches across China with its primary business focus on medium- and long-term lending to corporations, conducted primarily within major international financial centres.[4]

Morgan Stanley has its headquarters on New York's Broadway. The firm took its present form in 1997 after the merger of Morgan Stanley – which also began life in New York in 1935 – and Dean Witter, which opened its first office in San Francisco in 1924. Morgan Stanley currently employs over 50,000 people working on the production of investment banking services in more than 600 offices – including those in Beijing, Shanghai and Hong Kong – located within 27 countries throughout the world.[5]

Why should one of the world's leading investment banks establish a joint venture with a Chinese bank – even one as big as the China Construction Bank – and so extend an already complex global network of production still further? An obvious answer is the resurgence of Asia (including China, India and other parts of the region) as a major global producer. At the outset of the last millennium in 1000, Asia (excluding Japan) accounted for over two-thirds (67.6 per cent) of the value of total global production. By 1820, this share was still as high as 56.2 per cent, whilst that of the West (here defined as western Europe and its global off-shoots – the USA, Canada, Australia and New Zealand) had grown from less than one-tenth of the global total in 1000 to over a quarter in 1820. Then, despite the fact that between 1820 and 1998 the value of global production grew at an annual rate ten times that of the preceding 800 years, growth in Asia was scarcely half that of the West over the period.

Thus, whereas Asia's share of global production was only 15.5 per cent in 1950, that of the West was 56.9 per cent – almost the mirror image of the shares of these two regions in 1000. However, from 1950 onwards, Asia began to move back to its previous dominance. During the second half of the twentieth century, production in Asia grew at three times the rate of the West so that, by 2001, Asia accounted for over 31 per cent of global production compared with the 45.6 per cent located in the West. Over the same period, the share of Japan in global production had grown from 3 per cent to almost 8 per cent, whilst the shares of India and China grew from 4.2 per cent and 4.5 per cent to 12 per cent and 5 per cent respectively. In short, by 2001, India and China accounted for well over half the rapid growth in Asia's share of total world production, whilst Japan accounted for a further quarter.

These figures[6] point to major global shifts in the geography of production:[7] out of Asia from the early nineteenth century, followed by a return to Asia during the last century, and an acceleration of Asian growth into the third millennium.[8] Measured in terms of purchasing power parity,[9] China is now the second largest economy in the world after the USA. So it is hardly surprising that western investment banks – whose business includes the purchase and underwriting of new share offerings, their distribution in smaller parcels to investors, and advice to investors – should wish to extend their operations to the growth regions of Asia, and especially to China.[10] Neither is it accidental that such banks emerged as a response to the increasing complexity and dynamism of economic development in the West during the nineteenth and early twentieth centuries. Both Dean Witter and Morgan Stanley (in its original pre-merged form) were founded during the period of especially rapid economic growth that accompanied the emergence of the USA as the world's largest economy during the period between the two world wars.

As global companies, such banks are drawn to China because it is here that a major share of global economic growth will occur over the coming decades. If they are to maintain their global presence as financial producers, they have no choice but to extend their networks of production and to penetrate[11] the space of the Chinese economic geography. But this is also a tempting proposition, not least because of the expectation that the Chinese stock markets of Shanghai and Shenzhen will become increasingly attractive to the burgeoning domestic corporations in China within the next decade as regimes of corporate governance are improved and the *renminbi* becomes fully convertible. More immediately, a joint venture with a Chinese partner enables western banks greatly to extend the range of their financial services to both domestic and non-Chinese firms.[12]

Nevertheless, the involvement of these banks in China has been tortuous and complex. This is partly because of the extraordinary rates of growth in the Chinese economy during the past decade or so. But it is also because, if they are to engage with the economic geography of China, they have to cope with the social relations that shape Chinese economic practices and performances, which remain very different from those prevalent in the West. Foreign securities firms wishing to operate in China must do so as part of a joint venture and, even then, are not allowed to take more than a minority share (currently ranging from 33 per cent at the beginning of a venture to 49 per cent as it matures) of the joint company. Furthermore, foreign companies are banned from dealing in securities considered by the Chinese government to be economically strategic. And, even when joint ventures are established, they do not prevent the Chinese partner working with other, competitive, investment banks.

Economic geographies as social constructs

Circumstances like this help in understanding the significance of the quote at the head of this chapter. As a joint venture, CICC brings together Morgan Stanley and the Chinese Construction Bank: one privately owned and aggressively capitalist in its orientation and performance, the other state owned and with a history of involvement in national economic development; one located in a market-driven and financially dynamic centre like New York, the other emerging out of a bureaucratic process of economic planning; one with the experience of almost 80 years of the production of financial services in a highly competitive environment, the other scarcely 50 years old and isolated for many years from the competitive norms of capitalist financial markets; one used to operating within a culture of individualism, the other more attuned to collective endeavour with performance targets established elsewhere. Not surprisingly, then, the joint venture faced not just the problems of dealing in two languages and with a highly complex and dynamic economic geography but, even more profoundly, of coping with these quite different sets of social relations.

And this is fundamental, for economic geographies are **social constructions**. They do not arise automatically, nor are they merely physical or material sets of flows and transactions. They are shaped and directed by emergent but always contested sets of social relations. Social relations frame the shared or imposed understandings and values about the very nature, purpose and parameters of economic activity. They provide the interpretative context of economic life, so making sense of, legitimating and giving direction to it. They offer a framework of communication and evaluation (what is good/bad, better/worse, progress/regress) and so identify notions of normality and rationality. In effect, social relations are the social context in which people make their living and come to understand their relationship to the natural and social world, and they reflect relations of trust as well as of power, relations of control as well as of spontaneity. Above all, the social relations of economic life deny the possibility of the autonomous individual reacting mechanically and independently of external stimulae.[13] Thus the diversity

Social constructions

Relations, processes, practices, places, institutions created through conscious and unconscious action. Social constructions may, therefore, be both intended and unintended consequences of social behaviour and action. The critical point, however, is that social constructions are made by people in society and so may be transformed and re-made. This is a vital political possibility to which economic geographies are no exception.

of different sets of social relations represents one of the most significant sources of differentiation and of conflict (geopolitical as well as economic, secular as well as religious) in the contemporary world.

So it is hardly surprising that, in seeking to engage in economic performance across two very different sets of social relations, those involved face some profound difficulties.[14] They may be 'in the same bed' in the sense that they occupy the same place and seek to act jointly but the objectives, norms of practice and measures of performance they bring to the task – their dreams – are, initially at least, fundamentally different.

Geographies of production

This story illustrates a range of issues critical to the understanding of the performance of production (and economic life, more generally) and its geographies.

- *Production involves work – the intentional application of labour – in the creation (or, when undertaken in an inefficient fashion, the destruction) of value.* It therefore mobilizes a range of environmental relations but it is not limited merely to the creation of material goods. Value – which may be defined simply as things of worth – can take very different forms (e.g. processes, ideas, information, transactions . . .). For CICC, the production of value takes the form of the collection of data, the provision of knowledge and advice, and the raising of capital, all of which are value-full and, although none has a physical manifestation, all involve material transformations – not least, that of labour.
- *What is considered to be a value, to be of worth, is entirely dependent on the social context – on the social relations of economic life.* CICC produces value in the form of advice on extending capitalist social relations into, within and out of China. By contrast, the China Construction Bank was founded 50 years earlier in a very different China to oversee the management of over 150 infrastructural projects envisaged in the first national plan of China.
- Thus *production – and economic life more generally – are social processes shaped by prevailing* – but rarely uncontested and not necessarily locally derived – *social relations of value* which may be sustained or changed by conscious and unconscious action from near and far (Fig. 16.1). The formation of a joint venture between Chinese and American banks has the effect (intended and unintended) of moving China further in the direction of capitalist social relations. But the ruling Chinese Communist Party formulates regulations that have the intended effect of resisting, or at least restricting, that movement.
- Production is *subject to the norms of evaluation* (profitability in the case of capitalist economic geographies) *prevailing within these social relations.* The movement of capital and labour – but especially highly mobile capital – in response to geographies of profitability and risk exert a profound influence on the trajectory and geographies of production and development. Hence the continuing controls over foreign capital wishing to operate within China.
- The critical influence of social relations and norms of evaluation within

economic geographies raises a related question concerning the *social construction of the conditions in and through which production takes place.* 'You can't', a former Prime Minister of Britain was fond of remarking, 'buck the markets.'[15] The implications of this assertion are that economic geographies are somehow automatic and that market processes are mechanistic driving forces – beyond social control – of such geographies. And yet the very actions of Morgan Stanley and the China Construction Bank in setting up a joint venture precisely to shape the market for capital in China and the response of the Chinese state demonstrate that exactly the opposite is the case. So, far from being 'un-buckable', markets are social constructs purposefully shaped and regulated in various ways.

- Production has itself to be produced. The creation of a *geography* of production – here that of the joint venture involving highly articulated local and global geographies – is *an essential condition* of production. Thus the geography of production is *not merely an outcome* but *the means through which production takes place. It is a formative and determinant influence on the effectiveness of production.* CICC, for example, is headquartered in major financial centres in which it finds the conditions of existence it needs for effective production.
- This geography of production is highly complex. It involves 'a nexus of interconnected functions and operations by firms and non-firm institutions'[16] organized into *extended – even global – networks of value creation and transmission.* CICC, for example, is a bank based in China with several offices in widely dispersed locations and direct links to its partners elsewhere in the world.
- Such geographies are themselves – like all geographies – *space and path dependent.* They reflect the contours and temporal trajectories of past and existing geographies such as the uneven temporal and geographical development of regions like Asia. This spatial and path dependence of geographies of production may constrain future developments – but, as the changing geography of the world economy demonstrates, it certainly does not determine them.
- What is more, production itself is a dynamic process constantly changing in response to technological change and the demand for its products. *It is, therefore, very difficult to define 'industries' and to draw classificatory boundaries around them* as they flow into each other and are perpetually reshaped. Where the 'industry' of investment banking, information technology, financial research and dealing in securities begin and end is constantly changing and impossible to perceive.

These observations suggest that, in order to begin to understand production, we should reflect a little on the wider contexts and linkages – the networks and circuits of value – within and through which it takes place.

FIGURE 16.1
A Spanish post office acts as agent for the private German Deutsche Bank, Comillas, Cantabria, Spain. Photo © Roger Lee

Household production and reproduction
Household production is sometimes referred to as reproduction. However, to do so is to imply a distinction between production which is paid and that which is not. Yet both are forms of production. The latter is directed at the reproduction of the workforce and the ability of the household to consume, exchange and produce. As the figures show, household production is arguably far greater in size than production in the wider economy.

PRODUCTION AND CIRCUITS OF VALUE

Household production

No matter how revelatory it may be, one example cannot tell the whole story about production. A glaring omission from the account discussed above is one that is so often absent from stories of economic geographies of production. Most production takes place not in specialized spaces and places of paid and formal work – like global production networks – but in spaces of unpaid work, most notably the home.

Homes are the spaces within which the 'vast bulk of production in households'[17] takes place (Fig 16.2). Estimates – based on alternative assumptions of valuation – of the value of household production in the UK range from around 40 per cent to around 120 per cent of GDP. These figures are staggering. And yet the enormous quantitative contribution of domestic production remains largely unremunerated. Thus firms operating beyond the home are supported by a hidden subsidy of massive proportions, whilst 'much of what is presented in the national accounts as final consumption is in fact intermediate consumption by the household production industries'.[18]

FIGURE 16.2
Farm buildings, Asturias, Spain. Photo © Roger Lee

Economic diversity

The production and consumption of value, often based in and around the home, is necessary to reproduce the workforce and to enable its continued participation in production at work. However, the relationship between household production and paid labour is far from constant – varying from activity to activity, place to place (the ratio of paid to unpaid work in Denmark, for instance, is around 2:1, in the USA around 1:1 and in the Netherlands around 1:2) and from time to time in the same place. Household production thus points up the diversity of economic life, even in a globalizing world (see pages 238–9, below).

Gender

It also draws attention to the gendered nature of production. Despite the continuing convergence of the proportion of women and men in the paid labour force, it is women who remain primarily responsible for domestic production. Whilst the proportion of time spent in paid work by UK males is 15 per cent,[19] for women the equivalent figure is 9 per cent. By contrast, nearly a quarter (23 per cent) of the time of women is spent in unpaid, overwhelmingly domestic, work, whereas only 16 per cent of men's time is so spent. Thus, whilst work patterns are highly gendered, a form of quantitative equivalence exists: women in the UK spend 32 per cent of their time working in paid and domestic production whilst men spend 31 per cent of such time. Furthermore, the two sectors of production 'are as often substitutes as complements'.[20] The changing technology of domestic production may itself be a factor in the shift of certain forms of domestic work – like cleaning, for example – into the formal economy and the widespread growth of the paid female labour force. Given the rapidly growing (relative to men and in absolute terms) participation of women both in the formal economy and in non-passive activities outside it,[21] this gender-differentiated engagement in, and the shifting locus of, production are profound influences on the complex of changing relations between men and women in contemporary society.

Circuits of value

Economic geographies are not just about the *moments* of production, consumption and exchange in the sports grounds, offices, shops, households, factories, concert venues, art galleries, markets and all the other places in and through which they take place. Rather, they involve two forms of social struggle: (i) to construct sustainable *circuits* of value – through which the production, consumption (including the consumption of the productive value of means of production, for example, machines, communications networks, places and built environment of production) and exchange of values fundamental to the continuance of social life may be maintained across space and time – and (ii) to establish the social and environmental *relations* through which such circuits may be created, sustained and transformed[22] in location, scale, technology and sector.

Circuits of capital as circuits of value

The establishment of a specific and at least temporarily acceptable set of social relations of economic life sustainable across geographical space is an essential condition of existence for any circuit of value. As indicated above, social relations provide the bases for social communication and understanding by establishing norms of social action and indicators of progress and regress. Thus the form taken by a circuit of value and its objectives, meanings and purposes is defined and shaped by prevailing sets of social relations.

Within the contemporary world economic geography, the determinant – if not necessarily dominant and certainly not uncontested[23] – set of social relations are capitalist. The essential feature of **capitalism** is the separation of the ownership and control of capital (by capitalists) and labour power – the power to engage in productive work (by labour). Although such a representation of a binary divide between the two class positions of labour and capital is a gross over-simplification of contemporary capitalism, and much effort has been put into trying to reduce its ideological and political significance, the social relationships between capital and labour remain a critically powerful determinant of the trajectory of capitalist circuits of value and of the ways in which they work in practice.

As labour and capital are 'free' of each other under capitalist social relations, the only reason for advancing capital into the circuit is the prospect of **accumulation**. This involves the creation of surplus value through the production of **commodities** and the realization of this surplus in the form of a profit through their sale. The total amount of

Capitalism

an economic system in which the production and distribution of goods is organized around the profit motive (*see* CAPITAL ACCUMULATION) and characterized by marked inequalities in the social division of work and wealth between private owners of the materials and tools of production (capital) and those who work for them to make a living (labour) (*see* CLASS)

Capital accumulation

the prime goal of CAPITALISM as a MODE OF PRODUCTION. It involves the deployment of capital to convert it into new (and more) capital. This process is often designated by the simple formula MCM', where M is money or liquid capital, which is invested in C which is commodity capital (land, labour, machines) with a view to profit, realized as M' which is more money (or more technically 'expanded capital').

Commodity

something that can be bought and sold through the market. A commodity can be an object (a car, for example), but can also be a person (the car production worker who sells their labour for a wage) or an idea (the design or marketing concepts of the car). Those who live in capitalist societies are used to most things being commodities, though there are still taboos (the buying and selling of sexual intercourse or grandmothers, for example) (*see* CAPITALISM and COMMODIFICATION). This should not disguise the fact that the 'commodity state' is a very particular way of framing objects, people and ideas.

capital is, thereby, increased and may be re-advanced in its expanded form in a further circuit of value. The mutual 'freedom' of capital and labour creates highly competitive conditions. Each must seek the other out in competition with other units of capital and labour, and must combine within productive units (firms) at the highest possible level of productivity (the ratio of outputs to inputs in production) in order to sustain their competitive edge in selling the commodities produced.

Furthermore, the surplus value produced and realized through the sale of the commodities must be sufficiently high to enable firms to compete with others in attracting further capital investment. This means that capital must extract as large a quantity of surplus from the production process as possible. It may do this by constantly increasing productivity or, in an ultimately self-limiting fashion, by reducing the proportion of the surplus absorbed by labour in the form of wages. Thus the social relations of capitalism – the class relations between capital and labour – create inherently competitive and exploitative conditions in which the realization of a surplus and its extraction by capital are necessary features.

So, under capitalism, production, consumption and exchange are merely the means to the end of the production of a surplus – or profit – which can be accumulated by capital and then set in motion again in search of a further surplus. And the mutual freedom of labour and capital endows capital especially with great mobility in space and time. Geographies of capitalist circuits of value are, therefore, highly dynamic and expansionary. It is within this context of a mobile, dynamic and highly directed circuit of value that capitalist production takes place and geographies of production are constructed.

Production, circuits and social relations

- *Production is merely a moment* in circuits of value, which sustain networks of consumption, production and exchange across space and time.
- *Production takes place throughout these circuits* – most notably in the home where it is largely unpaid.
- Circuits of value are dependent upon *the establishment of social relations* – of communication, meaning and direction (including, for example, the diverse relations of household production), which guide participation in and understanding and evaluation of economic geographies – and of *sustainable environmental relations*.
- The particularly powerful and formative objectives and criteria brought to bear upon circuits of value by *capitalist social relations* are continuously resisted, replaced and supplemented by other, diverse sets of social relations, often practised by those who also engage in capitalist social relations.

GEOGRAPHIES OF PRODUCTION UNDER CAPITALISM

It is in and through spaces of production (see Fig I.i), including the home, that value is created or, more precisely, where value is transformed with the intention of its expansion. Material and mental inputs are combined within the labour process in ways that are directed at the enhancement of value by producing outputs, the value of which exceeds that of the inputs used to produce them. A haircut, for example, involves the productive combination of a place of production (the home, the street or a hairdressers, for example), the means of production (scissors, shampoo, water, electricity) and skilled labour brought together to produce the product: the haircut.

But that is far from the end of the story. The intention of the transaction is that the value of the haircut to the consumer (appearance, convenience, status) – its exchange value – should exceed the value of the inputs used up in the process of production and so generate a material surplus. This should also enhance the reputation of the haircutter – thereby increasing further the potential exchange value of her/his labour power – and, most importantly in terms of the evaluation of this productive activity, increase the value of capital embodied in the business. As argued above, the objectives of the capitalist production of value are its realization as profit and its accumulation as capital that may be used in further rounds of accumulation in the circuit of capital. The production (and consumption) of the haircut are simply the means to this end.

The production of production and of production networks

This does not imply that production itself is a simple or an incidental process. In order for production to take place and value to be created within capitalism, three sets of processes have to be set in motion.

1. Sources of finance and investment have to be identified and put in place. This is a highly selective and competitive, and hence regulative, process which is itself produced within spaces of financial hegemony (see Fig. I.i) in the circuit of capital.
2. A location – or, more normally, a set of interconnected locations – must be established and serviced in such a way that links with related sectors may be sustained, the **means and forces of production** (labour power, equipment and an appropriate built environment) may be established, assembled, combined and put to use in productive work, the most effectively to transform inputs into finished or semi-finished commodities in ways that produce value. The commodities produced must then be circulated to realize their (surplus) value.
3. These activities must be mobilized through the exercise of corporate power – not least that of the knowledge appropriate to the material (productivity), environmental (e.g. sustainability) and social (in capitalism, profitability) norms of the prevailing social relations of production.

Means of production

the resources that are indispensable for any form of production to occur. Typically this would include land, labour, machines, money capital, knowledge/information. In MARXIST thinking the means of production and labour power together constitute the 'forces of production'.

Transaction costs

the costs involved in engaging in transactions, normally between productive firms. Such costs (which normally do not include the costs of commodities being exchanged or the costs of transport between points of supply and points of demand) may be associated with factors like distance. Distance may serve to increase costs as delays or misinformation may be more common when transactions are taking place between partners located some way away from each other. By contrast, geographical and social proximity may help to reduce transaction costs.

Economies of scale are generated when the unit cost of output falls within a firm or a place with the increasing scale of output. Diseconomies occur when unit costs rise with increases in the level of output. Economies of scope exist when two or more activities can be carried out together within a single place, firm or unit of production more cheaply than if they were carried out separately. Diseconomies arise when it is cheaper to disintegrate the tasks to specialized production units, possibly in different locations.

Studies of production within economic geography have tended to focus on the second of these sets of processes, despite the fact that it can make little sense without the formative context of the first and the third. Thus economic geographies of production have tended to neglect the crucial importance of what Peter Dicken calls the 'production chain',[24] which he defines as 'a transactionally linked sequence of functions in which each stage adds value to the process of production of goods or services' and of 'production networks of inter-firm relationships'. These networks of production draw upon research and development and technology from within or outside the network to sustain the competitiveness of the production process, and on logistical services to circulate the values produced. And, in so doing, they incur **transaction costs**.

This draws attention to the interrelatedness and 'discontinuously territorial'[25] nature of production networks across and within geographical spaces. The networked production of commodities involves the bringing together, within or across territories, of diverse activities, materials and functions (hence the difficulty in defining 'industries', noted above) (see Chapter 40). Such networks link the different territories, or parts of territories, in which production takes place with others that may be far distant, and integrate them into specific trajectories of networks and production. A good example of this kind of geographical transformation is the process of outsourcing and its global variant, offshoring.[26] This involves the relocation of some or all of the production facilities in a firm, thereby creating new or extended geographies of production networks judged to be more profitable than the old.

The 'dramatic transformation' in the apparel sector of east central Europe during the 1990s is a case in point. It reflects the changing contractual strategies of 'EU-based retailers and buyers as they balance competing locational opportunities in the global economy within a context of intensive competition in domestic markets'.[27] The opportunity to extend supply chains and so reduce costs gives them significant competitive advantage. Thus the production networks of the European apparel sector have been *buyer driven* – the retailers have played the pivotal role – rather than *producer driven* – whereby the producers of value (like Morgan Stanley, for example, in finance) seek to transform production networks.[28] But they have also been shaped by the legacies of state socialist production capacities and skills in the region, not least a feminized and relatively skilled but low-wage labour force.[29]

Thus geographical patterns of economic development are shaped increasingly by the intersection (or what Neil Coe *et al.*[30] call 'strategic coupling') between non-territorial, globally dispersed and networked circuits of value, and local (city, regional, national and international spaces) territorial assets and conditions.[31] Whilst the economic development of places is dependent upon such strategic couplings, local circumstances condition production networks, as was illustrated by the case of CICC. Furthermore, production networks are often constituted of geographical concentrations of activity, often in marked localized clusters[32] sustained by **economies of scale and scope** (Fig. 16.3). Such clusters may be linked to each other and to outlying, less well-integrated places of production by flows of material (e.g. labour power, commodities, capital) and immaterial values.[33]

The evaluation and regulation of production and production networks

FIGURE 16.3
Private greengrocery stall set up in public space in the former Jewish ghetto of Podgorze, Kracòw, Poland. Photo © Roger Lee

The governance of circuits of value and networks of production involves their direction, co-ordination, **regulation** and, above all, evaluation against the norms of the social relations through which they take place. In **neo-liberal** versions of capitalism, the market and networks of firms dominate this process, whilst states withdraw as far as politically possible. However, the state – at local, national and international levels – remains indispensable to the production and circulation of value. States establish macro-economic conditions of, for example, monetary, fiscal and other economic policies. And in sustaining appropriate legal arrangements for capitalist reproduction, socializing the provision of certain forms of infrastructure and of the basic means of subsistence in the highly competitive environment of capitalism, and engaging in the geo-strategic use of the means of violence, they enhance and protect capitalist interests.

With the withdrawal of the state from a more interventionist role in the conduct of circuits of value, financial firms (like CICC) operating in and through financial markets have become increasingly important arbiters and directors – evaluators – of economic geographic performance and direction. The significance of financial markets and firms for the evaluation and regulation of circuits of value stems from their control over financial capital – the ability to advance or withdraw capital to particular activities and locations – and their hegemonic indifference to the particular location or type of economic activity affected by their decisions and actions. Thus they can affect the trajectory of whole networks of production and of uneven geographies of economic development. Hence, for example, the tight controls exerted by the Chinese state over the freedom of action of CICC in China.

Such evaluations have themselves to be produced.[34] Information is collected and processed by 'experts' (some would say 'believers' in a particular form of financial understanding), such as financial analysts, specialized in particular fields of reproduction (like oil production, for example, or grocery retailing) working in financial institutions. These firms both invest their own capital as profitably as possible and sell their expertise at a profit to other investors. Using their 'expert' knowledge (or belief), analysts look back across earlier rounds of accumulation to assess, amongst other things, the effectiveness of different locations, organizations and sectors of production against the goal of expected profitability. At the same time, they look forward to assess the risks and potential profitability of future rounds of accumulation. On the basis of such assessments, capital may be switched into certain spaces of production, withdrawn from them or withheld and invested in other

Regulation

the arrangement of an economy into more or less cohesive forms of production, consumption, monetary circulation and SOCIAL REPRODUCTION. Derived initially from a disparate group of French political-economists (*see* POLITICAL-ECONOMY) a 'regulationist approach' therefore attends to the different ways of socially, politically and culturally organizing economic activity, especially capitalist economic activity (*see* CAPITALISM). These different ways of regulating capitalist economies are identified both historically and geographically (*see also* FORDISM and POST-FORDISM).

Neo-liberalism, neo-liberal

pertaining to an economic doctrine that favours free markets, the deregulation of national economies, decentralization and the privatization of previously state-owned enterprises (e.g. education, health). A doctrine that, in practice, favours the interests of the powerful (e.g. TRANSNATIONAL CORPORATIONS) against the less powerful (e.g. peasants) within societies.

activities that may enable more profitable surplus extraction and optimize the relationship between risk and profitability.

Such work requires access to large amounts of (often up-to-the-second) data from around the world, and the ability and techniques to translate these data into meaningful information and to assess their significance. It is hardly surprising, then, that the geographies of evaluative production take place within spaces of hegemony (see Fig. I.i), located predominantly in highly localized clusters of financial activities within global financial centres such as London, New York and Tokyo, and within centres like Paris, Melbourne and Hong Kong with a more restricted geographical reach. It is in such centres that the data and highly specialized skills (and beliefs) needed for evaluations of the circuit are readily available. But that alone would not be a sufficient reason for localization of financial markets and production, as the wide and relatively cheap availability of information technology, that can disseminate information quickly and easily across geographical space in real time, creates the potential for the geographical decentralization of such activities. If they are to be useful, data have to be converted to information and information must be assessed. These requirements necessitate contact with other believers or knowledgeable others within and beyond the workplace. The value of face-to-face communication and access to the multifarious uses and users of information facilitate its evaluation and so promote the clustering of the productive activities engaged in this task.

If financial capitals operating within spaces of financial hegemony are able to influence the trajectory of multiple locations and circuits of value, the regulatory reach of those firms directly engaged in these networks extends primarily to the internal structure and dynamics of the network itself. And this is a highly complex task. Production is merely a moment – a complex, messy, dramatic, depressing and uplifting moment, but a moment nevertheless – in the lengthier and wider circuits of value. Individual capitals must organize and dynamize their activities in as effective (profitable) a way as possible. Thus firms are not only legal entities but the framework within which capital can operate, disperse its means of production across geographical space, hire and fire labour, store surplus capital and administer the complex processes of production. Above all, perhaps, firms are the major entities through which capital engages in competition. But at the same time, they operate within rationalities bounded by their own cultures and the imagination that they are able to bring to bear upon the formulation of strategy in the face of changed conditions of competition.[35] All firms are embedded in (i.e. their actions are contingent upon)[36] particular networks of production, particular sets of social relations, patterns and levels of cognition and particular territories with more, or less, distinctive legal and political institutions and cultures.

It is the embeddedness of firms and production networks that lies behind the power of geography to shape and drive production.[37] The *spatiality* – or spatial constitution – of production and production networks reflects the multiple scales of geographical organization and linkages that enable production to take place. And that is the point. Production *takes place*: 'every component in the production network – every firm, every economic function – is, quite literally, grounded in specific locations' (Fig. 16.3).[38]

This grounding involves not only the built environment – the kitchens, stadia, cinemas, factories, shops, restaurants, offices – in and through which production takes place, but the relationships with other firms, near and far and, as indicated above, the local social relations, institutions, practices and norms that shape the understanding and performance of economic activity in particular places (Fig. 16.4). Especially important in this regard – even within neo-liberal circuits of value – are the multiple scales of state (local, national, international) and quasi-state institutions (from the local to the global) that play a geographically and temporally uneven interventionist role in shaping the various elements of production and economic activity.

Against this complex and constantly changing background, firms must organize the production and circulation of value in ways that generate competitive advantage. The effectiveness of the organizational dynamics of firms in this regard is judged and evaluated within the spaces of hegemony (see Fig I.i). The evaluations made of their performance will then inform the decisions of financial capital in shaping future circuits of value and future geographies of production that reflect a range of formative circumstances.

FIGURE 16.4
Signposts to vineyards near Greve-in-Chianti, Italy. Photo © Roger Lee

Production spaces and development

- Production *creates value* through the consumption and *transformation of values* embodied in other goods (e.g. labour power, books, machines, knowledge, raw materials, finance).
- It involves *prior investment*, a *location* in which it may be organized and take place, and from which its products may be distributed, and the *exercise of corporate power* to articulate all of these processes.
- Production *takes place in and through networks of production* grounded in and across places.
- These complex processes are *evaluated, regulated and integrated within spaces of hegemony*.
- *Economic development in places* is closely influenced by their present, past and potential role as locations for the networks of production and circuits of value, whilst these locations, in turn, shape the functioning of the networks and circuits, and the processes of the production and circulation of value that take place within them.

STORY TWO: OF VALUE, NETWORKS AND THE DIVERSITY OF PRODUCTION

Between 1990 and 1996, during a period of intense transition from state socialism to capitalism, over 19 million jobs were lost in east central Europe (ECE).[39] This represents a fall in the number of jobs of no less than 14 per cent – or 2 per cent per annum over the seven years. In other words, more than one person in seven employed – and so connected to circuits of value – in 1990 was disconnected from such circuits during the period. The experience of this unemployment was geographically uneven and highly, but differentially, gendered across the region. However, even where officially recorded unemployment grew far less – as, for example, in the former Soviet Union – the downward pressure on wages exerted by economic decline in effect marginalized millions of workers and attenuated their links with emergent capitalist circuits of value. And for many – especially the elderly – long-term unemployment marked a possible final break with employment in the formal economy.

But human survival depends on being able to create, sustain and remain linked to circuits of value (Fig. 16.5). The response in many parts of ECE was the maintenance, re-creation and extension of non-capitalist circuits of value – notably of household food production, exchange and consumption – with their own distinctive and often locally extended geographies. In Bulgaria, for example, 45 per cent of respondents to the World Bank's Bulgarian Integrated Household Survey in 1995 'received some kind of cash or in-kind income from activity other than that derived from their place of work'. Some 30 per cent were engaged in some form of agricultural production and 10 per cent in a formally registered business other than their main job.

FIGURE 16.5
Producers awaiting hoped-for exchange and consumption, Xian, China. Photo © Lesley Lee

Furthermore, this production by households is differentially commodified. Work-rich households (head and spouse, or head of single-person households, employed) accounting for half of all households in 1995 and those households with one partner formally employed, were involved in formal market sales, whereas work-poor households (accounting for one-fifth of households) were more involved in individual or other forms of exchange. But at the same time – and reflecting the dominance of state-owned industry – over three-quarters of respondents were in the same job they had occupied in 1989. In other words, diverse sets of class positionalities are identifiable that place individuals in differentiated locations in relation to the appropriation and distribution of the various forms of surplus being produced within circuits of value.

Clearly, despite the apparent power of financial markets to shape production to narrowly defined ends, production is highly diverse.

And this diversity is not merely a response to austerity or the breakdown of established circuits of value. In Slovakia, as elsewhere in ECE and the world economy more generally, large but geographically uneven proportions of households engage in production outside the market economy. Furthermore, their reasons for doing so are not reducible merely to the material sustenance of circuits of value. Thus, agricultural production for self-provisioning, or the reciprocal provisioning of family and friends, for example, is undertaken partly because it is a traditional activity that, in terms of the time and labour involved, may be highly inefficient but enables access to better-quality, often organic, food; partly because it sustains long-held identities, local circuits of value and culinary practices; and partly because it is a physically demanding hobby undertaken primarily by women. In addition, it enables increased access for non-food commodities in the market economy, and links producers in reciprocal and mutually supportive ways with each other.

These examples point to the socially and culturally complex nature of the 'economy' and production. Circuits of value involve far more than the purely instrumental processes of consumption, exchange and production, but also connect with deep-seated cultural and social relations that shape and form the practices of circuits of value. All sorts of alternatives are, therefore, always possible. Hardly surprising, then, that the regulatory mechanisms implemented by financial markets and states are directed so closely at maintaining an economic conformity.

CONCLUSION

Production is a complex but intensely practical process directed above all at the production of values and thereby at the sustenance of circuits of value. But the nature of 'value' or 'worth' is defined by the social relations in and through which production operates, whilst engagement in production is subject to multiple determinations. Within capitalist societies, value is defined in terms of profitability whilst production is subject to evaluations of profitability or potential profitability made by financial analysts working in financial markets. These evaluations have both a direct and indirect influence over the geographical trajectories of highly mobile capital actually or potentially invested in production and the places through which production takes place.

A vigorous creator of landscapes, production is capable both of transforming the nature and levels of development, appearance and ways of life of those places and people caught up within it, and of enhancing or restricting the effectiveness of present and future production. Equally, the switching of capital away from certain landscapes of production and towards others is capable of wreaking enormous damage on these same people and places judged/valued as irrelevant to the continued profitable circulation of capital. Production can, simultaneously, endow and strip away identity through its capacity to integrate individuals and places within, or to disengage them from, networks of relations of production

FIGURE 16.6
A flower-seller outside the gates of the cemetery, Nowa Huta, Kraców, Poland with the Huta im. Sendzimira (the former Huta im. Lenina) steelworks in the background. Photo © Roger Lee

Alienation

a term with two interrelated meanings, the second being a more specific formulation of the first. First, then, alienation refers to a sense of estrangement or lack of power felt by people living in the MODERN world. In this respect it is often used to describe the experience of modern urban living, in which traditional forms of social cohesion and belonging supposedly break down. Second, and drawn from MARXIST social thought, alienation refers more particularly to the separation of labour from the MEANS OF PRODUCTION under CAPITALISM. To explain, since under capitalism it is capitalists who own the resources required for economic production (land, machinery, money, etc.) workers have no control over their productive lives: how production is organized, what is produced, what the product is used for and how they relate to other workers. They are therefore alienated from their work and its products.

whilst demanding – more, or less, insistently – conformity with corporate objectives (Fig. 16.6).

At a global level, the two-thirds or so of the world's population left outside effective circuits of value are – in the face of separation from such circuits and of social conflict and illegal and violent networks of production – often too weary trying to sustain life to mount serious resistance. Within the global North, the absence of production, or of access to production, for a substantial and growing minority of unemployed people – young and old men rather more than women in many western societies – often congregated together in particular localities and separated from effective circuits of value, is increasingly recognized as a major social problem. It engenders material deprivation and feeds a sense of **alienation** and disconnectedness in which social norms are seen both as personally irrelevant and as the cause of the plight of the unemployed. Such exclusionary tendencies of the multi-scalar geographical selectivity of production are not unconnected with the widespread and increasingly violent but, dreadfully enough, not unreasonable repudiation of secular norms and the rejection of democratic participation.

However, in those societies whose identity and history has not been completely obliterated by the demands of, or neglect by, contemporary global capitalist production, circuits of value and processes of production may be established on the basis of relations of production and exchange outside the formal, and often dominant, economy. And here the complex, profound, social and environmental influences of production and its involvement in the shaping of identities may be re-imagined.

DISCUSSION POINTS

1. Think of any economic activity in which you are engaged. Identify the material and the social aspects of it, and consider how the social and material are related.

2. In what diverse ways are you, your family and your friends connected to circuits of value?

3. Identify the ways in which the class positions of capital and labour have been modified in recent years. Think, for example, of the ways in which share ownership has been diversified.

4. Look for evidence of how production in your home area or your area of study is shaped by both local and non-local (including global) influences.

5. What criteria do you use to value things that are of value to you? Why is it that monetary measures are often used to quantify such values?

6. In what ways does the financial system evaluate you as a financial actor? Why are these evaluations made?

7. The clustering of production is a marked feature of the contemporary economic landscape. Clustering is said to be sustained by economics of scale and scope, but what kinds of socio-geographic interactions make those economies work in practice?

8. What kinds of work do you enjoy – and why – and what do you find less pleasant? Can answers to these questions be used to design the organization of productive work in circuits of value more generally?

9. Look through some recent issues of the financial media (e.g. *Financial Times*, *Wall Street Journal*, *The Economist*, *Business Week*) to compile further stories of the (trans)formation of geographies of production.

NOTES

1. Reported in the *Financial Times*, 10 December 2003, 14.

2. http://www.cicc.com.cn/english/about/, accessed 6 September 2004.

3. In terms of tier one capital assets (a measure of size of capital assets based on capital that may be accessed at short notice) the China Construction Bank was ranked 21st in the world's largest 1000 banks in the annual survey produced by *The Banker* (July 2004).

4. http://www.ccb.cn/portal/en/home/index.jsp, accessed 6 September 2004.

5. http://www.morganstanley.com/, accessed 6 September 2004.

6. Calculated from data in Maddison (2001; 2003).

7. However, this does not make the world a more equal place – quite the reverse. By 2004 income per head in the world's richest economy (the USA) was over 100 times greater than that in the world's poorest (the Dominican Republic). Whilst the ranking of countries has shifted repeatedly over the period, this ratio of inequality has been growing dramatically since the 1820s, during which period the world's economy has grown at unprecedented rates (see Lee, 2002).

8. For a fuller and far more detailed account see Dicken (2003: especially Chapter 3).

9. This is a measure of the value of production that takes account of the purchasing power of local currencies for the same range of commodities.

10. See, for example, Guerrera (2003).

11. The phallocentric language is intentional here. See Gibson-Graham (1996).

12. China accounted for over 9 per cent of global inflows of foreign direct investment in 2003.

13. For a discussion of the essential sociability of humankind and its central significance for economic geography, see Lee (1989).

14. 'We fight a little war everyday' is how Gian Maurizio Rodella, a senior manager at Naveco – a bus and truck joint venture between Fiat and the state-owned Nanjing Auto Group – describes relations between the partners (Marsh, 2004).

15. A quote attributed to Margaret Thatcher when challenging the way in which Nigel Lawson – her Chancellor of the Exchequer – was setting out to try to manage the exchange rate of the pound in 1989. Following neo-liberal discourses of economics, Thatcher insisted not only that economies were somehow naturally driven by markets but that they, in turn, were inevitable and natural and so beyond social construction and control thereby making (state) intervention not only pointless but harmful.

16. Coe *et al.* (2004); see also Smith *et al.* (2002).

17. Murgatroyd and Neuburger (1997: 63).

18. Murgatroyd and Neuburger (1997: 64).

19. This and the figures that follow refer to *all* males and females aged 16 and over.

20. Murgatroyd and Neuburger (1997: 64).

21. Lee (2000).

22. These ideas are explored by Lee (2002).

23. See, for example, Gibson-Graham (1996).

24. Dicken (2003: 14–17).

25. Dicken (2003: 21); see Storper and Walker (1989) for a discussion of the territorial organization of production.

26. See, for example, the accounts in the *Financial Times* (21 September 2004: 19) and Special Report on central and eastern Europe (21 September 2004: 4).

27. Begg *et al.* (2003: 2191, 2205); more generally, see the series of articles on the transformations of the global textile and clothing industries *Financial Times* (19–23 July 2004).

28. See Gereffi (1994).

29. See Begg *et al.* (2003, op. cit.).

30. Coe *et al.* (2004).

31. See Chapter 13 of this volume, on development.

32. For example, clustering to take advantage of economies of knowledge, creation, dissemination and use in the production of financial services in financial centres like New York, Tokyo and, especially, London, or of industrial production – like the case of 'motor sport valley' in the UK (Henry and Pinch, 2000).

33. Adrian Smith (2003) demonstrates the geographical and economic complexities involved in the creation and transformation of multi-scalar production networks. More generally, see Dicken (2003); Bryson *et al.* (1999: Part 3: 'Spaces of production',

34. Production takes place within spaces of financial hegemony as well as within spaces of production. Although it is convenient to distinguish spaces of production within the circuit of capital, the production of value is central to the functioning spaces of financial hegemony and realization as well as within spaces of production. Production of value within spaces of financial hegemony takes the form primarily of financial services and financial instruments; within spaces of realization, it takes the form of trade, retail and logistical services.

35. Schoenberger (1997).

36. Zukin and DiMaggio (1990).

37. However, the precise degree of influence of this embeddedness is itself contingent and presents a tricky empirical question. See, for example, Rutherford (2004).

38. Dicken (2003: op. cit., 20).

39. These accounts and data are drawn from Smith, A. (2000; 2002).

FURTHER READING

Dicken, P. (2003) *Global shift* **(4th edn). London: Sage Publications.**

Contemporary tendencies towards the globalization of networks of production are explored both theoretically and empirically and in a wide range of case studies in this classic account of the subject.

Hudson, R. (2001) *Producing places.* **New York: Guilford Press.**

Hudson, R. (2004) Conceptualising economies and their geographies: spaces, flows and circuits. *Progress in Human Geography*, **28(4), 447–71.**

A detailed examination of production and the places in and through which it takes place, and of geographies of circuits of value, is offered by these texts.

Bryson, J. *et al.* **(eds) (1999)** *The economic geography reader.* **Chichester: Wiley, Part 3.**

Provides a range of examples of different forms and sectors of production.

Stroper, M. and Walker, R. (1989) *The capitalist imperative: territory, technology and industrial growth.* **New York and Oxford: Blackwell.**

Explores the dynamics of production and shows how production shapes and disrupts social life and how, therefore, society is constituted geographically.

Hayter, T. and Harvey, D. (eds) (1993) *The factory and the city: the story of Cowley automobile workers in Oxford.* **London and New York: Mansell.**

Offers an insight into the significance of production in sustaining circuits of value and giving identity to localities and into the struggles involved in trying to establish and sustain alternative bases of decision-making to those founded merely in concepts of corporate rationality in the face of industrial restructuring are explored in diverse ways by the essays.

Leyshon, A., Lee, R. and Williams, C. (2003) *Alternative economic spaces.* **London: Sage.**

Explores alternative circuits of value and illustrates them through a series of wide-ranging examples.

CHAPTER 17
MONEY AND FINANCE

Adam Tickell

INTRODUCTION

FIGURE 17.1
KLF Poster. Source:
http://jumper.mcc.ac.uk/~ttl/klf/images/
kfposter.jpg

At the end of August 1994, police on the remote Scottish island of Jura were called out by a local fisherman who had discovered the charred remains of numerous £50 notes on the seashore. Shortly afterwards, the *Observer* newspaper reported that the K Foundation had unceremoniously burnt £1 million as part of their campaign of 'art terrorism' (see Fig. 17.1). Previously the Foundation, which was made up of the two members of the band The KLF, had planned an exhibition called 'A major body of cash', which would consist of £1 million hammered into a frame. As news of the K Foundation's actions on Jura seeped out, it was met with disbelief, bewilderment and anger. Burning such a large amount of money is in many ways incomprehensible. Even if the destroyers had no need for the money themselves, surely they could have found some constructive use for it. The poor are, after all, always with us.

And yet it was in many senses a creative destruction. The act of burning £1 million forces us to think about money. As Bill Drumond, one of the K Foundation, said in a rare interview, 'We created something there. That thing there now exists. The fact that one million pounds exists in the mind ... it'll gnaw away at you' (Brook and Gimpo, 1997: 12). Perhaps, compared to the billions that are spent on developing mechanisms to kill people more effectively or manipulating our tastes and preferences, the symbolic burning was money well spent. Perhaps. But whatever we think of it, it does remind us that although money has become fundamental to modern life, and it is worth remembering that the extent of this is both a recent development and not yet globally pervasive, few of us stop to think about what money actually is.

In some respects, the K Foundation's activities remind us that money is more than simply dollars, pounds, yen and euros, notes and coins, cheques and credit card slips, and digits on a screen whizzing around the world at the click of a financier's mouse. It is a special commodity that obscures the nature of production. When the Roman emperor Vespasian, who built the Coliseum, introduced a tax on the contents of the city's urinals his son, Titus, objected. Vespasian simply replied, 'Money does not smell.' In much the same way, today money hides the social and geographical processes that have gone into getting something on to a supermarket's shelves. Take an everyday item like chocolate, for example. The production of chocolate typically involves extraordinary levels of exploitation of West African cocoa workers; subsidies for European and North American sugar producers; the use of pesticides and insecticides on plants and hormones to stimulate overproduction of milk in cows; the wasteful use of energy to bring the beans to processing centres; low wages for shop workers, and so on. Yet none of this is important when we buy chocolate – all that we need is the right amount of money and the entire production process from raw materials to finished product is both mobilized for – and hidden from – us. Money is able to achieve this because it is a *store of value*, we exchange things for money because it allows us to buy other things with it later.[1]

In theory, money is not really geographical. Unlike most other products, and whilst inflation and currency fluctuations do affect its 'value', money neither rots nor rusts: a pound is the same in Aberdeen as in London, whilst a dollar is the same in San Francisco, New York and Bogotá. Furthermore, in the past 30 years or so, connections between financial markets in different countries have become far deeper, as governments have increasingly pursued 'liberal' economic policies and deregulated financial markets at the same time as technological advances in the telecommunications industry have facilitated global trading. These developments have led some commentators to believe that money no longer 'respects borders' and that the whole financial industry will cease to be a geographically variable one. In a highly influential book, for example, Richard O'Brien (1992: 1–2) claimed that the

> *end of geography, as a concept applied to international financial relationships, refers to a state of economic development where geographical location no longer matters in finance, or much less than hitherto. In this state, financial market regulators no longer hold full sway over their regulatory territory . . . For financial firms, this means that the choice of geographical location can be greatly widened, provided that an appropriate investment in information and computer systems can be made . . .*
>
> *There will be forces seeking to maintain geographical control . . . Yet, as markets and rules become integrated, the relevance of geography and the need to base decisions on geography will alter and often diminish.*

However, this chapter shows that finance has not reached an 'end of geography' state. Not only is finance an industry with a very particular geography, but it has marked geographic impacts. In this chapter I focus on the continued importance of international centres for the financial industry and on the ways in which geographical restructuring of the financial industry unwittingly contributes to the decline of inner cities.

THE GEOGRAPHY OF INTERNATIONAL FINANCE

With its intangible inputs and heavy reliance upon the 'liberating' telecommunications technologies, the financial industry should be free of the traditional constraints of location. Paradoxically, however, finance is highly spatially concentrated within a small number of international financial centres, and prominent amongst these are London, New York and Tokyo, which form the core of the international financial system. The overwhelming majority of international financial transactions take place in these cities and in secondary centres such as Singapore, Chicago and Frankfurt. In 1993, for example, there were 342 foreign banks in New York, 312 in London and 97 in Tokyo; the three cities accounted for over 40 per cent of international bank lending and headquartered 23 out of the 25 largest securities firms, although during the 1990s the number of overseas banks actually fell by 20 per cent (Choi *et al.*, 2003). International financial centres are able to maintain their dominance because their very size has become self-reinforcing. Part of the reason for this is that globally integrated financial markets, which are effectively open 24 hours a day, require a physical location in which to operate and are, according to Saskia Sassen (1990), co-ordinating centres which ensure that the markets retain an overall coherence (Meyer, 2003; Taylor, 2003; 2004). The historical and economic strengths of London, New York, Chicago and Tokyo gave the cities an initial competitive advantage in becoming the 'regional representatives' of the international financial system, whilst their continued strength rests in part because they are located in different time zones that allow round-the-clock trading. On the London Stock Exchange, for example, the trading of foreign equities has dwarfed trading in domestic stocks for some time.

However, it is not simply that international financial centres are conveniently located that explains their continued dominance. Within Europe, the authorities in Paris and Frankfurt are – with little success – continually attempting to grow their financial service infrastructure at the expense of London, whilst similar processes are under way – with more success – in Asia, as Singapore and Hong Kong position themselves as major participants in the international financial system (Choi *et al.*, 2003). Yet finance remains highly concentrated in a relatively small number of financial centres because the very nature of the industry positively promotes geographical concentration (Taylor, 2004). Economically, financial centres benefit from 'agglomeration' in terms of financial 'liquidity', technology and labour: simply the fact of having a large financial market attracts buyers and sellers of financial products (because they are likely to be able to easily sell and buy); the size of the client base means established centres such as London and New York have been at the cutting edge of innovation in information and telecommunication technologies; whilst large centres typically develop a pool of highly skilled – and highly paid – workers, which helps to draw in new financial institutions requiring skilled workers. Furthermore, an increasing number of banks in a financial centre not only increases the number of competitors for business, it also increases the total size of the market.

Less tangible factors also help to explain why technological change is unlikely to lead to the end of geography in international finance. Lenders of money want to be able to have access to their money quickly if they need it and large, established financial markets theoretically provide this. However, as Nigel Thrift (1994) has demonstrated, large markets are often made up of networks of smaller markets where prices can change quickly on unreliable information. Rather than undermining larger markets, however, this volatility underpins them, because social networks allow traders to interpret market movements reliably (see Fig. 17.2). In this sense, firms need to be 'sociable', because 'who you know' helps develop business relationships and profits, and developing relationships is easier if people are physically close to one another. Furthermore, as the financial sector grows larger and more complex, financial centres become more important as proving grounds for new products and as centres of trust (Abolafia, 1996; Clark *et al.*, 2004; Zaloom, 2003).

The development of integrated global financial markets has speeded up a tendency towards the 'flattening' of financial space, where time horizons have shortened and geographical distance has become less important in determining the price of goods. Although this process has been under way since at least the nineteenth century, the development of new financial products in the global markets means that although buyers and sellers 'may be very distant from one another in geographical space, the time–space distance between them may be negligible' (Leyshon, 1996: 70; Swyngedouw, 2000). One of the most significant developments

FIGURE 17.2
Crowded trading room in Chicago.
Credit: Scott Olson/Getty Images

has been the growth of 'derivative' financial products. Derivatives were developed in order to let companies manage risk and volatility in financial markets. The most common are 'futures' and 'swaps', and these essentially allow firms to know what rate of exchange or interest they will be paying at a given date in the future, in much the same way as individuals borrow money at fixed rates in order to be sure that they will not be subject to interest rate rises on loans.

Since the early 1970s, and particularly during the closing two decades of the twentieth century, the use of derivatives mushroomed and derivatives have become a ubiquitous feature of business life. As Table 17.1 shows, the value of derivatives contracts outstanding on organized exchanges (which are closely regulated) appears to grow exponentially. Furthermore, the staggering value of outstanding 'options' contracts is

Table 17.1 Market for selected financial derivatives (US$ billions)

	1986	1988	1990	1992	1994	1996	1998	2000	2002	2004
Futures	394	935	1541	3019	5976	6212	8355	8354	10328	19744
Options	8570	9322	22403	33055	14262	12986	18352	17074	50057	84139

Source: BIS (2004) 'BIS Quarterly Review: International Banking and Financial Market Developments'. Bank for International Settlements, Basel (http://www.bis.org/publ/quarterly.htm)

dwarfed by 'over-the-counter' derivatives deals (which in July 2004 had an outstanding value of $197,167 *billion*). However, although cautious use of derivatives allows firms to manage risk, they have also been implicated in a series of high-profile losses. Striking examples being the collapse of Barings Bank in 1995 when a trader in Singapore used derivatives, to disastrous effect, to back up his belief that the Japanese stock markets would stay relatively stable when, in fact, they fell rapidly, leading Barings to lose £900 million and its independence, and the collapse of Long Term Capital Management, a firm that had been set up by Nobel Prize-winning economists, which led central banks to launch a $3.5 billion rescue in order to prevent the global financial system from collapsing (de Goede, 2001; MacKenzie, 2000). The Barings crisis is particularly instructive about the changes that have occurred in the international financial system during the past century. In 1890, Barings had previously got into severe financial problems after lending in Argentina went sour, but the leisurely pace of life then meant that the crisis took years to come to a head, allowing the Bank of England to organize a rescue. The 1995 crisis took just days to blow up and once the Bank of England became aware of the problems it had less than 24 hours to act.

Tragic though the failures of institutions like Barings are for the people involved, a wider concern about the internationalization of financial markets and the development of new financial products is that they may have the potential to increase the levels of a widespread collapse of global financial markets. If a large financial institution suffered major losses using derivatives, the highly interconnected nature of firms and markets could result in losses being transmitted throughout the world. Furthermore, during the 1990s it became clear that two further factors increased risk in the international financial system. First, there was the emergence of large conglomerates with highly complex financial and corporate structures (one of the contributory factors in the collapse of Barings, for example, was the complex nature of the bank's corporate structure). Second, an increasing share of international financial transactions is dominated by a small number of institutions from a small number of countries. If one of these got into difficulty the contagion effect would be more serious than in a less concentrated market, whilst at the same time putting pressure on smaller companies to cut corners in order to develop their market share. For these reasons, the International Monetary Fund (IMF), the world's major central banks, and the Bank for International Settlements have increased their surveillance of the financial system and agreed a set of minimum regulatory standards.

Globalization

the economic, political, social and cultural processes whereby: (a) places across the globe are increasingly interconnected; (b) social relations and economic transactions increasingly occur at the intercontinental scale (*see* TRANSNATIONAL); and (c) the globe itself comes to be a recognizable geographical entity. As such, globalization does not mean everywhere in the world becomes the same. Nor is it an entirely even process; different places are differently connected into the world and view that world from different perspectives. Globalization has been occurring for several hundred years, but in the contemporary world the scale and extent of social, political and economic interpenetration appears to be qualitatively different to international networks in the past.

SUMMARY

- There has been a **globalization** of financial markets.
- Global markets are concentrated in a small number of major financial centres.
- The globalization of financial markets has contributed to higher levels of risk in the international financial system.

NATIONAL GEOGRAPHIES OF FINANCE

If financial services have internationalized over the past two decades, during the past two centuries, financial systems *within* capitalist countries have evolved from localized to being increasingly centralized. From an early stage this was particularly noticeable in the United Kingdom, whose governments have been happy to adopt a *laissez-faire* approach to business decisions, particularly in the financial sector. The nineteenth and early twentieth century saw the gradual erosion of regional financial systems that had developed their own banks and stock exchanges, as financial institutions merged with rivals based in London. This process left Britain with one of the most highly concentrated financial systems in the capitalist world – concentrated in terms of geography in London and concentrated in terms of power in the hands of a small set of banks and insurance companies. This centralization of control was reinvigorated during the 1990s – despite a relative decentralization of employment – as mutually owned building societies became private companies and merged with London-based banks. In terms of employment, in 1995 nearly 300,000 people worked in the financial sector in London and together with the rest of the south-east region this accounts for over half of all workers in the sector. Furthermore, London is the only place in Britain where more men work in finance than women, reflecting the relatively high status and maintenance of male power in the industry (see McDowell, 1997).[2] More recently, however, the deregulation of finance in other capitalist countries is increasingly leading to similar levels of economic and geographical concentration.

Yet it is not simply in terms of the geographical distribution of activities that the financial sector is geographical. Investment by pension and **venture capital** funds has for a long period reproduced geographical patterns of wealth and poverty (Martin and Minns, 1995; Mason and Harrison, 2002), but local governments and investor groups are increasingly active in marshalling pension funds for their social, economic and political aims (Clark, 2000; Clark and Hebb, 2004). If finance has a national geography that tends to reinforce existing patterns of relative wealth and poverty, perhaps of more significance to many people are the ways in which the geography of the financial system affects their daily lives. Until very recently, the extensive branch networks of the banks acted as highly effective barriers to entry by new competitors. Branches allowed banks to offer a range of services across a range of areas and provided them with access to information about their clients, which was then used to assess creditworthiness. Geographically, firms responded to this by ensuring that they had an extensive network, and success was partially measured in terms of the number of customers with accounts. However, mundane technologies like cash machines, the telephone and the internet mean that customers no longer have to go near their branch for money; the development of generic financial products and sophisticated databases has undermined the intelligence-gathering role of the branch; and banks have stopped cross-subsidizing customers with profits made from more lucrative clients.

Yet at the same time as the branches have become less important for the

Venture capital
the provision of finance by an investor to businesses not quoted on stock markets and in the form of shares. The aim of venture capitalists is to make a very high return on their investment by selling their shares at a later date. Venture capital is a highly risky way to invest and, partly because of this, investors typically expect returns of over 30 per cent.

banks, the new technologies have allowed new entrants into an already overcrowded market. On the one hand, brand names with little history in finance, such as Virgin or British Gas in the United Kingdom or General Motors in the United States, are targeting particular segments of the financial market, whilst on the other hand, established companies are establishing direct sales subsidiaries that rely primarily on the internet and telephone communication. These organizations have far lower operating costs, greater levels of accessibility and, on the whole, a much more affluent set of customers. Relatively well-off customers receive better rates of interest, but another outcome is that banks are increasingly 'rationalizing' their networks. Between 1989 and 1995 the 'big four' banks in Britain closed over 2000 branches, contracting their branch networks by more than 20 per cent (Pratt *et al.*, 1996). In the United States, poor neighbourhoods are increasingly becoming stripped of banks at the same time as more affluent areas are seeing growth. In Los Angeles, for example, the two largest banks closed 51 branches during the 1980s – over two-thirds of these were in low-income neighbourhoods (Pollard, 1996).

There are costs to these processes and – somewhat predictably – the costs are being felt by the poor and, particularly in the United States, people of colour. As insurance companies are able to price risk more accurately, whole areas of the inner cities face crippling premiums for house and car insurance, or simply cannot get quotes at all. Leyshon and Thrift (1997) have convincingly demonstrated that the restructuring of the banking sector is resulting in poorer people getting *reduced* access to the formal financial system at precisely the time that it is becoming more important (in terms of discounts on utility bills or in terms of pay). These processes have been going on for longest in the United States and the withdrawal of the 'financial infrastructure' from poor areas has resulted in a growth in the 'second tier' financial sector: pawnbrokers, money lenders, cheque-cashing firms and hire-purchase shops (Burton *et al.*, 2004; Leyshon *et al.*, 2004). Commenting on this, Gary Dymski and John Veitch have pointed out that:

> *Financial structures ... amplify growth and decay in urban neighbourhoods. Second-tier financial firms which service lower income communities provide no way to pool community savings to finance community investment in new human or physical assets that enhance future economic growth. These new non-banking financial firms meet the financial needs of a community in strictly limited ways. They charge higher fees for services and facilitate households' decumulation of their stock of assets to meet current income crises. In consequence, lower income, higher minority population communities are increasingly isolated from more prosperous communities. Social polarisation is the result.*

(1996: 1257)

At the same time, however – but also, more optimistically – there has been a growth in the number of 'ethnobanks', which are targeted at specific ethnic communities (Li *et al.*, 2002).

SUMMARY
- At the national level, financial services tend to be geographically concentrated.
- Financial service investment reproduces existing patterns of wealth and poverty.
- During the 1980s and 1990s, less affluent people were increasingly excluded from the formal financial system in the USA and, to a lesser extent, elsewhere.

CONCLUSION: A ROLE FOR GOVERNMENT?

This chapter has explored some of the ways in which geography affects, and is affected by, the financial sector. In particular, the development of risk in the system and the contribution of finance to uneven regional development have been highlighted. These raise fundamental questions about the ways in which governments should respond to financial sector restructuring. Should, for example, governments attempt to regulate international finance more closely? Any such moves would go against the thrust of policy over the past 20 years and would face a number of potentially insuperable barriers (not least that financial institutions would be likely to move to countries with lower levels of regulation). However, not to do so may result in a widespread financial meltdown that could plunge the world into a 1930s-style recession, and this explains why governments seem increasingly prepared to co-operate in framing very limited controls at the international level. Similarly, should governments attempt to control the local activities of financial institutions to ensure, for example, that they provide equal access to the poor or invest in inner-city areas? Such measures may meet resistance from the banks, who would almost certainly lose money from them. However, as access to financial services is increasingly a badge of citizenship, such measures may increase a sense of belonging (see Chapter 26) and begin to redress the trend towards social exclusion.

Acknowledgement

I would like to acknowledge the support of ESRC for its support of the research fellowship 'Regulating finance: the political geography of financial services' (H52427001394).

DISCUSSION POINTS

1. Is it possible to conceptualize a world without money?
2. Does geographical location still matter in international finance? If so in what ways?
3. How does the geography of financial services affect your daily life?
4. What do we mean when we claim that money is more than notes and coins, or credit cards and cheques?

252 Introducing Human Geographies

NOTES

1. Money also has other qualities that set it apart. It is not simply a means of exchange, it actually creates value through what Marxists term the circuit of capital (see Fig. I.i).

2. The data were obtained by the author from the Office for National Statistics' 1995 Census of Employment via NOMIS.

FURTHER READING

Leyshon, A. and Thrift, N.J. (1997) *Money/space*. London: Routledge.

Martin, R. (ed.) (1998) *Money and the space economy*. Chichester: John Wiley.

Corbridge, S., Thrift, N.J. and Martin, R. (1996) *Money, power and space*. Oxford: Blackwell.

Knorr Cetina, K. and Preda A. (eds) (2004) *The sociology of financial markets*. Oxford: Oxford University Press.

Research on the geography of finance remains in relative infancy. Although there are now a growing number of articles in academic journals (see, particularly,

Environment and Planning A, Economic Geography, Geoforum; Regional Studies; Annals, Association of American Geographers and *Transactions, Institute of British Geographers*), there is a limited number of books that deal with the issue. Three excellent collections of essays on the geography of finance have been published (the first three texts in the list above), whilst research by sociologists and anthropologists of finance is also relevant (the fourth).

McDowell, L. (1997) *Capital culture*. Oxford: Blackwell.

A more specialist book, which examines the essentially masculine nature of much of the City of London.

CHAPTER 18
CONSUMPTION GEOGRAPHIES

Jon Goss

INTRODUCTION

Geography's engagement with consumption is fairly recent. As a discipline, we have paid far more attention to the other two moments in the circuit of capital: finance and production. Now, however, there is an appreciation that consumption is an important dimension of the geographies of our everyday lives, from the intimate spaces of our homes to the public places of our cities and countryside. In fact, the urban environment is dominated by retail parks and shopping malls, as much as by factories and offices, and the countryside is a place of leisure and recreation as much as primary production. In this chapter I explore the new geography of consumption. I first examine the contradictory nature of consumption and then explore our complex relationship with objects. Next I describe the functions of consumption and its historical development. Finally, I consider the ways in which geography is implicated in consumption, moving from the geography of consumption to the peculiar consumption of geography.

THE CONTRADICTIONS OF CONSUMPTION

In its original sense consumption means to squander or destroy, and in the vernacular it was thus used to described pulmonary tuberculosis, an often fatal wasting disease. The term was partly rehabilitated in the specialist discourse of eighteenth-century **political economy**, from which it got its neutral meaning as the utilization of products of human labour. Even then, however, consumption was conceived as secondary to production. Adam Smith, for example, dismissed consumption as the unproductive investment of resources necessary to realize production, whilst Karl Marx argued that production simultaneously produced objects for consumption (commodities) and social subjects (classes) to consume them.

The view of consumption as negative or subordinate to production persisted amongst modern cultural critics, who lamented manipulation of consumers by the so-called 'consciousness industries' – mass media marketing, advertising and ancillary activities. There are almost endless variations on the theme, but the main points are that 'false needs' created by the consciousness industries corrupt basic human needs, hedonistic consumer identities replace real community, public life gives way to choreographed commercial spectacle, anonymous transactions of the department store displace interpersonal interaction of the traditional marketplace, private solutions are sought to social problems, and democratic politics degenerates into 'spin' and electoral role-playing. There is no doubt that commodity relations have penetrated into virtually all spheres of our lives and whether citizens or students, parents or patients, we increasingly adopt a 'consumer attitude', experiencing life as a series of challenges to be overcome by the acquisition of appropriate

Political-economic, political economy
the study of how economic activities are socially and politically structured and have social and political consequences. Political-economic approaches in Human Geography have paid particular attention to understanding capitalist economies and their geographical organization and impact (*see* CAPITALISM and also MARXIST GEOGRAPHY). Central to such analyses have been questions concerning the class-based nature of the human geographies of capitalist societies (*see* CLASS).

Commodification

this term is used in two interrelated ways: (a) as the conversion of any thing, idea or person into a COMMODITY (the term 'commoditization' is often preferred for this sense); and (b) a wider societal process whereby an ever increasing number of things, human relationships, ideas and people are turned into commodities. Both meanings see the process of commodification as symptomatic of the penetration of CAPITALISM into the everyday lives of people and things.

goods and services (Bauman, 1990: 204). Our consumer identities are themselves **commodified**, as when they are sold as television audiences or mass marketing lists, for example, and it seems plausible that objects possess us with their characteristics as much we possess them (Baudrillard, 1988b). It seems almost impossible to escape, and to give a flavour of the moral panic this engenders in recent literature: apparently, we live in an 'all-consuming' era (Cross, 2000) and are subjects of 'the consumer society' (Clarke, 2003) or 'consumer republic' (Cohen, 2003); in the United States, at least, we are addicted to shopping, credit cards, fast food and brand names (Klein, 2000; Manning, 2000; Schlosser, 2001; Schor, 2000); the rest of the world is rapidly being colonized, or rather 'McDonaldized', as authentic ways of life are reduced to empty rituals of consumption (Ritzer, 2004); and even dissent is co-opted and commodified to become just alternative 'styles' of consumption (Frank and Weiland, 1997). It seems that, for worse rather than better, we are all shoppers now (Hine, 2002).

Despite its dominance on the bestseller lists, there has recently been a backlash against this negative view amongst academics and within the discipline of geography. Research shows that consumers are not manipulated dupes of forces of production, but are in many ways 'unmanageable' (Gabriel and Lang, 1996). The vast majority of new products fail, and the consciousness industries cannot create markets, but compete to identify and meet our unpredictable desires (see box).

To a considerable extent consumers make their own meaning from products, displaying critical knowledge and discriminating skilfully between them. Consumption is not merely about using up stuff in response to the demands of producers, but about creatively appropriating their products to construct lifestyles expressive of individual and collective identity.

Women still dominate everyday consumption, of course, and misogyny may partly explain the contempt in which predominantly white male critics have traditionally held it, as they have held to the distinction

---

THE 'COOL' CONSUMER AND THE GEOGRAPHY OF 'COOL'

In an article in the *New Yorker*, Malcolm Gladwell shows how marketers identify emerging trends by employing 'coolhunters' to search out 'cool' consumers who pioneer style. There are three rules of cool:

1. cool cannot be defined, only felt
2. cool can only be observed by those who are cool
3. cool cannot be manufactured.

Cool customers cannot be told what to consume by advertising campaigns, but they set the trends, so marketers, who themselves are said to possess a sixth sense for 'coolness', visit the inner cities of North America to consult with selected street kids. There is an interesting geographical component to cool, and marketers talk in terms of the conventional innovation-diffusion model, recognizing innovators, early adopters and late adopters within the urban hierarchy and across the United States. In the market for Reebok shoes, for example, the main source of innovation is Philadelphia, and trends move along the East Coast, such that if Chicago, New York and Detroit adopt the innovation, then it spreads out from these major cities and is a guaranteed hit. Even within cities, some neighbourhoods are more cool than others. Within New York, for example, Harlem is most sophisticated and cool in terms of sneaker markets, while the Bronx is colourful and glitzy, and Brooklyn tends to be more 'preppy'.

(Gladwell, 1997: 84)

between their modern rational bases of behaviour, and the emotional and superstitious sensibilities of others. Recently, however, the housewife has been hailed as a 'global dictator', since her decisions determine outcomes in the international political economy, and as 'hero' due to her thrifty and loving management of the moral economy of the home (Miller, 1995b). Recent feminist histories have shown how consumer desire created public spaces and employment opportunities for women in department stores, transforming gender relations in the late nineteenth century. Consumerism and feminism go hand in hand, and shopping, once condemned as a frivolous female activity, has become a metaphor for citizenship in the modern world. Consumers collectively use the power of markets to influence corporate behaviour, government legislation and foreign policy. For example, the politics of consumption played a significant role in the 'collapse' of communism in the late 1980s and, immediately after the events of 11 September 2001, both the President of the United States and the Prime Minister of Great Britain are reported to have reminded their people of a patriotic duty to go shopping, in order to sustain consumer confidence, a vital support in the edifice of contemporary capitalist society.

Acknowledging the power of the consumer, academics now argue that 'consumption, and not production, is the central motor of society' or 'the vanguard of history' (Corrigan, 1997: 1; Miller, 1995b) and it is now possible for intellectuals to write 'in praise of commercial culture' (Cowen, 1998) and to confess their personal pleasures in consumption (Gregson and Crewe, 2003). Even as we celebrate the rationality of the housewife and joy of shopping, however, we admit the contradictory nature of consumption, and ultimately of our relations with the object world. Consumption actually depends upon the gap between what we know and want we wish to believe, which is why advertising, for example, moves between rational and fantastic motivations for acquisition of products, and why most of us are willing to suspend disbelief in the magical powers of mundane things, at the same time as we judge their value and efficiency against our material need. The magical system depends partly on the verbal rhetoric of advertising: have you ever noticed, for example, how advertising tries to persuade you that you are not merely like the rest of us – a modern shopper buying mass-produced objects – but that you are particularly discriminating of real value and uniquely deserving of the product? You cannot have escaped observation that commodities are supposed to possess qualities that in turn possess us – such as, for example, the brand of cigarette that brands the rugged man, and the designer label that labels the sophisticated woman. This system also depends on the visual rhetoric of advertising, and particularly upon the real or imaginary settings in which objects are presented – what the geographer Robert Sack (1992) calls the 'context of the commodity'. The context facilitates our fantasized dissociation from mundane objects and acts of consumption, so that whilst we are merely reading an advertisement, contemplating a store display or strolling in the mall, something entirely different is going on. Have you noticed that many advertisements and even the places you shop evoke somewhere else in space and time, a distant or past world where the natural value of objects putatively inheres and endures, or a fantastic realm where objects come to life? Of course, we know that the SUV perched atop the canyon cannot really climb rock walls, that a bite of chocolate bar cannot really transport us to paradise, and that the shopping arcade is not really a street in an nineteenth-century seaport, but then why does marketing persist in these claims? Why, when so many of us understand the general environmental and social consequences of consumption, do we still consume as if it were not so, and somehow believe in the innocence of our possessions. This capacity for simultaneously knowing and not-knowing, and for conflating the material and symbolic is captured by the difficult concept of fetishism, which describes how, despite our rational selves that know better, inanimate things are possessed with fantastic lives of their own. It is a remarkable capacity that all humans possess, and some marketing campaigns even play ironically on our self-conscious cleverness in 'having it both ways' or containing the contradictions of consumption (Fig. 18.1).

FIGURE 18.1
Advertising irony: the choice of watch that says that you are cool because you know that the watch you choose is not what makes you cool!
Source: Cross Watches USA

OUR DESIRE FOR OBJECTS

In the modern world things are literally not what they used to be, in that scientific rationality and world religions have resulted in a generalized 'disenchantment of the world' and the material world is no longer supposed to possess inherent meaning or to be animated by spirits. Our primitive tendencies are repressed, and the aura of objects – their ability to look at and engage us – is generally limited to an appreciation of the artist's vision or the genius behind modern technology, and is otherwise relegated to the realm of childish imagination, primitive religion, escapist fiction, or horror and science-fiction film genres. Contemporary consumption, however, purposely blurs boundaries between art and commerce, object and intelligence, and adopts practices functionally equivalent to the magic of fairy tales, and thus it is no coincidence that the word glamour, for example, originally referred to the casting of spells. The 'commodity aesthetic' asks us to believe in the transformative powers of material objects, such that the perfect slipper makes the princess, or in the modern version of the fairy tale, the perfect sportswalker makes the estate attorney (see Fig. 18.2).

Rationality tells us that the 'real' origin of power lies in social relations that legitimate possession of the object, not in the object itself. In this case, then, one might argue that a successful lawyer would necessarily possess the requisite taste, wealth and lifestyle to purchase this shoe, rather than that any young woman who purchases it will become possessed of these personal and social characteristics. Clearly, however, the advertisement plays on a residual faith in the transformative power of the object or its fetish character.

The term fetish originally applied to objects of so-called 'primitive' religions that were believed to possess animate powers, and the term was borrowed from early modern anthropology in the foundational theories of the capitalist economy and the modern psyche. Karl Marx, for example, used the notion of commodity fetishism to describe our failure to see that the value of commodities lies not in their inherent nature, but in the human labour they embody. His labour theory of value is controversial; nevertheless under conditions of competition it is generally true that the prices you pay at the supermarket are not determined by relative need, capacity to pay or particularistic social relations, but more or less by the costs of production. Moreover, the material origins of commodities are generally obscured, in the sense that they appear for sale with little evidence of their real geographic or social origins (see box).

As many will know from popular psychology, Sigmund Freud also borrowed the term to describe the displacement of sexual desire on to an arbitrary object. His argument is also controversial, but his concept usefully describes the ambivalence of the consumer, in that, like the fetishist, we know that the object is merely a substitute, but we temporarily take it for the presence of an original ideal that appears to have been lost.

The French philosopher Jean Baudrillard (1988b) problematizes the concept of fetishism, showing how it reproduces a modernist conviction that form obscures substance, that truth lies beyond the surface of display, and reality behind the mask. He argues that Marx's distinction between

Commodity fetishism

the process whereby the material origins of commodities are obscured and they are presented 'innocent' of the social and geographical relations of production that produced them.

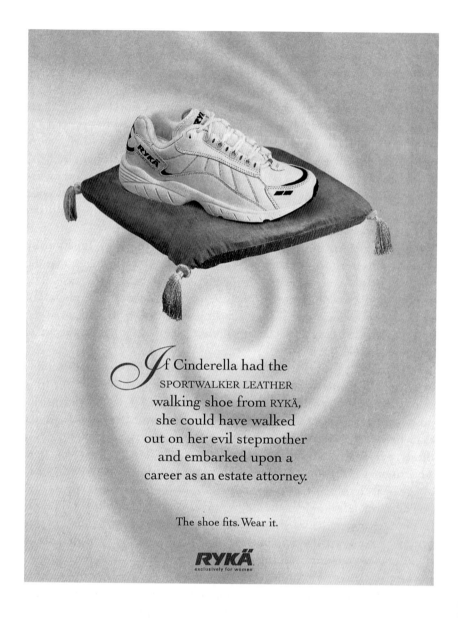

Figure 18.2
The magic object of the modern fairy-tale.
Source: Rykä

COMMODITY MAGIC

Whilst doing fieldwork in Mall of America I found two excellent examples of fetishism by which commodities are stripped of their real material origins and placed in an imaginary world. In the Love from Minnesota store there was a $155 stuffed bear for sale; the store's tag prominent on its right ear said 'Minnesotans who live deep in the north-woods among the loons, wolves and scented pine trees, listen to the gentle lapping of the waves of the shoreline while they handcraft unique mementos of our homeland, like this one, to share with you'; the manufacturer's label, hidden behind its other ear said 'Bear made by Mary Meyer Corp, Townshend, Vermont … Made in Indonesia.'

In COLORADO, an outdoor outfitter, I picked up a coat made in Sri Lanka and imported by Columbia Sportswear of Oregon and asked the assistant about the connection. I was told, 'It's just a name. Most people associate it with the outdoors. I mean, if we called it Iowa or something … who'd wanna come?' The store is headquartered in New York and has no outlet in Colorado itself, but the slogan of the store explains the connection: 'Remember COLORADO isn't only a store: it's a state … of mind.'

use-value and exchange-value is itself a form of mysticism, that material function and economic worth are abstractions and merely part of 'sign-value'. It is not so much the usefulness or price of objects that clinches sales, but the *image* of usefulness and price, neither of which are properties of objects per se. How else could we explain such phenomena as 'Pet Rocks', more or less valueless lumps of coal that sold several years ago as loveable low-maintenance concept-pets? It is clear that consumption is as much an act of imagination as the using up of things, and we are thus advised to 'forget that commodities are good for eating, clothing and shelter; forget their usefulness and try instead the idea that commodities are good for thinking; treat them as a nonverbal medium for the human creative faculty' (Douglas and Isherwood, 1979: 62).

In this sense commodities communicate both metaphorically and metonymically: they open up a whole world of associations. American automobiles, for example, are utilitarian objects quite similar in style and function from one manufacturer and model to another. Their names, however – from Colt to Cougar, and Falcon to Phoenix – are **metaphors** for powerful animistic forces associated with speed, the freedom of the wild, and mythical transformations. The logic is simple, but in case you do not get it, a Chrysler advertisement instructs: 'You are what you drive. Fantasize.' The car, like other commodities, is a prop in the performance of our cultural and personal fantasies of transcendence. Also, the context in which the automobile is presented evokes desirable elsewheres, such as when the latest SUV, surely more car than most drivers will ever need, splashes through a swollen stream and parks in the forecourt of a posh hotel. The fantasy car literally transports us: uncovering hidden parts of ourselves and opening up whole new worlds of possibility. Most of our expenditures are for more mundane household needs, but even everyday products possess transformative qualities, as in the 'cool' of particular cigarettes or the 'carefree' of particular toiletries. It needs stressing that, however tenuous the connection, one is not purchasing merely an abstraction, image rather than substance, because, however arbitrary, the sign is always also an object. The commodity is, in fact, a promised unity of materiality and meaning, souvenir of an immanent world that tragically we seem to have lost. Below, I will map the terrain of this world, but first we need to consider the functions of consumption in terms of social distinction, self-actualization and social reproduction, which will also allow us to explore something of its history.

Metaphor

the use of a word or symbol from one domain of meaning to apply to another. Thus a rose (a botanical term) is translated into the domain of human relationships to symbolize love. Metaphors involve this movement of concepts from their normal realm to a new realm.

THE OBJECT OF OUR DESIRES

The use of fashionable dress to mark social distinction was institutionalized in the 'first consumer revolution' in the sixteenth century, when Queen Elizabeth forced her nobles to attend court and so compete for her attention with flamboyant fashion (McCracken, 1988: 11–15). The progressive expansion of world trade and the intensification of industrial production in this early era of globalization increased opportunities for the acquisition of prestige goods, and what were once luxuries for elites became basic needs for the majority, so that by the end of the eighteenth century, not only clothing but also home furnishings

Class

a collection of people sharing the same economic position within society, and/or sharing the same social status and cultural tastes. The precise ways in which one's economic position – for example, as a worker, a capitalist or a member of the land-owning aristocracy – is related to one's social status or cultural tastes has been much debated. However, Human Geographers have studied class and its geographies from all these perspectives: as an economic, social and cultural structuring of society.

Fordism

a form of industrial capitalism dominating the economies of the US and western Europe from the end of the Second World War to the early 1970s. It was characterized by mass production and mass consumption, where high levels of productivity (often promoted by new assembly line production) sustained high wages, which in turn led to high levels of demand for industrial products. This demand fed into higher production, which supported higher productivity, and the 'virtuous circle' began all over again. It was an economic system that was often underpinned by a political compromise between capital and labour, and by subsequent state policies towards wages, taxes and welfare provision, which helped to sustain mass production and consumption. *See also* POST-FORDISM.

Capital accumulation

the prime goal of CAPITALISM as a MODE OF PRODUCTION. It is the deployment of capital to convert it into new (and more) capital. This process is often designated by the simple formula MCM', where M is money or liquid capital, which is invested in C which is commodity capital (land, labour, machines) with a view to profit, realized as M' which is more money (or more technically 'expanded liquidity').

and pottery fashionably expressed social status (McKendrick *et al.*, 1982). Subsequently, consumption expanded inexorably through envy and emulation, even as the leaders of fashion constantly innovated to stay ahead. Torstein Veblen (1899), an American economist and sociologist, was the first and most influential of many who railed against 'invidious distinction' made through 'conspicuous consumption'.

Distinctions of style, taste and 'class' are particularly important in urban society, which requires regular interaction amongst strangers, and in capitalist society where social status is determined by wealth, rather than, say, physical attributes or heritage, which are more apparent or familiar. Conspicuous consumption thus provides us with an immediately interpretable system of signs of social identity and status – think what you can tell about strangers on the train from the clothes they wear or the newspapers they read. Pierre Bourdieu (1984: 136), a French sociologist, says that consumer choices are never merely personal judgements, but constitute 'position-taking' within a hierarchy of competencies distributed largely according to education. Like Karl Marx, he sees consumption as ultimately determined by the status of consumers as producers. Consumption reproduces social distinctions, as suggested by popular expressions of contempt for objects that betray *poor* taste, such as 'I wouldn't be seen dead in that' or 'it's so common'. Objects serve to differentiate those 'in the know' from others, and we work hard to learn and apply knowledge of appropriate 'constellations of commodities' that define particular consumer identities (McCracken, 1988). As we have seen, marketing sometimes trades explicitly on distinction by poking fun at those who have to ask what it means (see Fig. 18.1).

Still, consumption is more than striving to 'keep up with the Joneses'. Partly because of the expansion of consumption choices, there is increasing horizontal differentiation of social groups, or segmentation of markets. Large and rigid status categories of mass consumption are said to have fragmented into specialist 'consumer tribes' (Maffesoli, 1996), which is a particularly apt analogy because it describes some key features of contemporary consumption: for example, that it is a communal activity defining coherent groupings and primary loyalties; that membership is conditional upon acquisition of knowledge, often quite arcane, and increasingly outside of formal institutions; that identity is performed in ritualized activities; that 'primitive' traits, captured by the concepts of the fetish and totem are conserved (a totem is a revered object that serves as a symbol of identity for a collectivity that shares its mystical qualities); and that contexts of consumption are where familiarity with the landscape and its meanings provide for a sense of belonging. In short, each consumer tribe has its totem and its territory.

A 'second consumer revolution' is said to have occurred in the eighteenth century as the Romantic movement, in reaction to industrialism and the 'Protestant ethic', extolled the virtues of self-expression and self-improvement, and the pleasures of art, craft and travel (Campbell, 1987). Popular media, particularly novels, and the new 'exhibitionary complex' of the nineteenth century (museums, world's fairs, panoramas and photography), told tales and showed images of romance, adventure and exotic lives. Marketing shifted from informational to associative techniques, combining sophisticated new technologies of colour, glass and light to persuade consumers to buy products for their transformative qualities. Illusions of exotic elsewheres and authentic times past were vital to displays in which commodities were presented as passports to imagined new worlds and souvenirs of fantastic experiences. This 'dream world of mass consumption' (Williams, 1982: 64) promised the possibility of self-realization and personal transformation through the simple possession of the right commodity.

Finally, in our modern consumer societies, we tend to think of consumption behaviour in terms of individual choice and consider that collective good results from the private pursuit of well-being. The fact is, however, that governments regulate exchange, define minimum standards for products and levels of consumption, and subsidize or directly organize health, housing, education and recreation services. There was perhaps a 'third consumer revolution' in the early to mid-twentieth century with the development of 'Fordism', a form of industrial capitalism based on mass production and consumption mediated by the state. Consider, for example, the massive suburbanization of capitalist economies since the Second World War, which could not have occurred without public investment in infrastructure, financial incentives, facilitating legislation and regulation. Suburbanization dramatically expanded production and capital accumulation, not only in construction but also in consumer durables, since each home required an automobile, washing machine and lawnmower. At the same time, it afforded independent lifestyles and pleasures of consumption to workers, compensating for increased overall productivity and intensified discipline in the workplace (Schor, 1998).

Without raising the spectre of determinism, as if consumption is simply the end of production, similar arguments can be made about the role of government in promoting the development of contemporary consumer landscapes, from shopping centres and festival marketplaces to sports arenas and cultural complexes, which both facilitate capital accumulation and publicly subsidize consumption. There is, of course, a very particular geography to these subsidies, which disproportionately enhance the consumer lifestyles of the middle classes: the countryside becomes their residential dormitories and the city their urban playgrounds. If there is a particular geography of consumption, however, there is also a peculiar consumption of geography, and it is to this that we now turn.

Modern, modernity, modernism

ideas of the modern are most commonly defined through their opposition to the old and the traditional. In this light, the adjective 'modern' is synonymous with 'newness'; 'modernity' refers both to the 'post-traditional' historical epoch within which 'newness' is produced and valued, as well as to the economic, social, political and cultural formations characteristic of that period; and 'modernism' applies more narrowly to artistic, architectural and intellectual movements that centrally explore ideas of 'newness' and develop 'new' aesthetics and ways of thinking to express these. Modernity has been most commonly located in Euro-American societies from the eighteenth century onwards, and thereby associated with their characteristic combination of capitalist economies (see CAPITALISM), political organization through NATION-STATES, and cultural values of secularity, rationality and progress (see ENLIGHTENMENT). However, increasingly, Human Geographers are recognizing that modernity is a global phenomenon that has taken many different forms in different times and places. See also MODERNIZATION.

> ### SUMMARY
> - Consumption is fed from our desires, and these in turn depend as much upon our images of the objects to be consumed as on the objects themselves.
> - Distinctions in taste and style are important in shaping these desires, and hence in shaping consumption.
> - Despite these distinctions, a form of mass consumption has emerged, increasingly regulated by the state.

LANDSCAPES OF CONSUMPTION

Under conditions of modernity, a nostalgic narrative tells of progressive alienation from the natural world and our true nature: rationality subordinating imagination, technology severing culture from nature, the cult of newness divorcing the present from the past, and mass media undermining genuine sociality. The retail built environment exploits this sad tale and creates idealized settings that stage restoration of lost innocence and authenticity through the redemptive powers of commodities. As we shall see, these settings include rather specific spatial and temporal archetypes, the former including public space, marketplace and festival setting, and the latter including nature, primitiveness, heritage and childhood. The spatial themes respectively evoke the possibility of community amongst strangers in an authentic public realm, social interaction and transaction in a free market, and the spontaneous drama of festivity. The temporal themes evoke memories of human origins in nature and primitive society, early commerce and national heritage in the nineteenth century, and of personal origins in childhood. Transport to these spatio-temporal realms occurs through imagination and memory, and via various 'vehicles': we go back to the past in restored sailing vessels and trains; we evoke memories and yearn for old times in photographs and 'authentic reproduction' antiques and handicrafts; and we imagine worlds of myth and magic in objects through characters of cartoons and fairy tales. Most shopping centres and many shops evoke these realms in multiple and complex ways.

1. Public space

Genuine urban life is thought to have disintegrated under the assault of the automobile, urban redevelopment and violent crime, and it is restored in forms reminiscent of pedestrian streets, avenues, parks, gardens and train stations, often from places distant in time and space – nineteenth-century European themes, for example, dominate North American malls, where nodal points quote plazas and piazzas, and food courts resemble street cafés. Despite private ownership and control, shopping centres evoke spaces of social aggregation, people-watching and public performance. In North America, they often host public institutions such as daycare centres, health clinics, religious centres, post offices, municipal services, police stations, and even high schools and colleges; they provide 'disabled access', family restrooms and community education programmes; and they raise funds for charity, sponsor special events and pioneer recycling programmes (Goss, 1993; 1999). The aim is to reconcile commerce and community, private property and the public interest, so restoring trust in

FIGURE 18.3
The costermonger barrow evokes traditional marketplaces. Credit: Jon Goss

our business institutions, which are generally perceived to have abandoned civic responsibility in the pursuit of wealth.

2. Marketplace

The modern economy purportedly undermines traditional markets characterized by unmediated exchanges born of custom, reciprocity and need. The retail built environment, therefore, exploits what I playfully call *agorafilia* – a nostalgic desire for the lost spirit of the marketplace – by evoking exotic and historic forms in designs reminiscent of bazaars, stylized historic shop fronts and detailing, and numerous variations on the 'Ye Olde Shoppe' theme, complete with paraphernalia such as costermonger barrows (Fig. 18.3). It highlights the artisanal **mode of production**, evoking the values of petty enterprise and the regional basis of traditional trade. Again, consumption blurs boundaries: even as cultural critics complain that the exploitation of nature and art commercializes aesthetics, the retail built environment aestheticizes commerce.

3. Festivity

According to the narrative of decline, we no longer assemble for real public rituals, but submit ourselves to spectacular simulacra of festival orchestrated by mass media. The contemporary retail built environment provides settings for its restoration in spaces conducive to circulation, aggregation and observation of people, on stages for public performances and in decor that changes according to ritual calendars (Fig. 18.4). It mobilizes the excitement of the crowd, the pleasures of performance and the erotics of the body, so tempting you to 'treat yourself', 'discover a new you' or to 'try it on'. Here, the transformative potential of commodities is reminiscent of the function of mask and costume in festival and carnival, and hence, perhaps, the popularity and profitability of festival market-places and fairground features in shopping centres.

4. Nature

In contemporary consumption, nature stands for an originary purity and contemporary scarcity, so the retail built environment exploits a pastoral or edenic aesthetic and evokes the fugitive nature, often focusing on fragile ecosystems and endangered species (Fig. 18.5). It seems to me that nature products are allegories of the fate of the commodity under contemporary capitalism, where we are exhorted to buy 'while stocks last'. Our predilection for stuffed animals, precious stones and dinosaurs naturalizes the relentless obsolescence of form and function under capitalist commodity production, but also promises potential restoration provided we have faith in commodity aesthetics and eternal value. Such objects are nature's equivalent of antiques and collectibles that decorate shopping centres and stores. It is as if, paradoxically, the very latest product will somehow never go out of style.

Mode of production
a term taken from MARXIST social thought, referring to the distinctive ways in which production has taken place in different types of society and in different historical epochs. Thus CAPITALISM is seen as one 'mode of production' distinguishable, for example, from feudalism and communism. In Marxist Geography, the mode of production is seen as the fundamental determinant of the kind of society and the kind of human geographies a person has to live with and through.

FIGURE 18.4
Shopping centres stage traditional public life.
Credit: Jon Goss

5. Primitiveness

In the modern imagination, pre-industrial peoples 'naturally' exhibit values and behaviours that civilization has long repressed, enjoying stewardship relations with nature, simple economies and, like the child (see below), an innocent faith in animate powers in the material world. Like nature, primitiveness is endangered, which of course enhances its value, and consumers, like tourists, seek signs of its authentic presence even as it ceases to exist. Primitiveness is evoked in exotic settings and native products – almost literally fetishes – often incorporating themes of historic travel and colonial adventure so that native products appear as poignant reminders or valuable souvenirs of disappearing ways of being in the world. They promise, literally, 'a bit of the Other'.

FIGURE 18.5
The nature theme often focuses on endangered species. Credit: Jon Goss

6. Heritage

According to the nostalgic narrative, a steep cultural decline has occurred since the late nineteenth century, a time associated with simple virtues of craft labour and local community, stable identity and public purpose. Contemporary contexts of consumption thus evoke early industrial cities, small towns and villages, in forms such as the commercial waterfront reproduced in festival marketplaces, main streets in shopping malls and village squares in speciality centres. They are decorated with antique tools and bric-a-brac, souvenirs of obsolete forms of production and testaments to the preservation of traditional value(s). The Museum Store in your local mall, or the gift store in your local museum, again blur conventional boundaries, both forms incorporating the display aesthetic to narrate how these respective institutions re-*store* the lost meaning and values of objects.

7. Childhood

As western civilization has developed or 'grown up', modern rationality and instrumentality has repressed our childlike impulses to believe in myth and fairy tale. Like the primitives, however, our children are not yet mature, and through them we can vicariously experience the imaginative realm, even as we adhere to adult values: the retail built environment is therefore often organized around the experience of the child, appealing directly to imaginative capacities for transcendence and instant gratification, as it also evokes the quality, efficiency, price and educational content of products and services. As an adult shopping for practical purposes, I might pooh-pooh the trickery of animation, gigantism and miniaturization mobilized in the shopping centre, and smile knowingly at games of dressing up, anthropomorphization of animals and superstition of magic objects. I dismiss birthday wishes and tooth fairies, and certainly do not believe in Santa Claus. But I do believe in the innocent belief of children, and I am reminded that I once shared their beliefs absolutely, and I feel nostalgic for my lost capacity for enchantment. More importantly, it is through our faith in children's innocence, that a lost part of ourselves can perhaps once again, even if fleetingly, glimpse the genius of things and believe in the alchemy of advertising and the magic of marketing. It is through children's eyes, in other words, that the adult can imagine a world of magic slippers and secret potions or the wizardry of washing powder, and it is thus that in the fantastic environment of the shopping centre I might be momentarily distracted from my practical purposes to make that 'impulse purchase' that is its whole intention.

SUMMARY

- The particular geography of consumption partly operates through a specific consumption of geography.

- The geographies that are consumed invoke very specific archetypes, ranging from public space and marketplace to nature, heritage and the spaces of childhood.

CONCLUSION

This chapter has argued that consumption provides compensation for the felt alienation of modernity and that the retail built environment seeks to restore our sense of well-being by creating an alternative reality constructed from geographical and historical archetypes of an originary, authentic and immanent world. In these contexts, it seems as if something other than mere consumption is going on, and fetishized commodities appear as other than merely material objects of human labour. Ironically, however, whilst offering images of authentic public life, marketplaces and festival settings, the increasingly privatized and socially controlled retail built environment undermines genuine urbanity, and whilst incorporating images of nature, primitiveness, heritage and childhood, its technical virtuosity seems to make increasingly redundant the realms of myth, memory and imagination. The cynical critic is right: it seems to present the world of commodities innocent of the commodification of the world, and the magic turns out to be an illusion. We all know that somehow the object loses its lustre when it leaves the perfect context of the advertisement, display or packaging. Nevertheless, the condemnation is not entirely fair, for even if our desire for authentic life has been transformed into demand for commodities, those commodities, properly understood, might possess the key to our self-understanding and ultimately our actualization. That is, by recognizing the fantasy content of these commodified objects and services we might, like the subject of psychotherapy, come to identify the impossibility of the originary object of collective desire, and embrace the messy and conflictual reality of global capitalist production.

DISCUSSION POINTS

1. Think about how you decide whether to buy one product rather than another. Are you influenced at all by advertising? If so, in what ways?

2. List some commodities that are supposed to possess particular qualities that they pass on to their owners. How is such an association fostered and maintained?

3. Choose a shopping centre you are familiar with. Sketch out the geographical settings within which consumption takes place.

4. Is mass consumption a positive or negative process? Argue why.

FURTHER READING

Cross, G. (2000) *An All-consuming century: why commercialism won in modern America.* New York: Columbia University Press.

Schor, J.B. (2000) *Do Americans shop too much?* Boston: Beacon Press.

These texts are good representatives of recent work on consumption in the USA.

Cohen, L. (2003) *A consumer's republic: the politics of mass consumption in postwar America.* New York: Knopf.

Klein, N. (2000) *No logo: taking aim at the brand bullies.* New York: Picador.

These offer useful information on the politics of consumption.

Clarke, D.B. (2003) *The consumer society and the postmodern city.* London and New York: Routledge.

Goss, J. (1999) Once upon a time in the commodity world: an unofficial guide to mall of America. *Annals of the Association of American Geographers*, 89, 1: 45–75.

Gregson, N. and Crewe, L. (2003) *Second-hand cultures*, Oxford and New York: Berg.

These are texts that provide a geographical take on consumption.

SECTION 4
ENVIRONMENTAL GEOGRAPHIES

INTRODUCTION

Early in 2004, several Greenpeace activists dressed as pantomime cows conducted protests outside Sainsbury's supermarkets under the banner 'There's something scary in the dairy' (see Fig. II.i). The protest was designed to highlight the annual sale in supermarkets of millions of pints of milk sourced from cows fed on genetically modified feed. Claiming that GM is threatening the environment with irreversible contamination, the protesters were seeking to influence both consumers, and supermarket managers, to go GM-free. Such protests, and the issues underlying them, now seem part of our everyday existence, with new threats to environment and health seeming to be brought constantly into our purview. A brief glance at Greenpeace's own website (http://www.green peace.org) reveals a range of current concerns, including the following.

FIGURE II.I
'Something scary in the dairy'.
Credit: Sam Tinson/Rex Features

- 'Hurricane devastation in the US, flash floods in Japan and a UK village washed in the sea. As climate change gathers pace, devastation caused by extreme weather is becoming more certain.'
- 'Thanks to the Bush Administration's disregard for global concerns about nuclear proliferation, two ships carrying some 150kg of weapons grade plutonium are en route from Charleston, South Carolina, to Cherbourg in France.'
- 'Activists on motorbikes are stopping bulldozers from destroying forest lands in Salta, Argentina. Cyberactivists around the world are picking up the phone and calling the Argentine embassies in their countries to demand a moratorium on forest destruction to stop the killing of rare wildlife and displacement of forest peoples.'

. . . the list of concerns goes on and on.

In many ways, environmental issues are a 'natural' area of concern for geographers. Indeed, traditional definitions of the subject have tended to emphasize the relationships between people and their environment, and geographers have for a long time been interested in the connections between human activity and environmental degradation, or environmental hazards. For many years, geographers tended to adopt rather formal approaches to studying these interconnections. For example, a 'science' of 'environmental impact assessment' has grown up that suggests methods either for cataloguing the environmental consequences of a particular project or for a more structured quantitative accounting of the costs and benefits to the environment of that project.

More recently, however, Human Geographers have turned their attention to environmentalism as a focus of study. Environmentalism collectively describes a wide range of ideas and practices that demonstrate a concern for nature–society relations. Many of these ideas and practices can be brought much closer to the geographies of our everyday life than the previous evaluative foci. For example, Human Geographers have been interested in different forms of environmentalism, from the deep ecology movement, which has exposed the principle of living in harmony with nature, to the different elements of the 'green' movement, which have used popular protest to highlight key environmental concerns, and the 'new age' movement, which has brought a range of personal and spiritual attachments to nature into sharp focus.

As we move further into the new millennium, the global and local consideration of different environmentalisms will become increasingly important. We have already seen how long-term shifts in public opinion towards quality-of-life issues, and the increasingly active and effective green pressure groups, have begun to result in a range of policy changes. These include green accounting, **environmental auditing**, strategic planning and some greater acceptance of intergenerational equity. However, there is a strong suspicion that these changes simply represent shades of **technocentrism** – the management of growth so as to permit the further exploitation of the environment by human beings for human beings – rather than any more **ecocentric** alternative.

The three chapters in this section demonstrate how Human Geography is getting to grips with the complex and often contentious nature of environmental issues. Sally Eden in Chapter 19 emphasizes how problems relating to the environment are presented as social constructions to the waiting world – constructions that are strongly influenced by powerful claims-makers who are able to define and publicize particular problems. Moreover the spatial and temporal context of any particular set of issues significantly influences the ways in which we make sense of our environment. Global issues, such as climate change and ozone depletion, illustrate the different ways in which environmental problems become contentious and 'fixable'. Local issues such as waste management attract a rather different politics and lend themselves to technological responses.

So, environmental geographies cannot simply be approached through the straightforward application of scientific principles. We need to recognize that the way in which environmental issues are discussed in the public arena matters enormously. Bill Adams illustrates this starkly in Chapter 20, in which he demonstrates how 'environmentalism' has been transformed into 'sustainability', which has been the subject of a meteoric rise to the status of global buzzword. He clearly shows how sustainability has become a powerful concept because of the lack of precision involved in its definition. Put simply, sustainability is defined in different ways by different interests, even though these interests might have opposing objectives! It follows that the introduction of sustainability ideas into

Environmental audit

the attempt to calculate, and list for comparison, all the likely effects of any proposed action on the surrounding ECOSYSTEMS and populations.

Technocentrism

an outlook of optimism towards any environmental or other geographical challenge on the basis of the adaptiveness and innovation of human endeavour and technological know-how.

Ecocentrism

a perspective favouring a humble and cautious outlook towards the scope for interfering with the planet, and arguing for a smaller-scale, more communitarian, style of living.

practical policy, such as in the principles of Agenda 21, means that every seemingly firm commitment to environmental action is likely to be accompanied by a get-out clause. There is definitely an exciting potential inherent in making environmental policy sustainable. For example, policies to preserve the quality of the environment, especially in the case of biodiversity, can be integrated with policies to ensure the livelihoods of the world's poorest people in truly sustainable ways. However, the potential for sustainability can be diminished if it is taken to mean all things to all people.

The power to influence the production, circulation and consumption of environmental knowledges has thus become paramount. After all, as Jacquie Burgess makes clear in Chapter 21, without the globalization of information there would be no global environmental crisis – it is the discovery and publicizing of the global reach of environmental hazards that has led us into the 'Risk Society'. The ways in which knowledge about the environment is presented to us are greatly influenced by the media and by 'experts' who help to frame the issues involved, and to 'spin-doctor' public perception of environment crisis. It is in this production of environmental knowledge that the communication of environmental problems is variously effective in persuading people to adopt sustainable lifestyles. Information is often globalized, but human response is often based in the home or work locality – hence 'think global, act local'.

The rise of sustainability has placed environmentalism in a broader field of coalition – building across a wide range of policy communities that were previously unconnected. Health and social care, crime prevention, family solidarity and environmental stewardship by business have become entwined across national borders and all levels of government. In this flux, outdated environmental outlooks are beginning to atrophy. The 'old guard' of environmental leaders is slowly and painfully being replaced by a more opportunist, managerialist class. As environmentalism tackles sustainability, however, the political stakes have become much more resistant to the demands of tax reform, economic and political redistribution, and spatial reorganization that the new agenda of sustainability is making. The nerve centres of power have recognized that sustainability needs to be tamed, and this process is now the centre of the struggle.

FURTHER READING

Park, C. (1997) *The environment: principles and applications.* **London: Routledge.**

Geographies of environment and environmentalism are both vast and multifaceted, yet there are relatively few texts that succeed in pulling together the various strands. This one is a lively introductory text.

Allen, S., Adam, B. and Carter, C. (eds) (2000) *Environmental risks and the media.* **London: Routledge.**

Dobson, A. (2000) *Green political thought* **(3rd edn). London: Routledge.**

These texts offer readable accounts of the important of politics and the media.

Bell, M. (1998) *An invitation to environmental sociology.* **Thousand Oaks: Pine Forge Press.**

O'Riordan, T. (1999) *Environmental science for environmental management* **(2nd edn). Harlow: Longman.**

Pepper, D. (1996) *Modern environmentalism: an introduction.* **London: Routledge.**

You might like to look at the above texts for more focused, but also more discursive, accounts.

CHAPTER 19

Sally Eden

GLOBAL AND LOCAL ENVIRONMENTAL PROBLEMS

INTRODUCTION

It's August in Yorkshire and it's raining – more than raining, it's blustery and wet and downright chilly for the time of year. Now, is this the tail-end of Hurricane Charley lashing across the Atlantic from its recent vandalism in Florida? Another manifestation of the disruption of our weather we can expect from climate change? In which case, should I be reducing my impact on climate change, such as by driving to work less often? Or is it just a typical British summer, in which case I should consider flying to sunnier places for my holiday next year? In other words, how do I – and all those other people sitting and looking at the rain – make sense of the environment, and how does this influence what we, as individuals and as a society, do in response?

Environmental problems have now become part of everyday life: recycling, deforestation, air pollution, genetically modified food – we experience them all through media reporting and household activities. They have also become part of Human Geography, both through curricula for teaching and agendas for research. And so they should, because geographers have often taken their cue from society's concerns. But what exactly do we mean by 'environmental problems'? This may seem an obvious question, but it is not until we are clear about our terms and thinking that we can be clear about how we might attempt to 'solve' such problems.

ENVIRONMENTAL PROBLEMS AND SOCIAL CONSTRUCTION

First of all, we should not see 'environmental problems' simply as reflections of 'real' environmental change. This is because we need to consider the theory of the **social construction** of reality (see Chapter 1). This idea has been around for 30 years now and seeks to understand how society makes sense of the world, particularly through endowing it with meaning and, often, changing that meaning as society changes. It is sometimes criticized as meaning that there is *no* reality except in our collective imagination. This is mistaken. Talking about the social construction of environmental problems does not mean that such problems are merely imaginary, but it does mean that we can only think about them in socially defined ways – and that it is on the basis of these social definitions, rather than on the 'real' conditions, that we act. Whether I see the rain outside as climate change or a British summer, the rain continues to fall. But the meaning that rain has for me might make me act differently – how we *perceive* things matters because it directly affects what we *do* about them. So, social construction is about meaning but it is also about action.

Social construct

a set of specific meanings that become attributed to the characteristics and identities of people and places by common social or cultural usage. Social constructs will often represent a 'loaded' view of the subject, according to the sources from which, and the channels through which, ideas are circulated in society.

These meanings are shared and can be greatly influenced by powerful groups: environmental problems have been fought over for decades in a tug-of-war between governments, businesses, scientists and pressure groups. Moreover, many environmental problems are distant from people or not measurable by them, for example, an oil spill in the North Atlantic or rainforest loss in the Amazon. For social problems like crime or unemployment, I would understand them through drawing on my own experiences or those of my neighbours but, sitting here in England, I rely on other people – particularly scientists and environmental activists – to tell me what is going on in the Atlantic or the Amazon, and why it matters. Applying social construction to environmental problems in this way focuses upon what we can think of as a 'claims-making' process (Hannigan, 1995), specifically:

- Who makes the claims that there is (or is not) an environmental problem?
- Who makes up the audience that is listening (or not listening) to these claims?
- How are these claims made and contested, using facts, rhetoric and **metaphor**?

We are influenced by various 'claims-makers', like pressure groups, scientists, industrial companies and journalists, who identify and define an environmental problem and bring it to our attention through the media (see examples in Hansen, 1993). They frequently 'encode' it in particular ways, to suit their own agenda and how they want to persuade their audience. Sometimes claims-makers tailor their information directly to their audiences, so that the coverage of environmental problems on the BBC's *Newsround* for younger viewers will be quite different to that on the BBC's *News at Ten* or *Newsnight*. Another example is school packs that help teachers by providing easy-to-use information, brightly coloured briefing sheets and well-organized tasks. But they are not neutral: they bring into the classroom the arguments that the pack's producers favour, often in very subtle ways. Similarly, environmental groups use newsletters, magazines and websites to speak to their members (who are already in a sense 'converts') and also to those not yet in tune with their views, without being filtered by newspaper or TV editors.

But claims-makers cannot control their audience's reaction. Some people will 'decode' the environmental meanings presented to them quite differently from how the producers intended. Geography matters: familiarity with and proximity to the environments being described may influence how people respond. People living around big factories and nuclear power plants understand the environmental impacts and risks of those sites in different ways, influenced negatively by 'folk memories' of smells, accidents and company PR, and positively by the employment provided, so their views may differ substantially from those of someone living far away. Some studies suggest that women, younger people, those with more education and those in more socially supportive occupations (teaching, healthcare, local government) tend to be more sympathetic to environmental messages. But other studies contradict this or show that sympathy does not translate into action. Lifestyle choices also matter:

Metaphor

the use of a word or symbol from one domain of meaning to apply to another. Thus a rose (a botanical term) is translated into the domain of human relationships to symbolize love. Metaphors involve this movement of concepts from their normal realm to a new realm.

some groups identify themselves as 'green consumers' whereas others are more concerned with fashion, for example, which means they will think about buying a new car in quite different ways, whatever claims the car manufacturers make. Together, the production and consumption of environmental meanings (Burgess, 1990) are critical in constructing and re-constructing environmental problems over time, as many layers of encoding and decoding accumulate.

A distinctive name or metaphor is often coined for an environmental problem, like 'the greenhouse effect' or 'Frankenstein foods', and this is a hugely effective shorthand way of conveying very complex ideas. Images are also important. Photogenic or visually arresting images, such as furry mammals or soaring birds to illustrate environmental stories, can thus influence TV producers in deciding whether and how to cover a story and persuade people to pay attention (Fig. 19.1). Timescale also matters. News coverage of chronic conditions – i.e. long-term but low-level – is difficult to keep exciting: 'pollution still happening' is not headline-grabbing, whereas flooding or oil spills have sudden drama. Claims are often geographical: global, national, local are all ways in which environmental problems are constructed. Local protests against development in the countryside are a good example and frequently make the news. Restoration of species to 'the British landscape' is a storyline that plays on national views of wildlife. All these images are part of constructing the urgency, impact and size of environmental problems, especially problems with which the audience is not familiar.

FIGURE 19.1
Photogenic wildlife make good visuals for environmental stories. Credit: Alaska Stock LLC/Alamy

SUMMARY

- Environmental problems do not simply reflect 'real' environmental change but are socially constructed.

- This construction is very much influenced by different 'claims-makers' – like pressure groups, scientists, industry and journalists – who identify and define an environmental problem and bring it to our attention through the media.

ENVIRONMENTAL PROBLEMS IN TIME AND SPACE

Environmental problems, moreover, are products of specific times and places. Let us take time first. Although we tend to think of environmental problems as modern, they are very old. Ancient Greek writers considered problems of soil erosion, and early laws against pollution (especially smoke) were enacted in London in the thirteenth century. Campaigners in Victorian England were concerned about the impact of increasing urbanization and industrialization on the environment and people's health, leading to campaigns for public sanitation, personal hygiene, nutrition, exercise and access to open space. In America, George Perkins Marsh's *Man and Nature* is sometimes cited as the first 'modern' take on environmental problems and a touchstone for geographers. First published in 1864, Marsh's book was before its time in not assuming that environmental resources were inexhaustible and the environment was resilient to human impact (Lowenthal, 1965; 2001). But although Marsh's book helped to inspire US forest protection in the late nineteenth century, it then fell into neglect until rediscovered in the 1930s, when another US environmental problem – agricultural erosion – gained public and political attention. In the UK in the 1930s, the rise of outdoor recreation generated a drive for public access to land and for national parks (first developed in the USA in the 1860s) that came to fruition in the 1949 National Parks and Access to the Countryside Act. These debates constructed environmental problems in social terms by portraying landscapes as national assets to be protected for the public.

Even what we might think of as 'modern' environmental problems have their origins in the 1960s, in concerns about nuclear weapons and energy, industrial pollution and endangered species, concerns that we think of today as **environmentalism** and associate with the environmental movement and pressure groups like Greenpeace, Friends of the Earth, the Sierra Club and WWF. However, there is a range of environmentalist views, some being more 'radical' and some more 'reformist', depending on how far they are willing to work with technology, with politicians and with companies and on the degree of change that they want to see in modern, industrialized systems (see Dobson, 1990). Despite this range, in most public debates environmental pressure groups tend to be simplified as collective representatives of environmentalism fighting against transnational companies – the 'green' activists standing symbolically against the forces of 'brown' capitalism. Greenpeace in particular has used this storyline very successfully since 1971 to obtain media coverage and public support for its environmental campaigns, sometimes symbolized as 'David versus Goliath' (Fig. 19.2).

Environmentalism, environmentalist

a social and political movement aimed at improving the relationship between humans and their natural environment.

Ecology

a way of studying living things (plants, animals or people) that emphasizes their complex and dynamic interrelationships with each other and the environment.

FIGURE 19.2
'David versus Goliath' in environmental action.
Credit: Argus/Still Pictures

In the late 1960s and early 1970s, public interest in environmental issues rose markedly, generating considerable support for environmental groups. This also drew on science – both the growth of **ecology**, which provided scientific evidence for environmental campaigns, and space travel, which nurtured modern ideas of the global environment as 'Spaceship Earth', a small, fragile ball in space, not least through the visual power of photographs from space (Cosgrove, 1994). Evidence of this successful construction of environmental problems is seen in the big international conference on environmental problems organized by the United Nations in 1972 (see Chapter 20). But researchers remained sceptical about claims of 'environmental crisis'. *The Limits to Growth* (Meadows *et al.*, 1972) reported the results of a 'world model' computer program run by researchers in the Massachusetts Institute of Technology to calculate future trends in population, industrial output, food production, resource use and pollution (Fig. 19.3). Although the crude modelling techniques were widely criticized at the time by geographers and others, the central argument was that environmental resources would become scarce, a point seemingly justified by the 1973 oil price crisis. The model constructed a world that (a) had limits to its growth that, once reached, would cause collapse, and (b) was moving closer to them. It was part of a new debate about shocking the world out of its complacency about the future, as a political and polemical act that was criticized by some as 'doom-mongering'.

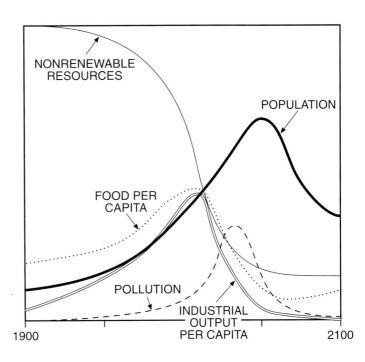

FIGURE 19.3
A graphic symbol of environmental crisis – the 'world model' results from *The Limits to Growth* (Meadows *et al.*, 1972)

Environmental problems are thus differently constructed over time. The climate is one example. In the 1970s, climate change was often constructed as a problem of global cooling, raising the prospect of 'the next ice age'. In the 1980s, as an undergraduate, I was taught about climate change through the concept of a 'nuclear winter' – what would happen to the climate if the **Cold War** turned into a nuclear war. In the 1990s, climate change was constructed as 'global warming' (see below). The point is that these three constructions reflect not rapid shifts in climate but rapid shifts in society and science that affected how environmental problems were seen and prioritized. In a classic paper, Downs (1972) suggested that environmental problems go through a 'life cycle': they rise from relative obscurity to reach a high public profile and enthusiasm for action, but then decline to a back-seat in people's minds. The claims-makers change too: the environmental pressure groups established in different periods have very different characters even now (Table 19.1).

As well as being products of specific times, environmental problems are products of specific places. Sometimes this is an effect of the physical sort of geography – for example, the concern since the 1980s over increasing pollution in the shallow, closely bounded North Sea on the part of those countries that surround it, or the 'dust bowl' agricultural problems in the USA in the 1930s, when soil erosion contributed to unemployment, massive migration and economic loss. At other times, it is the social and political sort of geography that matters. In Florida, USA, 16 people recently died in the damage caused by Hurricane Charley, which was covered extensively in the British news. A few weeks earlier, 2000 people died in flooding in Bangladesh, which received less than half as much coverage. Newspaper editors make choices like this every day, prioritizing places for coverage and thus influencing our global consciousness. Sometimes the politics comes to a head: European countries have been

Cold War

a period conventionally defined as running from the end of the Second World War until the fall of the Berlin Wall, during which the globe was structured around a binary political geography that opposed US CAPITALISM to Soviet communism. Although never reaching all-out military confrontation, this period did witness intense military, economic, political and ideological rivalry between the superpowers and their allies.

Table 19.1 The establishment of key environmental groups in England

	Year established
Manchester Association for the Prevention of Smoke	1843
Commons, Open Spaces and Footpaths Preservation Society	1865
National Trust	1895
(now Royal) Society for the Protection of Birds	1889
Wildlife Trusts (originally the Society for the Promotion of Nature Reserves)	1912
Ramblers Association	1925
Campaign to Protect Rural England (originally the Council for the Preservation of Rural England)	1926
Soil Association	1946
WWF	1961
Friends of the Earth	1969
Greenpeace	1971
Woodland Trust	1986

embroiled in heated debates over genetically modified crops since 1998, whereas the USA has been steadily planting them for ten years with little public debate, not least because of the huge power of agribusiness there. These different constructions are now at the heart of trade disputes about the legality of preventing the USA from exporting its crops to countries that have rejected this technology. Here, the shared meanings given to different environmental problems and solutions reflect cultural predispositions, political structures and, often, power.

As well as place, scale is important in constructing environmental problems. As geographers, we are of course interested in scale as an organizing principle and as a construct itself (see Chapter 3). I can illustrate scale in more detail through three examples (see below).

SUMMARY

- The social construction of environmental problems is influenced by specific times and places, because context strongly influences the way we make sense of our environment.

GLOBAL ENVIRONMENTAL PROBLEMS

Let us compare two famous global environmental problems: stratospheric ozone depletion and climate change. When I first began teaching environmental problems in 1991, ozone depletion was a very recent issue. Today, it has been largely superseded by others in the media and in curricula. Why?

Constructing the problem

Both stratospheric ozone depletion and climate change involve atmospheric chemistry and both are very dependent upon science and scientific claims-makers. The ozone 'layer' is in the stratosphere, about 15–22 km above our heads, where ozone is concentrated. Ozone (O_3) is created in sunlight as oxygen (O_2) molecules break down into two O atoms and then recombine unequally with others to form ozone. Ozone is broken down again when the reverse happens in sunlight, and catalysts such as chlorine and bromine encourage this destruction. Chlorine and other catalysts are largely anthropogenic, produced from the breakdown of chlorofluorocarbons (CFCs) and similar compounds emitted from human activities and products, such as air conditioners, freezers and fire extinguishers. So, the environmental problem that was identified was that emissions of CFCs and the like from human activities were destroying ozone in the stratosphere faster than it was being created.

In climate change, radiation (sunlight and heat) from the sun is partly reflected but mostly absorbed by the Earth, which then re-radiates it. Certain gases in the atmosphere absorb this heat and stop it escaping to space, making the lower atmosphere (troposphere) about 32°C warmer than it would be without these 'greenhouse gases'. The environmental problem that was identified was that emissions of greenhouse gases were increasing the amount of heat being retained – 'radiative forcing' – and thus causing 'global warming' or the 'enhanced' or 'anthropogenic' 'greenhouse effect'.

So far, so similar. But the trajectories of the two problems then diverge. The ozone 'hole' (this is shorthand of the sort I mentioned earlier – it is actually a 'thinning' of the layer, not a complete loss) over Antarctica was famously 'discovered' by the British Antarctic Survey in 1984 and confirmed by NASA scientists in 1985 (Fig. 19.4). These were big, very credible scientific groups and they quickly provided a clear, international consensus that CFCs emitted by human activities were threatening stratospheric ozone. Moreover, the consequences of stratospheric ozone depletion seemed to be primarily negative. Because the ozone layer absorbs and reflects ultraviolet rays from the sun, which can cause skin cancer, losses of ozone have been correlated with rises in skin cancers (approximately a 1 per cent rise for every 1 per cent ozone loss), eye cataracts and problems with the immune system in humans, as well as possibly reducing the productivity of agricultural crops and fisheries. Disagreements over the science did occur but were quickly quashed, not least when the large chemical industries, led by DuPont in the USA, decided to begin to replace ozone-depleting CFCs with other compounds.

The science of climate change has been much more contentious. There are massive uncertainties about how greenhouse gases behave and how clouds, ice sheets, oceans, forests, volcanoes and pollution will influence climate change in both direction and degree. This leaves several contentious questions. Has the climate changed already or not? Is climate change natural or our fault? How much change will happen and how fast?

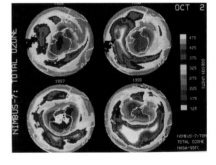

FIGURE 19.4
An international environmental problem seen through science: the ozone hole in 1985.
Credit: NASA/Getty Images

Where will the effects be and will they be dangerous or beneficial? People have turned to science to provide answers. The Intergovernmental Panel on Climate Change (IPCC) was set up in 1988 to bring together scientists to advise the United Nations. In producing its 1995 report, the IPCC scientists debated long and hard before stating that, on balance, there was evidence for a 'discernible' human influence on climate globally (quoted in Houghton, 1997: 50). Yet they also tried to recognize the uncertainty in their work (Fig. 19.5), which left plenty of scope for argument. For some commentators, the IPCC's reports are the definitive statements on the subject; for others, they are products of scientists who have been 'bought' by the political system or deluded by flawed results.

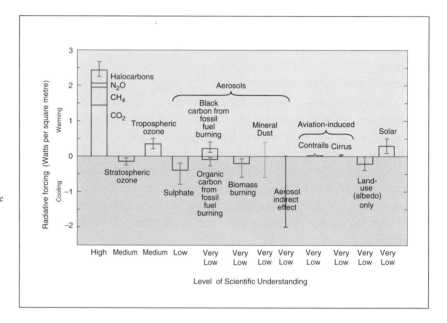

FIGURE 19.5

The global mean radiative forcing of the climate system for the year 2000, relative to 1750. Uncertainty in predicting climate change as seen by the IPCC. The bars show the IPCC's estimate of how much each gas retains heat in the atmosphere. No bar means that the uncertainty is too big to make a reasonable guess. The vertical lines show the range of estimates for each gas and are often very wide

Moreover, we talk about 'global warming' but the science shows that there will not be a simple global average but a highly complex geographical variability (Fig. 19.3). Some argue that climate change will be beneficial rather than damaging to some countries, not least in improving their agricultural and tourist industries. Others argue that the regions to suffer will be precisely those that can least afford it and thus are most vulnerable, yet will suffer at the hands of the richest, because they emit, per head, more greenhouse gases. Predictions of climate change and its impact therefore become highly politicized – the voices of the USA and Russia, which produce huge amounts of greenhouse gases, drown out the voices of the Association of Small Island States (AOSIS), which produce tiny amounts but are in the first line of any sea-level rise that climate change will cause.

To make the debate even muddier for the public, media stories about global warming sometimes bypass science completely in favour of extreme, but short-term weather events (see Fig. 21.2). The exceptionally wet months of 2000–01 in the UK, for example, were cited at the time in national newspapers as evidence of climate change – but so was the hot summer of 1995.

The business response has been quite different from that for ozone depletion. In the 1990s, business formed a club – the Global Climate Coalition (GCC) – to counteract claims about global warming. Involving companies in power, fuel, chemical and plastics, the GCC sought to protect the production and use of carbon-rich fossil fuels – oil, gas and coal (Rowell, 1996) – by TV advertising in the USA arguing that human-induced global warming was not proven, referring to it as the climate change 'hypothesis', and that any controls on greenhouse gases would cause unemployment and higher taxes for Americans. Although the GCC was later disbanded, the second Bush government subsequently followed a similar line and has even been accused of tampering with the scientific reports and distorting their conclusions to legitimate their position.

Constructing the solution

We have looked at how two environmental problems are constructed. But the essential reason to define something as a 'problem' in the first place is usually to argue for a particular 'solution'. Climate change is a good example: if the US government under Bush argues that there is no conclusive evidence that climate change is a problem, then there is no pressure on them to take action to solve it. Social construction like this can therefore be very useful politically.

There are two sorts of solution: mitigation and adaptation (and, of course, do nothing). Mitigation means you try to prevent or reduce the problem happening; adaptation means you work out a way to live with the problem without too much damage. Ozone depletion was constructed as a technological problem – there was a clearly identified and delineated culprit in CFCs and their like, and mitigation was possible through a technological solution or 'technofix': substitute the offending compounds with less damaging ones. The 1987 Montreal Protocol on Substances that Deplete the Ozone Layer was the global agreement to reduce CFCs and similar compounds and is now seen as a political success. All the major producing and consuming countries signed up to it and the extensive public and **NGO** support led to support from manufacturers to make products 'CFC-free'. This is why I have stopped teaching ozone depletion – the 'problem' is regarded as 'solved'. In the meantime, until the ozone layer has recovered sufficiently (perhaps by 2040), affected populations have been educated to 'live with' the problem by changing their behaviour in the sun. Public campaigns in Australia tell sunbathers how to protect themselves from the higher levels of ultraviolet radiation ('slip on a shirt, slop on some sun-cream, slap on a hat').

Climate change is far trickier. First, the 'culprits' are more complicated. Greenhouse gases include carbon dioxide, CFCs (again), methane and nitrous oxide (the big four) but also ozone (in this case in the troposphere) and water vapour, which have so far defied clear measurement and modelling. Moreover, unlike CFCs, the other greenhouse gases pervade all human activities and natural cycles to enable everyday life at a very basic level (heat, light, power, food) and are not easily replaceable. Climate change thus resists easy compartmentalization by industrial use – it is

Non-governmental organization (NGO)

an organization that belongs neither to the private for-profit sector, or the public or government sector.

implicated in everything we do and there are no easy substitutes in modern lifestyles.

The UN sponsored the 1992 Framework Convention on Climate Change and its famous upgrade, the 1997 Kyoto Protocol, but unlike the Montreal Protocol these have faced strong opposition, most notably from the presidents of the USA and Russia, two of the largest countries involved. Scientific uncertainties in the measurement and prediction of climate change are multiple and contentious, with a strong 'climate sceptic' community continuing to reject either the notion that climate change is human-induced rather than natural and/or the notion that climate change is necessarily bad. This is why climate change, unlike ozone depletion, is still very much a 'problem'.

SUMMARY

• Ozone depletion and climate change are both environmental problems related to atmospheric chemistry, but climate change has been far more contested, especially in terms of uncertainties and predictions, than ozone depletion, reflecting its more contentious construction and the importance of science in claims-making.

• The techno-fix solution to ozone depletion is largely seen as a success, whereas solutions to climate change have continued to be technologically and politically difficult.

LOCAL ENVIRONMENTAL PROBLEMS

By comparison with these two examples, environmental problems that are typically constructed as local often seem less glamorous. A good example is waste. Waste management is rarely subject to big modelling efforts, it does not dominate the agenda at international conferences run by the United Nations and it often, frankly, involves rather smelly and mundane questions. But it is hugely important (Fig. 19.6).

Constructing the problem

The environmental problem of waste is both simpler and more complicated than ozone depletion and climate change. For one thing, it is close at hand: where I live, everybody puts their rubbish out on Wednesday mornings in black plastic bags and, if I wanted to measure the amount of waste produced by my neighbours and myself, I could go out and weigh the bags – much easier than measuring ozone 22 km above my head. But in each bag will be a great variety of materials: broken glasses wrapped in newspapers, potato peelings, abandoned plastic toys and CDs, cardboard cereal boxes. The low-tech solution to all this for decades across the world has been to dump it in holes in the ground, often old quarries, cover it over and ignore it – more euphemistically referred to as 'landfilling'. Of the 400+ million tonnes of waste currently produced every year in the UK, most comes from construction, mining and other industries, only about 6 per cent comes from households and the vast majority of it all is landfilled.

Waste disposal has environmental and health effects. Landfill risks land contamination and leakage to the water table from the buried materials, or a build-up of methane gas from decomposition, which can explode or be emitted. Methane is also a greenhouse gas and about a third of it in the UK comes from landfill, which leads us right back to the argument above about climate change. Moreover, finding new landfill sites is getting more difficult as the UK runs out of holes to fill, particularly in the south-east. As this is also where most of the waste is produced, transport and its environmental impacts will also increase as waste is moved around the country in search of landfill space. Incinerating waste has health effects and risks environmental acidification when the emissions fall on surrounding land.

FIGURE 19.6
The increasing waste problem. Credit: Thomas Raupach/Still Pictures

All this is exacerbated by the simple fact that waste is growing – at about 3 per cent per year, which is faster than the economy. Indeed, waste is a proxy measure of human success: more production and more wealth means more consumption and more material things and packaging that eventually end up in the bin. Product design with 'in-built obsolescence', such as the laptop computer on which I typed this chapter, speeds up the process of waste creation and the amount produced over time, but can be hugely profitable.

Yet we know surprisingly little about waste: there are many uncertainties in waste management data and predictions, especially regarding new technologies and health effects. For example, a review commissioned by the UK government on the environmental and health effects of waste management options reported in 2004 that it could not decide which option was best because the information was simply not good enough. But modelling UK waste production is less glamorous than modelling climate change and far less likely to make the front pages of newspapers.

Constructing the solution

As with climate change and ozone depletion, the most permanent solution to waste disposal would be mitigation: reduce the problem by producing less waste. Failing that, adaptation involves dealing more effectively with the waste that *is* produced. Unlike climate change, the construction of waste as an environmental problem has no difficulty with natural variability: waste is constructed unambiguously as anthropogenic and bad, and there is no 'sceptic' argument to answer in this case. There is contestation, however, over the best solutions: whether recycling is better than waste-to-energy, for example, or whether the emissions from an incinerator are so damaging that they outweigh its advantages in disposing of waste and generating electricity in the process. Indeed, proposing incineration as 'waste-to-energy' is not necessarily a solution, because it will typically run into local opposition because of smells, visibility, emissions, increased traffic, and so on.

Recycling is often constructed as everyday common sense and therefore an obvious and well-established solution. But infrastructure, culture and geography matter. The Netherlands and Germany, for example, have had household recycling systems for decades, recycle twice as much material as Britain, recover over three times as much and correspondingly landfill half as much, as well as reducing the amount of waste they produce. The social construction of the solution in such countries is 'normalized' and has become part of daily routine, whereas recycling, particularly separating materials like glass, plastics and food waste inside the house, is often portrayed as difficult, inconvenient or just messy in Britain. Why is citizen responsibility better developed in some countries than others? And what can be done to make people in the UK construct the environmental problem of waste in similar terms?

Unlike climate change and ozone depletion, waste policy has been driven by Europe, especially through a common construct called the 'waste hierarchy'. This has the 'best' options at the top – waste minimization and reuse of waste – and the less good ones further down – recycling and recovery (usually through incineration that produces electricity) – with landfill last. The UK has had policies to try to 'move up the hierarchy' for years. In 1990, when the rate of recycling household waste was at only about 5 per cent, the government set a target of 25 per cent recycling by 2000. We failed to meet this by a long way, with household recycling rates still only 14 per cent in 2002–03, so the government has continually had to revise the target. Like climate change, waste is problematic because it is involved in everything we do, from building houses to cooking dinner. It is therefore politically difficult to ask people to buy less and thus to waste less, which leaves politicians in a dilemma: they want people to buy more (to help the economy) but produce less waste (to help the environment). We are therefore encouraged to participate in recycling schemes, but this is still entirely voluntary in the UK.

One solution adopted by the UK government in 1996 is a tax on landfill, paid by local authorities and companies, to make landfill more expensive and encourage them to consider other options. This constructs the waste problem as a waste of *money* as well as of resources and uses rhetoric like waste minimization, waste-to-energy, 'de-materialization' (such as using email instead of paper letters), industrial ecology and eco-efficiency. Lots of books have been written arguing that changing to more efficient (less wasteful) operations is not only possible but increasingly being implemented by business (e.g. von Weizsäcker *et al.*, 1997). By constructing environmental problems as to do with efficient technology (or lack of it), this avoids discussing the structural problems of underdevelopment, unequal access to resources and wasteful consumption.

Waste management is also a good example of a problem that gets relegated down to local government. Local authorities in the UK are responsible for collecting and disposing of household rubbish but, as planning authorities, they are also responsible for approving new disposal sites, such as incinerators. They are now charged with collecting and safely disposing of unwanted electrical goods and cars under the delightfully named WEEE Directive (Waste from Electronic and Electrical Equipment) and the End of Life Vehicles Directive respectively, both passed by the European Union in recent years. Both will prove major headaches for local authorities, with restricted budgets and facilities for recycling such large and complex consumer goods – fridges and freezers need to be safely disposed of to avoid releasing their CFCs, taking us back to ozone depletion. Researchers are currently grappling with how best to dismantle and reuse the tiny useful elements from unwanted computers, mobile phones and hairdryers that are thrown away every day in our wealthy country.

SUMMARY

- Waste is constructed as a local environmental problem, with less scientific and international controversy than climate change and ozone depletion.

- Solutions constructed for waste have been mainly to do with technology rather than consumption, and have been politically delegated to the more local level.

CONCLUSION

These three environmental problems have different geographies and histories. The same claims-makers are involved in all three, particularly environmental groups, the UK government and, for waste in particular, local governments. Science is an important claims-maker, although the individual scientists speaking to each issue differ and some areas of science are more contentious than others. Media coverage of the global issues has been frequent, but waste is rarely headline news – with the exception of abandoned cars, which made for striking images when editors decided to cover the End of Life Vehicles Directive. All the issues depend upon shorthand, whether this is 'global warming' or 'recycling', to summarize a set of complicated ideas, many of which are contested.

And the boundaries that we put around a 'problem' are socially constructed, because we tend to compartmentalize. I separated out 'local' and 'global' problems, but they are connected: greenhouse gases include CFCs that deplete ozone and are found in waste fridges, and landfills produce methane, another greenhouse gas. Emissions and waste production both tend to rise with development – the problems are products of success. More wealthy people, more diverse production processes, effective marketing mechanisms, better extractive technology – these all add up to more use of fossil fuels, driving more cars and further, running more electric appliances, buying more household products and then disposing of them more quickly. Yet constructions of the solution to these problems focus upon technology and politics, not on changing our lifestyles.

So, environmental problems are not just reflections of 'real' environmental change but reflections of how our society sees itself, its environment and the possibilities for improving both. Which is not to say that environmental problems are not important or worth addressing. As I said, sometimes critics of social construction argue that it denies external reality. Not so. What it does is show more clearly how little we know and how much our social and geographical context affects what we know and how we act.

DISCUSSION POINTS

1. Choose a recent environmental problem that you have seen or heard discussed in the media and make a list of the major 'claims-makers' involved. How influential is each one, in your view?

2. The contestation over global warming has been quite different to that over ozone depletion. What types of groups are involved in this contestation and what resources do they have at their disposal to make their arguments convincing?

3. What do you think are the main obstacles to (a) reducing waste and (b) increasing recycling in this country? How are these different to those in other countries?

FURTHER READING

Hannigan, J.A. (1995) *Environmental sociology: a social constructionist perspective.* **London: Routledge.**

This explains social construction and applies it to environmental cases.

Hansen, A. (ed.) (1993) *The mass media and environmental issues.* **Leicester: Leicester University Press.**

This has a variety of empirical studies of environmental stories in the media, within the approach of social construction, particularly the editor's own chapter on Greenpeace.

Houghton, J. (1997) *Global warming: the complete briefing.* **Cambridge: Cambridge University Press.**

This does just as the title says and was written by a key scientist in the IPCC, with authority and clarity.

Jackson, T. (1996) *Material concerns.* **London: Routledge.**

This introduces environmental management and covers recycling, waste minimization and pollution prevention, in a clear and non-technical way.

CHAPTER 20
SUSTAINABILITY

William M. Adams

INTRODUCTION

In 1999, the renowned conservation biologist John Terborgh complained that sustainable development had become the mantra of the conservation movement: like motherhood and apple pie, nobody could be against it, and yet because the word was seldom rigorously defined, it meant whatever anyone wanted it to mean (Terborgh, 1999). At first this vagueness of meaning is surprising, for indeed the idea of sustainability has become fundamental to any discussion of human impacts on the environment. It is hardly one of those secret words used only by academics and other toilers in the depths of libraries, for it peppers the speeches of politicians, teachers, business leaders and environmentalists and, of course, geographers.

It is worth remembering that the term sustainability has only recently become so widely used. The ideas for which it is so convenient (and, as we shall see, so slippery) a label have been around for many decades, but sustainability is very much a word of the 1990s. Specifically, it owes its global reach to the vast media roadshow surrounding the United Nations Conferences on Environment and Development (UNCED, or the 'Earth Summit') at Rio de Janeiro in Brazil in June 1992 (Chatterjee and Finger, 1994). Sustainability was UNCED's 'Big Idea'. Thus launched upon the world, its meteoric rise to global buzzword began. But what does sustainability mean? Why did it emerge at Rio? What use is it? These questions are rather harder to answer than it might at first appear.

Inter-generational equity

this term refers to the concept of equality in access to resources or wealth between one generation of people and another (usually a future generation, or people as yet unborn).

Intra-generational equity

this term refers to the concept of equality in access to resources or wealth within a single generation (usually between different groups of people today – for example, between rich and poor classes in one country, or between rich and poor countries such as between 'first world ' and 'third world' countries).

WHAT IS SUSTAINABILITY?

What does sustainability mean? Irritatingly, we could answer, 'everything and nothing'. It is a word that promises much. A dictionary definition offers a range of meanings, each of which captures something of the meaning of sustainability. Longman's *Dictionary of the English Language* (1991) gives the following definitions of the verb 'to sustain':

- to give support or relief to
- to supply with sustenance, nourish
- to cause to continue, prolong
- to support the weight of
- to bear up under, to endure (to suffer, to undergo).

They are all to do with continuity ('prolonging', 'nourishing', 'supporting', 'enduring'). They are also all basically positive, all things that might be thought of as broadly desirable or admirable. In public debate about environment and development, use of the word sustainability suggests that change can be allowed to happen (or made to happen), that the best of what has been done before is maintained, whether that change

Ecosystem

an ecosystem comprises: a set of plants, animals and micro-organisms amongst which energy and matter are exchanged; the physical environment with which, and within which, they interact. *See also* ECOLOGY.

is in an economy or society ('sustainable development') or in an **ecosystem** ('sustainable environmental management').

Internationally, the dominant definition of sustainable development has undoubtedly been that of the Brundtland Report, in *Our Common Future*: 'development that meets the needs of the present without compromising the ability of future generations to meet their own needs' (Brundtland, 1987: 43). This definition is both rhetorical and vague (Lélé, 1991), but it proved compelling as a way of pulling together concerns about environmental degradation and present and future poverty (often spoken of as **inter-** and **intra-generational equity**).

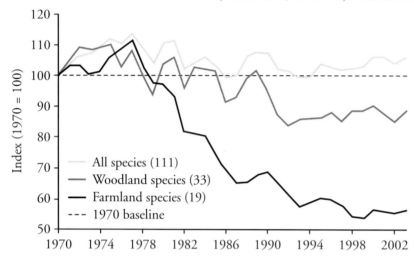

The word sustainability first appeared in British legislation in 1991, in the act establishing the conservation organization Scottish Natural Heritage (SNH). SNH was charged with achieving and promoting the conservation and enjoyment of landscapes and wildlife 'in a manner that is sustainable'. This apparent coup for environmental thinking caused some scratching of heads in the new agency, because whilst the word might have sounded wonderful in Parliament, its meaning was far from clear. Eventually, SNH suggested that sustainability should mean 'the ability of an activity or development to continue in the long term without undermining that part of the environment which sustains it' (SNH, 1993). Whilst heart-warming (and arguably very wise) as a general principle, this is hardly a sharply focused definition. When other UK national conservation agencies set up in 1991 got in on the act, their own definitions were no more specific.

In May 1999 the UK government published a strategy for sustainable development, *A Better Quality of Life*, to bring 'the environment, social progress and the economy alongside each other at the heart of policy making'. This expressed sustainable development as 'the simple idea of ensuring a better quality of life for everyone, now and for generations to come' (www.sustainable-development.gov.uk). Less simplistically, Forum for the Future (a UK non-governmental organization, or NGO) defines sustainable development as: 'A dynamic process which enables all people to realize their potential and improve their quality of life in ways which simultaneously protect and enhance the Earth's life support systems.'

FIGURE 20.1
The UK government has adopted as one of its indices of sustainability the population of farmland birds (indicator H 13)

SUMMARY

- Sustainability is an emotive word, with complex meanings.
- The concept of sustainability began to be used internationally in the 1980s (notably in the report of the Brundtland Commission in 1987), and first appeared in British law in 1993. Since 1999 it has been emphasized as a central feature of UK government policy.

SUSTAINABILITY: MORE THAN A BUZZWORD?

Almost as soon as it started to be widely adopted, in the early 1990s, sustainability was being criticized or dismissed as jargon. In the UK, for example, the Council for the Protection of Rural England described sustainable development as 'the latest buzz-phrase to hit the planning profession' (Jacobs, 1993: 8). By the end of the decade, it had become almost impossible to avoid using it. Geography has certainly not been free of its influence, as a glance through any mainstream publisher's catalogue, or a swift perusal of geography textbooks (including this one, of course!) would prove. Sustainability is therefore quite obviously important if one measures something's importance by the number of people talking about it. What is less clear, however, is whether anything much lies behind the glittery promise of the word.

Superficially, the concept of sustainability seems very simple, yet it can have a wide range of meanings attached to it. It is attractive to environmental campaigners and businesses as well as governments. The transnational company Rio Tinto speaks of sustainability in the context of its business of mining and mineral processing for profit, producing 'essential metals and minerals that supply the amenities of life and enhance living standards' in a manner that safeguards the natural resources in its care, be they water, air or land (see www.riotinto.com/community/). Similarly, the oil multinational Shell, which revised its 'Business Principles' in 1997 to include a commitment to contribute to sustainable development, defines it as 'engaging with our stakeholders to better understand and manage the impacts, both positive and negative, that our operations and products have on society and the environment today, and to identify business opportunities for the future' (www.shell.com/home). Such professions of enthusiasm for sustainability by global business corporations are obviously chiefly designed to reassure shareholders and head off critical public opinion. However, they can generate significant investment for other organizations such as universities. In July 2002, the Shell Oil Company Foundation announced an endowment of $3.5 million to establish a Shell Center for Sustainability at Rice University (Houston, Texas), while in May 2003, Shell International Exploration and Production announced a £0.5 million endowment to establish a Shell Chair in Sustainable Development in Energy at Imperial College, London.

However, the view of even an enlightened business leader of sustainability tends to be rather different from that of an environmental campaigner, or for that matter from that of someone who has suffered from gas flaring and heavy-handed oil companies and state security forces in Nigerian Ogoniland (see Fig. 20.2; for a local view of Shell's sustainability report, see www.nigeriavillagesquare1.com/Articles/bankarow.html). It tends to be different too from the view of governments. The UK Sustainable Development Commission, for example, see sustainable development as providing a framework for redefining progress and redirecting economies to enable people to meet basic needs and improve their quality of life, whilst maintaining and enhancing natural systems, resources and diversity (www.sd-commission.gov.uk).

This suggests a modestly radical vision of sustainability, where it drives changes in business-as-usual. The UK government itself places less emphasis on change. Its four objectives for sustainable development are:

1. social progress that recognizes the needs of everyone
2. effective protection of the environment
3. prudent use of natural resources, and
4. maintenance of high and stable levels of economic growth and employment.

A key principle of the UK's approach to sustainable development is the creation of 'an open and supportive economic system', involving the maintenance of economic growth: the government argues that 'sustainable development requires a global economic system which supports economic growth in all countries. We need to create conditions in which trade can flourish and competitiveness can act as a stimulus for growth and greater resource efficiency' (www.sustainable-development.gov.uk). This approach, seeking to maintain economic growth, whilst trying to restructure the economy, is typical of the mainstream thinking about sustainability that has won acceptance around the globe since the Rio Conference (Adams, 2001). However, there is a vast difference between 'sustainable development' and 'sustainable growth' (see box).

Environmentalists, government economic and political planners, and business people all use the word sustainability to express their own vision of how economy and environment should be managed. Use of the word does not end the debate about how society should exploit non-human nature, it simply re-labels it. Indeed, such is the power of sustainability to allow different ideas to be smuggled forward in its ample conceptual folds that it can effectively delay debate and pushes it underground. Radical opponents of roads and other infrastructure have literally taken to the ground (or the trees) as well as city streets in opposition (see Fig. 20.3). Although there has been a growing debate about sustainability and transport in the UK, it has not been the direct result of their protests, but of widespread alarm at clotting roads and the results of rail privatization. For a single neat word, sustainability hides a theoretical maze of great complexity (Lélé, 1991). It offers a verbal flourish, but arguably, at its core, lies a theoretical black hole (Adams, 2001; Redclift, 1987).

Of course, it is not strictly fair to say that sustainability has no theoretical core. Its intellectual roots lie in population biology, ecology and economics. Through the 1920s and 1930s, biologists were developing simple mathematical models of population growth and competition, from

FIGURE 20.2
Spills from oil wells, pipelines and gas flaring are major environmental problems in the Niger Delta in southeast Nigeria, where Shell is a leading operator. Ken Saro Wiwa, Nigerian playwright, was executed in 1996 following protests about pollution and demands for independence for Ogoniland. Credit: Detlef Pypke/Still Pictures

ECONOMIC GROWTH AND SUSTAINABLE DEVELOPMENT

" *Governments often speak of aiming for 'sustainable growth': they mean economic growth without inflation rather than without environmental degradation, and the usual interpretation of 'sustainable' is lasting about four years, or until the next election, whichever is the sooner.* "

(Jacobs, 1993: 9)

" *In the past, economic activity tended to mean more pollution and wasteful use of resources. We have had to spend to clean up the mess. A damaged environment impairs quality of life and, at worst, may threaten long term economic growth – for* "

example, as a result of climate change. And too many people have been left behind, excluded from the benefits of development but often suffering from the side-effects. "

(www.sustainable-development.gov.uk)

" *It needs to be remembered after all that sustainable development and sustainability were not originally intended as 'economic' terms. They were, and remain, essentially ethico-religious objectives, more like 'social justice' and 'democracy' than 'economic growth'. And as such, their purpose or 'use' mainly to express key ideas about how society – including the economy – should be governed.* "

(Jacobs, 1995: 65)

which, in time, grew the notion of maximum sustainable yield, that populations of organisms (initially fish, but the point was generally true) could be harvested at a rate that allowed the population to reproduce itself.

These scientific ideas about how animal populations fluctuated, and what happens when people start to harvest them, comprise one stream of biological ideas feeding into sustainability. A second is in ecology, particularly in the concept of the ecosystem (proposed in the 1930s), and in ideas about plant succession. As ecology became influenced by systems thinking in the 1960s, ideas of equilibrium in ecosystems provided a further natural science basis for ideas of sustainability. The science of ecology seemed to show the vulnerability of the environment to human impacts, and the need for those impacts to be moderated. Meanwhile, from economics came concepts of renewable (flow) and non-renewable (stock) resources. These are diverse enough roots, but on to them many other ideas were grafted from the emerging worldview of environmentalism, particularly about population growth, resource exhaustion, and the toxic and shocking effects of industrialization and urbanization (Adams, 2001).

FIGURE 20.3
Anti-globalization protestors carry their message to the streets in the USA. Credit: Joel Saget/Getty Images

SUMMARY

- Sustainability tends to be defined in different ways by different interests – for example, by environmental organizations and big business.

- The concept of sustainability draws on scientific studies of the dynamics of animal populations and ecosystem equilibrium, and ideas about the economics of renewable resource exploitation.

SUSTAINABILITY AND THIRD WORLD DEVELOPMENT

The concept of sustainability first emerged at the United Nations Conference on the Human Environment, held at Stockholm in 1972 (Adams, 2001; McCormick, 1992). This meeting was the direct forerunner of the Rio Conference 20 years later. Like Rio, it saw profound divisions between industrialized countries and the third world. The poorer non-aligned countries saw the first world's concerns about pollution and technology as the worries of an exclusive club of wealthy countries, and a potential threat to their ability to industrialize effectively. They also feared and resented the obsession of environmentalists in the first world with population growth (see box). The concept of sustainable development was coined explicitly to argue that an option existed that would allow appropriate (i.e. rapid) economic growth and industrialization without environmental damage. This happy outcome has been the target of all subsequent calls for sustainability.

Since Stockholm, different interests have emphasized different aspects of sustainability, and sought to claim the concept for their own. In 1980 the World Conservation Strategy (IUCN, 1980) took a strongly conservation-oriented position. It defined conservation as sustained resource use, and suggested three objectives for global conservation. The objectives of the World Conservation Strategy were:

FIGURE 20.4
It is estimated by the United Nations Environment Programme that between 5 and 20 per cent of the 14 million plant and animal species on earth are threatened with extinction. Human activities are believed to have increased 'background' extinction rates by up to 10,000 times. Amphibians like this golden toad of Costa Rica are particularly threatened. Credit: Arnold Newman/Still Pictures

1. to maintain essential ecological processes and life support systems (such as soil regeneration and protection, the recycling of nutrients and the cleansing of waters)
2. to preserve genetic diversity (the range of genetic material found in the world's organisms)
3. to ensure the sustainable utilization of species and ecosystems (notably fish and other wildlife, forests and grazing lands).

Six years later, the report of the World Commission on Environment and Development, *Our Common Future* (referred to as the Brundtland

POPULATION, ENVIRONMENT AND SUSTAINABILITY

In the 1970s, first world environmentalists placed particular emphasis on the problem of population growth, arguing that as populations rose, resource exploitation would inevitably become unsustainable. This argument was made particularly in connection with rural populations in the third world. Books like *The Population Bomb* by Paul Ehrlich (1972), and papers like Garrett Hardin's 'The tragedy of the commons' (published in *Science* in 1968), started a new and apocalyptic 'neo-Malthusian' debate about people and environment. Through the 1970s and 1980s, the drylands of Sub-Saharan Africa were singled out in particular as a place where rapid population growth was leading to environmental degradation. Drought and famine were both significant problems in this decade, but attention focused in particular on the problem of 'desertification' and human-made deserts. It was widely held (not least by geographers) that population growth inevitably led to desertification, as farmers and pastoralists pushed semi-arid ecosystems past some natural limit.

However, research in recent years has begun to show that, in several parts of Africa, agricultural systems appear to have coped with significant levels of population growth without loss of sustainability. The most important study of this kind was conducted in the Machakos District in Kenya (Tiffen *et al.*, 1994). In the 1930s, government officials despaired of Machakos, which was thought to be on the verge of ecological collapse due to over-population. Some 50 years later, the changes have been remarkable. The population has soared (from 0.24 m in 1930 to 1.4 m in 1990), but far from destroying the environment, farmers have developed it. Terracing is extensive, cattle are stall-fed and their manure applied to the land (see Fig. 20.5), and with the advent of cash crops (particularly coffee), the volume and value of output have increased to match population growth. It is an astonishing story, and whilst the experience of this area might not be a good model for the whole of Africa (amongst other things, the international city of Nairobi is not far from the borders of Machakos, and the main road to the coast passes through it), the same kinds of pattern have been identified elsewhere – for example, in southern Niger and the peanut basin of Senegal in the Sahel (Mortimore, 1998). It is clearly unwise to make the automatic assumption that rural population growth is unsustainable.

Report after its Chair), had a very different emphasis. It deliberately broadened the debate, locating environmental issues within the economic and political context of international development debates. It therefore linked basic development needs and environmental degradation, arguing that one could not be solved without the other. The way forward, it suggested, was through global multilateral co-operation between rich and poor countries to achieve development: sustainability achieved through careful economic growth.

FIGURE 20.5
Intensively cultivated, densely settled and terraced land in Mbooni, Machakos, Kenya, 1996. Credit: Bill Adams

The Brundtland Report, published in 1987, led directly to UNCED in two ways. First, it was debate of the report in the General Assembly of the UN that led to the resolution to hold what became the Rio Conference. Second, it was this message of adapted, or 'green', growth that provided the carrot to persuade both rich and poor countries to come to the negotiating table. Nonetheless, the task of finding common ground was

Herculean, and lasted through a full five years of preparatory meetings before the conference itself (Chatterjee and Finger, 1994). The documents produced by this 'Rio process' were the fruit of wearying debate far into the night by government delegations determined to produce a form of words that gave least away in terms of their own national interests.

Inevitably, divisions opened up between the distinction between countries in the industrialized 'North' and the underdeveloped 'South'. They disagreed over what the main global problems were (global atmospheric change, **biodiversity** loss and tropical deforestation in the industrialized countries, poverty and the environmental problems associated with it in unindustrialized countries), and they disagreed over who should pay for any action needed. Third world countries feared that their development would be stifled by restrictive international agreements on atmospheric emissions (just as at Stockholm in 1972), and they were jealous of their right to use the natural resources within their boundaries for development (notably tropical forests) without restriction by environmentalists in the first world (whose environmental concerns, arguably, were only possible because of a wealth itself created by polluting freely and consuming forests and other resources).

Eventually, some kind of agreement was patched together, and the conference agreed a slightly rambling set of 29 principles in the 'Rio Declaration', a much watered-down set of principles for forest management, and the vast compendium of good intentions in *Agenda 21*, which contains more than 600 pages of text in 40 separate chapters. These were divided into four sections, covering socio-economic and environmental aspects of sustainable development, the actors who could make it happen and the means of implementation (see box).

Agenda 21 has become a symbol of the term sustainability itself, worshipped but not examined in much detail. Because of the way it was written through negotiation, every commitment has a get-out clause

Biodiversity
describes the variability in nature, including of genes, individuals, species and ecosystems. Biodiversity exists both in particular living things (such as individual rare species) and also in biological processes and dynamic ecological systems.

THE CONTENTS OF *AGENDA 21*

Section 1   *Social and Economic Dimensions* Eight chapters, covering international co-operation, combating poverty, consumption patterns, population, health, settlements, and integrated environment and development decision-making.

Section 2   *Conservation and Management of Resources for Development* Fourteen chapters on the environment. These cover the atmosphere, oceans, freshwaters and water resources, land resource management, deforestation, desertification, mountain environments, sustainable agriculture and rural development. They also cover the conservation of biological diversity and biotechnology, toxic, hazardous, solid and radioactive wastes.

Section 3   *Strengthening the Role of Major Groups* Ten chapters discussing the role of women, young people and indigenous people in sustainable development; the role of non-governmental organizations, local authorities, trades unions, business and scientists, and farmers.

Section 4   *Means of Implementation* Eight chapters, exploring how to pay for sustainable development, the need to transfer environmentally sound technology and science; the role of education, international capacity-building; international legal instruments and information flows.

(Robinson, 1993)

somewhere nearby. It, therefore, contains within it most possible arguments, and is readily mined for nuggets of text that can be used to legitimate any given point of view.

In the late summer of 2002, the ten-year follow-up to Rio, the World Summit on Sustainable Development (WSSD), took place in Johannesburg, South Africa. This was attended by over 22,000 people, including 100 heads of state. Governments committed themselves to achieving poverty-related targets and goals, including those in *Agenda 21* and the United Nations Millennium Declaration. The meeting issued the Johannesburg Plan of Implementation (www.johannesburgsummit.org/). This addressed poverty eradication, the need to change unsustainable patterns of consumption and production, the protection and management of the natural resource base of economic and social development, the issue of sustainable development and globalization, and the links between health and sustainable development. It also addressed sustainable development of particular regions (for example, small-island developing states and Africa).

The WSSD updated the debates and conclusions of the Rio Conference, but it was Rio that was the critical watershed. From then on, governments and international agencies began to re-interpret their normal work of economic planning within the new, internationally agreed, terminology. There was a substantial shift in political and bureaucratic rhetoric, but the new language sometimes lay wafer-thin across old and not obviously 'sustainable' policies. A shift in the language of policy of this magnitude, of course, is no small matter. It was due to two related forces. First, it was a straightforward response by politicians (particularly in Europe and North America) to the surge of environmentalism that took place within western societies in the early 1990s. Behind that pragmatic (perhaps sometimes cynical) politics lay a perception of environmental limits, which had itself driven that rise of environmental concern. As Bill McKibben wrote in his bestselling book *The End of Nature*, 'The greenhouse effect is the first environmental problem we can't escape by moving to the woods' (McKibben, 1990: 188). Sustainability and sustainable development were the words people in the 1990s came to use to express that thought, and on which they tried to build arguments for reform.

FIGURE 20.6
Smoke plume from UK power station: concern about acid rain was one of the environmental problems that led to the Stockholm Conference in 1972. Credit: Jochen Tack/Still Pictures

Globalization

the economic, political, social and cultural processes whereby: (a) places across the globe are increasingly interconnected; (b) social relations and economic transactions increasingly occur at the intercontinental scale (*see* TRANSNATIONAL); and (c) the globe itself comes to be a recognizable geographical entity. As such, globalization does not mean everywhere in the world becomes the same. Nor is it an entirely even process; different places are differently connected into the world and view that world from different perspectives. Globalization has been occurring for several hundred years, but in the contemporary world the scale and extent of social, political and economic interpenetration appears to be qualitatively different to international networks in the past.

SUMMARY

- The key event in the development of thinking about sustainability was the Rio Conference in 1992.

- At Rio a series of agreements were signed, the most important of which was the massive *Agenda 21*.

SUSTAINABILITY, EQUITY AND BIODIVERSITY

FIGURE 20.7
The United Nations Development Programme estimate that more than a billion people continue to live and work in abject poverty with no access to clean and safe drinking water. Current expenditure of 16 billion dollars a year would need to be doubled to achieve the Millennium Development Goal target of halving the population lacking access to clean water by 2015.
Credit: T.C. Malhotra/ZUMA/Corbis

Issues of equity, between rich and poor today and between present and future generations, are fundamental to sustainable development. However, the radical element in thinking about sustainability for Human Geographers is its emphasis on the state of the environment. The 1990s saw a massive theoretical and practical engagement in debates about society and environment in the social sciences as a whole, and in geography in particular. Issues of environmental risk, environmental planning and policy, of the social construction of nature and the political ecology of resource exploitation have become increasingly central themes for research (for example, Castree and Braun, 2001; Keeley and Scoones, 2003; Peet and Watts, 1996).

There is an important tension in the way the conservation of the environment is portrayed within thinking about sustainability. It is obvious that human impacts and demands on the biosphere have become very significant (Palumbi, 2001). One response to this emphasizes the preservation of biodiversity – for example, through the creation of national parks and other protected areas. The other emphasizes the use of biodiversity to generate economic benefits, particularly the need for the environment to provide safe and productive livelihoods for the poor.

Sometimes preservation and economic exploitation can be closely aligned. There is growing awareness, for example, of the importance of 'ecosystem services', the economic benefits that flow from ecosystems (such as clean air and water; see Daily, 1997). However, in many instances these responses conflict. The creation of protected areas, often described as a policy of 'fortress conservation', has often involved the eviction of former land users, and has been an important factor in the impoverishment of local communities (Adams, 2004). On the other hand, the best strategies for the development of land from the point of view of poverty alleviation or economic growth may involve the loss of biodiversity (e.g. the conversion of forest to farms).

The area of national parks has grown very fast in the last 20 years. The 2003 UN World List includes 102,102 sites, covering an area of 18.8 million km, and technical expertise in selecting the best locations is also developing rapidly. Debate at the fifth World Parks Congress in Durban in September 2003 proposed further development of the global system of protected areas (PAs) and their integration into national development planning – for example, in an attempt to reach the Millennium Development Goals (see box). This continuing (indeed, growing) enthusiasm for PAs emphasizes the centrality of the question of whether it is possible to deliver conservation goals whilst also meeting poverty needs. The Director General of the World Conservation Union argued in 2003 that protected areas must be seen as 'islands of biodiversity in an ocean of sustainable human development', with their 'benefits extending far beyond their boundaries' (Steiner, 2003). But can this be done?

From the 1980s onwards, biodiversity conservation strategies based on

SUSTAINABILITY AND THE MILLENNIUM DEVELOPMENT GOALS

Sustainability was one of the eight Millennium Development Goals agreed at the United Nations Millennium Summit in September 2000 (www.developmentgoals.org/). The others goals are to eradicate extreme poverty and hunger, to achieve universal primary education, to promote gender equality and empower women, to reduce child mortality, improve maternal health, to combat HIV/AIDS, malaria and other diseases, and to build a global partnership for development. The goals are intended to be yardsticks for measuring improvements in people's lives, and are associated with 18 targets and 48 indicators.

Goal 7, to 'ensure environmental sustainability' involves three targets:

1. the integration of the principles of sustainable development into country policies and programmes, and reverse the loss of environmental resources
2. the halving of the proportion of people without sustainable access to safe drinking water by 2015
3. the achievement of a significant improvement in the lives of at least 100 million slum dwellers by 2020.

There are seven indicators relevant to these goals. Some have an obvious and direct development focus (e.g. the proportion of people with sustained access to an improved water source). Two have some relevance to biodiversity, the proportion of land area covered by forest (although the kind of forest is not specified – it could include plantations, of low biodiversity value) and the area of land protected to maintain biological diversity.

excluding local people have begun to be replaced with attempts to integrate conservation and economic development, particularly around national parks. New 'community conservation' strategies include Integrated Conservation and Development Projects, which attempt to combine biodiversity conservation and economic development by targeting development aid. Typical approaches are to develop wildlife tourism or safari hunting activities that yield significant benefits to local people. A well-known example of the latter approach is the CAMPFIRE model developed in Zimbabwe, where legal rights in wildlife can be granted to district councils, who can then allow communities to charge safari hunters for shooting rights.

Where economic development is on a larger scale, conflict between biodiversity and economic returns can be more difficult to reconcile. As we have seen above, the concept of sustainable development was precisely devised as a means of suggesting that this conflict can be avoided. One way to do this would be to recognize the manifold economic values of the environment and ensure they are taken into account in decision-making. To this end, a distinction is now commonly drawn between five different kinds of capital, one of which is 'natural capital', meaning natural resources and services; see box). Sustainability can then be defined in terms of the maintenance of the stock of natural capital over time. Some conservationists suggest treating vital conservation areas as 'critical natural capital', off-limits for development. These cannot be replaced if lost (or, at least, not within feasible time-frames), and cannot therefore be substituted for human capital or compensated for by positive projects elsewhere. However, some economists argue that this approach immobilizes important economic resources that are needed if the wider economic benefits of resource use (for example, to alleviate poverty) are to be realized.

FIVE FORMS OF CAPITAL

- **Financial capital:** the conventional meaning of capital – for example, in the form of shares, bonds or bank notes. Financial capital is central to the capitalist economy, for it enables the other form of capital to be owned and traded. However, unlike the other forms, it has no real value itself but is representative of natural, human, social or manufactured capital.
- **Human capital:** people's health, knowledge, skills and motivation.
- **Social capital:** the institutions that maintain and develop human capital – for example, in families, communities, businesses, trades unions, schools and voluntary organizations.
- **Manufactured capital:** material goods or fixed assets that contribute to the production process rather than being the output itself – for example, tools, machines and buildings.
- **Natural capital:** any stock or flow of energy and material that produces goods and services – including: *resources*, renewable and non-renewable materials; *sinks*, which absorb, neutralize or recycle waste, and *processes* such as climate regulation.

SUMMARY

- One aspect of sustainability emphasizes the importance of preserving the quality of the environment, particularly biodiversity. Another aspect emphasizes the flow of economic benefits through time, particularly the livelihoods of the poor. The concept of sustainability is attractive because it suggests that both these objectives can be achieved together.

- Biodiversity conservation strategies (such as national parks) are increasingly being designed to have a positive rather than a negative impact on local people.
- One approach to integrating environmental and welfare aspects of sustainability is through identifying the economic values of the environment, and treating biodiversity as 'natural capital'.

CONCLUSION: LIVING WITH SUSTAINABILITY

At Rio, Johannesburg and everywhere else, from street-corner demonstrations to corporate board rooms, debates about sustainability have often involved a large amount of hot air. However, behind this lies an extremely important set of issues for world leaders, and indeed for Human Geographers. Although, to date, the radical potential of sustainability as a political and policy tool has tended to be smothered, it has not yet been wholly lost. A critical question for geographers must be what happens when the over-inflated balloon of green rhetoric comes down to earth. Specifically, how will the challenge of sustainability posed at Rio and Johannesburg be taken up, and the fine words turned into policy by central and local government, businesses and non-governmental organizations?

Although it has exciting potential in policy terms, the concept of sustainability is less satisfactory in theoretical terms. It has little rigour to offer geographers anxious to get an intellectual grip on issues of environment and development. Here too, however, sustainability cannot be ignored, for it has few equals as a challenge to geographers to develop their theoretical ideas, and then to use them to engage in understanding the relations between society and nature, and perhaps even changing them for the better.

DISCUSSION POINTS

1. Does the fact that the meaning of sustainability is so difficult to establish make it useless as a way of talking about the relations between people and environment on either the national or international scale? (Think about what has been achieved at international conferences and in national reports on sustainability.)

2. Can activities that deplete finite natural resources (such as the exploitation or oil or metallic minerals) ever truly be 'sustainable' and, if not, what implications does this have for discussions about the 'greening' of industry? (Think about the gaps between efforts to improve present business practices and the requirements for genuine sustainability.)

3. Can the world economy continue to grow without destroying the planet, and, if so, how? (Think about the distribution of wealth and economic power, the problem of greenhouse gases, and the geography of flows of goods, services and pollution.)

4. To what extent do you think the Millennium Development Goals can be achieved and, if they are achieved, to what extent do you think they will have helped achieve global sustainability?

5. Discuss the geography of a world where extensive powered air flight is no longer possible.

FURTHER READING

Chatterjee, P. and Finger, M. (1994) *The earth brokers: power, politics and world development*. London: Routledge.

This thought-provoking and critical book provides useful insights on the Rio Conference and the political wrangling leading up to it. The failings of the 'Rio Process' have been shared by subsequent attempts to deliver sustainability on the international stage, notably the World Summit on Sustainable Development in Johannesburg in 2002. This book explains why this happened.

Holdgate, M. (1996) *From care to action: making a sustainable world*. London: Earthscan.

This book provides a valuable overview of the global challenge of sustainable development. It develops the ideas discussed in *Agenda 21*, and discusses how sustainable development could be delivered in the real world at international, national and local scales. It provides practical analysis and ideas for change.

McCormick, J.S. (1992) *The global environmental movement: reclaiming Paradise*. London: Belhaven.

John McCormick's book gives an excellent introduction to the history of the environmental movement. Ideas about sustainability became important internationally following the first peak of modern environmental concern in industrialized countries, although their roots (like those of environmentalism itself) are much older. The book sets sustainability in its historical context.

Adams, W.M. (2001) *Green development: environment and sustainability in the third world*. London: Earthscan.

This book provides an in-depth account of sustainable development in theory and practice. It describes the history of ideas of sustainability, and outlines ideas such as political ecology, environmental modernization and risk society that have become important to understanding it. The book discusses mainstream and radical approaches in the search for sustainability.

CHAPTER 21

ENVIRONMENTAL KNOWLEDGES AND ENVIRONMENTALISM

INTRODUCTION

The woman with the clipboard stops you in the street. It's an environmental survey. Could she ask you a few questions? 'OK, so long as it's quick.' So she starts by asking you how serious are each of the following problems.

'Global warming?'

And you think: *The IPCC statements. Global warming est arrivé – don't think it's chance variation any more. Um, Kyoto conference a few years ago (reminder to self: must look up an atlas and find out where Kyoto actually is). Hey, I remember reading recently that the UK government's Chief Scientific Adviser has gone on record saying that climate change was a greater threat to world order than international terrorism. Bet New Labour didn't want to hear that! Oh yes, and* The Day After Tomorrow. *Wasn't a bad movie as disaster movies go; great effects even if the story was a bit rubbish. Can't think of anything else. But this is a really weird winter. Dawn chorus in the middle of January; the bulbs are up in the parks, already.*

So you say: 'I think global warming is quite serious.'

'Local air quality?', she asks.

And you think: *We're standing on the pavement and I can hardly hear what she's saying because of the noise of the traffic. The smell is absolutely disgusting! Look at the fumes belching out of the back of that bus! I gave up riding my bike 'cos it's so bad. Can't afford the bus fares, though. Read somewhere that the cost of motoring has stayed constant since 1974 while public transport costs have increased by 20 per cent. Where was that? My little brother's got asthma. They say it's not traffic related, but they would say that, wouldn't they? Something's got to be done. The road protesters did a good job, got a lot of publicity. I wouldn't mind immobilizing a bulldozer – probably more interesting than the tutorial I'm late for . . .*

So you say: 'I think local air quality is a very serious issue.'

Then the interviewer says, 'Could you tell me whether you do any of the following and, if so, how often? Recycle your domestic waste?'

And you think: *What does she mean? Bottles? Well, mum does that at home, so I suppose that counts. Er, we had a compost heap but the smell was so bad we dug it in. Can't you get worms or something? Wonder what would happen if some escaped – or got 'liberated' by the animal rights people: TERROR IN THE TURF . . . Scientists warned today of a potential catastrophe as alien worms crunch through their mild-mannered English cousins. Come on, concentrate – this is serious. I always leave the newspaper on the bus so someone else can read it – that's a sort of recycling. But then again, what's the point? There was a story on the 6 o'clock News the other day that recycling actually uses more energy and it would be better to burn paper in one of those, um, what are they called, combined heat and light stations? Er, don't do that much really. But I ought to be doing more; over-consumption of resources; think about the third world and all that.*

So you say: 'I always recycle papers and bottles.'

You have just read a creative construction of how someone, not unlike you, might think as they respond to questions about environmental topics. We know very little about the internal deliberations, the arguments that go on inside people's heads, especially when they answer questionnaires. All researchers are able to capture on their survey forms are the bald responses. Contrast what my imaginary student was thinking with what was actually communicated and recorded. One of the major changes in geographical research over the last 15 years has been a shift towards qualitative, discursive forms of inquiry, where the aim is to engage people in extended conversation so as to better understand the nature of argument and evidence they draw upon to make sense of the world.

My student is imaginary but what she is thinking and how she is framing answers to questions is representative of the ways people understand environmental questions. Complex knowledges of different status and different levels of certainty come together as half-remembered items in the news and fuse with personal memories. The intense, sensory impacts of immediate experience take precedence over the discursive, abstract knowledges of experts. The imaginary student accords different kinds of authority to these different sources of knowledge. Her stream of consciousness is an example of what Michael Billig, a social psychologist interested in rhetoric and social dilemmas, calls 'witcraft' – the skill of argumentation, which includes thinking as much as speaking and writing. Witcraft is about asking, 'What are the crucial claims in this issue?', 'What is a persuasively structured argument?', 'What style of presentation is effective?', 'How did we get to this point?' or, in other words, 'What is the history of this topic?' A good place to start.

CONTEXTS

Geography claims much of its disciplinary identity from study of the relations between people and environment, although research that straddled the apparent divide between 'Physical' and 'Human' Geography became rather unfashionable in the late 1970s and 1980s. This was a pity, for it was at just this time that environmentalism emerged as a powerful new social movement, with the activities of campaigning groups such as Friends of the Earth and Greenpeace forcing environmental issues on to the front pages of newspapers and the agendas of national governments. Sociologists, political scientists, economists and philosophers have joined the debate, each discipline offering its own slant on the characteristics of modern environmentalism (Barry, 1999; Pepper, 1996).

In this chapter, I want to focus on one element of modern environmentalism: the production of environmental knowledges and the extent to which the communication of environmental problems is effective in persuading people to adopt more sustainable lifestyles. The movement to sustainable development involves major changes both to the structures of modern society and to individual identities. Over-consumption of resources, excessive levels of waste, and the release of pollutants into water and air are problems of the rich countries of the North. It is very hard to persuade people voluntarily to cut back on those things that, for so long, have been seen as central to 'the good life', and changes will only be achieved through programmes that combine education and persuasion with the development of new policies and regulations. In this first decade of the twenty-first century, like it or not, we are all participating in a massive social experiment as environmental and social scientists, campaign groups, governments and international agencies such as the UNEP seek to change the world.

Why now? There is growing appreciation that the meanings of 'nature' and 'environment' are socially constructed in both scientific and popular discourses (see Chapter 1). The late 1980s was the period when concerns about the possible consequences of global environmental change rose to the forefront of political and popular concern. It was a time when, to take the sociologist Anthony Giddens' (1991) apt phrase 'apocalypse became banal'. Through the development and widespread dissemination in the media of scientific theories about the impact of carbon dioxide and other gases on the atmosphere, the meaning of wind, rain and sun changed. No longer could extreme events be thought of as 'acts of God' or 'elemental nature', rather they became frightening consequences of apparently irrevocable, human-induced changes to nature (McKibben, 1990).

The mass media are playing a fundamental if too often neglected part in the social construction of environmental knowledges (Smith, 2000). Public awareness of global environmental problems such as climate change, the links between poverty and environmental degradation, and the collapse of global fish stocks comes primarily from the pages of the newspapers and the television news. But the media never provide a 'window on the world' – an unmediated view of events. Environmental news, like any other sort of news, is actively constructed, shaped by the professional, technical and economic demands of each medium. Because the environment has not traditionally been a mainstay of news-gathering practices, coverage tends to vary quite dramatically over time. Moreover, environmental problems do not fit easily within journalistic news values: the events are long term rather than immediate; they are complex, which makes stories harder to explain simply, and scientists tend to use long words and difficult concepts. In addition, competition for space in the paper or time on the television news is intense. One outcome of these different pressures is that, when events are running fast, environmental stories are radically reshaped to fit media judgements of newsworthiness, or they are simply ignored at other times.

SUMMARY

- Over the last 20 years or so, geographical studies of environmentalism have been joined by many other social sciences, each bringing their distinctive disciplinary perspectives to bear. A particularly important contribution is being made by academics interested in 'witcraft' – the deliberations that go on inside people's heads – as well as in public forms of communication.

- The production, circulation and consumption of environmental knowledges are of fundamental importance in understanding social constructions of 'the environmental crisis'; and the extent to which institutions and lay publics can be persuaded to change towards more environmentally friendly practices.

- The mass media are playing a central role in helping to frame environmental issues for the public and in shaping political agendas. However, the media are not neutral in these processes. As active mediators, environmental science is translated in accordance with news values.

GLOBALIZATION: A CENTRAL ISSUE IN THE PRODUCTION AND CONSUMPTION OF ENVIRONMENTAL COMMUNICATIONS

There is general agreement that the age we live in differs fundamentally from what has gone before. We are living in 'a runaway world', Anthony Giddens suggests (1991: 16), a world characterized by the speed, scope and depth of social changes. There are many reasons for the sense of uncontrollable dynamism and endless change that characterizes modern life that have profound implications for environmental knowledge. Probably the most important factor is the ever increasing capacity to produce, process and move information around the world. Information travels very fast across space and through time. It comes from everywhere and goes to everywhere else almost instantaneously (Morley and Robbins, 1995).

As a result, human consciousness of the relations between time and space is changing. Harvey (1989) famously called this process 'time–space compression' – the sense that the world is 'shrinking' and time is 'speeding up' through ever faster forms of electronic communications. Events in distant places now penetrate private, domestic spaces in particularly dramatic ways through television images, resulting in unpredictable fusions of global and local knowledges. For some people, the increasing penetration of the global into the local encourages a greater consciousness of the interdependencies of societies around the world and a corresponding global environmental sensibility. For other audiences, the outcome is a sense of hopelessness and 'compassion fatigue' (Philo, 1993).

The incredible power of the new information technologies lies at the heart of globalization, providing scientific evidence for processes of global environmental change as well as the means of communicating them to the world. Figure 21.1 provides an illustration of how the process works. In this article, an arbitrary event (New Year's Day, when few journalists are working and little 'hard' news is being produced) is used as a hook to bring together disparate sources of scientific and 'folk' evidence about the vagaries of the world's weather patterns. Through articles such as this, the mass media continuously bring distant worlds, events and individuals into people's living rooms, creating a world that is both unitary and present, fragmented and dispersed. The drama of the story in Figure 21.1 lies in the frisson of anxiety it creates – the rising thermometer; people being killed by extreme weather events in different parts of the world, the unpredictability of nature. The media, through the ways in which they frame environmental science stories, constantly provide their readers with interpretative scripts that guide ways of making sense of these events. But the challenge of reporting the weather in the late 1990s was the level of scientific uncertainty about the causes of such extreme events. Were they 'natural nature' (El Niño? sunspots?) or 'technological nature' (global warming)?

One striking feature of the reporting of climate change today is the way in which scientific opinion has hardened around anthropogenic change, a trend increasingly reflected in media reports and political rhetoric. We even see scientists embracing Hollywood's attempt to bring climate change to mass audiences (Fig. 21.2).

Dependence on experts: the downgrading of local knowledge

New technologies and practices mean that individuals and social institutions are also lifted out of their places of origin, or 'disembedded' in Giddens' (1991) terms. Pre-modern societies were characterized by secure, local places and communities where social relations were clearly demarcated, the workings of local nature were known intimately through everyday practices, and a moral order defined people's obligations to one another and to nature. These certainties have been replaced by scientific rationality and technological expertise which, paradoxically, create radical insecurity both individually and collectively. Individuals are now highly dependent on expert forms of knowledge, and in the proliferation of expertise all knowledge becomes hypothesis, subject to challenge and change. As one environmental adviser commented in a discussion group I was moderating: 'But how can we tell the truth when we don't know how long the truth will be for?' (Burgess *et al.*, 1998).

One consequence of the rise of expert systems is that new kinds of knowledge, new forms of thinking through and responding to problems are proliferating that leave people who lack expertise in these areas in a vulnerable position of feeling, and being, 'deskilled'. People often feel they no longer have sufficient control over their everyday lives. At the same time, the penetration of expert systems into people's everyday lives means individuals are constantly acquiring new kinds of knowledge; but these knowledges are always partial and fragmentary. They are also subject to expert revision and change in the light of new evidence, for example, or dispute between different experts. Again, the media play a particularly significant role in these processes as they communicate the findings of environmental science to the public. Researchers need the media to get their message across to the general public but, more importantly, to

A year in the weather

WINDY

November 2 ①
Super Typhoon Keith blows through the Northern Marriana Islands in the Pacific with a central pressure of 872mb, one of the deepest typhoons ever

February 22 ②
Gusts of up to 153mph are measured on the Cairngorm summit, and the mean wind speed is 110mph. (Hurricane strength is classified as anything above 74mph)

SNOW

April 2 ③
Record-breaking snow storms over New England with depths of up to 61cm over some parts of Boston

October 27 ④
Denver has the worst snow for 30 years, temperatures down to -14°C, and 35 inches of snow recorded in the city (50 inches in the mountains)

WET

October 17 ⑤
Eilat in Israel has 21mm of rain in 18 hours. This is 7 times the October average of 3mm, and some reports of hail too

December ⑥
El Nino washes against the American coasts There are floods in Ecuador, Paraguay and Peru

COLD

November 1 ⑦
Perth in Western Australia equalled its November lowest temperature with 6°C (average is 14°C)

October 28 ⑧
Germany freezes up. Hamburg recorded -6.8°C: the previous record was -5.9°C

July 6 ⑨
Rome records a record low temperature of 11.2°C. The previous record was 12.1°C, and the average minimum is 18.3°C

March 9 ⑩
Verhoyansk, in the Siberian Arctic, and known as the coldest place on earth, had a temperature of -46°C, but there is still 12°C more to drop to beat the March record minima!

HOT

November 24 ⑪
Western Australia bakes: Shay Gap at the edge of the Great Sandy Desert reached 45°C at 4am, 10°C above average

November 7 ⑫
Temperatures reached 20.2°C in the Austrian capital Vienna, beating the previous November record of 19.6°C

September 15 ⑬
Satellites confirm that El Nino is back. There are droughts, fires and famine in Indonesia.

June 18 ⑭
The afternoon temperature in Naples soared to 36°C, beating the previous June record of 35°C

June 13 ⑮
Bangkok reached a record high temperature of 40°C beating the previous record by 2°C

May 21 ⑯
Acapulco, Mexico had temperatures up to 36.3°C (the previous highest for May was 35.6°C)

May 1 ⑰
Britain's sunniest day of the year so far with London reporting 23.2°C. August then became our second hottest since records began.

Number key for map

Britain bakes in record summer temperatures

Clouds of haze cover Indonesia as a result of the fires

Snow storms in New England

El Nino causes flooding in South America

GRAPHIC: STEVE VILLIERS

Worst snow in Denver for 30 years

FIGURE 21.1 Hottest year for Planet Earth. Credit: *Guardian*; Associated Press; Reuters; Popperfoto/*Guardian*, 1 January 1998

News

Never mind the weather overkill: scientists praise Hollywood's global warning

The Guardian Thursday May 13 2004 **3**

The Statue of Liberty disappearing beneath the waves as New York suffers a succession of weather-related disasters and the royal family freezes to death at Balmoral in the Hollywood blockbuster movie, The Day After Tomorrow

FIGURE 21.2 Never mind the weather overkill: scientists praise Hollywood's global warming. Credit: *Guardian* 13 May 2004, 3

Environmental risk

real and imagined threats to existing human, social and ecological systems posed by physical events, such as earthquakes; or from the unforeseen consequences of human activity, such as releasing genetically modified organisms into the environment.

politicians, government and those responsible for making environmental policies. The media, in turn, need scientific stories that can be told simply, stories where there is conflict between different scientific claims and/or where the science can be placed in a political framing. In situations where decisions are required about politically contentious issues such as whether genetically modified crops should be allowed to be grown in the UK, for example, scientific evidence is often subordinated to more general concerns about the extent to which government can be trusted or not to act in the best interests of its citizens and nature (Fig. 21.3).

Environmental risks

Societies have always faced many kinds of natural hazards and disasters, but the contemporary environmental crisis is fundamentally different. Over the last decade, one of the most dynamic 'knowledge environments' has been that of **environmental risk**. The discovery of the unintended consequences of science, technology and industrialization for the natural and physical systems that support life on earth has prompted Ulrich Beck

(1992a) to describe contemporary society as Risk Society. The 'mega-hazards' associated with nuclear power, chemical and bio-techno-logical programmes and ecological destruction embody threats of environmental catastrophe. Further, and this is one of Beck's central arguments, it is simply not possible to insure against the risks of mega-hazards. Citizens can only place their trust in the claims of experts that the 'fail-safe' mechanisms of nuclear power plants are indeed safe; that there are in fact 'safe limits' of pollutants in air or water;

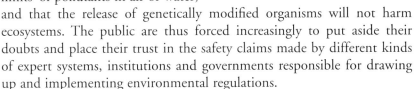

FIGURE 21.3
Greenpeace raiding a GM crop field.
Credit: David Hoffman Photo Library/Alamy

and that the release of genetically modified organisms will not harm ecosystems. The public are thus forced increasingly to put aside their doubts and place their trust in the safety claims made by different kinds of expert systems, institutions and governments responsible for drawing up and implementing environmental regulations.

Expert claims and assurances are articulated in the public sphere through the mass media but, once again, issues are represented within their own communicative rules and strategies (Adams *et al.*, 2000). The media are engaged in creative processes of risk translation as they make the news. Some commentators who take a rather pessimistic view of the power of the media in relation to the capacity of audiences to make sense for themselves, argue that public opinion is easily swayed by the amount of environmental coverage in the media and the style of reporting. Although it is not easy to get hold of data that matches volumes of media coverage of specific environmental issues with public understanding of those issues over time, there is a good example from the late 1980s/early 1990s.

Figure 21.4 shows a graph tracking people's responses to MORI opinion polls on the relative importance of environmental and other key economic and social problems over the period 1989–94. The very high levels of public concern recorded in 1989–90 fell away rapidly; thereafter, environmental issues bump along the bottom of the graph, having been superseded by economic and social welfare issues. Now compare the shape of the graph with those in Figure 21.5, which record the number of stories with the key words 'greenhouse effect' and 'global warming' published

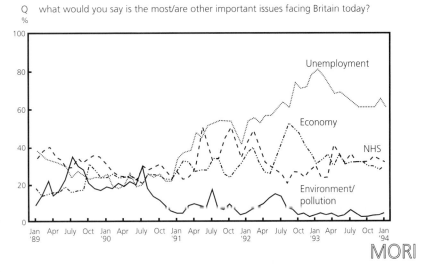

FIGURE 21.4
Public concern about the environment 1989–94. Credit: MORI

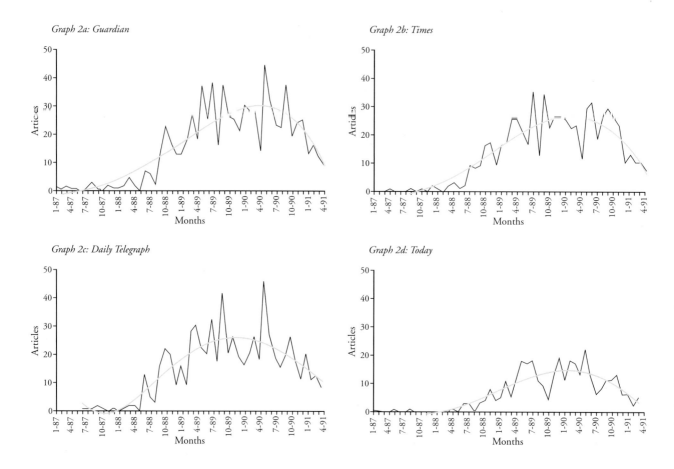

FIGURE 21.5
Global warming stories in the press. Credit:
Langman and Lacey, 1993

Linguistic (or cultural) turn

this phrase is used to describe changes
in the social sciences and Human
Geography over the last 30 years. It
refers to the adoption of interpretative
(qualitative) approaches to explore the
ways in which meanings, values and
knowledges are constructed through
language and other forms of
communication.

between 1987–91. Comparing these graphs, it is clear that as media coverage of environmental issues rises, so too does public opinion of the importance of those issues; when media coverage falls, public awareness of environmental problems similarly declines.

If we take more recent evidence from a major study of the coverage of climate change in the UK broadsheet press over the period 1985–2003 (Fig. 21.6), we can see how the peaks and troughs shown in Figure 21.5 are situated within a longer time frame. Climate change coverage has been on a consistently upward trajectory since 1995–96, and its saliency to the general public, at least as measured by public opinion surveys, has also increased once more. In the most recent survey of public attitudes published by the Department for Environment, Food and Rural Affairs in 2002 (Defra, 2002), climate change was the second highest environmental trend identified by respondents as likely to cause the most concern in 20 years' time (44 per cent of respondents).

The relationship between volume of media coverage and levels of concern, as measured by questionnaire surveys, suggests that public commitment to environmentalism is very shallow and fickle, being driven largely by media agendas. Others would disagree, seeing the media as instruments through which more positive and emancipatory public responses to risk may be achieved. The media, at least potentially, are able to create a public space where science and the judgements of expert systems can be subject to much wider and more democratic debate. After all, environmental reports do question science's achievements and thus raise doubts about the industrial structures that science legitimates (Adams *et al.*, 2000). From this perspective, people's responses to public opinion surveys about environmental issues are not especially helpful because, as we saw at the start of the chapter, if researchers want to understand how people think about environmental issues, and to find out more about why individuals answer questionnaires in the way they do, then the best strategy is to listen to them discussing the issues. The **'linguistic (or cultural) turn'**, commented on in several chapters in this book, has also penetrated environmental research. Most effort is being directed towards interpretation of ordinary people's knowledge, meanings, values and understanding of environmental issues. For example, several studies show that people's concerns about environmental issues encompass feelings of dread and fear, moral correctness and responsibility. There is also, however, an intensely political edge, as individuals express doubt and mistrust of those institutions responsible for creating and managing risk (Burgess *et al.*, 1998; Irwin, 2000).

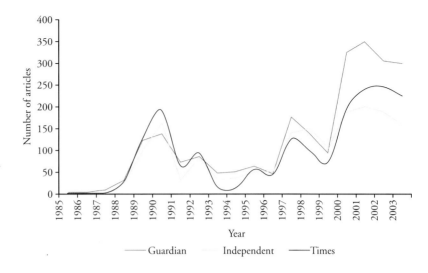

FIGURE 21.6
Annual totals of newspaper articles containing the phrase 'climate change', 'global warming' or 'greenhouse effect' in 3 UK broadsheet newspapers, 1985–2003. Credit: Burgess and Carvalho, 2004

SUMMARY

- The ever increasing capacity to produce, process and move information lies at the heart of globalization. Without the globalization of information there would be no global environmental crisis.

- In the last 150 years, a major feature of modernity has been the domination of local 'traditional' knowledge by a scientific rationality and technological expertise. We are now highly dependent on experts and their forms of knowledge; and in the proliferation of expertise, all knowledge becomes hypothesis, subject to challenge and change.

- Alarmed discovery of the global reach of mega-hazards has led to the concept of the Risk Society. There is no agreement about the extent to which members of the public understand the causes and consequences of contemporary mega-hazards. Either public opinion is shallow – merely reflecting the rise and fall in media coverage of these issues – or there is a subtle, rich understanding as individuals interpret environmental stories in the light of their personal and political experiences.

THINK GLOBAL, ACT LOCAL: THE CHALLENGE OF CHANGING LIFESTYLES

'Social learning' is the phrase increasingly being used to explain how societies are making use of the knowledges being produced by both

Reflexivity

a process through which we are able to reflect on what we know, how we come to know it, and how we interact with others. The key point is that we are able to change aspects of ourselves and the structures that make up society in the light of these reflections.

natural and social science, and the extent to which these new knowledges are leading to changes in current practices. In social theory, this kind of learning is described as **reflexivity** (Giddens, 1991). Reflexivity is central to an understanding of how individuals and institutions are changing under conditions of late modernity. In other words, individuals and institutions are both organized and able to transform themselves through knowledge and information. Reflexivity is now a fundamental element of individual and institutional identity: both individuals and organizations constantly monitor their behaviour and experiences, and thereby are caught up in a process of continual change.

Reflexivity lies at the root of arguments for sustainable development, for example. By becoming aware of the risky consequences of currently unsustainable practices, political, economic and social policies may be put in place to turn development to another path. *Think globally* – consider the mounting evidence about the consequences of human activity on the natural and physical systems of the world; of the effects of your actions on peoples distant from you in space; *act locally* – because what you can do at home, in your immediate environment will have a beneficial impact right through to the global level and thereby *change* the future. The old slogan of Friends of the Earth is an excellent example of reflexivity.

Environmentalists believe that the only logical response to mounting evidence of ecological catastrophe is to change, fundamentally, the ways in which societies use and abuse the natural and physical systems that support human life on earth (see Fig. 21.7). If people are given sufficient information about the consequences of continuing to live beyond the capacity of the environment to support them, then individuals and institutions can be reflexive in changing their values, beliefs and practices. The UK Labour government's 'Are you doing your bit?' campaign (Fig. 21.8) in the late 1990s is one recent example of the use of celebrities in mass advertising campaigns to try to promote more sustainable behaviour.

The strategy is based on an assumption that if people are given the 'right' information in the 'right way', they will change their behaviour accordingly. Public opinion surveys show a rise in the number of people claiming to take personal action 'on a regular basis', but measurable changes in, for example, the amount of waste sent to landfill or the rise in the number of short car journeys over the same period, suggest that these claims are not actually true. Respondents are answering such questions in terms of how they feel they *should* be behaving rather than being strictly truthful about what they do. Just like our student, in fact.

Unfortunately, research evidence suggests that people are rather more resistant to these rhetorical appeals than might be hoped; there is real and active resistance to exhortations for people to change their lifestyles (Burgess *et al.*, 2003). Two strands of argument are particularly important in people's rationalizations of why they are reluctant to change their lifestyles. The first relates to people's sense of agency – the belief that what they do can make a difference. Individuals need to be convinced that actions would be effective in achieving the desired aims. Global environmental problems often seem intractable and people often speak of compassion fatigue. 'You've got enough problems of your own, without taking on all of the world's all of the time', as people will say in small

IF YOU'RE MAD ABOUT WASTE, THERE ARE THINGS THAT YOU CAN DO.

Remember the 3'R's
Reduce waste - don't buy over-packaged goods. Lots of goods come wrapped in more packaging than they need. The picture shows one example. Can you think of any others?

Reuse things when you can instead of throwing them away. You can do this by mending things, sending old toys and clothes to jumble sales and by using jars, bottles, bags and envelopes again.

Recycle bottles, paper, cans and other goods if they can't be reused as this saves energy, resources, and means less waste is produced.

Why not read the other leaflets in the **Mad About...** series?

Air Pollution
Water Pollution
Tropical Rainforests
The Ozone Layer
Natural Habitats
Climate Change
Energy

FRIENDS *of the*
earth

June 1994 © Friends of the Earth 1994
Published by Friends of the Earth Trust Limited
Charity number 281681
Illustrated by John Watson
Friends of the Earth, 26-28 Underwood Street,
London N1 7JQ. Telephone (071) 490 1555
Partially funded by the Department of the
Environment.

FIGURE 21.7
Recycling campaign leaflet. Credit: Friends of the Earth

group discussions about environmental issues. Furthermore, people are unsure what to do for the best and have a sceptical relationship with environmental expertise. For example, is it better to save newspapers and bottles and drive to the waste tip once a fortnight, or does the increased pollution from using the car outweigh the benefits of not creating more landfill?

The second strand of argument concerns questions of democracy – in particular, the extent to which citizens trust local and national government, and feel there is a strong social contract between them. If such a political culture exists, then individuals are more likely to accept shared responsibility for environmental action. Environmental appeals fall on deaf ears when people can see no visible evidence of change in institutional lifestyles. Research suggests that public and private institutions of all kinds must demonstrate their own commitment to the need to change by underpinning their environmental rhetoric with visible, tangible actions of their own. Co-ordinated programmes of waste reduction, reduced water and energy demand, and increased public transport use are necessary at work, in government offices and at home, if public scepticism about the urgency of the environmental crisis, and the sincerity of those calling for changes in lifestyle, is to be overcome.

FIGURE 21.8
John Prescott promoting the 'Are you doing your bit?' campaign. Credit: PA Photos

SUMMARY

- Social learning (reflexivity) is a particularly important concept in sociology and social geography. It suggests that individuals and organizations constantly monitor their behaviour and experiences, and make adjustments in the light of new information.

- 'Think global, act local' is a reflexive injunction that, if obeyed, would lead to greater sustainability. However, there is dispute about the most effective means of achieving the changes in individual identity and practices required. Some, notably government organizations, believe top-down mass advertising campaigns will work. Others argue for a bottom-up strategy of working with members of the public and recognizing the psychological, social, economic and cultural barriers to change.

CONCLUSION: THE GEOGRAPHY OF ENVIRONMENTAL KNOWLEDGES

Public awareness and understanding of the causes and possible consequences of environmental degradation have increased dramatically over the last 30 years. The media have played important roles in this process, acting as translators of the environmental message as well as channels for communication – for both environmental pressure groups and national institutions. Academic research and environmental policy-making are being enriched by multi-disciplinary interests in society–environment relations. Of particular note are social theories to explain why the environmental crisis is an inevitable consequence of modernity and the move towards greater discussion and dialogue between elites and lay publics in deciding what should be done to enable societies to become more sustainable. And what should be geography's role in these developments? Geography is unique in having an internal dialogue between natural and social sciences – our own form of disciplinary 'witcraft'. At the same time, through our central concern with the distinctiveness of places and regions, with the specifics of how relations between people and environments vary across space and through time, we ensure that what the sociologists call the environmental *problematique* remains grounded in the real world of landfill sites, polluted drinking water, eroding soils and the specific impacts of climate change.

DISCUSSION POINTS

1. Using environmental stories from different newspapers or television news channels, can you identity any common features in the way the stories are reported? What might be important reasons to explain these similarities?

2. To what extent is 'think global, act local' still a meaningful slogan around which to mobilize people to support sustainable development?

3. How green are you and your family/friends? What are the main barriers and constraints preventing you from taking more action in support of the environment? What could be done to reduce or remove those constraints?

SECTION 5
HISTORICAL GEOGRAPHIES

INTRODUCTION

Many Geography students begin their university degrees with little experience of Historical Geography. Some may even be surprised by its existence, given the promotional emphasis placed by schools and universities alike on Geography's ability to speak to contemporary events and up-to-date issues. In this brief introduction we therefore want to say a little about why Historical Geography is such a central and important part of Human Geography.

A simple, but overly simplistic, definition of Historical Geography is that it is concerned with the geographies of the past. If it's dead, old or a little bit musty, it's Historical Geography. To the extent that this is true it means that Historical Geographers study a vast range of thematic issues, time periods and geographical areas from a variety of perspectives. Importantly, and happily, this also means that Historical Geography is not confined within some sort of intellectual ghetto. In this book, for example, you will find historical research being discussed in many chapters outside of this particular section.

But Historical Geography is distinctive. It has a special role to play in Human Geography more widely. Increasingly, this is seen as stemming less from its attention to the past per se than from its concern with 'historicity', or 'historical specificity and historical transformation' (Gregory, 1986: 197). In part this involves recognizing the potential difference of other times and places from our own, thereby widening our horizons and preventing us from making uncritical generalizations about how things can and might be. It might also involve discovering parallels in the past, thereby qualifying a frequent sense that we live in unheralded times, and helping to sharpen our sense of what may really be 'new' and different about our present circumstances. But more generally, it means reflecting on what role history plays in the present and how we relate those central historical notions, 'past', 'present' and 'future'.

Historical Geography is therefore far from a dry, antiquarian pursuit devoted solely to the archiving and organization of relics of the past. Not least, that's because any archiving of the past and its relics is something we do in the present, and often with an eye on the future. In fact, we think about history all the time, although often not in terribly rigorous ways. Historical notions infuse our ways of speaking about the world and its geographies (thus we talk of some things being traditional, others modern), we flock in our millions to museums and heritage sites; we discuss whether things now are different to how they used to be, and what role remembering the past might have.

Picking up on such issues, Nuala Johnson's opening chapter in this section focuses on those sites that connect history, heritage and memory in the present. Her discussion is framed through two case studies: first, a gallery devoted to trade and empire in the National Maritime Museum in

Historicity

to recognize the historicity of human geographies is to recognize their historical variability. This involves both an emphasis on historical specificity – on how historical periods differ from each other – and on historical change – on how human geographies are re-made and transformed over time.

Greenwich, London; second, sites that act as memorials to the Nazi Holocaust of European Jewry, in particular the Auschwitz death camp in Poland. In both cases, her analysis is particularly powerful in drawing out the constructed and contested nature of landscapes of the past and sites of memory.

Richard Phillips' discussion of colonialism and postcolonialism extends the thematic of how and why we should remember. We may think of colonialism as something that is now over. Certainly, at the level of formal political control, we might argue that the British Empire is largely a thing of the past. But Phillips sets out clear grounds for why we should neither forget colonialism nor romanticize it in 'pith helmet chic' (cf. Gregory, 2004). Colonialism was fundamental to the shaping of the modern world, he argues, establishing global geographies of power that still resonate today. Not only that, but it isn't over. British colonialism, for example, has not only left traces that have lasted beyond the Empire's decline and posed dilemmas that are still being grappled with (e.g. in the politics of land in settler colonies like Australia), but it has also been overtaken by other 'neo-colonialisms' (in particular associated with American power).

The final chapter in this section is by Miles Ogborn and deals directly with the dominant framing of world history in terms of a progression towards a modern present. Miles emphasizes how the notion of 'creative destruction', with its combination of both loss and invention, may better capture the experience of this 'modernization' than ideas of progress or development, illustrating his argument with reference to debates over the national modernization of Turkey and the urban development of nineteenth-century Paris. He also stresses how modernization is a profoundly geographical as well as historical process: involving the re-making of places and their landscapes so that they can embody modernity (in modern housing, roads, countryside, and so on); and working out across space in complex ways, so that whilst modernity is a global presence, particular places experience different 'global modernities'.

All chapters in this section demonstrate, then, that Historical Geography matters. History is important to our present-day human geographies; indeed to live in the present demands an understanding of past and future too. But, in turn, geography is important to those histories: we remember through sites such as museums and memorials; we understand the new and the past through creating places of modernity and tradition. Our geographies are always historical; our histories always geographical.

FURTHER READING

Journal of Historical Geography

It might be useful to have a look through some of the recent issues of this journal to get a feel for the variety of work done by historical geographers, as well as some of the key contemporary debates they are engaged in. It's an excellent journal.

Graham, B. and Nash, C. (eds) (1999) *Modern historical geographies.* **London: Longman.**

A collection that elaborates on the contents of the three brief chapters here, discussing in more depth the history of modernity.

Philo, C. (1995) History, geography and the still greater mystery of historical geography. In Martin, R., Gregory, D. and Smith, G.E. (eds) *Human geography: society, space and social science.* **London: Macmillan, 252–81.**

An exploration of the contribution Historical Geography can make to both Human Geography and History.

CHAPTER 22
MEMORY AND HERITAGE

Nuala C. Johnson

INTRODUCTION

Modern, modernity, modernism

ideas of the modern are most commonly defined through their opposition to the old and the traditional. In this light, the adjective 'modern' is synonymous with 'newness'; 'modernity' refers both to the 'post-traditional' historical epoch within which 'newness' is produced and valued, as well as to the economic, social, political and cultural formations characteristic of that period; and 'modernism' applies more narrowly to artistic, architectural and intellectual movements that centrally explore ideas of 'newness' and develop 'new' aesthetics and ways of thinking to express these. Modernity has been most commonly located in Euro-American societies from the eighteenth century onwards, and thereby associated with their characteristic combination of capitalist economies (*see* CAPITALISM), political organization through NATION-STATES, and cultural values of secularity, rationality and progress (*see* ENLIGHTENMENT).

Post-industrial

a description applied to the new economic, social and cultural structures emerging in late capitalist societies in the late twentieth century, highlighting in particular, trends away from manufacturing, manual work and the mass production of physical goods (*see* INDUSTRIALIZATION) and towards the tertiary sector, forms of service employment and the production of experiences, images, ideas and relationships.

The wreaths have been removed. The ceremonies are over. As Remembrance Sunday passes once again, the statue to fallen soldiers who were members of Queen's University in Belfast returns to its slightly invisible status as a memorial icon. During the days surrounding 11 November each year this monument, like many others around the country, assumes renewed significance in the maintenance and cultivation of a public memory dedicated to Ulster soldiers killed in the First World War and subsequent conflicts. This spectacle of remembrance amplifies Nijinsky's response to the Great War: 'Now I will dance you the war, with its suffering, with its destruction, with its death' (cited in Eksteins, 1990: 273). This dance takes the form of a seasonal ritual of wreath-laying, memorial services held in the churches, and the wearing of the poppy. All play a central role in the memory-work rehearsed annually in cities and towns across the United Kingdom. This memory-work, however, is not confined to the spaces of commemoration associated with the First World War but forms part of a larger network of sites that connect history, heritage and the geographies of identity in contemporary life.

There has been a huge expansion in the number of such heritage spaces over the past 20 years, coinciding with the expansion of tourist activity worldwide. Experiencing a growth rate of 5 to 6 per cent per annum (Williams and Shaw, 1988) tourism has become one of the largest employers in the twenty-first century. But tourism involves not only commercial transactions, it is as McCannell (1992: 1) notes, 'an ideological framing of history, nature and tradition; a framing that has the power to reshape culture and nature to its own needs'. Museums, stately homes, heritage centres, folk parks, memorials and the myriad of other sites designed to convey historical and geographical knowledge emphasize the ways in which our efforts to represent and remember the past are mediated through complex and sometimes contradictory lenses. Heritage usually denotes two related sets of meanings. On the one hand it refers to tourism sites with a historical theme that often have been preserved for the nation-state. On the other hand, heritage is used to refer to a suite of shared cultural values and memories, inherited over time and expressed through a variety of cultural performance – for example, song (Peckham, 2003). The following discussion will underline the contention that the relationships between heritage and history, between tradition and modernity continue to play a significant role in contemporary society. The heritage site itself frequently forms the epicentre upon which these issues are scrutinized. If histories are constructed and memories are mapped on to the past, the manner in which these stories and recollections of the past are related is constantly open to contestation, to alternative renderings of history and to the spaces in which histories are mediated and interpreted. This chapter has two main objectives: first, I will briefly outline some of the key themes anchoring discussions about the relationship between history and heritage; second, I will examine in detail two particular sites of memory – the Wolfson Gallery of Trade and Empire, at the National Maritime Museum, and the death camp at Auschwitz, Poland – as exemplars of the contested spaces in which history is materially and metaphorically translated to the public.

WHAT SHOULD WE MAKE OF HERITAGE?

The relationship between history, heritage and memory has been subject to much debate recently amongst geographers, historians, cultural critics and others. Conventionally a rigid line of demarcation ran between the past as narrated by professional historians on the one hand, and by the heritage industry on the other. Heritage, as a concept, begins with a highly individualized notion of what we either personally inherit or bequeath (e.g. through family wills and legacies). We are more concerned, however, with collective notions of heritage that link us as a group to a shared inheritance. The basis of that group identification varies in time and in space. It can, for instance, be based on allegiance derived from a communal religious tradition or a class formation or a 'nation'. Indeed, it is with respect to cultivating the 'imagined community' of nationhood that heritage is often most frequently linked. Three different, albeit interrelated, approaches to understanding heritage have gained currency in recent years. Briefly these comprise the view that: (a) heritage is a form of inauthentic history; (b) heritage is primarily part of a process of tourism expansion and **postmodern** patterns of consumption; and finally, (c) heritage is a contemporary manifestation of a longer historical process whereby human societies actively cultivate a social memory. The next few paragraphs will deal with each approach in turn.

Whilst the **nation-state's** origins may be relatively recent, the national state is based on the assumption that this group identity derives from a collective cultural inheritance that spans centuries. As Benedict Anderson (1983: 15) has put it, nations are collectively imagined because 'members of even the smallest nation will never know most of their fellow-members . . . yet in the minds of each lives the image of their communion'. And that communion is traditionally conceived as historical. National states therefore attempt to maintain this identity by highlighting the historical trajectory of the cultural group through the preservation of elements of the built environment, through spectacle and parade, through art and craft, through museum and monument. As Peckham notes (2003: 2), 'Many of the institutions through which heritage is promoted, including museums, folklore societies and other educational establishments, played a formative role in the nation-building project'. The heritage industry, then, is viewed as a mechanism for reinscribing nationalist narratives in the popular imagination (Wright, 1985). Lowenthal (1994: 43) claims

Nation-state

a form of political organization that involves (a) a set of institutions that govern the people within a particular TERRITORY (the state), and (b) that claims allegiance and legitimacy from those governed, and from other states, on the basis that they represent a group of people defined in cultural and political terms as a nation.

Multicultural, multiculturalism

multicultural is an adjective used to describe a place, society or person comprised of a number of different cultures. Multiculturalism is a body of thought that values this plurality. As the Human Geographer Audrey Kobayashi has noted, both the multicultural and multiculturalism can be conceived of in a number of ways: as 'demographic', i.e. simply reflecting a diversity of population; as 'symbolic', i.e. as about the presence or absence of the symbols associated with particular cultural groups within wider societal or national culture (for example, in the media, or in museums, or in school curricula); as 'structural', in so far as institutions are established to reflect a multicultural society and pursue multiculturalism; and 'critical', to the extent that multiculturalism itself critiques the assumptions of distinct, separate cultural groups sometimes attached to notions of the multicultural. Within Human Geography, increasing emphasis is being placed on developing this 'critical multiculturalism' through examining the HYBRID or SYNCRETIC cultural forms emerging within multicultural societies.

Postmodern, postmodernity, postmodernism

the British national newspaper, the *Independent*, sarcastically defined postmodernism thus: 'This word has no meaning. Use it as often as possible.' In fact, the main problem for a glossary entry such as this is that ideas of the postmodern have been used so often with so many different meanings! Nonetheless, one can generalize to say that notions of the postmodern (sometimes hyphenated, sometimes not) are used to suggest a move beyond 'modern' society and culture (*see* MODERN, MODERNITY, MODERNISM). More specifically: (a) postmodern is an adjective used to describe social and cultural forms that eschew 'modern' qualities of order, rationality and progress in favour of 'postmodern' qualities of difference, ephemerality, superficiality and pastiche; (b) 'postmodernity' is the contemporary epoch, after a period of 'modernity', in which such postmodern forms supposedly predominate, an epoch characterized both by the loss of an overall sense of social direction and order and by the triumph of the media image over reality (*see* HYPER-REALITY and SIMULACRUM); and (c) 'postmodernism' refers more narrowly to a collection of artistic, architectural and intellectual movements that promote postmodernist values, aesthetics and ways of thinking. If that is not complicated enough, whilst some view all things postmodern as signs of a radically new historical era of postmodernity, others see them more as recent twists to the history of modernity.

that 'heritage distils the past into icons of identity, bonding us with precursors and progenitors, with our own earlier selves, and with promised successors'. Heritage signifies, then, the politicization of culture where cultural forms are mobilized for ideological purposes. This contrasts with the work of professional historians where 'testable truth is [the] chief hallmark' and where 'historians' credibility depends on their sources being open to general scrutiny' (Lowenthal, 1996: 120). Many of the conventional assumptions about the nation-state, however, have been called into question at the beginning of the twenty-first century as globalization, **multiculturalism** and border change have all challenged the easy demarcation of 'us' and 'them'.

The expansion in the number of heritage sites over recent years has also been examined as exemplary of the postmodern cultural forms associated with **post-industrialism** and contemporary tourism. According to Urry (1990: 82), 'postmodernism involves a dissolving of boundaries, not only between high and low cultures, but also between different cultural forms, such as tourism, art, music, sport, shopping and architecture'. Consequently, the distinction between representations and reality, between genuine history and false heritage is made problematic. Baudrillard (1988a) suggests that meaning has been replaced with spectacle where historical and futuristic images coalesce. For instance, the Lascaux caves in France are now closed to the public but a replica of them can be visited 500 metres from the original. The original has become redundant as its replacement by a **simulacrum** provides a hyper-real representation of the caves. Consequently heritage tourism is seen as 'prefiguratively' post-modern because it has long privileged the visual, the performative and the spectacular for popular consumption. In this portrait, therefore, the past that is mediated through heritage is just one element, albeit an increasingly important one, in a whole suite of historical representations.

The links between memory and heritage are also important. The historian Nora (1989) suggests that before the nineteenth century memory was such a part of the practices of everyday life through storytelling that people were hardly aware of its existence. Whilst elite classes (e.g. the Church or aristocracy) had an institutionalized memory preserved through archives and biographies, ordinary people neither recorded nor objectified their past. This latter type of memory had taken 'refuge in gestures and habits, in skills passed down by unspoken traditions, in unstudied reflexes and ingrained memories' (Nora, 1989: 13). In contrast, from the nineteenth century onwards, modern memory became more democratized, and it became self-consciously preserved and archival. In this light, rather than viewing heritage as a false, distorted history imposed on the masses, we can view heritage sites as forming one link in a chain of popular memory. Whilst some critics have queried this 'museumification' of the past, the historian Samuel (1996) has celebrated such democratization, claiming that industrial museums and interiors of domestic life have been progressive developments in heritage preservation and have diminished the tendency for heritage to purvey a white, elite, European and male perspective on the past. Bearing these points in mind, I will now turn to analysing the first of my examples – the Wolfson Gallery of Trade and Empire – which challenges conventional popular representations of the British Empire.

SUMMARY

- There has been a long-standing debate about the authenticity of the historical narratives offered at heritage sites. It has frequently been suggested that heritage is merely a form of bogus history.

- Recent writing about heritage suggests that it is part of a much larger cultural transformation associated with postmodernism.

- Recognizing the evolution of a modern collective memory in the nineteenth century contributes to blurring the distinction between heritage as a site of history or as a site of memory.

MUSEUMS: BRINGING THE EMPIRE HOME

Since the eighteenth century, museums have served to augment, naturalize and locate national and imperial identities. As sites that collect and display objects, the processes involved in the evolution of museum cultures provides us with an important vehicle for understanding the development of collective meanings and values. Museums involve both the processes of disconnection and reconnection. Objects and narratives are shifted from the milieux in which they arise and are relocated, re-presented and made 'authentic' by their re-siting in the static context of a museum display. As Cosgrove (2003: 123) states, 'Preserving the heritage fragment inescapably involves its relocation, reconstruction and representation within the different landscape of the present'. Thus the museum acts as part of a process of **de-territorialization** and re-territorialization that is associated with modernity. In a museum display objects are removed from their original material social relations and are reintegrated into a new set of institutions and hierarchies. For instance, a weaving machine's meaning changes when it is removed from a linen factory in Belfast and relocated to a space on industrial heritage within the Ulster Museum. The reworking of objects in their new setting provides both constraints and opportunities for creative interpretations of the past. In their analysis of museum culture Sherman and Rogoff (1994) suggest four conceptual keystones in the arch of museum politics and practices that will help to throw light on how representation works. First, museums are comprised of a series of objects, which are ordered and classified in a specific sequence to offer a coherent meaning to the display. Second, these sequences of objects are woven into an external narrative that may relate, for instance, to local history, class relations or the nation. Third, museums are designed to serve a specified public and exhibits are structured to disclose the story to that public. Finally, the audience's response to a display becomes an integral part of the design process. I now wish to turn to consider these reworkings through the example of the Wolfson Gallery of Trade and Empire, which opened in 1999.

The gallery is located in the National Maritime Museum in London. Established in 1834 the Maritime Museum is at the centre of the old British Empire, located as it is on the prime meridian (Longitude 0) in Greenwich, south-east London. Greenwich lay at the symbolic heart of Britain's naval empire. It is the site of the National Observatory and the Greenwich Hospital. The latter, which was designed by Sir Christopher Wren, was established to support seamen and their families. It became a

Simulacrum

refers to the notion of a copy without an original. If we say at the first point we have an original object, then any image represents it, or replicas are copies of it. We thus have a pattern of original and copy. However, often it is the copies themselves that are copied. The products may begin to diverge from the original. The idea of a simulacrum, or of many simulacra, takes this a step further by emphasizing the presence in contemporary POSTMODERN landscapes of many copies with no original. An example might be the shopping-mall 'Parisian café' that clearly imitates a Parisian café, but for which there is no single original it imitates; or Disneyland's main street, which is again a REPRESENTATION for which there was no original. *See also* HYPER-REALITY.

De-territorialization

the uncoupling of political and economic processes from particular national spaces, as when banks move offshore or when economic decisions are entrusted to the World Bank or the G7 powers. *See also* TERRITORY.

Royal Naval College in 1873 and trained officers in the skills of naval science, navigation and geographical knowledge. In 1998 the Royal Navy left and the old Naval College became part of the UNESCO-designated Maritime Greenwich World Heritage Site; in following year the Wolfson Gallery of Trade and Empire was opened. Thus the space in which this exhibition is located has changed function and meaning over time, from being the epicentre of naval training and imperial naval planning to a place where Britain's history of empire is re-displayed and relayed to popular, public audiences. The empire exhibition, however, has proved controversial. Seeking to offer a radical critique of the exploitative and racist underpinning of Britain's overseas empire, it has aroused protest from a variety of different quarters within UK society.

The exhibition begins with two large posters that highlight the purpose and structure of the gallery. One poster claims that:

> *Although the British Empire was sometimes oppressive, its power was seldom absolute and there was always two-way traffic in wealth, ideas, goods and people along imperial trade routes.*

(Cited in Duncan, 2003: 20)

As Duncan observes, there is an attempt at the 'reconstruction of social memory … [to] tell the old story differently' (2003: 21). The story will be told differently by changing the narrative structure to one that emphasizes some of the negative consequences of empire and by telling the story from a variety of different perspectives (i.e. not just from the point of view of those building the Empire).

The gallery is roughly organized around four sections. It avoids a chronological approach and instead rotates the narratives and the displays around themes. In the first section the arrival to and impact of non-European migrants (Africans, African-Caribbeans and Asians) to

FIGURE 22.1
The interior of a tea house in 19th century China. Credit: The Art Archive/Musée Thomas Dobrée Nantes Dagli Orti

Britain is the focus. Referring to these migrants as 'Imperial Travellers' the exhibit disrupts our usual expectation of imperial travellers as British, white, male explorers. Instead the very positive impact of black and Asian culture on contemporary British society is emphasized (e.g. references to carnival). This first section, Duncan claims, 'explicitly seeks to restructure social memory by displacing the emphasis away from the British abroad and towards a celebration of the empire come home to Britain' (2003: 22).

The second part of the exhibition focuses on the tea trade from China and the West African slave trade (see Fig. 22.1). Using a variety of visual displays this section links the trade in tea, consumed by elegant eigh-

FIGURE 22.2
New Zealand All-Blacks performing the haka.
Credit: Getty Images/Scott Barbour

teenth-century British society, to the development of the trade in slaves. With a 'drawing room' forming the visual centrepiece of this part of the story, the links between commerce (global trade relations), slavery and exploitation, and ideas of an imperial civilizing mission are highlighted.

The third section of the gallery tacks between the eighteenth century and the present. At the centre of the field of vision is an embodiment of today's All-Blacks New Zealand rugby team performing the Maori ceremonial dance, the *haka* (see Fig. 22.2). There is some discussion as to whether the *haka* should be used at rugby matches as it 'appropriates' Maori tradition for a 'European' sport. The other element in this part of the gallery brings us back two centuries and to the British attempt to control the trade in palm oil in West Africa. Used as a lubricant in British industry and in the manufacture of margarine and soap, palm oil was important to British economic interests. The display therefore tells the story of palm oil through the actions and records of one minor British colonial official, Lt Walter Cowans. The exhibit highlights the attacks on local African chiefs, the destruction of settlements and local economies, the killing of native people and the looting of African artefacts later to be transported and displayed in European museums and galleries. This section draws the audience's attention to the banality of greed that undergirded this quest for palm oil; it also highlights the devastating social and cultural consequences of the competition to control the flow of this commodity.

The final part of the exhibition, relayed through a 12-minute film, documents how contemporary Britons saw their Empire and how it has been depicted through popular-culture media (e.g. movies). Narrated in a voice that seems to replicate BBC World Service English, and thus perhaps implying the authenticity of the report, this part of the story is directed towards a white British audience. It seeks to ask white Britons to reflect on their image and attitude towards their imperial past.

Whilst the opening section of this exhibition celebrates the economic, cultural and political contribution of people of colour to British society, the remainder of the gallery highlights 'the havoc caused by white British people abroad … what these exhibits do is refashion the social memory of trade and empire as a story of banality and violence' (Duncan, 2003: 24). So this particular museum re-presentation of empire shifts in tone from celebration to repentance. It highlights the indignities and suffering experienced by those subjected to imperial rule and it simultaneously celebrates the achievements and resilience of Britain's imperial subjects. Using a variety of visual media (e.g. maps, photos, text, film) this exhibition seeks to re-position the dominant narratives of empire.

The gallery provoked considerable response, especially from white Britons. In the letters pages of the national press, some viewers objected to the museum's representation of empire, deeming it to be biased, negative and 'politically correct'. Some saw it as overtly political and argued that museums should be 'neutral' relayers of culture. However, as the earlier part of this chapter has emphasized modern museums emerged often as arms of the state where the nation's 'heritage' could be put on display. Hostile commentators saw the gallery as suppressing 'the good and exalt[ing] the bad in our colourful past' (cited by Duncan, 2003: 25) or as an attempt 'to deprive our children of their national identity' (2003: 25). The directors of the gallery strongly defended the interpretation and representation of empire displayed at Greenwich.

The gallery did, however, make some revisions. First, it introduced the Royal George figurehead signifying the abolition of slavery and alluded to other positive aspects of empire. Second, it raised the issue of the museum acting as a contact space between different cultures, and thus it actively encouraged viewers to enter into debate about the meaning of heritage and its role in the construction of contemporary social memories. Whilst the museum may have sought to blur the boundaries between 'racial' categories and to emphasize the multicultural basis of British society, the very deployment of the black–white dualism in many parts of the exhibition gave 'authenticity' to these categories in everyday life. In that sense the very political project in which the museum was engaged and its practices of interpretation posed some contradictions. As Duncan (2003: 24) puts it, 'the contradiction is troubling, for it fails to address questions of complicity, collaboration and anti-racist dissent among the colonizers'. Nonetheless this exhibition does, at the very least, provide an image of Britain's Empire that is self-critical, thought-provoking and reflective.

LANDSCAPES OF DEATH: REMEMBERING THE HOLOCAUST

" *Memory is blind to all but the groups it binds. History, on the other hand belongs to everyone and to no one, whence its claim to universal authority.* "

(Pierre Nora, 1989)

From Rwanda to Armenia the silent landscapes of genocide perhaps present the most difficult task for society in general to remember and to record. This second example focuses our attention on the representational, political and moral questions raised by attempting to preserve sites of mass

SUMMARY
- At the National Maritime Museum exhibition on the history of trade and empire the meanings are derived from an interplay of object, narrative and audience.
- The museum challenges orthodox representations of Britain's empire by focusing on the experience of those who were colonized rather than colonizing.

human destruction for popular consumption. The term genocide was first coined in 1942 and after the 1960s the term 'holocaust' was adopted to describe the mass murder of European Jewry. It is worth noting, however, that attempts at premeditated extermination of a particular ethnic group did not originate with the Second World War. In the twentieth century alone the Great War had witnessed the mass murder of Armenians by Turks in Ottoman territory. The fact that this genocide receives less attention both in the canon of scholarly work and in public memory reminds us of the fragile processes involved in the making of history and memory. Indeed, the distinction between memory and history becomes intensely blurred when confronted with the challenge of representing large-scale murder. Whilst history texts can describe, document, diagnose Nazi policy and practice towards Jews and these insights can be incorporated into school curricula and university programmes, there is a danger that the Holocaust is then consigned solely to the past, to be accessed through the work of professional historians, and to be represented as an aberration of the human spirit or an iniquity bred from geopolitical and eugenicist imperatives. But, of course, genocide does not literally take place in the pages of a textbook or in the files of Nazi Chiefs of Staff, but in concentration camps scattered throughout Germany and Poland. Memory, then, is not just a recollection of times past, but it is an intense recollection of spaces past – spaces of mass death and destruction – where history is writ large on the landscape. These sites of memory have been subject to vociferous debate over the last decades and have been central to discussions about how to represent genocide. Whilst the landmarks of destruction – the death camps – seem to reveal a timeless property, their meaning is continuously bound up with new cultural and political demands on memory.

Between 1939 and 1945, 3.2 million of Poland's 3.5 million Jews were killed by Nazis and their sympathizers. This extermination took place primarily in the six Polish death camps established under the National Socialists (see Fig. 22.3). The surviving remnants of Jews largely evacuated Poland in 1946 due to post-war Polish pogroms. Three million non-Jewish Poles were also killed during the war and half of Poland's population was either killed, wounded or imprisoned during the conflict (Young, 1993). Consequently, for both Jews and Poles, the war represents an episode of unprecedented suffering, a fact that has both a unifying and divisive effect on the conjugation of a collective memory. Although the ruins of some of the death camps survived after the war it is their conversion from 'death' camps per se to 'memorial' camps that highlights the contested nature of public memory and popular interpretations of the past. Of the six death camps in Poland, only two – Majdanek and Auschwitz – had large portions of the complexes left intact after the war.

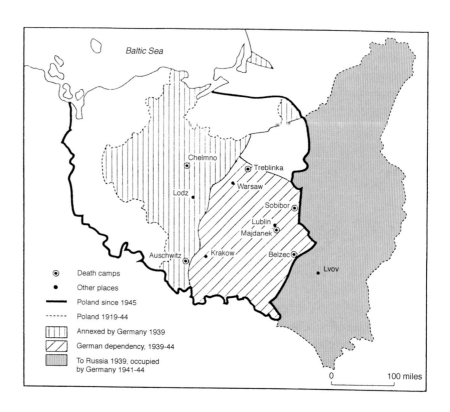

FIGURE 22.3

The location of the main Nazi death camps.
Credit: Pion

Both were camps where Jews, Poles, Romani, Sinti and Soviet prisoners of war had suffered. Both were turned into memorials and museums, although Auschwitz is commonly regarded as the central symbolic site of the Holocaust. In each case 'Guard towers, barbed wire, barracks, and crematoria – mythologized elsewhere – here stand palpably intact' (Young, 1993: 120).

In 1947 the Polish Parliament, dominated by a Soviet-style Communist Party, chose Auschwitz as the site that best represented the 'Nazi occupation from which the Soviet Union had liberated Poles' (Charlesworth, 1994: 581). In an attempt to combine memorialization of Jews and Poles, and to stress the role of the Soviet Union in defeating fascism, the site was seen as significant in nurturing Polish–Soviet relationships. Located closer to the German border than other death camps it underscored the Soviets' wish to situate Polish suffering solely in the context of German aggression. Second, although it is thought that 1.6 million people were killed at the camp and that 87 per cent of them were Jews, it turns out that less than one-third were Polish Jews. The significance of this fact is that the camp came to be represented as a site for international genocide that would link Poland to other Warsaw Pact countries (Charlesworth, 1994). The Polish Parliament declared that the camp would be 'forever preserved as a memorial to the martyrdom of the Polish nation and other peoples' (cited in Young, 1993: 130). Cold War geopolitical considerations were important in the maintenance of specific sites of memory.

Auschwitz comprises three main camps: Auschwitz I, which housed the administrative headquarters and a concentration camp (with one gas chamber/crematorium); Auschwitz II, also known as Birkenau, built as a death camp for the annihilation of Jews but also containing a concentration camp; and Auschwitz III, primarily a camp for prisoners working in the nearby industrial plant. The camp has been memorialized through a variety of strategies: the conversion of barracks into national pavilions documenting the deaths of different groups (e.g. Belgians); museum spaces; sculptures of remembrance; and exhibits of artefacts of the deceased, which include piles of suitcases, human hair (shorn from women), spectacles and prosthetic limbs belonging to Jews. It is this accumulation of artefacts that many tourists remember most clearly about their visit to the camp (see Fig. 22.4). It is also the **representation** of mass extermination through the paraphernalia of those on the eve of their death that raises questions about the types of history that the camp seeks to elucidate. The lives of those killed are literally represented as the clothes on their backs. Young (1993: 132) suggests that 'these remnants rise in a macabre dance of memorial ghosts . . . victims are known by their absence, by the moment of their destruction'. The difficulty lies in the fact that the varied and complex histories of those brought to Auschwitz are reduced to the collective geography of their death in the camp. Little attention, therefore, is devoted to the lives they had led – culturally, politically, spiritually – before the war. The complexity of their lives is masked by a representation that emphasizes the clinical manner in which their executions were orchestrated. Whilst it is important that the manner of their murder is visible, it is equally important that the roots and scale of European anti-Semitism be exposed.

There is also a blurring of the distinctions between those that were killed at Auschwitz. Whilst one may legitimately argue that each life taken at the camp is of equal value and worthy of equal inclusion in the narrative, there is a suggestion that an emphasis on Polish suffering under Nazi occupation undermines the specificity of the Jewish experience at Auschwitz. Charlesworth (1994) suggests that the site allows for a particularly Polish reading of the Holocaust that connects with a nationalism that focuses on Polish victimization by its neighbours over the previous centuries. The remit for the establishment of the museum in 1947 reads that 'a monument of the martyrdom of the Polish nation and of other nations is to be erected' (cited in Charlesworth, 1994: 584). The absence of any direct reference to Jews is revealing. More recently there have been efforts to Catholicize Auschwitz by the activities of Cardinal Karol Wojtyla (now Pope John Paul II). Through the beatification of Father Kolbe, a rabidly anti-Semitic priest who had exchanged his life for that of a Polish prisoner at Auschwitz, Cardinal Wojtyla suggested that the

Representation

the cultural practices and forms by which human societies interpret and portray the world around them and present themselves to others. In the case of the natural world, for example, these representations range from prehistoric cave paintings of the creatures that figured in the lives of early human groups to the televisual images and scientific models that shape our imaginations today. *See also* DISCOURSE.

FIGURE 22.4
Tourists visiting a site of memory at Auschwitz, Poland. Credit: AFP/Getty Images

martyrdom of this priest should be memorialized at Auschwitz through the erection of a church (Young, 1993). The establishment of a Carmelite convent inside the camp in 1984 complicates the issue further and illustrates the *contested* nature of the spaces of memory at Auschwitz. That Jews, the Church, the state, Polish nationalists, professional historians and the international community all have had influence on how the Holocaust is represented at Auschwitz underlines the contention that memory-work is rarely an act of mimesis – that is, imitation – but is woven through complex cultural, political and symbolic processes.

SUMMARY

- Genocide highlights the complex issues involved in creating, maintaining and representing sites of memory.

- The reading of history through a geographical space such as a death camp can simplify the complex lives of those exterminated by focusing primarily on the manner of their death.

- The case of the death camp at Auschwitz underscores how heritage spaces can be sites of contested memory. The distinctions between different groups of people killed at Auschwitz can become blurred and this raises the question of whose past is being recorded and remembered.

CONCLUSION: SPACES OF HISTORY OR SPACES OF MEMORY?

Geographers are increasingly concerned with the representation of landscapes and how the past can be read through landscape interpretation. Apart from a few exceptions, however, geographers have paid scant attention to the historical geography of heritage landscapes and how they represent the past. Criticisms of the heritage industry's attempts to narrate the past as little more than bogus history are often overdrawn and in the case of the Wolfson Gallery of Trade and Empire I have attempted to highlight how the past can be explored provocatively through a heritage installation. Rather than focusing on whether heritage conveys inaccurate history, the more interesting questions for geographers relate to examining the ways in which the spaces of heritage translate complex cultural, political and symbolic processes into the popular imagination. Through the example of Auschwitz, a provocative case certainly, an analysis of the site reveals how these processes are intermixed in complex ways; it also exemplifies the moral dilemmas that are thrown up by the seemingly contradictory desires to remember and forget the past.

DISCUSSION POINTS

1. The heritage industry is a modern replacement for serious, scholarly and objective history. Discuss.

2. The Wolfson Gallery of Trade and Empire is an exercise in 'political correctness'. Do you agree?

3. Space is central to understanding the development of memory places. Discuss using examples.

FURTHER READING

Lowenthal, D. (1996) *The heritage crusade and the spoils of history.* **London: Viking.**

This text offers the most comprehensive overview of the distinction between history and heritage by a geographer.

Urry, J. (1990) *The tourist gaze.* **London: Sage, Chapters 1, 2.**

Peckham, R.S. (2003) *Rethinking heritage: culture and politics in Europe.* **London: I.B. Taurus.**

McCannell, D. (1992) *Empty meeting grounds: the tourist papers.* **London: Routledge, Chapters 1, 4.**

Turn to these texts for general introductions to tourism, postmodernism and heritage in Britain, Europe and North America, respectively.

Young, J. (1993) *The texture of memory: Holocaust memorials and meaning.* **London: Yale University Press.**

This book deals with the issue of remembering the Holocaust.

CHAPTER 23

Richard Phillips

COLONIALISM AND POSTCOLONIALISM

INTRODUCTION: MAPPING EMPIRE

The world map shown in Figure 23.1 appeared in the opening pages of an official *Atlas of Canada*, published by the Dominion of Canada's Department of the Interior in 1915. It is typical of maps that were produced and consumed around much of the world in the first half of the twentieth century. People often see maps as straightforward representations of space – facts about geography. But the map makers have made all sorts of choices: what to include; how to depict it; what to leave out.

The first choice the cartographers have made, perhaps their most powerful device, is one of colour. In the Canadian world map, originally 40 cm by 60 cm, colour is used to represent colonial power, as the key makes clear. Each empire is a different colour. Above all, this is a map of colonial empires, most of them European. The map is cleanly printed. Its even blocks of colour cover regions, nations, even whole continents uniformly. They depict a world that is tidily, uniformly colonized.

The colour scheme is not arbitrary. The map makers have chosen colours that reinforce the colonial theme of the map. The colour red seems to occupy much of the land surface of the earth. The key shows that Britain and British colonies are coloured bright red. Other colonial powers appear in more delicate or demure colours: the French Empire, for example, is a gentle mauve. Each colour has a symbolic and graphic function within the map. Red symbolizes authority (think of 'red tape'), aggression (a red sports car), confrontation (like a 'red rag' to a bull) and England (England's flag, showing the cross of St George, is white and red); it is also the colour of blood. Graphically, too, it is an aggressive colour, appearing larger mile-for-mile than its more lightly shaded neighbours, also pushing out and spilling into their territory. Looking at this map – imaginatively 'losing oneself' in it – it is easy to imagine a time, not too far into the future, when the colour red will be everywhere. So it is not surprising that the map makers chose the colour red for themselves. Other map makers, including French and Germans, often did the same in their own maps.

Notice the words. They are in English. Canada is not and never has been a nation just of anglophones. When the map was made, many Canadians spoke French, as well as a host of other languages, some native North American, others imported from eastern and northern Europe, Asia and elsewhere. But the map is in English – the dominant, official language. The world is named with the place names chosen by English-speaking peoples; everywhere is what the English say it is. Thus the map asserts an English way of seeing the world.

Neither is composition merely factual, an innocent artefact of scientific cartography (see Harley, 1992). The map depicts a world with a centre and margins; it turns some places into centres and others into margins.

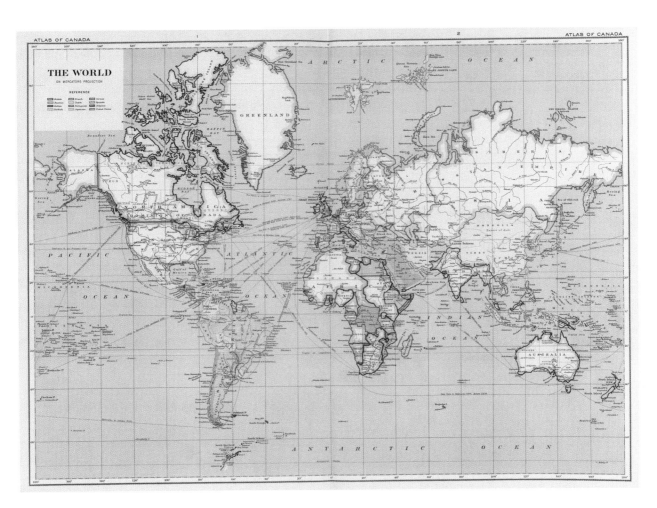

FIGURE 23.1
This map represents colonial power, and is a
vehicle of that power. World map, 1915.
Source: *Atlas of Canada*, Ottawa: Government
of Canada. Credit: The British Library, London

Anywhere could be at the centre – Fiji, France, the Falkland Islands. But
Europe, and specifically England, is at the centre. The centrality of
England is also formally marked through lines of longitude, which as most
people know centre on Greenwich, London. Before 1881 when England
got other nations to accept their own prime meridian, and thereby
established an international convention respected by many (but not all)
nations, most map makers drew lines of longitude that were centred upon
their own capitals or other cities. Americans, for example, generally used
Washington or Philadelphia. Persuading others to respect the Greenwich
meridian, the Europeans persuaded them to see London and
Britain/Europe as the centre of the world. In case any map reader should
miss the point, shipping lines were included, drawing the eye from all
corners of the world into Liverpool, Bristol, Southampton and the
Thames Estuary, towards a metropolitan centre. The shipping lines also
suggest the importance of England as a centre of trade and commerce;
every other nation seems to be measured and located according to its links
with England.

The projection of the map also adds to the importance of England and other northern countries. Here, the map makers have chosen to use the Mercator projection, which was developed in the Netherlands – a leading European imperial power – in the sixteenth century. The Mercator projection distorts space, making areas further from the equator appear bigger (by land area) than they really are. This makes western European nations appear disproportionately large. England, part of a small island in the North Atlantic, is exaggerated in geographical importance, as are British dominions such as Canada, New Zealand and Australia. The projection also serves as a reminder of England's competitor in eastern

Table 23.1 The colonial empires at the outbreak of war in 1914

	area in sq. km	pop. in '000s
1. In British possession		
A. Mediterranean	10	517
B. Asia	5,199	324,114
C. Africa	9,392	50,824
D. America	10,407	10,082
E. Australia/South Seas	8,267	2,508
F. Other	18	599
Total:	**33,293**	**388,644**
2. In French possession		
A. Asia	803	14,871
B. Africa	9,499	30,514
C. Other	116	807
Total:	**10,418**	**46,192**
3. In Dutch possession	2,036	38,248
4. In Russian possession	16,153	22,605
5. In Japanese possession	288	19,200
6. In German possession	2,954	13,784
7. In American possession	388	10,299
8. In Belgian possession	2,365	10,000
9. In Portuguese possession	2,244	9,146
10. In Italian possession	1,641	1,850
11. In Spanish possession	441	640

Source: Veit Valentin: Kolonialgeschichte der Neuzeit, Tübingen, 1915

Europe and Asia, the Russian Empire, which looks very imposing on the map. Conversely, it makes India appear much smaller, perhaps more easily ruled by the English, than it might otherwise appear.

SUMMARY

- The 1915 world map represents a world dominated by colonial power.

- It also functions as an ideological vehicle of that colonial power.

EXPERIENCES OF EMPIRE

European colonial empires reached their peak around 1914, before the First World War broke out. Amongst these empires, the British was the greatest, with the French in a relatively poor if absolutely large second place. Table 23.1 shows the breakdown of British, French and other possessions, by population and area. The British controlled huge areas of land in America (mainly Canada) and Australia, although it was its African and especially its Asian colonies (mainly India) that qualified Britain as the world's largest imperial power. Whilst British Canada and Australia accommodated just over 12 million increasingly self-governing people, the combined populations of British Africa and India numbered nearly 400 million, and these colonial subjects were subjected to something closer to absolute colonial rule.

Tables such as this group land and people into columns and aggregate statistics, categorizing them under labels such as 'empires', 'imperial' and 'colonial' – terms we have already found ourselves using. There is, at the outset, a need to clarify this vocabulary. Imperialism refers, very broadly, to 'The creation and maintenance of an unequal economic, cultural and territorial relationship, usually between states and often in the form of an empire, based on domination and subordination' (Dan Clayton in Johnston *et al.*, 2000: 375). Colonialism is defined more narrowly as 'The establishment and maintenance of rule, for an extended period of time, by a sovereign power over a subordinate and alien people' (Michael Watts in Johnston *et al.*, 2000: 93), whilst colonization, more specific still, involves the physical settlement of people (i.e. settlers) and the displacement of others: the resettlement of places.

Definitions and labels, like statistics and maps, make the world seem tidier, more ordered and more generic than experience tells us it is. Within the areas painted red, or listed in columns of British statistics, or labelled under headings such as 'colony', there remain a great variety of different experiences and perspectives. These differences – between colonizers, colonies and colonized peoples – must be remembered, because they are often greater than the similarities. As historian Ronald Hyam puts it in *Britain's Imperial Century* (1993: 1), 'When you think about it, there was no such thing as a greater Britain – India, perhaps apart. There was only a ragbag of territorial bits and pieces, some remaindered remnants, some pre-empted luxury items, some cheap samples.' Colonialism, he goes on to explain, is messier than our maps of it. Colonialism takes many different forms, and is experienced by different people in different ways.

The experiences of colonists have been many and varied, as a selection of British colonists illustrates. David Livingstone, a Scotsman, spent much of his life as a missionary and explorer in Africa (see Driver, 2001). Like many colonists, he was driven by faith in Christianity, civilization and commerce. He campaigned practically against slavery and for Christianity, in both cases by exploring the continent, thereby opening Africa to trade, development and (a British idea of) progress. As an explorer, Livingstone is remembered for the epic journey to the great waterfall that the British were to name after their Queen Victoria. Most colonists were less famous and less idealistic than Livingstone. Daisy Phillips, for example, was one of many who emigrated from England in search of a new home and a better livelihood in the colonies. Along with her husband, Jack, she embarked upon the long journey from England to the interior of British Columbia, where she did her best to set up home. Frontier life proved difficult and lonely, although Daisy was to remember it fondly. The couple returned to Europe when war broke out, and soon Jack died on the

Robinson Crusoe rescues Friday.

FIGURE 23.2
Imaginative geographies accommodated colonial encounters, such as that between Crusoe and Friday, which inspired and legitimized real colonial acts. Source: Frontispiece and title page of *Robinson Crusoe* in *Words of One Syllable* by Mary Godolphin (1868). Credit: The British Library, London

battlefield. Daisy's letters home, reprinted in *Letters From Windermere* (Harris and Phillips, 1984), tell a story of literate, middle-class colonial experience (see also Moodie, 1986). Other emigrants, whose colonial experiences were generally less well documented and considerably less comfortable than Daisy's, include the convicts transported to Australia in the late eighteenth and early nineteenth centuries. Most were Irish or English, six out of seven were male, and many were transported for petty offences. All found themselves in a brutal world of violence, hard labour and alienation, which Robert Hughes vividly describes in *The Fatal Shore* (1987). When they had served their sentences, few could afford the cost of a passage home, so they stayed as free colonists. Other British colonists had very different experiences, which were also shaped (like Livingstone's) partly by their faith and ideals, and (like Daisy Phillips's) by their class and gender, as well as by other aspects of their identities including their race and sexuality (see McClintock, 1995; Phillips, 2005).

Meanwhile, many other Britons experienced colonialism from an altogether different angle – they stayed at home. There they imagined the colonial empire from a distance, hearing or reading about it. Books such as *Robinson Crusoe* (see Fig. 23.2), with exotic settings and lively storylines, narrated and mapped colonial encounters between Europeans and others (Phillips, 1997). Popular geographical narratives such as *Robinson Crusoe* presented an acceptable and exciting face of colonialism to their British, French, German and other readers. They popularized empire, persuading many to support their governments' wider imperial projects and inspiring others to seek adventures of their own, many in actual and would-be colonies. So imaginative geographies of empire did not just represent the empire, they helped construct it (see Said, 1993, and Chapter 10 of this volume, in which Felix Driver examines imaginative geographies and their significance in the real world). European armchair and shop-floor imperialists did not just dream about empire; they also consumed it and produced goods for it. Europeans consumed colonial products such as tea from India, sugar from the Caribbean and furs from Canada. They helped to produce the manufactured goods such as railway engines, textiles and guns that Britain shipped to its colonial markets. They posted letters to friends and relatives in (what to them were) far-flung corners of the world. When they received replies, those who noticed stamps often also noticed the head of their own monarch. In their personal communications, as in their material life (as producers and consumers) and in their dreams, Europeans participated in a system that was both global and imperial.

The experiences of colonized peoples were equally varied; being colonized meant different things to different people. Chief Sechele, for example, was the only African known to have been converted by the famous British missionary, David Livingstone. Sechele followed his spiritual mentor's advice and agreed to change his polygamous ways, he annulled all but one of his marriages, and in 1848 he was baptized in front of hundreds of weeping spectators. Soon, however, he missed the three wives he had sent away, and resumed sexual relations with at least one of them. Louis Riel was also the leader of a people colonized and fundamentally changed by British imperialism, although of a very different sort. He emerged as leader of the Canadian Métis nation, a

Imaginative geographies

representations of place, space and landscape that structure people's understandings of the world, and in turn help to shape their actions. In the work of Edward Said, the term refers to the projection of images of identity and difference on to geographical space in a way that sustains unequal relationships of power.

LALLA ROOKH, OR TRUGANINA, THE LAST TASMANIAN WOMAN.
(*Photographed by* MR. WOOLLEY.)

LALLA ROOKH, OR TRUGANINA.
(*Photographed by* MR. WOOLLEY.)

FIGURE 23.3
Truganina, the last Tasmanian. Source: *The Lost Tasmanian Race* (1884) by James Bonwick (Fellow of the Royal Geographical Society)

Hybrid, hybridity, hybridization

hybrids are the products of the combination of usually distinct things. These terms are often used to describe new plant types but are used in Human Geography to emphasize the equal and positive mixing of cultures rather than negative ideas of cultural assimilation, dilution, pollution or corruption. *See also* SYNCRETIC.

hybrid people born through centuries of cultural and sexual contact between Amerindians and French-Canadian *voyageurs*. Riel led two uprisings against the British North American authorities, whose plans to settle western Canada threatened the Métis people's way of life. Riel was executed and his people were displaced, as colonists swarmed west. Unlike the Métis, some colonized peoples were entirely wiped out by colonists. This was the fate of many Australian Aboriginal peoples who were displaced by penal colonies. Truganina, the last Tasmanian, saw her countrymen and women broken by English colonists (see Fig. 23.3). The English hunted down some of the inhabitants and transported the others to an island reserve (Flinders Island, 40 miles to the north) that, for most, was to be their grave. Others experienced colonization in very different ways, which like those of the colonists depended partly upon – and in turn reshaped – their class, race, gender and sexuality. Some colonized people grew rich from the colonial encounter, whilst others lost their language, their livelihoods, even their lives. Like the colonists, many colonized peoples consumed stories and maps of the wider world, and participated in an increasingly global economic and cultural system. But unlike the European colonists they were not the principal architects of this world. Their colonial encounters were from positions of relative weakness.

Colonialism transformed the world, simultaneously producing a 'New World' and modernizing the 'Old World'. Changes in the non-European world are perhaps most evident. Some effects of colonialism were superficial – statues of Queen Victoria, for example. Other colonial imprints were more fundamental, and can never be reversed. Enormous population movements, both forced and free, scattered Europeans and Africans, particularly in the Americas. Some 20 million people left Britain and Ireland between 1815 and 1914, in a **diaspora** motivated variously by hunger (particularly during the Irish famine), displacement (notably in the Scottish clearances) and the desire for a better (freer and/or wealthier) way of life (by middle-class emigrants). Europeans and Euro-Americans also engineered an African diaspora, in which 12 million Africans were sold into slavery and shipped overseas, mainly to the Americas (see Chapters 36 and 37 on diaspora and contemporary migrations). Vast tracts of the world were partly or wholly resettled, as aboriginal peoples were deliberately or accidentally wiped out and replaced with free and/or forced immigrants. Movements of capital also transformed and integrated far-flung territories. Railways and shipping lines, which rapidly encircled the Victorian globe, were important both as capital investment, and as infrastructure through which capital and goods, people and information were moved. The result was an increasingly global society and economy, a global geography of development and underdevelopment (see Chapters 13–15 for introductions to geographies of development).

Whilst colonialism transformed the non-European world, it also reshaped Europe. Europeans, the principal architects of the modern **world-system**, constructed a modern world in which they were at the centre. Europe grew rich, and European lifestyles were enhanced by the non-European products, labour and markets that Europe controlled. Non-European economies supplied the raw materials and provided the markets that enabled Britain and other European countries to industrialize. Buoyed by prosperity, many Europeans grew arrogant, confident of their economic, political, religious and racial superiority. European confidence, expressed for example in its maps, redefined its place in the world and mapped out its future. This was not a stable or harmonious arrangement, however, as Winston Churchill, First Lord of the Admiralty and future Prime Minister, admitted before the outbreak of the First World War:

> " We are not a young people with an innocent record and a scanty inheritance. We have engrossed to ourselves … an altogether disproportionate share of the wealth and traffic of the world. We have got all we want in territory, and our claim to be left in the unmolested enjoyment of vast and splendid possessions, mainly acquired by violence, largely maintained by force, often seems less reasonable to others than to us. "

(Churchill, quoted by Ponting, 1994: 132)

Diaspora

the dispersal or scattering of people from their original home. As a noun it can be used to refer to a dispersed 'people' (hence the Jewish diaspora or the Black diaspora). However, it also refers to the actual processes of dispersal and connection that produce any scattered, but still in some way identifiable, population. In this light it also can be used as an adjective – diasporic – to refer to the senses of home, belonging and cultural identity held by a dispersed population.

World-system

an integrated international economic system, founded upon mercantile then industrial CAPITALISM, which originated in Europe around 1450 and spread to cover most of the world by 1900. World-systems analysis, which examines this system, treats the world as a single economic and social entity, the capitalist world economy.

SUMMARY

- European colonization was experienced in many different ways by many different peoples, but when Europeans encountered the peoples of Asia, the Americas, Oceania and Africa, they generally had the upper hand.

- European colonialism established and formalized unequal territorial relationships between peoples, ensuring that modern maps and modern geographies were and are colonial maps and colonial geographies.

'POST-COLONIAL' GEOGRAPHIES

Now compare the 1915 map (Fig. 23.1) with a more up-to-date map of the world (Fig. 23.4). What differences do you see? And what similarities? What evidence of colonialism do you see? You may need to look closely.

Perhaps the most striking difference between the two maps is the colour scheme. The domination of a few European colonial empires, symbolized in the handful of strong colours we have discussed, has gone. People often say that the sun has now set on the British Empire (a response to the old boast that it never would). In July 1997 the British handed over control of their last major colony, Hong Kong. Britain's *Guardian* newspaper (see Fig. 23.5) described the handover of Hong Kong as the end of an era of European empire building that began five centuries ago, 'the eclipse of an empire that lasted more than 400 years'. As European colonial empires were formally dismantled, a chapter of colonial history ended, and according to some observers a post-colonial chapter began. Post-colonial sometimes refers to that which is after or against colonialism – an ongoing colonial hangover, in which former colonies are plagued by relics and legacies of the defunct colonial order, as well as by some new forms of colonialism.

If you look closely at the new world map you will see relics, traces and new forms of colonialism. First the relics: not all of the old colonies have been handed back. The British, for example, retain dependencies around the world, mainly small islands ranging from Gibraltar (on the southern

FIGURE 23.4

Colonialism is less obvious in 2005 than in the 1915 world map. Credit: © Oxford Cartographers, 2005, www.oxfordcarto.com

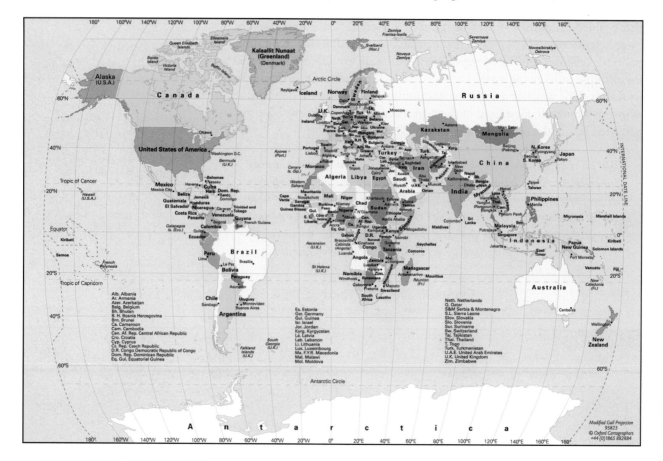

tip of Spain) to the Falkland Islands (off the coast of Argentina) and Montserrat (in the Caribbean). Britain also claims part of Antarctica. European powers have also held on to their 'internal' colonies. Notice, for example, how Brittany blends seamlessly into France, how Wales blends with its neighbour to the east into a single nation. To many people in Brittany and Wales, French and English colonialisms respectively are very much alive. Internal colonialism can also be seen outside Europe. For example, some people see Tibet and Hong Kong as colonies of China, and the North West Territories as a colony of Canada (Morris, 1988; 1992).

Now, looking, for example, at the configurations of states and national borders, you will see traces of European colonialism. Many present-day nations are legacies of colonialism. Canada, for example, is a nation born of British **hegemony** over territory settled by English and French emigrants, and the borders of present-day Canada are a fossil of Empire – albeit one that Quebec separatists would like to dismantle. Other borders reflect the colonial inheritance. The border between India and Pakistan was drawn by a British civil servant, Cyril Radcliffe, a stranger to British India who was given just 36 days to complete his momentous task. Armed only with a pile of outdated maps, some crude census returns and a case or two of claret, Radcliffe produced the 'Wiggly Line' that initiated one of the world's greatest population movements (15 million Muslims and Hindus crossed the new borders) and set the stage for half a century of animosity between the two nations (Khilnani, 1997). In Africa, as in India, many borders and states are essentially colonial creations transformed into independent states. Their boundaries, shapes and sizes are part of the colonial inheritance (as Griffiths shows in *The Atlas of African Affairs*, 1994). Bob Geldof, the Irish former pop star who now campaigns to help Africans living in hunger or with AIDS, attributes many contemporary African problems to the continent's geopolitical inheritance of empire. 'No country in Africa,' he told a human rights committee in 2004, 'is free from problems of access, security, and economic stability that is directly attributable to the boundaries they inherited from the colonial era' (Geldof, 2004).

However closely you look at the 2005 map (Fig. 23.4), though, you will not learn very much about new forms of colonialism. For, as overt enthusiasm for the imperial project has receded, map makers and others have tended to downplay and disguise continuing and new forms of colonialism. Strong, confident, aggressive colours are succeeded by an apparently arbitrary pattern of equal and different national colours. Still, even though colonial powers have lowered their flags over most former colonies, ending formal colonial rule, **decolonization** has not meant an end to 'unequal economic, cultural and territorial relationships'; in other words, it has not meant an end to imperialism (as defined above). As some old imperial powers have fallen, others have risen. A transformed imperial order was revealed in 1956, when Britain and France finally retreated from Egypt, which they had invaded to regain control of the Suez Canal. They retreated because the Soviets had told them to and because the Americans chose not to intervene. Those superpowers continued where their western European imperial ancestors left off. They did not generally set up formal colonial governments, nor did they tend to found new overseas colonial settlements, both of which their predecessors frequently did, so their

FIGURE 23.5
An empire closes down but is Hong Kong decolonized? Source: *Guardian*, 1 July 1997

Hegemony, hegemonic, hegemon

hegemony is an opaque power relation relying more on leadership through consensus than coercion through force or its threat, so that domination is by the permeation of ideas. For instance, concepts of hegemony have been used to explain how, when 'the ruling ideas are the ideas of the ruling class', other classes will willingly accept their inferior position as right and proper (*see* CLASS). Hegemonic is the adjective attached to the institution that possesses hegemony. For instance, under CAPITALISM the bourgeoisie are the hegemonic class. Hegemon is a term used when the concept of hegemony is applied to the competition between NATION-STATES: a hegemon is a hegemonic state. For instance, the USA has been described as the hegemon of the world economy in the mid-twentieth century.

Decolonization

this term has two meanings: (a) the ending of formal colonial rule by one power over another (*see* COLONIALISM); (b) the departure of a settler population from a colonized territory (*see* COLONIZATION). In both cases, however, processes of decolonization are in fact likely to be far less of a 'clean break' than these definitions suggest. Legacies from, and new forms of, colonialism are still central to POST-COLONIAL experiences.

Neo-colonialism

economic and political ties, continuing after formal independence, between metropolitan countries and the South, that work to the benefit of the North. *See also* COLONIALISM.

FIGURE 23.6
Call centre workers in India. Credit: Indranil Mukherjee/Getty Images

activities cannot always be labelled colonial. But the external influence and ventures of the USA and the USSR (until its break-up in 1990) can be described as imperial, and they are sometimes said to be **neo-colonial**. This term was coined by the first president of independent Ghana, Kwame Nkrumah (1965), who was disillusioned by the failure of decolonization to liberate Africans from the power of Europe and the United States. Colonial governments had been replaced by international monetary bodies, multinational corporations and a variety of educational and cultural organizations, reconfiguring what one US critic has called 'imperialism without colonies' (Magdoff, 2003).

Allegedly neo-colonial or imperial American ventures involve some of the same tactics that were used by former colonial powers such as the British, with many of the same objectives (including preferential access to resources, labour and markets). These tactics include occasional military intervention to protect investment and trade. In 2003, for instance, the United States and a few close allies invaded Iraq in what was officially presented as a defensive measure, provoked by global terrorism in the wake of the September 11th attacks, but which many saw as a war for oil and global domination (Epstein, 2003). The reasons for going to war were complex and contested, but consistent with a broad strategy made explicit by Richard Haass, a key figure in the US government. In a paper entitled 'Imperial America', presented in 2000, Haass advocated 'an imperial foreign policy' in which 'the US role would resemble nineteenth-century Great Britain' (Foster, 2003). Other senior US politicians, speaking through an organization known as the Project for the New American Century, directly argued that more overseas bases, particularly in the Gulf, were fundamental to any strategy to 'preserve *Pax Americana*' – a phrase that reiterated the parallel with British and before that Roman imperialism: *Pax Britannica* and *Pax Romana* (Foster, 2003).

In the neo-colonial order, American and other western corporations have access to global resources, markets (Coca-Cola and McDonald's, for example) and labour, which often comes cheap (see Fig. 23.6). Large companies tap cheaper foreign labour by setting up assembly plants or 'outsourcing' – subcontracting work to local producers. European countries have exported manufacturing and more recently call centre and other service jobs to former colonies, with which they retain many business contacts and share languages. The USA, with fewer former colonies as such, has invested in Asia and Latin America, and also joined British companies in India. As one British newspaper put it in 2003, 'The list of countries on a passage to India reads like a Who's Who of British business' (*Sunday Times*, 2003). If outsourcing enriches western (and other) investors, it does so at the expense of workers not only in developing countries, but also in the West. The secretary general of the British Trades Union Congress (TUC) estimated in 2004 that two million jobs could be outsourced from wealthy nations in the next five years (*Wall Street Journal*, 2004).

One response to their mutual vulnerability to international capital has been for workers and governments around the world to undercut and compete with each other; another has been to recognize shared experiences and interests, and to struggle against certain forces of globalization or neo-colonialism. Western workers and consumers have campaigned on behalf of their counterparts in developing countries, for example by using their buying – and boycotting – power to pressurize large companies to improve conditions and pay for workers and suppliers. Activists around the world have also co-ordinated their protests on issues such as the invasion of Iraq in 2003, multiplying efforts and impacts (Epstein, 2003). Interventions such as these – not only by dissident figures but also governments – rest upon understandings of global inter-dependence and inequality. The historical sensitivities of governments were evident in the early 2000s, when the USA, France and Britain all intervened to suppress bloody civil wars in West Africa. Each sent troops and aid to the nation with which it had a specific historical colonial connection and, it was felt, responsibility: the USA to Liberia (where African-Americans were settled in the eighteenth century), the French to the Ivory Coast (where slaves, ivory and plantation goods were once obtained) and the British to Sierra Leone (first a slave trading centre, later the base for Britain's campaign against slavery) (*Guardian*, 2003). Historical understandings of imperialism have also informed a range of other actions in the present, concerned with reconciliation between and within nations. Thus, for example, British prime minister Tony Blair apologized to the people of Ireland for centuries of oppression, and Australian prime minister John Howard apologized to Aborigines, whom the nation's school systems and adoption agencies had taken from their families and attempted to assimilate (Gooder and Jacobs, 2002). In some cases, this dialogue with the colonial past – informed by historical and post-colonial geographers – is being followed through in financial reparations, land claims and sovereignty disputes, in which colonized and native peoples are renegotiating their relationships with the descendants of colonists and inheritors of the colonial state (Harris, 2002). Mapping the colonial past, they implicitly address the post-colonial present.

SUMMARY

- Empires have shaped modern world maps, dictated and policed borders and configurations of states, controlled systems of production and consumption, and interfered with patterns of culture and settlement.
- Geographies of colonialism and imperialism are not necessarily historical geographies, since the demise of western European colonial empires has been matched by the rise of other, mainly western and northern, imperial and/or neo-colonial powers.
- An understanding of the colonial past, in which historical geographers have an important part to play, speaks to contemporary issues ranging from relationships between former colonial powers and colonies to aboriginal land disputes and racial identity politics.

CONCLUSION

Geographies of colonialism and postcolonialism begin in the past, but due to the inertia of old empires and the emergence of new ones, they continue into the present. European colonial empires have largely disappeared, but they live on in territorial boundaries and relationships, and within the social, political, economic and cultural ordering of the modern world. Whilst British, French and other European Empires have receded, leaving legacies, memories and material traces, others have advanced. In many ways the United States has taken over where the British left off, but *Pax Americana* is not simply a copy of *Pax Britannica*. The ongoing history of empire is one of continuity and change: continuity in patterns of unequal territorial relationships and (within the modern period) western domination; and change in the ways that this is organized, and in its ever increasing scope. Colonial and post-colonial perspectives draw together many traditional sub-fields of the discipline – including geographies of development, trade, economy, migration, language and culture – in an approach that is synthetic, historical and critical.

DISCUSSION POINTS

1. What are the legacies of European imperialism?

2. Discuss the relationships between geographical knowledge and imperial power.

3. How might it be possible to map colonial encounters from the perspectives of colonized peoples?

4. Discuss the relationships between imperialism and globalization.

5. Compare and contrast the British and American empires.

FURTHER READING

Blunt, A. and McEwan, C. (eds) (2002) *Postcolonial geographies*. London: Continuum.

An excellent introduction to new research on geographies of colonialism and postcolonialism, which reflects the mainly historical and cultural emphasis of this field.

Godlewska, A. and Smith, N. (eds) (1994) *Geography and empire*. London: Blackwell/IBG.

A series of essays on the relationships between geographical scholarship and empire. Read the editors' introduction and a selection of the others, including Crush's essay on 'Post-colonialism, de-colonisation and geography'.

Livingstone, D.N. (1992) *The geographical tradition*. Oxford: Blackwell.

This substantial contribution to the history and philosophy of geographical knowledge is a must for any undergraduate geographer. Livingstone pays particular attention to relationships between colonialism and the production and use of geographical knowledge.

Sidaway, J.D., Bunnell, T. and Yeoh, B.S.A. (2003) Geography and postcolonialism. Theme issue of *Singapore Journal of Tropical Geography*, 24(3).

This edited collection draws together some of the most exciting new research on colonial and post-colonial geographies, and makes useful and provocative connections between historical and contemporary forms of imperialism.

Phillips, R. (2005) *Sex, politics and empire: a postcolonial geography*, Manchester: Manchester University Press.

This book draws upon the colonial past – specifically the sex lives and sexual attitudes of colonists and colonial subjects – to envision a post-colonial geography, which shows how imperial power was and is both constituted and resisted geographically.

Said, E. (1993) *Culture and imperialism*. London: Chatto & Windus.

Real and imagined geographies are at the heart of Said's exploration of relationships between western culture and imperialism. The brief introductory section on 'Empire, geography, and culture' is particularly useful. This book develops ideas about 'geographical discourse' that Said first introduced in his influential if sometimes difficult *Orientalism* (1978).

CHAPTER 24

Miles Ogborn

MODERNITY AND MODERNIZATION

INTRODUCTION: THIS IS THE MODERN WORLD

What does it mean to call something 'modern'? In part it simply means that it is new, up to date or of the moment. This might relate to (modern) technology, art or life as a whole, and these descriptions are about understanding how the world is changing. Sometimes this idea of 'modernity' – the condition of being modern – is used to celebrate newness, perhaps to encourage people to adopt an innovation or, in the case of political parties (like the British Labour Party in the 1990s), to attract a wider range of voters to a new set of policies. Sometimes it is part of complaints that the modern world is moving on and leaving much that is valuable behind, as in some discussions of the difficulties found in understanding modern art. Whichever point of view is taken, the idea of 'modernity' situates people in time. It suggests that time is divided up into past, present and future. It gives a certain value or significance to the past (positive or negative), and it makes the present important as a time of change and of decisions about what the future should be. Calling something 'modern' makes people think about historical change (Baldwin *et al.*, 2004).

Understanding modernity as 'newness' allows an appreciation of the modernity of any point in time. It helps to explain the excitement that accompanied the coming of the railways, electricity, the cinema, or buildings made of concrete, steel and glass. It also helps in understanding the sense of danger they brought too – the fear that the world was changing too fast. In each case the relationship between past, present and future established by modernity is experienced by people and understood in terms of how it might change their lives for better or worse. For example, Raphael Samuel has examined the ideas of modernity in Britain in the 1950s to argue that '[t]he ruling ideology of the day was forward-looking and progressive, the ruling aesthetic one of light and space. Newness was regarded as a good in itself, a guarantee of things that were practical and worked' (1994: 51). He explores this by showing that post-war 'home improvement' meant – for those unlucky enough to live in 'ugly', 'old-fashioned' Georgian and Victorian houses – tearing out fireplaces, removing draughty sash windows, knocking down partition walls and covering over 'dust-collecting' plasterwork or banisters. In their place came central heating, fluorescent strip lighting, fixtures and fittings of easy-clean, smooth and colourful plastic, Formica and fibreglass, and kitchens and 'broom cupboards' full of labour-saving devices – washing machines, electric cookers and Hoovers (see Fig. 24.1). Houses and people's lives were to be transformed through this 'appetite for modernization' (1994: 56). This example shows both the intensity with which people experience modernity (in this case as something desirable) and its role in making new geographies. Here it is new domestic geographies. These houses were

Postmodern, postmodernity, postmodernism

the British national newspaper, the *Independent*, sarcastically defined postmodernism thus. 'This word has no meaning. Use it as often as possible.' In fact, the main problem for a glossary entry such as this is that ideas of the postmodern have been used so often with so many different meanings! Nonetheless, one can generalize to say that notions of the postmodern (sometimes hyphenated, sometimes not) are used to suggest a move beyond 'modern' society and culture (*see* MODERN, MODERNITY, MODERNISM). More specifically: (a) postmodern is an adjective used to describe social and cultural forms that eschew 'modern' qualities of order, rationality and progress in favour of 'postmodern' qualities of difference, ephemerality, superficiality and pastiche; (b) 'postmodernity' is the contemporary epoch, after a period of 'modernity', in which such postmodern forms supposedly predominate, an epoch characterized both by the loss of an overall sense of social direction and order and by the triumph of the media image over reality (*see* HYPER-REALITY and SIMULACRUM); and (c) 'postmodernism' refers more narrowly to a collection of artistic, architectural and intellectual movements that promote postmodernist values, aesthetics and ways of thinking. If that is not complicated enough, whilst some view all things postmodern as signs of a radically new historical era of postmodernity, others see them more as recent twists to the history of modernity. So perhaps a revised version of the *Independent*'s definition might be: 'This word has a host of meanings. This makes it interesting, but also means it should be used with care'!

made into different sorts of *places*; they looked and felt different. Indeed, the same impulse also transformed the geography of many cities and their inhabitants' lives and experiences. The motorways, housing estates and civic and shopping centres so characteristic of the urban planning of the 1950s and 1960s can also be seen as an attempt to make spaces that were new, clean and easy to use. In both cases modernization involves geographical change – transforming places, spaces and landscapes – as a part of historical change (Hubbard and Lilley, 2004).

These examples begin to suggest that modernity and modernization are about more than just 'newness'. There are particular sorts of historical and geographical change involved. Without setting this out too rigidly (for the many opinions about what 'modernity' is see Ogborn, 1998), important processes can be identified: the application of scientific principles to human and natural worlds; the development of industrial economies (capitalist and non-capitalist); and the formation of states that govern many aspects

FIGURE 24.1
Home improvement as modernization.

of life through their bureaucracies (Giddens, 1990). These are all both historical and geographical processes. They create particular forms of 'modern life' through specific (and often very rapid) types of historical change, and a crucial part of this is the transformation of spaces, places and landscapes. For example, Figure 24.2 shows a dramatic modern landscape: the Hoover Dam built across Black Canyon on the Arizona–Nevada border between 1931 and 1936. It is 725 feet high, incorporating 2.5 million cubic metres of concrete and creating a lake of 210 square miles. Understanding this dam in terms of modernity means seeing it as a product of the technological and scientific control of nature by geologists and engineers, funded largely from public money, and planned by one of the world's most powerful states to provide irrigation and hydro-electric power for the development of capitalist industry and agriculture. The Hoover Dam has not only transformed the physical geography of Black Canyon, but also the economic geography and environment of the western United States. It should also be understood in terms of the responses it provokes:

FIGURE 24.2
The Hoover Dam: a landscape of modernity.
Credit: Lester Lefkowitz/Corbis

> *Confronting this spectacle in the midst of emptiness and desolation first provokes fear, then wonderment, and finally a sense of awe and pride in man's skill in bending the forces of nature to his purpose. In the shadow of the Hoover Dam one feels that the future is limitless, that no obstacle is insurmountable, that we have in our grasp the power to achieve anything if we can but summon the will.*

(Stevens, 1988: 266–7)

The idea of 'man' against nature is raised again later, for now it is important to note the sense of wonder, excitement and fear in how the dam seems to open up the future. The Hoover Dam is a landscape that is the product of the scientific, industrial and political processes of modernization, and is experienced in terms of the challenges and dangers of modernity. It combines, therefore, the ideas of modernity as both 'newness' and as particular forms of historical and geographical change.

The historical geography of modernity and modernization (and the difficult question of '**postmodernity**') is a huge area. In many ways this whole book is about the geographies of the modern relationships between people, science and nature; industry, capitalism and space; and politics, power and territory. Instead I want to concentrate in this chapter on some of the different ways of understanding the historical and geographical changes involved in processes of modernization. I want to start with an idea that is there in both the examples of the Hoover in the 1950s house and the Hoover Dam: modernization as 'progress'.

SUMMARY

- Modernity is a matter of the experience of 'newness' and the specific understanding of historical time that involves.

- Modernity is also a matter of a specific set of interconnected economic, political, social and cultural changes.

- Modernization involves changes in people's lives and in geographies at all scales. These changes can be understood in a range of different ways.

MODERNITY AND MODERNIZATION AS PROGRESS

Understanding modernization in terms of 'progress' suggests that a society makes a clean break with a problematic past and does what is necessary to move forward into a better future. An influential version of this was the 'modernization theories' that were applied to Latin America, Asia and Africa after 1945. In his book *The Stages of Economic Growth* (1960) W.W. Rostow suggested that the history of each society could be understood through five stages: traditional society; the preconditions for take-off; take-off; the drive to maturity; and the age of high mass consumption. Britain, with its 'Industrial Revolution', had been through this process first and could be followed by the other countries of the world (see Fig. 24.3). Rostow argued that 'traditional society' prevented regular growth through its non-scientific attitude to nature, lack of social mobility, failure to see the potential for change, and non-centralized political power. This situation was to be changed in the 'preconditions' period by removing the technological, social and political constraints on economic growth through, for example, newly centralized states (controlled by new, often nationalist, elites keen on modernization) building roads and railways, and encouraging science, technology and key industries. These geographical changes in agriculture, industry, transportation and urbanization, combined with a positive attitude to 'modernization', would prompt 'take-off' – 'the great watershed in the life of modern societies . . . when the old blocks and resistances to steady growth are finally overcome' (1960: 7) – into a stage of continual growth and less state intervention. This economic growth would utterly transform the society into a complex modern industrial economy during the 'drive to maturity'. Eventually it would reach a final stage of 'high mass consumption' (modelled on the affluent parts of the USA in the 1950s) where production and consumption were based on consumer durables: a land of automobiles and suburban homes equipped with refrigerators and televisions.

Rostow presented modernization as progress. He argued that it was absolutely necessary for countries to make the decisions that would promote modernization or they would lose out to others. He also presented it – through the idea of 'take-off' – as a dramatic transformation. However, by understanding it as an orderly progression of stages that others had successfully gone through he was able to claim that there was only one path to follow for successful modernization, and that this break with the past and the move into a brighter future would be relatively painless and full of benefits in the long run. This meant that this form of modernization could be offered as the way forward for the countries of what people were starting to call the 'third world'. They could become like western Europe and the USA.

One country that modernized in this way was Turkey (although Rostow argued that the Turkish state pushed for 'take-off' too early). It is a useful example of some of the changes in people's lives and in geographies that 'modernization as progress' involves. It also suggests some of the problems with this version of modernity. Turkey's transformation involved opening

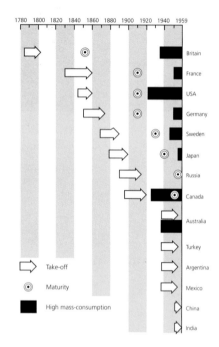

FIGURE 24.3
Rostow's stages of economic growth. Source: W.W. Rostow, 1960: *The stages of economic growth*, p. xii

Nation-state

a form of political organization that involves (a) a set of institutions that govern the people within a particular TERRITORY (the state), and (b) that claims allegiance and legitimacy from those governed, and from other states, on the basis that they represent a group of people defined in cultural and political terms as a nation.

itself up to the forces of western modernization. This began during the nineteenth-century Ottoman Empire, but was dramatically accelerated with the foundation of Turkey as a **nation-state** in 1923 under Mustapha Kemal (he later called himself Atatürk, 'Father of the Turks'). The modernization process was to be a total transformation of Turkish economy, society, politics and culture, and a total break with the past. Mustapha Kemal declared that 'the new Turkey has no relationship to the old. The Ottoman government has passed into history. A new Turkey is now born' (Robins, 1996: 68). Moving into this promising new future involved economic policies that transformed parts of the country. During the 1930s the state intervened to modernize the economy and to make it serve national ends rather than being oriented to the export of raw materials (see Fig. 24.4). Import controls were coupled with agricultural policies aiming at national self-sufficiency in food through scientific farming and irrigation schemes. A modern capital city was built at Ankara. Extensive railway construction produced a national network, and a Soviet-inspired five-year plan (1934–38) provided large textile, sugar, paper, cement and steel plants spread across the country in order to substitute Turkish goods for imports from the West. These were combined with earlier (1920s) policies designed to remove what were seen as cultural barriers to modernization. The influence of Islam on people's lives was to be reduced by separating state and religion, abolishing religious courts and centres of religious learning, and closing down shrines and religious brotherhoods. Turks were to be reoriented towards the West and its ideas by prohibiting the fez in favour of the western hat for men; the adoption of Latin rather than Arabic script, the metric system, family surnames and the Gregorian calendar; and, along with the westernization of new architecture, the playing of American jazz in public places. Finally, any identifications with causes other than that of the modern Turkish nation-state were prevented by the prohibition of internationalist organizations and programmes of repression and assimilation aimed at ethnic minorities (Kurds, Georgians and Armenians). Turkey's modernizers understood the process of modernization as one of making people make a clean break with the past and encouraging them to progress into a bright (western) future (Landau, 1984; Parker and Smith, 1940; Schick and Tonak, 1987).

There are clearly some very real problems with this single, progressive and western version of modernization. First, it can never be a matter of simply following a western model. These countries are not separate entities ranged along a developmental path, they are connected together so that the development of one has consequences for others (Taylor, 1989). Also, within Turkey, the adoption of a model from outside has meant that 'modernization has been an arid and empty affair' (Robins, 1996: 67) unconnected to the cultures of the place and lacking dynamism. Second, this version of modernization underplays the disruptiveness of the transformation for people and the landscapes that they live in. Robins shows how Kemalist policies that sought to achieve a western modernity by suppressing the past, the specific nature of Turkish society and the cultural differences within the country had very traumatic consequences, which are only now being dealt with.

Why modernization theorists put forward such ideas is best explained

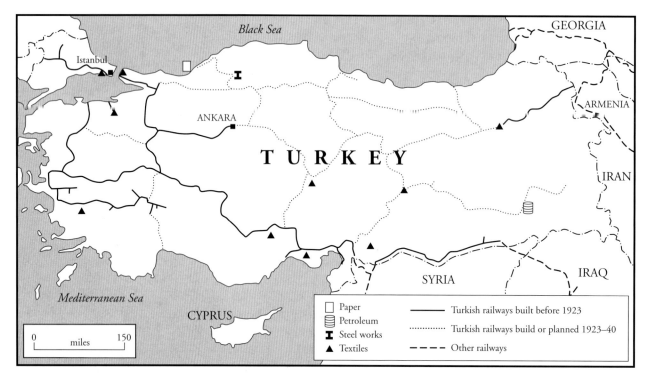

FIGURE 24.4
Turkish modernization: industry and transport

by their political context. In an era of decolonization, the Cold War and a post-war boom in western Europe and the USA the idea of modernization as westernization (and seeing that as orderly progress) was part of a political move to combat the appeal of communism to 'third world' countries. Rostow certainly saw himself as offering an alternative, and subtitled his book 'a non-communist manifesto'. In the next section I want to look at some of the ideas that Rostow was reacting against to see how modernization is understood in a different way: as 'creative destruction'.

SUMMARY

- Rostow's theory presented modernization as progress: a single (western) path to modernity that is positive, beneficial and relatively painless.

- Turkey's experience of 'modernization as progress' shows the changes in lives and geographies that it

involves, and that ideas like Rostow's simplified the difficulty, complexity and trauma of modernization.

MODERNITY AND MODERNIZATION AS CREATIVE DESTRUCTION

Understanding modernization as 'creative destruction' suggests that the changes involved are dramatic and unsettling ones, and that making a new future always means destroying many of the geographies and ways of life of the past and present. Marshall Berman (1982) has suggested that Karl Marx and Freidrich Engels' (1848) *Communist Manifesto* puts forward this view of historical and geographical change in its discussion of capitalism. He sums it up using a phrase (borrowed from Shakespeare) from the

Manifesto: in the modern world 'All that is solid melts into air'. This poetic image suggests the sense of constant change and uncertainty that Marx and Engels argued is necessary for **capitalism** to be successful. This arises from the continual need to develop the 'productive forces' – labour power, raw materials, machinery, science, communications and transportation – needed to produce **commodities** and make a profit. This generates the constant search for new materials and new markets that drove global exploration and settlement, and radically transformed the lives and landscapes of many in Africa, Asia and the Americas, as well as in Europe. It also meant a dramatic transformation in forms of work, most vividly seen in the coming of the factory system, where all sorts of labour – no matter how menial or prestigious – became activity that was done for wages and was often controlled by the workings of a machine. Finally, it involved radical geographical changes, the building of huge industrial cities, the making of modern nation-states, and what Marx and Engels described as the 'Subjection of Nature's forces to Man, machinery, application of chemistry to industry and agriculture, steam-navigation, railways, electric telegraphs, clearing of whole continents for cultivation, canalisation of rivers, whole populations conjured out of the ground . . .' (1848: 85). So, even though they opposed it, Marx and Engels were in awe of capitalism's capacity to make 'all that is solid melt into air', destroying entire ways of life and whole landscapes as it developed the forces of production. More importantly, they saw capitalism as destroying what it had itself previously created – factories, docks, whole cities – as they became unprofitable. For them the process of modernization is both dramatic and traumatic. It offers all sorts of possibilities for changing the world, but also destroys ways of life and places that had become known, accepted and familiar. This making and breaking of social relations and their geographies is modernization understood as 'creative destruction'.

An example can help here. Between 1850 and 1870 Paris was transformed by this sort of 'capitalist modernization'. Many of that city's best-known features – tree-lined boulevards, monumental architecture and pavement cafés – were constructed during that period. However, to create this new urban geography much of Paris had to be destroyed and many lives were seriously disrupted. How and why did this happen? David Harvey (1985) argues that the impetus was the economic crisis of the 1840s – the worst that France had experienced. There were many workers who could not find work and, at the same time, many investors who could find nowhere profitable to invest. In addition, Paris's eighteenth-century infrastructure made it more of a hindrance than a help in escaping from this crisis. The solution orchestrated by Emperor Louis Napoleon and his minister Baron Haussmann was a massive reorganization of the geography of France and its capital through a huge public works programme – building new railways, roads and telegraph systems across France and transforming Paris with new streets, water supply, sewers, monuments, public buildings, parks, schools and churches. The rebuilding programme would put people and capital to work in the short term, and, in the longer term, would provide the sort of modern city within which profitable investments in land, manufacturing or commerce could be made.

The most significant part of this new urban geography was

Capitalism

an economic system in which the production and distribution of goods is organized around the profit motive (*see* CAPITAL ACCUMULATION) and characterized by marked inequalities in the social division of work and wealth between private owners of the materials and tools of production (capital) and those who work for them to make a living (labour) (*see* CLASS).

Commodity

something that can be bought and sold through the market. A commodity can be an object (a car, for example), but can also be a person (the car production worker who sells their labour for a wage) or an idea (the design or marketing concepts of the car). Those who live in capitalist societies are used to most things being commodities, though there are still taboos (the buying and selling of sexual intercourse or grandmothers, for example) (*see* CAPITALISM and COMMODIFICATION). This should not disguise the fact that the 'commodity state' is a very particular way of framing objects, people and ideas.

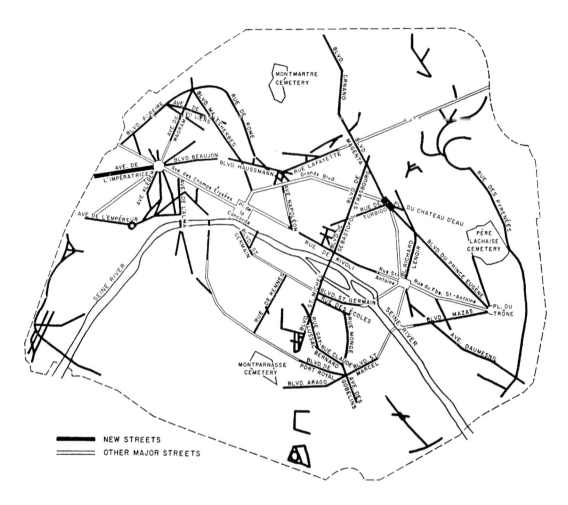

FIGURE 24.5

Principal new streets in Paris, 1850–70. Source: D.H. Pinckney, 1958: *Napoleon III and the rebuilding of Paris*, p. 73

Haussmann's boulevards. Figure 24.5 shows the streets built between 1850 and 1870. In all they were 85 miles long and, on average, three times wider than the ones they replaced (Pinckney, 1958). The extent of the remodelling of traffic flows is clear. The aim was to make Paris into a single, functioning unit rather than a series of separate neighbourhoods. Particularly significant is the cross at the heart of the city made by Rue de Rivoli, Boulevard de Strasbourg, Boulevard de Sébastopol and Boulevard Saint Michel, which linked both banks of the River Seine to an axis that ran right across Paris. Other boulevards connected new railway terminals to the city centre. These new streets brought other changes too. Building them combined modern science and engineering, as well as a lot of hard work (in the mid-1860s, 20 per cent of the working population of Paris was employed in construction). Their planning necessitated the first accurate topographic and land ownership maps for the city. They were also politically important. Haussmann ensured that the boulevards provided vistas of monuments or buildings that were symbols of France, religion and empire – like the Arc de Triomphe – so that the new city combined both tradition and modernity. It was also rumoured that these wide, straight roads made it harder for revolutionaries to put up barricades as they had done in 1830 and 1848, and easier for the army to ride their horses or fire their artillery down them. These huge streets certainly made it easier to travel faster through the city by horse and carriage, and pedestrians were now confronted with huge numbers of speeding vehicles (Berman, 1982). Finally, they provided new opportunities for private investment in the plush apartment buildings, exclusive hotels, fashionable pavement cafés and dazzling shops (including vast department stores) that lined the gas-lit boulevards. As Harvey argues, they 'became corridors of homage to the power of money and commodities, [and] play spaces for the bourgeoisie' (1985: 204). Paris was transformed – a new geography was created – and some people benefited from the opportunities for profitable investment and pleasure.

FIGURE 24.6
'But here is where I live - and I don't even find my wife.' Source: Honoré Daumier cartoon, 1852. In D.H. Pinkney, 1958: *Napoleon III and the rebuilding of Paris*

However, to build the boulevards, the old city of Paris had to be torn apart. The new streets carved their way straight through ancient districts of winding streets, hidden corners and higgledy-piggledy buildings housing vast numbers of Parisian workers. In 1850 the Ile de la Cité (the island in the Seine where Notre Dame cathedral stands) housed 14,000 people. By 1870 only a few hundred were left to defy Haussmann's plans to devote the island to institutions of law, religion and medicine. For 20 years the centre of Paris was a building site and thousands of people were displaced. They were either forced out to the suburbs, and had to walk for several hours to get to work, or they crowded into the remaining central areas and paid exorbitant rents for appalling accommodation. Figure 24.6 shows a contemporary cartoon that, whilst making fun of the situation, gives a sense of the disruption felt by many ordinary Parisians as their city was destroyed. As well as the elimination of neighbourhoods it also hints at the disruption of family relationships. This man's wife may not have been in the shell of what had been their home because, as Harvey shows, the economic restructuring that accompanied Paris's transformation meant that both men and women were forced to work, often very long hours, if they and their families were to survive. In Paris, therefore, we can see an example of the wider process of 'creative destruction' whereby the forces of modernization benefit some and disadvantage others as they dramatically transform lives and landscapes (Pred, 1990). However, this is not just a historical matter. The same processes and effects can be seen in many contemporary sites. For example, Figure 24.7 is an attempt to use a montage of images to capture the dramatic and contradictory transformations of the city of Berlin in the years since 1990.

FIGURE 24.7
Potsdamer Platz, Berlin. Montage by Michael Pryke. Source: Tracing economic rhythms through visual and audio montage (www.open. ac.uk/socialsciences/geography/research/berlin)

SUMMARY

- Understanding modernization as 'creative destruction' shows that it involves the destruction of lives and geographies as well as the construction of new geographies and new ways of life.

- The example of nineteenth-century Paris shows that some people benefit and some people lose out through the processes of modernization.

CONCLUSION: MANY MODERNITIES

'Modernization as progress' and as 'creative destruction' offer very different ways of understanding these historical and geographical changes. They give different versions of the relationship between past, present and future and, as presented by Marx and Rostow, suggest very different political responses. However, there are three points that can be made about both versions that help to develop the idea of modernity. First, they both present modernity as a radical break with the past. This may be true for some parts of Turkey in the 1920s and 1930s or for many Parisians in the 1850s and 1860s. However, it is worth thinking about more subtle ways of understanding these historical geographies of modernization which recognize that change happens at different rates in different places, and that instead of being eradicated by modernity past lives and landscapes are often remade, reinvented or reincorporated with new ways of doing things and new geographies. Second, they are both primarily concerned with economic transformations, and particularly with capitalism. Whilst this is clearly important we need to remember that historical geographies of modernity also need to be about political transformations (e.g. modern bureaucratic and territorial nation-states), technological transformations (e.g. the application of science to both nature and society), and social and cultural transformations (e.g. modernist art's attempts to deal with processes of modernization). All these processes shape the modern world together and they have done so in non-capitalist as well as capitalist economies.

These two issues lead towards the third point: that there are many different modernities. 'Modernity' is different at different times, and it has many different strands. It is also different in different places. Both versions discussed here see western Europe and North America as the most important places in these historical geographies of modernity. Instead, we might investigate other experiences of modernity that were connected to what went on in London, Paris and New York but were not simply the same (Miller, 1994). Robin's (1996) discussion of Turkey offers one possibility, as do studies of Shanghai (Ou-fan Lee, 1999), Calcutta (Chakrabarty, 1999) and Brasília (Tauxe, 1996). Another is Paul Gilroy's (1993a) argument that black Africans transported to the Americas and to Europe under slavery can be seen as the first modern people because of their experience of (and resistance to) globalization, industrial work on the plantations and attempts to use science to justify racism. There are, therefore, also different modernities for different social groups defined in terms of class, 'race' and gender. For example, this means that processes of modernization have different effects on, and are experienced differently by, men and women: modernity is often talked about in terms of dramatic confrontations between 'Man' and 'Nature' which present the whole process in gendered terms; Turkey's modernization programme meant that women were given the vote (as well as equal rights in many other areas); and, in Paris, the new pleasures and hardships of the modernized city were experienced differently by men and women who had different access to the new spaces of the city and very different expectations of them when they were on the streets or in the cafés or department stores (Pollock, 1988).

What we end up with, therefore, are many different modernities. There are various processes of modernization that have been transforming lives and landscapes across the globe in different ways for hundreds of years and that are experienced differently by different sorts of people. Each one makes for a different historical geography of modernity and raises different questions about understanding the past, present and future.

DISCUSSION POINTS

1. Try and find examples of policies being put forward to change particular geographies (perhaps regenerating parts of a city, or for development in areas of the global South) which offer different versions of the future. What forms of 'modernity' are being promoted here?

2. Is modernization ever only a matter of 'progress', or does it always involve 'creative destruction'?

3. Is it possible to understand historical and geographical change without thinking of it in terms of 'modernization'?

FURTHER READING

Given that is a good idea to read original works and make up your own mind, the two books that I use for this discussion are as follows.

Rostow, W.W. (1960) *The stages of economic growth: a non-communist manifesto.* **Cambridge, Cambridge University Press.**

Especially Chapters 1 to 4, which cover the stages up to 'take-off'.

Marx, K. and Engels, F. (1967, originally published in 1848) *The communist manifesto.* **Harmondsworth: Penguin Books.**

Section 1, 'Bourgeois and proletarians', includes the material discussed here.

Other, more general treatments of the issues raised are covered in the following texts.

Berman, M. (1982) *All that is solid melts into air: the experience of modernity.* **London: Verso.**

Offers a discussion based on the idea of 'creative destruction' that covers Marx (Chapter 2) and Paris (Chapter 3). Quite a difficult book to read, but has many interesting insights and examples.

Ogborn, M. (1998) *Spaces of modernity: London's geographies 1680–1780.* **New York: Guilford Press.**

Chapter 1 contains an overview of theories of modernity that relates them to questions of Historical Geography.

SECTION 6
POLITICAL GEOGRAPHIES

INTRODUCTION

The statement that the 'personal is political' has achieved quite widespread currency since it was first used as part of the feminist movement in the 1960s. It neatly sums up the idea that politics is to be found in each and every aspect of our daily lives, and is not restricted to the more formal machinery of parliament and government. The latter concern with formal politics dominated political geography for many years and led to an emphasis on a seemingly distant and specialized sphere of activity to do with political parties, elections, governments and public policy. Although there was the notion that everyday life was affected by such processes, there was little conception that politics was actually part of our day-to-day lives. It was something that was carried out by other people (politicians and civil servants) and that went on elsewhere (in government institutions).

More recently, however, this view has changed in two key ways. First, there has been a realization that the formal politics of government and the state have much more impact on our daily lives than hitherto thought and, second, there has been a far broader examination of a whole host of informal politics – taking place in the home, in the workplace in the street and in the community. The three chapters in this section all examine these twin developments, but do so at different levels of enquiry. Initially, in Chapter 25, Joanne Sharp takes a global perspective by concentrating on the issue of geopolitics or the relations between states. She shows how these relations are not fixed, but instead are fluid and always specific to particular historical and cultural circumstances. She then looks at how the geography of international relations is constructed through particular sets of discourses, and at how even these very distant formal politics are connected to our everyday lives via elements of popular culture such as Hollywood movies and computer games. These elements in turn help to shape the 'geographical imaginations' that we all hold of the world and its political interrelationships at a global level.

In Chapter 26, Mark Goodwin examines the twin concepts of governance and citizenship, and in doing so moves the scale of analysis down to the more local level. He shows how the two themes are related and how, together, they cover the issues of what it means to be a citizen, of what rights and obligations one has as a citizen and of the ways in which we as citizens are governed. The chapter points out how both citizenship and governance are experienced differently by different social groups, and examines how these divisions create differential spaces where different degrees of citizenship and governance are experienced and played out. Crucially, these differential geographies have become critical to the building and sustaining of new forms of participatory citizenship around localized community issues.

In Chapter 27 Pyrs Gruffudd helps to show that the scale of analysis is also fluid by looking at the contested notions of the 'nation' and nationalism. He shows that what for some people is only a region within a bigger entity, is to others a fully fledged 'nation'. Often the tension between these two views boils over into war and turmoil, as witnessed by events in the Middle East and in the former Yugoslavia. Pyrs looks at how the symbolic role of geography is hugely implicated in the very construction of national identity and nationalist movements, which are often centred on a struggle for land and territory.

Taken together, these chapters provide excellent examples of the movement of political geography away from a concentration on formal politics to an exploration of the myriad spaces of informal politics. Yet they also show the continued importance of the formal political sphere. The challenge for the future, perhaps, is to examine these two spheres together, by looking at how each affects the shaping of the other, rather than continuing to see them as separate. Each chapter gives a pointer to the very exciting areas of enquiry that emerge if this is done.

FURTHER READING

Jones, M., Jones, R. and Woods, M. (2004) *An introduction to political geography: space place and politics.* London: Routledge.

This is the best recent introductory textbook on political geography.

Taylor, P. and Flint, C. (2000) *Political geography.* Harlow: Pearson.

Cox, K. (2002) *Political geography: territory state and nation.* Oxford: Blackwell.

Two other very good textbooks on political geography.

For the most up-to-date writings on economic geography you should scan recent editions of the journal *Political Geography*. This will give you a sense of the current topics being pursued in this field.

CHAPTER 25
CRITICAL GEOPOLITICS

INTRODUCTION

For many people, the downfall of the Soviet Union, symbolized so dramatically by the destruction of the Berlin Wall and the toppling of statues of communist leaders, heralded a new world order of peace and stability after the fear and anxiety of the **Cold War**. The moral global battle of the previous half-century – the ultimate battle between freedom and the 'Evil Empire' as it was often put – was over. Images of world leaders shaking hands at global summits seemed to offer an image of a unified world. Rather than seeing images of stability, however, some commentators quickly started to sense danger lurking in this New World Order. The multipolarity of the post-Cold War order seemed to offer the potential for greater dangers to world peace. One commentator suggested that we would soon miss the stability of the superpower opposition of the Cold War (Mearsheimer, 1990), while another suggested that the emerging world 'is likely to lack the clarity and stability of the Cold War and to be a more jungle-like world of multiple dangers, hidden traps, unpleasant surprises and moral ambiguities' (Huntingdon, quoted in Ó Tuathail, 1996: 242). The events of 11 September 2001 have changed the dominant image once again. Despite evidence which suggests that Al Qaeda is a global network, in his rhetoric of the 'axis of evil' President George W. Bush redrew clear lines of good and evil on to the global political map.

Each of these models of the contemporary world order is structured by a geographical imagination of some sort. During the Cold War the free world was pitted against the communist world (if you happened to live in the USA) with maps geared towards proving the military superiority of the Soviet Union and her allies, and demonstrating the inevitability of countries falling under communism like dominoes unless the Soviet Union was contained behind the Iron Curtain. Following the end of the Cold War, theorists offered new visions of a globe of chaos and fragmentation offering threats and dangers from all around. The imagined geography of the War on Terror re-establishes a globe in which it seems that each country is either for the USA or for the terrorists, there is no in-between space. The use of geographical imaginaries in global political models like this is called 'geopolitics'.

The *Dictionary of Human Geography* defines geopolitics as an element of the practice and analysis of statecraft that considers geography and spatial relations to play a significant role in the constitution of international politics. Certain 'laws' of geography, such as distance, proximity and location are understood to influence the development of political situations. In geopolitical arguments, the effect of geography on politics is based upon 'common sense', rather than ideology: the 'facts' of geography are seen to have predictable influences upon political processes.

However, recently certain authors have challenged such arguments about the political innocence of geography to suggest that rather than

Cold War

a period conventionally defined as running from the end of the Second World War until the fall of the Berlin Wall, during which the globe was structured around a binary political geography that opposed US CAPITALISM to Soviet communism. Although never reaching all-out military confrontation, this period did witness intense military, economic, political and ideological rivalry between the superpowers and their allies.

FIGURE 25.1
Al Qaeda leader Osama Bin Laden. Credit: Reuters/Corbis

being a timeless concept, geographical relationships and entities are specific to historical and cultural circumstances: the nature of the influence of geography on political events can change. Given this, the meaning of geography can be *made to* change: there is a politics to the use of geographical concepts in arguments about international relations. After a brief introduction to traditional geopolitical concepts, this chapter will explore the alternative political arguments of 'critical geopolitics'. It will use various examples from the Cold War to the more recent War on Terror to explore the uses and critiques of geopolitical concepts.

THE GEOPOLITICAL TRADITION: GEOGRAPHY AS AN AID TO STATECRAFT

The term 'geopolitics' was first used by the Swedish political scientist Rudolf Kjellen in 1899, but did not become popular until used in the early twentieth century by British geographer and strategist Halford Mackinder. Mackinder wanted to promote the study of geography as an 'aid to statecraft', and he believed that geopolitics offered one such way in which geographers could inform the practices of international relations. The study of geopolitics focused on the ways in which geographical factors shaped the character of international politics. These geographical factors included the spatial layout of continental masses and the distribution of physical and human resources. As a result of geography, certain spaces are seen as either easier or harder to defend, distance has effects on politics (proximity leading to susceptibility to political influence), and certain topographical features promote security or lead to vulnerability.

The concept of security is fundamental to the study of geopolitics. This refers to the maintenance of the state in the face of threats, usually from external powers. Geopoliticians argue that they can aid national security by explaining the effects of a country's geography, and that of potential conquerors, on future power-political relations. A student of geopolitics claims to be able to predict which areas could strengthen a state, helping it to rise to prominence, and which might leave it vulnerable. An oft-quoted line from Nicholas Spykman illustrates the necessity of a geopolitical vision by insisting that 'geography is the most important factor in international relations because it is the most permanent' (quoted in Nijman, 1994: 222). As a result, geopolitics has traditionally been considered to be a very practical and objective study: the actual *practice* of international relations has been seen to be quite separate from political theory.

One central feature of geopolitical reasoning is that it presents the world as one closed and interdependent system. It is perhaps not accidental that the rise of geopolitics as a way of understanding the world occurred at a time when global space was 'closing', the entire world was now fully explored by western colonists and imperialists so that it was now all available for state territorial and economic expansion (see Agnew, 1998). European **colonialism** had reached its height. Geopolitics offered a way states could protect territorial holdings at a time when the 'blank spaces' on the world map were finally all filled in by European powers.

Colonialism

the rule of a NATION-STATE or other political power over another, subordinated, people and place. This domination is established and maintained through political structures, but may also shape economic and cultural relations. *See also* NEO-COLONIALISM and IMPERIALISM.

Mackinder's best-known geopolitical argument is presented in his 'Heartland Thesis', which insisted upon the importance of the Asian Heartland to the unfolding history of great powers (see Fig. 25.2). Mackinder believed that controlling the territory of the Heartland provided a more or less impenetrable position and could thus lead to world domination. For Mackinder, unless checked by power in the 'outer rim' of territory proximate to the Heartland, the occupying power could quite easily come to control first Europe and then the world. In 1919 Mackinder famously stated that:

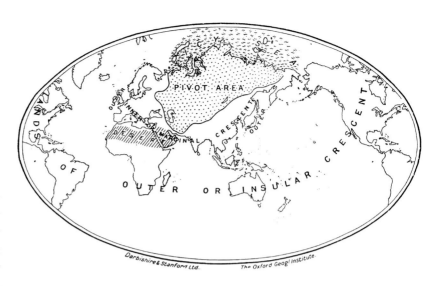

FIGURE 25.2
Mackinder's Heartland map

" *Who rules East Europe commands the Heartland;*

Who rules the Heartland commands the World Island;

Who controls the World Island commands the World. "

(Quoted in Glassner, 1993: 226–7)

His conclusion was that British statesmen would need to be wary of powers occupying the Heartland, and should create a 'buffer zone' around the Heartland to prevent the further accumulation of power that might challenge the hegemony of the British Empire.

Such geopolitical reasoning was heady stuff indeed, and there is evidence that it has both influenced foreign policy and the popular imagination. However, despite geopoliticians' insistence upon their geographical laws, their conclusions to the location of power differed. For example, whereas Mackinder promoted the power of territory, American strategist Mahan viewed control of the sea as paramount, and later others highlighted the importance of air power. Each came up with different core areas from which political dominance could be exercised.

Associations with Nazi expansionist *Geopolitik* policies (also inspired by Kjellen's work), meant that geopolitics, expressed formally in formal spatial models, fell out of use. Models still remained in textbooks, however, and were periodically updated to keep up to date with changing technology (especially the dominance of airpower and the introduction of inter-continental ballistic missiles). More significantly, a form of implicit geopolitical reasoning persisted in international relations theory and state practice throughout the Cold War.

COLD WAR GEOPOLITICS

One of the formative documents of the Cold War was sent as a telegram from Moscow, by George Kennan – 'Mr X' – a US official in the Soviet

Union at the end of the Second World War. Kennan argued that the Soviet Union was so different from the USA that there could not be compromise between the two. This image of two distinct and incompatible territorial blocs was reinforced by the political rhetoric of various political figures: in Stalin's pronouncements of the threat of capitalist expansion, Churchill's image of an Iron Curtain dividing Europe and, more recently, Reagan's depiction of the Soviet Union as an Evil Empire. A number of interrelated geopolitical concepts reiterated this binary geography in political discourse. These were, most importantly, containment, domino effects, and disease metaphors.

Containment, first outlined by Kennan, referred to the military and economic sequestration of the Soviet Union. Russia's historical geography, and not simply its political and cultural difference, was invoked to give this argument scientific respectability: the USSR was seen as an inherently expansionary force that had to be kept in check. Pietz suggests that in Cold War rhetoric, the USSR was presented as nothing more than traditional Oriental despotism plus modern police-state technology (Pietz, 1988: 70).

The inevitability of Soviet expansion was also expressed in metaphors of dominoes or disease. Such metaphors saw the spread of communism or socialism not as a complex political process of adaptation and conflict but instead merely as a result of proximity to territory ruled by Soviets. The Domino Theory assumed that Soviets, communists and socialists everywhere 'were, and are, unqualifiedly evil, that they were fiendishly clever, and that any small victory by them would automatically lead to many more' (Glassner, 1993: 239). For US Admiral Arthur Redford, speaking in 1953, for example, an American nuclear strike on Vietnam was essential in order to halt a Viet Minh victory, which would set off a chain reaction of countries falling to the communists, 'like a row of falling dominoes' (in Glassner, 1993: 239). The Domino Effect can actually be seen to underlie the Vietnam War more generally. As Glassner (1993: 241) put it: 'The argument went that the United States had to fight and win in Vietnam, for if South Vietnam "went communist," then automatically, like falling dominoes, Cambodia, Laos, Thailand, Burma, and perhaps India would as well.' This process would not stop until it reached the last standing domino, the USA, and made future political action appear inevitable, unless proactive action – such as containment or pre-emptive strike – were enacted here and now.

The domino metaphor simultaneously embodied a power-political system where only two forces existed (the USSR and the USA), where only force could oppose force and where the unfolding of the process was inevitable – once started, the continuing fall of states was as unavoidable as stopping a line of dominoes from toppling once the first had been pushed. Disease metaphors were structurally very similar, relying upon notions of contagion or the malign spread of infection, again depending upon a simple notion of geographical proximity as the basis for social and political change. Even more so than with dominoes, disease metaphors illustrated the necessity for immediate action in order to prevent the further spread of the malady.

SUMMARY

• Traditional geopolitical models explain the effects of geography on international relations.

• Especially important was the question of territorial security and the danger of proximity to territory ruled by an opposing power.

• Traditional geopolitics were seen to represent a very practical application of geographical 'laws' to understanding international politics.

CRITICAL GEOPOLITICS

Some recent approaches to geopolitics, sometimes called 'critical geopolitics', refuse to accept the objectivity and timelessness of the effects of geography on political process. Critical geopolitics encompasses a range of engagements with more traditional forms of geopolitics. Some have highlighted geopoliticians' over-emphasis on the state as the main, or only, actor in international politics. Clearly other powers are involved both at the sub-state level, such as ethnic, regional and place-based groups, and at the supra-state level, such as transnational corporations and international organizations including the UN and NATO.

Critical geopolitics has been especially interested in questioning the language of geopolitics, or 'geopolitical **discourse**'. Language is not unproblematic, somehow *simply* describing what is there. Language is metaphorical, explaining through reference to other, known, concepts. Thus, there is always a choice of words and metaphors. The type of terms used – the conceptual links made – affects the meaning of what is being described. There is, as a consequence, a politics of language.

Geopolitical discourse

Critical geopolitics is influenced by postmodern concerns with the politics of representation, with 'the use of particular modes of discourse in political situations in ways that shape political practices' (Dalby, 1990: 5). To Gearoid Ó Tuathail (1996: 1), geography is not a collection of incontrovertible facts but is instead about power. What he means is that geography is not an order or facts and relationships 'out there' in the world awaiting description. Instead, geographical orders are created by key individuals and institutions and then imposed upon the world. Geography is thus the product of cultural context and political motivation.

Critical geopolitical approaches seek to examine how it is that international politics are imagined spatially or geographically and in so doing to uncover the politics involved in writing the geography of global space. Ó Tuathail (1996) calls this process 'geo-graphing' – earth-writing – to emphasize the creativity inherent in the process of using geographical reasoning in the practical service of power. Those adopting critical geopolitical approaches grant a range of power to language, from Agnew and Corbridge (1989) who see language becoming out of sync with the geopolitical reality it seeks to describe and so causing inappropriate state practice, to a figure like French philosopher Jean Baudrillard for whom language and representation are everything (he

Discourse, discursive

drawing on the work of the French philosopher Michel Foucault, Human Geographers define discourses as ways of talking about, writing or otherwise representing the world and its geographies (*see also* REPRESENTATION). Discursive approaches to Human Geography emphasize the importance of these ways of representing. They are seen as shaping the realities of the worlds in which we live, rather than just being ways of portraying a reality that exists outside of language and thought. They are also seen as connected to questions of practice – that is, what people actually do – rather than being confined to a separate realm of images or ideas. More specifically, Human Geographers have stressed the different ways in which people have discursively constructed the world in different times and places, and examined how it is that particular ways of talking about, conceptualizing and acting on people and places come to be seen as natural and common-sensical in particular contexts.

famously suggested that the Gulf War only occurred on television; see Norris, 1992).

Rather than arguing over the true effects of geography on international relations – whether land or sea powers are strongest, as Mackinder and Mahan might have debated – critical geopolitics asks whose models of international geography are used, and whose interests these models serve. This approach owes much to the work of Michel Foucault (1980), who argued that power and knowledge are inseparable. For geopoliticians, there is great power available to those whose maps and explanations of world politics are accepted as accurate because of the influence that these have on the way the world and its workings are understood, and therefore the effects that this has on future political practice.

Critical geopolitics aims to challenge the objectivity of the geopolitician. For example, the privileging of sight (especially with the use of maps and diagrams) over other senses in geopolitical reasoning allows the geopoliticians to write as if from afar, as if somehow unconnected to the world being surveyed. This reinforces the idea of an objective account rather than one written from a position grounded within the events being discussed. It hides the fact that the geopolitician has his or her own point of view and loyalties. Although it is generally accepted that Nazi *Geopolitik* had a political agenda, this is considered to be an aberration of the 'science' of geopolitics. Yet other geopoliticians have not been innocent of interest. For example, Mackinder wanted to help maintain the British Empire and its **hegemony** over world affairs and Mahan, a naval historian, was interested in building up the US Navy at a time when other technologies seemed to make naval power less important.

Critical geopolitics looks to analyse the geography in any political description of the world. As Ó Tuathail and Agnew (1992: 194) have suggested, 'geopolitics is not a discrete and relatively contained activity confined only to a small group of "wise men" who speak in the language of classical geopolitics'. Simply to describe a foreign policy is to engage in geopolitics and so normalize particular worldviews. Any statement concerning international relations involves an implicit understanding of geographical relationships or a worldview.

Similarly, any geographical description can influence political perception. Descriptions of other places and the character of the people who inhabit them can be as significant as measurements of distance and calculations of location in constructing people's geographical imaginations. For example, the constant use of terms such as 'Evil Empire' to describe the USSR in America reinforced a binary geography of superpower stand-off that legitimated US military build-up and intervention.

Hegemony, hegemonic, hegemon

hegemony is an opaque power relation relying more on leadership through consensus than coercion through force or its threat, so that domination is by the permeation of ideas. For instance, concepts of hegemony have been used to explain how, when 'the ruling ideas are the ideas of the ruling class', other classes will willingly accept their inferior position as right and proper (*see* CLASS). Hegemonic is the adjective attached to the institution that possesses hegemony. For instance, under CAPITALISM the bourgeoisie are the hegemonic class. Hegemon is a term used when the concept of hegemony is applied to the competition between NATION-STATES: a hegemon is a hegemonic state. For instance, the USA has been described as the hegemon of the world economy in the mid-twentieth century.

Critical geopolitics and identity

Perhaps the most important claim of critical geopolitics is that traditional geopolitical arguments are in fact profoundly a-geographical. Rather than being concerned with understanding geographical process, geopolitics reduces spaces and places to concepts or **ideology**. Space is reduced to units that singularly display evidence of the characteristics that are used to

Ideology

a meaning or set of meanings that serves to create and/or maintain relationships of domination and subordination, through symbolic forms such as texts, landscapes and spaces.

define the spaces in the first place (Asia *is* exoticism, the USSR *is* communism, Iran *is* fundamentalism, the USA *is* freedom and democracy, and so on).

In the contemporary political system, dominated by the territorial state, the geography of geopolitics tends to reduce the complex workings of politics into two spheres: the domestic sphere under the control of the modern territorial state and the international realm facing anarchy without higher power to control it. Thus the state invokes discourses of security through which any different characteristics are excluded through practices of territorial control, such as patrol of borders. In security discourse, it is difference that threatens the states so that, for critic Simon Dalby (1990: 185),

> the essential moment of geopolitical discourse is the division of space into 'our' place and 'their' place; its political function being to incorporate and regulate 'us' or 'the same' by distinguishing 'us' from 'them,' 'the same' from 'the other.'

In arguing this, critical geopolitics suggests that geopolitics is not something simply linked to describing or predicting the shape of international politics, but is central to the ways in which identity is formed and maintained in modern societies. National identity is not simply defined by what binds the members of the nation together but also – perhaps even more importantly – by defining those who exist outside as different from members of the nation. Drawing borders around territory to produce 'us' and 'them' of the nation and those who are different, does not simply reflect the divisions inherent in the world but helps to create differences. Again, geopolitics does not simply reflect the facts of geography but in dividing the world into a state and the international realm helps to form geographical orders and geographical relationships.

The construction of 'otherness', and particularly the sense of danger that this presents, has implications for the practice of domestic affairs in addition to foreign policy. Thus Dalby (1990: 172) suggests that geopolitics is 'about stifling domestic dissent; the presence of external threats provides the justification for limiting political activity within the bounds of the state' (see Fig. 25.3). The construction of otherness simultaneously presents a normative image of identity. So, for example, when the USSR was constructed as being completely unlike the USA, any description of the USSR as evil, aggressive and unreasonable implies goodness, tolerance and reason on the part of Americans.

FIGURE 25.3
Nice to have an enemy again. Credit: © Joel Pett, *Lexington Herald*

Critical geopolitics and popular culture

As a result of the influence of cultural context, different countries' geopolitical traditions draw upon specific metaphors to create images of international geography. Political elites must use stories and images that are central to their citizens' daily lives and experiences. By reducing complex processes to simple images with which their audiences would be familiar, geopoliticians could render political decisions quite natural, or could make the result of the process appear predetermined (as the domino example has demonstrated). For example, sport metaphors have been particularly prominent in the USA. Such language points to the 'essential' differences between national potentials for world-class performance and naturalizes a global arena in which the rules of the game are understood, and within which there are clear (unequivocal) winners and losers. Agnew (1998) argues that in so doing, the ambiguities of conflict are reduced to technicalities in game play. Michael Shapiro (1989: 70) points out that comparing world politics to sporting contests serves the geopolitical purpose of emptying world space of any particular content: places lose their uniqueness and world politics becomes a strategy played out on a familiar sports field.

One of the effects of broadening the scope for analysis in critical geopolitics is a consideration of a wide range of sources for analysis. More traditional approaches to geopolitics have concentrated upon the writings and pronouncements of political leaders and their academic advisers. More recently, some theorists have considered popular culture to be an important source of information.

It is possible to see the influence of popular culture on state practice, whether directly in the central role of CNN as a source of information during the Gulf War for American leaders, or indirectly in the role of popular culture in the construction of hegemonic cultural values that shape both the actions of politicians and the expectation of societies. Popular culture is entwined with more formal geopolitical visions as James Der Derian (1992: n1) explains:

> We are witnessing changes in our international, intertextual, interhuman relations, in which objective reality is displaced by textuality (Dan Quayle cites Tom Clancy to defend anti-satellite weapons) ... representation blurs into simulation ... imperialism gives way to the Empire of Signs (the spectacle of Grenada, the fantasy of Star Wars serve to deny imperial decline).

For example, it is accepted that the film *The Manchurian Candidate* (1962) encouraged the CIA to pursue the possibility of controlling secret agents without their knowledge, and to envisage methods of combating the prospect of the Soviets having already developed such technology. The film starts from the plausible premises of both the Cold War exchange of spies, and the 'brainwashing' of soldiers in the Korean War. It then develops the possibility of the programming of people who are unknowing of their condition and therefore undetectable: the perfect spy. Ultimately the film influenced the political situation that it initially sought to reflect. President Reagan suggested enthusiastically after seeing *Rambo: First Blood Part II* (1985) that the next time American hostages were taken in the Middle East he would know what to do about it. More recently, Der Derian (2002: para. 27) has reported that American government intelligence specialists 'have been secretly soliciting terrorist scenarios from top Hollywood filmmakers and writers'.

Whether in films, TV programmes or in print culture, the opposition between a heroic and moralistic America and the communist Evil Empire was taken as a given. Although never using the term, the American magazine the *Reader's Digest* frequently invoked geopolitical reasoning in its explanation of world affairs to its readership (see Sharp, 1993; 1996; 2000). The *Reader's Digest* believed in the limitless expansive potential of communism, and that only power could effectively oppose power, so that the USSR 'will not stop at international frontiers unless it is opposed' (Chennault, 1948: 121). The magazine used geopolitical arguments to warn its readers about their country's vulnerability: 'The United States is naked – incredibly naked – against a Russian atom-bomb attack' (Taylor, 1951: 85).

New technologies invite more active participation on the part of audiences. In response to George W. Bush's War on Terror, a computer game company launched the game *America's 10 Most Wanted* in the summer of 2004 (see Fig. 25.4). The developers enthuse that the game

> enlists the military expertise of CIFR's [Criminal Interdiction & Fugitive Recovery] top agent in the hunt for US fugitives listed on the FBI website, including the notorious leader of the Al 'Qaeda terrorist network Osama Bin Laden and the ousted leader of Iraq Saddam Hussein. Commentary is provided by Dan Rathner, star news anchor for the US television network CBS over licensed news footage from CNN ... [It] draws its inspiration from a real concern which is engulfing the world – the need to stamp out terrorism and violent crime. ... We invite you to take the patriotic challenge and join the ranks of CIFR.

(Xbox solution, 2003)

The narration of territory and identity then emerges from the formal arena of politics but also through spaces of media (movies, magazines, computer games). But these spheres are not separate: the well-known news anchorman lends reality effect to games, while movie plot writers and directors are consulted by the state for suggestions on possible future scenarios.

Feminism and critical geopolitics

Critical geopolitics has also begun to address feminist concerns. Some feminist commentators have remarked on the lack of women in the history of geopolitics and contemporary theory and practice of international relations. Cynthia Enloe suggests that women have been

Gender

Gender a criterion of social organization that distinguishes different groups of people on the basis of femininity or masculinity. In any one location, many masculinities and femininities interact. As a concept, gender is usually used in Human Geography in distinction to that of sex (i.e. femaleness and maleness) in order to emphasize the SOCIAL CONSTRUCTION of women's and men's roles, relations and identities. Human Geographers' accounts of the world have always been shaped through understandings of gender (*see* MASCULINISM) but explicit analyses of the geographies of gender and the gendering of geographies are comparatively recent, and associated with the growth of Feminist Geography (*see* FEMINISM).

written out of international politics. The story of international politics has traditionally been one of the spectacular confrontation of mighty states led by powerful statesmen, of the speeches and heroic acts of the elite, and the specialist knowledge of 'intellectuals of statecraft'. Enloe (1989) refuses to accept this story as covering the full extent of the workings of international relations, and instead focuses on those elements the traditional story excludes and silences: the role of international labour migration, the availability of cheap female labour for transnational corporation investment, the availability of sex workers for the tourist industry in South East Asia, and so on. Enloe's is a very different account of international politics than the traditional story, and certainly one that lacks its glamour. She links international geopolitics to everyday geographies of **gender** relations. Her account links the personal and the political, arguing that these alternative political geographies need to be

FIGURE 25.4
Advert for the computer game *America's 10 Most Wanted*.

uncovered because, 'if we employ only the conventional, ungendered compass to chart international politics, we are likely to end up mapping a landscape peopled only by men, most elite men' (Enloe 1989: 1).

SUMMARY

- Critical geopolitics understands geography to be a 'discourse', created by powerful individuals and institutions, and used as a map or script with which to make sense of the world.

- Critical geopolitics seeks to denaturalize geographical statements in international relations which appear to be so self-evident as to be 'common sense'.

- Critical geopolitics recognizes the power of geopolitical arguments not only in the context of elite debates but also in popular accounts which help to form the 'geographical imaginations' that all people hold of the world and its political interrelationships.

CONCLUSION

Geopolitics continues to be a powerful form of geographical reasoning, used in support of powerful political interests. While the content of geopolitical arguments may change (the enemy is different, the location of the heartland may move), the structure of the argument is relatively stable – geopolitics can confidently produce moral maps of the world, and locate enemies beyond the borders of the familiar. Critical geopolitics represents an important challenge to the common-sense production of these political representations, and offers the possibility for imagining alternative connections and linkages between people and groups around the world.

DISCUSSION POINTS

1. What geographical laws are used in geopolitics? Is this how you understand 'geography'? How else might you think about geographical influences on international relations?

2. What have been the most significant changes in the shift from Cold War to post-Cold War geopolitics? What has stayed the same?

3. What are the main criticisms that critical geopolitics levels at traditional geopolitics?

4. In what places are geopolitical arguments created and communicated to others?

5. What kind of people are included in geopolitical representations? Who is excluded from them?

FURTHER READING

Ó Tuathail, G. (1996) *Critical geopolitics.* Minneapolis: Minnesota University Press.

This text offers the best examination of traditional forms of geopolitics and recent critical approaches.

Special issue, *Political Geography* (1996) vol. 15(6/7).

Take a look at this special issue to see the range of work going on under the title of 'critical geopolitics'.

Campbell, D. (1992) *Writing security: United States foreign policy and the politics of identity.* Minneapolis: University of Minnesota Press.

Dalby, S. (1990) American security discourse: the persistence of geopolitics. *Political Geography Quarterly*, 9(2): 171–88.

The above texts explore the interdependencies between geopolitics and American identity.

Der Derian, J. (2002) The war of networks. *Theory and event*, 5(4).

Smith, N. (2001) Ashes and aftermath. *The Arab World Geographer* forum on 11 September events.

See these texts for discussions of post-September 11th geopolitics.

Enloe, C. (1989) *Bananas, beaches and bases: making feminist sense of international relations.* Berkeley: University of California Press.

Hyndman, J. (2003) Beyond either/or: a feminist analysis of September 11th. *ACME*, 2(1).

The above texts offer a different map of international relations that includes everyday processes and gendered images rather than just high-profile events and confrontations.

CHAPTER 26
CITIZENSHIP AND GOVERNANCE

Mark Goodwin

INTRODUCTION

Issues of citizenship and governance have recently assumed a prominent position in political and academic debates. Indeed, during the summer of 2004 when this chapter was being written, fierce arguments were raging, in the UK for example, over the questions of closer European integration, the powers of devolved governments in Wales and Scotland, the introduction of elected assemblies in the English regions, the restoration of an elected assembly in Northern Ireland, the involvement of the private sector in running underperforming schools, the introduction of a ban on hunting wild animals with dogs, the legal position of asylum seekers and the charging of tuition fees to university students. Move outside the UK and the debates become even fiercer, ranging from the right of Muslim schoolgirls in France to wear the Islamic headscarf in school, to the legitimacy of the USA's occupation of Iraq. Running through these and other similar debates are the twin themes of citizenship and governance – covering the issues of what it means to be a citizen, of what rights and obligations one has as a citizen, and of the ways in which we, as citizens, are governed. A good example of how these twin themes come together has recently been provided by the debates over Scottish and Welsh **devolution**. At the heart of these debates are concerns about how different parts of the United Kingdom are governed, and about the different identities felt by those who are citizens of this supposedly 'united' nation. Recent research, for instance has shown that in Scotland, 68.0 per cent of people claim either exclusively or mainly Scottish identity, and only 8.9 per cent claim to be exclusively or mainly British (Scottish Social Attitudes Survey, 2003). In Wales, 51 per cent claim to be exclusively or mainly Welsh, but 19 per cent still claim to be exclusively or mainly British. Some 30 per cent of people in Wales claim to be equally Welsh and British (Wales Life and Times Survey, 2003). In Northern Ireland only 24 per cent of people claim to feel Northern Irish, with 41 per cent claiming a British identity (Northern Ireland Life and Times Survey, 2003).

Asking these relatively simple questions about identity raises a host of issues about the complex mixtures of states and territories, and areas of government, within which we all live, and about how these relate to our shared understandings of what it means to be a citizen of one or other of these spaces. The huge difference between the percentage of people who feel British in Scotland and Northern Ireland stems from a host of political, cultural, social and economic processes, which stretch back some 500 years, but which have a very obvious contemporary manifestation. These questions promise to become more complex as we progress through the new millennium. This chapter explores such complexity by investigating the twin notions of citizenship and governance. It looks at the ways in which geography is bound up with both concepts and with

Devolution

the process of devolving some political power to more local levels of government, often associated with the formation of local and regional assemblies. This can take place at many scales: at a supranational scale, for example within the European Union, power can be devolved to individual nations or to regions; and within the NATION-STATE power can be devolved to regions and localities.

how they operate in practice, and at how an appreciation of these issues helps to broaden the way we look at Human Geography.

THE CONTESTED SPACES OF CITIZENSHIP

Issues of citizenship are usually seen as the province of political science, and not geography, and the usual definition of citizenship is provided in political terms as referring to 'the terms of membership of a political unit (usually the nation-state) which secure certain rights and privileges to those who fulfil particular obligations. Citizenship is a concept, rather than a theory, which formalizes the conditions for full participation in a community' (Smith, 1994: 67). A moment's thought, however, will indicate that even this narrowly political definition is bound up with geography. The political unit that one is a member of has a certain territory – thus, by definition, one is a citizen of a particular place. Also, the community, or communities, that one participates in, whether fully or not, are bounded too, and geographically situated. Indeed, the whole concept hinges around notions of inclusion and exclusion – to be a citizen is to be included in both a social and spatial sense, and this has offered fertile ground for geographical work.

In particular, geographers have questioned the basis on which such inclusion and exclusion takes place. The political definition of citizenship stresses the inclusive nature of the term – it implies that anyone within a certain territory who meets certain obligations will be included as a citizen, with corresponding rights and privileges. Yet matters are not this simple and the act of residence within a definable and bounded space does not necessarily secure citizenship. Somewhat paradoxically, the **globalization** of both capital and labour that has led to increased flows of people around the world (see Chapters 37, 38 and 42) has resulted in attempts by many governments to legislate for tighter immigration controls. This has two main implications: some people are excluded from residence altogether, and others are denied full citizenship rights. In Britain, for example, there is an explicit link between immigration and those means-tested benefits that, as part of the social security system, should be available to all citizens. As Oppenheim points out (1990: 89), claiming income support, family credit or even access to housing under the homeless legislation can endanger the chances of bringing the rest of one's family to the UK, or create problems for the claimant themselves or their sponsor. The Immigration Act 1971 meant that the wives and children of Commonwealth citizens could only enter the country if a sponsor could support and accommodate them 'without recourse to public funds', defined clearly for the first time in 1985 to include the three major means-tested benefits referred to above. Thus people who may have worked and paid taxes here for decades, are only allowed to be joined by their families on condition that they do not claim benefits for them or turn to the welfare state for accommodation. More surreptitiously, perhaps, the increasing frequency of passport checks on black claimants at benefit offices – regardless of whether they were born in the United Kingdom – helps to create a climate of opinion that views welfare as the entitlement of white Britons rather than of black 'outsiders' (Oppenheim, 1990).

Globalization

the economic, political, social and cultural processes whereby: (a) places across the globe are increasingly interconnected; (b) social relations and economic transactions increasingly occur at the intercontinental scale (*see* TRANSNATIONAL); and (c) the globe itself comes to be a recognizable geographical entity. As such, globalization does not mean everywhere in the world becomes the same. Nor is it an entirely even process; different places are differently connected into the world and view that world from different perspectives. Globalization has been occurring for several hundred years, but in the contemporary world the scale and extent of social, political and economic interpenetration appears to be qualitatively different to international networks in the past.

What we might term the bounded spaces of citizenship within the nation-state are therefore not 'straightforwardly inclusionary' (Painter and Philo, 1995: 112). Divisions along racial or ethnic lines as referred to above are fairly widespread and long established – in Germany, for instance, migrants who arrived to fill labour shortages in the 1950s and 1960s were labelled as 'guest workers' and denied social rights and freedom of movement. This labelling denied them even the status of ethnic-minority migrants – they were expected to return 'home' when no longer needed. Figure 26.1 shows the abject living conditions many such workers endured, often in spatially segregated 'ethnic enclaves'. The denial of full citizenship rights to 'guest workers', and their geographical and social marginality in special hostels or dormitories have played no small role in the rise of racism and fascism in the newly unified Germany. This is one example of the ways in which inclusionary citizenship is actually riddled with divisions that are at once spatial and social.

Other examples of these divisions have emerged as recent debates about the term have broadened the scope for new avenues of geographical enquiry. It quickly became apparent that many groups who seem to enjoy full citizenship are actually limited in terms of the places and spaces in which this can be exercised. A highly visible example has been provided by the recent debates about sexuality. Geographers have increasingly been investigating the links between sexuality and citizenship by exploring what Bell (1995: 139) has called 'the spaces of sexual citizenship'. His starting point for this exploration is to ask the question, quoting Diana Fuss, 'What does it mean to be a citizen in a state which programmatically denies citizenship on the basis of sexual preference?' (1995: 139). His answer begins from the fact that such preferences can be played out in some locations and not in others. What it does mean to be a citizen in this case is partly dependent on where you are. As Bristow observes, 'In Britain, it is possible to be gay [only] in specific places and spaces: notably, the club scene and social networks often organized around campaigning organizations' (quoted in Bell, 1995: 141). It is only in these spaces that those who are gay can feel comfortable, and as Painter and Philo (1995: 115) put it, 'if citizenship is to mean anything in an everyday sense, it should mean the ability of individuals to occupy public spaces in a manner that does not compromise their self-identity, let alone obstruct, threaten or even harm them more materially'.

Valentine (1993b), in her exploration of the geographies of gay friend-ships, has confirmed that gay people are often forced to inhabit marginal spaces. The result is the growth of 'dense and heterogeneous networks formed around a limited geographical base [which] foster a sense of com-munity' (Valentine, 1993b: 113). As this suggests, the more marginal spaces of sexual citizenship can be positive as well as negative. Valentine goes on to explain that 'because lesbians find it difficult to make friends and express their lifestyles outside these gay contexts . . . their identities can become embedded in the networks formed in and around these places'. In some senses, then, we can see how these restricted geographies can offer the chance for a reconstituted citizenship to emerge around a series of 'alterna-tive' or 'underground' spaces. In the case of gay people, whole neighbour-hoods have now grown up as places of deliberate congregation, such as

Sexuality

sexual attitudes, preferences, desires and behaviours. Human Geographers have emphasized how our sexualities are not simply a biological given but complex socio-cultural constructs (*see also* SOCIAL CONSTRUCTION). They have examined how, on the one hand, these constructs sexualize our encounters with places and environments in personally and socially significant ways and, on the other hand, how our sexualities themselves are shaped through experiences and understandings of the geographies of the body, the home, the city, the nation, travel, etc.

(a)

(b)

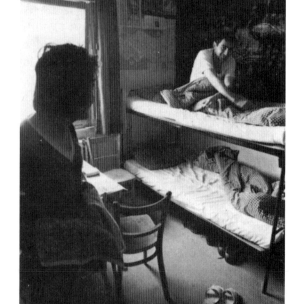

(c)

FIGURE 26.1
The social and spatial marginality of migrant
workers denied full citizenship. Source: J.
Berger and J. Mohr (1975) *A Seventh Man*.
Harmondsworth: Penguin Books

Castro in San Francisco (see Castells, 1983), West Hollywood in Los Angeles (Forest, 1995), Soho in London or the City of Amsterdam (Binnie, 1995). In these areas we can find a clustering of bars, restaurants, bookshops, theatres, clothes shops and other retail outlets all catering for a gay clientele (see Fig. 26.2). In these spaces we can see the flowering of an alternative culture, which can act as the basis for an alternative kind of citizenship, in which members of certain groups can establish rights and obligations to each other. Through this type of work, the notion of citizenship has been expanded beyond a somewhat narrow concern with rights and responsibilities bestowed by the nation-state. As Desforges puts it, 'rather, citizenship is conceptualized as a set of social processes in which individuals and social groups negotiate, claim and practice not only rights, responsibilities and duties but also a sense of belonging which enables full participation within a multiplicity of "communities"' (2004: 551).

This 'negotiation of belonging' within multiple communities has led geographers to look at the multiple spaces within which such negotiation takes place (Desforges, 2004; MacKian, 1995). Attention has turned away from the nation-state to examine the practice of citizenship within the home (Fyfe, 1995; McEwan, 2000), the neighbourhood (Pile, 1995), the urban (Brown, 1997) the rural (Parker, 2002) and the global (Desforges, 2004). Other geographers are looking at how the emergence of notions of sustainable development and the 'sustainable citizen' has led to the development of a stretched or 'distanciated' mode of citizenship. Such distanciation involves an 'enlargement of the public sphere within which citizenship is conceived of and then practiced' (Bullen and Whitehead, 2004: 7). This enlargement is three-fold. It covers not just a stretching beyond the nation-state to encompass an engagement with others across the globe, but also a sense of obligation towards future generations and a concern with environmental rights and responsibilities. As geographers explore these new spaces of citizenship, it has become apparent that they have been used to develop alternative forms of what we may call 'participatory citizenship'. A collection of writings from the USA documents how different marginal groups have refashioned spaces of social control into sites of resistance, and how in this process have been able to contest dominant views and assumptions about their 'place' in society (Smith, 1995). The groups include squatters resisting urban development in Michigan; the homeless campaigning for decent housing in Chicago; an anti-gentrification coalition seeking to preserve low-cost housing in New York; low-income African-American women living in a public housing project in New Orleans involved in community development; and immigrant Mexican agricultural labourers in California campaigning for employment rights. All the groups are using the appropriation of space to claim what they see as legitimate citizenship rights for their section of society.

One chapter describes the setting up of 'Tranquility City', a homeless encampment of 22 plywood 'huts' in a run-down industrial district of West Chicago. The author concludes that:

“ *for a brief period Tranquility City became a mini-movement area in which a different way of living poor was experimented with: a possibility was created for the formation of a homeless community free*

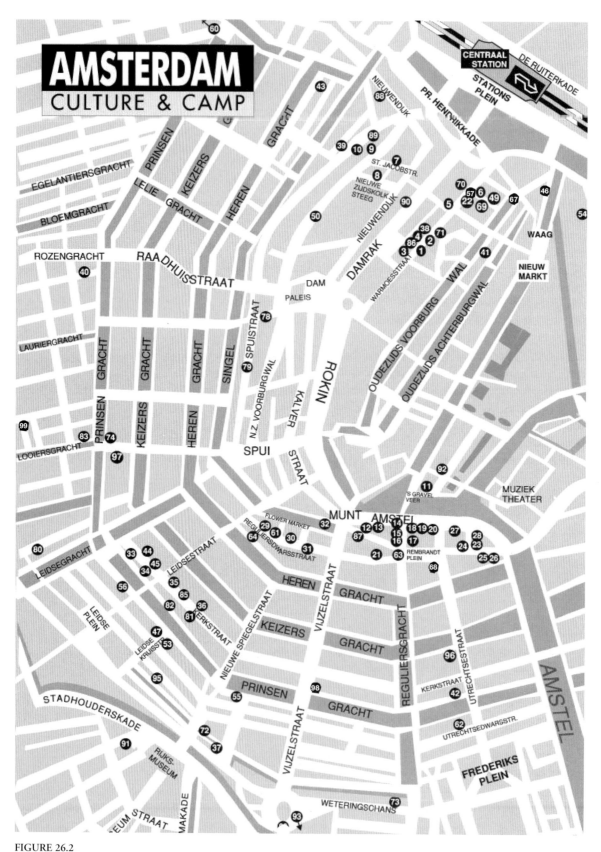

FIGURE 26.2
The alternative spaces of sexual citizenship – the clustering of gay bars, clubs, hotels, restaurants, shops, cinemas and fitness centres in Amsterdam.
Source: www.matchoman.com/gay/community/map

of institutional shelter restraints. Within this <u>mini-movement area</u>, residents of Tranquility City were able to construct a collective identity centred around issues of social justice for other homeless individuals and collective action in helping each other acquire housing and needed services. **"**

(Wright, 1995: 39, original emphasis)

As this suggests, the spaces that such groups inhabit can be crucial in helping to form a group identity, which helps to underpin a localized community that can experiment with different ways of living, which in turn is able to campaign around issues of social justice and citizens' rights. In this way geography becomes critical to the establishment of new forms of participatory citizenship.

SUMMARY

- The concept of citizenship is inherently geographical, hinging around social and spatial inclusion and exclusion.

- Such inclusion is never straightforward and is riddled with divisions.

- These divisions create differential spaces where different degrees of citizenship are experienced and played out by different groups in society.

- These spaces can be positive as well as negative, and can be used for resistance as well as control.

THE CHANGING GEOGRAPHIES OF GOVERNANCE

The renewed interest in issues of citizenship within both academic and policy circles can be viewed as evidence of a rethinking of the relationship between individuals, the communities they are part of, and government. Citizenship lies at one pole of this relationship, concerning as it does the rights and obligations of those being governed. At the other pole are the processes and institutions of government, and the actions of those who do the governing. And just as new forms of citizenship have emerged as part of this rethinking, so too have new forms of government. Indeed, so prevalent are these new forms that the term governance, and not government, is now used to describe these new structures. The use of governance is widely accepted across a variety of academic and practitioner circles. It is also routinely heard in the speeches of politicians from across the political spectrum. Put simply, it 'refers to the development of governing styles in which boundaries between and within public and private sectors have become blurred' (Stoker, 1996: 2). Thus the term governance is not simply an academic synonym for government. Its increasing use signifies a concern with a change in both the meaning and the content of government. As Rhodes puts it (1996: 652–3), the term is now used to refer 'to a new process of governing, or a changed condition of ordered rule, or the new method by which society is governed'. Where government signals a concern with the formal institutions and structures of the state, the concept of governance is broader and draws attention to the ways in which governmental and non-governmental organizations work together, and to the ways in which political power is distributed, both internal and external to the state.

The way in which we are governed touches all aspects of our lives. It determines the type of education we receive, from nursery school to university. It dictates the level of healthcare we are provided with, and it concerns the provision of housing and the provision of jobs and training. It concerns planning and environmental issues, as well as transport and social services. In the UK, and indeed in many western European countries, for much of the post-war period these services were mainly provided by central, regional and local governments. These elected institutions would set the policy agenda, and be largely responsible for the delivery of services. The new structures of governance that have emerged during the past two decades have transformed this system into one that now involves a wide range of agencies and institutions drawn from the public, private and voluntary sectors. They will still include the institutions of elected government, at central, regional and local level, but will also involve a range of non-elected organizations of the state, as well as institutional and individual actors from outside the formal political arena, such as voluntary organizations, private businesses and corporations and supranational institutions such as the European Union (see Goodwin and Painter, 1996: 636). The concept of governance focuses attention on the relations between these various actors, and crucially from our perspective draws attention to the complex geographies now involved in the act of governing any particular area. The governing of localities is no longer exclusively, or even mainly, a local matter, but instead is a complex, fragmented and multi-scale process.

Geographers have investigated these issues at a variety of levels. Some have studied the international scale and looked at the emergence of multinational or global forms of governance. Others have looked at the way subnational or regional governance is developing, both in Britain and elsewhere, and many have looked at the changing nature of local governance, especially at the urban level. Some common threads can be discerned running through many of these studies. In particular the new emphasis on governance raises questions about:

- the purpose of the new governing mechanisms – how and why were the particular agencies involved brought together, and what are their interests and rationales
- the effectiveness of the various agencies involved at working together – how does each blend its particular capacities with the others
- the links between different forms of governance and different rates of economic and social development
- how do the new mechanisms of governance cope with uneven development and with the specific problems that might emerge in one place rather than another
- the nature of democracy and accountability in non-elected agencies – just how does the public influence what are in the main unelected and appointed institutions, and how is the declining scope of elected state activity squared with the fashionable political notions of inclusion and empowerment.

We can illustrate these concerns by reference to some of the new work on urban governance, which has investigated these new ways of governing our cities. Table 26.1 charts the growing proliferation of those institutions involved in urban regeneration in the UK, and the centre and right-hand columns show the various initiatives that have been introduced by the New Labour government since 1997. The Audit Commission depicted urban policy in the late 1980s as a 'patchwork quilt' of unco-ordinated policy initiatives (Audit Commission, 1989; see also Atkinson and Moon, 1994, and Duncan and Goodwin, 1988, on how this patchwork quilt developed). Some 15 years later, New Labour's 'initiativitus' (Johnstone and Whitehead, 2004: 14) had resulted in an altogether more complex picture, which Lord Rooker, a junior government minister, described as a 'bowl of spaghetti'. The difference between the two metaphors is instructive. Patchwork quilt conjures up images of spatial complexity, with various initiatives being placed side by side without ever quite being joined up seamlessly. As Johnstone and Whitehead point out (2004: 5), 'the metaphor of spaghetti denotes an altogether higher-order of urban policy complexity: a diverse landscape of strategies and initiatives that cross different spaces, scales and policy arenas'. In each case, the geography of these new forms of urban governance is critical – their uneven and somewhat disjointed appearance is the surface manifestation of a situation where some communities are benefiting from public intervention, whilst others go unnoticed and unrewarded. By definition not all communities can share in the public resources that are being deployed through these new systems of governance. Indeed, the vast bulk of urban regeneration money is selectively allocated via competitive bidding – resources are not distributed as of right, but are given to those areas that prevail through the bidding process.

Many of the new initiatives set out in Table 26.1 are delivered through a particular form of governance called a **partnership**. Indeed, in many cases government resources are only given to partnerships that involve the public, private and voluntary sectors working together. Local authorities cannot bid on their own for the resources associated with these initiatives, and thus by definition governance replaces government as the guiding force behind urban policy. The attraction of partnerships results from their apparent potential to bring interested local organizations and agents of government together to pool their resources (financial, practical, material or symbolic), leading to the development of consensual strategies to address issues of service delivery. Partnerships, it is claimed, can offer a blending of resources from the public, private and voluntary sectors, which adds up to more than the sum of the parts, can provide a forum in which local communities can make their voices heard, and can help foster a shared sense of objectives and direction at a local level. From this perspective they are portrayed as a mechanism for bringing together the issues of community involvement and local empowerment. Here we return almost full circle to the ideas of citizenship with which we began the chapter. New Labour is based on a philosophy that emphasizes both the rights and responsibilities of citizens and local communities. Even in opposition, New Labour was emphasizing the sharing of powers *and* responsibilities between local government and the communities they

Partnerships

an arrangement between a number of agencies and institutions in which objectives are shared and a common agenda is developed in pursuit of a common purpose. The partnership approach encourages collaboration and integration, and the aim is that by blending and pooling their resources the different agencies will be able to produce a capacity for action that is more than simply the sum of their individual parts.

Table 26.1 Regeneration initiatives 1989 and 2003 – from the 'patchwork quilt' to the 'bowl of spaghetti'

'Patchwork quilt' (1989)	'Bowl of spaghetti' (2003)	
• City grant	• Action team for jobs	• Health action zones
• Derelict land grant	• Active community programme	• Healthy living centres
• English estates	• Capital modernization fund	• Healthy schools programme
• Enterprise allowance	(small retailers)	• Neighbourhood management
• Enterprise Zones	• Children's fund	• Neighbourhood nursery centres
• Estate action	• City growth strategies	• Neighbourhood renewal fund
• Regional selective assistance	• Coalfields task force	• Neighbourhood support fund
• Section 11	• Community champions	• Neighbourhood wardens
• Task forces and CATs	• Community chest	• New deal for communities
• Technical and vocational	• Community empowerment	• New entrepreneur scholarships
education initiative	fund	• Playing fields and community
• Urban development	• Community legal partnerships	green spaces
corporations	• Creative partnerships	• Positive futures
• Urban programme	• Crime reduction programme	• Regional centres for
• Welsh development agency	• Drug action teams	manufacturing excellence
• Work-related NAFE	• Early excellence centres	• Safer communities initiative
	• Early years development and	• Single regeneration budget
	childcare partnerships	• Spaces for sport and arts
	• Education action zones	• Sport action zones
	• Employment zones	• StepUp
	• European regional development	• Street wardens
	fund	• Sure start
	• Excellence challenge	• Sure start plus
	• Excellence in cities	• Urban regeneration companies
	• Fair share	• Youth inclusion programme
	• Framework for regional	• Youth music action zones
	employment and skills action	

Source: C. Johnstone and M. Whitehead (eds) (2004) *New horizons in British urban policy*. Aldershot: Ashgate.

served. The Labour Party's Commission for Social Justice, for instance, suggested in 1994 that

> *the aim [of policy] must be to build among local people the capacities and institutions which enable them to take more responsibility for shaping their own futures … small and local initiatives, based on a partnership of public, private and voluntary sectors, are the essential foundation of lasting empowerment.*

(Cited in Raco and Imrie, 2000: 2192)

It is easy to pick out similar statements from almost any official document on partnership working, and government rhetoric seems to assume that within any given community 'there is a degree of *latent* citizenship to be nurtured and institutionalized as a resource in the governance of policy' (Raco and Imrie, 2000: 2192). For the New Labour government, partnerships provide an organizational framework within which this latent citizenship can be both nurtured and institutionalized. They can be said to offer a governance form that not only resonates with, but also provides a vehicle for, the emblematic New Labour themes of 'citizenship', 'rights and responsibilities' and 'community'.

Recently, however, attention has shifted from the joined-up nature of partnership working to joining up the partnerships themselves. The proliferation of partnerships, local initiatives and individual projects represented by the 'bowl of spaghetti' has led to a concern with issues of co-ordination and rationalization. As a result, the New Labour government in the UK has obliged local authorities to establish Local Strategic Partnerships, in order to 'rationalize and simplify existing partnerships' (DETR, 2001: 4). However, these attempts to co-ordinate the profusion of partnerships might be better understood not as a continuation of governance but as a response to the problematics of governance regimes. According to Jessop (2000: 334), 'the development of [governance] mechanisms ... adds further layers of complexity to the social world. It thereby risks adding governance failure to market failure and state failure as problems to be confronted'. In succinct terms, what we are witnessing with the development of these strategic partnerships is an attempt to govern the structures of governance.

Viewing the new arrangements of urban governance in these terms allows us to ask questions about who is holding the levers of power in our contemporary cities, and about how they are using that power. By definition we can also ask questions about who is not represented in the partnerships, and about why they have been excluded. The networks and partnerships that are emerging in British cities can be investigated in these terms. We can ask questions about the interests each member of the partnership brings to the table and about the goals they intend to achieve from their membership. Thus if we use the governance perspective, we can open up a whole host of research questions about the exercise of power at the urban level.

This promises to be crucial, because urban-based governance will become more rather than less complex in the years to come, as places will increasingly have to sell themselves and their partnerships – whether to central government or the private sector – if they wish to remain competitive in an era of global competition. However, in an era of reducing state support and increasing capital mobility this competition is a zero-sum game. This means that existing resources are simply shifted around rather than new resources being added. The places that win can only do so at the expense of those who lose. Territorial competition and difference can only serve to deepen rather than reduce uneven development, which means that a geographical perspective will continue to be invaluable in analysing the trajectory of the new urban governance.

FIGURE 26.3
Urban regeneration partnerships: the new Bull Ring complex in Birmingham, including the architecturally innovative Selfridges department store (seen here), was developed by a partnership including the City Council, the private sector, community groups and market stall holders from the old Bull Ring

SUMMARY

- The concept of governance refers to new ways of governing society involving a range of participants drawn from the public, private and voluntary sectors.

- The new mechanisms of governance are operating at a variety of scales, from the local to the global.

- There is no guarantee of governance success, and in many instances there are concerns over the co-ordination, accountability and legitimacy of governance structures.

CONCLUSION: SPACES OF CITIZENSHIP AND GOVERNANCE

There are very real concerns over the nature of contemporary citizenship and governance that promise to keep these issues at the forefront of geographical inquiry. Official policy statements, concerning many areas of economic and social development at all levels from the local to the European, emphasize the important role that is envisaged for partnerships and networks operating beyond the formal structures of government. Yet once these new mechanisms of governance are in place they raise a number of critical questions about participation and citizenship. In many instances the new structures of governance, especially those that involve the private sector, are blurring the distinction between the public as citizen and the public as customer. Yet the citizen has rights that differ from the customer, and in the long term the legitimacy of the new structures of governance will rest on the granting of consent and support from the public. Moreover, if groups are unable to achieve their goals through these formal citizen rights, they will often set up alternative forms, and spaces, of participatory citizenship, which offer a chance to build new communities of interest based on shared and collective identities that lay beyond that of the formal citizen.

A crucial issue, however, is the territory to which the citizen feels they belong. Increasingly, as we saw at the very beginning of the chapter, people are identifying not with the established nation-state but with entities that are either supranational (such as the EU) or subnational (such as the region, or the locality). The debates over devolved government in Scotland and Wales, over elected mayors and regional assemblies in England, and over an increasingly integrated Europe are evidence of this. As this uncertainty indicates, the very complexity of the new structures of governance may well ensure that all kinds of new spaces of citizenship will emerge to replace those previously linked only to the nation-state. As we saw, many of these spaces will be created and defined by those who presently feel that they can only exercise partial citizenship. Already there are signs that, as a response to new management structures, self-organization by user groups in the fields of health and social services is redefining the relationship between previously excluded citizens, their communities and processes of governance (Barnes, 1997). These kinds of redefinitions point to the ways in which the processes of citizenship and governance will continue to impact upon one another, and they indicate that these issues will be of continuing importance for the political geographer.

DISCUSSION POINTS

1. Which area, or country, do you identify with? To which place do you feel you belong? Of where do you consider yourself a citizen? Why do you think you have this identity?

2. Can you identify in your area of residence the formation of new forms of participatory citizenship? Who is involved, and why did they seek these new spaces of engagement?

3. How is your city governed? Make a list of the agencies and institutions that are responsible for running the city, and think about who is involved in them.

4. Which groups are excluded from these agencies? What does this tell you about the structures of power in contemporary capitalism?

FURTHER READING

Smith, S. (1989) Society, space and citizenship; a Human Geography for the 'new times'? *Transactions of the Institute of British Geographers*, 14(2), 144–56.

This is the paper that set the original agenda for the study of geography and citizenship, and it is still worth reading for the suggestive links it draws between geography and social justice.

Painter, J. and Philo, C. (1995) Spaces of citizenship. *Political Geography*, 14(2).

This is a special edition of the journal, which contains nine separate articles on various aspects of geography and citizenship.

Esin, I. and Turner, B. (2002) *Handbook of citizenship studies*. **London: Sage.**

This is the definitive collection of papers on citizenship and covers a huge range of contemporary issues and debates. It is useful in shedding light on the perspectives of other disciplines outside geography.

Johnstone, C. and Whitehead, M. (2004) *New horizons in British urban policy*. **Aldershot: Ashgate.**

This is the most comprehensive collection of material on New Labour's urban policy. It contains several chapters that explicitly seek to investigate the new forms of urban governance described in this chapter.

International Journal of Urban and Regional Research, **19(1) (1995);** *Urban Studies,* **33(8) (1996), with Alan Cochrane;** *Transactions of the Institute of British Geographers,* **21(4) (1997).**

For excellent case studies of the emergence of new urban partnerships in the UK in the 1990s, see any one of a series of papers by Jamie Peck and Adam Tickell on urban politics and urban governance in Manchester. Articles by them on this theme appear in the above journals.

CHAPTER 27
NATIONALISM

INTRODUCTION

According to the sociologist Anthony Smith (1991: viii) 'Nationalism provides perhaps the most compelling identity myth in the modern world'. Feelings of identification with, even loyalty to, a particular 'nation' remain powerful despite the emergence of 'global culture' and transnational movements or appeals to other forms of identity like class, gender and ethnicity. If anything, the appeal of national identity is growing. On the one hand, UK politics are frequently dominated by the relationship with the rest of Europe, with much of this defined in terms of threats to national sovereignty. On the other hand, we have witnessed the relatively peaceful re-emergence of small nations in eastern Europe – Estonia, Latvia and Ukraine – whose identities had been suppressed for generations by the Soviet Union, but also the bloody re-emergence of Serbs, Croats and Muslims in Bosnia following the break-up of the former Yugoslavia. And simmering away for decades, and occasionally bursting into violent life, are separatist conflicts in places like Northern Ireland, the Basque region of Spain and the Russian republic of Chechnya (see Fig. 27.1).

FIGURE 27.1
Demonstrators – including two in traditional costume – carry the Ikurrina (the Basque flag) to protest at the banning of a separatist political party by the Spanish state, 2003. Credit: Rafa Rivas/Getty Images

This chapter tries to highlight some of the complexities of nationalism. The first concerns precisely which situations are commonly considered 'nationalist'. Billig (1995: 5) argues that

> *In both popular and academic writing, nationalism is associated with those who struggle to create new states or with extreme right-wing politics. According to customary usage, George Bush is not a nationalist; but separatists in Quebec or Brittany are; so are the leaders of extreme right-wing parties such as the Front National in France.*

Ideological
a meaning, idea or thing is ideological in so far as it helps to constitute and maintain relations of domination and subordination between two or more social groups (CLASSES, GENDERS, age groups, etc.).

He claims that this narrow understanding of nationalism always locates it on the colourful periphery whilst overlooking the nationalism of established western states. Members of those states often suggest that they are 'patriotic' whereas others are 'nationalistic'. But that distinction might usefully be collapsed. In its broadest sense, nationalism is simply an **ideological** movement that draws upon national identity in order to achieve certain political goals. It therefore covers a far wider range of contexts and narratives than we might, as a gut reaction, suppose. The usual tendency is to imagine that nationalism is a negative phenomenon characterized by bigotry or racism, violence (be it terrorism or warfare), and aggressive social exclusion. For many others, however, nationalism can refer to a positive celebration of identity in the face of oppression or marginalization and the eventual attainment of social and political liberation. The conditions against which nationalist groups struggle can be extreme – racial or religious intolerance, for instance – but they can also be simple dissatisfaction with the structure of government. Nationalist struggle can, therefore, be carried through by force of arms, but also through democratic process.

NATIONALISMS

Nationalism is such a complex phenomenon that we may be better off thinking in terms of nationalisms. In this section I will try to highlight some key concepts that can help us recognize and make sense of these nationalisms. The first is the distinction between civic nationalism and ethnic nationalism. Civic nationalism (sometimes called 'territorial nationalism') is a modern, liberal phenomenon geared towards the creation and regulation of an efficient social, economic and political unit. Its origins lie in eighteenth- and nineteenth-century Europe when states such as France and Britain modernized, industrialized and sought to create homogeneous societies around the capitalist system. This form of nationalism, according to Ignatieff (1993: 3–4),

> *maintains that the nation should be composed of all those – regardless of race, colour, creed, gender, language or ethnicity – who subscribe to the nation's political creed. This nationalism is called civic because it envisages the nation as a community of equal, right-bearing citizens, united in patriotic attachment to a shared set of political practices and virtues.*

Civic nationalism is often seen as a set of state-building practices, concerned with the political, economic and cultural systems that serve to bind a people together. Sometimes, however, its lack of conceptual regard to race, creed, colour and so forth can be problematic when the nation assumes that cultural homogeneity is desirable and refuses to acknowledge difference. Ethnic nationalism, on the other hand, replaces this formal, rationalistic language of 'rights' and 'systems' with the language of 'belonging'. What makes the nation a place to which people feel they belong and to which they pledge allegiance is 'not the cold contrivance of shared rights, but the people's pre-existing ethnic characteristics: their language, religion, customs and traditions' (Ignatieff, 1993: 4). Modern nations are often built on ancient ethnic origins, and the myths and

Ethnicity

a criterion of social categorization that
distinguishes different groups of people
on the basis of inherited cultural
differences. Ethnicity is a very complex
idea that needs careful consideration.
For instance, in popular usage ethnicity
often becomes a synonym for RACE,
but in fact there is a crucial distinction
in so far as race differentiates people on
the grounds of physical characteristics,
and ethnicity on the grounds of learnt
cultural differences. Moreover, whilst
everyday understandings of ethnicity
often treat it as a quality only possessed
by some people and cultures (for
instance, 'ethnic minorities' and their
'ethnic foods' or 'ethnic fashions') in
fact these differential recognitions of
ethnicity themselves need explanation.
The complexities of the concept are
further emphasized by recent debates
within and beyond Human Geography
over the extent to which new forms of
ethnicity are emerging through the
cultural mixing associated with
processes of GLOBALIZATION (*see also*
HYBRID and SYNCRETIC).

Socialization

the relations through which human
beings learn about acceptable social
norms and moral standards in a given
society. Socialization can occur through
different institutions and spaces such as
the family, schools or the media.

FIGURE 27.2
Unisonality: Welsh rugby fans sing the national
anthem at the Millennium Stadium, Cardiff.
Credit: Photolibrarywales.com

legends of that ethnicity are resilient and powerful. This form of nationalism can be a positive celebration of cultural heritage and diversity, often in the face of an oppressive regime, but it can also be exclusionary and can promote intolerance. An ethnic group that is denied autonomy by an existing state of which it is a part will often build its nationalism around ethnic identity and, as 'national separatists', will seek political autonomy as a vehicle for protecting and expressing its ethnicity. In truth, however, most nationalisms combine both 'civic' and 'ethnic' elements – either at different times, in different proportions, or according to the different audiences to whom messages are being addressed. Smith (1991) suggests that we think, rather, in terms of the functions that these various types of nationalism perform for a people. He draws a distinction between 'external' functions, which govern the territorial, economic and political relationships with the rest of the world, and 'internal' functions that socialize members into a national community.

Some of the most interesting recent work has addressed these 'internal' processes – the ways in which we come to feel we 'belong' to a particular community. Benedict Anderson (1991) argues that the nation is not 'real' as such, but that subtle mechanisms work on us and blend us into what he calls an 'imagined community'. The nation is 'imagined' because you will only ever meet, or even be aware of, a minuscule proportion of your fellow 'nationals' but you have a strong image in your mind of the nation as existing simultaneously nonetheless. And that image is one of communality, which often masks very real differences and fractions: 'regardless of the actual inequality and exploitation that may prevail in each, the nation is always conceived as a deep, horizontal comradeship' (Anderson 1991: 7). These processes include overt forms of national bonding like the singing of national anthems, which provide an experience of simultaneity: 'At precisely the same moments, people wholly unknown to each other utter the same verses to the same melody. The image: unisonance. Singing 'La Marseillaise', 'Waltzing Matilda' and Indonesian 'Raya' provide occasions for unisonality, for the echoed physical realization of the imagined community' (1991: 145) (see Fig. 27.2). Famously, Anderson also suggests that 'national newspapers' provide a daily, visible and shared reminder of the imagined nation. We might extend this to the 'national news' on television or radio, particularly at times of 'national crisis', 'national mourning' (see, for example, McGuigan, 2000) or 'national rejoicing'.

Michael Billig goes even further than Anderson in highlighting the very mundaneness or banality of this process of national socialization. He argues (1995: 8) that 'because the concept of nationalism has been restricted to exotic and passionate exemplars, the routine and familiar forms of nationalism have been overlooked. In this case, "our" daily nationalism slips from attention'. For Billig, 'banal nationalism' is not the flag being passionately waved, it is the flag hanging unnoticed on public buildings like schools and post offices in the United States. He extends his analysis to language, to politicians' clichés, even to newspapers' sport and weather coverage and their unquestioned references to 'the country' or 'the nation'. Together, these banalities make the homeland look 'homely, beyond question and, should the occasion arise, worth the price of sacrifice' (Billig, 1995: 175). Similarly, Tim Edensor (2002: 2) argues that we need to understand the ways in which popular culture and everyday life can be 'expressed as national'. His analysis ranges from material objects like cars, foods and clothing to our bodily performances of identity in language, gesture and time–space routines. Crucially, it has been argued (Thompson, 2001) that we are far from passive 'dupes' of national identity but are, rather, knowing agents who make the nation real in the course of our own deliberations and interactions, and signify this in our 'common sense' understandings of the world around us. In a geographical sense, this means that most of us make sense of the national at a local scale (see, for example, Jones and Desforges, 2003).

SUMMARY

- National identity is, arguably, becoming more – rather than less – significant in the modern world, despite appeals to 'global culture', etc.
- Nationalism is a phenomenon whose complexity has often been overlooked. It can, for instance, be both a positive and a negative social force.
- There is a major distinction between 'ethnic' and 'civic' nationalism. The former is concerned with citizenship, laws, rights, etc., whilst the latter is

concerned with ethnicity, culture and belonging. In most cases, nationalism is a blend of both types, perhaps at different times.

- Some of the most interesting recent studies of nationalism examine its day-to-day presence in our lives – its 'banality' or its role in creating 'imagined communities'. These studies also redress the balance towards popular culture and human agency.

GEOGRAPHIES OF NATIONALISM

There are several reasons why nationalism is of critical interest to geographers. Patterns of electoral support for nationalist parties, for instance, are open to geographical analysis (e.g. Levy, 1995). But I will concentrate here on the symbolic role of geography for national identity and nationalist movements. This is a major role, for nationalism is primarily a territorial ideology that derives its logic and inspiration from the relationship between a particular group of people and a particular parcel of land. This leads on to a whole raft of cultural relationships though which a people make *a* land *their* land.

One of the best summaries of this relationship is still Williams and Smith's (1983) article in which they identify eight major dimensions of national **territory** – habitat, folk culture, scale, location, boundaries, autarky (self-sufficiency), the idea of 'homeland', and processes of nation-building. Some of these dimensions are 'external' in that they refer to attempts to distinguish one nation from another. Attempts may be made to 'solidify' or 'confirm' national space by delimiting and maintaining borders. The changing of place names from an earlier phase of occupation serves to harden the identity of that piece of land and to deny the claims of others upon it. 'Internally', however, territory and landscape can become symbolic of national identity and powerful agents of social cohesion. This process frequently draws on an awareness of history:

Territory
a more or less bounded area over which an animal, person, social group or institution claims and attempts to enforce control.

" *The nation's unique history is embodied in the nation's unique piece of territory – its 'homeland', the primeval land of its ancestors, older than any state, the same land which saw its greatest moments, perhaps its mythical origins. The time has passed but the space is still there.* "

(Anderson, 1988: 24)

Legends are therefore placed within the nation's space and national heroes and heroines are located through their birthplaces, graves or the site of their greatest act, thus confirming the link between a particular people and that place. More generally, such sites of memory can often become places of pilgrimage at which explicitly or implicitly 'national' political ceremonies might be staged (see, for example, Johnson, 2003; Withers, 1996).

Landscape and specific physical features can also become emblematic of national identity. As Stephen Daniels (1993: 5) puts it, 'Landscapes, whether focusing on single monuments or framing stretches of scenery, provide visible shape; they picture the nation. As exemplars of moral order and aesthetic harmony, particular landscapes achieve the status of national icons'. In many cases, rural landscapes are imagined as the 'real', 'authentic' essence of the nation. This idealization also extends to the people – or folk – living within them in idealized, organic communities. Many nationalist movements had close ties with groups protecting the legacy of the 'folk', be it their customs and way of life or simply their buildings, costume or music. Some nationalist groups went so far as to advocate moves 'back to the land' – that is, to resettle the population away from the cities and in the rural 'heart' of the country – in order to regain some essential, and lost, form of national identity (e.g. Gruffudd, 1994). Daniels (1993) argues that the gentle, pastoral lowlands of southern England – and paintings of them by artists like John Constable – have come to symbolize 'Englishness' and have been used at times of social tension (the two world wars, for instance) as emblems of national identity. In the United States, a more rugged sense of national identity coalesces around the idea of the frontier (e.g. Slotkin, 1992).

There are few better examples of this mythologizing and politicization of territory than Israel. Hooson (1994: 10) argues that

" *The endowment of religious symbolism upon a piece of land ... precipitated by the establishment of Israel after the Second World War ... alongside the Moslem religious significance of the area, will make that tiny piece of land a tortured example of multiple overlapping national identities for a long time.* "

The maintenance of Israel's external and internal borders has assumed immense significance since the creation of the new state in 1947. Newman (1989) argues that this maintenance has been achieved not only through military action but also through civilian settlement in farms, *kibbutzim* and industrial villages in border regions. More recently, the controversial and frequently violent building and defence of Jewish settlements in areas hitherto exclusively or overwhelmingly Arab-Palestinian transfers this spatial form of nation-building to the internal space of the Israeli state (see Falah, 1989). Elements within the Israeli state have also, at various times, used history and myth as a form of nation-building, and geography has been a potent factor in that process. Zerubavel (1995) notes how Zionists sought to legitimate Jewish nationalist ideology though the recovery and reinvention of a settler history. The 'science' of archaeology played a prominent part in this recovery as it did in other aspects of Israeli life – uncovering traces of Jewish settlement in Jerusalem, for instance, thus adding to claims about the legitimacy of present-day settlement and control (Silberman, 2001). One of the most dramatic elements of this historical reconstruction is the legend of Masada, a mountain-top fortress established above the Dead Sea by King Herod and whose Jewish occupants were besieged by the Romans at the end of the first century AD Legend has it that, as the Romans were about to break through the defences, the occupants of the city committed mass suicide rather than be enslaved by them. The production of modern translations of the legend 'led to its reconstruction as a major turning point in Jewish history, a locus of modern pilgrimage, a famous archaeological site, and a contemporary political metaphor' (Zerubavel, 1995: 63). Despite its grisly and ultimately hopeless end, the legend became symbolic of Jewish resistance in the face of overwhelming odds. Hebrew teachers – socializing their charges into a new language and, thus, a new nation – organized youth trips to Masada from the 1930s onwards, and a pilgrimage to Masada and a pledge that it will not fall again were part of Israeli military training until the late 1980s (see Fig. 27.3).

FIGURE 27.3
Israeli soldiers taking their oath of allegiance in a ceremony on top of Masada. The Hebrew inscription reads 'Never again shall Masada fall'. Source: Israel Defence Forces' Spokesman's Office

SUMMARY

- Nationalist ideology is nearly always 'geographical' in that it is based around a territorial claim and it proclaims a clear sense of place.

- This geographical aspect can be manifested equally in material acts of nation-building (e.g. road networks) and in cultural forms like landscape painting, etc.

- History and folk culture provide a nation with a long-standing imaginary bond to the land. Apparently 'neutral' conservation policies and 'sciences' like archaeology can thus play a role in nationalist movements by defining the authorized 'national past'.

INFLECTING NATIONALISM

Smith argues that the key to understanding nationalism is an appreciation of its multidimensionality. It is this 'that has made national identity such a flexible and persistent force in modern life and politics, and allowed it to combine effectively with other powerful ideologies and movements, without losing its character' (1991: 15). This is partly what Edensor

(2002) means when he refers to the 'matrix' of national identity. To illustrate this I will look briefly at inflections of nationalism in different contexts and countries. This will also help us grasp the distinctions between civic and ethnic, external and internal, even positive and negative forms of nationalism. I will consider, briefly, issues of economics, 'race', and language.

Some of the most influential early writings on nationalism sought an explanation for its persistence or re-emergence in relative socio-economic conditions. Hechter (1975), for instance, saw nationalism as a phenomenon born out of poverty and oppression. His historical analysis of Britain identified a developed economic core and an underdeveloped periphery, with the latter concentrated in the 'Celtic fringes' of Wales and Scotland. Because capitalism had flowed along ethnic divides to the disadvantage of the minority Celtic groups it heightened ethnic consciousness due to a growing awareness of disadvantage. Similarly, Tom Nairn (1977) claimed that nationalist cultural resurgence in Scotland and Wales was a romantic and populist response to uneven development. There are parallels in David Harvey's (1989: 306) argument that the insecurity caused by capitalist globalization in part explains the resurgence of nationalism: 'there are abundant signs that localism and nationalism have become stronger precisely because of the quest for the security that place always offers in the midst of all the shifting that flexible accumulation implies'.

But there is no inevitable correlation between poverty, ethnic identity and nationalism. In Spain, the regions with the most overtly developed senses of identity are the traditionally more prosperous ones. The Basque country and Catalonia have been for centuries the core regions of the Spanish economy, but modernization actually served to heighten – rather than diminish – their senses of regional identity. The Spanish state came to be seen as a parasite. The Basque country was, however, hit by an economic recession in the 1980s and this *did* give Basque nationalism a new surge of energy, including a dramatic upturn in the activities of the terrorist group ETA (*Euskadi Ta Azkatasuna* – Basque Homeland and Liberty), established in 1959. Catalonia, on the other hand, has established itself as one of the core regions of the European economy, and its own parliament projects it as a self-confident, dynamic and creative 'nation' within Europe, rather than region within Spain. There is a strong – though less attractive – echo of this in Italy and its long-standing disparity between the affluent north and the poorer south. There the *Lega Nord* (the Northern League), formed in 1991 – and its charismatic leader Umberto Bossi – harnessed northern grudges against the south and its supposedly 'corrupt' politicians that preyed on the industrious north. In a ceremony on the banks of the River Po in 1996 Bossi declared an independent north Italian state called Padania, with its capital in Venice, and demanded a separate currency (see Fig. 27.4). The League's electoral success has lagged way behind its historically inspired rhetoric, though (see Agnew, 2002).

The *Lega Nord*, however, is also notable for its racist rhetoric and opposition to immigration. As I have already noted, nationalist politics are frequently articulated around the issue of ethnic 'belonging', with 'ethnic cleansing' in Bosnia – the forcible construction of ethnically

FIGURE 27.4
Supporters of the Lega Nord demonstrate on the Grand Canal, Venice – proposed capital of Padania. Credit: Pizzoli Alberto/Corbis SYGMA

homogeneous areas – perhaps the most painful recent example in Europe. Whilst the origins of Basque nationalism were, in part, based on racial distinctiveness and superiority (Conversi, 1990), very few of the 'mainstream' nationalist movements in Europe (i.e. those organizing as political parties) are now overtly racist. However, this does not mean that issues of 'racial belonging' are not prescient in any understanding of the nation. At the level of the state, immigration policy serves to exclude and include primarily on ethnic lines, and below that level a whole range of popular discourses about race are also woven together with nationality (see Jackson and Penrose, 1993). Contemporary debates about British identities in the wake of devolution have highlighted the fact that many ethnic minorities feel uncomfortable about assuming the identity of the constituent nations (Wales, Scotland, etc.) as opposed to a hyphenated sense of, say, 'Asian-British' (Bryant, 2003). The most overtly exclusionary alliance between racialism and nationalism is, however, the use of the Union Flag as a symbol by right-wing racist groups including the British *National* Party (BNP).

Ethnicity more generally is, however, central to any understanding of the vast majority of nationalist situations, but that ethnicity may be expressed as the politics of language or of religion, rather than some crude notion of 'racial belonging'. Often, we need to think of these nationalisms in terms of the celebration of ethnic diversity in the face of homogenizing or oppressive forces, rather than in terms of aggressive exclusion. Recent Spanish nationalisms can be partly understood as a response to the ethnic suppression that characterized the fascist dictatorship of General Franco from 1935 until 1975. Franco abolished the historic parliaments and legal rights of both Catalonia and the Basque country and ruthlessly repressed their regional identities and languages. Books in Catalan were destroyed and the names of villages and towns changed to Castilian (what we call 'Spanish'). Despite this, Catalan nationalism was almost entirely peaceful and based around the maintenance of folk culture. Since the restoration of Catalan autonomy in 1980 the language has regained its status in all aspects of life. According to the first leader of the new regional government in the 1980s, 'If some issue is crucial to Catalonia, it is language and culture, because they are core elements of our identity as a people … Catalonia did not want autonomy for political or administrative reasons, but for reasons of identity' (quoted in Conversi, 1990: 56).

Welsh nationalism, too, has historically been a predominantly cultural movement. *Plaid Cymru* (the Party of Wales) was formed in 1925 in response to the perceived decline of traditional Welsh rural life and, crucially, the Welsh language. The language had been marginalized and outlawed by the British state since Wales's incorporation under the Act of Union of 1536, but the modern world (radio, tourism, etc.) further threatened the language. *Plaid Cymru* believed Welshness to be primarily rural and idealized the *gwerin* (folk). Many of its campaigns therefore opposed the British state's incursions (for water, military training, even tourism) into those parts of rural Wales imagined as the cultural heartlands of the nation. Since the 1970s, campaigns by the more radical nationalist groups against holiday homes and in-migration to rural Wales attempted the same kind of defence, though using direct action such as arson attacks. For most of the century, then, Welsh nationalism operated within a linguistic definition of identity. More recently, however, this ethnic stress on cultural maintenance has been assisted by government support for bilingualism through education and broadcast policies. A growing civic nationalism has also emerged in Wales, newly confident about issues of identity and language, and critical of the unaccountable systems of government that emerged in the 1980s and early 1990s. Remarkably, the Welsh referendum on devolution in September 1997, which produced a narrow vote in favour of the establishment of a Welsh Assembly was, on the surface at least, less to do with national identity than it was with governance. Though this does not mean that tensions around the issue of identity have gone (and the closeness of the result proves that) they have, at least, been placed within a wider spectrum of national concerns.

SUMMARY

- Nationalism is a very flexible or multidimensional ideology that can be manifested in a number of contexts. It is, perhaps, best thought of as existing within a matrix of concerns and identities.

- It has frequently been associated with groups highlighting poverty and economic and social injustice along ethnic lines, although several nationalist movements represent 'rich' areas.

- More commonly, nationalism interacts with ideas of ethnicity, race, language, religion, and so forth. In these forms it can be either culturally repressive or a reaction against cultural repression.

CONCLUSION

Nationalism, then, is an extremely complex – and even bewildering (see Fig. 27.5) – phenomenon, and one that is not always (as the popular use of the term implies) reducible to simple measures of 'good' and 'bad'. It can be liberating as well as oppressive, peaceful as well as violent, progressive as well as reactionary, traditional as well as modern, even rural as well as urban. Little surprise then that it has often been characterized as 'Janus-faced', after the dual-faced Roman god. Also wrong is the tendency within established western states to think of nationalism as something 'out there' on the margins. As Billig and Anderson have shown, nationalism (though maybe in the apparently more neutral and benign form of 'national identity') is as much a feature of those established states as it is of those nationalist groups struggling for expression and for sovereignty. A thorough and sensitive analysis of nationalism, then, should consider the context within which it is being expressed, the issues that it identifies as central, the balance between ethnic and civic strategies, and – importantly – the way in which these factors evolve over time. It should also look at how national identity – or competing identities – come to be politicized. And, of course, for geographers, considerations of space, territory, landscape and scale are not only crucial but also open avenues of study that reveal in fascinating detail how powerful, creative and often destructive, nationalism can be.

FIGURE 27.5
Let's go ahead and partition all of the former Yugoslavia. Credit: MacNelly/*Chicago Tribune*

DISCUSSION POINTS

1. Do you agree with those who argue that nations and nationalism are, if anything, more important nowadays despite globalization?

2. In how many ways can nationalism be thought of as 'Janus-faced'?

3. How is national identity manifested in popular culture and material culture in everyday life?

4. Why is nationalism nearly always a spatial ideology?

5. What is meant by the 'matrix of national identity', and to what other forms of identity is a national one related?

FURTHER READING

Guibernau, M. and Hutchinson, J. (eds) (2001) *Understanding nationalism.* Cambridge: Polity Press.

A useful survey of the sometimes bewildering debates on how best to understand nationalism.

Harvey, D., Jones, R., Milligan, C. and McInroy, N. (eds) (2002) *Celtic geographies: old culture, new times.* London: Routledge.

On how the idea of 'the Celtic' serves to underpin cultural and political identification and action in a variety of places around the world.

Lowenthal, D. (1998) *The heritage crusade and the spoils of history.* Cambridge: Cambridge University Press.

A provocative study of how history – commodified or packaged as 'heritage' – has been used to legitimate or gloss over certain political points of view.

Short, J. (1991) *Imagined country: society, culture and environment.* London: Routledge.

A very readable introduction to the environmental myths of England, America and Australia, covering everything from city planning to westerns.

Spillman, L. (1997) *Nation and commemoration: creating national identities in the United States and Australia.* Cambridge: Cambridge University Press.

A series of studies of the role of history and memory in shaping and sustaining national identities and nationalisms.

SECTION 7
SOCIAL GEOGRAPHIES

INTRODUCTION

'There is no such thing as society', the former British Prime Minister Margaret Thatcher once famously proclaimed. It is understandable that people want to be seen as individuals. Certainly Mrs Thatcher understood this, to devastating electoral effect. We tend to resent being reduced to crude social determinants of class, gender, race, age, sexuality or nationality. Whilst we may often be guilty of stereotyping others, we don't want it done to us. On the other hand, with just a little reflection, it is also fairly obvious that we only possess and express our individual identities through wider social dimensions: through the relations we have to others (the three of us writing this could not be lecturers without students, men without women); through the organizations and social settings that we inhabit (our families, our friendships, our haunts); through our senses of collective identification. Strip all that away and most of us would fall apart (which is why solitary confinement is a such a brutal form of discipline and has such powerful effects on individuals).

Social geographers are also wary of simplistic ideas of society. But they know the social matters. We only exist as individuals through social labels and categories, however much we may chafe against them at times. Think about our gendering. It is quite right to question simplistic judgements about all men or all women having certain kinds of characteristics. But being women or men (or something beyond these options) is something that we all have to deal with. It is a part of what makes us who we are, both to ourselves and others. In conjunction with our class, ethnicity, age, sexuality, dis/ability, and so on, it structures our lives, too, impacting on how we are treated, the life chances we have, the expectations placed upon us. Generally, then, we cannot be ourselves outside of these social dimensions; and these social dimensions have crucial effects on who and what and where we can be.

The 'where' matters here. Social geographers are especially interested in understanding how social processes operate through spaces, places and environments. This is worth emphasizing (see also Chapter 2 for a sustained analysis of this point). Social Geography goes far beyond detailing the spatial distributions or environmental impacts of social groups, whilst leaving direct investigation of these groups to others such as sociologists and anthropologists. Instead, it emphasizes how geography is central to social processes and relations.

In this section, we begin with the idea of 'identities' and its suturing of the individual and the social. Peter Jackson, one of the founding figures of the revitalized Social Geography that emerged in the 1980s, argues against over-simplifying identity into fixed (and fixing) labels. Our identities are multiple, he suggests. They are 'relational' too, formed in relation to others rather than stemming from innate characteristics of our own. What is more, how we 'form' our identities is shaped by wider historical currents and processes. One might argue, for example, that one set of currents and processes that Mrs Thatcher tapped into and promoted was a shift towards forming identities through our consumption practices rather than through work (Chapter 18 has obvious resonance here). We might also think about how our identities increasingly form around materials and spaces that transcend national boundaries (an issue pursued further in Chapter 36). Peter concludes by thinking about how complex, relational identities can be portrayed and researched, suggesting biographical narratives or life stories as one particularly promising method.

In Chapter 29 Sarah Holloway picks up on the relational nature of identity, and homes in on the role of socially constructed differences in defining who we are. Drawing on recent work in Social Geography on age, sexuality and dis/ability, Sarah examines how social differences are both socially produced and intensely, personally felt. She also provides a range of examples that illustrate how social identities and relations come into being through particular geographies. She concludes by suggesting that Social Geography's attention to 'different' identities has been invaluable, shaking up a host of assumptions, but that the sub-discipline also needs to beware of being silent on those identities that are in some way seen as 'the norm'.

In Chapter 30 Jon May deploys the relational understandings of identity discussed by Jackson and Holloway to explore the processes and politics of social 'exclusion'. Jon deliberately brings together more abstract work on the urges people have to get away from (or more likely, push away) those seen as problematically different to themselves with social policy debates on social polarization. In his approach, and in the specific work on homelessness that he discusses, Jon represents a broader quality of Social Geography, the combination of theoretical sophistication with practical commitment and applicability.

FURTHER READING

Social and Cultural Geography

As the title suggests, this journal is not limited to Social Geography alone. In this, it represents wider confluences of Social and Cultural Geography, especially in the UK. But a survey of recent volumes will give you a feel for a breadth of anglophonic Social Geography; and you can consult the excellent reports on Social and Cultural Geography in non-anglophonic countries too.

Pain, R. *et al.* (2001) *Introducing social geographies.* London: Arnold.

A recent textbook that will let you read further on how Social Geographers have studied various dimensions of social difference and identity, and on how these insights have been applied to social policy debates, including crime, housing and socio-economic exclusion.

Valentine, G. (2001) *Social geographies: space and society.* London: Prentice Hall.

Rather than being organized around social categories or aspects of social identity, this book foregrounds their geographies through an analysis of spatial scales ranging from the body to the nation. Discussion focuses on how social identities and relations are constructed and contested in these spaces. Typically well written, by one of the leading authors in the field.

CHAPTER 28
IDENTITIES

TAKE 1

I'd like to start by looking at a work by the contemporary artist Antony Gormley (whose statue *The Angel of the North* you may already know). He calls this piece *Field for the British Isles* (see Fig. 28.1). It was made in September 1993 and consists of thousands of unglazed, fired, small clay figures, packed closely together, staring mutely at the viewer and filling every inch of the available space. I saw this piece at the Mappin Art Gallery in Sheffield but it has been on tour to a number of different galleries in Dublin, Edinburgh, Liverpool, London and elsewhere. At first glance, all you see is a crowd of relatively undifferentiated figures – a sea of anonymous figures who together occupy our field of vision. After a while, you begin to notice the patterns they create: an undulating landscape, varying by height and colour, creating waves of light and shade, with different hues amongst the terracotta landscape. Gradually, too, you begin to pick out individual differences between the figures: some are taller than others, some are thinner; some look happy, others sad; some gaze straight ahead, others stare up at the sky.

For me at least, Gormley's *Field* challenges us to think about our personal and collective identity: who we are and how we differ from those around us, both near and far. We may feel a sense of empathy with Gormley's figures, or we may be a little intimidated by all those anonymous faces, a potentially hostile crowd. Identity issues raise many such emotions (fear and fascination, desire and dread), based on our sense of similarity and difference. Initially, at least, Gormley's figures all look the same. With time, though, we begin to discern patterns and groupings and, with sufficient patience, we become aware of individual expressions and bodily imperfections. We may also start to ask questions about who shaped this particular *Field*, whose ideas it represents, how it came to assume this particular shape and how it relates to other communities elsewhere. In fact, the figures in *Field for the British Isles* were made by a community of families in St Helens using clay and kilns provided by a local brick-making company. Similar versions have been made by families of brick makers in Mexico, by children from the Amazon basin, and by students and families in Sweden. We may also begin to ask questions about our own engagement with this particular work. With 40,000 figures filling the gallery space, we can only engage with it in visual terms: we cannot walk round the exhibition or touch the figures. As one art critic writes of Gormley's work:

> *Looking at art is never a passive act. It is we, the spectators, who must do the work of bringing these forms to life, and in doing so discover something about our own lives, our own space and place in the world.*

(Searle, 1996: 5)

TAKE 2

If someone stopped you in the street and asked you about your identity, you'd probably find it hard to answer their questions. 'Identity' isn't something you can easily express in words and our answer would probably depend on who was asking the question (a census enumerator, a police officer or a market researcher). Your answer might also vary in different times and places. When I'm on holiday abroad, for example, I'm often quite conscious of being 'British', aware of other British holidaymakers around me and of all the other nationalities who come together for a week or two in some 'foreign' place. When I'm back home in England, I often describe myself as a Londoner (although I was born just south of London in Surrey and have lived in Yorkshire for the last ten years). In other situations, I might be more conscious of my age or sex, or how I dress, or the kind of music I enjoy. These subjective 'lifestyle' issues are just as central to my sense of identity (who I am and how I differ from other people) as more objective issues like nationality or place of birth. All this suggests that it's usually better to talk about *multiple identities* than to try and reduce complex identity issues to a single 'dimension' (such as age or class). As the cultural historian Frank Mort once remarked:

> *We are not in any simple sense 'black' or 'gay' or 'upwardly mobile'. Rather we carry a bewildering range of different, and at times conflicting, identities around with us in our heads at the same time. There is a continual smudging of personas and lifestyles, depending where we are (at work, on the high street) and the spaces we are moving between.*

(Mort, 1989: 169)

I've started this chapter with two different 'takes' on identity to emphasize that it is a complex and contested term. This is no surprise, perhaps, given the political intensity associated with ideas of identity and belonging. Identity can sometimes be, quite literally, a matter of life and death as in the case of 'ethnic cleansing' in the former Yugoslavia or the genocide in Rwanda (to name just two recent conflicts where 'ethnic' identities became highly politicized). Identity has been a constant source of debate within the social sciences and there is no single 'right way' to approach these issues. A good way of engaging with them is to ask questions and think of examples of your own, relating the different theories of identity that we'll discuss in this chapter to your own experience.

Conventional approaches to identity have tended to assume that we each inhabit a particular, relatively fixed, identity. So, for example, we might talk about the identity of 'single mother' or 'black youth'. Within this perspective, identities might be made up of multiple strands (such as age, gender, ethnicity or marital status). But each individual's identity is assumed to be singular and relatively stable over time and there are assumed to be a finite number of identity positions. The assumption that groups of people share a common identity position and that we can 'read off' their attitudes and characteristics from that position (that women are natural homemakers or West Indians are good at dancing, for example) is often described as essentialism. Within the social sciences, particularly from feminist scholars, there have been many criticisms of essentialist thinking (see Fuss, 1989) that, as in the previous examples, is often regarded as a form of racism or sexism. This chapter therefore adopts a different position, arguing that identities are plural and fluid, complex and contested. We should not assume that all single mothers share any common characteristics beyond their marital and parental status, and we should be particularly wary of categorizations like 'black youth' as such labels are often applied indiscriminately to demonize whole groups of people.

The approach that is taken in this rest of this chapter can best be described as *relational*, arguing that our identities are constructed in relation to perceived similarities and differences. Some of these differences relate to the most intimate scale of the body (to notions of sexual and racial difference, for example) whilst others (such as citizenship or nationality) relate to the wider scales of the nation and the world. Questions of identity are politically and emotionally charged because they are simultaneously about the most personal issues of embodiment and subjectivity, but also they relate directly to processes of inclusion and exclusion where inequalities of power often result in discrimination and injustice (Sibley, 1995). The chapter concludes that identities are rarely fixed or stable because they are always in process of formation.

Essentialism

the belief that identities, such as class, gender and race, as well as age, dis/ability and sexuality, are directly determined by biology. This view is opposed by SOCIAL CONSTRUCTIONISTS, who argue that these differences between us are shaped through the interweaving of wider socio-spatial processes and individual biographies. The term is often used negatively to emphasize the stereotyping that it can produce.

A *relational approach* to identity starts from the position that our identities are formed in relation to others. Identities are not defined in terms of individual characteristics that are 'innate' to particular groups of people. Thinking relationally implies much less bounded notions of the self. We become aware of who we are through a sense of shared identity with others (those who speak the same language or share our tastes and ideas, for example) and by a process of setting ourselves apart from those we consider different from ourselves. A relational sense of identity implies a sense of fluidity and flux, where identities are subject to porous boundaries and changing alliances. Relational thinking opposes fixed and antagonistic notions of identity, where people define themselves through assumptions of innate difference (such as ideas of racial superiority) or where social and cultural differences are equated with differences of power (as in most theories of social class). Relational approaches to identity challenge essentialist definitions, emphasizing the 'play of difference' between people and their (human and non-human) environments.

SUMMARY
- This chapter argues for a relational approach to identity in contrast to traditional (essentialist) approaches.
- Identities involve the most intimate aspects of our personal lives but are also related to wider notions of social inclusion and exclusion.

FORMATIONS OF IDENTITY

Modernization

a process of social transformation in which technological change plays a leading role and in which scientific rationality becomes widely accepted. Often associated with the rise of industrial CAPITALISM, modernization has far-reaching implications for processes of identity formation and change.

As well as understanding identities as always in formation at any point in time, it is also important to think about how identity formations change over time. Many social theorists have argued that questions of identity became a particularly salient issue through the process of **modernization**. In pre-modern societies, people's social reach was relatively limited and their day-to-day interactions were generally conducted on a face-to-face basis with already familiar people (in the family and immediate community around the home). With the modernization of society, individuals increasingly came into contact with relative strangers, where questions of sameness and difference had to be negotiated on a daily basis. Structures rapidly emerged that enabled individuals to handle these issues, including class-based identities at work and gender-based identities at home (with clear overlap between these and other forms of identity). Authors such as Ulrich Beck have argued that in late modernity, the hold of these traditional bases of identity has weakened through a process of 'reflexive modernization' (Beck, 1992b; Beck *et al.*, 1994). Beck argues that post-industrial society is characterized by the decreasing constraints of social structures associated with class, gender, family and work, and that a process of increasing individualization is taking place. This process of de-traditionalization, where old structures of authority are increasingly questioned, leads to increased uncertainty and risk. This, in turn, requires new forms of self-management where individuals are (to varying degrees) able to construct their own personal narratives that enable them to understand themselves and control their future lives. For sociologists like Anthony Giddens, who have developed Beck's ideas about 'reflexive modernity', self-identity becomes a 'project' whereby individuals sustain their notions of identity through a constantly revisable and future-orientated 'narrative of the self' (Giddens, 1991).

While it is easy to overstate the demise of earlier forms of work-based identity associated, for example, with notions of social class, it is clear that modern life now revolves around a host of other identity markers. Authors such as Maffesoli (1995) have talked about the present day as the 'time of tribes', referring to the proliferation of ephemeral social groupings that come together for temporary social interaction at a nightclub or other social gathering. Sociologists like Pierre Bourdieu (1984) have explored the way that social distinctions are based on issues of **cultural capital** as well as economic capital, with tastes in music, food and leisure serving as markers of collective identity and social differentiation. Many of these distinctions are rooted in people's consumption practices rather than in their connection to the worlds of work, which were the defining feature of class-based models of social identity. As 'traditional' sources of identity have declined in significance, new sources of authority have risen to guide

Cultural capital

a term invented by the French sociologist Pierre Bourdieu, who argued that distinctions based on the judgement of taste were as important in marking social differences as access to economic capital. Some people may be high in cultural capital but low in economic capital (and vice versa).

people through the potential minefield of consumer choice (examples would include the proliferation of consumer lifestyle magazines and the popularity of TV 'makeover' programmes such as *Changing Rooms* and *Ground Force*).

Other authors have insisted on the continued salience of class in contemporary accounts of identity formation, particularly in association with other identity markers such as gender. A particularly good example is Beverley Skeggs' study of *Formations of Class and Gender* (1997), based on long-term ethnographic work with 83 white, working-class women in north-west England. The subtitle of Skeggs' book, 'becoming respectable', provides a good introduction to the subtle ways in which class continues to shape women's everyday lives, whether in terms of their childcare practices or how they dress when going out for the evening. As one of Skeggs' informants told her:

> *All the time you've got to weigh everything up: is it too tarty? Will I look a right slag in it? What will people think? It drives me mad that every time you go to put your clothes on you have to think 'do I look dead common? Is it rough? Do I look like a dog?'*

(Skeggs, 1997: 3)

Skeggs argues that contemporary formations of class and gender involve a complex process of identification and dis-identification (including the refusal to be identified as working class) as social judgements are constantly being made and re-made. Her account shows how class operates at an intimate and emotional level even whilst others have argued that its effects are disintegrating at a wider structural level.

Collective identities are also being reshaped by new communications media such as the internet, the mobile phone and satellite television. These media are particularly significant in a context of increasing mobility where many people (such as migrants, asylum seekers and refugees) typically conduct their lives over long distances, often involving a series of transnational connections (Hannerz, 1996). David Morley and Kevin Robins (1995) have argued that new 'spaces of identity' are emerging in response to these diasporic conditions where Europe's relations with its most significant others (America, Islam and the Orient) are being redefined. Others have argued that increasing numbers of people now inhabit this diasporic or transnational space (see Chapter 37). Moreover, this space is not just occupied by those who are themselves members of specific transnational migrant communities (Brah, 1996; Jackson *et al.*, 2004). Examples would include the growing popularity of 'Indian' food or 'Asian'-inspired music and fashion amongst white British consumers, many of whom participate in the symbolic and material spaces associated with other cultures without ever leaving home.

As these examples show, new conceptions of space and place, associated with ideas of **diaspora** or transnationality, are giving rise to new ideas about personal and collective identity (see also Chapter 37). Though we have grown accustomed to thinking about places as coherent and bounded entities, recent work has challenged these ideas. Doreen Massey (1991), in particular, has argued for a more 'progressive' sense of place in which the

Transnational

an adjective used to describe processes that have escaped the bounded confines of the NATION-STATE. These have been identified in the realms of the economy (*see* TRANSNATIONAL CORPORATIONS), in politics (for instance, through the political agency of groups in relation to a nation-state they do not reside in; e.g. Kurdish exiles campaigning for Kurdish nationalism) and in culture (for example, through the identification of 'transnational communities' that have dispersed from an originary homeland into a number of other countries but that also have strong linkages across this DIASPORA).

Diaspora

the dispersal or scattering of people from their original home. As a noun it can be used to refer to a dispersed 'people' (hence the Jewish diaspora or the Black diaspora). However, it also refers to the actual processes of dispersal and connection that produce any scattered, but still in some way identifiable, population. In this light it also can be used as an adjective – diasporic – to refer to the senses of home, belonging and cultural identity held by a dispersed population.

emphasis is on the connections between places, looking outwards, rather than on the assertion of internal coherence, looking inwards. This assertion of the flows and networks through which places are made and re-made is entirely consistent with relational notions of identity, seen as multiple and contingent, rather than notions of a fixed or singular identity, based on some allegedly intrinsic characteristic. As Roger Rouse has argued (in the context of Mexican migration to the USA).

> *The comfortable modern imagery of nation-states and national languages, of coherent communities and consistent subjectivities, of dominant centers and distant margins no longer seems adequate ... [D]uring the last 20 years, we have all moved irrevocably into a new kind of social space.*

(Rouse, 1991: 8)

I would suggest that a similar argument about the porous boundaries of place and identity can be made in many different parts of the world, not just in those that are characterized by high levels of transnational migration as in the case discussed by Rouse. In a world 'on the move', identities are increasingly complex and unstable, and our theories need to adjust to these changing circumstances.

SUMMARY

- Modern formations of identity are often said to be more complex and reflexive than those in the past.
- As traditional sources of identity (associated with work, family and religion) have waned, new forms of identity have emerged (around consumption issues, for example).
- Place-based identities are increasingly complex (diasporic, transnational, etc.).

NARRATIVES OF IDENTITY

Narrative

narratives are particular kinds of stories that are subject to cultural conventions about authorship, plot, style and audience. Narrative approaches in the social sciences attempt to recover the way that social life is 'storied' in terms of a series of events and how we 'make sense' of those events. Borrowed from historical and literary sources, narrative methods often involve the collection of life-history interviews that use personal testimony to relate the particularities of individual biography to their wider social context.

In this section I'd like to think through the implications of taking a relational approach to identity in terms of how we might put these ideas into practice (for an undergraduate project or dissertation, for example). One implication of my earlier argument is that direct questions, such as are asked in national population censuses and social surveys, are of only limited use in relation to complex issues of identity. The UK National Office of Statistics had enormous difficulty devising an appropriate question about 'ethnic identity' in 2001, with the result that over 600,000 people identified themselves as of 'Mixed' ethnic group and over 200,000 as 'Other' (see Table 28.1). Censuses and surveys are usually better at asking for objective data (such as nationality or birthplace) with qualitative methods usually better suited to more subjective issues such as ethnic or religious identity. This is particularly true where such labels are politically contested as is undoubtedly the case with religion and ethnicity. Whilst many different approaches are possible (see Limb and Dwyer, 2001), I'd like to focus on just one set of methods which I shall call **narrative** approaches to identity.

Giddens' (1991) account of 'reflexive modernization' (referred to

Table 28.1 The UK's minority ethnic population, 2001

	Population	%
White	54,153,898	92.1
Mixed	677,117	1.2
Asian or British Asian		
Indian	1,053,411	1.8
Pakistani	747,285	1.3
Bangladeshi	283,063	0.5
Other Asian	247,664	0.4
Black or Black British		
Black Caribbean	565,876	1.0
Black African	485,277	0.8
Black Other	97,585	0.2
Chinese	247,403	0.4
Other	230,615	0.4
All minority ethnic	4,635,296	7.9
Total population	58,789,194	100

Source: National Office of Statistics (http://www.statistics.gov.uk)

above) describes identity as a reflexive project, shaped by the institutions of late modernity and sustained through narratives of the self that are continually monitored and constantly revised. But Giddens says very little about how these ideas might be put into practice in terms of empirical research. For that we need to turn to other sources, such as Margaret Somers' (1994) account of identity as a discursively constituted social relation, articulated through narratives of the self. According to Somers:

> Narrative identities are constituted by a person's temporally and spatially variable place in culturally constructed stories composed of (breakable) rules, (variable) practices, binding (and unbinding) institutions, and the multiple plots of family, nation, or economic life. Most importantly, however, narratives are not incorporated into the self in any direct way; rather, they are mediated through the enormous spectrum of social and political institutions and practices that constitute our social world.

(Somers, 1994: 635)

There are a number of important features to Somers' account of the narrative construction of identity. An individual's narration must always be located within wider stories associated with family life and wider social institutions. From this it should be apparent that we do not simply construct our own narratives on an individual basis. We are also located within narratives that are not of our own choosing. Second, narrative identities involve a range of discursive practices that go beyond the textual construction of individual biographies. Narratives are culturally constructed, emplotted within the context of other lives and mediated by a range of external factors. Narratives are subject to social regulation through cultural norms and expectations (as in Skeggs' account of respectability, referred to above). Finally, our sense of self is socially and spatially constituted: *who* we are is related in fundamental ways to *where* we are (cf. Bell and Valentine, 1997; Keith and Pile, 1993).

A good way of exploring the relational construction of narrative identities is through the method of life-history interviewing. I'd like to take just one example that demonstrates how our personal identities are crafted in relation to a range of wider forces. The following interview extracts were recorded by Polly Russell in the course of her PhD research on British culinary culture (Russell, 2003). The interviewee, Stephen Hallam, was born in 1956 in Bulwell, Nottinghamshire, and is currently Managing Director of Dickinson & Morris. The company has made pork pies since 1851 and places great emphasis on the quality and authenticity of its products. Despite its commitment to tradition and authenticity, however, to satisfy demand the production process at Dickinson & Morris is becoming increasingly automated and a lot of its pies are now mass produced. During the interview, Stephen Hallam reflected critically on this process, reconciling the inevitability of technological change with his own passionate commitment to traditional craft skills:

> *The pastry case is raised by a machine, the meat is deposited by a machine, the lid is then initially secured, so a stamp comes down to make sure it is well and truly attached to the pie, then it's a pair of hands that puts the crimp on the top, it's a pair of hands that puts the hole in the top, it's a hand that puts the glaze on the top ... Yes, it's a compromise but I don't think you'll ever get a machine that does it all ... You can't substitute that technical knowledge, that knowledge with the hands, the eyes, the nose. You will smell a pie baking and your nose will tell you if something is wrong. Now you tell me a machine that can do that ... As long as you still embody the essence of the heritage there's nothing amiss to using technology to assist you with that.*

(Tape 11, Side B)

Stephen Hallam's interview also emphasizes the significance of place in the construction of personal and institutional identities. Dickinson & Morris's website proudly proclaims that it is 'the oldest pork pie bakery and the last remaining producer of authentic Melton Mowbray pork pies based in the town' (http://www.porkpie.co.uk, accessed 17 August 2004). Dickinson & Morris projects this image to the public through its shop in Melton, Ye Olde Pork Pie Shoppe (see Fig. 28.2), which was renovated following a disastrous fire in 1992. Today, however, as Stephen Hallam readily admits, most of its pies are made in a larger bakery in nearby Leicester:

> *To a lot of consumers, a lot of people, Dickinson & Morris is just the pork pie shop and they believe all these packets of pork pies and sausages you see in the supermarket on shelves come from the shop but in reality they can't. We don't have the space, it's impossible. So we utilise the*

There is an extensive literature on oral history interviewing, with established guidelines on ethics and etiquette, ways of preparing for an interview and putting respondents at ease (see Perks and Thomson, 1998, for a critical introduction). As well as recording the interview on tape, researchers usually prepare a tape summary and/or full transcript of the interview. The challenge is then the interpretative one of making sense of the data – see Limb and Dwyer (2001) for some guidelines.

FIGURE 28.2
Ye Olde Pork Pie Shoppe in Melton Mowbray

resources of our sister companies and divisions in the group ... And the branded products, i.e. all those that are in supermarkets, come from the pork pie bakery facility just on the outskirts of Leicester. **"**

(Tape 4, Side A)

These short extracts cannot do justice to the richness of the longer interview. But, hopefully, they do demonstrate how Stephen Hallam's personal identity is wrapped up in wider processes of social and technological change, including those associated with particular place identities. Hopefully, too, they demonstrate how interviewees are able to reflect critically on the significance of these wider changes in shaping their own identities.

SUMMARY

- Identities often assume a narrative form, in the sense that individual biographies are emplotted within wider contexts.

- One useful way of understanding narrative identities is through the analysis of life histories, an approach that sets personal biographies in their wider relational context.

DISCUSSION POINTS

1. What are the most important aspects of your own identity, and can you articulate this in terms of similarities to and differences from other people?

2. To what extent have identities become more complex in recent years and how would you account for these changes?

3. To what extent are identities related to particular places and how does this work at different spatial scales (from the body to the home, from the neighbourhood to the nation)?

4. How far are our identities fixed (through biological notions of sex or age, for example) and how much scope is there to alter our identities?

5. Using a narrative approach, plan out how you would conduct a life history interview in order to gain a better understanding of your respondent's identity.

FURTHER READING

Jenkins, R. (1996) *Social identities*. London: Routledge.

Part of the 'key ideas' series, this is an accessible introduction to theories of identity, written from the perspective that identities are always social, involving the interplay of similarity and difference.

Pile, S. and Thrift, N. (eds) (1995) *Mapping the subject: geographies of cultural transformation*. London: Routledge.

An important collection of essays by geographers and other social scientists that addresses the subjective dimensions of human experience and the geographies of identity formation at a variety of scales.

Skeggs, B. (1997) *Formations of class and gender*. London: Sage.

A compelling and passionately written research-based account of how working-class women in north-west England negotiate the demands of 'respectability'.

Woodward, K. (ed.) (1997) *Identity and difference*. London: Sage.

Produced as part of the Open University's 'Culture, Media and Identities' series, this is a commendably accessible introduction to theories of identity and difference with chapters on the body, sexualities, motherhood and diaspora.

CHAPTER 29

IDENTITY AND DIFFERENCE: AGE, DIS/ABILITY AND SEXUALITY

INTRODUCTION

Geographical debates about identity and difference have taken two forms in recent decades. One approach has been to dispute **essentialist** assumptions about identity, and argue instead that the differences between us are **socially constructed**. You were introduced to this idea in the previous chapter where we saw that identities are not simply grounded in our individual biology, but are socially constituted through the interleaving of wider processes and the individual's biographical narratives. This social rather than natural constitution of identities means that they are not universal but vary across time and space, reflecting temporal and spatial variations in social relations. Laurie *et al.* (1999) demonstrate, for example, that what it means to be a woman varies over time and space, by tracing changing hegemonic forms of femininity in Britain over the past 200 years, and contrasting these notions with the very different understandings of women's capabilities and responsibilities in communist East Germany and Latin America. Interestingly, as well as varying between times in history and places in the world, socio-spatial relations also shape our ideas of where particular groups are seen to be in and out of place. For example, women's place has, at some points in British history been idealized as in the home, whereas men are seen to be more at home in the workplace (Laurie *et al.*, 1999).

A second contrasting, but not necessarily contradictory, approach to the study of identity and difference draws on **psychoanalytic** traditions. Sibley (1995) is a prominent figure in the use of such approaches. Drawing on Klein (1960), he argues that a sense of border developed in infancy forms the basis from which the Self seeks to distance itself from objects and people defined as abject, as **Other**. These ideas of Self and Other are not innate, but are culturally produced through interaction with the social milieu. One important way in which the subject mediates interaction with this social milieu is through stereotypical understandings of good and bad objects and people. These stereotypical representations of Others not only define the Self (by representing what it is not), they also inform social practices of inclusion and exclusion, processes through which different social groups come to be constructed as in and out of place in particular settings (Sibley, 1995). For example, romantic representations of gypsy travellers as an exotic race living in harmony with nature in gaily painted, horse-drawn caravans construct them as perfectly at home on the highways and byways of rural England; this unreal picture based somewhere in a mythical past works against contemporary city-based gypsy travellers who are often considered out of place in urban space (Kenrick and Clark, 1999; Sibley, 1995).

What is striking is that, despite their very different starting points, both social constructionist and psychoanalytic research on identity suggest a need to pay attention to questions of place and space. On the one hand,

Essentialist/ists/m

the belief that identities, such as class, gender and race, as well as age, dis/ability and sexuality, are directly determined by biology. This view is opposed by SOCIAL CONSTRUCTIONISTS, who argue that these differences between us are shaped through the interweaving of wider socio-spatial processes and individual biographies. The term is often used negatively to emphasize the stereotyping that it can produce.

Socially constructed

a catch-all term that emphasizes how the differences between us are made and remade through the interweaving of wider socio-spatial processes and individual biographies. An emphasis on social construction has been widely drawn upon in Human Geography in order to emphasize how: (a) the things, situations and ideas that surround us are not innate but the products of social forces and practices that require explanation; and (b) nor are they inevitable, instead being open to the possibility of critique and change.

both approaches reject essentialist understandings of identity and emphasize that the constitution of identity and difference is a cultural process and is therefore specific to time and space. On the other hand, they both highlight that these processes can produce highly spatialized understandings of difference, for example as we hold spatially specific understandings of where particular social groups are in or out of place.

This chapter explores these approaches to identity and difference through a focus on three axes of identity: age, dis/ability and sex-

FIGURE 29.1
Credit: Zigy Kaluzny/Getty Images

uality. As we shall see during the course of the chapter, social constructionist approaches to identity have been more important in geographical studies of age, bodily ability and sexuality to date; however, psychoanalytic approaches are becoming increasingly popular. The chapter now considers age in more detail, before moving on to look at the growing literature on dis/ability, and finally sexuality.

AGE

Age as a concept has been, and continues to be, paid relatively little attention within the discipline of geography. Despite some innovative attempts to inspire interest in the geographies of the life course (Katz and Monk, 1993), the most common way in which geographers have engaged with age-related issues is through a focus on those at the extremes of the age spectrum, with children and young people attracting somewhat more attention that older adults.

The 1990s, in particular, saw a rapid increase in the attention paid to children's and young people's geographies (Aitken, 2001; Holloway and Valentine, 2000a; Skelton and Valentine, 1998), and since 2003 this sub-disciplinary field has had its own journal, entitled *Children's Geographies*. Most of the research in this period has been allied to broader social studies of childhood. Researchers in this field argue that child, far from being a biological category, is a socially constructed identity (James *et al.*, 1998). Not only has historical research shown the category child to be a recent invention (it did not exist in the same way in the middle ages, for instance, when young people were regarded as miniature adults rather than conceptually different from adults (Ariès, 1962)), but the qualities supposed natural in children have changed over time. Historically, some

Psychoanalysis, psychoanalytic

largely associated with the work of Freud, psychoanalytic theory concerns itself with the mental life of individuals rather than with any overt observable behaviour, and argues that the most important elements of such mental lives are the unconscious ones. It posits that the unconscious parts of the mind (the 'id') are in perpetual conflict with both the more rational and conscious elements (the 'ego') and with those parts of the mind concerned with conscience (the 'superego'). Psychological disturbances can then be traced to these conflicts, and can be remedied through psychoanalytical therapy, which is able to give an individual insight into their unconscious mental life.

Other, Otherness

usually typographically capitalized, an Other is that person or entity that is understood as opposite or different to oneself; Otherness is the quality of difference which that Other possesses A rather abstract conceptual couplet, potentially applicable at scales varying from the individual person to the global political bloc, these terms have been used in Human Geography to emphasize how ideas about human and geographical difference are structured through oppositions of the Self/Same versus the Other/Different.

versions of Christian doctrine viewed children as 'little devils', as inherently naughty, unruly, unsocialized beings who need to be saved through strict discipline and a religious upbringing (Newson and Newson, 1974; Schnucker, 1990); in contrast, Enlightenment thinkers such as Rousseau imagined children as 'little angels' with natural talents and virtues that could be developed though gentle coaxing by adults (Jenks, 1996). Recognition that childhood is a socially constructed phenomenon has fuelled research into its construction, contestation and consequences, as well prompting a focus on children as competent social actors in their own right rather than simply a concentration on forces of socialization such as school and family (Holloway and Valentine, 2000a).

Geographers have made a distinctively spatial contribution to social studies of childhood (Holloway and Valentine, 2000b). One important contribution has been geographers' insistence that socially constructed ideas about childhood are not only time but also place specific. This means that many of the 'normal' assumptions that we hold about childhood in the West – that children are less able and less competent than adults and thus need to be educated into their future adult roles at the same time as they should be allowed a childhood of innocence and freedom from adult responsibilities – are culturally specific. For example, whilst childhood in the Global North is often seen as a time of dependence, in the Global South many children make essential contributions to the economic and social reproduction of their households through domestic, agricultural and paid work (Punch, 2001; Robson, 1996). Geographical research can thus expose the Eurocentrism of many of our ideas about childhood, assumptions that underpin advances such as the UN convention on the rights of the child. Whilst it is important to recognize cultural difference and avoid judging countries of the South by northern norms, we must balance this with the imperative to ask questions about the global distribution of resources, which means that some children must work to ensure household survival whilst others are faced with an 'epidemic' of obesity and ill-health through reduced physical activity and over-consumption.

In addition to this focus on place, geographers have also considered the everyday spaces in and through which children's identities are made and remade, in so doing considering the ways our ideas of childhood inform, or are informed by wider spatial discourses about home, school, city, rural idyll and nation (see Holloway and Valentine, 2000a, for a more extensive review). One example of this is research on children's use of public space. There is a relatively long history of research into children's attachment to and use of space (Hart, 1979; Ward, 1978), but in the 1990s this began to chime with growing public concern about children's presence in public space. This concern centred on the twin fears that some children (little angels) are vulnerable to dangers in public places, whilst the unruly behaviour of other children (little devils) can risk adult control of public space (Valentine, 1996a; 1996b). Geographic research has considered how parents and children conceive of and negotiate these risks in socio-economically mixed urban and rural areas, emphasizing both the importance of local parenting cultures and children's agency in the construction and contestation of family rules about use of the street

(Valentine, 1997a; 1997b; 1997c). More recent research emphasizes the continuing importance of societal concerns about children's independent use of public space, as well as the importance of these spaces to children of diverse ages, genders, class backgrounds and locations (Lees, 2003; Skelton, 2000; Tucker and Matthews, 2001). This emphasis on age, gender, class, and so on, draws attention to the importance of differences between children within the global North, which exist alongside those differences between North and South that were discussed earlier.

At the other end of the age spectrum, research on older people has numerous parallels with the field of children's geographies. Research into older people's geographies has a relatively long history of geographical research (Rowles, 1978a) and witnessed an expansion of interest (though not of a comparable size) from the mid-1990s (Harper, 1997; Harper and Laws, 1995; Laws, 1994; 1997). Here, too, researchers base their work on social rather than biological understanding of identity, and consider the articulation of age with other social differences:

> Rather than defining and employing old age as a chronological descriptor, many now argue that the socially and economically constructed aspects of old age have most influence on the condition of older people's lives.

(Pain et al., 2000: 377)

Pain et al.'s (2000) study of the way discourses of old age intersect with class, bodily ability and gender in the framing of older people's leisure spaces is an interesting example of this type of work. In this, Pain and her co-authors explore the ways some older people frame their leisure activities in ways that maintain positive images of themselves through contrast with other groups of older adults. For example, some of the retired men in her study who attended a senior men's club organized around educational lectures saw themselves as maintaining a mentally active lifestyle they had been used to at work, and reinforced this positive image of themselves by contrasting their own club with one aimed at retirement-aged middle-class women, which they constructed simply as a place for tea and gossip (despite the fact that it, too, had a talk each week).

Children's and young people's geographies have now been established as a vibrant field, and there is considerably more scope for research on older adults. However, a note of caution needs to be sounded as the current practice of focusing on either end of the age spectrum inadvertently

SUMMARY

- Childhood is a socially constructed identity: it is a recent invention and the qualities supposed natural in children have varied over time.

- Geographers have emphasized the importance of place as well as the sites of everyday life in and through which diverse children's identities are made and remade.

- Old age has attracted less attention, though past and present studies demonstrate the potential for future research into the social construction of old age and its articulation with other axes of identity.

- The focus on the twin extremes of the age spectrum inadvertently normalizes those in the intervening years.

suggests that those in the middle are unmarked by age. This not only establishes this middle group as a norm against which young and old are Othered, it also means that an analysis of the meaning of age for those in the middle years is missing from the geographical research agenda.

DIS/ABILITY

Geographical research on illness, impairment and disability has a complex relation to debates about the social construction of identity. To date research in this fairly diverse field has been shaped by two contrasting models of disability, and by subsequent attempts to move the latter of these two positions forward.

The first, the medical model of disability, has wide social currency within the global North (Parr and Butler, 1999). In this model, disability is regarded as an 'individual medical tragedy' (Shakespeare, 1993, cited in Parr and Butler, 1999: 3). Medical problems are seen to impair some people's bodies such that they cannot undertake activities regarded as normal for a human being; for example a baby born blind cannot see, or someone paralysed as the result of a road traffic accident cannot walk. This is regarded as an individual tragedy, and the person disabled by their medical condition is often seen as deserving of sympathy and dependent on help from able-bodied society (although social discomfort and discrimination are also common reactions to disability – see box).

The response from the medical establishment is to provide interventions that aim to give the individual as normal a life as possible, for example through the provision of cochlea implants to some deaf people or prosthetic limbs to those missing an arm or leg. In some circumstances medical intervention can improve the quality of life for people with disabilities, but it is not universally welcomed. For example, some deaf people are against cochlea implants, arguing that the procedure – which gives some though not full hearing but involves the risk of invasive surgery, potentially destroying any residual hearing, and possible side-effects such as headaches – is an attempt by hearing society to make deaf people conform to their norms, and as such is an attack on well-developed deaf signing culture. The best-known geographer to adopt the medical model is Golledge (1993); he argues that disabled people's experience of space is fundamentally different to that of the able-bodied population; that as geographers we need to understand these different ways of knowing the world; and that having done so we will be able to suggest useful interventions, ranging from the spatial criteria to be included in the assessment of learning disabilities to tactual maps suitable for visually impaired users.

A second approach, which has had wider currency in activist and academic circles, draws on the social model of disability. This model recognizes bodily differences in terms of impairment, but locates disability as a product of society. This is evident in the oft-cited definitions of the terms impairment and disability by the Union of Physically Impaired Against Segregation (UPIAS 1976: 3–4; see Hall, 1995; Holt, 2003; Parr and Butler, 1999):

> " *Impairment – Lacking all or part of a limb, or having a defective limb, organism or mechanism of the body.*
>
> *Disability – The disadvantage or restriction of activity caused by a contemporary social organization which takes no or little account of people who have physical impairments and thus exclude them from the mainstream of social activities.* "

In this model, disability is seen to be a social construction, as the organization of society rather than an individual's medical condition is identified as the root cause of any problems. It is thus society, rather than the individual, that is seen to be in need of change.

One popular way in which this model has been utilized in geography is in studies that seek to show how the current social organization of the built environment disables people with impairments (Imrie, 1996). In a classic piece early in these debates Hahn (1986) discusses a range of problems the urban environment presents for people with impairments, ranging from insufficient provision of dropped kerbs (which enable wheelchair users to get on and off pavements), to a lack of accessible public transport, to poor-quality housing provision. These he locates squarely within a social model of disability:

> " *the major problems resulting from a disability can be traced to a disabling environment; and the solution must be found in laws and policies to change that milieu rather than in unrelenting efforts to improve the capacities of a disabled individual.* "

(Hahn, 1986: 274)

OTHERING PEOPLE WITH DISABILITIES

Notwithstanding the dominance of debates about the medical and social model of disability, there have been some attempts to understand the Othering of people with disabilities through a psychoanalytic lens (Dear *et al.*, 1997; Holt, 2003; Kitchin, 1998; Pain *et al.*, 2001). Holt (2003) provides a particularly useful review of these developments: she argues that the discourses that comprise the medical model of disability parallel the symbolism of abjection in contemporary western society. Abjection, part of the process through which Self defines itself as separate from Other, involves both elements of attraction and repulsion. These twin understandings can be seen in respect to disability: on the one hand we have 'positive' representations of disabled heroes overcoming adversity; on the other, 'negative' narratives in which people with impairments are seen as abnormal, dependent, frightening and unattractive beings. In different ways both these types of 'stories' harm people with disabilities, as neither extreme represents the everyday, ordinariness of living with an impairment.

Dear *et al.* (1997, cited in Holt, 2003) argue that this construction of an abject category disabled reflects a desire on the part of the Self to impose an artificial distinction of disabled/non-disabled on a continuum of human capacity and thereby distance and protect itself from its Other. This distancing is also seen in broader socio-spatial relations, as Holt (2003: 19), in a review of the literature in this field, explains: 'disabled people's historical geographies of socio-spatial exclusion in asylums are [now] being replicated on a smaller scale by the new geographies of "de-institutionalisation"' (see also Dear and Wolch, 1987; Gleeson, 1997).

Source: Holt (2003)

Though not universally embraced, this social model of disability has had a far greater influence on geographic studies of disability than its medical counterpart. However, as Parr and Butler (1999) make clear:

> *in acknowledging the undeniable value of the social model, it is easy to forget that it too is not without fault ... At present society plays the dominant role in constructing disability, but the role of different physical and mental impairments cannot be ignored by the social model if it is to continue to be valued and respected.*

Embodied, embodiment

this concept suggests that the self and the body are not separate, but rather that the experiences of any individual are, invariably, shaped by the active and reactive entity that is their body – irrespective of whether this is conscious or not. The argument, then, runs that the uniqueness of human experience is due, at least in part, to the unique nature of individual bodies.

Much contemporary research on disability thus starts with an appreciation of the social model of disability but also seeks to nuance it in important ways. One way in which this is achieved is to reincorporate appreciation of the pain and physical difficulties impairments can cause into more recent work, thus treating disability both as a social construct and as an **embodied** experience. Equally important has been the move away from an overemphasis on physical impairments and the incorporation of a focus on chronic illness (Dyck, 1999; Moss, 1999) as well as mental difference, including mental ill-health, learning disabilities and, most recently, emotional and behaviour difficulties (Hall and Kearns, 2001; Holt, 2003; Lemon and Lemon, 2003; Parr, 1999). Underlying all of this is an appreciation that dis/ability inevitably articulates with other social differences (Parr and Butler, 1999).

SUMMARY

- The medical model locates disability as an 'individual medical tragedy'. Geographical studies based on this model aim to identify ways in which disabled people can be helped to cope with their problems.

- The social model posits disability as a socially constituted problem, stemming from the current organization of society. Geographical studies based on this model aim to expose the ways in which the environment currently disables people, and suggest alternative ways forward.

- Most current research favours the social over the medical model of disability, but suggests that it needs to incorporate an appreciation of disability as an embodied experience, and broaden its focus to include chronic illness, mental health and learning disabilities.

- Dis/ability articulates with other forms of social difference.

SEXUALITY

Geographers focusing on sexuality have tended to pay less explicit attention to debates about essentialism. Those who have addressed this highlight the difficult issues it raises for activists and academics alike (Bell and Valentine, 1995a). On the one hand, some lesbians and gay men are happy to support scientific research that seeks to uncover a genetic basis for sexual orientation. Finding a 'gay gene' would substantiate claims that homosexuality is 'natural', and thus ought not to be cause for discrimination and abuse. On the other hand, these essentialist arguments are rejected both by some lesbian feminists who argue that sexuality is a choice, and more broadly by social constructionists who argue that sexuality, like all other identities, is socially constituted. For some, strategic essentialism is a way out of this dilemma: academics and activists employing this tactic hold a broadly constructionist approach to identity but deploy essentialist arguments when these are politically useful (Bell and Valentine, 1995a; see also Hubbard, 2002, on the possibilities of marrying social constructionist and psychoanalytic approaches). Regardless of whether opposite-sex or same-sex attraction has some basis in biology, however, the way hetero-, bi- and homosexual identities are shaped, experienced and performed is inevitably (also) shaped by socio-spatial relations, such that what it means to be a heterosexual, a bisexual, a lesbian or a gay man varies not only over time but also between places and spaces.

One of the first ways in which geographers began to look at sexuality was through an exploration of the formation and impact of 'gay neighbourhoods' in the urban landscape of the global North (Binnie and Valentine, 1999). Paralleling early research on the segregation of racialized minorities, initial studies examined the choice and constraint factors that produced clusters of commercial gay venues and drew gay men to the city (Castells, 1983; Lyod and Rowntree, 1978; Weightman, 1981; Winchester and White, 1988). As this approach developed researchers sought to explore the links between capitalism and gay space: this has included studies of the gentrifying role some gay men have played in the urban land market (Knopp, 1990), and research into the impact business marketing has on sexualized space – for example, the implications of branding Manchester's Gay Village as a cosmopolitan spectacle, authentically gay but open to all consumers regardless of sexual orientation (Binnie and Skeggs, 2004).

By the 1990s the exclusion of lesbians from debates about 'gay neighbourhoods', on the grounds that as women they had less economic power and fewer territorial aspirations than gay men (Castells, 1983), was no longer tenable. Rothernberg's (1995) study of Park Slope, Brooklyn, New York, demonstrates that there are indeed 'lesbian neighbourhoods', and questions the orientation of previous work that emphasized commercial venues, by demonstrating the importance of social networks in community formation (see also Adler and Brenner, 1992; Peake, 1993; Valentine, 1993a; as well as Williams Paris and Anderson, 2001, on faith-based queer spaces). The overwhelming urban emphasis of these studies is increasingly being counterbalanced by research that focuses on 'the gay experience' in suburban and rural landscapes (Kirkey and Forsyth, 2001; Kramer, 1995; Smith and Holt, 2004); however, there is still a paucity of research on lesbian and gay geographies in the global South (Visser, 2003).

The inclusion of a focus on women marked a broadening in the way geographers look at lesbian and gay landscapes. Valentine's (1993c) work was key in this respect: through a study of lesbians in an unnamed UK town she explored the ways in which everyday spaces such as the street, the workplace, social spaces, service environments and the home are often 'heterosexed' – that is, shaped by normative expectations of heterosexuality with 'aberrant' behaviour being policed through stares and gestures, as well as verbal and physical abuse. For example, the heterosexing of public space means that whilst heterosexual couples can

Capitalism

an economic system in which the production and distribution of goods is organized around the profit motive (*see* CAPITAL ACCUMULATION) and characterized by marked inequalities in the social division of work and wealth between private owners of the materials and tools of production (capital) and those who work for them to make a living (labour) (*see* CLASS).

FIGURE 29.2
A heterosexual geography of home.
Credit: Lorna Ainger

hold hands or kiss goodbye in the street, the same behaviour from same-sex couples is likely to attract attention, and sometimes verbal or physical sanctions against them. Understanding of the heterosexing of society and space, and challenges to this, have been taken forward through research on everyday residential, employment, shopping and social spaces (Kitchin and Lysaght, 2003; Podmore, 2001) as well as more out of the ordinary events such as parades (Brickell, 2000; Marston, 2002).

In contrast, heterosexuality has received less attention from geographers. In the past there was a 'general silence' concerning marginal forms of heterosexuality (Jackson, 1989: 115), with Symanski's (1981) study of prostitution being the best-known exception to this trend. Contemporary work exploring the importance of sex work in the city, including studies of residents' reactions to prostitution in their neighbourhood and legal attempts to cleanse the streets of sex advertising, has now been mainstreamed (Hubbard, 1999; 2002; Hubbard and Sanders, 2003). However, there is still an under-representation of research on 'moral' forms of sexuality, not least because it is harder (for heterosexuals at least) to see how schools, churches, supermarkets and the like are shaped by these normative forms of heterosexuality (Hubbard, 2000). Some studies that seek to explore 'moral' versions of heterosexuality do so as it has emerged as important in the context of broader projects: McDowell's (1995) research on heterosexuality in the City of London, and Holloway *et al.*'s (2000) study of the heterosexual economy of the IT classroom fall into this category. However, other researchers are taking heterosexuality as their primary focus: Little (2003), for example, examines normative heterosexuality in a rural context, whilst Nast (2000) theorizes the links between racism and the oedipal family.

SUMMARY

• Sexual identities are shaped by socio-spatial relations, such that what it means to be a heterosexual, a bisexual, a lesbian or a gay man varies over time and space.

• Geographers have explored the formation and implications of 'gay and lesbian neighbourhoods' in the urban landscape. This is now being matched by research on rural areas.

• The (contested) heterosexing of public, work, residential and other spaces is also a key focus of concern.

• Marginal forms of heterosexuality have attracted more attention than their 'moral' counterparts, prompting calls for more studies of normative heterosexuality in the future.

CONCLUSION

Each of the axes of social difference discussed in this chapter has witnessed a blossoming of research from the last decade of the twentieth century onwards. Although age, dis/ability and sexuality are widely assumed in society to be biological givens, researchers in each of these fields have teased out the ways these identities are made and remade through socio-spatial relations. Most of this has been informed by social constructionist thinking as the use of psychoanalytic approaches, though increasing, is still less common in respect to age, dis/ability and sexuality than for some other forms of social difference. Regardless of which approach is adopted, all the axes of identity discussed in this and the previous chapter are mutually articulated such that, for example, an older person's experience of age is shaped by their social class, just as a gay man's sexuality is experienced through his dis/ability, ethnicity, and so on. The challenge for social geographers in the future is to explore normalized, unmarked identities (the middle years on the age spectrum, abled identities, moral heterosexuality) in the same depth as we have considered more marginal identity positionings. In doing so, we need to redress the balance and pay at least as much attention to the Global South as we do the North.

DISCUSSION POINTS

1. There is a bias in the geographical research agenda towards studying identity in the Global North. Why is this problematic and what areas for future research can you identify focusing on the Global South?

2. How might a psychoanalytic approach usefully inform geographical research on age?

3. Why do social differences such as age, class, ethnicity, gender and sexuality matter in geographical research on disability?

4. Why is it important for geographers to study heterosexuality, and how might we set about studying normative versions of this particular sexual orientation?

FURTHER READING

Holloway, S.L. and Valentine, G. (2000) *Children's geographies: playing, living, learning.* **London: Routledge.**

Chapter 1 provides a detailed introduction to the field of children's geographies; it is followed by empirical studies focusing on the global North and, to a lesser extent, the South.

Pain, R. (2001) Age, generation and lifecourse. In R. Pain, M. Barke, D, Fuller, J. Gough, R. McFarlane and G. Mowl, *Introducing social geographies.* **London: Arnold, 141–63.**

A nice introductory textbook chapter specifically about age.

Canadian Geographer **(2003) Special issue on disability in society and space, 47(4).**

A recent, wide-ranging special issue on dis/ability.

Kitchin, R. and Lysaght, K. (2003) Heterosexism and the geographies of everyday life in Belfast, Northern Ireland. *Environment and Planning A*, 35, 489–510.

This paper on the sexual production of space draws on interviews with gay, lesbian, bisexual and transgender individuals, and covers a diversity of sites, including the home, work and social space.

Little, J. (2003) 'Riding the rural love train': heterosexuality and the rural community. *Sociologia Ruralis*, 43, 401–17.

A paper specifically devoted to 'moral' forms of heterosexuality in a rural context.

Sibley, D. (1999) Creating geographies of difference. In D. Massey, J. Allen and P. Sarre (eds) *Human Geography today.* **Cambridge: Polity, 115–28.**

A good introduction to psychoanalytical approaches to difference.

CHAPTER 30
EXCLUSION

Jon May

INTRODUCTION

'Exclusion' is a word that many people are familiar with but may find difficult to define. These difficulties arise, in part, from the very different ways in which the word is used – both in everyday life and within the rather more restricted (but no less confusing) world of academic geography.

For those with an interest in British politics, for example, the word may be familiar from the seemingly endless references by politicians and pundits to the new mantra of 'social exclusion': a phrase that suggests a concern with material inequalities – of healthcare, education, housing or employment, for example. For others, the word may have quite different connotations. Speaking more strongly of the symbolic rather than the material world, here the notion of 'exclusion' is strongly connected to the idea of **stigma** – referring to the way in which particular individuals or groups may come to be viewed as standing apart from and as posing a threat to 'normal' society.

A useful way through this confusion is to turn to the definition of 'exclusion' provided by the social geographer Chris Philo. For Philo, exclusion refers to: 'A situation in which certain members of society are, or become, separated from much that comprises the normal "round" of living, and working within that society', and should be thought of

> *as simultaneously social and spatial. Indeed, excluded individuals will tend to slip outside, or even become unwelcome visitors within, those spaces which come to be regarded as the loci of 'mainstream' social life (e.g. middle class suburbs, upmarket shopping malls, or prime public space).*

(Philo, 2000: 751)

It is the role that *space* plays in processes of exclusion that holds most interest for social geographers and is the focus of the current chapter. Within the growing body of work by social geographers exploring themes of exclusion, however, two broad trajectories can be traced.

Mirroring the distinction drawn above, the first has focused mainly upon the ways in which certain individuals or groups come to be constructed as 'different' to 'normal' society. That is, it is concerned with the role of the symbolic, and with the kinds of questions relating to identity explored in the previous two chapters.

The second is more obviously concerned with the causes and consequences of the various material inequalities alluded to in discussions of 'social exclusion'. Part of a long-standing interest by social geographers in questions of inequality and social justice, this second body of work connects more strongly to current political debates and with the concerns of social policy.

Stigma

a social process leading to the devaluation of an individual or group(s) who over time come to be identified as embodying negative traits such as dirt, disorder, laziness, criminality or mental illness. Human Geographers are especially interested in the spatial practices by which stigmatized groups come to be separated from mainstream society – thus re-enforcing the boundaries between the 'normal' and the 'deviant'.

Because social geography is a relatively 'broad church', the current chapter explores the ideas associated with both bodies of work. It also points to some of the exciting possibilities that emerge when the two are brought together.

A GEOGRAPHY OF OUTSIDERS

The first person to explore the notion of the geographies of exclusion in any detail was the social geographer David Sibley. In his *Outsiders in Urban Society* (1981), he noted how stigmatized groups commonly inhabit the geographical margins of society. Through a detailed investigation of the lifeworlds of 'gypsies', 'travellers' and the North American Inuit, Sibley investigated the role that spatial boundaries play in maintaining social boundaries. As he recognized, as those considered socially 'marginal' are either pushed towards or, in an attempt to avoid confrontation and abuse, seek out geographically marginal spaces, space emerges as both an expression of and a means by which exclusionary practices gain purchase and meaning.

Developing these ideas further, in *Geographies of Exclusion* (1995) Sibley set out to explain the dynamics of such practices. Drawing upon the ideas of Objects Relations Theory (a body of work associated with the psycho-analysts Melanie Klein and Julia Kristeva), Sibley argued that western identities are structured by an innate need to differentiate between those considered to be broadly the same and those identified as fundamentally Different – or 'Other'. Having constructed such a distinction in their infancy, people are then engaged in a life-long struggle to maintain this distinction lest that which is Different undermines a clear and coherent sense of 'Self' (what Sibley refers to as the fear of pollution, or 'abjection'). One way of maintaining this distinction is to ensure a suitable physical distance is also maintained between 'Self' and 'Other' though, as Sibley recognizes, distance per se is rather less important than the fact that a clear and unambiguous boundary be established between the two.

Though in Object Relations Theory these ideas are mainly developed at the inter-personal level, it is not difficult to see how they can be applied at a broader scale, or why they might be attractive to social geographers. In fact, geographers have drawn on Sibley's work in two main ways. First, inspired by his more general call to explore the social geography of 'outsiders', an increasing body of work has begun to unpack the experiences of those positioned outside of 'mainstream' society, with studies of children and elderly people, the physically disabled, the mentally ill, and so on. Second, drawing on his reading of Object Relations Theory, geographers have turned to Sibley in an attempt to better understand the role that spatial boundaries play in maintaining the distinctions between outsider groups and mainstream society.

Whilst we could think of numerous examples of such 'boundary marking' one of the most obvious concerns the nature and design of prisons. Whilst prisons are in one sense designed to keep people *in*, they are also understood as a way of keeping prisoners at a *safe distance from* 'decent society'. This is one reason why prisons housing the most dangerous prisoners (the 'criminally insane', for example) are often built some distance away from centres of population (in places like Dartmoor – see below). The use of space as a way of separating the 'good' from the 'bad' continues within prisons themselves: with those who break prison rules consigned to solitary confinement.

SUMMARY

- Western identities are structured by an innate need to differentiate between 'Self' and 'Other'.
- To avoid contamination of the 'Self' by the 'Other' people strive to establish clear and unambiguous boundaries between the two. These boundaries often take physical form.
- Spatial boundaries therefore play an important role in maintaining social boundaries.

LIFE AT THE MARGINS

As Sibley also recognized, one of the earliest and most powerful sources of 'abjection' is the fear of bodily residues (Sibley, 1995). As such, it is not surprising that particularly reviled individuals and groups may in turn also come to be associated with 'dirt' or 'shit', and hence be shunned by mainstream society. Alternatively, a process of 'stigma by spatial association' may come in to play, whereby those who live or work in 'dirty' environments may themselves come to be viewed as 'dirty' and treated accordingly.

Exactly such a process is explored by Chris Philo in his study of tin workers in the south-west of England. For Philo, the exclusions suffered by 'tinners' can be understood as a result of the associations drawn between tinners and the harsh and unusual environment in which they lived and worked.

From the mid-fifteenth to the closing decades of the nineteenth century, British tin mining was concentrated on Dartmoor, a wild and remote upland area in the far south-west of England. Because of its remoteness from surrounding towns and cities, the tinners of Dartmoor led a relatively isolated life: living and working in small settlements, cut off for long periods of time from their wives and families and from the rest of society.

FIGURE 30.1
The physical exclusion of the socially marginal.

This geographical isolation encouraged a perception of tinners as likewise socially remote. Such ideas were in turn fuelled by the associations that were drawn between the relatively 'wild' environment in which tinners worked and the wild nature of tinners themselves (see box).

Such apparent wildness positioned tinners in an ambiguous light. For some contemporaries, the unusually close relationship between tin miners

THE WILD TINNER

In the extract below, the 'wildness' of the miner is presented as a product of the dangers of mining (with 'rough work' producing 'rough characters'). But the extract also hints at a certain closeness of fit between the relatively wild environment in which the miners work and the character of the miners themselves: as they forego the 'civilized' pleasures of a cup to drink directly from their shovels, for example. This construction of miners as 'close to nature' placed miners in an ambiguous light.

" *[H]is apparel is course [sic], his dyet sklender, his lodginge harde, his feedynge commonly course breade and hard cheese, and hi drincke is water, and for lacke of a cupe he drynketh it out of his spade or shovell ... his lyffe most commonly is in pyttes and caves under the grounde of a great depth and in greate danger because the earthe above his hedd is in sundry places crossed and posted over with tymber to keepe the same from falling.* "

Greeves, 1981: 79–80, quoted in Philo, 1998: 165)

and the environment in which they worked positioned tinners as 'close to nature' and thus as enjoying a lifestyle to be envied. Hence, in 1630 Thomas Westlake noted how the ability of the tinners to work according to the rhythm of 'nature's demand' enabled them to 'sleep soundly without careful thoughts' (quoted in Greeves, 1981: 80, in Philo, 1998: 166). Re-working the nature–culture binary (see Chapter 1), for others this same wildness invoked only the obvious distance between the tinners' lives and the moral order of settled society. In stark contrast to Thomas Westlake, then, nineteenth-century commentators drew a series of disparaging comparisons between the productivity and moral fortitude of local farming communities and the idleness and immorality of those in the mining camps.

Importantly, however, the exclusions suffered by tinners did not go unchallenged. More specifically, whilst the isolation of the mining settlements was a major factor in the stigma that came to be attached to tin mining it also provided mine workers with certain freedoms not enjoyed elsewhere. In contrast to colleagues in less specialized industries, for example, tinners were able to exert considerable control over their pay and working conditions. Under the remit of what was called 'Stannary Law', miners also stood beyond the reach of Common Law: being tried and sentenced by specialist 'stannary courts' instead – in front of a jury made up entirely of local tinners.

Though such freedoms should not be overestimated (and there is good evidence to suggest that the stannary courts were anything but lenient)

SUMMARY

- One of the most powerful sources of 'abjection' is the fear of bodily residues. As a result, especially reviled individuals or groups may also come to be viewed as 'dirt' or 'shit'.
- Those living or working in 'dirty' environments may also come to be viewed as 'dirty' via a process of 'stigma by spatial association'.
- Such groups often come to inhabit marginal spaces and places – whether because pushed there, or as they seek some reprieve from confrontation and abuse.
- Processes of socio-spatial exclusion rarely go unchallenged.
- Marginal spaces may provide marginalized groups with a certain autonomy over their lives.

they are important. Not least, they remind us that whilst processes of exclusion may on occasions be vigorously resisted, a life at the margins may also, in some cases at least, offer those cast as 'outsiders' the chance to exercise a certain autonomy over their lives.

FROM POVERTY TO SOCIAL EXCLUSION

Whilst the notion of 'exclusion' was placed upon the geographical agenda by the work of David Sibley, discussions of 'social exclusion' emanated in policy circles – first in France, and more recently in Britain and the USA. Its rise to pre-eminence in the UK can be traced back to June 1998, when the New Labour government announced the formation of its Social Exclusion Unit.

Though definitions of social exclusion vary, the term can best be understood as an attempt to broaden discussions of poverty and inequality so as to take account of the range of life opportunities that are systematically denied to those at the bottom of society. A useful working definition in this regard is provided by Eisenstadt and Witcher, for whom social exclusion refers to 'the outcome of processes and/or factors which bar access to participation in **civil society**', including access to 'legal justice, the labour market and political processes' (1998: 6).

Crucially, then, the experience of social exclusion is understood to be multidimensional: such that those excluded from the labour market are also likely to be those living in the worst housing, suffering problems of ill-health or little engaged in the political process. Any responses to the problems of social exclusion must therefore be likewise multifaceted, working to confront problems of social exclusion on a number of fronts at once.

One of the main reasons behind the setting up of the New Labour government's Social Exclusion Unit was the recognition that a new kind of response to the problems of social exclusion necessitated new ways of working for those in government. Rather than have different government departments all pulling in different directions, one of the key aims of the Social Exclusion Unit was to encourage government departments to work together: with new programmes from the Department of Health working alongside projects by the Department for Education and Science, for example.

The extent to which such aims have been realized is open to debate. For Ruth Levitas (1998), for example, one of the problems with discussions of social exclusion is that the concept remains so broad that it enables politicians to pick and choose which aspects of the problem they wish to focus upon according to political expediency. Developing this point, Levitas has suggested that despite paying lip-service to the idea of social exclusion as a multifaceted problem, the approach of the New Labour government to these problems has remained curiously one-dimensional: focused almost entirely on attempts to get more people back in to paid employment. More generally, Levitas suggests that New Labour's attempts to tackle problems of social exclusion have been hampered by a tendency to work with quite different, and competing, understandings of the term, each of which suggests quite different policy responses (see box).

Civil society

a concept with a long and changing history of meanings, civil society has been used in the last decade to emphasize a realm of social life and a range of social institutions that are separate from the NATION-STATE.

COMPETING DISCOURSES OF SOCIAL EXCLUSION

Rather than a single understanding of social exclusion, Ruth Levitas (1998) has suggested that we can trace three different and competing **discourses** of social exclusion in circulation in Britain today.

A *redistributive discourse* (RED) understands people to be excluded as a result of the limited material resources available to them. The way to tackle social exclusion is therefore to raise the income of the poorest groups in society, whether through increased wages or benefits.

By contrast, a *social integrationist discourse* (SID) stresses the rights *and* responsibilities of excluded groups. Rather than simply increase benefits (and thus maintain people's position on the 'edge' of society) it holds that the best way to reintegrate the excluded in to mainstream society is by encouraging people back in to paid work – irrespective of the nature, or quality, of that work.

Finally, a *moral underclass discourse* (MUD) sees social exclusion as the result of the individual failings and moral degeneracy of the excluded themselves. Here the poorest members of society become represented as idle scroungers and benefit cheats who have no one to blame for their position but themselves. The appropriate response to such people is understood to be a punitive one: tightening the eligibility requirements placed on benefit receipt and lowering the real value of benefits so as to 'encourage' people in to the workplace.

As Levitas argues, though RED, SID and MUD suggest the need for quite different responses to social exclusion, New Labour's discussions of social exclusion contain elements of all three (though leaning more strongly to SID and MUD). This confusion may be one reason that the government's responses to the problems of social exclusion have been less successful than it would have hoped.

Discourse, discursive

drawing on the work of the French philosopher Michel Foucault, Human Geographers define discourses as ways of talking about, writing or otherwise representing the world and its geographies (*see also* REPRESENTATION). Discursive approaches to Human Geography emphasize the importance of these ways of representing. They are seen as shaping the realities of the worlds in which we live, rather than just being ways of portraying a reality that exists outside of language and thought. They are also seen as connected to questions of practice – that is, what people actually do – rather than being confined to a separate realm of images or ideas. More specifically, Human Geographers have stressed the different ways in which people have discursively constructed the world in different times and places, and examined how it is that particular ways of talking about, conceptualizing and acting on people and places come to be seen as natural and common-sensical in particular contexts.

Though there is much to be said for Levitas's critique, it does not tell the whole story. Other initiatives by the British government have been much more obviously in tune with the idea of 'joined up solutions' to a 'joined up problem'. Interestingly, the programmes most obviously in accord with the understandings of social exclusion outlined at the beginning of this section are those that have taken an areal approach: targeting resources towards particular neighbourhoods. Thus, government programmes like New Deal for Communities, Health Action Zones and Educational Action Zones have tended to overlap, enabling teams working at the local level to target a range of problems in the same neighbourhood.

Given the geographical focus of these kinds of programmes, and geographers' long-standing interest in questions of inequality and social justice, it is hardly surprising that social geographers have found much to interest them in debates around social exclusion. Hence, there now exists a whole host of studies tracing the growing gap in a range of indicators of well-being and social exclusion between the wealthiest and poorest neighbourhoods in both Britain and the USA, with studies addressing everything from differences in levels of employment and income (Clark and McNicholas, 1996), early mortality and ill-health (Dorling, 1997), to educational attainment (Gordon, 1999).

Yet it is also fair to say that geographers in both countries have tended to concentrate on particular aspects of social exclusion rather than attempting to understand it 'in the round'. They have also exerted more energy in tracing its consequences than on developing new ways of understanding its causes.

A notable exception is provided by Wacquant (1999). Setting debates about social exclusion in their broader context, Wacquant has developed a framework for understanding the emergence of what he calls 'advanced marginality' in the heart of the major western cities. The emergence of such problems, he suggests, can be put down to four intersecting 'dynamics': the resurgence of social inequality, or what Wacquant calls the 'macro-social dynamic'; changes in the world of work (notably the growth of both high-paid and low-paid employment, and rising unemployment) – the 'economic dynamic'; the restructuring of state welfare systems (the 'political dynamic'); and a greater tendency towards a geographical concentration of both the richest and poorest households in particular neighbourhoods, and the growing stigmatization of the poor and poorer neighbourhoods – the 'spatial dynamic'. Whilst these dynamics can be traced across most advanced western countries, differences in *intensity* and in the way in which they *combine* in different places means that their outcome also differs from one place to another.

FIGURE 30.2
Credit: courtesy of North Huyton New Deal for Communities/Geoff Roberts

Wacquant's framework is useful for a number of reasons. Not least, by including a discussion of stigma, Wacquant offers a means of bringing together two previously distinct sets of debates around 'exclusion' and 'social exclusion': the one dealing with questions of 'culture' and 'identity', the other with the 'nitty-gritty' of poverty and inequality.

In the final section of this chapter, I examine the value of Wacquant's framework with an examination of the exclusions suffered by homeless people.

SUMMARY

- The notion of 'social exclusion' emerged in policy circles in France. It has become a major organizing theme for the provision of welfare in Britain under the New Labour government.

- Social exclusion is a *multidimensional* phenomenon, with those excluded from the labour market also likely to be living in the worst housing, suffering problems of ill-health, etc. Any responses to the problems of social exclusion must therefore be likewise multifaceted.

- The New Labour government's response to problems of social exclusion has been criticized as being confused and one-dimensional. The most effective responses have taken an 'areal approach' – tackling a number of interrelated problems in a single neighbourhood.

- Social geographers have traced the *consequences* of social exclusion across a range of domains (including employment, housing, health and education).

- The best attempts to explain the *causes* of social exclusion combine an emphasis on recent changes in employment and welfare with an account of the increasing concentration of poor households in particular areas, and of the growing sense of *stigma* experienced by the poorest members of society.

LIFE ON THE STREETS

Wacquant's framework is especially useful when trying to make sense of the nature of, and responses to, the crisis of homelessness that began to unfold in Britain in the mid- to late 1980s and that continues to the present day. As Wacquant suggests, the roots of this crisis can be traced to changes in the British labour market and to the restructuring of Britain's welfare system.

With regards to the former, in the early 1980s the then Conservative government embarked upon a major restructuring of the British space-economy, encouraging the growth of service-sector and high-tech employment at the expense of Britain's traditional manufacturing base. The result was a steady rise in the number of high-paid, service-sector jobs alongside rising unemployment. Particular sections of Britain's workforce were hit especially hard by such changes. By 1990, for example, almost a third of Britain's long-term unemployed consisted of people aged between 16 and 24 years of age (Heddy, 1990).

The impact of such changes was amplified by changes to Britain's welfare system. Following a sharp reduction in the money made available for the construction of new local authority housing (down from some £7.2 billion in 1978/79 to just £1.6 billion in 1989/90) and the sale of existing local authority stock, poorer groups began to face a severe shortage of affordable accommodation (Blake and Dwelly, 1994). For others it became increasingly difficult to keep a roof over their heads, even when accommodation was available. Following the passage of the Social Security Act 1986, for example, 16 and 17 year olds became ineligible for Income Support, leaving thousands of young people with no visible means of support (Hutson and Liddiard, 1994).

As a result of these changes, levels of homelessness began to rise dramatically. By 1990, some 140,350 households – or approximately 420,000 people – were officially registered as 'homeless' by local authorities across England and Wales (up from 80,500 households in 1984). Adding to these, some 20,000 or so single people were staying in night shelters and hostels, and a further 3000 sleeping rough, in central London alone by the turn of the decade. Significantly, a growing proportion of those staying in night shelters and hostels were young people, with those under the age of 30 accounting for almost four out of ten of all hostel residents by 1990 (Anderson et al., 1993).

The consequences of such developments were disastrous. As the number of people sleeping rough soared so too did the number of people dying on the streets of Britain. By the mid-1990s, for example, one charity famously reported the average age of death of a person sleeping rough in London to be just 47. As more and more people were forced to take refuge in increasingly crowded shelters, levels of tuberculosis also rose, sparking fears of a new epidemic (Shaw et al., 1999). And on the streets themselves, members of the public were confronted daily with the spectre of people begging for food and change.

Whilst Wacquant's framework can help us understand the roots of Britain's homelessness crisis, however, it also enables a better understanding of the limited response that the crisis generated. Most obviously, responses to homelessness are powerfully shaped by the *stigma* suffered by homeless people.

The American geographer Louis Takahashi (1996) has suggested four main roots to this stigma. First, in so far as they are usually under- or unemployed, homeless people tend to be viewed as *unproductive*. In a society that accords a privileged status to economic productivity homeless people are therefore afforded at best a marginal position and at worst come to be viewed as a drain on collective resources. Second, having apparently lost contact with friends and family, homeless people are commonly perceived as 'disaffiliated' – as existing outside the comforts (and constraints) of mainstream social life. Third, whether because of their own habits or because of stereotyping, homeless people often come to be associated with other stigmatized, and threatening groups: drug addicts, alcoholics and the mentally ill, for example. Fourth, as by necessity those living on the streets do in public that which is usually done in private (eating, sleeping and bathing, for example) the sense of Difference homeless people articulate and the apparent threat they pose is heightened by their greater visibility and poor personal aesthetics.

As Takahashi also recognizes, however, the degree of stigma suffered by homeless people differs according (in part) to the extent to which a person might be understood as responsible for the circumstances in which they find themselves. Hence, whilst a homeless child might be afforded considerable sympathy, a single homeless man is likely to engender a far less charitable response.

Exactly such a distinction is evident in responses to Britain's homelessness crisis. Under the provisions of the Housing (Homeless Persons) Act 1977, people with dependants who become homeless have a right to be rehoused by their local authority. No such duty of care is extended to single people, however. Understood as responsible for their own plight, single people who become homeless must rely instead upon the generosity of the charitable sector for the provision of emergency accommodation.

Despite the scale of the crisis unfolding before them through the 1980s and 1990s, successive British governments failed ever to challenge this basic distinction. Rather than offer housing to all, Conservative and New Labour governments alike offered only a minimal response to the problems faced by Britain's single homeless people: providing some £430 million to local charities to increase the supply of emergency accommodation for those sleeping rough between 1990 and 2002. When set against the £5.6 billion cut from the local authority housing budget over the course of the previous decade it is clear that the needs of single homeless people do not figure highly on the government agenda.

When set against other responses to the crisis of street homelessness unfolding in Britain through the 1990s, however, the response of central government looks positively progressive. In June 1990, for example, the Metropolitan Police launched the first of a series of co-ordinated sweeps aimed at clearing beggars from the streets of central London, resulting in the arrest of no fewer than 1445 homeless people between 1991 and 1992 alone. Similar such campaigns followed in cities across the UK – in Bristol,

FIGURE 30.3
Credit: Lorna Ainger

Brighton, Manchester, Oxford and Cambridge. Though Britain has yet to follow the example of cities in the United States (a number of which have passed 'anti-camping' ordinances that effectively criminalize rough sleeping) numerous UK cities have now augmented a crackdown on begging with new by-laws designed to restrict the movements of homeless people and make it more difficult to survive on the streets – banning the consumption of alcohol in certain parts of the city, for example, or closing down the soup kitchens on which homeless people rely (Johnsen *et al.*, 2005).

Such developments need to be understood as part and parcel of a broader strategy aimed at clearing homeless people from the streets lest their presence disrupts the image of a 'vital' and 'prosperous' city promoted by local businesses and city managers (Mitchell, 2003). Rendered homeless by processes of social exclusion, then, the stigma suffered by Britain's single homeless has resulted in their clearance from the very streets to which they have been consigned. (For an extended account of the rise of and responses to Britain's crisis of street homelessness, see May *et al.*, 2005.)

CONCLUSIONS

The study of exclusion and social exclusion has reinvigorated social geography. Spurred on by Sibley's call to consider the geographies of 'outsiders', social geographers have begun to explore the experiences of a range of groups excluded from mainstream society. Work has mainly focused upon the spatial exclusions suffered by such groups, and the role that space plays in maintaining the distinction between mainstream society and those constructed as Different or Other. Studies have been conducted at a variety of scales: examining everything from the design of prisons and asylums, to the marginal status of those living and working in marginal areas of the British landscape.

The emergence of a discourse of social exclusion in UK and US policy circles has likewise led geographers to examine a variety of the material inequalities shaping the lives of the poorest members of society in both countries. The best of such work combines an examination of the growing structural inequalities evident in British and US society with an account of the growing sense of stigma experienced by those locked outside 'mainstream life'.

DISCUSSION POINTS

1. Identify particular groups you feel might suffer from exclusion (for example, children, elderly people). In what domains is their exclusion articulated (for example, housing, health, leisure spaces, and so on)? At what *scale* is their exclusion articulated?

2. Identify a particular institution (for example, prisons, schools, universities, hospitals). How is the space of this institution organized so as to promote the exclusion/inclusion of different groups?

3. What kinds of *methods* are best suited to the study of exclusion?

FURTHER READING

Sibley, D. (1995) *Geographies of exclusion: society and difference in the West.* **London: Routledge.**

Still the most comprehensive account of the theories of exclusion explored here, and very readable.

Geoforum **(1998) Special issue on 'Exclusion', 29(2).**

Useful examples of studies of the geographies of exclusion inspired by Sibley's work.

Levitas, R. (1998) *The inclusive society: social exclusion and New Labour.* **Basingstoke: Macmillan.**

Quite taxing, but a powerful critique of New Labour's rhetoric on social exclusion.

Mohan, J. (2000) Geographies of welfare and social exclusion. *Progress in Human Geography,* **24(2), 291–300.**

Mohan, J. (2002) Geographies of welfare and social exclusion: dimensions, consequences and methods. *Progress in Human Geography,* **26(1), 65–75.**

Two comprehensive reviews of work by geographers on social exclusion, and a great source of references.

www.homeless-research.org.uk

A useful website providing free-to-download academic articles exploring the problems of single homelessness in Britain.

Mitchell, D. (2003) *The right to the city: social justice and the fight for public space.* **New York: The Guilford Press.**

A powerful and easy-to-read book offering detailed examples of attempts to exclude homeless people from the streets of the American city.

Ruddick, S. (1996) *Young and homeless in Hollywood.* **New York: Routledge.**

A useful counterpoint to Mitchell, providing important (if rare) examples of homeless people's attempts to resist expulsion from the streets of Los Angeles.

SECTION 8
URBAN AND RURAL GEOGRAPHIES

INTRODUCTION

Urban and rural are two of those taken-for-granted concepts we use all the time in an almost unthinking manner. Indeed, the everyday use of the terms betrays an almost self-evident acceptance of the distinction between them – we know what 'rural' means, we know what 'urban' means, and we know how they differ. Geography has played on this distinction and for much of its post-war history has tended to study the two as separate entities. It was able to do this, partly because the division between urban and rural was premised around a physical distinction, and partly because the rural became conflated with agriculture. But this physical reading of both urban and rural was increasingly challenged, and gradually replaced by an emphasis on process. As Harvey put it with reference to the urban,

> " *The study of urbanization is not the study of a legal political entity or of a physical artefact. It is concerned with processes of capital circulation; the shifting flows of labour power, commodities and money capital; the spatial organization of production and the transformation of space relations; movements of information and geopolitical conflicts … I prefer to … concentrate on urbanization as a process.* "

(Harvey, 1995: xvii)

Freed from the moorings of studying the urban and rural as somewhat fixed and distinct physical entities, the scope emerged for all kinds of research that explored the two in terms of process. For if urbanization could be studied as a process, so too could rurality. A number of key themes soon became prevalent in work on both – the role of economic restructuring in shaping town and country, and the influence of each on that restructuring; the social recomposition of each, sometimes as a response to economic restructuring and sometimes as a precursor to it; the role of the state and structures of governance, in both responding to economic and social change and trying to shape it. The cultural turn across the social sciences brought a concern with different sets of processes – those to do with the ways in which both 'urban' and 'rural' are key socio-cultural constructs. Both act as **signs, signifiers** and **referents**, and have been increasingly interpreted as a set of **social constructions** that convey a host of social, moral and cultural values. Through these processes both urban and rural lose their geographical anchors – socio-cultural spaces of rurality do not necessarily coincide with the countryside, and socio-cultural spaces of urbanism are not confined to the city. Instead each reaches out to pervade wider society. Indeed, some have claimed that with ever sharpening processes of counter-urbanization, migration and commuting, and increasing flows of goods, services and people between the two, the social and cultural views which are thought to be attached to

Sign, signification, referent

these are ideas relating to the DISCURSIVE construction of geographical worlds. The sign is a concept or word that is significant in the understanding of everyday meanings and places and people (for example, 'rurality'). Signification is the process by which significant meanings are attached to signs (for example, social representations and interpretations of 'rurality'). The referent is the geographical phenomenon that is being signalled (for example, rural localities).

Social construct

a set of specific meanings that become attributed to the characteristics and identities of people and places by common social or cultural usage. Social constructs will often represent a 'loaded' view of the subject, according to the sources from which, and the channels through which, ideas are circulated in society.

rural and urban provide clearer grounds for distinguishing between the two than do their geographic differences.

The chapters in this section take up and explore all these themes. In so doing they introduce you to some exciting contemporary themes in both urban and rural studies. We have chosen to hold the two separate, with distinctive chapters on each, although you will see there are several points at which such distinctions become blurred. Initially, in Chapter 31, Chris Hamnett explores some of the key aspects of recent urban change. One of these is counter-urbanization – the movement of people away from the city towards the suburbs and countryside. Others are the trends of ghettoization and gentrification, the latter exploiting images of loft living and urban renaissance. Underlying each is a worsening inequality that plays on, and sharpens, social and racial divides, and produces distinctive sets of urban experiences. In Chapter 32 Lisa Law draws out what it means to experience the city. Using Singapore as an example she explores the way in which different groups visualize and feel the city, through a combination of senses. She reminds us that there is more to the city than its material construction. In Chapter 33 Paul Cloke also considers some of these themes, but in relation to the countryside. He, too, examines how the countryside is commodified and sold as an image, and also how it is experienced. He also shows how geographers are exploring social divisions in the countryside, by looking at rural poverty and marginalization. It is interesting that these themes of inequality, experience and commodification crop up across the chapters – showing how geographers are now looking at similar sets of processes within the country and the city. Exactly how they operate in each setting will be different of course, but this only brings us back to the richness of contemporary work on both.

FURTHER READING

Williams, R. (1985 [1973]) *The country and the city.* **London: Hogarth Press.**

As it says on the back, 'From the moment of its first publication this book has been hailed as a masterpiece'. For once the blurb is true. This is a classic book that sets about unpacking the shifting meanings of city and country from the sixteenth to the twentieth century.

Barnett, A. and Scruton, R. (eds) (1998) *Town and country.* **London: Jonathan Cape.**

Wilson, A. (1992) *The culture of nature.* **Oxford: Blackwell.**

Two books that blur commonly held distinctions between the city and the country.

Woods, M. (2005) *Rural geography: processes, responses and experiences in rural restructuring.* **London: Sage.**

An excellent contemporary textbook on the countryside.

Knox, P. and Pinch, S. (1998) *Urban social geography: an introduction.* **Harlow: Pearson.**

And an excellent contemporary textbook on the urban.

CHAPTER 31
URBAN FORMS

Chris Hamnett

INTRODUCTION: LIVING IN AN URBAN WORLD

We are living in an increasingly urbanized world. In Britain over 80 per cent of the population live in urban areas, and in most developed western countries the proportion is over 70 per cent. Although there has been rapid suburbanization and urban population decline in recent years, most people in western countries live in urban environments. Nor is the process of urbanization confined to western countries. The most recent UN figures (2004) suggest that 60 per cent of the world's population will be living in cities by the year 2030. Much of this growth will be in the 'third world' and much of it will be in large cities such as Mexico City, São Paulo, Lagos, Jakarta and Shanghai. Urban living will be a defining characteristic of life in the twenty-first century for the majority of the world's population. Consequently, the changing form, economic base and social structure of cities will continue to be of immense importance. We need to know how cities are changing, and what the implications for urban life are now and will be in the future. These issues are frequently a subject of Hollywood movies ranging from *Escape from New York*, Woody Allen's *Manhattan*, Tom Wolfe's *Bonfire of the Vanities*, *Wall Street*, *Working Girl*, *Do the Right Thing* and *Desperately Seeking Susan*, to list just a few that focus on life in New York.

Films and novels give us an insight into urban life, or representations of it, but as geographers we want to probe a little more deeply under the surface.

In this chapter, I want to concentrate on the changing nature of urban form in the contemporary developed western world, focusing on three very different aspects of urban living: first, counter-urbanization and the rise of ex-urban 'edge cities'; second, the experience of urban economic decline in the black ghettos of Chicago; third, the 'back to the central city' movement seen in some major western cities where it is associated with gentrification and the rise of what Sharon Zukin (1982) termed 'loft living'. Finally, I want to look briefly at the growth of inequality in global cities, focusing on Jonathan Raban's journalistic view of New York.

Gentrification

an urban geographical process commonly taken to have two main attributes. The first is the invasion (or replacement) of traditional inner-city working-CLASS residential areas by middle-CLASS in-migrants; the second is the upgrading, improvement and renovation of the existing housing, whether done by the new residents or by developers. Commercial gentrification refers more specifically to the replacement of older, traditional, low-rent, retail and other uses by new, stylish, fashionable boutiques, cafés, bars and other retail outlets.

Global city

a term used by Saskia Sassen in the early 1990s to denote those cities that play a key role in the operation of the capitalist world economy, particularly in terms of financial and business services. The term builds upon the concept of 'world city', put forward by Freidmann and Wolff, to capture the command and control centres of late CAPITALISM, particularly in terms of the concentration of headquarters of multi- and TRANSNATIONAL CORPORATIONS.

FROM URBANIZATION TO COUNTER-URBANIZATION

Urbanization in many western countries peaked in the early decades of this century. In Britain, 70 per cent of the population lived in cities by 1900. Although urbanization has grown in many eastern and southern European countries in the post-war period, with rapid rural depopulation and urban growth in Spain, France, Portugal, Italy and other countries,

White flight

this term refers to the ethnically specific nature of out-migration from urban areas, particularly in the USA. In many of the major metropolitan areas, large-scale ethnic immigration into the inner cities from the 1950s onwards was followed by the out-migration of affluent whites. The result has been a growing ethnic differentiation of urban space between poor minority urban areas and white suburbs. *See also* ETHNICITY.

Discourse, discursive

drawing on the work of the French philosopher Michel Foucault, Human Geographers define discourses as ways of talking about, writing or otherwise representing the world and its geographies (*see also* REPRESENTATION). Discursive approaches to Human Geography emphasize the importance of these ways of representing. They are seen as shaping the realities of the worlds in which we live, rather than just being ways of portraying a reality that exists outside of language and thought. They are also seen as connected to questions of practice – that is, what people actually do – rather than being confined to a separate realm of images or ideas. More specifically, Human Geographers have stressed the different ways in which people have discursively constructed the world in different times and places, and examined how it is that particular ways of talking about, conceptualizing and acting on people and places come to be seen as natural and common-sensical in particular contexts.

much of north-west Europe has experienced a process of rapid suburbanization and counter-urbanization (Champion, 1989; Cheshire, 1995) and urban population decline. A growing share of population and employment have moved out of what were frequently seen as dirty, declining, derelict and crime-ridden central and inner cities, first to the growing suburbs but, more recently, aided by a rapid increase in car ownership levels, to smaller towns and villages, far beyond the city boundary. This trend was accurately foreseen by H.G. Wells, the novelist and science fiction writer, almost 100 years ago in his book *Anticipations*, published in 1902. As Wells put it:

> *We are – as the Census returns for 1901 quite clearly show – in the early phase of a great development of centrifugal possibilities. And since it has been shown that a city of pedestrians is inexorably limited by a radius of about four miles, and that a horse using city may grow out to seven or eight, it follows that the available area of a city which can offer a cheap suburban journey of thirty miles an hour is a city with a radius of 30 miles . . . But 30 miles is only a very moderate estimate of speed and the available area for the social equivalent of the favoured season ticket holders of today will have a radius of over 100 miles . . . Indeed, it is not too much to say that the London citizen of the year 2000 may have a choice of nearly all England and Wales south of Nottingham and east of Exeter as his suburb . . . The country will take to itself many of the qualities of the city. The old antithesis will disappear . . . to receive the daily paper a few hours late, to wait a day or two for the goods one has ordered, will be the extreme measure of rusticity save in a few remote islands and inaccessible places.*

What Wells anticipated has come to pass, and the trend towards population deconcentration was discussed by Berry (1970) in another perceptive paper that envisaged the urban population of the USA becoming increasingly dispersed by the year 2000 into low-density, ex-urban settlements, with their own shopping malls, factories, office parks and entertainment facilities. In the USA Garreau (1991) terms these 'edge cities', and in Britain Herrington (1984) coined the term the 'outer city'.

There is no doubt that, in aggregate terms, population dispersal and counter-urbanization have been the single most important trend in urban structure in many western countries, particularly in North America, Australia and north-west Europe. There has been a major redistribution of the population in the USA from the older, industrial 'snow-belt' cities of the north-east such as Detroit and Pittsburgh, towards the 'sun-belt' cities of the south and west, such as Phoenix, Tucson, Las Vegas, Atlanta, Dallas and Houston. This has been aided by what Beauregard (1994) in his book *Voices of Decline* views as a long-standing and powerful **discourse** of urban decline concerning the nature, causes and consequences of urban change in older, industrial, cities. In Beauregard's view, this discourse has often functioned as a rationalization of, and a response to, racial change in American inner cities.

The magnitude of this change is indisputable. In the space of a few decades, the racial and ethnic composition of American cities has changed dramatically as a result of both high levels of immigration, particularly into key 'gateway' cities (Clark, 1995) and **white flight** to the suburbs (Massey and Denton, 1993). The changing ethnic composition of the city of Los Angeles has been clearly shown by Bill Clark of UCLA. The Los Angeles of the 1930s or the 1950s, depicted in films such as *Chinatown* and *Back to the Future*, has been replaced by a Los Angeles more akin to that of *Blade Runner* in ethnic composition. Los Angeles is now a 'majority minority' city, the second-biggest Spanish-speaking city outside Mexico City, and what Ed Soja terms 'the capital of the Third World'. The Anglo population has fallen from 80 per cent to 33 per cent of the total, whilst the Hispanic population has risen from 10 per cent to 45 per cent, and Asian-Americans make up another 12 per cent. Similar trends characterize Miami, which has the highest rate of immigration in the USA. In 1960 Latin Americans accounted for just 5 per cent of the metropolitan population but 50 per cent by 1990, whilst the Anglo share of the population decreased from 80 per cent to 32 per cent (Nijman, 1996) as many of the Anglo population moved north out of the city in the 1980s. Almost half of the present population was born abroad and 60 per cent do not speak English at home. Nijman states that Miami has made the transformation from a 'southern US city' to a 'northern Latin American city'. In Detroit (Deskins, 1996) the white population fell by 71 per cent in 1970–90, from 851,000 to 250,000, but rose by 240,000 in the suburbs. As a result, Detroit is now 75 per cent black against 43 per cent black in 1970. Similar trends have characterized Washington, DC, and other cities (Knox, 1991). A black inner city is surrounded by a predominately white suburban ring.

One of the defining characteristics of edge cities in the USA is the emergence of what are termed 'gated communities': safe, socially selective, high-security residential environments in which the predominantly white, upper-middle-class residents can turn their backs on the growing social and economic problems of the ethnically diverse central cities and retreat behind the walls, protected by security staff, electronic surveillance and 'rapid response' units. The rise of such gated communities is particularly marked in California and the south and west, though white suburbanization is common in many large American cities. This phenomenon has been documented by Mike Davis (1990) in his book *City of Quartz*, and by Ed Soja (1992) who discusses the growth of Mission Viejo and other gated communities in the southern half of Orange County, south of Los Angeles. Davis suggests that we are seeing the emergence of what he terms 'Fortress LA' characterized by the withdrawal of the affluent behind defensive walls and the erosion of public space. One of the best commentaries is by Christopher Parkes (1997) in a *Financial Times* article entitled 'The birth of Enclave Man' (see Fig. 31.1). He argues, like Davis, that the growth of gated communities is undermining any notion of the USA as a mixed society and is leading to the hardening of social divisions in space as social protectionism firmly excludes minorities from suburban homes and jobs. We are now seeing the rise of gated luxury residential developments in parts of some British cities – for example, London's Docklands – where developers perceive potential demand from buyers concerned about

Postmodern, postmodernity, postmodernism

the British national newspaper, the *Independent*, sarcastically defined postmodernism thus: 'This word has no meaning. Use it as often as possible.' In fact, the main problem for a glossary entry such as this is that ideas of the postmodern have been used so often with so many different meanings! Nonetheless, one can generalize to say that notions of the postmodern (sometimes hyphenated, sometimes not) are used to suggest a move beyond 'modern' society and culture (*see* MODERN, MODERNITY, MODERNISM). More specifically: (a) postmodern is an adjective used to describe social and cultural forms that eschew 'modern' qualities of order, rationality and progress in favour of 'postmodern' qualities of difference, ephemerality, superficiality and pastiche; (b) 'postmodernity' is the contemporary epoch, after a period of 'modernity', in which such postmodern forms supposedly predominate, an epoch characterized both by the loss of an overall sense of social direction and order and by the triumph of the media image over reality (*see* HYPER-REALITY and SIMULACRUM); and (c) 'postmodernism' refers more narrowly to a collection of artistic, architectural and intellectual movements that promote postmodernist values, aesthetics and ways of thinking. If that is not complicated enough, whilst some view all things postmodern as signs of a radically new historical era of postmodernity, others see them more as recent twists to the history of modernity. So perhaps a revised version of the *Independent*'s definition might be: 'This word has a host of meanings. This makes it interesting, but also means it should be used with care'!

The birth of Enclave Man

Growth of US gated communities is imperilling the social contract, says **Christopher Parkes**

Even after dark the children of Avalon Gardens whirl and chatter in their new playground. Adults mingle over barbecues and in fitness facilities. All are relishing the unfamiliar sense of security and community that comes from the new 12ft iron fence, security floodlights and bullet-proof guard boxes ringing their homes.

Such simple freedoms are increasingly attainable throughout the US, as Americans, exhausted by urban violence and disintegration, retreat to the cosy sanctuary of so-called gated communities. There are now 30,000 such fortresses, home to some 8m people. In some parts of America a third of all new houses are being built behind walls.

So common have such communities become that they are now spreading even to ganglands like Avalon Gardens, a former free-fire zone in South Central district of Los Angeles.

The gang "tags" spray-painted on walls, and menacing clusters of young men loitering inside the fence betray this pilot scheme as a pale imitation of suburbia's orderly walled communities. But its ambitions are identical.

The fortress community has come to represent in the popular imagination a safe haven for people who want to live among their own kind in a compound shuttered against outsiders. The mainly black residents of Avalon Gardens – who include members of this local chapter of the Crips gang – now have an unprecedented measure of protection from the Bloods who dominate the surrounding districts. The shooting sprees have stopped.

Another housing project on Bloods turf in nearby

Watts has since asked for similar privileges. Their request has awakened local politicians to the danger of sanctioning the establishment, at public expense, of unruly fiefdoms reminiscent of medieval Europe.

Others see even more danger in the cosy middle-class version of these communities. The prospect that the number of such developments may double within five years dismays social scientists. In the suburban separatism, defensive localism or plain Balkanisation that lies behind the trend, they see a rejection of the sense of mutuality on which the country was founded.

Whites-only segregation, buried by federal legislation more than 30 years ago, is being restored by consumer demand for orderly, safe living conditions. Although anyone can buy a home in a gated community, today's inhabitants are predominantly white, earning between $60,000 and £200,000 a year.

In most aspects, they mirror the people who led the so-called "white flight" to the suburbs in the 1970s and 1980s. Most proceeded to fight for, and win, municipal incorporation for their bedroom communities, thus escaping the obligations and taxes of the fast-rotting cities they left behind. To some observers, the rise of the gated community marks a critical further stage in the process of white flight.

According to Edward Blakely, dean of the University of Southern California urban planning school, the

retreat from the "basic ethic of mutuality which is the notion behind the US" is nowhere more apparent than in California, Texas, Arizona and Florida – the main points of arrival and concentration of Latino immigrants.

"You will see the walls go up wherever you see large numbers of immigrants," he says. "We will get to the point where [white] people will not feel safe unless they live in one of these places."

The mass retreat is well under way in parts of California, according to Dale Maharidge of Stanford University, who has logged what he calls "the browning" of the state and the withdrawal of monied whites to walled and gated developments in Orange County which keep "those people" out.

"No white society of the industrial world has ever evolved into a mixed culture," he writes in his recent apocalyptic book, *The Coming White Minority*.

According to state data, whites will account for less than half California's population in two years. The simultaneous rise of Latino political power – as 150,000 people of Hispanic origins reach voting age each year – foreshadows an unprecedented upheaval, Mr Maharidge argues.

Mr Blakely, co-author of *Fortress America: Gated Communities in the US*, concedes that the browning of California represents a "deep psychological threat" to some. But he is more concerned about the white withdrawal, which he believes

could threaten the very structure of democracy.

This is a hefty charge to lay against what others, especially in the building and property business, see as simply a trendy lifestyle choice: one formerly restricted to the rich and famous and now affordable for the middle classes. Mr Blakely bases his fears on the argument that "fragmentation undermines the very concept of *civitas* – organised community life".

Most gated developments pay for their own private

police patrols and security guards. Traditionally communal services such as schools, parks, entertainment facilities and even street cleaning and maintenance are often privatised within the enclaves. The inhabitants are ever more reluctant to pay higher taxes to maintain government and city services outside their walls.

Such reluctance has already capped Californian property taxes. In New Jersey some community-dwellers have won abatements on

local levies after arguing that they already pay for their own private services.

According to Mr Blakely's theories, such tendencies threaten the social contract. The lack of social contact fostered by exclusive lifestyles serves only to accentuate the peril. Economists say one result of social protectionism is to cut ambitious minorities off from the contacts and opportunities they need to advance up the economic scale.

On the available evidence, these are not issues that

impinge greatly on the thinking of the enclave-dwellers. Instead of a social contract – a bewildering concept in places such as California where more than 100 languages and cultures mingle – gated communities offer a straightforward option.

Membership of the homeowners' association and the payment of monthly dues to cover the cost of maintaining amenities – whether the newcomer chooses to use them or not – are mandatory. Association rules, typically drawn up by the builders and strictly enforced, establish a code of conduct.

In return for the security and other benefits offered by the community, people will commonly be required to sacrifice many of the freedoms available in the world outside. Rules may dictate the colour of their front door, curtains or other indoor furnishings visible from the street. Sticking political posters in front windows is usually forbidden. In some places homeowners may plant only shrubs from an approved list, and may not station gnomes in their gardens, make noise after 10pm, or own a dog weighing more than 20lbs.

"In effect," according to Jo Anne Stubblefield, a community governance specialist, "the property owner becomes a citizen of the association, subject to its governing and assessment powers."

This "contractual government" – in the words of a recent economic analysis of the gated community phe-

nomenon – "appears to be the closest thing to a real-world social contract that can be found".

This is a curious development in a country where generations have been brought up on the concept of limited government. As Evan McKenzie, professor of political science at Illinois University, pointed out in a recent radio broadcast, the Bill of Rights, which protects a citizen's right to hang out a flag or put a wishing well on the front lawn, is ineffective inside the confines of a private community.

"We teach [people] that they have rights that are protected against intrusion from government authorities," Mr Mckenzie says. "But what nobody told them was that local government was going to be privatised to this degree."

In spite of these disadvantages, the desire of ordinary Americans to live in walled communities is far from slackening. Some planners say that, in parts of Orange County, Montgomery County, Maryland and southern Florida, the concentration of gated communities is so dense that middle-class home buyers have little choice but to move into one of them.

One result is that the economic and social segregation characteristic of societies worldwide is, in the US, taking on a physical form. "Social barriers have always been there, but Americans climb over them," says Mr Blakely. "That's what America's always been about."

But walls, gates and armed guards – the essential elements of a prison – present more substantial impediments: both to those trying to get in and those who want to get out.

FIGURE 31.1

The birth of the Enclave Man. Credit: © Ingram Pinn. Source: *Financial Times*, 21 September 1997

crime and security. The social implications of this are arguably negative as such developments imply greater residential segregation of the well-off, the exclusion of other groups, and a reduction in overall social trust and integration. This means that the use of the term 'gated *community*' is actually problematic as such developments tend to lessen rather than increase a sense of community.

SUMMARY

- In many northern European and American cities, counter-urbanization has proceeded apace in recent years, with population decentralizing from the old urban cores to new suburbs and, most recently, to ex-urban centres.

- This out-migration has been very socially and racially selective in the USA, with large-scale ethnic immigration into the cities accompanied by

a growing suburbanization of the white middle class.

- Many American cities, particularly in the southern and western states, have seen the growth of 'gated communities', which are highly socially selective by income, in an attempt to shut out the problems of crime and violence.

WHEN WORK DISAPPEARS: GHETTO POVERTY IN CHICAGO

Many large western cities have experienced dramatic transformations in their social and residential structure in recent decades as a result of a combination of a massive decline of manufacturing employment, large-scale

immigration, rapid suburbanization, white flight, inner-city decay
and social despair. This transformation has been particularly marked
in many of the older American
cities of the mid-west and north-
east such as Pittsburgh,
Philadelphia, New York, Detroit
and Chicago. The transformation
of New York has been well studied
by Mollenkopf and Castells in their
book *Dual City*, but the city I want
to concentrate on here is Chicago,
which has been the subject of major
research by the black sociologist
William Julius Wilson (1987;
1996) in his books *The Truly
Disadvantaged* and *When Work
Disappears: The World of the New
Urban Poor*.

FIGURE 31.2
A gated development in London.
Credit: Lorna Ainger

Wilson's work is important for a number of reasons, but first and
foremost it addresses a crucial urban social issue: that of the new black
urban poor and the social dislocation and breakdown that follow from it.
In this respect, his work is committed to real social issues, not to the
intellectual games of **postmodernism**. This is the social world treated in
gritty and demanding films such as Spike Lee's *Do the Right Thing*, *Grand
Canyon* and *Boyz n the Hood*. The latter focuses on two talented young
blacks who live in the ghetto of South Central Los Angeles and struggle
against the forces of crime, violence and despair to get a college education.
The French equivalent – *La Haine* – is the world of young immigrant
males in one of the big social housing estates. They are depressing films,
but worth seeing. *Trainspotting* offers a less bleak and more humorous
Scottish equivalent set in Edinburgh's social housing estates.

Wilson takes on two sets of intellectual opponents: the social conservatives who attribute the problems of the black ghetto to the attitudes and
behaviour of its residents who are seen to be irresponsible, criminal and
feckless welfare dependants, thinking only of the moment and happy to
live by a combination of crime and welfare handouts. The second set of
opponents comprises the liberals who ignore or deny the reality of anti-
social behaviour in the black ghetto and have yielded the field to
conservative popularizers such as Charles Murray in his book *Losing
Ground*. Wilson argues that ghetto social problems are only too real and
cannot be ignored or brushed aside; he argues instead that they are a result
of the changing employment, racial and demographic structure of
American inner cities aided by systematic discrimination, and he argues
that the attitudes and behaviours found in black poverty areas are a
response to the problems faced by their residents rather than reflecting an
innate culture of lawlessness, criminality and immorality, as conservatives
often believe.

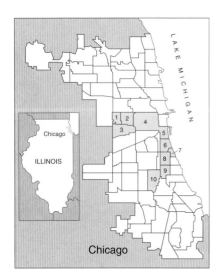

Community Areas in Chicago's Black Belt

1. West Garfield Park
2. East Garfield Park
3. North Lawndale
4. Near West Side
5. Near South Side
6. Douglas
7. Oakland
8. Grand Boulevard
9. Washington Park
10. Englewood

FIGURE 31.3
Chicago black belt. Source: Wilson 1996

De-industrialization

this term usually refers to a decline in manufacturing industry. It can designate either a fall in manufacturing output or, more commonly, a fall in the number and share of employees in manufacturing industry as a result of plant closures, lay-offs, etc. It is possible for de-industrialization to occur at the same time as manufacturing output, and exports rise if automation is associated with jobless growth. Areas that have suffered from de-industrialization are characterized by large numbers of vacant derelict factories. *See also* POST-INDUSTRIAL.

As Wilson (1996) points out:

" *It is important to understand and communicate the overwhelming obstacles that many ghetto residents have to overcome just to live up to mainstream expectations involving work, the family and the law. Such expectations are taken for granted in middle-class society. Americans in more affluent areas have jobs that offer fringe benefits; they are accustomed to health insurance that covers paid sick leave and medical care. They do not have to live in neighbourhoods where attempts at normal child rearing are constantly undermined . . . and their family's prospects for survival do not require at least some participation in the informal economy . . . I argue that the disappearance of work and the consequences of that disappearance for both social and cultural life are the central problems in the inner city ghetto.* "

(Wilson, 1996: xix)

Wilson's research is set in the neighbourhoods of Chicago's Black Belt (see Fig. 31.3) and incorporates a powerful mixture of quantitative and qualitative sources. He points out that less than one in three of the poor in the United States lived in metropolitan central cities in 1959 but by 1991 the figure had risen to almost half, and that much of the increase in concentrated poverty has occurred in African-American neighbourhoods. In the ten communities that constitute the historic core of the Black Belt, eight had poverty rates in 1990 that exceeded 45 per cent, three had rates over 50 per cent and three of over 60 per cent. In 1970 only two neighbourhoods had poverty rates of over 40 per cent. Overall, the poverty rate in the Black Belt rose from one-third in 1970 to half in 1990. The increase in poverty has a simple explanation according to Wilson: the rapid growth of joblessness. In 1990 only one in three adults held a job in the Black Belt in 1990 compared to 60–70 per cent in the 1950s. The increase in joblessness is, in turn, a result of **de-industrialization** and the replacement of manufacturing, transportation and construction jobs, traditionally held by males, by jobs in high technology and services that hire more women. These changes, says Wilson, are related to the decline of mass production in the USA or, perhaps more accurately, the automation of mass production, and the consequent job losses. He points out that in the 20-year period from 1967 to 1987, Philadelphia, Chicago, New York City and Detroit each lost between 50 and 65 per cent of their manufacturing jobs. These manufacturing job losses particularly affected black males, who disproportionately worked in the sector and had lower education levels that did not equip them for the new jobs in business services and high technology. In addition, many of the new jobs are either located in the city centre or in the expanding suburbs. He notes that, in the last two decades, 60 per cent of the new jobs created in the Chicago metropolitan areas have been located in the north-west suburbs of Cook and Du Page counties in which African-Americans comprise less than 2 per cent of the population. Consequently, blacks living in the inner city have less access to employment, and they are far less likely to own a car to enable them to get to the new jobs in a country where public transport is particularly poor. As one of his respondents, a 29-year-old unemployed South Side black male noted:

> *You gotta get out in the suburbs, but I can't get out there. The bus go out there but you don't want to catch the bus out there, going two hours each ways. If you have to be at work at eight that mean you have to leave for work at six, that mean you have to get up at five to be at work at eight. Then when wintertime come you be in trouble.*

> (Wilson, 1996: 39)

Wilson notes that nearly half the housing stock in the black neighbourhood of North Lawndale has disappeared since 1960 and the remaining units are mostly run-down or dilapidated. And whereas in the past the Hawthorne plant of Western Electric employed 43,000 workers, International Harvester employed 14,000 and the world headquarters of Sears Roebuck, the mail-order firm, employed 10,000, all have now closed. The departure of the big plants, says Wilson,

> *triggered the demise or exodus of the smaller stores, the banks, and other businesses that relied on the wages paid by large employers . . . In 1986, North Lawndale, with a population of over 66,000, had only one bank and one supermarket; but it was home to forty-eight state lottery agents, fifty currency exchanges, and ninety-nine licensed liquor stores and bars.*

> (Wilson, 1996: 35)

Another of his interviewees, a 29-year-old unemployed black male, stated that:

> *Jobs were plentiful in the past. You could walk out of the house and get a job. Maybe not what you want but you could get a job. Now you can't find anything. A lot of people in this neighborhood, they want to work but they can't get work. A few, but a very few, they just don't want to work: but the majority they want to work but they can't find work.*

> (Wilson, 1996: 36)

The social consequences of mass joblessness are profound. Wilson argues that: 'Neighborhoods plagued by high levels of joblessness are more likely to experience low levels of social organization' and 'High rates of joblessness trigger other neighborhood problems that undermine social organization, ranging from crime, gang violence and drug trafficking to family breakups' (1996: 21).

The decline of job opportunities amongst inner-city residents has increased the incentives to sell drugs, and addiction to crack cocaine has been paralleled by the rise of violent crime amongst young black males. Wilson points out that whereas the homicide rate for white males aged 14 to 17 increased from 8 to 14 per 100,000 between 1984 and 1991, the rate for black males more than tripled over the same period from 32 per 100,000 to 112; he argues that neighbourhoods plagued by high levels of joblessness and disorganization are unable to control the volatile drug market and the violent crimes related to it. As the informal social controls weaken, so the social processes that regulate behaviour change and Wilson instances the spread of gun culture:

> *Drug dealers cause the use and spread of guns in the neighbourhood to escalate, which in turn raises the likelihood that others, particularly youngsters will come to view the possession of weapons as necessary or desirable for self-protection, settling disputes, and gaining respect from peers.*

(Wilson, 1996: 21)

Wilson argues that many inner-city ghetto residents clearly see the social and cultural effects of living in high-jobless and impoverished neighbourhoods, particularly the effects on attitudes and behaviour. A 17-year-old black male living in a poor ghetto neighbourhood on the West Side stated that:

> *Well, basically, I feel that if you are raised in a neighborhood and all you see is negative things, then you are going to be negative because you don't see anything positive … Guys and black males see drug dealers on the corner and they see fancy cars and flashy money and they figure: 'Hey, if I get into drugs I can be like him'.*

(Wilson, 1996: 55)

The problem of the black ghettos, as Wilson sees it, is one of historic racial discrimination and segregation compounded by de-industrialization, which has dramatically reduced the formal employment opportunity structure and led to destructive social behaviours that are pulling neighbourhoods down.

It is sometimes asserted that European cities are being Americanized and that some areas are becoming ethnic ghettos. But, as Loic Wacquant (1993) and Peach (1996) have argued, this is a fundamental misconception. The overall proportion of ethnic minorities in European cities is far smaller than in the USA, and there is nothing approaching the levels of ethnic concentration in American cities. In answer to the question 'Does Britain have ghettos?', Peach unequivocally says 'No'. There are areas with high minority concentrations in some British cities such as Leicester and Bradford but minorities comprise a majority of the population in only a relatively small number of enumeration districts. Nonetheless, the ethnic minority population of London rose by over 50 per cent between 1991 and 2001, and ethnic minorities comprised 29 per cent of the population in Greater London in 2001 and 34 per cent in Inner London. In two boroughs (Brent and Newham) the non-white population now exceeds 50 per cent, and in Tower Hamlets is reaching 50 per cent with several other boroughs such as Hackney over 40 per cent (Hamnett, 2003b). Although these figures are considerably lower than in American cities such as New York and Los Angeles, they suggest that London may be moving more towards the levels of ethnic diversity found in some American cities. It is rare in most European cities, however, to find the extensive concentrations of ethnic minorities that are found in American cities. This is not to deny that some groups fare badly in labour and housing markets (Madood, 1997), but this is not the same as the concentration of ghetto poverty found in the USA. The scale of the problem is quantitatively and qualitatively different.

SUMMARY

- In the predominantly black inner cities of the north-eastern United States, large-scale de-industrialization has been associated with a massive increase in unemployment and poverty. These problems are found to a lesser extent in some British and European inner-city areas.
- The collapse of inner-city manufacturing jobs, particularly for males, and the growth of predominantly low-wage service-sector jobs, linked to the out-migration of jobs to the white suburbs, have generated major social problems.
- The social and behavioural problems found in inner-city black areas are very real, but they should be seen as the consequence of de-industrialization and discrimination rather than innate social characteristics. They represent a response to a changed set of economic and social conditions.

GENTRIFICATION AND LOFT LIVING IN THE CENTRAL CITY

The economic decline of older, industrial cities such as Detroit, Pittsburgh, Manchester, Liverpool, Glasgow, Lille and the Ruhr, has been paralleled by the rise of a small number of major world or global cities (Sassen, 1990) as the command and control centres of the world economy and finance system. These cities, which include London, New York, Paris, Tokyo, Toronto and others, have all experienced massive deindustrialization, but they have also seen the rapid expansion of business and financial services such as banking, legal services and management consultancy as well as the continued growth of a number of creative industries such as advertising, film and video, music, fashion and design. The cultural and creative industries are becoming increasingly important in global cities both in terms of production and attracting visitors.

These cities have been characterized by the transformation of their industrial, occupational, income and residential structure. As Ley (1996) shows in the context of Toronto and Vancouver, the rise of a service-based economy has been paralleled by the growth of a new professional, managerial, technical and creative middle class, generally highly educated and highly paid. The rise of this group, with its cultural interests and housing market demands has, in large part, been responsible for the growth of gentrification in post-industrial inner cities. Many of them work in business or creative industries in the central city or its environs, have long or irregular hours and want to live close to work and the cultural and entertainment facilities offered by the central city. But traditional central and inner-city high-status residential areas are expensive and in short supply. Consequently, the new middle class have sought out new living opportunities in the inner city, aided by developers and estate agents who have seen the prospects for profitable transformation of these areas.

Moving in and up

More of us are middle class and we're flooding back to the city, says Chris Hamnett

Gentrification has become a widespread phenomenon. The movement of the middle classes into previously working class or run-down inner city areas has occurred from New York, London, Paris, Sydney and Toronto to Budapest, Prague and even Moscow.

The term has passed effortlessly into common parlance but, although many people know intuitively what it means, few probably know where it originated. The answer lies with a London-based émigré Jewish journalist turned urban sociologist called Ruth Glass.

Glass noticed that something strange was happening in run-down areas of central London such as Chelsea and Pimlico in the late 1950s and early 1960s. Small privately rented mews cottages and larger multiple-occupied terraced houses (generally Georgian or Victorian) were being sold when their leases expired to be converted by the middle classes for owner occupation.

As readers of Jane Austen will know, in 18th and 19th century England the gentry occupied an intermediate position in the class structure between the landed aristocracy, typified by Mr Darcy at the top, and yeoman farmers below. In 1963 Glass ironically termed the process "gentrification": the coming of a new urban gentry.

From Chelsea, the process has spread rapidly over the past 40 years, first to the select areas of imposing, centrally located period housing such as Barnsbury in Islington, parts of Camden Town, Notting Hill and Primrose Hill, and then onwards and outwards. These areas are now expensive but in the late 1960s much of Notting Hill was run-down and decaying, with stucco peeling off the collapsing porticos.

In New York, Greenwich Village in downtown Manhattan became attractive to artists in the 1960s, as did Georgetown in Washington, and property prices began to creep up. By 1974, the process of converting buildings in run-down but centrally located areas had begun to spread to old iron-framed industrial buildings and warehouses in New York's SoHo and the loft apartment was born. This was followed by TriBeCa, Chelsea, and most recently the old downtown meatpacking district.

In Paris at around the same time a similar, though superficially rather different process was beginning to take place in the Marais district, east of the centre. An area of imposing aristocratic town houses, including the majestic Place des Voges, which had been in decay since the court moved westwards and was finished off in the Revolution, saw the start of a process of renovation that has led to the area becoming the Covent Garden of Paris.

Now the process has spread southwards and eastwards, out to the Bastille and beyond and into the previously working class 19th and 20th *arrondissements.*

In Sydney, the old inner city working-class areas around the Harbour such as Glebe, Redfern and Paddington have been spruced up, as have the 19th century terraced houses in Boston, Melbourne, Toronto and San Francisco. In the last 10 years gentrification has grown in eastern Europe. After the Berlin Wall came down the middle classes began to make their way back towards the old, attractive housing found in places such as Prenzlauerberg in east Berlin, or the inner city areas of Budapest and Prague.

So why has gentrification become so commonplace. Theories range from the availability of cheap domestic technologies to changes in the relationship between property prices and land prices, and the coming of age of the postwar baby boomers.

The most convincing explanation is in the relationship between changes in the structure of the economy, in class structure and changing tastes. Go back 40 years and almost all the cities mentioned above had large industrial sectors employing

> City centres are much more attractive, convenient places to live

large numbers of manual workers. The middle classes were relatively small.

In the interim, much of the old industrial base has disappeared and with it the manufacturing workforce. In its place is the rapidly growing financial, business services (law, advertising, management consultancy) and creative industries that employ large numbers of professionals and managers. The social class structure of big western cities has changed dramatically.

The result was predictable. Increasing numbers of the middle-class, many aged in their 20s and 30s, began to hit the housing market in the early 1970s. Many worked in or near the city centre, they were university educated and enjoyed the cultural buzz of the inner city. Last, but not least, decaying old terraced houses in inner city areas were cheap.

Will gentrification continue and if so where? If one accepts the argument that it is simply a product of postwar baby boomers looking for a cheap place to live, it should already have peaked. Most of this group are already in their 40s and 50s and are well established in the housing market. But the evidence is against this. Gentrification is thriving and spreading to some of the older industrial cities such as Manchester, Leeds and Liverpool.

Much more likely is that rising real incomes and the continuing trends towards smaller households will intensify the demand for city-centre living, aided by the fact that to many city centres and inner cities are much more attractive, convenient places to live.

The evidence points to the expansion and extension of gentrified areas.

In London, the process has spread from Islington to neighbouring Hackney, and Tower Hamlets, and south of the river into Lambeth and north Southwark. Leafy Crouch End and Finsbury Park have undergone the process. In New York, parts of Brooklyn have been gentrified and pioneers are moving into southern Harlem.

Rising demand and limited supply leads to price rises and the gradual colonisation of areas further from the centre. Meanwhile, what remains of the working class and those who cannot afford the high prices? They are either squeezed into the remaining council housing or into the outer suburbs.

Gentrification has remade the social structure of the post-industrial city. The middle classes fled the inner cities in the late 19th century and first half of the 20th centuries. Now they are back and it looks like they will remain for a while yet.

The tests will be crime and education. Young middle-class households enjoy social mix but they also require safety and the ability to ensure a good education for their children. If either requirement becomes too difficult to achieve gentrification could stall.

Chris Hamnett is professor of geography at King's College London and the author of 'Unequal City: London in the Global Arena'

Village life: Greenwich Village was at the forefront of gentrification in New York Corbis

FIGURE 31.4
Article from the *Financial Times*, 10 July 2004

FIGURE 31.5
New River Head Development. Credit: The Berkeley Group Holdings plc

There is a large literature on traditional forms of gentrification (Butler, 1997; Hamnett, 2003b; Ley, 1996; Smith, 1996), which commonly involve conversion of nineteenth-century multi-occupied rental housing (much of it originally built for middle-class occupancy) back into single family houses or apartments.

In New York and London, however, there has been a trend towards conversion of older industrial buildings into spacious if expensive city-centre apartments. In New York, this was first concentrated in the SoHo area of downtown Manhattan, adjacent to the financial district and characterized by elegant late nineteenth-century multi-storey industrial lofts, but it has since spread into Tribeca and other areas where industrial buildings are available (Zukin, 1982). Unlike the gentrification of single family housing, conversion of such buildings generally involves property developers who have the finance and expertise to carry out the work. An insight into loft living in SoHo is seen in the film *Desperately Seeking Susan* featuring Madonna and Rosanna Arquette.

In London, the process got under way in the 1980s in Docklands with the conversion of some the old riverside warehouses along the Thames in Wapping and elsewhere, aided by the efforts of the London Docklands Development Corporation to socially transform the area (Goodwin, 1991). But in the last few years, there has been a dramatic expansion of loft conversions in the Clerkenwell area of London, just west of the City of London, and north of the Inns of Court. This area was formerly one of the industrial districts of London, as SoHo was for New York, but with the rapid decline of manufacturing in the 1960s onwards, it became increasingly derelict and empty. One or two pioneering developers, such as the aptly named Manhattan Loft Corporation, saw their potential and their proximity to the City and initiated the process of conversion. They have been an instant success, and many of the buildings sell out immediately, often straight from the plan, with prices ranging from £300,000 to £750,000 per unit.

FIGURE 31.6
Price's Candle Factory, Clapham, London, has been converted into luxury apartments. Credit: Lorna Ainger

Some of the conversions are very dramatic, such as the old headquarters of the New River Company (Thames Water) in Rosebery Avenue, near Sadlers Wells just south of the Angel, Islington. The conversion was undertaken by a consortium of Kennet Properties, a subsidiary of Thames Water, Berkeley Homes and the Manhattan Loft Corporation, and it includes 129 flats as well as some spectacular private public space (see Fig. 31.5).

As the area has increased in desirability, aided by marketing and promotion as a fashionable place to live, prices have soared as they did in SoHo in the 1970s. Clerkenwell lofts have become home to bankers, lawyers and highly paid creative workers, and the process has spread rapidly in recent years into Shoreditch, Spitalfields and Hoxton, as well as south of the river to Borough Market. In many ways the creative centre of gravity of London has shifted sharply eastwards with many new bars, galleries and restaurants in the old city fringe. Similar developments are also taking place in a number of other cities such as Manchester, Liverpool, Leeds and Newcastle. The conversion of old industrial and office buildings into luxury apartments has been one of the defining characteristics of changing urban form in recent years.

SUMMARY

- In addition to the rise of edge cities and ex-urban development, and inner-city decline, there has a been a widespread growth in the middle classes in the central and inner areas of some major cities where economic change in the structure of employment has created new jobs in the creative industries and financial services.

- Many of the workers in these new growing industries have chosen to live in the central cities, leading to the growth of gentrification and 'loft living'. This latter trend has been associated with the conversion of industrial buildings to residential uses.

- Areas such as SoHo in New York and Clerkenwell in London have become fashionable residential areas for the new wealthy professional middle classes.

INEQUALITY IN THE GLOBAL CITY

It is clear from the discussion of the loft conversion market in London and New York, and ghetto poverty in Chicago that the modern city is marked by sharp inequalities. Recent analyses of earnings in London (Hamnett, 2003b), New York (Mollenkopf and Castells, 1992) and Paris (Preteceille, 2001) reveal that inequalities have grown very sharply in recent years, aided by the rapid rise in earnings and bonuses in financial and legal services where earnings of hundreds of thousands of pounds are not uncommon. Friedmann and Wolff (1982) and Sassen (1991) argue that these trends are inscribed in the global city rather than being merely incidental. These cities, says Friedmann, are run for the benefit of the transnational elite, and social polarization is an integral and inevitable part of such cities: the prosperity of the elite rests on the exploitation of the poor.

In his book on America *Hunting Mr Heartbreak*, Jonathan Raban (1990) makes the brilliant distinction between the 'air people' and the 'street people' of Manhattan in terms of the total separation of their economic and social circumstances and their ways of life. Although his treatment is journalistic, and perhaps rather overdrawn, he puts his finger on the massive inequality that characterizes contemporary cities (see box).

Raban's picture of New York is impressionistic journalism and travel writing, not social science, and for a more considered approach you should look at Mollenkopf and Castells' (1992) book *Dual city? Restructuring New York*, which provides an excellent overview of trends and inequalities. But Raban's piece is one of the most powerful and vivid insights into New York today, as is Tom Wolfe's novel *Bonfire of the Vanities*, since made into a film. Getting to grips with the form and culture of the modern city is as much about film, video and novels as it is about census data, interviews and questionnaire surveys. What matters is that we try to understand what is going on, and writers, journalists and film-makers provide us with powerful visions and interpretations that can stimulate social scientific research.

CONCLUSION

Contemporary cities are changing in complex and often contradictory ways. Continuing suburbanization is paralleled, in some cities, by inner-city urban decline (the two are frequently causally linked) and by central city urban regeneration and gentrification. As a consequence, modern western cities are frequently characterized by growing inequality – both between rich and poor and between different ethnic groups. In some cities this is accompanied by growing social segregation between those with greater resources and choice, and those with limited resources and limited choice. Whilst some changes are clearly the result of a degree of choice and preference for different lifestyles and environments, others are often unwilling victims of economic and social processes largely outside their influence and control. Whilst some people may be living in a postmodern urban lifestyle playground, others have to live in a post-industrial wasteland.

AN EXTRACT FROM JONATHAN RABAN'S *HUNTING MR HEARTBREAK* (1990)

"*The beggars slept much of the day away on benches on the subway platform. By night, they scavenged. Returning home late after dinner, I would meet them on the cross streets around East 18th, where small knots of them went tipping over trashcans in search of a bit of half-eaten pizza, or the lees of someone's can of Coors. . . .*"

"*The current term for these misfortunes was 'street people', an expression that had taken over from bag ladies, winos and bums. The Street People were seen as a tribe, like the Beaker Folk or the Bone People, and this fairly reflected the fact that there were so many more of them now than there had been a few years before. In New York one saw a people, a poor nation living on the leftovers of a rich one. They were anthropologically distinct, with their skin eruptions, their wasted figures, poor hair and bony faces. They looked like the Indians in an old Western . . .*"

(pp. 77–8)

"*There were the Street People and there were the Air People. Air People levitated like fakirs. Large portions of their day were spent waiting for, and travelling in, the elevators that were as fundamental to the middle class culture of New York as gondolas had been to Venice in the Renaissance. It was the big distinction – to be able to press a button and take wing to your apartment . . . access to the elevator was proof that your life had the buoyancy that was needed to stay afloat in a city where the ground was seen as the realm of failure and menace.*"

"*In blocks like Alice's, where doormen kept up a 24 hour guard against the Street People, the elevator was like the village green. The moment that people were safely inside the cage, they started talking to strangers with cosy expansiveness . . .*"

(p. 80)

"*Everyone I knew lived like this. Their New York consisted of a series of high-altitude interiors, each one guarded, triple locked, electronically surveilled. They kept in touch by flying from one interior to the next, like sociable gulls swooping from cliff to cliff. For them, the old New York of streets, squares, neighbourhoods, was rapidly turning into a vague and distant memory. It was the place where TV thrillers were filmed. It was where the Street People lived . . .*"

(p. 81)

"*For Diane, places like Brooklyn and the Bronx were as remote as Beirut and Teheran. Nobody went there. The subway system was an ugly rumour – she had not set foot in it for years . . . I sometimes joined her on evenings when she was dining out uptown – evenings that had the atmosphere of a tense commando operation. At eight o'clock, the lobby of her building was full of Air people waiting for their transport. A guard would secure a cab, and we'd fly up through New York to the West 60's or the East 80's . . .*"

(p. 84)

"*It was a white knuckle ride. Diane sat bolt upright, wordless, clinging to the grab-rail in front of her, while the cab flew through the dismal 30s. At this level, at this hour, all of New York looked ugly, angular, fire-blackened, defaced – bad dream country. The sidewalks were empty now of everyone except Street People. This was the time when things began to happen that you'd see tomorrow on breakfast television, and read about, in tombstone headlines, in the Post and Daily News . . .*"

(p. 85)

"*Few of these journeys last more than ten or eleven minutes: they were just long enough to let you catch a glimpse of the world you feared. Then, suddenly, there was another guard, dressed in a new exotic livery, putting you through Customs and Immigration in another lobby.*"

(p. 86)

DISCUSSION POINTS

1. Some commentators have suggested that western cities are being turned inside-out. What do you think this means, and what are the processes contributing to this?

2. Discuss whether gated communities make positive or negative contributions to urban life.

3. Why are cities becoming increasingly unequal places to live?

4. What do you think should be done to lessen this social and economic inequality?

FURTHER READING

Wilson, W.J. (1987) *The truly disadvantaged.* **Chicago: University of Chicago Press.**

Wilson, W.J. (1996) *When work disappears: the world of the new urban poor.* **New York: Alfred A. Knopf.**

To understand what is happening in the black inner areas of some American cities you can do no better than read one of W.J. Wilson's two major books. The second is particularly interesting as it combines quantitative and qualitative material in an illuminating way. The urban poor are given voices and outline their situation in their own words.

O'Loughlin, J. and Friedrichs, J. (eds) (1996) *Social polarization in post-industrial metropolises.* **Berlin and New York: De Gruyter.**

Deskin's chapter in the above text gives a powerful picture of the changes that have affected Detroit in recent decades.

Clark, W. (1998a) *The California cauldron: immigration and the fortunes of local communities.* **New York: The Guilford Press.**

Clark, W. (1998b) Mass migration and local outcomes: is international migration to the United States creating a new urban underclass. *Urban Studies,* **35(3), 371–84.**

These texts offer an insight into the impact and implications of large-scale immigration in the United States.

Peach, C. (1996) Does Britain have ghettos? *Transactions of the Institute of British Geographers,* **21(1), 216–35.**

Read this article for an assessment of the scale of ethnic segregation in Britain.

Ley, D. (1996) *The new middle class and the remaking of the central city.* **Oxford: Oxford University Press.**

Hamnett, C. (2003) *Unequal city: London in the global arena.* **London: Routledge.**

Smith, N. (1996) *The new urban frontier: gentrification and the revanchist city.* **London: Routledge.**

These texts present an analysis of gentrification, its causes and effects.

Sorkin, M. (ed.) (1992) *Variations on a theme park: the new American city and the end of public space.* **New York: The Noonday Press.**

Davis, M. (1990) *City of quartz.* **London: Verso.**

These provide an understanding of the changes taking place in the edge cities of America.

Champion, A.G. (1989) Counterurbanisation in Europe. *The Geographical Journal,* **155, 32–59.**

Cheshire, P. (1995) A new phase of urban development in western Europe: the evidence for the 1980s. *Urban Studies,* **32(7), 1045–64.**

Rigorous social scientific analyses of counter-urbanization.

Beauregard, B. (1994) *Voices of decline: the post-war fate of US cities.* **Oxford: Blackwell.**

A good textual analysis of the representation of urban decline in the USA.

CHAPTER 32

Lisa Law

SENSING THE CITY: URBAN EXPERIENCES

INTRODUCTION

Take a moment to think about what the word 'city' means to you. Where does your imagination begin? Do you think of what a city looks like? Do you visually map it, picturing its architecture and urban form? Do you look down at it from above or do you imagine yourself wandering through the streets? Perhaps instead of seeing the city, and conjuring it from your visual imagination, you contemplate the city's distinctive aromas or sounds. Do you smell car exhaust fumes, bakeries, coffee, perfume? Do you hear traffic, mobile phones, music, multiple languages? Or perhaps you have a disability and think of the city in a haptic register, possibly as a difficult place to get around. Do any of these senses evoke negative feelings, such as fear, or positive associations such as freedom or pleasure? How do we begin thinking about the city and the different experiences it evokes? Can we connect these seemingly routine experiences to culture and politics? This chapter encourages you to think about the senses – sight, smell, sound, touch and taste – as one possible way to investigate these issues.

Geography is conventionally understood as a visual discipline, with an emphasis on optic methods and techniques such as observation and mapping. Our cartographic roots encouraged our reliance on sight, but this has had a profound impact on the way we contemplate the world around us. Recall various geography texts you have read (or are now reading) and consider how we describe our research and our knowledge:

> " *Questions are 'looked at' in a particular way, pilot studies are completed 'with a view' to developing a larger project, things are kept in 'perspective', events are 'seen' in one way or another, futures are 'envisaged', empirical research 'sheds light' on theoretical concerns, 'insights' are gained, problems are 'looked into'.* "

> (Smith, 2000: 615)

Seeing, in other words, is equated with believing; we assume vision is clear and transparent. Until recently geographers have unwittingly associated this visual world with reliable knowledge, without considering how the other senses might shape our everyday lives and geographies. But in the past few decades some geographers have suggested that looking and seeing – although dominant in the discipline – are only one of several possible pathways to knowledge and understanding.

Cultural and **feminist** geographers first brought questions of the reliability of vision to the fore, querying how vision helps produce geographic knowledge. Denis Cosgrove (1984; 1985b; 2001), a cultural geographer, has examined how 'perspective' shapes our seemingly innocent depictions of landscape. He explains how landscape descriptions – whether in written texts, paintings or photographs – have evolved through time, and how

Feminism

a series of perspectives, which together draw on theoretical and political accounts of the oppression of women in society to suggest how GENDER relations and Human Geography are interconnected (*see also* PATRIARCHY).

Colonialism

the rule of a NATION-STATE or other political power over another, subordinated, people and place. This domination is established and maintained through political structures, but may also shape economic and cultural relations. *See also* NEO-COLONIALISM and IMPERIALISM.

Positionality

the personal experiences, beliefs, identities and motives of the Human Geographer, which influence her or his work and the way in which her or his knowledge is situated.

Gender

a criterion of social organization that distinguishes different groups of people on the basis of femininity or masculinity. In any one location, many masculinities and femininities interact. As a concept, gender is usually used in Human Geography in distinction to that of sex (i.e. femaleness and maleness) in order to emphasize the SOCIAL CONSTRUCTION of women's and men's roles, relations and identities. Human Geographers' accounts of the world have always been shaped through understandings of gender (see MASCULINISM) but explicit analyses of the geographies of gender and the gendering of geographies are comparatively recent, and associated with the growth of Feminist Geography (see FEMINISM).

Sexuality

sexual attitudes, preferences, desires and behaviours. Human Geographers have emphasized how our sexualities are not simply a biological given but complex socio-cultural constructs (see also SOCIAL CONSTRUCTION). They have examined how, on the one hand, these constructs sexualize our encounters with places and environments in personally and socially significant ways and, on the other hand, how our sexualities themselves are shaped through experiences and understandings of the geographies of the body, the home, the city, the nation, travel, etc.

they are more akin to a 'way of seeing' than a 'true' depiction of what is actually seen. 'We *learn* to see through the communicative agency of words and pictures', he argues, 'and such ways of seeing become "natural" to us' (Cosgrove, 2003: 250). Landscape descriptions are thus not clear or transparent; they are a visual ideology that expresses what the world looks like from particular 'points of view'. No one view is omniscient, and there are multiple perspectives on any one phenomenon. Think again about your images of the city when you began reading this chapter, and compare them with those of your classmates. Presumably you have different ways of representing urban spaces. Yet it is likely that at least one of your images would include a bird's eye view with abstract symbols for landforms, roads and significant buildings. Geographers suggest this depiction occurs repeatedly in western culture, and is linked to the West's scientific and cultural histories (especially the cartographic project of colonialism). We *learn* to see the city this way, from above, like a map. But is this portrayal innocent? What is at stake when we represent the world in a particular way? Cultural geographers ask us to contemplate the relationship between vision and power: who is looking, what do they see, what conditions enable this point of view to be obtained?

These questions of positionality also interest feminist geographers. They sensitize us to how different people interpret and represent landscapes, and thinking about *whose* images predominate in any one culture provides clues to power. Gillian Rose (1993b; 1997b), a feminist geographer, suggests that the dominant 'way of looking' in geography has been normalized as white, male and heterosexual. That is, the way geographers look at landscapes has been informed by the vantage point of a group that has considerable economic, political and social power. It is a position that assumes its vision is clear and objective, without bearing in mind how it might exclude the viewpoints of different genders, sexualities, races, and so on. But let us consider this argument in relation to urban planning, as the work of geographers is often implicated in state power. Urban planners imagine our cities from above – with the aid of zoning, land use and other maps – building into designs an idealized city. This might include a tree-lined boulevard to introduce nature and aesthetic beauty to your neighbourhood, but the feelings this evokes for a range of people would likely be quite different. As Gill Valentine (1989) discusses, women can find tree-lined boulevards frightening at night as they increase shadows and reduce the possibility of being seen. She calls these 'geographies of fear' that shape women's access to public space. If women find dark boulevards frightening, we might also consider how senior citizens or minority ethnic groups experience these spaces. Green environmental ideals are now internalized in the planning process and help this desire for green spaces appear unproblematic, objective and 'natural'. But, as we will discuss in relation to our case study below, the street *looks* and *feels* different depending on the perspectives of those inhabiting urban spaces; in other words, it depends on whether you view it from 'above' or 'below'.

Rather than tackling the question of vision on its own terms, as geographers such as Cosgrove and Rose have done, other geographers consider geographies of the broader sensorium. After all, what our eyes see does not encapsulate the totality of our experience; we learn about and become **embodied** in the world through our whole bodies and the several senses. Perhaps the distancing, objective (read 'rational') reliance on vision has been opposed to the more embodied, intuitive (read 'irrational') reliance on other forms of knowledge. But challenging the dominance of vision has been more straightforward than efforts to include other sensory experiences in our understanding of geography. We might intuitively know how the feel of the subway, the smell of food cooking, the sound of music, and so on, is crucial to the making of place, but how do we include these experiences in our research? Geographers had not developed a vocabulary to describe sensory experiences until recently, partly because of our reliance on sight but also because they are difficult to record in fieldwork. Geographers are now generating new terms such as 'smellscapes' (Porteous, 1985), 'soundscapes' (Ingham, 1999; Leyshon *et al.*, 1998; Revill, 2000; Smith, S.J., 1997; 2000) and 'sensory landscapes' more generally (Law, 2001; Rodaway, 1994), in the hope that new language will aid in our comprehension of more embodied geographies. The importance of **ethnography** in addressing people's lives and experiences cannot be overstressed; embodied senses of place are difficult to observe from a distance. Whilst some studies of the senses have been inspired by abstract critiques of vision, people with disabilities have initiated other research. The latter have asked geographers to consider how those without the capacity for sight, or who are deaf (for example), might have different experiences of place (see Kitchen *et al.*, 1997). Until recently, these people have been marginalized in our discussions of the city.

In this chapter we examine how thinking about the senses can help us understand our urban experiences, using a case study of Singapore to illustrate these ideas. We begin with 'sight', and visions of Singapore as a global city, and briefly recount the history of Singapore's development using the perspectives of its urban planners and politicians. These perspectives draw on a modernist, utopian view from above, but tell us more about state power than about people's everyday lives. Views of the urban planning landscape are like a freeze-frame, and deny the practices that make the city lively and give it meaning. We thus turn to de Certeau's (1984) ideas of 'spatial practices' that lie below planners' thresholds of visibility and consider urban living as enacted through our everyday routines. We consider a more embodied sense of place in Singapore's famous hawker centres (outdoor restaurants), with their distinctive sounds, aromas and tastes. Here we find alternative maps and views of the city, and can connect a range of senses to urban life and to an unconventional conception of politics.

Race

a criterion of social categorization that distinguishes different groups of people on the basis of particular secondary physical differences (such as skin colour). Human Geographers have studied questions of race in a number of ways including: (a) the extent, causes and implications of the spatial segregation of different racial groups within cities, regions or nations; (b) the role played by geographical understandings of place and environment in the construction both of ideas of race per se and of ideas about particular races; and (c) the forms of racism and inequality that operate through these geographical patterns, processes and ideas. Increasingly, Human Geographers have emphasized how racial categories, whilst having very real consequences for people's lives, cannot simply be assumed as biological realities, having instead to be recognized as SOCIAL CONSTRUCTIONS. *See also* ETHNICITY.

Embodied, embodiment

this concept suggests that the self and the body are not separate, but rather that the experiences of any individual are, invariably, shaped by the active and reactive entity that is their body – irrespective of whether this is conscious or not. The argument, then, runs that the uniqueness of human experience is due, at least in part, to the unique nature of individual bodies.

Ethnography, ethnographic

the research processes that use qualitative methods to provide in-depth explorations and accounts of the lives, interactions and 'textures' associated with particular people and places.

SUMMARY

- The way we experience urban places is not only shaped by vision; a whole range of senses embody us as subjects.
- Geography has tended to rely on vision for the acquisition of knowledge, although feminist and cultural geographers have challenged this tradition.
- Understanding the urban as a sensory landscape – which includes, but is not limited to, vision – can provide insights to the everyday politics of cities.

SEEING SINGAPORE

Looking at Singapore from the 72nd floor of the Raffles City complex is an extraordinary sensation (see Fig. 32.1). Your gaze is drawn unavoidably south, beyond the old colonial Padang and Cricket Club, to the glittering skyscrapers of Shenton Way. Here lies Singapore's stock exchange and the headquarters of many multinational institutions and corporations. Much like other **global cities**, this is where Singapore's business and financial services compete in the world economy. At the south-eastern edge of the business district lies a row of gentrified shop-houses along Boat Quay, a waterfront lined with riverboats until the 1980s but now home to cosmopolitan eating places and nightclubs. Shift your gaze north-east to see the recently completed 'Esplanade: Theatres on the Bay'. Locals have nicknamed this world-class performing arts centre 'The Durians' (a spiked, fragrant fruit), as if to give such internationally inspired architecture a local flavour. Esplanade is part of Singapore's vision to become a 'global centre for the arts' and, together with places like Boat Quay, is imagined as transforming Singapore's erstwhile image as monotonous and uncreative (Chang, 2000; Chang and Lee, 2003; Kong and Yeoh, 2003). Global cities are now thought to maintain their competitiveness by fostering creativity and entrepreneurship, a principle embraced by Singapore's politicians. Places like Esplanade and Boat Quay are being promoted as sites to be creative and have fun. Continue your gaze along the coastline to see condominiums with spectacular sea views, stretching almost as far as Singapore's first-class Changi Airport. It's a city obsessed with being 'global', 'first' and 'world class'.

Participating in the global economy means building cities that can compete with others in the global capitalist economy. Thus places like Singapore – or Tokyo, London, Paris, and so on – have changing urban forms that shape and reflect new kinds of urban spaces, but also new kinds of experiences. In some cities this has meant demolishing the old to make way for the new, and this is certainly true in Singapore. In Boat Quay, for example, the redevelopment of this site all but erases its history. No longer is it a bustling anchorage where immigrants arrive, or where

FIGURE 32.1
Raffles City and view: Raffles City is a massive I.M. Pei-designed complex that includes shops, restaurants, offices, conference facilities and a luxury hotel; the top floor of the hotel is touted as offering the best views of Singapore.
Credit: Kevin R. Morris/Corbis

goods are sold and exchanged, although a few riverboats still ply the river on scenic cruises and statues commemorate this history. The nearby redevelopment of Chinatown has been most controversial, however, as gentrification has brought an entirely different life to what was initially a bustling community of Chinese migrants. No longer is this where Chinese culture is *lived*, it is a place where it is *seen*. The visual *look* of the

Global city

a term used by Saskia Sassen in the early 1990s to denote those cities that play a key role in the operation of the capitalist world economy, particularly in terms of financial and business services. The term builds upon the concept of 'world city', put forward by Freidmann and Wolff, to capture the command and control centres of late CAPITALISM, particularly in terms of the concentration of headquarters of multi- and TRANSNATIONAL CORPORATIONS.

FIGURE 32.2
HDB housing: the majority of Singaporeans live in public housing; the architecture of these buildings is often criticized as excessively repetitive and anonymous.
Credit: Dean Conger/Corbis

architecture has been given highest priority, in preference to the daily practices of trades and lifestyles that made this an ethnic neighbourhood (Yeoh and Kong, 1994). It is now a place for tourists, complete with hotels, museums and upmarket restaurants. This morphing of Singapore's urban form is not a new phenomenon, and could be said to reflect a privileging of 'time' over 'space' (Koolhaas, 2000). Since independence, Singapore's restless landscape has reflected the state's desire to join the ranks of the world's most developed nations.

Let us continue with our Raffles City vista, but shift our focus north and west, where there are views less familiar to visitors (see Fig. 32.2). They also tell stories of Singapore's developmentalism and provide immense insight into the everyday life of its inhabitants. High-rise government flats of various shapes and sizes dominate the panorama; almost 80 per cent of Singapore's inhabitants live in public housing. Unlike in places such as North America and Europe, where public housing is targeted at low-income groups, in Singapore the majority of the population aspire to own their own flats and eventually upgrade them. The state's Housing Development Board

Fordism

a form of industrial capitalism dominating the economies of the USA and western Europe from the end of the Second World War to the early 1970s. It was characterized by mass production and mass consumption, where high levels of productivity (often promoted by new assembly line production) sustained high wages, which in turn led to high levels of demand for industrial products. This demand fed into higher production, which supported higher productivity, and the 'virtuous circle' began all over again. It was an economic system that was often underpinned by a political compromise between capital and labour, and by subsequent state policies towards wages, taxes and welfare provision, which helped to sustain mass production and consumption. *See also* POST-FORDISM.

Space of flows

a term first coined by the urban theorist Manuel Castells in distinction to the 'space of places', this self-confessed 'cumbersome expression' emphasizes how the character and dynamics of a bounded place are reliant upon a host of connections and flows that go beyond its boundaries. These include flows of people (through many forms of travel and migration), of capital and money (think of the impacts of the global networks of the international financial system, for example), of ideas, of media imagery and of objects, amongst many others. The notion of the 'space of flows' is therefore a complement and corrective to Human Geographers' long-standing interest in bounded places and territories (*see* TERRITORY), perhaps particularly important in an age of intensified GLOBALIZATION.

(HDB) administers the scheme, an institution originally established in 1960 to provide mass housing to Singapore's low- and middle-income households (Perry *et al.*, 1997). The HDB's early mandate was to redevelop the squalor that had become concentrated in the inner-city area – a relic of the colonial administration that neglected to address racialized inner-city neighbourhoods and urban sprawl. The goal was to transform the housing landscape into one representing a 'well-planned modern metropolis', whilst at the same time integrating Chinese, Indian, Malay and other ethnic groups into less segregated neighbourhoods (Goh, 2001: 1589). The landscape is thus shaped by state ideologies of modernity and multiculturalism.

Whilst the state did rapidly transform living conditions, providing mass housing to the population, the shift to new accommodation was stressful for those relocated to these sites. It broke up communities and dramatically changed ways of life. Furthermore, because housing is shaped so strongly by state ideology, policy decisions have discernible impacts on people's everyday lives. Class and racial mixing are built into HDB neighbourhoods, for instance, and ideologies of what constitutes the 'Asian family' also shape people's access to housing. Preventing singles from buying government flats, and preferential treatment for extended families, are two examples found in the history of HDB policies. Chua (1995: 139) suggests that the sheer material presence of countless blocks of flats are 'powerful symbolic monuments to [the] government's efficacy', visually reinforcing the state's legitimacy and achievements. Public housing thus tends to be a powerful sign in the landscape that overpowers other meanings, such as the extent to which ideology regulates people's everyday sense of class, race, gender, sexuality, and so on. Whilst there is resistance to state housing policies in popular culture, as in Eric Khoo's film *12 Storeys* (see box), Chua (1995: 140) suggests that alternatives to the current system generally fail to become incorporated into people's 'everyday rationalisation of their life-world'. We will return to this idea of state planning and architecture, and people's capacity to resist dominant meanings, in our discussion of hawker centres.

Our touristic view of Singapore tells us much about how the state manipulates the landscape to accord with its own, idealized, vision of Singapore. The early housing landscape, with its minimalist and anonymous architecture, mirrored **Fordist** modes of production that were driving the economy of the time (Goh, 2001). The contemporary central business district, with its multinational headquarters and cosmopolitan sites, illustrates the state's desire to network itself into a global **space of flows**. Singapore's landscape thus tells a story of the state's ongoing desire to compete in the global economy, organize its population and rationalize its spheres of production and reproduction (De, 2002). It is a vision from above, available from vantage points like Raffles City, but tells us little about the people who inhabit and make sense of the city at street level. As Michel de Certeau (1984: 383–4) once observed in relation to the view of New York City from the (now destroyed) World Trade Center, to be lifted to such heights is

" *to be lifted out of the city's grasp … one's body is no longer clasped by the streets … nor is it possessed … by the rumble of so many differences*

... It transforms the bewitching world ... into a text that lies before one's eyes. It allows one to read it ... looking down like a god. "

This vision from above fixes the landscape into a static image that denies its lived complexity.

Michel de Certeau (1984), a theorist of the everyday as counter-concept in western societies, has written about how urban practices can interrupt the hegemony of state ideologies of urban development. His interest lies in disrupting totalitarian systems that become incorporated into our sense-making activities and routines, and in exploring the possibilities of **human agency** that are foreclosed when we focus too narrowly on reading representational systems in the urban landscape. In Singapore, a country stereotypically known as a surveillant state, it is important to understand how state power is established through a mechanism such as urban planning. We can 'read' in the landscape how the state organizes its economy and society, finding evidence of how ideologies materialize in urban space. People live in mixed neighbourhoods, labour at cosmopoli-

Human agency

usually indicates self-conscious, purposeful action. Geographers have used this term to stress the freedom and capacity of people to generate, modify and influence the course of everyday and world events.

ERIC KHOO'S *12 STOREYS*

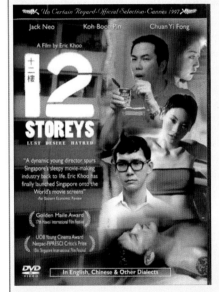

Eric Khoo's film, *12 Storeys*, premiered in Singapore and at Cannes in 1997. Touted as Singapore's return to the world screen, the film offers a critique of Singapore's archetypal image as clean, efficient and upwardly mobile. *12 Storeys*, as the title implies, is set within a typical working-class HDB block (many of which have 12 storeys). Khoo portrays the worlds of three households inhabiting the block, and whose experience of HDB living is claustrophobic and full of loneliness and alienation: a dutiful but repressed brother obsessed with disciplining his siblings' work ethic and sexuality; a frustrated, sexless relationship between a bucktoothed noodle seller and his acquisitive China bride; and an

overweight daughter of a malicious Cantonese immigrant woman who devoted her life to raising other people's children. One thread holding the stories together is the spirit of a young man who commits suicide at the beginning of the film; he witnesses these people's dramas, but never speaks to them. Another thread is a group of unemployed men that collectively idle at the local coffee shop (a phenomenon discussed further in the main text of this chapter). The characters express the 'nightmarish contradictions in self-understanding and interpersonal relations' that Khoo believes haunt modern Singapore, and reveal what most Singaporeans just 'know' (De, 2002: 196).

Khoo's characters are ordinary Singaporeans in a dysfunctional society; they are 'representative types of Singaporeans who have fallen out of step with the Singapore Success Story' (Chua and Yeo, 2003: 119). As disaffected HDB-dwellers, they do not symbolize the state-promoted imagery of happy families, efficiency and economic prowess. In this way, Khoo provides us with an alternative portrayal of everyday life and an oblique critique of the state. He does so from the margins of the modern metropolis, however, and this is reflected in the audience he reaches: *12 Storeys* is not mainstream cinema and has limited circulation in the art-house circuit. Without engaging Singapore's mass audience, and without empathizing with (rather than merely representing) their worlds, Khoo stands accused of 'superficial ethnography' and an inability to represent the 'embodied psychological dramas' of life in Singapore (Chua and Yeo, 2003: 120).

tan workplaces and have fun in places like Boat Quay. At the same time, Singaporeans do not necessarily carry out their lives in ways intended by the state; we might also consider how people resist, subvert and/or transgress state ideology. Drawing on our critiques of vision discussed earlier, we might ask ourselves: What does Singapore look like from the sidewalks of the city and suburbs? Is living in Singapore akin to living within the confines of a city-planning map? De Certeau advises that we should not undervalue the capacity of the everyday pedestrian walking in the city to craft new meanings into spaces designed by planners. He terms these subversions and transgressions 'spatial practices' that make up the 'lived space' of the city.

Everyday life contains habits, or what de Certeau terms 'spatial practices', that interrupt – rather than resist – state or other ideologies. He describes these fragmentary routes through the city as 'tactics' in that they are not resistant in the conventional sense; rather, they are enacted through a myriad of footsteps that undermine state ideology. Pedestrians recreate even the most highly planned city by living in it, by weaving new stories into the urban landscape that can transgress the narratives preferred by the state. Even though pedestrians transgress ideologies in ways that are small, individual and non-confrontational, de Certeau suggests these practices do create another 'mobile' city within the highly planned one. He suggests that spatial practices are not *separate* from the administration of everyday life by the state, but they are '*foreign* to the "geometrical" or "geographical" space of the visual, panoptic, or theoretical constructions' that preoccupy urban planners (de Certeau, 1984: 93, emphasis added). Using de Certeau's ideas allows us to think about what the city looks like 'from below', and thus to understand the complex engagement Singaporeans have with state ideology. As we will see in our discussion of hawker centres shortly, de Certeau's conceptualization works particularly well in Singapore, where people find individual (and collective) ways to survive life under an interventionist state.

Everyday life
a notoriously difficult term to define, as it has meant many different things to a great many different philosophers, theorists and practitioners. We can generalize that it is an arena of social life that includes repetitive daily cycles and routines that we learn but eventually take for granted.

SUMMARY

- Seeing the city from above, as urban planners do, fixes the city's meaning and denies its lived complexity.
- State ideology is built into the city's built form, and can inscribe a dominant meaning into space.
- State ideology is not the only meaning inscribed in urban landscapes. De Certeau suggests that the everyday pedestrian can craft new and sometimes subversive meanings into the urban environment. His idea of 'spatial practices' allows us to consider the possibilities of human agency.

SENSING EVERYDAY GEOGRAPHIES

Let us now shift our attention to the lived space of Singapore, and consider how state ideology and human agency are practised in an everyday environment. One space of considerable significance is the ubiquitous hawker centre, an open-air food court typically attached to a wet market or HDB housing estate (see Fig. 32.4). Hawker centres have several stalls selling a variety of ethnic fare, including Chinese, Indian,

Malay and even western food. Customers order and pay at their chosen stall, where food/drink is served immediately or soon thereafter to a numbered table in an open seating area. Because the price of food at hawker centres is reasonable, and because there are so many of them (more than 130 centres with almost 18,000 individual stalls are regulated by the government) many families across socio-economic groups take advantage of hawker fare to supplement or even replace home cooking. Frequent patronage makes hawker centres an important social space in Singapore, whether it be for family meals, housewives stopping for a chat, couples on dates, youths having coffee or men gathering to drink beer. Hawker centres are thus densely meaningful sites, where state ideology meets the practices of everyday life.

Hawker centres have been regulated by the state since their planned construction in Singapore after independence. Their history can be traced to the state's ideology of a well-ordered modernity, and to the sanitization of the city bound up in the garden city movement of the time. Mobile hawkers that once plied their trade on the streets were gradually moved into state-regulated centres complete with electricity, rubbish disposal, water and sewerage facilities. Their relocation into purpose-built centres was thought to be a solution to the problems of pollution, the spread of food-borne diseases and 'the encumbrance of land for other national development projects' (Perry *et al.*, 1997: 210). Whilst regulations have changed over time, the state maintains a surveillant role in managing these sites. For example, each stall must be granted a permit to commence operation, which allows the

state to ensure a mix of hawker fare at any one centre. As in the case of HDB estates, the state favours racial mixing and can ensure hawker centres are reflective of Singapore's multicultural population and sensitive to religious dietary restrictions (e.g. providing halal sections for Muslims). Furthermore, each food handler must take a state-run course and pass various health examinations, and each stall is officially 'graded' according to state-defined sanitary conditions (ranging from 'A' to 'D', with 'A' being the cleanest). Hawker centres are important everyday sites that could be 'read' as a powerful inscription in the landscape. Their design and form corresponds to the state's ideology of class and racial mixing and orderliness. But do Singaporeans merely live out the state's ideals of order and cosmopolitanism in hawker centres?

If we return to de Certeau's ideas of spatial practices, we can rethink hawker centres as part of the everyday lived experience of the city. Because hawker centres are so ubiquitous, and frequented by people across different social groups, they form an important part of the rhythm of daily

FIGURE 32.4
Hawker centres. Credit: Michael S. Yamashita/Corbis

life. They are spaces where people gather for many reasons, from the functional act of eating a meal to renewing social networks or simply stopping to chat and gossip. But patronage does not mean adhering to state ideology, as people's visits are harnessed to different everyday lives and routines. If we drew a map of people's everyday routes we would have a sense of how important hawker centres are to the flow of daily life, but we would not be able to tell the meanings people attach to their visits. We would not know, for instance, if they experience pleasure, apprehension or different degrees of feeling in or out of place. Hawker centres look and feel different depending on who you are.

For the purposes of our discussion, let us take one group that forms a regular feature of life in hawker centres, especially at the ever present *kopi tiam* (literally, 'coffee shop'). The *kopi tiam* is an important meeting place for blue-collar men in HDB neighbourhoods, where they gossip and tell stories in vernacular groups. Conversations range from idle banter to discussions of world affairs, and the men 'freely mingle current historical information and rational knowledge with folk wisdom' thus rejuvenating 'a heterogeneous tradition of conversation characteristic of ethnic village life in colonial Singapore' (De, 2002: 201; see also Chua, 1997). By upholding village life in the midst of the modern metropolis, the men sustain traditions that subtly undermine (rather than overtly resist) state ideology. They do not gather in groups that imply class or racial mixing, and they speak in ethnic languages or in Singlish – a dialect spoken colloquially in Singapore but officially discouraged by the government (see box). These 'traditional' practices are antithetical to the state's 'modern' ideals. The vernacular soundscapes of hawker centres thus offer us different possibilities in terms of thinking about power and resistance, but require listening to – and not just looking at – what is taking place.

Whilst soundscapes provide important clues to the everyday world of hawker centres, this does not mean that vision remains irrelevant. What

SINGLISH IN SINGAPORE

Singlish is spoken vernacularly in Singapore and can be thought of as an Asian dialect of the English language. It is a mixture of British (and increasingly American) English with some grammar and vocabulary drawn from Chinese (especially Hokkien), Malay and Tamil languages. Singlish is influenced by the grammatical and tonal structure of Chinese, making it difficult to imitate for non-Chinese or non-Singaporean speakers. Importantly, Singlish is officially denounced by the state, as it is understood as unrefined pidgin that impedes equality and Singapore's access to the outside world. On the other hand, many Singaporeans think:

'Bladi Garmen si peh kaypoh one, why always so bedek kacang hor?'

According to www.free-definition.com this sentence can be broken down as follows:

- 'bladi Garmen' – bloody government
- 'si peh' – very (from Hokkien, a Chinese dialect)
- 'kaypoh' – busybody (from Hokkien)
- 'one' – extraneous modifier
- 'why always so' – indication of harboured displeasure
- 'bedek kacang' – lit. 'aiming at peanuts' (Malay); in this sentence, can probably be taken to mean 'meddlesome' or 'annoying'
- 'hor?' – Chinese prompt for affirmation, somewhat like *n'est-ce pas?* in French.

Since the late 1990s schools have carried out Speak English Campaigns and a broader Speak Good English Movement was initiated in 2000. It is unlikely that Singlish can be eradicated by the state, however.

blue-collar men see at the *kopi tiam* is not the glittering skyscrapers of Shenton Way, the orderly HDB landscape or the more general vision of Singapore as well-planned metropolis. Instead they watch people pass by, sometimes making disparaging comments about today's modern youth (e.g. the bizarreness of dyed hair), or they scan the landscape for lucky numbers to enter into the next 4D lottery (illegal bookies are in close proximity to take their wager). This is not what the state *wants* them to see, nor is this how it *wants* hawker centres to be used. These textures of place 'from below' are multifaceted, and require a degree of ethnographic awareness.

Yao Souchou (2001), an ethnographer, argues that an important feature of a *kopi tiam* gathering is the social pleasure of poking fun at the state: a sophisticated yet informal practice of bitching about the government. He suggests that by 'eating air' and 'talking cock', the men enact a visceral condition that tells us much about everyday life in Singapore. In local parlance 'eating air' evokes leisurely evening strolls that provide respite from the tropical heat, as well as opportunities to chat with friends and share a meal. 'Talking cock' is a Singlish term for the informal, artful verbal exchanges that embellish social facts with a mixture of humour and wisdom. Yao argues that in the cool of the evening these men 'eat air' and 'talk cock' as an everyday, subversive practice that tells us much about the pleasure and burden of life under a robust state. Crucial to these exchanges – which introduce everything from the price of cars to the enduring fortunes of the Lee family – is their seasoning with food and drink. Food arrives in bite-sized pieces small enough not to inhibit talking, and alcohol lubricates the discussion. Eating air and talking cock thus represent a visceral embodiment that can be connected to discussions of politics in Singapore, but this is not a politics that understands talking cock as formal, conscious resistance. Instead, it is an embodied form of political engagement that subtly undermines the state (which, in any case, talks cock too).

Understanding these textures of place and sensory embodiments provides important clues to life in everyday Singapore, where resistance is not generally 'seen'. In this context it might be more important to understand phenomena such as idling in hawker centres, where more subtle politics unfold through the everyday habits of gathering and sharing a meal. Such communal assembly is a spatial practice (in de Certeau's sense) that helps rewrite Singapore's landscape in ways that are more meaningful to its inhabitants. These everyday geographies lie below the state's threshold of visibility, and summon a whole range of senses to give them meaning: the soundscapes of vernacular language, the taste of ethnic food and the feel of the cool evening air. Whilst these everyday practices might not alter the political world most Singaporeans live in, they do provide alternative

SUMMARY

- Hawker centres in Singapore are one example of a state narrative inscribed in the landscape, but people craft new meanings into these sites. They are thus the 'lived spaces' that tell us about urban experience.

- Whilst spatial practices are about vision, it is also important to remember that a range of senses embody people at these sites; the senses work in tandem to produce everyday, embodied experiences.

maps and views of a city undergoing profound transformation. To access these worlds geographers must move beyond optic methods and techniques, and learn to hear, taste and smell their meanings.

CONCLUSION

Although the discipline of geography has historically relied on vision for its understanding of urban experience, there is another world of understanding that lies beyond (within?) that which is in view. We must not rely solely on our sense of sight, or on the visions of powerful others. Otherwise we end up investigating only 'remarkable' and 'elite' landscapes, ones that are more readily seen from above than below. As Cresswell (2003: 280) argues, our challenge is to produce 'geographies that are lived, embodied, practiced; landscapes which are never finished or complete, not easily framed or read'. The senses can provide geographers with fresh insights to the complexity of everyday urban life, and new opportunities for embodied research.

DISCUSSION POINTS

1. What are some of the problems encountered when thinking about urban experience from above?

2. Why is it important to move beyond geographers' critiques of vision?

3. What methods would you use to investigate the link between the senses and urban experience?

4. Does an understanding of the senses provide us with insight to human agency?

FURTHER READING

Rodaway, P. (1994) *Sensuous geographies: body, sense and place.* London and New York: Routledge.

Pocock, D. (1993) The senses in focus. *Area*, 25(1), 11–16.

These texts offer a good introduction to how the senses are relevant to geography.

Ingham, J. (1999) Hearing places, making spaces: sonorous geographies, ephemeral rhythms, and the Blackburn warehouse parties. *Environment and Planning D: Society and Space*, 17, 283–305.

Law, L. (2001) Home cooking: Filipino women and geographies of the senses in Hong Kong. *Ecumene*, 8(3), 264–83.

Smith, S. (2000) Performing in the (sound)world. *Environment and Planning D: Society and Space*, 18, 615–37.

These three articles examine the senses and our urban experiences.

De Certeau, M. (1984) *The practice of everyday life.* Berkeley: University of California Press.

Michel de Certeau's ideas about 'spatial practices' are to be found in this book.

Lefebvre, H. (1971) *Everyday life in the modern world.* New York: Harper & Row.

Geographers interested in everyday life will find the work of Henri Lefebvre useful.

Howes, D. (ed.) (2004) *Empire of the senses: the sensual culture reader.* Oxford and New York: Berg Publishers.

Outside geography, this is an excellent collection of essays on the senses.

CHAPTER 33
THE COUNTRY

Paul Cloke

INTRODUCTION: THE COUNTRYSIDE COMES TO TOWN?

In July 1997, and again in March 1998, more than 100,000 people gathered in Hyde Park, London, to protest about the gradual encroachment of urban-based bureaucracy into country life, as epitomized by the government's proposal to ban fox hunting (see Fig. 33.1). In the words of the *Daily Telegraph*,

> *in the annals of popular protest, there can seldom have been a noisier plea to a British government to do absolutely nothing than yesterday's Countryside Rally ... they had come from farms, moors and fells, emptying villages and leaving nature to its own devices for a day in order to let the urban majority know that the rural minority wishes to be left alone.*

(*Daily Telegraph*, 11 July 1997)

Such protests have continued, largely under the political banner of the Countryside Alliance, but also involving acts of civil disobedience by the so-called Real Countryside Alliance, even though a ban on hunting wild animals with dogs has now been passed.

In many ways such a protest is indicative of a peculiarly British collection of landscapes, traditions and cultural practices associated with the countryside. Here we are offered the view of a somewhat timeless, highly valued and all-embracing country life that needs to be preserved at all costs from the ravages of urbanism. It is, however, the view of a small but powerful minority, which can grab the imagination about what country life stands for. Our geographical imaginations of the country are often produced and reproduced from 'stuff' such as this. By contrast the distinguished travel writer, Jonathan Raban, records a visit to rural Alabama in his book *Hunting Mr Heartbreak*. Here he emphasizes the shock experienced by some Europeans when they encounter some of the countrysides of America. The scale, colour and 'savagery' of nature in the American outdoors do not easily accommodate direct comparisons with more familiar European landscapes.

Geographical imagination

an awareness of the role of space, place and environment in human life. This phrase is sometimes used in the definite singular – the geographical imagination – to refer to the distinctive intellectual concerns and contributions of Geography. It is also used in the plural – geographical imaginations – to emphasize the many different ways in which academics, students and lay publics alike can develop their sensitivities to human geographies.

FIGURE 33.1
The country comes to town.
Credit: Dan Chung/Reuters/Corbis

Idyll-ized

the process by which dominant myths about places and spaces come to reflect circumstances of picturesque beauty, tranquillity and harmonious living conditions. The term is often used in relation to rural spaces, where social problems can be hidden by the impression of idyllic life in close-knit communities and close to nature.

Gender

a criterion of social organization that distinguishes different groups of people on the basis of femininity or masculinity. In any one location, many masculinities and femininities interact. As a concept, gender is usually used in Human Geography in distinction to that of sex (i.e. femaleness and maleness) in order to emphasize the SOCIAL CONSTRUCTION of women's and men's roles, relations and identities. Human Geographers' accounts of the world have always been shaped through understandings of gender (*see* MASCULINISM) but explicit analyses of the geographies of gender and the gendering of geographies are comparatively recent, and associated with the growth of Feminist Geography (*see* FEMINISM).

Sexuality

sexual attitudes, preferences, desires and behaviours. Human Geographers have emphasized how our sexualities are not simply a biological given but complex socio-cultural constructs (*see also* SOCIAL CONSTRUCTION). They have examined how, on the one hand, these constructs sexualize our encounters with places and environments in personally and socially significant ways and, on the other hand, how our sexualities themselves are shaped through experiences and understandings of the geographies of the body, the home, the city, the nation, travel, etc.

> " *It was how Europeans had always seen American nature – as shockingly bigger, more colourful, more deadly, more exotic, than anything they'd seen at home. When the urban European thought of the countryside, he imagined a version of pastoral that was akin to, if a good deal less exaggerated than, that on offer in Ralph Lauren's Rhinelander Mansion on Madison Avenue. The 'country' was an artefact – hedged, ditched, planted, well patrolled . . . The European landscape was a mixture of park, farm and garden; the nearest we come to wilderness was the keepered grouse moor and the occasional picturesque crag. We were astonished by America, its irrepressible profusion and 'savagery'.* "

(Raban, 1990: 153)

In highlighting these differences, Raban also shows us that rural areas represent a vivid and often specific facet of the geographical imagination. Not only do we carry around with us an idyll-ized sense of what our rural areas look like, and therefore of what they are like to live in and visit, but we are often shocked when encountering other stereotypes of our countrysides or other countrysides.

In this chapter, I want to discuss how rural areas have become exciting contexts for study in Human Geography. There has been, over recent years, something of a resurgence of interest in rural studies, partly as it has embraced the 'cultural turn' that is evident in the broader social sciences, but also in part because the significance of 'nature' and 'rurality' has gone beyond rural geographical space. Rural areas themselves have offered fertile ground for the study of more mainstream cultural ideas, of which three have been of particular importance.

1. *A focus on landscape*, emphasizing the meanings, myths and ideologies that are represented therein. Geographical study of landscape can range from deep countryside to urban street and from deep history to the imaginative futuristic landscapes of science fiction. However, countryside landscapes demonstrate particular power relations as well as being objects of desire that many would wish to conserve.
2. *A focus on how nature relates to space*. Again, nature is by no means confined to rural areas, but countrysides are often represented as the 'obvious' spaces of nature. Here the relations between culture and nature (see Chapter 1) are often a visible element of country life – as in the 'hunting' debate mentioned above – and consequently the country provides fertile ground for the study of how humans and non-humans interact.
3. *A focus on 'hidden others'*. Countrysides are rich in myth, and they represent territories where an overriding cultural gloss on life can mask very significant socially excluded groups. Issues of gender, sexuality, poverty and alternative lifestyles are important in this context.

What links these themes together is the importance of an idyll-ized view of the rural. Countrysides are seen as places where people can live close to nature and in harmony with surrounding landscapes. Country living is characterized by a happy, healthy and close-knit community and a problem-free existence that differs markedly from urban life. Such an idyll reflects the power of those who can afford to buy into and enjoy rural life, and deflects any 'problems' that don't fit the image. And it is this idyllic cultural image that transfers itself into broader society such that the country is no longer confined to the spatial boundaries of recognizably rural areas. Through the **commodification** of nature and rurality within contemporary consumption (as indicated not only through media attention and in advertising but also in 'country' consumer goods ranging from four-wheel drive vehicles to furnishings and clothing) the importance of the country, and the meanings attached to it, have spread throughout society.

It is important to note that these cultural themes of the country are not the only geographies to be told of rural areas. Indeed, these more recent cultural geographies are being overlaid on to existing accounts of behavioural and political studies of economic change, and demographic and relational studies of social change. What makes the country important in Human Geography, however, is a combination of the idyll-ized imagined geographies peddled by media and advertising and held by people as significant reference maps for spatial behaviour, and the specific material changes occurring in rural geographical areas. This mix of imagined and spatialized countrysides begs questions about how we recognize rurality when we see it, and it is important here to reflect briefly on these debates surrounding the nature of rurality.

Commodification

this term is used in two interrelated ways: (a) as the conversion of any thing, idea or person into a COMMODITY (the term 'commoditization' is often preferred for this sense); and (b) a wider societal process whereby an ever increasing number of things, human relationships, ideas and people are turned into commodities. Both meanings see the process of commodification as symptomatic of the penetration of CAPITALISM into the everyday lives of people and things.

THE BLURRING OF COUNTRY AND CITY

When we study rural geographies we have to keep hold of two rather different kinds of change. First, there are the changes that are occurring in rural areas themselves. For example, over the past 25 years there has been a hugely significant reversal of the trend of the previous century whereby population had been concentrating into urban centres in most western countries. In the United States, for example, the 1950s and 1960s saw a strong positive correlation between settlement size and population growth rate, but during the 1970s 'smallness' became associated with growth. In the UK, the 1981 census revealed that rural districts had begun to experience demographic growth over the previous decade, and this trend continued over the next 20 years (Table 33.1). Although this broad picture of rural in-migration masks a diversity of localized patterns of growth and decline, it suggests important changes in rural society. In-migrant populations were at one and the same time seeking out the perceived advantages of rural lifestyles, and bringing with them attributes of urban living and expectations that were likely to transform the very communities they had been attracted to. Traditional rural life had already been transformed by the near universal availability of urban-based media, and now this has been reinforced by the infusion of migrants, often from urban places, who were seeking to live out imagined geographies of rural life in particular geographical places and spaces, often leading to some turbulence with more 'indigenous' populations.

Demographic change has usually gone hand in hand with economic change. As the size of the agricultural workforce has diminished, the notion that rural areas are dominated by agriculture has in many places

Table 33.1 Population change in rural and urban districts of England, 1981–2001

	1981–1991	1991–2001	1981–2001
Rural districts	+7.1%	+4.9%	+12.4%
Urban districts	+1.4%	+0.9%	+2.4%
England total	+3.0%	+2.0%	+5.0%

Source: Woods (2004), drawing on data from the Countryside Agency

become more applicable to the dominance of agricultural landscapes than to the agricultural economy. Counter-urbanization was often accompanied by an urban-to-rural shift in new manufacturing growth, and although the economic impact of this shift has sometimes been short-lived, new forms of service-sector employment have often added to the economic potential of these non-metropolitan areas. Indeed it is now commonly assumed that the growing importance of telecommunications and information technology will metaphorically 'shrink' the geographic distances between rural areas and major urban centres and thereby favour service-sector growth in rural areas. An online personal computer allows many contemporary work tasks to be performed from the rural home, although the degree to which such 'telecottaging' will obviate the need for face-to-face work contact more generally is as yet arguable.

This general picture of change itself masks considerable variation both within and between nations. Indeed, there is evidence, for example in parts of the United States and in different European countries (see Fig. 33.2), that the 'population turnaround' may have a limited duration. So, it is useful to talk of rural geographies rather than a rural geography. It is an obvious but often forgotten fact that what we regard as western or 'developed' nations vary enormously in scale. As Figure 33.3 demonstrates, the scale of influence exerted by major metropolitan areas differs widely, such that the urban pressure on the country in Britain will be far more intense than those on certain areas of the United States and Australia. Such variation means that particular places will be located rather differently in the mosaic of change described above. For some, it would be no exaggeration to suggest that they reflect suburban characteristics, performing a dormitory role for metropolitan labour markets. Elsewhere, agriculture will remain as the dominant economic as well as landscape feature. Elsewhere again, extreme geographical marginality reflects characteristics of 'outback', 'wilderness' or even desert – each posing particular questions of nature–culture relations, and of the potential for commodification. So, the changes occurring in rural areas themselves are

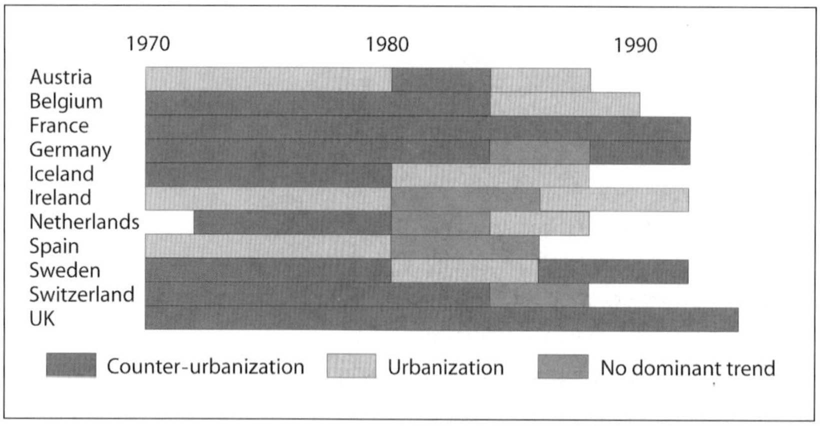

FIGURE 33.2
Predominance of counter-urbanization and urbanization for 11 European countries (Woods, 2004)

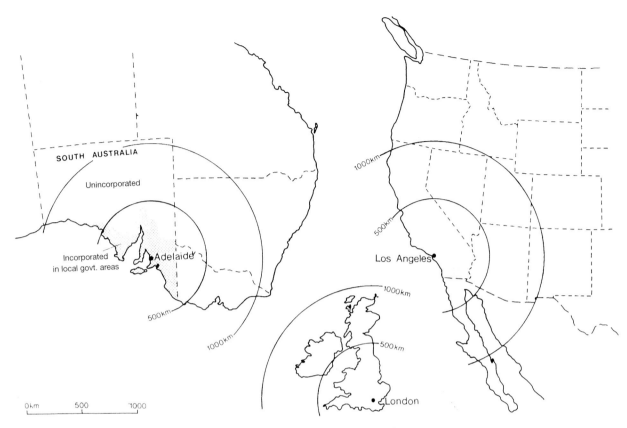

FIGURE 33.3
Different scales of urban influence. Source: G. Hugo and P. Smailes (1985) Urban rural migration in Australia. *Journal of Rural Studies*, 1, 19

irregular, and particular attention has to be given to the geographies of particular places within the overall framework of change.

Accepting the importance of these differences in nature–culture relations, Marc Mormont (1990) has suggested that another key question about rural change concerns the changing relationship between space and society, and it is increasingly clear that this relationship is no longer only about the traditional divisions between rural and urban, or town and countryside. He argues that such dualisms have been completely overtaken by events, and outlines a series of changes relating to personal mobility, and new economic uses of the countryside that indicate the outmoded nature of any view that sees rural society and rural spaces as being welded together. Mormont's analysis of change relates to Belgium, but appears relevant to many countrysides as is his conclusion, which is to suggest that there is no longer a single rural space, but rather a multiplicity of social spaces that overlap the same geographical area. The supposed opposition between the geographic spaces of city and countryside is being broken down, but oppositions between the social significances of city and countryside remain. For Mormont, then, rurality is a category of thought – a social construction – and in contemporary society the social and cultural views that are thought to be attached to rurality provide clearer grounds for differentiating between urban and rural than do the differences manifest in geographic space.

Other commentators (see, for example, the seminal writings of Raymond Williams in the British context) have also noted the blurring of the country and the city. A very interesting contributor to this debate is Alexander Wilson (1992), who in his book *The Culture of Nature* suggests

FIGURE 33.4
West Edmonton Mall.
Credit: Simon Grosset/Alamy

that recent land development in North America – suburbs, theme parks, shopping centres, executive estates, industrial parks, tourist developments and the like – has served to reproduce misleading ideas about city and country. He argues that the form of this development fragments geographies into those devoted to work and leisure, and production and recreation, which are oppositions that obscure more than they reveal about the nature of city and country. He cites the West Edmonton Mall (Edmonton, Canada – see Fig. 33.4) as an example of this jumble of country/city compromises. Its suburban location, 45-hectare size, and 2.5-kilometre-long concourse suggest the monstrous urbanism of an indoor shopping centre. However, it includes a 1-hectare lake with dolphins, sharks (and four full-size submarines, which give rides in the lake). Moreover, the mall also houses an 18-hole golf course, a water park with 6-foot surfing waves, and hundreds of animals in aquariums and cages.

> " *The relentless mission of the West Edmonton Mall is to bring everything into its climatized, commodified space, especially objects and species from the natural world. There are hundreds of animals – 'hand-picked specimens,' the brochures say – in aquariums and cages. The species chosen are displayed in the ways that we've come to know them. First come the most glamorous and evil beasts, familiar from James Bond movies: piranhas, octopuses, alligators, and sharks. Then there are the performers: seals and penguins, peacocks, flamingos, and dolphins. Then there are the cute animals: spider monkeys, emus, and angel fish. And the 'wild' ones we know from TV: black bears, mountain lions, jaguars, iguanas, ostriches. Some of the animals are available for photos. A sign at one stall says:*
>
> > *Have your photo taken with a live cougar cub, $5.99. Extra persons in photo, $2.00 each. Small cub $5.99. Large cub $7.99. Special cuddly cougar prints, regular $30.00 value, now only $5.00 while they last. Lovable lynx prints only $5.00.*
>
> *There is little effort wasted on contextualization at the Mall. Why bother recreating the pre-industrial farm or a simulated jungle, conceits insisted on in Disney environments? Here the animals are just another commodity form, alongside Yves St Laurent and Shoppers Drug Mart. As if to emphasize the point, the mall maintains a 'retreat' for the animals at an undisclosed suburban site in Edmonton. There the animals can rest from their work at the mall, a fact that hasn't discouraged the local gossip that these non-human employees have a very short lifespan. See them while they last!* "

(Wilson, 1992: 198–9)

Here, then, is nature, but in a controlled, climatized, commodified space (see also Chapter 18). The 'landscape' is artificial, but the control over nature is very much part of the attraction. In yet another way, the binary opposition between city and country, and indeed culture and nature is blurred in such place-making.

These examples suggest that the assumed differences between the geographical spaces of city and country have been somewhat undermined by changes occurring in the social, economic and built environments concerned. It is again important to emphasize that such changes differ in scale and intensity in different places. Some countrysides will appear relatively untouched whilst others will have been visibly transformed. Nevertheless, the increasing importance of rurality as a social rather than geographical construct applies very widely. These factors constitute the first set of changes that rural geographers have to grasp.

The second kind of change relates to the way in which geographers have offered different ways of understanding rurality itself. Any given rural geographical space can appear different according to the theoretical perspectives adopted. For example, geographers have traditionally mapped rurality by equating it with particular functions: thus rural areas are dominated (currently or recently) by extensive land uses, such as agriculture and forestry, or large open spaces of undeveloped land; rural areas contain small, lower-order settlements that demonstrate a strong relationship between buildings and surrounding extensive landscapes, and are thought of as rural by most of their residents; and rurality engenders a way of life that is characterized by a cohesive identity based on respect for the environment and behavioural qualities of living as part of an extensive landscape.

This type of analysis has been useful in generating indicators of rural territory, and remains useful, especially in those areas that are less transformed by the process of blurring described above. However, different theoretical epochs in the social sciences have produced critiques of these definitions of rural space. From political–economy approaches came the insight that rural areas were increasingly linked into changing international economies, with the causes of 'rural' change usually stemming from outside of the rural areas concerned. From this viewpoint 'rural' places were not particularly distinct, and for some, this realization led to a call to do away with rural as an analytical category. Recent moves to highlight the theoretical power of *actor networks* give a different perspective to these spatial linkages (see Cloke, 2005; Murdoch, 2003). Here there is a recognition that human and non-human actors are bound together relationally into *hybrid collectifs* (see Chapter 1) that transcend simple spatial and temporal boundaries. Thus the here and now of rural areas may not reflect the complexity of the networks concerned.

Other windows on rurality have focused on the power of the rural as a significant category of the imagination. Drawing on more *postmodern* and *poststructural* ways of thinking, rural researchers (see, for example, Marc Mormont's work discussed above) have suggested that rurality can be regarded as a **social construct**, and that the importance of the 'rural' lies in the fascinating world of social, moral and cultural values that are thought to be significant there. Far from 'doing away with' the rural, then, the idea of rurality as a social construct invites researchers to study how behaviour and decision-making are influenced by the social and cultural meanings attached to rural places. In particular, there is considerable interest in how meanings of rurality are constructed, negotiated and experienced (Cloke and Milbourne, 1992). While such meanings may have much in common, there will be many different versions of rurality perceived by different individuals and organizations.

Leaning on the philosophical writings of Baudrillard, Keith Halfacree

Social construct

a set of specific meanings that become attributed to the characteristics and identities of people and places by common social or cultural usage. Social constructs will often represent a 'loaded' view of the subject, according to the sources from which, and the channels through which, ideas are circulated in society.

(1993) discusses these multiple meanings of 'rural' in terms of three levels of divergence. The sign (= rurality) is increasingly being detached from the signification (= meanings of rurality) as social representations of rurality become more diverse. Equally, sign and signification are also becoming more divorced from their referent (= the rural geographical space). He points out that it is a characteristic of postmodern times that symbols are becoming more detached from their referential moorings, and therefore that socially constructed rural space is becoming increasingly detached from geographically functional rural space. Indeed, Jonathan Murdoch and Andy Pratt (1997) believe that we have reached the stage of 'post-rural' studies, reflecting a willingness to believe in an idea of countryside that we realize may no longer be authentic in terms of the material reality of rural society and space.

These different approaches to 'mapping' or 'knowing' the country introduce a constructive tension to rural studies, especially when held together with the material changes occurring in what are commonly recognized as rural geographical spaces. For some, the country will be seemingly knowable, and apparently atheoretical. For others, the complexities of power, practice and process will render the category 'rural' unknowable as any kind of geographical or social entity. The more postmodern the country seems, the more blurring seems to occur between country and city. Many residents and visitors do appear to act as if the countryside exists in some knowable form. Others, however, appear to know their 'rural' places differently seeing them in other regional (e.g. 'The Borders') or local (e.g. as specific settlements) ways.

SUMMARY

- Rural areas themselves are changing demographically, socially and economically. A geographically 'rural' space may now be overlapped by many different social spaces, thus transforming traditional countrysides.
- Many new land developments – theme parks, shopping centres, tourist developments, etc. – also blur the difference between country and city.
- Geographers have also changed the ways in which

they have sought to understand rurality itself. Defining rural space by the functions that go on there has been challenged by those who view rurality as a social construct – a category of thought.

- The cultural meanings associated with the country have become increasingly detached from rural geographical space and are now important throughout society.

COMMODIFYING THE COUNTRYSIDE

There is evidence that the continuing importance of the country will in part lie in attempts to commodify the countryside as a particular type of attraction within postmodern consumption. Popular culture now serves us up with what Raymond Williams referred to as 'a continuing flood of sentimental and selectively nostalgic versions of country life'. Films such as *The Remains of the Day*, *A River Runs Through It* and *Four Weddings and a Funeral*; television series such as *Heartbeat*, *Peak Practice* and *Pride and Prejudice*; children's favourites such as *Postman Pat* and *Sylvanian Families*; magazines such as *Country Life* and *Countryman*; all merely add to classics in art, literature and media in their focus on cosy and nostalgic aspects of countryscape.

Moreover, the advertising industry repeatedly borrows from the treasure chest of positive meanings vested in the countryside – the 'goodness' of nature, to sell bread; the 'classiness' of the country house to sell cars; the 'pioneer spirit' of rural America to sell jeans or cigarettes – and in so doing reinforces these references to nature, heritage, nostalgia, and so on, in popular constructions of contemporary rural life. In this way, the meanings of country are attached to products that are themselves often aspatial. The country escapes from its geographical referent and inhabits the wider world of taste and consumption. An excellent example of this escape can be found in the way in which the Laura Ashley company purposefully commodified the appeal of country tradition to create a style that is applicable to many kinds of geographical space. In this example the past rustic traditions are sieved through the 'colourful mixture of prints and textures' and the Welsh farmhouse, Long Island house and Swiss chalet are made available to anyone, anywhere. Rustic tradition becomes contemporary commodity, and nature's countryside is bought and sold as fabric and furnishings.

The country is thus being commodified within both the geographical spaces and social spaces it inhabits. Part of the background to the significant shift in the nature and pace of commodification in rural areas in many developed nations is the perceived transition from productivist agriculture, where industrialization and scientization of farming have been deployed to generate increasingly efficient production outputs, to post-productivist agriculture. Although such a transition is far from clear-cut (there are many complexities and ambiguities that defy a simple translation from an overall productivist scheme to an overall post-productivist scheme – see Evans *et al.*, 2002), there are some common underlying changes occurring in rural land use, often encouraged by state regulation, such as the reforms to the Common Agricultural Policy of the EU. One aim has been to extensify food production, by using fewer chemical inputs; witness, for example, the growth in organic food production. Another has been to recognize and reward the role of farmers as guardians of landscape and environment, capable of switching to farm practices that are conducive to broader goals of sustainability and conservation. A third trend has been to diversify farming, promoting a more pluriactive countryside in which farmers are seeking both to enhance the value of their food products (for example, through the growth of local farmers' markets) and to engage in new enterprises, notably in the tourism and leisure sectors. Alongside this farm-based commodification, rurality more generally has given rise to a series of new markets for countryside commodities: the countryside as an exclusive place in which to live; rural communities as a context to be bought and sold; rural lifestyles that can be colonized; icons of rural culture that can be crafted, packed and marketed; rural landscapes with a new range of potential, from 'pay-as-you-enter' national parks, to sites for the theme park explosion, and so on.

As the country becomes commodified, particular meanings and characteristics are emphasized that come to represent its very essence. For example, in a study of how new and revamped rural tourist attractions were being advertised in parts of Britain, it was found that particular meanings, signs and symbols of countryside were clearly being represented (Cloke, 1993). These socially constructed ruralities reflected the perhaps predictable themes of nature, outdoor fun and history. They also reflected the slightly less predictable themes of family safety, 'hands-on' or 'up-close' experiences of nature; and the specific commodity links with souvenir craft and particular foods and drinks that form integral components of the packaged day out in the countryside. The study demonstrated that many of these new countrysides were based on the production of a spectacle for visitors. For example, Morwellham Quay on the border of Devon and Cornwall recreates a Victorian copper port (see Fig. 33.5a) and in so doing offers an outdoor theatre of rural history. According to the brochure,

> the quay workers, cooper, blacksmith, assayer and servant girls dressed in period costume, recreate the bustling boom years of the 1860s . . . Chat with the people of the past. Sample for yourself the life of the port where a bygone age is capture in the crafts and costumes of the 1860s . . . Try on costumes from our 1860s wardrobe.

The invitation is to spectate and participate in the history that is 'captured' by the attraction and presented to visitors in the form of spectacle.

Examples of commodification of country spaces abound. Indeed, Howard Newby (1988) has suggested that rural Britain in general has become a theatre for visiting townsfolk, with rural people, and especially farmers, being the scene-changers and bit-part actors for that theatre. In other nations, this commodification of often reconstructed ruralities is also strongly represented in the changing rural scene. Alexander Wilson (1992) discusses examples in southern Appalachia:

> Scattered along the roads of Tennessee, Kentucky, and the western part of North Carolina are restored villages that recall and reconstruct ideas about the way things once were in those mountains. Some are within nature parks, some are part of theme parks, some are simply an assemblage of buildings that evolved out of someone's backyard, some promote religion, others consumerism.

(Wilson, 1996: 206)

His examples range from gaudy theme parks such as 'Dollywood' (The Dolly Parton story – see Fig. 33.5b) to 'authentic' museums, but each attempts to recreate a lost time and culture in this part of rural America. Here, too, then, the nostalgia of rural life – and in this case the pioneerism and specific culture of rural mountain folk – are commodified as attractions for visitors to the contemporary countryside. Once again, the character of the present is vested in the symbols and meanings of the past.

At this point, though, we need to appreciate that the process and practices of commodification do not always reinforce nostalgic countryside notions of English rural idylls or the pioneerism of rural America. Although rural areas will usually be trading on their past, there are interesting examples now whereby the commercialism of place-making has begun to forge new identities for the country. An example of this can be

(a)

FIGURE 33.5
Rural attractions: (a) Morwellham Quay, and
(b) Dollywood. Credit: Pat O'Hara/Corbis

drawn from rural New Zealand, where the growth and commodification of adventure tourist facilities, practices and subcultures have added new dimensions to the lives of many of its people, and to its landscape (Cloke and Perkins, 1998). Adventure tourism has influenced the production and reproduction of new imagined geographies of the country in South Island, New Zealand. In particular, whatever the activity and place being advertised, there are repeated allusions and references to freshness:

(b)

FIGURE 33.6
The Awesome Foursome: helicopter, bungy, jet-boat and white water rafting experience near Queenstown, New Zealand

1. *a fresh look at spectacular environments* – what was previously thought to be the spectacular scenery of New Zealand can be made more spectacular by participation in (or watching others participate in) adventurous pursuits in places of natural or historical significance
2. *fresh, youthful thrills* – adventure tourists are provided with the white-knuckle excitement of contemporary theme parks, but in a 'natural' outdoor setting
3. *the freshness of eager experimentation* – rural areas of New Zealand are being 'branded' by continual experimentation with bigger, better and more exciting thrills in the outdoors environment.

Invitations to 'crack the canyon with the Awesome Foursome' (see Fig. 33.6) reflect a different form of countryside commodification, where the relationship between tourist and landscape reflects a far more active, participatory and 'embodied' experience of nature relations than is provoked by conventional countryside nostalgia.

This account of commodification in the reshaping (yet often reinforcing) of countrysides has tended to emphasize the natural and positive cultural attitudes of rural areas. Against these potentially idyllic representations of rurality, however, can be set rather more dystopian narratives of rural life and landscape (see, for example, David Bell's (1997) analysis of 'horror' films set in small-town America). Commodified rurality is not unambiguous. The glorious isolation of 'wilderness' or 'outback' can also be attractive to those wishing to dump hazardous waste that is unwanted in more populated regions (see Fig. 33.7).

SUMMARY

- Rural commodification is linked to changes from productivism to post-productivism.
- The country is being made into a commodity in many different ways, and this process contributes to the emphasis on particular meanings and symbols as being important indicators of rurality.
- Some meanings reflect a nostalgic representation of the country as being dominated by the virtuous values of the past, involving closeness to nature and close-knit community. These meanings are often presented in various kinds of spectacle.
- Other commodification has led to new 'country' meanings such as the fresh and adventurous encounters with nature sponsored by the rise of adventure tourism in New Zealand.

OUT OF SIGHT AND OUT OF MIND: RURAL OTHERS?

Figure 33.7 also emphasizes that beneath the innocent idyll of the country there lie other characteristics that hit the headlines less often. The underbelly of idyll-ized countrysides is rarely exposed. Indeed, the stories used to promote the country as idyll usually serve to mask any contradictory social conditions. Unemployment or underemployment, the scarce availability of affordable housing, the rationalization of local services into larger centres, and the shrinking of public transport services have all served to disadvantage low-income households in rural areas. Moreover, two recent volumes (Cloke and Little, 1997; Milbourne, 1997) have emphasized different processes and practices by which certain rural people can be marginalized. Here the emphasis is on individuals and groups that are 'other' than the mainstream, with identities characterized by gender, race, sexuality, age, class, alternativeness, and so on. I use the 'otherness' relating to rural poverty as an example here, but the story of how a rural problem is hidden discursively away in public discourses as well as geographically could just as easily refer to the rural homeless, or indeed any of the identity groupings listed above.

" REMEMBER WHEN THEY USED TO SEND US POVERTY PROGRAMS!..."

FIGURE 33.7
Issues in rural Appalachia. Source: *The Charlotte Observer*, © Doug Marlette

A recent study has shown that the percentages of households in or on the margins of poverty in 12 case study areas in England ranged between 39.2 per cent and 12.8 per cent, with 10 of the 12 areas having more than 20 per cent levels of poverty (see Table 33.2). Yet, in successive government policy documents for rural areas, the word poverty does not appear. Two reasons may be advanced for this. First, the political propaganda of 1980s and early 1990s Britain has effectively pronounced the end of poverty, claiming that absolute poverty has been eradicated by economic success, and that relative poverty is a figment of the academic imagination and should more properly be labelled as 'inequality'. Second, despite the censorship of the word 'poverty' from government pronouncements, there is a strong sense in which it has been easier to deny the existence of poverty in rural areas than in the cities. Here, we can link the imagined geographies of idyll-ized rural lifestyles with the idea that poverty in rural areas is being hidden or rejected in a cultural dimension both by decision-makers with power over rural policy, and by rural dwellers themselves (including those who appear, normatively, to be poor). Rural people can be recognized as 'deprived' of ready access to the advantages of urban life, but are not as such impoverished by such deprivation because rural living somehow offers perceived compensations for any such disadvantage. In this way, rurality appears to signify itself as a poverty-free zone, and constructs of rural idyll at the same time exacerbate and hide poverty in rural geographic space.

Poverty in other developed nations, such as rural America, is an equally important issue, and one that is also influenced by the impact of dominant cultural constructions of rurality. In contrast to Britain, the United States does have an official poverty line, and so by state-defined statistics, levels of rural poverty are currently reckoned to be around 20 per cent of households. Rather than attempting to deny poverty politically, the emphasis has been to differentiate between the deserving and the undeserving poor. In this way, urban underclasses are signalled as 'undeserving' whilst non-metropolitan low-income workers are cast as

Table 33.2 Percentage of households in or on the margins of poverty* in 12 case study areas in rural England

Nottinghamshire	39.2	North Yorkshire	22.0
Devon	34.4	Shropshire	21.6
Essex	29.5	Northamptonshire	14.8
Northumberland	26.4	Cheshire	12.8
Suffolk	25.5	West Sussex	6.4
Wiltshire	25.4	Across 12 areas	23.4
Warwickshire	22.6		

Note: * measured as less than 140 per cent income support entitlement
Source: P. Cloke *et al.* (1994) *Lifestyles in rural England*. London: Rural Development Commission.

'deserving'; the spotlight of publicity falls on the former not the latter. As a result, cultural construction of poverty in America has a distinct spatial outworking, with impoverished rural Americans being lost in the shadows. And even when poverty is recognized as an issue in rural areas, there is a tendency to assume that it is restricted to key problem areas, notably Appalachia and the south. But as McCormick (1988) graphically indicates: 'Today, the problem has no boundaries. A tour of America's Third World can move from a country seat in Kansas to seaside Delaware, from booming Florida to seemingly idyllic Wisconsin' (1988: 22).

The tendency to regard social problems in the country as out of sight and out of mind is directly related to the dominance of prevailing social constructions of rurality. These in turn are essentially interconnected with the relations of power at work in and beyond rural areas. It is unsurprising, then, that the most significant demonstration of 'rural' opinion in Britain in recent years should be focused on the specific issue of fox hunting, and the more general issues of being left alone to exercise personal freedom in the idyllic villages, farms, moors and fells. Neither is it surprising that the major demand of demonstrators is that nothing should change. Such is the conservatism of the powerful, not the powerless.

SUMMARY

- Low-income households in rural areas are disadvantaged by changes to job markets, housing markets and the provision of services.
- 'Other' individuals and groups are marginalized in rural society on the grounds of gender, race, sexuality, age, and so on.
- The example of rural poverty demonstrates how idyllic representations of the country mask the occurrence of significant social problems and nullify the perceived need for policy responses to those problems.

CONCLUSION: POWERFUL GEOGRAPHIES OF COUNTRYSCAPES?

These complex and often ambiguous relations between nature and culture, and society and space, which underpin the mosaic of geographical space of the country make for an important and exciting territory of geographic enquiry. It should be made clear that there are many specific fascinations within these countryscapes that have hardly been touched on here – for example, the restructuring and reregulation of agricultural landscapes in a 'post-productivist' era; the cultural importance of food; the conservation of valued landscape and habitat; the evolution of community and social relations in countrysides; the power relations and governances that pertain there; and so on. Those wishing to delve into particular issues such as these might like to use the further reading suggested at the end of this chapter. None of these concerns, however, is immune from the emerging core of significance in rural studies that has been outlined in this chapter – namely, the interconnections between the socio-cultural constructs of 'country', 'rurality' and 'nature' that seem to be so important in (re)producing our geographical imaginations of rural space (geographical and social), and the actual experiences of how lives are practised within these spaces. Such practices will need to be viewed both from the outside looking in (taking full account of 'structuring' influences) and from the inside looking out (taking full account of individual difference, embodiment and identity). Chris Philo (1992) catches the mood of these significances in his review of what he regards as neglected rural geographies in Britain. His contention is that most accounts of rural life have viewed the mainstream interconnections between culture and rurality from the perspective of typically white, male, middle-class narratives. There is therefore an urgent need to look through other windows on to the rural world.

Myths of rural culture often marginalize a range of individuals and groups from a sense of belonging to, or in, the rural. We need to make our geographies of the rural more open to the circumstances and voices of other people in order to overcome the neglect of 'other' geographies. Such a conclusion is exciting, but not unproblematic. As Jonathan Murdoch and Andy Pratt (1993) have suggested, simply by 'giving voice' to others we do not necessarily uncover the power relations that lead to marginalization or neglect. A range of important questions arises here, relating in particular to the power of the researcher, the potential reinforcement of marginalized identities by labelling them as 'other', and the potential for flippant rather than politically grounded engagement with marginalized people. However, the mosaic geographies of the country will be richer for the addressing of these questions than for their neglect. After all, when the huntsmen come to town, are they really the voice of the country?

DISCUSSION POINTS

1. Evaluate the arguments for and against 'doing away with rural' (Hoggart, 1990) as an appropriate geographical category.

2. In what way does the blurring of the urban–rural divide consist of different processes of urbanizing the rural and ruralizing the urban?

3. How appropriate is the idea of a transition from productivist and post-productivist in the understanding of contemporary rural areas?

4. Why is it important to recognize the increasing range and scale of commodification in rural areas?

5. How useful is it to think about rural 'others'? Using the example of a particular social group, explore how exactly rurality is associated with rendering that group 'out of sight and out of mind'.

FURTHER READING

Cloke, P. (ed.) (2002) *Country visions*. Harlow: Pearson.

Cloke, P., Marsden, T. and Mooney, P. (eds) (2005) *Handbook of rural studies*. London: Sage.

Murdoch, K., Lowe, P., Ward, N. and Marsden, T. (2003) *The differentiated countryside*. London: Routledge.

Woods, M. (2004) *Rural geography: processes, responses and experiences in rural restructuring*. London: Sage.

These texts offer comprehensive accounts of the parallel importance of the changing nature of rural areas and the changing ways in which geographers and others have sought to interpret rurality.

Bunce, M. (1993) *The countryside deal*. London: Routledge.

A view of the idyll-zation of the country in North America and Britain.

Barnett, A. and Scruton, R. (eds) 1998 *Town and country*. London: Jonathan Cape.

Wilson, A. (1992) *The culture of nature*. Oxford: Blackwell.

These texts discuss the blurring of the country and the city.

Cloke, P. and Little, J. (eds) (1997) *Contested countryside cultures*. London: Routledge.

Deals, amongst other things, with the issue of marginalized 'others' in the country.

Part three

ISSUES

INTRODUCTION

Part 1 of this book considered some of the foundational concerns that inspire and preoccupy Human Geographers. Part 2 offered illustrated reviews of how these concerns are being translated into more specific geographical research agendas, organized in terms of thematic sub-disciplines and topics. This third part now goes on to show how the questions and approaches developed within the different sub-disciplines of the subject are brought together in the study of places, spaces and issues that don't easily fall within one sub-disciplinary terrain.

More specifically, this part of the book gives us and our authors licence to show, even more explicitly than hitherto, how Human Geography speaks to issues that matter. It also lets us highlight areas of geographical research that are particularly innovative and/or where much more work needs to be done. This final part of *Introducing Human Geographies* aims, then, to give you insights into some of the key geographical issues that matter today and will matter tomorrow.

We deliberately begin with Hester Parr's account of a whole realm of life all too often deemed not to matter in Human Geography: emotions. Hester looks at how human–environment relations are emotional; and what it might mean for Human Geography to recognize this. We deliberately end with Clive Barnett's account of the geographies of 'care'. Here Clive reflects on how caring is central to any practice of morality or ethics, and thus as well as being a deeply personal and emotional process is also one that rests and impacts upon much wider social and political forms. To put that another way, care is both about intimacy and close relationships and some translation of this into the wider world, so that we can care for 'distant strangers' as well as our 'nearest and dearest'. The intervening chapters also manifest this concern with the interleaving of scales as they move from the local to the global. From the geographies of the heart we move on to Tim Cresswell's account of place and its role in the organization of our social lives. Place, he argues, both embodies dominant ways of seeing and being in the world (through judgements of what and who is in and out of place, moral and immoral) and offers possibilities to challenge those dominant views (through practices of what he terms 'transgression', deliberately breaking place-based conventions and crossing boundaries).

The next three chapters develop these ideas of mobility between places at a larger scale. Claire Dwyer looks at 'diasporas' or dispersed peoples, and what their experiences suggest about the need for rethinking ideas of place and boundary. Khalid Koser, in his account of migrants and refugees, looks at how those more traditional bounded ideas of place still matter, through powerful designations of people as various kinds of migrant. In so doing, he also casts a refreshingly calm eye over issues that, at least in his study area of the UK, often generate far more heat than light. Luke Desforges discusses a different kind of migrant: the tourist. In some ways this is a painful juxtaposition. Migrants who generate acres of negative newsprint are followed by people who as tourists expect to move without opposition and demand hospitality. And yet in many ways Luke's argument parallels Khalid's, in suggesting that criticisms of tourists' impacts on the geographies of place are often overblown.

Diasporas, migrants and tourists operate in and through place; but they also constitute what Manuel Castells has called 'spaces of flows' (see, for example, Castells, 1989). And it is not only people who flow around the world. Michael Watts looks at the complicated geographies of commodities, the things we buy and sell. James Kneale looks at the geographies produced through mass media, reflecting on how the television in the living room is, in David Morley's telling phrase, a place 'where the global meets the local' (Morley, 1992). For us at least, Scott Kirsch's concern with the new geographies of war and peace in the twenty-first century is something we also experience through our televisions and other media. Here, too, relations between global networks and territorial states are played out, ending up with a global war on terror located in Iraq, at least for now. It is stating the obvious, but what we also see here is emotional geographies (what could be more emotional than war and terror?) playing out on the grandest of scales. Jane Wills' chapter on globalization and those who protest (aspects of) it addresses the other metanarrative of contemporary global politics. Globalization, though, is not only global; it is local too, as Jane demonstrates through an analysis of the importance of place to both its impacts and the responses it generates. Nonetheless, in so-called anti-globalization movements there is a new internationalism emerging, one that has to grapple with how to care for local concerns whilst looking more broadly too.

So the contents of this third part of *Introducing Human Geographies* vary greatly: from accounts of how dancing makes us feel, to attitudes to prostitutes in rural areas, to British-Asian music and fashion, to debates over immigration in the UK, to watching the TV, to global geographies of war and capitalism. All the chapters have their own, specific claims on your attention. They matter in different ways, because there is not only one criterion for what makes a geography important. But at the same time, one can see resonant preoccupations of contemporary Human Geography running through them: of how we relate the near and far, the local and global, the here and there, the sensed and the more distantly perceived.

Space of flows

a term first coined by the urban theorist Manuel Castells in distinction to the 'space of places', this self-confessed 'cumbersome expression' emphasizes how the character and dynamics of a bounded place are reliant upon a host of connections and flows that go beyond its boundaries. These include flows of people (through many forms of travel and migration), of capital and money (think of the impacts of the global networks of the international financial system, for example), of ideas, of media imagery and of objects, amongst many others. The notion of the 'space of flows' is therefore a complement and corrective to Human Geographers' long-standing interest in bounded places and territories (*see* TERRITORY), perhaps particularly important in an age of intensified GLOBALIZATION.

GEOGRAPHY AND EMOTIONS

The idea that Human Geography is concerned with emotions – or that we can discuss 'emotional geographies' – may seem rather surprising. Certainly, geographers have struggled to come to terms with the notion that emotions are central to our experience of spaces and places. This chapter offers a basic introduction to emotional geographies, charting a generalized and partial disciplinary account of the different ways in which geographers have encountered emotions as a focus of study. It also offers some examples of how thinking and writing with attention to emotions can reveal new geographical insights into human–environment relations.

It has often been mooted that Geography is a discipline built upon so-called 'objective' scientific truths and investigations, whereby the 'subjectivity' of the geographer is actively ignored, dismissed and written out of accounts of the physical and human world that are produced by such knowledge. In this construction, Human Geography can be seen as a 'rational' discipline, predicated on notions of a scientific order that is (supposedly) devoid of any human emotional content. By implication, Human Geographical work that does not simply represent the 'facts' of the world in a detached, scientific and objective manner runs the risk of being 'irrational' and therefore not as valuable a form of knowledge. What counts as irrational knowledge? For some geographers, irrationality has been a category linked with disorder, chaos, corporeality, femininity and, crucially, emotionality. Therefore geographical research that is seen to work with notions of disorder, the body, gender and emotion could be deemed irrational knowledge that is not valuable in the canons of the discipline. In other words, Human Geography can be considered built on the basis of a profound binary dualism. This dualism is effected, on the one hand, through constantly reproducing so-called objective, rational scientific knowledge that is considered valuable and, on the other, through ignoring and not reproducing so-called irrational and worthless knowledges (see also Chapter 7). There are specific **feminist** readings of this dualism that we address further below.

There has hence been a reluctance to encounter emotions in geography. There has not been, for example, a widely recognizable 'geography of emotions' (with some small exceptions such as a literature on 'the geography of women's fear', of which more below). This *could* have even incorporated a 'rational', spatial-scientific analysis of emotions as a quasi-measurable object (as revealed by, say, rating scales in a social survey relating to the answering of such questions as 'How afraid are you of the back streets of town on a scale of 1 to 5?'), but such research has still been limited across a range of emotional states. Likewise, until recently, there has also been a reticence about incorporating emotions into Geography as a component of our own knowledge production. Overall, then, unless you

Feminism

a series of perspectives, which together draw on theoretical and political accounts of the oppression of women in society to suggest how GENDER relations and Human Geography are interconnected (*see also* PATRIARCHY).

Psychoanalysis, psychoanalytic

largely associated with the work of Freud, psychoanalytic theory concerns itself with the mental life of individuals rather than with any overt observable behaviour, and argues that the most important elements of such mental lives are the unconscious ones. It posits that the unconscious parts of the mind (the 'id') are in perpetual conflict with both the more rational and conscious elements (the 'ego') and with those parts of the mind concerned with conscience (the 'superego'). Psychological disturbances can then be traced to these conflicts, and can be remedied through psychoanalytical therapy, which is able to give an individual insight into their unconscious mental life.

look carefully at the discipline, it is difficult to find both a geography *of* emotions and emotions *in* Geography. Disciplinary knowledges are never static, however, and in recent times this silence has been addressed. Partly as a result of more women entering the western academy and more geographers responding to associated debates about a 'politics' of knowledge (see the section on 'feminist geographies' below), there has been a critique of so-called rational and objective knowledge production (Rose, 1992). Although this critique has taken many forms, one effect of this questioning of knowledge production has been an increasing interest in and validation of subjective knowledges, ones that privilege 'insider' accounts of the human world. In doing so, new research work has opened up different understandings of everyday human lives and the ways in which everyday geographies contain complicated relations between selves,

Embodied, embodiment

this concept suggests that the self and the body are not separate, but rather that the experiences of any individual are, invariably, shaped by the active and reactive entity that is their body – irrespective of whether this is conscious or not. The argument, then, runs that the uniqueness of human experience is due, at least in part, to the unique nature of individual bodies.

DEFINING EMOTIONS

Despite there having been no *explicit* body of work related to 'emotional geographies' (spatial knowledge written with and/or on emotions) or the 'geography of emotions' (a mapping of different emotional states), much work in Human Geography speaks in various ways about the complicated manner in which different people emotionally embody space and place. Generally speaking, references to 'emotions', 'feelings' and 'affect' in academic work indicate an interest in intense physical, mental and social experiences (commonly represented as 'love', 'happiness', 'sadness', and so on) that have profound impacts on individuals, their relations with others and with things in the world. Human geography has encountered these intensities in different ways as we see below.

In order to understand this encounter between Geography and emotions, it is helpful to be more specific about the terms being used here. Indeed, what are 'emotions'? Pringle (1999: 68–9) argues that emotions combine 'mental, social, cultural and bodily dimensions', and signals that there are debates about whether emotions are universal or culturally specific. She argues that emotions are different from feelings in that 'they exist relative to human social acts'. In other words, it is possible to associate feelings with intense and immediate bodily states (which is why people refer to shivering with excitement, for example), and differentiate emotions as 'cultural acquisitions' that are 'part of the conscious relations, actions and experiences of selves'. 'Affect', for

which 'there is no stable definition' (Thrift, 2004a: 57), is also variously associated with these two explanations, although is possibly better understood as a kind of emotionally 'moving' force. Pringle (1999) also points out that in the western world we have become very conscious of our emotions as part of an age of popular psychological and therapeutic practice, meaning that our emotions are thoroughly drawn through such social institutions. Academics in disciplines such as psychology, sociology and those influenced by **psychoanalytic** thinking (see below) may further differentiate the terms emotions, feelings and affect, although there is often slippage between them in research. It is notable that there is a wealth of writing about the 'sociology of emotions', and one of the reasons for this is the difficulty academics have in pinning down emotions and their relative significance in social life. It seems that for many:

> *emotion is a complex, multidimensional multifaceted human compound, including irreducible biological and cultural components, which arise or emerge in various socio-relational contexts. As a thinking, moving, feeling 'complex' – rather than a static uni-dimensional 'thing' emotion is embodied through and through.*

(Williams, 2001: 132, original emphasis)

So, emotions are hard to define and complex, but nonetheless central to the ways in which we live in the world.

bodies and spaces. A key part of this recent re-evaluation has been the analysis of subjective *emotional geographies* (Davidson and Bondi, 2004; Davidson and Milligan, 2004), as part of a disciplinary struggle to encounter emotion in different ways. The reminder of this chapter characterizes some of those encounters.

SUMMARY

- Emotions have been neglected in the discipline of Human Geography and this is partly explainable by the construction of so-called rational and objective knowledge.
- In constructing rational knowledge, an opposite irrational knowledge category is created, the latter being considered less valuable to the canons of the discipline.

- Geographical work that focuses on emotions, gender, the body and disorder have been constructed as irrational knowledge in the past.
- New research values subjectivity and subjective emotional knowledge as the result of debates about the politics of knowledge construction.

MOVING EMOTIONS INTO GEOGRAPHY: HUMANISTIC GEOGRAPHY

Humanistic Geography

a theoretical approach to Human Geography that concentrates on studying the conscious, creative and meaningful activities and experiences of human beings. Coming to prominence in the 1970s, Humanistic Geography was in part a rebuttal of attempts during the 1960s to create a law-based, scientific Human Geography founded on statistical data and analytical techniques (*see* SPATIAL SCIENCE). In contrast, it emphasized the subjectivities of those being studied and, indeed, the Human Geographers studying them. Human meanings, emotions and ideas with regard to place, space and nature thus became central.

One of the first sustained attempts to incorporate emotions as part of geographers' thinking became apparent through the project of **humanistic geography** in the 1970s. Humanistic geography emerged as a critical reaction to the perceived *dehumanizing* effects of an increasingly technical Human Geography as *spatial science*, involving the translation of the human world from a language of 'substance' (involving rich textures of people and places) to one of 'geometry' (involving mapped and graphed [X, Y] co-ordinates). Part of this critique was to incorporate versions of the philosophical base of humanism into Geography. The result was an explicit agenda that sought to validate and centre subjective understandings of the relations between humans and world. As the famous humanistic geographer Yi Fu Tuan claimed early on, 'humanistic geography achieves an understanding of the human world by studying people's relations with nature, their geographical behaviour, *as well as their feelings and ideas* as regards space and place' (Tuan, 1976: 266). Tuan and others like him produced work that investigated deeply held attachments to place. However, creating a human(istic) geography that was about 'feelings' was no simple task, and humanistic geographers articulated the need for the incorporation of feelings and emotions in geographical analysis through an appeal to a complex set of humanist philosophies known as existentialism and phenomenology. This is not the place to explain these influences in any great detail (for this see Cloke *et al.*, 1991, and Peet, 1998), but suffice to say that core geographical concepts such as place were re-evaluated through a deliberate appeal to subjective human experience:

Within this humanist perspective concepts of traditional significance in geography are given existential meaning or a focus of human emotional attachment ... for example, place is defined as the centre of meaning or a focus of human emotional attachment.

(Entrikin, 1976: 616)

Existentialism ... deals with the emotional life, the feelings, the moods, and affects through which people are involved in the world. Existentialism, then, differs from positivist science in its emphasis on inner experience, knowledge by participation rather than observation and its celebration of subjectivity over objectivity.

(Peet, 1998: 36–7)

A clear conceptual agenda was established that centred 'feelings, emotions, moods and affects', although how these were actually differentiated and written through as part of substantive geographical study is more controversial. Humanistic geography has been criticized as a search for essences: *essential* human emotional responses to place, for example, that were largely *undifferentiated* by location, gender, age, class or race and generally structured on mythical masculine norms (Rose, 1992). Some have also criticized humanistic geographers for only really trying to consider *their own* emotions towards places, and only then partially, whilst others criticize these geographers for reducing human subjectivity to feelings that are somehow 'beyond rational scrutiny' (Daniels, 1985: 151).

Certainly, much of the work is partial and often abstract. However, Rowles' work on ageing, personal and social environments is more accessible (Rowles, 1978b), despite his acknowledgement of the difficulties of writing emotion in humanistic geography and discussing 'the frustration stemming from clumsy efforts to convey mood ... [in which] the problem of translation was clearly revealed' (Rowles, 1978b: 188). In one study, Rowles interviews an elderly woman (Maria) about the emotions engendered by the spatial restrictions she experiences as a result of impaired physical functioning and reduced social networks. Examining rich subjective data in the form of multiple interview narratives and conversations about her apparently shrinking place-in-the-world, Rowles was to understand her emotional relations with her immediate social space as not just negatively diminished by ageing (as he had first assumed). Rather, Maria's relationship with objects in her immediate home environment (like old photographs and a clock), her contact with distant family, her garden and the various associations these held with positive memories, other times

FIGURE 34.1
Grandma Nelly feeling emotionally secure in home-space.

and spaces, and her sense of identity acquired over her life-course and life-geographies, led to a surprisingly secure emotional environment predicated on an expansive geographical imagination and a 'vicarious immersion in the places of the past and in displaced contemporary locations' (Rowles, 1978b: 183). Maria was hence shown to maintain a positive emotional relationship to her world through her complex geographical experience:

> *Geographical experience for these older persons was not just locomotion through timeless Cartesian space. It was a complex dynamic immersion in a 'lived space' with temporal depth and meaning as well as spatial extent. I began to see more clearly why a prevalent societal image of a progressively shrinking geographical lifespace with advancing years was such a demeaning oversimplification.*

(Rowles, 1978b: 183)

Rowles's humanistic approach was perhaps atypical in the 1970s, given his more sociological emphasis (literally placing emotions in everyday lives, spaces and social networks), although the style of this work would be more recognizable now. Although not beyond critique, then, humanistic geography served a purpose in terms of enabling the validation of subjective emotional experience that was then placed at the heart of some versions of Human Geography.

SUMMARY

- Humanistic geographers validated subjective knowledge as a means to understanding human–world relations.
- Place, and the emotions it evokes for people, was a central focus of this work.
- However, humans, their bodies and emotions were largely undifferentiated by humanistic geographers.
- Rowles' work on ageing and personal social environments is something of an exception.

FEMINIST GEOGRAPHIES

As argued by many feminist geographers, the western academy, including the Geography discipline, is dominated by white, heterosexual, non-disabled men, and this is reflected in the form and content of the knowledge produced by this academy. Feminist geographers have critiqued how, in particular, valued geographical knowledge is inscribed by gender relations. Here, a valued rational Human Geography is also understood as a masculinist knowledge, although many feminists have tried to destabilize the binary distinctions and associations between masculinist rationality and feminine irrationality. In the context of this chapter, feminist analyses of a rational geography discipline suggest subjective emotional matters may be ignored or essentialized by masculinist knowledge productions.

For the likes of Gillian Rose (1992: 60), the possible 'overlaps between humanistic geography and feminist geography were more apparent than real', and feminism offered a more complicated understanding of emotional subjectivity and geography. Feminist geography work, especially since the 1990s, contributes to 'offer[ing] distinctive … perspectives on the human subject' in ways that 'unsettle and move beyond the denial and neglect of emotion and corporeality characteristic of most social research' (Bondi, 2002: 6), including that of humanistic geography. There are many examples of the work of feminist researchers who have sought to centre emotions as part of a re-assertion of unstable subjectivity within the discipline. Studies of fear, embodied panic, feelings associated with music, childbirth, pregnancy and illness, have all contributed to the multiple ways in which both men and women's emotional lives are 'alternative sources of knowledge' for geographers (WGSG, 1997: 87). The turn to write through explicit and substantive emotional geographies (Davidson and Bondi, 2004) is still an ongoing project; although one of the key ways in which a concern for emotions has been translated within and beyond feminist writings is in the realm of research practice (the 'doing' of geography).

Although, as Rebecca Widdowfield (2000: 200) argues, and Graham Rowles' work shows above, there is nothing 'inherently feminist about recognizing the influence of emotions in academic research', feminist geography has been enormously influential in the exposure of emotional relations in research *practice* (WGSG, 1997). Widdowfield discusses the importance of acknowledging her own emotions in research on lone parents in run-down council estates in northern England. Adopting a multi-method approach (drawing on both quantitative and qualitative materials), she relates the emotional experience of conducting interviews in places where the physical and social environment seemed like 'a desolate landscape', and where:

> Going into the LDNs ('less desirable neighbourhoods'), I was angry at the injustice and inequality in society … I was upset at the unpleasant and unhappy circumstances in which many people live and distressed by the fact that I could not see a solution …

(Widdowfield, 2000: 204)

Whilst acknowledging that it is not always appropriate that researchers should detail their feelings in each piece of research they undertake, Widdowfield argues that reflecting on her 'demoralized' and 'disillusioned' emotional state, allowed her some insights into the reality of the social circumstances of her interviewees in Newcastle's deprived estates. At the same time, noting the 'positive feelings' amongst some of her interviewees and their strong sense of community challenged her own emotional responses charted above. Over the course of the research project, her own negative feelings changed somewhat as she became more familiar and less threatened by the environments she researched and, through this process, became aware of the danger of 'outsider perspectives in making policy prescriptions' based on particular emotive readings of place (2000: 205). In attempts to expose knowledge production (and even policy-making) as subjectively constituted, Widdowfield (2000: 205) argues that 'writing emotions into research accounts can facilitate a better understanding of the work undertaken and forms an important part of situating

Masculinism, masculinist

a form of thought or knowledge that, whilst often claiming to be impartial, comprehends the world in ways that are derived from men's experiences and concerns. Many Feminist Geographers have argued that Human Geography has traditionally been masculinist (*see* FEMINISM).

Essentialist/ists/m

the belief that identities, such as class, gender and race, as well as age, dis/ability and sexuality, are directly determined by biology. This view is opposed by SOCIAL CONSTRUCTIONISTS, who argue that these differences between us are shaped through the interweaving of wider socio-spatial processes and individual biographies. The term is often used negatively to emphasize the stereotyping that it can produce.

Reflexivity

a process through which we are able to reflect on what we know, how we come to know it, and how we interact with others. The key point is that we are able to change aspects of ourselves and the structures that make up society in the light of these reflections.

knowledge'. There are now other accounts of the personal and relational nature of gaining geographical knowledge, broadly addressing this call to 'emotional writing' (see examples in Limb and Dwyer, 2001).

Apart from reflecting on the researcher's experiences, discussing emotions as part of the research process is an increasingly appropriate activity given that qualitative methods are often used to 'empathize with' the relationships between people, social groups and their everyday environments. Building upon humanistic geography traditions that validate the inclusion of emotionally subjective experiences in the world, and also the feminist mantra of 'the personal is political', it has become commonplace for Human Geographers to seek out 'insider' accounts of everyday life. Key methods for eliciting these accounts have been the use of in-depth interviews, biographical life histories and ethnography. Such methods are best understood as a means to collect in-depth and intensely personal understandings of lived geographies, and it should come as no surprise that such methods produce encounters that are laden with a powerful emotional content, both for the researcher and the researched. Feminist scholarship has been at the forefront of a call to acknowledge these emotional exchanges in academic work, in ways that hopefully enlighten us as to how and whether our research methods and the emotions they evoke are implicated in the knowledges produced. Some geographers have written of the difference that 'emotionally safe' interview space can make to knowledge production (Parr, 1998), whilst others have

SITUATED KNOWLEDGES

This term is most associated with feminist geographers and their critiques of the process of knowledge production. Drawing inspiration from the philosopher Donna Haraway (1991b), who comments critically on the construction of powerful scientific knowledge, feminists have challenged the truth claims of detached, disembodied means of knowing the world. Haraway argues for a 'situated knowledge', which refers to the notion that knowledge can be partial, located and embodied – in other words, and put simply, knowledge always comes from someone, somewhere. Conventionally, the western academy has constructed the most valuable forms of knowledge as ones that are impartial and deeply authoritative because of 'the god trick of seeing everything from nowhere' (Haraway, 1991b: 189) and the refusal to situate claims relative to personal, social and geographical contexts. Feminist researchers argue that situating knowledge enables more critical thinking whereby 'transcendent' knowledge is replaced by 'a politics and epistemologies of location, positioning and situating where partiality and not universality is the condition of being heard to make rational knowledge claims' (Haraway, 1991b: 195).

Feminist geographical research has been particularly influenced by such critiques of knowledge production and this has been evident in debates about research methods, reflexivity and power relations in the discipline (England, 1994). These debates in turn have influenced feminist research practice, as researchers have tried to employ a range of qualitative research techniques that enable sensitive, non-exploitative and embodied encounters with a range of actors and agents in a variety of locations. Such encounters and the knowledges that they produce 'do not depend on a logic of discovery, but a social relation of conversation, [and hence] the world neither speaks for itself nor disappears in a favor of a master coder' (Peet, 1998: 269). Producing situated knowledge also entails processes of **reflexivity**, itself a kind of 'self conscious analytic scrutiny' (England, 1994: 82) in order to avoid the 'god trick' of the objective master gaze. However, such processes are fraught with difficulties, as Rose (2002: 257) argues when asking 'in what terms can we describe our "situation"? what is our "position"?' in a world often conceptualized as constituted by fluid and uncertain boundaries. Haraway's account of 'situating knowledge' hence challenges feminist and other researchers to destabilize taken-for-granted forms of academic authority, but without 'fixing' our positions and differences.

problematized the emotive power relations that are always present in the management of interviews (Limb and Harrison, 1988b), for example.

Criticisms of this 'emotional turn' have included the accusation that such research runs the risk of being self-indulgent, a charge also occasionally levied at the humanistic geographers. Rose (1997a) has also questioned our abilities to be able to envision clearly and lay bare our multiple feelings and relations in research encounters, and asks whether such a project has hallmarks of a rationalist geographical knowledge, in so far as emotional subjectivity is ordered and made intelligible. Similarly, others worry that a concern with emotionality is being increasingly ghettoized within certain parts of Human Geography, as 'what little talk of emotion there is occurs squarely in the cultural (and often feminist) corners of the discipline' (Anderson and Smith, 2001: 7), and that this runs the risk of reinforcing a wider divide between a perceived rational, relevant and a 'frothy', irrelevant geographical knowledge (Hamnett, 2003a).

SUMMARY

- Some feminist geographers read the dualism of rational and irrational knowledge as gendered, and seek to destabilize this construct.
- Acknowledging the emotional subjectivity of the researcher can help situate geographical knowledge.
- Qualitative methods can evoke powerful emotions for respondents.
- Writing emotional geographies is an emerging tradition, but there are worries about the 'ghettoization' of this approach within feminist and cultural geography.

PSYCHOANALYTIC GEOGRAPHIES

" *In 1993 in the Transylvanian village of Haderni, three Gypsies were murdered and thirteen Gypsy houses were destroyed in retaliation for the killing of a Romanian by a Gypsy during a fight. Commenting on the deaths of the Gypsies, one resident said: 'We did not commit murder – how could you call killing Gypsies murder? Gypsies are not real people, you see. They are always killing each other. They are criminals, subhuman vermin.'* "

(*Independent*, 19 October 1993, cited in Sibley, 1999: 121)

" *It's very good that they [Romanian asylum seekers dispersed to Glasgow] are going, because we have had enough. The Kosovans who came last year are very nice people – but that lot are dirty thieves.* "

(*Scottish Sun*, 17 March 2000: 12)

There are still other ways in which geographers have recently encountered emotions. In work influenced by psychoanalytic thinking, they have shown how reflecting on the psyche and theories of the self can serve to connect the unconscious, emotions and the social and material world (Sibley, 1995). Psychoanalysis has proved attractive to geographers who want to understand more about the ways in which anxieties and desires structure social life in what has been called 'psycho-social geographies'. The quotes above relate how strong emotions are often central to material social geographies (making them very 'relevant' to study). As David Sibley (1999: 116) argues,

> *In mapping the topography of the mind, the psychoanalyst is necessarily concerned with feelings. Feelings of repulsion and desire, of nervousness, elation and so on, contribute to ... the avoidance of certain places and people, or conversely, attraction to particular place and social milieu.*

Using insights from 'object relations' theory, Sibley (1999: 117) argues that certain people and places can be constituted as 'good' or 'bad' objects in the world, and that they can then be depositories for feelings of pain and anxiety, pleasure and excitement. It has hence been possible to appreciate more about how negative emotional states are provoked and sustained in relation to certain human groupings in certain places (see Chapters 29 and 30 for examples).

In general, psychoanalytic geographers would argue that adult emotional behaviour cannot be understood outside of the ways in which early psychological conflicts are experienced. In other words, how we develop as infants and children has a massive impact on our adult social and spatial relationships. Reflecting on this process helps us to see how humans relate to their world through the formation of strong beliefs about who and what is acceptable and who and what is not ('the Self' and 'the Other'). The latter represents a category that is rejected and distasteful. The significance of infant development in this theory is as follows. In the western world our infant development has common features, in that we usually experience the world in clean, safe, warm environments, and the way in which we are **socialized** into the world by our parents in infanthood is deemed important. In particular, we are often socialized into keeping things clean from an early age. We learn to distance ourselves from dirty things all the time when we are young, such as bodily waste, nasty things in the garden, and people designated as dirty. This has a huge significance for psychoanalytic geographers, who maintain that how we learn about purity and cleanliness when young holds meanings for later adult life and the creation and maintenance of social and spatial boundaries between people and places. Strong feelings and fears about the possible pollution of the self and body (ideas learned in childhood) come to the fore when adult people are presented with people and places that they deem to be 'dirty'. Who and what is deemed dirty is often the result of different social stereotypes in western society, but the results are often the same. Feelings of fear and anxiety about pollution and dirt result in social and spatial distancing between groups:

> *The sense of border in the infant in Western society [e.g. border between pure/dirty] becomes the basis for distances from 'others' ... [this feeling] assumes a much wider cultural significance [in adulthood].*

(Sibley, 1995: 7)

Socialization

the relations through which human beings learn about acceptable social norms and moral standards in a given society. Socialization can occur through different institutions and spaces such as the family, schools or the media.

So Sibley argues that the stereotypes or categories that societies assign to people constructed as 'ugly, dirty or imperfect' are associated with the border between Self and Other, reflecting deep, ultimately unconsciously rooted feelings that make some people distance themselves from others. Extreme forms of spatial purification based on such strong feelings include examples of 'ethnic cleansing' whereby one ethnic group actively seeks the exclusion of another from particular spaces (usually nation-states).

FIGURE 34.2
Emotional borders and boundaries.
Credit: Kael Alford/Getty Images

This thus becomes a very geographical argument about the constitution of human identity and emotional relations as these relate to the constitution of space. Geographers hence argue that there is an explicit link between the inner workings of the human mind (the psyche), and the social landscape and how it is organized spatially. In particular, proximity to 'otherness' (other groups or people deemed 'different' by social stereotypes) can constitute a challenge to the security of emotional stability and self-identity, and so individuals strive to separate themselves from that they deem different: in order to try to sustain a pure identity: 'Separation is a large part of the process of purification – it is the means by which defilement or pollution is avoided' (Sibley, 1995: 37).

Psychoanalysis has provided geographers with a distinctive theoretical basis for understanding the emotional and psychic processes that fuel geographies of social exclusion, such as those hinted at in the above quotations (see also Chapter 30). This work deals directly with embodied irrationality in ways that complement but also differ from humanistic and feminist geographies.

Social exclusion

a state of being that is perceived as being outside of, or marginalized from, mainstream social relations and the attendant resources and opportunities that this involves.

SUMMARY

- Psychoanalytic geography explores the connections between unconsciousness, social selves and spaces.
- Through socialization as infants we learn what is unclean and clean, pure and impure.
- As adults we apply this knowledge to people and places, and those deemed impure are avoided.
- Society often labels people and places as impure and 'Other' through symbolic stereotyping.
- Emotional and physical distancing can result from this symbolic stereotyping.

NON-REPRESENTATIONAL EMOTIONS

In the work above, geographers have sought to represent emotional processes and subjective experiences in various ways, normally as meaningful entities that hold data about human–environment relations.

Non-representational theory

introduced into Human Geography by the Geographer Nigel Thrift, this phrase – which he has since accepted may not have been 'the best-chosen of phrases' – seeks to highlight various understandings that emphasize the practical, active and EMBODIED character of the world. Rather than denying the importance of REPRESENTATIONS, non-representational theory has sought to resist an undue obsession with them (see LINGUISTIC (OR CULTURAL) TURN) through a direct focus on actions, events, moments, things.

Discourse, discursive

drawing on the work of the French philosopher Michel Foucault, Human Geographers define discourses as ways of talking about, writing or otherwise representing the world and its geographies (see also REPRESENTATION). Discursive approaches to Human Geography emphasize the importance of these ways of representing. They are seen as shaping the realities of the worlds in which we live, rather than just being ways of portraying a reality that exists outside of language and thought. They are also seen as connected to questions of practice – that is, what people actually do – rather than being confined to a separate realm of images or ideas. More specifically, Human Geographers have stressed the different ways in which people have discursively constructed the world in different times and places, and examined how it is that particular ways of talking about, conceptualizing and acting on people and places come to be seen as natural and common-sensical in particular contexts.

Yet emotions are such complex phenomena that some researchers are beginning to problematize whether they can be represented. An emerging body of challenging work linked to '**non-representational theory**' concerns itself with 'mundane everyday practices that shape the conduct of human beings towards others and themselves in particular sites' (Thrift, 1997: 126–7). Developing a non-representational theory involves 'not a project concerned with representation and meaning, but rather the performative 'presentations', 'showings' and manifestations of everyday life' (1997: 126–7). The emphasis in this style of work, as Catherine Nash (2000: 655) argues, is on practices 'that cannot adequately be spoken of, that words cannot capture, that texts cannot convey'. Emotional geographies, and the bodily, sensual, instinctive moments and practices that constitute them, seem to be a possible case in point.

Central to this literature is a specific proposition that the words of human language cannot adequately do the work of representing many interior mental and emotional states. Here the assumption is that emotions can never be reconvened in words that somehow represent their interiority, nor their intangible threads of connection with everyday spaces, thus pointing to the 'ineffability' (or unspeakability) of emotions. Reflecting more specifically on emotions in a non-representational mode, Paul Harrison (2002: 3–4) elaborates as follows:

> *Emotions, it seems relatively uncontroversial to claim, always threaten to overwhelm language beyond a communicative function. Emotions constantly threaten to disrupt and break-up our everyday use of language … this 'failure' of language, this inability of language to absorb emotions, may not be a failure of accuracy or representation, as if we simply lacked the 'right' words, as if the issue were simply to find the appropriate phrase or cliché then our problems would be solved …*

Harrison then speculates that the difficulty is 'not due to our lack of accurate concepts, but due to a constitutive resistance within emotions [to] words', and hence to 'meaning and representation'. Such ideas have promoted some geographers to try and encounter emotions not through exhaustive self-reflection or interview data, but rather through exploring new ways to 'attend to' smiles, movements, gestures, in order to participate in emotional practice. In elaborating this when researching movement and emotion in the context of Dance Music Therapy (DMT), Derek McCormack (2003: 495) makes an important distinction between 'emotions' and 'affect'. Emotion, he claims, 'works in an already established field of **discursively** constituted categories in relation to which the felt intensity of experience is articulated'. In other words, we all more or less know how to behave and represent our feelings in relation to what we perceive after the event as sadness, happiness or anxiousness. However, when working with the notion of 'affect', a notion that is not reducible to emotion, the focus becomes the sensational properties of embodied experience *before* they are registered by conscious thought (and thus represented as readily identifiable emotions). The argument is that thinking in terms of 'affect', researchers are more attuned to practices and not representations of everyday life, and that this effectively opens up exciting possibilities for new understandings of human being-in-the world.

Attention to such matters also potentially involves styles of knowledge with attendant experimental delivery to a wider audience (see McCormack's use of diagrams, for example).

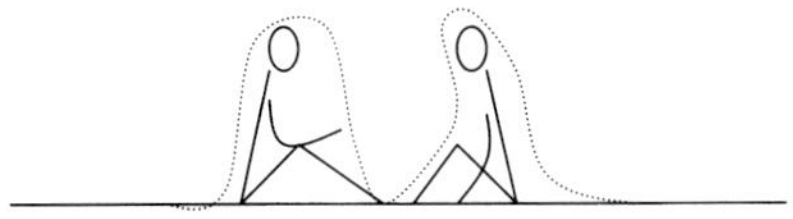

As a geographer, McCormack was interested in DMT in order to explore some links between emotions, bodies and therapeutic spaces in order to witness how the intersection between geography and particular practices 'facilitate[s] a kind of transformation in awareness, thinking, feeling and relating' (2003: 490–1). McCormack participated in DMT for two hours a week for 18 months. During this time he abandoned a quest to interview participants of his classes about emotions and geography, as he felt that 'this tended to get people to provide some interpretative after-the-event sense to something that, as it was playing out, did not seem to require such sense to happen' (2003: 493). Rather, McCormack sought to 'become responsive to different surfaces of attention rather than seeking to go behind or beyond them' (2003: 493). In moving away from simply representing the thought-out reflections of his fellow class members, McCormack effectively becomes more involved in the spaces he is researching in order to encounter emotion and, more particularly, affect, as *it happens*. Writing about or drawing such 'happenings' afterwards, is, of course, a form of representation, but trying to witness relational emotional moments differently in research practice, and then later, through for example the use of the diagrams above, is just one way in which such moments might be shared in innovative ways.

Critics of these new geographical ideas have bemoaned a return to notions of essentialized emotional embodiment reminiscent of some versions of humanistic geography (Nash, 2000), in which pre-cognitive habitual practices (including feelings) seem curiously asocial (not marked by gender, race, and so on). In particular, this approach has raised fundamental questions about *how and why* to study emotional geographies, as Nash articulates as she asks

> *how can the pre-cognitive body [and embodied affects] be known? … are ethnographic research methods as redundant as textual and visual sources, since they invite people to speak and therefore cannot access the pre-verbal? What happens to the project of 'giving voice' to the marginalized, if the concern is with what cannot be expressed rather than what can?*

Even accepting that our affective lives are partly pre-cognitive and pre-verbal, critics may argue that this should not reduce us as geographers to silence about the imperative of such emotional groundings to our socio-spatial lives, practices and worlds. Despite these criticisms, non representational geographers do much to challenge researchers to think differently both about how they encounter the world and how they communicate those encounters to others.

FIGURE 34.3
Encountering emotional practices through dance movement therapy

Representation

the cultural practices and forms by which human societies interpret and portray the world around them and present themselves to others. In the case of the natural world, for example, these representations range from prehistoric cave paintings of the creatures that figured in the lives of early human groups to the televisual images and scientific models that shape our imaginations today. *See also* DISCOURSE.

SUMMARY

- Non-representational geographies focus on what people do as opposed to what they say they do.
- In research work attention is drawn to practices rather than **representations**.
- Pre-cognitive feelings and sensations are of more interest than emotions (a cultural construction).
- There is controversy about how to research the non representational.

CONCLUSION

Despite being an academic discipline forged on oppositions of rationality and irrationality, and objectivity and subjectivity, geographers have seemingly encountered emotions in exciting and different ways throughout the recent past. Although there are important differences in terms of how different geographers have understood emotions and how they are relevant to geographical enquiry, collectively humanistic, feminist, psychoanalytic and non-representational approaches have all sought to validate the place of emotions in the discipline.

DISCUSSION POINTS

1. Why have emotions been ignored by geographers in the past?

2. What are the dangers in researching and writing emotional geographies?

3. What emotions has your own research work evoked for you?

FURTHER READING

Bondi, L., Davidson, J. and Smith, M. (forthcoming 2004) *Emotional geographies*.

This is an edited book of chapters relating to a range of work on emotions and geography, arising from the first ever conference on 'emotional geographies'.

Davidson, J. and Milligan, C. (2004) Embodying emotion, sensing space: introducing emotional geographies. *Social and Cultural Geography*, 5(4), 523–32.

This article introduces a theme issue on geography and emotions, and reviews recent geographical work that has recognized the significance of emotion at a range of spatial scales.

Widdowfield, R. (2000) The place of emotions in academic research. *Area*, 32(2), 199–208.

This article is clear and straightforward. It was discussed in the main text of this chapter and highlights how the doing of research is an emotional activity and that reflecting on such matters can be useful.

Bondi *et al.* (2002) *Subjectivities, knowledge and feminist geographies*. Oxford: Rowman and Littlefield.

This is an edited collection that includes contributions from postgraduate students. The text is accessible and contains interesting case studies about the role of emotion in spaces of human subjectivity.

CHAPTER 35
PLACE

Tim Cresswell

PLACE, ORDER AND CATEGORIZATION

Place is one of the central terms in Human Geography. It is a term that eludes easy definition and has been used in a number of disparate ways throughout Geography's history (see Entrikin, 1991; Massey, 1993; Sack, 1997; Tuan, 1977). Place has been used as an alternative to 'location'. Whilst location refers to position within a framework of abstract space, often indicated by 'objective' markers such as degrees of longitude and latitude, or distance from another location, place has come to refer to a mixture of 'objective' and 'subjective' facets including location but adding other, more subtle, attributes of the world we inhabit. John Agnew (1987) has argued, for instance, that place consists of:

- location – a point in space with specific relations to other points in space
- locale – the broader context (both built and social) for social relations
- sense of place – subjective feelings associated with a place.

Sense of place refers to the subjective feelings evoked by a place for both insiders (people who live there) and outsiders (people who visit). We can see, then, that place is a much richer idea than its precursor, location. It is not surprising, therefore, that Geographers have studied place and places in a number of ways. Whilst the importance of meaning to the definition of place has made it central to the concerns of cultural geographers, it has appeared throughout the sub-disciplines of Human Geography. Political geographers, for instance, have looked at the construction of particular kinds of politics influenced by specific local places such as the north of Italy or Cornwall (Agnew, 2002; MacLeod and Jones, 2001). Economic geographers, meanwhile, have enquired into why and how specific places become sites of clusters of particular kinds of economic activity. Place's central role in Human Geography means that it transcends sub-disciplines. In this chapter I focus on places as ways of seeing and framing the world according to what and who is said to belong where. This approach is only one possible way of thinking about place.

Place is more than an academic term – it is a word we frequently use in our everyday lives. Some of the ways we use it point to the richness of place as an idea. Here are some examples:

- He knew his place.
- She was put in her place.
- Everything in its place.

Terms such as these point towards the social and cultural significance of place. In each of these phrases the word place suggests simultaneously a geographical location and a position on a social hierarchy. Think, for example, of a dinner table, either at home or in a more formal setting such as an annual dinner of an organization. Everything from the flowers to the

FIGURE 35.1
A woman's place is in the home?/A stereotypical image of a post-war US housewife. Credit: Bettman/Corbis

position of the cutlery to the seating arrangement is in some way related to place in the social sense. Old-fashioned notions of the patriarch sitting at the head of the table live on in households today and are formalized in the formal business dinner with its 'head table' and peripheral space for secretaries and janitors. A place for everything and everything in its place.

The human mind makes sense of the world by dividing it up into categories. As the examples above reveal, place and space are fundamental forms of categorization. Philosophers (most famously Kant) have insisted that the two basic dimensions of life are space and time, which form the basis for all other forms of categorization. Indeed, our conceptions of space and time are so fundamental they appear to pre-exist our conception and **representation** of them – that is to say they appear as nature. When we say that something is natural we are saying that it is not social – it 'just is' and is therefore unchangeable. This makes categories of space and time potent **ideological** weapons. They are ideological because they are laden with meanings that tend to create and reinforce relations of domination and subordination. As the French theorist Pierre Bourdieu (1984; 1990) has claimed, categorization schemes that remain unarticulated (seemingly as nature) inculcate adherence to the established order of things. This is the case because categorizations in space and time, for the most part, are not recognized discursively (we do not speak about them, write about them or even think about them) but practically (we act upon them). As we cannot possibly think about everything we do throughout our lives, the vast majority of our actions are fairly uncritical acts that conform to the expectations of those around us. In the remainder of this chapter I will examine the way in which place acts as a category that serves to reproduce the existing 'order of things'. In addition, we will see how challenges to the taken-for-granted relations between place and actions provide profound challenges to the 'order of things'.

Representation

the cultural practices and forms by which human societies interpret and portray the world around them and present themselves to others. In the case of the natural world, for example, these representations range from prehistoric cave paintings of the creatures that figured in the lives of early human groups to the televisual images and scientific models that shape our imaginations today. *See also* DISCOURSE.

Ideological

a meaning, idea or thing is ideological in so far as it helps to constitute and maintain relations of domination and subordination between two or more social groups (CLASSES, GENDERS, age groups, etc.).

PRIVATE PLACES AND PUBLIC PLACES

Mothers of the disappeared

Ideology

a meaning or set of meanings that serves to create and/or maintain relationships of domination and subordination, through symbolic forms such as texts, landscapes and spaces.

Nation-state

a form of political organization that involves (a) a set of institutions that govern the people within a particular TERRITORY (the state), and (b) that claims allegiance and legitimacy from those governed, and from other states, on the basis that they represent a group of people defined in cultural and political terms as a nation.

Public space is often simultaneously the site of the assertion of power and **ideology** by the **nation-state**, corporations and local governments and counter-ideological practices. Just as power is spatialized as place is given meaning, resistance can take the form of spatialized disobedience. A case in point is the actions of the Plaza de Mayo Madres (sometimes called the Mothers of the Disappeared) in Buenos Aires, Argentina, during the late 1970s and early 1980s. The application of meaning to space (the creation of place) is a supremely political process that tends to inscribe a particular idea of order on the lives of the people who inhabit (but do not build) that space (Duncan, 1990). The creation of public places such as streets, parks and public squares are often acts of ordering of the first magnitude. These spaces are constructed in order to convey the legitimate order to citizens.

One of the master codes by which such places are constructed is the division of public and private. The public spaces are supposed to be non-political. Proper politics is supposed to occur in designated political spaces

– the chambers and corridors of government. Similarly, public space is supposed to be masculine space. Public spaces are thus material manifestations of masculine ideas of order and authority. A 'feminine' presence on the street, in public space, is often seen as threatening (Wilson, 1991).

Jennifer Schirmer recounts some of the history of this attitude in western spaces. She tells the story of the French eighteenth-century assertion of freedom for men to speak, move and think, which arose at the same time as the banishment of women's public speech and polit-

FIGURE 35.2
A protest by the Plaza de Mayo Madres (the Mothers of the Disappeared) in Buenos Aires 1985. More than 10,000 attended. Credit: Micheline Pelletier/Corbis SYGMA

ical life. Women in public were 'out of place'. The best kind of woman, the most virtuous woman, was one who knew her place and did not speak out of turn: 'Boundaries between the public and private, the political and social, the productive and reproductive, and justice and family were established, and justified by women's absence in the first and presence in the second' (Schirmer, 1994: 188).

Schirmer goes on to tell the story of women who have taken it upon themselves to transgress the boundary of public and private space in order to make political points (in places supposedly non-political). Thus the Plaza de Mayo Madres inserted their bodies into the public space of Plaza de Mayo in order to protest against the 'disappearance' of family members (see Fig. 35.2). In the period 1976–82 the military junta of General Videla fought against a so-called International Conspiracy of Subversion that was said to be against all the (western) values that Argentina stood for. This included getting rid of all those who were out of place in Argentina – the 'alien bodies' who sought to subvert the state. Over 30,000 people became targets for official and unofficial state security forces to abduct, torture and disappear. The victims were erased from public consciousness. In protest, the Plaza de Mayo Madres began to circle the main square in Buenos Aires in 1977.

The square itself, like many grand squares around the world, had been built to symbolize elements of official history and ideology. In this case it was a symbol of the Inquisition in addition to contemporary ideas of governance. Every Thursday at 3.30 pm they would walk arm in arm, their heads covered, demanding the return of their disappeared relatives and the punishment of the people responsible. The presence of these women in public space is an immediate transgression of two place-based categorizations – the association of public space with masculinity and the association of such places with an absence of politics. In addition to these transgressions, however, the women used many of the symbols of motherhood and domesticity to make their case.

Gender

a criterion of social organization that distinguishes different groups of people on the basis of femininity or masculinity. In any one location, many masculinities and femininities interact. As a concept, gender is usually used in Human Geography in distinction to that of sex (i.e. femaleness and maleness) in order to emphasize the SOCIAL CONSTRUCTION of women's and men's roles, relations and identities. Human Geographers' accounts of the world have always been shaped through understandings of gender (see MASCULINISM) but explicit analyses of the geographies of gender and the gendering of geographies are comparatively recent, and associated with the growth of Feminist Geography (see FEMINISM).

" *The Plaza de Mayo is flanked by monumental buildings that are incongruous with the private lives of domesticity: the presidential palace (the Casa Rosada), which was used by the juntas; the cathedral; and the Ministry of Social Welfare. This site of masculinist power is demystified by older women, humbly circling the plaza wearing on their heads diapers first, and later white headscarves, embroidered with the names of their disappeared son or daughter or husband, together with worn photographs of their loved ones pinned on their breasts or placed on large placards at marches and demonstrations.* "

(Schirmer, 1994: 203–4)

Here the Madres are confusing the relationship between place and meaning in complicated ways, both transgressing the expectations of **gender** and politics; public and private space, and reaffirming (strategically) the 'normal' and 'proper' association between femininity and the nexus of the family and the domestic. A similar process has been identified at Greenham Common, where peace protesters in the 1980s pinned symbols of domesticity and reproduction such as nappies and sanitary pads to the fence at the monumental and masculine airbase that housed Cruise missiles (Cresswell, 1994; Schirmer, 1994). Relations between genders are not the only social relations that are maintained through the division of places into public and private. Other geographers have shown how the same divisions are used to construct the relations between adults and children.

The place of children

Childhood as a social category varies over time and place. In the western world, childhood is a lifestage associated with the home, which is constructed as a safe space that children leave when they become adults. Gill Valentine has noted how parents associated public space with potential danger for their children, ranging from abduction to traffic accidents. She suggests that the equation of stranger = danger, in particular, helps to reproduce the idea of the street and public space in general as a space 'populated by "deviant" others, a space in which the male body (particularly the black male body) is saturated with threat and danger' (Valentine, 1996b: 210).

The restrictions placed on the activities of children by their parents equate types of behaviour with categories of place. Because children are seen to be dependent, incompetent and under threat, they are protected through segregation and the restriction of access to 'dangerous places' in the public realm. Public places are thus constructed as adult spaces where children are 'naturally' absent. It is not just adults that produce public places in this way, however. Children internalize expectations about danger in public places and withdraw from interaction with adults in places such as playgrounds and parks. Thus 'children contribute through their own performative acts, towards producing public space as an adult space where they are not able to participate freely' (Valentine, 1996b: 211). The inverse, Valentine suggests, is that children no longer produce their own street space in the way they once did.

FIGURE 35.3A
Press coverage of traveller children in the UK during the 1980s. Source: *Daily Mirror* 2 June 1986, p. 4

FIGURE 35.3B
Press coverage of traveller children in the UK during the 1980s. Source: *Daily Mirror* 30 June 1983, p. 23

It is not just the streets of cities where children have been labelled out of place. Some of the labels of deviance in 1980s Britain were partly built on images of misplaced children. The convoys of travellers (New Age and otherwise) that have become a part of rural life in many parts of the United Kingdom have been met with considerable hostility by the media, some local residents and government at both the local and national level. One story used to indicate their manifest deviance concerned 'Emma', a young child who travelled with one of the groups attempting to reach Stonehenge in 1986. She was shown to be dirty, 'not toilet trained at four' (*Sun*, 7 June 1986: 4–5) and having no place to go. She was called 'Emma, the Kid from Nowhere' (*Daily Mirror*, 30 June 1986: 23) (see Fig. 35.3). Emma was made out to be indicative of the 'dirtiness' and 'lack of discipline' amongst traveller children. In an article entitled 'The Convoy Kids' (*Daily Mirror*, 2 June 1986: 4) we are informed at some length of children 'their faces streaked with mud, wearing tattered denims and even bovver boots'. The travellers were accused of depriving their children of a 'normal family environment'. The theme developed by these stories was the out-of-placeness of the children and the nomadic travellers as a group. Children are particularly associated with a so-called 'normal family environment' and thus the existence of children such as Emma amongst the travellers pointed towards the travellers' transgression of the place-based norms of home, family, work and privacy.

SUMMARY

- Place is a complicated term that refers to both objective location and subjective meanings attached to it.
- Place is simultaneously geographical and social.
- The division of the world into private and public places denotes particular relationships between geography, social group and behaviour.
- Examples of the way in which public and private places are implicated in the construction of acceptable behaviour can be seen through investigations of the social divisions between, for instance, men and women and adults and children.

RURAL AND URBAN

So far we have focused on the relationship between place and categories surrounding the important dualism of public and private. As we have seen, relationships between men and women and adults and children are constructed through this dualism at a number of scales. It is certainly not the only dualism that gets mapped on to particular places though. Another dominant spatialized dualism is that of urban and rural.

In Chapter 33 Paul Cloke discusses the march on London by British people claiming to represent the 'rural way of life'. A significant part of their complaint is that present attitudes to rural pursuits are driven by urban perceptions of the rural. Thus the claim is made that fox hunting is an age-old rural tradition under threat from urban do-gooders who do not understand the intricacies of country life. Indeed, there is a long tradition of people and actions labelled 'urban' being labelled out of place in the country, just as there are things associated with the rural that are labelled out of place in the city.

Prostitution in the country

A television advertisement for Hovis bread in the late 1970s and early 1980s featured a little boy struggling up a steep hill with his bicycle, complete with freshly baked wholesome brown bread and Dvorak's 'New World Symphony' playing in the background (see Fig. 35.4). The place was more than a backdrop in this advertisement – it was a central actor that suggested a simpler and more wholesome and honest life of rural innocence. In the advertisement we are led to believe by the voiceover that the town is in the north of England but, as it turns out, the location was Shaftesbury in the southern county of Dorset. The street up the hill in the middle of Shaftesbury was already a tourist attraction before the Hovis advertisement appeared on television. Since then thousands of tourists every year have climbed the hill or simply taken a picture of it. When people see it they recognize it as the site where the little boy pushed his bicycle up the hill. It has become a place where a certain view of rural and rustic Englishness is reproduced.

FIGURE 35.4
Shaftesbury, Dorset, as featured in an advertisement for Hovis bread. Credit: The Advertising Archive

In the autumn of 2002 a policeman noticed a website called 'Complete Excellence', which advertised the sexual services of a Shaftesbury resident who was described, in bucolic terms, as an 'English rose' who lived in a 'beautiful home deep in the West of England'. Potential clients were offered an overnight stay followed by 'sensuous morning tea in bed'. The police raided the Shaftesbury home and arrested Michael Chubb, the husband of 'English rose' Jilly Bywater, for running a brothel. The arrest of pimps is not usually front-page news in Britain but the arrest of Chubb and the revelations about Bywater's activities made all the newspapers. The press expressed surprise at the existence of prostitution in rural Britain. In one *Guardian* article (28 July 2003: 6) the Shaftesbury area is referred to as both 'Hovisland' and 'Thomas Hardy country':

> But this 'English Rose' is not advertising in the red-light district of London, Manchester or Edinburgh. She lives 'in a discreet cottage in the Shaftesbury area of Dorset', … Thomas Hardy country is not the place you'd expect to find a hooker, but Rosie is no normal lady of the night …
>
> Almost everyone in Shaftesbury and the surrounding villages is now talking about how all is not wholesome in Hovisland. 'What did she do for £500 a night? The ladies in my bridge circle want to know,' says Janet Brady, 48, her dog, Max, by her feet as she sips coffee in the Rose Café. This part of Englande is the land of the tea shoppe.

Thus the disclosure that Jilly Bywater (like several other rural prostitutes) had resorted to prostitution following the failure of farming in the area in order to pay for her daughter's private boarding school fees is framed within implicit understandings of what it means to be a rural place in England. People have 'bridge circles' and England is spelled Englande. As the *Guardian* points out, prostitution would not be surprising if it occurred in 'London, Manchester or Edinburgh' but when it occurs at the top of Gold Hill, where the Hovis advert was filmed, it becomes national news. Shaftesbury is not simply any place in the English countryside but, thanks to Hovis, a place that has become an icon of the countryside and an imagined way of life. Such is the power of place and the rural–urban distinction in framing expectations about behaviour.

Animals in the city

The division between urban and rural mirrors the more fundamental division between culture and nature (see Chapter 1). Cities are supposed to be places of culture and society whilst rural landscapes have often been thought of as natural landscapes. Particular problems arise, therefore, when 'nature' appears in the city. Animals, for instance, are subjected to many of the place-based forms of control that marginalized social groups experience. Animals, like people, have their place. Chris Philo (1995) has examined the 'possible responses of a social geographer when confronted by the intrusive reality of (say) cows, sheep, and pigs mingling with people in the spaces of a large urban area' (Philo, 1995: 657). Philo discusses how various aspects of domesticated animal behaviour intrude upon ideas about the 'proper' place of animals. During the nineteenth century, just as the urban poor and other marginal groups became the object of sanitary and environmental discussion, animals and the places associated with them (abattoirs, meat markets, etc.) began to be removed from the city due to, amongst other things, the 'odours, flies and unseemly sights associated with animal husbandry' (Fielding, cited in Philo, 1995: 666). As the city became progressively segmented into functional containers for people and activities, animals became matter-out-of-place. Whilst some animals became acceptable urbanites, such as cats and dogs, others were expelled to the country where they apparently 'naturally' belonged. Of particular concern was the meat industry and the spaces associated with it. Most cities had large areas devoted to the slaughtering and processing of meat products by the early nineteenth century. In Britain, Smithfield Market in London was the most prominent of these (see Fig. 35.5). Philo reveals how as the century progressed people surrounding Smithfield became disturbed by the mixing of people and animals in the city. Take, for instance, the account of a shop assistant:

FIGURE 35.5
Smithfield Market during the nineteenth century, London. Credit: Mary Evans Picture Library

"
On Monday last we had one beast put its head through the window; we are obliged to have a person at the door to keep them off; and last Monday week we had a sheep got into the shop and fell down the cellar steps into the cellar amongst the workmen: I think that fewer customers

come to the shop on Monday; the ladies would not come to the shop if there was a crowd of bullocks . . . "

(Padmore, cited in Philo, 1995: 667)

Alternatively there is the case of a Mr J.T. Norris, the owner of a printing establishment located near Smithfield. When asked by a committee looking into the presence of animals in the city if he had seen any immorality in and around the market he replied:

" *I . . . know that I have seen that which to me in a refined city is very unbecoming: I have seen bullocks driven from the market, which have been imperfectly operated upon, jumping on the backs of the cows in public streets, in the presence of passengers of both sexes. I think that it is an offence to decency: it is unbecoming in a great city, and forms a reason in my mind why such scenes should be at a distance, and out of the way of the observation of females and children.* "

(Norris, cited in Philo, 1995: 669)

Here we have the obvious displeasure of people observing the country in the city, nature in culture, animals out of place. Philo charts the way in which the natural behaviour of animals in the city was seen to be a threat to human morality. Smithfield Market was not just associated with people out of place but with people engaged in immoral acts, spurred on by the sight of animals copulating. Nature and animals needed to be put in their place as they increasingly transgressed the links between space and behaviour.

So whilst prostitutes have been seen as the urban in the rural, the animals of Smithfield Market were seen as the rural in the urban. Both provoked responses that sought to define the 'proper' activities for such places and expel the intruding transgressors. Both responses reveal how place is implicated in the construction of particular kinds of morality – the production of moral geographies.

SUMMARY

- As with the conceptual division between private and public, the categories of urban and rural are signified by particular places and particular actions.

- Whilst prostitution has often been associated with urban space it becomes newsworthy when it is discovered in a rural area. Rural places have been associated with wholesome innocence, and the

location of prostitution in a rural town confounds normal expectations of the links between commercial sex and place.

- Certain kinds of animals were progressively seen as out of place in the city during the eighteenth and nineteenth centuries as their behaviour was too close to nature for an ordered, civil urban life.

CONCLUSION: PLACE, CATEGORIZATION AND TRANSGRESSION

In the introduction to this chapter I discussed the way in which the association between place as meaningful location and categories of people and actions is often invisible because it is so deeply engrained. Knowing one's place thus seems 'natural' or 'inevitable'. In the examples that followed, the relationship between place and categories became most apparent when the relationships were transgressed – when people (or animals) were said to be 'out of place'. Thus the construction of public space as adult space becomes obvious when children appear in it. Likewise beliefs about what happens and belongs in the countryside are underlined when something (such as prostitution) is described as 'out of place' there. The order that is constructed by and through place is not inevitable and is often transgressed. It is in these moments of transgression that a great deal is said (in the media, by politicians and figures of authority) about what and who belongs where. Transgression, then, is a key concept for geographers who want to describe and explain the construction of 'normality' through the creation and maintenance of particular types of place.

DISCUSSION POINTS

1. How is place different from location?

2. In addition to distinctions between public and private places and urban and rural places, what other kinds of binary distinctions characterize our thinking about place?

3. In what ways can places be given meaning?

4. How do pre-existing images of place affect our judgement of events located in them?

5. How might place be thought of as ideological?

6. How might places be used to resist dominant forms of power?

FURTHER READING

Cresswell, T. (2004) *Place: a short introduction.* Oxford: Blackwell.

This book surveys, in greater depth, the variety of ways place has been used in geography and beyond. It explores the development of the concept and provides concrete examples of the role of place in a variety of social and cultural processes.

Cresswell, T. (1996) *In place/out of place: geography, ideology and transgression.* Minneapolis: University of Minnesota Press.

In this book I expand upon the connections between place, meaning and power through an examination of events and people labelled out of place. It includes discussions of graffiti, travellers and Greenham Common Peace Protesters.

Sibley, D. (1995) *Geographies of exclusion: society and difference in the West.* London: Routledge.

David Sibley develops a similar theme in this excellent book. His focus includes a consideration of psychoanalytic

theory and he provides numerous examples of how space and place are implicated in the exclusion of people and actions defined as 'Other'.

Philo, C. (1995) Animals, geography, and the city: notes on inclusions and exclusions. *Environment and Planning D: Society and Space*, 13(6), 655–81.

Schirmer, J. (1994) The claiming of space and the body politic within national-security states. In Boyarin, J. (ed.) *Remapping memory: the politics of timespace.* Minneapolis: University of Minnesota Press, 185–220.

Valentine, G. (1996) Children should be seen and not heard: the production and transgression of adult's public space. *Urban Geography*, 17(3), 205–20.

Some of the case studies presented in this chapter are discussed in more depth in the above-named texts.

CHAPTER 36
DIASPORAS

Claire Dwyer

> " *Nazneen walked a step behind her husband down Brick Lane. The bright green and red pendants that fluttered from the lamp-posts advertised the Bangla colours and basmati rice. In the restaurant windows were clippings from newspapers and magazines with the name of the restaurant highlighted in yellow or pink. There were smart places with starched white tablecloths and multitudes of shining silver cutlery. In these places the newspaper clippings were framed. The tables were far apart and there was an absence of decoration that Nazneen knew to be a style. In the other restaurants the greeters and waiters wore white, oil-marked shirts. But in the smart ones they wore black.* "
>
> (Monica Ali, *Brick Lane*, 2003: 208)

Essentialist/ists/m

the belief that identities, such as class, gender and race, as well as age, dis/ability and sexuality, are directly determined by biology. This view is opposed by SOCIAL CONSTRUCTIONISTS, who argue that these differences between us are shaped through the interweaving of wider socio-spatial processes and individual biographies. The term is often used negatively to emphasize the stereotyping that it can produce.

INTRODUCTION

In her recent and hugely popular novel *Brick Lane* (2003) Monica Ali tells the story of the Ahmed family, Bengali migrants who live in the East End of London. The novel centres on the thoughts and aspirations of Nazneen, weaving a narrative between her childhood in Bangladesh, the life of her sister Hasina who remains in Dacca and the migrant community of Brick Lane in London to which Nazneen comes on her marriage to Chanu. The novel encompasses the pains and possibilities of migration – her husband's humiliation and struggle to find employment and status, her daughters' adept negotiation of the differing demands of Bengali and British societies, racism and the response to racism by Bengali young men on the estate, who form new political Islamist organizations, and Nazneen's own awakening as she charts a new life in a foreign country.

Whilst *Brick Lane* is a work of fiction, and open too to charges of sentimentalism or essentialism, the novel captures movingly some of the issues and experiences provoked by migration. Other recent novels have similarly found inspiration in migration stories. Zadie Smith's *White Teeth* (2000) engages in a wry depiction of the possibilities of multicultural London in a story about the intersections between the lives of three different families. In *Transmission* (2004) Hari Kunzru puts the connections, transfers and cross-overs of migration at the heart of his tale of life for an Indian migrant and computer analyst in Silicon Valley, California. All these novels are, in different ways, stories about migration or the aftermath of migrations. They are also stories that raise questions about place, identity, belonging and home. These are, of course, profoundly geographical questions, and it is perhaps not surprising that diasporic fiction has been a focus in some recent geographical writing (Jazeel, 2003; Sharp, 1994).

In this chapter I want to explore how migration flows and the transnational connections they produce are involved in rethinking how we

Globalization

the economic, political, social and cultural processes whereby: (a) places across the globe are increasingly interconnected; (b) social relations and economic transactions increasingly occur at the intercontinental scale (*see* TRANSNATIONAL); and (c) the globe itself comes to be a recognizable geographical entity. As such, globalization does not mean everywhere in the world becomes the same. Nor is it an entirely even process; different places are differently connected into the world and view that world from different perspectives. Globalization has been occurring for several hundred years, but in the contemporary world the scale and extent of social, political and economic interpenetration appears to be qualitatively different to international networks in the past.

think about places. In particular, I want to use the concept of diaspora and some examples of the cultural, social, economic and political practices associated with diaspora populations to emphasize geographies of flows and connections between places. I will argue that theories of diaspora offer new ways of thinking about the connections between global–local geographies (see Chapter 3).

I begin by emphasizing the links between migration and globalization suggesting the ways in which these two processes are linked. I then provide a more detailed discussion of the concept of diaspora and the different kinds of geographies it might suggest. In the second half of the chapter I discuss some examples of what I define as diaspora cultures and diaspora spaces to illustrate some of the different ways in which geographers and others have used this concept.

GLOBALIZATION AND MIGRATION

Transnational

an adjective used to describe Human Geographical processes that have escaped the bounded confines of the NATION-STATE. These have been identified in the realms of the economy (*see* TRANSNATIONAL CORPORATIONS), in politics (for instance, through the political agency of groups in relation to a nation-state they do not reside in; e.g. Kurdish exiles campaigning for Kurdish nationalism) and in culture (for example, through the identification of 'transnational communities' that have dispersed from an originary homeland into a number of other countries but that also have strong linkages across this DIASPORA).

Migration study has long been of interest to geographers. However contemporary studies of migration have revealed new issues (see Chapter 37). In particular, less attention is being paid to models of migration which suggest that migration is theorized as a permanent move from one place to another, and geographers are emphasizing the extent to which new forms of migration are associated with webs of transnational linkages and connections. Migration movements can be seen as an integral part of **globalization** – those economic, social, cultural and political processes whereby places across the globe are increasingly interconnected (Giddens, 1990) through the compression of time and space (Harvey, 1989). Migration results in the 'stretching out' of social relations between people across space (Massey and Jess, 1995) as individuals retain links within a community that is spread out across national boundaries.

Whilst links are maintained through visits or the exchange of letters, the globalization of telecommunications means that communities can be linked much more immediately. So, for example, families may communicate frequently with each other via the internet or telephone. Marie Gillespie's study of British-Punjabi families in Southall emphasized the importance of the exchange of home videos with family members in India (Gillespie, 1995). In another study, of the mainly female domestic workers from Latin America working in the USA, the women phoned their relatives in Mexico or El Salvador frequently to advise and discipline their children, described as 'transnational mothering' (Hondagneu-Sotelo and Avila, 1997). Satellite television is also increasingly important in creating shared transnational cultural experiences – viewers in Germany, Turkey and Britain may all watch the same programmes on the same channel (Robins and Aksoy, 2003) whilst the Bollywood film industry is now orientated as much to the lucrative audience of Indians living outside India as to the domestic audience (Shah, 2002). The internet and email electronic bulletin boards can prove a rapid form of communication, for example between Indians residing in the United States and in India (Adams and Ghose, 2003; Rai, 1995). Telecommunications may not simply facilitate closer familial contact, they also enable citizens living outside their country of origin to participate in political debates and exchanges as Koser's study of the relationship between Eritreans abroad and the Eritrean state illustrates (Koser, 2003).

These forms of transnational relations raise important questions about culture and place. If social, political and cultural relations are stretched out across space, then ideas about culture or cultural identity can no longer be thought of as being bounded in one place – transported by migrants from one place to another. Instead, these transnational links suggest a more dynamic conceptualization of cultures being formed and transformed across and between national boundaries.

One way of thinking about this might be through the words of Gloria Anzaldúa (1987), a Chicano (Mexican-American) woman, who reflects on her own identity in relation to the border between Mexico and the United States, a very important boundary for transnational immigration.

Gloria Anzaldúa
'To Live in the Borderlands Means You . . .'

To live in the Borderlands means you
    are neither *hispana india negra espanōla*
    ni gabacha, eres mestiza, mulata, half-breed
    caught in the crossfire between camps
    while carrying all five races on your back
    not knowing which side to turn to, run from;

To live in the Borderlands means knowing
    that the *india* in you, betrayed for 500 years,
    is no longer speaking to you,
    that *mexicanas* call you *rajetas,*
    that denying the Anglo inside you
    is as bad as having denied the Indian or Black;

Cuando vives en la frontera
    people walk through you, the wind steals your voice,
    you're a *burra, buey,* scapegoat,
    forerunner of a new race,
    half and half – both woman and man, neither –
    a new gender;

To live in the Borderlands means to
    put *chile* in the borscht,
    eat whole wheat *tortillas,*
    speak Tex-Mex with a Brooklyn accent;
    be stopped by *la migra* at the border checkpoints;

Living in the Borderlands means you fight hard to
    resist the gold elixer beckoning from the bottle,
    the pull of the gun barrel,
    the rope crushing the hollow of your throat;

In the Borderlands
    you are the battleground
    where enemies are kin to each other;
    you are at home, a stranger,

FIGURE 36.1
Credit: Lorna Ainger

the border disputes have been settled
the volley of shots have shattered the truce
you are wounded, lost in action
dead, fighting back;

To live in the Borderlands means
the mill with the razor white teeth wants to shred off
your olive-red skin, crush out the kernel, your heart
pound you pinch you roll you out
smelling like white bread but dead;

To survive the Borderlands
you must live *sin fronteras*
be a crossroads.

gabacha a Chicano term for a white woman
rajetas literally, 'split,' that is, having betrayed your word
burra donkey
buey oxen
sin fronteras without borders

Source: *Borderlands/La Frontera: the New Mestiza*, pp. 194–5. San
Francisco: Spinsters/Aunt Lute (1987)

Anzaldúa reflects on a Chicano identity that is 'in between' – neither Mexican nor American – reflected in her mixing of languages between Chicana, Spanish and English. It is also an identity that is not rooted in one place but draws upon an evocation of several different geographies at the same time. The poem suggests both the transformative possibilities associated with a speaking position on the border but also the struggles entailed for those who do not appear to 'belong' in one place or another. A concept that is helpful in understanding these 'stretched out' or 'extroverted' geographies of flows and connections between people, culture and places is the idea of *diaspora*.

SUMMARY

- Geographers increasingly understand migration as a complex system of transnational movements rather than a permanent move from one country of residence to another.
- Migration movements are integral to the processes of globalization whereby different places across the globe are increasingly interconnected.
- Migrant communities have 'stretched out' social relations and networks that cross-cut national boundaries and borders.

DIASPORAS

The term diaspora is an attempt to encompass the different and complex belongings of peoples who may be dispersed across geographical boundaries and may have connections to several different places they call 'home' (Clifford, 1994). Whilst the term 'diaspora' has sometimes suggested a fixed point of origin from which a group of people initially dispersed, the evocation of 'diaspora' is more often understood as a challenge to the idea of identities as rooted in fixed places of origin and instead an attempt to explore the ways in which diaspora cultures are created through the fusion and mixing of different cultural elements.

The word diaspora derives from the Greek verb *speiro* (to sow, or to scatter) and the preposition *dia* (over, or through). In ancient Greece the term referred to the process of migration and colonization. A dictionary definition states that the term diaspora refers to 'dispersion from', suggesting an original homeland from which dispersion occurs. This definition resonates with the biblical description of the dispersion of the Jewish people after their exile in Babylon, often seen as the original use of the term diaspora. Whilst some writers have defined the ancient Jewish diaspora as an 'ideal type' (Safran, 1991), the term now has a much wider currency to describe a variety of different kinds of diasporas. What all these diaspora communities share, however, is the memory of shared journeys or migrations and a recognition that another place, another 'homeland', has some claim on their emotions and loyalties. Since the term diaspora has been used to evoke a range of different historical experiences there has been much debate about its theoretical reach. As James Clifford (1994) reflects, there is often slippage between diaspora as a theoretical concept, the discursive evocation of diaspora and distinct historical experiences of diaspora. In order to engage with this tension I want to briefly outline a few different examples of diasporas, recognizing that each has a specific history and geography. However, I then move beyond this delineation of different types of diasporas and their different geographies to explore the theoretical possibilities of the term diaspora for reconceptualizing the relationships between people and place.

In his book *Global Diasporas* (1997) Robin Cohen produces a typology of different kinds of diasporas. His starting point is the Jewish expulsion from Babylon which, like Safran (1991), he uses as a model with which to compare other diasporas. He suggests that the common features of diaspora include: 'dispersal from an original homeland, often traumatically, to two or more foreign regions'; 'a collective myth and memory about the homeland'; 'a strong ethnic group consciousness sustained over a long time and based on a sense of distinctiveness, a common history'; 'a sense of empathy and solidarity with co-ethnic members in other countries of settlement'; 'a troubled relationship with host societies suggesting a lack of acceptance' (Cohen, 1997: 26). A forced population movement that conforms most closely to Cohen's typology, and that he defines as a 'victim diaspora', is the slave movement that transported millions of Africans to the Caribbean, and North and South America to work in tropical plantations in the eighteenth and nineteenth centuries. Whilst the term African diaspora was not really used until the 1950s, evocations of the Jewish exile recur in the musical cultures that have developed within this transatlantic African diaspora (see below).

A second example of a global diaspora associated with coerced population movement is the indentured Indian labour associated with the plantation colonies of the British Empire. In the nineteenth century, slavery was replaced by the movement of indentured labourers from the British Empire in India to work on colonial plantations in Africa and the Caribbean. The legacy of this population movement can be seen most forcibly in another forced population movement – the expulsion from

Uganda in 1972 of Ugandan Asians who were the diaspora descendants of indentured labourers. Many of these expelled Ugandan Asians came to Britain, where they still held citizenship, thus completing another process of migration within the Asian diaspora, as 'twice migrants' (Bhachu, 1985).

Cohen also includes other important examples of diasporas shaped by trade movements – such as the migration of Chinese traders to other parts of South Asia and North America, or Lebanese traders' migration to Europe and North America. In the late twentieth and early twenty-first century, processes of globalization have transformed population movements. At the same time, however, many contemporary population movements have close associations with their historical antecedents. The new diasporas formed through labour migrations of central American and Caribbean workers to the USA (like the Latina domestic workers mentioned above) are a legacy of historical trade and labour patterns with North America. In the post-war period of labour recruitment in Britain new migrations took place from South Asia and the Caribbean. Whilst this migration was voluntary rather than forced or enslaved migration, it continued the historical connections established under the labour conditions of the Empire and established new webs of diaspora connections.

Tracing the geographical dimensions of particular historical diasporas is helpful in understanding the complexity of the migration movements involved. However, I want to now move beyond the typology established by Cohen to open up some more expansive ways of thinking about diaspora. As I suggested above, writers like James Clifford have argued that in addition to the mapping out of distinctive historical diasporas we can also use the term diaspora as a theoretical tool to note a particular understanding of the relationship between people and place. For Clifford, a diasporic identity is one that encompasses both a consciousness of displacement and a recognition of multi-locational attachment. It is also a form of resistance, a cultural politics, opposed to nationalism and assimilation. Avtar Brah (1996), a British Asian writer interested in questions of identity and belonging, has also sought to theorize the term diaspora. Brah argues that the term diaspora is about holding in 'creative tension' the idea of 'home' and 'dispersion' (1996: 192). What she means by this is that whilst we can recognize a 'homing desire' we should also challenge discourses about fixed origins. So diaspora thinking is a challenge to *essentialist* and often even racist discourses that imagine the world in relation to fixed identities, borders and even nations. Instead it is a celebration of the possibilities of cross-border thinking and making connections and networks. Diasporic identities also produce new kinds of geographies. Diaspora identities involve social, cultural, political and economic relationships with others who share the same identity but are widely dispersed in different places. As Brah suggests: 'Diaspora identities are at once local and global. They are networks of transnational identifications' (1996: 196).

Whilst many of the writers who use the term diaspora may not be geographers, we can see how the term is a key geographical notion. It sketches out a way of thinking about geography that emphasizes connections, flows and networks. This is perhaps a different kind of geography to that which emphasizes boundaries and borders. In the words of Paul Gilroy (1994) it is about *routes* not *roots*. In the next two sections I want to look at some examples of different ways of thinking about geographies of diaspora. First, I give two examples of diaspora cultures, I then focus on what I term diaspora spaces.

SUMMARY

- Diaspora describes dispersed communities that share multiple belongings to different places or 'homes' in different national spaces.

- Diaspora identities challenge the concept of fixed 'roots' or origins, and emphasize instead transnational connections and linkages.

DIASPORA CULTURES

The black Atlantic

As I outlined above, one of the most important migrations in history was the 'triangular trade' of slaves, which dispersed black people from Africa across the Americas. This forced migration formed the basis for what Paul Gilroy (1994) describes as a black Atlantic diaspora. This is a diaspora culture that links African-Americans, Caribbeans, black British people and peoples in Africa. In his exploration of the cultures of the black Atlantic diaspora, Gilroy uses metaphors of travel – recalling the ships that first took slaves to America as well as those that brought Caribbean migrants to Europe in the post-war period. He argues that the cultures of the black Atlantic are characterized not by a return to African 'roots' but by the interconnection of many interlinked 'routes' between different places.

This is emphasized through his exploration of the connections between different kinds of musical forms. He argues that the music of the black Atlantic diaspora – blues, reggae, jazz, soul, rap – have all been produced through particular fusions of influences in different places. Thus on the plantations African music was transformed particularly through a fusion with other kinds of music such as European religious music. When slaves later migrated to the cities, new musical forms such as rhythm 'n' blues and jazz were created, and in each case these were created through new interconnections. Thus New Orleans jazz was a different music from other forms of jazz such as Afro-Cuban jazz. Gilroy traces these connections to music produced in Britain by post-war migrants including British adaptations of Jamaican reggae, whilst noting reggae itself was born of fusions between Jamaican folk music and American rhythm 'n' blues. Similarly, the production of contemporary black music, such as rap, had its origins in the 1970s, in the fusion of the music of the Jamaican sound systems with the 'talk-over' of New York Bronx DJs (Hall, 1995).

Gilroy's argument is that all these musical forms are the results of fusions of different cultural traditions within the black Atlantic diaspora. Whilst all of the musical forms retain some distinctive elements of what might be deemed 'African', they have been transformed within different geographical and national contexts. Through these connections Gilroy

Syncretic
an adjective applied to a culture or cultural phenomenon that is composed of elements from different sources, and that combines them in such a way as to create something new and different from those sources. Drawn from anthropological literatures, notions of the syncretic are very similar to those of HYBRIDITY, but are often preferred for their less biological undertones.

FIGURE 36.2
Winner of the Mercury Music Prize in 2003,
Dizzee Rascal, from Bow in East London, is a
black British rap artist whose distinctive take on
British garage music draws on his experience of
growing up in a tough urban environment (*Boy
in da Corner*, Dizzee Rascal, 2003, XL
Recordings)

unsettles a notion of tradition or fixed origins. The musical forms are not
diluted forms of 'traditional' African music but are new **syncretic** forms
produced within a diasporic culture through cultural flows or
interconnecting routes. And indeed these routes are not simply one-way –
American and British black music is also played and bought in Africa,
influencing the ways in which contemporary African music is produced.

Gilroy (1987) also traces these interconnections within black British
youth cultures – black styles, music, dance, fashion and language –
emphasizing the extent to which black British culture must be understood
as an integral part of a black Atlantic diaspora. He argues that black
cultures

> *draw inspiration from those developed by populations elsewhere. In
> particular, the culture and politics of black America and the
> Caribbean have become raw materials for creative processes which
> redefine what it means to be black, adapting it to distinctively British
> experiences and meanings.*

(Gilroy, 1987: 154)

In this way, black British youth culture is actively made and re-made
within a diasporic community of connection across the black Atlantic. At
the same time black youth cultures are created within a distinctive British
context and increasingly lead the production of a British youth culture
that itself becomes part of a transformative diasporic culture.

There are other examples of diaspora musical cultures that we could
also draw on here, such as bhangra and other musical forms produced
within the Asian diaspora (see Sharma *et al.*, 1996). However, I want to
turn to an alternative cultural space, that of fashion, for my next example.

Transnational fashion

Fashion is a rich, but also complicated, cultural space for examining the
making of diaspora cultures. On the one hand, we can think of the ways
in which clothes are often used as fixed markers or boundaries for 'ethnic'
identities. Think of the ways in which 'traditional' costume is used at key
international events likes sports competitions to denote national
identities, or the marketing of costumed dolls as touristic
commodifications of place. Whilst seemingly fixing ethnic identity on
the body – and often on a female body – anthropological accounts
demonstrate the extent to which dress codes are never fixed and are
constantly open to change and redefinition (Eicher, 1995). On the other
hand, there has been much debate about the 'appropriation' of different
forms of ethnic dress by elite fashion designers in the current vogue for
cross-over or hybrid designs (Niessen *et al.*, 2003). How fashion operates
as a site of cultural exchange and fusion is therefore complex. Here I want
to consider some examples from a case study of the British-Asian fashion
industry to demonstrate the possibility of diaspora cultures.

In a recent book about Asian fashion in Britain, Parminder Bhachu
(2004) emphasizes the *diaspora economies* within which the making and
marketing of Asian clothing in Britain are being transformed. Bhachu

Commodification
this term is used in two interrelated
ways: (a) as the conversion of any thing,
idea or person into a COMMODITY
(the term 'commoditization' is often
preferred for this sense); and (b) a
wider societal process whereby an ever
increasing number of things, human
relationships, ideas and people are
turned into commodities. Both
meanings see the process of
commodification as symptomatic of the
penetration of CAPITALISM into the
everyday lives of people and things.

traces a 'cultural narrative' of the salwaar-kameez, or Punjabi suit, from an item of negatively coded 'ethnic clothing' to a highly fashionable garment that was given particular prominence on the global fashion stage when worn by the late Princess Diana. Bhachu's analysis of these diaspora economies focuses on two groups of women entrepreneurs, those involved in design and retail, and the home-based seamstresses who produce outfits on a much smaller scale. Her argument is that the making of these suits involves complex, dialogic and diasporic processes, for example in the adaptation of patterns, fabrics and designs for different markets. The older African-Asian women she interviews were pioneers in adapting patterns, sharing designs with relatives abroad and procuring fabrics from different places, producing unique garments that represented all these diasporic connections and networks. Younger Asian designers combine British and Asian sensibilities to produce 'fusion' designs that are both highly fashionable and ethnically inflected. Like the musical cultures described by Gilroy these garments only make sense at this crossroads of cultural space. To illustrate this further I want to use the examples of two different designers I interviewed as part of a wider research project on South Asian commodity culture and transnationality (see Crang *et al.*, 2003; Dwyer, 2004).

Raishma is a fashionable boutique selling designer Asian fashion in East London. The eponymous designer, a young British-Pakistani woman, is a fashion graduate with experience in both the mainstream bridal fashion industry and the specialist Asian fashion industry. She specializes in evening and wedding wear and has high-profile clients including the comedy actress Meera Syal. Raishma's designs are evident of a diasporic aesthetic – she describes them as 'East/West' emphasizing that they represent a combination of both 'western fashion', evident in the styles and shapes used, and 'eastern traditions', evident in the fabrics and the traditional hand-beaded embroidery. For example, her wedding outfits (see Fig. 36.3) deliberately use colours like cream and white rather than the more traditional red, whilst also developing variations on more conventional outfits such as her separate bodices and skirts, or her backless, 'sari-dress'. In her marketing Raishma also self-consciously challenges expectations by putting Asian models in rural, 'English' landscapes.

Raishma's clothes are bought by young British-Asian women seeking outfits that reflect their syncretic identities as simultaneously British *and* Asian, but they are also bought by a wider clientele as Raishma capitalizes on the current enthusiasm for an Asian aesthetic. For example, Raishma obtained widespread media coverage when one of her outfits was worn by Ffion Hague, wife of the then Conservative Party leader William Hague, at a political dinner in 1999 (see Fig. 36.4).

If Raishma's clothes reflect a diasporic aesthetic in their fusion of different influences they are also evident of a process of production that depends upon Raishma's own positioning within the Pakistani diaspora. Raishma's clothes are produced in Pakistan and design sketches are faxed back and forth between Lahore and London as the transnational process of production is competed.

Liaqat Rasul is the owner of the designer label Ghulam Sakina, which was launched in 1999 with Liaqat's degree show (for an extended

FIGURE 36.3
Asian Wedding magazine, autumn 1999.
Photograph: Vincent Dolman

FIGURE 36.4
William and Ffion Hague. Credit: PNS/Rex Features

discussion of this case study see Dwyer and Crang, 2002). Unlike Raishma, Liaqat's clothes are not sold within the specialist Asian retail market; they are sold particularly in the London department store Liberty as well as a number of different outlets including some in Japan, thus reaching a diverse market. However, like Raishma, Liaqat's fashion designs can be understood within a diasporic cultural space. British born of Pakistani parents, Liaqat seeks through his clothes to develop a 'multicultural aesthetic'. He defines this as a juxtaposition of different elements 'jarring against each other'. His clothes are also about 'longevity and nostalgia', they are made from natural fibres that are dyed using traditional block-printing techniques and hand embroidery. The resulting garments represent complex combinations of different elements. In the dress shown in Figure 36.5 these include old packing fabric printed with Hindi script, a cutting taken from a borrowed paisley duvet, and a decoration based on the Bengali Kantha, or running stitch, traditionally used to recycle materials by sewing them together.

If Liaqat's garments are a fabrication of diasporic cultures in their weaving together of many different cultural elements, their production also emphasizes a diaspora culture. Liaqat uses contacts gained through his work in India with Indian designer Ritu Kumar, and specialist handicraft producers Anokhi to produce clothes in collaboration with Indian craftsmen as well as in more commercial workshops. Like Raishma he is constantly involved in a transnational dialogue, and travels between London and Delhi, to monitor the production process.

These two examples illustrate the emergence of a diaspora material culture. Like the musical cultures of the black Atlantic these fashion spaces only emerge out of the crossroads of the diaspora history representing both an aesthetics of fusion and syncretism and a material production process shaped by diasporic networks. These fashion stories are also shaping the wider fashion economy within which fusion styles like those described here are increasingly part of the 'mainstream' western fashion market. Whether or not this commodification of difference can be straightforwardly interpreted as politically progressive and evident of a broader diasporic consciousness is, of course, complex and contested (Jackson, 2002). Some of these issues of commodification recur in my final example, which returns to *Brick Lane*, as an example of a diaspora space.

FIGURE 36.5
Liaqat Rasul Graduate Collection 1999
'Observational Composite'. Photograph:
Masoud Golsorkhi

SUMMARY

- Diaspora cultures are characterized by interconnections, fusions and links that cut across or transform geographical boundaries.

- It is in music, art, fashion other cultural forms that diaspora cultures have been most readily recognized.

DIASPORA SPACES

The previous section emphasized that geographies of diaspora are characterized by networks, flows and connections which link multiple locations. These networks are also characterized by specific global–local connections (see Chapter 3). However, it is also important to look at the nexus within which these global–local connections take place. Avtar Brah's work provides a very useful understanding of this in her description of what she defines as 'diaspora spaces'. For her diaspora spaces are 'the point at which boundaries of inclusion and exclusion, of belonging and otherness, of "us" and "them" are contested' (Brah, 1996: 209). What is particularly interesting about Brah's definition is that she includes within these spaces not only those who have migrated and their descendants but also those who are constructed or represented as 'indigenous'. She argues that this concept of diaspora space (as opposed to that of diaspora) includes 'the entanglement, the intertwining of the genealogies of dispersion with those of 'staying put' (1996: 209). What she means by this is that the multiple connections characteristic of diaspora communities also affect those who have not migrated. So, for example, British youth cultures are bound up with and inflected by the transnational exchanges of black British 'black Atlantic' cultures even for those who are not part of these diasporas. Similarly, English men and women who remained 'at home' during Britain's imperial reign in India did not remain unaffected by the social, political, cultural and economic relationships that developed between Britain and India. Indeed, as contemporary **post-colonial** scholarship emphasizes, those who remained in the metropolitan centres of Empire, were also interlinked into colonial relationships, for example through the consumption of colonial products like cotton or tea, or the consumption of images and other 'imagined geographies' embodied in entertainment or education (Ploszajska, 2000; Ryan, 1997). In this final section I want to look at how we might understand local–global connections within which particular places might be evoked or imagined as diaspora spaces.

Post-colonial, post-colonialism

sometimes hyphenated, sometimes not, this term has two distinct meanings: (a) the post-colonial era, i.e. the historical period following a period of COLONIALISM (*see also* DECOLONIZATION); (b) post-colonial political, cultural and intellectual movements, and their perspectives, which are critical of the past and ongoing effects of European and other colonialisms.

Banglatown

Returning to the example with which I began this chapter, I want to consider Banglatown in the East End of London as a diaspora space. Banglatown refers to the area around Brick Lane in the Spitalfields area of the London Borough of Tower Hamlets. Spitalfields is characterized by a history of in-migration and settlement from the French Huguenots in the eighteenth century, Jews and Irish in the nineteenth century and early twentieth century, to Bengalis since the 1970s, and the area is emblematic of the multicultural history of the city of London (Merriman, 1993). Spitalfields, which remains one of the poorest wards in London, is approximately 80 per cent Bengali and the economy of the area is characterized by small family businesses, particularly textiles and restaurants. Banglatown was a local name used to describe the area around Brick Lane with its collection of restaurants, music and sari shops. This name creates a space for a Bengali diaspora where individuals assert their identities as simultaneously British and Bengali (Eade, 1997), as one local restaurateur remarks, 'Why not call it Banglatown? If anyone comes here they don't see England. They see India, Bangladesh and Pakistan in Europe' (cited by Waugh, 1997). These diasporic connections were reworked in 1980 when the Bangladeshi president, Ziaur Rahman visited Spitalfields and was presented with a street sign for Brick Lane, with which he promised to name a street in Dhaka (cited in Jacobs, 1996b: 96).

In 1997 Banglatown was used as a 'concept' (the term used by the development company, Cityside Regeneration Limited) to drive redevelopment in the Spitalfields area, drawing self-consciously on the examples of 'Chinatowns' in London and elsewhere. As regeneration of the Spitalfields market takes place, particularly through the introduction of city investment (see Jacobs, 1996b), Tower Hamlets Council is backing an initiative to develop Brick Lane and the surrounding area in partnership with private investment. Whilst this development encompasses shops, businesses, office spaces and housing, it is linked together through the imaginative geography of 'Banglatown' – symbolized by the arch that acts as a gateway into Brick Lane, which joins together Indian, Islamic and classical European architectural styles. Projects planned for the area include the 'Rich-Mix' centre. Launched in April 2002 this new building will provide a space for the exhibition and production of a range of cultural activities including film, art and music. The ethos of the centre is to provide a creative focus for the continued 'globalization of cultures and peoples' building on both the history of migration and exchange, which characterizes the East End of London, and Spitalfields more recent emergence as a site for the cultural industries.

Banglatown celebrates the possibilities of diaspora connections in creating new and vibrant cultural and social spaces in British cities. Investment in Banglatown raises the visibility of Bangladeshi-Britons and provides an important site upon which to centre key celebrations such as the annual Brick Lane Festival or *mela*. Banglatown might also be celebrated as a representation of a multicultural British landscape – with its signposts in sylheti script and its symbolic archway. The use of the concept of Banglatown has been supported by many local Bengalis, who see it as an opportunity to bring much needed investment to the area. They recognize the need to attract city investment into the Tower Hamlets area and therefore have been keen to embrace the concept of Banglatown as a marketing tool.

At the same time, there are also fears that the marketing of Banglatown simply becomes a means by which Bengali identities and cultures are essentialized or commodified as exotic or stereotypical. A recent study of Brick Lane (Carey, 2004) described the touristic encounters between the overwhelmingly white city visitors who come to Brick Lane curry restaurants, and the poorer, predominantly male, Bengali workers. These questions of representation were also highlighted in response to the novel *Brick Lane*. Some Bengali community leaders protested that the novel portrayed Bangladeshis as 'uneducated and unsophisticated' (*Independent*, 4 December 2003: 21). These debates highlight some of the complex politics of diaspora negotiations. Diaspora theories have been celebrated because of the possibilities they offer for challenging fixed and narrow conceptions of identity and belonging, and the opening up of more plural, more multicultural forms of citizenship that might displace or transform older national identities. However, there is also scepticism about the extent to which the celebration of multiculturalism promoted by the 'cultural industry' is merely another manifestation of capitalism and does nothing to challenge racism (Hutnyk, 2000).

SUMMARY

- Diaspora spaces are those within which a nexus of global–local connections can be recognized, contested and celebrated.
- Diaspora spaces suggest the possibility for new cartographies of diaspora identity and belonging

that may transform placed identities such as Britishness.
- Diaspora spaces can be created or 'invented' through the commodification of cultural difference as 'exotic'.

CONCLUSION: POSSIBILITIES OF DIASPORA?

In this chapter I have suggested that the globalization of migration has produced diasporas. Diasporas are defined as peoples dispersed across geographical boundaries but linked through connections to particular places that are imagined as multiple 'homes'. I have emphasized the ways in which thinking about diasporas challenges many geographical notions. The evocation of multiple 'homes' unsettles fixed geographical and national boundaries and the association of culture with particular places. Instead diasporic cultures are celebrated for their fusion of differences, both across different borders but also coming together within particular places to create distinctive syncretic cultures. Thus the geographies of diaspora are about the flows and connections between particular places and of networks that link up global and local spaces. Whilst diaspora cultures are characteristic of particular groups, I have also suggested that diaspora cultures may be transformative of all national cultures since they challenge the very notion of fixed national cultures within geographical boundaries.

DISCUSSION POINTS

1. What kinds of possibilities and opportunities are presented by diaspora populations? What difficulties might be raised by the presence of large diaspora populations?

2. Can you think of other diaspora cultures or diaspora spaces than those presented here? To what extent are such spaces simultaneously 'global' and 'local'? How can researchers identify the geographies of such spaces?

3. Are diaspora spaces inherently progressive?

FURTHER READING

Hall, S. (1995) New cultures for old. In Massey, D. and Jess, P. (eds) *A place in the world?* **Open University Press: Milton Keynes, 175–214.**

Stuart Hall, a sociologist, is one of the foremost writers associated with ideas about diaspora and cultural transformation. This article, part of a student reader, gives further examples, such as cricket, of the notion of diaspora cultures.

Gillespie, M. (1995) *Television, ethnicity and cultural change.* **London: Routledge.**

This is an ethnography of young British Punjabis living in Southall. Worth dipping into as an example of the 'everyday' ways in which the transnational linkages of a diasporic community are maintained. It focuses particularly on the role of television.

Hutnyk, J. (2000) *Critique of exotica: music, politics and the culture industry.* **London: Pluto Press.**

This is a provocative, if a little polemical, critique of the celebration of 'diaspora culture' focusing in particular on the music industry.

CHAPTER 37 MIGRANTS AND REFUGEES

Khalid Koser

INTRODUCTION

Human geography inevitably engages with issues that are controversial, emotive and politically charged. One challenge for students is to see beyond the news headlines and political 'spin' – properly to understand the central issues, and objectively to assess the facts and figures in reaching their own conclusions. Indeed these are amongst the key 'transferable skills' of any Geography degree.

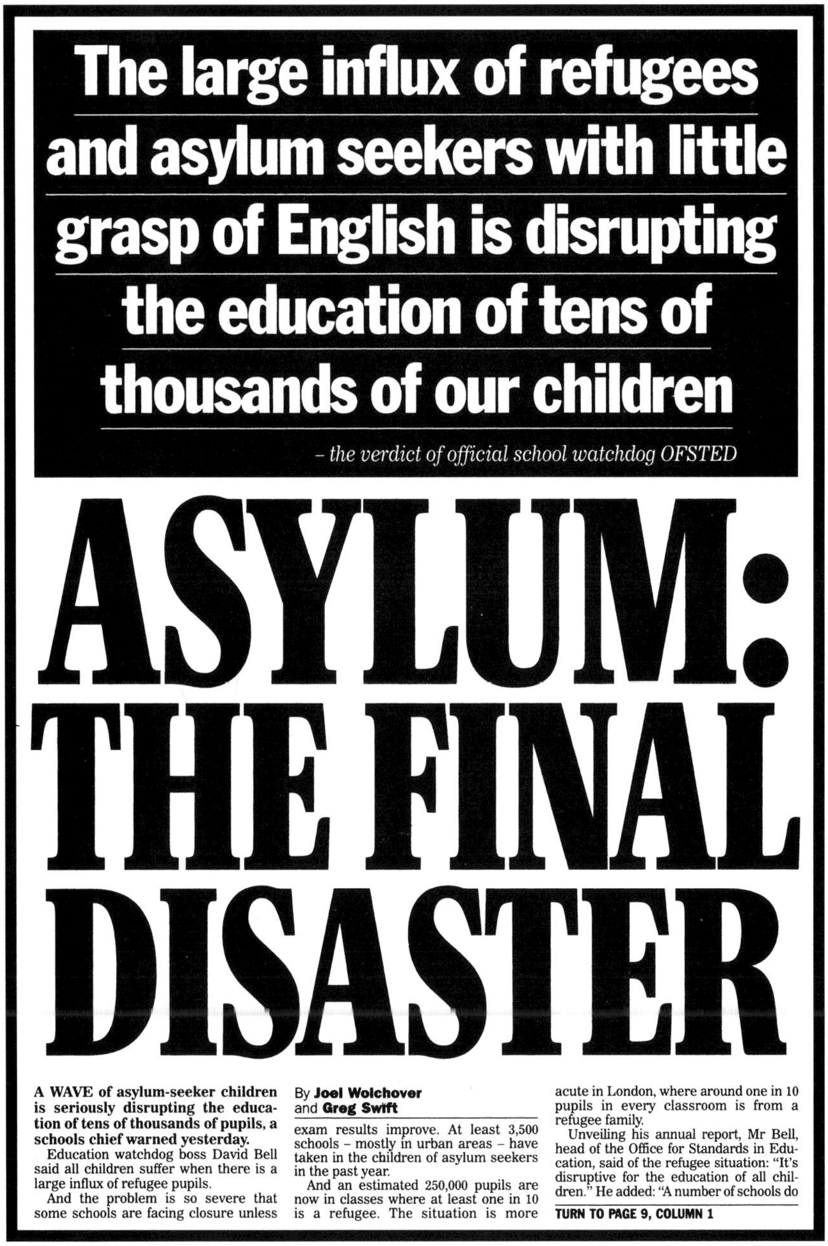

The large influx of refugees and asylum seekers with little grasp of English is disrupting the education of tens of thousands of our children

– the verdict of official school watchdog OFSTED

ASYLUM: THE FINAL DISASTER

A WAVE of asylum-seeker children is seriously disrupting the education of tens of thousands of pupils, a schools chief warned yesterday.

By **Joel Wolchover** and **Greg Swift**

Education watchdog boss David Bell said all children suffer when there is a large influx of refugee pupils.

And the problem is so severe that some schools are facing closure unless exam results improve. At least 3,500 schools – mostly in urban areas – have taken in the children of asylum seekers in the past year.

And an estimated 250,000 pupils are now in classes where at least one in 10 is a refugee. The situation is more acute in London, where around one in 10 pupils in every classroom is from a refugee family.

Unveiling his annual report, Mr Bell, head of the Office for Standards in Education, said of the refugee situation: "It's disruptive for the education of all children." He added: "A number of schools do

TURN TO PAGE 9, COLUMN 1

FIGURE 37.1
Front page of the *Daily Express*, 6 February 2003. Credit: John Frost Newspapers

Migration

migration can be considered a sub-category of a wider concept of 'movement', which embraces a whole range of forms of human mobility, from daily commuting at one end of the spectrum to permanent emigration at the other.

Asylum seeker

an asylum seeker is someone seeking protection under the terms of the 1951 United Nations Convention relating to the Status of Refugees.

Refugee

a refugee is someone who, 'owing to a well-founded fear of being persecuted for reasons of race, religion, nationality, membership of a particular social group or political opinion, is outside the country of his [or her] nationality'.

There are probably few greater contemporary challenges in the UK in this respect than the study of migrants and refugees. In recent years migration has charged to the top of political agendas in the UK and elsewhere in western Europe, and it has also become something of an obsession in the media, especially for more right-wing newspapers. Such papers uniformly portray migration negatively, and in so doing often misrepresent the realities of migration. Concepts are unclear – the terms 'asylum seeker', 'refugee' and 'illegal migrant' are regularly used interchangeably. Statistics are quoted in ways that alarm rather than inform. Only a very partial picture of migration is presented – by no means, for example, are all the migrants entering the UK today asylum seekers. Overall, the real diversity and complexity of migration is ignored.

Against this background, the purpose of this chapter is to try to cut through the hype and provide students with the sort of information they require to understand and analyse migration, and hopefully to engage in reasonable debate. It focuses on four key questions.

1. What is migration?
2. What do the statistics mean?
3. How many migrants are there?
4. What are the main types of migrant?

WHAT IS MIGRATION?

Illegal migrant

there are at least three ways an individual might be classified as an illegal migrant. First, they can enter a country illegally, without passing through an immigration checkpoint. Such entrants are often also referred to as 'irregular' migrants. Second, they can enter a country legally for a limited period of time – for example with a short-term visa – but then stay illegally after the expiry date of their visa. These are also described as 'undocumented' migrants. Third, they can be legally resident but involved in illegal activities.

The answer to this question is by no means straightforward. International migration can be considered a sub-category of a wider concept of 'movement', which embraces a whole range of forms of human mobility, from daily commuting at one end of the spectrum to permanent emigration at the other. What is defined as migration thus becomes an arbitrary choice, and may be time-specific. In the UK, for example, a migrant is defined as someone who has been living abroad continuously for one year or more – whereas in the Netherlands the time period is only six months.

The concept of permanent migration has been epitomized in the idea of new lands of opportunity, perhaps typified by Australia (Castles and Miller, 1998). Today, however, what is meant by 'permanent' migration is less clear. Even people who have lived abroad for most of their lives often retain a 'dream to return' to the place of their birth, and it is now relatively rare for people to migrate from one country to another and remain there for the rest of their lives. Despite this, the phenomenon of return migration remains sorely under-studied and poorly understood (see box).

In addition to the time period concerned, there are three main ways that migrations are categorized. A common distinction is between voluntary and involuntary (or forced) migration. The Office of the United Nations High Commissioner for Refugees (UNHCR) estimates that, worldwide, there are about 10 million people who have been forced to leave their home countries – usually as a result of conflict or persecution. There are far more migrants in the world today who have moved voluntarily – perhaps 100 million worldwide.

A second distinction often drawn is between people who move for

RETURN MIGRATION

Writing in the geographical journal *Area* in 1978, Russell King lamented the lack of data, theory and analysis concerning the phenomenon of return migration (King, 1978). Over 25 years later his comments are largely still valid – return migration remains a neglected aspect of population geography, even though millions of people return to their countries of origin each year. Return seems set to become even more important in the UK and elsewhere for some of the following reasons.

- Return is increasingly viewed as one way of reversing the so-called 'brain drain', whereby skilled people leave poorer countries to work in richer countries.
- Return is viewed as one way of combating irregular migration.
- There is growing pressure to return rejected asylum seekers.
- As conditions in their countries settle, some refugees may consider going home – in recent years it has become safer to return to the Balkans, Somaliland and Sri Lanka.
- Increasingly, work permits are only issued for short periods of time, with the expectation that migrants will return home at the end of the permit period.

economic and those who move for political reasons. The former are often described as labour migrants, and the latter as refugees.

The final main distinction is between legal and illegal migrants. There are at least three ways an individual might be classified as an 'illegal migrant'. First, they can enter a country illegally, without passing through an immigration checkpoint. Such entrants are often also referred to as 'irregular' migrants. Second, they can enter a country legally for a limited period of time – for example, with a short-term visa – but then stay illegally after the expiry date of their visa. These are also described as 'undocumented' migrants. Third, they can be legally resident but involved in illegal activities.

Categorizations always simplify reality, and this is true of the above migration categories in at least three main ways. First, there is some overlap *between* the different categorizations. Thus most voluntary migrants are also economic migrants, and most involuntary migrants are political migrants or refugees. Second, individuals can transform from one type of migrant to another *within* the different categorizations. A legal migrant may overstay his or her visa and become an illegal migrant; or an individual might leave his or her country voluntarily but then not be able to return, as a result for example of the start of a war, and thus effectively become an involuntary migrant.

Third, the sharp distinctions drawn between migrants within each categorization are often more blurred in reality. Very few migrations, for example, are purely voluntary or involuntary. Many large corporations, for instance, consider moving staff between international offices to be part of their training. So whilst employees moving within, say, IBM from London to Tokyo are ostensibly moving voluntarily, they may have no option if they want to keep their job in that company (Koser and Salt, 1997). At the other end of the spectrum, even refugees have choices other than to migrate – they might, for example, stay and take a risk, or move internally to a neighbouring village or town, or join one side of a conflict or the other.

The same blurring applies to distinctions between economic and political migration. Consider the case of someone who leaves their home because they lose their job. Ostensibly they are moving for economic reasons. But what if they have lost their job because of their race or religion, or because the factory where they worked has been bombed during a conflict. In that case you might argue they are fleeing for political reasons. The analytical challenge here is to distinguish between underlying causes of migration and its immediate precipitants.

SUMMARY

- International migration can be considered a sub-category of a wider concept of 'movement'.
- There are three main ways of categorizing migration, distinguishing voluntary from involuntary, economic from political, and legal from illegal migrants.
- These categorizations oversimplify reality; there is overlap between the different categorizations and blurred boundaries within them.

WHAT DO THE STATISTICS MEAN?

Perhaps the most potent weapon in the ongoing debate about migration in the UK, and often elsewhere, is statistics. They are often used selectively by the press and occasionally by politicians too, in order to paint a particular – normally negative – picture of immigration.

There are three very important observations to make about statistics on migration in the UK. First, although they are the most accurate available, even official migration statistics cannot provide a complete picture of international migration in the UK. To put this rather more bluntly, not even the government can state with any certainty exactly how many people enter or leave the country each year. The most obvious reason is that official migration statistics do not include numbers on illegal migrants. Statistics on illegal migrants in the UK are no more than guesses, and really should not be used to sell newspapers or, worse, make policy (see box).

Second, there are important reservations surrounding the statistics on migration that the government does record. Most published statistics on migration into and out of the UK are based on the International Passenger Survey (IPS). This is a small sample survey (about 2200 contacts) conducted at sea and airports. Passengers are interviewed about their intentions of staying in the UK (or abroad, if emigrating). Those who intend to stay in or out of the UK for a year or more, having lived abroad or in the UK for a year or more, are counted as migrants. One problem is coverage: only a small fraction of the population is interviewed and the results are scaled up. Another is that people's intentions change – they may or may not stay as long as they intended. Adjustments are made to the IPS figures to try to take account of such factors.

There are two other main sources of data on migration flows. Work permits issued measure the entry of workers, but only from outside the European Economic Area. Asylum statistics show how many people apply for protection in the UK, but care is required in interpreting them, as sometimes they include dependants (spouses and children) and sometimes not. Alternative indicators of numbers of foreign migrants entering the

COUNTING ILLEGAL MIGRANTS

Counting illegal migrants is an imprecise science. One reason is conceptual – as we saw in the first part of this chapter, the term covers a range of people who can be in an illegal situation for different reasons. Another is methodological – people without legal status are likely to avoid speaking to the authorities for fear of detection, and thus go unrecorded.

Various methods have been used to try to at least estimate the size of the illegal migrant population, although it needs to be emphasized that none of these is comprehensive:

- in some countries – though not the UK – amnesties are periodically declared, whereby foreign nationals residing or working illegally can regularize their status
- direct surveys of illegal migrants have taken place
- it is possible to compare different sources of recorded migration data and population data to highlight discrepancies that might be accounted for by illegal migration
- Surveys of employers can indirectly reveal foreign workers without legal status.

UK include the Labour Force Survey, which records nationality and address a year ago, but again is based only on a sample of households. The national census also records address a year ago, but it does not record nationality, only country of birth, and it takes place only once every decade.

A third observation, which is of course true of any statistics, is that migration statistics can be presented in different ways with different implications. In 2002 about 100,000 asylum seekers arrived in the UK. This figure can be portrayed very negatively indeed – it was higher than the figure for any other country in western Europe; and it amounts to the population of a small city like Cambridge arriving each year. Alternatively, it can be made to seem really rather insignificant if placed in a different context. If the number of asylum seekers is taken as a ratio of the total population of the country in which they arrive, the UK ranks only eighth in western Europe with a ratio of about 1.5 asylum seekers per 1000 population – Austria comes in first with a ratio of 4.5 per 1000. Taking a longer-term perspective, the UK received only about 25 per cent of the number of asylum seekers received in Germany between 1990 and 2000 – and a total of 100,000 per year pales into real insignificance in a global context in which very poor countries like Iran and Pakistan currently host almost two million refugees each.

SUMMARY
- Statistics on migration are often used to alarm rather than inform.
- Even the UK government cannot state with any certainty exactly how many people enter or leave the country each year, and a particular problem is recording illegal migrants.
- There are reservations about the statistics even for migration that is recorded regularly.
- Depending on the way statistics are presented, migration can be portrayed positively or negatively.

HOW MANY MIGRANTS ARE THERE?

KEY STATISTICS RELATING TO MIGRATION IN THE UK

- In 2001, 480,000 people came to the UK as immigrants and 308,000 left as emigrants; the net balance was 172,000.
- In 2001, 120,000 foreign students entered the UK to begin their first year of study in a higher education institution.
- In 2002, 84,100 applications were received for asylum, compared with 71,400 in 2001. The main countries of origin of applicants in 2002 were Iraq, Zimbabwe, Somalia and China.
- In 2001, 4.3 per cent of the UK population (around 2.3 million people) were foreign nationals; of whom 46 per cent were from Europe, 24 per cent from Asia, 13 per cent from Africa, 11 per cent from the Americas and 4 per cent from Oceania.

Reading the press, it is easy to run away with the idea that the UK already has been, or is about to be, overrun by migrants. But how many migrants are there in reality? As we have just seen, data problems mean that it has never been easy to say how many people come to stay in the UK or leave to live elsewhere. Following the 2001 census, the Office for National Statistics produced a revised set of international migration estimates. From these, it appears that in 2001 about 480,000 people arrived to live in the UK for at least a year, and this is the last year for which statistics are currently available.

Once again, it is worth taking a moment to look behind this bald statistic. Media portrayals of 'floods' of immigrants rarely acknowledge, for example, that substantial numbers of people leave the UK too – it is estimated that they numbered 308,000 in 2001. This means that the net balance of migration in the UK in 2001 was 172,000. A longitudinal perspective reinforces this perspective. It was not until the mid-1980s that the UK became a net immigration country, after more than a century of losing people. Today recorded migratory movements both in and out of the UK are greater than they have ever been.

Similarly, the media often concentrates undue attention on immigrants originating in poorer countries. In fact, of those arriving in the UK in 2001, just over one-fifth were British citizens, most of whom would, earlier, have been emigrants. Another 14 per cent were from Australia, New Zealand, Canada and South Africa, 13 per cent from the rest of the European Union, 18 per cent from the rest of the Commonwealth and the remainder from other foreign countries. Meanwhile a little over half of all emigrants were British.

SUMMARY

- It is important to consider how many migrants leave the UK each year as well as how many arrive, in order to arrive at a figure for net immigration.

- A good proportion of those arriving in and leaving the UK each year are British citizens.
- Immigrants arrive in the UK from around the globe, and not just from poor countries.

WHAT ARE THE MAIN TYPES OF MIGRANT?

Political and media discourse in the UK tends towards a simplistic view of international migration. It focuses mainly on asylum seekers, and to a lesser extent illegal migrants, and often confuses the two categories. This section is concerned with trying to introduce some clarity to the asylum debate.

The first point to emphasize is that most immigrants in the UK are not asylum seekers. In 2001 about 92,000 people, including their dependants, applied for asylum in the UK. That compares with about 120,000 foreign students who entered the UK to commence their first year of study, and almost 200,000 who entered the UK to work, including work permit holders. The media – and more surprisingly the government – rarely publicize the immigrant doctors and nurses who help maintain the National Health Service, or the foreign students whose fees help fund universities, or the highly skilled migrants who contribute to the financial and industrial sectors in the UK.

The second point is that the category asylum seekers, just like all other migrant categories, covers a wide diversity of people. Asylum seekers are not all the same. They come to the UK for a variety of reasons; they originate in a wide range of countries; they have diverse educational backgrounds and skills; some come alone and others with family members; and there are increasing numbers of unaccompanied children claiming asylum (Bloch, 2002).

We have seen that media coverage fails to place asylum seekers in the context of other immigration in the UK, and underestimates the diversity of people who are asylum seekers. Perhaps most importantly, however, there is a lack of clarity over precisely who is an asylum seeker.

An asylum seeker is simply a person who has applied for protection in the UK. Most do so upon arrival in the UK, although it is also possible to apply for asylum in the UK at a British Embassy in another country. Asylum seekers' applications are judged by the criteria of the 1951 United Nations Convention relating to the Status of Refugees (see box).

In the UK over the last decade, about 10–20 per cent of asylum seekers have been considered to satisfy the criteria in the Convention, and are granted refugee status. A further 20–30 per cent do not satisfy the Convention criteria, but are granted 'Exceptional Leave to Remain' because it is accepted that it is currently unsafe for them to return to their country of origin. This means that somewhere in the region of 50–70 per cent of asylum seekers are not recognized as in need of any form of protection. Those rejected have the right to appeal, and some are subsequently granted protection. The majority have their appeals rejected, and are then expected to return to their countries of origin. Many, however, do not, and remain in the UK illegally.

It is simply misleading, it follows, to conflate the categories 'asylum seeker' and 'illegal migrant'. Some asylum seekers arrive in the UK illegally, others break the law once they are here, and many rejected asylum seekers stay on without authorization. But the majority of asylum seekers are not also illegal migrants. And, conversely, most illegal migrants in the UK are not asylum seekers.

WHO IS A REFUGEE?

The most widely used definition of a refugee is that employed in the 1951 Convention relating to the Status of Refugees, according to which a refugee is someone who '... owing to a well-founded fear of being persecuted for reasons of race, religion, nationality, membership of a particular social group or political opinion, is outside the country of his nationality ...'.

One observation worth making is that this is an explicitly geographical definition – you need to be outside your own country in order to qualify for refugee status. The many millions of people who have fled for reasons similar to those that displace refugees, but have not left their countries, are referred to as internal displaced persons (IDPs).

Many critics argue that it is not just IDPs, but many other people of concern that are also excluded by this definition. It does not, for example, cover people who have been persecuted on the basis of their sex or sexuality.

SUMMARY
- Media and political discourses ignore the true complexity and diversity of immigration.
- The majority of immigrants arriving in the UK are not asylum seekers, and even within the single category 'asylum seeker' there is great diversity.
- Far clearer and more consistent terminology is needed in the asylum debate.

CONCLUSIONS

This brief chapter has tried to show the complexity of migration flows into and out of the UK. People come for different reasons, stay for different periods and fulfil different roles. There are inflows from all parts of the globe. Simultaneously, thousands of people each year return to their country of origin or migrate elsewhere. And British citizens are part of the movement in both directions.

The UK is not being 'flooded' with immigrants from the poorer parts of the world. Most immigrants are not asylum seekers. And most asylum seekers are not illegal migrants. If a rational debate about migration is to take place, it is essential to consider the totality of population movements and not to focus on one group, still less to demonize it. The debate needs to involve, amongst other things:

- considering the definition of a migrant, and using the word in a clear, consistent and non-discriminatory way understanding the value and limitations of statistics
- having a balanced overview of migration patterns and trends in the UK, and
- considering all the different strands of migration, and the circumstances and contributions of each.

DISCUSSION POINTS

1. What is migration?

2. Why is migration so hard to measure?

3. Who is a refugee?

FURTHER READING

Bloch, A. (2002) *The migration and settlement of refugees in Britain.* **London: Palgrave.**

Focusing on refugees from Somalia, Sri Lanka and the Democratic Republic of Congo, this book demonstrates the wide diversity of the asylum-seeking experience and analyses the impact of UK policy.

Castles, S. and Miller, M. (1998) *The age of migration: international population movements in the modern world.* **Basingstoke: Macmillan.**

This is probably the key text on international migration. It places contemporary migration in historical and global perspective, and analyses the causes and consequences of immigration for receiving countries.

King, R. (1978) Return migration: a neglected aspect of population geography. *Area,* **10, 175–82.**

Although dated, this brief article by geographer Russell King is still the best overview of return migration.

UNHCR (annual) *State of the world's refugees.* **Oxford: Oxford University Press.**

This is an annual review of the world's refugees, providing the most authoritative data and analysis available.

CHAPTER 38
TRAVEL AND TOURISM

Luke Desforges

INTRODUCTION

It is not difficult to justify the inclusion of studies of travel and tourism as part of Human Geography. An interest in 'other places' has long stimulated the study of Geography, and travel stimulates many Geography students' interest in tourism. Travel and its accompanying industries are caught up in the formation of human geographies across the world, enmeshed with the environmental, social, economic, cultural and political fabric of the lives and landscapes of literally millions of people. One way of presenting the importance of tourism to Human Geography is through figures concerning its economic role in the contemporary world. The direct and indirect impact of the travel and tourism economy is estimated at 10.4 per cent of global GDP in 2004, and many countries throughout the world gain significant income from tourism (see Fig. 38.1). Annual growth in tourism is predicted to be 4–5 per cent between 2005 and 2014 (WTTC, 2004). In 2000 there were 698 million international passenger arrivals, compared with 25 million in 1950 (WTO, 2000, quoted in Urry, 2002: 3). In 2003 there were 70 million jobs in the tourism industry worldwide, and 8.1 per cent of global employment is dependent on tourism and travel (2004).

Perhaps because of the sheer scale of these numbers, the treatment of the expansion of tourism within geography has often been orientated towards the process of planning and policy. Indeed many geographers have seen their role as providing information about the development of tourism to agencies such as pressure groups, **non-governmental organizations**, and local and central governments. This chapter takes a different tack. Tourism Geography's practical bent has often led it to be divorced from other insights that have been developed within Human Geography at a more conceptual and theoretical level. In this chapter I argue that these insights encourage us to think through some of the criticisms that have been directed at tourism itself. Theoretical insights from Human Geography offer a way of rethinking the geography of tourism and travel. The chapter starts by outlining some of the criticisms of tourism and travel that circulate in both academic texts and popular culture (such as newspaper articles). It then looks at some of the theoretical insights offered by Human Geography, before applying these to tourism geography through the use of some recent case studies of tourism out in 'the field'.

Non-governmental organization (NGO)

an organization that belongs neither to the private for-profit sector, or the public or government sector.

CRITICISMS OF TOURISM AND TRAVEL

In contemporary commentaries on tourism, common criticisms are circulated across a number of different arenas, from academic writing to non-governmental organizations to broadsheet journalism. To give an example, concern is voiced about the growth of long-haul travel to countries such as Nepal, which in common with many developing

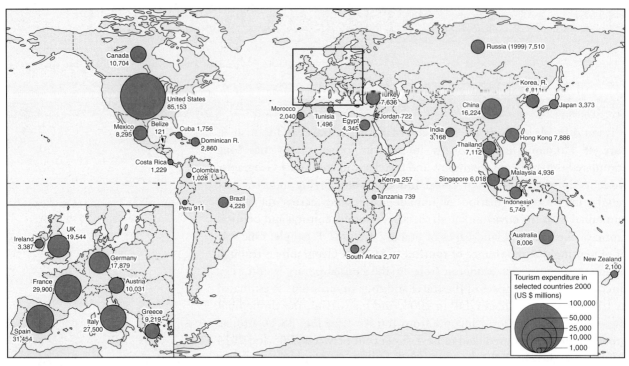

FIGURE 38.1

Tourism expenditure in selected countries, 2000
Source: World Tourism Organization 2002

countries has used tourism in the quest to fulfil its development goals. In 1970 a total of 1500 tourists visited the country (Nicholson-Lord, *Independent on Sunday*, 3 October 1993), but in 2000 more than 464,000 travellers spent $167 million (WTO, 2002), providing 24 per cent of Nepal's foreign exchange earnings (Uprety, 2002). Commentators on Nepal identify a number of areas where tourism is seen as causing detrimental effects. First, there are important concerns about tourism's impact upon the natural environment. The author Sanjay K. Nepal (1997) has researched the main impacts visitors have on the environment of the Sagarmartha National Park, a key tourist destination in the area around Mount Everest. He states that 'an average trekking group of 15 generates 15 kg of non-biodegradable, non-burnable garbage in 10 trekking days', which has led to the area being labelled as 'the world's highest trash pit'. The relative lack of sanitary infrastructure has also meant that trekkers who are unsure of their route are advised to follow the 'toilet paper trails'. Even more problematic is the deforestation of the Nepalese forest. Sanjay K. Nepal cites evidence that 'visitors' demand for firewood in the Park is estimated to increase local demand by roughly 85 percent', partly due to the demand for hot showers and cooked food, and partly because of the building materials needed to construct new lodges for trekkers. The soil erosion resulting from forest clearance is compounded by further localized environmental degradation on trails that are heavily used by trekkers.

In addition to these environmental problems, tourism's impact on the economies of holiday destinations has also been criticized. Whilst advocates of tourism point towards its role in increasing incomes, and particularly in increasing foreign exchange earnings in developing countries, other authors point out that the industry's economic benefits are not so clear-cut. In Nepal, the independent organization NepalNet argues that much of the money spent by foreign visitors 'leaks' away from tourist sites, as goods and services are supplied by international companies and urban entrepreneurs. NepalNet argues that tourism development in the country has been led by the external demands of visitors, rather than local people developing products that could tap into the tourism economy. An additional factor in this leakage is that where local jobs are created, they are often low-paid and menial tasks. In the mountain areas of Nepal, portering on tourist treks is an example of such work, where poor employment conditions combine with the seasonality of the labour market to create a relatively low annual income. At the same time, pre-existing economic networks, in the form of local agricultural and herding livelihoods, can become disrupted as labour is transferred to the tourism industry at certain key periods in the farming year (International Centre for Integrated Mountain Development, 1998; Price, 1996). The result is that, despite the tourism industry being one of the biggest earners on the planet, economic development does not necessarily take place in the immediate destinations visited by travellers.

FIGURE 38.2
On the tourist trail in Nepal
Credit: (above) David Woodfall/WWI/Still Pictures; (below) Macduff Everton/Corbis

Critics of tourism also identify a number of social problems caused by tourism to a 'Nepali' way of life. Tourist guides often sound warnings about the difficulties caused by tourists, for example the author of MyTravelGuide.com (2004) states that:

> The damage that has been done to the valley's culture in the name of progress is less easy to quantify [than environmental problems], but is arguably more profound. Traditional architecture is no longer valued. Members of the younger generation are drifting away from the religion of their parents. Guthi (charitable organizations) are in decline and have been forced to leave the upkeep of many temples to foreign preservationists. Tourism has robbed crafts of their proper use, and many performance arts of their meaning. Work outside the home has

disrupted family life, and the influx of strangers has introduced social tensions and crime."

Academic authors often concur with this analysis of tourism. For example, David Zurick argues that although traditional Nepalese handicrafts can be seen in the villages, 'tourism may safeguard the artefacts of a culture but destroy the spirit that created them' (1992: 618). Similarly the wealth of the tourism means that more 'traditional' ways of life, such as local agricultural lifestyles, are made less attractive than the tourism industry. Researchers reporting for the International Centre for Integrated Mountain Development argue that Nepal is particularly problematic because 'Mountain communities have evolved the ensembles of their culture through centuries of isolation and compulsions of their survival strategies'. They conclude by arguing that 'tourism can accelerate an otherwise slow process of change in directions that may not be desirable'.

SUMMARY

- Important critiques of tourism are circulated by sources such as non-governmental organizations, journalists, guide books and academics.
- Tourism is represented as adversely affecting the nature and culture of places throughout the world.
- In the case of Nepal, tourism is presented as causing environmental, economic and socio-cultural problems.
- Critics of tourism often base their disapproval on unfavourable comparisons between the present-day state of tourism destinations and their condition prior to the arrival of tourism.

RETHINKING CRITIQUES OF TOURISM

The argument that tourism impacts adversely on local environments and societies has long been voiced by critics of the industry in their analysis of tourism destinations across the world. The strong feelings engendered by tourism are evident in the vocabulary of some of the earliest academic commentaries: Mishan (1969), for example, depicts a battleground where there is a clear division between 'on the one hand, the tourists, tourist agencies, traffic industries and ancillary services, to say nothing of governments anxious to raise foreign currency; and all those who care about preserving natural beauty on the other' (quoted in Urry, 2002: 39). The seemingly endless spread of tourism is presented as 'a competitive scramble to uncover all places of once quiet repose, of wonder, of beauty and historic interest to the money flushed multitude, [which] is in effect literally and irrevocably destroying them' (Mishan, 1969, quoted in Urry, 2002: 40).

Strong condemnations of tourism have continued amongst academics. Urry, for example, points out that the metaphor of tourism as a form of **colonialism** (1995: 190) is commonplace. What is worth highlighting here is the way in which a particular model is used to critique tourism. When faced with the very real problems of tourism in places such as Nepal, there is a temptation to base criticisms of tourism on a desire to return to a pre-tourist culture and environment that have been left untouched by the presence of 'western' bodies and money. To provide a further example of this model, Davydd Greenwood's account of the ways

Colonialism

the rule of a NATION-STATE or other political power over another, subordinated, people and place. This domination is established and maintained through political structures, but may also shape economic and cultural relations. *See also* NEO-COLONIALISM and IMPERIALISM.

in which tourism 'spoils' local cultures by **commoditizing** them follows a similar line:

> *Treating cultures as a natural resource or a commodity over which tourists have rights is simply perverse, it is a violation of the people's cultural rights … what must be remembered is that in its very essence [culture] is something people believe in implicitly. By making it part of the tourism package it is turned into an explicit and paid performance and no longer can be believed in the way it was before. Thus, the commoditization of culture in effect robs people of the very meaning by which they organise their lives.*

(1989: 179)

Here the advent of tourism is presented as commoditizing and 'spoiling' pre-existing cultural practices. Because the desire to critique tourism through reference to an ideal pre-tourist model is so strong, it is worth considering it in more detail. Not all criticisms of tourism use this argument, and indeed many geographers and policy-makers are concerned with the 'proper management' of tourism and its consequences, rather than its suppression. But theoretical insights from Human Geography and elsewhere mean that these kinds of criticisms of the impact of global tourism on local cultures and environments may need to be rethought.

In particular, rethinking tourism means addressing the idea that places are either 'authentic' or 'inauthentic'. I have placed these two words in inverted commas to signify that their original meaning has come to be questioned by many who deal with tourism, and it is through thinking about these terms that critiques of tourism have been reworked. 'Authentic' places are often associated with 'the primitive, the folk, the peasant and the working class' (Frow, 1991: 129; see also Wang, 1999; Coleman and Crang, 2002) whose culture is seen as sticking to its roots and traditions in an unselfconscious way. In particular authentic places are thought to contain cultural objects and practices that have not been produced for sale, but for other members of the local community. Such places are represented as having a shared culture that is untouched by outside forces. They are captured in phrases such as 'the real India' or 'unspoilt France'. Conversely, 'inauthentic' places are characterized by a sense of self-conscious design for others – for example, making souvenirs for sale to tourists, rather than for the use of the local community. 'Inauthentic' places have been 'spoilt' by their contact with people from 'outside'.

What is being presented here is a relationship between culture and place that is criticized by Human Geographers in this book and elsewhere. The idea that places are either 'authentic' or 'inauthentic' implies that to remain unspoilt a culture must be 'bounded off' from neighbouring influences, particularly globalizing western cultures. 'Authentic' cultures are those that emerge 'organically' from a place without the interference that 'corrupts' their original form. The differences between places, then, are seen as created internally. In Chapter 3, Philip Crang uses the metaphor of 'mosaic' to discuss this way of thinking about places and their differences.

As Crang argues, the idea that spatial differences are the result of boundaries around places can be questioned factually, and this is as true of

Commodification

this term is used in two interrelated ways: (a) as the conversion of any thing, idea or person into a COMMODITY (the term 'commoditization' is often preferred for this sense); and (b) a wider societal process whereby an ever increasing number of things, human relationships, ideas and people are turned into commodities. Both meanings see the process of commodification as symptomatic of the penetration of CAPITALISM into the everyday lives of people and things.

the spaces of tourism as any other. To give an example, the area in which I live and work, in and around Aberystwyth, is renowned as a bastion of Welsh cultural difference. According to the 2001 census, around 61 per cent people living in Ceredigion are conversant in Welsh, the constituency has a Welsh nationalist Plaid Cymru Member of Parliament, and the town of Aberystwyth is often presented as a regional capital for Welsh culture. The heart of Welsh-speaking Wales is associated with the small villages and towns of Ceredigion, which have fostered Welsh-speaking communities for generations.

This image of Welsh culture is used to market Ceredigion as a tourist destination (see Fig. 38.3). The tourist office brochure talks of a warm Welsh welcome, of local hospitality and friendliness, and of a landscape that is unspoilt and natural. Visiting Ceredigion provides the opportunity to escape the stresses and strains of modern life in the city, a chance to spend a week away from it all. And yet the character of Ceredigion is very much the result of links to elsewhere. In cemeteries up and down the Cardigan Bay coast is evidence on gravestones showing that Ceredigion men in the nineteenth century earned their wages by sailing to and from the United States, Australia and South America, with many dying abroad. The improved pasturelands and quaint cottages typical of Ceredigion were built on the back of these connections (Jenkins, 1982). Likewise, slightly further south in Pembrokeshire, the shipping of roadstone to England and the rest of Europe built communities associated with quarrying, ports and boats. More recently, in the early to mid-twentieth century, when the railways used to run directly from London to the west coast, profits were made by sending family members to open dairies, which supplied the capital with milk. Cows in milk were sent down to London, and those that needed to calve again were sent back (Colyer, 1976; Knowles, 1997: 71–87).

In addition to west Wales's connections elsewhere, the rest of the world has long come to west Wales. Travellers have visited Ceredigion for centuries, bringing their own 'impacts' and 'influences' recorded in travel books from Giraldus Cambrensis's eleventh-century *A Journey through Wales* to George Borrow's nineteenth-century *Wild Wales* (1989) to Jan Morris's twentieth-century *The Matter of Wales* (1986). Aberystwyth as a town, with its pier and promenade, was built on the back of the railway from Birmingham and its countless holidaymakers. Tourism as a social formation is older than is often realized (see Adler, 1989).

The point of these details is that whilst west Wales's unique culture and landscape are seemingly the result of isolation, and resistance to forces of **homogenization**, in fact the very characteristics of the place that are used to attract tourists are a result of Ceredigion's connections to the rest of the world. Tourist places, then, like all other places, have never been 'authentic' because they have never been bounded places shut off from the rest of the world. Their character and difference have been formed through a whole series of connections.

In fact, as Coleman and Crang note (2002: 2), criticisms of tourism that draw on notions of spoilt authenticity are as old as tourism itself. Divisions between the 'real' traveller who encounters authentic places, and mere tourists who only get to see the spoilt remains are not only popular

Homogenization

a term used to describe the process whereby places and social characteristics become more similar to each other, so that they eventually become indistinguishable. For example, the spread of global brands such as McDonald's (McDonaldization) through the world is thought to cause places to look and feel the same, thus reducing local difference.

FIGURE 38.3
Ceredigion tourist office brochure

figures quoted by holiday shows and travel guide books alike, but also by John Ruskin who in 1865 complained that 'Going by railroad I do not consider as travelling at all; it is merely being "sent" to a place, and very little different from being a parcel' (quoted in Boorstin, 1992a: 87). Whilst this may seem a bit odd today, when travelling by steam train is considered a quintessential symbol of 'real travel', it illustrates the point that a yearning for 'untouched' places has long been a feature of commentary on tourism.

To round off this section: in critiquing tourism, we cannot refer back to a 'golden age' of authenticity that existed before tourists 'invaded'. Tourism and travel are merely a new form of interconnection between places. If we take the view that places are formed through their interconnections (Massey, 1994), then the character of places clearly changes as their relationship with the global become mediated through tourism. The role of Tourism Geography has been to understand what happens to places when they become connected to the global tourism industry. What sorts of places does tourism produce? How do the interconnections forged by tourism differ from other social processes? And what are the results of these connections for the Human Geography of the contemporary world?

SUMMARY

- Critiques of tourism have often revolved around notions of 'authentic' places and the ways in which tourism 'spoils' them.

- The idea of a place as 'authentic' relies on a conceptualization of places as bounded. Such notions have been criticized in Human Geography.

- Tourist places have always been interconnected to other places – for example, a tourist destination such as west Wales has long been connected to London, Birmingham, Europe, the former British Empire and beyond.

- Criticisms of tourism as a harbinger of inauthenticity are as old as tourism itself. Critiques of tourism that refer back to a pre-tourist 'golden age' are difficult to sustain.

TOURIST PLACES AND TRAVEL INTERCONNECTIONS

In this final section I look at some recent work on tourism that tries to tease out what it means for places to be interconnected via the global tourist industry. To do this we need to think about the ways in which these interconnections are entangled in the formation of tourist places, and the livelihoods and landscapes of those who live and work in them. It would seem obvious from the figures presented in the introduction to this chapter that tourism is often associated with a profound shift in the intensity of relationships with the global. But it is worth identifying the ways in which the nature of tourism produces very specific sorts of interconnections and places.

Tourism produces a distinctive set of interconnections between places because of its relationship between producers and consumers. The transfer of material goods often forms the nature of interconnections between places (see Philip Crang's pineapple example in Chapter 12, or think of west Wales's export of roadstone and cows). Consumers of those goods are influential in the formation of far distant communities and their livelihoods. But they will probably never meet or even know about each other. In tourist places, by contrast, tourist consumers and the producers of tourist experiences often meet face to face (they are **spatially** and temporally **co-present**).

In addition, the product that is sold at tourist sites is very often intangible. The tourist product is an experience that cannot physically be taken home. Urry (2002) argues that tourism involves the visual consumption of place through 'the tourist gaze', in which as tourists we experience place destinations through our eyes. Lash and Urry (1994) describe tourism as part of an 'economy of signs', where the tourism industry is part of a post-industrial sign economy in which incomes are earned through the flow of images and information rather than hard goods. Edensor (2000) is one of a number of authors who argue that there is more to tourism than the visual: tourist destinations are also fabricated to meet demands for bodily activities such as sunbathing, eating or hiking. Nevertheless, whether visual or tactile, the experiential nature of tourism production and consumption shapes the material and socio-cultural characteristics of tourism places.

Spatial co-presence

a term used to describe a situation when several people or objects are found in the same location at the same time. For example, a holidaymaker and a tour guide are spatially co-present during a guided tour, but a farmer and the consumer who finally eats his/her product are usually spatially distant.

Tourism Geographers have therefore been interested in the key actors and social processes involved in shaping the spaces of travel and tourism. How and why do travel spaces such as seasides and mountains come into existence? How did 'must-visit' places, such as the Eiffel Tower or the Taj Mahal, become shaped by travel? For the sake of clarity, it is worth breaking down the key actors involved in these processes into producers, consumers and regulators.

The production of tourism is shaped by actors ranging from large travel companies (Papatheodorou, 2003), such as those deciding on which country to 'open up' for mass tourism, to individual guides or waiters (Crang, 1994) moulding the experience of consumers. Tourism production can be conceptualized as both material and imaginative. It is material in that it involves the production of the concrete infrastructure of the industry: in the form of transport, accommodation, companies, working conditions, and the management of built and rural environments (Agarwal *et al.*, 2000). Understanding the economic, social and cultural resources needed to produce the materiality of travel spaces is an important component of Tourism Geography. Tourism production is also imaginative in that it involves the production of geographical imaginations: the ways in which we understand places. Endowing places such as Paris with characteristics such as 'romantic', Goa with 'relaxing' and the latest club resort with 'coolness' requires cultural work on the part of tourism producers. Travel advertisements, guide books, photographs and films all construct space in ways that structure its subsequent development as a tourist place (Mellinger, 1994).

The consumption of tourist destinations similarly shapes the development of travel spaces (Shaw *et al.*, 2000). The geographical imaginations and performative expectations that travellers bring to and develop through tourism destinations are an essential component of the connections between travel spaces and elsewhere. The historical shifts in consumption have been traced by authors such as Adler (1989), from the European Grand Tour to Shields' (1991) account of the rise of the seaside holiday. Urry (1995) argues that the patterns and practices of tourism consumption continue to change, particularly as the demand for more 'niche-marketed', as opposed to mass-produced products, has become a strong feature of the travel scene. Such changes involve whole new ways of encountering tourism spaces, such as the adventure travel practices of bungee jumping and white water rafting analysed in the context of New Zealand by Cloke and Perkins (1998).

Finally, understanding the regulation of tourist space is about analysing how particular practices are sanctioned and legitimated within space. The state plays a large role in this process – for example, in designating particular areas as protected areas in which the visual consumption of nature is the only legitimate commercial and cultural practice for tourism producers and consumers. The role of the state is often an under-researched area of tourism, despite the fact that it is often writ large through travel destinations. D'Hauteserre (1999), for example, examines how the French state was instrumental in regulating the development of Disneyland Paris, from its built landscape to its management of waste to the rights of workers (even down to the right of employees to wear lipstick, contra to Disney rules in the USA).

Cloke and Perkins' research on the development of adventure tourism in New Zealand illustrates some of the key actors involved in the production of tourism space. The New Zealand tourist board invested in a new country-wide marketing strategy known as 'Brand New Zealand' in order to develop its tourism economy. Private companies in the Queenstown region were able to build on the imagined characteristics of New Zealand as an appropriate place for an encounter with an 'exhilarating', 'fresh', 'unsullied' environment in the context of new adventure tourism products such as white water rafting, bungee jumping, jetboating and helicopter rides (known as the 'Awesome Foursome'). A group of consumers increasingly attracted to New Zealand, young independent travellers were instrumental in transforming the built landscape and cultural 'feel' of Queenstown into a renowned centre for adventure tourism.

FIGURE 38.4
New spaces of tourism and travel: the 'Awesome Foursome'. Credit: Queenstown Combos/New Zealand

SUMMARY

- Tourism provides a set of interconnections between the global and the local, which are different from many other interconnections.
- Tourism Geographers are interested in how the specific practices of travel shape the contemporary world.
- Key actors in the sphere of tourism and travel include producers, consumers and regulators, all of whom shape the geography of travel spaces.

CONCLUSION

In summary, this chapter has made the case that those interested in understanding tourism cannot focus exclusively on the popular analysis that tourism 'spoils' previously untouched places. Insights from Human Geography and elsewhere suggest that notions of authenticity rely on the idea of 'bounded places'. In fact, tourism is merely one more way in which places are connected to the wider world. That said, tourism interconnections do structure places in unique ways. In order to discover the ways in which tourism and travel shape the Human Geography of the contemporary world, we need to turn to empirical work on the specific social, economic and cultural practices of producers, consumers and regulators, and the ways in which tourism entangles itself into the lives and landscapes of those living and working in tourist destinations.

DISCUSSION POINTS

1. What are the main criticisms levelled at tourism?

2. What role does the concept of 'authenticity' play in critiques of tourism?

3. What are the main factors that influence the production of tourism space?

4. How have travel and tourism spaces changed over time?

5. What sort of research projects might be useful in examining the role of travel and tourism in the production of contemporary human geographies?

FURTHER READING

Urry, J. (2002) *The tourist gaze.* **London: Sage.**

A key introduction to the main themes in research into tourism and travel.

Franklin, A. (2003) *Tourism: an introduction.* **London: Sage.**

Provides a strong overview of the impact of key theoretical developments for our understanding of tourism and travel.

Mowforth, M. and Munt, I. (2003) *Tourism and sustainability.* **London: Routledge.**

Gives a strong grounding in contemporary changes in tourism and their associated environmental and social challenges.

CHAPTER 39
COMMODITIES

Michael Watts

> " *A commodity appears at first glance a self-sufficient, trivial thing. Its analysis shows that it is a bewildering thing, full of metaphysical subtleties and theological capers.* "
>
> (Karl Marx, *Capital*, Vol. 1, 1867)

A COMMODITY IS A BEWILDERING THING: THE CAPITALIST COSMOS AND THE WORLD OF COMMODITIES

With its price tag, said the great German critic Walter Benjamin, the commodity enters the market. In the capitalist societies, that is to say the market economies, that we inhabit this appears perfectly obvious. The *Oxford Dictionary* defines a commodity as something *useful* that can be turned to *commercial advantage* (significantly, its Middle English origins invoke profit, property and income); it is an article of trade or commerce, a thing that is expedient or convenient. A commodity, in other words, is self-evident, ubiquitous and everyday; it is something that we take for granted.

Commodities surround us and we inhabit them as much as they inhabit us. They are everywhere, and in part define who and what we are. It is as if our entire cosmos, the way we experience and understand our realities and lived existence in the world, is mediated through the base realities of sale and purchase. This cosmos, one might say, is dominated by shopping. But the commodity economy is *more* than retailing and it is this surfeit that led Marx to refer to the metaphysical subtleties of the commodity. Virtually *everything* in modern society *is* a commodity: books, babies (is not adoption now a form of negotiated purchase?), debt, sperm, ideas (intellectual property), pollution, a visit to a national park, and human organs are all commodities. An Italian tourist company offered the experience of war – a two-week tour of ethnic cleansing in Yugoslavia – as a commodity for sale; a group of internationally known models ('the commodified face') put their ova up for auction ($80,000.00 and up!). The advent of the internet and the rise of eBay and electronic auctions of various sorts have, of course, vastly expanded the ability to engage in commodity exchanges – to bring buyer and seller together virtually – for of a bewildering array of detritus. Even things that do not exist as such appear as commodities. For example, I can buy a 'future' on a basket of major European currencies, which reflects the average price (the exchange rate) of those national monies at some distant point in time. Other commodities do not exist in another sense; they are illegal or 'black' (heroin, stolen organs). Others are fictional (for example, money scams

Capitalism

an economic system in which the production and distribution of goods is organized around the profit motive (*see* CAPITAL ACCUMULATION) and characterized by marked inequalities in the social division of work and wealth between private owners of the materials and tools of production (capital) and those who work for them to make a living (labour) (*see* CLASS).

Modern, modernity, modernism

ideas of the modern are most commonly defined through their opposition to the old and the traditional. In this light, the adjective 'modern' is synonymous with 'newness'; 'modernity' refers both to the 'post-traditional' historical epoch within which 'newness' is produced and valued, as well as to the economic, social, political and cultural formations characteristic of that period; and 'modernism' applies more narrowly to artistic, architectural and intellectual movements that centrally explore ideas of 'newness' and develop 'new' aesthetics and ways of thinking to express these. Modernity has been most commonly located in Euro-American societies from the eighteenth century onwards, and thereby associated with their characteristic combination of capitalist economies (*see* CAPITALISM), political organization through NATION-STATES, and cultural values of secularity, rationality and progress (*see* ENLIGHTENMENT). However, increasingly, Human Geographers are recognizing that modernity is a global phenomenon that has taken many different forms in different times and places. See also MODERNIZATION.

and fraud). Visible or invisible, legal or illegal, real or fictive, commodities saturate our universe.

As someone once said: in America virtually everything is for sale . . . which means virtually everything is a commodity. This may be of little comfort to you. But one way of thinking about contemporary capitalist societies like the United States or the United Kingdom, in which virtually everything is a commodity (i.e. for sale), is that it is a *commodity economy*. It is, in other words, a system of commodities producing commodities. So why examine commodities if they are so trivial and ubiquitous? And why might they be of interest to geographers?

Well, one issue is that commodity-producing societies – by which I mean the dominating principle is commodities producing commodities – are quite recent inventions historically speaking, and many parts of the world, whilst they may produce for the market, are not commodity societies in the same way as our own. Socialist societies (and perhaps parts of China and Cuba today), stood in a quite different relationship to the commodity than so-called advanced capitalist states. Low-income countries, or the so-called third world, are 'less developed' precisely because they are not mature commodity-producing economies (markets are undeveloped or incomplete, as economists might put it). In the peasant village in which I lived in northern Nigeria in the 1970s, much of what was produced by family farmers (i.e. peasants) did not pass through the market at all. It was directly consumed or entered into complex circuits of gift-giving and non-market exchange. The rural household as a unit of production was not a commodity producer; it was not fully *commoditized*.

So the full commodity form as a way of organizing social life has little historical depth; that is to say it appeared in the West within the last 200 years. It is derivatively part of what Max Weber called the 'spirit of modern **capitalism**', but it remains an unfinished project if viewed globally. Over large parts of the earth's surface the process of *commodification* – of ever greater realms of social and economic life being mediated through the market as a commodity – is far from complete. Perhaps there are parts of our existence, even in the heart of **modernity** (see Chapter 24), that never will take a commodity form. I, after all, do not purchase my wife's labour, power or affection . . . yet; neither do I buy the chance to go biking with my young son . . . yet. But in a commodity economy in which the logic of the market rules, the prospect of converting social intimacy into a commodity is always present. Indeed, it is happening before our eyes. Adoption is part of a market in babies; child and elderly care is sustained through market transaction. My neighbour's pet canine is walked by a paid and 'professional' dog walker.

Another peculiarity of a commodity economy is that some items are traded as commodities but are not intentionally produced as commodities. Cars and shoes are produced to be sold on the market. But labour, or more properly labour power, is also sold – I sell something of myself to my employer, the University of California – and yet it (which is to say me as a person) was not conceived with the intention of being sold. Since I am not a slave, I was not in any meaningful sense produced, like a manufactured good or a McDonald's hamburger. This curious aspect of labour as a commodity under capitalism is as much the case for land or Nature. These sorts of curiosities are what Karl Polanyi in his book *The Great Transformation* (1947) called 'fictitious commodities'. Polanyi was of the opinion that market societies that do not regulate the processes by which these fictitious commodities become commodities will assuredly tear themselves apart. The unregulated, free market, commodity society would eat into the very fabric that sustains it by destroying Nature and by tearing asunder the most basic social relationships. We need look no further than the booming trade in human organs. In her book *Contested Commodities*, Margaret Radin shows how the fact that a poor Indian woman sells her kidney and other organs out of material desperation 'threatens the personhood of everyone' (1996: 125).

And, not least, there is the tricky matter of price, which after all is the *meaning* of the commodity in the capitalist marketplace, how it is fixed, and what stems from this price fixing. For example, the running shoe that a poor inner-city kid yearns for is Air Nike, which costs slightly more than the Ethiopian GNP per capita and perhaps more than his mother's weekly income; or the fact that a great work of art, Van Gogh's *Wheat Field*, is purchased for the astonishing sum of $57 million as an investment.

The problem of the determination of prices and their relations to *value* lay at the heart of nineteenth-century classical **political economy**, but it is an enormously complex problem that really has not gone away or in any sense been solved. The 'metaphysical subtleties' that Karl Marx refers to are very much about the misunderstandings that arise from the way we think about prices (doesn't it have something to do with supply and demand?) and what we might call the sociology or social life of commodities. But if there is more to commodities than their physical properties and their prices, which are derived from costs of production or supply and demand curves, then there is a suggestion that commodities are not what they seem. Commodities have strange, perhaps 'metaphysical', effects. For example, the fact that a beautiful Carravagio painting is a commodity – and correlatively, that it is private property and only within the means of the extravagantly rich – fundamentally shapes my experience of the work, and of my ability to enjoy its magnificent beauty in some unalloyed way. Its commodity status has tainted and coloured my appreciation of it. Commodities cannot escape the grip of money and money carries a particular odour (of shit, said Sigmund Freud!) and a cool, glacial quality (Simmel, 1895).

A commodity, then, appears to be a trivial thing – here's a car for sale, it has these fine qualities – but it is in fact bewildering, even theological. The commodity, said Walter Benjamin, has a phantom-like objectivity, and it leads its own life after it leaves the hands of its maker. What on earth might this mean?

Political-economic, political economy

the study of how economic activities are socially and politically structured and have social and political consequences. Political-economic approaches in Human Geography have paid particular attention to understanding capitalist economies and their geographical organization and impact (*see* CAPITALISM and also MARXIST GEOGRAPHY). Central to such analyses have been questions concerning the class-based nature of the human geographies of capitalist societies (*see* CLASS).

SUMMARY

- A commodity is something useful that enters the market.
- Commodification refers to the process by which more and more of the material, cultural, political, biological and spiritual world is rendered as something for sale.
- A commodity-producing economy is one in which the logic of commodification is dominant.

A COMMODITY BIOGRAPHY: THE SOCIAL LIFE OF THE CHICKEN AND US CAPITALISM

" *A century ago you'd eat steak and lobster when you couldn't afford chicken. Today it can cost less than the potatoes you serve it with. What happened in the years between was an extraordinary marriage of technology and the market.* "

(John Steele Gordon)

Once in a while I will bring into my undergraduate class a freshly dressed chicken – oven-ready in poultry parlance – and ask students to identify this cold and clammy creature that I've tossed upon the lectern. After five minutes of 'it's a chicken', 'it's a dead bird', 'it's a virtual Kentucky Fried Chicken', I solemnly pronounce that it is none of the above: it is in fact a bundle of social relations.

So let's examine the humble chicken. According to the latest Agricultural Census, almost 9 billion chickens were sold in the United States in 2004 (more than 30 per person). In 1991, chicken consumption per capita exceeded beef, for the first time, in a country that has something of an obsession with red meat. The fact that each American man, woman and child currently consumes roughly 1.5 pounds of chicken each week reflects a complex vectoring of social forces in post-war America. First, a change in taste driven by a heightened sensitivity to health matters and especially the heart-related illnesses associated with red meat consumption. Second, the fantastically low cost of chicken meat, which has in real terms *fallen* since the 1930s (a century ago Americans would eat steak and lobster when they could not afford chicken). And not least the growing extent to which chicken is consumed in a panoply of forms (Chicken McNuggets, say) which did not exist 20 years ago and which are now delivered to us by the massive fast-food industry – a fact that, itself, points to the reality that Americans eat more and more food outside of the home (food consumption 'away from home' is, by dollar value, 40 per cent of the *average* household food budget).

The vast majority of chickens sold and consumed are broilers (young chickens) which, it turns out, are rather extraordinary creatures. In the 1880s there were only 100 million chickens. In spite of the rise of commercial hatcheries early in the century, the industry remained a sideline business run by farmers' wives until the 1920s. Since the first commercial sales (by a Mrs Wilmer Steele in 1923 in Delmarva, who sold 357 in one batch at prices five times higher than today), the industry has been transformed by the feed companies, which began to promote integration and the careful genetic control and reproduction of bird flocks, and by the impact of big science, often with government backing. The result is what was called in the 1940s the search for the 'perfect broiler' (Boyd, 2001). Avian science has now facilitated the mind-boggling rates at which the birds add weight (almost five pounds in as many weeks!). The average live bird weight has almost *doubled* in the last 50 years; over the same period the labour input in broiler production has fallen by 80 per cent! The broiler is the product of a truly massive R&D campaign; disease control and regulation of physiological development have fully industrialized the broiler to the point where it is really a cyborg: part nature, part machine. The chicken is industrial and fully commodified: its genome is mapped, particular breeds owned through intellectual property rights, and its shape and form the product of human intervention (a featherless chicken has recently been 'invented' in Israel, and Pfizer owns the patent on a rooster developed

FIGURE 39.1
Battery farm chickens.
Credit: UNEP/Still Pictures

for massive combs (the red fleshy growth – hyaluronan – on its head) which is used in various surgical operations and for reconstructive surgery). Our understanding of chicken nutrition now exceeds that of any other animal, *including* humans! Applied poultry science and industrial production methods have also been the key to the egg industry. A state-of-the-art hen house holds 100,000 birds in minuscule cages stretching the length of two football fields; it resembles a late twentieth-century high-tech torture chamber (see Fig. 39.1). The birds are fed by robot in carefully controlled amounts every two hours around the clock. In order to reduce stress, anxiety and aggression (which increases markedly with confinement), the birds wear red contact lenses, which for reasons that are not clear reduce feed consumption and increase egg production. It's pretty weird.

Broilers are overwhelmingly produced by family farmers in the USA, but this turns out to be a deceptive statistic. They are grown by farmers under contract to enormous transnational corporations – referred to as 'integrators' in the chicken business – who provide the chicks and feed. The growers (who are not organized into unions and who have almost no bargaining power) must borrow heavily in order to build the broiler houses and the infrastructure necessary to meet contractual requirements. Growers are not independent farmers at all. They are little more than underpaid workers – what we might call 'propertied labourers' – of the corporate producers who also dominate the processing industry. Work in the poultry processing industry, in which the broilers are slaughtered and dressed and packaged into literally hundreds of different products, is some of the most underpaid and dangerous in the country (in the *New York Times* of 9 February 1998, p. A12, government report cited almost two-thirds of all poultry processing plants as in violation of overtime payment procedures). Immigrant labour – Vietnamese, Laotian, Hispanic – now represents a substantial proportion of workers in the industry. The largest ten companies account for almost two-thirds of broiler production in the USA. Tyson Foods, Inc., the largest broiler producer, accounts for 124 million pounds of chicken meat per week, and it controls 21 per cent of the US market with sales of over $5 billion (two-thirds of which go to the

Transnational corporations

very large companies with offices or plants in several countries; and/or companies that make decisions and accrue profits on a global basis (sometimes called multinational or global corporations).

Post-Fordism

refers to the forms of production, work, consumption and REGULATION that emerged out of the crisis of mass, standardized forms of capitalist production (FORDISM) during the 1970s. In terms of production and work, post-Fordism turns on the importance of flexibility in work and other institutional forms of productive organization. Economic Geographers have analysed how this flexibility has been driven both by versatile and programmable machines, and by forms of 'vertical disintegration' of some firms in some sectors that make greater use of strategic alliances and subcontracting. Accompanying these changes in production are changes in consumer demand (the centrality of quality over standardization), in labour markets, in finance and legal structures, and in the broad social contract that characterized post-war Fordism.

fast-food industry). According to Don Tyson, CEO of Tyson Foods, his aim is to 'control the center of the plate for the American people'. Yet it is an industry on the verge of crisis. Disease resistance to the massive chemically based nutrition and health regimen associated with confinement and industrial production, the worldwide threats of massive avian flu (as I write, in January 2004, a major outbreak is in train in Thailand and China), and the documentation of extraordinary levels of toxins in chicken meat (most recently terrifying levels of arsenic ingestion), all speak to the rickety structure of the contemporary chicken industry.

The heart of the US chicken industries is in the ex-slave-holding and cotton-growing south. Until the Second World War the chicken industry was located primarily in the Delmarva peninsula in the mid-Atlantic states (near Washington, DC). During the 1940s and 1950s the industry moved south and with it emerged the large integrated broiler complexes – what geographers call flexible or post-Fordist capitalist organization. The largest producing region is Arkansas – the home state of former US President Bill Clinton – and the chicken industry has been heavily involved in presidential political finance and lobbying, including a case in which the Secretary of Agriculture was compelled to resign. The lowly chicken reaches deep into the White House.

The USA is the largest producer and exporter of broilers, with a sizeable market share in Hong Kong, Russia and Japan. Facing intense competition from Brazil, China and Thailand, the chicken industry is now global, driven by the lure of the massive Chinese market and by the newly emerging and unprotected markets of eastern Europe and the post-Soviet states. Actually, the world chicken market is highly segmented: Americans prefer breast meat, whilst US exporters take advantage of foreign preference for leg quarters, feet and wings to fulfil the large demand from Asia. The chicken is a thoroughly global creature – in its own way not unlike the global car or global finance.

You start with a trivial thing – the chicken as a commodity for sale – and you end up with a history of post-war American capitalism.

The commodity

It is in this sense that a product is a commodity; it is simultaneously a use value for the other, and a means of exchange for the producer.

(M. Postone, *Time, Labour and Social Domination*, 1993)

One way to think about the commodity is derived from Karl Marx who begins his massive treatise on capitalism (Volume 1 of *Capital*) with a seemingly bizarre and arcane examination of the commodity, with what he calls the 'minutiae' of bourgeois society. The commodity, he says, is the 'economic cell form' of capitalism. It is as if he is saying that in the same way that the DNA sequence holds the secret to life, so the commodity is the economic DNA, and hence the secret of modern capitalism. For Marx the commodity is the general form of the product – what he calls the generally necessary form of the product and the general elementary form of wealth – *only* in capitalism (Postone, 1993). A society in which the commodity is the general form of wealth – the cell form – is characterized by what Postone (1993: 148) calls 'a unique form of social inter-dependence': people do not consume what they produce, and produce and exchange commodities to acquire other commodities.

But the commodity itself is a queer thing because whilst it has physical qualities and uses, and is the product of physical processes that are perceptible to the senses, its *social* qualities – what Marx calls the social or value form – are obscured and hidden. 'Use value' is self-evident (this is a chair, which I can use as a seat and has many fine attributes for the comfort of my ageing body) but value form – the social construction of the commodity – is not. Indeed this value relation – the ways in which commodities are constituted, now and in the past, by social relations between people – is not perceptible to the senses. Sometimes, says Marx, the social properties things acquire under particular circumstances are seen as inherent in their natural forms (that is, in the obvious physical properties of the commodity). The commodity is not what it appears. There is, then, a hidden life to commodities and understanding something of this secret life might reveal profound insights into the entire edifice – the society, the culture, the political economy – of commodity-producing systems.

Let's return to the chicken as a commodity. It has two powers. First, it can satisfy some human want (my need for a chicken curry). This is what Adam Smith called a *use value*. Second, it has the ability to command other commodities in exchange. This power of exchangeability Marx called *exchange value* or value form. Use values coincide with the *natural form* of the commodity – its chicken-ness – whereas the value form expresses its *social form*. Use values express the qualitative incommensura-bility of commodities – the uses of chicken can never be commensurable with the uses of a car – whereas exchange value expresses quantitative commensurability (I can exchange 20,000 chickens for one car). But com-modity exchange in turn requires a universal equivalent to facilitate this quantitative commensurability: which is to say, money. The commensura-bility of commodities is expressed phenomenally through money – that is, in the form of a price (a chicken is $1.00 per pound and turkey is $2.00 per pound, which means that chicken exchanges for turkey at the rate of two chickens for one turkey). *Commodity circulation* refers to the process by which a commodity is exchanged for money, which in turn permits the purchase of another, different, commodity.

But the basis of comparing commodities through price is only its phenomenal form. The real basis is *value*. But what is value? For Marx it turns on what he calls abstract labour – any labour whatsoever viewed as a process of consumption of human energy – so that value is expended labour. Capitalism, however, is a reality not an abstraction, and rests upon commodities producing commodities in quite specific sorts of ways. More specifically, a capitalist starts with money, purchases labour power and the means of production, and produces commodities that are sold for money. This process generates more money for the capitalist than he began with (i.e. profit). Put differently, money and commodities circulate as expressions of the expansion of capital (not just the circulation of commodities) which rests upon the existence of a commodity-producing

Means of production

the resources that are indispensable for any form of production to occur. Typically this would include land, labour, machines, money capital, knowledge/information. In MARXIST thinking the means of production and labour power together constitute the 'forces of production'.

Dialectic, dialectical

a dialectic is a process through which two opposites are generated, interrelated and eventually transcended. This process can be purely intellectual, in so far as it is a procedure of thought. Examples in this vein would include the opposites used as the starting points for all the chapters in Part 1 of this collection (nature–culture, society–space, and so on), which are then worked through and beyond in the course of each chapter. Dialectical processes can also be identified in the wider world, though. An example would be the combination in a COMMODITY of both use and exchange values, in which opposites become interpenetrated in the commodity form.

system and the emergence of a universal equivalent (money) (see Part 2).

Exchange value is, to summarize, bound up with the particular form of social labour as it exists in a commodity-producing economy (capitalism). This particular form of social labour is wage labour – that is to say there is a class of individuals (workers) who sell their labour power to another class (capitalists), which organizes production. It is this aspect of labour – as a commodity, labour power, sold to someone else at a price called the wage – that is unique to a commodity-producing economy. A commodity can thus be seen as being composed of three aspects or relations: variable capital (that paid to labour as wages), constant capital (that covering fixed capital costs such as machines) and surplus value (profits). Marx tried to explain where this surplus came from and how it emerged from the disparity between the value that the workers embody in the commodities they produce and the value they require for their own reproduction.

Whether Marx's theory of value or account of the origins of profit is right or wrong is of less relevance than the fact that the commodity allows us to analyse the forms that arise on the basis of a well-developed or full commodity economy. Capitalism is unique because it rests upon commodities that are fictitious. Labour, capital and money are all commodities (the wage, rate of interest and exchange rates determine their respective market value) but are not produced as commodities. The commodity is the way into the problem of value (its origins and its forms) and it establishes a sort of toolkit with which we can understand something of the distinctiveness of living in capitalist societies. Property, money, value in its various forms, class interests, the circulation of commodities, they are all implied in the 'dialectical union' of use and exchange value that the commodity contains.

SUMMARY

- A commodity is a unity of exchange value and use value.
- Exchange value expresses the social, and hidden, form of the commodity.
- Commodity exchange requires a universal equivalent (money).

THE COMMODITY CIRCUIT

As tangible, physical things – as the embodiment of particular uses and values – commodities have lives, or *biographies*. They are made, born or fabricated; they are fashioned and differentiated in a variety of ways; they are sold, retailed, advertised and ultimately consumed or 'realized' (and perhaps even recycled!). The life of the commodity typically involves movement through space and time, during which it adds values and meanings of various forms. Commodities are therefore pre-eminently geographical objects.

Let's return to the US chicken. It is possible to construct a diagrammatic 'biography' of the broiler from production to consumption, which depicts many of the actors involved in the commodity's complex movements and valuations. This is a *commodity circuit* or a *commodity*

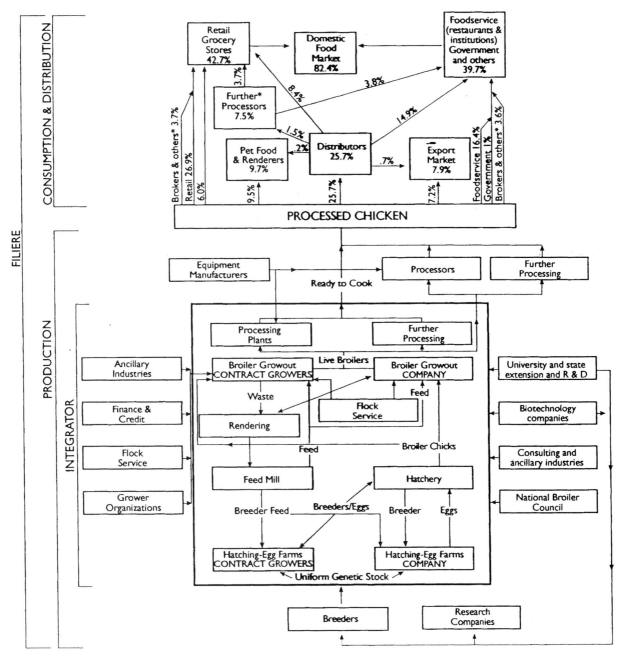

FIGURE 39.2
The broiler *filière*, *c.* 1999. Source: Boyd and Watts, 1996, p. 205

chain (in French it is referred to as a *filière*) (Friedland *et al.*, 1981). Figure 39.2 depicts the US broiler *filière* (Boyd and Watts, 1996). At the centre of this figure is the broiler complex and the large transnational integrator – Tyson Foods, Perdue Farms, ConAgra, and so on – but there are obviously a multiplicity of other actors: the public extension systems, the R&D sector, the fast-food chains, the exporters, the retailers, the service providers, the state and local government. The starting point of the commodity circuit might be the breeding units, but this itself is a collaborative effort that has involved a half-century of genetics research to produce breeding flocks. What is bred is a peculiar creature that has been 'industrialized' to maximize productivity (but with the danger of massive

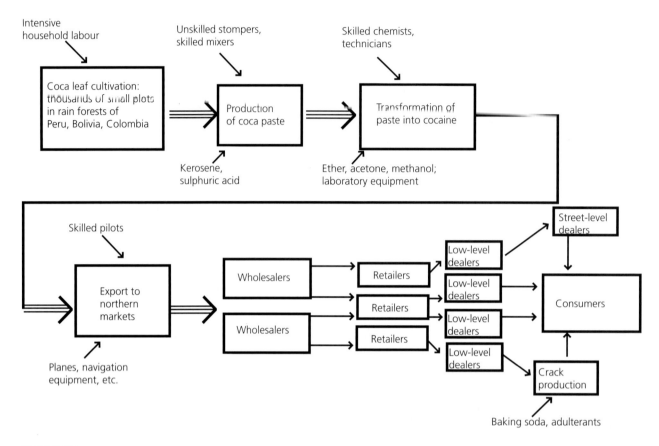

FIGURE 39.3
Cocaine commodity chain. Source: Morales, 1989, p. 104

disease problems, which itself generates one large part of the commodity circuit devoted to chicken 'health care'). The terminus is the consumption of chicken in a bewildering array of forms: as a complement to other foods in a TacoBell burrito, as an 'organic free range chicken' bought ready to cook in a yuppy store, or as 'mass' chicken parts destined for institutions like schools or hospitals. The chicken as a commodity has, in short, been further commodified. And the process is seemingly endless. At all points along the commodity circuit there are opportunities for the creation of all manner of new forms of chicken commodity.

Commodity circuits can depict different types of commodity chains and contrasting commodity dynamics. Figures 39.3 and 39.4 depict global commodity circuits for cocaine and for the apparel and automobile sectors. In the former the peasant grower of coca leaf in Colombia is linked through a series of agents (processors, wholesalers, transporters) to the street dealer in, say, Detroit. It is an *illegal* commodity chain, which links the third world as producer to the first world as consumer. This has historically been the case for many third world drug commodity circuits (tea, coffee, sugar) which are, however, usually typically legal and dominated by rather different agents and actors (agribusiness companies rather than the Medellin Cartel). Figure 39.4 reveals different dynamics within two contrasting commodity circuits (Gereffi, 1995). The buyer circuit for which the apparel industry is the prime case is dominated by the retailers. The high-end fashion retailers (Armani, Donna Karan) typically produce apparel in sweatshops in the core countries or in newly industrialized countries like Hong Kong. Low-end supermarket retailers

Producer-driven commodity chains

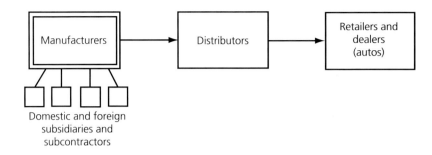

Buyer-driven commodity chains

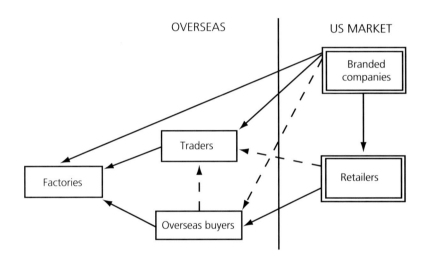

FIGURE 39.4
Producer-driven commodity chain. Source: G. Gereffi, 1995, p. 114

(Wal-Mart) have producers in particularly poor and low-wage countries (Sri Lanka, Philippines). Producers and retailers are often held together by complex subcontracting arrangements. In producer-driven chains, conversely – the automobile is an exemplar – transnational companies (TNCs), as integrated industrial enterprises, play the central role. Toyota or Ford have integrated production complexes embracing literally thousands of parent, subsidiary and subcontractor firms dotted around the world. The producer-driven commodity chain produces the 'world car' in which component parts are produced in multiple locations, although the final commodity – say, the Ford Fiesta – is assembled at one single site.

My earlier discussion of the US chicken industry highlights a number of key geographical aspects of commodity circuits. First, that different actors and agents in the circuit are linked together in complex market *and* non-market relations. At particular locations ('nodes') within the commodity circuit there are especially dense sets of social and institutional relations: contracts between growers and integrators, co-operative relations between companies and government, and so on. Second, throughout the course of the circuit the commodity itself is differentiated in enormously complicated ways into a panoply of new products and processes. According to the industry there are now literally hundreds of 'chicken products'. Third, the process of moving through the commodity chain is simultaneously a process of adding value. Growers command a low proportion of the final product price, which raises the question of who captures the value-added (in cocaine it is clearly the wholesalers and not street-level dealers or peasant growers). And finally, within each commodity chain there are particular *nodes* – which can be seen as 'sinks' of especially intense activity – in which the commodity acquires particular meanings and attributes (these are values but not necessarily economic values). In the broiler *filière*, for example, these qualities may have to do with freshness, or the acquisition of a brand name (the 'Rocky Road' chicken), or the attachment of 'quality'. Quality is typically about status (think of the cachet of Michael Jordan Air Nikes), and the **semiotics** of the commodity (this is a *real* Stilton cheese produced *traditionally* in Leicestershire). A commodity circuit can, then, display both the space–time attributes of the commodity – many of which are now global, of course – and also of what Marx called the 'social' (and partially hidden) qualities of commodities: their value, their meanings and their fetish qualities.

COMMODITIZATION/COMMODIFICATION

" *[T]he idea of a self-adjusting market implied a stark utopia. Such an institution could not exist for any length of time without annihilating the human and natural substance of society.* "

(Karl Polanyi, *The Great Transformation*, 1947)

The process by which everything becomes a commodity – and therefore everything comes to acquire a price and a monetary form (*commoditization/commodification*) – is not complete, even in our own societies where transactions still occur outside of the marketplace. Perhaps one might say that the process can never be complete, but history will always throw up new frontiers for the commodity process to penetrate. The reality of capitalism is that ever more of social life is mediated through and by the market. Karl Polanyi referred to this process as the *embedding* of social relations in the economy. On the one hand, he said more of social life is embedded in the logic of a commodity economy – industries are given permits to pollute, which can be bought and sold. Nature is patented by private companies – and, on the other, the market itself, if left to its own devices, becomes *disembedded* from social institutions.

Karl Polanyi was concerned to show that societies dominated by the self-adjusting market, in which individuals relentlessly pursued their own interests as Adam Smith suggested, would be no society at all. Rather, every person is pitted against each other in a state of quasi-war. Smith recognized the costs of unbridled accumulation, and saw civil society as the necessary saviour of a market system whose powers he so admired. If the genesis of market-regulated societies carries the prospect of disembedded markets and economically embedded social relations, they remain tendencies rather than inevitabilities. The case of the chicken industry revealed, of course, that in a highly competitive and market-driven broiler industry, markets

Semiotics

this term has two interrelated meanings: (a) the study of forms of human communication and the ways they produce and convey meaning; and (b) those forms of human communication and systems of meaning themselves. Whilst including spoken and written language, semioticians deliberately also analyse how other social phenomena – including dress, architecture and the built environment, visual art, social gatherings and events, landscapes – are communication systems whose 'languages' can and should be analysed. Human Geographers have drawn on ideas from semiotics (*see* SIGN, SIGNIFICATION, REFERENT) but parallel work in art history on the language of painting has been more directly influential (*see* ICONOGRAPHY).

and commodities are indeed socially embedded. Economics is, as Polanyi put it, *an instituted process*. This institutedness takes the forms of social alliances, networks and studied forms of trust between actors in the commodity system (see also Chapter 16). Firms build up relations of trust and co-operation between one another; the relationship between grower and integrator is contractual, and not a pure market relationship. The vertically integrated, patrimonial Korean conglomerates (*chaebol*) such as Daewoo and the Taiwanese flexible, contractually linked, family firms are the socially embedded forms of market, commodity-producing behaviour associated with the so-called Asian miracle. Commodities are always fashioned in institutional and cultural ways.

In the far-flung corners of the globe, there are societies that are not commoditized at all, or at least the pursuit of 'commercial advantage' represents a minor part of their social existence. Some contemporary Indian communities in the Amazon, for example, or hunter-gatherer communities in Zaire, produce almost nothing for the market and buy little in the way of consumer goods. Some back-to-the-land communes in northern California also aspire to self-sufficiency. However, even these non-market (or non-capitalist) societies are typically commodified in some way. When I worked amongst isolated pastoral nomads in West Africa in the 1970s – small mobile families who depended entirely on livestock for their survival – these seemingly traditional communities did view cattle and other animals as property, and indeed would sell limited numbers of animals, particularly during the dry season when lactation rates of their animals had fallen due to the deterioration of pasture, in order to buy grain, tea and sugar. Similarly, the communards on Albion ridge in northern California participate in a moral economy of barter and exchange with other communes (what Polanyi would have called a sort of administered trade).

Statistically speaking, one of the largest classes of people in the world is the peasantry, and they are defined specifically by their *partial commoditization*. Peasants own the means of production – they directly work their land with their own family labour, which means that they do sell their labour power as a commodity. But peasants *are* involved with the market to some degree, selling part of what they grow (often export crops such as cotton or tea) to acquire money to buy clothes, pay taxes and cover school fees for their children. This partial commoditization can have some unusual consequences. Henry Bernstein (1978) pointed out that in such circumstances, a peasant family may produce commodities in order to gain cash but should the price of this commodity fall (the price of bananas on the world market falls by, say, 40 per cent), the peasant may be forced either to produce more of a commodity whose price is falling or work harder just to meet the irreducible family needs. For a family with a small plot of land this may mean working longer and harder and exploiting the soil in order to, as it were, stay in the same place. Bernstein referred to this conundrum of price squeezes (commodity prices falling) and partial commoditization (household enterprises with irreducible consumption goals) as 'the simple reproduction squeeze'.

Polanyi's 'great transformation' was the process by which economy and society were separated during the course of the rise of the self-adjusting market: the emergence of the market economy as a *totality* in contradistinction to the patchwork market economy prior to the Industrial Revolution. The reach of the market – which is to say the extent to which everything has become a commodity – has deepened since the 1750s. What Marx called the 'vulgar commodity rabble' now encompasses much of what we do and feel. Human life has become dependent upon the market, and commoditization inevitably charges inward into the refuges of social life. My colleague Nancy Scheper-Hughes, an anthropologist at the University of California, Berkeley, has been a major voice in the exposure of the so-called 'rotten trade' in human organs (Scheper-Hughes, 2002). Commercialization has entered almost every sphere of contemporary medicine and biotechnology, and practices such as mortuary practices, and tissue and DNA harvesting represent what she calls 'human strip farming'. Heart valves, cornea, bone fragments and other body parts are traded as a basis for research and teaching. Hughes has documented a new kind of organ trade emerging within the interstices of the global economy, what she calls 'transport tourism', which has its brokers and outlaws who short-circuit the problem of long waiting lists or donors and international codes of ethical conduct by acquiring organs from poor sellers illegally and sometimes by outright theft (kidneys stolen from Chinese prison inmates, for example). Organ brokers freely advertise on the internet, able to provide 'a living donor next week'. Jürgen Habermas (1993) calls this the 'colonization of the lifeworld'.

But this process is always resisted, especially in societies undergoing a radical and rapid transition to a market economy. The **moral economy** – the embeddedness of economic relations – in pre-capitalist or partially capitalist societies (whether peasant communities in contemporary Borneo or in late eighteenth-century France) breaks down slowly and unevenly in the face of the onslaught of commodity production (Thompson, 1991). In my peasant community in Nigeria, for example, land was rarely sold in large part because of the cultural and spiritual meanings attached to the land and the anti-social character of land sale (this remains an issue, for example, in Native American Indian communities in the United States). Poor families would steadfastly deny that they sold their labour because of the shame surrounding the fact of being perceived to be not self-sufficient. These are elements of a larger moral economy in which there is some effort to guarantee subsistence rights and also strong sentiments for a just price (for bread, for example). The process by which this moral economy has been undercut by the commodity economy – by growing commoditization – has often generated social conflict and strife. Some have argued that the great peasant rebellions of this century – Tonkin in the 1930s, Mexico earlier in the century – were efforts to defend the moral economy of the peasantry against the onslaught of the world market and the irrepressible logic of the commodity economy (Scott, 1976; Thompson, 1991). Of course, the moral economy is still not entirely dead; something of this remains in English villages or the crofting communities of the Hebrides. The efforts by the state to provide services (i.e. unemployment relief) outside of the market and through moneyless exchange can also be seen as an effort to *decommoditize* some realms of social life (Offe and Heinze, 1992).

Moral economy

a term used by the historian Edward Thompson to describe the fact that economic relations have a normative aspect. For instance, the moral economy in the peasant economy would refer to the idea of a subsistence ethic in which the social relations of the poor attempt to provide forms of local security and support to prevent starvation. The concept of the moral economy has connections to Karl Polanyi's idea that the economy is an instituted process embedded in social relations.

COMMODITY FETISHISM AND THE COMMODITY SPECTACLE

" It is an enchanted, perverted, topsy-turvy world in which Monsieur Le capital and Madame La Terre do their ghost walking as social characters and at the same time directly as things. "

(Karl Marx, *Capital*, III, 1894)

In 1993, in a media stunt for her animal rights book, Rebecca Hall offered four men $2500 each to live like battery hens for a week – in other words, barefoot in a small wire cage with a sloping floor, with 24-hour light, automated food delivery and a cacophonous noise (see Fig. 39.5). They lasted 16 hours. Two years later one of the major US broiler firms hired a nationally known chef to use 'fresh' oven-ready chicken to play bowls outside of the US Congress, to demonstrate the fact that its competitors were in fact selling purportedly fresh chickens that were frozen as hard as titanium. Or take a look at the advertisement in Figure 39.6 for an 89 Male broiler: top 'livability', superior growth, excellent efficiency. Chicken as machine.

These chicken tales are each speaking to quite different aspects of the commodity under capitalism, namely the spectacular and the fetishistic. A fetish is a material object invested with magical powers. Marx invoked *commodity fetishism* to describe the ways in which commodities have a phantom objectivity. The social character of their making is presented in a 'perverted' form. By this he meant a number of complex things. First, that the social character of a commodity is somehow seen as a natural attribute intrinsic to the thing itself. Second, that the commodities appear as an independent and uncontrolled reality apart from the producers who fashioned them. And third, in confusing relations between people and between things, events and processes are represented as timeless or without history, they are **naturalized**. Another way to think about this is that commodity production – the unfathomable swirl of commodity life – produces particular forms of **alienation** and **reification**. Let me elaborate.

We come to accept the creature we buy as an oven-ready chicken as a natural product that stems from its use-value (as food). In fact, it is a sort of machine, something created by science to be an input (of particular proportion, colour, efficiency, and so on) into industrial manufacture; something that, far from being natural, is a social artefact containing many and complex forms of value. Moreover, the social value of the chicken appears, as it is under capitalism, in terms of relations between things (growth, efficiency, white meat). In our society virtually all of our existence appears as a thing – it is reified – but these reified things interact with us to give the impression that the social really *is* natural. The chicken futures market is 'up' this week – as though the market has a life of its own – which is confirmed to me because my shares in Tyson Foods carry increased dividends. This confusion or obfuscation of relations between people – the huge number of people involved in the community *filière* –

Naturalization, naturalized

this term has two distinct and different meanings: (a) the way in which social relations, cultural norms or institutions are made to seem 'natural' rather than SOCIAL CONSTRUCTIONS; and (b) the process through which species become established in new environments, sometimes also applied to human life to refer to the formal integration of immigrants in new societies.

Alienation

a term with two interrelated meanings, the second being a more specific formulation of the first. First, then, alienation refers to a sense of estrangement or lack of power felt by people living in the MODERN world. In this respect it is often used to describe the experience of modern urban living, in which traditional forms of social cohesion and belonging supposedly break down. Second, and drawn from MARXIST social thought, alienation refers more particularly to the separation of labour from the MEANS OF PRODUCTION under CAPITALISM. To explain, since under capitalism it is capitalists who own the resources required for economic production (land, machinery, money, etc.) workers have no control over their productive lives: how production is organized, what is produced, what the product is used for and how they relate to other workers. They are therefore alienated from their work and its products.

Reification

the act of transforming human properties, relations and actions into properties, relations and actions that are seen to be independent of human endeavour, and that then come actually to govern human life. The term can also refer to the transformations of human beings into 'thing-like' beings. Reification is therefore a form of ALIENATION.

FIGURE 39.5
Four men attempt to live like chickens in
Rebecca Hall's cage. Credit: Martin
Argles/Guardian

with relations between things is central to the alienation rooted in a world
in which everything is for sale, and everything is a thing.

In his book *Society of the Spectacle* (1977) Guy Debord argues that in a
world of total commodification, life presents itself an as immense
accumulation of *spectacles*. The spectacle, says Debord, is when the
commodity has reached the total occupation of social life and appears as a
set of relations mediated by images (*see* Fig. 39.7 and Chapter 18). The
great world exhibitions and arcades of the nineteenth century were
forerunners of the spectacle, celebrating the world as a commodity. But in
the contemporary epoch in which the representation of the commodity is
so inextricably wrapped up with the thing itself, the commodity form
appears as spectacle, or as a spectacular event, whether four men trying to

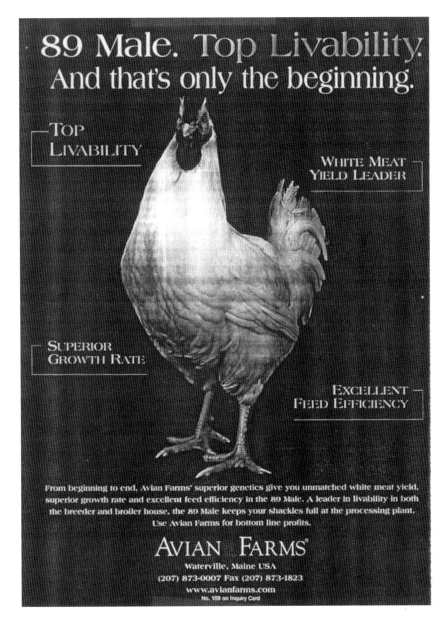

FIGURE 39.6
The Industrial Chicken advert. Source: *Broiler Industry*, August 1997

be chicken or a chef playing bowls with a frozen broiler. Whatever else it may be, the terrifying events of September 11th 2001 and the collapse of the Twin Trade Towers represented an enormous spectacle in the Debordian sense; and a spectacle for which there could be no spectacular response of equal measure. Necessarily this spectacle of spectacles was a product of commodification and necessarily has become a commodity itself. Within weeks of the attacks, ground zero in New York City had become a small marketplace for September 11th T-shirts and other mementoes, just as shirts bearing the image of Osama and the falling towers were selling like hot cakes in Bangkok, Jakarta and the West Bank as icons of anti-imperialism.

Once they leave the confines of their makers, commodities take on a life of their own.

In the cities in which we live, all of us see hundreds of publicity images every day of our lives. No other kind of image confronts us so frequently.

In no other form of society in history has there been such a concentration of images, such a density of visual messages.

One may remember or forget these messages but briefly one takes them in, and for a moment they stimulate the imagination by way of either memory or expectation. The publicity image belongs to the moment.

FIGURE 39.7
Society as spectacle. Source: John Berger, 1972: *Ways of Seeing*, p. 129, Penguin. Credit: © Sven Blomberg

SUMMARY

- A commodity circuit is a methodological device to reveal a commodity as an organized space–time system.

- Commodification always involves complex processes of economic and social embedding and disembedding.

- Commodity fetishism refers to the ways in which alienation and reification operate in commodity-producing societies.

COMMODITIES AND THE IMMENSE COSMOS OF CAPITALIST ACCUMULATION

> *Commodity production in its universal, absolute form [is] capitalist commodity production . . .*
>
> (Karl Marx, *Capital*, II, 1885)

We began with the commodity as a trivial thing and have ended with a world of commodities that 'actually conceals, instead of disclosing, the social character of private labour, and the social relations between the individual producers' (Marx, *Capital*, I: 75–6). But this hidden history of the commodity allows us to expose something unimaginably vast, namely the dynamics and history of capitalism itself. The proliferation of commodities as exchange values presupposes a universal equivalent – that is, money as an expression of value (see Chapter 11). But this itself has its own preconditions – property is implied by money-mediated exchange and correlatively the entire superstructure that sustains property relations – and poses the knotty problem of the relations between price and value. In exploring the question of value we have seen that it turns in large part on the peculiarities of labour and money being themselves commodities. Whether Marx was right that labour is a special commodity that has the ability to produce greater value than it has, the relations between commodity, price and value do nonetheless lead inexorably to the centrality of class relations between labour and capital as a fundamental aspect of capitalism. This itself poses the question of how capital and wage labour come to be and how they are reproduced under conditions of contradictory interest (profit versus wage). We may as reasonable men and women differ in our accounts of how capitalism as a class system secures the conditions of its own reproduction, and at what cost, but the commodity as its 'cellular form' is surely one of the keys to unlocking the secrets of what Max Weber (1958) called the capitalist cosmos.

DISCUSSION POINTS

1. What does it mean to say that a product bought and sold in the marketplace can take on a life of its own, or that a commodity might have a 'social life' or a 'biography'?

2. Why is it that 'fictitious' commodities are so charged? That is to say, why is the commodification of land, labour, space and money often the object of furious social reaction?

3. As a sort of thought experiment, take the idea that the commodity is the 'cell form' of the modern capitalist world; how might you explain to someone that such a line of reasoning can shed light on the make-up or the way in which capitalism in experienced?

4. Take a global commodity (the Sony Walkman, the Nike running shoe, say) and construct a commodity chain in which you try to understand key nodal points in which 'value' and 'quality' are created.

FURTHER READING

Appadurai, A. (ed.) (1987) *The social life of things.* Cambridge: Cambridge University Press.

Buck-Morss, S. (1990) *The dialectics of seeing.* Cambridge, MA: MIT Press.

Comaroff, J. and Comaroff, J. (1990) *Ethnography and the historical imagination.* Boulder, CO: Westview Press.

Harvey, D. (1982) *The limits to capital.* Oxford: Blackwell.

Mintz, S. (1985) *Sweetness and power.* New York: Viking Books.

Ollman, B. (1972) *Alienation.* Cambridge: Cambridge University Press.

Postone, M. (1993) *Time, labour and social domination.* Cambridge: Cambridge University Press.

Pred, A. and Watts, M. (1992) *Reworking modernity.* New Brunswick: Rutgers University Press.

Taussig, M. (1980) *The devil and commodity fetishism in Latin America.* Durham, NC: University of North Carolina Press.

Weiss, B. (1997) *The making and unmaking of the Haya lived world.* London: Duke University Press.

CHAPTER 40
THE MEDIA

James Kneale

INTRODUCTION

The mass media seem rather trivial compared to other geographical issues like the exploitation of the South by neo-colonialism. In fact, what have they got to do with Geography at all? In this chapter I want to argue that the media do have a place in our studies because they can help us to understand wider social and cultural issues – including the example above.

The media are significant because they are so commonplace. Stephen Heath asks 'Can anyone in our societies be outside television, beyond its compulsions?' and other mass media are nearly as ubiquitous (1990: 283). In the UK, around 85 per cent of men and women watched television every day in 2002 (ONS, 2004: 198) and, in 1996/97, 58 per cent of men and 71 per cent of women asked had read a book in the four weeks before the survey (ONS, 2000: 210).

This significance is not restricted to western(-ized) societies, either. The media play a vital role in globalization (see Chapter 3) by diffusing products and ideas across space, and act as global commodities in their own right. The television in the living room is one place 'where the global meets the local' (Morley, 1992), and from Marshall McLuhan's global village (1964) to David Harvey's 'time–space compression' (1989) the media are credited with shrinking the world.

The global reach of the media is extensive (Barker, 1999) but local experiences of globalization vary widely (Massey, 1994) and the homogenizing power of western media should not be exaggerated. India's Bollywood film industry and public access cable both represent 'local' challenges to Hollywood and the big television networks. And the media are bound up in questions of national and diasporic identities, as the examples of the BBC World Service, pan-European broadcasting, and the consumption of Hindi videos in Southall (Gillespie, 1995) make clear. Even a cursory consideration shows that the media play a part in a number of interesting geographical issues.

We should also consider the arguments put forward by Jacquie Burgess in a key piece of research in media geography (1990). She argues that we need to get to grips with the media because they are an important source of environmental knowledge (see Chapter 21) as well as using representations of nature to sell commodities. Burgess concludes that 'media texts are, in fact, saturated with geographical messages and meanings' (1990: 141), and this observation underlies one strand of geographical research into the media, which tries to uncover the ideology of mediated representations (see, for example, Burgess and Gold, 1985).

There is another way we can look at the media, though. Burgess notes that media texts are produced and consumed; they are part of a social process of creating meaning. And what they do is *mediate social relations*. The fact that TV signals, books, and so on, move through space means

Neo-colonialism

economic and political ties, continuing after formal independence, between metropolitan countries and the South, that work to the benefit of the North. *See also* COLONIALISM.

Representation

the cultural practices and forms by which human societies interpret and portray the world around them and present themselves to others. In the case of the natural world, for example, these representations range from prehistoric cave paintings of the creatures that figured in the lives of early human groups to the televisual images and scientific models that shape our imaginations today. *See also* DISCOURSE.

Ideology

a meaning or set of meanings that serves to create and/or maintain relationships of domination and subordination, through symbolic forms such as texts, landscapes and spaces.

Social capital

the notion of social capital is used to suggest that people's social networks have wider value through the relations of trust, reciprocity, co-operation and information exchange that they engender. Models of social organization and social space that involve high levels of social interaction and hence social capital – whether that be neighbourhood communities or internet-based support groups – are counterposed positively to examples of individualistic and passive existence.

that we can extend social life across space and time. The media do not simply carry these social relations, though; they also *transform* them (Thompson, 1995). These geographies concern the ways that the media connect different sites, flowing through space to diffuse ideas to different groups of people in different places. Of course this can mean that different kinds of relations get mixed up. For example, when you watch television with your friends you are relating to them *and* to the TV programme.

This has been a source of concern for quite a while. Robert Putnam's study of American **social capital** blames TV as a major cause of the apparent decline in civic participation and sociable interaction: 'between 1965 and 1995 we gained an average of six hours a week in added leisure time, and we spent almost all six of those additional hours watching TV' (2000: 222–3). He also notes that Americans are increasingly watching TV alone; three-quarters of all US homes possess more than one set and one-third of all viewing is done alone. Are the media destroying the home through this restructuring of social relations? Should we worry that our relationships with media like TV are one-sided – in the sense that most of us are passive consumers rather than active producers? And might the meaning of media texts be affected by the relations we have with other members of the audience?

This chapter considers these arguments through a number of historical and contemporary examples.

GEOGRAPHIES OF THE BOOK

FIGURE 40.1
Engraving by Marillier of reading in public in eighteenth century France. Source: A. Manguel 1996: *A History of Reading*. London: HarperCollins. Credit: © Bibliotheque Nationale/Paris/Archives Ceuil

Recent histories of the book can tell us a great deal about the geography of knowledge as well as about the relationships between media and social change.

Most people who could read did so out loud, often to an audience, until the sixteenth and seventeenth centuries. This means that the shift to private and silent reading also represented a change in the way that people related to one another; public reading produced social capital through communities of readers and listeners (see Fig. 40.1). In particular, 'reading aloud was a way of structuring family life' (Chartier, 1989: 152) since it served to reproduce the authority of parent and patriarch. Private reading contributed to the changing nature of the family, though this was a complicated process; silent reading allowed individuals to cut themselves off from one another whilst reading. This even created new spaces within the home, like the private library and the nineteenth-century study, places for seclusion where readers (particularly men) could retreat from the outside world.

Histories of the book can also tell us something about wider geographies of knowledge. For example, the European book market after 1500 illustrates how particular areas became well supplied with books and information, whilst others remained outside of this circulation of media (Martin, 1994). To broaden the range of their stock, booksellers developed collective networks of exchange with other sellers, sometimes bartering books for other books. Regional and then national networks began to appear, like the one in northern France organized by Parisian printers (1994: 249).

In Germany the rise of a national book network followed the Reformation; the immense appetite for books and tracts for or against Martin Luther meant that popular titles outstripped scholarly ones, and booksellers' networks had to extend into rural areas through peddlers (1994: 253–4). Because of this 'a cleavage opened between regions won over to Lutheranism (or Calvinism) and southern lands that had remained faithful to the Roman Church and that would be inundated with a mass literature of their own during the Catholic revival' (1994: 254).

Later mappings of the circulation of books in society show a similar picture. Robert Darnton (1979) shows that the eighteenth-century distribution of Diderot's *Encyclopédie* indicates that most purchasers would have been well-educated members of the urban upper and middle classes (see Fig. 40.2). Nigel Thrift suggests that this meant that knowledge about the world was strongly localized (both spatially and socially), forming a map of places with 'stocks' of information and spaces with relatively little (1996b). And since the *Encyclopédie* contained a treasury of **Enlightenment** thinking, this revolution in thought was also highly unevenly distributed.

The Enlightenment itself was built on books – rediscoveries of classic texts and the production and circulation of new ones. The men and women whose writing was part of this great shift – not only in how people thought about the world but how they related to it – recommended books to one another, wrote them for one another, exchanged them, and passed on information about booksellers and publishers. The movements of these books across Europe (and outside it) is part of a wider history of social change, but these changes themselves partly depended on the accumulation of knowledge by a particular class of people.

Enlightenment

a philosophical and intellectual movement usually dated to the seventeenth and eighteenth centuries and centred in Europe, which advanced the view that the world could be rendered knowable and explained systematically by the application of rational thought (science). Revolutionary in its challenge to the religious beliefs and superstitions that then held sway, it has since been much criticized for projecting rationality as a universal, rather than situating reasoning processes in particular social and material contexts.

SUMMARY

- Changes in print culture played their part in the 'privatization' of the household.
- European networks of bookselling were geographically uneven and socially unequal, and show us geographies of print-based knowledge.
- The geography of the book can help us to understand the nature of the social changes associated with the Enlightenment.

CIRCUITS, FLOWS AND SPACES

How exactly do the media link places together? Perhaps the best way of thinking about this is through Richard Johnson's 'circuit of culture' (see Fig. 40.3; 1986: 283) which illustrates the changing meaning of a media text as it moves through society. Let's take the British BBC soap opera *EastEnders* as an example. This text contains geographical meanings: the programme begins and ends with a map of the East End of London, and is situated in Walford, a mythical part of this area; it is also largely restricted to particular public and private spaces within this setting, like Albert Square, the Queen Vic, and so on. But this text is only one of the 'moments' in the circuit of this particular programme.

EastEnders is produced by a whole host of people – scriptwriters and

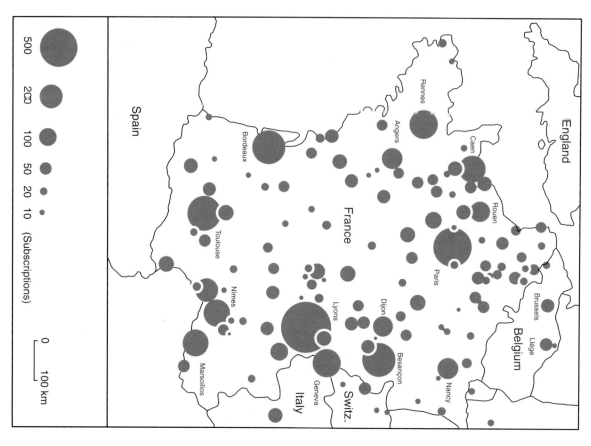

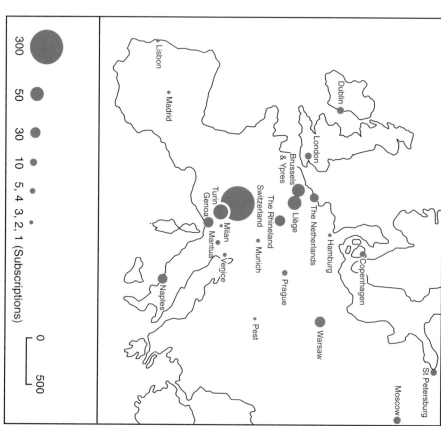

FIGURE 40.2
Diffusion of Diderot's *Encyclopédie* in and
outside France, 1777–82. Source: N. Thrift
1996b: *Spatial Formations*. London: Sage,
112–13.

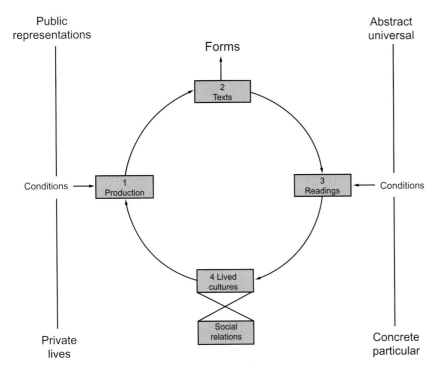

Public
representations

Abstract
universal

Forms

Conditions → 1 Production

3 Readings ← Conditions

4 Lived cultures

Social relations

Private
lives

Concrete
particular

FIGURE 40.3
The circuit of culture. Source: R. Johnson 1986: The story so far. In D. Punter (ed.) *Introduction to Contemporary Cultural Studies.* Harlow: Longman.

continuity people, directors and sound technicians, and many others. The finished product is the text, the transmitted programme. The audience for *EastEnders* – which is exported around the world – consumes the text, making their own meanings from it. These meanings are then taken away from the TV set, into the lived culture; viewers talk about it on the bus or at work, for example. The circuit then begins again, as producers draw upon this culture to see how popular the programme is, commissioning market research to gather feedback from viewers: Is a character working out? Is a storyline unpopular?

Obviously, we can use the circuit to track transformations in the geographical meanings of media texts, as Burgess suggests. But it also shows us how the media join spaces together. *EastEnders* flows through scriptwriters' studies at home, BBC offices, Pinewood Studios and on to the audience's screen; in living rooms, kitchens, bedrooms and pubs the programme is consumed; and in countless other spaces it is discussed, criticized and picked over.

Seen in this way, media texts are just like other commodities: they flow through social spaces, sometimes altering them, sometimes being transformed themselves. Writing about the history of the book, Roger Chartier notes 'their peregrinations . . . about the social world' (1994: x). It is these wanderings that I want to concentrate on now, rather than the

SUMMARY

- Media flow around the 'circuit of culture', from production to consumption and into wider social life.

- They therefore connect different places and people together as they flow through them.

- Media shape spaces and places, but spaces and places shape media.

geographical meanings of texts. Two geographies of the media are particularly interesting: the household, because it tells us something about the way that the media affect particular 'bounded' spaces; and, second, some of the networks that connect these spaces together and flow across their boundaries.

DOMESTIC MEDIA

Having already noted the globalizing effects of the media, it might seem rather parochial to concentrate upon the home – and the western home at that. However, most of the research that examines social spaces of the media is based upon the households of the 'first world', examining the interrelationships between media and social space.

There is a very important reciprocal relationship between domesticity and the media in these household spaces. Take television, for example:

> Television is a domestic medium. It is watched at home. Ignored at home. Discussed at home. Watched in private and with members of family or friends. But it is part of our domestic culture in other ways too, providing in its programming and its schedules models and structures of domestic life, or at least of certain versions of domestic life.

(Silverstone, 1994: 24)

This domestic life is already shaped by power relationships, like those existing in families.

> When media consumption takes place in the family . . . it takes place in a complex social setting in which different patterns of cohesion and dispersal, authority and submission, freedom and constraint, are expressed in the various sub-systems of conjugal, parental or sibling relationships and in the relationships that the family has between itself and the outside world.

(Silverstone, 1994: 33)

Domesticity depends especially upon particular forms of gender relations and upon a gendered division of labour; 'Men dominate the television at home because home is where they relax, where they are looked after' (Silverstone, 1994: 39). Many women, on the other hand, have to fit their media consumption around a schedule of domestic housework: watching TV with the children not because they want to watch it but because they might be needed, or keeping one eye on a daytime magazine programme while preparing a meal.

We can look at the relationships between TV and domesticity in a number of ways. First, TV, like radio before it, produces a routine for living because it is scheduled on an hourly, daily and weekly basis. In particular these media are associated with women's domestic work: 'the schedules of radio and television were not arbitrary, but were designed in accordance with certain structures associated with housework itself' (Seiter *et al.*, 1989: 229). TV schedules still fix our days – a process sometimes called 'clocking'. Though the family meal is an increasingly rare occurrence, household members may still gather to watch the news, evening soaps or sitcoms. These meetings are like the public reading of the early modern period; they reproduce the structures of the family and domestic life around the 'electronic hearth' (see Fig. 40.4). Finally, the content of some programmes reinforces domesticity; soaps and sitcoms usually rely on family life for their material, even when the families represented are far from happy ones.

There are three main objections that can be made to these arguments. First, I've been using the words 'family', 'household' and 'domesticity' fairly loosely; the overlap between them is not as neat as it might be. In 2003 only 28 per cent of UK households were 'nuclear families' (a couple plus at least one child); another 28 per cent were just couples, and 29 per cent were one-person households (Social Trends 34, 2004: 26). Different kinds of households represent different social spaces.

Second, haven't video and digital recorders weakened the 'clocking' power of television, by allowing us to watch what we want when we want? Though viewers do make good use of these 'timeshifting' technologies, some researchers have suggested that they are not 'innocent' technologies, available to all. Ann Gray found that the VCR tends to be controlled by men (1992), just like the remote control (Morley, 1986). I'll come back to this in the next section.

FIGURE 40.4
Who is in control? Credit: Angela Martin

Finally, the media can also threaten domesticity by connecting the household to the wider world, bringing the public into the private. Moral panics about the media are highly self-reflexive: Chris Morris' satirical UK series *Brass Eye* prompted a panic when it parodied media coverage of paedophiles (see Fig. 40.5). And when the media aren't blaming each other, they are blaming parents for not keeping children away from inappropriate material and calling for regulatory mechanisms (from 'watersheds' to child locks on VCRs) to keep threatening material away from susceptible members of the audience.

SUMMARY
- The relationship between the media and domesticity is a reciprocal one.
- Media consumption is incorporated into and may reproduce the inequalities of gender, age and class that make up families and households.
- However households take many forms, may use technologies to resist 'clocking', and may fear the media as an invasive presence.

HOGGING THE REMOTE

This image of the home as a haven from conflict does of course ignore the fact that relationships within households are often not equal. Gauntlett and Hill's research showed that whilst it was rare for men to openly 'hog' the TV, 'it was more common for men . . . to get their way insofar as their own choices were viewed on the household's main TV set, whilst women's choices were videoed, or were viewed on a secondary set in another room' (1999: 244). The dispersal of the household away from the electronic hearth seems to confirm Robert Putnam's fears about family life, but it seems rash to assume that it is the fault of the TV set; conflicts about what can be watched and where still negotiate and reproduce power-laden social relations within the household. In fact Tim Dant's review of a number of studies suggests that TV viewing is often done in a highly distracted way; viewers only look at the TV for about two-thirds of the time that they are in its presence, and between 15–19 per cent of the time that the set is on there is no one present to watch it (1999: 170). Maybe other people and other activities are just as fascinating as the TV.

FIGURE 40.5
Troublesome TV – Chris Morris of *Brass Eye* fame in *The Day Today*. Credit: © BBC

Janice Radway's study of American women readers provides us with another good example (1984). Many of them saw it as a guilty pleasure, because (unlike TV) reading cannot usually be combined with domestic work. Women in the UK are more likely to read than men, and more likely to say that they read to relax or because they are bored (ONS, 2004: 202). Radway's interviewees valued their reading as 'time for oneself' but worried that it meant neglecting their 'duties' – a feeling often strengthened by the hostility of their partners towards reading. The privacy of reading is, in fact, often an ambiguous pleasure:

> *Something in the relationship between a reader and a book is recognized as wise and fruitful, but it is also seen as disdainfully exclusive and excluding, perhaps because the image of an individual curled up in a corner, seemingly oblivious of the grumblings of the world, suggests impenetrable privacy and a selfish eye and singular secretive action.*

(Manguel, 1996: 21)

A less guilty group of women can be found in Henry Jenkins' study of US science fiction television fandom (1992). Discussing their first encounters with the TV series *Beauty and the Beast*, members of the programme's Boston area fan club clearly identified its importance in terms of 'neglecting' their domestic work:

> *I was sitting there and I didn't get any work done! My chin was on the ground! I couldn't believe what I was seeing.*

(Jenkins, 1992: 58)

> *I sat there and I sat there and I'm like this and my kids come in and I remember them going past me vaguely but I didn't let it distract me at all.*

(Jenkins, 1992: 58–60)

The relationship between the media and domesticity is more complicated than commentators like Putnam would have us believe, even before we move to the next moment on the circuit.

SUMMARY

- Disagreements about media consumption provide a space in which power relationships are reproduced and negotiated.
- Reading can be exclusive, provoking guilt in the reader and resentment in other members of the household.
- However, viewers and readers do recognize the value of claiming 'time for oneself' through media consumption.

AUDIENCES AS SOCIAL NETWORKS

As Silverstone reminds us, households are 'leaky' social spaces in the sense that they aren't enclosed and self-sufficient. Members must leave the home to work, socialize, and so on. It is at this point that media are carried into the lived culture of Johnson's circuit.

Media texts flow away from the original site of consumption and are re-used elsewhere, in social networks outside the household. One of the best examples of this comes from Dorothy Hobson's interviews with women soap viewers, where she points out that 'talking about soap operas forms part of the everyday work culture of both men and women. It is fitted in around their working time or in lunch breaks', becoming part of their experience of work spaces (1989: 150). As Silverstone points out, 'the life of the soap opera pervades life in the home, life over the garden wall, on the street, in the pub, in the canteen and in the factory' (1994: 74).

In fact these social relationships can actually lead people to watch television when they might not have otherwise bothered. Hobson interviewed one woman who began watching *EastEnders* because her colleagues discussed it so much at work:

> *When a storyline is so strong that it is a main topic of conversation it is reason enough to get someone watching it so as not to be left out of the conversation which takes place at work.*

(1989: 161)

FIGURE 40.6
Riot Grrrl zines. Source: T. Skelton and G. Valentine (eds) 1998: *Cool Places: Geographies of Youth Cultures*. London: Routledge. Credit: © Rob Strachan

These kinds of conversations about media take on a new significance in fan culture, where relationships between fans become organized to the extent that they operate as important social networks in their own right. The extent of these networks is much further than a chat over the garden wall; fans receive letters and fan produce from other countries around the world. And these networks are formed primarily because of the media, as opposed to the media fitting into networks established at work or elsewhere. Jenkins discusses one aspect of this:

> *The exchange of videotapes has become a central ritual of fandom, one of the practices helping to bind it together as a distinctive community . . . No sooner do two fans meet at a convention than one begins to offer access to prized tapes and many friendships emerge from these attempts to share media resources.*

(1992: 71)

A similar network underpins the riot grrrl subculture; young women produce fanzines and distribute them to one another, becoming friends in the process (Leonard, 1998). The fanzine (see Fig. 40.6) allows a sense of community to develop: 'whilst [they] may reach people in other countries, their content and scale of production give the impression of conversing with a close group of friends' (1998: 108).

Both riot grrrls and SF fans also use the internet; but both media SF fans (mostly women – literary SF fans are mostly men) and riot grrrls express suspicion of this forum because of its masculine character. Jenkins usefully compares *Star Trek* fandom and *Twin Peaks* internet discussion groups to show that the two communities seek different things from these programmes, talk about them in different ways, and form different kinds of social relationships with them precisely because the former group is made up mainly of women whilst the latter are mostly men (1998: 77–9, 109–15). Here **gender** is crucial to an understanding of these dispersed geographies.

One of the challenges facing geographers interested in the media is evaluating the role that they play in constituting social networks, and the ways that these networks cross space and link places.

Gender

a criterion of social organization that distinguishes different groups of people on the basis of femininity or masculinity. In any one location, many masculinities and femininities interact. As a concept, gender is usually used in Human Geography in distinction to that of sex (i.e. femaleness and maleness) in order to emphasize the SOCIAL CONSTRUCTION of women's and men's roles, relations and identities. Human Geographers' accounts of the world have always been shaped through understandings of gender (*see* MASCULINISM) but explicit analyses of the geographies of gender and the gendering of geographies are comparatively recent, and associated with the growth of Feminist Geography (*see* FEMINISM).

SUMMARY

- Media flow out from households into places of work and leisure.
- Talking about the media forms an important part of social relationships outside the home.
- If these networks are more formalized, as is the case for fan culture, they can acquire a global reach.

CONCLUSION

The media saturate the social spaces of many people around the world with representations of places and landscapes. However, they also shape and are shaped by other geographies. In particular they help to construct domestic or family spaces, where they reproduce (and sometimes transform) gender relations as well as ideas of the 'public' and the 'private'.

These spaces are not isolated from the outside world, however; by talking about media texts, consumers make them part of their lives outside the home. Many social relationships involve discussions of the media; some are initially built upon a shared interest in a programme, whilst others draw upon the media as one of many resources for producing social spaces. In some cases, like fan communities, this goes beyond talking about media at work, and the geographies created by video exchanges, writing to fanzines, or going to conventions span international distances. Of course the real question is whether these sorts of mediated communities can ever have the strength of the face-to-face networks that Putnam thinks are withering away.

Finally I've discussed these media geographies and the interpretation of the geographical meanings of texts as if they are separate concerns. However, to fully understand the meanings of texts, we need to know how their meanings are transformed as they circulate through space and around the circuit of culture. There are a few examples of work of this sort – like Secord's tremendous study of the many readings of a single book produced by different audiences in Victorian Britain (2000). In many ways, though, this remains an under-explored area of Human Geography. Maybe we'd rather watch TV than write about it . . .

DISCUSSION POINTS

1. Putting to one side arguments about media *content*, should we be worried that we spend so much time with the mass media?

2. How do you feel about the gendered patterns of media consumption discussed in this chapter (Silverstone, Morley, Gray, Gauntlett and Hill, Radway)?

3. Do established forms of media already allow for a dialogue between producers and audiences, or will this only happen through emerging, 'interactive', media?

4. Does it matter that books and TV transmissions travel through social space differently?

5. What kinds of research projects might allow us to examine media consumption in different social spaces?

FURTHER READING

Burgess, J. (1990) The production and consumption of environmental meanings in the mass media: a research agenda for the 1990s. *Transactions of the Institute of British Geographers*, **15: 139–61.**

A clear and powerful argument for geographical work on the media.

Morley, D. (1992) *Television, audiences and cultural studies.* **London: Routledge.**

Collects and reviews earlier work from *Family Television* through to 'Where the global meets the local' – worth reading to get a feel for media studies research with an eye for space.

Silverstone, R. (1994) *Television and everyday life.* **London: Routledge.**

Quite taxing in places, but a sustained investigation that has a great deal to say about domesticity and the role of the media in everyday social space.

Thompson, J. (1995) *The media and modernity: a social theory of the media.* **Oxford: Polity Press.**

A sustained discussion of the role of the media that draws upon a wide range of work in social theory.

Stevenson, N. (2002) *Understanding media cultures.* **London: Thousand Oaks and New Delhi: Sage.**

A useful overview of work on the media that covers a number of important topics from a social science perspective.

INTRODUCTION: A NEW TYPE OF WAR?

Speaking to airline workers at Chicago's O'Hare airport in late September 2001, American President George W. Bush assured his audience, ten days before the start of the war on the Taliban and Al Qaeda in Afghanistan, that their nation was already 'adjusting to a new type of war'. In the weeks following the September 11th 2001 attacks on the World Trade Center and Pentagon, Bush had been at pains to evoke this notion of a *different type of battlefield*, a *different type of war* and a *new type of struggle*, in speeches and photo opportunities with foreign leaders, forecasting an ambiguously 'long campaign' to be carried out, in military and intelligence operations as well as in finance and law enforcement, against an enemy, terrorism, which 'knows no borders' and 'has no capital' (Ó Tuathail, 2003). At O'Hare, a busy hub airport on the newly recognized front lines of a war, Bush continued:

> " *This isn't a conventional war that we're waging. Ours is a campaign that will have to reflect the new enemy. There's no longer islands to conquer or beachheads to storm. ... These are people who strike and hide, people who know no borders ...* "

The new war was to be fought, instead, 'wherever terrorists hide, or run, or plan. Some victories will be outside of public view', the President added in a national radio address two days later, 'in tragedies avoided and threats eliminated. Other victories will be clear to all' (Bush, 2001).

No borders, no capitals, no islands, no beachheads. Battles to be fought 'wherever'. Some victories 'unseen', and apparently unmappable. Judging by the President's statements throughout the month, the American-led global war on terrorism was going to have to be prosecuted *beyond* geography in new and important ways.

This chapter, nevertheless, is about the geographies of war, security, and the 'global war on terrorism', including those spatialities that may be troubling, as Bush portrayed, precisely because of their invisibility and apparent lack of geography (a 'geography of no geography'). But neither the rhetoric nor the violence of the emerging dynamics of contemporary war, security and terror could exist without drawing on existing real and imaginative geographies and, at the same time, producing powerful new ones (for related points, see Chapter 10 by Felix Driver, on imaginative geographies, and Chapter 27 by Pyrs Gruffudd, on imagined national communities). The very absence of beachheads and islands to storm in Bush's remarks, for example, evoked geographical images of America's Second World War battlefields in Europe and the Pacific, thus serving as markers of a common national history and identity forged in a different great historical moment. The notion that the September 11th hijackers 'knew no borders', on the other hand, reflects a more curious erasure of

Spatiality

socially produced space. This term is used by Human Geographers to emphasize how space is socially constructed and experienced, rather than being an innate backdrop to social life (*see also* SOCIAL CONSTRUCTION). As such it is a central concept of contemporary Human Geography. It is sometimes used in the plural, spatialities, in order to stress the many different ways in which space can be constructed and experienced.

Imaginative geographies

representations of place, space and landscape that structure people's understandings of the world, and in turn help to shape their actions. In the work of Edward Said, the term refers to the projection of images of identity and difference on to geographical space in a way that sustains unequal relationships of power.

Representation

the cultural practices and forms by
which human societies interpret and
portray the world around them and
present themselves to others. In the
case of the natural world, for example,
these representations range from
prehistoric cave paintings of the
creatures that figured in the lives of
early human groups to the televisual
images and scientific models that shape
our imaginations today. *See also*
DISCOURSE.

geography, for each had presumably crossed international boundaries to
enter the USA, amongst other borders passed through, well before they
boarded the airplanes that morning, and were well aware of the
geographical differences that such boundaries marked off in terms of
jurisdictions, surveillance, rights and opportunities (such as abundant
flight training schools). Even the suggestion of spaces such as airports and
train stations as the new front lines of a war, rather than places secured by
the 'thin blue line' of policing and law enforcement, presented a kind of
new geography that was at once highly localized and fully globalized, a
world wherein the entire planet was suddenly to be conceived as an
internal threat for the USA. Geographies of the new war, in the weeks
following the 9/11 attacks, were not so much missing, then, as they were
'over-coded' (see Pickles, 2003).

The diverse geographical **representation** of war and security has continued in a number of ways, from map-rich media coverage of the war in
Afghanistan beginning October 2001, to the landscapes of war footage
transmitted through journalists 'embedded' with American and British
troops in Iraq in 2003, to subsequent mappings of a 'Sunni Triangle'
region in which, at times, insurgency movements in Iraq have been said to
be concentrated (see Fig. 41.1). War, security, and the spectacle (or public
representation) of war, however, whilst related, are not the same things;
there are rather clear differences, for example, between new security practices adopted in the West and those used to besiege the cities of Fallujah
and Najaf, Iraq, where as I write two seemingly intractable conflicts
between occupying American forces and separate groups of Iraqi insur-
gents have engendered front lines of urban siege and insurgency that are
more easily recognized as war than the ones that many of us stand in, with
varying degrees of patience, at security checkpoints at our local airports
(see Fig. 41.2).

FIGURE 41.1
Geographically locating violence within a
'Sunni Triangle' in Iraq was, for a time, how
popular media made sense of the Iraqi
insurgency. Source: NewsHour with Jim Lehrer,
'Attacks in the Sunni Triangle', April 2004

The evolving dynamics of war and security, if not exactly war and peace, are circulated across media networks at virtually the same time as they are realized on the ground, wars of both emotional affect and brutal material effect. But the ways that war and security are produced and reproduced, as we will explore in this chapter, are more constructively understood as highly geographical than lacking in geography. Geographical concepts of territoriality, boundaries, scale, spatial representation, variation, place and landscape provide a grammar that helps us to make

FIGURE 41.2

Military occupation: An American Bradley fighting vehicle on the streets of Baghdad, September 2004. Credit: Sabah Arar/Getty Images

sense of war's uneven distributions, whilst more focused geographical perspectives and debates on the nature of contemporary American **hegemony** in particular allow us to further pull apart some of the geographical specificities of the global war on terrorism, as it was dubbed by the Bush administration, so that we might gain a better sense of how they fit together.

GEOGRAPHIES OF WAR AND SECURITY

We need not look beyond the conditions of our own lives to begin to grasp not only the fact that war has a geography (or many different, intersecting geographies), but also that the geographies of war and security that we produce and reproduce are extremely consequential. Most obviously, one's everyday safety from the dangers of war, terrorism and other forms of systematic political violence (i.e. the risks of death or severe injury from derelict land mines, of forced conscription of juveniles, or of battle deaths for soldiers and civilians) varies to a great extent depending on where one happens to live. John O'Loughlin's (2004) map of the geography of conflict since the Second World War – in which geographical locations of battle deaths are plotted against three classes of United Nations Human Development Index scores – illustrates this point well (see Fig. 41.3). Seen from this global perspective, the geographical articulation of war with poverty over the past six decades is evident. The implications are equally clear: security from the localized effects of war, with a few notable exceptions, has become something that those living in the world's wealthier regions – the upper third of the HDI represented in dark blue on the map – are more likely to afford, in a sense, than those living in the middle and lower HDI classes, in light blue and yellow on the map (see also O'Loughlin and van der Wusten, 1993).

This is not to suggest that the comparatively peaceful territories of the North Atlantic powers are therefore disconnected from conflicts occurring elsewhere. It is meant to show that geographical knowledge – achieved in this case by comparing the geographical distribution of war deaths against

Hegemony, hegemonic, hegemon

hegemony is an opaque power relation relying more on leadership through consensus than coercion through force or its threat, so that domination is by the permeation of ideas. For instance, concepts of hegemony have been used to explain how, when 'the ruling ideas are the ideas of the ruling class', other classes will willingly accept their inferior position as right and proper (*see* CLASS). Hegemonic is the adjective attached to the institution that possesses hegemony. For instance, under CAPITALISM the bourgeoisie are the hegemonic class. Hegemon is a term used when the concept of hegemony is applied to the competition between NATION-STATES: a hegemon is a hegemonic state. For instance, the USA has been described as the hegemon of the world economy in the mid-twentieth century.

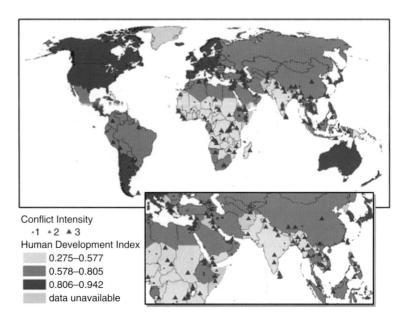

FIGURE 41.3
Mapping the geographic distribution of conflict against the UN Human Development Index scores. Conflict intensity is measured in three classes: (1) 25–1,000 total battle deaths; (2) over 1,000 battle deaths in the conflict but fewer than 1,000 per year; and (3) 1,000 or more battle deaths per year of conflict.
Source: O'Loughlin (2004)

Cold War

a period conventionally defined as running from the end of the Second World War until the fall of the Berlin Wall, during which the globe was structured around a binary political geography that opposed US CAPITALISM to Soviet communism. Although never reaching all-out military confrontation, this period did witness intense military, economic, political and ideological rivalry between the superpowers and their allies.

that of poverty or human development – often serves to open many more questions than it closes: Why are wars (including terrorist wars) so much more likely to occur in poor regions than in wealthy ones? How have these patterns changed over time? To what extent are geographies of war and security produced by regional dynamics and processes, and to what extent, on the other hand, do they reflect differing regional effects of global dynamics and processes? In the still evolving wake of the **Cold War**, in which the USA has consolidated its position as the sole military superpower, what is the role of American economic and geopolitical power in producing and maintaining the geographies of war and security, and what work do its partners and allies do in enabling, inflecting, or transforming these processes? How are existing geographical arrangements of military power nevertheless resisted, in a variety of ways, by actors and institutions operating at different scales, and to what effects? Did the September 11th attacks shatter a long-standing geography of war and security, or have they served instead to reinforce that geography? Answers to these questions would no doubt require a much more sustained inquiry than can be presented in this chapter, and a piling on of many more questions, but it is worth turning to the final question in the litany, for it is largely in the American reaction to, and geopolitical leveraging of, the 9/11 attacks that the 'global war on terrorism' has taken shape in many different regional contexts.

'Somehow,' as Neil Smith has described it (2001: 634),

> *through nearly a century in which the US rose to global hegemony, none of the brutal wars – 20 million in World War I, more than 30 million in World War II, and many tens of millions of other wars on four continents – seriously touched the national territory of the United States. ... No other country has been so immune to the terror that made the 20th century the most violent in history, yet so implicated in it.*

Against this historical backdrop, the 2001 World Trade Center attack – and the large red triangle over New York in Figure 41.3 – now appears remarkably like the 'geographical exception' that proves the rule, especially in considering American military actions undertaken afterwards. In Afghanistan, as O'Loughlin (2004; after Shaw, 2002) notes, 'between October and December 2001 (the period of heaviest warfare), the so-called collateral damage of civilian deaths amounted to between 4200 and 5000; deaths of US allies' – including the 'Northern Alliance' and other armies associated with regional warlords empowered to call in US air strikes – totalled in the hundreds; deaths of 'enemy combatants' numbered in the thousands or perhaps even tens of thousands, whilst the number of US military deaths during the same period was one. The trend of high civilian casualties has continued in the American and British invasion and occupation of Iraq (see www.iraqbodycount.org 2004).

The invasion of Iraq, we recall, had originally been justified by the USA and UK on the basis of its alleged weapons of mass destruction (WMD) in connection with its alleged ties to terrorist groups, and more generally for the (also alleged) 'imminent threat' that it posed; the whole operation was thus cast as part of the global war on terrorism. In fact, polls suggest that at the time of the invasion a majority of Americans had been led to believe that Saddam Hussein had at least something to do with the 9/11 attacks themselves. A politics of affect over intellect, as Gerard Toal (Ó Tuathail, 2003) has argued, was thus critical to the generation of consent for the Iraqi war amongst the US electorate, despite widespread international opposition:

" *Although the secular Iraqi regime of Saddam Hussein had no connection to the 9/11 attacks, was condemned by Osama bin Laden, and was deterred from using weapons of mass destruction, it was the object of a 'pre-emptive war' made possibly by their channeling of the public affect unleashed by 9/11. In the geopolitical window of opportunity generated by September 11, 2001, the Bush administration interpreted the attacks in a sweeping, simplistic, and politically opportunistic manner, and after a brief war against Afghanistan, turned its 'war against terrorism' into a campaign against the regime of Saddam Hussein.* "

(Ó Tuathail, 2003: 857)

After the failure to find evidence of WMD in Iraq following the toppling of the regime, the war, interestingly, is still referenced as part of the global war on terrorism (in fact, its 'central front'), but now, without missing a beat, in reference to insurgencies engendered by the invasion itself and against the military occupation (cf. Bush, 2004). In justifying foreign military operations, the apparent need for democratic governments to generate consensus amongst a polity defined by the territorial boundaries of the nation-state reflects the continuing importance of a politics of scale in geographies of war and security. The cultural politics of affect geared for audiences inside these guarded geographies of national security are indeed powerful forces in the manufacturing of consent for wars conducted, and peaces policed, in strategic regions outside zones of greater security from war. And yet the emotional scripting of (new) war, risk and geopolitics has scarcely gone unnoticed or uncontested, as the American cartoonist Tom Tomorrow's critique of the pre-emptive 'Bush Doctrine', on the eve of the war on Iraq, makes plain. In 'The Moon' (January 13, 2003, on www.thismodernworld.com), President Bush announces that 'Because the Moon MAY someday break out of orbit and crash into the Earth – I have decided to use our nookyalur arsenal to destroy it NOW!' Soon, the narration continues, the 'destruction of the moon seems like the ONLY sensible option,' and liberal critics, unable to transcend the logic of preemption and fear, are effectively marginalized, as seen in a conversation between two men in the street:

> 'They whine and complain about destroying the moon—but do THEY have any solutions?'
>
> 'THEY probably just want us all to sit around wait for the moon to fall right on our HEADS!'
>
> 'Crazy moon lovers!'

Human Geographers, with long standing interests in the relations between places and between processes occurring at different spatial scales, are well positioned to ask critical questions about how wars of affect in the world's more powerful countries, in which analytical critiques of war policies are either silenced or marginalized serve to authorize wars of violent effect taking place elsewhere.

For O'Loughlin (2004), writing on the nature of 'civil wars in the hegemonic shadow', it is clear that a geography of contemporary conflict must come to grips with conditions of disproportionate American economic and military power as they are coupled with the asymmetric nature of modern warfare itself. 'While there is little doubt that the USA tries to avoid needless civilian loss of life', he argues that

> the disturbing numbers of civilians killed in 'accidents' illustrates another fact of US-style modern war. In order to reduce the risk to US troops, weapons are fired from even greater distances. The advances in the electronic battlefield, combined with the use of global positioning systems, has pushed US military technology far ahead of any other country … These distances lead to more 'accidents' since they allow the US to fight wars at little risk to its troops. (How risky is it to drop laser-guided bombs from 29,000 feet against an enemy with weak air defenses?)

(O'Loughlin, 2004)

With US military spending roughly equal to that of the next 25 countries combined, the effects of such 'risk transfer wars' indeed reflect broader asymmetries of power, even though the bloody dynamics of occupation and insurgency on the ground in Iraq, whilst still unequal, may yet temper the American utilization of asymmetric force in the future, as did the limits of American power (and far greater American casualties) realized in Vietnam 30 years earlier. Regardless, the trend in American high-tech weapons development, as O'Loughlin points out, will continue, from long-distance, high-speed cruise missiles to the long promised missile defence shield, which, whilst by no means guaranteed of success, will continue to figure in the reproduction of geographies of war and security for many years to come, even as conflicts in regions peripheral to US interests, such as Congo, where 3.1 million to 4.7 million people have died as a result of civil war in the past decade, are largely left to languish.

For some commentators, like Michael Klare (2002), who sees a new 'strategic triangle' emerging around the geography of oil reserves and transit routes from the Persian Gulf/Arabian Peninsula in the west to the Caspian Sea in the north to the South China Sea to the east, such a pattern of strategic choices for the US is hardly surprising, although the revival of traditional geopolitical thinking under the Bush administration 'neo-cons' following 9/11, he maintains, has worked largely as self-fulfilling prophecy (on the geopolitical tradition, see Chapter 25 by Joanne Sharp).[1] The geographical expansion and restructuring of American military bases (and basing rights) into these strategic oil regions alongside military conflicts in recent years, as seen in Figure 41.4, does make clear that, in the restructuring and expansion of a global geography of American military power, there is in effect far more at stake in recent conflicts in both Afghanistan and Iraq than the future of terrorist organizations of global reach, the stated American enemy in the war on terrorism (Lawson, 2004).

None of this is to say that the risks posed by Al Qaeda and like-minded terrorist organizations are not real, nor that the worst-case scenarios of chemical, biological, nuclear or 'dirty bomb' terrorist attacks should not be taken seriously and guarded against. Rather, the point is that the very existence of such dangers *within* – apparently possible anywhere, but in fact geographically specific: New York and Washington, Madrid or a westernized tourist enclave in Indonesia – has been mobilized to support a war on terrorism that is both absolute (we are all in danger) and highly specific. James Sidaway (2003: 646) has suggested that the 9/11 attacks 'embodied the collapse of a geopolitics of the inside/outside binary – a *homecoming* of the violent world that the West might seek to keep at a distance (or ignore), but in the violence of which it is complicit'. It is striking to consider, though, how rapidly those geopolitics of inside/outside are now being reconfigured. For instance, what new forms of inside/outside geopolitics would a 'star wars'-style missile defence shield produce, if successful, and how might the very idea of such a shield, as well as that of the American 'virtual border' programme linking immigration, customs and counter-terrorism databases with the collection and analysis of biometric data, serve to produce new insides and outsides? How, if at all, will the emergence of new geographies of a 'war' conducted by territorial nation-states against the transnational network structure of 'terrorist organizations of global reach' work to recast the very norms of territorial sovereignty, as well as such competing territorial jurisdictions as world energy markets, privatized security and warfare, international policing, and national and international courts? In the next section, we will begin to approach these questions in a discussion of the changing

Geopolitics

an approach to the theory and practice of statecraft, which considers certain laws of geography (e.g. distance, proximity and location) to play a central part in the formation of international politics. Although the term was originally coined by Swede Rudolf Kjellen in 1899, it was popularized in the early twentieth century by British geographer Halford Mackinder.

dimensions of American extra-territorial power, before turning to question how geographies of war and security are perhaps already being reconfigured in geographically differentiated, hybrid landscapes of both war and peace.

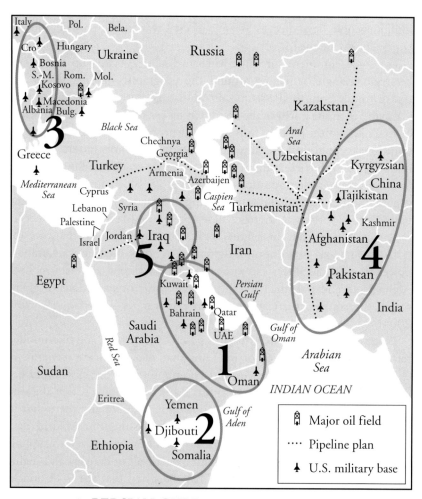

FIGURE 41.4
Expansion in US military basing rights preceding and following conflicts, 1990–2003. Map by Zoltan Grossman

1. **PERSIAN GULF** 1990
2. **SOMALIA** 1992–93 / **YEMEN** 1996–2000
3. **BALKANS** 1995, 1999
4. **CENTRAL ASIA** 2001
5. **IRAQ** 2003

SUMMARY

- There is a very definite geography to issues of war and security.
- These geographies include critical connections between 'wars of affect' in the world's more powerful countries and 'wars of effect', which largely take place elsewhere.

- Wars are increasingly fought 'at a distance', minimizing the risk to powerful countries and their soldiers, but increasing the risk to civilian populations in the theatre of war.

PEACE, *IN OTHER WORDS*, WAR ...[2]

Following the American atomic bombings of Hiroshima and Nagasaki at the end of the Second World War, the argument that the possibility of total annihilation in the atomic age called for new forms of world governance and co-operation gained widespread currency, not least amongst a group of politically active, guilt-driven émigré scientists who had worked on the USA's secret Manhattan Project. In the face of such an absolute risk, some argued, a new international atomic order, and perhaps ultimately even a unitary world state, were the best hopes for preventing both an international arms race and a devastating nuclear war (Boyer, 1994). The ultimate foreclosure of such arguments, however, constituted an important moment in the politics of geographical scale; by the time the USSR detonated its first atomic bomb in a 1949 test, a thorough retrenchment of atomic (and, soon, thermonuclear) weaponry within the nation-state took root as an underlying condition of the emergent Cold War world order. Rather than a 'world risk society' in which shared dangers served to mobilize new forms of democratic governance of technology (Beck, 1999), the nuclear threat instead was mobilized to constitute a dynamic scientific and high-tech arms race; it continues only partly abated, as depleted uranium 'bunker busters' and other 'mini' and 'tactical' nuclear weapons still under development are now designed for terrorists and rogue state leaders hiding from American air assaults deep underground or inside mountains instead of Moscow and Leningrad.

To the extent that the risk of terrorism is presented as universal and free-floating, uprooted from any specific geographical locations and disconnected from real historical processes, it also can seem absolute – albeit the absolute risk of random violence rather than total annihilation. Whether this particular risk is dealt with as a permanent 'just war' on terrorism or, as Beck alternately suggests, an 'alliance against terrorism' to be governed in a world space of law and justice (Beck, 2002), remains an open question, a politics of geographical scale not yet foreclosed upon in the long term.

Writing in 2002, as the USA was still endeavouring to win both national and international support for an invasion of Iraq, the Director of the Stockholm International Peace Research Institute (SIPRI) cautiously assessed the US position in an emerging, post-9/11 global security environment:

> The USA can play a decisive role. It has a position unprecedented in history in terms of military, economic, and technological capabilities. ... This preponderance both tempts and permits the USA to act unilaterally. However, security is based on interdependence rather than independence or preponderance. While this understanding is reflected in official US statements, in practices the US tendency towards unilateralism in decision making prevails. The world needs the USA as never before and the USA needs the world, too. Neither domination and hegemony nor neo-isolationism offer an adequate response to the new challenges.

(Rotfeld, 2002)

Two years later, and writing from a similar liberal internationalist perspective, the next Director of SIPRI reflected on the lessons of Iraq in illuminating both the extent and the limits of American extra-territorial power (Bailes, 2004). On the one hand, that the USA (the UK is not mentioned) could so swiftly occupy a distant country, despite having various bases and routes closed off to it by allies Saudi Arabia and Turkey, over the objections of fellow UN Security Council members, and without any substantial military resistance from other countries in the region, certainly suggests unique resources and capabilities, and, under Bush, a willingness to use them. On the other hand, the failure to 'win the peace' afterwards, compounded by the USA and UK failure to win UN or even NATO support in advance of the war, has revealed limitations of such unilateral and bilateral uses of power, just as the political, military and moral dangers of occupation will continue to pose challenges that are characteristically unwinnable by military means (as students of wars of occupation and decolonization, such as Algeria, Indochina/Vietnam and Israel/Palestine, have for long understood).

Once again, important lessons can be drawn from the geographies in which these strengths and limitations have been expressed. For Colin Flint (2004b), the US tendency to define terrorism as a matter of global geopolitics rather than domestic (or international) policing reflects a potentially important spatial mismatch in the 'meta-geographies' in conflict in the US war on terrorism – that is, the world of **territorial** nation-states, on the one hand, and the transnational network structure of religious terrorism, on the other. 'To counter networks in its war on terrorism,' Flint argues,

> the United States must impose a territorial presence – in other words it has been forced to occupy sovereign spaces. The geopolitical dilemma facing the USA is that part of the motivation behind the terrorist attacks is their presence in sovereign spaces in the first part – Saudi Arabia being the most important venue. In other words, occupying sovereign spaces to destroy terrorist networks may well be counter-productive counter-terrorism.

The meta-geographies may differ, then, but they intersect in a kind of territorial trap; if there is a global war being waged between the USA and its allies, on the one hand, and Al Qaeda and sympathetic groups on the other, then it might reasonably be argued that, based on its getting sucked into a dangerous, costly and demoralizing occupation in Iraq (whatever the actual motivation for the invasion of Iraq), the USA may be losing that war. Whilst it may be tempting to interpret the American reaction to (and/or leveraging of) the 9/11 attacks as another retrenchment of power at the national scale, geographical perspectives are also useful in raising questions about how American power, which we have observed as the key guarantor in contemporary geographies of war and security (not only in wars waged but in basing rights spread across the planet), is not only limited but also transformed in potentially new ways. Will the first decade of the twenty-first century be looked back upon by future historians as a moment of American 'imperial overstretch' and hegemonic decline (Flint,

Territory
a more or less bounded area over which an animal, person, social group or institution claims and attempts to enforce control.

2004b), as a key moment in the emergence of new forms of global power and sovereignty, with its basis in the international policing of terrorism, or merely as a geopolitical restructuring of existing trends in American geostrategic hegemony?

It is also possible to examine the geography of war by raising questions about the meaning of peace. In the global war on terrorism, a war carried out, purportedly, on diplomatic, legal, financial, humanitarian, as well as military grounds, has peace become, as Alliez and Negri (2003: 110) claim, 'merely a deceptive illusion fostering the power of disorder and its threat – *urbi et orbi* – against the security of the world'? The notion of 'peace, *in other words,* war' thus signifies, for these theorists, the extent to which (secured) peace and war have become 'absolutely contemporary with one another' – a hybrid condition wherein 'peace no longer appears as anything other than *the continuation of war by other means*'. Has the very idea of peace been reduced to that of militarized security and a justification for new wars? And, if we are engaged in a more or less permanent war on terrorism, what does this fusion of the concepts of war and peace mean in light of the clear geographical variations in the geographies of war that we have observed? Hybrids of war and peace are indeed proliferating – the ballyhooed American sorties that dropped some 2,360,000 individually packaged vegetarian meals – 'Humanitarian Daily Rations' – across Afghanistan from October to December 2001, amidst an otherwise hazardous bombardment, provides one rather spectacular example. But, again, it is important to recognize that whilst war and peace may be absolutely contemporary with one another, such war/peace hybrids are nevertheless highly differentiated geographically; the risk of encountering terrorism at O'Hare airport in autumn 2001 was still far below that of encountering violence whilst scavenging for prepackaged lentils in an active war zone.

Another example of peace serving as an extension of war – and war premised on the extension of secured peace – is the Iraq Local Governance Project, a three-year, $167 million development programme contracted through RTI International, a North Carolina, USA-based non-profit scientific research and services firm. Setting up local offices in 17 of 18 Iraqi governorates, the Local Governance Project is, as its title suggests, a highly scalar enterprise, a 'capacity-building project' organized around improving 'the quality of governance in Iraq's governorates, cities, and towns in order to bring concrete improvements to the quality of life of Iraqi Citizens' (RTI International, 2004). But whilst advocates stress the project's accomplishments in improving access to basic services and participation of civil society organizations in local government, critics charge that, in their close collaboration with the Coalition Provisional Authority and American Government, their work matches closely not only with the American geopolitical agenda, as RTI contractors endeavour to win the peace at local and regional levels, but also with a neo-liberal agenda in which handpicked transitional governments are encouraged to facilitate the privatization (and internationalization) of Iraqi resources and services (Klein, 2004). Interestingly, the very reliance of the American government on private contractors – from RTI to the oil and war services firm Halliburton to the private paramilitary firms such as Blackwater, Inc.

(which pays an international army of mercenaries and truck drivers perhaps $20,000 per month to protect and supply American troops) to privately contracted intelligence collectors at Abu Ghraib prison near Baghdad – may reflect an important trend in the *neo-liberalization* of war/peace which, whilst evidently designed as a means of reducing public accountability and increasing efficiency of military operations, may yet serve to undermine American geopolitical entrenchments in unexpected ways. Investigating the complexly intertwined geographies of war and peace provides an important venue for critically examining such changes as the grounds shift beneath our feet, and for exploring their implications.

SUMMARY

- It is important to raise questions about the meaning of peace in any geographical examination of war.

- Conditions of peace frequently serve as extensions of war.

- War is now often premised on the extension of secured peace.

CODA

Still a few days before the American bombing of Afghanistan was initiated on 7 October 2001, I was invited to participate on a panel at my university, amongst four faculty from the social sciences and history, addressing the question of 'What kind of US response will make us most secure?'[3] Like many university campuses across the USA at the time, mine had been the site of vigils, demonstrations, teach-ins and debates in the month following the September 11th attacks, and so it was, presumably, a talk that I had given at one of these events about the need to develop alternative politics and practices to those of a 'war on terrorism', including international policing and institutions of justice, that led to my inclusion on the panel. In the event, however, my co-panellists (for various reasons) had little desire to consider an international justice regime not yet in existence as an answer to the question of security, nor to engage in a conversation about what relevant political issues might be opened up by evaluating differences between institutions of war and those of justice in what suddenly seemed, at the time, such a different world. Most obviously, though, in war civilian casualties are more or less expected and thus acceptable, whereas in the everyday work of policing and law enforcement they are in principle *not*. Yet when I raised the question of repercussions of civilian deaths in Afghanistan on other aspects of the problem of security and terrorism that our panel was supposed to address, it provoked a sharp exchange with one interlocutor:

> '*Why do you assume that striking Afghanistan will kill a lot of people?*'
>
> '*Why do you assume it won't?*' I replied.
>
> '*Because we've already waited three weeks. It's quite clear that we are preparing a strike that is not going to be a lash out, but is going to be very carefully calibrated precisely because, it seems to me, the*

administration understands that, unlike traditional military actors, terrorists act in part to bait you into a response that will kill a lot of people. That's part of what terrorists want you to do. And I think the very fact we did not respond on the 12th is evidence of the fact that the administration understands that. "

Three weeks of planning, then, and the greatest horror of modern warfare – the killing of large numbers of innocents – would be prevented? Now that would be a new type of war.

Whilst my arguments perhaps gained little traction that day, I have continued to pose them to Geography students since, in lectures and now in this chapter, asking them (you) how it is that geographies of peace and security depend, or are made to depend, on geographies of war. This chapter has sought to investigate and explore this critical interrelationship chiefly in the context of the American-led 'global war on terrorism', a term that has itself been mobilized to support a wide range of activities, including new airport security practices in many parts of the world as well as the 'pre-emptive' invasion of Iraq. As we have seen, contemporary warfare is characteristically geographical in a number of important ways, from the changing location of battle deaths over time to the geopolitics of troop deployments and basing rights. It is also, since the end of the Cold War, characterized by a highly disproportionate geography of power in terms of overwhelming US military and technological capabilities, the geographical scales around which political authorization and consent for war are organized (and contested), and the changing nature of the inside/outside binary of secured peace that transnational terrorist networks seek to challenge. Only by grasping the geographies of war/peace as interrelated and mutually implicated, but still profoundly differentiated, can we understand how alternative political arrangements might be possible, what they might look like and what obstacles prevent their emergence.

DISCUSSION POINTS

1. What risks do war and terrorism pose to you as an individual? How do these compare to other risks that you encounter in your everyday life (for example, from toxic substances, traffic accidents or crime)?

2. How does the question of where you live condition the risks that you as an individual face? What does this tell us about the geography of war and peace?

3. Since the end of the Cold War in 1991, how has the USA changed in its projection of military power beyond its borders? What do you expect for the future?

4. What is the significance of the UK–US alliance to contemporary geographies of war and peace? And the significance of the European Union?

5. What are the different connotations of a 'war on terrorism' and an 'alliance against terrorism'?

NOTES

1. The neo-conservative or neo-con political movement in the USA, as geographer David Harvey (2003: 190) observes, seeks to impose 'a different agenda from that of neo-liberalism. Its primary objective is the establishment of and respect for order, both internally and upon the world stage. This implies strong leadership at the top and unwavering loyalty at the base, coupled with the construction of a hierarchy of power that is both secure and clear.'

2. Subtitle quoted from Alliez and Negri (2003, 110). Italics and ellipsis in original.

3. The event was moderated but had no live audience; instead the discussion was audio-taped, transcribed, edited and published in abridged form in the university's newspaper and unabridged on the internet.

FURTHER READING

Flint, C. (ed.) (2004) *The geography of war and peace: from death camps to diplomats.* **Oxford and New York: Oxford University Press.**

A recent edited volume that explores the changing political geographical dimensions of war and peace from a number of different perspectives and scales, with case studies that include Afghanistan, Bosnia-Herzegovina, Israel and Palestine, and Northern Ireland.

Harvey, D. (2003) *The new imperialism.* **Oxford and New York: Oxford University Press.**

Offers a Marxist argument that traces the historical and geographical roots of contemporary American imperialism as global 'accumulation by dispossession'.

Forum (2001) *Arab World Geographer,* 4(2): 77–103.

Antipode (2003), 35(5): 839–97.

The post-9/11 environment of global security, terror and counter-terror has been the subject of much commentary and debate amongst geographers. The above texts are just two examples.

http://www.iwpr.net

The website of the London-based Institute for War & Peace Reporting is well worth visiting for war coverage that encourages and facilitates locally produced representations of ongoing conflicts in Central Asia, the Middle East, Africa, the Caucasus and the Balkans.

CHAPTER 42
GLOBALIZATION AND PROTEST

Jane Wills

INTRODUCTION

We live in a world in which there is a tremendous amount of contact and exchange across geographical borders. The goods we buy and consume are likely to be produced by workers many thousands of miles away working for a transnational corporation based outside the UK; the food we eat is likely to consist of a wide variety of different 'national' dishes, being airlifted to our shores from a galaxy of different locations; and our cultural references will probably be music, films, books and art from many different locations. Transport and communication technologies, combined with political efforts to erode existing barriers to transnational investment and trade, have stimulated the set of changes that we now call globalization. Whilst such transnational exchange is not new (as is particularly evident in the chapters looking at colonialism and post-colonialism in this book for example), contemporary globalization is characterized by an extension and deepening of connections across space. International links stretch wider and with more local intensity than has been the case in the past. As is already clear from many of the chapters in this book (such as those looking at the local–global, development and post-development, finance, production, consumption and culture), understanding globalization is critical to making sense of our contemporary world. Transnational relationships and the particular model of political-economy that has driven such changes are now integral to understanding economy, politics and culture right across the world. This chapter explores what is meant by globalization, and then goes on to look at the socio-political protest movement that has grown up to contest various aspects of globalization.

Globalization

the economic, political, social and cultural processes whereby: (a) places across the globe are increasingly interconnected; (b) social relations and economic transactions increasingly occur at the intercontinental scale (*see* TRANSNATIONAL); and (c) the globe itself comes to be a recognizable geographical entity. As such, globalization does not mean everywhere in the world becomes the same. Nor is it an entirely even process; different places are differently connected into the world and view that world from different perspectives. Globalization has been occurring for several hundred years, but in the contemporary world the scale and extent of social, political and economic interpenetration appears to be qualitatively different to international networks in the past.

GLOBALIZATION

The word globalization is often used as a 'catch-all' phrase to describe a wide variety of things, all of which concern the acceleration of exchange across geographical borders. People use the term to describe changes in the way goods and services are produced and delivered; the ways in which political ideas and practices are translated across space; and the nature of cultural production and consumption (for a rich account of globalization in all its diversity see Held *et al.*, 1999). As the World Bank puts it: 'Globalisation can be summarized as the global circulation of goods, services and capital but also of information, ideas and people' (cited in Perrons, 2004: 1). Many have also highlighted the way in which globalization connects increasing numbers of people across national borders, even if they never meet face to face. As the UNDP (1999: 1) suggests, 'Globalisation is not new, but the present era has distinctive features. Shrinking space, shrinking time and disappearing borders are linking people's lives more deeply, more intensely, more immediately than

Time–space compression

coined by the Geographer David Harvey, this phrase has been more widely used to express (a) the transformations in TEMPORALITY and SPATIALITY produced in a world of ever more rapid turnover and ever quicker forms of communication; and (b) the subjective experience of these changes.

ever before.' New technologies have facilitated this contact across geographical space, compressing the time it takes to transmit goods, ideas and people across space in what David Harvey has called time–space compression.

Although globalization involves much more than economic activity, the development and impact of transnational corporations (TNCs) provides a good illustration of the types of changes involved in the shift towards a more globalized world. There are now at least 60,000 TNCs, directly employing many millions of workers across the world (see Figs 42.1 and 42.2). As is evident from Figure 42.1, the number of such global companies has increased dramatically during the twentieth century, and although most have their roots in Europe and North America, there are growing numbers that originate in South America and South East Asia. In the early days, such companies tended to make direct investments in resource extraction or productive capacity outside their home country but, increasingly, they operate through subcontracted relationships, buying the goods and services they require from independent suppliers. This allows large companies to be more flexible in the production and management of goods, and gives them greater opportunity to lever economic advantages by promoting competition between suppliers, and to benefit from geographical differences in production costs and state legislation. This approach also cuts down on the risks borne by large companies as they rely on their suppliers to employ staff, to meet production deadlines and to manage the logistics of getting the products to market on time.

This organizational structure is sometimes called a global commodity chain or a global production network and, as indicated in Figure 42.3, it increases pressure on those furthest down the supply chain. Leading TNCs have tended to retain direct control of their product development, marketing and brand management, whilst outsourcing production so that they can operate at the global scale without losing the flexibility, cost and risk advantages they need to make the most profit they can (see Klein, 2000). Thus, a branded garment that you buy in the shops is likely to have been made by an independent supplier in a low-cost location – often in the developing world – that, in turn, might have cut costs by further outsourcing the work to small local workshops and homeworkers (see Hale and Wills, 2005; Oxfam, 2004).

As an example, Figure 42.4 illustrates the complex global relations involved in the production of a pair of Lee Cooper jeans. In this case, a pair of jeans that were bought in Ipswich, Suffolk, were sewn at a factory in Tunisia and then shipped to the UK. In addition, however, Lee Cooper was able to source the components involved in producing each pair of jeans – such as the cotton, denim, dyes, thread and zips – from the most competitive and suitable suppliers worldwide. As a result, the jeans were the product of a complex geography of commodity movements and labour that spanned the world. Such global networks lie behind most of the goods we consume, each having its own particular impact on place and on the geographical relationships forged across space (for a good example of geographical work in this field, see Cook, 2004).

Capitalism

an economic system in which the production and distribution of goods is organized around the profit motive (*see* CAPITAL ACCUMULATION) and characterized by marked inequalities in the social division of work and wealth between private owners of the materials and tools of production (capital) and those who work for them to make a living (labour) (*see* CLASS).

This model of capitalism has prompted the scholar Manuel Castells to argue that we live in a network society – one in which capitalism depends

1914

☐ Hong Kong
☐ Singapore

3,077 total parent corporations

1994

▨ Hong Kong
☐ Singapore

39,463 total parent corporations

2000

▨ Hong Kong
☐ Singapore

63,321 total parent corporations

☐ 1–100
☐ 100–500
▨ 500–1,000
▨ 1,000–2,000
▨ 2,000–5,000
■ 7,000–9,500
☐ No parent companies

FIGURE 42.1
Number of multinational corporations
1914–2000 (Parent companies by country)
Source: Gabel and Bruner (2003: 31)

Employment by multinational corporations 1975–98

Source: Gabel and Bruner (2003: 122)

FIGURE 42.2

on information that travels via computer technology along networks orchestrated at global dimensions (see Castells, 1996). As we have seen, the capacity of informational networks allows TNCs to access new production locations and new markets, co-ordinating activity across vast geographical distance. Such developments have a profound impact on national economies by affecting patterns of economic investment, trade, employment, tax revenues and prices; on the capacity

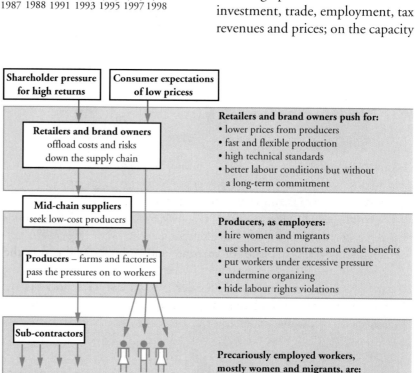

FIGURE 42.3
Supply chain pressures create precarious employment

Source: Oxfam (2004: 35)

of national political institutions, which are less able to control capital movements and economic activity than they were in the past; and on the way in which people experience and make sense of their lives. Yet in evaluating the development and impact of globalization, it is important to remember that this model of capitalism is the product of very particular circumstances and very conscious political choices that have been made by those in charge of key institutions over the past 30 years. The end of the post-war boom in western economies from the early 1970s, the collapse of the Soviet bloc in the 1990s and political experiments in Britain and the

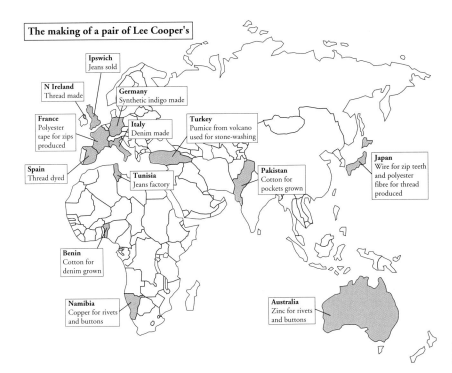

The making of a pair of Lee Cooper's

Ipswich Jeans sold

N Ireland Thread made

Germany Synthetic indigo made

France Polyester tape for zips produced

Italy Denim made

Turkey Pumice from volcano used for stone-washing

Spain Thread dyed

Tunisia Jeans factory

Pakistan Cotton for pockets grown

Japan Wire for zip teeth and polyester fibre for thread produced

Benin Cotton for denim grown

Namibia Copper for rivets and buttons

Australia Zinc for rivets and buttons

FIGURE 42.4
Source: Abrams and Anstill (2001)

USA during the 1980s and 1990s, all contributed to the development of what is now known as neo-liberal ideology by those in key positions of power. Adherence to neo-liberal political economy moved from the fringe to the mainstream of policy-making in a very short space of time, coming to create much of what we now call globalization. Proselytizing 'free' trade, flexible labour, a reduced role for the state and active individualism, the prophets of neo-liberalism made it easier for capital to move, for governments to justify reduced intervention in social standards and welfare, and for the emphasis to be placed on the individual to make their own way in the world (see Peck and Tickell, 2002). Since the 1980s, such policy ideas have come to influence organizations like the World Trade Organization (WTO), International Monetary Fund (IMF) and World Bank, and their prescriptions for change, rolling out neo-liberalism to the developing world.

Those politicians, business leaders and academics who have promoted the neo-liberal model of globalization have suggested that it provides the only route to development. In a global version of the argument for 'trickle-down', they have argued that the increased economic investment and growth that results from the erosion of national barriers will create increased taxation revenue, new employment opportunities and further development for the country concerned. As Paul Krugman (in Gabel and Bruner, 2003: 16; see also Wolf, 1997, Legrain, 2002, and Fig. 42.5) has declared:

> The raw fact is that every successful example of economic development this past century – every case of a poor nation that worked its way up to a more or less decent, or at least dramatically better, standard of living – has taken place via globalization; that is, by producing for the world market rather than for self-sufficiency.

Neo-liberalism, neo-liberal

pertaining to an economic doctrine that favours free markets, the deregulation of national economies, decentralization and the privatization of previously state-owned enterprises (e.g. education, health). A doctrine that, in practice, favours the interests of the powerful (e.g. TRANSNATIONAL CORPORATIONS) against the less powerful (e.g. peasants) within societies.

In contrast, critics of neo-liberal globalization question the extent to which taxes are paid by transnational corporations, the nature of the employment created, the impact of insecure work and the low wages paid. Moreover, they argue that this model of globalization has fuelled a damaging increase in inequality as the rich have got richer on the backs of the poor (see Fig. 42.5). Since the 1960s there has certainly been a striking increase in inequality and, as Table 42.1 indicates, the ratio of wealth held by the richest 20 per cent of the world population relative to the poorest 20 per cent has increased from 30:1 to 74:1 between 1960 and 1997. Although globalization will not be the sole reason for such inequality, not least because national regulation and culture remain critical to the distribution of wealth, it is clear that the economic growth associated with increased global investment and trade is not leading to reduced inequality within or between nation-states. Indeed, when 'freed' from any social obligations by the shift to neo-liberal forms of governance, those with wealth are able to invest and exploit it to better effect. Moreover, the power of those with capital to invest, particularly when reinforced by the lending policies of organizations such as the IMF, can intensify competitive pressures on nation-states to reduce social regulation and controls over the production of wealth. As the UNDP (1999: 2) put it: 'When the market goes too far in dominating social and political outcomes, the opportunities and rewards of globalization spread unequally and inequitably – concentrating power and wealth in a select group of people, nations and corporations, marginalizing the others.'

As a result, and despite the wealth that is generated, the world's

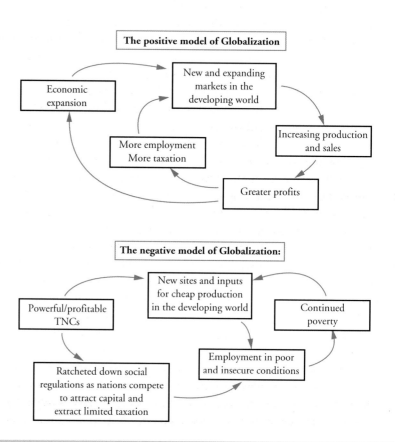

FIGURE 42.5

resources are now more unequally distributed than at any time in history. Statistics indicate that in 1999 the world's richest 200 people had the combined income of almost half (41 per cent) of the world's people. This means that a group of people who can be accommodated in a large lecture theatre on your university campus had the wealth of literally billions of their fellow human beings outside. Furthermore, in 2002 the richest 1 per cent of the global population (50 million households – a figure that may well include a certain number of Human Geography undergraduates and their teachers in Europe and North America) had as much income as the poorest 57 per cent of the global population (2.7 billion households). And as you read this, most of the world's people still have to live on less than $5 a day (see Perrons, 2004: 35).

Table 42.1 Share of global income over time

Year	Richest 20%	Poorest 20%	Ratio of Rich/Poor
1960	70.2	2.3	30:1
1970	73.9	2.3	32:1
1980	76.3	1.7	45:1
1989	82.7	1.4	59:1
1997	90.0	1.0	74:1

Source: Ellwood (2001: 101)

Of course, global integration has provided new opportunities to a small number of developing countries, but at the same time, a greater number of countries and people have experienced economic decline. Data indicate that although 40 countries had growth of more than 3 per cent between 1990 and 1999, as many as 55 countries saw real incomes decline (particularly those in Sub-Saharan Africa, and eastern Europe) (UNDP, 1999: 3). In practice, globalization produces 'winners' and 'losers' within and between different places. In the older industrialized countries, for example, unskilled manual workers have been undercut and forced out of employment by the relocation of capital, whereas those with informational skills have done rather well. Likewise, in developing countries, there are new job opportunities for relatively unskilled manual workers – many of them women – and some real advantages for entrepreneurs, but at the same time, processes of globalization mean that many jobs are vulnerable to relocation whilst subsistence economies are simultaneously being eroded by market relations, making it harder for the poor to survive. In short, globalization has benefited the rich and powerful but has often left the poor and disadvantaged lagging behind in all parts of the world.

To conclude this brief introduction, it is important to recognize that globalization is an economically and politically driven process that is taking place in an uneven world with geographically differentiated effects. Peter Dicken has pioneered research into the shift towards global production and trade, arguing that it is important to study these new networked relationships in the context of existing political structures, cultural practices and established patterns of everyday life (a complexity that he usefully represents diagrammatically; see Fig. 42.6). As he puts it:

> Globalization is … a complex syndrome of processes, in which actor-networks and macro-structures interconnect in extremely complex ways. We need to map, and to analyse in detail, concrete manifestations of these processes: for example, the production networks and the migration

networks, and the flows within and between them. Such processes are not only geographically grounded and embedded (in the sense of deriving some of their characteristics and resources from place-specific contexts), but they also generate geographically specific, highly uneven, concrete outcomes. "

(Dicken, 2004a: 16)

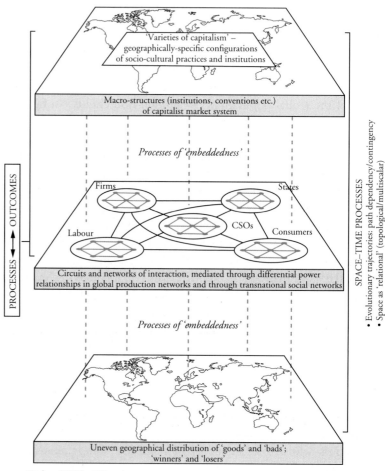

FIGURE 42.6   Source: Dicken (2004a: 10)

SUMMARY

- Although such transnational developments are not new, globalization means the widening and deepening of relationships across national borders, involving economic, political and cultural relations and change.

- Globalization has been stimulated by new information technologies that allow the development of networked capitalism in conjunction with a shift towards neo-liberal policy that promotes 'free' trade and a reduced role for the state. As such, what we call globalization is really neo-liberal globalization and it has been both economically and politically driven.

- Globalization is what Peter Dicken calls a 'syndrome of processes' and comprises networks operating across prevailing macro-economic, political and socio-cultural structures and systems.

- The effects of globalization are uneven, both within and between places: whilst some have benefited, most have not, and inequality continues to rise.

This argument highlights the importance of geography to globalization. The characteristics of global networks depend upon the way in which they are geographically embedded and their impact is differentiated by place. Moreover, as we will see in the following section, geography is also important in resisting aspects of contemporary globalization.

PROTEST

In spring 1999 a new political movement had its 'coming-out party' on the streets of Seattle, USA (Klein, 2002: 3). Apparently appearing from nowhere, a coalition of various groups, famously including 'teamsters and turtles' (labour and environmental activists; see Fig. 42.7), gathered to protest about the trade rules being applied and renegotiated by the WTO. Coming from a range of different perspectives, including development activists, trades unionists, feminists, human rights activists and environmentalists, thousands of campaigners found common ground in their opposition to global corporations and the 'policies that give them free reign' (Klein, 2000: 338). This protest has been called the anti-globalization movement in the media, but for many participants it is neo-liberal policy (including unfair trade rules, the erosion of state welfare provision, privatization, anti-trades union practices and restrictions on the free movement of people) and corporate power (the might of TNCs, their enclosures and their impact on the environment) that are the real cause for concern. As such, many now refer to this emerging alliance of different groups and interests as the global justice movement. In reality, most participants in the movement welcome increased transnational integration, but not of a neo-liberal hue.

FIGURE 42.7
'Teamsters and Turtles': protesting against neo-liberal globalization, Seattle, USA, 1999.
Credit: Patrick Hagerty/Corbis SYGMA

This new global justice movement has important antecedents in a number of political developments during the 1980s and 1990s. Most obviously, it has grown because the 'old' ways of doing politics no longer sufficed. In the face of neo-liberal globalization, people were instinctively responding to developments defensively. Rather than linking struggles together, there was a tendency to campaign on single issues and to try and defend a communal or cultural identity in the face of rapid change from 'outside'. Examples include the way some labour activists tried to prevent capital moving abroad and to defend home-based TNCs against those based abroad or to resist privatization (Figure 42.8 illustrates this type of protest in the challenge that was made to the privatization of naval bases in the UK); the way some sections of the trades union movement sought to develop partnerships with national capital in the hope that this would keep jobs in place (see Moody, 1997); and the way some have sought refuge in

FIGURE 42.8
Challenging privatization: the naval bases in the UK. Credit: P.A. Photos

a 'pure' national and/or religious culture, most clearly demonstrated by the growth of the British National Party (BNP) in the UK but also in the popularity of fundamentalist religious groups (see Giddens, 1999).[1] Such protest has proved largely futile in protecting people from the impact of globalization. National legislatures have not been willing to intervene and protect jobs, capital will not be tied down to place unless it makes business sense, and racial and religious purity flies in the face of a world that is increasingly integrated and diverse. In this context, out of necessity, some political activists began to develop other ideas, drawing in particular on some of the decentralized networking traditions of the feminist, environmentalist and anarchist movements.

As a counter to capitalist networks, these political activists began to grasp the opportunities of the internet to share ideas, build links and co-ordinate activity at the international scale. Rather than relying on the national or local state to defend and advance their interests as had been done in the past, activists began to create transnational networks and alliances around the need for solidarity in the face of neo-liberal global reform. Early initiatives in this vein included the groups of NGOs that held meetings at various UN conferences during the 1980s; the trades unionists who began to develop their own 'bottom-up' networks around particular campaigns; and the inspiration provided by the Zapatista uprising in Chiapas, Mexico, from 1994 (Brecher *et al.*, 2000; Waterman and Wills, 2002; see box). As De Angelis (2000; see Table 42.2) argues in counterposing this emerging new internationalism with that practised by 'old' social movements in the

Table 42.2 A comparison between 'old' and 'new' internationalisms

	Relation between national and international struggles	Relation between labour movement and other movements
'Old' internationalism (nineteenth and twentieth centuries)	International dimension of struggle is instrumental to the national dimension	They are distinct movements that involve the subordination of others to the labour movement (the working class is seen as the vanguard of change)
'New' internationalism (twenty-first century?)	National and international distinctions lose their sharpness; the national (as well as the 'regional', 'local', etc.) is seen as a moment in the global and vice-versa	The aim is to build alliances/bridges between movements

Source: adapted from De Angelis (2000: 11)

THE ZAPATISTA UPRISING IN CHIAPAS, MEXICO (1994), AND ITS INFLUENCE ON THE GLOBAL JUSTICE MOVEMENT

The Zapatista National Liberation Army (EZLN) responded to the impact of neo-liberal policy stemming from the Mexican government and the North America Free Trade Agreement (NAFTA) by rising up against the Mexican army in the state of Chiapas in Mexico on 1 January 1994 (the day that the NAFTA agreement came into effect). The movement sought to resist the further marginalization and immizeration of the local population, but rather than being a liberation struggle in the old vein, this movement became a model for others to follow. Even though they have their own battles to win with the Mexican government, the Zapatistas became emblematic of a new approach to protest. Rather than simply promote their own cause, they have tried to speak to all those negatively affected or disenchanted with neo-liberal globalization, using the internet to promote a new way to resist.

As Naomi Klein (2001: 11) puts it:

" *In Canada, where I'm from, indigenous uprising is always symbolized by a blockade: a physical barrier to stop the golf course from being built on a native burial site, to block the construction of a hydroelectric dam or to keep an old growth forest from being logged. The Zapatista uprising was a new way to protect land and culture: rather than locking out the world, the Zapatistas flung open the doors and invited the world inside. Chiapas was transformed, despite its poverty, despite being under constant military siege, into a global gathering place for activists, intellectuals, and indigenous groups.* "

In 1996 they hosted the first Encuentro (meeting) for Humanity and Against Neo-Liberalism and at least 3000 people attended from around the world. These meetings were hugely significant for the evolution of the movement for global justice; a number of participants set up a new network called People's Global Action (PGA), many of those early participants went on to lead the protest that erupted on the streets of Seattle, and the Zapatistas' model of decentralized organization, liberation from the state and direct action has been emulated elsewhere (for more on the PGA, see Routledge, 2003b). In his opening remarks to that first Inter-continental Encuentro Subcommandante Marcos, the unnamed leader of the Zapatistas, declared:

Brothers and sisters of Asia, Africa, Oceania, Europe and America,
Welcome to the mountains of the Mexican Southeast.
Let us introduce ourselves.
We are the Zapatista National Liberation Army.
For 10 years, we lived in these mountains, preparing to fight a war.
In these mountains, we built an army.
Below, in the cities and plantations, we did not exist.
Our lives were worth less than those of machines or animals.
We were like stones, weeds in the road.
We were silenced.
We were faceless.
We were nameless.
We had no future.
We did not exist.
For the powers that be, known internationally by the term 'neo-liberalism', we did not count, we did not produce, we did not buy, we did not sell.
…
Brothers and sisters:
We have invited you to this meeting to seek for and find yourselves and us.
You have all touched our hearts, and you can see we are not special.
You can see we are simple and ordinary men and women.
You can see we are the rebellious mirror that wants to be a pane of glass and break.
You can see we are who we are so we can stop being who we are to become the you, who we are.
We are the Zapatistas.

(Cited in Klein, 2001: 16)

past, activists came to see the importance of a global perspective and the need to build alliances between equals at the international scale.

Over time, the development of this new form of alliance building at the international level and successful popular protests such as that held in Seattle in 1999 and Cancun, Mexico, in 2003 have shifted the debate about globalization. Organizations like the WTO now acknowledge the need for greater equity in the trade rules applied to the developing world; many TNCs have adopted codes of conduct that commit them to minimal labour and environmental standards along their corporate chains; and the fair trade movement continues to grow as consumers get behind the campaign. In this context, the global justice movement has gained momentum and begun to use social forums at global and regional scales as a way to take stock, share ideas and co-ordinate activity and protest events. As a counter to the World Economic Forum, an annual meeting of political and corporate leaders in Davos, Switzerland, the first World Social Forum (WSF) was held in Porto Allegre, Brazil, in January 2001. Held under the slogan 'Another World is Possible', increasingly large social forums (up to 120,000 attended the fourth WSF in Mumbai, India, in January 2004, for example) have become 'a means for social movement activists from around the world to express their emergence and attempted convergence as a global movement' (Anderson, 2003: 197; see also Waterman, 2002, and Fig. 42.9).

As might be expected, these forums contain a wide range of political opinion, ranging from those who seek to regulate capitalism more tightly – in some form of transnational democratic governance – to those who promote revolution and the development of some form of socialist or non-capitalist society (and many who are somewhere in between such extremes, see Callinicos, 2003; Monbiot, 2003; Wainwright, 2003). Held and McGrew (2002: 106–15) distinguish between reformists, nationalists (who seek to defend the role and power of the nation-state) and grassroots radicals in the movement. All are invited to take part in the debate, which whilst ideological, does not promote any one particular ideological position: there is a common adversary, but no shared vision of alternatives to neo-liberal globalization. The emphasis has been on allowing space for everyone who wants to take part, and to focus on what is common rather than the issues that divide.

A number of geographers are beginning to engage with and evaluate this new movement, its geographical and institutional manifestations, and its significance for academic theory and political practice (Featherstone, 2003; Fisher and Ponniah, 2003; Ponniah, 2004; Routledge, 2003b). It can be argued that successful protest demands a heightened sense of geography, an understanding of the way in which local politics can challenge the global and an ability to map the arteries of neo-liberal globalization in order to identify key nodes for intervention and action. As Massey (2004: 11) has recently argued:

> [D]ifferent places are of course constructed as various kinds of nodes within globalization; they each have distinct positions within the wider power-geometry of the global. In consequence, both the possibilities for intervention in (the degree of purchase upon), and the

ANOTHER WORLD IS POSSIBLE

FOR GLOBAL JUSTICE

european social forum
14–17 October 2004, London ✳ www.fse-esf.org
stop the war ✳ no to racism ✳ end privatisation

FIGURE 42.9
The European Social Forum, London, 2004

nature of the potential political relationships to (including the degree and nature of responsibility for) these wider constitutive relations will also vary. 〞

Developing political strategy thus depends on some analysis of this geographical differentiation of the local in the global. Moreover, it requires that political activists understand the way in which globalization is rooted in place so that the local can be defended and celebrated in a progressive rather than a conservative way (Ainger *et al.*, 2004; Gibson-Graham, 2002). Thus far, the movement for global justice has created new opportunities for having this debate, for testing out strategies and tactics, but as yet it is difficult to see how things will develop in future. Charting the development and significance of the global justice movement is a task for future research.

SUMMARY

- If we see contemporary globalization as being made by a particular form of politics in particular circumstances, it allows us to consider making it in other ways too. Neo-liberal globalization can become a target for protest.

- During the 1990s a new movement for global justice has emerged to contest many aspects of globalization, and although there is a common adversary, the movement is built on alliances and has no shared vision of alternatives to neo-liberal globalization.

- This new movement uses the internet to develop alternative networks to share ideas and co-ordinate protest. The movement has also started to use global and regional social forums as points of convergence, providing spaces for debate and the development of political action.

- Geographically, the movement raises some very important questions. Not least, the way in which the politics of local action and globalization interrelate, the way the new spaces of the global protest movement can be used and the way struggles can be linked across space.

CONCLUSION

This chapter has examined the forces of globalization, and has shown that this somewhat catch-all term covers a host of complex processes. It has tried to uncover some of these key processes, and has pointed out how economic and political aspects of globalization are often entwined – and indeed how they often reinforce each other. But the chapter has also shown how the processes of globalization are not inevitable and predetermined. We have witnessed the recent emergence of a range of protest groups fighting to contest the dominant neo-liberal agenda. These groups are raising key issues that geography is just beginning to engage with – not least the critical question of how the local and the global can be connected. The familiar activist phrase 'Think globally, act locally' has perhaps more resonance than ever in the current era of globalization.

DISCUSSION POINTS

1. What is new about contemporary globalization?
2. What is the relationship between neo-liberal politics and globalization?
3. Who are the winners and losers of globalization?
4. Why does geography matter to the movement for global justice?
5. What are the political prospects of the movement against neo-liberal globalization and for global justice?

NOTE

1. For a further elaboration on these arguments it is useful to explore David Harvey's (1996) suggestion that these political responses represent a militant particularism, a defensive response to change, which he contrasts with the universalism that is necessary to effect progressive reform. Similarly, Castells (1997) argues that such politics is based on 'resistance' identities and to alter the direction of global neo-liberalism it is necessary to turn such struggles into 'project' identities that look out to form links with others fighting for change. It is also important to note that many popular political protests remain purely defensive today (and for a useful debate about this in relation to the differences between British and French rural politics, see Ainger et al., 2004).

FURTHER READING

Dicken, P. (2003) *Global shift: reshaping the global economic map in the twenty-first century* **(4th edn). London: Sage.**

This text offers a rich account of economic globalization.

Held, D., McGrew, A., Goldblatt, D. and Perraton, J. (1999) *Global transformations: politics, economics and culture.* **Cambridge: Polity.**

A book that provides a wealth of data on all aspects of globalization, its history and implications.

Monbiot, G. (2003) *The age of consent: a manifesto for a new world order.* **London: Flamingo.**

There is a growing body of literature that explores the global justice movement. This is an excellent place to start.

In the geographical literature, the papers published in the *Transactions of the Institute of British Geographers* (2003) by David Featherstone and Paul Routledge listed in the Bibliography at the end of the book are very useful, and highlight the type of research that geographers are starting to do.

CHAPTER 43
WHO CARES?

Clive Barnett

INTRODUCTION: WHO CARES?

This chapter examines a range of philosophical and social-scientific issues that fall under the rubric of 'care'. The theme of care raises questions about how the needs of people are defined, and how responsibility for meeting those needs is distributed between different social actors. Care is often thought of as a positive value that designates values of co-operation, sociability and collective responsibility. Thus, it is easily aligned on one side of a set of evaluative oppositions between individual and society, autonomy versus community, or rights and responsibilities. Care easily becomes associated with the latter terms in each of these pairs, but this tends to simplify what is in fact a much more complicated set of relationships. By keeping in mind the question 'Who cares?', this chapter will focus attention on the contested process of defining the nature and scope of needs, and of defining where obligations to meet needs should fall.

Care has become an important topic of research in Human Geography (see Conradson, 2003; Smith, 2005; Staeheli and Brown, 2003). There are three ways in which questions of care are connected to issues of space, place and scale. First, there is a tendency in discussions of care to suggest that the value of caring is necessarily partial – that it follows from intimate concerns for concrete others, rather than an abstract concern for others in general. This implies that care is associated with spatial relations of proximity, and makes it very difficult to imagine how care can be extended over spatial distance. Second, geographers have recognized that caring tends to take place in particular spatial locations – in the home, at school, in hospitals. Indeed, spaces of care are often sequestered away from the spaces of ordinary life, and this gives the impression that care is something that only special classes of vulnerable people – children, the sick, the elderly, and so on – are in need of. Third, once one recognizes the diversity of caring practices, then the geography of care can be seen to involve not only specific practices in particular locations, but also the co-ordination of these specific practices into spatially and temporally complex routines of care. Each of these geographical dimensions is dealt with in this chapter. The chapter is divided into three main sections. In 'The value of care', feminist arguments about a so-called 'ethic of care' are discussed, with particular attention given to the extent to which the value of care is at odds with the value of justice. In 'Spaces of care', the chapter considers a more complex account of the different practices that go to make up care, and then considers how the geographies of the caring practices can usefully be analysed using the concept of 'carescapes'. In 'Care unbound', the chapter considers the extent to which values of care can be extended across space and to strangers. The chapter then concludes with a reflection on the main points covered.

Feminism

a series of perspectives, which together draw on theoretical and political accounts of the oppression of women in society to suggest how GENDER relations and Human Geography are interconnected (*see also* PATRIARCHY).

THE VALUE OF CARE

A feminine ethic of care?

One place to start our consideration of care is by looking at a set of debates amongst feminist social theorists and philosophers on the moral significance of care. This will help us clarify what is at stake in contested definitions of the scope and location of responsibilities to provide care. Feminist thinkers have been at the forefront of promoting the value of care, or what is often called an ethic of care. An ethic of care is often contrasted with the supposedly abstract principles of justice and autonomy. The idea of an ethic of care is most closely associated with the work of Carol Gilligan (1982). There are, she suggested, two ways of thinking about the self in relationship with others (Gilligan, 1986). One of these ways supposes a separate and autonomous individual, and thinks about responsibility in terms of a commitment to abstract obligations. The other supposes 'a psychology of love', or what is sometimes called a 'relational' notion of the self. This view sees the self as thoroughly interdependent, and is rooted in the experiences of attachment and vulnerability, which are in turn rooted in the parent/child relationship (1986: 282). Drawing on extensive empirical work on the ways in which men and women, and boys and girls, discuss notions of moral responsibility, Gilligan argued that these two moral dispositions – of a self defined through separation, and of a self defined through connection – were fundamentally incompatible (1982: 35). She further argued that women were inclined towards thinking and acting in relation to the injunction to care, whilst men were inclined to accord highest value to respecting the rights of others, a principle of non-interference (1982: 100). Gilligan presented an ethic of care (based on values of attachment, engagement and intimacy) as more contextual than abstract notions of justice, rights and obligations. Through this comparative analysis of the way in which different social actors talk about morality, Gilligan arrived at a specific definition of care: 'the ideal of care is thus an activity of relationship, of seeing and responding to need, taking care of the world by sustaining the web of connection so that no one is left alone' (Gilligan, 1982: 62).

Gilligan's arguments concerning the tendency of men and women to display different moral dispositions towards their responsibility to others have been highly influential in social psychology, in educational theory and also in moral philosophy. The strongest and most important emphasis of Gilligan's work was on the ways in which people's moral dispositions emerged from the social roles in which they were involved. There are not naturally 'feminine' or 'masculine' dispositions to favour care or justice, but rather socially constructed dispositions. Nonetheless, despite this emphasis, this line of work does affirm the value of relations of care by reproducing an image of relationships of intimacy and attachment off-set from a realm of abstract, impersonal relations. In so doing, the value and meaning of care is, however inadvertently, associated with a longer tradition that conflates care with an apparently natural pattern of obligations whose model remains family relations. This inadvertent idealization of caring is evident in the work of the other key theorist of a feminine ethic of care, the educational theorist Nel Noddings. For Noddings, caring is about being focused on and absorbed by other people. It implies a sensitivity to the specificity of the needs of other people. On this definition, the value of care seems to mitigate against the extension of care to anonymous others. Accordingly, Noddings makes a distinction between 'caring for' others and 'caring about' others:

> " *I can 'care about' the starving children of Cambodia, send five dollars to hunger relief, and feel somewhat satisfied. I do not even know if my money went for food, or guns, or a new Cadillac for some politician. This is a poor second-cousin to caring. 'Caring about' always involves a certain benign neglect. One is attentive just so far. One assents with just so much enthusiasm. One acknowledges. One affirms. One contributes five dollars and goes on to other things.* "

(Noddings, 1984)

There is a clear spatial inflection to this distinction – caring-for is direct, up close and implies relationships of close proximity. Caring-about is, on the other hand, indirect, mediated and undertaken over distance. Caring-about others seems to be a little too easy. The strong implication of Noddings' rendition of this distinction is that caring-for is a more authentic disposition, based in direct and unmediated response to the cared-for and a detailed attentiveness to how caring is received by the cared-for. Caring-about, in contrast, can actually lead to self-righteousness, she suggests, because it can be undertaken out of a self-interested motivation to be seen to be a good person. This intrusion of self-interest into the scene of care is enough to disqualify this style of concern from being a form of authentic care.

FIGURE 43.1
A mother caring for her child. Credit: Wides & Holl/Getty Images

Justice and the relational value of care

The feminist political theorist Joan Tronto has challenged the association of caring with women's distinctive moral disposition that Gilligan and Noddings have been so important in establishing as an element of feminist thought. Tronto's argument (1987; 1993) is that this line of work, rooted in the empirical methodologies of social psychology and educational theory (which emphasize dynamics of interpersonal interaction), tends to ignore the wider political frameworks that help to determine which matters are defined as matters of public or private concern, and in turn help define these matters in distinctively gendered ways. In particular, Tronto challenges the tendency of this version of feminist theory to present caring as necessarily an intimate and direct practice rooted in specific relations of dependence and vulnerability. She suggests that the relationship between values of care and justice, interdependence and autonomy, need not be thought of as a clear and stark opposition. Rather, it is a matter of clarifying the appropriate contexts for the application of different normative principles in particular contexts: When is it appropriate to act out of partial concerns towards concrete others, and when is it appropriate to act out of impartial concerns towards others?

With respect to this question, it is worth considering the moral philosopher Bernard Williams' argument that the deepest loyalties of human life should not be expected to be governed by the sorts of justification that theories of morality tend to favour. Williams' (1981) famous example is that of whether a husband, faced with the choice of saving his own drowning wife or the life of a drowning stranger, could justify saving his wife. Williams suggests that the idea that the husband requires such a justification is, as he famously put it, 'one thought too many'. Williams' point here is that what it means to be a good person, to act ethically, exceeds the model of a person whose actions are only guided by adherence to moral principles or rules. Indeed, Williams' suggestion is that in lots of situations, an excessive concern with principle can actually get in the way of caring and acting out of concern for others.

Now this seems, on the face of it, to support the distinction between care and justice, contextual ethics and abstract judgement, discussed already. However, the idea that the value of care should be elevated over the abstract value of justice might easily turn into an excuse for caring only for a narrowly defined range of people – one's family or friends, or perhaps an exclusively defined set of members of the same ethnic or national group as oneself (see Smith, 2000: 97). A narrow delimitation of the scope of caring relations might be embedded into broader institutional structures such that the pursuit of the positive values of care by individuals can, nonetheless, lead to the reproduction of unjust and unequal outcomes. This indicates that the significance of Williams' argument is not that matters of principle or moral rules are never relevant, only that one needs to be sensitive to when it is appropriate to apply them, and when other 'virtues' such as compassion, generosity or care are more appropriate responses.

In short, the value of relationships of care cannot be separated from the judgements of social justice. If care is embedded in concrete networks of social relationships, from which its distinctive moral value is derived, then nonetheless there are situations in which acting according to this positive imperative might lead to outcomes that are difficult to square with our broader moral intuitions about what is right and good. If one were to think of relations of care – of loyalty, mutual obligation, friendship, reciprocal attachment and trust – as morally good in and of themselves, then this would imply thinking of organizations such as the Mafia or the Ku Klux Klan as the epitome of moral worth. In contrast, it would imply that sitting on a jury along with a series of anonymous fellow citizens and casting judgement on another person based solely on the evidence before you is somehow not a morally worthy practice; and nor is voting, which is a practice undertaken wholly in secret and, furthermore, one in which one's own actions are not tied to any expectation of reciprocal obligation (voters are not normally held responsible to the governments they elect into power). In short, judgement about the value of particular care relationships depends on the broader webs of social relationships and institutional structure into which these partial relationships are embedded.

We seem to have arrived at the point where we can see that impartial values of justice, equality and fairness, and partial values of care, concern and responsibility, might not be so easy to separate as the distinction between justice and care itself might imply. Nor do these two families of values map straightforwardly on to matters of public concern versus matters of personal or private concern. The relationships between care and justice, individualism and community, partial concern and impartial judgement, the private sphere and the public sphere are, in fact, ones of multiple and cross-cutting connections. The importance of the feminist literature on an ethics of care is that it points towards the embeddedness of moral dispositions in social practices and inter-subjective relations.

SUMMARY

- Taken in isolation, care can be seen to be an important, perhaps even necessary, element of any practice of moral or political judgement. But the key issue is to track the broader patterns of inter-subjective, social and institutional relations in which caring is learnt and practised.

- Practices of care are necessarily embedded in wider patterns of social, economic, political and cultural power.
- If the value of care lies in its being a set of partial relations, then this raises the problem of how to square the value of care with other values such as justice, altruism and humanitarianism.

SPACES OF CARE

Unpacking care

In the previous section, we saw that it is important to locate the analysis of care in wider patterns of social life, rather than idealize particular sorts of intimate social relationship as the essence of caring:

> ... caring is a process that can occur in a variety of institutions and settings. Care is found in the household, in services and goods sold in the market, in the workings of bureaucratic organizations in contemporary life. Care is not restricted to the traditional realm of mother's work, to welfare agencies, or to hired domestic servants but is found in all of these realms. Indeed, concerns about care permeate our daily lives, the institutions in the modern marketplace, the corridors of government. Because we tend to follow the traditional division of the world into public and private spheres and to think of caring as an aspect of private life, care is usually associated with activities of the household. As a result, caring is greatly undervalued in our culture – in the assumption that caring is somehow 'women's work' in perceptions of caring occupations, in the wages and salaries paid to workers engaged in provision of care, in the assumption that care is menial ...

(Tronto, 1998)

At its simplest, care has a dual set of associations and meanings: it refers to both a disposition to be concerned, and also to the actual practices that follow from these concerns (Tronto, 1993). There is a tendency in discussions of care to emphasize one of these dimensions over the other – to focus upon the emotional and intellectual capacities to be moved to care about other people or particular needs; or to focus on the actual work that goes into caring, and underplay the motivations that they are a response to in the first place. Fisher and Tronto (1990) argue that one can break caring down into four phases, each of which is associated with distinctive moral qualities and motivations.

1. *Caring about*: this involves becoming aware and paying attention to the needs of others; the key moral quality here is attentiveness, being able to acknowledge the needs in others as well as in oneself.
2. *Caring for*: this involves actually taking responsibility for meeting a need; this might involve organizing resources, paying for work, and so on. The key moral quality here is that of assuming responsibility.
3. *Caregiving*: this refers to the actual practices of meeting needs; it requires the effective performance of various tasks; the key moral quality here, then, is competence – this is important, given that a great deal of caregiving is undertaken in organized and organizational contexts, by nurses, doctors, teachers, policemen, social workers, and so on; it is important not to assume that questions of professionalism, competence and technical capability are somehow foreign to the values associated with care.
4. *Care receiving*: this refers to the response of the person, thing or group that receives caregiving; this requires the moral quality of responsiveness – responsiveness is not only about those who have received care, it also requires the attention of those doing caring work and those who have assumed responsibility; this, then, is the phase at which the process of caring generates further needs for care, further calls for attentiveness and further demands to assume responsibility.

This might seem like a linear sequence, but as should be clear from the fourth 'phase' in this list, there is in fact a constant interaction between each of these elements, so that care is better thought of as a negotiated process. It is important to keep in mind that integrating each of these aspects of care into any specific practice of caring is always likely to be a highly complex achievement. Above all, there are likely to be all sorts of moments of conflict embedded in this process of integration. Caring involves all sorts of practices – listening, feeding, giving advice, administering medicine, and so on – and it is hard work for all those involved, work that is both physical and emotional in character. The co-ordination of these four phases implies the integration of different sorts of actors (family members, friends, professionals, and so on) and the integration of a series of different spaces of social life (the home, certainly, but also the routines of paid work, and the geographies of modern living spaces, with their characteristic separation of home, work, school, and so on).

This four-phase model suggests that care is intimately related to questions of power. The relative power of a group is manifest in its ability

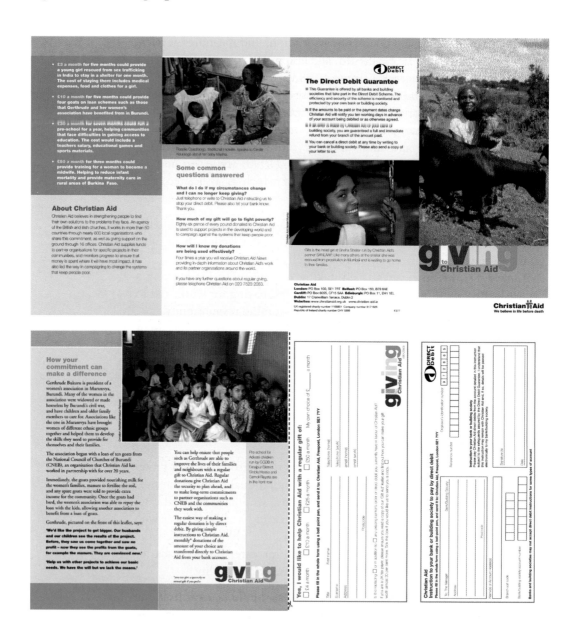

FIGURE 43.2
A direct debit form for Christian Aid.
Credit: Christian Aid

to have other people provide its own care needs. In turn, whilst some groups benefit from the care of others, it is also common for them to devalue care in general. The key to this devaluation of care, Tronto argues, is an unwillingness to acknowledge one's own vulnerability. This leads to particular groups being defined as particularly vulnerable – young children, or the elderly – and therefore as particularly in need of being cared for. This in turn reproduces the sense that 'normal' adults are free from the needs and vulnerabilities that call for care – that they are fully independent, so that care becomes associated with dependence. Tronto argues, in contrast, that care and the issues of vulnerability and need that it raises affect everyone – the ability to act autonomously depends on the carework of other people, in both personal spaces of intimate family relations as well as more public spaces such as schools or hospitals. Care, then, is not merely a private matter, and nor is it only concerned with 'moral' dispositions to be nice to other people. It is, rather, a fully public issue of political significance, not least because our understanding of what counts as a public issue or a political issue is defined in part by understandings of how caring should be distributed.

Tronto (1998) distinguishes between three possible relationships of care. First, care can occur amongst equals – between friends for example. Second, care can be provided by one set of people for others who could, in fact, provide this care for themselves. Third, some care is based on asymmetries of competence that are quite fundamental to the need and provision of care concerned, because the caregiver has some ability, knowledge or resource the care receiver does not. The most obvious example is the sorts of care that young children require. These are relationships of dependence, where the vulnerability to which care is a response is clear. In practice, of course, these three types of relationship are likely to be mixed up. So, for example, the needs arising out of the dependency of children on adults (the third sort of relationship above) can be distributed between parents and friends (a version of the first kind of relationship where care is provided amongst equals), but it is also likely to involve schoolteachers, doctors and various experts (that is, relationships of the second kind, where care is delegated) and, in some cases, this can involve significant inequalities. In such cases, wealthy or privileged groups are able to take advantage of socio-economic inequalities to displace caregiving on to poor or disadvantaged groups.

'Carescapes'

The topic of care has become an important focus of research in Human Geography. This is particularly the case in areas of the discipline where care has always been an implicit concern – for example, in medical geography or in geographies of housing, or more broadly in areas of research interested in changing patterns of welfare provision. In these sorts of fields, the set of relationships between caring about, caring for, caregiving and care receiving are central to understanding the history and contemporary transformation of, for example, mental healthcare provision, or changing patterns of housing tenure and housing need, or changing policies towards the welfare entitlements of children, the unemployed or the elderly.

In order to understand the ways in which relations of care are related to questions of space and time, McKie *et al.* (2002) develop the notion of carescapes. If care involves the co-ordination of a complex variety of tasks undertaken by a range of different individual and collective actors, then the idea of carescapes adds an appreciation that care therefore involves the co-ordination of the different spaces and different times in and across which these tasks and actors are distributed. Taking childcare as their example, these researchers point out that childcare in western societies involves the combination of the spaces of the family home (where lots of informal and unpaid caring for children, especially young children, takes place), with the public spaces of paid work, schools, hospitals and nurseries. People therefore develop distinctive carescapes in order to combine these different spatial and temporal patterns, and this involves a complex negotiation and renegotiation of the schedules of everyday routines such as going to work, doing the shopping, picking kids up from

FIGURE 43.3
Parents escorting their children to school.
Credit: John Birdsall

Temporality

socially produced time. This term is used by Human Geographers to emphasize how time is socially constructed and experienced, rather than being an innate backdrop to social life (*see also* SOCIAL CONSTRUCTION).

school, and so on. The development of particular carescapes is neither just a simple matter of connecting the private sphere of the home to the public sphere of the workplace, however. Nor is it just a matter of isolated parents juggling their responsibilities to their own children. Rather, the sequencing and co-ordination of paid work and care takes place in a variety of spaces and often involves a range of actors, including 'childminders, friend's homes, school, local shops, parks, doctors, regional shopping centres, leisure centres and so on' (McKie *et al.*, 2002: 912).

An important feature of the idea of carescapes is not just the emphasis on the geographies of caring, but on the connection between these routine everyday geographies and the complex temporalities of caring. The responsibilities of caring involve at least three different temporalities:

> *the temporality of the human life course with its different and differing dependencies (childhood, pregnancy, illness, old age and interaction with family and friends); the temporality of paid work career paths (within the context of regional, national and global economies) and the temporality of the daily routines of the people and institutions with whom a person habitually interacts (education, welfare, health and training).*

(McKie *et al.*, 2002: 905)

This emphasis on the longer-term temporality of the life course and of careers helps to underscore the complex task of developing and sustaining carescapes. This involves not only the establishment of everyday routines of co-ordination, but must also be able to adjust to various 'crisis' situations – sudden illness, cars that won't start, trips away from home – as well as shifts in the requirements of care as, for example, children grow up and move schools, or when parents lose jobs, change careers, split up or divorce, and so on.

SUMMARY

- Care is far from a private matter, either in the sense that practices of care are contained only in spaces of the home and the family, or in the sense that they are not shaped by and impact upon public issues of employment, social policy and welfare provision.

- The ways in which care is organized are quite fundamental in shaping social understandings of what is a public issue and what is a private issue – that is, with defining the nature of needs and where the burdens for meeting them fall.

CARE UNBOUND

The paradox of care

The notion of carescapes pinpoints the importance of thinking through the different locations where care takes place. I want now to turn to the question of how the impulse or imperative to care is motivated – to the question of how caring about others arises in the first place. We have already seen that for Noddings, caring-about was considered secondary and derivative of a more immediate, authentic form of *caring-for*. It is easy to assume that authentic care is necessarily partial – that it is care for one's 'nearest and dearest' that is automatically expected and offered, and in turn it is necessarily up-close-and-personal, based on relations of proximity and familiarity. In turn, *caring-about* would appear to be less authentic because it is assumed to be more passive, and in turn therefore implies a more distanced relationship. The implicit assumption in Noddings' distinction is that as care is extended to more people over greater distance, the degree of authenticity and involvement is steadily diluted.

The simplistic distinction between 'authentic' care and more diluted forms of care, and the assumed association of these two with relations of proximity and of distance respectively, is misleading because it leads us to ignore the problems of co-ordination that the idea of carescapes highlights. It also makes it very difficult to think about the forms of care that might be extended to people one does not know or who might be a long way away as anything but pale imitations of proper forms of care. If one opposes caring-for to caring-about, then authentic care is assumed to be really about relationships with people one is personally involved with in a quite intense fashion. This leaves the question of how to respond to the needs of strangers or to people who live somewhere else a difficult one to conceptualize.

The emphasis on the partiality of care is an important reminder that one cannot, in practice, actually care equally for everyone, not because of some moral deficit but precisely because care is the sort of value that is tied to the value of partiality. Care is something one is moved to provide, rather than being rationally calculated as an obligation. But there is a paradox at the heart of the value we ascribe to care. The moral concerns that motivate love or caring derive their value from very partial and personal situations, and yet these concerns also inform a felt sense of responsibility to people we do not know or have not met who are in need. But by definition, care is the sort of value that cannot simply be aggregated and extended to just anyone – its value lies in it being wrapped up in relations of recognition and attentiveness.

Some philosophers make a distinction between two kinds of caring: intimate caring, based on personal relations with people one knows very well, and humanitarian caring, extended towards others one only knows about. But this still seems to suggest that the model of intimate care is naturally given in some way. The problem is whether it is possible to maintain the sense of intense partiality and attentiveness that underwrites the value of care (as distinct, say, from justice, whose value lies in impartiality), whilst combining it with an extension over larger areas of social and geographical space.

The four-phase model of care suggests that caring-for is never simply immediately forthcoming, that it always requires some form of attentiveness to the needs of others. Caring-for and caring-about are not necessarily opposed in the way often implied. Rather than assuming that caring-for is a natural disposition against which other forms of care should be judged, thinking about care as a combination of attentiveness, responsibility, acting and responsiveness suggests that no form of care is just spontaneously given without first of all being called for. By putting caring-about before caring-for in the four-phase model described above, we see that an important element of the value of care is that it is a response of being called upon to care about, that it requires that a carer is attentive to the needs of other people. Without this element of attentiveness and responsiveness on the part of the carer, the value of care as a relationship would be undermined, in so far as it would become mechanical and automatic.

Once we have identified this fundamental aspect of care – that it is something that is called forward by the expression of needs by others – then we can begin to reassess the **imaginative geographies** that underlie the problem of caring for distant others. David Smith (2000: 97–106), the geographer who has written most widely about this problem, argues that extending the scope of care in a humanitarian fashion requires more than the forms of partiality that both feminist theorists of care and communitarian theorists value, which remain embedded in the personal sentiments that motivate care for one's nearest and dearest. These discussions often maintain a sense that one needs to find some principle of identity or similarity before one can extend care. Geographers have argued that responsibilities to care at a distance in fact arise from other sources. For example, the complexity of causal relationships that connect people living in different places through market transactions, supply chains, displaced pollution effects and the like, means that we are in fact bound up with and implicated in the lives of all sorts of people living in all sorts of different places (see Chapter 40). So, just as 'intimate care' is based on relations of mutuality and dependence, this would support the argument that we are morally obliged to care for distant others with whom we are likewise connected in relations of mutual benefit and dependence. If this sounds a little too intellectual – it makes it appear that one could calculate the extent and number of one's caring obligations by tracking all the lines of connection that intersect in one's everyday life – it is worth noting that campaigning organizations and charities that have been successful in organizing care at a distance through sophisticated media and marketing campaigns do so not by making epistemological arguments about causal connections, but more through organizing the same range of sentiments – laughter, pity, shame, respect, and so on – that underwrite the attentiveness and responsiveness of 'intimate care' (Silk, 1998).

Care structures

We seem to have got to the point where we can see that any simple distinction between intimate care exercised in relations of spatial proximity and humanitarian care exercised over relations of distance, which tends to elevate the former over the latter as the more authentic model of care, needs to be unpicked. All forms of care are mediated in various ways, and stretched out over various spaces and times. Intimate care can be and is exercised over long distances – through mobile phone calls between children and parents, emails between friends, the exchange of gifts between lovers, or the sending of remittances from one family member who has migrated to those still living at home. The preceding discussion about the carescapes of childcare should already have alerted

Imaginative geographies
representations of place, space and landscape that structure people's understandings of the world, and in turn help to shape their actions. In the work of Edward Said, the term refers to the projection of images of identity and difference on to geographical space in a way that sustains unequal relationships of power.

us to the fact that even this most personal and intimate form of care involves both face-to-face contact and various forms of action mediated by other actors and institutions. So, whilst some forms of care require that the carer and the cared-for be in physical proximity to one another, it is also quite normal for care to be provided at a distance in various ways:

> *While much childcare requires face-to-face interactions and bodily contact, some parents are using mobile phones as a means of 'staying in touch' with and monitoring older children while spending longer at work, which much media alarm is voiced over the use of the TV as a babysitter. Car travel allows us to move children quickly from one context to another, to be close in time if not in miles.*

(McKie *et al.*, 2002: 911)

This reminds us that both the experience and understanding of what counts as care and how well it is provided are shaped by both the social and technological organization of relations of caring. The notion of carescapes is valuable because it moves us away from thinking about certain spaces as uniquely spaces of care in contrast to others, and instead points out that care is always distributed across different times and spaces.

It is also worth remembering that we learn about how and what to care for in all sorts of mediated ways – it is difficult to imagine the experience of falling in (and out of) love without recognizing that whilst being a deeply personal experience, it is also 'modular' in the sense that the rituals and practices that go to make up this type of experience are learnt and transformed by reading stories in books, watching soaps on television, listening to pop music on the radio, and by talking about all of these things to other people. Caring for others is neither as immediate nor as direct as a simple distinction between caring-for and caring-about would seem to imply. Care requires an interactive context of deliberation in which people can decide what the appropriate response to expressions of needs should be, who is responsible and what sort of action should be taken, and so on.

The implication of this argument is that the scope, content and form of our concern for others is shaped in important ways by cultural infrastructures, which work up and maintain even the most personal and intimate dispositions to care for others. There is no reason in principle that intense feelings of commonality or responsibility with others should be contained at a particular spatial scale – the home or, perhaps, the nation. For example, what is notable about the sorts of international humanitarian media events that have been developed in the past three or four decades is how they seem to be re-scaling feelings of care at a global level, leading perhaps to forms of 'global feeling'. Now, it is tempting to suppose that televisually mediated care is not all that we would want genuine care to be – it can easily seem to conform to Noddings' model of indifferent caring-about. But this interpretation assumes that television is a medium that is impersonal and indifferent. The media theorist and historian Paddy Scannell (1995) argues quite the opposite. He argues that radio and television have a characteristic 'care-structure' that accounts for their ethical significance. Care refers to the very conditions of being concerned at all about the world around us:

> *That things matter for us (no matter what), the ways in which they matter and the extent to which they do so, mark out the boundaries of our concerns. Concern is all such things as noticing, remarking upon, attending to, observing, picking out, foregrounding and bringing to bear a focused attentiveness upon phenomena (upon each other and our selves and circumstances) in such ways as to find and make the matter to hand significant and meaningful in some way or other.*

(Scannell, 1995: 144)

The care-structures of modern mass media vastly expand the range of matters that one can be concerned about and care for (see Chapter 41). More importantly, they transform this range of publicly available material into the sorts of things that people feel involved with and competent to talk about and pass judgement over: 'not just weighty matters as they appear in news, current affairs and social concern documentaries' but also 'the goings on in soaps', and 'fun things and odd things, and sporting "moments" and last night's movie and a great deal else besides' (Scannell, 1995: 163).

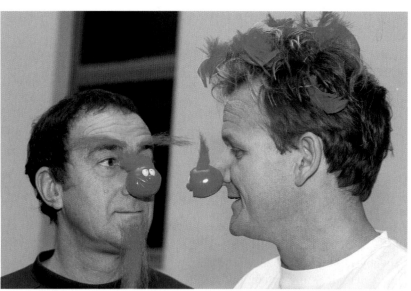

FIGURE 43.4
Angus Deayton and Gordon Ramsay promote Red Nose Day. Credit: Tony Kyriacou/Rex Features

The range of public matters is thus extended, but in so doing, the way in which these matters are considered things to be concerned about and care for is also transformed, so that ordinary norms of sincerity, sociability and authenticity become the terms through which matters of public importance are evaluated.

SUMMARY

- The scope and the practices of care are historically variable – they depend on policies, technologies and, above all, on the complexities of social relations and cultural meanings.
- There are different social and technological modalities of care, through which people learn how to be attentive and sensitive, how to listen, how to respond appropriately and how to act in response to need – whether this means bearing witness to someone's suffering, giving them some form of material comfort, donating to an intermediary care organization or trying to do one's own caring work – paid or unpaid – more competently.

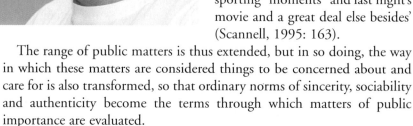

CONCLUSION: WHO CARES?

Thinking about care geographically can be helped by decomposing care into four sets of activities: being attentive, being responsible, being competent and being responsive. These four activities raise a range of analytical questions.

1. *Attentiveness*. What care is necessary? Are there basic human needs? What types of care now exist; how adequate are they? Who gets to articulate the nature of needs and to say which and how problems should be cared about?

2. *Responsibility*. Who should be responsible for meeting the needs for care that do exist? How can and should such responsibility be attributed? Why?

3. *Competence*. Who actually are the caregivers? How well do they do their work? What conflicts exist between them and care receivers? What resources do caregivers need in order to care competently? Who pays attention to changes in care receivers' needs?

4. *Responsiveness*. How do care receivers respond to the care that they are given? How well does the care process, as it exists, meet their needs? If needs conflict with one another, who resolves these conflicts?

Actual practices of care involve the complex integration of all four of these activities, and this in turn involves the co-ordination of activities over various spaces and diverse temporalities – leading to the development of distinctive 'carescapes'. The lesson of Gilligan's work is that the activities of care – 'being there, listening, the willingness to help, and the ability to understand' – all of which reflect injunctions 'to pay attention and not to turn away from need', are all shaped by social practices that are crossed by power relationships (Gilligan, 1986: 249). This implies that issues of care are not only matters of ethics and morality, they are also big public issues of deciding about what matters, about what to care about, and about the distribution of the burdens and benefits of care.

DISCUSSION POINTS

1. Why should geographers care about care?

2. How important is the issue of distance in understanding different types of care?

3. Discuss different types of care. Are there different geographies associated with these?

4. Discuss and describe a 'carescape' that you are familiar with.

FURTHER READING

Smith, D.M. (2000) *Moral geographies: ethics in a world of difference.* **Edinburgh: Edinburgh University Press.**

The best introduction to the ways in which issues of justice, care and ethics are relevant to geography, and to the ways in which a geographical perspective makes a difference to how these things are thought about in the first place.

Tronto, J. (1993) *Moral boundaries.* **London: Routledge.**

The best introduction to the topic of care in moral philosophy and political theory.

We started this book by talking about how beginning to study Human Geography at the university level involved confronting unfamiliar ideas and topics. But Human Geography is never just a distant body of knowledge that you have to be introduced to. It is part of your life already, and it is something you can contribute to. It is not just 'ours' on this side of the word processor, but yours too. You are doing and thinking about Human Geography already. Those of us lucky enough to teach the subject know that we don't just pass ideas on to our students. The ways they respond to the ideas we present, the arguments they raise, the examples they talk about, all end up making us rethink those ideas. Human Geography is, or certainly should be, a meeting ground for many voices, not a series of monologues. It has therefore been our intention that much of the material in this book should intersect with the everyday lives of those who read it.

Of course, it is also important that we learn about things that we do not directly experience, whether because they are part of other people's daily lives (and not ours) or because they operate at levels of reality that are hard to grasp directly. Certainly, the Human Geography presented in this book is no less complicated, contentious or difficult to understand than areas of knowledge that are explicitly framed in more abstract forms. We don't know everything we need to know about geography simply through our experiences of living in the world. But nor are those wider experiences unimportant or illegitimate resources as you engage with academic Human Geography and Human Geographers.

So, on the basis of what you have read in this book, we would urge you to be much more sensitive to the human geographies going on around you. Don't become resigned to thinking that the subject is done by other-worldly academics writing about purely abstract ideas in obscure languages. Instead, start with your own experiences and then work outwards from that. Be aware of the human geographies wrapped up in and represented by the food you eat, the news you read, the films you watch, the music you listen you, the television you gaze at. Be aware of the places you live in, or travel to, or see images of. Be aware of the person you are, the company you keep, the society you live in, the nature of your and others' living, working and play spaces. And in your being aware, take note of what or who is being omitted, marginalized or 'othered' in your narratives. Take note of the power of discourse; how stories are told, and how people or places are categorized, are powerful processes. Take care to listen to voices other than your own and those who agree with you. Think about how what you read in books and articles connects, or doesn't, to your everyday life, and why that might be. Have you been unaware of issues that are important to your academic studies, and if so why? Or are those academic ideas and accounts out of touch with your life, and if so, how would you change them? Think about the wider implications of the arguments you read, not just their academic logics. Try to avoid just looking for the 'right' answer you think someone else wants you to give them, and instead figure out (this isn't easy!) what you really think about the issues you are studying. Let your academic work speak to you, and let your own voice come through as you speak about it.

In the end, all introductions to Human Geography are partial, even those as large as this. All come from particular perspectives, times and places. Ours presents an anglophonic Human Geography early on in the twenty-first century. We hope you are inspired by it, but we do not ask that you agree with all the ideas and interpretations in it. Rather, we encourage you to think through and spell out your own. The Human Geographies introduced here are yours to learn from, but also yours to contribute to. Geography matters, you matter, your geography matters. Having been introduced to Human Geography by this book, why not start to practise Human Geography for yourself?

GLOSSARY

This glossary provides brief definitions of key terms used but not explained fully in the course of this collection's chapters. The terms listed in the glossary are marked in bold when first used in a particular chapter; definitions of these emboldened terms also appear in the margin adjacent to the text. Here, in the glossary itself, cross-referencing between entries is facilitated by capitalizing terms that are separate glossary entries in their own right.

ALIENATION: a term with two interrelated meanings, the second being a more specific formulation of the first. First, then, alienation refers to a sense of estrangement or lack of power felt by people living in the MODERN world. In this respect it is often used to describe the experience of modern urban living, in which traditional forms of social cohesion and belonging supposedly break down. Second, and drawn from MARXIST social thought, alienation refers more particularly to the separation of labour from the MEANS OF PRODUCTION under CAPITALISM. To explain, since under capitalism it is capitalists who own the resources required for economic production (land, machinery, money, etc.) workers have no control over their productive lives: how production is organized, what is produced, what the product is used for and how they relate to other workers. They are therefore alienated from their work and its products.

ASYLUM SEEKER: an asylum seeker is someone seeking protection under the terms of the 1951 United Nations Convention relating to the Status of Refugees.

AUTOETHNOGRAPHY: the processes by which the Human Geographer chooses to make explicit use of her or his own POSITIONALITY, involvements and experiences as an integral part of ETHNOGRAPHIC research.

BIODIVERSITY: describes the variability in nature, including of genes, individuals, species and ecosystems. Biodiversity exists both in particular living things (such as individual rare species) and also in biological processes and dynamic ecological systems.

CAPITAL ACCUMULATION: the prime goal of CAPITALISM as a MODE OF PRODUCTION. It is the deployment of capital to convert it into new (and more) capital. This process is often designated by the simple formula MCM′, where M is money or liquid capital, which is invested in C which is commodity capital (land, labour, machines) with a view to profit, realized as M′ which is more money (or more technically 'expanded liquidity').

CAPITALISM: an economic system in which the production and distribution of goods is organized around the profit motive (*see* CAPITAL ACCUMULATION) and characterized by marked inequalities in the social division of work and wealth between private owners of the materials and tools of production (capital) and those who work for them to make a living (labour) (*see* CLASS).

CIVIL SOCIETY: a concept with a long and changing history of meanings, civil society has been used in the last decade to emphasize a realm of social life and a range of social institutions that are separate from the NATION-STATE.

CLASS: a collection of people sharing the same economic position within society, and/or sharing the same social status and cultural tastes. The precise ways in which one's economic position – for example, as a worker, a capitalist or a member of the land-owning aristocracy – is related to one's social status or cultural tastes has been much debated. However, Human Geographers have studied class and its geographies from all these perspectives: as an economic, social and cultural structuring of society.

COLD WAR: a period conventionally defined as running from the end of the Second World War until the fall of the Berlin Wall, during which the globe was structured around a binary political geography that opposed American CAPITALISM to Soviet communism. Although never reaching all-out military confrontation, this period did witness intense military, economic, political and ideological rivalry between the superpowers and their allies.

COLONIALISM: the rule of a NATION-STATE or other political power over another, subordinated, people and place. This domination is established and maintained through political structures, but may also shape economic and cultural relations. *See also* NEO-COLONIALISM and IMPERIALISM.

COLONIZATION: the physical settling of people from a colonial power within that power's subordinated colonies (*see* COLONIALISM). *See also* DECOLONIZATION.

COMMODIFICATION: this term is used in two interrelated ways: (a) as the conversion of any thing, idea or person into a COMMODITY (the term 'commoditization' is often preferred for this sense); and (b) a wider societal process whereby an ever increasing number of things, human relationships, ideas and people are turned into commodities. Both meanings see the process of commodification as symptomatic of the penetration of CAPITALISM into the everyday lives of people and things.

COMMODITY: something that can be bought and sold through the market. A commodity can be an object (a car, for example), but can also be a person (the car production worker who sells their labour for a wage) or an idea (the design or marketing concepts of the car). Those who live in capitalist societies are used to most things being commodities, though there are still taboos (the buying and selling of sexual intercourse or grandmothers, for example) (*see* CAPITALISM and COMMODIFICATION). This should not disguise the fact that the 'commodity state' is a very particular way of framing objects, people and ideas.

COMMODITY FETISHISM: the process whereby the material origins of commodities are obscured and they are presented 'innocent' of the social and geographical relations of production that produced them.

CULTURAL CAPITAL: a term invented by the French sociologist Pierre Bourdieu, who argued that distinctions based on the judgement of taste were as important in marking social differences and class as access to economic capital. Some people may be high in cultural capital but low in economic capital (and vice versa).

CULTURAL ETHNOCIDE: the permanent disappearance of a particular ethnic group, associated with the eradication of their cultural practices, brought about by the effects of economic and/or political policies. *See also* ETHNICITY.

CULTURAL LANDSCAPE: traditionally this phrase has meant the impact of cultural groups in fashioning and transforming the natural landscape. More recently it has been suggested that landscape itself is a cultural image, a way of symbolizing, representing and structuring our surroundings.

CULTURAL POLITICS: a phrase that emphasizes the implications of culture in questions of power. On the one hand, this means reflecting on how cultural forms and judgements involve relations of power. On the other hand, it means recognizing that politics are in part undertaken through cultural relations and realms (resulting in what in the USA, especially, have been termed 'culture wars'). More specifically, a focus on cultural politics centres questions about whose culture is dominant, the role of culture in practices of resistance, whose REPRESENTATIONS portray the world, and about the IDEOLOGY of cultural forms.

CYBERSPACE: the forms of space produced and experienced through new computational and communication technologies. Exemplary are the SPATIALITIES of phenomena such as the internet, virtual reality programs, hypertext and hypermedia, or the science-fictional accounts that draw on these for inspiration. Human Geographers have approached these spatialities in at least three distinct ways: in terms of the kinds of places users encounter within them; by analysing the kinds of communicational networks they facilitate; and in terms of the geographical location of their infrastructures.

DE-INDUSTRIALIZATION: this term usually refers to a decline in manufacturing industry. It can designate either a fall in manufacturing output or, more commonly, a fall in the number and share of employees in manufacturing industry as a result of plant closures, lay-offs, etc. It is possible for de-industrialization to occur at the same time as manufacturing output, and exports rise if automation is associated with jobless growth. Areas that have suffered from de-industrialization are characterized by large numbers of vacant derelict factories. *See also* POST-INDUSTRIAL.

DECOLONIZATION: this term has two meanings: (a) the ending of formal colonial rule by one power over another (*see* COLONIALISM); (b) the departure of a settler population from a colonized territory (*see* COLONIZATION). In both cases, however, processes of decolonization are in fact likely to be far less of a 'clean break' than these definitions suggest. Legacies from, and new forms of, colonialism are still central to POST-COLONIAL experiences.

DEPENDENCY THEORIES: theories that explain levels of economic and social DEVELOPMENT with reference to global economic structures. In particular, dependency theories emphasize the idea that southern countries are exploited by those of the North and will remain in subservient or dependent positions until the global economic system is changed.

DE-TERRITORIALIZATION: the uncoupling of political and economic processes from particular national spaces, as when banks move offshore or when economic decisions are entrusted to the World Bank or the G7 powers. *See also* TERRITORY.

DEVELOPMENT: a highly contested term that, in its most general sense, means change (usually positive change) over time. It has often been used to describe processes of becoming MODERN or ideas of progress. More specifically, development has often been defined from a particular EUROCENTRIC viewpoint, such that progress is assessed in relation to the experiences of western European societies and economies. Thus, development encompasses INDUSTRIALIZATION, urbanization and increasing standards of living in relation to health, education and housing, for example. Constructions of development are not value-free. POST-DEVELOPMENT theorists, amongst others, have highlighted the way definitions and DISCOURSES of development reflect and reinforce existing power relations.

DEVELOPMENTALISM: a set of propositions or policies that demand (or provide for) the transformation of pre-modern societies into MODERN societies. INDUSTRIALIZATION is often considered to play a key role in the process of development. *See also* POST-DEVELOPMENTALISM.

DEVOLUTION: the process of devolving some political power to more local levels of government, often associated with the formation of local and regional assemblies. This can take place at many scales: at a supranational scale, for example within the European Union, power can be devolved to individual nations or to regions; and within the NATION-STATE power can be devolved to regions and localities.

DIALECTIC, DIALECTICAL: a dialectic is a process through which two opposites are generated, interrelated and eventually transcended. This process can be purely intellectual, in so far as it is a procedure of thought. Examples in this vein would include the opposites used as the starting points for all the chapters in Part 1 of this collection (nature–culture, society–space, and so on), which are then worked through and beyond in

the course of each chapter. Dialectical processes can also be identified in the wider world, though. An example would be the combination in a COMMODITY of both use and exchange values, in which opposites become interpenetrated in the commodity form.

DIASPORA: the dispersal or scattering of people from their original home. As a noun it can be used to refer to a dispersed 'people' (hence the Jewish diaspora or the Black diaspora). However, it also refers to the actual processes of dispersal and connection that produce any scattered, but still in some way identifiable, population. In this light it also can be used as an adjective – diasporic – to refer to the senses of home, belonging and cultural identity held by a dispersed population.

DISCOURSE, DISCURSIVE: drawing on the work of the French philosopher Michel Foucault, Human Geographers define discourses as ways of talking about, writing or otherwise representing the world and its geographies (*see also* REPRESENTATION). Discursive approaches to Human Geography emphasize the importance of these ways of representing. They are seen as shaping the realities of the worlds in which we live, rather than just being ways of portraying a reality that exists outside of language and thought. They are also seen as connected to questions of practice – that is, what people actually do – rather than being confined to a separate realm of images or ideas. More specifically, Human Geographers have stressed the different ways in which people have discursively constructed the world in different times and places, and examined how it is that particular ways of talking about, conceptualizing and acting on people and places come to be seen as natural and common-sensical in particular contexts.

ECOCENTRISM: a perspective favouring a humble and cautious outlook towards the scope for interfering with the planet, and arguing for a smaller-scale, more communitarian, style of living.

ECOLOGY: a way of studying living things (plants, animals or people) that emphasizes their complex and dynamic interrelationships with each other and the environment. As well as their use in Biogeography, ecological theories about competition for resources, invasion and distribution have also been applied in Urban Geography.

ECOSYSTEM: an ecosystem comprises: a set of plants, animals and micro-organisms amongst which energy and matter are exchanged; the physical environment with which, and within which, they interact. *See also* ECOLOGY.

EMBODIED, EMBODIMENT: this concept suggests that the self and the body are not separate, but rather that the experiences of any individual are, invariably, shaped by the active and reactive entity that is their body – irrespective of whether this is conscious or not. The argument, then, runs that the uniqueness of human experience is due, at least in part, to the unique nature of individual bodies.

ENLIGHTENMENT: a philosophical and intellectual movement usually dated to the seventeenth and eighteenth centuries and centred in Europe, which advanced the view that the world could be rendered knowable and explained systematically by the application of rational thought (science). Revolutionary in its challenge to the religious beliefs and superstitions that then held sway, it has since been much criticised for projecting rationality as a universal, rather than situating reasoning processes in particular social and material contexts.

ENVIRONMENTAL AUDIT: the attempt to calculate, and list for comparison, all the likely effects of any proposed action on the surrounding ECOSYSTEMS and populations.

ENVIRONMENTAL DETERMINISM: a school of thought which holds that human activities are controlled by the environment in which they take place. Especially influential within Human Geography at the end of the nineteenth and beginning of the twentieth centuries, when the approach was used in particular to draw a link between climatic conditions and human development. Some authors used this link to argue that climate stamps an indelible mark on the moral and physiological constitution of different races (*see* RACE). This in turn was used to assert the superiority of western civilization, and hence to justify and support the imperial drive of nineteenth-century Europe (*see* COLONIALISM and IMPERIALISM).

ENVIRONMENTAL RISK: real and imagined threats to existing human, social and ecological systems posed by physical events, such as earthquakes; or from the unforeseen consequences of human activity, such as releasing genetically modified organisms into the environment.

ENVIRONMENTALISM, ENVIRONMENTALIST: a social and political movement aimed at harmonizing the relationship between human endeavour and the presumed limits to interference of planetary life support systems.

EPISTEMOLOGY, EPISTEMOLOGICAL: epistemology is the study of knowledge, particularly with regard to its methods, scope and validity. This technical term from philosophy refers to differing ideas about what it is possible to know about the world and how it is possible to express that knowledge. Different academic disciplines and different general approaches in Geography are marked by distinctively different epistemologies. Human Geographers are interested in the epistemological questions raised by the geographical knowledges held both by academics and by ordinary people. In studying these epistemological questions Human Geographers seek to connect up questions of content (what kinds of things people know) with structures of belief (how and why they claim to know) and issues of authority (how and why these knowledges are valued and justified).

ESSENTIALIST/ISTS/M: the belief that identities, such as class, gender and race, as well as age, dis/ability and sexuality, are directly determined by biology. This view is opposed by SOCIAL CONSTRUCTIONISTS, who argue that these differences between us are shaped through the interweaving of wider socio-spatial processes and individual biographies. The term is often used negatively to emphasize the stereotyping that it can produce.

ETHNICITY: a criterion of social categorization that distinguishes different groups of people on the basis of inherited cultural differences. Ethnicity is a very complex idea that needs careful consideration. For instance, in popular usage ethnicity often becomes a synonym for RACE, but in fact there is a crucial distinction in so far as race differentiates people on the grounds of physical characteristics, and ethnicity on the grounds of learnt cultural differences. Moreover, whilst everyday understandings of ethnicity often treat it as a quality only possessed by some people and cultures (for instance, 'ethnic minorities' and their 'ethnic foods' or 'ethnic fashions') in fact these differential recognitions of ethnicity themselves need explanation. The complexities of the concept are further emphasized by recent debates within and beyond Human Geography over the extent to which new forms of ethnicity are emerging through the cultural mixing associated with processes of GLOBALIZATION (*see also* HYBRID and SYNCRETIC).

ETHNOCENTRIC: an adjective describing the tendency for people to think about other cultures, societies and places through the assumptions of their own culture, society or place. An example of ethnocentricism is the production of theories about the whole world based on the specific model of western development (*see also* DEVELOPMENTALISM).

ETHNOGRAPHY, ETHNOGRAPHIC: the research processes that use qualitative methods to provide in-depth explorations and accounts of the lives, interactions and 'textures' associated with particular people and places.

EUROCENTRIC: adjective that describes the characteristic of believing that the western European experience is the only correct way to progress. This may be because there is no awareness of alternatives, or it may reflect a belief in European superiority. Is often used now to refer to theories and perspectives coming more generally from the global North.

EVERYDAY LIFE: a notoriously difficult term to define, as it has meant many different things to a great many different philosophers, theorists and practitioners. We can generalize that it is an arena of social life that includes repetitive daily cycles and routines that we learn but eventually take for granted.

FEMINISM: a series of perspectives, which together draw on theoretical and political accounts of the oppression of women in society to suggest how GENDER relations and Human Geography are interconnected (*see also* PATRIARCHY).

FORDISM: a form of industrial capitalism dominating the economies of the USA and western Europe from the end of the Second World War to the early 1970s. It was characterized by mass production and mass consumption, where high levels of productivity (often promoted by new assembly line production) sustained high wages, which in turn led to high levels of demand for industrial products. This demand fed into higher production, which supported higher productivity, and the 'virtuous circle' began all over again. It was an economic system that was often underpinned by a political compromise between capital and labour, and by subsequent state policies towards wages, taxes and welfare provision, which helped to sustain mass production and consumption. See *also* POST-FORDISM.

GENDER: a criterion of social organization that distinguishes different groups of people on the basis of femininity or masculinity. In any one location, many masculinities and femininities interact. As a concept, gender is usually used in Human Geography in distinction to that of sex (i.e. femaleness and maleness) in order to emphasize the SOCIAL CONSTRUCTION of women's and men's roles, relations and identities. Human Geographers' accounts of the world have always been shaped through understandings of gender (*see* MASCULINISM) but explicit analyses of the geographies of gender and the gendering of geographies are comparatively recent, and associated with the growth of Feminist Geography (*see* FEMINISM).

GENTRIFICATION: an urban geographical process commonly taken to have two main attributes. The first is the invasion (or replacement) of traditional inner-city working-CLASS residential areas by middle-CLASS in-migrants; the second is the upgrading, improvement and renovation of the existing housing, whether done by the new residents or by developers. Commercial gentrification refers more specifically to the replacement of older, traditional, low-rent, retail and other uses by new, stylish, fashionable boutiques, cafés, bars and other retail outlets.

GEOGRAPHICAL IMAGINATION: an awareness of the role of space, place and environment in human life. This phrase is sometimes used in the definite singular – the geographical imagination – to refer to the distinctive intellectual concerns and contributions of Geography. It is also used in the plural – geographical imaginations – to emphasize the many different ways in which academics, students and lay publics alike can develop their sensitivities to human geographies.

GEOPOLITICS: an approach to the theory and practice of statecraft, which considers certain laws of geography (e.g. distance, proximity and location) to play a central part in the formation of international politics. Although the term was originally coined by Swede Rudolf Kjellen in 1899, it was popularized in the early twentieth century by British geographer Halford Mackinder.

GLOBAL CITY: a term used by Saskia Sassen in the early 1990s to denote those cities that play a key role in the operation of the capitalist world economy, particularly in terms of financial and business services. The term builds upon the concept of 'world city', put forward by Freidmann and Wolff, to capture the command and control centres of late CAPITALISM, particularly in terms of the concentration of headquarters of multi- and TRANSNATIONAL CORPORATIONS.

GLOBALIZATION: the economic, political, social and cultural processes whereby: (a) places across the globe are increasingly interconnected; (b) social relations and economic transactions increasingly occur at the intercontinental scale (*see* TRANSNATIONAL); and (c) the globe itself comes to be a recognizable geographical entity. As such, globalization does not mean everywhere in the world becomes the same. Nor is it an entirely even process; different places are differently connected into the world and view that world from different perspectives. Globalization has been occurring for several hundred years, but in the contemporary world the scale and extent of social, political and economic interpenetration appears to be qualitatively different to international networks in the past.

GRAVITY MODEL: a mathematical model based on a rather crude analogy with Newton's gravitational equation, which posited a constant relationship between the gravitational force operating between two masses, their size and the distance between them. Geographers have used this model to predict and account for a range of flows between two or more points, especially those to do with migration and transport (*see also* SPATIAL SCIENCE).

HEGEMONY, HEGEMONIC, HEGEMON: hegemony is an opaque power relation relying more on leadership through consensus than coercion through force or its threat, so that domination is by the permeation of ideas. For instance, concepts of hegemony have been used to explain how, when 'the ruling ideas are the ideas of the ruling class', other classes will willingly accept their inferior position as right and proper (*see* CLASS). Hegemonic is the adjective attached to the institution that possesses hegemony. For instance, under CAPITALISM the bourgeoisie are the hegemonic class. Hegemon is a term used when the concept of hegemony is applied to the competition between NATION-STATES: a hegemon is a hegemonic state. For instance, the USA has been described as the hegemon of the world economy in the mid-twentieth century.

HISTORICITY: to recognize the historicity of human geographies is to recognize their historical variability. This involves both an emphasis on historical specificity – on how historical periods differ from each other – and on historical change – on how human geographies are re-made and transformed over time.

HOMOGENIZATION: a term used to describe the process whereby places and social characteristics become more similar to each other, so that they eventually become indistinguishable. For example, the spread of global brands such as McDonald's (McDonaldization) through the world is thought to cause places to look and feel the same, thus reducing local difference.

HUMAN AGENCY: usually indicates self-conscious, purposeful action. Geographers have used this term to stress the freedom and capacity of people to generate, modify and influence the course of everyday and world events.

HUMANIST: an outlook or system of thought that emphasizes human, rather than divine or supranatural, powers in understanding the world. Associated with the ENLIGHTENMENT, humanism marks human beings off from other animals and living things by virtue of supposedly distinctive capacities for language and reasoning. Whilst underscoring progressive social changes, like the idea of human rights, it is criticized for making universal claims about human nature; privileging the individual over the social relations of human being; and licensing human abuse of the natural world.

HUMANISTIC GEOGRAPHY: a theoretical approach to Human Geography that concentrates on studying the conscious, creative and meaningful activities and experiences of human beings. Coming to prominence in the 1970s, Humanistic Geography was in part a rebuttal of attempts during the 1960s to create a law-based, scientific Human Geography founded on statistical data and analytical techniques (*see* SPATIAL SCIENCE). In contrast, it emphasized the subjectivities of those being studied and, indeed, the Human Geographers studying them. Human meanings, emotions and ideas with regard to place, space and nature thus became central.

HYBRID, HYBRIDITY, HYBRIDIZATION: hybrids are the products of the combination of usually distinct things. These terms are often used to describe new plant types but are used in Human Geography to emphasize the equal and positive mixing of cultures rather than negative ideas of cultural assimilation, dilution, pollution or corruption. *See also* SYNCRETIC.

HYPER-REALITY: a phrase most associated with the Italian semiotician (*see* SEMIOTICS) and novelist Umberto Eco, which suggests the development of simulated events and representations that out-do the 'real' events they are meant to be depicting. Thus in hyper-reality the REPRESENTATION exceeds the original, being more sensational, more exciting or so forth. *See also* SIMULACRUM.

ICON: a visual image, landscape feature or other material form that comes to symbolize or stand for a wider set of meanings or phenomena.

ICONOGRAPHY: this term means both: (a) the study of the symbolic meanings of a picture, visual image or landscape; and, less often, (b) the system of visual meaning thereby being studied. Developed in particular within disciplines such as art history, Human Geographers have extended iconography to the analysis of landscape symbolism and meaning. This analysis combines examination of the symbolic elements of a landscape with consideration of the social contexts in which a landscape is produced and viewed (*see also* SEMIOTICS).

IDEOLOGICAL: a meaning, idea or thing is ideological in so far as it helps to constitute and maintain relations of domination and subordination between two or more social groups (CLASSES, GENDERS, age groups, etc.).

IDEOLOGY: a meaning or set of meanings that serves to create and/or maintain relationships of domination and subordination, through symbolic forms such as texts, landscapes and spaces.

IDYLL-IZED: the process by which dominant myths about places and spaces come to reflect circumstances of picturesque beauty, tranquillity and harmonious living conditions. The term is often used in relation to rural spaces, where social problems can be hidden by the impression of idyllic life in close-knit communities and close to nature.

ILLEGAL MIGRANT: there are at least three ways an individual might be classified as an illegal migrant. First, they can enter a country illegally, without passing through an immigration checkpoint. Such entrants are often also referred to as 'irregular' migrants. Second, they can enter a country legally for a limited period of time – for example with a short-term visa – but then stay illegally after the expiry date of their visa. These are also described as 'undocumented' migrants. Third, they can be legally resident but involved in illegal activities.

IMAGINATIVE GEOGRAPHIES: representations of place, space and landscape that structure people's understandings of the world, and in turn help to shape their actions. In the work of Edward Said, the term refers to the projection of images of identity and difference on to geographical space in a way that sustains unequal relationships of power.

IMPERIALISM: a relationship of political, and/or economic, and/or cultural domination and subordination between geographical areas. This relationship may be based on explicit political rule (*see* COLONIALISM), but need not be.

INDUSTRIALIZATION: the process through which societies develop an economy based on the mass and mechanized production of goods. *See also* DE-INDUSTRIALIZATION and POST-INDUSTRIAL.

INTER-GENERATIONAL EQUITY: this term refers to the concept of equality in access to resources or wealth between one generation of people and another (usually a future generation, or people as yet unborn).

INTRA-GENERATIONAL EQUITY: this term refers to the concept of equality in access to resources or wealth within a single generation (usually between different groups of people today – for example, between rich and poor classes in one country, or between rich and poor countries such as between 'first world ' and 'third world' countries).

LINGUISTIC (OR CULTURAL) TURN: this phrase is used to describe changes in the social sciences and Human Geography over the last 30 years. It refers to the adoption of interpretative (qualitative) approaches to explore the ways in which meanings, values and knowledges are constructed through language and other forms of communication.

MARXIST: social and economic theories influenced by the legacy of the leading nineteenth-century political philosopher, Karl Marx. Highly influential in the framing of critical geography, these theories focus on the organization of capitalist society and the social and environmental injustices that can be traced to it. *See also* CAPITALISM, MODE OF PRODUCTION, ALIENATION and COMMODIFICATION for examples of the influence of Marxist thinking in Human Geography.

MASCULINISM, MASCULINIST: a form of thought or knowledge that, whilst often claiming to be impartial, comprehends the world in ways that are derived from men's experiences and concerns. Many Feminist Geographers have argued that Human Geography has traditionally been masculinist (*see* FEMINISM).

MEANS OF PRODUCTION: the resources that are indispensable for any form of production to occur. Typically this would include land, labour, machines, money capital, knowledge/information. In MARXIST thinking the means of production and labour power together constitute the 'forces of production'.

MENTAL MAP: a mental map describes our everyday notions about our spatial location. People rarely picture their spatial location to themselves through the images of a formal map. But of course we are all spatially located and aware. A mental map thus relates the elements we see as important and misses places we do not visit. Studies have shown that instead of a bird's eye view mental maps are organized around paths and landmarks that help us find our way in daily life. *See also* PERCEPTION.

METAPHOR: the use of a word or symbol from one domain of meaning to apply to another. Thus a rose (a botanical term) is translated into the domain of human relationships to symbolize love. Metaphors involve this movement of concepts from their normal realm to a new realm.

MIGRATION: migration can be considered a sub-category of a wider concept of 'movement', which embraces a whole range of forms of human mobility, from daily commuting at one end of the spectrum to permanent emigration at the other.

MODE OF PRODUCTION: a term taken from MARXIST social thought, referring to the distinctive ways in which production has taken place in different types of society and in different historical epochs. Thus CAPITALISM is seen as one 'mode of production' distinguishable, for example, from feudalism and communism. In Marxist Geography, the mode of production is seen as the fundamental determinant of the kind of society and the kind of human geographies a person has to live with and through.

MODERN, MODERNITY, MODERNISM: ideas of the modern are most commonly defined through their opposition to the old and the traditional. In this light, the adjective 'modern' is synonymous with 'newness'; 'modernity' refers both to the 'post-traditional' historical epoch within which 'newness' is produced and valued, as well as to the economic, social, political and cultural formations characteristic of that period; and 'modernism' applies more narrowly to artistic, architectural and intellectual movements that centrally explore ideas of 'newness' and develop 'new' aesthetics and ways of thinking to express these. Modernity has been most commonly located in Euro-American societies from the eighteenth century onwards, and thereby associated with their characteristic combination of capitalist economies (*see* CAPITALISM), political organization through NATION-STATES, and cultural values of secularity, rationality and progress (*see* ENLIGHTENMENT). However, increasingly, Human Geographers are recognizing that modernity is a global phenomenon that has taken many different forms in different times and places. *See also* MODERNIZATION.

MODERNIZATION: a process of social transformation in which technological change plays a leading role and in which scientific rationality becomes widely accepted. Often associated with the rise of industrial CAPITALISM, modernization has far-reaching implications for processes of identity formation and change.

MORAL ECONOMY: a term used by the historian Edward Thompson to describe the fact that economic relations have a normative aspect. For instance, the moral economy in the peasant economy would refer to the idea of a subsistence ethic in which the social relations of the poor attempt to provide forms of local security and support to prevent starvation. The concept of the moral economy has connections to Karl Polanyi's idea that the economy is an instituted process embedded in social relations.

MULTICULTURAL, MULTICULTURALISM: multicultural is an adjective used to describe a place, society or person comprised of a number of different cultures. Multiculturalism is a body of thought that values this plurality. As the Human Geographer Audrey Kobayashi has noted, both the multicultural and multiculturalism can be conceived of in a number of ways: as 'demographic', i.e. simply reflecting a diversity of population; as 'symbolic', i.e. as about the presence or absence of the symbols associated with particular cultural groups within wider societal or national culture (for example, in the media, or in museums, or in school curricula); as 'structural', in so far as institutions are established to reflect a multicultural society and pursue multiculturalism; and 'critical', to the extent that multiculturalism itself critiques the assumptions of distinct, separate cultural groups sometimes attached to notions of the multicultural. Within Human Geography, increasing emphasis is being placed on developing this 'critical multiculturalism' through examining the HYBRID or SYNCRETIC cultural forms emerging within multicultural societies.

NARRATIVE: narratives are particular kinds of stories that are subject to cultural conventions about authorship, plot, style and audience. Narrative approaches in the social sciences attempt to recover the way that social life is 'storied' in terms of a series of events and how we 'make sense' of those events. Borrowed from historical and literary sources, narrative methods often involve the collection of life-history interviews that use personal testimony to relate the particularities of individual biography to their wider social context.

NATION-STATE: a form of political organization that involves (a) a set of institutions that govern the people within a particular TERRITORY (the state), and (b) that claims allegiance and legitimacy from those governed, and from other states, on the basis that they represent a group of people defined in cultural and political terms as a nation.

NATURALIZATION, NATURALIZED: this term has two distinct and different meanings: (a) the way in which social relations, cultural norms or institutions are made to seem 'natural' rather than SOCIAL CONSTRUCTIONS; and (b) the process through which species become established in new environments, sometimes also applied to human life to refer to the formal integration of immigrants in new societies.

NEO-LIBERALISM, NEO-LIBERAL: pertaining to an economic doctrine that favours free markets, the deregulation of national economies, decentralization and the privatization of previously state-owned enterprises (e.g. education, health). A doctrine that, in practice, favours the interests of the powerful (e.g. TRANSNATIONAL CORPORATIONS) against the less powerful (e.g. peasants) within societies.

NEO-COLONIALISM: economic and political ties, continuing after formal independence, between metropolitan countries and the South, that work to the benefit of the North. *See also* COLONIALISM.

NON-GOVERNMENTAL ORGANIZATION (NGO): an organization that belongs neither to the private for-profit sector, or the public or government sector.

NON-REPRESENTATIONAL THEORY: introduced into Human Geography by the Geographer Nigel Thrift, this phrase – which he has since accepted may not have been 'the best-chosen of phrases' – seeks to highlight various understandings that emphasize the practical, active and EMBODIED character of the world. Rather than denying the importance of REPRESENTATIONS, non-representational theory has sought to resist an undue obsession with them (see LINGUISTIC (OR CULTURAL) TURN) through a direct focus on actions, events, moments, things.

OTHER, OTHERNESS: usually typographically capitalized, an Other is that person or entity that is understood as opposite or different to oneself; Otherness is the quality of difference which that Other possesses. A rather abstract conceptual couplet, potentially applicable at scales varying from the individual person to the global political bloc, these terms have been used in Human Geography to emphasize how ideas about human and geographical difference are structured through oppositions of the Self/Same versus the Other/Different. They also stress how the Other is often defined in terms of its relations to that Self – as its negative, everything it is not – rather than in its own terms. For example, a number of studies have examined how dominant ideas about GENDER are based on a logic in which Woman is Other to Man; how ideas about global politics and culture frame the East as Other to the West, and the South as Other to the North; and so on.

PARADIGM: a stable consensus about the aims, shared assumptions and practices of a particular academic discipline. The term can be used in a narrow technical sense to fit the model of change in scientific disciplines such as Physics and Chemistry proposed by Thomas Kuhn in *The Structure of Scientific Revolutions* (1962). Kuhn argued that most scientific activity works within a stable consensus that he called 'normal science' and does not challenge these fundamental assumptions. Eventually normal science becomes disrupted by anomalies or issues that cannot be explained within the existing framework, and new innovative work may trigger a 'paradigm shift' to a new set of shared assumptions and practices. The term 'paradigm' has entered popular usage in a looser sense and is now used regularly to refer to general approaches, theoretical frameworks and methodologies held by significant groups both within disciplines and, particularly in the social sciences and humanities, across disciplines. It is difficult to fit the development of Human Geography to a strict model of paradigms and paradigm shifts, but the terminology is often used to draw attention both to communities of geographers who share general approaches, theoretical frameworks and methodologies, and to the episodic nature of change in the discipline.

PARTNERSHIPS: an arrangement between a number of agencies and institutions in which objectives are shared and a common agenda is developed in pursuit of a common purpose. The partnership approach encourages collaboration and integration, and the aim is that by blending and pooling their resources the different agencies will be able to produce a capacity for action that is more than simply the sum of their individual parts.

PATRIARCHY: a social system in which men oppress and exploit women. The term was first coined in analyses of households headed by men and organized to the benefit of those 'patriarchs' (for example, through an unequal division of domestic work, or through women's marriage vows 'to obey', or through the legality of rape by husband of wife). However, the term is now used in a wider sense to think about how unequal power relations between men and women are established through realms stretching from the social organization of reproduction and childcare, to the organization of paid work, the operations of the state, cultural understandings of GENDER differences, the regulation of human SEXUALITY, and men's violence towards women.

PAUPERIZATION: the progressive impoverishment of people owing to the impacts of certain development programmes. For example, the displacement of peasant and tribal peoples from their sources of livelihood (e.g. land) to make way for the construction of hydro-electric dams.

PERCEPTION: the process through which people form mental images of the world. Often assumed to be both one-directional (from the world to us) and biological (neurologically controlled), many academic studies have emphasized the role of cultural filters or frames in altering how we form pictures of the world.

POLITICAL-ECONOMIC, POLITICAL ECONOMY: the study of how economic activities are socially and politically structured and have social and political consequences. Political-economic approaches in Human Geography have paid particular attention to understanding capitalist economies and their geographical organization and impact (*see* CAPITALISM and also MARXIST GEOGRAPHY). Central to such analyses have been questions concerning the class-based nature of the human geographies of capitalist societies (*see* CLASS).

POSITIONALITY: the personal experiences, beliefs, identities and motives of the Human Geographer, which influence her or his work and the way in which her or his knowledge is situated.

POST-COLONIAL, POST-COLONIALISM: sometimes hyphenated, sometimes not, this term has two distinct meanings: (a) the post-colonial era, i.e. the historical period following a period of COLONIALISM (*see also* DECOLONIZATION); (b) post-colonial political, cultural and intellectual movements, and their perspectives, which are critical of the past and ongoing effects of European and other colonialisms.

POST-DEVELOPMENTALISM: a radical critique of DEVELOPMENTALISM, which demands the self-empowerment of poor or marginalized people in opposition to the powers of the state or capital.

POST-FORDISM: refers to the forms of production, work, consumption and REGULATION that emerged out of the crisis of mass, standardized forms of capitalist production (FORDISM) during the 1970s. In terms of production and work, post-Fordism turns on the importance of flexibility in work and other institutional forms of productive organization. Economic Geographers have analysed how this flexibility has been driven both by versatile and programmable machines, and by forms of 'vertical disintegration' of some firms in some sectors that make greater use of strategic alliances and subcontracting. Accompanying these changes in production are changes in consumer demand (the centrality of quality over standardization), in labour markets, in finance and legal structures, and in the broad social contract that characterized post-war Fordism.

POST-INDUSTRIAL: a description applied to the new economic, social and cultural structures emerging in late capitalist societies in the late twentieth century, highlighting in particular, trends away from manufacturing, manual work and the mass production of physical goods (*see* INDUSTRIALIZATION) and towards the tertiary sector, forms of service employment and the production of experiences, images, ideas and relationships.

POST-MATERIALIST: a philosophy relating the quality of existence, and peaceful relations between people and between people and the planet, to the manageable acquisition of material goals.

POSTMODERN, POSTMODERNITY, POSTMODERNISM: the British national newspaper, the *Independent*, sarcastically defined postmodernism thus: 'This word has no meaning. Use it as often as possible.' In fact, the main problem for a glossary entry such as this is that ideas of the postmodern have been used so often with so many different meanings! Nonetheless, one can generalize to say that notions of the postmodern (sometimes hyphenated, sometimes not) are used to suggest a move beyond 'modern' society and culture (*see* MODERN, MODERNITY, MODERNISM). More specifically: (a) postmodern is an adjective used to describe social and cultural forms that eschew 'modern' qualities of order, rationality and progress in favour of 'postmodern' qualities of difference, ephemerality, superficiality and pastiche; (b) 'postmodernity' is the contemporary epoch, after a period of 'modernity', in which such postmodern forms supposedly predominate, an epoch characterized both by the loss of an overall sense of social direction and order and by the triumph of the media image over reality (*see* HYPER-REALITY and SIMULACRUM); and (c) 'postmodernism' refers more narrowly to a collection of artistic, architectural and intellectual movements that promote postmodernist values, aesthetics and ways of thinking. If that is not complicated enough, whilst some view all things postmodern as signs of a radically new historical era of postmodernity, others see them more as recent twists to the history of modernity. So perhaps a revised version of the *Independent*'s definition might be: 'This word has a host of meanings. This makes it interesting, but also means it should be used with care'!

PSYCHOANALYSIS, PSYCHOANALYTIC: largely associated with the work of Freud, psychoanalytic theory concerns itself with the mental life of individuals rather than with any overt observable behaviour, and argues that the most important elements of such mental lives are the unconscious ones. It posits that the unconscious parts of the mind (the 'id') are in perpetual conflict with both the more rational and conscious elements (the 'ego') and with those parts of the mind concerned with conscience (the 'superego'). Psychological disturbances can then be traced to these conflicts, and can be remedied through psychoanalytical therapy, which is able to give an individual insight into their unconscious mental life.

QUALITATIVE METHODS: research methods that involve the production and analysis of data that do not take a numerical form.

QUANTITATIVE METHODS: research methods that involve the production and analysis of numerical data.

RACE: a criterion of social categorization that distinguishes different groups of people on the basis of particular secondary physical differences (such as skin colour). Human Geographers have studied questions of race in a number of ways including: (a) the extent, causes and implications of the spatial segregation of different racial groups within cities, regions or nations; (b) the role played by geographical understandings of place and environment in the construction both of ideas of race per se and of ideas about particular races; and (c) the forms of racism and inequality that operate through these geographical patterns, processes and ideas. Increasingly, Human Geographers have emphasized how racial categories, whilst having very real consequences for people's lives, cannot simply be assumed as biological realities, having instead to be recognized as SOCIAL CONSTRUCTIONS. *See also* ETHNICITY.

REFLEXIVITY: a process through which we are able to reflect on what we know, how we come to know it, and how we interact with others. The key point is that we are able to change aspects of ourselves and the structures that make up society in the light of these reflections.

REFUGEE: a refugee is someone who, 'owing to a well-founded fear of being persecuted for reasons of race, religion, nationality, membership of a particular social group or political opinion, is outside the country of his [or her] nationality'.

REGULATION: the arrangement of an economy into more or less cohesive forms of production, consumption, monetary circulation and SOCIAL REPRODUCTION. Derived initially from a disparate group of French political-economists (*see* POLITICAL-ECONOMY), a 'regulationist approach' therefore attends to the different ways of socially, politically and culturally organizing economic activity, especially capitalist economic activity (*see* CAPITALISM). These different ways of regulating capitalist economies are identified both historically and geographically (*see also* FORDISM and POST-FORDISM).

REIFICATION: the act of transforming human properties, relations and actions into properties, relations and actions that are seen to be independent of human endeavour, and that then come actually to govern human life. The term can also refer to the transformations of human beings into 'thing-like' beings. Reification is therefore a form of ALIENATION.

REPRESENTATION: the cultural practices and forms by which human societies interpret and portray the world around them and present themselves to others. In the case of the natural world, for example, these representations range from prehistoric cave paintings of the creatures that figured in the lives of early human groups to the televisual images and scientific models that shape our imaginations today. *See also* DISCOURSE.

SEMIOTICS: this term has two interrelated meanings: (a) the study of forms of human communication and the ways they produce and convey meaning; and (b) those forms of human communication and systems of meaning themselves. Whilst including spoken and written language, semioticians deliberately also analyse how other social phenomena – including dress, architecture and the built environment, visual art, social gatherings and events, landscapes – are communication systems whose 'languages' can and should be analysed. Human Geographers have drawn on ideas from semiotics (*see* SIGN, SIGNIFICATION, REFERENT) but parallel work in art history on the language of painting has been more directly influential (*see* ICONOGRAPHY).

SEXUALITY: sexual attitudes, preferences, desires and behaviours. Human Geographers have emphasized how our sexualities are not simply a biological given but complex socio-cultural constructs (*see also* SOCIAL CONSTRUCTION). They have examined how, on the one hand, these constructs sexualize our encounters with places and environments in personally and socially significant ways and, on the other hand, how our sexualities themselves are shaped through experiences and understandings of the geographies of the body, the home, the city, the nation, travel, etc.

SIGN, SIGNIFICATION, REFERENT: these are ideas relating to the DISCURSIVE construction of geographical worlds. The sign is a concept or word that is significant in the understanding of everyday meanings and places and people (for example, 'rurality'). Signification is the process by which significant meanings are attached to signs (for example, social representations and interpretations of 'rurality'). The referent is the geographical phenomenon that is being signalled (for example, rural localities).

SIMULACRUM: refers to the notion of a copy without an original. If we say at the first point we have an original object, then any image represents it, or replicas are copies of it. We thus have a pattern of original and copy. However, often it is the copies themselves that are copied. The products may begin to diverge from the original. The idea of a simulacrum, or of many simulacra, takes this a step further by emphasizing the presence in contemporary POSTMODERN landscapes of many copies with no original. An example might be the shopping-mall 'Parisian café' that clearly imitates a Parisian café, but for which there is no single original it imitates; or Disneyland's main street, which is again a REPRESENTATION for which there was no original. *See also* HYPER-REALITY.

SOCIAL CAPITAL: the notion of social capital is used to suggest that people's social networks have wider value through the relations of trust, reciprocity, co-operation and information exchange that they engender. Models of social organization and social space that involve high levels of social interaction and hence social capital – whether that be neighbourhood communities or internet-based support groups – are counterposed positively to examples of individualistic and passive existence.

SOCIAL CONSTRUCT: a set of specific meanings that become attributed to the characteristics and identities of people and places by common social or cultural usage. Social constructs will often represent a 'loaded' view of the subject, according to the sources from which, and the channels through which, ideas are circulated in society.

SOCIAL EXCLUSION: a state of being that is perceived as being outside of, or marginalized from, mainstream social relations and the attendant resources and opportunities that this involves.

SOCIAL REPRODUCTION: the processes through which societies sustain themselves in social and material terms across space and time. In purely material terms, people need to consume various commodities (housing, food, clothing, recreation, etc.) in order to sustain (reproduce) themselves, and these commodities have to be made available through various forms of exchange (e.g. wholesaling, retailing, sites of consumption like cinemas, concert venues, clubs). But, crucially, social reproduction is necessarily also a social process. It involves the development and transmission of norms and 'rules' of behaviour around the circuits of social reproduction that give direction to, and make sense of, their activities within such circuits. Social reproduction also suggests that the purpose of economic activity is not the generation of particular moments of production, consumption or exchange but the sustenance (the reproduction) of these activities over space and time.

SOCIALIZATION: the relations through which human beings learn about acceptable social norms and moral standards in a given society. Socialization can occur through different institutions and spaces such as the family, schools or the media.

SOCIALLY CONSTRUCTED/ION/ISTS: a catch-all term that emphasizes how both human geographies in the world 'out there' and the knowledges Human Geographers have of these geographies are the outcome of socio-spatial relations. For example, in debates about identity and difference social constructionists have opposed ESSENTIALIST conceptions which suggest that the differences between us are grounded in nature and emphasize instead how they are made and remade through the interweaving of wider socio-spatial processes and individual biographies. Whilst it runs the risk of reproducing a crude society/nature dichotomy, an emphasis on social construction has been widely drawn upon in Human Geography in order to emphasize how: (a) the things, situations and ideas that surround us are not innate but the products of social forces and practices that require explanation; and (b) nor are they inevitable, instead being open to the possibility of critique and change.

SPACE OF FLOWS: a term first coined by the urban theorist Manuel Castells in distinction to the 'space of places', this self-confessed 'cumbersome expression' emphasizes how the character and dynamics of a bounded place are reliant upon a host of connections and flows that go beyond its boundaries. These include flows of people (through many forms of travel and migration), of capital and money (think of the impacts of the global networks of the international financial system, for example), of ideas, of media imagery and of objects, amongst many others. The notion of the 'space of flows' is therefore a complement and corrective to Human Geographers' long-standing interest in bounded places and territories (*see* TERRITORY), perhaps particularly important in an age of intensified GLOBALIZATION.

SPATIAL CO-PRESENCE: a term used to describe a situation when several people or objects are found in the same location at the same time. For example, a holidaymaker and a tour guide are spatially co-present during a guided tour, but a farmer and the consumer who finally eats his/her product are usually spatially distant.

SPATIAL SCIENCE: an approach to Human Geography that became influential in the 1960s by arguing that geographers should be concerned with formulating and testing theories of spatial organization, interaction and distribution. The theories were often expressed in the form of models – of, for instance, land use, settlement hierarchy, industrial location and city sizes. If validated, these theories were then accorded the status of universal 'laws'. Through this manoeuvre, the advocates of spatial science claimed that Human Geography had been shifted from an essentially descriptive enterprise concerned with the study of regional differences to a predictive and explanatory science. Critics claim that in its attempts to formulate universally applicable laws, spatial science ignored the social and economic context within which its spatial variables were located.

SPATIALITY: socially produced space. This term is used by Human Geographers to emphasize how space is socially constructed and experienced, rather than being an innate backdrop to social life (*see also* SOCIAL CONSTRUCTION). As such it is a central concept of contemporary Human Geography. It is sometimes used in the plural, spatialities, in order to stress the many different ways in which space can be constructed and experienced.

STIGMA: a social process leading to the devaluation of an individual or group(s) who over time come to be identified as embodying negative traits such as dirt, disorder, laziness, criminality or mental illness. Human Geographers are especially interested in the spatial practices by which stigmatized groups come to be separated from mainstream society – thus re-enforcing the boundaries between the 'normal' and the 'deviant'.

STRUCTURATION: an approach to social theory that stresses the interconnection between knowledgeable human agents and the wider social structures within which they operate. Although used across the social sciences, the notion of structuration is most closely associated with the British sociologist Anthony Giddens, who developed structuration theory in a number of writings in the late 1970s and early 1980s. A key point of such theory is that the wider structural properties of social systems are both the medium and the outcome of the social practices that constitute the systems.

SYNCRETIC: an adjective applied to a culture or cultural phenomenon that is composed of elements from different sources, and that combines them in such a way as to create something new and different from those sources. Drawn from anthropological literatures, notions of the syncretic are very similar to those of HYBRIDITY, but are often preferred for their less biological undertones.

TECHNOCENTRISM: an outlook of optimism towards any environmental or other geographical challenge on the basis of the adaptiveness and innovation of human endeavour and technological know-how.

TEMPORALITY: socially produced time. This term is used by Human Geographers to emphasize how time is socially constructed and experienced, rather than being an innate backdrop to social life (*see also* SOCIAL CONSTRUCTION).

TERRAINS OF RESISTANCE: the material and/or symbolic ground upon which collective action (e.g. by social movements) takes place. This can involve the economic, political, cultural and ecological practices of resistance movements, as well as the physical places where their resistance occurs.

TERRITORY: a more or less bounded area over which an animal, person, social group or institution claims and attempts to enforce control.

TIME–SPACE COMPRESSION: coined by the Geographer David Harvey, this phrase has been more widely used to express (a) the transformations in TEMPORALITY and SPATIALITY produced in a world of ever more rapid turnover and ever quicker forms of communication; and (b) the subjective experience of these changes.

TRANSACTION COSTS: the costs involved in engaging in transactions, normally between productive firms. Such costs (which normally do not include the costs of commodities being exchanged or the costs of transport between points of supply and points of demand) may be associated with factors like distance. Distance may serve to increase costs as delays or misinformation may be more common when transactions are taking place between partners located some way away from each other. By contrast, geographical and social proximity may help to reduce transaction costs.

TRANSNATIONAL CORPORATIONS: very large companies with offices or plants in several countries; and/or companies that make decisions and accrue profits on a global basis (sometimes called multinational or global corporations).

TRANSNATIONAL: an adjective used to describe Human Geographical processes that have escaped the bounded confines of the NATION-STATE. These have been identified in the realms of the economy (*see* TRANSNATIONAL CORPORATIONS), in politics (for instance, through the political agency of groups in relation to a nation-state they do not reside in; e.g. Kurdish exiles campaigning for Kurdish nationalism) and in culture (for example, through the identification of 'transnational communities' that have dispersed from an originary homeland into a number of other countries but that also have strong linkages across this DIASPORA).

VENTURE CAPITAL: the provision of finance by an investor to businesses not quoted on stock markets and in the form of shares. The aim of venture capitalists is to make a very high return on their investment by selling their shares at a later date. Venture capital is a highly risky way to invest and, partly because of this, investors typically expect returns of over 30 per cent.

WHITE FLIGHT: this term refers to the ethnically specific nature of out-migration from urban areas, particularly in the USA. In many of the major metropolitan areas, large-scale ethnic immigration into the inner cities from the 1950s onwards was followed by the out-migration of affluent whites. The result has been a growing ethnic differentiation of urban space between poor minority urban areas and white suburbs. *See also* ETHNICITY.

WORLD-SYSTEM: an integrated international economic system, founded upon mercantile then industrial CAPITALISM, which originated in Europe around 1450 and spread to cover most of the world by 1900. World-systems analysis, which examines this system, treats the world as a single economic and social entity, the capitalist world economy.

BIBLIOGRAPHY

ABOLAFIA, M. (1996) *Making markets: opportunism and restraint on Wall Street*. MA: Harvard University Press.

ABRAMS, F. AND ANSTILL, J. (2001) Story of the blues, *Guardian* (G2), 29 May, 2–4.

ADAMS, P.C. AND GHOSE, R. (2003) India.com: the construction of a space between. *Progress in Physical Geography*, 27(4), 414–37.

ADAMS, V. (1992) Tourism and Sherpas, Nepal: reconstruction of reciprocity. *Annals of Tourism Research*, 19, 534–54.

ADAMS, W. (1990) *Green development: environment and sustainability in the Third World*. London: Routledge.

ADAMS, W. (1996) *Future nature*. London: Earthscan.

ADAMS, W.M. (2004) *Against extinction: the story of conservation*. London: Earthscan.

ADLER, J. (1989) Origins of sightseeing. *Annals of Tourism Research*, 16, 7–29.

ADLER, S. AND BRENNER, J. (1992) Gender and space: lesbians and gay men in the city. *International Journal of Urban and Regional Research*, 16, 24–34.

AGARWAL, S., BALL, R., SHAW, G. AND WILLIAMS, A. (2000) The geography of tourism production: uneven disciplinary development, *Tourism Geographies*, 2, 241–63.

AGNEW, J. (1987a) *Place and politics*. Boston: Allen & Unwin.

AGNEW, J. (1987b) *The United States in the world economy: a regional geography*. Cambridge: Cambridge University Press.

AGNEW, J. (1989) The devaluation of place in social science. In Agnew, J. and Duncan, J. (eds) *The power of place*. London: Unwin Hyman.

AGNEW, J. (1995) The rhetoric of regionalism: the northern league in Italian politics, 1983–94. *Transactions of the Institute of British Geographers*, 20(2), 156–72.

AGNEW, J. (1998) *Geopolitics*. London: Routledge.

AGNEW, J. (2002) *Place and politics in modern Italy*. Chicago: Chicago University Press.

AGNEW, J. AND CORBRIDGE, S. (1989) The new geopolitics: the dynamics of geopolitical disorder. In Johnston, R. and Taylor, P. (eds) *A world in crisis?* (2nd edn). Oxford: Blackwell.

AGNEW, J. AND CORBRIDGE, S. (1995) *Mastering space: hegemony, territory and international economy*. London: Routledge.

AGNEW, J.A., LIVINGSTONE, D. AND ROGERS, A. (EDS) (1996) *Human geography: an essential anthology*. Oxford: Blackwell.

AINGER, K., FOOT, J., JOY, C., MASSEY, D. AND RUTHERFORD, J. (2004) Thinking the globally locally: a roundtable. *Soundings*, 26, 46–58.

AITKEN, S. (2001) *Geographies of young people: the morally contested spaces of identity*. London: Routledge.

AITKEN, S. AND ZONN, L. (1993) Weir(d) sex: representations of gender-environment relations in Peter Weir's *Picnic at Hanging Rock* and *Gallipoli*. *Environment & Planning D: Society and Space* 11, 191–212.

ALBERS, P. AND JAMES, W. (1988) Travel Photography – a methodological approach. *Annals of Tourism Research*, 15, 134–58.

ALLAN, S., ADAM, B. AND CARTER, C. (EDS) (2000) *Environmental risks and the media*. London: Routledge.

ALLEN, J. (1995) Global worlds. In Allen, J. and Massey, D. (eds) *Geographical worlds*. Oxford: Oxford University Press.

ALLEN, J. AND MASSEY, D. (EDS.) (1995) *Geographical worlds*. Oxford: Oxford University Press.

ALLEYNE-DETTMERS, P. (1997) Tribal arts: a case study of global compression in the Notting Hill Carnival. In Eade, J. (ed.) *Living the global city*. London: Routledge.

ALLIEZ, E. AND NEGRI, A. (2003) Peace and war. *Theory, Culture and Society*, 20(2), 109–118B.

AMIN, S. (1990) *Maldevelopment: anatomy of a global failure*. London: Zed Books.

AMSDEN, A. (1989) *Asia's next giant: South Korea and late-industrialisation*. New York: OUP.

ANDERSON, A. (1997a) *Culture, media and environmental issues*. London: UCL Press.

ANDERSON, B. (1983) *Imagined communities: the origins and spread of nationalism*. London: Verso.

ANDERSON, B. (1991a) *Imagined communities: reflections on the origins and spread of nationalism*. London: Verso.

ANDERSON, B. (2003) Porto Allegre: a worm's eye view. *Global Networks*, 3, 197–200.

ANDERSON, I., KEMP, P. AND QUILGARS, D. (1993) *Single homeless people*. London, HMSO.

ANDERSON, J. (1988) Nationalist ideology and territory. In Johnston, R.J., Knight, D.B. and Kaufman, E. (eds) *Nationalism, self-determination and political geography*. London: Croom Helm.

ANDERSON, J. (1996) The shifting stage of politics: new medieval and postmodern territorialities. *Environment and Planning D: Society and Space*, 14(2), 133–53.

ANDERSON, K. (1991b) *Vancouver's Chinatown: racial discourse in Canada 1875–1980*. Montreal: McGill-Queen's University Press.

ANDERSON, K. (1997b) A walk on the wildside. *Progress in Human Geography*, 21(4), 463–85.

ANDERSON, K. AND DOMOSH, M. (eds) (2002) North American spaces/postcolonial stories. *Cultural Geographies*, 9(2), themed issue.

ANDERSON, K. AND GALE, F. (EDS) (1992) *Inventing places: studies in Cultural Geography*. London: Longman.

ANDERSON, K. AND GALE, F. (EDS) (1999) *Cultural geographies* (2nd edn). London: Longman.

ANDERSON, K. AND SMITH, S. (2001) Emotional geographies. *Transactions of the Institute of British Geographers*, NS, 26, 7–10.

ANDERSON, K., DOMOSH, M., PILE, S. AND THRIFT, N.J. (EDS) (2002) *Handbook of Cultural Geography*. London: Sage.

ANG, I. (1985) *Watching Dallas*. London and New York: Methuen.

ANG, I. (1991) *Desperately seeking the audience*. London and New York: Routledge.

ANSPRENGER, F. (1989) *The dissolution of the colonial empires*. London: Routledge.

ANZALDÚA, G. (1987) *Borderlands/La Frontera: the new Mestiza*. San Francisco: Aunt Lute.

APPADURAI, A. (ED.) (1986) *The social life of things. Commodities in cultural perspective*. Cambridge: Cambridge University Press.

APPADURAI, A. (ED.) (1987) *The social life of things*. Cambridge: Cambridge University Press.

APPADURAI, A. (1990) Disjuncture and difference in the global cultural economy. *Theory, Culture and Society*, 7, 295–310.

ARBLASTER, A. (1984) *The rise and fall of western liberalism*. Oxford: Blackwell.

ARIÈS, P. (1962) *Centuries of childhood*. New York: Vintage Press.

ARMSTRONG, J. (2004) The body within, the body without. *Globe and Mail*, 12 June, F1, F6.

ARREOLA, D.D. (1988) Mexican American housescapes. *Geographical Review*, 78, 299–315.

ARRIGHI, G. (1990) The three hegemonies of historical capitalism. *Review*, 13, 365–408.

ARRIGHI, G. (1994) *The long twentieth century*. London: Verso.

ASSOCIATION OF AMERICAN GEOGRAPHERS (2002) The geographical dimensions of terrorism: action items and research priorities. www.aag.org/news/godt.html, viewed 22 May 2002.

ATKINSON, R. AND MOON, G. (1994) *Urban policy in Britain*. London: Macmillan.

AUDIT COMMISSION (1989) *Urban regeneration and economic development: the local government dimension*. London: HMSO.

AUFDERHEIDER, P. (2000) *The Daily Planet: a critic on the capitalist culture beat*. Minneapolis: University of Minnesota Press.

AUGÉ, M. (1995) *Non-places: introduction to an anthropology of supermodernity*. Trans. John Howe. London: Verso.

AUGÉ, M. (1998) *A sense for the other*. Trans. A. Jacobs. Stanford, CA: Stanford University Press.

AZARYAHU, M. (2001) Water towers: a study in the Cultural Geography of Zionist mythology. *Ecumene. A journal of cultural geographies*, 8, 317–39.

BACK, L. (1995) X amount of Sat Siri Akal! Apache Indian, reggae music and the cultural intermezzo. *New Formations*, 27, 128–47.

BAIER, L. (1991/92) Farewell to regionalism, *Telos* 90 (winter), 82–8.

BAILES, A.J.K. (2004) Lessons of Iraq. Moscow, 20 April 2004, lecture. Downloaded 21 May 2004, from http://www.sipri.org/people/alyson_bailes/2004042001.html.

BAKER, N.C. (1984) *The beauty trap*. London: Piatkus.

BAKER, S. (1993) *Picturing the beast: animals, identity and representation*. Manchester: Manchester University Press.

BALDWIN, E., LONGHURST, B., MCCRACKEN, S., OGBORN, M. AND SMITH, G. (1999) *Introducing cultural studies*. Hemel Hempstead: Prentice Hall, Chapter 5, Culture, time and history.

BALDWIN, E., LONGHURST, B., MCCRACKEN, S. OGBORN, M. AND SMITH, G. (2004) *Introducing cultural studies* (revised 1st edn). Harlow: Pearson Education, Chapter 5: Culture, time and history.

BARBIER, E.B., BURGESS, J.C. AND FOLKE, C. (1994) *Paradise lost? The ecological economics of biodiversity*. London: Earthscan.

BARKER, C. (1999) *Television, globalization and cultural identities*. Buckingham: Open University Press.

BARNES, C. (1991) *Disabled people in Britain and discrimination*. London: Hurst and Company.

BARNES, M. (1997) *Care, communities and citizens*. Harlow: Longman.

BARNES, T.J. AND DUNCAN, J.S. (EDS) (1992) *Writing worlds: discourse, text and metaphor in the representation of landscapes*. London: Routledge.

BARNETT, A. AND SCRUTON, R. (EDS) (1998) *Town and country*. London: Jonathan Cape.

BARRELL, J. (1980) *The dark side of the landscape: the rural poor in English painting 1730–1840*. Cambridge: Cambridge University Press, 1–33.

BARRELL, J. (1990) The public prospect and the private view: the politics of taste in eighteenth-century Britain. In Pugh, S. (ed.) *Reading landscape: country – city – capital*. Manchester: Manchester University Press, 19–40.

BARRY, J. (1999) *Environment and social theory*. London: Routledge.

BARTHES, R. (1972) The great family of man. In *Mythologies*. London: Jonathan Cape.

BARTON, H. (1996) The Isles of Harris superquarry: concepts of environment and sustainability. *Environmental Values*, 5, 97–122.

BAUDRILLARD, J. (1988a) *America*. London: Verso.

BAUDRILLARD, J. (1988b) Consumer society. In Poster, M. (ed.) *Selected writings*. Cambridge: Polity Press.

BAUMAN, Z. (1990) *Thinking sociologically*. Cambridge, MA: Blackwell.

BAUMAN, Z. (1996) On communitarians and human freedom, *Theory, Culture and Society*, 13(2), 79–90.

BAUMANN, G. (1990) The re-invention of bhangra. *World Music*, 32(2), 81–95.

BEAUREGARD, B. (1994) *Voices of decline: the postwar fate of US cities*. Oxford: Blackwell.

BEAUREGARD, R. (1999) Break dancing on Santa Monica Boulevard. *Urban Geography*, 20(5), 396–9.

BEBBINGTON, A. AND BATTERBURY, S. (EDS) (2001) Transnational livelihood and landscapes: political ecologies of globalisation. *Ecumene. A journal of cultural geographies*, 8(4), special issue.

BECK, U. (1992a) From industrial society to the risk society: questions of survival, social structure and ecological enlightenment. *Theory, Culture and Society*, 9, 97–123.

BECK, U. (1992b) *Risk society: towards a new modernity*. London: Sage.

BECK, U. (1999) *World risk society*. Cambridge: Polity Press.

BECK, U. (2002) The silence of words and political dynamics in the world risk society. *Logos*, 1.4(Fall), 1–18.

BECK, U., GIDDENS, A. AND LASH, S. 1994. *Reflexive modernization: politics, tradition and aesthetics in the modern social order*. Cambridge: Polity Press.

BEGG, B., PICKLES, J. AND SMITH, A. (2003) Cutting it: European integration, trade regimes, and the reconfiguration of east-central European apparel production. *Environment and Planning A*, 35, 2205.

BELL, D. (1995) Pleasure and danger: the paradoxical spaces of sexual citizenship. *Political Geography*, 14(2), 139–54.

BELL, D. (1997) Anti-idyll: rural horror. In Cloke, P. and Little, J. (eds) *Contested countryside cultures*. London: Routledge.

BELL, D. AND VALENTINE, G. (1995a) *Mapping desire: geographies of sexualities*. London: Routledge.

BELL, D. AND VALENTINE, G. (1995b) Queer country: rural lesbian and gay lives. *Journal of Rural Studies*, 11, 113–22.

BELL, D. AND VALENTINE, G. (1997) *Consuming geographies: you are where you eat*. London: Routledge.

BELL, M. (1998) *An invitation to environmental sociology*. Thousand Oaks: Pine Forge Press.

BELL, M., BUTLIN, R. AND HEFFERNAN, M. (EDS) (1994) *Geography and imperialism, 1820–1940*. Manchester: Manchester University Press.

BENJAMIN, W. (1978) *Reflections*. New York: Harcourt Brace Jovanovitch.

BENNETT, B. AND ROUTLEDGE, P. (1997) Tibetan resistance 1950–present. In Powers, R.S., Vogele, W.B., Kruegler, C. and McCarthy, R.M. (eds) *Protest, power, and change*. New York: Garland Publishing.

BERGER, J. (1972) *Ways of seeing*. Harmondsworth: Penguin.

BERMAN, M. (1982) *All that is solid melts into air: the experience of modernity*. London: Verso.

BERNSTEIN, H. (1978) Notes on capital and peasantry. *Review of African Political Economy*, 10, 53–9.

BERNSTEIN, R. (1992) *The new constellation: the ethical – political horizons of modernity/postmodernity*. Cambridge, MA: MIT Press.

BERRY, B.J.L. (1970) The geography of the United States in the year 2000, *Transactions of the Institute of British Geographers*, 51, 21–54.

BHABHA, H.K. (1994) *The location of culture*. London: Routledge.

BHACHU, P. (1985) *Twice migrants*. London: Tavistock Publications.

BHACHU, P. (2003) *Dangerous designs: Asian women fashion the diaspora economies*. London: Routledge.

BHATTACHARYYA, D. (1997) Mediating India: an analysis of a guidebook. *Annals of Tourism Research*, 24(2), 371–89.

BILLIG, M. (1995) *Banal nationalism*. London: Sage.

BINNIE, J. (1995) Trading places: consumption, sexuality and the production of queer space. In Bell, D. and Valentine, G. (eds) *Mapping desire*. London: Routledge.

BINNIE, J. AND VALENTINE, G. (1999) Geographies of sexuality – a review of progress. *Progress in Human Geography*, 23, 175–87.

BLAKE, L. AND DWELLY, T. (1994) *Home front*. London: Shelter.

BLAIR, T. (2004) Message to the Commissioners from the Rt Hon. Tony Blair, Prime Minister of the United Kingdom, 24 May 2004. http://213.225.140.43/commission/message_to_comm.htm, accessed 30 June 2004.

BLAUT, J. (1993) *The colonizer's model of the world*. New York: Guilford.

BLOCH, A. (2002) *The migration and settlement of refugees in Britain*. London: Palgrave.

BLUNT, A. (1994) *Travel, gender, and imperialism: Mary Kingsley and West Africa*. New York: Guildford.

BLUNT, A. (2003) Geography and the humanities tradition. In Holloway, S., Price, S. and Valentine, G. *Key concepts in geography*. London: Sage.

BLUNT, A. AND MCEWAN, C. (EDS) (2002) *Postcolonial geographies*. London: Continuum.

BLUNT, A. AND VARLEY, A. (2004) Introduction: geographies of home. *Cultural Geographies*, 11, 3–6.

BLUNT, A. AND WILLS, J. (2000) *Dissident geographies: an introduction to radical ideas and practice*. London: Longman.

BONDI, L. *ET AL.* (2002) *Subjectivities, knowledge and feminist geographies*. Oxford: Rowman & Littlefield.

BONDI, L., DAVIDSON, J. AND SMITH, M. (forthcoming 2004) *Emotional geographies*.

BONNETT, A. (1997) Geography, 'race' and whiteness: invisible traditions and current challenges. *Area*, 29, 193–9.

BONWICK, J. (1884) *The lost Tasmanian race*. London: Sampson Low, Marston, Searle and Rivington.

BOORSTIN, D. (1992a) *The image: a guide to pseudo-events in America*. New York: Vintage Books (Random House, 2nd edn).

BOORSTIN, D. (1992b) From traveller to tourist: The lost arts of travel. In *The image: a guide to pseudo-events in America* (2nd edn). New York: Vintage Books, Random House.

BOOTH, D. (ED.) (1994) *Rethinking social development: theory, research and practice*. Harlow: Longman.

BORDEN, I. (2001) *Skateboarding, space and the city. Architecture and the body*. Oxford: Berg.

BORROW, G. (1989) *Wild Wales: the people, language and scenery*. Century Hutchinson.

BOUQUET, M. (1987) Bed, breakfast and an evening meal: commensality in the nineteenth and twentieth century farm household. In Bouquet, M. and Winter, M. (eds) *Who from their labour's rest? Conflict and practice in rural tourism*. Aldershot: Avebury.

BOURDIEU, P. (1984) *Distinction: a social critique of the judgement of taste*. Cambridge, MA: Harvard University Press.

BOURDIEU, P. (1990) *The logic of practice*. Stanford, CA: Stanford University Press.

BOYCE, J.K. (1992) Of coconuts and kings: the political economy of an export crop. *Development and Change*, 23(4), 1–25.

BOYD, W. AND WATTS, M. (1996) Agro-industrial just-in-time: the chicken industry and postwar American capitalism. In Goodman, D. and Watts, M. (eds) *Globalizing food*. London: Routledge.

BOYD, W. (2001) Industrial meat. *Technology and Culture*, 42, 153–78.

BOYER, P. (1994) *By the bomb's early light: American thought and culture at the dawn of the atomic age* (2nd edn). Chapel Hill and London: University of North Carolina Press.

BRADSHAW, M. AND STENNING, A. (EDS) (2004) *East Central Europe and the former Soviet Union*. London: Pearson Prentice Hall.

BRAH, A. (1996) *Cartographies of diaspora*. London: Routledge.

BRANTLINGER, P. (1985) Victorians and Africans: the genealogy of the myth of the Dark Continent. *Critical Inquiry*, 12, 166–203.

BRECHER, J. AND COSTELLO, T. (1994) *Global village or global pillage*. Boston: South End Press.

BRECHER, J., COSTELLO, T. AND SMITH, B. (2000) *Globalization from below: the power of solidarity*. Cambridge, MA: South End Press.

BRICKELL, C. (2000) Heroes and invaders: gay and lesbian pride parades and the public/private distinction in New Zealand media accounts. *Gender, Place and Culture*, 7, 163–78.

BROHMAN, J. (1996) *Popular development: rethinking the theory and practice of development*. Oxford: Blackwell.

BROOK, C. AND GIMPO (1997) *K Foundation burn a million quid*. London: Ellipsis.

BROWN, K., TURNER, R.K., HAMEED, H. AND BATEMAN, I. (1997) Environmental carrying capacity and tourism development in the Maldives and Nepal. *Environmental Conservation*, 24, 316–19.

BROWN, M. (1997) *Replacing citizenship: AIDS activism and radical democracy*. New York: Guilford Press.

BRUNDTLAND, H. (1987) *Our common future*. Oxford: Oxford University Press.

BRYANT, C.G.A. (2003) These Englands, or where does devolution leave the English? *Nations and Nationalism*, 8(3), 393–412.

BRYSON, J. *ET AL.* (eds) (1999) *The economic geography reader*. Chichester: Wiley.

BUCHLI, V. (ED.) (2002) *The material culture reader*. Oxford: Berg.

BUCK-MORSS, S. (1990) *The dialectics of seeing*. Cambridge, MA: MIT Press.

BULL, M. (2000) *Sounding out the city. Personal stereos and the management of everyday life*. Oxford: Berg.

BULLEN, A. AND WHITEHEAD, M. (2004) Negotiating the networks of space, time and substance: a geographical perspective on the sustainable citizen. Unpublished paper available from authors at Institute of Geography and Earth Sciences, University of Wales, Aberystwyth.

BUNCE, M. (1993) *The countryside deal*. London: Routledge.

BUNGE, W. (1971) *Fitzgerald: geography of a revolution*. Cambridge, MA: Schenkman Publishing.

BUNGE, W. (1973) The geographer. *Professional Geographer*, 25, 331–7.

BUNN, D. (1994) 'Our wattled cot': mercantile and domestic space in Thomas Pringle's African landscapes. In Mitchell, W.J.T. (ed.) *Landscape and power*. Chicago, IL: University of Chicago Press, 127–74.

BURGDORF, M.P. AND BURGDORF, R. (1975) A history of unequal treatment: the qualifications of handicapped persons as a suspect class under the equal protection clause. *Santa Clara Lawyer*, 15, 855–910.

BURGESS, J. (1985) News from nowhere: the press, the riot and the myth of the inner city. In Burgess, J. and Gold, J. (eds) *Geography, the media and popular culture*. London and Sydney: Croom Helm.

BURGESS, J. (1990) The production and consumption of environmental meanings in the mass media. *Transactions of the Institute of British Geographers*, 15, 139–61.

BURGESS, J. (1993) Representing nature: conservation and the mass media. In Goldsmith, B. and Warren, A. (eds) *Conservation in progress*. Chichester: John Wiley.

BURGESS, J. AND GOLD, J. (EDS) (1985) *Geography, the media and popular culture*. London and Sydney: Croom Helm.

BURGESS, J. AND UNWIN, D. (1984) Exploring the living planet with David Attenborough. *Journal of Geography in Higher Education*, 8(2), 93–113.

BURGESS, J., BEDFORD, T., HOBSON, K., DAVIES, G. AND HARRISON, C.M. (2003) (un) sustainable consumption. In Berkhout, F., Leach, M. and Scoones, I. (eds) *Negotiating environmental change: new perspectives from social science*. Cheltenham: Edward Elgar, 261–92.

BURGESS, J., HARRISON, C.M. AND FILIUS, P. (1998) Environmental communication and the cultural politics of environmental citizenship. *Environment and Planning*, A, 30, 1445–60.

BURGESS, J., LIMB, M. HARRISON, C.M. (1988a) Exploring environmental values through the medium of small groups 1: theory and practice. *Environment and Planning A*, 20, 309–26.

BURGESS, J., LIMB, M. HARRISON, C.M. (1988b) Exploring environmental values through the medium of small groups 2: illustrations of a group at work. *Environment and Planning A*, 20, 457–76.

BURTON, D., KNIGHTS, D., LEYSHON, A., ALFEROFF, C. AND SIGNORETTA, P. (2004) Making a market: the UK retail financial services industry and the rise of the complex sub-prime credit market. *Competition and Change*, 8, 3–25.

BUSH, G.W. (2001) News releases for September 2001. http://www.whitehouse.gov/news/releases/2001/09/.

BUSH, G.W. (2004) *President outlines steps to help Iraq achieve democracy and freedom. Remarks by the President on Iraq and the War on Terror*. United States Army War College, Carlisle, Pennsylvania, 24 May 2004. http://www.whitehouse.gov/news/releases/2004/05/20040524-10.html.

BUTLER, R. (1998) Rehabilitating the images of disabled youths. In Skelton, T. and Valentine, G. (eds) *Cool places: geographies of youth culture*. London: Routledge.

BUTLER, R. AND BOWLBY, S. (1997) Bodies and spaces: an exploration of disabled people's use of public space. *Environment and Planning D: Society and Space*, 15(4), 411–33.

BUTLER, T. (1997) *Gentrification and the middle classes*. Aldershot: Ashgate.

CAIRNCROSS, F. (1977) *The death of distance*. Cambridge, MA: Harvard Business School Press.

CALLINICOS, A. (2003) *An anti-capitalist manifesto*. Cambridge: Polity.

CAMBRENSIS, G. (1978) *The journey through Wales and the description of Wales*. Harmondsworth: Penguin.

CAMPBELL, C. (1987) *The romantic ethic and the spirit of modern consumption*. Oxford: Blackwell.

CAMPBELL, D. (1992) *Writing security: United States foreign policy and the politics of identity*. Minneapolis: University of Minnesota Press.

CANADIAN GEOGRAPHER (2003) Special Issue on Disability in Society and Space, 47(4).

CAREY, J. AND QUIRK, J. (1970a) The mythos of the electronic revolution. *American Scholar*, Winter, 219–41.

CAREY, J. AND QUIRK, J. (1970b) The mythos of the electronic revolution. *American Scholar*, Summer, 395–424.

CAREY, S. (2004) *Curry capital*. London: Institute of Community Studies.

CARNEY, G. (1998) *Baseball, barns and bluegrass: a geography of American folklife*. Oxford: Rowman and Littlefield.

CARR, E.H. (1961) *What is history?* London: Macmillan.

CARSON, R. (1964) *Silent spring*. Boston: Little, Brown.

CASTELLS, M. (1983) *The city and the grassroots*. London: Edward Arnold.

CASTELLS, M. (1989) *The informational city*. Oxford: Blackwell.

CASTELLS, M. (1996) *The rise of the network society. Volume I, The information age: economy, society and culture*. Cambridge, MA and Oxford: Blackwell.

CASTELLS, M. (1997) *End of millennium: Volume III, The information age: economy, society and culture*. Oxford: Blackwell.

CASTLES, S. AND MILLER, M. (1998) *The age of migration*. Basingstoke: Macmillan.

CASTREE, N. (1995) The nature of produced nature. *Antipode*, 27(1), 12–48.

CASTREE, N. AND BRAUN, B. (EDS) (2001) *Social nature: theory, practice and politics*. Oxford: Blackwell.

CASTREE, N. AND MACMILLAN, T. (2004) Old news: representation and academic novelty. *Environment and Planning A*, 36, 469–80.

CASTREE, N. AND SPARKE, M. (2000) Professional geography and the corporatization of the university: experiences, evaluations and engagements, *Antipode*, 32(3), 222–9.

CELL, J. (1982) *The highest stage of white supremacy*. Cambridge: Cambridge University Press.

CHAKRABARTY, D. (1999) Adda, Calcutta: dwelling in modernity. *Public Culture*, 11, 109–45.

CHAMPION, A.G. (1989) Counterurbanisation in Europe, *The Geographical Journal*, 155, 52–9.

CHANG, T.C. (2000) Renaissance revisited: Singapore as a 'global city for the arts'. *International Journal of Urban and Regional Research*, 24(4), 818–31.

CHANG, T.C. AND LEE, W.K. (2003) Renaissance city Singapore: a study of arts spaces. *Area*, 35(2), 128–41.

CHANT, S. (1997) *Women-headed households: diversity and dynamics in the developing world*. Basingstoke: Macmillan.

CHAPLIN, M. (1998) Authenticity and otherness: the Japanese theme park. *Architectural Design*, 131, 76–9.

CHARLESWORTH, A. (1994) Contesting places of memory: the case of Auschwitz. *Environment and Planning D: Society and Space*, 12, 579–93.

CHARTIER, R. (1989) The practical impact of writing. In Chartier, R. (ed.) *Passions of the Renaissance*. Cambridge, MA: Belknap Press.

CHARTIER, R. (1994) *The order of books: readers, authors, and libraries in Europe between the fourteenth and fifteenth centuries*. Cambridge: Polity.

CHATTERJEE, P. (1986) *Nationalist thought and the colonial world*. London: Zed Books.

CHATTERJEE, P. AND FINGER, M. (1994) *The earth brokers: power, politics and world development*. Routledge: London.

CHENNAULT, C. (1948) Why we must help China now. *Reader's Digest*, April, 121–2.

CHERTOW, M. AND ESTY, D. (EDS) (1997) *Thinking ecologically: the new guardians of environmental policy*. New Haven, CT: Yale University Press.

CHESHIRE, P (1995) A new phase of urban development in western Europe: the evidence for the 1980s, *Urban Studies*, 32(7), 1045–64.

CHOI, S.R., PARK, D. AND TSCHOEGL, A.E. (1996) Banks and the world's major banking centres 1990. *Weltwirtschaftliches Archiv*, 132, 774–93.

CHOI, S.R., PARK, D. *ET AL.* (2003) Banks and the world's major banking centers, 2000. *Review of World Economics*, 139(3), 550–68.

CHRISTIAN AID (2004) *Trade justice*. London: Christian Aid.

CHUA, B.H. (1995) *Communitarian ideology and democracy in Singapore*. London: Routledge.

CHUA, B.H. (1997) *Political legitimacy and housing: stakeholding in Singapore*. New York: Routledge.

CHUA, B.H. AND YEO, W.W. (2003) Singapore cinema: Eric Khoo and Jack Neo – critique from the margins and mainstream. *Inter-Asia Cultural Studies*, 4(1), 117–25.

CHURCHILL, W. (1993) *Struggle for the land*. Monroe, ME: Common Courage Press.

CLARK, G., GERTLER, M. AND FELDMAN, M. (2000) *The Oxford handbook of economic geography*. Oxford: Oxford University Press.

CLARK, G.L. (2000) *Pension fund capitalism*. Oxford: Oxford University Press.

CLARK, G.L., THRIFT, N. AND TICKELL, A. (2004) Performing finance: the industry, the media and its image. *Review of International Political Economy*, 11(2), 289–310.

CLARK, G.L. AND HEBB, T. (2004) Pension fund corporate engagement – the fifth stage of capitalism. *Relations Industrielles-Industrial Relations*, 59(1), 142–71.

CLARK, W. AND MCNICHOLAS, M. (1996) Re-examining economic and social polarisation in a multi-ethnic metropolitan area: the case of Los Angeles. *Area*, 28, 56–63.

CLARK, W.A.V. (1996) Scale effects of international migration to the United States. *Regional Studies*, 30, 589–600.

CLARK, W.A.V. (1998a) *The California cauldron: immigration and the fortunes of local communities*. New York: Guilford Press.

CLARK, W.A.V. (1998b) Mass migration and local outcomes: is international migration to the United States creating a new urban underclass. *Urban Studies*, 35, 3, 371–84.

CLARKE, C. (2002) The Latin American structuralists. In Desai, V. and Potter, R.B. (eds) *The Companion to Development Studies*. London: Arnold, 92–6.

CLARKE, D.B. (2003) *The consumer society and the postmodern city*. London and New York: Routledge.

CLASTRES, P. (1998) *Chronicle of the Guayaki Indians*. Trans. by P. Auster. London: Faber and Faber.

CLIFFORD, J. (1994) Diasporas. *Cultural Anthropology*, 9(3), 302–38.

CLOKE, P. (1993) The countryside as commodity: new spaces for rural leisure. In Glyptis, S. (ed.) *Leisure and the environment*. London: Belhaven.

CLOKE, P. (1997) Poor country: marginalization, poverty and rurality. In Cloke, P. and Little, J. (eds) *Contested countryside cultures*. London: Routledge.

CLOKE, P. (ED.) (2002) *Country visions*. Harlow: Pearson.

CLOKE, P. (2004) Exploring boundaries of professional/personal practice and action: being and becoming in Khayelitsha township, Cape Town. In Fuller, D. and Kitchin, R. (eds) *Radical theory/critical praxis: making a difference beyond the academy*. Praxis (e) Press, 92–102.

CLOKE, P. (2005) Conceptualising rurality. In Cloke, P., Marsden, T. and Mooney, P. (eds) *Handbook of rural studies*. London: Sage.

CLOKE, P. AND LITTLE, J. (EDS) (1997) *Contested countryside cultures*. London: Routledge.

CLOKE, P. AND MILBOURNE, P. (1992) Deprivation and lifestyles in rural Wales II: rurality and the cultural dimension. *Journal of Rural Studies*, 8, 360–74.

CLOKE, P. AND PERKINS, H. (1998) 'Cracking the canyon with the Awesome Foursome': representations of adventure tourism in New Zealand. *Environment and Planning D: Society and Space*, 16, 185–218.

CLOKE, P., MARSDEN, T. AND MOONEY, P. (EDS) (2005) *Handbook of rural studies*. London: Sage.

CLOKE, P., CRANG, P. AND GOODWIN, M. (EDS) (2004a) *Envisioning human geographies*. London: Arnold.

CLOKE, P., COOK, I., CRANG, P., GOODWIN, M., PAINTER, J. AND PHILO, C. (2004b) *Practising Human Geography*. London: Sage.

CLOKE, P., JOHNSEN, S. AND MAY, J. (2004c) Journeys and pauses: tactical and performative spaces in the homeless city. Unpublished manuscript available from authors at the University of Bristol.

CLOKE, P., PHILO, C. AND SADLER, D. (1991) *Approaching Human Geography*. London: Paul Chapman Publishing.

COCKBURN, C. (1997) Domestic technologies: Cinderella and the Engineers. *Women's Studies International Forum*, 20, 361–71.

COE, N.M., HESS, M., WAI-CHUNG YEUNG, H., DICKEN, P. AND HENDERSON, J. (2004) Globalizing regional development: a global production networks perspective. *Transactions of the Institute of British Geographers 2004*, 7.

COHEN, A. (1982) A polyethnic London carnival as a contested cultural performance. *Ethnic and Racial Studies* 5, 23–41.

COHEN, L. (2003) *A consumer's republic: the politics of mass consumption in postwar America*. New York: Knopf.

COHEN, R. (1997) *Global diasporas: an introduction*. London: UCL Press.

COHEN, S. (1980) *Folk devils and moral panics: the creations of the Mods and Rockers* (2nd edn). Oxford: Martin Robertson.

COLEMAN, S. AND CRANG, M. (2002) *Tourism: between place and performance*. Oxford: Berghahn.

COLYER, R. (1976) *The Welsh cattle drovers: agriculture and the Welsh cattle trade before and during the nineteenth century*. Cardiff: University of Wales Press.

COMAROFF, J. AND COMAROFF, J. (1990) *Ethnography and the historical imagination*. Boulder, CO: Westview Press.

COMMISSION OF THE EUROPEAN COMMUNITIES (1986) Television and the audiovisual sector: towards a European policy. *European File*, 14(86), August–September.

CONE, C. (1995) Crafting Selves: the lives of two Mayan women. *Annals of Tourism Research*, 22(2), 314–27.

CONRADSON, D. (2003) Geographies of care: spaces, practices, experiences. *Social and Cultural Geography*, 4(4), 451ff.

CONVERSI, D. (1990) Language or race? The choice of core values in the development of Catalan and Basque nationalisms. *Ethnic and Racial Studies*, 13(1), 50–70.

COOK, I. (2000) Social sculpture and Shelley Sacks's 'Exchange Values'. *Ecumene*, 7, 338–44.

COOK, I. (2004) Follow the thing: papaya. *Antipode*, 36, 642–64.

COOK, I. AND CRANG, P. (1996) The world on a plate: culinary culture, displacement and geographical knowledges. *Journal of Material Culture*, 1, 131–53.

COOK, I. AND HARRISON, M. (2003) Cross over food: re-materializing postcolonial geographies. *Transactions of the Institute of British Geographers*, NS28, 296–317.

COOMBES, A.E. (1994) National unity and racial and ethnic identities: the Franco–British Exhibition of 1908. In *Reinventing Africa*. New Haven, CT: Yale University Press.

COOPER, A., LAW, R., MALTHUS, J. AND WOOD, P. (2000) Rooms of their own: public toilets and gendered citizens in a New Zealand city, 1860–1940. *Gender, Place and Culture*, 7(4), 417–35.

CORBETT, J. (1994) A proud label: exploring the relationship between disability politics and gay pride. *Disability and Society*, 9(3), 343–57.

CORBRIDGE, S. (1993) Colonialism, post-colonialism and the political geography of the Third World. In Taylor, P. (ed.) *Political geography of the twentieth century*. London: Bellhaven Press.

CORBRIDGE, S. (ED.) (1995) *Development studies – a reader*. London: Arnold.

CORBRIDGE, S., THRIFT, N.J. AND MARTIN, R. (1996) *Money, power and space*. Oxford: Blackwell.

CORRIGAN, P. (1997) *The sociology of consumption: an introduction*. Thousand Oaks: Sage.

COSGROVE, D. (1984) Prospect, perspective and the evolution of the landscape idea. *Transactions of the Institute of British Geographers*, 10, 45–62.

COSGROVE, D. (1985a) Prospect, perspective and the evolution of the landscape idea. *Transactions of the Institute of British Geographers*, 10, 45–62.

COSGROVE, D. (1985b) *Social formation and symbolic landscape*. London: Croom Helm.

COSGROVE, D. (1989) Geography is everywhere: culture and symbolism in human landscapes. In Gregory, D. and Walford, R. (eds) *Horizons in Human Geography*. Basingstoke: Macmillan.

COSGROVE, D. (1994) Contested global visions: one-world, whole-earth and the Apollo space photographs. *Annals of the Association of American Geographers*, 84, 270–94.

COSGROVE, D. (1997) Prospect, perspective and the evolution of the landscape idea. In Barnes, T. and Gregory, D. *Reading Human Geography*. London: Edward Arnold, 324–41.

COSGROVE, D. (2001) *Apollo's eye: a cartographic genealogy of the globe in the western imagination*. Baltimore: Johns Hopkins University Press.

COSGROVE, D. (2003) Heritage and history: a Venetian geography lesson. In Peckham, R.S. (ed.) *Rethinking heritage: culture and politics in Europe*. London: I.B. Taurus, 113–23.

COSGROVE, D. AND DANIELS, S. (EDS) (1989) *The iconography of landscape: essays on the symbolic, design and use of past environments*. Cambridge: Cambridge University Press.

COTGROVE, S. AND DUFF, A. (1980) Environmentalism, middle class radicalism and politics. *Sociology Review*, 28, 335–51.

COULOUBARITSIS, L., DE LEEUW, M., NOEL, E. AND STERCKX, E. (1993) *The origins of European identity*. Brussels: European Interuniversity Press.

COWEN, T. (1998) *In praise of commercial culture*. Cambridge, MA: Harvard University Press.

COX, K. (2002) *Political geography: territory state and nation*. Oxford: Blackwell.

CRANG, M. (1998a) *Cultural geography*. London: Routledge.

CRANG, M. (1998b) Places of practice, and the practice of science. *Environment and Planning A*, 30, 1971–4.

CRANG, M. AND THRIFT, N. (2000) *Thinking space*. London: Routledge.

CRANG, M., CRANG, P. AND MAY, J. (EDS) (1999) *Virtual geographies*. London: Routledge.

CRANG, P. (1994) It's showtime: on the workplace geographies of display in southeast England. *Environment and Planning D: Society and Space*, 12, 675–704.

CRANG, P. (1997) Performing the tourist product. In Rojek, C. and Urry, J. (eds) *Touring cultures: transformations of travel and theory*. London: Routledge.

CRANG, P. (ED.) (2003) Field cultures. *Cultural Geographies*, 10, special issue, 251–378.

CRANG, P. (2004) The geographies of consumption. In Daniels, P., Bradshaw, M., Bryson, J. and Sidaway, J. (eds) *Introduction to Human Geography* (2nd edn). Harlow: Prentice Hall.

CRANG, P., DWYER, C. AND JACKSON, P. (2003) Transnationalism and the spaces of commodity culture. *Progress in Human Geography*, 27, 438–56.

CRESSWELL, T. (1994) Putting women in their place: the carnival at Greenham Common. *Antipode*, 26(1), 35–58.

CRESSWELL, T. (1996) *In place/out of place: geography, ideology and transgression*. Minneapolis: University of Minnesota Press.

CRESSWELL, T. (2001) The production of mobilities. *New Formations*, 43, 4–28.

CRESSWELL, T. (2003) Landscape and the obliteration of practice. In Anderson, K., Domosh, M., Pile, S. and Thrift, N. (eds) *Handbook of Cultural Geography*. London: Sage, 269–81.

CRESSWELL, T. (2004) *Place: a short introduction*. Oxford: Blackwell.

CRONON, W. (1995) The trouble with wilderness: or getting back to the wrong nature. In Cronon, W. (ed.) *Uncommon ground: towards reinventing nature*. New York: W.W. Norton.

CROSS, G. (2000) *An all-consuming century: why commercialism won in modern America*. New York: Columbia University Press.

CUGOANO, O. (1787) *Thoughts and sentiments on the evil and wicked traffic of slavery and commerce of the human species*. London: T. Becket.

CULLER, J. (1988) *Framing the sign: criticism and its institutions*. Oxford: Basil Blackwell.

CUNNINGHAM, H. (1992) *Children of the poor: representations of childhood since the seventeenth century*. Oxford: Polity Press.

CUTTER, S. (2000) Why didn't geographers map the human genome? *AAG Newsletter*, 35(9), 3–4.

DAILY, G.C. (1997) (ed.) *Nature's services: societal dependence on natural ecosystems*. Washington: Island Press.

DALBY, S. (1988) Geopolitical discourse: the Soviet Union as Other. *Alternatives*, XIII.

DALBY, S. (1990) American security discourse: the persistence of geopolitics. *Political Geography Quarterly*, 9(2), 171–88.

DALBY, S. (1994) Gender and geopolitics: reading security discourse in the new world order. *Environment and Planning D: Society and Space*, 12(5), 525–46.

DALY, H.E. (1990) Toward some operational principles of sustainable development. *Ecological Economics*, 2, 1–6.

DANIELS, S. (1982) Humphry Repton and the morality of landscape. in Gold, J.R. and Burgess, J. (eds) *Valued environments*. London: Allen & Unwin, 124–44.

DANIELS, S. (1985) Arguments for a humanistic geography. In R.J. Johnston (ed.) *The future of Geography*, 143–58.

DANIELS, S. (1993) *Fields of vision: landscape imagery and national identity in England and the United States*. Cambridge: Polity Press.

DANIELS, S. AND LEE, R. (EDS) (1996) *Exploring Human Geography: a reader*. London: Arnold.

DANIELS, S. AND COSGROVE, D. (1993) Spectacle and text: landscape metaphors in Cultural Geography. In Duncan, J.S. and Ley, D. (eds) *Place/culture/representation*. London: Routledge, 57–77.

DANIELS, S. AND SEYMOUR, S. (1990) Landscape design and the idea of improvement 1730–1900. In Dodgson, R.A. and Butlin, R.A. (eds) *An historical geography of England and Wales*. London: Academic Press, 187–520.

DANN, G. (1996) The people of tourist brochures. In Selwyn, T. (ed.) The tourist image: myths and myth making in tourism. London: Wiley, 61–82.

DANT, T. (1999) *Material culture in the social world: values, activities, lifestyles*. Buckingham: Open University Press.

DARBY, H. (1962) The problem of geographical description. *Transactions of the Institute of British Geographers*, 30, 1–14.

DARDEN, J. (2004) *The significance of white supremacy in the Canadian metropolis of Toronto*. Edwin Mellon Press.

DARNTON, R. (1979) *The business of the Enlightenment: a publishing history of the encyclopaedia*. Cambridge, MA: Harvard University Press.

DAVIDSON, B. (1992) *The black man's burden*. New York: Times Books.

DAVIDSON, J. AND BONDI, L. (2004) Emotional geographies of gender and sexuality: spatialising affect; affecting space. *Gender, Place and Culture*, 11(3), 373–4.

DAVIDSON, J. AND MILLIGAN, C. (2004) Embodying emotion, sensing space: introducing emotional geographies. *Social and Cultural Geography* 5(4), 523–32.

DAVIES, G. (1999) Science, observation and entertainment: competing visions of postwar British natural history television, 1946–1967. *Ecumene. A journal of cultural geographies*, 7.

DAVIS, M. (1990) *City of quartz: excavating the future in Los Angeles*. London: Verso.

DE ANGELIS, M. (2000) New internationalism and the Zapatistas. *Capital and Class*, 70, 9–36.

DE CERTEAU, M. (1984) *The practice of everyday life*. Berkeley: University of California Press.

DE GOEDE, M. (2001) Discourses of scientific finance and the failure of long-term capital management. *New Political Economy*, 6, 149–70.

DEAR, M. (1999) The relevance of postmodernism. *Scottish Geographical Magazine*, 115(2).

DEAR, M. AND FLUSTY, S. (1998) Postmodern urbanism. *Annals of the Association of American Geographers*, 88, 50–72.

DEAR, M. AND WOLCH, J. (1987) *Landscapes of despair: from deinstitutionalization to homelessness*. Princeton: Princeton University Press.

DEBORD, G. (1977) *Society of the spectacle*. Detroit: Black and Red Books.

DEFRA (2002) The environment in your pocket: key facts and figures on the environment of the United Kingdom. Available free from www.defra.gov.uk.

DELANTY, G. (1995) *Inventing Europe: idea, identity, reality*. Basingstoke: Macmillan.

DELYSER, D. AND STARRS, P. (2001) Doing fieldwork. *The Geographical Review*, 91, iv–viii.

DEPARTMENT FOR INTERNATIONAL DEVELOPMENT (1997) *Eliminating world poverty: a challenge for the 21st century*. London: UK Government Stationery Office.

DER DERIAN, J. (1992) *Anti-diplomacy: spies, terror, speed and war*. Oxford: Blackwell.

DER DERIAN, J. (2002) The war of networks. *Theory and event*, 5, 4.

DERY, M. (1993) Flame wars. In Dery, M. (ed.) *Flame wars: the discourse of cyberculture*. Durham, NC: Duke University Press.

DESFORGES, L. (2004) The formation of global citizenship: international non-governmental organizations in Britain. *Political Geography*, 23, 549–69.

DESKINS, D.R. (1996) Economic restructuring, job opportunities and black social dislocation in Detroit. In O'Loughlin, J. and Friedrichs, J. (eds) *Social polarization in post-industrial metropolises*. Berlin and New York: de Gruyter.

DETR (2001) *Local strategic partnerships: government guidance*. London: HMSO.

DEVERTEUIL, G. (2003) Homeless mobility, institutional settings, and the new poverty management. *Environment and Planning A*, 2003, 35, 361–79.

D'HAUTESERRE, A.-M. (1999) The French mode of social regulation and sustainable tourism development: the case of Disneyland Paris. *Tourism Geography*, 1, 86–107.

DICKEN, P. (1998) *Global shift* (3rd edn). London: Paul Chapman.

DICKEN, P. (2003) *Global shift* (4th edn). London: Sage Publications.

DICKEN, P. (2004a) Geographers and globalisation: (yet) another missed boat? *Transactions of the Institute of British Geographers*, 29, 5–26.

DICKEN, P. (2004b) Globalization, production and the (im)morality of uneven development. In Lee, R. and Smith, D. (eds) *Geographies and moralities: international perspectives on development, justice and place.* Oxford: Blackwell.

DICKEN, P. AND THRIFT, N. (1992) The organization of production and the production of organization: why business enterprises matter in the study of geographical industrialization. *Transactions of the Institute of British Geographers*, NS 17(3), 279–91.

DIXON, D. AND JONES, J.P. (2004) Guest editorial: What next? *Environment and Planning A*, 36, 381–90.

DOBSON, A. (2000) *Green political thought* (3rd edn). London: Routledge.

DODD, L. (1992) Heritage and the 'Big House': whitewash for rural history. *Irish Reporter*, 6, 9–11.

DODD, L. (1993) Interview by Nuala Johnson, Strokestown Park House, 2 September.

DOEL, M. (1994) Deconstruction on the move: from libidinal economy to liminal materialism. *Environment and Planning A*, 26, 1041–59.

DOHMEN, R. (2004) The home in the world: women, threshold designs and performative relations in contemporary Tamil Nadu, south India. *Cultural Geographies*, 11, 7–25.

DOMOSH, M. (1994) The symbolism of the skyscraper: case studies of New York's first tall buildings. In Foote, K.E., Hugill, P.J., Mathewson, K. and Smith, J.M. (eds) *Re-reading Cultural Geography*. Austin: University of Texas Press, 48–63.

DOMOSH, M. (1996) A 'feminine' building? Relations between gender ideology and aesthetic ideology in turn-of-the-century America. *Ecumene. A journal of environment, culture and meaning*, 3, 305–24.

DOMOSH, M. (1999) Corporate cultures and the modern landscape of New York. In Anderson, K. and Gale, F. (eds) *Cultural geographies*. London: Longman, 95–111.

DOMOSH, M. AND SEAGER, J. (2001) *Putting women in place: feminist geographers make sense of the world.* New York: Guildford Press.

DORLING, D. (1997) *Death in Britain: how local mortality rates have changed 1950s–1990s.* York: Joseph Rowntree Foundation.

DORRA, M. (1996) La traversée des apparences, *Le Monde Diplomatique*, June, 32.

DOUGLAS, M. AND ISHERWOOD, B. (1979) *The world of goods.* New York: Basic Books.

DOWNS, A. (1972) Up and down with ecology: the issue-attention cycle. *The Public Interest*, 28, 38–50.

DRAKULIC, S. (1996) *Café Europa*. London: Abacus.

DRIVER, F. (1992) Geography's empire: histories of geographical knowledge. *Environment and Planning D. Society and Space*, 10, 23–40.

DRIVER, F. (2001) *Geography militant: cultures of exploration and empire.* Oxford: Blackwell.

DRIVER, F. (2003) The geopolitics of knowledge and ignorance. *Transactions of the Institute of British Geographers*, 27, 131–2.

DRIVER, F. AND GILBERT, D. (1998) Heart of empire? Landscape, space and performance in imperial London. *Environment and Planning D: Society and Space*, 16, 11–28.

DRIVER, F. AND MARTINS, L. (2002) John Septimus Roe and the art of navigation, c.1815–1830. *History Workshop Journal*, 54, 144–61.

DRIVER, F., NASH, C., PRENDERGAST, K. AND SWENSON, P. (2002) *Landing: eight collaborative projects between artists and geographers.* Egham: Royal Holloway, University of London.

DRYZEK, J. (1997) *The politics of the earth*. Oxford: Oxford University Press.

DU GAY, P., HALL, S., JONES, L., MACKAY, H. AND NEGUS, K. (1997) *Doing cultural studies: the story of the Sony Walkman.* London: Sage.

DUNBAR, G. (1974) Geographical personality. *Geoscience and Man*, V, 25–33.

DUNCAN, J. (1990) *The city as text: the politics of landscape interpretation in the Kandyan kingdom.* Cambridge: Cambridge University Press.

DUNCAN, J. (2003) Representing Empire at the National Maritime Museum. In Peckham, R.S. (ed.) *Rethinking heritage: culture and politics in Europe.* London: I.B. Taurus, 17–28.

DUNCAN, J. (1995) Landscape geography 1993–94. *Progress in Human Geography*, 19, 414–22.

DUNCAN, J.S. (1973) Landscape taste as a symbol of group identity: a Westchester County village. *Geographical Review*, 63, 334–55.

DUNCAN, J.S. (1999) Elite landscapes as cultural (re)productions: the case of Shaughnessy Heights. In Anderson, K. and Gale, F. (eds) *Cultural geographies*. London: Longman, 53–70.

DUNCAN, J.S. AND DUNCAN, N.G. (2004) *Landscapes of privilege: the politics of the aesthetic in an American suburb.* New York: Routledge.

DUNCAN, S. AND GOODWIN, M. (1988) *The local state and uneven development.* Cambridge: Polity Press.

DWYER, C. (2004) Tracing transnationalities through commodity culture: a case study of British-South Asian fashion. In Jackson, P., Crang, P. and Dwyer, C. (eds) *Transnational Spaces*. London: Routledge.

DWYER, C. AND CRANG, P. (2002) Fashioning ethnicities: the commercial spaces of multiculture. In *Ethnicities*, 2(3), 410–30.

DWYER, C. AND JACKSON, P. (2003) Commodifying difference: selling EASTern fashion. *Environment and Planning D: Society and Space*, 21, 269–91.

DYCK, I. (1999) Body troubles: women, the workplace and negotiations of a disabled identity. In Butler, R. and Parr, H. (eds) *Mind and body spaces: geographies of illness, impairment and disability.* London: Routledge, 119–37.

DYER, R. (1997) *White*. London: Routledge.

DYMSKI, G.A. AND VEITCH, J.M. (1996) Financial transformation and the metropolis: booms, busts and banking in Los Angeles. *Environment and Planning A*, 28, 1233–60.

EADE, J. (1997) Identity, nation and religion: educated young Bangladeshi Muslims in London's East End. In Eade, J. (ed.) *Living the global city*. London: Routledge.

EBODA, M. (1997) Rum do as Reggae Boyz blow hot. *The Observer*, 18 November 1997, 12.

ECO, U. (1985) How culture conditions the colours we see. In Blonsky, M. (ed.) *On signs*. Oxford: Blackwell, 157–83.

ECO, U. (1987) *Travels in hyper-reality*. London: Picador.

ECOLOGIST, THE (1972) *A blueprint for survival*. Harmondsworth: Penguin.

EDENSOR, T. (2000) Staging tourism: tourists as performers. *Annals of Tourism Research*, 27, 322–44.

EDENSOR, T. (2002) *National identity, popular culture and everyday life.* Oxford: Berg.

EDWARDS, E. (1996) Postcards: greetings from another world. In Selwyn, T. (ed.) *The tourist image: myths and myth making in tourism.* London: Wiley, 197–222.

EDWARDS, M. AND HULME, D. (EDS) (1995) *Non-governmental organisations performance and accountability. beyond the magic bullet.* London: Earthscan.

EHRLICH, P.R. (1972) *The population bomb.* London: Ballantine.

EICHER, J. (ED.) (1995) *Dress and ethnicity: change across time and space.* Oxford: Berg.

EISENSTADT, N. AND WITCHER, S. (1998) Social exclusion and poverty. *Outlook: the quarterly journal of the National Council of Voluntary Child Care Organisations,* 1, 6–7.

EKSTEINS, M. (1990) *Rites of spring, the Great War and the birth of the modern age.* New York: Bantum Books.

ELLWOOD, W. (2001) *The no-nonsense guide to globalization.* London: Verso.

ELSAESSER, T. (1994) European television and national identity: or 'what's there to touch when the dust has settled'. Paper presented to the European Film and Television Studies Conference, London, July.

EMMER, P. (1993) Intercontinental migration as a world historical process. *European Review,* 1(1), 67–74.

ENGLAND, K. (1994) Getting personal: reflexivity, positionality and feminist research. *Professional Geographer,* 46, 80–9.

ENGLISH NATURE (1993) Position statement on sustainable development. November.

ENLOE, C. (1989) *Bananas, beaches and bases: making feminist sense of international relations.* Berkeley, CA: University of California Press.

ENTRIKIN, J.N. (1976) Contemporary humanism in geography. *Annals of the Association of American Geographers,* 66, 615–32.

ENTRIKIN, J.N. (1991) *The betweeness of place: towards a geography of modernity.* London: Macmillan.

ENTRIKIN, J.N. (1994) Place and region. *Progress in Human Geography,* 18(2), 227–33.

EPSTEIN, B. (2003) Notes on the antiwar movement. *Monthly Review,* 55(3), 109–16.

ESCOBAR, A. (1992) Culture, economics, and politics in Latin American social movements theory and research. In Escobar, A. and Alvarez, S.E. (eds) *The making of social movements in Latin America.* Boulder, CO: Westview Press, 62–85.

ESCOBAR, A. (1995) *Encountering development: the making and unmaking of the Third World.* Princeton: Princeton University Press.

ESIN, I. AND TURNER, B. (2002) *Handbook of Citizenship Studies.* London: Sage.

EVANS, N., MORRIS, C. AND WINTER, M. (2002) Conceptualising agriculture: a critique of post-productivism as the new orthodoxy. *Progress in Human Geography,* 26, 313–23.

FALAH, G. (1989) Israeli 'Judaization' policy in Galilee and its impact on local Arab urbanization. *Political Geography,* 8(3), 229 54.

FEATHERSTONE, D. (2003) Spatialities of transnational resistance to globalisation: the maps of grievances of the Inter-Continental Caravan. *Transactions of the Institute of British Geographers,* 28, 404–21.

FISHER, A. (1996) Deutsche Bank in Asia facing a rough ride in the East. *Financial Times,* 13 November, 25.

FISHER, A. (1997) A reluctant departure. *Financial Times,* 13 May, 21.

FISHER, A. (1998) Deutsche Bank warns of lower profits. *Financial Times,* 29 January, 36.

FISHER, B. AND TRONTO, J. (1990) Towards a feminist theory of care. In Abel, E. and Nelson, M. (eds) *Circles of care.* Albany: State University of New York Press,

FISHER, W.F. AND PONNIAH, T. (2003) *Another world is possible: popular alternatives to globalisation at the World Social Forum.* London: Zed Books.

FLINT, C. (ED.) (2004a) *The geography of war and peace: from death camps to diplomats.* Oxford and New York: Oxford University Press.

FLINT, C. (2004b) Dynamic meta-geographies of terrorism: the spatial challenges of religious terrorism and the 'war on terrorism. In Flint, C. (ed.) *The geography of war and peace: from death camps to diplomats.* Oxford and New York: Oxford University Press.

FLORIDA, R. AND SMITH, D.F. (1993) Venture capital formation, investment and regional industrialisation. *Annals of the Association of American Geographers,* 83, 434–51.

FOOTE, K.E., HUGILL, P.J., MATHEWSON, K. AND SMITH, J.M. (EDS) (1994) *Re-reading Cultural Geography.* Austin: University of Texas Press.

FOREST, B. (1995) West Hollywood as symbol: the significance of place in the construction of gay identity. *Environment and Planning D: Society and Space,* 13, 133–57.

FOSTER, J.B. (2003) The new age of imperialism. *Monthly Review,* 55(3), 1–14.

FOUCAULT, M. (1980) *Power/knowledge.* London: Harvester Wheatsheaf.

FOX, J. (1996) How does civil society thicken? The political construction of social capital in rural Mexico. *World Development,* 24, 1089–103.

FRANK, A.G. (1967) *Capitalism and underdevelopment in Latin America.* London: Monthly Review Press.

FRANK, T. AND WEILAND, M. (1997) *Commodify your dissent: salvos from the baffler.* New York: W.W. Norton and Company.

FRANKLIN, A. (2003) *Tourism: an introduction.* London: Sage.

FRIEDLAND, W., BARTON, A. AND THOMAS, R. (1981) *Manufacturing green gold.* Cambridge: Cambridge University Press.

FRIEDMANN, J. AND WOLFF, G. (1982) World city formation: an agenda for research and action. *International Journal of Urban and Regional Research,* 6, 3, 309–44.

FROW, J. (1991) Tourism and the semiotics of nostalgia. *October,* 57, 123–51.

FUSS, D. (1989) *Essentially speaking: feminism, nature and difference.* London: Routledge.

FYFE, N. (1993) The police, space, and society: the political geography of policing. *Progress in Human Geography,* 15, 249–67.

FYFE, N. (1995) Law and order policy and the spaces of citizenship in contemporary Britain. *Political Geography,* 14, 177–89.

FROW, J. (1991) Tourism and the semiotics of nostalgia. *October,* 57, 123–51.

GABEL, M. AND BRUNER, H. (2003) *Global Inc.. an atlas of the multinational corporation.* New York: The New Press.

GABRIEL, Y. AND LANG, T. (1996) *The unmanageable consumer: contemporary consumption and its fragmentations.* Thousand Oaks: Sage.

GADGIL, M. AND GUHA, R. (1995): *Ecology and equity.* London: Routledge.

GAME INFO (2003) 'America's 10 Most Wanted' coming to consoles in 2004. Posted on 5 December 2003 @ 23:28:18 EST by xbox, http://www.xboxsolution.com/article1083.html, viewed 2 February 2004.

GARITAONANDÍA, G. (1993) Regional television in Europe. *European Journal of Communication*, 9(3), 277–94.

GARREAU, J. (1991) *Edge city: life on the new frontier*. New York: Doubleday.

GARTON ASH, T. (1998) Europe's endangered liberal order. *Foreign Affairs*, 77(2), 51–65.

GAUNTLETT, D. AND HILL, A. (1999) *TV living: television, culture, and everyday life*. London: Routledge.

GEDICKS, A. (1993): *The new resource wars*. Boston: South End Press.

GELDOF, B. (2004) The bitter legacy colonialism left to Africa. *Independent*, 21 April 2004, 29.

GEOFORUM (1998) Special Issue on Exclusion, 29(2).

GEREFFI, G. (1994) The organisation of buyer-driven commodity chains: how US retailers shape overseas production networks. In Gereffi, G. and Korzeniewicz, M. (eds) *Commodity chains and global capitalism*. Westport, CT: Praeger, 95–122.

GEREFFI, G. (1995) Global production systems and Third World development. In Stallings, B. (ed.) *Global change, regional response*. Cambridge: Cambridge University Press.

GERTLER, M. (1997) The invention of regional culture. In Lee, R. and Wills, J. (eds) *Geographies of economies*. London: Arnold.

GIBSON, W. (1984) *Neuromancer*. New York: Ace.

GIBSON-GRAHAM, J.K. (1996) *The end of capitalism (as we knew it)*. Cambridge, MA: Blackwell.

GIBSON-GRAHAM, J.K. (2002) Beyond global vs local: economic politics outside the binary frame. In Herod, A. and Wright, M. (eds) *Geographies of power: placing scale*. Oxford: Blackwell, 25–60.

GIDDENS, A. (1990) *The consequences of modernity*. Cambridge: Polity Press.

GIDDENS, A. (1991) *Modernity and self identity: self and society in the late modern age*. Cambridge: Polity Press.

GIDDENS, A. (1993) *Sociology* (2nd edn). Cambridge: Polity.

GIDDENS, A. (1999) *Runaway world: how globalisation is reshaping our lives*. London: Profile Books.

GILBERT, D. (1999) 'London in all its glory – or how to enjoy London': guidebook representations of imperial London. *Journal of Historical Geography*, 25(3), 279–97.

GILBERT, E.W. (1951) Geography and regionalism. In Taylor, G. (ed.) *Geography in the twentieth century*. London: Methuen.

GILBERT, E.W. (1960) The idea of the region. *Geography*, 45(3), 157–75.

GILBERT, E.W. (1972) British regional novelists and Geography. In *British pioneers in geography*. Newton Abbot: David and Charles.

GILDERBLOOM, J.I. AND ROSENTRAUB, M.S. (1990) Creating the accessible city: proposals for providing housing and transportation for low income, elderly and disabled people. *American Journal of Economics and Sociology*, 49(3), 271–82.

GILLESPIE, M. (1995) *Television, ethnicity and cultural change*. London: Routledge.

GILLIGAN, C. (1982) *In a different voice: psychological theory and women's development*. Cambridge, MA: Harvard University Press.

GILLIGAN, C. (1986) Remapping the moral domain: new images of the self in relationship. In Heller, T. *et al.* (eds) *Reconstructing individualism*. Stanford: Stanford University Press. 237–52.

GILROY, P. (1987) *There ain't no black in the Union Jack*. London: Routledge.

GILROY, P. (1993a) *The black Atlantic: modernity and double consciousness*. London: Verso.

GILROY, P. (1993b) *Small acts*. London and New York: Serpent's Tail.

GILROY, P. (1994) *The black Atlantic*. London: Verso.

GINSBURG, F. (1991) Indigenous media: Faustian contract or global village? *Cultural Anthropology*, 94–114.

GINSBURG, F. (1993) Aboriginal media and the Australian imaginary. *Public Culture*, 5, 557–78.

GLADWELL, M. (1997) The coolhunt. *The New Yorker*, March 17: 78–88.

GLASSNER, M.I. (1993) *Political geography*. Chichester: John Wiley.

GLOBE AND MAIL (2003) Merit found amid video-game mayhem: violence aside researchers argue skills can be gained by playing regularly, 29 May, A3.

GODLEWSKA, A. AND SMITH, N. (EDS) (1994) *Geography and empire*. London: Blackwell/IBG.

GODOLPHIN, M. (1868) *Robinson Crusoe in words of one syllable*. London: George Routledge.

GOFFMAN, E. (1963) *Stigma*. Englewood Cliffs, NJ: Prentice Hall.

GOH, R. (2001) Ideologies of 'upgrading' in Singapore public housing; postmodern style, globalization and class construction in the built environment. *Urban Studies* 38(9), 1589–1604.

GOODER, H. AND JACOBS, J.M. (2002) Belonging and non-belonging: the apology in a reconciling nation. In Blunt, A. and McEwan, C. (eds) *Postcolonial geographies*. London: Continuum, 200–13.

GOODWIN, M. (1991) Replacing a surplus population: the policies of London Docklands Development Corporation. In Allen, J. and Hamnett, C. (eds) *Housing and Labour Markets*. London: Unwin and Hyman.

GOODWIN, M. AND PAINTER, J. (1996) Local governance, Fordism and the changing geographies of regulation. *Transactions of the Institute of British Geographers*, 21(4), 635–49.

GOPINATH, G. (1995) 'Bombay, UK, Yuba City': Bhangra music and the engendering of diaspora. *Diaspora*, 4(3), 303–22.

GORDON, I. (1999) Family structure, educational achievement and the inner city. *Urban Studies*, 36, 407–23.

GORDON, J.S. The chicken story. *American Heritage*, September 1996.

GOSS, J. (1993) The magic of the mall: form and function in the retail built environment. *Annals of the Association of American Geographers*, 83(1), 18–47.

GOSS, J. (1999) Once upon a time in the commodity world: an unofficial guide to Mall of America. *Annals of the Association of American Geographers*, 89(1), 45–75.

GOULD, P. (1985) *The geographer at work*. New York: Routledge.

GOULD, S.J. (2004) *The hedgehog, the fox, and the magister's pox: mending and minding the misconceived gap between science and the humanities*. London: Vintage.

GOWAN, P. AND ANDERSON, P. (EDS) (1997) *The question of Europe*. London: Verso.

GRAHAM, B. AND NASH, C. (EDS) (1999) *Modern historical geographies*. London: Longman.

GRAY, A. (1992) *Video playtime: the gendering of a leisure technology*. London: Routledge.

GREGSON, N. AND CREWE, L. (2003) *Second-hand cultures*. Oxford: Berg.

GREEN, D. (1991) *Faces of Latin America*. London: Latin America Bureau.

GREEN, E., HEBRON, S. AND WOODWARD, W. (1990) *Women's leisure, what leisure?* Basingstoke: Macmillan.

GREENWOOD, D. (1989) Culture by the pound: an anthropological perspective on tourism as cultural commoditization. In Smith, V. (ed.) *Hosts and guests* (2nd edn). Philadelphia: University of Pennsylvania Press.

GREGORY, D. (1994) *Geographical imaginations*. Oxford: Blackwell.

GREGORY, D. (1995) Imaginative geographies. *Progress in Human Geography*, 9, 447–85.

GREGORY, D. (2003) Emperors of the gaze: photographic practices and productions of space in Egypt, 1839–1914. In Ryan, J. and Schwartz, J. *Picturing place: photography and the geographical imagination*. London: I.B. Tauris, 195–225.

GREGORY, D. (2004) *The colonial present: Afghanistan, Palestine and Iraq*. Oxford: Blackwell.

GREGSON, N. AND CREWE, L. (2003) *Second-hand cultures*. Oxford and New York: Berg.

GRIFFITHS, I. (ED.) (1993) *The atlas of African affairs*. London: Routledge.

GRIFFITHS, J. (1997) F1 probe says threat to relocate racing was groundless. *Financial Times*, 15 December, 1.

GRUFFUDD, P. (1994) 'Back to the land': historiography, rurality and the nation in inter-war Wales'. *Transactions of the Institute of British Geographers*, 19(1), 61–77.

GUARDIAN (2003) Did we make it better? *Guardian*, London, 29 May, G2, 10.

GUBACK, T. (1974) Cultural identity and film in the European Economic Community. *Cinema Journal*, 13(1), 2–17.

GUERRERA, F. (2003) Wall Street's drive to scale the Great Wall. *Financial Times*, 10 December, 14.

GUHA, R. (1989) The Problem. *Seminar*, March, 12–15.

GUIBERNAU, M. AND HUTCHINSON, J. (EDS) (2001) *Understanding nationalism*. Cambridge: Polity Press.

GUPTA, A. (1998) *Postcolonial developments: agriculture in the making of modern India*. London and Durham: Duke University Press.

HABERMAS, J. (1970) *Toward a rational society: student protest, science, and politics*. Boston: Beacon Press.

HABERMAS, J. (1993) *The structural transformation of the public sphere*. Cambridge, MA: MIT Press.

HAGGETT, P. (1972) *Geography: a modern synthesis*. London: Harper Row.

HAHN, H. (1986) Disability and the urban environment: a perspective on Los Angeles. *Environment and Planning D: Society and Space*, 4, 273–88.

HALE, A. AND WILLS, J. (EDS) (2005) *Threads of Labour: a workers' view of the global garment industry*. Oxford: Blackwell.

HALFACREE, K. (1993) Locality and social representation: space, discourse and alternative definitions of the rural. *Journal of Rural Studies*, 9, 23–38.

HALFACREE, K. (1996) Out of place in the country: travellers and the 'rural idyll'. *Antipode*, 28 (1), 42–72.

HALL, E. (1995a) Contested (dis)abled identities in the urban labour market. Paper presented to the Tenth Urban Change and Conflict Conference, Royal Holloway, University of London, UK.

HALL, S. (1991) Old and new identities, old and new ethnicities. In King, A.D. (ed.) *Culture, globalization and the world system*. London: Macmillan.

HALL, S. (1992a) The question of cultural identity. In Hall, S., Held, D. and McGrew, T. (eds) *Modernity and its futures*. Oxford: Polity.

HALL, S. (1992b) The West and the rest. In Hall, S. and Gieben, B. (eds) *Formations of modernity*. Oxford: Polity.

HALL, S. (1995b) New cultures for old. In Massey, D. and Jess, P. (eds) *A place in the world?* Milton Keynes: Open University Press.

HAMNETT, C. (2003a) Contemporary Human Geography: fiddling while Rome burns? *Geoforum*, 34, 1–3.

HAMNETT, C (2003b) *Unequal city: London in the global arena*. London: Routledge.

HAMNETT, C. AND CROSS, D. (1998) Social polarisation and inequality in London: earnings evidence, 1979–95. *Environment and Planning C, Government and Policy*, 16, 659–80.

HANNERZ, U. (1996) *Transnational connections: culture people places*. London: Routledge.

HANNIGAN, J.A. (1995) Environmental sociology: a social constructionist perspective. London: Routledge.

HANSEN, A. (ED.) (1993) *The mass media and environmental issues*. Leicester: Leicester University Press.

HANSON, S. (1999) Is feminist geography relevant? *Scottish Geographical Journal*, 115(20), 133–41.

HANSON, S. AND PRATT, G. (1995) *Gender, work and space*. New York and London: Routledge.

HARAWAY, D.J. (1991a) *Simians, cyborgs and women: the reinvention of nature*. London: Routledge.

HARAWAY, D.J. (1991b) Situated knowledges: the science question in feminism as a site of discourse of the privilege of partial perspective. In Haraway, D.J., *Simians, cyborgs, and women: the reinvention of nature*. London and New York: Routledge.

HARAWAY, D.J. (1996) Situated knowledges: the science question and the privilege of portal perspective. In Agnew, J. *et al.* (eds) *Human Geography: an essential anthology*. Oxford: Blackwell, 108–28.

HARDIN, G. (1968) The tragedy of the commons. *Science*, 162, 1243–8.

HARDING, S. (1991) *Whose science? Whose knowledge? Thinking from women's lives*. Ithaca, NY: Cornell University Press.

HARLEY, B. (2001) *The new nature of maps: essays in the history of cartography*. Baltimore: Johns Hopkins University Press.

HARLEY, J.B. (1992) Deconstructing the map. In Barnes, T. and Duncan, J. (eds) *Writing worlds: discourse, text and metaphor in the representation of landscape*. London: Routledge.

HARPER, S. (1997) Contesting later life. In Cloke, P. and Little, J. (eds) *Contested countryside cultures*. London: Routledge, 189–96.

HARPER, S. AND LAWS, G. (1995) Rethinking the geography of ageing. *Progress in Human Geography*, 19, 199–221.

HARRIS, C. (2002) *Making native space: colonialism, resistance, and reserves in British Columbia*. Vancouver: UBC Press.

HARRIS, N. (1995) *The new untouchables: immigration and the new world order*. Harmondsworth: Penguin.

HARRIS, R.C. AND PHILLIPS, E. (EDS) (1984) *Letters from Windermere 1912–1914*. Vancouver: UBC Press.

HARRISON, C.M., BURGESS, J. AND FILIUS, P. (1996) Rationalising environmental responsibilities: a comparison of lay publics in the UK and the Netherlands. *Global Environmental Change*, 6(3), 215–34.

HARRISON, P. (2002) 'How shall I say it ...?' Emotions, exposure and compassion. Paper given at the Emotional Geographies Conference, Lancaster 2002, typescript provided by author.

HARRISS, J., HUNTER, J. AND LEWIS, C. (EDS) (1995) *The new institutional economics and Third World development*. London: Routledge.

HART, R. (1979) *Children's experience of place*. New York: Irvington.

HARVEY, D. (1969) *Explanation in geography*. London: Edward Arnold.

HARVEY, D. (1973) *Social justice and the city*. London: Edward Arnold.

HARVEY, D. (1982) *The limits to capital*. Oxford: Blackwell.

HARVEY, D. (1985) Paris, 1850–1870. In Harvey, D. *Consciousness and the urban experience*. Oxford: Blackwell, 63–220.

HARVEY, D. (1989) *The condition of postmodernity: an enquiry into the origins of cultural change*. Oxford: Blackwell.

HARVEY, N. (1995) Rebellion in Chiapas: rural reforms and popular struggle. *Third World Quarterly*, 16(1), 39–72.

HARVEY, D. (1996) *Justice, nature and the geography of difference*. Oxford: Blackwell.

HARVEY, D. (2003) *The new imperialism*. Oxford: Oxford University Press.

HARVEY, D., JONES, R., MILLIGAN, C. AND MCINROY, N. (EDS) (2002) *Celtic geographies: old culture, new times*. London: Routledge.

HAYTER, T. AND HARVEY, D. (EDS) (1993) *The factory and the city: the story of Cowley automobile workers in Oxford*. London and New York: Mansell.

HEALY, P. (1992) A planner's day: knowledge and action in communicative practice. *Journal of the American Planning Association*, 58, 9–20.

HEATH, S. (1990) *Representing television*. In Mellencamp, P. (ed.) *Logics of television*. Bloomington: Indiana University Press.

HEBDIGE, D. (1988) Object as image: the Italian scooter cycle. In *Hiding in the light. On images and things*. London: Comedia, 77–115.

HECHTER, M. (1975) *Internal colonialism: the Celtic fringe in British national development, 1536–1966*. London: RKP.

HEDDY, J. (1990) *Housing for young people: a survey of the situation in selected European Community countries*. Paris: Union des Foyers des Jeunes Travailleurs.

HEFFERNAN, M. (2003) Histories of Geography. In Holloway, S, Price, S. and Valentine, G. *Key concepts in Geography*. London: Sage.

HELD, D. AND MCGREW, A. (2002) *Globalisation/anti-globalisation*. Cambridge: Polity.

HELD, D., MCGREW, A., GOLDBLATT, D. AND PERRATON, J. (1999) *Global transformations: politics, economics and culture*. Cambridge: Polity.

HENRY, N. AND PINCH, S. (1997) *A regional formula for success? The innovative region of motor sport valley*. Edgbaston: University of Birmingham.

HENRY, N. AND PINCH, S. (2000) Spatialising knowledge: placing the knowledge community of motor sport valley. *Geoforum*, 31, 191–208.

HENRY, N., PINCH, S. AND RUSSELL, S. (1996) In pole position? Untraded interdependencies, new industrial spaces and the British Motor Sport Industry. *Area* 28.1, 25–36.

HERRINGTON, J. (1984) *The outer city*. London: Harper & Row.

HINE, T. (2002) *I want that: how we all became shoppers*, New York: HarperCollins.

HOBSBAWM, E. (1983) Introduction: inventing traditions. In Hobsbawm, E. and Ranger, T. (eds) *The invention of tradition*. Cambridge: Cambridge University Press.

HOBSON, D. (1989) Soap operas at work. In Seiter, E. *et al.* (eds) *Remote control*. London and New York: Routledge.

HOCHSCHILD, A. (1983) *The managed heart: commercialisation of human feeling*. Berkeley, CA: University of California Press.

HODGE, D. (ED.) (1995) Should women count? The role of quantitative methodology in feminist geographic research. *The Professional Geographer*, 47, 426–66.

HOGENDORN, J.S. AND SCOT, K.M. (1981) The East African Groundnut Scheme: lessons of a large-scale agricultural failure. *African Economic History*, 10, 81–115.

HOGGART, K. (1990) Let's do away with rural. *Journal of Rural Studies*, 6, 245–57.

HOLDGATE, M. (1996) *From care to action: making a sustainable world*. London: Earthscan.

HOLLOWAY, L. AND HUBBARD, P. (2000) *People and place: the extraordinary geographies of everyday life*. New Jersey: Prentice Hall.

HOLLOWAY, S.L. AND VALENTINE, G. (2000a) *Children's geographies: playing, living, learning*. London: Routledge.

HOLLOWAY, S.L. AND VALENTINE, G. (2000b) Spatiality and the new social studies of childhood. *Sociology*, 34, 763–83.

HOLLOWAY, S.L. AND VALENTINE, G. (2000c) Corked hats and *Coronation Street*: British and New Zealand children's imaginative geographies of the other. *Childhood*, 7, 335–57.

HOLLOWAY, S., PRICE, S. AND VALENTINE, G. (2003) *Key concepts in Geography*. London: Sage.

HOLLOWAY, S.L., VALENTINE, G. AND BINGHAM, N. (2000) Institutionalising technologies: masculinities, femininities and the heterosexual economy of the IT classroom. *Environment and Planning A*, 32, 617–33.

HOLT, L. (2003) (Dis)abling children in primary school spaces. Unpublished PhD thesis, Loughborough University, UK.

HONDAGNEU-SOTELO, P. AND AVILA, E. (1997) 'I'm here but I'm there': the meanings of Latina transnational motherhood. *Gender and Society*, 11(5), 548–71.

HOOKS, B. (1990) *Yearning: race gender and cultural politics*. London: Turnaround.

HOOKS, B. (1992) Eating the other. In b. hooks (ed.) *Black looks: race and representation*. Boston: South End Press.

HOOSON, I.D. (ED.) (1994) *Geography and national identity*. Oxford: Blackwell.

HOUGHTON, J. (1997) *Global warming: the complete briefing*. Cambridge: Cambridge University Press.

HOWES, D. (ED.) (2004) *Empire of the senses: the sensual culture reader*. Oxford and New York: Berg Publishers.

HOWLEY, K. (2001) Envision television: charting the Cultural Geography of homelessness. *Ecumene*, 8, 345–50.

HUBBARD, P. (2000) Desire/disgust: mapping the moral contours of heterosexuality. *Progress in Human Geography*, 24, 191–217.

HUBBARD, P. (2002) Sexing the self: geographies of engagement and encounter. *Social and Cultural Geography*, 3, 365–81.

HUBBARD, P. AND LILLEY, K. (2004) Pacemaking the modern city: the urban politics of speed and slowness. *Environment and Planning D: Society and Space*, 22, 273–94.

HUBBARD, P. AND SANDERS, T. (2003) Making space for sex work: female street prostitution and the production of urban space. *International Journal of Urban and Regional Research*, 27, 75–89.

HUDSON, B. (1977) The new geography and the new imperialism, 1870–1918. *Antipode*, 9(2), 12–19.

HUDSON, R. (2001) *Producing places*. New York: Guilford Press.

HUDSON, R. (2004) Conceptualising economies and their geographies: spaces, flows and circuits. *Progress in Human Geography*, 28(4), 447–71.

HUGGINS, J., HUGGINS, R. AND JACOBS, J.M. (1995) Kooramindanjie: place and the postcolonial. *History Workshop Journal*, 39, 164–81.

HUGHES, A. AND REIMER, S. (EDS) (2004) *Geographies of commodity chains*. London: Routledge.

HUGHES, R. (1987) *The fatal shore: a history of the transportation of convicts to Australia*. London: Collins Harvill.

HUGHES, R. (1988) *The fatal shore*. New York: Vintage.

HULME, D. AND EDWARDS, M. (EDS) (1997) *NGOs, states and donors: too close for comfort?*, Basingstoke: Macmillan in association with Save the Children.

HUNT, D. (1989) *Economic theories of development: an analysis of competing paradigms*. London: Harvester Wheatsheaf.

HUTNYK, J. (2000) *Critique of exotica: music, politics and the culture industry*. London: Pluto Press.

HUTSON, S. AND LIDDIARD, M. (1994) *Youth homelessness: the construction of a social issue*. London: Macmillan.

HYAM, R. (1990) *Empire and sexuality*. Manchester: Manchester University Press.

HYAM, R. (1993) *Britain's imperial century, 1815–1914*. Basingstoke: Macmillan.

HYNDMAN, J. (2003) Beyond either/or: a feminist analysis of September 11th. *ACME*, 2(1).

IGNATIEFF, M. (1993) *Blood and belonging: journeys into the New Nationalism*. London: BBC Books/Chatto & Windus.

IMRIE, R. (1996) *Disability and the city: international perspectives*. London: Paul Chapman Publishing.

INGHAM, J. (1999) Hearing places, making spaces: sonorous geographies, ephemeral rhythms, and the Blackburn warehouse parties. *Environment and Planning D: Society and Space*, 17, 283–305.

INGLEHART, R. (1977) *The silent revolution*. Princeton, NJ: Princeton University Press.

INKELES, A. AND SMITH, D.H. (1974) *Becoming modern*. Cambridge, MA: Harvard University Press.

INTERNATIONAL CENTRE FOR INTEGRATED MOUNTAIN DEVELOPMENT (1998) Environment, culture, economy, and tourism: dilemmas in the Hindu Kush-Himalayas. *Issues in Mountain Development*, 3, http://www.icimod.org/publications/imd/imd983.htm, accessed 12 July 2004.

IRWIN, A. (1995) *Citizen science: a study of people, expertise and sustainable development*. London: Routledge.

IRWIN, A. (2000) *Sociology and the environment*. Cambridge: Polity Press.

IUCN (1980) *The world conservation strategy, international union for the conservation of nature and natural resources*. Gland: World Wildlife Fund and United Nations Environment Programme.

JACKSON, P. (1989) *Maps of meaning*. London: Routledge.

JACKSON, P. (1999a) Commodity cultures: the traffic in things. *Transactions of the Institute of British Geographers*, NS24, 95–108.

JACKSON, P. (1999b) Postmodern urbanism and the ethnographic void. *Urban Geography*, 20(5), 400–2.

JACKSON, P. (2000) Rematerialising Social and Cultural Geography. *Social and Cultural Geography*, 1, 9–14.

JACKSON, P. (2002) Commercial cultures: transcending the cultural and the economic. *Progress in Human Geography*, 26, 3–18.

JACKSON, P. AND PENROSE, J. (EDS) (1993) *Constructions of race, place and nation*. London: UCL Press.

JACKSON, P., CRANG, P. AND DWYER. C. (EDS) (2004) *Transnational spaces*. London: Routledge.

JACKSON, T. (1996) *Material concerns*. London: Routledge.

JACOBS, J. (1994) Earth honoring: western desires and indigenous knowledges. In Blunt, A. and Rose, G. (eds) *Writing women and space: colonial and postcolonial geographies*. New York and London: Guildford, 169–96.

JACOBS, J.M. (1988) Politics and the cultural landscape: the case of Aboriginal land rights. *Australian Geographical Studies*, 26, 249–63.

JACOBS, J.M. (1996a) Authentically yours: de-touring the map. In Jacobs, J.M. *Edge of empire: postcolonialism and the city*. London: Routledge, 132–56.

JACOBS, J.M. (1996b) *Edge of empire: postcolonialism and the city*. London: Routledge.

JACOBS, M. (1993) *Sense and sustainability: land use planning and environmentally sustainable development*. London: Council for the Protection of Rural England.

JACOBS, M. (1995) Sustainable development, capital substitution and economic humility: a response to Beckerman. *Environmental Values*, 4, 57–68.

JAMES, A., JENKS, C. AND PROUT, A. (1998) *Theorizing childhood*. Cambridge: Polity.

JAROSZ, L. (1992) Constructing the dark continent: metaphor as geographic representation of Africa. *Geografiska Annaler*, 74B, 105–15.

JAZEEL, T. (2003) Unpicking Sri Lankan 'island-ness' in Romesh Gunesekera's *Reef. Journal of Historical Geography*, 29(4), 582–98.

JENKINS, H. (1992) *Textual poachers: television fans and participatory culture*. London and New York: Routledge.

JENKINS, J.G. (1982) *Maritime heritage: the ships and seamen of southern Ceredigion*. Llandysul: Gomer Press.

JENKINS, R. (1996) *Social identities*. London: Routledge.

JENKS, C. (1996) *Childhood*. London: Routledge.

JESSOP, B. (2000) The crisis of the national spatial-temporal fix and the tendential ecological dominance of globalising capitalism. *International Journal of Urban and Regional Research*, 24, 2, 323–60.

JOHNSEN., S., CLOKE, P. AND MAY, J. (2005) Transitory spaces of care: serving homeless people on the street. *Health and Place* (forthcoming).

JOHNSON, J. AND SALT, J. (1992) *Population migration*. Walton-on-Thames: Thomas Nelson.

JOHNSON, N.C. (1996) Where geography and history meet: heritage tourism and the big house in Ireland. *Annals of the Association of American Geographers*, 86, 551–66.

JOHNSON, N.C. (2003) *Ireland, the Great War and the geography of remembrance*. Cambridge: Cambridge University Press.

JOHNSON, R. (1986) The story so far: and further transformations? In Punter, D. (ed.) *Introduction to contemporary cultural studies*. London and New York: Longman.

JOHNSTON, R. (1997) *Geography and geographers: Anglo-American Human Geography since 1945* (5th edn). London: Arnold.

JOHNSTON, R.J., GREGORY, D. AND SMITH, D.M. (EDS) (1994) *The dictionary of Human Geography* (3rd edn). Oxford: Blackwell.

JOHNSTON, R.J., GREGORY, D., PRATT, G., SMITH, D.M. AND WATTS, M.J. (EDS) (2000) *The dictionary of Human Geography* (4th edn). Oxford: Blackwell.

JOHNSTONE, C. AND WHITEHEAD, M. (2004a) *New horizons in British urban policy*. Aldershot: Ashgate.

JOHNSTONE, C. AND WHITEHEAD, M. (2004b) Horizons and barriers in British urban policy. In Johnstone, C. and Whitehead, M. (eds) *New horizons in British urban policy*. Aldershot: Ashgate.

JONES, J.-P. (2003) Reading Geography through binary oppositions. In Anderson, K., Domosh, M., Pile, S. and Thrift, N., *Handbook of Cultural Geography*. London: Sage.

JONES, J.-P. AND MOSS, P. (1995) Democracy, identity, space. *Environment and Planning D: Society and Space*, 13, 253–7.

JONES, M., JONES, R. AND WOODS, M. (2004) *An introduction to political geography: space place and politics*. London: Routledge.

JONES, R. AND DESFORGES, L. (2003) Localities and the reproduction of Welsh nationalism. *Political Geography*, 22(3), 271–92.

JORDAN, T. (1994) Cultural preadaptation and the American forest frontier: the role of New Sweden. In Foote, K.E., Hugill, P.J., Mathewson, K. and Smith, J.M. (eds) *Re-reading Cultural Geography*. Austin: University of Texas Press, 215–36.

JORDAN, T. AND KAUPS, M. (1989) *The American backwoods frontier: an ethnic and ecological interpretation*. Baltimore: Johns Hopkins University Press.

KARP, I. AND LAVINE, S. (1991) (eds) *Exhibiting cultures: the poetics and politics of museum display*. Washington DC: Smithsonian Institute.

KATZ, C. AND MONK, J. (EDS) (1993) *Full circles: geographies of women over the life course*. London: Routledge.

KEELEY, J. AND SCOONES, I. (2003) *Understanding environmental policy processes: cases from Africa*. London: Earthscan.

KEITH, M. AND PILE, S. (EDS) (1993) *Place and the politics of identity*. London: Routledge.

KENRICK, D. AND CLARK, C. (1999) *Moving on: the gypsies and travellers of Britain*. Hertfordshire: University of Hertfordshire Press.

KERN, S. (1983) *The culture of time and space, 1880–1918*. Cambridge, MA: Harvard University Press.

KHILNANI, S. (1997) *The idea of India*. London: Hamish Hamilton.

KING, R. (1978) Return migration: a neglected aspect of population geography. *Area*, 10, 175–82.

KING, R. (1995) Migrations, globalisation and place. In Massey, D. and Jess, P. *A place in the world?* Oxford: Oxford University Press.

KINNAIRD, V., MORRIS, M., NASH, C. AND ROSE, G. (1997) Feminist geographies of environment, nature and landscape. In Women and Geography Research Group, *Feminism and geography: diversity and difference*. London: Longman, 146–89.

KINSMAN, P. (1995) Landscape, race and national identity: the photography of Ingrid Pollard. *Area*, 27, 300–31.

KIRKEY, K. AND FORSYTH, A. (2001) Men in the valley: gay male life on the suburban–rural fringe. *Journal of Rural Studies*, 17, 421–41.

KITCHEN, R.M., BLADES, M. AND GOLLEDGE, R.G. (1997) Understanding spatial concepts at the geographic scale without the use of vision. *Progress in Human Geography*, 21(2), 225–42.

KITCHIN, R. AND LYSAGHT, K. (2003) Heterosexism and the geographies of everyday life in Belfast, Northern Ireland. *Environment and Planning A*, 35, 489–510.

KLARE, M. (2002) Resource wars: the new landscape of global conflict. New York: Holt.

KLEIN, M. (1960) *Our adult world and its roots in infancy*. London: Tavistock Pamphlet 2.

KLEIN, N. (2000) *No logo: taking aim at the brand bullies*. New York: Picador.

KLEIN, N. (2001) The unknown icon. *Guardian*, 3 March, 9–16.

KLEIN, N. (2002) *Fences and windows*. London: Flamingo.

KLEIN, N. (2004) How Bush told his lie. *The Nation*, 23 February.

KNEALE, P. (2003) *Study skills for geographers*. London: Arnold.

KNIFFEN, F.B. (1965) Folk housing: key to diffusion. *Annals of the Association of American Geographers*, 55, 549–77.

KNIFFEN, F.B. (1990) Cultural diffusion and landscapes: selections by Fred B. Kniffen. In Walker, J.H. and Detro, R.A. (eds) *Geoscience and Man*,. Baton Rouge: Louisiana State University, Department of Geography and Anthropology 27.

KNOPP, L. (1990) Some theoretical implications of gay involvement in an urban land market. *Political Geography Quarterly*, 9, 337–52.

KNORR CETINA, K. AND PREDA, A. (EDS) (2004) *The sociology of financial markets*. Oxford: Oxford University Press.

KNOWLES, A. (1997) *Calvinists incorporated: Welsh immigrants on Ohio's industrial frontier*. Chicago: University of Chicago Press.

KNOX, P. (1991) The restless urban landscape: economic and sociocultural change and the transformation of Metropolitan Washington DC. *Annals of the Association of American Geographers*, 81(2), 181–209.

KNOX, P. AND PINCH, S. (1998) *Urban social geography: an introduction*. Harlow: Pearson.

KONG, L. AND YEOH, B. (2003) *The politics of landscapes in Singapore: constructions of 'nation'*. Syracuse: Syracuse University Press.

KOOLHAAS, R. (2000) Singapore songlines: portrait of a Potemkin metropolis … or thirty years of tabula rasa. In Miles, M., Borden, I. and Hall, T. (eds) *The city cultures reader*, London: Routledge, 22–25.

KOSER, K. (2003) Long-distance nationalism and the responsible state: the case of Eritrea. In Ostsergaard-Nielsen, E. (ed.) *International migration and sending countries*. London: Palgrave Macmillan, 171–84.

KOSER, K. AND SALT, J. (1997) The geography of highly-skilled international migration. *International Journal of Population Geography*, 3, 285–303.

KRAMER, J.L. (1995) Bachelor farmers and spinsters: gay and lesbian identities and communities in rural North Dakota. In Bell, D. and Valentine, G. (eds) *Mapping desire: geographies of sexualities*. London: Routledge, 200–13.

KRISTEVA, J. (1980) *Powers of horror: an essay in abjection*. New York: Colombia University Press.

KRISTEVA, J. (1992) Le temps de la dépression. *Le Monde des Débats*, October.

KRISTEVA, J. (1993) *Nations without nationalism*. New York: Columbia University Press.

KUHN, T. (1962) *The structure of scientific revolutions*. Chicago: University of Chicago Press.

KUHN, T. (1970) *The structure of scientific revolutions*. Chicago: University of Chicago Press.

KUHN, T. (1977) Second thoughts on paradigms. In Suppe, F. (ed.) *The structure of scientific theories*. Urbana: University of Illinois Press.

LACEY, C. AND LONGMAN, D. (1993) The press and public access to the environmental debate. *Sociological Review*, 41, 207–43.

LAKATOS, I. AND MUSGRAVE, A. (EDS) (1970) *Criticism and the growth of knowledge*. Cambridge: Cambridge University Press.

LANDAU, J.M. (ED.) (1984) *Atatürk and the modernization of Turkey*. Boulder, CO: Westview Press.

LASH, S. AND URRY, J. (1994) *Economies of signs and space*. London: Sage.

LATOUR, B. (1987) *Science in action: how to follow scientists and engineers through society*. Cambridge, MA: MIT Press.

LATOUR, B. (1993) The proliferation of hybrids. In *We have never been modern*. Harlow: Pearson Education.

LATOUR, B. AND WOOLGAR, S. (1979) *Laboratory life: the construction of scientific facts*. Princeton: Princeton University Press.

LAURIE, N., DWYER, C., HOLLOWAY, S.L. AND SMITH, F.M. (1999) *Geographies of new femininities*. London: Routledge.

LAW, J. (1986) On the methods of long-distance control: vessels, navigation and the Portuguese route to India. In Law, J. (ed.) *Power, action and belief. A new sociology of knowledge?*. London: Routledge, 254–63.

LAW, L. (2001) Home cooking: Filipino women and geographies of the senses in Hong Kong. *Ecumene* 8(3), 264–283.

LAWS, G. (1994) Ageing, contested meanings, and the built environment. *Environment and Planning A*, 26, 1787–1802.

LAWS, G. (1997) Spatiality and age relations. In Jamieson, A., Harper, S. and Victor, C. (eds) *Critical approaches to ageing and later life*. Milton Keynes: Open University Press, 90–100.

LAWSON, F.H. (2004) Political economy, geopolitics and the expanding US military presence in the Persian Gulf and Central Asia. *Critique: Critical Middle Eastern Studies*, 13(1), 7–31.

LEE, R. (1989) Social relations and the geography of material life. In Gregory, D. and Walford, R. (eds) *Horizons in Human Geography*. London: Macmillan, 152–69.

LEE, R. (1998) Shelter from the storm? Mutual knowledge and geographies of regard (or legendary economic geographies). Paper presented to the RGS-IBG Annual Conference. University of Surrey, Guildford, 6 January.

LEE, R. (1999) *Access to the gods? Social relations and geographies of material life*. Routledge: London.

LEE, R. (2000) Shelter from the storm? Geographies of regard in the worlds of horticultural consumption and production. *Geoforum*, 31, 137–57.

LEE, R. (2002) Nice maps, shame about the theory? Thinking geographically about the economic. *Progress in Human Geography*, 26(3), 333–55.

LEE, R. (2005) The old economy. In Daniels, P.W., Beaverstock, J.W., Bradshaw, M.J. and Leyshon, A. (eds) *Geographies of the new economy*. London: Routledge, Chapter 2.

LEES, L. (2003) The ambivalence of diversity and the politics of urban renaissance: the case of youth in downtown Portland, Maine, USA. *International Journal of Urban and Regional Research*, 27(3), 613–34.

LEFEBVRE, H. (1971) *Everyday life in the modern world*. New York: Harper & Row.

LEFTWICH, A. (1993) Governance, democracy and development in the Third World. *Third World Quarterly*, 14(3), 605–24.

LEFTWICH, A. (1995) Governance, the state and the politics of development. *Development and Change*, 25, 363–86.

LEGRAIN, P. (2002) *Open world: the truth about globalisation*. London: Abacus.

LEHMANN, D. (1997) An opportunity lost: Escobar's deconstruction of development. *Journal of Development Studies*, 33(4), 568–78.

LÉLÉ, S.M. (1991) Sustainable development: a critical review. *World Development*, 19, 607–21.

LEMON, C. AND LEMON, J. (2003) Community-based cooperative ventures for adults with intellectual disabilities. *The Canadian Geographer*, 47, 414–28.

LEONARD, M. (1998) Paper planes: travelling the new grrrl geographies. In Skelton, T. and Valentine, G. (eds) *Cool places: geographies of youth cultures*. London and New York: Routledge.

LEVITAS, R. (1998) *The inclusive society: social exclusion and New Labour*. Basingstoke: Macmillan.

LEVY, R. (1995) Finding a place in the world economy. Party strategy and party vote: the regionalization of SNP and Plaid Cymru support, 1979–92. *Political Geography*, 14(3), 295–308.

LEWIS, M. AND WIGEN, K. (1997) *The myth of continents: a critique of metageography*. Berkeley: University of California Press.

LEWIS, P. (1979) Axioms for reading the landscape. In Meinig, D.W. (ed.) *The interpretation of ordinary landscapes: geographical essays*. New York: Oxford University Press, 11–32.

LEWIS, P. (1994) Common houses, cultural spoor. In Foote, K.E., Hugil, P.J., Mathewson, K. and Smith, J.M. (eds) *Re-reading Cultural Geography*. Austin: University of Texas Press, 82–110.

LEWIS, W.A. (1955) *The theory of economic growth*. London: George Allen and Unwin.

LEY, D. (1974) The black inner city as frontier outpost: images and behaviour of a Philadelphia neighbourhood. *Association of American Geographers, Monograph Series 7*, Washington DC.

LEY, D. (1977) Social geography and the taken-for-granted world. *Transactions of the Institute of British Geographers* NS 2, 498–512.

LEY, D. (1995) Between Europe and Asia: the case of the missing sequoias. *Ecumene. A journal of environment, culture, meaning*, 2, 185–210.

LEY, D. (1996) *The new middle class and the remaking of the central city*. Oxford: Oxford University Press.

LEY, D. AND CYBRIWSKY, R. (1974) Urban graffiti as territorial markers. *Annals of the Association of American Geographers*, 64, 491–505.

LEY, D. AND MOUNTZ, A. (2001) Interpretation, representation, positionality: issues in field research in Human Geography. In Limb, M. and Dwyer, C. (eds) *Qualitative Methodologies For Geographers: Issues and Debates*. London: Arnold, 234–47.

LEY, D. AND SAMUELS, H. (EDS) (1978) *Humanistic geography: prospects and problems*. London: Croom Helm.

LEYSHON, A. (1996) Dissolving difference? Money, disembedding and the creation of global financial space. In Daniels, P. and Lever, W.F. (eds) *The global economy in transition*. London: Longman.

LEYSHON, A. AND THRIFT, N.J. (1997) *Money/space*. London: Routledge.

LEYSHON, A., BURTON, D., KNIGHTS, D. *ET AL.* (2004) Towards an ecology of retail financial services: understanding the persistence of door-to-door credit and insurance providers. *Environment and Planning A*, 36, 625–45.

LEYSHON, A., LEE, R. AND WILLIAMS, C. (2003) *Alternative economic spaces*. London: Sage.

LEYSHON, A., MATLESS, D. AND REVILL, G. (EDS) (1998) *The place of music*. New York: Guilford.

LIEBES, T. AND KATZ, E. (1990) *The export of meaning: cross-cultural readings of Dallas*. Oxford: Oxford University Press.

LILLEY III, W. AND DE FRANCO, L.J. (1997) No guarantees for F1's 'Sport Valley'. *Financial Times*, 31 December.

LIMB, M. AND DWYER, C. (EDS) (2001) *Qualitative methodologies for geographers*. London: Arnold.

LIPSITZ, G. (1994) Kalfou Dangere. In *Dangerous crossroads: popular music, postmodernism and the poetics of place*. London: Verso.

LITTLE, J. (2003) 'Riding the rural love train': heterosexuality and the rural community. *Sociologia Ruralis*, 43, 401–17.

LITTLE, J., PEAKE, L. AND RICHARDSON, P. (1988) *Women in cities*. London: Macmillan.

LIVINGSTONE, D. (2000) Putting Geography in its place. *Australian Geographical Studies*, 38, 1–9.

LIVINGSTONE, D.N. (1992) *The geographical tradition*. Oxford: Basil Blackwell.

LIVINGSTONE, D.N. AND HARRISON, R.T. (1981) Hunting the snark: perspectives on geographical investigation. *Geografiska Annaler*, 63B, 69–72.

LLEWELLYN, M. (2004) Designed by women and designing women: gender, planning and the geographies of the kitchen in Britain 1917–1946. *Cultural Geographies*, 11, 42–60.

LOGAN, J. AND MOLOTCH, H. (1987) *Urban fortunes*. Beverley, CA: University of California Press.

LONGHURST, R. (1995) The body and geography. *Gender, Place and Culture*, 2(1), 97–105.

LONGMAN (1991) *Dictionary of the English language*. London: Longman.

LOWE, P. AND RUDIG, R. (1986) Political ecology and the social sciences: the state of the art. *British Journal of Sociology*, 16, 513–50.

LOWENTHAL, D. (1991) British national identity and the English landscape. *Rural History*, 2, 205–30.

LOWENTHAL, D. (1994) Identity, heritage and history. In Gillis, J.R. (ed.) *Commemorations: the politics of national identity*. Princeton, NJ: Princeton University Press.

LOWENTHAL, D (1996) *The heritage crusade and the spoils of history*. London: Viking.

LOWENTHAL, D. (1997) *Geographical Journal*, 163, 355.

LOWENTHAL, D. (1998) *The heritage crusade and the spoils of history*. Cambridge: Cambridge University Press.

LUKE, T. (1997) At the end of nature: cyborgs, 'humachines' and environments in postmodernity. *Environment and Planning A*, 29, 1367–80.

LUTZ, C. AND COLLINS, J. (1993) *Reading National Geographic*. Chicago, IL: University of Chicago Press.

LYOD, B. AND ROWNTREE, L. (1978) Radical feminists and gay men in San Francisco: a social space in dispersed communities. In Lanegran, D. and Palm, R. (eds) *An invitation to Geography*. New York: McGraw-Hill.

MACCANNELL, D. (1989) *The tourist: a new theory of the leisure classes* (2nd edn). New York: Schocken.

MACCANNELL, D. (1992) *Empty meeting grounds: the tourist papers*. Routledge: London.

MACKENZIE, D. (2000) Fear in the markets. *London Review of Books*, 13 April, 1–5 (http://www.lrb.co.uk/v22/n08/mack01_.html).

MACKENZIE, J. (1995) *Orientalism: history, theory and the arts*. Manchester: Manchester University Press.

MACKIAN, S. (1995) That great dust-heap called history: recovering the multiple spaces of citizenship. *Political Geography*, 14, 209–16.

MACLEOD, G. AND JONES, M. (2001) Renewing the geography of regions. *Environment and Planning D: Society and Space*, 1(6), 669–95.

MADDISON, A. (2001) *The world economy: a millennial perspective*. OECD.

MADDISON, A. (2003) *The world economy: historical statistics*. OECD.

MADOOD, T. AND BERTHOUD, R. (1997) *Ethnic minorities in Britain: diversity and disadvantage*. London: Policy Studies Institute.

MAFFESOLI, M. (1995) *The time of the tribes: the decline of individualism in mass society*. London: Sage.

MAFFESOLI, M. (1996) *The time of the tribes: the decline of individualism in mass society*. Trans. D. Smith. Thousand Oaks: Sage.

MAGDOFF, H. (2003) *Imperialism without colonies*. New York: Monthly Review Press.

MANGUEL, A. (1996) *A history of reading*. London: HarperCollins.

MANNING, R.D. (2000) *Credit card nation: the consequences of America's addiction to credit*. New York: Basic Books.

MANSFIELD, B. (2003) 'Imitation crab' and the material culture of commodity production. *Cultural Geographies*, 10, 176–95.

MARCUS, G.E. AND MYERS, F.R. (1995) The traffic in art and culture: an introduction. In Marcus, G.E. and Myers, F.R. (eds) *The traffic in culture. Refiguring art and anthropology*. Berkeley: University of California Press, 1–51.

MARSH, G.P. (1965 [originally 1864]) *Man and nature*. Introduction by David Lowenthal. Cambridge, MA: Bellknap Press.

MARSH, P. (2004) Where partners fight a little war everyday. *Financial Times*, 22 June, 13.

MARSTON, S. (2000) The social construction of scale. *Progress in Human Geography*, 24, 219–42.

MARSTON, S.A. (2002) Making difference: conflict over Irish identity in the New York City St Patrick's Day parade. *Political Geography*, 21, 373–92.

MARTIN, D.-C. (1992) Le choix d'identité. *Revue Française de Science Politique*, 42(4), 582–93.

MARTIN, H.-J. (1994) *The history and power of writing*. Chicago: University of Chicago Press.

MARTIN, R. (ED.) (1998) *Money and the space economy*. Chichester: John Wiley.

MARTIN, R. (2001) Geography and public policy: the case of the missing agenda. *Progress in Human Geography*, 25(2), 189–201.

MARTIN, R. AND MINNS, R. (1995) Undermining the financial basis of regions: the spatial structure and implications of the UK pension fund system. *Regional Studies*, 29, 125–44.

MARTINEZ-ALLIER, J. (1990) Ecology and the poor: A neglected dimension of Latin American history. *Journal of Latin American Studies*, 23, 621–39.

MARTINUSSEN, J. (1997) *Society, state and the market: a guide to competing theories of development*. London: Zed Books.

MARX, K. (1976 [1867]) *Capital*. Volume 1. Harmondsworth: Penguin Books.

MARX, K. (1981) *Surveys from exile*. Harmondsworth: Penguin.

MARX, K. AND ENGELS, F. (1967 [1848]) *The communist manifesto*. Harmondsworth: Penguin Books.

MASLOW, H. (1970) *Motivation and personality*. New York: Harper and Row.

MASON, C. AND HARRISON, R. (1998) Financing entrepreneurship: venture capital and regional development. In Martin, R.L. (ed.) *Money and the space economy*. Chichester: John Wiley.

MASSEY, D. (1991) A global sense of place. *Marxism Today* (June), 24–9; reprinted in D. Massey (1994) *Space, place and gender*. Cambridge: Polity Press, 146–56.

MASSEY, D. (1993) Power-geometry and a progressive sense of place. In Bird, J., Curtis, B., Putnam, T., Robertson, G. and Tickner, L. (eds) *Mapping the futures: local cultures, global change*. London: Routledge.

MASSEY, D. (1994 [1991]) A global sense of place. In *Space, place and gender*. Oxford: Polity Press.

MASSEY, D. (1995a) The conceptualization of place. In Massey, D. and Jess, P. (eds) *A place in the world?* Oxford: Oxford University Press.

MASSEY, D. (1995b) *Spatial divisions of labour: social structures and the geography of production* (2nd edn). Basingstoke and London: Macmillan.

MASSEY, D. (2004) Geographies of responsibility. *Geografiska Annaler*, 86B, 5–18.

MASSEY, D. AND JESS, P. (1995) Places and cultures in an uneven world. In Massey, D. and Jess, P. (eds) *A place in the world?* Oxford: Oxford University Press.

MASSEY, D. AND JESS, P. (EDS) (1995) *A place in the world?* Oxford: Oxford University Press.

MASSEY, D.S. AND DENTON, N.A. (1993) *American apartheid*, Cambridge, MA: Harvard.

MASSEY, D., ALLEN, J. AND SARRE, P. (EDS) (1999) *Human geography today*. Cambridge: Polity Press.

MATLESS, D. (1992) An occasion for geography: landscape representation and Foucault's corpus. *Environment and Planning D: Society and Space*, 10, 41–56.

MATLESS, D. (1994) Moral geography in Broadland. *Ecumene*, 1(2), 127–56.

MATLESS, D. (1995) 'The Art of Right Living': landscape and citizenship, 1918–39. In Pile, S. and Thrift, N. (eds) *Mapping the subject: geographies of cultural transformation*. London and New York: Routledge, 93–122.

MATLESS, D. (1998) *Landscape and Englishness*. London: Reaktion Books.

MATLESS, D. (2000) Action and noise over a hundred years: the making of a nature region. *Body and Society*, 6, 141–65.

MATTHEWS, M.H. (1987) Gender, home range and environmental cognition. *Transactions of the Institute of British Geographers N.S.*, 12, 43–56.

MAY, J. (1996) A little taste of something more exotic: the imaginative geographies of everyday life. *Geography*, 81, 57–64.

MAY, J., CLOKE, P. AND JOHNSEN, S. (2005) Re-phasing neo-liberalism: New labour and Britain's crisis of street homelessness. *Antipode*, 37(4).

MAYER, T. (2005) Nation, gender, and boundaries: feminist political geography and the study of nationalism. In Staeheli, L., Kofman, E. and Peake, L. (eds) *Mapping women, making politics,* London and New York: Routledge, forthcoming.

MCCANNELL, D. (1992) *Empty meeting grounds: the tourist papers*. London: Routledge.

MCCLINTOCK, A. (1995) *Imperial leather: race, gender and sexuality in the colonial contest*. New York: Routledge.

MCCORMACK, D. (2003) An event of geographical ethics in spaces of affect. *Transactions of the Institute of British Geographers*, 28(4), 488–507.

MCCORMICK, J. (1988) America's third world. *Newsweek*, 8 August, 20–24.

MCCORMICK, J. (1991) *British politics and the environment*. London: Earthscan.

MCCORMICK, J.S. (1992) *The global environmental movement: reclaiming paradise*. London: Belhaven.

MCCRACKEN, G. (1988) *Culture and consumption: new approaches to the symbolic character of consumer goods and activities*. Bloomington: Indiana University Press.

MCDOWELL, L. (1995) Body work: heterosexual gender performances in city workplaces. In Bell, D. and Valentine, G. (eds) *Mapping desire: geographies of sexualities*. London: Routledge, 75–95.

MCDOWELL, L. (1997) *Capital culture*. Oxford: Blackwell.

MCEWAN, C. (2000) Engendering citizenship; gendered spaces of democracy in South Africa. *Political Geography*, 19, 627–51.

MCGREGOR, A. (2000) Dynamic texts and the tourist gaze: death, bones and buffalo. *Annals of Tourism Research*, 27(1), 27–50.

MCGUIGAN (2000) British identity and the 'people's princess'. *Sociological Review*, 48(1), 1–18.

MCINTYRE, M., PETER EILERS, H. AND MAIRS, J. (1991) *Physical Geography*. Chichester: John Wiley.

MCKENDRICK, N., BREWER, J. AND PLUMB, J.H. (1982) *The birth of a consumer society: the commercialization of eighteenth-century England*. London: Europa Publications.

MCKIBBEN, B. (1990) *The end of nature*. Oxford: Oxford University Press.

MCKIE, L., GREGORY, S. AND BOWLBY, S. (2002) Shadow times: the temporal and spatial frameworks and experiences of caring and working. *Sociology*, 36, 897–924.

MCLAFFERTY, S. (2002) Mapping women's worlds: knowledge, power and the bounds of GIS. *Gender, Place and Culture*, 9, 263–9.

MCLUHAN, M. (1964) *Understanding media*. London: Routledge and Kegan Paul.

MCNAMEE, S. (1998) Youth, gender and video games: power and control in the home. In Skelton, T. and Valentine, G. (eds) *Cool places: geographies of youth cultures*. London and New York: Routledge, 195–206.

MCNAY, L. (1994) *Foucault: a critical introduction*. Cambridge: Polity Press.

MEADOWS, D.H. *ET AL.* (1972) The limits to growth: a report for the Club of Rome's project on the predicament of mankind. London: Pan.

MEARSHEIMER, J. (1990) Why we will soon miss the Cold War. *The Atlantic*, 266(2), 35–50.

MEINIG, D. (ED.) (1979) *The interpretation of ordinary landscapes*. Oxford and New York: Oxford University Press.

MELLINGER, W. (1994) Toward a critical analysis of tourism representations. *Annals of Tourism Research*, 21, 756–79.

MERRIMAN, N. (ED.) (1993) *The peopling of London: fifteen thousand years of settlement from overseas*. London: Museum of London.

MERRIMAN, P. (2004) Driving places: Marc Augé, the dynamics of place and motorway travel in the late 1950s. *Theory, Culture and Society*, 21(4), in press.

MERTES, T. (ED.) (2004) *The movement of movements: a reader*. London: Verso.

MEYER, D.R. (2003) The challenges of research on the global network of cities. *Urban Geography*, 24(4), 301–13.

MEYROWITZ, J. (1985) *No sense of place: the impact of electronic media on social behaviour*. Oxford: Oxford University Press.

MILBOURNE, P. (ED.) (1997) *Revealing rural others*. London: Pinter.

MILLER, D. (1987) *Material culture and mass consumption*. Oxford: Blackwell.

MILLER, D. (1988) Appropriation of the state on the council estate. *Man*, 23, 353–72.

MILLER, D. (1992) The young and the restless in Trinidad. A case study of the local and the global in mass consumption. In Silverstone, R. and Hirsch, E. (eds) *Consuming technologies*, London: Routledge.

MILLER, D. (1994) *Modernity: an ethnographic approach*. Oxford: Berg.

MILLER, D. (1995a) Consumption and commodities. *Annual Review of Anthropology*, 24, 141–61.

MILLER, D. (1995b) Consumption as the vanguard of history. In Miller, D. (ed.) *Acknowledging consumption: a review of new studies*. London: Routledge.

MILLER, D. (1997) *Capitalism: an ethnographic approach*. Oxford: Berg.

MILLER, D (1998a) Coca-cola: a black sweet drink from Trinidad. In Miller, D. (ed.) *Material cultures. Why some things matter*. London: UCL Press, 169–87.

MILLER, D. (ED.) (1998b) *Material cultures. Why some things matter*. London: UCL Press.

MILLER, D. (ED.) (2001) *Home possessions. Material culture behind closed doors*. Oxford: Berg.

MILLS, S. (1989) Tourism and leisure – setting the scene. *Tourism Today*, 6, 18–21.

MILWARD, A. (1992) *The European rescue of the nation state*. London: Routledge.

MINTZ, S. (1985) *Sweetness and power*. New York: Viking Books.

MISHAN, E. (1969) *The costs of economic growth*. Harmondsworth: Penguin Books.

MITCHELL, B. AND DRAPER, D. (1982) *Relevance and ethics in Geography*. London: Longman.

MITCHELL, D. (2000) *Cultural geography: a critical introduction*. Oxford: Blackwell.

MITCHELL, D. (2003) *The right to the city: social justice and the fight for public space*. New York: Guilford Press.

MITCHELL, D. AND STAEHELI, L. (forthcoming) Clean and safe? Property redevelopment, public space and homelessness in downtown San Diego. In Lowe, S. and Smith, N. (eds) *The politics of public space*. New York: Routledge.

MITCHELL, W.J.T. (1994a) Introduction. In Mitchell, W.J.T. (ed.) *Landscape and power*, Chicago and London: University of Chicago Press.

MITCHELL, W.J.T. (1994b) Imperial Landscape. In Mitchell, W.J.T. (ed.) *Landscape and power*. Chicago and London: University of Chicago Press.

MOHAN, G., BROWN, E., MILWARD, B. AND ZACK-WILLIAMS, A.B. (2000) *Structural adjustment: theory, practice and impacts*. London: Routledge.

MOHAN, J. (2000) Geographies of welfare and social exclusion. *Progress in Human Geography*, 24(2), 291–300.

MOHAN, J. (2002) Geographies of welfare and social exclusion: dimensions, consequences and methods. *Progress in Human Geography*, 26(1), 65–75.

MOHANTY, C. (1991) Cartographies of struggle, Third World women and the politics of feminism. In Mohanty, C., Parker, A. and Russo, A. (eds) *Cartographies of struggle, Third World women and the politics of feminism*. London: Routledge.

MOLLENKOPF, J. AND CASTELLS, M. (1992) *Dual city? Restructuring New York*. Russell Sage Foundation.

MONBIOT, G. (2003) *The age of consent: a manifesto for a new world order*. London: Flamingo.

MONK, J. AND HANSON, S. (1982) On not excluding half the human in geography. *The Professional Geographer*, 34, 11–23.

MOODIE, S. (1986) *Roughing it in the bush* (with Introduction by Margaret Atwood). London: Virago.

MOODY, K. (1997) *Workers in a lean world*. London: Verso.

MOODY, R. (ED.) (1988) *The indigenous voice*. (2 vols.) London: Zed Books.

MOORE, R. (1992) Marketing alterity. *Visual Anthropology Review*, 8(2), 10–26.

MORALES, E. (1989) *Cocaine*. Tucson: University of Arizona Press.

MORLEY, D. (1986) *Family television: cultural power and domestic leisure*. London: Comedia.

MORLEY, D. (1991) Where the global meets the local: notes from the sitting room. *Screen*, 32, 1–15.

MORLEY, D. (1992a) *Television, audiences and cultural studies*. London: Routledge.

MORLEY, D. (1992b) Where the global meets the local: notes from the sitting room. In Morley, D. *Television audiences and cultural studies*. Routledge.

MORLEY, D. AND ROBBINS, K. (1995) *Spaces of identity: global media, electronic landscapes and cultural boundaries*. London: Routledge.

MORMONT, M. (1990) Who is rural? Or how to be rural: towards a sociology of the rural. In Marsden, T., Lowe, P. and Whatmore, S. (eds) *Rural restructuring*. London: David Fulton.

MORRIS, J. (1986) *The matter of Wales: epic views of a small country*. Harmondsworth: Penguin Books.

MORRIS, J. (1988) *Hong Kong, Xiang Gang*, London: Viking.

MORRIS, J. (1990) *Hong Kong: epilogue to an empire*. London: Penguin Books.

MORRIS, J. (1991) *Pride against prejudice*. London: The Women's Press.

MORRIS, J. (1992) *O! Canada*. London: Hale.

MORT, F. (1989) The politics of consumption. In Hall, S. and Jacques, M. (eds) *New times: the changing face of politics in the 1990s*. London: Lawrence and Wishart, 160–72.

MORTIMORE, M. (1998) *Roots in the African dust: sustaining the drylands*. Cambridge University Press.

MOSER, C. (1993) *Gender planning and development*. Routledge, London.

MOSS, P. (1999) Autobiographical notes on chronic illness. In Butler, R. and Parr, H. (eds) *Mind and body spaces: geographies of illness, impairment and disability*. London: Routledge, 155–66.

MOSS, P. (ED.) (2002) *Feminist geography in practice: research and methods*. Oxford: Blackwell.

MOUNTZ, A. (2003) Human smuggling, the transnational imaginary, and everyday geographies of the nation-state. *Antipode*, 622–44.

MOWFORTH, M. AND MUNT, I. (2003) *Tourism and sustainability.* London: Routledge.

MURDOCH, J. (2003) Co-constructing the countryside: hybrid networks and the extensive self. In Cloke, P. (ed.) *Country visions.* London: Pearson, 263–82.

MURDOCH, J. AND PRATT, A. (1993) Rural studies: modernism, postmodernism and the 'post-rural'. *Journal of Rural Studies,* 9, 411–28.

MURDOCH, J. AND PRATT, A. (1997) From the power of topography to the topography of power: a discourse in strange ruralities. In Cloke, P. and Little, J. (eds) *Contested countryside cultures.* London: Routledge.

MURDOCH, K., LOWE, P., WARD, N. AND MARSDEN, T. (2003) *The differentiated countryside.* London: Routledge.

MURGATROYD, L. AND NEUBURGER, H. (1997) A household satellite account for the UK. *Economic Trends,* 527, October, 63–71.

MYTRAVELGUIDE.COM (2004) Kathmandu Valley problems, http://www.mytravelguide.com/city-guide/Asia/Nepal/Kathmandu-Valley-problems, accessed 27 July 2004.

NAIRN, T. (1977) *The break-up of Britain.* London: New Left Books.

NAIRN, T. (1995) Breakwaters of 2000: from ethnic to civic nationalism. *New Left Review,* 214, 91–103.

NANDY, A. (1984) Culture, state and rediscovery of Indian politics. *Economic and Political Weekly,* 19(49), 2078–83.

NASH, C. (1996) Reclaiming vision: looking at landscape and the body. *Gender, Place and Culture: A Journal of Feminist Geography,* 3, 149–69.

NASH, C. (2000) Performativity in practice: some recent work in Cultural Geography. *Progress in Human Geography,* 24(4), 653–64.

NAST, H.J. (2000) Mapping the 'unconscious': racism and the oedipal family. *Annals of the Association of American Geographers,* 90, 215–55.

NATIONAL PORTRAIT GALLERY (1996) *David Livingstone and the Victorian encounter with Africa.* London: National Portrait Gallery.

NEPAL, S. (1997) Sustainable tourism, protected areas and livelihood needs of local communities in developing countries. *The International Journal of Sustainable Development and World Ecology,* 4, 123–35.

NEWBY, H. (1988) *The countryside in question.* London: Hutchinson.

NEWHOUSE, J. (1997) Europe's rising regionalism. *Foreign Affairs,* 76(1), 67–84.

NEWMAN, D. (1989) Civilian and military presence as strategies of territorial control: the Arab-Israeli conflict. *Political Geography,* 8(3), 215–28.

NEWSON, J. AND NEWSON, E. (1974) Cultural aspects of childrearing in the English-speaking world. In Richards, M.P.M. (ed.) *The integration of a child into a social world.* Cambridge: Cambridge University Press.

NIESSEN, S., LESHKOWICH, A.M. AND JONES, C. (2003) *Re-orienting fashion: the globalisation of Asian dress.* Oxford, Berg.

NIJMAN, J. (1994) Nicholas Spykman. In O'Loughlin, J. (ed.) *Dictionary of geopolitics.* Westport, CT: Greenwood Press.

NIJMAN, J. (1996) Ethnicity, class and the economic internationalization of Miami. In O'Loughlin, J. and Friedrichs, J (eds) *Social polarization in post-industrial metropolises.* Berlin and New York: de Gruyter.

NIYOGI DE, E. (2002) The city between the global state: architecture and the people in Singapore's gendered imaginations. In Sarker, S. and Niyogi de, E. (eds) *Trans-status subjects: gender in the globalisation of South and Southeast Asia.* Durham and London: Duke University Press, 189–210.

NKRUMAH, K. (1965) *Neo-colonialism: the last stage of imperialism.* London: Nelson.

NODDINGS, N. (1984) Caring: a feminine approach to ethics and moral education. Berkeley: University of California Press.

NORA, P. (1989) Between memory and history: *Les Lieux de Mémoire. Representations,* 26, 7–25.

NORRIS, C. (1992) *Uncritical theory: postmodernism, intellectuals and the Gulf War.* Amherst, MA: University of Massachusetts Press.

NOTES FROM NOWHERE (ED.) (2003) *We are everywhere.* London: Verso.

NYE, D. (1991) The emergence of photographic discourse: images and consumption. In Nye, D. and Pedersen, C. (eds) *Consumption and American culture.* Amsterdam: VU University Press.

OAKLEY, A. (1981) *Subject women.* London: Martin Robertson.

O'BRIEN, R. (1992) *Global financial integration: the end of geography?* London: Pinter/ RIIA.

OFFE, K. AND HEINZE, R. (1992) *Beyond employment.* London: Polity Press.

OFFICE FOR NATIONAL STATISTICS (2000) *Social Trends 30.* London: The Stationery Office.

OFFICE FOR NATIONAL STATISTICS (2004) *Social Trends 34.* London: The Stationery Office.

OGBORN, M. (1998) *Spaces of modernity: London's geographies 1680–1780.* New York: Guilford Press.

OGBORN, M. (2002) Writing travels: power, knowledge and ritual on the English East India Company's early voyages. *Transactions of the Institute of British Geographers,* 27, 155–71.

OLLMAN, B. (1972) *Alienation.* Cambridge: Cambridge University Press.

O'LOUGHLIN, J. (2004) The political geography of conflict: civil wars in the hegemonic shadow. In Flint, C. (ed.) *The geography of war and peace.* New York: Oxford University Press.

O'LOUGHLIN, J. AND FRIEDRICHS, J. (EDS) (1996) *Social polarization in post-industrial metropolises.* Berlin and New York: De Gruyter.

O'LOUGHLIN, J. AND VAN DER WUSTEN, H. (1993) Political geography of war and peace. In Taylor, P.J. (ed.) *Political geography of the twentieth century.* London: Belhaven Press.

OPENSHAW, S. (1991) A view on the GIS crisis in geography, or, using GIS to put Humpty-Dumpty together again. *Environment and Planning A,* 23, 621–8.

OPENSHAW, S. (1992) Further thoughts on geography and GIS: a reply. *Environment and Planning A,* 24, 463–6.

OPPENHEIM, C. (1990) *Poverty: the facts.* London: Child Poverty Action Group.

O'RIORDAN, T. (1976) *Environmentalism.* London: Pion.

O'RIORDAN, T. (1988) The politics of sustainability. In Turner, R.K. (ed.) *Sustainable environmental management.* London: Belhaven Press.

O'RIORDAN, T. (1999) *Environmental science for environmental management* (2nd edn). Harlow: Longman.

O'RIORDAN, T. AND JORDAN, A, (1998) Kyoto in Perspective. *ECOS,* 18, 314, 38–42.

O'RIORDAN, T. AND VOISEY, H. (EDS) (1998) *The transition to sustainability.* London: Earthscan.

OSBORNE, P. (1996) Modernity. In Payne, M. (ed.) *A dictionary of cultural and critical theory.* Oxford: Blackwell.

Ó TUATHAIL, G. (1996) *Critical geopolitics.* Minneapolis: Minnesota University Press.

Ó TUATHAIL, G. (2003) 'Just out looking for a fight': American affect and the invasion of Iraq. *Antipode*, 35(5), 856–70.

Ó TUATHAIL, G. AND AGNEW, J. (1992) Geopolitics and discourse: practical geopolitical reasoning in American foreign policy. *Political Geography*, 11(2), 190–204.

OU-FAN LEE, L. (1999) *Shanghai modern: the flowering of a new urban culture in China, 1930–1945*. Cambridge, MA: Harvard University Press.

OVERTON, M. (1994) Historical geography. In Johnston, R.J., Gregory, D. and Smith, D.M. (eds) *The dictionary of Human Geography* (3rd edn). Oxford: Blackwell.

OWENS, S. (1997) Negotiated environments: needs, demands, and values in the age of sustainability. *Environment and Planning A*, 29, 571–80.

OXFAM (2004) *Trading away our rights: women working in global supply chains*. London: Oxfam.

PACIONE, M. (1999) Relevance in Human Geography: special collection of invited papers. *Scottish Geographical Journal*, 115(2).

PAIN, R (2001) Age, generation and lifecourse. In Pain, R., Barke, M., Fuller, D., Gough, J., McFarlane, R. and Mowl, G. (eds) *Introducing social geographies*. London: Arnold, 141–63.

PAIN, R. (2004) Social geography: participatory research. *Progress in Human Geography* (forthcoming).

PAIN, R., MOWL, G. AND TALBOT, C. (2000) Difference and the negotiation of 'old age'. *Environment and Planning D: Society and Space*, 18(3), 377–94.

PAIN, R. *ET AL.* (2001) *Introducing social geographies*. London: Arnold.

PAINTER, J. AND PHILO, C. (1995) Spaces of citizenship: an introduction. *Political Geography*, 14(2), 107–20.

PALUMBI, S. (2001) Humans as the world's greatest evolutionary force. *Science* 293 (7 September), 1786–90.

PAN-AMERICAN HEALTH ORGANIZATION (PAHO) (2002) *Health in the Americas. Volume II, 2002 Edition*. Washington, DC: PAHO.

PAPATHEODOROU, A. (2003) Corporate strategies of British tour-operators in the Mediterranean region: an economic geography approach. *Tourism Geographies*, 5, 280–304.

PARK, C. (1997) *The environment: principles and applications*. London: Routledge.

PARK, R. (1926) The urban community as a spatial pattern and a moral order. In Burgess, E.W. (ed.) *The urban community*. Chicago, IL: University of Chicago Press, 3–18.

PARKER, G. (2002) *Citizenships, contingency and the countryside*, London: Routledge.

PARKER, J. AND SMITH, C. (1940) *Modern Turkey*. London: George Routledge & Sons.

PARKER, K., PARKER, A. AND VALE, T. (2001) Vertebrate feeding guilds in California's Sierra Nevada: relations to environmental condition and change in spatial scale. *Annals of the Association of American Geographers*, 91(2), 245–62.

PARR, H. (1998) The politics of methodology in 'post-medical geography': mental health research and the interview. *Health and Place*, 4(4), 341–53.

PARR, H. (1999) Delusional geographies: the experiential worlds of people during madness/illness. *Environment and Planning D: Society and Space*, 17, 673–90.

PARR, H. AND BUTLER, R. (1999) New geographies of illness, impairment and disability. In Butler, R. and Parr, H. (eds) *Mind and body spaces: geographies of illness, impairment and disability*. London: Routledge, 1–24.

PARR, H., PHILO, C. AND BURNS, N. (2004) Social geographies of rural mental health: experiencing inclusion and exclusion. In *Transactions of the IBG*, 29(4), 401–19.

PEACH, C. (ED.) (1975) *Urban social segregation*. London: Longman.

PEACH, C. (1996) Does Britain have ghettoes? *Transactions of the Institute of British Geographers*, 21(1), 216–35.

PEAKE, L. (1993) Race and sexuality: challenging the patriarchal structuring of urban social space. *Environment and Planning D: Society and Space*, 11, 415–32.

PEARCE, D. *ET AL.* (1988) *Blueprint for a green economy*. London: Earthscan.

PEARCE, D. *ET AL.* (1993) *Blueprint three: measuring sustainable development*. Earthscan: London.

PEARCE, S. (ED.) (1994) *Interpreting objects and collections*. London: Routledge.

PEARCE, S. (1999) *On collecting: an investigation into collecting in the European tradition*. London: Routledge.

PECK, J. AND TICKELL, A. (2002) Neoliberalizing space. *Antipode*, 34, 380–404.

PECK, J., BARNES, T.J., SHEPPARD, E. AND TICKELL, A. (EDS) (2003) *Reading economic geography*. Oxford: Blackwell.

PECKHAM, R.S. (2003) *Rethinking heritage: culture and politics in Europe*. London: I.B. Taurus.

PEET, R. (1998) *Modern geographical thought*. Oxford: Blackwell.

PEET, R. (1989) World capitalism and the destruction of regional cultures. In Johnston, R.J. and Taylor, P. (eds) *The world in crisis?* (2nd edn). Oxford: Blackwell.

PEET, R. (WITH E. HARTWICK) (1999) *Theories of development*. London: The Guilford Press.

PEET, R. AND THRIFT, N. (1989) Political economy and Human Geography. In Peet, R. and Thrift, N. (eds) *New models in geography: volume 1. The political-economy perspective*. London: Unwin Hyman.

PEET, R. AND WATTS, M. (EDS) (1996) *Liberation ecologies: environment, development and social movements*. London: Routledge.

PEPPER, D. (1984) *The roots of modern environmentalism*. London: Routledge.

PEPPER, D. (1996) *Modern environmentalism: an introduction*. London: Routledge.

PERKS, R. AND THOMSON, A. (EDS) (1998). *The oral history reader*. London: Routledge.

PERLMUTTER, T. (1993) Distress signals: a Canadian story – an international lesson. In Dowmunt, T. (ed.) *Channels of resistance: global television and local empowerment*. London: BFI/Channel 4, 16–26.

PERRONS, D. (2004) *Globalization and social change: people and places in a divided world*. London: Routledge.

PERRY, M., KONG, L. AND YEOH, B. (EDS) (1997) *Singapore: a development city state*. New York: John Wiley.

PHILLIPS, R. (2005) *Sex, politics and empire: a postcolonial geography*. Manchester: Manchester University Press.

PHILLIPS, R.S. (1997) *Mapping men and empire: a geography of empire*. London: Routledge.

PHILO, C. (1992) Neglected rural geographies: a review. *Journal of Rural Studies*, 8, 193–207.

PHILO, C. (1995) Animals, geography, and the city: notes on inclusions and exclusions. *Environment and Planning D: Society and Space* 13(6), 644–81.

PHILO, C. (1997) Of other rurals. In Cloke, P. and Little, J. (eds) *Contested countryside cultures: otherness, marginality and rurality*. London: Routledge.

PHILO, C. (1998) A 'lyffe in pyttes and caves': exclusionary geographies of the west country tinners. *Geoforum*, 29(2), 159–72.

PHILO, C. (2000) Social exclusion. In Johnston, R.J., Gregory, D., Pratt, G. and Watts, M. (eds) *The dictionary of Human Geography*. Oxford: Blackwell, 751–2.

PHILO, C. AND WILBERT, C. (2000) *Animal spaces, beastly places: new geographies of human–animal relations*. London: Routledge.

PHILO, G. (1993) From Buerk to Band Aid: the media and the 1984 Ethiopian famine. In Eldridge, J. (ed.) *Getting the message: news, truth and power*. London: Routledge.

PICKLES, J. (ED.) (1995) *Ground truth: the social implications of geographical information systems*. New York: Guilford.

PICKLES, J. (2003) A history of spaces: cartographic reason, mapping and the geo-coded world. London and New York: Routledge.

PIETZ, W. (1988) The 'post-colonialism' of Cold War discourse. *Social Text*, 19/20(Fall), 55–75.

PILE, S. (1995) 'What we are asking for is decent human life' SPLASH, neighbourhood demands and citizenship in London's docklands. *Political Geography*, 14, 199–208.

PILE, S. AND THRIFT, N. (1995) *Mapping the subject: geographies of cultural transformation*. London: Routledge.

PINCKNEY, D.H. (1958) *Napoleon III and the rebuilding of Paris*. Princeton, NJ: Princeton University Press.

PLATTEAU, J.-P. (1994) Behind the market stage where real societies exist: Parts I and II. *Journal of Development Studies*, 30, 533–77 and 753–817.

PLOSZAJSKA, T. (2000) Historiographies of geography and empire. In Graham, B. and Nash, C. (eds) *Modern historical geographies*. London: Prentice Hall.

POCOCK, D. (1981) Place and the novelist. *Transactions of the Institute of British Geographers*, NS 6, 337–47.

POCOCK, D. (1993) The senses in focus. *Area*, 25(1), 11–16.

PODMORE, J.A. (2001) Lesbians in the crowd: gender, sexuality and visibility along Montréal's Boul. St-Laurent. *Gender, Place and Culture*, 8, 333–55.

POLANYI, K, (1947) *The great transformation*. Boston: Beacon Books.

POLLARD, J.S. (1996) Banking at the margins: a geography of financial exclusion in Los Angeles. *Environment and Planning A*, 28, 1209–32.

POLLOCK, G. (1988) Modernity and the spaces of femininity. In Pollock, G. *Vision and difference: femininity, feminism and the histories of art*. London: Routledge, 50–90.

PONNIAH, T. (2004) Democracy vs empire: alternatives to globalisation presented at the World Social Forum. *Antipode*, 36, 130–3.

PONTALIS, J.-B. (1990) *La force d'attraction*. Paris: Seuil.

PONTING, C. (1994) *Churchill*. London: Sinclair-Stevenson.

PORTEOUS, J.D. (1985) Smellscape. *Progress in Human Geography*, 9(3), 358–9.

POSTONE, M. (1993) *Time, labour and social domination*. Cambridge: Cambridge University Press.

POWER, M. (2003) *Rethinking development geographies*. London: Routledge.

PRATT, G. (2004) *Working feminism*. Edinburgh: Edinburgh University Press; and Philadelphia: Temple University Press.

PRATT, G. AND HANSON, S. (1994) Geography and the construction of difference. *Gender, Place and Culture*. 1, 5–29.

PRATT, J., LEYSHON, A. AND THRIFT, N.J. (1996) Financial exclusion in the 1990s II: geographies of financial inclusion and exclusion. *Working Papers on Producer Services*, 38.

PRATT, M.L. (1986) Scratches in the face of the country; or, what Mr Barrow saw in the lands of the Bushmen. In Gates, H.L. Jr (ed.) *'Race', writing and difference*. Chicago, IL: Chicago University Press, 138–62.

PRED, A. (1990) *Lost words and lost worlds: modernity and the language of everyday life in late nineteenth-century Stockholm*. Cambridge: Cambridge University Press.

PRED, A. AND WATTS, M. (1992) Reworking modernity. New Brunswick: Rutgers University Press.

PRENDERGAST, K. AND NASH, C. (2002) Mapping emotion again. In Driver, F., Nash, C., Prendergast, K. and Swenson, P. (eds) *Landing: eight collaborative projects between artists and geographers*. Egham: Royal Holloway, University of London.

PRESTON, P.W. (1996) *Development theory: an introduction*. Oxford: Blackwell.

PRETECEILLE, E. (2001) *Inegalites et contrastes sociaux en Ile de France*. Paris: IRESCO.

PRICE, M. (1996) Taming the tourists. *People and the Planet*, 5, http://www.oneworld.org/patp/pap_info.html, accessed 4 April 2004.

PRINGLE, R. (1999) Emotions. In McDowell, L. and Sharp, J. (eds) *A feminist glossary of Human Geography*. London: Arnold, 68–9.

PROBYN, E. (1993) *Sexing the self: gendered positions in cultural studies*. London: Routledge.

PUNCH, S. (2001) Household division of labour: generation, gender, age, birth order and sibling composition. *Work, Employment and Society*, 15, 803–23.

PUTNAM, R. (2000) *Bowling alone: the collapse and revival of American community*. New York: Simon & Schuster.

RABAN, J. (1990) *Hunting Mr Heartbreak*. London: Pan Books.

RACO, M. AND IMRIE, R. (2000) Governmentality and rights and responsibilities in urban policy. *Environment and Planning A*, 32, 2187–204.

RADCLIFFE, S. AND WESTWOOD, S. (EDS) (1993) *Viva: women and popular protest in Latin America*. London: Routledge.

RADCLIFFE, S.A. (1990) Ethnicity, patriarchy and incorporation into the nation: female migrants as domestic servants in Peru. *Environment and Planning D: Society and Space*, 8, 379–93.

RADIN, M. (1996) *Contested commodities*. Cambridge, MA: Harvard University Press.

RADWAY, J. (1984) *Reading the romance: women, patriarchy, and popular literature*. Chapel Hill, NC: University of North Carolina Press.

RAI, A. (1995) India on-line: electronic bulletin boards and the construction of a diasporic Hindu identity. *Diaspora*, 4, 31–58.

RAWCLIFFE, P. (1998) *Swimming with the tide: environmental groups in transition*. Manchester: Manchester University Press.

REDCLIFT, M. (1984) *Development and the environmental crisis: red or green alternatives?* London: Methuen.

REDCLIFT, M. (1987) *Sustainable development: exploring the contradictions*. London: Methuen.

REDCLIFT, M. (2004) *Chewing gum. The fortunes of taste*. New York: Routledge.

REDISCOVERING GEOGRAPHY COMMITTEE, NATIONAL RESEARCH COUNCIL (1997) *Rediscovering geography: new relevance for science and society*. Washington: National Academy Press.

REED, H.C. (1981) *The pre-eminence of international financial centers*. New York: Praeger.

RELPH, E. (1976) *Place and placelessness*. London: Pion.

RENGERT, G., MATTSON, M. AND KENDERSON, K. (2001) *Campus security: situational crime prevention in high-density environments*. Monsey, NY: Criminal Justice Press.

REVILL, G. (2000) Music and the politics of sound: nationalism, citizenship and auditory space. *Environment and Planning D: Society and Space*, 18, 597–613.

RHOADS, B. AND THORN, C. (EDS) (1996) *The scientific nature of geomorphology*. London: Routledge.

RHODES, R. (1996) The new governance: governing without government. *Political Studies*, XLIV, 652–67.

RIEFF, D. (1993) Notes on the Ottoman legacy written in a time of war. *Salmagundi*, 100, 3–15.

RIGG, J. (2003) *Southeast Asia* (2nd edn). London: Routledge.

RILEY, R. (1994) Speculations on the new American landscapes. In Foote, K., Hugill, P., Mathewson, K. and Smith, J. (eds) *Re-Reading Cultural Geography*. Austin: University of Texas Press.

RITZER, G. (2004) *The globalization of nothing*, Thousand Oaks, CA; and London: Pine Forge Press.

ROBINS, K. (1996) Interrupting identities: Turkey/Europe. In Hall, S. and du Gay, P. (eds) *Questions of cultural identity*. London: Sage, 61–86.

ROBINS, K. AND AKSOY, A. (2003) Banal transnationalism: the difference that television makes. In Karim, K.H. (ed.) *The media of diaspora: mapping the global*. London: Routledge, 89–104.

ROBINSON, N. (ED.) (1993) *Agenda 21: Earth's action plan*. New York: Ocean Publications (IUCN Environmental Policy and Law Paper No. 27).

ROBSON, E. (1996) Working girls and boys: children's contribution to household survival in West Africa. *Geography*, 81, 403–7.

RODAWAY, P. (1994) *Sensuous geographies: body, sense and place*. London and New York: Routledge.

RODNEY, W. (1974) *How Europe underdeveloped Africa*. Washington, DC: Howard University Press.

ROSE, D. AND CARRASCO, P. (2000) The 1996 census as a tool for measuring unpaid household labour: reflections on a controversy and preliminary explorations for the case of the Montreal region. Paper presented at the annual meetings of the Association of American Geographers, Pittsburgh.

ROSE, G. (1992) *Feminism and geography: the limits of geographical knowledge*. London: Polity Press.

ROSE, G. (1993a) *Feminism and geography: the limits of geographical knowledge*. Cambridge: Polity Press; and Minneapolis: University of Minnesota Press.

ROSE, G. (1993b) Looking at landscape: the uneasy pleasures of power. In Rose, G. *Feminism and geography: the limits of geographical knowledge*. Cambridge: Polity Press; and Minneapolis: University of Minnesota Press, 86–112.

ROSE, G. (1995) Place and identity: a sense of place. In Massey, D. and Jess, P. (eds) *A place in the world?* Oxford: Oxford University Press.

ROSE, G. (1997a) Looking at landscape: the uneasy pleasures of power. In Barnes, T. and Gregory, D. (eds) *Reading Human Geography*. London: Arnold.

ROSE, G. (1997b) Situating knowledges: Positionality, reflexivities and other tactics. *Progress in Human Geography*, 21(3), 305–20.

ROSE, G. (2001) *Visual methodologies: an introduction to the interpretation of visual materials*. London: Sage.

ROSE, G. (2002) Conclusion. In Bondi *et al.* (eds) *Subjectivities, knowledges and feminist geographies*. Oxford: Rowman and Littlefield, 253–8.

ROSE, G. (2003) Family photographs and domestic spacings: a case study. *Transactions of the Institute of British Geographers*, NS28, 5–18.

ROSS, J. (1995) *Rebellion from the roots*. Monroe, ME: Common Courage Press.

ROSTOW, W. (1960) *The stages of economic growth: a non-communist manifesto*. Cambridge: Cambridge University Press.

ROTFELD, A.D. (2002) Introduction: global security after 11 September 2001. In *SIPRI yearbook 2002: armaments, disarmament, and international security*. Oxford: Oxford University Press.

ROTHENBERG, T. (1995) 'And she told two friends': lesbians creating urban social space. In Bell, D. and Valentine, G. (eds) *Mapping desire: geographies of sexualities*. London: Routledge, 165–81.

ROUSE, R. (1991) Mexican migration and the social space of postmodernism. *Diaspora*, 1, 8–23.

ROUTLEDGE, P. (2003a) Voices of the dammed: discursive resistance amidst erasure in the Narmada Valley, India. *Political Geography*, 22, 3, 243–70.

ROUTLEDGE, P. (2003b) Convergence space: process geographies of grassroots globalisation networks. *Transactions of the Institute of British Geographers*, 28(3), 333–49.

ROWLANDS, J. (1997) *Questioning empowerment: working with women in Honduras*. Oxford: Oxfam.

ROWLES, G. (1978a) *Prisoners of space? Exploring the geographic experience of older people*. Boulder, CO: Westview Press.

ROWLES, G. (1978b) Reflections on experiential fieldwork. In Ley, D. and Samuels, M. (eds) (1978) *Humanistic geography: prospects and problems*. London: Croom Helm.

RTI INTERNATIONAL (2004) The Local Governance Project in Iraq. Downloaded from www.rti.org, 19 May 2004.

RUDDICK, S. (1996) *Young and homeless in Hollywood*. New York: Routledge.

RUDDICK, S. (2004) Activist geographies: building possible worlds. In Cloke, P., Crang, P. and Goodwin, M. (eds) *Envisioning human geographies*. London: Arnold, 229–41.

RUSHKOFF, D. (1994) *Cyberia: life in the trenches of hyperspace*. New York: HarperSanFrancisco.

RUSSELL, P. (2003) Narrative constructions of British culinary culture. Unpublished PhD dissertation, University of Sheffield.

RUTHERFORD, T. (2004) Convergence, the institutional turn and workplace regimes: the case of lean production. *Progress in Human Geography*, 28(4), 425–46.

RYAN, J. (1997) *Picturing empire: photography and the visualization of the British Empire*. London: Reaktion Books.

SACK, R. (1992) *Place, modernity and the consumer's world: a relational framework for geographical analysis*. Baltimore: Johns Hopkins University Press.

SACK, R. (1997) *Homo Geographicus*. Baltimore: Johns Hopkins University Press.

SAFRAN, W. (1991) 'Diasporas in modern societies: myths of homeland and return. *Diaspora*, 1(1), 83–99.

SAID, E. (1993) *Culture and imperialism*. London: Chatto & Windus.

SAID, E. (1995 [1978]) *Orientalism*. London: Penguin Books.

SAMUEL, R. (1996) *Theatres of memory. Volume 1: past and present in contemporary culture*. London. Verso.

SASSEN, S. (1988) *The mobility of capital and labour*. Cambridge: Cambridge University Press.

SASSEN, S. (1990) Finance and business services in New York City: international linkages and domestic effects. *International Social Science Journal*, 42, 287–306.

SASSEN, S. (1991) *The global city: New York, London, Tokyo*. Princeton, NJ: Princeton University.

SAUER, C.O. (1925) The morphology of landscape. *University of California Publications in Geography*, 2, 19–54.

SCANNELL, P. (1988) Radio times: the temporal arrangements of broadcasting in the modern world. In Drummond, P. and Paterson, R. (eds) *Television and its audience: international research perspectives*. London: BFI, 15–31.

SCANNELL, P. (1995) *Radio, television, and modern life*. Oxford: Blackwell.

SCHAMA, S. (1987) The Enlightenment in the Netherlands. In Porter, R. and Teich, M. (eds), *The Enlightenment in national context*. Cambridge: Cambridge University Press.

SCHECH, S. AND HAGGIS, J. (2000) *Culture and development: a critical introduction*. Oxford: Blackwell.

SCHEPER-HUGHES, N. (2002) The end of the body. *SAIS Review*, XXII/1, 61–80.

SCHICK, I.C. AND TONAK, E.A. (EDS) (1987) *Turkey in transition: new perspectives*. New York: Oxford University Press.

SCHIRMER, J. (1994) The claiming of space and the body politic within national-security states. In Boyarin, J. (ed.) *Remapping memory: the politics of timespace*. Minneapolis: University of Minnesota Press.

SCHIVELBUSCH, W. (1986) *The railway journey. The industrialization of time and space in the nineteenth century*. Berkeley: University of California Press.

SCHLESINGER, P. (1994) Europe's contradictory communicative space. *Daedalus*, 123(2), 25–52.

SCHNUCKER, R.V. (1990) Puritan attitudes towards childhood discipline, 1560–1634. In Fildes, V. (ed.) *Women as mothers in pre-industrial England*. London: Routledge.

SCHOENBERGER, E. (1997) *The cultural crisis of the firm*. Cambridge, MA and Oxford: Blackwell.

SCHOR, J.B. (1998) *The overspent American: upscaling, downshifting and the new consumer*. New York: Basic Books.

SCHOR, J.B. (2000) *Do Americans shop too much?* Boston: Beacon Press.

SCHROEDER, R. (1996) *Possible worlds: the social dynamic of virtual reality technology*. Boulder, CO: Westview Press.

SCHUMACHER, E.F. (1973) *Small is beautiful: a study of economics as if people mattered*. London: Blond and Briggs.

SCHWARTZ, J. AND RYAN, J. (EDS) (2003) *Picturing place: photography and the geographical imagination*. London: I.B. Tauris.

SCHWARTZ, J.M. (1996) 'The Geography Lesson': photographs and the construction of imaginative geographies. *Journal of Historical Geography*, 22, 16–45.

SCOTT, J. (1976) *The moral economy of the peasantry*. New Haven, CN: Yale University Press.

SCOTT, R.A. (1969) *The making of blind men: a study of adult socialization*. London: Transaction Books.

SCOTTISH NATURAL HERITAGE (1993) *Sustainable development and the natural heritage: the SNH approach*. Edinburgh: Scottish Natural Heritage.

SEAGER, J. (1994) *Earth follies*. London: Routledge.

SEAGER, J. (2000) 'And a Charming Wife': gender, marriage, and manhood in the job search process. *The Professional Geographer*, 52, 709–21.

SEAGER, J. (2003) *The state of women in the world atlas* (3rd edn). New York: Penguin; London: Women's Press; Paris: Autremont Editions.

SEARLE, A. (1996) *Antony Gormley: 'Field for the British Isles'*. London: Arts Council of Great Britain (Spotlight Series).

SECORD, J. (2000) *Victorian sensation: the extraordinary publication, reception, and secret authorship of Vestiges of the natural history of creation*. Chicago and London: University of Chicago Press.

SEHGAL, R. (1995) *The black diaspora*. New York: Farrar, Straus and Giroux.

SEITER, E., BORCHERS, H., KREUTZNER, G. AND WARTH, E.-M. (1989) 'Don't treat us like we're so stupid and naïve': towards an ethnography of soap opera viewers. In Seiter, E. *et al.* (eds) *Remote control*. London and New York: Routledge.

SELF, C. AND GOLLEGE, R. (1994) Sex-related differences in spatial ability: what every geography educator should know. *Journal of Geography*, 93, 234–43.

SEN, G. AND GROWN, C. (1987) *Development crises and alternative visions. Third World women's perspectives*. New York: Monthly Review Press.

SEYMOUR, S., DANIELS, S. AND WATKINS, C. (1994) Estate and empire: Sir George Cornewall's management of Moccas, Herefordshire and La Taste, Grenada, 1771–1819. Working Paper 28, University of Nottingham, Department of Geography, and *Journal of Historical Geography*, 24, 313–51.

SHAH, D. (2002) Hooray for Hollywood. *Observer*, 24 March, 5.

SHAKESPEARE, T. (1993) Disabled people's self organisation: a new social movement? *Disability, Handicap and Society*, 8, 249–64.

SHAKESPEARE, T. (1994) Cultural representations of disabled people: dustbins for disavowal? *Disability and Society*, 9(3), 283–99.

SHAPIRO, M. (1989) Representing world politics: the sport/war intertext. In Der Derian, J. and Shapiro, M.J. (eds) *International/intertextual relations: postmodern readings of world politics*. Lexington MA: Lexington Books.

SHARMA, S., HUTNYK, J. AND SHARMA, A. (1996) *Dis-orienting rhythms: the politics of the new Asian dance music*. London: Zed Books.

SHARP, J. (1993) Publishing American identity: popular geopolitics, myth and the *Reader's Digest*. *Political Geography*, 12(6), 491–503.

SHARP, J. (1994) A topology of 'post' nationality: (re)mapping identity in *The Satanic Verses*. *Ecumene*, 1(1), 65–76.

SHARP, J. (1996) Hegemony, popular culture and geopolitics: the *Reader's Digest* and the construction of danger. *Political Geography*, 15(6/7), 557 70.

SHARP, J. (2000) *Condensing the Cold War: Reader's Digest and American identity*. Minneapolis: University of Minnesota Press.

SHAW, G., AGARWAL, S. AND BULL, P. (2000) Tourism consumption and tourist behaviour: a British perspective. *Tourism Geographies*, 2, 264–89.

SHAW, M. (2002) Risk-transfer militarism, small massacres and the historic legitimacy of war. *International Relations*, 16, 343–59.

SHAW, M., DORLING, D. AND BRIMBLECOMBE, N. (1999) Life chances in Britain by housing wealth and for the homeless and vulnerably housed. *Environment and Planning A*, 31, 2239–48.

SHEAHAN, J. (1987) *Patterns of development in Latin America*. Princeton: Princeton University Press.

SHEPPARD, E. AND BARNES, T. (2003) *A companion to economic geography*. Oxford: Blackwell.

SHERMAN, D.J. AND ROGOFF, I. (1994) *Museum culture: histories, discourses and spectacles*. Minneapolis: University of Minnesota Press.

SHIELDS, R. (1991) *Places on the margin: alternative geographies of modernity*. London: Routledge.

SHILLING, C. (1993) *The body and social theory*. London: Sage.

SHORE, C. (1996) Transcending the nation-state? The European Commission and the (re)-discovery of Europe. *Journal of Historical Sociology*, 9(4), 473–96.

SHORT, J. (1991) *Imagined country: society, culture and environment*. London: Routledge.

SHORTRIDGE, B.G. AND SHORTRIDGE, J.R. (EDS) (1999) *The taste of American place: a reader on regional and ethnic foods*. New York: Rowman & Littlefield.

SHORTRIDGE, J.R. (1991) The concept of the place-defining novel in American popular culture. *The Professional Geographer*, 43, 280–91.

SHURMER-SMITH, P. AND HANNAM, K. (1994) *Worlds of desire, realms of power: a Cultural Geography*. London: Edward Arnold.

SIBLEY, D. (1981) *Outsiders in urban societies*. Oxford: Blackwell.

SIBLEY, D. (1995) *Geographies of exclusion: society and difference in the West*. London: Routledge.

SIBLEY, D. (1998) The problematic nature of exclusion. *Geoforum*, 29(2), 119–21.

SIBLEY, D. (1999) Creating geographies of difference. In Massey, D., Allen, J. and Sarre, P. (eds) *Human Geography today*. Cambridge: Polity, 115–28.

SIDAWAY, J.D. (2003) Banal geopolitics resumed. *Antipode*, 35(4), 645–51.

SIDAWAY, J.D., BUNNELL, T. AND YEOH, B.S.A. (2003) Geography and postcolonialism. Theme issue of *Singapore Journal of Tropical Geography*, 24(3).

SILBERMAN, N.A. (2001) 'If I forget thee, O Jerusalem': archaeology, religious commemoration and nationalism in a disputed city, 1801–2001. *Nations and Nationalism*, 7(4), 487–504.

SILVERSTONE, R. (1994) *Television and everyday life*. London: Routledge.

SIMMEL, G. (1990) *The Philosophy of Money*. London: Routledge.

SIMMONS, I. (1996 [1st edn 1989]). *Changing the face of the earth. Culture, environment, history*. Oxford: Basil Blackwell.

SIMON, D. (1997) Development reconsidered: new directions in development thinking. *Geografiska Annaler*, 79B(4), 183–201.

SKEGGS, B. (1997) *Formations of class and gender*. London: Sage.

SKELTON, T. (2000) 'Nothing to do, nowhere to go?': teenage girls and 'public' space in the Rhondda Valleys, South Wales. In Holloway, S.L. and Valentine, G. (eds) *Children's geographies: playing, living, learning*. London: Routledge, 80–99.

SKELTON, T. AND VALENTINE, G. (1998) *Cool places: geographies of youth cultures*. London: Routledge.

SLOTERDIJK, P. (1995) World markets and secluded spots: on the position of the European regions in the world-experiment of capital. In Büchler, P. and Papastergiadis, N. (eds) *Random access: on crisis and its metaphors*. London: Rivers Oram Press.

SLOTKIN, R. (1992) *Gunfighter nation: the myth of the frontier in 20th century America*. New York: Macmillan.

SMITH, A. (2000a) Employment restructuring and household survival in 'postcommunist transition': rethinking economic practices in eastern Europe. *Environment and Planning A*, 32, 1759–80.

SMITH, A. (2002) Culture/economy and spaces of economic practice: positioning households in post-communism. *Transactions of the Institute of British Geographers*, NS(27), 232–50.

SMITH, A. (2003a) Power relations, industrial clusters and regional transformations: pan-Europe integration and outward processing in the Slovak clothing industry. *Economic Geography*, 79, 17–40.

SMITH, A., RAINNIE, A., DUNFORD, M., HARDY, J., HUDSON, R. AND SADLER, D. (2002) Networks of value, commodities and regions: reworking divisions of labour in macro-regional economies. *Progress in Human Geography*, 26(1), 41–63.

SMITH, A.D. (1991a) *National identity*. Harmondsworth: Penguin Books.

SMITH, B. (1985) *European vision and the South Pacific* (2nd edn). New Haven and London: Yale University Press.

SMITH, D. (2004) Morality ethics and social justice. In Cloke, P., Crang, P. and Goodwin, M. (eds) *Envisioning human geographies*. London: Arnold, 195–209.

SMITH, D. AND HOLT, L. (2004) Lesbian migrants and the cultural consumption of greentrified rurality. Paper available from the authors. University of Brighton, Cockcroft Building, Lewes Road, Brighton BN2 4GJ.

SMITH, D.M. (2000b) *Moral geographies: ethics in a world of difference*. Edinburgh: Edinburgh University Press.

SMITH, J. (2000c) 'The Daily Globe': environmental change, the public and the media. London: Earthscan.

SMITH, J.M. AND FOOTE, K.E. (EDS) (1994) How the world looks. In Foote, K.E., Hugill, P.J., Mathewson, K. and Smith, J.M. (eds) *Re-reading cultural geography*. Austin: University of Texas Press, 27–163.

SMITH, M.P. (ED.) (1995) *Marginal spaces*. New Brunswick, NJ: Transaction Publishers.

SMITH, N. (1987) 'Academic war over the field of geography': the elimination of Geography at Harvard, 1947–1951. *Annals of the Association of American Geographers*, 77(2), 155–72.

SMITH, N. (1990 [1st edn 1984]) *Uneven development*. Oxford: Basil Blackwell.

SMITH, N. (1994a) Geography, empire and social theory. *Progress in Human Geography*, 18(4), 491–500.

SMITH, N. (1996) *The new urban frontier: gentrification and the revanchist city*. London: Routledge.

SMITH, N. (2001) Ashes and aftermath. *The Arab World Geographer* forum on 11 September Events.

SMITH, N. (2003b) Scales of terror and the resort to geography: September 11, October 7. *Society and Space*, 19, 631–7.

SMITH, N. AND GODLEWSKA, A. (1994) Introduction: critical histories of Geography. In Godlewska, A. and Smith, N. (eds) *Geography and empire*. Oxford: Blackwell.

SMITH, S. (2000d) Performing in the (sound)world. *Environment and Planning D: Society and Space*, 18, 615–37.

SMITH, S.J. (1989) *The politics of 'race' and residence*. Cambridge: Polity Press.

SMITH, S.J. (1993) Residential segregation and the politics of racialisation. In Cross, M. and Keith, M. (eds) *Racism, the city and the state* London: Routledge.

SMITH, S.J. (1994b) Citizenship. In Johnston, R., Gregory, D. and Smith, D.M. (eds) *The dictionary of Human Geography* (3rd edn). Oxford: Blackwell.

SMITH, S.J. (1997) Beyond geography's visible worlds: a cultural politics of music. *Progress in Human Geography*, 21, 502–29.

SMITH, S.J. (2005) States, markets and an ethic of care. *Political Geography*, 24.

SMITH, S. J. AND EASTERLOW, D. (in press) The strange geography of health inequalities. *Transactions, Institute of British Geographers*.

SMITH, S.J. AND MALLINSON, S. (1996) The problem with social housing: discretion, accountability and the welfare ideal. *Policy and Politics*, 24, 339–58.

SMITH, W.D. (1984) The function of commercial centres in the modernisation of European capitalism: Amsterdam as an information exchange in the seventeenth century. *Journal of Economic History*, 44, 985–1005.

SNOW, C.P. (1959) *The two cultures and the scientific revolution*. Cambridge: Cambridge University Press.

SOJA, E. (1992) Inside exopolis: scenes from Orange County. In Sorkin, M. (ed.) *Variations on a theme park*. New York: Noonday.

SOJA, E.W. (1996) *Thirdspace*. Oxford: Blackwell.

SOMERS, M.R. (1994) The narrative constitution of identity: a relational and network approach. *Theory and Society*, 23, 605–49.

SORKIN, M. (ED.) (1992) *Variations on a theme park: the new American city and the end of public space*. New York: The Noonday Press.

SPILLMAN, L. (1997) *Nation and commemoration: creating national identities in the United States and Australia*. Cambridge: Cambridge University Press.

SPOONER, B. (1986) Weavers and dealers: the authenticity of an oriental carpet. In Appadurai, A. (ed.) *The social life of things. Commodities in cultural perspective*. Cambridge: Cambridge University Press, 195–235.

STAEHELI, L. AND BROWN, M. (2003) Where has welfare gone? Introductory remarks on the geographies of care and welfare. *Environment and Planning A*, 35, 771–7.

STAEHELI, L. AND MITCHELL, D. (forthcoming), The complex politics of relevance in geography. *Annals of the AAG*.

STALLYBRAS, J. (1996) *Gargantua: vision and mass culture*. London: Verso.

STEINER, A. (2003) Trouble in paradise. *New Scientist*, 18 October, 21.

STEVENS, J.E. (1988) *Hoover Dam: an American adventure*, Norman, OK: University of Oklahoma Press.

STEVENS, S. (1993) Tourism, change and continuity in the Mount Everest region. *Geographical Review*, 83, 410–27.

STEVENSON, N. (2002) *Understanding media cultures*. London: Thousand Oaks; New Delhi: Sage.

STODDART, D. (1986) Geography, exploration and discovery. In *On geography and its history*. Oxford: Blackwell.

STODDART, D. (1987) To claim the high ground: geography for the end of the century. *Transactions of the Institute of British Geographers*, NS 12, 327–36.

STOKER, G. (1996) Governance as theory: five propositions. Mimeo (available from the author at the Department of Government, University of Strathclyde).

STORPER, M. AND WALKER, R. (1989) *The capitalist imperative*. New York and Oxford: Basil Blackwell.

SUI, D. (1999) Postmodern urbanism disrobed: or why postmodern urbanism is a dead end for urban geography. *Urban Geography*, 20(5), 403–11.

SUNDAY TIMES (2003) The great Indian takeaway. London: *Sunday Times*, 8 June, 3.5.

SWYNGEDOUW, E. (2000) The Marxian alternative: historical-geographical materialism and the political economy of capitalism. In Sheppard, E. and Barnes, T. (eds) *A companion to economic geography*. Oxford: Blackwell.

SYMANSKI, R. (1981) *The Immoral landscape: female prostitution in western societies*. Toronto: Butterworths.

SYNNOTT, A. (1993) *The body social: symbolism, self and society*. London: Routledge.

TAKAHASHI, L. (1996) A decade of understanding homelessness in the USA: from characterization to representation. *Progress in Human Geography*, 20(3), 291–310.

TAUSSIG, M. (1980) The devil and commodity fetishism in Latin America. Durham, NC: University of North Carolina Press.

TAUXE, C.S. (1996) Mystics, modernists and constructions of Brasília. *Ecumene, 3, 43–61*.

TAYLOR, G. (1949) *Urban Geography*. London: Methuen.

TAYLOR, H. (1951) No watchdog for America. *Reader's Digest*, February, 85–7.

TAYLOR, P. (1989) 'The error of developmentalism in Human Geography. In Gregory, D. and Walford, R. (eds) *Horizons in Human Geography*. Basingstoke: Macmillan, 303–19.

TAYLOR, P. (1990) Editorial comment: geographical knowledge systems. *Political Geography Quarterly*, 9, 211–12.

TAYLOR, P. AND FLINT, C. (2000) *Political geography*. Harlow: Pearson.

TAYLOR, P. AND OVERTON, M. (1991) Further thoughts on geography and GIS. *Environment and Planning A*, 23, 1087–9.

TAYLOR, P.J. (1996) *The way the modern world works: world hegemony to world impasse*. Chichester: John Wiley.

TAYLOR, P.J. (2004) *World city network: a global urban analysis*. London and New York: Routledge.

TAYLOR, P.J., CATALANO, G. AND GANE, N. (2003) A geography of global change: cities and services, 2000–2001. *Urban Geography*, 24(5), 431–41.

TENDLER, J. (1997) *Good government in the tropics*. Baltimore: Johns Hopkins University Press.

TERBORGH, J. (1999) *Requiem for nature*. Washington, DC: Island Press.

THEDE, N. AND AMBROSI, A. (EDS) (1991) *Video the changing world*. Montreal and New York: Black Rose Books.

THEE DATA BASE (1996) The K Foundation: why we burnt a million pounds. *thee data base* [online], 7, Available from http://members.xoom.com/databass/KFound.htm.

THOMAS, H. (1997) *The slave trade*. London: Macmillan.

THOMAS, W., SAUER, C., BATES, M. AND MUMFORD, L. (1956) *Man's role in changing the face of the earth*. Chicago, IL: University of Chicago Press.

THOMPSON, A. (2001) Nations, national identities and human agency: putting people back into nations. *Sociological Review*, 49(1), 18–32.

THOMPSON, E. (1991) Customs in common. London: Penguin Books.

THOMPSON, J. (1995) *The media and modernity: a social theory of the media*. Oxford: Polity Press.

THRIFT, N. (1983) On the determination of social action in space and time. *Environment and Planning D: Society and Space*, 1, 23–57.

THRIFT, N. (1994) On the social and cultural determinants of international financial centres. In Corbridge, S., Thrift, N.J. and Martin, R. (eds) *Money, power and space*. Oxford: Blackwell, 327–55.

THRIFT, N. (1996a, orig. 1985) 'Flies and Germs: a geography of knowledge'. In Thrift, N., *Spatial formations*. London: Sage.

THRIFT, N. (1996b) *Spatial formations*. London: Sage.

THRIFT, N. (1996c) Inhuman geographies: landscapes of speed, light and power. In Thrift, N., *Spatial formations*. London: Sage, 256–310.

THRIFT, N. (1997) The still point: expressive embodiment and dance. In Pile, S. and Keith, M. (eds) *Geographies of resistance*. London: Routledge, 124–51.

THRIFT, N. (1999) Steps to an ecology of place. In Massey, D., Allen, J. and Sarre, P. (eds) *Human geography today*. Cambridge: Polity Press.

THRIFT, N. (2001) Chasing capitalism. *New Political Economy*, 6, 3, 375–80.

THRIFT, N. (2004a) Intensities of feeling: towards a spatial politics of affect. *Geografiska Annaler*, 86B(1), 55–76.

THRIFT, N. (2004b) Summoning life. In Cloke, P., Crang, P. and Goodwin, M. (eds) *Envisioning human geographies*. London: Arnold, 81–103.

THRIFT, N.J. (2003) Closer to the machine? Intelligent environments, new forms of possession and the rise of the supertoy. *Cultural Geographies*, 10, 389–407.

TICKELL, A. AND PECK, J. (1996) The return of the Manchester men: men's words and men's deeds in the remaking of the local state. *Transactions of the Institute of British Geographers*, 21(4), 595–616.

TIFFEN, M., MORTIMORE, M.J. AND GICHUGI, F. (1994) *More people, less erosion: environmental recovery in Kenya*. Chichester: John Wiley.

TOYE, J. (1993) *Dilemmas of development: the counter-revolution in development theory and policy* (2nd edn). Oxford: Blackwell.

TRELLUYER, M. (1990) La télévision regionale en Europe. *Dossiers de l'Audiovisuel*, 33, 10–55.

TRONTO, J. (1987) Beyond gender differences in a theory of care. *Signs*, 12, 644–63.

TRONTO, J. (1993) *Moral boundaries: a political argument for an ethic of care*. London: Routledge.

TRONTO, J. (1998) An ethic of care. *Generations*, 22(3), 15–20.

TUAN, YI-FU (1976) Humanistic geography. *Annals of the Association of American Geographers*, 66, 266–76.

TUAN, YI-FU (1977) *Space and place: the perspective of experience*. Minneapolis: University of Minnesota Press.

TUCKER, F. AND MATTHEWS, H. (2001) 'They don't like girls hanging around there': conflicts over recreational space in rural Northamptonshire. *Area*, 33: 161–8.

TURNER, T. (1991) The social dynamics of video media in an indigenous society: the cultural meaning and personal politics of video-making in Kayapo communities. *Visual Anthropology Review*, 7(2), 68–76.

UK GOVERNMENT (1999) *A Better Quality of Life: a strategy for sustainable development for the UK*, Cm 4345, The Stationery Office, London: ISBN 0-10-143452-9.

UN CENTRE FOR HUMAN SETTLEMENTS (1996) *An urbanizing world: global report on human settlements 1996*. Oxford: Oxford University Press.

UNHCR (annual) *State of the world's refugees*. Oxford: Oxford University Press.

UNITED NATIONS DEVELOPMENT PROGRAMME (UNDP) (1997) *Human development report 1997*. Oxford: OUP-UNDP.

UNITED NATIONS DEVELOPMENT PROGRAMME (UNDP) (1999) *Human development report: Globalisation with a human face*. New York: Oxford University Press.

UNITED NATIONS DEVELOPMENT PROGRAMME (UNDP) (2002) *Human Development Report 2002*, Oxford: Oxford University Press.

UPIAS (1976) *Fundamental principles of disability*. London: Union of the Physically Impaired Against Segregation.

UPRETY, R. (2002) Impact of tourist industry in Nepal. *Nepal Weekly Telegraph*, 14 August, http://www.nepalnews.com.np, accessed 25 April 2004.

URRY, J. (1990) *The tourist gaze: leisure and travel in contemporary society*. London: Sage.

URRY, J. (1995) *Consuming places*. London: Routledge.

URRY, J. (1999) *Sociology beyond societies: mobilities for the twenty-first century*. London: Routledge.

URRY, J. (2002) *The tourist gaze (2nd edn). London: Sage.

VAKIL, A.C. (1997) Confronting the classification problem: toward a taxonomy of NGOs. *World Development*, 25(12), 2057–70.

VALENTINE, G. (1989) The geography of women's fear. *Area*, 21(4), 385–90.

VALENTINE, G. (1993a) Desperately seeking Susan: a geography of lesbian friendships. *Area*, 25(2), 109–16.

VALENTINE, G. (1993b) Negotiating and managing multiple sexual identities: lesbian time-space strategies. *Transactions of the Institute of British Geographers*, 18, 237–48.

VALENTINE, G. (1993c) (Hetero)sexing space: lesbian perceptions and experiences of everyday spaces. *Environment and Planning D: Society and Space*, 11, 395–413.

VALENTINE, G. (1996a) Angels and devils: moral landscapes of childhood. *Environment and Planning D: Society and Space*, 14, 581–99.

VALENTINE, G. (1996b) Children should be seen and not heard: the production and transgression of adult's public space. *Urban Geography*, 17(3), 205–20.

VALENTINE, G. (1997a) 'Oh Yes I Can.' 'Oh No You Can't': Children and parents' understandings of kids' competence to negotiate public space safely. *Antipode*, 29, 65–89.

VALENTINE, G. (1997b) 'My Son's a Bit Dizzy' 'My Wife's a Bit Soft': gender, children and cultures of parenting. *Gender, Place and Culture*, 4, 37–62.

VALENTINE, G. (1997c) A safe place to grow up? Parenting, perceptions of children's safety and the rural idyll. *Journal of Rural Studies*, 13(2), 137–48.

VALENTINE, G. (1998) 'Sticks and Stones May Break My Bones': a personal geography of harassment. *Antipode*, 30(4), 305–32.

VALENTINE, G. (1999) Imaginative geographies. In Massey, D., Allen, J. and Sarre, P. (eds) *Human geography today*. Cambridge: Polity Press.

VALENTINE, G. (2001) *Social geographies: space and society*. London: Prentice Hall

VAN ROOY, A. (1998) *Civil society and the aid industry*. London: Earthscan.

VARLEY, A. (1996) Women-headed households: some more equal than others? *World Development*, 24, 505–20.

VEBLEN, T. (1899) *The theory of the leisure class: an economic study in the evolution of institutions*. New York: Macmillan.

VEIJOLA, S. AND JOKINEN, E. (1994) The body in tourism. *Theory, Culture and Society*, 11, 125–51.

VERTOVEC, S. (1996) Berlin Multikulti: Germany, 'foreigners' and 'world-openness'. *New Community*, 22(3), 381–99.

VIDAL, J. (1997) The long march home. *The Guardian Weekend*, April 26, 14–20.

VISSER, G. (2003) Gay men, leisure space and South African cities: the case of Cape Town. *Geoforum*, 34, 123–37.

VISVANATHAN, N. *ET AL.* (eds) (1987) *The women, gender and development reader*. London: Zed.

VON WEIZSÄCKER, E., LOVINS, A.B. AND LOVINS, L.H. (1997) Factor Four: doubling wealth – halving resource use the new report to the Club of Rome. London: Earthscan.

WADE, R. (1990) *Covering the market: economic theory and the role of government in East Asian industrialisation*. Princeton: Princeton University Press.

WAINWRIGHT, H. (2003) *Reclaim the state: experiments in popular democracy*. London: Verso.

WALL STREET JOURNAL (2004) Outsourcing concerns some globalisation backers. *Wall Street Journal Europe*, 26 January, A6.

WALLERSTEIN, I. (1979) *The capitalist world economy*. Cambridge: Cambridge University Press.

WALLERSTEIN, I. (1984) *The Politics of the World-Economy*. Cambridge: Cambridge University Press.

WALVIN, J. (1996) *Fruits of empire: exotic produce and British trade, 1660–1800*. London: Macmillan.

WACQUANT, L. (1993) Urban outcasts: stigma and division in the Black American ghetto and the French urban periphery. *International Journal of Urban and Regional Research*, 17(3), 366–83.

WACQUANT, L. (1999) Urban marginality in the coming millennium. *Urban Studies*, 36, 1639–47.

WANG, N. (1999) Rethinking authenticity in tourism experience. *Annals of Tourism Research*, 26, 349–70.

WARD, C. (1978) *The child in the city*. London: Architectural Press.

WARF, B. (1988) Regional transformation, everyday life, and Pacific Northwest lumber production. *Annals of the Association of American Geographers*, 78, 326–46.

WARK, M. (1994) *Virtual geography*. Bloomington and Indianapolis: Indiana University Press.

WATERMAN, P. (2002) The 'call of social movements' of the Second World Social Forum, Porto Allegre, Brazil, 31 January–5 February 2002. *Antipode*, 34, 625–32.

WATERMAN, P. AND WILLS, J. (2002) (eds) *Place, space and the new labour internationalisms*. Oxford: Blackwell.

WATSON, J.L. (ED.) (1997) *Golden arches east: McDonald's in East Asia*. Stanford: Stanford University Press.

WAUGH, P. (1997) Banglatown. *Evening Standard*, 23 January, 15.

WEBER, M. (1958) *The Protestant ethic and the spirit of capitalism*. New York: Scribners.

WEIGHTMAN, B. (1980) Gay bars as private places. *Landscape*, 23, 9–16.

WEISS, B. (1997) The making and unmaking of the Haya lived world. London: Duke University Press.

WELLS, H.G. (1902) *Anticipations of the reaction of mechanical and scientific progress upon human life and thought*. London: Chapman and Hall.

WELLS, H.G. (1920) *The outline of history*. London: Cassell.

WEX, M. (1979) *'Let's take back our space': 'female' and 'male' body language as a result of patriarchal structures*. Berlin: Frauenliteratureverlag Hermine Fees.

WHICH? (1989) No entry. October, 498–501.

WHITE, S. (ED.) (2003) Participatory video: images that transform and empower. London: Sage.

WIDDOWFIELD, R. (2000) The place of emotions in academic research. *Area*, 32(2), 199–208.

WILLIAMS, A. AND SHAW, G. (EDS) (1988) *Tourism and economic development*. London: Belhaven.

WILLIAMS, B. (1981) *Moral luck*. Cambridge: Cambridge University Press.

WILLIAMS, C.H. AND SMITH, A.D. (1983) The national construction of social space. *Progress in Human Geography*, 7(4), 502–18.

WILLIAMS, J. (1982) *Dream worlds*. Berkeley: University of California Press.

WILLIAMS, R. (1983) *Keywords. A vocabulary of culture and society*. New York: Oxford University Press.

WILLIAMS, R. (1985 [1973]) *The country and the city*. London: Hogarth Press.

WILLIAMS, S. (2001) *Emotions and social theory*. London: Sage Publications.

WILLIAMS PARIS, J. AND ANDERSON, R.E. (2001) Faith-based queer space in Washington, DC: the Metropolitan Community Church-DC and Mount Vernon Square. *Gender, Place and Culture*, 8, 149–68.

WILLIS, K. (2005) *Theories and practices of development*. London: Routledge.

WILSON, A. (1992) *The culture of nature*. London: Routledge.

WILSON, E. (1991) *The Sphinx in the city*. Berkeley, CA: University of California Press.

WILSON, W.J. (1987) *The truly disadvantaged, the inner city, the underclass and public policy*. Chicago: University of Chicago Press.

WILSON, W.J (1996) *When work disappears: the world of the new urban poor*. New York: Alfred A. Knopf.

WINCHESTER, H. AND WHITE, P. (1988) The location of marginalised groups in the inner city. *Environment and Planning D: Society and Space*, 6, 37–54.

WITHERS, C.W.J. (1996) Place, memory, monument: memorializing the past in contemporary Highland Scotland. *Ecumene*, 3(3), 325–44.

WOLCH, J. AND DEAR, M. (1993) *Malign neglect: homeless in an American City*. San Francisco, CA: Jesse-Bars.

WOLCH, J. AND DEVERTEUIL, G. (2001) Landscapes of the new poverty management. In May, J. and Thrift, N. (eds) *TimeSpace*, London: Routledge, 149–67.

WOLCH, J. AND EMEL, J. (EDS) (1998) *Animal geographies*. London: Verso.

WOLF, M. (2000) Why this hatred of the market? in Lechner, F.J. and Boli, J. (eds) *The globalization reader*. Oxford: Blackwell, 9–11.

WOMEN AND GEOGRAPHY STUDY GROUP (WGSG) (1997) *Feminist geographies: explorations in diversity and difference*. Harlow: Longman.

WOOD, D. (1992) *The Power of Maps*. New York: Guilford Press.

WOODS, M. (2005) *Rural geography: processes, responses and experiences in rural restructuring*. London: Sage.

WOODWARD, K. (ED.) (1997) *Identity and difference*. London: Sage.

WORCESTER, R.M. (1993) Public and elite attitudes to environmental issues. *International Journal of Public Opinion Research*, 5, 315–34.

WORLD BANK (1992) *World development report, 1992*. Oxford: Oxford University Press/World Bank.

WORLD BANK (1993) *The East Asian Miracle*. Oxford: OUP.

WORLD BANK (1994) *Adjustment in Africa: reforms, results and the road ahead*. Oxford: Oxford University Press/World Bank.

WORLD TOURISM ORGANIZATION (2002) *Compendium of tourism statistics*. Madrid: World Tourism Organization.

WORLD TRAVEL AND TOURISM COUNCIL (2004) global travel and tourism poised for robust growth in 2004, http://www.wttc.org/News31.htm, accessed 29 July 2004.

WRIGHT, P. (1985) *On living in an old country*. London: Verso.

WRIGHT, T. (1995) Tranquility city: self organisation, protest and collective gains within a Chicago homeless encampment. In Smith, M.P. (ed.) *Marginal spaces*. New Brunswick, NJ: Transaction Publishers.

WRIGLEY, N. (1998) Leveraged restructuring and the economic landscape: the LBO wave in US food retailing. In Martin, R.L. (ed.) *Money and the space economy*. Chichester: John Wiley.

WYNNE, B. (1993) Public uptake of science: a case for institutional reflexivity. *Public Understanding of Science*, 2, 321–37.

YAO, S. (2001) 'Eating air', 'talking cock': food, pleasure and the art of lying in Singapore. Paper presented to the Foodscapes: the cultural politics of food in Asia Conference, National University of Singapore, 13–15 June.

YAPA, L. (1996) What causes poverty? A postmodern view. *Annals of the Association of American Geographers*, 86, 707–28.

YEOH, B. AND KONG, L. (1994) Reading landscape meanings: state constructions and lived experiences in Singapore's Chinatown. *Habitat International*, 184, 17–35.

YOUNG, I.M. (1990a) The ideal of community and the politics of difference. In Nicholson, L. (ed.) *Feminism/postmodernism*. London: Routledge.

YOUNG, I.M. (1990b) Throwing like a girl: a phenomenology of feminine body comportment, motility and spatiality. In *Throwing like a girl and other essays in feminist philosophy and social theory*. Bloomington: University of Indiana Press.

YOUNG, J. (1993) *The texture of memory: holocaust memorials and meaning*. London: Yale University Press.

ZALOOM, C. (2003) Ambiguous numbers: trading technologies and interpretation in financial markets. *American Ethnologist*, 31, 258–72.

ZERUBAVEL, Y. (1995) *Recovered roots: collective memory and the making of Israeli national tradition*. Chicago, IL: Chicago University Press.

ZUKIN, S. (1982) *Loft living: culture and capital in urban change*. Baltimore: Johns Hopkins University Press. (London: Radius, 1988).

ZUKIN, S. AND DIMAGGIO, P. (1990) Introduction. In Zukin, S. and DiMaggio, P. (eds) *Structures of capital. The social organization of the economy*. Cambridge, New York and Sydney: Cambridge University Press.

ZURICK, D. (1992) Adventure travel and sustainable tourism in the peripheral economy of Nepal. *Annals of the Association of American Geographers*, 82(4), 608–28.

INDEX

Orders: please contact Bookpoint Ltd, 130 Milton Park, Abingdon, Oxon OX14 4SB.
Telephone: (44) 01235 827720.
Fax: (44) 01235 400454.
Lines are open from 9.00 - 6.00, Monday to Saturday, with a 24 hour message answering service.
You can also order through our website www.hoddereducation.co.uk

British Library Cataloguing in Publication Data
A catalogue record for this title is available from the British Library

ISBN-10: 0 340 88276 X
ISBN-13: 978 0 340 88276 4

First Published 1999
Second edition 2005
Impression number   10 9 8 7 6 5 4 3
Year   2009 2008 2007 2006

Copyright © 2005 Hodder Arnold

Cover photo from The Image Bank / Getty Images
Typeset by Phoenix Photosetting, Chatham, Kent
Printed in Dubai for Hodder Arnold, an imprint of Hodder Education, a member of the Hodder Headline Group, 338 Euston Road, London, NW1 3BH.

If you have any comments to make about this, or any of our other titles, please send them to the feedback section on www.hoddereducation.co.uk

INTRODUCING HUMAN GEOGRAPHIES

Second Edition

Edited by Paul Cloke, Philip Crang and Mark Goodwin

Hodder Arnold

A MEMBER OF THE HODDER HEADLINE GROUP